A Practical
Commentary on
HOLY
SCRIPTURE

Chapel of the Holy Sepulchre at Jerusalem
(Phot. Bruno Hentshel, Leipzig)

A Practical Commentary on HOLY SCRIPTURE

By Most Rev.

Frederick Justus Knecht, D.D.

LATE AUXILIARY BISHOP OF THE ARCHDIOCESE OF FREIBURG

TRANSLATED AND ADAPTED FROM THE
SIXTEENTH GERMAN EDITION

TAN BOOKS AND PUBLISHERS, INC.
Rockford, Illinois 61105

#56603385

Imprimatur: Dr. Mutz
             Vicar General
             Freiburg-im-Breisgau
             July 28, 1923

Published in 1923 by B. Herder, London and St. Louis, Missouri, Publisher to the Holy Apostolic See, as *A Practical Commentary on Holy Scripture For the Use of Those Who Teach Bible History*. All rights reserved.

Reprinted from the Fourth English Edition by TAN Books and Publishers, Inc. in 2003.

ISBN 0-89555-757-6

Cover photo of stained-glass window "Moses and the Ten Commandments" copyright © 1998 Alan Brown. Cover photo of Our Lord from stained-glass window "Last Supper—very close" copyright © 1993 Alan Brown. Both photos used by arrangement with Al Brown Photo, 3597 N. Roberts Rd., Bardstown, KY 40004.

Printed and bound in the United States of America.

TAN BOOKS AND PUBLISHERS, INC.
P.O. Box 424
Rockford, Illinois 61105
2003

SOME APPROBATIONS.

We strongly recommend Bishop KNECHT'S "Practical Commentary on Holy Scripture". It contains an Appendix, called a Concordance of Scripture Aids to the Catechism, by reference to which the teacher will find himself in possession of Holy Scripture to illustrate every part of the Catechism. The work has gone through 19 editions, and is the most complete and the most valuable book for its purpose in any language. The English translation has been exceedingly well done, and is preceded by a Preface by the Rev. M. GLANCEY, of the Diocese of Birmingham, in which there are valuable hints on teaching Holy Scripture in combination with the Catechism.

  Lenten Letter 1903.   † *HERBERT* CARDINAL *VAUGHAN*,
               ARCHBISHOP OF WESTMINSTER.

I have devoted as much time as I could afford occasionally to a perusal of this admirable work, and always felt that my spare moments were well spent. The method adopted in explaining the Holy Scripture is plain and simple, and consequently can be easily understood by any one of ordinary capacity. The division of each Chapter into Narrative and Explanation, Commentary, and Application, will render the work of the highest utility to those who are engaged as Catechists or as Teachers in Schools. I can recommend the work strongly, as affording, in the simplest form, a great amount of information on the History of the Old and New Testament.

  Catholic Cathedral, Madras, September 20. 1894.

               † *J. COLGAN*,
             ARCHBISHOP OF MADRAS.

The translation of Dr. KNECHT'S celebrated "Practical Commentary" is a most valuable and welcome addition to our English literature. Brimful of interest and practical instruction, it should be in the hands not only of every Priest and Catechist, but of the heads of every Catholic family. In a few days we shall have our annual Retreat and Synod. I shall not fail to recommend it strongly to all my Priests and Religious Communities. Wishing the admirable work all the success it deserves,

  Christchurch, New Zealand, December 27. 1894.

             † *J. J. GRIMES, S. M.*,
             BISHOP OF CHRISTCHURCH.

I have perused Dr. KNECHT's "Commentary" with much pleasure, interest, and profit. I have no hesitation in pronouncing it to be a most useful handbook for teachers and priest, and to supply a want in English Catholic literature. No doubt, Bible History, bearing as it does on the doctrines of faith, is capable of rendering most valuable service to the teacher of Religion, as proof, illustration, and expansion of doctrinal truth, It becomes an object-lesson, nay a pictorial catechism, setting forth the isolated texts of Scripture found in the Catechism in the full light of their context and surroundings, exhibiting religious truth in its practical bearing on the varied states and conditions of life. To effect all this, it must be read not as a mere story-book, but in close connection with the Catechism, hand in hand with it—Catechism being the guide and Bible History the handmaid. Dr. KNECHT's "Commentary" seems to have been composed with such objects in view, and hence I feel sure of its receiving a most hearty welcome in English-speaking countries, and of its proving to be of the greatest service to priest and catechist by pointing out so ably the bearing of the Bible History on faith and morals. Catholics need more than esteem and love for the Holy Scriptures—they should know how to use them to the best practical advantage; and Dr. KNECHT's work is a valuable aid in that direction. I expect it will have a wide circulation, and I should like to see it in the hands of all my priests and teachers, to whose notice I shall bring it by an official channel.

    St. Mary's Cathedral, Wellington, N. Z., August 31. 1894.

† *FRANCIS REDWOOD, S. M.,*
ARCHBISHOP OF WELLINGTON.

I beg to assure you that I shall bring Dr. KNECHT's "Practical Commentary" under the favourable notice of the Clergy of Cashel, at the earliest opportunity that offers.

    The Palace, Thurles, August 9. 1894.

† *J. W. CROKE,*
ARCHBISHOP OF CASHEL.

The plan of Dr. KNECHT's "Practical Commentary" seems excellent and the execution no less so. Whatever system may be adopted by the individual Catechist, he cannot fail to find this Scripture Narrative and Commentary of great practical utility. I shall be very happy to recommend it to my clergy.

    42, Greenhill Gardens, Edinburgh, August 9. 1894.

† *ANGUS MACDONALD,*
ARCHBISHOP OF ST. ANDREWS AND EDINBURGH.

I hope Dr. KNECHT's Commentary on Holy Scripture may meet a wide and ready sale. I am sure it will be found most useful in Catholic families and schools.

    Wexford, August 11. 1894.

† *JAMES BROWNE,*
BISHOP OF FERNS.

I have read a good portion of the second volume of Dr. KNECHT'S "Practical Commentary", and I am more than pleased with the work. It deserves the title "celebrated", which you give to it. It will be a most useful book for Teachers as well as for the Clergy. I shall have great pleasure in recommending it strongly to both.

Bishop's House, Leeds, July 23. 1894.

† WILLIAM,
BISHOP OF LEEDS.

I like very much the plan of Dr. KNECHT'S "Practical Commentary", and think it well adopted to attain the end in view — an intelligent acquaintance with Scriptural History and Doctrine and a practical application of their lessons to the duties of life.

I shall be happy to recommend it to my clergy as a valuable aid to Religious Teaching in our schools.

Spring Hill, Claughton, Birkenhead, July 22. 1894.

† EDMUND,
BISHOP OF SHREWSBURY.

The "Commentary for the use of Catechists and Teachers" by Dr. F. J. KNECHT, now Auxiliary Bishop of Freiburg, Baden, has been received with the greatest welcome by the Clergy in Germany. It is considered by them as one of the best and most useful works for Catechists and Teachers. I am glad to learn that an English translation of this most excellent work is to be published by you, and I do not hesitate to say that the English edition will become as popular as the original German. It deserves strong recommendation.

Belleville, Ill., April 5. 1894.

† JOHN JANSSEN,
BISHOP OF BELLEVILLE.

I like extremely the Chapters I have read of Dr. KNECHT'S Bible Narrative and Commentary. With an admirable method he combines with the Narrative brief explanatory notes, which he follows up with suitable reflections. To a Catechist in want of a Manual for teaching Bible History this work will be found invaluable.

St. Mary's Seminary, Oscott: Birmingham, March 8. 1894.

† EDWARD,
BISHOP OF BIRMINGHAM.

KNECHT'S "Practical Commentary" is an excellent and useful book. It is written in an interesting, methodical, and instructive manner. I consider it as eminently calculated to inspire its readers with a real love for Holy Scripture and to show them, as Cardinal Vaughan says, in what ways the

Inspired Writings are of a practical use to Christian life. Such a book ought to be a welcome and revered guest in all Catholic families, and it deserves to occupy a place of honour in the libraries of catechists, teachers and priests. I strongly recommend it to the Faithful and Clergy of my Archdiocese.

Calcutta, April 2. 1895.   † *PAUL, S. J.,*
                                          ARCHBISHOP OF CALCUTTA.

I consider Dr. KNECHTS "Practical Commentary" one of the best handbooks of its kind. Its admirable method accounts for its great popularity. I shall continue to recommend it to my priests and teachers.

Fort Chapel, Bombay, June 14. 1895.

                                   † *THEOD. DALHOFF, S. J.,*
                                        ARCHBISHOP OF BOMBAY.

Allow me to take the opportunity of assuring you that Dr. KNECHTS Commentary on Holy Scripture is well known to me as a most valuable aid both to the catechist and the preacher, and I shall be only fulfilling a pleasant duty in bringing it before the notice of the Clergy. The fact that this English Edition is taken from the 16th German edition is a sufficient guarantee that the book is up to date, and adds very materially to its usefulness in the hands of the Clergy.

Bishop's House, Middlesbrough, November 13. 1901.

                                          † *RICHARD,*
                                  BISHOP OF MIDDLESBROUGH.

PREFACE
TO THE FIRST ENGLISH EDITION.

I.

IN no country, perhaps, has the study of Catechetics made such rapid strides, or its importance been so much appreciated, as in Germany. That country can boast of a band of writers who have enriched the world with a most valuable catechetical literature, treating the subject in a way at once scientific and practical. Gruber, Krawutzcky, Overberg, Barthel, Hirschfelder, and Benda are names deservedly honoured by those who can appreciate the importance of Catechetics; but more honourable still are the names of Schuster and Mey, to which must now be added the name of Dr. KNECHT, Auxiliary Bishop of the Archdiocese of Freiburg, the author of several pamphlets on state education and the school question, but better known as the author of the *Practical Commentary*, which entitles him to a place in the front rank of Catechists. Besides issuing Catechisms and Histories, these writers have done what in them lay to elevate Catechetics into a science, and to build it up from a solid foundation. They were quick to see that Catechetics is both a science and an art, and that like every other science it must rest on certain broad principles, and move along certain fixed lines. They recognized that Catechisms must be constructed not at hap-hazard, but on a definite plan and principle, and according to rule. Hence, for years past, the principles underlying Catechetics, its various branches — e. g. Bible History and Catechism — and their mutual interdependence, the catechetical method itself — viz. the mode of imparting the several branches, and the rules to be followed by the Catechist — all, in a word, that goes to constitute the science, has passed through the sieve of exhaustive discussion.

And where do we stand in England? Have we advanced thus far? Or have we so much as grasped the truth that Catechetics is a science at all? On looking into the dictionary I found, indeed, the word Catechetics, but it was marked with an obelus or death-mark, to show that it was either dying or dead. The thing is not, perhaps, quite as lifeless as its name; but if Catechetics, as a science, still barely lives, it is the utmost that can be said. I am far from saying that there is a lack of earnestness amongst us, or that we have no experienced Catechists who have attained a fair, or, if you will, a large measure of success. Nor am I insinuating that we are not alive to the vast consequences with which success or failure in catechizing is fraught for the future. On the contrary, the steady, if slow, growth of a catechetical literature amongst us points to a growing interest in the subject, and a deepening sense of its importance. All this, however, while proving that we are in point of fact catechizing, only serves to bring out in greater prominence the fact that we are still without the science. Are our tools rusty? Are our weapons broken or blunted? In a word, are our methods right or wrong? Are the instruments we are using adapted to the purpose for which they are intended? Are our Catechisms correctly adjusted, that is, are they set in a manner best calculated to secure their aim? All these are questions on which our future success turns, and which clamour for an answer. If our methods and our instruments are perchance wrong, we are but wasting our energies in attempting to naturalize mistakes, by forming them into a regular system. And what answer can be given to these questions? Until lately no answer has been attempted, even if the question has been asked. But recently an enterprising clerical journal, *Pastoralia* by name, has been rife with discussions that have yet only touched the fringe of these great questions; still I am not without hopes that when the mass of nebulous matter condenses, it may prove to be the beginning of a solid catechetical system.

We in England, then, seem to be just entering on the preliminary stage of discussion. In Germany the stage of discussion has long been passed. And, it will naturally be asked, has the discussion proved as barren of practical fruit as many German discussions have undoubtedly been? What has been the net result? Is any advantage likely to accrue from a discussion? Is not the catechetical system that is stereotyped in practice good enough? These are, I submit, questions that may be profitably discussed, even if the discussion entail no change. At any rate, it can do no harm, if it only strengthen our self-assurance that we are travelling on the right road. For it is not a little singular that the Germans, who have discussed these matters, and we, who have not, move in many respects on totally distinct planes. The Germans, for instance, use a graduated series of Catechisms. There are lower Catechisms, middle Catechisms, and upper Catechisms. In England.

on the other hand, we have practically but one Catechism, which is learnt alike by infants on the gallery, and by youths in the upper forms. Is it better to have one Catechism or a graduated series adapted to the several capacities of those who use them?[1] Surely, it would not be futile to discuss the respective merits or demerits of the two systems. For without presuming to say that either is better than the other, I may safely affirm that ours is not so obviously superior as to be outside the pale of discussion.

Another question closely bound up with the former is to determine what should be the setting and frame-work and general characteristics of a Catechism. Should a Catechism, in a word, be a *Summa Theologica* in miniature? a compendium of Theology? a condensed essence of theological treatises? Should it be couched in technical language? Should it bristle with definitions? Should the definitions be framed with such studied accuracy that the most fastidious philosopher shall be unable to detect the slightest flaw or imperfection? Should they be such that "only a philosopher can read them without a groan"? Or should a Catechism be a *religious primer?* Should its language be plain and simple, but accurate withal, though without straining after minute shades of accuracy? Should there be more explanations and fewer definitions? By way of illustrating the two methods I will transcribe two answers to the question: What is God? One answer occurs in the English Catechism, the other in Deharbe's Small Catechism, a translation of which is extensively used in the United States.

ENGLISH CATECHISM.	DEHARBE'S CATECHISM.
What is God?	What is God?
God is the supreme Spirit, who alone exists of Himself and is infinite in all perfections.	God is the Lord and Master of heaven and earth, from whom all good things come.

The English definition is made up of a number of ideas of such a hard metaphysical cast as to be wholly impervious to the ordinary mind, to say nothing of the child-mind. Nay, it may be affirmed without exaggeration that only those who have undergone a philosophical and a theological training can ever hope to understand it. The very explanation involves a course of theology. For the definition is the whole treatise *De Deo* in a nut-shell. Deharbe's answer immediately stoops to lowly intelligences, and thereby it stoops to conquer. Being adapted to the capacity of children, it will give them, at least, some idea of God, whereas the English definition cannot but leave a blank. And

---

[1] One and the same Catechism might serve for all grades, if it were printed with some distinction analogous to large and small type.

yet, as Frassinetti rightly contends, the first and chiefest step in catechizing is to give children a grand and exalted idea of God. Even the
Middle Catechisms do not require their pupils to soar to such metaphysical heights as we expect our infants to scale.

To some it will seem that both methods are right, if each be kept
in its place: that we need both a digest of theology and a religious
primer. At the same time it is respectfully insisted that the two works
are so different in scope und material that any attempt to fuse them
into one is foredoomed to failure. Surely, all must allow that religious
teaching comes first, theological explanation a long way second, and
theological terms are to be admitted only when they cannot be kept out.

Thus we have again veered round to the previous question: whether
it is better to have one Catechism or several? Those who maintain the
necessity of having several Catechisms, or several grades in the one
Catechism, can at all events appeal to the example of St. Paul, who
prescribed milk for the weak and solid food for the strong.

There is yet a third point on which we need light, and that is the
disposition and order in which the material should be set. In what
order should the Catechism be arranged? On a metaphysical or a practical plan? The order followed in the English Catechism is severely metaphysical, and consequently children do not learn till late many things
that they require to know early. Take, for instance, the Sacrament of
Penance and the Christian's Daily Exercise. These occur in the latter
part of the Catechism. And yet, children require these long before
this stage in the Catechism is reached, that is, if the present order be
followed. And what is the result? That children have to be learning
two parts of the Catechism concurrently: one for school-work, and
another to fit them for the Sacraments they are about to receive. Thus
the school-work is a drag on the Sacraments, and the Sacraments a
drag on the school-work, whereas they should be a mutual help one to
the other. A question proper to be discussed in Catechetics is how
far this double system is a waste of energy, and how far it would be
advantageous to arrange the school Catechism on a more useful principle,
that is, broadly speaking, in the order in which it is required [1]. In the
Catechism for the Diocese of Rottenburg the Sacraments follow immediately on the articles of the Creed. This, at all events, is a step in
the right direction. For obviously children receive the Sacraments, and
therefore require to know about them, before they need a detailed
knowledge of the commandments. But still greater advance has been
made in the Diocese of Salford. In the manuals of Religious Instruction

---

[1] Catechisms of this kind are in use in the Dioceses of Birmingham and
Salford.

used in that diocese, and approved by Cardinal Vaughan when Bishop of Salford, the questions and answers are arranged, not in the mechanical order with which we are familiar in the ordinary Catechism, but in *subjects*. Here we have, I submit, a valuable hint which, if judiciously acted upon, cannot but greatly simplify the work of learning and, what is more important, of understanding the Catechism.

The incidental mention of the Catechism for the Diocese of Rotten-burg suggests another point — and it shall be the last — on which I wish now to touch. This Catechism has in common with our own one nota-ble feature. Underlying both is the remarkable principle of embodying the question in the answer. When this principle was first introduced into the English Catechism, it was looked upon as the golden key that would unlock the portals of knowledge. It was imagined that the auto-matic action of dovetailing the question into the answer would serve as a sort of plastic medium for transferring to the mind of the child the connexion between question and answer that exists on paper. The physic process by which this result was to be achieved was doubtless wrapped in mystery; but as an expedient for bridging over the abyss between mind and matter, the device was certainly ingenious. It looked very plausible, and no one could say that it might not succeed. Its short-lived existence, however, has but confirmed the old axiom that an automaton will never produce life or intelligence. No one nowadays dreams that it has realized the great expectations that were formed from it. Nay, if I may speak as one less wise, I should say that the sound-ness of the principle is very widely called in question. Instead of smoothing away, as many object, it has multiplied the difficulty of learning the Catechism by increasing the matter of the answers, already in many cases too bulky [1]; and, what is far worse, by giving such undue prominence to the question, it has thrust the answer into the background, and thus the answer is smothered or strangled in the question. Now, which is the more important factor in a Catechism: the question or the answer? The answer to this question is too obvious to need stating; for surely there can be no doubt that the answer is of primary, and the question of only secondary importance. The question is of value only inasmuch as it draws out the answer. It is the answer, therefore, that should be to the front, and the question in the background. Whereas when the question is put in front, and the answer in the rear — when the question is made to overshadow the answer — the natural order is inverted.

---

[1] Bulky not merely in words, but chiefly in ideas. An answer should contain one fact or one idea; not a fact and a reason for the fact; or a fact and an ex-ception, and a reason for the exception. Questions with a multiplicity of ideas (e. g. What is an Indulgence?), if split up into several, may be made intelligible.

I have said that the English and Rottenburg Catechisms share this principle in common. But, after all, the agreement between the two Catechisms is only apparent. For there is this difference between the two, that in the English Catechism the question was framed before the answer, whereas in the Rottenburg Catechism the answer was framed before the question. Thus in the latter the true principle appears as a living force.

This is a matter of greater import than at first blush it may seem. Not only is this mode of procedure a courageous assertion of the true principle on which I have been insisting; not only is the true proportion between question and answer thereby observed; but it also gives us a glimpse of yet another truth which we seem barely to have realized: viz. that answers gain in clearness and directness when they are unhampered by the stilted phraseology of a preformed question. How much plainer and simpler would Catechisms be, if all were constructed on this plan! Still, if the Rottenburg principle is right, we may reasonably go a step farther and ask, how far it is advisable to have stereotyped questions at all. Will the Catechism of the future — if Catechism it can be called — consist merely of sets of plain simple consecutive statements? That some chapters in the Catechism lose in effectiveness by being put in the form of question and answer, is to me painfully evident. Take, for instance, the last chapter — the Christian's Daily Exercise. Will anyone say that the beautiful instructions therein contained would not be far more telling, if written in the form of pithy childlike statements? But, as they stand, they are positively handicapped by the questions to which they form a pendant. And it is to be feared that, in consequence, children often think of the duty inculcated only in connexion with its question in the Catechism.

2.

Leaving the domain of general Catechetics, we now come to that branch which is the subject-matter of the present volume, viz. Bible History. And, first of all, it may be asked: what place does Bible History hold in a course of religious instruction? Bible History is not the foundation on which religious instruction rests, nor the centre round which it revolves, nor the goal towards which it tends. Our religion centres in our faith, which is not a condensed extract from Bible History, but comes from the Church. Not Bible History, then, but the teaching of the Church must, on Catholic principles, be at once the beginning, middle and end of religious instruction. Hence Bible History, to claim a place in religious instruction, must do so only inasmuch as it bears on the doctrines of faith. If this principle be kept steadily in view, Bible History may be made to render most valuable service in religious instruction. The illustrative light it throws on doctrinal truths makes them more easily intelligible. They become invested with a concrete form, are clothed with flesh and blood, breathe the breath of life, and move like living truths before our eyes. In the Catechism, they appear as cold abstracts and mere outlines. Thus Bible History becomes an object-lesson in faith, a veritable pictorial Catechism. How powerfully, for instance, is the truth of an all-ruling Providence illustrated by the histories of Joseph and Abraham! What, again, is better calculated to teach the power of prayer than the stories of Moses praying while the Israelites fought, and of the Church praying for the imprisoned Peter? On the other hand, the fate of Judas and the rejection of Juda show forth, in all their hideous deformity, the terrible consequences of resistance to grace; while the history of the fall of Eve and of Peter brings out the necessity of avoiding dangerous occasions. In this way, Bible History at once proves and illustrates doctrinal truth. And it likewise develops and expands such truth. The Catechism tells us, indeed, how and why Christ suffered, but Bible History gives a full and detailed account of His sufferings, and so enables us better to realize the infinite love of God and the enormity of sin. The texts of Scripture that in the Catechism stand isolated and shorn of their context, are now seen in the light of their surroundings, and speak to us with a new force and meaning. Moreover, Bible History serves to complete the Catechism. The Catechism, for example, is silent about miracles, about God's mercy and forbearance, His patience and long-suffering. Of humility, and indeed of many other virtues, it is also silent, except that it arranges them over against the opposing vices. But would we learn their nature and properties, and how pleasing they are to God, it is to Bible History that we must turn. The Catechism is monosyllabic in stating the duties that children owe to their parents, masters to their servants, and vice versa; whereas the history of the centurion's servant, of Heli's sons, and of Tobias surrounds these duties with a halo of interpreting light. Again, Bible History exhibits religious truth in its bearing and action on the most varied states and conditions. Virtue and vice stand before us, with life-blood coursing through their veins, in attractive beauty or repellent ugliness. The Good Samaritan invites to mercy; Job, in his resignation to God's will, is a beacon-light to the sorrowing; the Apostles going forth from the scourges, and rejoicing that they were accounted worthy to suffer for Christ, invest with a startling reality the beatitude: Blessed are they that suffer persecution for justice' sake.

From all this it is clear that Bible History is not to be read, as too often it is, merely as a story-book; that it is to be studied, not on its own account, but because it imparts life and vigour, picturesqueness and comprehensiveness to religious instruction; because it elucidates, proves, enforces and illustrates the truths that go to make up religious instruction. But, as Dr. Knecht insists, in order that Bible History may be in a position to render these services, it must be "taught in the closest connexion with the Catechism". "Catechism and Bible History must mutually interpenetrate [1], for only in this way is a systematic course of religious instruction possible". Catechism and Bible History must go hand in hand, but Catechism must be in the van. Catechism is the guiding principle, and Bible History its hand-maid.

These are the principles, weighty though elementary, on which Dr. Knecht and all writers on Catechetics are generally agreed. And how does practice harmonize with principles? Is practice attuned to principle? Or are the two in hopeless discord? To begin with, how many teachers have mastered the reason why Bible History has a place in religious instruction? How many, or how few, realize the fact that Bible History and Catechism should be "taught in the closest connexion"? And what percentage of those who have grasped this truth put it into practice? There is no denying the patent fact that, as a rule, the two are not taught concurrently, and are not made to run on parallel lines. Ten to one, the Bible History set down for a class in a given year has no connexion whatever with the doctrinal instruction of that year. Thus, while children are being instructed in the Holy Eucharist, their Scripture History turns on that singularly uninspiring period embraced by the reigns of the kings of Israel and Juda! All this comes from being enslaved to the chronological system. This is the root of the evil to which the axe must be laid. Forgetting the plain principle that should underlie the teaching of all Bible History, and utterly ignoring the profit or loss to the children, we have stumbled over the crooked idea that Bible History must be taught chronologically even in our poor schools. I am far from denying, nay, I affirm that a systematic course of Bible History should be given when time and facilities are not wanting, as in our upper schools and colleges. But in our poor schools, where the time barely suffices to give the necessary instruction and to drive it home with religious effect, a slavish adhesion to chronology is to sacrifice realities to figures. To talk of a systematic course in this sense, under such circumstances, is nothing short of preposterous. In the chronological system, Bible History cannot, except by a happy accident, enforce and illustrate the religious instruction. Far from being a help, it is a drawback. Instead of elucidating, it obscures. No longer the hand-maid, it seeks to be on an equality with the mistress. For

---

[1] "In inniger gegenseitiger Durchdringung".

religious instruction to succeed in its great purpose it must, as Dr. Knecht rightly says, be conducted on a "unitive" plan. The unit is the doctrinal instruction, with which the Bible History must be brought into line, unless we are to fly in the teeth of all our principles. Let me now briefly illustrate what I mean by this unification or concentration of subject that I am advocating, lest perhaps I be twitted with pulling down without attempting to build up. Instead, therefore, of teaching children who are being instructed in the Blessed Eucharist about the kings of Israel and Juda, I would teach them the Scripture History of the Blessed Eucharist, as in the following plan [1]:

THE HOLY EUCHARIST.

I. Types of the Holy Eucharist:
   1. The Sacrifice of Melchisedech.
   2. The Paschal Lamb.
   3. The Manna,
   4. The Food of Elias.
   5. The Jewish Sacrifices.
II. The Prophecy of Malachias.
III. Christ promises a new Sacrifice:
   1. At Jacob's Well.
   2. After the multiplication of the loaves.
IV. The Last Supper.—Institution of the Blessed Eucharist.
V. The two disciples going to Emmaus.
VI. Miracles illustrative of the Blessed Eucharist:
   1. Water made wine at Cana.
   2. Multiplication of loaves.
   3. Christ walking on the waters.
   4. The Transfiguration.

The important subject of the Church may be treated somewhat similarly.

THE CHURCH.
Part I. THE OLD TESTAMENT.

I. Introductory.
II. The Church a Family.
   1. Noe. The ark.
   2. Call of Abraham.—The promises to Abraham, Isaac and Jacob.
III. The Church a People.
   1. Moses.
   2. Giving of the Law.
   3. The Tabernacle.
   4. Entrance into the Promised Land.

---

[1] From *Scripture History for Schools* (No. 3). Approved for use in the Diocese of Birmingham.

IV. The Church a Kingdom.
  1. David.
  2. Solomon.—Building of the Temple.
  3. The kingdom broken up.
V. God promises to set up a New Kingdom.

PART II. THE GOSPELS.

VI. Introductory.
VII. Christ the King.—The Kingdom of God.
VIII. Parables on the Kingdom of God.
  1. The Hidden Treasure.
  2. The Pearl of Great Price.
  3. The Wheat and the Cockle.
  4. The Drag-net.
  5. The Leaven.
  6. The Mustard Seed.
  7. The Good Shepherd.
IX. Jesus calls Disciples.
X. The first Miraculous Draught of Fishes.
XI. Peter's Confession of Faith.—The Foundation of the Church of Christ.
XII. Christ promises that Peter's faith shall not fail.
XIII. The second miraculous Draught of Fishes. — Christ makes Peter Chief Shepherd.
XIV. The Mission of the Apostles.

PART III. HISTORY OF THE CHURCH AFTER OUR LORD'S ASCENSION.

XV. The Opening of the Church.
XVI. Peter cures the Lame Man.
XVII. The First Christians.
XVIII The Apostles work miracles; are imprisoned &c.
XIX. Conversion of St. Paul.
XX. Peter visits the Churches.
XXI. Peter's vision.—Cornelius.
XXII. Peter imprisoned and set free by an angel.
XXIII. The Council of Jerusalem.
XXIV. Primacy of St. Peter.—Summary.

In a word, the Scripture History should be grouped round the central doctrines of our faith.

3.

A subject largely discussed in Catechetics is the *method* of teaching Bible History. Catechists are now agreed that five factors go to make up the teaching of Bible History: 1. narrative, 2. explanation, 3. repetition, 4. commentary, 5. application. Not to be needlessly prolix, I assume that this is also the order in which they are to be taken. A few words must be said on each.

Narrative. The first stage in teaching Bible History is the narrative. The teacher *tells* the story briefly and pithily, in such a way, however, as to make the actors stand out as living beings, and enable the children to see with their eyes and hear with their ears what is said and done. This is what Fénelon called the "fundamental law" in teaching Bible History. Neglect or slip-shod observance of this rule is prolific in failures. And yet, in defiance of this "fundamental law", children are often set to learn the History *in the first instance* from a book! What is the result? The child, failing to understand the story aright at the outset, receives a blurred impression which is never wholly effaced. And no wonder. The negative was bad; and no amount of subsequent dilutions and retouchings will produce a good photograph from a bad negative. It is essential that the first impression should be a good one. If the child fails at first to catch the points of interest, it is bored by the story ever afterwards. But if the story is well told, the child's interest is awakened, and it is all ears to know something further. The narrative is the peg on which all that follows is to hang. Unless the nail be firmly driven in, it will not hold the picture; so unless the points of the story are clearly fixed in the child's mind, it is labour wasted to overlay it with explanations or to attach pendant commentaries.

Explanation. A story well told is half explained. In telling the story, hard words are, as far as possible, to be avoided; but from time to time, words and phrases, usages and customs that need explaining, will find their way into the story. This is all that Catechists mean by the explanation, viz., making clear all that is absolutely necessary for understanding the story aright. It does not mean branching off into learned digressions, or talking over the children's heads. All vapid display of learning confuses rather than explains.

Repetition. So far books have been on the shelf. And often they remain there much longer. Some teachers, taking their stand on high principles, rise to heights of virtuous indignation in denouncing all employment of Bible Histories as pernicious. Books, they say, degrade the learning of Bible History to the clumsiest mechanical operation, and deal a death-blow at intelligence. But surely this denunciation proceeds from a wrong conception of the time and place when books are to be used. If the children are made to learn the history in the first instance from a book, undoubtedly the objection has some force. Then, however, not books but wrong methods are to blame. How can the book rightly used be fatal to intelligence, since intelligence has been brought into play before the book is used at all? For surely it is bringing violence to bear against common sense to contend that reading a story after it has been understood, obliterates intelligence.

After the story has been told, the children open their books, and one or more read it aloud — the teacher adding any further explanations that may be necessary. Teachers — this is important — in telling the story should endeavour to adhere pretty closely to the words of the book. Otherwise, if the language differs notably from that in the book, the children, when reading the story for themselves, will be puzzled and perplexed. Considerable variety in language will only confuse them.

So far the children have listened to the story with attention, and have understood it. But the impression, like lines written in water, will quickly disappear, unless measures be taken to fix it in the memory. This is the next process. Our knowledge is co-extensive with our memory. We know as much or as little as we remember. Memory, says Hirschfelder, is the mortar that holds the bricks together. Without memory, the combined action of understanding, heart and will, can succeed in erecting only a pile of loose stones. Furthermore, many Catechists of note insist that the text should be committed to memory, word for word, at least by young children. Thus Alleker argues that a free reproduction is beyond the capabilities of all but advanced pupils, and that it is far easier for children to reproduce the matter in the form set before them. Hirschfelder truly observes that children are unequal to improving on the form given in the book, and that, when the lesson is not exacted word for word, the tendency, especially in the quicker and brighter children, is to learn it in the most slip-shod fashion. Perhaps time will throw light on this question. Meanwhile teachers may do much towards facilitating the by-heart and making it intelligent, by pointing out the natural divisions of the story, the connexion between the several parts, and so forth.

As regards the *repetition in class,* I cannot do better than give in substance Dr. Knecht's words: The repetition consists in the children telling the story independently, and in a connected fashion. It should be no parrot-prattle, no mechanical outpouring of sentences conned by rote; but the story should be told intelligently, with correct expression and emphasis. In particular, teachers should beware of letting the children either speak too quickly, or fall into a sing-song, drawling, or hum-drum style.

Commentary. Hitherto all our efforts have been concentrated on the Bible story in itself. The children have seized the right points of the story; they have learnt the course of events, and have gained an insight into the motives that impelled the actors in the drama; they understand the immediate meaning of the phrases in which the story is told. But the deeper meaning of the story is still hidden from them. The commentary is the key that opens the gate of this wider knowledge.

The Bible narrative is no longer to be viewed as a story, but as a revelation from God, disclosing God's will and God's attributes. Every Bible story contains dogmatic and moral truths. One might almost say that the events happened for the sake of the truths. To draw out these truths, and bring them vividly before the children, is the most important part of instruction in Bible History. And this is the function of the commentary. Thus the commentary brings out the *typical* character of persons and things; it unearths the truths buried in our Lord's parables; it unfolds the spiritual meaning underlying His miracles. But, most of all, it shows what bearing Bible stories have on doctrines of faith and morals, on the cultus and institutions of the Church. Thus the teacher has to hand an instrument which, if wisely used, is admirably adapted for deepening the religious knowledge and strengthening the religious convictions of the children, and for arming their faith at all points. Such is Dr. Knecht's account of the function of the commentary. And he goes on to point out the qualities that the commentary should have if it is to be effective. 1. It must be according to the mind of the Church, whom Christ has appointed to guard and expound Holy Scripture. The commentary is not intended for a platform on which the teacher can air his own crude opinions. 2. It must be catechetical. Both in matter and manner it must conform to the rules of Catechetics, i. e. it must be adapted to the class to which it is given. All platitudes, vague generalities, and scattered reflections wide of the mark are to be carefully shunned, as they leave only a nauseating effect. 3. The teacher must keep steadily in view the close connexion that should subsist between Bible History and religious instruction. On this point sufficient has already been said.

Application. On this last factor little need be said. It consists in holding up the mirror to nature; in making the children realize that the events recorded, though happening ten thousand miles away and some thousands of years back, have an interest and a concern for them, and are part and parcel of their own lives. The temptations and struggles, the falls and conversions, the unkept promises here depicted, are a reflection of our own conduct, and are written for our warning and encouragement and self-knowledge. Moreover, in the application, the truths elicited in the commentary are brought home to the individual child, and are held up to him as a rule of life and conduct.

4.

Such, in short, is the programme that Dr. Knecht has mapped out for himself in his *Practical Commentary.* A programme most inviting and comprehensive! To many, doubtless, it will appear too vast to be carried out successfully. But I have no hesitation in saying that Dr. Knecht's success is as great as his programme is vast. His work first saw the light in 1883, and since then twelve large editions have been exhausted. This fact alone speaks volumes for his success. His work marks an immense advance on anything that has been published in this country. In fact, we have nothing in any way like it; nothing that approaches it within a measurable distance. Our text-books, at their best, give but a good narrative; at their worst, I fear to say what they do. But best and worst alike have entered into an unholy covenant to give next to nothing beyond the narrative. Now, thanks to Dr. Knecht and his translator, we have a work that, in addition to a good narrative, supplies a good explanation and an excellent commentary. The very idea that Bible History needs an explanation and a commentary will, I suspect, come to many like a bolt from the blue. But I trust that after the appearance of Dr. Knecht's work we shall be ashamed to issue any more Bible Histories in the good old dry-as-dust style.

The narrative in the *Practical Commentary* is Dr. Schuster's Bible History. This work itself has already been translated into eighteen languages, and has run into I know not how many editions. Let it, however, be noted that the *Practical Commentary* is not inextricably bound up with any particular form of narrative, and it will be found equally serviceable with any other narrative that teachers may prefer to take as the groundwork.

In particular, I would call attention to the excellent "Concordance between Holy Scripture and the Catechism", as it is called, given in the Appendix. In it the teacher will find ready to hand an invaluable repertory of Bible stories and explanations for illustrating his catechetical instructions.

In conclusion, I wish to re-echo with all earnestness the words of a writer in the *Schweizer Pastoralblatt*: "I consider this *Commentary* the best and most useful hand-book of its kind . . . I am happy to think that every day strengthens my conviction of its great worth, and I should like to see it in the hands of every priest and every teacher." I will only add that it is indispensable to every teacher who would be abreast of his work. To priests it will be most useful, not only in the school, but also in the pulpit, as it supplies-most suggestive material for courses of sermons. And I make bold to affirm that no one, be he priest or teacher, can take up without profit this excellent manual, not the least merit of which is that it has imparted a thoroughly *religious* character to the teaching of Bible History.

MICHAEL F. GLANCEY.

STANLEY HOUSE, ECCLESHALL.
    May 17. 1894.

PREFACE

TO THE SECOND ENGLISH EDITION.

———

WHEN the first English edition was published in 1894, the original German work had reached the twelfth edition; it is now in the eighteenth. The present English edition has been revised according to the sixteenth German edition, and has been as far as possible brought into line therewith, though some freedom has been allowed in adding, altering and omitting portions, in order to adapt them to the circumstances of English readers. The passages of Scripture on which the narrative is based are indicated at the head of each chapter; all notes are placed at the foot of the page; the illustrations are new; and various improvements in matter and form have been effected in both text and notes.

The Revision of the present edition is due to the Right Rev. Monsignor V. J. SCHOBEL, D. D., whose judgment upon Bishop KNECHT'S Commentary deserves to be here recorded. He writes: "I have read the Commentary with genuine pleasure and profit. How it brings home to one the real scope and purpose of the Bible! 'For what things soever were written, were written for our learning: that, through patience and the comfort of the Scriptures, we might have hope' (Rom. 15, 4). The Practical Commentary will prove the very best antidote to the poison of Biblical Criticism now spreading among the masses. Its value, therefore, goes far beyond its immediate scope."

MICHAEL F. GLANCEY.

St. Augustine's, Solihull
May 1. 1901.

PREFACE

TO THE THIRD ENGLISH EDITION.

THE statements made in the Preface to the Second apply with still greater force to the Third Edition. From the many changes, chiefly verbal, that have been introduced, it is hoped that the work will gain in clearness and conciseness. The present Edition, like its predecessor, has had the advantage of being revised by Monsignor Schobel.

MICHAEL F. GLANCEY.

INSTITUTE OF ST. CHARLES, BEGBROKE, OXFORD.
May 1. 1910.

CONTENTS.

FIRST PART.

THE OLD TESTAMENT.

HISTORY OF THE PRIMITIVE AGES OF MAN.

THE TIME FROM ADAM TO ABRAHAM.

HISTORY OF THE PEOPLE OF ISRAEL.

I. EPOCH: THE TIME OF THE PATRIARCHS.

II. Epoch: THE AGE OF MOSES.

III. Epoch: JOSUE AND THE JUDGES.

IV. Epoch: THE KINGS.

V. EPOCH: THE BABYLONIAN CAPTIVITY.

VI. EPOCH: JUDÆA AFTER THE BABYLONIAN CAPTIVITY.

SECOND PART.

THE NEW TESTAMENT.

FIRST SECTION.

HISTORY OF JESUS CHRIST.

SECOND SECTION.

THE ACTS OF THE APOSTLES.

APPENDIX:

LIST OF ILLUSTRATIONS.

Frontispiece: Chapel of the Holy Sepulchre at Jerusalem.

A Practical
Commentary on
HOLY
SCRIPTURE

FIRST PART
THE OLD TESTAMENT

HISTORY OF THE PRIMITIVE AGES OF MAN.

THE TIME FROM ADAM TO ABRAHAM.

(About 4000—2100 B. C.)

CHAPTER I.

THE CREATION OF THE WORLD.

[Gen. 1, 1 to 2, 3.]

IN the beginning[1] God created heaven and earth[2]. The earth was void[3] and empty[4]; darkness was on the face of the deep[5], and the Spirit of God[6] moved over the waters. And God said[7]: "Be light made!" and light was made. This was the first day[8].

---

[1] *In the beginning* of time.

[2] *Heaven and earth.* i. e. both the visible and invisible worlds. This sentence relates to the whole of creation generally; what follows, to the creation of the earth in particular.

[3] *Void.* Which means that it was an unformed mass, all confusion and chaos.

[4] *Empty.* Without life in it, or without any plants, animals, or men on it.

[5] *Deep.* i. e. on the unformed mass of primeval matter. This mass was wrapped in gloom and darkness; and, being soft and fluid, is styled "the waters".

[6] *Spirit of God.* i. e. God, who is a pure Spirit in opposition to the unformed and lifeless mass of mere matter, breathed upon it in order to give life, movement and form to it, and to prepare it for a dwelling-place of men and beasts.

[7] *Said.* i. e. commanded.

[8] *First day.* The sacred writer divides the whole work of Creation, as we now see it before our eyes, into six days followed by the Sabbath or day of rest, in order to impress upon his readers that man should follow the example of God, and work six days and rest in God on the seventh. He consequently apportions a work to each day. By "day" he means exactly the same as we mean, namely, a space of time consisting of twelve hours of work and twelve of rest.* God Himself does not work in time, but He can be likened to a man who works six days and finishes all

---

* On June 30, 1909 the Pontifical Biblical Commission issued a response stating that the word "day" in the first chapter of *Genesis* can be taken "either in its proper sense as a natural day, or in the improper sense of a certain space of time." (D 2128). —*Publisher*, 2003.

3

On the second day God said: "Let there be a firmament[1] made amidst the waters; and let it divide[2] the waters from the waters." And it was so[3]. God called the firmament heaven[4].

On the third day God said: "Let the waters that are under the heaven[5] be gathered into one place[6]; and let the dry land[7] appear." And it was so done. God called the dry land earth; and the gathered waters, seas. He also said: "Let the earth[8] bring forth the green herb, and such as may seed, and the fruit-tree yielding fruit after its kind." And it was so done[9].

The fourth day God said: "Let there be lights[10] made in the firmament of heaven, to divide the day and the night, and

---

his work in one week. As to the real space of time which the formation of the world required and about which Geologists inquire, the sacred writer says nothing at all. His dramatic narrative is quite independent of it.

[1] *Firmament.* In other words, the atmosphere which surrounds our earth to the height of about 45 miles, and looks to our eyes like a blue dome.

[2] *Divide.* The firmament was to divide one part of the waters from the other part in this way: God made a considerable body of water to ascend, in the form of moisture (clouds), into the atmosphere, thus separating it from the water which remains and flows on the earth.

[3] *It was so.* i. e. it was as God had commanded.

[4] *Heaven.* This is not the heaven where the angels and saints dwell, and contemplate God. A distinction must be made between that heaven, and the visible, natural heaven, i. e. the firmament.

[5] *Under the heaven.* i. e. below the atmosphere, or, in other words, the waters that are on the earth.

[6] *One place.* This one place is the great ocean, out of the midst of which the five parts of the earth rise.

[7] *Dry land.* God made the water to gather itself together into rivers, lakes, and seas, and the dry land to appear. How this happened is described in Psalm 103, 6 and 8: "Above the mountains shall the waters stand. . . . The mountains ascend, and the plains descend into the place which Thou hast founded for them." The whole earth was covered with water. Then at the command of God, certain parts of the earth's surface raised themselves up. These became dry, because the water ran off them; and the lower parts of the earth's surface, towards which the water flowed, became the sea. About a quarter of the surface of the globe (accurately 27 per cent) is dry land, and nearly three quarters (accurately 73 per cent), water.

[8] *Earth.* Which was now dry.

[9] *So done.* God made plants of every kind to grow out of the dry ground, and gave them the power of producing their own seed. From these seeds there sprang new plants, and thus the world of plants never died out.

[10] *Lights.* God made the sun, the moon, and the stars, to give light and warmth to the earth. The heavenly bodies were to serve also as measures of time. The rising of the sun brings day to the earth, and its setting, night. According to the relative position of the sun and moon to the earth, time is divided into years, and seasons, and months.

let them be for signs, and for seasons, and for days and years."
And it was so done. God made the sun, moon, and countless
stars, and set them in the firmament of heaven, to shine upon
the earth, and to rule the day and the night.

The fifth day God said: "Let the waters bring forth the
creeping creatures having life, and the fowl that may fly over
the earth under the firmament of heaven." And God created
fish and birds of every kind, and He blessed them saying: "Increase and multiply." [1]

On the sixth day God said: "Let the earth bring forth the
living creature [2] in its kind: cattle and creeping things, and beasts
of the earth according to their kinds." And it was so done. At
last God created man, and gave him dominion over all the rest.
And God saw all the works that He had made, and they were
very good [3].

The seventh day God rested [4], and He blessed [5] that day
and made it holy.

COMMENTARY.

The beautiful Order of Creation. The very manner and order in
which the sacred writer relates the creation, serves to bring out the
order and mutual relation of things created. God had already created
light on the first day, but this light was not the light of the sun. It
was on the fourth day that God made the sun, to be the giver of light
to the earth. God made light first, because without light and without
warmth, which is connected with it, there could be no growth, no life,
no order in nature.

---

[1] *Multiply.* They were to multiply of themselves, ever increasing in number.
As plants propagate themselves by means of their seeds, so birds and fishes can,
by the blessing of God, lay eggs, which in their turn become birds and fishes.

[2] *Living creature.* i. e. God created the mammals which are the highest race
of beasts. God first created the lower and then the higher classes of animals; and,
last of all, He created man, the highest of all visible creatures. How God created
man, will be told in the third chapter.

[3] *Very good.* Everything was as God's goodness and wisdom desired it to be;
everything fulfilled the end for which He had created it. He disposed everything
in such a way that nothing could be better or more exactly adapted to its purpose
than it was.

[4] *Rested.* Man requires rest after he has worked hard, because he is tired.
Can God then be tired? No, God could create thousands of worlds, without being
tired. The words, 'He rested', mean this: that after the sixth day, after the creation
of man, God created no new kind of being.

[5] *Blessed.* He ordained that this day should bring a blessing both to soul
and body on those who keep it holy.

God made the atmosphere on the second day, because neither plants, nor animals, nor men can live without air. Sound also is impossible without air, so that without it there could have been neither speech nor hearing.

On the third day God made the earth to be dry, and plants to grow on it. But plants, to live and thrive, require something besides light and air. Therefore it was that God had already on the second day caused part of the water to remain in the air, to supply the plants with moisture from above, either by means of dew or rain.

The works of the first three days, and those of the last three, are thus related to each other as the general to the particular, or as the place and its furniture.

1st day. The light.	4th day. The bodies of light.
2nd day. The atmosphere which divided the waters.	5th day. The inhabitants of the air and water: the birds and fishes.
3rd day. The dry land.	6th day. The inhabitants of the dry land: the beasts and man.

Time began with the world. Once nothing existed but the Eternal God alone. "Before the mountains were made, or the earth and the world was formed, from eternity and to eternity Thou art, God" (Ps. 89, 2). Why does not the Psalmist say, 'Thou wast, God', instead of 'Thou art, God?' Because God is Eternal. He is not subject to the changes of time, for with God there is no past, no future, nothing but an everlasting present. "I am who am", God said to Moses (Exod. 3, 14). God exists of and by Himself. Everything else is made by God.

God is Almighty. God created the whole world, visible and invisible, material and spiritual, out of nothing by His almighty will. His almighty power is manifested to us in creation. By His word, that is, by His will, He called into existence the earth, moon, and the whole, to us immeasurable universe, with its millions and millions of heavenly bodies. "God spoke, and they were made; He commanded, and they were created" (Ps. 32, 9).

God works unceasingly. What then do the words, 'He rested on the seventh day', mean? They mean that God rested from this particular work, i. e. from creating, because the universe was finished and complete; but God does not cease from the work of conservation and of natural and supernatural providence. Our Lord says: "My Father works till now and I work" (New Test. XXVI). God is continually working for the good of His creatures, for only He who called the world into existence can sustain and govern it. If Almighty God were to withdraw His hand from the world, at that moment it would collapse and fall into ruin. Every day, every hour of life is a gift of Almighty God.

The Sabbath. With the creation of man, God's plan of creation was completed, and the great work of His creative love was crowned; for man is the most perfect of visible creatures. Then God rested, and appointed the seventh day for man's rest in Him. On the Sabbath, man was to contemplate the wonders of creation, and the preservation and government of the world, and to praise and thank God. On this account the seventh day is also called "the Lord's day", i. e. the day set apart for the service and worship of God. On this day we ought to put aside all worldly business, and think only of our souls and their welfare, for in God alone can our souls find peace and rest. The commandment to keep holy the Sabbath is the oldest commandment that there is. Ever since the world has stood as it is, this commandment has stood with it. The very fact that the sacred writer represents God as working a week, makes Him our pattern and example, and implies a commandment for us to do the same. The law was thus given by God at the creation of the world, and hence it is that among all, even heathen, nations we find one day of rest observed in the week. It is a great impiety to desecrate God's day.

The Nature of God. God is described as a Spirit, existing from all eternity, having life in Himself and being the cause of all created life; an omnipotent Spirit who by the sole act of His will gives existence and life to His creatures. God the Creator of heaven and earth is one God, not two or three. In the Old Testament it was above all necessary to inculcate this unity of God. The people of Israel were not yet ripe to learn the full truth of one God in three persons. But, all the same, in several passages of the Old Testament it is, as it were, hinted that there are more persons than one in God, e. g. in the first part of the history of the creation: "The Spirit of God moved over the waters."

The Wisdom of God. Holy Scripture, or, in other words, the Holy Spirit ~~Ghost~~, says explicitly that all that God made was very good. Short-sighted man should not, therefore, be audacious enough to criticise God's work. Almighty God made everything to fulfil the end for which He destined it. The whole of creation testifies to the wisdom of God, but I will call your attention only to one or two instances. Rivers and streams, many of which are of considerable breadth, are ceaselessly flowing into the sea, carrying into it, even in one single day, a tremendous volume of water. This goes on all the year round, and has been going on for thousands of years, and yet the sea does not overflow! How is this? God has so made it that as much water is incessantly rising into the air from the sea as is being poured into it. But how is it, then, that the streams and rivers do not dry up? Whence comes that volume of water which they are continuously pouring into the sea? The mists and clouds which rise from the sea are driven over the land by the wind, and fall back on the earth in the form of either dew, fog, rain or snow. This moisture collects in the ground and forms springs. These springs feed the streams and rivers which carry the water back again to the sea. It is owing to this continuous circulation of water that the sea does not overflow, or the rivers dry up. Moreover, those damp exhalations supply the air with that moisture which is necessary to the life of men and beasts, and to the growth of plants. One thing more. You know that water turns foul when it remains for some time without being stirred. How is it that though it is shut in one place, the water of the sea never turns foul? The goodness of God has provided against this by the constant motion of the sea. Twice every day the water flows from the centre of the sea towards the shore, and back again. Besides this, from time to time God sends winds and storms which stir the sea to its very depths. Such phenomena as these show us the wonderful wisdom manifested in the creation and preservation of the world. In like manner all other creatures bear witness to the wisdom of God. Bees, ants, ears of corn, leaves of the trees—in a word, all things teach us to admire His wisdom. Whether we contemplate nature in its greater or lesser aspects, we must exclaim with David: "How great are Thy works, O Lord! Thou hast made all things in wisdom. The earth is filled with Thy riches" (Ps. 103, 24)[1].

The infinite Greatness and Majesty of God are also revealed to us by creation. Think how enormous this earth is! It is 24,899 miles in circumference; the total area of its surface covers 197,000,000 of square miles, the corresponding volume is 260,000 millions of cubic miles. Enormous as this seems, the sun is 1,400,000 times as large as the earth, though it is not so dense. The number of stars, most of which can be seen only through a telescope, amounts to millions, though their number cannot be accurately fixed by man. The nearest fixed star is about twenty billions of miles away from us. If, then, the universe is so great, how much greater must He be who called all these spheres into existence, and who keeps and sustains them in space, pointing out its path to each one! He "telleth the number of the stars, and calleth them all by their names. Great is our Lord, and great is His power, and of His wisdom there is no number" (Ps. 146, 4. 5). Full of awe and reverence we ought to pray in some such words as these: "Great God, we praise Thee! We praise Thy power, O Lord! The earth bows down before Thee in wonder at Thy works! Even as Thou wast in all time, so wilt Thou be to all eternity. Heaven and earth, sky and sea are full of Thy glory. All things are Thine!"

APPLICATION. God being so infinitely great and wise, we ought to be filled with the deepest reverence for His divine majesty. He is, indeed, the Eternal, the Most High, the Creator

---

[1] This theme is well treated in the so-called *Bridgewater Treatises*.

and Lord of the whole universe. And yet how little reverence you have borne Him hitherto! Have you not often prayed to Him carelessly? Have you never dishonoured His holy name? Have you not often transgressed His commandments? Firmly resolve, then, that you will for the future honour the Lord your God more, and serve Him more zealously. We pay honour to God by often thinking about Him and by adoring Him with reverence and devotion. St Patrick used to worship God on his knees three hundred times every day. Think more about your Lord and Creator, both to-day and for the future, and pray to Him devoutly and from your heart. Let everything you look at impel you to say thus to yourself: 'I praise Thee, O great God, and worship Thy power and wisdom. As many stars as there are in the heavens, as many flowers as grow in the field, as many leaves as there are on the trees, as many drops as there are in the ocean, so many times may God be praised and magnified!"

God made the earth to be the dwelling-place of man, and has adorned it for him with divine prodigality. He has given us much more than is necessary for our existence. Are the numberless flowers which grow, necessary for life? Could we not live without the many sorts of fruit that there are? Take to heart, then, how good and generous God is towards us. Thank Him heartily for His gifts, and resolve that you will from this day forward say your grace before and after meals very devoutly.

CHAPTER II.

CREATION AND FALL OF THE ANGELS.

[Gen. 3, 1 to 5, 24. Apoc. 20, 1—2. Jude 6 ff.]

BESIDES the visible world, God also created an invisible world, namely, innumerable spirits, called angels. They all came forth from the hand of God good [1] and holy, being endowed with excellent gifts [2] of nature and grace, whereby they might persevere in that state and thus obtain everlasting happiness in union with God. But they did not all continue in that state, for, being possessed of free will, a great many of them abused it, lost the grace of God, and became wicked. They rebelled against God—Lucifer, their leader, saying: "We shall be like unto

---

[1] *Good.* They loved and wished for only what was good. and pleased God.

[2] *Gifts.* God has endowed them with such pre-eminent gifts that they are superior to all other created beings. Their chief gifts are sublime understanding, great strength, and, above all, sanctifying grace.

the Most High; we will place our throne above the stars." Then
there was a great strife in heaven. Michael[1] and the other angels
who had remained faithful to God, fought against the bad and
rebellious spirits, whose chief is now called Satan, or the devil.
The bad angels were conquered, and cast from heaven down to
hell. The angels who remained faithful[2] were rewarded with everlasting happiness[3]. They ever see the face of God in heaven.

COMMENTARY.

The angelic nature, and the infinite perfections of God. The angels
are spirits; God is also a Spirit, but there is an infinite difference
between Almighty God and the highest angel. The angels have a
sublime understanding, great wisdom, and much knowledge, but their
understanding, wisdom, and knowledge are finite. Their wills are holy,
and are much more powerful than ours, but they are not infinitely
holy, nor are the angels almighty. They have received all their great
qualities from God. He alone has His perfections of Himself, and from
all eternity: the angels were created by God in the beginning of time,
and received everything from Him. The angels are, indeed, wondrous-
ly perfect, but they are not infinitely perfect. Their perfections
have a limit, a measure, a number. God's perfections, on the other
hand, are infinitely great, without limit, measure, or number.

The office of the Angels. Like everything else the angels were
created for the honour and glory of God. They love and praise God,
and fulfil His holy will without ceasing. Hence the meaning of the
words in the Our Father: "Thy will be done on earth as it is in
heaven." The name of angel signifies messenger or envoy; this name
is given to the good spirits, because God sends them to take care
of men and make known to them His will. The angels, being pure
spirits, cannot be seen with our bodily eyes, but if it is God's will
that men should see and hear them, when they are sent as messengers
from Him, they are able to assume a human form. Take, for example,
the holy archangel Gabriel who appeared to Zachary and to our Lady.

Pictures of Angels. You have often seen pictures of the holy
angels. They are often represented as boys with wings and playing

---

[1] *Michael.* An archangel, and the leader of the good angels.

[2] *Faithful.* i. e. to the Lord God.

[3] *Everlasting happiness.* The angels had been happy from the beginning, but
their happiness was not yet final and complete, because it could be lost. As we
have seen, it was lost by the bad angels. But after the good angels had proved
steadfast, and had overthrown the bad angels, they received as a reward the
supernatural and eternal happiness of heaven, which they could never again lose.

on harps; or again, the holy archangel Gabriel is represented as a youth with wings, holding a lily in his hand, and with a glory round his head. Why should they be drawn like that? They are represented as boys or youths, because they never grow old, but are everlastingly young, and are immortal. The wings signify that the angels are swift as thought, and fulfil God's commands quickly and willingly. The harps are to remind us that the angels ceaselessly sing God's praises. The lily signifies their purity, and the glory, their heavenly splendour. Very often angels are pictured as children's heads without bodies, to signify that they have understanding and free-will, but that they are spirits without bodies.

God is good. Of His love God created the angels, and loaded them with natural and supernatural gifts.

God is just. God's justice is manifested by the punishment of the bad angels and the reward of the good. How did God punish the bad angels? For how long must they remain in hell? For ever and ever! They must suffer everlasting torments! They are rejected by God and are banished from Him for ever and ever! They hardened themselves against Him, therefore repentance was impossible. "God spared not the angels that sinned: but delivered them, drawn down by infernal ropes to the lower hell, unto torments to be reserved unto judgment" (2 Pet. 2, 4).

The evil of mortal sin. God punishes us according to our deserts: He never punishes us too severely. If, therefore, He condemned the fallen angels to the eternal torments of hell, we can see what a terrible evil sin is in His sight. One single mortal sin deserves everlasting punishment.

The consequences of sin. Just think what befell the angels through sin! Before their fall they were the friends and beloved of God, most beautiful, most holy, full of the love of what is good, and rich in their happiness and glory. But since their fall they have been enemies of God, horrible, hideous, and eternally miserable devils! Who, after contemplating this ruin caused by sin, could possibly think that sin, and especially mortal sin, is a trifle which God will not deal with severely? No! mortal sin, far from being a trifle, is the greatest of all evils. It changed angels into devils, and cast them into hell!

Pride. What was the cause of the fallen angels' disobedience? Instead of giving glory to God, from whom they had received all things, they became proud of their great gifts, and, with their leader, said: "We will ascend above the heights of the clouds, we will be like the Most High" (Is. 14, 14). Therefore, Holy Scripture says: "Pride is the beginning of all sin" (Ecclus. 10, 15).

Happiness of the Angels. Almighty God richly rewarded those angels who remained faithful. They gaze upon Him face to face, they rejoice unceasingly in His infinite beauty and majesty, and are thereby made inexpressibly happy. They have lived in this state of rapture for thousands of years, and will do so for all eternity. It is thus that God rewards those who are faithful to Him, and overcome evil.

The number of the Angels created by God is inconceivably great. The prophet Daniel saw them in spirit, and wrote thus: "Thousands of thousands ministered to Him (i. e. to God), and ten thousand times a hundred thousand stood before Him" (Dan. 7, 10). The prophet means by these words that the angels cannot be counted. And as the stars in heaven vary in size and splendour, so are there differences of degree among the holy angels. They are divided into nine choirs, according to each one's degree of wisdom, power and glory. These are, beginning with the lowest: Angels, Archangels, Virtues, Powers, Principalities, Dominations, Thrones, Cherubim, Seraphim.

Probation of the Angels. The angels are by their nature like to God, being highly gifted and pure spirits. To these natural gifts God added the supernatural gift of sanctifying grace, by means of which they became sons of God, thoroughly holy, and wonderfully beautiful. Their state was, even at first, one of great happiness; but by faithfulness in the service of God they were capable of winning for themselves an eternal happiness in the beatific vision of God. God will not have any forced service; so He gave to the angels the gift of free-will, by which they were at liberty to choose between good and evil, and could freely side either with God or against Him. When the decisive moment came, a portion of the angels made a bad use of their freedom, rebelled against God, lost sanctifying grace, and were cast into hell, their wills having become perverted and bad. But the good angels, who stood the test, were admitted into the immediate presence of God, and were confirmed for ever in supernatural happiness.

***

APPLICATION. God is just and punishes sin. How is it, then, that you think so little of sinning and offending God? You are still young, but you have committed many sins, and have deserved punishment at God's hands. Repent, therefore, of your sins, ask pardon of God, and never say again to yourself: "It is only a trifle!" It never could be a trifle to intentionally offend the great, holy and just God! Resolve, then, most firmly never again to sin wilfully. If you are ever tempted to commit a mortal sin, think of the fallen angels and their eternal torment. Die rather than commit a mortal sin! Fear the just God, and keep His commandments faithfully.

The fall of the bad angels should be a warning to you, and the faithfulness of the good angels should be an encouragement to you. If you are disobedient to God, and do not observe His laws, and if you think lightly of sin, you will some day join the lost spirits in hell. But if you are faithful in the service of God, and guard against sin as much as you can, you will some day join the angels in their everlasting happiness. Which of the two have you imitated hitherto, the good or the bad angels?

Above all things guard against pride; it is, as Holy Scripture says, hateful before God and men (Ecclus. 10, 7). Do not be conceited or vain about your clothes, or your appearance, or your knowledge, or your parents' position, but give glory to God in all things; for you have received everything from Him. The more God has given you, the more you should thank Him. Drive away all vain thoughts, and say very often: "Every good gift comes from Thee, O God; I thank Thee for all that I am and for all that I have!"

CHAPTER III.

CREATION OF THE FIRST MAN.—PARADISE.—THE FIRST COMMANDMENT.—CREATION OF EVE.

[Gen. 2]

WHEN God created man, He said: "Let Us[1] make man to Our image[2] and likeness, and give him dominion[3] over all animals and over the whole earth." He then formed[4] a human body of the slime of the earth, breathed into his face the breath of life[5], and man became a living soul[6]. At the same moment God added to the nature of man many favours, and, especially, sanctifying grace, whereby He raised man to a higher likeness of Himself. Thus was made the first man, who was named Adam, that is to say, man taken from the earth. By his nature, man was the image of God: by grace, he was the likeness of God.

---

[1] *Let Us.* i. e. We will make. When God called into existence the rest of the visible world, He simply said: "Let it be!" But in making man, He took, as it were, counsel with Himself, and said: "Let Us make &c." Why did He speak in that way before creating man? It was in order to prove that man was to be superior to other visible creatures, the first among them all.

[2] *Our image.* i. e. let him be a picture or image of Us, and like unto Us.

[3] *Dominion.* i. e. and let him be lord over all the earth.

[4] *Formed.* To form means to make something skilfully. God Himself made the human body most perfectly out of the earth.

[5] *Breath of life.* The soul, therefore, is not made from the earth, but is a breath of God.

[6] *Living soul.* By what means did man become a living being? God breathed a soul into the human body. The soul is the cause of the body's life; without it the body cannot live. When the soul is separated from the body, the body dies.

By a special effect of His goodness the Lord God created expressly for man a garden of pleasure, called Paradise [1]. There were in it all sorts of beautiful trees, covered with delicious fruit; and in the middle of the garden stood the Tree of Life [2], and the

Fig. 1. Assyrian representation of the Tree of Life. Relief from Nimrud. London, British Museum.
(Phot. Mansell.)

Tree of Knowledge [3] of good and evil. A river, divided into four branches, watered the whole garden. It was in this garden of delights that God placed man, that he might cultivate it for his own pleasure and occupation [4]. God then commanded [5] man,

---

[1] *Paradise.* This Paradise was on earth (in Asia), for which reason it is called the earthly paradise. Heaven, the place of eternal happiness, is also called paradise, but it is the supernatural and heavenly paradise.

[2] *Tree of Life* (Fig. 1). The tree was thus named, because its fruit had life-giving power, preserving the body of man in health and vigour.

[3] *Tree of Knowledge* of good and evil. So called from the fact that God had forbidden man to eat of this tree, and that, if he transgressed the commandment, he would learn by a sad and terrible experience the difference between good and evil.

[4] *Occupation.* In Paradise man worked for his own pleasure, and devoted his strength to the care of the beautiful garden of delights.

[5] *Commanded.* Almighty God imposed a command on man, in order to prove whether he were thankful and obedient. This command was very easy to obey, because there was an abundance of every kind of fruit in the garden.

saying: "Of every tree of Paradise thou shalt eat, but of the Tree of Knowledge of good and evil thou shalt not eat; for in what day soever thou shalt eat of it, thou shalt die the death." [1]

Adam was still alone on the earth. Hence God said: "It is not good [2] for man to be alone; let Us make him a help like unto himself." Then, God caused all the animals to come before Adam, that he might give to each its name. But for Adam there was not found a help like to himself; therefore, casting a deep sleep [3] upon Adam, God took one of his ribs and formed of it a woman. When Adam awoke, God brought to him his wife; and Adam rejoiced to see another being like himself. He called her Eve, that is, the mother of the living [4].

COMMENTARY.

God is good. To know this, you have only to count up the benefits and graces which He conferred upon Adam and Eve.

The twofold likeness of God. Man is the first among all God's creatures on earth, because he was created to the image of God, and is, therefore, like unto Him. This likeness is, however, a twofold one, a natural and a supernatural one, for which reason the two words, image and likeness, are used. For something to be the image of a person or of some other thing, it must be, to a certain degree, like that person or thing; but "likeness" signifies a still closer degree of resemblance. If one person is almost the same as another, we say they are *alike*.

---

[1] *Die the death.* i. e. become mortal, or subject to death. God added this threat to ensure the keeping of the command. By the threatened penalty of death it was easy for man to perceive how great his sin would be, if he ate the forbidden fruit.

[2] *It is not good.* This is the only time that God said of His work: "It is not good", because the work was still incomplete. The human race required not only a father, but also a mother. The two form the head and centre of the family. Hence it was not good for Adam to be alone. Furthermore no social life was possible for Adam without a companion like himself. He could not converse with the beasts of the earth that are devoid of reason and language. But why did God call all the animals before Adam? (1) In order that Adam might exercise his dominion over them by giving to each one a name suitable to its character; (2) to prove to him that none of the animals were like himself and that his nature was far higher than theirs; (3) that Adam, by finding himself lonely in the midst of all the beasts, might feel the want of a companion like himself, and might be the more grateful to God for creating Eve.

[3] *A deep sleep.* It was a sleep of ecstasy, during which he was aware of the significance of God's action, both to himself and to all future generations.

[4] *Living.* i. e. of all men. Adam is the father, and Eve the mother of all men, because all men are descended from them.

Thus the word "image" applies to the natural, and "likeness" to the supernatural resemblance of man to God. The natural likeness of man to God consists in this, that man has a spiritual soul, which not only makes his body live, but is also immortal, reasonable, and gifted with free-will. By these three qualities, it is, in a measure, like unto God, who is eternal, whose intelligence is supreme, and whose will is infinitely free.

These gifts are called natural gifts, because they belong to the nature of the human soul, and cannot be lost by it, though they can be marred and disfigured. The first man's supernatural likeness to God consisted in those gifts which do not belong to the nature of man, but soar far above it, for which reason they are called supernatural gifts. The chief among these gifts was sanctifying grace, whereby the Holy Ghost dwelt in the soul of the first man, and made him a child of God and an heir of the kingdom of heaven. The indwelling of the Holy Ghost carried with it many other gifts, such as the three theological virtues: faith, hope and charity, as well as the seven gifts of the Holy Ghost; the gifts also of freedom from ignorance, sorrow, and concupiscence or evil desires and inclinations. The body also of the first man possessed supernatural gifts. The natural body is frail and subject to sickness and death, because it is made from the earth, and, like every other earthly thing, is perishable. But so long as the first man remained in a state of grace, his body was immortal, and free from all sickness and need of labour. If our first parents had remained in a state of grace, they would not have died, but would have been translated, body and soul, from the earthly to the heavenly paradise.

The body of man, indeed, bears no likeness to God, for God has no body; but all the same it has high prerogatives. It is the dwelling-place and instrument of an immortal soul. It is more delicate and beautiful, more complete and better adapted to every kind of work than the bodies of any of the beasts. It stands erect, and raises its eyes to the heaven for which man was created. It is the masterpiece of the visible creation. Man should, therefore, hold his body in honour and not pollute it by sin. "Glorify and bear God in your body" (1 Cor. 6, 20).

Man is made to rule over the beasts and over the whole earth. The earth belongs to God. "The earth is the Lord's, and the fulness thereof, the world and all they that dwell therein" (Ps. 23, 1). But He has made it over to man that he may use its good things according to God's will. The rivers and mountains, the fields and woods, the plants and beasts, were made for the use of man, to preserve and gladden his life. We must therefore use the good things of this earth such as gold, silver, meat, drink etc., for a good end, and not abuse them. We should rule over the things of this world, and not make ourselves their slaves, like, for instance, the miser, who is not master of his possessions, but is their slave. Our thoughts and aspirations should soar beyond this world towards those things which are supernatural and eternal. We must make such use of earthly treasures, as not by their abuse to lose everlasting treasures. It is, moreover, God's will that man should have dominion over the beasts, but it is not God's will that he should be cruel to them. "The just regardeth the lives of his beasts, but the bowels of the wicked are cruel" (Prov. 12, 10). Therefore, be on your guard against cruelty to animals!

Twofold death. By the words: "What day thou eatest thereof, thou shalt die the death", Almighty God threatened man with a twofold death, the death of the soul and the death of the body. This last did not take place immediately after the sin was committed, for Adam lived on earth till he was 930 years old; but all the same, from the moment he sinned, his body became liable to death. The death of the soul, on the contrary, took place the very instant the sin was committed. A distinction must, of course, be made between the natural and the supernatural life of the soul. It cannot lose its natural life, because it is an immortal spirit; but it loses its supernatural life, founded on sanctifying grace and friendship with God, the moment it commits a grievous sin. The loss of grace is the soul's spiritual death, and leads to its eternal death, on which account grievous sins are called mortal or deadly sins.

The Blessed Trinity. The words: "Let Us make &c.", imply that there are more persons than one in God.

The unity of the human race. Why did God form Eve out of one of Adam's ribs? Firstly, because all mankind, even Eve, was to proceed from Adam. Secondly, because husband and wife ought to belong to one another, and to be but one heart and soul by their love and unity.

The happiness of Heaven. The life of our first parents in the earthly paradise was a type of the life of the blessed in heaven. They were perfectly happy in paradise. Peace reigned within and around them, because they were at peace with God. They had abundance of everything; they knew no pain, no want, no vexation, and lived in undisturbed joy and friendship with God and with each other. So also the life of the blessed in heaven is one of supreme happiness: there is no complaint nor sorrow there, nothing but peace, joy and glory. In the earthly paradise God held intercourse with our first parents, as a father does with his children. In heaven the blessed gaze on God face to face, and are united to Him by the closest love. But now comes the difference: the happiness of the earthly paradise could be lost, but the happiness of the blessed in heaven must be theirs for ever.

The probation of man. Man, like the angels, was gifted with free-will, and like them he had to undergo a probation. God gave him a command, by means of which he could freely choose either to side with Him or against Him. Adam being the representative and father of the human race, there rested on his decision not only his own fate, but the fate of all his posterity. An illustration of this we see in the case of a father who by gambling away his fortune makes his children losers as well as himself.

Marriage. When God gave Eve to Adam to be his companion, and pronounced His blessing on both, He instituted marriage. Being instituted by God, it is in any case a holy state, but Jesus Christ sanctified it still more and raised it to the dignity of a Sacrament. God Himself joins together man and wife. "What God hath joined together, let no man put asunder" (Mat. 19, 6). Marriage, therefore, is indissoluble, i. e. a man and his wife must remain joined together till death. Divorce is a crime.

The man is the head of the family. God Himself named Adam, but it was Adam who gave Eve her name. Why did God ordain this so? Because the husband is the head of the wife, and the wife is to obey her husband.

The Tree of Knowledge a type of the Cross of Christ. As by the Tree of Knowledge it was to be decided whether man would choose good or evil, so is Christ the Crucified "set for the fall and for the resurrection of many" (Luke 2, 34). They who believe in Him crucified, and follow Him, will obtain eternal life; but those who will not believe in the crucified Saviour, and will not follow Him, will be eternally lost. The devil conquered by means of the Tree of Knowledge; but by the Cross he was conquered. With the one, sin began; with the other, redemption and salvation.

The Tree of Life a type of the Blessed Sacrament. Even as the life of the body was preserved by this tree, so by the Blessed Sacrament grace, the supernatural life of the soul, is increased and preserved in it, and the soul made worthy of everlasting life. "If any man eat of this bread he shall live for ever", said our Lord (New Test. XXXIV). (About the Tree of Life in the paradise of heaven, see Chapter XCIX. New Testament.)

APPLICATION. God's goodness to man is infinitely great. Just think how He has raised and elevated him! He created him to His own image, and gave him the whole earth for his use. He gave him an immortal soul and sanctifying grace, placed him in the beautiful garden of paradise, and in addition to this gave him the promise of eternal happiness in heaven; for man was intended to occupy those thrones in heaven which the fallen angels had lost. And all this was destined not only for the first man, but for all his posterity. Just think, then, how loving were God's intentions towards man! "Praise the Lord, for He is good, for his mercy endureth for ever!" (Ps. 117, 1.) "Let us, therefore, love God, because God first hath loved us" (1 John 4, 19). Whatever you may be doing to-day, say: "I do it for love of Thee, O my God!"

CHAPTER IV.

PART I.

THE FALL OF OUR FIRST PARENTS.

[Gen. 3, 1—13.]

OF all the animals that God had placed upon the earth, none was more cunning than the serpent [1]. Hence the devil, who was envious of the happiness of our first parents, made use of him in order to seduce them. Eve, prompted by curiosity, approaching the forbidden tree, saw a serpent near it. He began to speak [2], and said to her: "Why [3] has God commanded you that you should not eat of every tree [4] of paradise?" Eve answered: "Of the fruit of the trees of paradise we do eat; but of the fruit of the tree which is in the midst of paradise, God has commanded us that we should not eat, and that we should not

---

[1] *Serpent.* The devil, full of envy at the happiness possessed by Adam and Eve, and made more envious still by the thought that they were intended to attain to the everlasting happiness which he himself had forfeited, made use of the serpent by entering into it and speaking by its mouth. God allowed him no other tool, and, indeed, the cunning serpent was admirably suited for his spiteful and evil purpose.

[2] *To speak.* The serpent into which the devil had entered spoke.

[3] *Why.* Satan did not betray his intention by saying at once: "Eat of the fruit", but he began by cunningly asking: "Why &c.?" in order that Eve might be induced to hesitate and question whether the prohibition to eat of the tree of knowledge were a legitimate one, and whether God had really meant it. Eve knew that an ordinary snake can neither reason nor speak; so she must have known that it was some spirit who spoke through the serpent. She ought to have at once perceived that it was no good spirit who thus spoke, for an angel would not have questioned God's will, being quite certain that whatever He had commanded was for the best. Now, what ought Eve to have done? She ought either to have made no answer and fled, or she ought to have said: "God has willed it so. I do not ask why, because God knows best what is good for us." Instead of this, Eve let herself be drawn into conversation with the devil, and thereby he had already gained half his object.

[4] *Of every tree.* By these words the devil sought to make the woman feel the burden of the restriction and its arbitrariness on the part of God.

touch it[1], lest, perhaps[2], we die." The serpent said to the woman: "No, surely, you shall not die[3] if you eat of the fruit of the tree; but, rather[4], your eyes[5] shall be opened, and you shall be as gods[6], knowing good and evil." Hearing this, Eve gave way to pride, and she saw that the fruit was good and pleasant to behold. She took and ate of the fruit, and gave to her husband, and he also ate. Thus was the first sin committed.

By this first sin they lost sanctifying grace, which was the life of their soul; they lost the immortality of their body; their eyes were opened[7], and they saw with shame that they were naked. In their shame and confusion they began to sew fig-leaves together, in order to cover their nakedness. But soon they heard the voice of God calling them, and they hid themselves[8] among

---

[1] *Not touch it.* Why this command? So that they might keep away from even the occasion of sin.

[2] *Lest, perhaps.* In this sentence there occur two remarkable words: "lest, perhaps": for God had not said: "*Perhaps* you may die", and we can see by this answer of Eve that she already half doubted whether God's threat had been meant seriously.

[3] *Shall not die.* Now the devil becomes more bold, and directly contradicts what God had said, making the Lord God to be a liar.

[4] *Rather.* i. e. on the contrary.

[5] *Your eyes.* The eyes of their spirit. How had their eyes been closed hitherto? They possessed great knowledge, but all the same they knew nothing about sin; and therein lay their happiness. By holding out to Eve the prospect of attaining to a further knowledge, Satan wished to excite in her a sinful curiosity.

[6] *As gods.* Not only like to God, but as God. By this lie the devil wished to make Adam and Eve proud. He represented Almighty God as a deceiver, who withheld this knowledge from them, not out of love, but out of a jealous fear lest they should become like to Him. He wished to destroy Eve's faith in the love and truth of God, and arouse in her instead a mistrust of Him, pride, and sinful curiosity. Alas, he succeeded in his purpose. Instead of being indignant at Satan's blasphemous speech, Eve took pleasure in the prospect held out to her. She allowed a presumptuous desire and sinful curiosity to take possession of her heart; and because it promised so much to her, she now saw that the fruit of the tree was good and pleasant to behold. She longed for it now, and taking some, she ate, and then she persuaded Adam to eat of it also. Revelation has given us no explanation of how Adam was induced to eat of the forbidden fruit. It is left to our conjecture.

[7] *Opened.* But not in the way they had intended. They knew evil, but this knowledge brought them no happiness, only restlessness, fear and misery. They now knew that they had been deceived, that they had sinned grievously, and had deserved punishment. Having lost their innocence, they were ashamed of being naked, and covered their bodies with fig leaves.

[8] *They hid themselves.* It was formerly their greatest happiness when God condescended to speak with them. Now they trembled when they heard His voice and

the trees. And God said: "Adam, where art thou?"[1] And Adam answered: "I heard Thy voice, and I was afraid, because I was naked[2], and I hid myself." And God said: "Who has told[3] thee that thou art naked, but that thou hast eaten of the tree whereof I commanded thee that thou shouldst not eat?" Adam replied: "The woman whom Thou gavest me to be my companion, gave me of the fruit, and I did eat." And the Lord said to the woman: "Why hast thou done this?" She replied: "The serpent deceived me[4], and I did eat."

COMMENTARY.

Sin. Adam and Eve transgressed the law of God. It is true that they were persuaded to do so, but still the devil did not force Eve to eat of the forbidden tree, nor did Eve oblige Adam to do so. It was of their own free-will that they sinned.

The manifold sin of Eve, its origin and process. She first sinned by *thought,* in a twofold way: she doubted of God's love, "why has He forbidden us" without any apparent reason? and next she doubted of His veracity, "lest *perhaps*" we shall die. Then she sinned by *desire,* a desire of pride wishing to be like God, and a desire of the flesh wishing to eat of the fruit, because it looked tempting. Lastly she sinned by *deed.* Eating of the fruit she boldly and proudly disobeyed God's commandment, and then inveigled Adam into the same grave sin of disobedience.

Was their sin a grievous sin? Our first parents undoubtedly transgressed the law of God in an important matter, for the prohibition to eat of the fruit was the only positive law which God had given them.

---

tried to hide themselves. We cannot hide ourselves from God; therefore, it was folly on their part to try to do so. From whence did this folly come? From sin. Sin blinds man and makes his understanding dull, so that he can no longer rightly understand the most elementary religious truths.

[1] *Where art thou?* This meant not only: In what place art thou? but also: In what condition art thou? What has happened to thee? Where is thine innocence? Where is thy good conscience?

[2] *Naked.* It was not only their bodies which were naked, but also their souls, which had lost their robe of innocence and sanctifying grace.

[3] *Who has told?* Why did God ask this? Did He not already know what had taken place? Yes, but He wished Adam to confess his guilt. Adam did so; he acknowledged and did not deny his sin, but at the same time he excused himself and tried to lay the blame on Eve. She, in turn, laid the blame on the serpent.

[4] *Deceived me.* Eve knew now that she had been deceived. The serpent had pretended that they would be much greater and happier through their disobedience, instead of which they already felt abased and miserable!

Moreover, on its observance depended their own happiness and that of their descendants, for Almighty God had threatened them with death if they disobeyed Him. They also transgressed the command wilfully, as explained above. Their sin was, therefore, a mortal sin, and a very grievous one. It was not only one sin, but many. It was a sin of proud revolt, of unbelief, of lust, of disobedience, and of ingratitude. God had shown them so much love and had given them so much that they owed Him the greatest gratitude; instead of which they repaid Him with the grossest ingratitude. Moreover, the command was one which they could easily have kept; for they were possessed of greater knowledge than we are, and knew God's infinite love, holiness, and justice much better than we do.

The consequences of their sin were very grave. Satan had pretended that by their disobedience they would be raised, and become as God; but the very opposite took place. They were now cast down from their former high position, and were less like God than they had been, because they had lost sanctifying grace and all other supernatural gifts. Having renounced God by their sin, they were no longer His children and heirs of heaven, but had become children of the devil and heirs of hell! They still retained the natural gifts which made them like to God, but even these gifts were marred. Their reason was obscured, so that they could no longer recognize the truth as they had done, as was proved by the foolish way in which they tried to hide themselves from God. Their hearts and wills were now infected by evil; sinful inclinations were kindled in their hearts, of which they felt ashamed, and which made them hide themselves. Their happiness was gone. They were still in paradise, and paradise was as beautiful as ever, but they felt miserable, because their consciences were guilty and their hearts were full of fear and unrest. "Tribulation and anguish is on every soul of man that worketh evil" (Rom. 2, 9). Those only are happy who have a good conscience, and the peace of God in their hearts. All the possessions in the world cannot make a man happy if he has not got inward peace. But there is no peace for the wicked.

Original sin. The sin of our first parents injured not only themselves but also all their posterity. Their supernatural gifts were given to them not for themselves alone, but for all those who were to come after them. If Adam and Eve had preserved these gifts, their children would have inherited them, and would have come into the world in a state of grace. But our first parents having sinned, and being no longer in a state of grace, their sinfulness has passed down to their children, so that men are now born into the world in a state of sin. The loss of grace with all its supernatural gifts in the children born of Adam is a matter of great displeasure and wrath to God, because contrary to His divine will and institution. Thus they are children of wrath.

APPLICATION. The devil induced Adam and Eve to sin by means of lies. Therefore our Lord says: "The devil is a liar and the father of lies" (John 8, 44). He is the father, i. e. the origin of lies. Have you never imitated him? Hate lies, for they come from the devil! Have nothing to do with them, or you will be a child of the devil. God is truth, and desires and loves only what is true. Stick to the truth if you wish to be a child of God.

Perhaps you think that, if you had been in Eve's place, you would not have allowed yourself to be overcome by temptation. Have you never then taken anything which you have been forbidden to take, such as sugar, fruit &c.? Has not God forbidden you to pilfer or to be greedy, quite as much as He forbade Adam and Eve to eat of the tree of knowledge? Further, did not God give you sanctifying grace in holy Baptism? Has He not placed you in the paradise of His holy Church, in order that you may live a holy life, and attain to the heavenly paradise? Have you not by means of your religious instruction acquired great knowledge, so that you know perfectly well what is right and what is wrong? Therefore, when you offend against the law of God, you have quite as little excuse as Eve. Guard against sin, and firmly resolve never again to offend God wilfully.

Eve's first temptation came from without. We too, as long as we live, shall have to encounter various temptations. They come partly from without, such as those arising from bad companions or other external occasions of sin, and partly from within, from our own bad inclinations, such as anger, sloth, self-will &c. They can also come from the direct suggestions of the evil one. Eve's fall should be a warning to us not to allow ourselves to be seduced by temptations to sin. Had Eve kept away from the forbidden tree, she would not have fallen. Keep away, therefore, from all occasions of sin, or else you are meeting sin half-way. If a bad thought occurs to you, do not dwell on it, but drive it from you, or bad desires will follow bad thoughts. If the Tempter or your own passions whisper to you; "Such and such a thing would not be a great sin! God would not treat it severely!" turn your thoughts at once to the just and holy God who would be outraged by that sin, and remind yourself that sin is the greatest of all evils! Above all things, beware of sinful curiosity. He who wishes to see and hear everything, and who does not shut his eyes and ears when he sees or hears anything evil, will soon have his heart corrupted, and will lose his innocence. Say often and devoutly: "Lead us not into temptation. Defend me, my God, against temptations to evil. Give me the grace to resist them steadfastly!"

CHAPTER IV.

PART II.

GOD'S PUNISHMENT AND CURSE.—PROMISE OF A REDEEMER.

[Gen. 3, 14—24.]

THEN God said to the serpent[1]: Because thou hast done this thing[2], thou art cursed[3] among all the beasts of the earth. Upon thy breast shalt thou go, and dust shalt thou eat all the days of thy life. I will put enmities[4] between thee and

---

[1] *To the serpent.* Adam had laid the blame on Eve; and she had excused herself by pleading the deception of the serpent. As a matter of fact, all three were guilty, and on that account God pronounced sentence on each of them. He began, it is true, by the serpent who had beguiled the woman; He then proceeded to the woman who had led Adam into sin; and finished with Adam himself. The devil had received his supreme punishment when he was cast down into hell with the other fallen angels; but, because he had deceived man and cheated him out of his happiness, God cursed him anew and with him cursed the serpent which had been his instrument.

[2] *This thing.* i. e. because you seduced Eve by your lies and deceit.

[3] *Cursed.* The language of the divine sentence applies immediately to the actual serpent which was the devil's tool. Being cursed by God, it is hated by man on account of its creeping, cunning, and poisonous ways. But in reality the words apply principally to the devil, and signify that he and his followers would be degraded below all other creatures, and would crawl in the filth of sin and base passions, these being, as it were, the very breath of their life.

[4] *Put enmities.* These clauses are directed only against the invisible and infernal serpent, the devil. Satan had hoped that once he had succeeded in separating man from God, man would make friends with him, serve him, and remain in his power. But, instead of this, God announced that his very punishment would lie in being overcome by the woman. The seed of the devil are all those who are born in sin and give themselves over to sin. The seed of the woman is the divine Saviour who as Man was descended from her. She, therefore, would tread on the head of Satan, would trample him under foot and overcome him, taking away from him his power over man. But the serpent, i. e. the devil, would resist, and seek to injure the woman. He would not, however, materially injure her, but would lie in wait for her heel; in other words, he would prepare sufferings for her, but would not overcome her. — Mary has overcome the devil through her Son, our divine Redeemer, who has saved first of all her from original sin [Immaculate Conception], and next the whole world from original and actual sins and from the power of Satan. But how, then, has the infernal serpent wounded her heel? The devil caused our Lord much suffering. He it was who prompted Judas to betray his Master. He it was who incited the Jewish priests and Pharisees to cry out: Crucify Him, crucify Him! The devil did this, and yet it is by our Lord's very death on the Cross that the devil has been overcome and the world redeemed!

the woman, and thy seed and her seed; she shall crush thy head, and thou shalt lie in wait for her heel."

To Eve [1] He said: "In sorrow and pain shalt thou bring forth thy children. Thou shalt be subject [2] to thy husband, and he shall have dominion [3] over thee." And to Adam [4] He said: "Because thou hast hearkened to the voice of thy wife, and hast eaten of the tree, whereof I commanded thee, that thou shouldst not eat, cursed is the earth [5] in thy work, with labour and toil shalt thou eat thereof all the days of thy life. Thorns and thistles shall it bring forth to thee. In the sweat [6] of thy face thou shalt eat bread, till thou shalt return to the earth, out of which thou wast taken; for dust [7] thou art, and into dust thou shalt return."

Then "the Lord God made for Adam and his wife garments of skin and clothed them. . . . And He cast Adam out of the

---

[1] *To Eve.* The sentence of punishment which Almighty God pronounced on Eve did not apply only to her, but to all women after her.

[2] *Subject.* Eve was subject to Adam before the fall, as a wife must always be to her husband. But this subjection only implied good order, not any hardship or any abuse on the part of man. It was different after the fall. Subjection became servitude and liable to all sorts of abuses.

[3] *Dominion.* Among pagans women were and still are very degraded, and cruelly treated. It is only since the Incarnation and the rise of Christianity that the treatment of women has improved.

[4] *To Adam.* The sentence that now follows was pronounced on Adam and all men after him.

[5] *Cursed is the earth.* Adam, the lord of the earth, having sinned, the curse upon him extended to all nature. As a consequence of the curse, the beasts which, before the fall, were attached to man, have become either shy and intractable, or positively ferocious towards him. Even the elements and forces of nature are very often hostile to him, and destroy the work of his hands. Moreover, the devil has obtained a certain dominion over them, and can injure man through them.

[6] *In the sweat.* i. e. it will be only by the most severe toil that you will be able to obtain bread, or, in other words, what is necessary for the life of yourself and your family. Thorns, thistles, and all kinds of weeds grow naturally from the earth, but corn, which is the chief staple of man's food, can only be made to grow by means of the cultivation bestowed by man on the ground; and this cultivation requires very severe toil.

[7] *Dust.* Man's body is made of the earth. The name Adam means "made of earth". He lost the gift of the immortality of the body when he lost sanctifying grace. From henceforth his body was to be subject to death and to the diseases which are the precursors of death. When he dies, his body turns to dust, mingling itself with the earth.

paradise of pleasure and placed before it Cherubim[1] and a flaming sword, turning every way to keep the way of the tree of life".

COMMENTARY.

God is the very Truth. He had threatened Adam and Eve with death if they ate of the forbidden fruit, and what He threatened was brought to pass. Of His mercy, Almighty God did not make our first parents die immediately, for they were not hardened in sin, and were capable of amendment; but, all the same, from that moment their bodies lost the supernatural gift of immortality, and their souls lost that grace which was their life.

The Justice of God. The punishment of Adam and Eve reveals to us the infinite justice of God. Their sin is the sin of the whole human race; therefore, the evil consequences of their sin have passed down to all mankind. We are by birth "children of wrath" (Eph. 2, 3). The image of God is defaced in each one of us. Our reason is obscured, our will is weakened, and the lusts of the flesh refuse to obey the spirit. We are all subject to suffering and death, and no one could attain to heaven, if our divine Redeemer had not died for us. — Think of the many passions which hold sway over man! Think of the countless diseases to which he is prone; the countless tears which are shed by him! Think of the bitter pangs of the dying; and of the terrible disasters by fire, water and earthquake! All this is the consequence of sin. How terrible, then, is the justice of Almighty God!

Sin is the greatest of all evils, for all other evils came into the world by sin.

Pride comes before the fall. Adam and Eve having sinned through pride, were humbled by the degrading sentence: "Dust thou art, and into dust thou shalt return."

The first promise of the Messias. Before Almighty God drove our first parents out of paradise into the misery of the outside world, He gave them the promise of a Redeemer. The thought that by their sin they had condemned themselves to misery in this world and eternal ruin in the next, would have driven them to despair, had not God awakened in their hearts the hope of a coming Saviour. The curse pronounced on the infernal serpent contained a consolation for fallen man. The words: "I will put enmities between thee and the woman &c.", told Adam and Eve that sin and the devil would be overcome

---

[1] *Cherubim.* Angels of one of the higher degrees, who were to prevent Adam and Eve from attempting to return to fetch of the fruit of the tree of life. If they had partaken of this means of immortality in a state of sin, it could only have brought them damnation.

some day, and that the gates of the heavenly paradise would be thrown open to them. We can see by this how merciful God was even to fallen man. "The Lord is gracious and merciful, patient and plenteous in mercy" (Ps. 144, 8). God punishes man in mercy, and imposes temporal punishments on him, so as to save his soul and make him eternally happy.

The penalties of sin are also its remedies. Work, whether mental or physical, keeps evil desires and passions at bay. If men were not obliged to work, they would live more in accordance with their bad passions, and evil would be rampant. "Idleness hath taught much evil" (Ecclus. 33, 29). Furthermore, if there were no pain or death, men would sink into mere sensuality, would not trouble themselves about eternity, and would quite forget their higher destiny. Sickness and death are always preaching thus to us: "All earthly things pass away; take heed for the affairs of your soul!" On Ash-Wednesday the Church reminds us in an especial manner that we are but dust and ashes, and that we shall surely die.

Adam, a type of Jesus Christ (Rom. 5, 14). Adam is the father of all men according to the flesh; Jesus Christ is the spiritual Father of the faithful, for through Him alone do they receive life. Through Adam sin and death came to all men; through Jesus Christ we have received grace and eternal life. Sin and misery came into the world by Adam's disobedience; but our redemption has been wrought by Jesus Christ, who became obedient even unto the death of the Cross.

Eve, a type of our Lady. Eve consented to sin; Mary consented to redemption, by consenting to become the mother of the Redeemer. Eve, by her sin, brought misery on mankind; Mary, through her Son, has brought salvation. Eve was, in a natural sense, the mother of the living; Mary is so in a supernatural sense.

The Immaculate Conception. Mary trampled under foot the infernal serpent, not only by giving birth to the divine Saviour, but also by this, that she was always free from the stain of sin, even of original sin. Had she, like the rest of mankind, come into the world with the stain of original sin on her, she would have been, for a time, under the dominion of Satan, and her victory over him would not have been complete. Therefore God, by a special grace, and in view of the merits of her divine Son, preserved her whom He had chosen to be that Son's mother from the taint of original sin.

Why did not God cast Adam and Eve straight into hell, as he did the fallen angels? Because, firstly, their sin, grievous as it was, was not so great as that of the rebellious angels, the angels being richer in grace and knowledge than were Adam and Eve; and moreover, the fact of the fall of these last having been caused by the deception of Satan, was in some measure an excuse for them. Secondly, our first parents were not hardened in sin, but confessed their guilt and repented of it.

Adam and Eve not eternally lost. They received pardon on account of their belief in the future Saviour; and, on account of their repentance and long life of expiation, were delivered from Limbo by our Lord, and taken by Him to heaven. In the Book of Wisdom (10, 2) it is expressly said that the divine wisdom "drew him (Adam) out of sin".

The curse which, as a consequence of sin, rests on irrational creatures, is removed by the blessing which the Church, in the name of our Lord Jesus Christ, bestows on natural objects.

Unworthy Communion. Adam and Eve, being in a state of sin, did not dare to eat of the fruit of the tree of life; for, had they done so, they would have been eternally damned. He who receives the Blessed Sacrament (which is prefigured by the tree of life) in a state of sin, draws damnation on himself.

———

APPLICATION. Sin is the greatest of all evils, and the source of all other evils. You are afraid of lesser evils, such as sickness, danger, or death; why are you so little afraid of the greatest of all evils? Guard against sin, for it leads to sorrow and misery. If you do right, you will have a joyful spirit, a good conscience, and peace and happiness in your innocent heart. But if you do wrong, your heart will be unhappy and uneasy, and the pains of remorse and fear will pursue you, as they pursued Adam and Eve after the fall. Therefore, set enmity between yourself and sin; detest it and flee from it. And often pray devoutly thus: "Deliver us from evil, from the greatest of all evils, sin!"

CHAPTER V.

CAIN AND ABEL.

[Gen. 4, 1—16.]

ADAM and Eve had many children; the first two were Cain and Abel. Cain was a husbandman, or tiller of the earth; Abel was a shepherd. Abel was just[1], but the works of Cain were evil. Now it happened one day that they offered a sacrifice[2] to God in gratitude for the benefits He had bestowed upon them.

———

[1] *Just.* He feared and loved God, and believed in the future Saviour.

[2] *Sacrifice.* i. e. visible gifts for the purpose of thanking God for the benefits already received, and of imploring further blessings from Him.

Abel offered the firstlings[1] of his flock, and Cain, fruits of the earth. The Lord regarded Abel and his gifts with favour, but for Cain and his offerings He had no regard[2]. Seeing this, Cain was exceedingly angry, and his countenance fell[3].

And the Lord said to Cain: "Why[4] art thou angry, and why is thy countenance fallen? If thou do well, shalt thou not receive? but if ill, shall not sin forthwith be present at the door?[5] But the lust thereof shall be under thee[6], and thou shalt have dominion over it." But Cain did not heed[7] the Lord. One day he said to his brother: "Let us go forth abroad." Abel, suspecting no evil, went out with him; and when they were in the field, Cain rose up against Abel, his brother, and slew him.

Then the Lord said to Cain: "Where[8] is thy brother Abel?" Cain replied in an insolent manner: "I know not; am I my

---

[1] *Firstlings.* i. e. the first born and best and finest of his flock.

[2] *No regard.* We are not told how Almighty God manifested His pleasure and displeasure. Probably, as at the sacrifice of Elias (Old Test. LXIII), He sent down fire from heaven, which consumed Abel's offering, whereas Cain's, notwithstanding every effort on his part, remained unconsumed.

[3] *His countenance fell.* i. e. it became dark and pale with anger. Envy was the cause of his anger. He envied his brother for being in God's favour, and feared that he would receive greater benefits than himself. Instead of winning God's approval by contrition and amendment, he was seized with rage against his innocent brother, although God lovingly warned him in time.

[4] *Why.* By these questions God wished to bring Cain to self-knowledge, and a realization of the terrible condition of his soul.

[5] *At the door.* i. e. it will swiftly overtake you.

[6] *Under thee.* i. e. you must not let these evil passions of envy and anger master you, but subdue them at once and rule over them.

[7] *Did not heed.* He did not take God's warning to heart. He did not subdue his anger, and therefore it gained more and more mastery over him, till it grew into the fiercest hatred. He could no longer endure the sight of his brother, and at last resolved to kill him. His evil passions quite blinded him. He did not think of the grief which his act would cause his parents, nor did he remember the threats of Almighty God. He enticed his brother into the field, and turning on him struck him dead. What must Adam and Eve have felt when they saw their dear Abel lying dead in his blood, slain by his own brother's hand? Perhaps, blinded by bitter tears, they exclaimed: "Alas, that we must survive this, our son's crime! Woe to us that we ever sinned! Cain has got his bad passions from us: this terrible deed is the consequence of our sin!"

[8] *Where.* By asking this question God wanted to give Cain the opportunity of honestly and contritely confessing his crime. Had he done so, God would have forgiven him and lessened his punishment. But instead of doing this, Cain made an insolent and defiant reply.

brother's keeper?"[1] And the Lord said to him: "What hast thou done? The voice of thy brother's blood crieth to me[2] from the earth. Now, therefore, cursed shalt thou be upon the earth, which hath opened her mouth[3] and received the blood of thy brother from thy hand. When thou shalt till it, it shall not yield to thee its fruit. A fugitive[4] and a vagabond[5] shalt thou be upon the earth."

And Cain, in despair, said to the Lord: "My iniquity is greater[6] than that I may deserve pardon. Behold! Thou dost cast me out this day from the face of the earth. Everyone, therefore, who findeth me, will kill me." The Lord said to him: "No, it shall not be so; but whosoever shall kill Cain shall be punished sevenfold."[7] And He set a mark[8] upon Cain, that whosoever found him should not kill him. And Cain went out from the face of the Lord, and dwelt as a fugitive[9] on the earth.

---

[1] *Keeper.* This was as much as to say: "Why dost thou ask me? I am not his keeper!" Being blinded by his passions, Cain believed that he could hide his crime from God, and defiantly lied to Him. After that, God reproached him for what he had done, and pronounced sentence on him.

[2] *Crieth to me.* Can blood cry out? Almighty God meant this: "Your evil deed is such that it demands punishment from heaven; in other words, it cries out to heaven for punishment and vengeance.

[3] *Mouth.* i. e. thou hast with thine own hand shed thy brother's blood which, flowing on to the ground, has been sucked up by it.

[4] *Fugitive.* i. e. without a home.

[5] *Vagabond.* i. e. thou shalt never find rest, but shalt always wander to and fro on the earth.

[6] *Greater.* Cain's defiance changed to despair. He believed that he could not obtain forgiveness, and despaired of God's mercy. He would have liked to hide himself from God. Why did Cain wish to hide himself from God? Because he no longer regarded Him as a loving father, but only as a severe judge; and now the thought of the presence of that God whom he had so offended was torture and terror to him. Having no longer any hope of attaining to eternal life, he clung the more anxiously to this earthly life, and was filled with dread, lest others should kill him, as he had killed Abel. As the expulsion of Adam and Eve from paradise had taken place about 120 years before, there were probably a great number of people on the earth by this time.

[7] *Sevenfold.* It was God's will to preserve the life of this murderer, in order that he might serve as a warning to other men.

[8] *Mark.* This mark was a sign on his face or brow, by which everyone might know who Cain was: that he was a man punished by the hand of God, and on account of his sins condemned to wander about on the earth, and that, being punished by God, he might not be killed by any man.

[9] *Dwelt as a fugitive.* Weighed down by the curse of God, and tormented by his evil conscience, the fratricide thenceforward led a most miserable life. Day and night the image of his murdered brother was before his eyes, and he wandered

COMMENTARY.

God is omniscient. God knew the minds of both Cain and Abel. He saw Cain's envy and bloodthirstiness, and knew what crime he had committed, even though Cain would not acknowledge it.

God is holy. Therefore the offering of the righteous Abel was well-pleasing to Him, but He took no pleasure in the offering of the evil-minded Cain.

God is just. In what way did God show His justice in this story? First by the words: "If thou do well, shalt thou not receive?" and those other words: "The voice of thy brother's blood crieth unto me." Secondly by the fact that He punished the murderer most terribly.

Envy is a capital sin, because, as we have seen in the case of Cain, it leads to many other sins. Cain began by being envious of his brother, and then, because he did not check this feeling, there grew up in his heart a fierce anger against Abel. He did not resist this anger, but rather cherished it, so that it turned into bitter hatred, and kindled in his heart the terrible desire to kill his brother. Then, as he did not resist this thirst for blood, it grew, until at last it led him to commit the horrible crime of fratricide.

Murder. The deadly blow which Cain dealt Abel was intentional and premeditated; and such an action is called murder. Cain was not only a murderer, but also a fratricide, i. e. the murderer of his brother.

The sins which cry to heaven for vengeance. We can see by this story of Cain and Abel, whence comes the expression of sins crying to heaven for vengeance. Wilful murder is counted among them, because of the words of God: "The blood of thy brother crieth &c."

The forgiveness of sins. Is it true that Cain might have obtained forgiveness if he had done penance? His sin was indeed great, but God's mercy is infinitely greater; and the murderer would have been forgiven by God if he had but repented and confessed his terrible sin. Our faith teaches us explicitly that all sins can be remitted if only they are confessed with the proper dispositions. It was Cain's own fault that he did not obtain forgiveness. He would not confess his sin, though God Himself questioned him. We cannot get our sins forgiven

---

to and fro on the earth, without comfort and without joy. The punishment of Cain was threefold. In the selfishness of his envy he had believed that, if Abel were dead, he would, firstly, receive more blessings from God, secondly, that the earth would produce more under his cultivation, and, thirdly, that he himself would be happier. The exact opposite took place. Firstly, God cursed him; secondly, the earth was barren under his touch; thirdly, he was a prey to constant fear and unrest, and never knew another happy moment.

unless we confess them. Moreover, Cain had no true contrition, and all
hope of pardon depends on that. He, however, had given up hope,
and despaired of God's mercy.

Free-will. There are those who yield to their evil passions, and
then say that they could not help it. Is it true that they could not
have helped it? Could not Cain have acted differently from what he
did? God Himself had said to him: "Keep your lust under." We are
not obliged to follow our evil inclinations, for we have free-will, and
can overcome our passions if we choose.

The necessity of grace. Grace is, however, necessary to enable
the free-will of man to choose what is right. Cain had received
sufficient grace, and if he had corresponded with it, he would have
been quite able to overcome his envy and hatred, and would never
have become a murderer. Even after his sin he would have been able
to obtain pardon, if he had not resisted the grace of God which urged
him to repent.

The wonderful working of divine grace for the good of man is
shown to us very plainly in this story of Cain. Think how much God
did both to keep him from sinning, and to bring him to repentance,
after he had sinned, so that his soul might be saved. First, He drew
Cain's attention to his ruling passions of envy and anger, in order to
bring him to a knowledge of himself. Then He promised him a reward
and blessing if he would correct himself, and threatened him with speedy
punishment if he let himself be led on to do an evil deed. Lastly, He
stirred him up, and exhorted him not to be led away by his evil desires,
but to have dominion over them. Even after the terrible deed was
done, Almighty God did not at once reject the murderer, and even
while reproaching him for his crime, tried to move his heart. He wished
Cain to recognise the horror of his deed, to abhor it, and repent of it.
He even asked him where his brother was, in order to make the confession of his guilt easier to him. It was only when Cain proved to be
hard-hearted and impenitent that God pronounced judgment on him.
Even then, the sentence was not an eternal one; it was only temporal
("cursed be thou on the earth"), and might have led him to repentance
and amendment. God protected the life of this wretch by a special
mark, in order to give him more time for repentance. How good and
merciful is God who, as it were, pursues the sinner so indefatigably,
and tries in so many ways to move his heart, so as to save him from
eternal damnation!

Resistance of grace. Sins against the Holy Ghost. Man, having
free-will, is able to resist grace which, much as it may move him and
incline him towards what is good, does not force him. Cain's terrible
example shows us to what resistance of grace can lead. He would
not listen to God's loving exhortation to overcome his envy and anger,
but cherished them in his heart, till his anger waxed fiercer and turned

to hatred, and, finally, led him to murder his own brother. Once again, after his crime, Cain resisted the promptings of God's grace. He hardened his heart and sinned directly against God by his lies, defiance and impenitence. It was only after God had pronounced sentence on him, and he already felt its effects, that he acknowledged his guilt. He did not, however, implore for pardon contritely and confidently, but despaired of God's mercy. Which of the sins against the Holy Ghost did he commit? First, he envied his brother on account of the grace God had given him; secondly, he hardened his heart against God's admonitions; and, finally, he despaired of God's mercy.

A right intention is the chief thing. St Paul says (Hebr. 11, 4): "By faith Abel offered to God a sacrifice exceeding that of Cain." What was wanting in Cain's sacrifice? His faith in God and in the promised Saviour was not firm and living, and therefore his worship of God was wanting in reverence and thankfulness. He worshipped Him outwardly, but not inwardly. The gifts which he offered were good, but the intention with which he offered them was not good. Let us learn from this that God does not look merely on our outward works and gifts, but that He looks especially to our intention. "The Lord seeth the heart."

The worship of God by sacrifice. Cain and Abel both brought gifts to God. What did they offer? Fruits and beasts. How did they offer these visible gifts? They burnt them, i. e. destroyed them by fire. They wished to express by this that they kept back nothing of these gifts for themselves, that they desired to offer them wholly to God, from whom all good things come, and to whom all things belong. From whom had Cain and Abel learnt how to offer sacrifice to God? Obviously, from their parents, Adam and Eve. We see, therefore, that men offered sacrifice to God from the very first: that so long as there have been men to worship Him, there have been sacrifices. Sacrifice is the highest and most perfect form of worship, and is essential to religion. The Catholic religion, being the most holy and perfect of all religions, must possess the most holy and perfect of sacrifices. What is this holiest sacrifice, most pleasing to God? It is Jesus Christ Himself, who once sacrificed Himself on the Cross in a bloody manner, and who continually offers Himself for us in the holy Mass in an unbloody manner.

Abel is the second type of Jesus Christ. Abel was just; a shepherd; envied by his brother; slain by him; and his blood cried for vengeance. Jesus Christ is the Most Just, and the Good Shepherd of mankind. Out of envy He was persecuted and slain by His brethren, the Jews. His Blood cries continually for grace and pardon for sinful man.

The homeless, wandering *Cain is a type of the Jewish people* who resisted God's grace, and who, since they slew their God, have been homeless and scattered over the whole earth.

Eve, weeping over the body of her beloved son, slain by the hand of his brother, *is a type of the sorrowful Mother of God* who stood, sorrowing, at the foot of the Cross on which hung her divine Son, slain by His brethren, the Jews.

APPLICATION. Envy is very easily aroused in our hearts. Have you never felt envious when others have been praised or rewarded? Detest envy, and overcome all temptations to it, for it is a hateful sin, and the source of many other sins. "Through the envy of the devil death came into the world, and they follow him who are of his side" (Wisd. 2, 24). If you let envy get possession of you, you are imitating the devil, and are his child. Do you wish to be a child of the devil? If not, be not envious and jealous of others, but rather rejoice when good befalls them. Drive away envy, for from envy came the first murder.

The divine admonition to overcome the desire to sin applies to everybody. If God required of Cain that he should master his evil desires, how much more does He require it of us Christians, to whom so many graces have been given? Examine yourself and see what sin you are most inclined to, whether it be lying, or greediness, or laziness, or disobedience, or anger, or sinful curiosity, and resolve never to give way to it, but to overcome it at once. Resist the beginnings of sin. If Cain had stifled his envy in the beginning, he would not have become a fratricide! God warns you through your conscience, in the same way that He warned Cain. Do not resist these warnings, or you will grow up ·hard-hearted.

If you have sinned through thoughtlessness or weakness, go at once and confess your sin to the priest, who is the representative of God, and God will forgive you. He who does not make a good confession, is hard-hearted, like Cain.

CHAPTER VI.

THE DELUGE.

(About 2400 B. C.)

[Gen. 5—7.]

ADAM lived nine hundred and thirty years. He had many sons and daughters to whom he announced the law of God and the coming of the Redeemer [1]. His immediate descendants also lived to a very great age. Mathusala, the oldest of them,

---

[1] *Redeemer.* According to the promise that the seed of the woman would overcome sin and the devil.

lived nine hundred and sixty-nine years. The people became very numerous. Some were herdsmen and lived in tents; others built cities and became mechanics[1] and musicians. The descendants of the pious Seth[2], whom God had given to Adam instead of Abel, were good, feared God, and hence were called the children of God. The descendants of Cain, however, turned away from God[3], were wicked, and were called the children of men.

Henoch[4], one of the children of God, was noted for his faith and piety, and was taken up[5] alive to heaven. Unhappily, the children of God began to associate[6] with the children of men, and soon they themselves became wicked. Then God said: "My spirit shall not remain in man for ever, because he is flesh, and his days shall be one hundred and twenty years."

"And seeing that the wickedness of men was great on the earth and that all the thought of their heart was bent upon evil at all times, God repented[7] that He had made man on earth, and He said: I will destroy man, whom I have created, from the face of the earth."

---

[1] *Mechanics.* They practised various arts and trades, such as building, stone-cutting, carpentering, weaving, forging, and the making of musical instruments.

[2] *Seth.* Seth, being just and holy like Abel, was a compensation to his parents for his loss. God chose Seth to be the heir of the promises, and the forefather of the people of God, and later on of the Redeemer Himself who, according to St Luke (3, 38), was, as Man, descended from Seth.

[3] *From God.* i. e. they did not seek God or serve Him. They were called sons of men, or of this world, in contradistinction to the children of the just Seth, who were called the sons of God, because they loved and honoured God as their Lord and Father.

[4] *Henoch.* He "walked with God", i. e. lived in God's presence, prayed without ceasing, and was united to God by the most intimate love. He was the saint of the primitive ages. His zeal for the glory of God, and his sincere love of his neighbour, urged him to convert sinners, so as to save them from eternal loss.

[5] *Taken up.* He did not die, but was translated to paradise with his body and soul, as happened later on to the prophet Elias. He, too, was a holy preacher of penance, and was translated without dying.

[6] *Associate.* In the course of centuries, the children of God intermarried with the children of men, and let themselves be led into their godless ways, so that impiety increased, and at last became general. Then God resolved to exterminate the human race, which was now living so shamelessly in accordance with its own evil passions. But He gave them a hundred and twenty years for repentance and amendment.

[7] *Repented.* This is a human way of speaking of God who, because He foresees all, does not change or regret His plans. But in order to express that God felt in His divine heart the terrible ingratitude of man and that it deserved punishment, the sacred writer says beautifully "it repented Him that He had made man".

But among these wicked men there was one just and virtuous man, who was called Noe. Noe found favour[1] with the Lord, and the Lord said to him: "Make thee an ark[2] of timber-planks; thou shalt make little rooms in the ark, and thou shalt pitch it within and without with bitumen. The length of the ark shall be three hundred cubits, and the breadth of it fifty cubits, and the height of it thirty cubits[3]. Thou shalt make a window in the ark, and a door in its side; and thou shalt divide the ark into lower, middle, and third[4] stories. Behold, I will bring the waters of a great flood upon the earth, to destroy all flesh wherein is the breath of life. But I will establish my covenant[5] with thee. Thou shalt enter into the ark, thou and thy sons, and thy wife and the wives of thy sons with thee. And of every living creature[6], of all flesh, thou shalt bring two of a sort into the ark that they may live with thee. Thou shalt take unto thee of all food which may be eaten, and thou shalt lay it up with thee."

Noe did all that the Lord had commanded him to do. He spent a hundred years in building[7] the ark (Fig. 2), during which time he preached[8] penance to the people. But men heeded not the warning. They ate, drank, and were married just as before, without a thought of the terrible punishment that was to come upon them. Then the Lord said to Noe: "Go in, thou and all

---

[1] *Found favour.* It was God's will to spare him, and not punish the just with the unjust.

[2] *Ark.* A great house, resting on a sort of raft made of wood, shaped and fitted together.

[3] *Cubits.* The Hebrew cubit was about 18 inches.

[4] *Third.* i. e. upper.

[5] *Covenant.* Of what did this bond or covenant consist? Almighty God promised to save Noe in the ark; and Noe, on his part, undertook to serve God faithfully with his family.

[6] *Every living creature.* Of clean beasts he was to take seven pair. Those beasts were styled clean which lived on herbage; and especially domestic animals were thus classed. Only clean beasts could be offered in sacrifice. Unclean beasts included (besides swine) all beasts of prey (because they shed blood), all vermin and creeping things.

[7] *Building.* With the help of his sons.

[8] *Preached.* Foretelling the coming punishment. The building of the ark ought to have confirmed his words, for each person must have said to himself: "Surely Noe would never have undertaken this great and laborious work if he did not believe in this coming judgment." But they would not allow any serious thoughts to interfere with their impious frivolity, and went on with their pleasure, refusing to believe Noe's words, and scoffing at his warnings. Thus they let the hour of grace go by without profiting by it.

thy house, into the ark; and after seven days I will cause rain to fall upon the earth for forty days and forty nights, and I will destroy every substance that I have made, from the face of the earth." Noe entered into the ark, with all his family, taking with him all the beasts[1] that the Lord had commanded him, and the Lord shut him in on the outside.

Fig. 2. The Ark. Reconstruction. (After Calmet)

And when the seven days were passed, the fountains of the great deep[2] were broken up, and the flood-gates[3] of heaven were opened, and the rain fell upon the earth for forty days and forty nights. The waters continued to increase till they rose fifteen cubits above the highest mountains. Thus every living being was destroyed, that moved upon the earth, both of fowl, of cattle, of beasts, and all men. Noe only remained, and they that were with him in the ark.

---

[1] *Beasts.* God made the animals to flock into the ark in the same way that He gathered them together to be named by Adam, and in the same way that He still draws the birds of passage every year towards the south.

[2] *Great deep.* That is, the waters under the earth came to the surface.

[3] *Flood-gates.* The water which was gathered in the air, and which God kept back, as it were, by flood-gates, broke loose and poured on to the earth. Many of you have seen flood-gates or sluices in a mill-stream, and you know what the water does when they are opened. In the same way, the water burst out of the clouds, and poured unceasingly on to the earth for forty days.

COMMENTARY.

The terror of God's judgment. Picture to yourself the horror of this terrible judgment of God. In sixteen hundred years the human race had increased to millions of beings, and now all were destroyed! Many of them were drowned when the Flood first began, while others saved themselves for a time in high trees or on the roofs of houses. But the houses were swept away and the trees uprooted, and all who were on them were swallowed up in the waters. Many fled to the mountains, but the flood followed them there. With deadly fear they watched the waters rising higher and higher, till the very mountain-tops were swallowed up, and one by one those who had sought safety on them were engulfed in the roaring waves. Mothers saw their children, brothers their sisters, husbands their wives, drowning before their eyes, and were powerless to help them. Black clouds covered the sky, and the earth was wrapped in darkness. Beasts roared, and men wailed and cried aloud to heaven for mercy. But the day of mercy was past; the day of retribution had come. And, behold, while the storm raged fiercer and fiercer, and the waters rose above the highest mountains, burying all mankind in a watery grave, the ark floated securely on the top of the horrible flood, protected by the hand of God, neither injured by the fallen trees which were hurled against it, nor dashed to pieces against the sunken rocks.

The four last things. The patriarchs lived to a great age, but they had to die at last. Of each one, with the exception of Henoch, it is said that he lived to such and such an age, and then died. By this they fulfilled the words of God: "Dust thou art, and into dust thou shalt return." So it is with man still, and so it will be till the end of the world: all men must die, because they are the inheritors of Adam's curse. "It is appointed unto men once to die, and after this the judgment" (Hebr. 9, 27). The four last things are death, judgment, heaven, hell.

The sons of God and the sons of men. The opposition between the sons of God and the sons of men continues to this day, and will continue to the end of the world. The children of men are those who either have no faith, or who do not live up to their faith, but follow the desires of their own corrupt hearts, and without shame transgress God's commandments. They love the world above all things, as if it were their God. They struggle after the honours, pleasures, and riches of this life, and do not trouble themselves about eternal life. But who are the children of God? They are those who do God's will, who live in the grace and love of God, and who strive after heavenly things. As Christians, we are all children of God. Let us live as such, and try to do the will of our Father, who is in heaven.

The long life of the Patriarchs. As the earth before the Flood produced larger plants and larger beasts than it does now, so men in primeval times were taller and stronger than the men of later ages. They lived a simple, temperate life, and therefore reached a great age. This long life of the patriarchs was ordained by God to serve several ends. The first was that they might have a great many children, and that the human race might multiply and spread itself. Another was that the patriarchs might be able to transmit the divine revelation of the history of creation, of the original state and fall of man, the promise of the Saviour, the story of Cain and Abel &c., to later generations, pure and unfalsified. Adam himself was able to teach these truths to his descendants down to the time of Lamech, who at the time of Adam's death was fifty years old. Lamech was the father of Noe, and died a few years before the Deluge. He instructed Noe (who lived 950 years) and Sem, the son of Noe. Sem (who lived 600 years) was able to instruct his descendants down to the time of Jacob. Jacob transmitted the divine revelation to his descendants, one of whom was Moses, who wrote the first five books of Holy Scripture, containing the revelation of God from the Creation onwards. There was no Holy Scripture between the time of Adam and that of Moses; the faith being preserved and spread by means of oral tradition and living witnesses.

The Forbearance of God. Although all men, with the exception of Noe and his family, had become impious and vicious, God gave them a hundred and twenty years in which to repent, before He let loose His wrath upon them. We call God long-suffering, because He waits such a long time before He will punish a sinner. Good men often complain thus: Why does God put up so long with impiety? Why does He not punish the sinner who defies Him? Almighty God is patient, because He is eternal. He waits for the sinner to repent; but if he will not repent, the punishment falls upon him at last, if not in this world, then in the world to come.

God's Holiness and Justice shine forth most clearly in this story. The sins of men are powerless to hurt the Lord God, or disturb His infinite peace and happiness. Why then did He repent of having made man? Because He is holy, and, sin being opposed to His very essence, He could no longer endure the wickedness of man. He also wished, by this destruction of sinful man, to reveal His detestation of sin to all future generations, and thereby to keep them from sinning. Because God is holy, He is also just, as is shown by His reward of the righteous Noe, and His punishment of the wicked.

The Mercy of God. God reveals to us His mercy as well as His justice in this story of the Deluge. He did not allow the Flood to come suddenly, but by degrees. When the rain began to fall, it is probable that many believed in Noe's warnings of the coming judgment and began to pray and repent of their sins, and cried to God for pardon. Such as did this were saved, and were not cast into hell, but sent to Limbo (1 Pet. 3, 19).

"Others do the same thing." Sinners often speak thus in excuse for themselves. But the Deluge teaches us that such words avail nothing with God. Sin remains sin, and mortal sin remains mortal sin, whether committed by few or many. When everybody was wicked, as in the days of Noe, everybody was punished. At the Last Day we shall not be judged according to the opinions and easy-going principles of the world, but according to the holy Commandments of God and of His Church.

The fortitude of Noe. Among all his other virtues we must admire this the most. He remained virtuous in the midst of a corrupt world, and did only that which was pleasing to God. The wicked people around him did all in their power to lead him astray. They mocked him, because he did not do as they did; but he did not let himself be moved to do evil. He firmly resisted the attractions of the wicked world, and remained true to what was right.

Noe's love of his neighbour. For a hundred and twenty years he laboured for the salvation of the souls of his fellow-creatures, who were walking on the road to ruin. His love of his neighbour was real, practical, and entire.

The Ark a type of the Catholic Church. All those who were in the ark, were saved from death: whosoever is a true child of the Catholic Church, will be saved from everlasting death. There was only one ark of safety: so is there only one true Church in which there is salvation. The ark was designed and built according to God's directions; so was the Church founded by our Lord. The ark did not sink amid the storms of the Deluge, being protected and guided by God; even so the Catholic Church does not sink amid the storms of persecution, being invisibly protected and governed by God the Holy Ghost.

The Last Judgment. The terrors of the Deluge are a type of the Last Day, for our Lord has said (Mat. 24, 37): "As in the days of Noe, so shall also the coming of the Son of man be" (i. e. when He comes again to judge the world). Great were the fear and lamentation when the Deluge broke forth, but greater far will be the terror felt at the approach of the Last Day. "There shall be then great tribulation such as hath not been from the beginning of the world until now" (Mat. 24, 21). And yet many men behave about the Last Judgment precisely as those of Noe's time behaved about the Deluge, passing their lives in frivolity, and fearing nothing. The very same thing which happened to these last will happen to them. The men of Noe's time would not listen to his warnings: they scoffed at him and refused to believe in the judgment that was to overtake them. But when the Flood came, and certain destruction lay before them, they cursed their folly and frivolity, and bitterly envied Noe's safety in the ark. So will it be with men when the Last Day comes. "Then will they say within themselves, repenting and groaning for anguish of spirit: These are they whom we had some time in derision, and for a parable of reproach. We fools esteemed their life madness, and their end without honour. Behold, how they are numbered among the children of God, and their lot is among the saints" (Wisd. 5, 3—5).

APPLICATION. You became children of God by holy Baptism. Have you always lived as such? Have you always prayed willingly and devoutly, and hated sin? Think very often about God, who is everywhere, and sees into your hearts. Henoch took delight in meditating about God. Wherever he went, and whatever he was doing, he had God before his eyes. Each time to-day that you hear the clock strike, or the bell ring, make short acts of faith, hope, and charity.

The children of God became corrupt, because they mixed with the children of the world. Man, being naturally inclined to evil, follows bad example very easily. "Evil communications corrupt good manners." One bad apple taints a hundred sound ones, but a hundred sound apples cannot make the bad one good again. Beware, in future, of bad companions. They are not true friends, but the enemies of your soul. Seek the company of pious, God-fearing people. "My son, if sinners shall entice thee, consent not to them" (Prov. 1, 10).

Noe's preaching was all in vain, because the frivolous people heard him indeed with their ears, but did not take to heart what he said. In what way do you listen to sermons and instructions?

Noe feared God, but did not fear the impious world. Very often you fear men more than God. Have you never been ashamed to make the sign of the cross, or to kneel down to say your prayers, or to take holy water? Do not ever again be so cowardly! Pay no attention to the scoffs of bad people, but be strong, and fearlessly confess your faith! Pray earnestly to God the Holy Ghost for the gifts of fortitude and holy fear!

CHAPTER VII.

NOE'S OFFERING.—HIS CHILDREN.

[Gen. 8—10.]

NOW God remembered [1] Noe and all that was in the ark, and He sent a wind upon the earth. This moved the waters, and after a hundred and fifty days they began to abate. At length, the ark rested upon a mountain in Armenia, called Mount

---

[1] *Remembered.* i. e. God saw that now was the time to bring about a change in the condition of Noe.

Ararat [1], and the tops of the hills began to appear. Noe perceived this with great joy, for he had been now three hundred and fifty days shut up in the ark.

Fig. 3.

Noe in the Ark with the returning dove. Early Christian painting. Catacomb of St. Domitilla, Rome.

In order to see whether the waters had subsided on the earth, he opened the window and sent forth a raven [2] which did not return. He next sent forth a dove, but she, not finding a spot whereon to rest her foot, returned to the ark. After seven days he again sent forth the dove. She came back to him, in the evening, carrying in her mouth a bough of an olive-tree [3] with green leaves (Fig. 3). Noe, therefore, understood that the waters had abated from off the face of the earth. He stayed in the ark yet other seven days, and he sent forth the dove again, which did not return [4] to him.

God then said to Noe: "Go out of the ark." So Noe went out of the ark with his wife, his sons and their wives, together with all the living creatures which he had placed in it. Filled with gratitude [5] towards the Lord who had so wonderfully pre-

---

[1] *Ararat.* This was a chain of mountains in Asia, south of the Caucasus, between the Black Sea and the Caspian Sea. The highest mountain in the chain is 17,230 feet high, and is called Ararat, which, in Persian, means the "mountain of Noe", because it was on it that the ark of Noe rested. Naturally, the waters sank slowly. When the tops of the mountains were uncovered, Noe had been 220 days in the ark, and it was a very long time after that, before the level parts of the earth were dry.

[2] *Raven.* It found quite enough food among the dead bodies floating about, and was able to settle on the mountain-tops. It had, therefore, no wish to return to the confinement of the ark.

[3] *Olive-tree.* i. e. a branch of an olive-tree, from the fruit of which sweet oil is made. Noe perceived by this that the earth, or at any rate the slopes of Mount Ararat, on which olive-trees grow, were dry.

[4] *Did not return.* She did not return, because by this time the plains were dry. Noe, however, did not leave the ark of his own accord, but waited for the command of God to whose guidance he had entirely abandoned himself.

[5] *With gratitude.* Noe was more than a year in the ark (cp. Gen. 7, 2 and 8, 14). What must he have felt when he once more trod on the earth? Whichever way he turned, there was desolation and death: no living creature to be seen, no house nor human habitation! Scattered about were the bones of those who had been drowned: the whole earth was one vast graveyard! Sorrow filled his heart

served him, he built an altar[1] to the Lord and offered on it a sacrifice[2] of clean animals. The sacrifice of Noe was pleasing to the Lord. He blessed Noe and his sons, and said to them: "Increase[3] and multiply, and fill the earth." God made a covenant[4] with Noe that He would never again destroy the earth with water. The rainbow, which we see in the clouds, is the sign of this covenant between God and the earth.

The sons of Noe were Sem, Cham, and Japhet[5]. Now Noe began to cultivate the earth. He planted a vineyard, and, drinking of the wine, he fell asleep[6], and was uncovered in his tent[7]. Cham, seeing his father thus exposed[8], spoke of it in a jesting way to his brothers. They, however, filled with a chaste and holy fear, put a cloak upon their shoulders, and, going backwards[9] so as not to look upon him where he lay, covered their father's nakedness. And Noe, awaking and hearing what had happened, said: "Cursed be Chanaan; a servant of servants shall he be unto his brethren." But he blessed Sem and Japhet.

---

when he thought of the terrible end of those who had perished; but thankfulness, inexpressible thankfulness, rose up within his soul, as he said to himself: "What would have become of me and mine, if God had not so mercifully taken care of me!"

[1] *Altar.* Of stones.

[2] *Sacrifice.* Of those species of animals of which seven pair had been taken into the ark.

[3] *Increase.* Almighty God had said these same words when He blessed Adam and Eve. Noe being the second parent of the human race, God gave him and his sons the same blessing, and in the same words.

[4] *Covenant.* The covenant was a covenant of friendship. Almighty God promised to be gracious to man, and never more to send a Deluge on the earth, or let the succession of seasons, interrupted by the Flood, be again upset. The rainbow was to be a sign of this covenant, and to remind us of God's mercy and promises.

[5] *Sem, Cham,* and *Japhet.* From these three all mankind descended. The children of Sem spread principally through Asia, those of Cham through Africa, and those of Japhet through Europe.

[6] *Fell asleep.* Sufficiently intoxicated to sleep an uneasy sleep. During his restless movements, the covering fell from his body. But how came holy Noe to be drunk? For drunkenness is a sin! He did not drink too much wine intentionally, but through ignorance, not knowing its potency.

[7] *Tent.* He had no house, only a tent which could be easily taken down and carried away.

[8] *Thus exposed.* Cham gazed without shame on his father's uncovered body, and went and told his brothers mockingly what had happened, so that they too might go and mock their father.

[9] *Going backwards.* So that they might have their faces turned, not towards Noe's couch, but towards the entrance of the tent.

COMMENTARY.

The Goodness of God. Almighty God, in His loving mercy, remembered not only Noe, but the beasts in the ark; for He hateth nothing
that He hath made. We, too, should be merciful, and carefully avoid
cruelty to animals. He who wantonly ill-treats dumb beasts, proves that
he has a hard, cruel heart.

God's Faithfulness. Just as the punishment with which God threatened sinful man, was brought to pass in the most terrible way, so the
promise which He made after the Deluge, never again to destroy the
world by water, has been kept for more than four thousand years.

Confidence in God. In Noe we have a glorious example of this
virtue. Full of a living faith in God's presence, wisdom and power,
he gave himself over entirely to the direction of divine Providence.
Full of confidence in God, and in complete submission to His will, he
built the ark and shut himself up in it; nor did he leave it, till God
Himself told him to do so. Fear might very well have seized him,
and he might very well have asked himself how the animals would
fare in the ark, and so forth: and when the ark was driven about
hither and thither, the anxious thought of how long it would be able
to resist the beating of the waves, might very well have occurred to
him. But he allowed no such fears to take possession of him, and
confided himself entirely to the Lord God and His holy word. Belief
in the wisdom and power of the ever present God ought to fill us also
with courage and comfort in time of tribulation, and make us trust in
God, and be content with whatever He wills. "Commit thy way to the
Lord, and trust in Him, and He will do it" (Ps. 36, 5). He who puts
his trust in God, builds on a sure foundation.

Gratitude to God. Why was God well pleased with Noe's sacrifice? Firstly, because it was offered with faith in the future Saviour;
and, secondly, because it was offered in thanksgiving. You may imagine
and picture to yourself how Noe and his family knelt round the altar,
praying with fervour and devotion, thanking God from the bottom
of their hearts, and promising Him that they would serve Him all the
days of their life, and avoid those sins which had called down such a
terrible punishment. Gratitude to God is a holy and essential part of
our worship of Him.

The reward of gratitude. Noe's thankfulness pleased the Lord
God, so that He gave him still greater blessings. When we thank God
for benefits we have received, we prepare the way for new ones.

The olive-branch, brought back to the ark by the dove, showed
those who were inside that the destruction on the earth had ceased, and
that the time of their liberation was at hand. On this account, the
olive-branch has ever since been a token of peace and joy.

Intemperance. Noe's drunkenness was excusable, because he was ignorant of the strength of wine. This is now known to everybody, so that it is a great sin to drink enough to obscure the senses and reason. Drunkenness leads to many other sins, such as quarrelling, fighting, swearing &c., and is, therefore, one of the capital sins. Man may drink wine &c. in moderation, for the purpose of refreshing and strengthening himself. But children should never drink wine, still less, spirits. Such drink is unwholesome for children, and those who indulge in it are pale and sickly, and often stupid and stunted in their growth. But milk and bread make rosy cheeks!

Cham's sin. What Commandments did Cham sin against? Firstly, against the sixth Commandment, by his immodesty. Secondly, against the fourth Commandment. Cham scoffed at, and failed in respect to his father, and spoke evil of him, by needlessly repeating to his brothers what he had seen. What ought Cham to have done when he accidentally found his father in that state? He ought to have turned away his eyes, covered up his father, and not told any one about it.

The blessing and curse of parents. When Noe learnt about Cham's conduct, he pronounced a curse on him and his descendants, and promised a blessing to Sem and Japhet. He foresaw, by the inspiration of the Holy Spirit, that Cham's descendants would, like those of Cain, turn away from God, and be punished by Him. The African negroes are descended from him, and they are to this day sunk in the lowest state of superstition, governed by cruel tyrants, treated as slaves, and often bought and sold as such. Their way of living is very barbarous, and they are very hard to convert to Christianity. The blessing on Sem and Japhet and their children has been fulfilled as completely as has been the curse on Cham. Sem was the heir of the divine promise, for the chosen people of God sprang from him, and of his race was born the Messias. The children of Japhet formed great and powerful nations, and were early converted to Christianity, some of them even in the time of the apostles. You can see by this story that children who are wanting in respect to their parents, are punished by God, but that those who love and honour them, are blessed and rewarded by Him.

Detraction. Just as Sem and Japhet covered their father's nakedness with a cloak, so ought we to cover the faults of our fellow-men with the mantle of charity, and never reveal them except in case of necessity. You commit the sin of detraction, if you reveal the sins of others without necessity.

Noe, the third type of Jesus Christ. Noe was the only just man in a sinful world: Jesus Christ is alone, and of and by Himself, most just, most holy. Noe built the ark for the saving of the human race: Jesus Christ founded the Church in order that in her men might find salvation. Noe preached penance and foretold the Deluge: our Lord preached penance and foretold the Last Judgment. Noe offered a sacrifice to God, which was so well-pleasing to Him that He made a covenant with him and his posterity: our Lord, by His death on the Cross, offered the most perfect sacrifice, and obtained for all men pardon, grace and everlasting peace. Noe saved the human race by the ark: Jesus Christ saves men by His Church.

APPLICATION. Say a hearty "Deo gratias" (thanks be to God) whenever you have escaped a danger or received a blessing or succeeded in some undertaking. As Noe's first act on leaving the ark was one of thanksgiving, so let your first act, when you wake in the morning, be one of thanksgiving.

Noe was saved in the ark on account of his justice. What have you done to deserve being received into the one ark of salvation, the Church, almost as soon as you were born? Thank God very often for having made you a member of the one true Church. There is, says St Augustine, no greater treasure than the Catholic faith.

Cham's conduct was very wrong. Would it not be wrong of you to look at anything indecent? Be on your guard, therefore, against curious looks, and be modest in dressing and undressing.

Honour your father and your mother. Do not despise them even if they have faults. "The eye that mocketh at his father or that despiseth his mother, let the ravens of the brooks pick it out, and the young eagles eat it" (Prov. 30, 17).

CHAPTER VIII.

THE TOWER OF BABEL.

[Gen. 11, 1—9.]

THE descendants of Noe soon multiplied[1], and again became as wicked as men had been before the Deluge. Now they were unable[2] to live together any longer, and they said: "Come, let us make a city and a tower[3], the top whereof may reach to heaven; and let us make our name famous, before we be scattered abroad in all lands." But God frustrated their foolish design. He

---

[1] *Multiplied.* They had left the mountains of Armenia, and dwelt in the large, fruitful plain between the Euphrates and the Tigris.

[2] *Unable.* To live together, because of their number.

[3] *Tower.* They wished to found an united kingdom, the centre and fortress of which should be this city with its high tower.

said: "Let Us confound their tongue[1] that they may not understand one another's speech." Till then there had been but one
language spoken amongst men. So the Lord scattered them from
that place into all the lands, and they ceased to build the city.
Therefore, the city was called Babel[2], which signifies confusion,
because there the language of the whole earth was confounded.

The children of Sem remained in Asia, and from them descended the Israelites, the chosen people of God. Most of the

Fig. 4. Birs Nimrud (Tower of Confusion). (After Oppert.)

descendants of Cham settled in Africa, while those of Japhet took
up their abode in Europe. Thus were different nations founded.
The more men multiplied on the earth, the more wicked they

---

[1] *Confound their tongue.* God introduced various languages among them.
Hitherto they had all spoken one language, because they were all the children,
first, of Adam, then, of Noe. In the course of time, with the extension of the
human race and the development of nationalities, this one original language would
naturally have split itself into divers dialects, just as the mental and physical
development of the race would have differed according to the different localities
in which they were placed. But in order to punish their presumption and compel
them to disperse, God brought the change about in a sudden and wonderful manner,
while they were still all together, and at work building their tower. They could
no longer understand each other, and had to give up their undertaking and separate into different bodies.

[2] *Babel.* Or Babylon. Among the ruins of this once great city the stupendous
foundations of a tower are still to be seen, which are considered to be the remains
of the Tower of Confusion (Fig. 4).

became. Their sins darkened their heart and mind, and thus they lost the true knowledge of God, and fell into idolatry. They began to adore a multitude of false gods [1]. Some worshipped the sun, moon and stars, others worshipped men and beasts, and even the works of their own hands. To these false divinities even human victims were offered, and sometimes innocent children, who were made to endure the most cruel torments. God left them to go their own way [2].

COMMENTARY.

Idolatry is a grievous sin against the first Commandment. It is, moreover, unreasonable and foolish, and is a sad proof of the evil effects on man of original sin.

Necessity of grace. God gave the idolaters over to their own evil desires and inclinations. As evil inclinations are rife in man, in consequence of original sin, it is only by God's grace that he is able to keep the commandments. As God withdrew His grace from these men who had rejected Him, they gave themselves over to the desires of their hearts, and were led by their unbridled passions into the most horrible sins.

Pride. This story shows us how man's apostasy from God began by pride. At the time that Noe's descendants built the Tower of Babel, they had increased to some millions in number. They began to build in defiance of God, relying on their own strength and numbers. They did not give glory to God, by acknowledging that they had received all things from Him, and could do nothing without Him. On the contrary, they intended to build a tower which would reach to heaven and make their name famous in all ages. Thus it was pride that prompted this sinful undertaking.

---

[1] *False gods.* Because men gave themselves over to their bad passions and were further and further removed from God by their sins, they at last lost the knowledge of Him and began to worship the creature instead of the Creator. This worship of false gods is called idolatry, and the people who so worship are called idolaters.

[2] *Their own way.* Their sin grew and grew, because God gave them over to the desires of their hearts. When Cain began to yield to the passions of envy and hatred, God did not give him over to these passions unwarned. When the children of Cain, the "sons of men", turned away from the true God, He, in His goodness, urged them to penance and conversion through holy Henoch. And immediately before the Deluge, He made the just Noe stand forth and proclaim the punishment which was hanging over mankind. Each of these times God warned sinners and manifested Himself to them: but now when, after the building of the Tower of Babel, men fell away from Him, though He neither destroyed nor punished them, He no longer revealed Himself to them, but gave them over to the desires of their hearts. Because they forsook God, He forsook them; and they had to learn by experience to what they would come when left by God to themselves.

God's Blessing the one thing necessary. This story of the Tower of Babel shows us the truth of the Psalmist's words: "Unless the Lord build the house, they labour in vain that build it" (Ps. 126, 1).

Necessity of supernatural or revealed religion. The majority of men fell into idolatry about 2000 years after the creation. However, there were always a few just men who, with their families, preserved the faith in the true God, and His revelation; such, for instance, were Abram, Melchisedech, Job &c. But the true faith would have been lost even in those families, unless God had revealed Himself anew, as you will learn He did in the stories which follow. Divine revelation was necessary, or else even man's natural knowledge of God would have been lost. The men of the time of the Tower of Babel possessed a revealed religion, for Noe had faithfully delivered to his descendants the revelation of God handed down by Adam. But as men followed their evil inclinations more and more, their faith became weak. They believed, indeed, but their faith was not living: they lived as if there were no God, until at last they lost the supernatural gift of faith. But, you will say, they could still know God by the light of their natural reason; "for the invisible things of Him, from the creation of the world, are clearly seen, being understood by the things that are made: His eternal power also and divinity, so that they (i. e. the heathens) are inexcusable" (Rom. 1, 20). But they lost even the natural knowledge of God, because their hearts and wills were so corrupt that they were no longer capable of knowing Him. They spoke thus, as it were, to God: "Depart from us: we desire not the knowledge of Thy ways" (Job 21, 14). When they turned their hearts from God, their reason became more and more blinded by their evil passions, and they fell into the utmost spiritual ignorance, and into the most foolish idolatry. Pride and vice still lead many men to unbelief.

The punishment of dispersion was at the same time a benefit to mankind. If all men had remained together much longer, they would have destroyed each other by civil war and fighting among themselves. (See the strife between the shepherds of Abram and Lot. Old Test. X.)

The re-union of mankind in the Church. People of all tongues are gathered together in unity of faith in the Catholic Church; for all Catholics over the whole face of the earth are joined together in one faith, one hope, one love. This unity of spirit is expressed by the unity of faith and partly also by the unity of language (Latin), used by the Church. In the Catholic Church, therefore, which is governed by the Holy Ghost, the very opposite has taken place to that which took place in the City of Confusion. There, the speech of men was confounded, and they were scattered: in the Church, men of every land and every tongue are gathered together, in unity of faith and speech, by the Holy Ghost whom Jesus Christ sent on Whitsunday. On that day there were collected together many men of different countries, and yet they all understood

the speech of the apostles, and 3000 of them became Christians. On
that day was built a city which rests upon earth and reaches to heaven;
in which men speak one tongue, and have one faith, and with which
God is well pleased. That city is the Holy Catholic Church.

APPLICATION. There are still on this earth 800,000,000 heathens
who do not know God and His only-begotten Son, Jesus Christ.
Pray earnestly for the conversion of the heathens.

Your forefathers, too, were heathens, and were converted by
missionaries sent by the Holy See. Thank God for your holy
faith, and confess it by word and deed. Pray fervently to the
Holy Ghost to keep you and yours firm in the light of the faith.

HISTORY OF THE PEOPLE OF ISRAEL[1].

I. EPOCH:

THE TIME OF THE PATRIARCHS.

(About 2100—1500 B. C.)

―――――

CHAPTER IX.

THE CALL OF ABRAM.

[Gen. 12, 1—9.]

AMONGST the wicked there was one just and upright man. He was called Abram[2]. The Lord chose him in order that through him and his posterity the true faith[3] and hope in the promised Redeemer might be preserved and propagated on the earth. He said to him: "Go forth out of thy country and from

―――――――――――――

[1] *People of Israel.* Hitherto we have been engaged in a brief study of the primitive history of man. In the last chapter we were told that the larger portion of mankind fell away from God into the grossest idolatry. Of those heathen nations whom God "gave up to the desires of their heart", we hear no more in Sacred History, with the exception of chance accounts of those with whom the people of Israel came in contact. Henceforth Scripture relates only the history of the people of Israel, to whom God revealed Himself again and again. This history is divided into six sections: 1. The time of the patriarchs, 2. the age of Moses, 3. Josue and the judges, 4. the kings, 5. the Babylonian captivity, 6. the time after the Babylonian captivity. The first section, therefore, treats of the patriarchs, or first parents of the children of Israel, and covers a period of 600 years, namely from 2100 to 1500 B. C. It begins with the narrative of the call of Abram which contains the account of how God chose him to be the father of the whole Israelite people (and of the Divine Redeemer).

[2] *Abram.* Living in the midst of idolaters, he had remained faithful to God. It was on account of his faithfulness that God favoured him, by revealing Himself to him, and by choosing him to be the father of the faithful.

[3] *True faith.* i. e. the faith in the true God which had been handed down ever since the days of Adam.

thy kindred, and out of thy father's house [1], and come into the
land which I will show thee, and I will make of thee [2] a great
nation. I will bless thee, and magnify thy name, and thou shalt
be blessed, and in thee shall all the nations of the world be
blessed." [3]

The father of Abram had gone from Ur in Chaldea, and
taken up his abode in Haran [4], with his relatives; but as idolatry
had at last made its way even into that family, the Lord called
Abram forth from amongst his kindred. Abram believed the word
of the Lord, and instantly set out for Chanaan, taking with him
Sarai, his wife, and Lot [5], his nephew, and his servants and his
herds of cattle. After a long journey, he arrived in the land of
Chanaan, and came to Sichem (Fig. 5). He was then seventy-
five years old. Chanaan, on account of its beauty and fertility,
was called a land flowing with milk and honey. There the Lord
appeared again to Abram and said to him: "To thy seed will
I give this land." Henceforth [6] Chanaan was also called the Promised Land [7]. Abram, wishing to show his gratitude, raised in that
place an altar to the Lord.

---

[1] *Thy father's house.* God commanded Abram to do this, because idolatry
prevailed in his own country, and even among his own kindred. He wished
moreover to test Abram's obedience and trust in Him.

[2] *Make of thee.* i. e. thy descendants shall be a great nation.

[3] *Blessed.* From Abram was to descend the Redeemer who would bring
grace and blessing to all mankind.

[4] *Haran.* On the upper Euphrates. See Gen. 11, 31—32.

[5] *Lot.* i. e. his brother's son. Lot's father was dead.

[6] *Henceforth.* i. e. from the time God promised it to Abram's descendants.

[7] *Promised Land.* We Christians call it the Holy Land, because it was there
that our Lord lived, laboured and suffered. In geography it is called Palestine. This
important country is situated at the east end of the Mediterranean Sea, and occupies a very small space in the eastern hemisphere. It is only about 140 miles
long from north to south, and 40 miles broad, and is about as large as Wales.
It is bounded on the north by the mountains of Lebanon; on the south by the
deserts of Arabia; on the west by the Mediterranean; and on the east by the
Syrian deserts. God, in His wisdom, appointed this land to be the abode of His
chosen people, because it was so well suited to their peculiar vocation. The land
of Chanaan is pretty well shut in on all sides by mountains, sea and deserts, and
this seclusion made it more easy for the people of God to keep themselves aloof
from heathen nations, and preserve intact the true faith. On the other hand Chanaan was situated in the centre of the then known world, so that it was easy to
spread among all nations, first, the promise of the Redeemer, and later on, the
preaching of the Gospel.

Fig. 5. View of Nabulus (Sichem).

53

COMMENTARY.

The second promise of the Messias. The words: "In thee shall all the kindred of the world be blessed", contain the second promise of the Messias. The second promise is more explicit than the first, for it says that the Divine Redeemer shall be born of the seed of Abram.

Necessity of faith. With good reason we are told so explicitly that Abram believed God, for faith is the first and most necessary of virtues. Faith brought Abram into the Promised Land; and it is only through faith that we can attain to the promised land of heaven.

Grounds of faith. Abram believed in God, and in His word, because God is the very truth.

The characteristics of faith. The faith of Abram had all the characteristics of true faith, being entire, firm, steadfast, and living. His faith was *entire*, because he believed all that God told him. It was *firm*, because he doubted nothing, but believed unreservedly in the words of the Lord. It would have been quite natural for him to ask how it was possible for a great nation to spring from him who yet had no child; but he gave ear to no such thought, and simply stood firm by the word of God. His faith was *steadfast*, because he did not allow it to be shaken either by the ridicule and arguments of his unbelieving relations, or by the difficulties and dangers of the journey before him. Finally, his faith was *living*, because he acted up to it, and did all that God required of him.

Obedience to God. Abram's cheerful obedience to God was a fruit of his living faith. God's command to leave his home was not an easy one to obey, for the natural love of home and kindred is a very strong one. Moreover, God did not tell him whither He was going to lead him. He was commanded to go into an unknown country, among strange people, and was entirely ignorant as to his future fate. Nevertheless, he obeyed God's command promptly and cheerfully. "By faith Abram obeyed to go out into a place which he was to receive for an inheritance, and he went out not knowing whither he went" (Hebr. 11, 8). He has given us a grand example of obedience, which we ought to imitate. "He that believeth God, taketh heed to the commandments" (Ecclus. 32, 28).

APPLICATION. God has not asked of you anything so hard as He asked of Abram; and yet how often you disobey Him! Whenever you tell lies, or fly into a passion, or neglect your prayers, or do not do as your parents tell you, you are disobeying God. Be sorry for your disobedience, and when you say your morning prayers, make a resolution to obey promptly and cheerfully those who are set over you.

Having a firm faith, Abram trusted himself cheerfully to the guidance of divine Providence. A childlike confidence in the Providence of our Heavenly Father is a great support and comfort to us in all the circumstances of our lives. Unhappy he who has not got this confidence! We do not know what will happen to us in the future; but we do know that our Father in heaven cares for us, and that not a sparrow can fall to the ground without His knowledge and consent. So whatever happens to you, say: "Whatever God does, is well done, even though I cannot understand it." Say constantly: "God's will be done!" "Thy will be done on earth as it is in heaven!"

CHAPTER X.

ABRAM'S LOVE OF PEACE.—HIS VICTORY OVER THE FOUR KINGS.—THE BLESSING OF MELCHISEDECH.

[Gen. 14, 1—24.]

GOD blessed Abram and increased his herds[1] and those of Lot in such a manner that the pasture in that country was not sufficient for them. On this account a strife arose between the herdsmen of Abram and those of Lot. And Abram said to Lot: "Let there be no quarrel, I beseech thee, between me and thee, and between my herdsmen and thy herdsmen; for we are brethren[2]. Behold, the whole land is before thee[3]: depart from me, I beseech thee. If thou wilt go to the left hand, I will take the right; if thou choose the right hand, I will pass to the left." Lot chose the fertile country about the Jordan[4], and dwelt in Sodom. Abram dwelt in Hebron, and built there an altar to the Lord.

---

[1] *His herds.* He had become very rich. A little further on it is mentioned that he had three hundred and eighteen men-servants whom he employed as soldiers. He had camels, asses, sheep, and oxen. The camels are used as beasts of burden in the East (Fig. 6, p. 56). There, a good camel costs a great deal of money. The ass is also a valuable beast in those parts, being much larger and stronger than our asses. They do the work of horses, yield very good milk, and their flesh is eatable.

[2] *Brethren.* Lot was Abram's brother's son, not his brother; but among the Israelites all near relations were called brothers and sisters. Thus, in the New Testament, the relatives of our Lord were called His brethren, though He had no brother.

[3] *Before thee.* i. e. you may go into any part of the country you choose. Thus Abram left the choice to Lot.

[4] *Jordan.* The Jordan is the principal river of the Promised Land. It takes its rise in Mount Lebanon, flows through Chanaan from north to south, and runs into the Dead Sea. The country about the Jordan which Lot chose was not the

Some time after this, strange kings, having come into the land, began to rob and plunder the cities of Sodom and Gomorrha, took Lot captive, and seized all his substance [1]. As soon as Abram heard [2] that Lot had been taken captive, he, with three hundred and eighteen well-armed men, his servants, pursued the kings, overtook them, rescued Lot from their hands, and brought him back with all his possessions. As Abram returned victorious, Melchisedech, king of Salem [3], and the king of Sodom went out to meet him. Melchisedech, being a priest of the Most High,

Fig. 6. Bedouins riding on their Camels.

offered to the Lord a sacrifice of bread and wine, as a sacrifice of praise and thanksgiving for Abram and his servants. He blessed him and said: "Blessed be Abram by the Most High God, by

valley north of the Dead Sea, but what is now the southern part of the Dead Sea itself, south of the peninsula. This part was not sea then, but a beautiful valley, watered by springs, in which lay the towns of Sodom and Gomorrha. It is only since the destruction of those cities that the beautiful plain has become a part of the Dead Sea.

[1] *All his substance.* i. e. all that he possessed.

[2] *Heard.* From one of Lot's people, who had fled from Sodom to Abram at Hebron. Abram immediately collected together those of his servants who were strong and able to fight, pursued the kings, who had retreated towards the north, surprised them in the night, defeated them, and set free Lot and the other prisoners.

[3] *Salem.* This was later called Jerusalem. Melchisedech believed in the true God, and was at the same time king and priest. As priest, he blessed Abram, and returned thanks to God for his victory over an enemy, who was so much stronger than himself. His sacrifice was, therefore, a thank-offering.

whose protection the enemies are in thy hands." [1] Abram gave him the tithes [2] of the booty. The king of Sodom then said to Abram: "Give me the persons, and the rest take to thyself." But Abram would accept of no reward [3].

COMMENTARY.

Peacemaking. Abram was a lover of peace. He was older than Lot and, moreover, the head of the family; yet he withdrew in his favour, and gave him the choice of the best pasturage, rather than that there should be any further strife. We ought to love peace in the same way, and prevent quarrelling and fighting, as far as we can. We ought to give up an advantage, and suffer some loss, rather than begin a quarrel; for we are all brethren in Jesus Christ. "Blessed are the peace-makers, for they shall be called the children of God."

Abram's disinterestedness was shown by his conduct on two occasions; first, towards Lot, and next, towards the king of Sodom. When Abram found it necessary to separate from Lot, he did not consult his own interests by keeping the best part of the country for himself, though it was to him and not to Lot that God had promised the whole land; but he gave Lot his free choice of the best pasturage. Then, when the king of Sodom offered him all his booty as a reward, he refused to keep anything for himself. He had undertaken the dangerous war out of pure love, without any thought of his own profit or advantage. His love was, therefore, quite disinterested.

This noble disposition of Abram puts to shame those Christians who are always seeking their own advantage, and who will not even show a kindness to anyone, without hope of reward. But did Abram, then, receive no reward? Yes, he received the reward of a good conscience. The consciousness that he had done a good work, and had deserved a reward of God, filled his heart with very great joy. We, too, ought to value the approbation of our own consciences and of Almighty God, far more than the praise and rewards of this world.

Real love of our neighbour. When Abram learnt the misfortune which had overtaken his nephew, he decided at once to go to his help. He remembered no more Lot's selfish and ungrateful conduct, but only remembered his present necessity and misfortune. He sincerely loved Lot, and wished to help him, even at the risk of great danger; for, after all, these powerful kings might easily have defeated him, and killed or taken him prisoner.

---

[1] *In thy hands.* i. e. in thy power.

[2] *Tithes.* i. e. the tenth part of everything that he had taken from the enemy. He gave him this, because he was a priest.

[3] *No reward.* Abram would not keep anything for himself, but he asked that the men, who had fought with him and risked their lives, should have their due share of the booty.

Inordinate self-love. Lot did not behave well to Abram. Firstly, he ought never to have accepted Abram's generous offer, and ought rather to have given the preference to his uncle. His love of himself was inordinate, therefore he became selfish. Lot believed he had chosen the best portion, and yet his very choice soon brought misfortune upon him. Secondly, he ought not to have gone so far away from his loving uncle and protector. Thirdly, he ought not to have gone to live in Sodom, full as it was of impious and vicious men. There was great danger there both to himself and his family, who might be led away by the bad example around them. We ought not to throw ourselves into the company of the wicked, and we ought to avoid all occasions of sin. We ought to care more for our souls and their eternal interests, than for our bodies and their temporal interests. Lot, therefore, did wrong in going to Sodom, and putting his soul into danger, for the sake of mere temporal advantages. And God punished him for this by letting the strange kings rob him and take him prisoner.

Melchisedech, the fourth type of Jesus Christ. Melchisedech's name signifies the king of justice, and he was king of Salem, which name means peace: Jesus Christ is in a far higher sense King of justice, and the Prince of peace who bought for us everlasting peace. Melchisedech was not only a king, but also a priest: Jesus Christ is our sovereign king and priest. Melchisedech offered bread and wine to God as an unbloody sacrifice: Jesus Christ offered Himself to His Eternal Father at the Last Supper, under the form of bread and wine, and continues to do so in the holy mass. Melchisedech, after the sacrifice, blessed Abram and his servants: Jesus Christ, by the hand of His priest, blesses the faithful at the end of mass. This will make you understand the meaning of the words which God spoke to the Divine Redeemer by the mouth of the prophet David: "Thou art a priest for ever after the order of Melchisedech" (Ps. 109, 4 and Hebr. 7, 1—28).

You have now learnt *four types of our Lord,* namely, Adam, Abel, Noe, and Melchisedech. These types show that our Divine Redeemer is, firstly, our Head; secondly, the Just One who suffered and was slain; thirdly, our Saviour from the destruction of sin and hell; and fourthly, an eternal King and Priest who, like Melchisedech, offers an unbloody sacrifice.

APPLICATION. Do you love peace as Abram did? What is the principal reason why you quarrel with other children? Try to be more unselfish. "Behold, how good and how pleasant it is for brethren to dwell together in unity"! (Ps. 132, 1.) If you have hitherto been quarrelsome, check that evil habit as soon as possible.

Abram gave tithes of his spoils to Melchisedech, because he was a priest. Reverence the priesthood. Priests are the messengers of God.

CHAPTER XI.

ABRAM'S FAITH AND ELECTION.—COVENANT OF CIRCUMCISION.—VISIT OF THREE ANGELS.

[Gen. 17—18.]

AFTER these things the word of the Lord came to Abram in a vision, saying: "Fear not[1], I am thy protector[2], and thy reward exceeding great."[3] On a certain night, Abram was called by a voice from heaven which said: "Look up to the heaven and number the stars, if thou canst. So shall thy seed be." Abram believed, and his faith justified him before God. Again, in the 99th year of his age, the Lord appeared to Abram and said to him: "I am the Almighty God. Walk before Me[4] and be perfect[5]. Neither shall thy name be called any more Abram [a high father], but Abraham [father of a multitude], because I have made thee a father of many nations. I will establish my covenant between thee and Me. And this is my covenant which you shall observe between me and you and thy seed after thee: All the male kind of you shall be circumcised.[6] Sarai [my princess], thy wife, shall be called Sara [princess], and she shall bear thee a son whose name thou shalt call Isaac."

Again when Abraham was one day, about noon, sitting at the door of his tent in the vale of Mambre, he saw three men ap-

---

[1] *Fear not.* Abram feared that the kings whom he had defeated would revenge themselves on him.

[2] *Protector.* I will take care of thee under all circumstances.

[3] *Exceeding great.* I will give Myself to thee by the eternal vision, as a reward. God promised Himself to be Abram's reward, because he had refused to take any earthly one for what he had done. The possession and contemplation of God is the highest of all rewards.

[4] *Walk before Me.* Have Me always before thine eyes, and remember that I am always with thee.

[5] *Perfect.* i. e. do only that which is right in My sight: lead a holy life in My presence.

[6] *Circumcised.* All male infants of eight days old among their own children, as well as all servants bought for household service (Gen. 17, 12) had to be circumcised. The covenant of God was to be (marked) in the flesh, and the soul of the male not so marked was to be destroyed out of his people. Circumcision, then, was instituted by God as a religious rite and as a sacred sign (Sacrament) of admission among the people of God. According to its deeper meaning, it pointed backward to our fallen nature and vitiated origin of life, and forward to the spiritual circumcision of the heart and the new birth through Jesus Christ.

proaching. He ran to meet them, bowed down before them, and invited them[1] to rest in his tent and partake of some refreshment. Calling Sara, his wife, he told her to make some cakes of the finest flour. He caused the best calf of his herds to be killed for the entertainment of the unknown visitors. Butter, milk and honey were also placed before them, Abraham himself waiting upon his guests. After the meal, when they were about to depart, one of the strangers said to Abraham that after a year he would return, and that Sara, his wife, would have a son. Then Abraham understood that the Lord God Himself[2], accompanied by angels, was his guest.

COMMENTARY.

Faith. At the time that Almighty God told Abraham that his descendants would be as numerous as the stars in the heavens, he and his wife Sara had no children, and both of them were growing very old. Therefore it seemed almost impossible that Abraham and Sara should have a son. Nevertheless, Abraham believed firmly in God's promise that He would give him a son, that his descendants would become a great nation, and that of his family would be born the Redeemer. On account of his faith in God's word, and especially in the promise of the future Saviour, Abraham was justified, i. e. he received sanctifying grace. Without faith no man can be justified, for "without faith it is impossible to please God" (Hebr. 11, 6). "The just man liveth by faith" (Rom. 1, 17).

Hope. With firm confidence Abraham waited for everything that God had promised him, and gave himself over calmly to His guidance. "By faith he abode in the (strange) land", says St. Paul, "dwelling in tents, for he looked for a city that hath foundations (i. e. the heavenly Jerusalem), whose builder and maker is God" (Hebr. 11, 9. 10). He therefore regarded himself as a stranger and a pilgrim, and looked forward to his heavenly home and the eternal possession and vision of God.

Charity. Abraham's faith was living, and active through love. He loved God above all things, as he proved in the story you will hear in Chapt. XIII. In the last chapter we saw how he loved his neighbour, and he again proved this by his behaviour to the three

---

[1] *Invited them.* He begged the strangers, as a favour to himself, to come and be entertained by him. He also brought water for them to wash their feet. In the East, in those days, people did not wear shoes or boots as we do, but only soles or sandals, bound to their feet by straps. The feet, being bare, became covered with dust, and had to be washed very often. To wash the feet of another was a service of love.

[2] *God Himself.* He knew this, because the stranger revealed things to him which only God could have known.

strangers. Abraham, the rich shepherd-prince, to whom Almighty God had made such great promises, ran to meet the three strangers, bowed down before them, and begged them to stay with him. He washed their feet and served them, while they were eating, though he had servants in abundance. Did not this show a great love of his neighbour, and great humility? As a reward of his virtue, God promised him that in a year he should have a son.

Walking in the presence of God. Thinking constantly of God's presence is a powerful motive for the practice of what is good, and the avoidance of what is evil. Wherever we are, there is God with us, seeing everything we think and do! We ought, therefore, to live with Him, to meditate on His universal presence, and lift up our hearts to Him. By doing this we shall avoid sin and grow in virtue.

The Old Covenant. Almighty God made His covenant first with Abraham, as being the father of His chosen people. Later (on Mount Sinai) He confirmed and renewed it with all the people of Israel. He instituted the rite of circumcision as an outward and visible sign of this covenant, that it might be, as it were, cut into the flesh of His chosen people, so that it could not be forgotten. This sign was to speak to the soul of every man of Israel, saying: "You are a member of the chosen people. You belong to God, and are to serve Him only!"

Circumcision a type of holy Baptism. By circumcision man belonged to the Old Covenant: by Baptism he belongs to the New. By the first he pledged himself to observe the Old Law: in Baptism we pledge ourselves faithfully to observe the Christian Law. Circumcision impressed an indelible mark on the body; Baptism does the same to the soul. The difference lies in this, that circumcision could not, like Baptism, cleanse man from sin, and make him pure and holy of heart.

Heaven. God gives Himself to the blessed as their reward exceeding great. They gaze for ever on His infinite majesty, and are eternally united to Him in love and happiness. Oh, what joy to possess God Himself, who is infinite goodness, beauty and holiness. Could God give us more than Himself?

APPLICATION. Almighty God is near each one of us, and yet how little we think about Him! Do not ever again be so forgetful of God, but put yourself in His presence several times each day. Whenever any one whose opinion you respect is looking at you, you gather yourself together, and are careful to do nothing wrong. Should you not have much more respect for God's presence?

You were put into this world to love and serve God. How have you served Him hitherto? Could you not serve Him better? Renew your baptismal vows to be faithful to Him unto death.

CHAPTER XII.

DESTRUCTION OF SODOM AND GOMORRHA.

[Gen. 19.]

ABRAHAM went[1] part of the way with the strangers, who were going to Sodom. As they journeyed along together, the Lord[2] said to Abraham: "The cry of Sodom and Gomorrha is multiplied, and their sin[3] is become exceedingly grievous." He told him that He would destroy the two cities. Abraham was struck with fear; for, although the men amongst whom he lived were wicked, he loved them as neighbours. At last, drawing near to the Lord, he said: "Wilt Thou destroy the just with the wicked? If there be fifty just men in the city, shall they perish withal? and wilt Thou not spare that place for the sake of the fifty just, if they be therein?" The Lord replied: "If I find in Sodom fifty just men within the city, I will spare the whole place for their sake." And Abraham said: "Seeing I have once begun, I will speak again to my Lord, whereas I am but dust and ashes[4]. If there be five less than fifty just persons in the city, wilt Thou destroy it?" And the Lord said to Abraham: "I will not destroy it, if I find five and forty." Abraham continued to plead in this manner, till at last the Lord said to him: "I will not destroy it for the sake of ten." Then the Lord disappeared, and Abraham returned to his tent.

The ten just men were not found in Sodom, and the two angels were sent to destroy it. They reached Sodom in the evening, and found Lot sitting at the gate of the city. Lot invited them into his house, and the angels said to him: "Arise, get you out of this place, for the Lord will destroy it. Lot went that night to two young men who were to marry his daughters, and told them to arise and go forth, for the Lord would destroy the city. But they thought that he spoke in jest. At the first

---

[1] *Went.* A sign that he not only waited on the three strangers, but also accompanied them on their way.

[2] *Lord.* One of the three Angels bore the name of God in him, and is addressed as such by Abraham.

[3] *Sin.* Their sins were many; but those of unnatural impurity were the chief.

[4] *Dust and ashes.* i. e. though I, a sinful, mortal man, am not worthy to speak to the Lord my God.

Fig. 7. The Dead Sea. (Phot. Bonfils.)

dawn of day the angels pressed Lot to depart, saying: "Take thy wife and thy two daughters, lest you also perish in the wicked city." And, as Lot still lingered[1], they took him by the hand, and, as it were against his will, led him and his family out of the city, warning them all not to look back, under pain of death. Lot's wife, however, looked back, and was instantly changed into a pillar of salt. The sun had just risen, when Lot entered the neighbouring city of Segor. Then the Lord rained down from heaven fire and brimstone, and utterly destroyed[2] those two wicked cities, with all their inhabitants.

COMMENTARY.

God's Holiness and Justice are most plainly shown to us by the terrible fate of the wicked cities. The attack made on them by the strange kings was a visitation, permitted by God for the conversion of their wicked inhabitants. But they remained impenitent, and were quite as wicked after, as they were before that visitation. Lot's good example might also have been to them a means of conversion, but they paid no heed to it. Then Almighty God could no longer endure their shameful state of vice, for sin is infinitely abhorrent to the Most

---

[1] *Lingered.* Hesitating, and unable to make up his mind.

[2] *Utterly destroyed.* Picture to yourself this terrible judgment which overtook the wicked cities. As the sun rose in the east, and the inhabitants of Sodom and Gomorrha woke from sleep, thick clouds gathered over them, out of which fire fell which kindled every part of the town. The whole air was full of smoke and sulphur; the flames roared and licked up everything. The people, full of fear, rushed from their houses, hoping to escape from the city, but it was impossible to get out. The very air was aglow, and the earth itself, full of pitch and petroleum, was on fire. Their clothes caught fire, and they died a terrible death, shrieking in agony. The whole country round was burnt up, and remains unfruitful to the present day. The earth sank, and the waters of the Dead Sea rushed in, and covered the place where the wicked cities once stood, and formed what has since then been the southern part of the Dead Sea. Lot's wife, who, against the angel's express command, looked back, was suffocated and seized by the fire, covered with the molten bitumen, so that her corpse stood up as a pillar of salt. The *Dead Sea,* the southern portion of which covers the ancient sites of Sodom and Gomorrha, is a peculiar and most ghastly lake (Fig. 7, p. 63). It lies very low, 900 feet below the level of the Mediterranean, and its water is so thick and bitter that no fish or creeping thing can live in it. If the Jordan, which flows into it, carries to it any fish, they die at once and come up to the surface. Therefore, the lake is called the Dead Sea. Objects thrown into it are covered at once with a salt-crust, and the stones on its shores are covered with bitumen. On the surface of the water, and on the shores, great flakes of bitumen are often found. The northern part of the lake is 1300 feet deep, but the southern part, where the wicked cities once stood, is only thirteen feet deep. This Dead Sea, which covers the once beautiful site of Sodom and Gomorrha, is a terrible monument of divine justice.

Holy God. He utterly destroyed the wicked cities from off the face of the earth, and made the whole neighbourhood desolate so that all men might know and fear His terrible justice. "Reducing the cities of the Sodomites and Gomorrhites to ashes, God condemned them to be overthrown", says Saint Peter, "making them an example to those that should after act wickedly" (2 Pet. 2, 6). The punishment of Sodom and Gomorrha is, therefore, always held up as an example of the divine justice.

God's hatred of impurity. This sin having been the chief cause of the destruction of the cities, you can see how hateful it is in the eyes of God, and how severely He punishes it. Impurity is the most shameful of all sins, and an abomination before God. It leads to many other sins, and easily results in impenitence and impiety, as was the case with the inhabitants of Sodom and Gomorrha. Almighty God does not always punish it in this world, but He will certainly do so in the next world. "Do not err; neither fornicators nor adulterers shall possess the kingdom of God" (1 Cor. 6, 9).

The duty of intercessory prayer. Intercession for the living and the dead is a spiritual work of mercy. Love prompted Abraham to pray for the wicked Sodomites: love should prompt you to pray for others, for your parents, brothers and sisters, and for your spiritual and temporal superiors; but especially for sinners, that they may have the grace of conversion, and may not be eternally lost. "Pray for one another that you may be saved" (James 5, 16).

The characteristics of prayer. Abraham prayed with fervour, with humility, with confidence, and with perseverance, making his petition six times.

The power of prayer. Abraham's prayer was not made in vain, for Almighty God granted it, in so far that, had there been ten just men in Sodom, the whole city would have been spared. "The continual prayer of a just man availeth much" (James 5, 16).

Lot's steadfastness is worthy of our admiration. He lived for twenty years in the wicked city, and did not let himself be led away into sin, but remained firm in what was right, and brought up his children in the holy fear of God. Therefore, Holy Scripture, in allusion to him, says: "The Lord knoweth how to deliver the godly from temptation" (2 Pet. 2, 9); because they pray and co-operate with grace.

Sorrow on account of sin. Lot's fellow-citizens in Sodom "vexed his just soul with unjust works" (2 Pet. 2, 8). The sins and crimes which he was obliged to witness hurt his holy soul, because God was offended by them, and many souls were eternally lost. We, far from jesting about the sins of others, should mourn over them. We shall know by our conduct in such cases, whether or no we have a true love for God and our neighbour. "Blessed are they who mourn."

Guardian angels. Holy angels protected Lot and his family. Lot's wife did not take heed to their warning; therefore, she perished.

The torments of hell. The burning of the wicked cities gives us a faint idea of that hell into which the impenitent Sodomites were cast for ever. The torments of the burning inhabitants of Sodom and Gomorrha were very terrible; but the torments of the lost souls in hell are far more terrible. The fire of Sodom was kindled from heaven; the fire of hell is kindled by the anger of God. The shrieks of the burning Sodomites were very terrible, but the wailing and gnashing of teeth of the damned are far worse. The bodies of the Sodomites were burnt and the fire was extinguished; but the damned burn and are never consumed, nor is the fire ever quenched.

Intercession. This story shows us how dear the just are in the sight of God. Because Abraham was just, Almighty God heard his prayer, and would have spared the cities for the sake of ten just men. Holy people living in any town or country bring a blessing on the sinners among whom they live, even though they may be scorned and persecuted by them. For their sake, many a temporal punishment is averted. Monasteries and religious houses bring a blessing on the places where they exist.

Inordinate love of temporal possessions. Lot's wife was punished by the death of her body, because, being too much attached to her possessions which she had been obliged to leave behind her in Sodom, she paid no heed to the angel's injunctions, but stopped and looked behind her. Was it not foolish of this woman to weigh the very best of earthly gifts, life, in the balance against her paltry household goods? But those act with still greater madness who, from an inordinate love of honours, riches, pleasures &c., forget the salvation of their souls, and lose the possessions and joys which are eternal.

Temporal punishment. God rewarded the virtue of Lot by saving him from the destruction of Sodom. But he lost all his possessions which were destroyed with the city, and he was thus punished for his selfish conduct towards his uncle. By this punishment of Lot and his wife, we see that God punishes the venial sins and imperfections even of the just. Temporal punishment must be suffered either in this world or in the next, i. e. in purgatory.

The sin of Sodom. The Sodomites committed horrible and un-natural sins of impurity which called down the judgment of God. They are, therefore, counted among the sins which cry to heaven for vengeance.

APPLICATION. How can you imitate Lot's steadfastness?

A just man is wounded by the sins of his fellow-men. He laments their wickedness, and prays for their conversion. How have you behaved hitherto in this respect? How will you behave in future? At the end of this lesson we will say three Our Fathers for the conversion of sinners.

Detest and fear sin, especially sins of impurity. Set hell before your eyes, think of its horrible torments, and carefully avoid all temptations to such sins. Say thus: "What will the whole world profit me, if I follow my own inclinations, and suffer eternally in hell!"

CHAPTER XIII.

BIRTH OF ISAAC AND ABRAHAM'S SACRIFICE.

[Gen. 21.]

SARA gave birth to a son, as the Lord had promised. He was named Isaac, and circumcised on the eighth day. Abraham loved this son very tenderly, and the Lord wished to see whether he loved his son more than God. When the boy had grown up[1], the Lord said to Abraham: "Take thy only-begotten son Isaac, whom thou lovest, and go into the land of vision, and there thou shalt offer him[2] for a holocaust[3] upon one of the mountains which I will show thee." Abraham instantly[4] arose, and by night saddled his ass, taking with him two young men, and Isaac, his son. And when he had cut the wood for the holocaust, he went to the place which God had shown him. On the third day he came in sight of Mount Moria, where he was to sacrifice his son; and he said to the servants: "Stay you here with the ass; I and the boy will go with speed as far as yonder, and, after we have worshipped[5], will return to you." Then he took the wood for the holocaust, and laid it upon the shoulders of Isaac. He himself carried in his hands fire[6] and a sword. As they went along, Isaac said: "My father." And Abraham

---

[1] *Grown up.* He was perhaps about twenty or twenty-five years old.

[2] *Offer him.* Almighty God wished to prove whether his faith were firm and living, and if he really loved Him above all things.

[3] *Holocaust.* In that kind of sacrifice the victim had to be first killed, and then wholly burnt.

[4] *Instantly.* Abraham obeyed immediately, although the required sacrifice tore his heart. Since the destruction of Sodom he had lived at Bersabee which lay to the south of Hebron. From Bersabee to Mount Moria, which was near Salem, was about twenty-five miles. It was on this mountain that, in after years, king Solomon built his splendid Temple.

[5] *Worshipped.* i. e. when they had offered their sacrifice in worship of God.

[6] *Fire.* i. e. red-hot coals in a vessel.

answered: "What wilt thou, son?" "Behold", said the son, "fire and wood: where is the victim[1] for the holocaust?" Abraham replied: "God will provide Himself a victim for the holocaust, my son." So they went on together.

When they reached the top of the mountain, Abraham erected an altar, placed the wood upon it, bound his son, and laid him on the altar. Then he put forth his hand and took the sword to sacrifice his son. And behold! an angel from heaven cried out to him, saying: "Abraham, Abraham!" And he answered: "Here I am." And the angel said: "Lay not thy hand on the boy, neither do thou anything to him! Now I know that thou fearest God, and hast not spared thy only-begotten son for My sake." Abraham lifted up his eyes and saw behind him a ram[2], sticking fast by his horns in the bushes; him he took and offered, instead of his son. The angel of the Lord spoke again unto Abraham, saying: "By My own self[3] have I sworn, saith the Lord; because thou hast done this thing[4], and hast not spared thy only-begotten son for My sake, I will bless thee, and will multiply thy seed as the stars of heaven, and as the sand that is by the sea-shore. And in thy seed[5] shall all the nations of the earth be blessed, because thou hast obeyed[6] My voice." And Abraham returned home with his son.

COMMENTARY.

Strength of faith. Abraham's faith was put to a most severe test. Almighty God had promised him a numerous posterity, and that in his seed all the nations of the earth should be blessed; and yet now He

---

[1] *Where is the victim?* How the father's heart must have bled at these questions of his son! And what must Isaac have felt, when his father told him that he himself was to be the victim! He was so young, and now he was to die by the hand of his own father! Nevertheless, he submitted to God's will, when he learnt that it was He who had commanded it.

[2] *Ram.* i. e. a male sheep. Abraham saw that it was by the will of God that the ram was on that spot; so he took him and sacrificed him, instead of his son.

[3] *By My own self.* God, being the Most High, can swear by nothing higher than Himself.

[4] *This thing.* i. e. because thou hast obeyed the command of God, and wert willing to offer up thy son.

[5] *In thy seed.* i. e. in Jesus Christ, who is the son of Abraham (Matthew 1, 1).

[6] *Because thou hast obeyed.* As a reward for his obedience God now solemnly repeats the same promise which He had made when He first called Abraham, that is, the promise of a numerous posterity, and that the Saviour should be born of his family.

commands him to sacrifice that son through whom alone he could have any descendants! Was not this an apparent contradiction? Nevertheless, Abraham's faith in the word of the Lord was unshaken, and he doubted neither the goodness nor the faithfulness of God. He did not murmur and say: "How can God ask of me such a hard and unnatural sacrifice? How can His promises possibly be fulfilled, if my only son is slain?" No, on the contrary, he said to himself: "God is good, faithful and true: His promise will surely be fulfilled, though how, or in what way, I know not! God is almighty: He is able to raise up Isaac even from the dead" (Hebr. 11, 19). Abraham believed so firmly that he is called a man of faith, and the father of the faithful. His example ought to lead us to believe firmly in God's word, and trust in His goodness and faithfulness, whatever our temptations and trials may be.

The love of God above all things. Abraham had a living faith, that is, he lived up to his faith, and consequently loved God above all things. His love of God had to stand a very severe test. He dearly loved the son whom God had given him, and the command which Almighty God gave him to sacrifice this son, was given to prove whether he loved God more than his son. Abraham, however, did not hesitate for an instant. He got up at once in the middle of the night, and made his preparations for the required sacrifice. He had interceded for the wicked cities, but he had no word to say for his son. He travelled along with the boy for three long days, and his heart must have sorely ached, as he looked upon Isaac and said to himself: "Very soon you will no longer be among the living, for you will have died by the hand of your own father!" However, his resolution never failed. He lifted up his heart to God and said: "Thou, O God, didst give me this son. Thou hast bidden me sacrifice him to Thee. So be it! Thy holy will be done! For love of Thee I will sacrifice him, however hard it be to me!" — Thus, during those three days' journey he offered up his son a thousand times on the altar of his heart, before he actually bound him and laid him as a victim upon the wood, and raised his hand to slay him. What great, what mighty love! Isaac was dearer to him than anything on earth, and on him he had set all his hopes; but he loved God. more than he loved Isaac, and for love of Him he offered up his son. He proved that he loved God above all things.

The object of trials. Why did God try Abraham? Was this trial necessary to show Him Abraham's dispositions? Did He not know beforehand that Abraham's faith was firm, and that he was quite ready to sacrifice his son for love of Him? Yes; God knew all this, because He is omniscient, and for Him, therefore, the test was not necessary: He need never prove men in order to discover their faith, obedience &c. Almighty God did not prove Abraham for His own sake but for Abraham's, in order to give him the opportunity of practising his virtues of faith, love &c., and of thus increasing his merits, and drawing down on himself fresh graces and blessings. This is why Almighty God so often tries us with all sorts of sufferings and adversities, these tests being of great benefit to ourselves.

The third promise of the Messias. The words: "In thy seed shall all the nations of the earth be blessed", contain a renewed promise of the Redeemer.

Isaac, the fifth type of Jesus Christ. (We have already studied the first four types: Adam, Abel, Noe, and Melchisedech.) In what way was Isaac a type of our Blessed Lord? The birth of Isaac was promised repeatedly: so was the coming of Jesus Christ. Isaac was the only and dearly beloved son of his father: Jesus Christ is the only-begotten and beloved Son of God, in whom His Father is well pleased. Isaac was obedient to his father, and was willing, out of obedience, to give up his life, letting himself be bound, and waiting patiently for his death-stroke: Jesus Christ was obedient to His Heavenly Father, unto death, even unto the death of the Cross. "As a sheep He was led to the slaughter, and like a lamb without a voice before his shearer, so opened He not His mouth." Isaac himself carried up the mountain the wood on which he was to be slaughtered: Jesus Christ carried up to Calvary the Cross on which He was to die. Isaac was saved from death by the wonderful intervention of an angel: Jesus Christ was brought back to life by the greatest of all miracles, His resurrection. You see in how many ways Isaac was a most plain type of our Redeemer, of His death and of His resurrection; but the sacrifice of Isaac, all the same, is not a perfect type of the Sacrifice of our Lord, for no figure can perfectly show forth the infinite love of God in giving His Son to die for us. In one main point Isaac's sacrifice was very different from the Sacrifice of Jesus Christ. Abraham was quite ready, out of love for God, to offer up his beloved son; but Almighty God would not permit the sacrifice to be completed, because sinful man could not be redeemed by a human sacrifice; and therefore the angel of God cried out to him, just as he was going to slay his son: "Hold thy hand!" God spared the son of Abraham, but He did not spare His own Son, but gave Him over to a painful death for our sakes. When, on Calvary, the executioners raised their hammers to nail to the Cross the Hands and Feet of God made Man, no angel cried out: "Hold thy hand!" The Sacrifice was completed, and the Son of God died for us on the Cross in unutterable agony of Soul and Body. "God so loved the world as to give His only-begotten Son, that whosoever believeth in Him, may not perish, but may have life everlasting" (John 3, 16).

The Vicarious Sacrifice of Jesus Christ. The ram whose head was caught in the thorns, which was sacrificed instead of Isaac, is a type of Jesus Christ, who was crowned with thorns, and offered Himself for us on the Cross.

APPLICATION. Abraham obeyed without any questioning, when God demanded of him the hardest of sacrifices. God asks nothing very hard of you, and yet you are often disobedient, and transgress those commandments which, by the help of His grace, you might very easily keep. When you disobey your parents, you disobey God, for it is His will that you should obey your parents and superiors.

Abraham practised the three theological virtues of faith, hope and charity in a most perfect way. Try to kindle them in your own heart. Let us conclude this lesson by making acts of faith, hope and charity.

CHAPTER XIV.

ISAAC MARRIES REBECCA.

[Gen. 24.]

NOW Abraham was advanced [1] in years, and the Lord had blessed him in all things. He, however, wished, before his death, to see his son wedded to a virtuous wife. But as the daughters of the land [2] were wicked, he said to his old servant Eliezer: "Go to my own country [3] and kindred, and take a wife thence for my son Isaac, but beware lest thou take one of the daughters of the Chanaanites, among whom I dwell." The serv ant promised faithfully all that Abraham had commanded him. He then took ten camels of his master's herd, loaded them with rich presents, and set out for Haran, where Nachor, the brother of Abraham, dwelt. Arriving there, he let his camels rest near a well outside the city. It was in the evening, the time when the young women were wont to come out to draw water from the well. Then he prayed fervently within himself that heaven might prosper his undertaking: "O Lord, I beseech Thee, show kindness to my master Abraham. Behold, I stand nigh the spring, and the daughters of the inhabitants of the city will come out to draw water. Now, therefore, the maid to whom I shall say: 'Let down thy pitcher that I may drink', and she shall answer: 'Drink, and I will give thy camels drink also', let it be

---

[1] *Advanced.* Abraham was now 140 years old, and Isaac 40.

[2] *The daughters of the land.* The inhabitants of Chanaan did not believe in the true God, but worshipped idols.

[3] *My own country.* Before Abraham lived in Chanaan he had lived with his father in Haran of Mesopotamia. Haran was several hundred miles from Bersabee.

the same whom Thou hast provided for thy servant Isaac; and by this I shall understand that Thou hast shown kindness to my master."

He had not yet ended his prayer when Rebecca, a beautiful and modest maiden, came out, carrying a pitcher. She went down [1] to the well, filled the pitcher, and was returning, when Eliezer ran to meet her and said: "Give me a little water to drink out of thy pitcher." · She answered him kindly: "Drink, my lord." And quickly she let down the pitcher upon her arm, and gave him to drink. And when he had drunk, she said: "I will draw water for thy camels also till they all drink." Then, pouring water [2] into the troughs, she let the camels drink. After they had drunk, the servant presented her with golden ear-rings and bracelets, saying to her: "Whose daughter art thou? Tell me, is there any place in thy father's house to lodge?" She answered: "I am the daughter of Bathuel, the son of Nachor. We have a good store of both straw and hay, and a large place to lodge in." Then Eliezer bowed down and adored the Lord, saying: "Blessed be the Lord God of Abraham, who hath not taken away His mercy and truth from him, and hath brought me the straight way into the house of my master's brother!"

He was then invited to the house, and bread was set before him, but he refused to eat, until he had delivered his message. When he had stated the object of his coming, Laban, the brother of Rebecca, and Bathuel, her father, answered: "The word hath proceeded from the Lord [3]: we cannot speak any other thing but His pleasure. Behold! Rebecca is before thee: take her and go thy way, and let her be the wife of thy master's son, as the Lord hath spoken." Then the servant bowed down to the ground, adored the Lord and, bringing forth vessels of gold and silver, with garments of the finest texture, presented them to Rebecca. He also presented rich gifts to her brother and mother. Then, full of joy, he partook of the refreshments offered to him. Next morning, after Rebecca had received the blessing of her parents

---

[1] *Down.* The place for drawing water from wells was generally below the surface of the ground and reached by steps leading down to it. But the drinking trough for cattle was above ground.

[2] *Pouring water.* This was hard work, for there were ten camels, each of which drank a great quantity of water, which had to be carried up to the trough.

[3] *From the Lord.* God has so ordained it.

Fig. 8. View of Hebron. (Phot. Bonfils.)

73

and brother, she set out with her maidens for her destined home, and on arriving there became the wife of Isaac. Abraham lived many years after Isaac's marriage. He died, aged one hundred and seventy-five years, and was buried by his son at Hebron [1], where Sara, his wife, had been buried before.

COMMENTARY.

Unity of faith the chief thing in married life. Almighty God chose Abraham in order that through him and his descendants the true faith might be preserved and spread. Therefore Abraham was very particular to choose for his son Isaac a wife who believed in and served the true God. He was resolved that Isaac should not marry any of the daughters of the heathen Chanaanites, however beautiful or rich they might be, for fear that either he or his children should become weak and wavering in their faith. His first care was that his son's wife should hold the true faith. It should likewise be the first thought of all Catholics, for unity of faith is, above all things, necessary to a happy marriage. Married people who look on religion as a secondary consideration are on the high road to indifference about their faith, and even to the loss of it altogether.

Eliezer the model of a faithful servant. Eliezer fulfilled his master's commission not only with prudence, but also with zeal, for he would not even eat until he had delivered his message, and wished to return to his master as soon as possible after having done so. He, like Abraham, was remarkable for his piety and confidence in God. He prayed fervently for guidance in making a good choice, and thanked God for the gracious guidance vouchsafed to him.

The virtues displayed by Rebecca. She was kind and hospitable to Eliezer, and compassionate towards the thirsty camels. She voluntarily offered to draw water for the beasts, without waiting for Eliezer to ask her to do so. He knew by this action that she had a kind heart, as well as that she was the bride destined by God for Isaac. God looks to the heart and not to the outward appearance, and chose Rebecca, on account of her virtues, to be the wife of the patriarch Isaac, from whom the Divine Redeemer was to descend.

A summary of Abraham's virtues. Faith and hope, love of God and his neighbour, hospitality, obedience, love of peace, disinterestedness and final perseverance.

---

[1] *Hebron.* Hebron (Fig. 8, p. 73) was twenty-five miles to the south of Jerusalem. Near this town was a double cave which Abraham had bought for a family burial-place. This cave was the only possession which Abraham had in the Promised Land. Sara, who had died three years before Isaac's marriage, was buried there.

Limbo. Where did Abraham's soul go after death? "He was gathered to his people" (Gen. 25, 8), i. e. he joined the souls of the just (such as Adam, Abel, Seth, Henoch, Noe &c.), in Limbo. There they rested in the blessed hope and expectation of the coming Redeemer who would deliver them from that prison and take them with Him into the eternal joy of the beatific vision of God.

APPLICATION. Begin and end each day, or any important undertaking, with a prayer for God's blessing. Begin with God and end with God; that is the best rule of life.

Are you obliging to your friends, and to strangers, as Rebecca was? Think in what way you can help others, whether brothers, companions, friends, or strangers, and resolve to make use of your opportunities. God will reward each little service you perform.

CHAPTER XV.

ESAU AND JACOB.

[Gen. 25, 20 to 27, 41.]

ISAAC and Rebecca remained twenty years without children. At length God heard their prayer[1], and gave them two sons. The first-born, Esau, was red and hairy, and of a rough, harsh temper. Jacob, the second, was smooth in appearance and gentle in his bearing. Esau became a skilful hunter and husbandman. Jacob was a plain man, and dwelt in tents. Isaac loved Esau, and ate with pleasure the game that he had killed. Rebecca, on the other hand, loved the mild and gentle Jacob. She loved him the more, because she knew by God's revelation (Gen. XXV, 23) that he, instead of Esau, had found favour with God[2]. One day Jacob was cooking a mess of pottage[3], when Esau, coming home from the field, faint with hunger, said to his brother: "Give me of this pottage, for I am hungry." Jacob said to him: "Sell me thy first birthright." Esau replied: „Lo, I die[4] of hunger: what

---

[1] *Their prayer.* They had prayed for many years that they might have a son who would be heir of the promises made to Abraham his father.

[2] *Favour with God.* i. e. that it was God's will that he should have precedency over Esau; that he was to be the heir of the promises, the forefather of the chosen people and of the Divine Redeemer.

[3] *Pottage.* A soup of lentils.

[4] *I die.* This was evidently an exaggeration. He might have appeased his hunger with other food; but he had set his heart on this particular mess of lentils, and would have nothing else.

will the first birthright avail me?" Jacob answered: "Swear,
therefore, to me." Esau swore[1] and sold his birthright. And
taking bread and the mess of pottage, he ate and drank and went
away, making little account of having sold his birthright.

Now Isaac was old[2] and had lost his eyesight. One day he
called Esau, his son, and said to him: "My son, thou seest I am
old, and I know not the day of my death. Take thy arms, thy
quiver[3] and bow, and go abroad[4]; and when thou hast taken
something by hunting, make me savoury meat thereof, as thou
knowest I like, and bring it that I may eat, and my soul may
bless thee before I die." Esau promptly obeyed the command of
his father, and went to the fields to hunt. Rebecca had over-
heard the words of Isaac, and fearing that, contrary to the will
of God, Esau might be preferred to Jacob, she said to him:
"Now, my son, follow my counsel. Go to the flock and bring
me two of the best kids, that I may make of them meat for thy
father, such as he gladly eateth; so that, after having eaten it,
he may bless thee before he die." Jacob hastened to the flock
and brought two kids. Rebecca prepared them as though they
were game, and then clothed Jacob in Esau's best garments, and
covered his neck and hands with the skin of the kids[5], and sent
him to his father with the meats she had prepared. Isaac asked:
"Who art thou, my son?" Jacob answered: "I am Esau, thy
first-born; I have done as thou hast commanded; arise, sit, and
eat of my venison that thy soul may bless me." Isaac said again:

---

[1] *Swore.* He swore to give over to Jacob his birthright, or his right of
eldest son. The first-born son received a double portion of his father's inheritance,
and after his father's death he became the head and priest of the family. In
the time of the patriarchs, it entailed not only these temporal advantages, but
spiritual advantages also, for by his father's blessing the first-born was made the
heir of the divine promises. Hence in those old and venerable patriarchal days
children esteemed their father's blessing very highly. It was to them the most
valuable part of the paternal inheritance, and was like a sacrament, by means of
which God conveyed to them the blessing which He had imparted to their forefathers, and made them the heirs of the promises (*Dupanloup,* De l'Éducation).
It was, therefore, most foolish and frivolous of Esau to sell these important rights
for a mere mess of pottage!

[2] *Old.* He was 137 years old and quite blind.

[3] *Quiver.* A sheath in which arrows are placed, something like the sheath
into which a soldier puts his sword.

[4] *Abroad.* Out hunting.

[5] *Skin of the kids.* The skins of the Angora-goat, the hair of which is very soft.

"Come hither that I may feel thee [1], my son, and may prove whether thou be my son Esau or no." Jacob then drew near to his father, and Isaac touching him said: "The voice, indeed, is the voice of Jacob, but the hands are the hands of Esau." [2] And he gave him his blessing.

Scarcely had Jacob gone out when Esau came with the game he had taken and cooked for his father. "Arise, my father, and eat," said he. Isaac, in surprise, asked him: "Who art thou?" and he answered: "I am thy first-born son Esau." And Isaac saw that Jacob had deceived him. Then Esau roared out with a great cry, saying: "He hath already taken from me [3] my birthright, and now he hath robbed me of my father's blessing." [4] Then he said to his father: "Hast thou kept no blessing for me?" And as he continued to cry out and lament, Isaac, moved with compassion, said to him: "In the fat of the earth, and in the dew of heaven from above, shall thy blessing be. Thou shalt live by the sword, and shalt serve thy brother [5]; but the time shall come when thou shalt shake off and loose his yoke from thy neck." From this time Esau hated his brother.

COMMENTARY.

Jacob's selfishness. Jacob did not behave either nicely or rightly when he turned his brother's desire for the pottage to his own advantage, and asked such a high price for it. He behaved very selfishly, and not at all like his unselfish grandfather, Abraham.

Lies and dissimulation. Jacob sinfully deceived his father in a twofold way. To begin with, he told a direct lie; but he also lied to his father in another way, by dissimulating, putting on Esau's clothes which smelt of the field, and covering his hands with the hairy skins. It is quite possible to lie without speaking a word. When you dissimulate,

---

[1] *Feel thee.* That I may know by the touch.

[2] *Hands of Esau.* They are as hairy as the hands of Esau.

[3] *Taken from me.* Was that true? No, for he himself had sold it to Jacob. Now, in his anger, he laid all the blame on his brother.

[4] *My father's blessing.* i. e. the blessing to which I, as the eldest son, have the right. But he no longer had a right to it, having sold his birthright, and sworn with an oath that he gave up all claim to it. He ought to have told his father this, when Isaac announced his intention of giving him his blessing.

[5] *Serve thy brother.* Isaac fully understood and realised that it was by God's special providence that Jacob received the blessing of the first-born, and that this could not be altered.

and lie by your actions, you sin against the eighth Commandment quite as much as if you told a lie in so many words.

Sharing the guilt of another's sin. The fact that his mother induced him to deceive his father, was a partial excuse for Jacob. Jacob, indeed, carried out the deception, but Rebecca instigated him, so that she shared in his sin. But Jacob was not compelled to obey his mother when she told him to act thus deceitfully.

The end does not justify the means. Rebecca and Jacob's intention in deceiving Isaac was good. They knew that Almighty God had chosen Jacob to be the heir of the promises, and they feared that His will would not be accomplished if Esau succeeded in obtaining the blessing of the first-born. True; but ought they to have committed a sin to attain this end? No! sin remains sin even if you have the best of intentions in committing it, and the noblest of ends to attain. Rebecca and Jacob ought, like Abraham, to have had confidence in God, and said: "The Almighty and All-wise God will carry out His own will even if we cannot see how." Instead of this, they took divine providence into their own hands and committed a sin. Thus, want of faith and confidence in God was the real cause of their sin [1].

Temporal punishment. Esau's indifference was punished by the loss of the rights of the first-born, not only to himself, but to all his descendants, the Edomites. Rebecca and Jacob were also punished in this world. Jacob confessed and repented of his sin, therefore God forgave him, but he did penance for it during many a long year. As you will read in the following chapters, he had to flee from his brother, and serve for twenty years in a strange land. Later in his life he was caused much grief by his own sons, who deceived him even more cruelly than he deceived Isaac, making out that a wild beast had devoured his dear son Joseph. Thus severely had he to expiate his one sin! Rebecca, who had sinned through love of Jacob, was punished by having to part with him, and she never saw him again in this life. In all this the divine justice is most clearly seen.

The Wisdom of God, which makes good come out of evil, can be learnt from this story. Almighty God had from the beginning, or rather from all eternity, chosen Jacob to be the heir of His promises. The faults of men (such as Isaac's preference for Esau, Jacob's deceit, and Esau's hatred) could not alter what He had ordained; on the contrary, they served, under the divine guidance, for the accomplishment

---

[1] It is but fair to mention that so great an interpreter of Scripture as St. Augustine hesitated to condemn the conduct of Rebecca and Jacob. "It is a mystery", he said, "and not a lie", meaning that the whole transaction was a kind of *drama* wherein a divine truth was acted in a human scene in which the actors were but *dramatis personae*. Anyhow their moral guilt is not so evident as the author might lead us to suppose. Another interpretation is possible. Indeed the author shifts the sin to something else. (E. E.)

of it. Jacob, especially, was strengthened in confidence in God, and purified by the very consequences of his deceit, his long exile and servitude. He was by them confirmed in humility and piety, and trained to be a holy man of God, and the worthy heir of the promises.

The frivolity and greediness of Esau. The elder brother sinned by longing too greedily for the mess of pottage, and by selling, in order to gratify a desire of the moment, his birthright, to which were attached such great privileges. He ought not to have given up his right to be the heir of the promises, and the forefather of the Divine Redeemer, for any price which the world could offer him. By giving way to a momentary and sensual desire, he proved how little he valued the good things of a higher kind which were held out to him. St. Paul, therefore, calls him "a profane person" (Hebr. 12, 16). Esau should have overcome his inordinate appetite. In order to attain to the virtue of temperance we must carefully deny ourselves.

Sinful oaths. Esau also sinned by lightly taking an oath which was not necessary.

Anger is a capital sin. Even as Esau was outwardly rough and hairy, so also was his character harsh and ungovernable. He conceived a great anger towards his brother; his anger turned to hatred; and hatred induced him to form the wicked project of killing his brother. In his blind passion he quite forgot how the murderer Cain had been punished, and gave no thought to the grief which his hatred was causing his parents (compare Commentary on the envy of Cain. Chapter V).

The prophecy of Isaac. While blessing Jacob he said: "And let peoples serve thee and tribes worship thee; be thou lord of thy brethren and let thy mother's children bow down before thee. Cursed be he that curseth thee, and let him that blesseth thee be filled with blessings." This promise has found its most complete fulfilment in our Divine Saviour who, by His human nature, was descended from Jacob. To Him all Christian nations bow down as to their supreme Lord.

The folly of sinners. Many men, alas, imitate foolish, frivolous Esau, who sold such great treasures for a mere mess of pottage. Every Christian who commits a mortal sin acts more foolishly than Esau; for he barters away treasures which are priceless and eternal for a passing, sinful desire. He renounces the grace of God, inward peace and joy, and all his merits; and draws down on himself the curse of God and eternal damnation. Therefore St. Paul says: "Look diligently, lest any man be wanting in the grace of God, lest there be any profane person like Esau who for one mess sold his birthright" (Hebr. 12, 15 &c.). Esau wept loudly for the loss of his father's blessing; but how will the children of this world mourn and wail on the great Day of Judgment? Stupefied by their passions, they bartered away their claim to heaven and all the imperishable treasures of the children of God, for the passing pleasures of sin; and on that day they will find themselves, in very deed, shut out from heaven and condemned to everlasting torments.

APPLICATION. Esau sinned through his greedy desire for the pottage. Have you never sinned by gluttony? Try for the future to overcome your greedy desires. Bear hunger and thirst for a short time with cheerfulness; and be not dainty about your food. He who does not tame his appetites, and deny himself, cannot be virtuous or happy.

Jacob ought to have given the mess willingly to his hungry brother. Have you never been selfish towards your brothers and sisters, and wished to keep everything for yourself, or chosen the best or largest portion for yourself?

Do you ever tell lies? Some day you must make satisfaction for every lie. God hates lies, because He is the very truth. If you wish to be a child of God, always tell the truth. "Lying lips are an abomination to the Lord" (Prov. 12, 22).

CHAPTER XVI.

JACOB'S FLIGHT.—HIS VISION OF THE LADDER AND SOJOURN WITH LABAN.

[Gen. 27, 42 to 29, 19.]

ESAU was very angry, because he had lost the blessing. He resolved to kill Jacob. Rebecca knew [1] the evil intentions of Esau, and saw that the life of Jacob was in danger. She therefore called Jacob and said to him: "My son, flee to Laban [2], my brother, and dwell with him, till the wrath [3] of thy brother hath passed away." Jacob at once set out [4]. As he went on, it

---

[1] *Knew.* Rebecca knew this by the threatening looks and hostile bearing of Esau.

[2] *Laban.* In Haran. You know already that Abraham had lived for a long time in Haran, before he came to Chanaan. Nachor, Abraham's brother, had remained there. His son was Bathuel, and Rebecca and Laban were his grandchildren. It was to this Laban, her brother, that Rebecca now told her son to go.

[3] *Wrath.* Esau's anger had passed into hatred, and hatred into fury and thirst for his brother's blood. Rebecca rightly hoped that, when Esau no longer saw his brother, this fury would die away.

[4] *Set out.* How sad Jacob must have felt when he bade farewell to his beloved parents, and went out into an unknown land. Sad at heart, and with his staff in his hand, he started forth, not knowing whether he would ever reach the end of his journey, or ever return home again. At that time Isaac was living at Bersabee, on the southern borders of Chanaan, and from thence to Haran was several hundred miles.

happened that night overtook him in an open plain. Being tired
from the journey, he lay down[1] on the ground and slept, having
a stone for a pillow. In his sleep he saw a ladder standing upon
the earth, the top touching heaven; and by it the angels of God
ascended and descended. The Lord was leaning upon the ladder

Fig. 9. Bethel. (Phot. Bonfils.)

and said to him: "I am the Lord God of Abraham, thy father,
and the God of Isaac[2]. The land wherein thou sleepest I will
give to thee and to thy seed. And thy seed shall be as the dust
of the earth; and in thee and thy seed all the tribes of the earth
shall be blessed."

---

[1] *He lay down.* Jacob had already travelled for several days, and when he
arrived, tired out, at Bethel (four hours' journey north of Jerusalem; Fig. 9), he had
to sleep in the open air. Wild beasts might have devoured him, or hostile men
might have seized him and taken him prisoner. But Jacob trusted in God: he
prayed fervently, and commended himself to the care of the Almighty. Then God
comforted him by revealing Himself to him in a dream.

[2] *God of Isaac.* i. e. the same God who appeared to thy grandfather Abraham
and thy father Isaac, and gave them the promises. Almighty God then repeated to
Jacob the same promises, namely, that the land of Chanaan should belong to his
descendants; that his posterity should be very numerous, and that of his family
should be born the Redeemer.

And when Jacob awoke from sleep, he said: "Indeed, the Lord is in this place[1], and I knew it not. How terrible[2] is this place! This is no other but the house of God[3] and the gate[4] of heaven." As soon as morning dawned, he took the stone upon which his head had lain during the vision, and set it up as a monument; he also poured oil[5] upon it, in honour of God, and changed the name of the place from Luza to Bethel, that is to say, the house of God. He also made a vow, saying: "If God shall be with me, and I shall return prosperously to my father's house, the Lord shall be my God; and of all things that Thou shalt give me I will offer tithes to Thee."

This being done, he continued his journey, and having come to a well near which three flocks of sheep were lying, he addressed the shepherds who were tending their flocks, saying: "Brethren, whence are you?" They answered: "Of Haran." He then asked them if they knew Laban, the son of Nachor. They replied: "We know him: and behold! Rachel, his daughter cometh with his flock." When Rachel drew near, Jacob met her in a friendly manner, and rolled the stone from the mouth of the well so that her flock might drink. He informed Rachel that he was the son of Rebecca, her father's sister. She joyfully ran home and announced the glad tidings to her father who, coming out, embraced Jacob and then conducted him to his house. Jacob remained[6] twenty years[7] with Laban, tending his flocks with

---

[1] *In this place.* i. e. the Lord is in a special manner in this place, not only in the general manner in which He is everywhere by His Omnipresence. God chose this place to make this grand revelation and promise to Jacob.

[2] *How terrible.* Jacob cried out in this way, because the fear of God had seized him.

[3] *House of God.* Because Almighty God had shown Himself visibly there.

[4] *Gate of heaven.* He calls the place the gate or door of heaven, because heaven had there opened itself before him, and he had gazed upon God and His holy angels.

[5] *Poured oil.* He placed the stone on which he had rested his head upright, to serve as a memorial of the wonderful vision of God; and, anointing it with oil, he consecrated it to God. By virtue of God's promises to him, Jacob had become a patriarch, and the patriarchs were not only the *heads,* but also the *priests* of their families, and offered sacrifice. It was only in the time of Moses that God instituted a special priesthood (Old Test. XXXIX). It was by right of his priestly dignity that Jacob consecrated the memorial stone.

[6] *Remained.* And God increased Laban's riches, for Jacob's sake. He, being blessed of God, brought a blessing on the master whom he served.

[7] *Twenty years.* Fourteen of which (seven for each) he had to serve in order to obtain Lia and Rachel, daughters of Laban, for his wives.

great care and fidelity. But Laban tried, by various unjust means, to withhold from Jacob a part of the hire to which he was justly entitled. Nevertheless, God blessed Jacob, and he became rich in flocks, and herds, and servants.

COMMENTARY.

All good things come from God. When Jacob made his vow, he did not say: "Of all things that I shall gain I will offer tithes to Thee", but: "of all things that Thou shalt give me". By these words the holy servant of God expressed his conviction that any riches or possessions which he might acquire, would all be a gift from God. Every true believer in God ought to say thus: "From Thee, O God, comes every gift. I thank Thee for what I am, and what I have."

The fourth promise of the Messias. The promise of the Redeemer was made to Jacob in these words: "In thy seed shall all the tribes of the earth be blessed", i. e. by one of your descendants shall grace and blessings be brought to all mankind. This Descendant of Jacob is Jesus Christ.

Our holy Guardian Angels. What does the heavenly ladder signify? Do the holy angels require a ladder, by which to ascend into heaven and descend to the earth? No! for they can pass to and from heaven with the swiftness of thought. God made this heavenly ladder to appear to Jacob so that he might understand that he was not forsaken; and that the holy angels had him in sight, took his prayers and good works to the throne of God, and returned to earth in order to stand by him and protect him. The angels help us in the same way, being, as St. Paul tells us, "ministering spirits, sent to minister to them who shall receive the inheritance of salvation" (Hebr. 1, 14). "That which Almighty God showed visibly to Jacob for his comfort, takes place continually, in an invisible manner, with those whom God loves. Day and night, even when they are asleep, God looks down on them, well pleased, and has given His angels to them to be their guardians. These holy angels ascend and descend the heavenly ladder. They ascend to carry the sighs and prayers of the just, to offer them as fragrant incense before the throne of God; they descend to bring back to them help, strength and consolation from above" (Overberg). See Old Test. LXIX, where the Archangel Raphael says to Tobias: "When thou didst pray with tears, and didst bury the dead, I offered thy prayer to the Lord" The holy angels are, therefore, ever working for our good.

Every Catholic church is a house of God and a gate of heaven. The words of Jacob: "How terrible is this place! This is no other but the house of God and the gate of heaven!" apply to every Catholic church still more than they applied to Bethel. For every Catholic church is, in very deed, a house of God, because every day, in the holy sacrifice of the Mass, our Divine Saviour descends on the altar, is there present under the form of bread and wine, and remains there with us, day and night, in the Most Blessed Sacrament. Every Catholic church is, also, a gate of heaven, because in it the one true faith is taught, and the Sacraments of Baptism, Penance and the Holy Eucharist are continually administered, through which we receive the remission of our sins, and obtain grace and life everlasting. Those words of the God-fearing Jacob might well be written over the entrance of every one of our churches. And, as for us, we ought to be very devout and re-collected in the house of God.

Vows. Jacob vowed to God that, if he returned safe to Chanaan, he would build an altar at Bethel and offer sacrifices to God; and you will see that, later on, Jacob faithfully kept his vow. We learn by this vow of Jacob that, even in quite ancient days, God-fearing men used to make vows to God, and that He was well pleased with such holy vows; for He gave Jacob everything for which he prayed, when he made that vow.

Diligence. Jacob served his uncle diligently and faithfully. All who love and fear God try to fulfil faithfully the duties of their state of life. Diligence is a virtue, if we are working, each one in his state, for the glory of God. Sloth is a sin, and one of the seven capital sins.

The efficacy of penance. Jacob's separation from his parents, and his long and hard servitude were a penance for his sin; and as he practised these penances willingly, they were pleasing to God, who forgave him his sin, and bestowed many blessings on him. Jacob left home quite poor, and returned a rich man. His confidence in God was richly rewarded. Nothing avails without the blessing of God.

The ladder of Jacob's vision, a type of the Redemption. This ladder stood on the earth, and its top reached to heaven, even to the throne of God; and thus it joined earth to heaven. By sin, this earth (or the men living on earth) had separated itself from heaven (from God). Men had become the enemies of God, and had lost all means of attaining to heaven. It is impossible to reach heaven by any human strength or effort, as the men who built Babel tried to do: heaven must first come down to earth, and draw men back to God. Therefore the Son of God came down from heaven, and, by so doing, put an end to the enmity between heaven and earth. He made satisfaction for us, and regained for us the grace and inheritance of heaven which we had lost. Jesus Christ is the true heavenly ladder. By His teaching He has shown us the way to heaven, and by His death He has won for us grace, in the strength of which we may climb up. Almighty God showed Jacob, by this vision, that some day the Redeemer would come and restore the union between heaven and earth, and would open to all men the way to heaven.

Oil is the type of grace. Even as oil illuminates, softens, strengthens, and heals, so does the grace of the Holy Ghost illuminate, comfort, strengthen, and heal the human soul. Thus, under the Old Law, men (priests and kings), as well as things, which were dedicated to the service of God, were anointed with oil. Under the New Law, Jesus Christ has made oil to be a great means of grace in the holy Sacraments of Confirmation, Extreme Unction and Holy Orders. The holy oils are blessed on Maundy-Thursday.

APPLICATION. Jacob had a great reverence for the place where God had appeared to him. Our churches are still holier places, and yet you often behave irreverently in church; your thoughts wander, you look about you, and you even laugh and talk! Examine your conscience on this point, and make resolutions of amendment. "The Lord is in His holy temple: let all the earth keep silence before Him!" (Hab. 2, 20.) Each time you enter a church, say to yourself: "This is the house of God; this is the gate of heaven."

Are you as diligent as Jacob was? Do you learn your lessons, and especially your catechism, diligently? Are you willing to help your parents, or your brothers and sisters, in their work? Resolve to overcome slothfulness, and to fulfil your duties faithfully for the love of God.

CHAPTER XVII.

JACOB RETURNS HOME AND IS RECONCILED WITH HIS BROTHER.

[Gen. 31—35.]

WHEN Laban saw that Jacob had become very rich, he began to envy him, and ceased to regard him with favour. Then God said to Jacob: "Return into the land of thy fathers[1]. I will be with thee."[2] Jacob rose up without delay, and set out with his family and all he possessed. He had reached the banks of the river Jordan when he began to fear on account of his brother. He sent messengers before him to say to Esau: "Let me find favour[3] in thy sight!" The messengers returned, saying to Jacob: "Esau cometh with speed to meet thee, with four hundred men." Then Jacob was sore afraid[4], and he thus prayed:

---

[1] *Thy fathers.* To the land of Chanaan where his grandfather Abraham had lived, and where his father Isaac still lived.

[2] *Be with thee.* I will protect thee. God said this, because Jacob was still in fear of the fury of Esau.

[3] *Find favour.* Act not as an enemy to me, but forgive me the wrong I did you.

[4] *Sore afraid.* Jacob had every reason to be afraid that Esau was coming at the head of four hundred men to take him prisoner, or kill him.

"God of my fathers, O Lord, who saidst to me, 'Return to thy land', I am not worthy of the least of all Thy mercies, and of Thy truth which Thou hast fulfilled to Thy servant. With my staff I passed over this Jordan, and now I return with two companies. Deliver me from the hand of my brother!"

During the night[1] an angel appeared to Jacob with whom he wrestled[2] till morning. And Jacob said to the angel: "I will not let thee go, except thou bless me."[3] The angel said to him: "Henceforth thy name shall not be called Jacob, but Israel (i. e. strength of God), for if thou hast been strong against God, how much more shalt thou prevail against men?"

He then divided his children, his servants, and his flocks into companies, and putting himself at the head of one of them, he advanced to meet his brother, bowing[4] seven times to the ground

---

[1] *Night.* Jacob had made all those with him go forward, while he himself remained alone behind, so as to begin this most eventful day by fervent prayer.

[2] *Wrestled.* Wrestling is that kind of combat in which, without the giving of any blows, one man tries to throw the other to the ground. The angel could easily have overthrown Jacob, if he wished it, for "he touched the sinew of Jacob's thigh, and forthwith it shrivelled up, and Jacob, from that time forward, limped on one foot, because the sinew of his thigh was shrunken". This lameness was to be to him a constant reminder of his strife, and a warning to be humble. Jacob was aware that he had to do with a supernatural being, on which account he asked for his blessing.

[3] *Bless me.* The mysterious being who appeared to Jacob while he was praying, and wrestled with him, was the "Angel of the Covenant", i. e. the Son of God, who, assuming a human form, allowed Himself to be apparently overcome by Jacob, as an encouragement to him, and a proof that he need fear nothing from Esau. Therefore the angel said: "If thou hast been strong against God, how much more shalt thou prevail against men" (Gen. 32, 28). The following explanation may help you to a deeper understanding of this mysterious event. A very important and decisive day lay before Jacob, and he might well ask: Would he reach the Promised Land in safety; and would God's promises, so all-important for the salvation of the world, be fulfilled? These questions did not only affect himself, but the whole of mankind, to the remotest future. At that moment Almighty God condescended to his chosen servant. The struggle to which he was subjected was a trial, similar to that mortal struggle which Abraham had to go through, when commanded to sacrifice his only son — a struggle for life and death, such as our Lord, the great Wrestler with God, had to endure in His Agony in the Garden. Jacob overcame, because his faith was invincible, and he came out of the struggle, strengthened and encouraged to live for his own and our salvation.

[4] *Bowing.* He humbled himself before his brother in order to awaken kindly feelings in Esau.

before him. But Esau, rejoicing to see his brother Jacob, ran to meet him and embraced him with many tears. Then, perceiving the children, he asked: "Whose are those?" Jacob replied: "They are the children which God hath given to me." And, making a sign to them, they all advanced, and bowed down before Esau. Jacob then presented Esau with several flocks. But Esau refused them, saying: "I have plenty, my brother; keep what is thine for thyself!" Jacob insisted, and said: "I beseech thee take of the blessing which

Fig. 10. Rachel's Tomb near Bethlehem. (Phot. Bonfils.)

God hath given me!" Then Esau yielded[1] to his prayer, and Jacob, full of gratitude for the protection of God, continued his journey, and arrived in the land of Chanaan. He came to Salem, a city of the Sichemites, where he bought a field; and then, mindful of his vow, he repaired to Bethel to offer sacrifice to the Lord. Thence he went south to Hebron, where his aged father lived. On the way (near Bethlehem) his wife Rachel died after having given birth to Jacob's youngest son Benoni or Benjamin (Fig. 10).

---

[1] *Yielded.* By this acceptance of gifts, the reconciliation was finally sealed.

Isaac was happy that his son had returned, and lived after this about twenty years. Finally, enfeebled by age, he died, one hundred and eighty years old. Esau and Jacob buried him at Hebron[1].

COMMENTARY.

All things come from God. When Jacob offered several flocks to his brother, he uttered these beautiful words: "Take of the blessing which God hath given me." He confessed thereby that it was God who had given, preserved, and increased his flocks.

Faithfulness of God. This story shows how God fulfilled His promise: "I will be thy keeper, and will bring thee back into this land."

Keeping vows. Jacob, too, was faithful, and kept his vow. After he had parted from Esau, he went to Bethel, and made there an altar. Picture to yourself how he knelt down before the altar, with all his household, and thanked Almighty God from the bottom of his heart.

Necessity makes people pray. In his great fear Jacob had recourse to God. We, too, ought to turn to God for help, comfort and strength in times of trial, fear and need. "Our help is in the name of the Lord who made heaven and earth" (Ps. 123, 8). The holy apostle James says: "Is any of you sad? Let him pray" (James 5, 13).

Prayer does not dispense us from helping ourselves. Jacob did not only pray to God, but he did all that lay in his own power to propitiate his brother. He sent messengers to beg his favour; he sent him presents, and humbled himself, bowing down seven times before him. We should act as he did, in our times of need or trouble. We should, indeed, pray, but we should not sit with our arms folded, but should use every lawful means to help ourselves.

Prayer must be persevering. The holy patriarch, wrestling with God, is a figure of persevering prayer. As Jacob wrestled and cried out: "I will not let thee go, except thou bless me"; so ought we never to give up praying, until we have been heard. Almighty God wills that we should, as it were, wrestle with Him in prayer, do violence to Him, and storm Him with our petitions. By doing so, we become more worthy to obtain what we ask. See the parable of the importunate friend (New Test. XLIX).

The power of prayer. We can see by Esau's conduct how powerful and effective Jacob's prayer was. For Esau still bore his brother a grudge, and came with four hundred men to seize him. But, on account of Jacob's prayer, God changed Esau's hard heart, and he became friendly towards his brother, and fell on his neck and kissed him, weeping with emotion. See in what manner God can change the hearts

---

[1] *At Hebron.* In the cave where Abraham and Rebecca were already buried.

of men! "As the division of waters, so the heart of the king is in the hand of the Lord: whithersoever He will He shall turn it" (Prov. 21, 1).

Hatefulness of envy. Not only was Jacob blessed by God, but, for his sake, God prospered Laban as well. And yet Laban envied his son-in-law, and was unfriendly to him. We can see by Laban's conduct what a foolish, hateful, and unjust vice envy is.

It is noble to forgive. What is the feeling of your heart, as you picture to yourself those two brothers weeping, and embracing one another? Is it not a moving sight? Is not Esau, forgiving and weeping, a thousand times better than Esau, angry and vindictive? Is it not, there-fore, a beautiful and noble thing to forgive those who have injured us? "Forgive us our trespasses, as we forgive them that trespass against us."

Parents are the representatives of God to their children. Jacob said, speaking of his children: "They are the children which God hath given to me." God gives children to their parents to bring them up for Him, to love and serve Him. On this account, parents are to their children the representatives of God, and children ought to honour them as such.

Jesus Christ, the Author of all grace. The blessing which Jacob wrung from God is a figure of the great gift of grace which Jesus Christ, the true Israel, wrung from heaven for us by His sufferings and death.

———

APPLICATION. Do you ever refuse to make friends with your brothers and sisters, or any other children who have injured you? Do you not nurse a feeling of resentment? Are you not ill-natured to them? Do you not wish them evil? Do you ask pardon of others (as, for example, your parents) when you have done wrong, and grieved them? Do you easily begin a quarrel? Forgive everyone from your heart! Be at peace with everybody, and especially with your brothers and sisters! Do not aggravate or strike anyone! It is far better to suffer wrong than to do wrong. Say to-day an "Our Father" for all those who have done you any injury!

CHAPTER XVIII.

JOSEPH SOLD BY HIS BRETHREN.

[Gen. 37.]

JACOB had twelve sons, and he loved Joseph[1] above all the others, because he was young and very good. And Jacob made him a coat[2] of divers colours. One day, when the brothers

———

[1] *He loved Joseph.* Jacob's preference for Joseph was justifiable, because the boy was so innocent and pious, but his father ought to have had the good sense not to prefer him to his brothers so openly.

[2] *Coat.* A coat of many-coloured and rich materials.

were all tending their flocks, some of them committed a most
wicked crime. Joseph, being shocked and angry, told his father,
on his return home, what he had seen. From that time forward,
his brothers hated Joseph, and could not speak to him kindly.
Joseph had once a remarkable dream [1] which he thus related to
his brothers: "Hear my dream: I thought we were binding sheaves
in the field, and my sheaf arose, as it were, and stood, and your
sheaves, standing about, bowed down before my sheaf." His
brothers replied: "Shalt thou be our king? Or shall we be subject to thy dominion?" And they hated him [2] more than ever.
Joseph also dreamed that the sun, the moon and eleven stars
worshipped him. His father rebuked [3] him, saying: "What meaneth
this dream? Shall I, and thy mother, and thy brethren, worship
thee upon the earth?" But Jacob [4] thought within himself that
perhaps God had destined Joseph for great things.

One day, when the sons of Jacob had gone with their flocks
to Sichem [5], Jacob said to Joseph: "Go and see if all things be
well with thy brethren and the cattle!" He obeyed, and went
in search of them. When they saw him afar off, they said: "Behold, the dreamer cometh. Let us kill him and cast him into
some old pit, and we will say some evil beast hath devoured
him; and then it shall appear what his dreams avail him."
Reuben, the eldest of the brothers, hearing this, sought to deliver
Joseph out of their hands, and said to them: "Do not take away
his life, nor shed his blood, but cast him into this pit." [6] This
he said, because he wished to restore the boy to his father.

---

[1] *Dream.* This was a supernatural dream, not an ordinary one.

[2] *They hated him.* His brothers envied him, first, for the preference shown
him by their father, as exemplified by the gift of the beautiful coat; secondly,
they hated him for having revealed their misdeeds to Jacob; and, lastly, their
hatred of him was increased by the fact that Joseph's dreams seemed to foreshadow
that he would one day rule over them.

[3] *Rebuked.* Jacob scolded him for repeating his dreams to his brothers, and
tried to remove the idea from his mind that these dreams meant anything.

[4] *Jacob.* He pondered over the meaning of Joseph's dreams. He suspected
that they had been sent by God, and that God destined Joseph for something great.
But he did not reveal his thoughts to Joseph, for fear of making him vainglorious.

[5] *Sichem.* Jacob, as we have seen, had property at Sichem. From Hebron
to Sichem was a distance of fifty-five miles.

[6] *Pit.* A deep pit walled in, in which rain-water was collected, and which
was then covered over with a stone. At the time that Reuben made his proposal,
it was dry.

When Joseph drew near to his brothers, they forthwith stripped him of his coat of divers colours, and cast him into the pit[1], in which, happily, there was no water. Then they sat down to eat bread, and saw some foreign merchants passing by, with camels, carrying spices, balm and myrrh into Egypt. Juda then said to his brothers: "What will it profit us to kill our brother? It is better that he be sold, and that our hands be not defiled, for he is our brother." The others agreed, and, the merchants having come up, they drew Joseph out of the pit, and sold him for twenty pieces of silver[2]. Joseph wept and besought them to have pity upon him, but in vain. The merchants took him away with them into Egypt[3].

Reuben, being absent at the moment, knew nothing of this wicked bargain. On going to the pit into which Joseph had been cast, and not finding him there, he rent his garments in despair, saying: "The boy doth not appear, and whither shall I go?" The other brothers remained quite unconcerned. Having killed a kid, they dipped Joseph's coat in it, and sent it to their father, saying: "This we have found; see, if it be thy son's coat, or no." The father, knowing the coat, said: "It is my son's coat; a wild beast hath devoured Joseph." Then he rent his garments, and putting on sackcloth, mourned his son a long time. His children gathered around and strove to soothe his grief, but he would not be comforted, saying: "I will go down[4] to my son into the grave[5], mourning."

---

[1] *Cast him into the pit.* Imagine to yourself how Joseph must have wept, and prayed for mercy: "Ah, spare me, my brothers! Am I to die of hunger and thirst in that pit! Think of our old father, how he will mourn, if I do not return to him! Think of the justice of God, and how He will punish you as He punished Cain! What have I done to harm you?" But his brothers had no compassion, and cast him without mercy into the pit; and then sat down to eat, just as if nothing had happened.

[2] *Twenty pieces of silver.* This was the usual price of a young slave. His brothers sold him as a slave, out of covetousness. As a slave, his owner could do as he pleased with him, and he was no more thought of than a beast, or any other piece of merchandise which could be had for money.

[3] *Egypt.* This country lies to the N.-E. of Africa, and was inhabited by pagans.

[4] *I will go down.* i. e. I care no more to live. I wish to die, so that I may join my beloved Joseph. Jacob thus expressed his belief in the immortality of the soul.

[5] *Grave.* To Limbo, where the souls of the just were detained.

COMMENTARY.

Innocent youth. It is impossible not to love the innocent and obedient Joseph, who did not follow his brothers' evil example, and who was such a joy to his father! Nothing is more beautiful than a holy, untarnished youth. God's blessing rests on him as it did on Joseph; for it was on account of Joseph's holy and innocent youth that God chose him for such high things. He who passes his youth in innocence, and is a joy to his parents, will look back to his young days with pleasure, even when he is an old man. On the contrary, if a man stains his beautiful youth with sins and vices, and is a grief to his parents, the memory of his early days will be as a gnawing worm to him for the rest of his life.

Revealing the faults of others. Now, was it nice or right of Joseph to tell his father about his brothers' sin? One says 'Yes', and another says 'No'; and both are apparently right. If Joseph had taken pleasure in revealing his brothers' sin, and had hoped to bring punishment on them by doing so, he would have acted very wrongly. He would also have sinned, had he revealed the wrong done to anyone but his father; for that would have been a sin of detraction. Joseph, however, had no bad intention, when he told his father what he knew, but acted out of true love both for God and his brothers, in order that his father might warn them and exercise supervision over them, and that thus his brothers might mend their ways, and not offend God any more. The revelation being necessary, it was Joseph's duty to make it. If he had kept silence about his brothers' sin, he would have shared the guilt of it. Had he not told his father, he would have been to blame, if his brothers had sinned again in the same way. You can learn an important rule from Joseph's conduct on this occasion: Never reveal the faults of others without necessity; but you must (and more especially, if you are asked) reveal them to those who have the right to know, such as your parents, masters &c.; and this, in order that the wrong-doing may be stopped.

Dreams. Joseph's dreams are called supernatural, because they were sent by God, and had a prophetical meaning. God has often shown men His will by means of dreams. Take, for example, the three kings whom God commanded in a dream not to return to Herod (New Test. VIII). Such dreams are supernatural, because they have a hidden meaning, and God reveals His will through them. It might happen, even now, that God should make known something to some holy person by means of a dream; but in a general way, dreams mean nothing, and are quite ordinary and natural. We possess the teaching of Jesus Christ, by which to know the will of God; and we must pay no attention to dreams and omens, or we shall sin by superstition.

The power of passion. The example of Joseph's brethren shows us, once more, to how many sins one passion can lead. The beginning of these men's sin was envy. Hatred, abusive language, and thirst for blood grew from it. They were heartless and cruel, turned a deaf ear to Joseph's lamentation, and sold him into the miseries of slavery. They lied to their father ("We have found this coat &c."), embittered his life, and counterfeited compassion for his grief. What a multitude of sins; and they all sprang from envy! Therefore, envy is a capital sin.

The evil consequences of one venial sin. This story teaches us that small causes (such as little faults and venial sins) produce great effects, and have very evil consequences. It was weak-minded and foolish of Jacob to parade his preference for Joseph; but this, in itself, was not a great sin. However, it roused the envy of his other sons, and brought much suffering and sorrow both upon Jacob and Joseph. So let us be on our guard against even the smallest faults.

Omission of what we ought to do. Reuben and Juda were the two brothers who sinned less than the others. Juda, at least, saved Joseph's life; and, as for Reuben—well, it might be said that he had no share in his brothers' sin, because he wished to save Joseph, and took no part in selling him. Nevertheless, he cannot be exonerated from blame. He ought to have openly and decidedly opposed his brothers' blood-thirsty plan, and boldly protected Joseph. Then, after he learnt that Joseph had been sold, he ought to have told the truth to his sorrowing father, who would have sent to Egypt, to seek and ransom Joseph. Reuben, therefore, sinned by omitting to do what he ought to have done.

God can make good come out of evil. Joseph's brethren said to themselves: "If we sell Joseph to be a slave in Egypt, his dreams will come to nothing, and he will never rule over us." But God's wisdom decreed that it was in Egypt that Joseph was to be exalted, and his brethren humbled before him.

Immortality of the soul. Jacob knew and believed that he would, one day, rejoin Joseph, even though he were dead. He knew that everything does not finish with death, but that there is an eternal life to come after this passing one.

APPLICATION. Take great pains to deserve the love of your parents by your conduct.

Do you wish for smart clothes? Do you wish to be distinguished from other children by your finery? God does not look to the clothes, but to the heart adorned with many virtues.

Perhaps you have often published abroad the faults of others without any necessity. On the other hand, you may have concealed what you know, from those set over you, who have a right to know. By doing so you have shared in the guilt of others.

You see in Jacob's case how very strong is the love which parents have for their children. Should not children be very grateful for the love and care shown them by their parents, and try to be a joy to them? Ask yourself if you have ever vexed, irritated, or grieved your parents, and resolve that, for the future, you will be a joy to them by your obedience and diligence. And do not forget to pray every day for them.

Joseph's brethren scoffed at him as a dreamer. Do you not often tease your brothers and sisters or companions, and give them abusive names? You must not let this bad habit take possession of you, for you do not like others to give you such names. Do unto others as you would they should do to you!

CHAPTER XIX.

JOSEPH IN THE HOUSE OF PUTIPHAR.

[Gen. 39, 1—20. Ps. 104, 17—22.]

ON arriving in Egypt, the merchants sold Joseph to Putiphar, the captain of the royal guard[1]. And the Lord was with Joseph, blessing him in all he did; wherefore he found favour with his master, who gave him charge of all his household[2]. And the Lord blessed the house of the Egyptian, for Joseph's sake, and multiplied his riches. But, after some time, Joseph was severely tried in his new home. The wife of Putiphar urged him to commit a most grievous sin. But Joseph would not consent, and said: "Behold, my master hath delivered all things to me. How, then, can I do this wicked thing, and sin against my God?" But even this decided refusal did not prevent the wicked woman from renewing her attacks on Joseph's virtue, and every day she importuned him[3] anew. But Joseph would not listen to her.

Now, it so happened that Joseph was, one day, alone in the house, attending to some business, when the woman took hold of the skirt of his cloak, and renewed her shameful proposal. But Joseph fled, leaving his cloak in her hands. The woman, seeing herself thus slighted, began to hate Joseph and to falsely denounce him to all the household and to her husband on his return saying: "The Hebrew servant whom thou hast brought, came to me to

---

[1] *Royal guard.* The soldiers whose duty it was to defend the king's life, and see to his safety.

[2] *Charge of household.* He made Joseph the overseer or steward of his house.

[3] *Importuned him.* Day after day, she tried to persuade him to sin; and this was wearisome and hateful to him.

abuse me, and when he heard me cry, he left the garment which I held, and fled out."

Putiphar, believing his wife too easily [1], was very angry and caused the innocent young man to be cast into prison [2].

COMMENTARY.

Piety. The fate of Joseph was a hard one, being thus torn away from his home and father, and taken to the market, to be sold as a slave. But Joseph did not despond. No doubt, the wrong he had suffered made his heart ache; but he trusted in God, prayed diligently, and submitted himself to God's will. He was a true worshipper of God. The end proved that his trust in Him was justified. By Almighty God's Providence, Joseph was bought by Putiphar, who began to love him on account of his virtues, and placed him, the least among his slaves, in a position of trust over his whole household. Therefore, St. Paul says: "Godliness is profitable to all things, having the promise of the life that now is, and of that which is to come" (1 Tim. 4, 8).

Performance of the duty of our state in life. Because Joseph feared God, he served his master so faithfully and zealously that Putiphar loved and praised him, and made him his steward over everything. He who wishes to serve God must, before all things, fulfil the duties of his state of life, faithfully and conscientiously.

Holy fear of God. A deep fear of God, and a hatred of sin were the fruits of Joseph's piety. When tempted to sin, he cried out, full of horror: "How can I do this wicked thing, and sin against my God!" He said to himself: "Mortal sin is the greatest of all evils. How could I offend the Lord my God who has so graciously created, preserved and protected me!" The fear of God is one of the seven gifts of the Holy Ghost.

The blessing attending piety. In the same way that God blessed Laban, for Jacob's sake, so did He bless Putiphar, for the sake of the God-fearing Joseph. Holy servants and holy children are sure to bring a blessing on a house.

Scandal. Putiphar's wife tried to induce Joseph to sin against the Sixth Commandment. Had he listened to this bad woman, he would have lost the grace and friendship of God. She wished to do him a spiritual injury, and thereby sinned also against the Fifth Commandment.

Calumny. Putiphar's wife calumniated Joseph, and accused him falsely to her husband, so as to revenge herself on him for having

---

[1] *Too easily.* Without examining the case, or hearing Joseph's version of the story.

[2] *Into prison.* In the state-prison. There Joseph, who was then twenty-six years old, was loaded with fetters (Ps. 104, 18).

resisted her evil suggestions. By this, she was the guilty cause of the innocent Joseph being deprived of his liberty, and cast into prison.

Rash judgment. Putiphar sinned by condemning Joseph, without careful investigation of the accusation brought against him. Such a sin is called rash judgment.

Means of preserving chastity. The sin which Putiphar's wicked wife wished to induce Joseph to commit was one against chastity. This temptation was a severe one to Joseph, considering her position and her shameless importunity. She was the mistress of the house, and he was but a poor slave. She would argue that the sin would not be a very great one; that no one need know about it, and so forth. She, furthermore, would flatter him and promise him riches, if he would consent, and threaten to do him great injury if he refused. Nevertheless, Joseph remained firm, and would not yield to the temptation. He loved the virtue of purity. He knew that impurity is the most shameful of all sins, and he carefully guarded himself against it. To do so, he used the following means: 1. He kept as much as he could out of this woman's way. He would not have been in her house that day, had not business called him there; and when she tried to detain him, he fled. 2. Before going into the house, he armed himself against the temptation by praying to God for strength. 3. Each time this wicked woman tempted him, he thought of God who sees everything, and who has a special hatred of sins against chastity. If you wish to preserve your innocence, dear children, you must do as Joseph did. You must avoid the occasions of sin, bad companions, and all unclean thoughts. You must appeal for help to God and His holy Mother; and you must think of God's presence, of death, and hell. You have far more powerful means of preserving your innocence than Joseph had in Egypt, for you have the holy Sacraments of Penance and of the Altar. If you receive these often and worthily, you will be able to resist all temptations. Joseph remained chaste, though he did not possess these mighty means of grace. Your sin will be far greater than his would have been, if you lose your innocence in spite of them.

APPLICATION. Joseph's temptation was a severe one, and yet he stood firm. Have you not let yourself be led into sin by far lesser temptations? Joseph paid no heed to the threats of this wicked woman, but feared God more than her. He preferred to suffer anything, even death, rather than offend God. Repent of your sins, and say often to God: "I will die rather than offend Thee."

Do you love purity as dearly as Joseph loved it? Would you preserve your innocence at any cost? Your innocence should be dearer to you than anything in the world, for it is the most priceless treasure you possess. Avoid, therefore, all occasions of

sin, bad companions, and impure things. "My son, if sinners shall
entice thee, consent not to them! If they shall say, 'Come with
us', walk not thou with them!" (Prov. 1, 10 &c.) Say every day
a Hail Mary for the preservation of your innocence.

CHAPTER XX.

JOSEPH IN PRISON.

[Gen. 39, 21—40.]

JOSEPH was now pining in prison, among criminals. But even
here God did not abandon him, and caused him to find
favour in the sight of the keeper of the prison, who gave him
charge of all the prisoners. Amongst these were the chief butler [1]
and the chief baker [2] of Pharao, accused of treason against their
king. After some time, they both, on the same night, had a
dream which perplexed them and made them sad.

Joseph, perceiving their sadness, asked them [3], saying: "Why
is your countenance sadder to-day than usual?" They answered:
"We have dreamed a dream, and there is nobody to interpret it
to us." Joseph said to them: "Doth not interpretation belong to
God? [4] Tell me what you have dreamed."

The chief butler first told his dream: "I saw before me a
vine on which were three branches which by little and little sent
out buds; and afterwards the blossoms brought forth ripe grapes.
And the cup of Pharao was in my hand, and I took the grapes,
and pressed them into the cup which I held, and I gave the cup
to Pharao."

Joseph answered: "This is the interpretation of the dream:
The three branches are yet three days, after which Pharao will
restore thee to thy former place, and thou shalt present him the
cup as before. Only remember me, when it shall be well with
thee, and do me this kindness, to put Pharao in mind to take me
out of this prison!"

---

[1] *Chief butler*. This was the name given to that officer in the king's court
whose duty it was to examine and pour out the wine which the king drank.

[2] *Chief baker*. The duty of the chief baker was to bake the bread for the
king, and, above all, to examine it, before the king ate it.

[3] *Asked them*. Full of sympathy for their trouble.

[4] *Belong to God*. By this Joseph meant: "Only those dreams which are sent
by God have any special meaning, and God alone can interpret such· dreams."

Fig. 11. Gathering grapes.

Fig. 12. Treading the grapes.

Then the chief baker, seeing that Joseph had so wisely interpreted the dream, said: "I, also, dreamed a dream that I had three baskets of meal upon my head; and that in one basket which was uppermost I carried all kinds of pastry, and that the birds ate out of it."

Joseph said to him: "This is the interpretation of the dream: The three baskets are yet three days, after which Pharao will take thy head from thee and hang thee[1] on a cross, and the birds shall tear thy flesh." The third day after this was the birthday of Pharao.

At the banquet[2] he remembered the chief butler and chief baker. The former he restored to his place; the latter[3] he caused to be hanged on a gibbet. The chief butler rejoiced in his good fortune, but he thought no more of Joseph.

COMMENTARY.

Fig. 13. Wine-press.
Fig. 11—13. Wine-making in Egypt.
Ancient Egyptian wall-paintings.

The object of suffering. Joseph really had a great deal to endure. At home, after being derided by his brethren, he was sold to be a slave in a strange land. Then, though innocent, he was thrown into prison and bound with chains, as if he were the worst of criminals.

[1] *Hang thee.* In olden times a criminal was first beheaded, and then his body was hung on a gibbet, as a warning to others.

[2] *Banquet.* At the feast, given by Pharao on this occasion.

[3] *The latter.* Apparently, the chief butler's offence was not so great as that of the chief baker, and therefore the king pardoned him on his birthday.

He had, apparently, lost everything now, home, freedom and honour, but he still kept what was best of all, his innocence and his confidence in God. Every kind of external misfortune had befallen him, but he still had a good conscience, and the peace of God in his heart, so that, in spite of everything, he was still inwardly happy. But we ask: "Why did Almighty God allow this holy, innocent man to be burdened by so many troubles?" The answer is: "He allowed it in order that Joseph might be confirmed in virtue, and prepared by these humiliations for his future exalted position. All the sufferings which God allows to befall the just are for this same end; only their exaltation does not always take place in this world, but generally in the next."

God does not forsake his servants. God was with Joseph, that is, He comforted and upheld him in his sufferings and enabled the jailer to recognise his innocence and usefulness, and thus to lighten his captivity. We learn by this story of Joseph that Almighty God does not forsake those who are His, and that we ought always to trust in Him, have recourse to Him, and submit ourselves to His will. You can see now why the Church (by the mouth of her priests) says "Dominus vobiscum" to us so often; for these words express her wish that God may always be with us by His grace. The response: "And with thy spirit", equally expresses the wish that God may, by His grace, dwell in the soul of the priest.

Compassion. When he was set over the other prisoners, Joseph was not rough and harsh with them, but, on the contrary, sympathised with them, and comforted those who were in trouble. "Blessed are the merciful, for they shall obtain mercy."

Humility. Joseph at once gave it to be understood that the interpretation of the dreams must come from God, and that of himself he could give none. He thus gave the glory to God.

Ingratitude. The chief butler behaved most ungratefully towards Joseph by forgetting him in the time of his own prosperity. Was not that horrible? But to whom is it that we owe most gratitude? Is it not to God? Thanksgiving is a necessary part of the worship of God. We should not thank Him by words only, but also by deed, and by doing His holy will. He who offends God grievously proves that he is thoroughly ungrateful.

APPLICATION. You have often been ungrateful to God, and also to your parents and superiors, by vexing and grieving them. Think of all the benefits both to soul and body which you have received from God! Say your morning and night prayers, and your grace at meal-times devoutly.

The chief butler forgot Joseph who, all the time, was lingering in prison. Christians are very apt to forget their departed

friends and benefactors who are suffering in the prison of purgatory. Has it been so with you? Pray every day for the holy
souls, and especially for your relations and benefactors.

CHAPTER XXI.

JOSEPH'S EXALTATION.

[Gen. 41, 1—52.]

AFTER two years, Pharao had a dream. He thought he
stood by the river Nile [1] out of which came seven cows,
very beautiful and fat; and they fed in marshy places. After them
came also seven others that were lean and ill-favoured, and they
devoured the fat ones. Then the king awoke.

He slept again and dreamed another dream in which he saw
seven ears of corn growing upon one stalk; and the ears were
full and fair. After these came up seven other ears, thin and
blighted, devouring all the beauty of the former. Pharao awoke
the second time and, morning having come, he sent for all the
soothsayers [2] and wise men of Egypt, and related to them his
dreams. But no one was found who could interpret them.

Then the chief butler remembered Joseph, and was sorry [3]
that he had so long forgotten him. He told the king that there
was in the prison a Hebrew [4] youth who had interpreted dreams
for him and the chief baker, and that all had come to pass just
as he said.

The king's curiosity being excited, he ordered the youth to
be brought before him. Then he addressed him, saying: "I have
dreamed dreams, and there is no one that can expound them.

---

[1] *Nile.* This is the only river in Egypt, and the lower part of it is divided
into many branches and channels. It is to this river that Egypt owes its fertility.
In the summer (from August to October) the Nile overflows its banks, and inundates
the whole plain with its slimy waters (Fig. 14). This water provides the sandy
plain with necessary moisture, and the slime, left behind by the inundation, acts
as a powerful manure. The crops are sown after the annual overflow, and the
ground produces corn in abundance, each stalk bearing from three to seven ears.
When the Nile does not overflow, nothing grows, and there is a famine.

[2] *Soothsayers.* The men who gave themselves out as capable of interpreting
dreams and foretelling the future.

[3] *Was sorry.* The duty of gratitude ought to have made him think of Joseph
as soon as ever he had received his pardon.

[4] *Hebrew.* He called Joseph a Hebrew, because the descendants of Abraham
were known by that name.

Now, I have heard that thou art very wise at interpreting them."
Joseph answered: "God alone can give Pharao a prosperous answer."
Pharao then related what he had seen.

Having heard the dreams, Joseph said: "God hath shown[1]
to Pharao what He is about to do. The seven beautiful kine,
and the seven full ears, are seven years of plenty; the seven lean
and thin kine, and the seven blasted ears, are seven years of

Fig. 14. Inundation of the Nile.

famine. There shall come seven years of great plenty in the
whole land of Egypt, after which shall follow seven other years
of so great a scarcity that all the abundance before shall be forgotten; for the famine shall consume all the land, and the greatness of the scarcity shall destroy the greatness of the plenty.

---

[1] *Hath shown.* i. e. these dreams have been sent to you by God in order
to show you what is, by His divine Providence, to happen in the future.

Now, therefore, let the king provide a wise and industrious man [1] and make him ruler over the land of Egypt that he may appoint overseers over all the countries, and gather into barns the fifth part of the fruits during the seven fruitful years that shall now presently ensue, and let all the corn be laid up under Pharao's hands and be reserved in the cities."

This counsel was pleasing to Pharao, and he said to his courtiers: "Can we find such another man that is full of the Spirit of God?" [2] Then the king said to Joseph: "Can I find one wiser and like unto thee? Thou shalt be over my house, and at the commandment of thy mouth all the people shall obey. Only in the kingly throne [3] will I be above thee."

Then the king, having made Joseph ruler over all the land of Egypt, took his ring [4] from his own hand, and placed it on that of Joseph. He also put on him a robe of silk, and a chain of gold around his neck, and caused him to be seated in a triumphal chariot next to his own, the crier proclaiming that all should bow their knee [5] before him and that they should know he was made governor over the whole land of Egypt (Fig. 15). He also changed his name, and called him saviour [6] of the world. Joseph was thirty years [7] old when he was made ruler of Egypt.

COMMENTARY.

Humility. When Pharao said to Joseph: "I have heard that thou art very wise at interpreting dreams", Joseph replied that it was God alone who could give the interpretation. This was as much as to say:

---

[1] *Industrious man.* A prudent, active man who would be capable of carrying out such a great work.

[2] *Spirit of God.* From the wonderful gift of interpreting the dream, Pharao knew that the Spirit of God was with Joseph.

[3] *Kingly throne.* Kings sit on a throne, and a throne, therefore, is the type of kingly power. The king meant: I will remain king, but next to me yours shall be the highest authority in Egypt, and you shall govern the country in my name. Joseph was, in fact, made the Vice-roy or Prime Minister of the king.

[4] *His ring.* Pharao gave Joseph his signet-ring, as a sign that Joseph was empowered to give orders in the king's name, and to seal them with the king's seal.

[5] *Bow their knee.* Pharao commanded that all men should bow the knee to Joseph, as a test whether they were ready to obey and honour him.

[6] *Saviour.* Because he had saved Egypt and the neighbouring countries from the horrors of famine.

[7] *Thirty years.* Joseph was now thirty years old. He was sixteen when his brothers sold him: therefore, he had been a slave for fourteen years, three or four of which had been passed in prison.

"Of myself I can do nothing: I can only interpret dreams by the inspiration of God." Thus he was humble, and gave the glory to God. "Not to us, O Lord, not to us, but to Thy name give glory" (Ps. 113, 9).

The reward of virtue. Joseph had suffered for a long time, but his troubles came to an end at last, his patience and trust in God were richly rewarded, and he was fully compensated for all his past sufferings. Once his brothers tore his clothes from his back: now he is clad in a robe of silk. Once he was degraded to a state of slavery: now he is raised to the highest dignity. Once he was loaded with chains in prison: now he is distinguished by a chain of gold round his neck. Once he was dragged off to prison like the worst of criminals: now he is led through the streets in the king's chariot, and all men bow before him. "Behold, thus shall the man be blessed that feareth the Lord" (Ps. 127, 4).

Fig. 15. King sitting on his throne, giving audience to a governor. Ancient Egyptian wall-painting from Thebes.

The Wisdom of Divine Providence is clearly to be seen in this story of Joseph's abasement and exaltation. What were Almighty God's intentions about Joseph? He had signified by the dreams which Joseph had dreamt as a boy, that he would one day be a great lord, and that his brethren would bow down before him. Man did everything possible to hinder this exaltation. His brothers sold him as a slave on account of those very dreams. The merchants took him far away; Putiphar had him cast into prison like a criminal; the chief butler, who was deeply indebted to him, forgot all about him. Humanly speaking, there was no prospect of either his freedom or his honour being restored to him; much less of his becoming a great Lord. But God made everything which was apparently a misfortune and humiliation conduce step by step to his future exaltation. By being sold, he was taken to the very land where he was to be exalted. By being put into prison, he became known to the chief butler who, later on, introduced him to the king. Even the chief butler's ingratitude, which must have deeply wounded Joseph, led, under God's Providence, towards the desired end; for if the chief butler had remembered him sooner, and got him taken out of prison at once, Joseph would not have remained in Egypt, but would have returned to Chanaan, to his sorrowful old father. Thus all these misfortunes led, under divine Providence, to the future exaltation of Joseph. Moreover, by his troubles he was confirmed in prayer, confidence, humility, and love of his neighbour, and was thus prepared for the important post for which God had destined him. When we think of all this, we can only exclaim with St. Paul: "How incomprehensible are God's judgments, and how unsearchable His ways!" (Rom. 11, 33.)

Joseph, the sixth type of Jesus Christ. Joseph, the beloved, obedient, and innocent son of his father, was envied by his brethren, illtreated by them, sold, and given over to the Gentiles: so also Jesus. Joseph was repeatedly tempted, and yet did not sin: so also Jesus. Joseph was falsely accused and unjustly condemned. Jesus suffered patiently and resignedly between two malefactors, to one of whom he foretold pardon: Jesus, crucified between two thieves, said to the one on His right hand: "This day shalt thou be with Me in Paradise." Joseph was set free from prison, and made ruler over the whole land: Jesus was raised from the prison of the tomb, and sitteth at the right hand of His Father. Joseph was called the saviour of the world, because he saved the Egyptians from famine; Jesus is indeed the Saviour of the world, because He has redeemed the whole world from sin and hell. The Egyptians bowed the knee before Joseph to testify the homage they owed him. "In the name of Jesus every knee should bow, of those that are in heaven, on earth, and under the earth, and every tongue should confess that the Lord Jesus Christ is in the glory of God the Father" (Phil. 2, 10. 11). (Repeat the first five types.)

Joseph's exaltation is a type of the glory of the just in heaven. God does not always reward the just in this world; for we were created, not for a temporal, but for an eternal happiness. But we may be sure that He will reward them in the next world by an "eternal weight of glory" (2 Cor. 4, 17). The just have to pass through many trials on earth. They may, like Joseph, be persecuted and ridiculed for their faith, piety, or conscientiousness, but some day they will be exalted, and rewarded with everlasting happiness. The more good a man has done on earth, and the more he has suffered for the love of God, the greater will be his reward in heaven. "Blessed are they that suffer persecution for justice' sake, for theirs is the kingdom of heaven. Blessed are ye when they shall revile you and persecute you, and speak all that is evil against you untruly, for My sake. Be glad and rejoice, for your reward is very great in heaven" (Mat. 5, 10—12). "Blessed is the man that endureth temptation, for, when he hath been proved, he shall receive the crown of life" (James 1, 12). "The sufferings of this time are not worthy to be compared with the glory to come" (Rom. 8, 18).

APPLICATION. Men often take that to be a misfortune which is really the contrary. Never complain of the ways of God, but always, and in all things, submit to His holy will. Have you ever complained? Are you not cowardly and desponding under suffering? Say to yourself: "God knows what is best for me. Not my will, but Thine be done!"

CHAPTER XXII.

THE SONS OF JACOB GO INTO EGYPT.

[Gen. 41, 53 to 42.]

THE seven years of plenty came, as Joseph had foretold. There was great abundance everywhere. And Joseph gathered the surplus of the grain[1] every year, and stored it up in the granaries. But, after the years of plenty, the seven years of scarcity set in, and a famine prevailed in all the countries. The people of Egypt cried to the king for bread, but he answered them: "Go to Joseph, and do all that he shall say to you."

Fig. 16. Egyptian wheat.

Joseph opened all the granaries and sold to the Egyptians. Likewise the people from other countries came to Egypt to buy corn. At last the famine reached Chanaan, and Jacob, having heard that there was wheat in Egypt for sale, sent ten of his sons with money to buy food. But Benjamin, the youngest, he kept at home, fearing lest some evil might befall him on the way.

The ten sons of Jacob arrived safely in Egypt, and seeing Joseph, they bowed down before him, not knowing[2] that he was their brother. But he at once recognized them, and remembered

---

[1] *Grain.* Corn, wheat &c. (Fig. 16).

[2] *Not knowing.* Joseph was a boy of sixteen, when they sold him, and was now thirty-eight years old. He would have changed a great deal in appearance in twenty-two years. Besides that, they could never have dreamt that their young slave-brother could have become this great ruler.

the dreams [1] he had dreamed. He wished to know whether they were now sorry [2] for their sin; so he spoke to them, as if they were strangers to him, and said: "You are spies." [3]

They answered: "It is not so, my lord, but we have come to buy food. We, thy servants, are twelve brethren, the sons of one man in the land of Chanaan. The youngest is with our father; the other [4] is not living. Joseph then cast them into prison [5] for three days.

On the third day, he brought them out and said: "If you be peaceable men, let one of your brethren be bound in prison, and go ye your ways, and carry the corn, that you have bought into your houses; and bring your youngest brother to me, that I may find your words to be true, and you may not die."

Then they said one to another: "We deserve [6] to suffer these things, because we have sinned against our brother, seeing the anguish of his soul when he besought us, and we would not hear; therefore is this affliction come upon us." They thought that Joseph did not understand them, for he spoke to them through an interpreter [7]. But he understood all that they said, and his heart was moved with pity, so that, turning aside from them, he wept [8].

But in order to see if their repentance was sincere, he returned to them and ordered Simeon [9] to be bound before their

---

[1] *Dreams.* The first of which was then fulfilled.

[2] *Sorry.* And if they had improved. Above all things, he wished to find out if they treated his younger brother Benjamin as harshly and unlovingly as they had treated him. This was why he forced them to bring Benjamin back with them, so that he might be convinced with his own eyes that he was still alive.

[3] *Spies.* i. e. you are foreign informers, and wish to find out how this country could be most easily invaded and conquered.

[4] *The other.* The brothers might well have hesitated and wondered what to say about Joseph.

[5] *Into prison.* He did this, so that they might have time to enter into themselves, and confess the sin which they had committed against him.

[6] *We deserve.* We can see by these words that they had entered into themselves in prison, and now confessed their guilt towards Joseph.

[7] *Interpreter.* A man who understood and translated both the Hebrew and Egyptian languages. In order not to betray himself to his brethren, he spoke to them in Egyptian, and the interpreter translated what he said to his brethren.

[8] *He wept.* He was moved by the penitent dispositions of his brothers. We can see by Joseph's tears that his harshness to his brothers arose from no desire of revenge, but from the very best intentions.

[9] *Simeon.* Simeon was the brother next in age to Reuben. Joseph would not have Reuben bound, because he had wished to save him; therefore he kept

eyes. Then he commanded his servants to fill their sacks with wheat, and put each man's money[1] secretly in his sack, and give them, besides, provisions for their journey. This being done, they loaded their asses with the corn, and returned home.

They related to their father all that had happened, and, on opening their sacks, every man found his money tied in the mouth of his sack. Seeing this, they were troubled and afraid[2]. And Jacob said to them: "You have made me childless. Joseph is not living, Simeon is kept in bonds, and Benjamin ye will take away. My son shall not go down with you, for, if any evil befall him, you will bring my grey hairs in sorrow to the grave."

COMMENTARY.

Admonishing sinners. Joseph treated his brethren severely, not out of revenge, but out of love. He wished to bring them to self-examination, repentance and amendment of life. To admonish sinners, so as to convert them and lead them to see their sins and repent of them, is a duty of brotherly love and one of the spiritual works of mercy. St. James says (5, 20): "He who causeth a sinner to be converted from the error of his way, shall save his soul from death, and shall cover a multitude of sins."

The object of sufferings. God, in His love, inflicts temporal sufferings on sinners, so that they may thereby be saved from the eternal sufferings of hell. These sufferings, such as sicknesses, misfortunes &c., ought to have the effect of turning the sinner's thoughts to God, death, judgment and eternity, of teaching him to see the vanity of earthly things, and of leading him to repent of his sins, do penance, and care for the things of his soul. Such troubles are called visitations, for it is in this way that God visits His wandering children, and seeks to bring them back to the right way. "For, whom the Lord loveth, He chastiseth" (Hebr. 12, 6). Millions of the blessed would not now be in heaven, if God had not visited them with tribulations in this world.

The strictness of parents. Parents must punish their children sometimes, so as to keep them from evil. They do so, and must do so, out of love. Parents who indulge their children in everything have no true love for them, because they spoil them. Happy the child,

---

the next eldest as a hostage. Very likely Simeon had been the chief instigator of Joseph's ill-treatment, and therefore a longer captivity was necessary to bring him to repentance.

[1] *Each man's money.* He would not take money for the bread, which was to feed his own family.

[2] *Afraid.* They feared that the great Egyptian governor would take them for thieves, and would be more severe than ever with them.

whose parents are strict. "He that spareth the rod, hateth his son, but he that loveth him, correcteth him betimes" (Prov. 13, 24).

Economy. Joseph practised economy in the time of plenty, in order to be able to help others in the time of need. The wise son of Sirach says: "Remember poverty in the time of abundance, and the necessities of poverty in the day of riches" (Ecclus. 18, 25).

Feeding the hungry. On one hand, we should guard against extravagance, on the other, against the detestable vice of avarice. Joseph fed the hungry Egyptians with bread: we too ought to be willing to help those in need.

A bad conscience. It was really from kindness that Joseph secretly returned their money to his brothers, and gave them provisions for their journey. But his generosity caused them no joy, only anxiety and fear, because their consciences were guilty. They feared that God meant to punish them for the crime they had committed against Joseph, and had brought it about that their money should be left in their sacks, so that they might be regarded and punished as thieves. An evil conscience spoils every joy. It fills the sinner with fear, and follows him about wherever he goes.

The treasury of Christ's merits. Even as Pharao said to the hungry Egyptians: "Go to Joseph", so does the Heavenly King say to all those who are laden with sin and misery: "Go to Jesus, and do all that He tells you", even as He said at the Transfiguration: "This is My beloved Son, hear ye Him." If we obey this command, we shall be saved from death. Jesus Christ bequeathed to His Church a treasury of His superabundant merits and graces, from which, by means of the seven Sacraments, we can draw for all our needs.

St. Joseph. The Church applies those words: "Go to Joseph", to the holy foster-father of our Lord, to whom the Joseph of Egypt bore much resemblance. St. Joseph was holy, chaste, and innocent, received revelations from God, was put in charge of the Holy Family, and is now in heaven, the true guardian and protector of every child of Jesus. His powerful intercession opens to us the treasury of divine grace. He is the special patron of Holy Church. We ought to venerate St. Joseph very much, follow his virtuous example, and implore his intercession.

APPLICATION. If you have any pain to bear, such as toothache &c., offer it to God, and resolve to lead a better life for the future. If you are punished by your parents, say to yourself: "It is what I deserve."

Have you not often been extravagant? Do not waste anything, and do not spend money unnecessarily, for instance, on sweets. Do not purposely spoil your clothes, books &c.; and willingly give of your savings to the poor.

CHAPTER XXIII.

BENJAMIN'S JOURNEY TO EGYPT.

[Gen. 43.]

BUT after some months the corn which the sons of Jacob had brought from Egypt was consumed, and the famine still continued. Therefore Jacob said to his sons: "Go again into Egypt and bring us a little food." Juda told his father that the governor had forbidden them to come back to Egypt, unless they brought Benjamin with them. And Juda added: "Send the boy with me that we may set forward, lest both we and our children perish. I take the boy upon me; require him at my hand." [1]

So Jacob consented to let Benjamin go. And he told his sons to take some of the best fruits of the country as presents to the governor of Egypt, and also to return the money, which they had found in their sacks, lest perhaps it was done by mistake. Then he prayed that God might prosper their journey, and make the governor of Egypt favourable [2] to them, and send them back with Simeon and Benjamin.

Then they went down to Egypt, and stood before Joseph. When Joseph saw them, and Benjamin in their midst, he commanded his steward to conduct them to his house, and prepare a banquet [3]. The steward obeyed. But the brothers, on finding themselves in the governor's house, were seized with fear, and said one to another: "Because of the money, which we carried back the first time in our sacks, we are brought in that he may bring upon us a false accusation, and by violence make slaves of us."

Therefore, they went to the steward at the door, and said: "We cannot tell who put that money in our bags." But he said to them: "Peace be to you; fear not." And he brought Simeon out to them. Joseph having now entered the house, they bowed down before him and offered their gifts. He kindly saluted them in return, and asked if their aged father [4] was still living.

---

[1] *At my hand.* I will be surety for him. I myself will stay in Egypt rather than that Benjamin should not return to you.

[2] *Favourable.* Favourably inclined, or kindly disposed towards them.

[3] *Banquet.* As soon as Joseph had convinced himself that Benjamin was alive, he resolved to receive his brothers cordially, and have a feast prepared.

[4] *Their aged father.* How beautiful and touching it is that Joseph's first thought should be to ask after his father.

They told him that their father lived, and was in good health. Then Joseph, seeing Benjamin, inquired if that was their youngest brother. They answered: "He is our youngest brother." Then Joseph said: "God be gracious to thee, my son"; and, going out, he wept, for his heart was deeply touched[1] at the sight of his younger brother. Having dried his tears and washed his face[2], he returned to his brethren and ordered food to be placed before them. Then they were ordered to sit before him, and he placed them according to their age, the first-born first, and the youngest last. All received gifts, but Benjamin received five times more[3] than the rest. And they wondered[4] much.

COMMENTARY.

God rules over everything, even the hearts of men. For this reason Jacob said when he sent his sons back to Egypt: "May Almighty God make the man favourable to you." God governs the hearts of men by His grace. "As the division of the waters, so is the heart of the king in the hand of the Lord. Whithersoever He will, He shall turn it" (Prov. 21, 1).

Love for parents. The first thing Joseph did was to ask after his father. While he was at home, Joseph had loved, honoured and obeyed him, and been a joy to him; and now, though he had become so distinguished, rich and powerful, he still loved his father dearly, and was most anxious for news of his welfare. He thus observed the Fourth Commandment.

Love for brothers and sisters. Joseph sincerely loved his brothers. He meant well by them, and was severe to them only for the purpose of doing them good. As soon as he was sure that Benjamin had suffered no harm from them, he was kind to them. He did not return evil for evil, but rather good for evil. They had sold him for money, and he, in return, gave them plenty of corn. They had thrown him into a pit and nearly starved him: he took them into his house, and feasted them royally. They had treated him as a rogue and a slave: he had them waited on like princes. They remained unmoved, when he prayed for

---

[1] *Touched.* Benjamin had been quite a little child when Joseph was sold.

[2] *Washed his face.* So that they might not see that he had been weeping.

[3] *Five times more.* By doing this, Joseph not only wished to distinguish and favour his younger brother, but he also wished to see if his brothers envied Benjamin, as they had envied him.

[4] *They wondered.* They could not understand how this Egyptian governor could know which was eldest &c. With the exception of Benjamin, they were all grown men of over forty, and, at that time of life, it is not easy to judge the difference of age.

mercy: he was so moved by the sight of them and their anxieties that he could not restrain his tears. Is he not a noble and beautiful character? Would that all brothers and sisters loved each other like that!

Restitution. Jacob bade his sons take back with them the money which they had found in their sacks; the reason which he gave being that it might have been put there by mistake. Jacob was, we can see by this, upright and conscientious, and wished to restore what he had found to its owner. "If", said he to himself, "this Egyptian governor refuses to take money for the corn, and has had the money returned in the sacks on purpose, then we can keep it with a clear conscience; but if it has been given back by mistake, I will, anyhow, return it, and then my conscience cannot reproach me."

APPLICATION. How do you behave to your brothers and sisters? Do you provoke or strike them? And are you angry and revengeful when they have injured you? Do you often quarrel with them? Where, then, is your love for them? You ought to love all your neighbours; and surely your brothers and sisters are nearer to you than any one else, and you ought to love them more than any one else.

Do you really love your parents? Do you ever vex or grieve them? You will have neither happiness nor blessing in life, if you do not honour your parents.

Have you kept anything which does not belong to you? Have you always restored anything you have found to its owner, or returned the money when too much change has been given to you &c.?

CHAPTER XXIV.

JOSEPH'S SILVER CUP.

[Gen. 44.]

THEN Joseph commanded the steward to fill their sacks with corn, and to put each one's money in the top of his sack; but to place in the mouth of Benjamin's sack Joseph's own silver cup. This was done, and the brothers set out on their journey.

But they had scarcely gone forward a little way, when Joseph sent his steward after them, who, overtaking them, accused them of stealing his master's cup. He said: "Why have ye returned evil for good?" [1] Struck with terror, and angry at being suspected of theft, the brothers replied: "With whomsoever the cup shall

---

[1] *Evil for good.* Why have you thus repaid the hospitality of my master?

be found, let him die [1], and we will be the bondsmen of my lord."
The steward replied: "Be it according to your words."

They immediately took down their sacks and opened them,
and when the steward had searched them all, beginning with that
of the eldest, he found the cup in Benjamin's sack. The brothers,
rending [2] their garments, loaded their asses again and returned to
the city [3].

And falling down [4] before Joseph, they said: "Behold, we
are all bondsmen [5] to my lord." But Joseph answered: "God forbid! He that stole the cup, he shall be my bondsman, and go
you away free to your father."

Then Juda told Joseph how much it had cost their father
to part with Benjamin. They would rather die, all of them, he
said, than return to their aged father without his youngest son.
Juda [6], moreover, offered to remain, and be the governor's slave
till death, if he would allow Benjamin to go back safe to his father.

COMMENTARY.

Sin is an ingratitude to God. Almighty God might well say to us,
what the steward said to Joseph's brethren: "Why have you returned
evil for good? I have done good to you; I have given you life and
health and grace, and you have repaid my bounties with ingratitude.
You have done a very evil thing each time you have sinned." Mortal
sin, especially, is a base act of ingratitude towards God, our Father.

Love for our parents, brothers and sisters. Juda had evidently a
very sincere love both for his father and for his brother Benjamin.

---

[1] *Let him die.* This they said, each feeling quite certain that no one of the
others was capable of such an act.

[2] *Rending.* With grief.

[3] *To the city.* i. e. the city where Joseph dwelt. With what feelings of
fear, grief and repentance must they have returned!

[4] *Falling down.* When, on other occasions, they had come into Joseph's
presence, they had bowed down to the ground before him, but this time, they
prostrated themselves, for they felt that everything depended on propitiating this
great man.

[5] *Bondsmen.* When first accused, they had said: "With whomsoever the
cup shall be found, let him die." But Juda makes no mention of this now. Once
it is a question of Benjamin, they would all prefer being slaves, rather than that
he should perish.

[6] *Juda.* Juda's conduct was very noble. He was quite ready to give himself
to be a slave, in Benjamin's stead, so as to spare his father sorrow for the boy's
loss. It was no longer possible for Joseph to doubt the change in his brothers'
dispositions.

Children should show their love for their parents by never annoying or grieving them, and by helping them in their necessities. And, in the same way, brothers and sisters ought to love one another.

———————

APPLICATION. In order to spare his old father grief, Juda offered to be a slave, instead of Benjamin, for the rest of his life. Have you ever caused sorrow to your parents? Repent of this, and take every pains to be a joy to them by your obedience, diligence &c. "Son, grieve not thy father" (Ecclus. 3, 14).

Juda protected Benjamin. You ought to take up the cause of your younger brothers and sisters, and help them to pray and learn to keep from evil and love what is good. But are you not, on the contrary, cross with them, and do you not, sometimes, encourage them to do wrong?

CHAPTER XXV.

JOSEPH MAKES HIMSELF KNOWN TO HIS BRETHREN.

[Gen. 45.]

JOSEPH could no longer restrain himself, and, therefore, he commanded his officers and servants to retire[1]. Then, with tears[2] and sobs, he said: "I am Joseph. Is my father[3] yet living?" His brothers could not answer him, being struck with exceeding great fear[4]. But Joseph said mildly to them: "Come nearer to me. I am Joseph, your brother, whom you sold into Egypt. Fear nothing, for God sent me[5] before you into Egypt for your preservation."

Then he said: "Make haste, and go ye up to my father, and say to him: 'Thus saith thy son Joseph: Come down to me; linger not; and thou shalt dwell in the land of Gessen; and thou

———————

[1] *Retire.* They were all Egyptians. He wished to talk undisturbed with his brothers, and also not to make known their guilt to others.

[2] *Tears.* His heart was so moved that he had to weep, before he could utter a word.

[3] *My father.* How he loved his father! He asked repeatedly after him, in order to hear over and over again the glad news that he was still alive.

[4] *Great fear.* Their guilty consciences made them fear that Joseph would now revenge himself on them.

[5] *God sent me.* He meant: It was by God's Providence that I came here, and became governor over Egypt, in order to save you and the Egyptians from starvation. He wished to comfort them and find excuses for them, and thus give them courage.

shalt be near me, thou and thy sons.'" Then, falling upon the neck of Benjamin, he wept, and Benjamin wept also in like manner. Then he embraced all his brethren, and wept over them, after which they were emboldened to speak to him.

The news went abroad in the king's court: The brethren of Joseph are come. And Pharao, with all his family, was glad. He told Joseph to invite his father and his brethren to come to Egypt. Joseph gave his brothers chariots and provisions for the way. He ordered two robes to be given to each of them, but to Benjamin he gave five robes of the best, with three hundred pieces of silver. Besides, he gave them rich presents for their father, and warned them not to be angry[1] on the way.

COMMENTARY.

Providence. "Not by your counsel was I sent hither, but by the will of God", said Joseph to his brothers. He understood that it was by God's permission that he was sold by them. It was, indeed, a great crime which the brothers committed. It was not by God's will that the evil was done, because He, being holy, can will no evil; but He permitted it, and so guided matters that good came out of evil. The good that came out of it was threefold. Firstly, Joseph's virtue was tried and strengthened, and subsequently rewarded by his exaltation. Secondly, his own relatives and all the Egyptians were saved from starvation. Thirdly, his brothers were converted.

Forgiveness of others. Just think how cruelly his brothers had behaved to the innocent Joseph. Being the powerful governor of Egypt, he could easily have had them cast into prison or killed, or he could have kept them as his slaves. Instead of this he freely forgave them. He did not even reproach them, but, on the contrary, made excuses for them, and loaded them with presents. Was not that beautiful and magnanimous?

Joseph as a type of Jesus Christ. We saw in chapt. XXI in how many ways Joseph is a type of our Blessed Lord. In this present chapter we can see a still further resemblance in him to the Divine Saviour. As Joseph forgave and excused his brethren, so did our Lord, hanging on the Cross, forgive His enemies, and pray for them: "Father, forgive them, for they know not what they do!"

The terror of sinners at the Last Judgment. When Joseph said to his brethren: "I am Joseph!" they were so full of fear that they could

---

[1] *Not to be angry.* He feared that they might begin to reproach one another, and each one make out that the others had had the greater share in the cruelty practised on Joseph. On this account, he admonished them to keep the peace.

not speak. How much greater will be the fear of sinners at the Last Judgment, when Jesus appears in power and majesty, and says: "I am Jesus, whom you have persecuted, and injured and crucified by your sins!"

APPLICATION. Joseph's example teaches us that we should from our hearts forgive those who have injured us, and return good for the evil they have done to us. The love of our enemies is, therefore, a beautiful and great virtue, which we Christians are bound to practise.

Brothers and sisters ought to love one another. Joseph's exhortation to his brethren: "Be not angry in the way", applies especially to them.

CHAPTER XXVI.

JACOB GOES INTO EGYPT.

[Gen. 45, 25 to 46.]

WHEN Joseph's brethren returned to their father, they told him: "Joseph, thy son, is living, and he is ruler in all the land of Egypt." But Jacob did not believe them, till they showed him the chariots and all the presents that Joseph had sent. Then he awoke, as it were, from a deep sleep[1]; his spirit revived[2], and he said: "It is enough for me, if Joseph, my son, be yet living[3]. I will go and see him, before I die."

And he set out for Egypt, with his whole family[4] and all his possessions. When he had reached the confines of Chanaan, he offered a sacrifice[5] to God, who spoke to him in a vision of

---

[1] *Sleep.* When a person dreams something terrible and alarming, and then wakes up and finds that there is no real cause for fear, he feels relieved and consoled. Jacob had hitherto mourned for his son Joseph, as for one dead — and now he heard that he was alive! His former grief was like a terrible dream of the past, and it was as if a heavy load were removed from his heart. However, it seemed so wonderful that Joseph, whose blood-stained coat he had seen with his own eyes, should be alive, and a great ruler in Egypt, that he could not believe it to be true, until he saw the waggons and costly gifts he had sent.

[2] *Revived.* His spirit, crushed by grief, recovered itself, and he felt happy.

[3] *Yet living.* It is quite enough for me to know that my son is alive. That he is rich and powerful is but a secondary consideration. I do not want anything in this world except to see him once more.

[4] *His whole family.* Jacob's sons were nearly all married, and had children. In all, Jacob's family, without counting the wives, amounted to seventy persons.

[5] *Sacrifice.* Jacob found himself on the point of again leaving the land which God had promised to give to him and his descendants, and of going with

the night, saying: "Fear not, go down into Egypt, for I will make a great nation of thee there, and will bring thee back again from thence." Consoled by the vision, Jacob continued his journey, and arrived in Egypt.

Juda went on in advance to apprise Joseph of his father's approach. Joseph immediately made ready his chariot, and went out to meet his father. As soon as he saw him coming, he descended from his chariot and embraced him, weeping.

And Jacob said to Joseph: "Now I shall die with joy, because I have seen thy face, and leave thee alive." Joseph presented his father to Pharao, who asked him: "How many are the years of thy life?" Jacob answered: "The days of my pilgrimage [1] are a hundred and thirty years, few [2] and evil [3], and they are not come up to the days of the pilgrimage of my fathers." Then Jacob, having blessed the king, retired. And Joseph gave his father and his brothers possessions in the land of Gessen [4], the most beautiful and fertile part of Egypt.

COMMENTARY.

The love of parents for their children. You can see by the example of Jacob, how very strong is the love which parents have for their children. He had mourned for Joseph for twenty-three long years, and the moment he heard that he was alive, full of fatherly love, he cried out that he asked for nothing more on earth than to see his son Joseph once more. Then, too, how troubled he was about the prisoner Simeon, and how anxious about Benjamin! He proved his love for Joseph by his actions, for out of love for him he left his home, notwithstanding his infirmities, and undertook a long and difficult journey. Parents are only too willing to do all they can for their children.

---

all his family into a strange country. Very likely the doubt arose in his mind, whether he were doing right. He desired that Almighty God would make known His will to him, and he wished, in case he were acting rightly, to ask the Lord's gracious protection for his journey. God heard Jacob's prayer, and gave him a threefold assurance: firstly, that he might without fear proceed on his way; secondly, that his descendants would become a great people in Egypt; and thirdly, that God would bring his people back to Chanaan.

[1] *My pilgrimage.* i. e. my life.

[2] *Few.* In comparison with those of his fathers. Abraham lived to be 175, Isaac 180, and Noe 950 years old.

[3] *Evil.* He called his days evil, because he had had so much trouble in his life.

[4] *Gessen.* The north-eastern part of Egypt.

Love and respect for parents. This story shows us the love and respect which Joseph had for his father. Joseph acted as he did, although his father was a shepherd, and shepherds were despised in Egypt. Moreover, by reason of the famine, Jacob had become poor; Joseph, however, was not ashamed of the humble and poor condition of his father, but showed him every open mark of respect that he could.

Respect for old age. King Pharao paid respect to Jacob, not only because he was Joseph's father, but because of his old age. We should always respect old age. "Rise up before the hoary head, and honour the person of the aged man" (Lev. 19, 32).

Prayer for light. Jacob prayed and offered up a sacrifice, in order to learn God's will. If we are in doubt, we should seek counsel not only from our parents, confessor &c., but we should pray to the Holy Ghost for light.

Consolation in suffering. Once both Jacob and Joseph wept for sorrow; now they wept for joy. After the rain comes sunshine, and after sorrow comes joy, often in this world, but most certainly in the next, if the sufferings are borne with patience and resignation. "God shall wipe away all tears from their eyes: and death shall be no more, nor mourning nor crying" (Apoc. 21, 4).

Life is a pilgrimage. God's servants know that they are strangers and pilgrims on earth. "The years of my pilgrimage have been few and evil", said old Jacob. His life had, indeed, been one of unrest, pain, and danger. He had had to leave his home, when he was quite young, and live for many years in exile and servitude. After his return home, there fell on him the heavy blow of Joseph's loss. Then came the great famine; and now, towards the end of his life, he found himself once more in a strange country, far from the Promised Land. He looked back sadly on his years of pilgrimage, and told the king that they had been evil. But, at the same time, he looked onward to that better and imperishable home, which is the aim and end of our earthly pilgrimage. Comparing his life in this world with that which is eternal, he said that his long years of pilgrimage had been few. "For we have not here a lasting city" (Hebr. 13, 14); we are but pilgrims on the road to eternity. Heaven is our home. We should not, therefore, cling to the things of this earth, but should, above all things, seek the kingdom of God. St. Peter writes: "I beseech you, as strangers and pilgrims, to refrain yourselves from carnal desires" (1 Pet. 2, 11).

God's Wisdom, shown by His guidance of the Israelites. Why did Almighty God's wise Providence send Jacob and his family into Egypt? In order that Jacob's descendants, His chosen people, should not be led into idolatry. The danger of this would have been very great in Chanaan, where they lived surrounded by idolaters. Esau had already made himself one with the children of Heth. Had Jacob's descendants

remained in Chanaan, they would either have got scattered among the
heathen, or they would have died out. They could not have developed
into an independent nation. In Egypt it was different. The Israelites
lived in a district of their own, cut off from and despised by the
Egyptians, on account of their being shepherds: thus the danger of
falling away from the true God was less. Besides this, God knew
that His chosen people would be purified by their long course of
servitude and suffering, and would be, as it were, forced by want
and persecution, to place all their confidence in God and look to Him
as their only Helper and Saviour. Lastly, Jacob's descendants would
learn much that was valuable from the Egyptians, these being far
ahead of the Chanaanites in agriculture, the arts, and all social laws
and institutions. By this means, the Israelites would be educated for
their high vocation.

APPLICATION. Say the first words of the Our Father: "Our
Father who art in heaven", with great devotion. Excite in yourself a longing for heaven, and say: "Thy kingdom come." To
win heaven is the most important business of our lives.

CHAPTER XXVII.

THE PROPHECY AND DEATH OF JACOB AND JOSEPH.

[Gen. 47—50.]

JACOB lived seventeen years in Gessen. When the day of
his end approached, Joseph, with his two sons, Ephraim and
Manasses[1], went to visit him. Jacob kissed the boys, blessed
them, and prayed that the angel, who had delivered him from
evil during life, might protect the sons of Joseph. To Joseph he
said: "Behold, I die, and God will be with you, and bring you
back into the land of your fathers."

Then, his children and grandchildren having assembled round
his couch, he blessed them all. To Juda[2] he gave a special

---

[1] *Ephraim and Manasses.* "Thy two sons shall be mine", Jacob said to
Joseph, "and shall inherit with mine." What should they inherit? Joseph was
much richer than his father, and neither he nor his sons required that which Jacob
possessed in Gessen. The inheritance which he meant, was that which God had
promised to his descendants, namely, the Promised Land. Of this land the two
sons of Joseph were to have equal shares with the eleven brothers of their father,
and thus Joseph was to have a double portion. In chapter XLV you will learn
how precisely these last wishes of Jacob were carried out.

[2] *Juda.* Who, after Joseph, was the noblest of his sons.

blessing. "Juda", said he, "thy hand shall be on the neck of thy enemies. The sons of thy father shall bow[1] down to thee, and the sceptre[2] shall not be taken away from Juda, till He come[3] that is to be sent, and He shall be the expectation[4] of nations."

Then, having told them to bury him with his fathers in the land of Chanaan, he died.

When Joseph saw this, he fell upon his father's face, weeping and kissing him. He then ordered the body to be embalmed[5]. And Pharao commanded that all Egypt should mourn Jacob for seventy days. When the time of mourning was passed, Joseph, accompanied by all the elders of the house of Pharao, set out for the land of Chanaan, and buried the remains of his father at Hebron[6]. Now, Jacob being dead, the brothers feared that Joseph would remember the wrong they had done him, and therefore they came to him and begged forgiveness. Joseph received them kindly, saying: "You thought[7] evil against me, but God turned it into good."

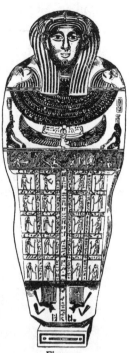

Fig. 17.

Egyptian painted coffin for depositing the embalmed body.

Joseph lived one hundred and ten years, and saw his children's children to the third generation. When his end drew near,

---

[1] *Shall bow.* Thy brothers will be subject to thee, i. e. the tribe of Juda will be the dominant tribe of the twelve.

[2] *Sceptre.* The sceptre, next to the crown, is the sign of royalty.

[3] *Till He come.* i. e. the royal dignity will last in Juda, until the Redeemer comes. Reuben, by an evil deed, had made himself unworthy of his birthright; hence, the double portion went to Joseph, and the rulership to Juda.

[4] *Expectation.* Expected with longing by all the people of the earth. As they were the heirs of the promises, God inspired the patriarchs, Noe, Isaac and Jacob, in the making of their last testaments, and they foretold the will of God, as if it were their own. The blessings they gave, and the arrangements they made, were in reality prophecies about the future destiny of the people of God.

[5] *Embalmed.* This was a custom among the Egyptians. Balm and sweet smelling drugs were introduced into the body, and the limbs tightly bandaged up. By this means the body was preserved from corruption (Fig. 17).

[6] *At Hebron.* In the double cave, where Abraham, Sara, Isaac and Rebecca were already buried.

[7] *You thought.* Your intention was to do evil.

he said [1] to his brethren: "God will visit you [2] after my death, and will make you go up out of this land, to the land which he swore to Abraham, Isaac and Jacob. Carry my bones [3] with you out of this place." He then died, and they embalmed him and laid him in a coffin (Fig. 18).

COMMENTARY.

The fifth promise of the Messias. Jacob's dying prophecy treated, firstly, of Juda's precedence over his brethren, and secondly, of the coming of the Redeemer. Both prophecies have been fulfilled. Even in the time of Moses, the tribe of Juda was the most numerous of the twelve. To this tribe belonged the royal race of David; and with it remained the capital, Jerusalem, with the Temple and the High-Priest.

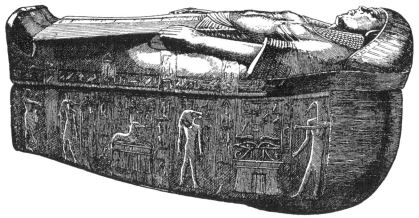

Fig. 18. Egyptian mummy-coffin. Paris, Louvre.

After the Babylonian captivity, this tribe gave its name to the whole nation, all its people being thenceforward known by the name of Jews. Finally, from the tribe of Juda sprang the Messias (Hebr. 7, 14), to whom the second part of Jacob's prophecy refers. In this wonderful prophecy, uttered 1900 years B. C., the very time of our Lord's coming was foretold, namely that in which the dominion of Juda should cease. This came to pass exactly as foretold, for, at the time of our Lord's birth, the foreigner, Herod, placed as king over the subjected people, ruled in Judæa. Jacob also prophesied that the Redeemer would be expected by all nations, i. e. that not only the children of Abraham, but all the nations would be looking for Him. This also came to pass.

---

[1] *He said.* Filled with a prophetical spirit.

[2] *Visit you.* First with servitude, sufferings and persecutions, then with deliverance.

[3] *My bones.* The splendour of Egypt had not made Joseph forget the Promised Land. He always looked on that as his country, and wished to have his body buried there.

Conduct towards aged parents. Joseph had always been a good son, and he honoured and loved his father as long as he was alive, and faithfully carried out his last wishes. His example shows us that we ought to support our parents in their old age; to visit and comfort them when they are sick; to be by their side at the hour of death; to faithfully carry out their last wishes; to pray diligently for the repose of their souls, and always have a grateful remembrance of them. "Son, support the old age of thy father, and grieve him not in thy life" (Ecclus. 3, 14).

The reward of virtue. Almighty God often visibly rewards virtue, and especially that which is shown by children to their parents. We can see this in the case both of Joseph and of Juda. a) Joseph loved and honoured his father; therefore, he was blessed by God even in this world. He lived fifty-four years after his father's death, rejoiced in his children and grandchildren, was protected and enlightened by God, and died a happy death. b) Next to Joseph, Juda was the best of Jacob's sons. He saved Joseph from death, saying: "It is better he be sold than that our hands be defiled, for he is our brother." He made himself surety for Benjamin, and when Joseph wished to keep the latter as a slave, he said: "I will stay, instead of the boy; for, if he is not with us, we shall bring our father's grey hairs with sorrow to the grave." Juda was rewarded for this generous conduct; for his tribe was the dominant one, and of it was born the Saviour. "Honour thy father in work and word and all patience. The father's blessing establisheth the houses of children: but the mother's curse rooteth up the foundation" (Ecclus. 3, 9 11).

Happy death. Is not Jacob's death striking and beautiful? Surrounded by his children, he gives his blessing to each one, foretelling God's will concerning them. Dying in a strange land, he fixes his mind on the divine promises, and leaves this world calm and joyous, solemnly proclaiming his belief in the coming Redeemer. Joseph, too, died a holy and happy death, mourned by his brothers, children, grandchildren and great-grandchildren. He died firm in the hope that his people would possess the Promised Land, and that, some day, the Redeemer would come. Both Jacob and Joseph had led holy, God-fearing lives; therefore they both died happy, peaceful deaths, firm in the hope of the future Saviour. As they lived, so they died. "With him that feareth the Lord, it shall go well in the latter end, and in the day of his death he shall be blessed" (Ecclus. 1, 13).

The words of Jacob to his son Juda refer to the Saviour, who was expected by the nations, and who was descended from Juda. The patriarch Joseph is a figure of St. Joseph, the foster-father of Christ. The one was ruler in Egypt; the other is the protector of the Catholic Church.

The twelve sons of Jacob were a type of the twelve Apostles. As from Jacob's twelve sons sprang the whole chosen people, even so, in

a spiritual way, have the chosen people of the New Testament, the
faithful, sprung from the twelve Apostles, who converted both Jews and
Gentiles, receiving them into the Church of Christ.

APPLICATION. If you wish to die a happy death, you must
fear God from your youth upward, and pray diligently for the
grace of final perseverance, because this most important of all
graces can only be obtained by prayer. Only the foolish and
cowardly hope for a sudden death. The Church teaches us to
pray: "From sudden and unprovided death, Lord, deliver us."
It is a great blessing *not* to die suddenly, but to watch death
approaching as Jacob did, and be able to prepare ourselves for it.
"Holy Mary, Mother of God, pray for us sinners now, and at
the hour of our death."

Some day you will stand by the death-bed of your father
or mother. How you will then grieve, if you have caused them
sorrow or suffering in their life-time!

CHAPTER XXVIII.

JOB'S PATIENCE.

[Book of Job 1—42.]

IN the time of the patriarchs[1], there lived in Arabia[2] a man,
whom God wished to give as a perfect model of patience
to all mankind, and for all time. This man's name was Job. He
had seven sons and three daughters. He owned seven thousand
sheep, three thousand camels, five hundred yoke of oxen, five
hundred she-asses, and had a great number of servants.

On this account, and still more because of his singular piety,
he was held in high esteem among the people of the East. One
day when the sons of God[3] came to stand before the Lord, Satan
also was present among them, and the Lord said to him[4]: "Hast
thou considered my servant Job, that there is none like him in

---

[1] *Patriarchs.* This was the name given to the founders of the people of
Israel, Abraham, Isaac, Jacob and his twelve sons. Job lived during the time of
the later patriarchs, after the death of Jacob.

[2] *Arabia.* South-east of the Dead Sea.

[3] *The sons of God.* i. e. the angels, who are witnesses and ministers of God's
Providence.

[4] *Said to him.* The dialogue or speech must be understood as between Spirit
and spirit. It is a spiritual manifestation and communication of thought.

the earth?" Satan, answering, said: "Doth Job fear God in vain?[1] Thou hast blessed the work of his hands, and his possession hath increased on the earth. But stretch forth Thy hand, and take away his possessions, then Thou shalt see that he will bless Thee to Thy face."

Then the Lord said to Satan: "All that he hath is in thy hand; only put not forth thy hand upon his person." So it came to pass upon one occasion, when the sons and daughters of Job were feasting in the house of their eldest brother, a messenger came to Job, exclaiming: "The oxen were ploughing, and the asses feeding beside them, and the Sabeans rushed in and took all away, and slew the servants with the sword, and I alone have escaped to tell thee."

While he was[2] yet speaking, another messenger came to tell Job that fire fell from heaven which struck the sheep and the shepherds, and that he alone had escaped. Whilst he was yet speaking, there came a third messenger, who announced to Job that the Chaldeans had taken away his camels and slain all the servants but himself.

Then came a fourth messenger who, entering in, said to Job: "Whilst thy sons and daughters were eating and drinking in the house of their elder brother, a violent wind came on a sudden from the side of the desert, and shook the four corners of the house, and it fell[3], and crushed thy children, and they are dead, and I alone have escaped to tell thee."

Then Job rose up and rent his garments, and, having shaved his head, fell down upon the ground and worshipped[4], saying: "The Lord gave, and the Lord hath taken away. As it has pleased the Lord, so is it done. Blessed be the name of the Lord." In all these things Job sinned not by his lips, nor spoke he any foolish thing against God.

And the Lord said to Satan: "Hast thou considered my servant Job that there is none like him in the earth?" Satan replied:

---

[1] *In vain.* Satan means that Job's holiness arises entirely from selfishness and greed of temporal prosperity.

[2] *While he was.* Thus quickly did the disasters fol'ow, one after the other.

[3] *It fell.* The beams gave way, and the stones fell, crushing and burying the children of Job.

[4] *And worshipped.* He did not murmur, but fell on the ground and adored.

"Skin for skin and all that a man hath will he give for his life[1];
but put forth Thy hand, touch his bone and his flesh, and then
Thou shalt see, if he will not curse Thee."

The Lord said: "Behold, he is in thy hand, but yet save his
life." So Satan struck Job with a most grievous ulcer[2] from the
sole of the foot even to the top of his head. And Job sat on
a dung-hill and scraped the ulcerated matter with a potsherd.
Then his wife[3] came, not to comfort, but rather to tempt him,
for she mockingly said: "Bless God[4] and die!"

But Job said to her: "Thou hast spoken like one of the
foolish women. If we have received good things at the hand of
God, why should we not receive evil?" Again, in all these things
Job did not sin with his lips or his heart.

Now when Job's three friends heard of the evils that had befallen him, they came to visit him. When they saw him afar off,
they knew him not, and crying out, they wept, and rending their
garments, they sprinkled ashes[5] on their heads. They sat with
him on the ground seven days and seven nights, and no man
spoke to him a word; for they saw that his grief was very great.

But when Job began at length to complain of the excess of
his misery, they reproached him, saying that secretly he must
have been a great sinner, or the just God would not have afflicted
him in so grievous a manner. But Job loudly and firmly asserted
his innocence, and consoled himself with the hope of the resur-

---

[1] *For his life.* Satan having been foiled in his first charge against Job, now
urges that indeed he cares not so much for worldly possessions which he can
easily acquire, but does care for health and outward appearance—for his skin.

[2] *Grievous ulcer.* He sickened suddenly with leprosy, a loathsome and painful
disease (Fig. 19). His body was covered with ulcers, and all men shunned him
on account of the horror and contagion of his disease.

[3] *His wife.* Job's wife was so prostrated and embittered by the loss of her
children, that she doubted God's mercy and justice. All her happiness was destroyed,
all her children were taken from her, so what good, said she, was the thought of
God to her! The sight of her husband's patience was more than she could understand, or put up with. By giving way to such feelings, she was obeying the
suggestions of the devil.

[4] *Bless God.* She meant to say: "What have you gained by all your piety?
Nothing remains for you but to die a miserable death. Therefore, leave God!
Why should you cling to Him who has rewarded your services in such a way?"

[5] *Sprinkled ashes.* As a sign of their horror, they threw ashes into the air,
which fell back on their heads. When they began to shower reproaches on him,
he had literally no human consolation left. Nothing remained to him but the hope
of the future Saviour and of the resurrection of the body.

rection of the body, saying: "I know that my Redeemer liveth; and, in the last day, I shall rise out of the earth; and I shall be clothed again with my skin, and in my flesh[1] I shall see my God, whom I myself shall see and not another. This my hope is laid up in my bosom."

When they had finished their reproaches, the Lord revealed Himself in a whirlwind to Job, and mildly reproved him, because, in defending his innocence, he had spoken some imprudent words. God's wrath, however, was kindled against the three friends, and

Fig. 19. Lepers in Palestine. (Phot. Bruno Hentschel. Leipzig.)

He commanded them to offer a holocaust for themselves, whilst Job should pray for them. And the Lord looked graciously on Job's humility[2], and granted his prayers on behalf of his friends. The Lord rewarded Job's faith and patience by healing his body and restoring to him double what he had lost. And new sons and daughters were born to him.

---

[1] *In my flesh.* Or my body.

[2] *Job's humility.* And contrition for the imprudent words for which God rebuked him.

COMMENTARY.

The moral of the story. Job, practising virtue while happy and wealthy, was admired by the angels, but he was not yet feared by the devils; but when he remained free from sin even in the depths of misery and affliction, then the devils began to tremble before him. By this we learn that wrong, patiently endured for God's sake, is the highest virtue. The friends of Job knew not that God sends afflictions even to His Saints, to make them more holy, and give them greater glory in heaven. Job also said that he would not live to see the Saviour promised to Adam, to Abraham, to Isaac and to Jacob, but that he would see Him on the day of the general resurrection. From Job we may also learn how pleasing to God, and how powerful is the intercession of the Saints.

The sufferings of the just. The chief lesson taught by the history of holy Job is that God does not send sufferings only for the punishment and conversion of sinners, but also as visitations to the just, for the purpose, firstly, of cleansing them from their small faults and imperfections; secondly, of · confirming them in the virtues of confidence, patience, humility &c.; thirdly, of enabling them to merit more, and therefore to receive a higher reward in heaven; fourthly, of making them shining examples for the imitation of their fellow-men. Lastly, for the purpose of confounding the devil, men's chief accuser before God.

All things come from God. Job first lost all his flocks and servants, then all his children, and lastly, his health. He did not complain; all he said was: "The Lord gave; the Lord taketh away; blessed be the name of the Lord!" But was it God, who took all these things from him? Had not our enemy, the devil, despoiled Job, and brought about all the disasters that we hear of? But Job believed and knew that nothing happens by chance, and that everything must take place by the guidance or permission of God, so that, in that sense, it was God, who had taken away all that he had. Believing firmly that God had sent him his sufferings, he resigned himself entirely to His holy will, and praised Him in the midst of his tribulations.

Patience in suffering is the work of faith. The trial of holy Job was, indeed, a severe one. Almost at one blow he was made poor, childless, and a leper! Forsaken by all, tortured with pain, taunted and tempted by his wife, who ought to have consoled him, he sat on a dung-heap, a very man of sorrows, with nothing to look forward to but a painful death. Even the arrival of his faithful friends did not lighten his burden, for they heaped on him reproaches for having brought these sufferings on himself by some secret sin. He fully realized what he suffered, and made it known to his friends by his sad complaints. He was not callous to his torments, but bore them with exemplary patience, without a murmur against Almighty God. From whence did Job draw these powers of heroic endurance? In a word, from his strong, living faith. He looked forward to nothing in this world except to a grave, in which to lay his diseased body; but this made him believe all the more firmly in the promised Saviour and in the future life. He knew and proclaimed that his Redeemer was living. Job could not know this, as he had never seen Him; but all the same he believed it, and also that God Himself, Who is eternal, would come as our Saviour. He believed, furthermore, that he himself would rise from the earth, and in his risen body would see God in heaven.

Resentment against Almighty God. Job's wife sinned grievously against the love of God. She loved her children more than she loved God, and could not resign herself to His having taken them all from her. She listened to the suggestions of Satan, and allowed herself to murmur against the ways of God, and even against God Himself. She also sinned against the love of her neighbour; for by her bitter scorn she tried to move her husband to renounce the service of God, as being that of an unjust Master.

Rash judgment. Job's friends also sinned. It was kind of them to visit Job in his misery, but they judged their friend uncharitably and without cause, reproaching him with having some secret sin on his conscience, without which God would not have visited him with these tribulations. Their main idea that "all evil is due to sin" was true, but they should have distinguished between original sin and personal sins.

The invocation of Saints. God was angry with these three friends, and bade them offer sacrifice and ask Job to intercede for them. Thus we can see that it is right and pleasing to God to ask for the intercession of the Saints; and we can also see that their intercession is efficacious, for God pardoned Job's friends, because he prayed for them.

Satan's power is limited. We see by the story of Job that *Satan can injure us only so far as God allows it.* Under the Old Law the devil had more power over men than he has now; for under the New Law Jesus Christ has crushed the head of the devil, and the suggestions of the evil enemy can hurt no one who clings to our Lord. Therefore, in her exorcisms, and in the blessing of creatures (as for instance of water), the Church prays our Divine Saviour to protect us from the attacks of Satan.

Job, the seventh type of Jesus Christ. Job, suffering the most profound grief of soul, seeing nothing but a miserable death before him and robbed of all human consolation, fell down on the ground, praying and humbly resigning himself to God's will. In this he is a type of our Lord in the Garden of Gethsemani.

APPLICATION. Job was not a Christian, and had not, as we have, the example of Christ's patient sufferings before him; yet how patient and resigned he was in the midst of his great trials! But you are a Christian, and in spite of being so you are often impatient, and incessantly complain and bewail your lot when anything goes wrong. Resolve for the future to look on all troubles as visitations from God; offer them up to God and bear them patiently, resigning yourself entirely to God's will. In all times of adversity you should, like Job, praise God, and say with our Lord: "Father, not my will, but Thine be done!" In all your temporal losses say with Job: "The Lord gave and the Lord hath taken away. Blessed be the name of the Lord."

II. EPOCH:

THE AGE OF MOSES.

(From the year 1500 to 1450 B. C.)

CHAPTER XXIX.

THE BIRTH OF MOSES.

[Ex. 1 to 2, 10.]

GOD had made two promises to the patriarchs Abraham, Isaac and Jacob: first, that they should be the fathers of a great nation; second, that the Saviour would be a descendant of theirs. The first promise was now fulfilled. In the space of two hundred years the descendants of Jacob in Egypt had become a great people. In the meantime a new king had arisen, "who knew not[1] Joseph", and who said to the Egyptians: "Behold, the children of Israel[2] are stronger than we. Come, let us oppress them, lest they join with our enemies and depart out of the land."

Now the Egyptians hated the children of Israel, and mocked them and made their life bitter, both by hard words and also with hard work in brick and clay (Fig. 20). And the king placed

---

[1] *Knew not.* i. e. did not care to remember the services he had rendered to Egypt.

[2] *Israel.* They took this name from Jacob's second name, Israel.

overseers [1] over them, to oppress them with labour. But the more they were oppressed, the more numerous they became. The king, seeing this, issued a decree that all the male children born of Hebrew parents should be cast into the river [2]; hoping, by this means, either to destroy the Hebrew people, or at least to prevent their increasing in number.

Now it came to pass that a Hebrew mother bore a son, and, seeing that he was very beautiful, she hid him for three months. At the end of that time, not being able to keep him any longer [3], she laid the babe in a basket of reeds and placed it in the sedges [4] by the river's bank. The sister of the child stood a little way off, to see what would happen.

And behold, at that time the daughter of Pharao went down to bathe in the Nile. Seeing the basket amongst the bulrushes

Fig. 20. Israelites forced to labour in Egypt (brick-making). Old Egyptian wall-painting.

by the river-bank, the princess sent one of her maids to bring it to her. On opening it, they saw within it a lovely infant, crying piteously. She had compassion on it, and said: "This is one of the babes of the Hebrews." The child's sister [5] then, taking courage, drew near and asked: "Shall I go and call to thee a Hebrew woman to nurse the babe?" She answered: "Go!" The maid went and called her mother.

---

[1] *Overseers.* Or task-masters, so called because they forced the Israelites to labour and build great houses, dams, canals and monuments.

[2] *The river.* i. e. the Nile.

[3] *Any longer.* The king had given orders that the houses of the Israelites should be searched from time to time.

[4] *The sedges.* Or bulrushes. She did this in order that the floating basket might not be carried down the river by the current.

[5] *Sister.* Miriam (Mary).

When the mother came, the princess said to her: "Take this child and nurse him for me, and I will give thee wages." The woman then took the child and nursed him. And when he was grown up, he was brought to Pharao's daughter, who adopted him [1] as her own, and called him Moses, which means rescued from the waters.

COMMENTARY.

The Wisdom of Divine Providence. God destined Moses to be the deliverer of His chosen people. Pharao's cruel command to drown all the male children of the Israelites could not nullify what He had decreed. On the contrary, it served, under His guidance, for the accomplishment of His designs; for Moses, being brought up in the king's court, was educated in the knowledge of the Egyptians, and was thus prepared for his high vocation of leader and deliverer of God's people.

The uses of tribulation. God permitted the Israelites to be oppressed, in order that they might begin to yearn for the Promised Land and the future Saviour, and might keep aloof from the Egyptians. All our various troubles in this life ought to detach our hearts from earthly things, and turn them towards heaven and eternity. If earth were a paradise, who would long for heaven?

The love of parents for their children. If it had been discovered that Moses' parents had hidden away a son, they would have been severely punished, and most likely put to death. Parents are willing to expose themselves to a great deal of danger for the sake of their children.

The confidence in God shown by Moses' parents. They did what they could to save the child, and prayed, full of confidence, to God to help them. Their confidence was not misplaced. He who trusts in God, builds on a sure foundation.

Compassion. The king's daughter was a pagan, and yet she had a kind, compassionate heart. How much more compassion ought we Christians to show! "Blessed are the merciful, for they shall obtain mercy." The Society of the Holy Childhood is an example of what can be done. By means of it, heathen children are saved from death, baptized and brought up as Christians.

Moses saved in his infancy from the cruel edict of Pharao is a type of Christ saved in His infancy from the slaughter ordered by Herod.

APPLICATION. God has preserved you, too, from many a danger. In order to save your soul, God has, so to speak, made you pass through the waters of Baptism, and has adopted you to

---

[1] *Adopted him.* She clothed him, educated him, and had him altogether treated as if he were her own son.

be the child of the Most High King. "Behold, what manner of love the Father hath bestowed on us" (1 John 3, 1). You are, therefore, another Moses. Serve God, then, as faithfully as Moses served Him.

CHAPTER XXX.

THE FLIGHT OF MOSES.

[Ex. 2, 11—22.]

MOSES was reared at the court of Pharao, and instructed in all the learning of Egypt. But when he was grown up and saw the misery of his people, the Hebrews, he resolved to help them. For he would rather be afflicted and despised with the people of God, than live in the palace of a wicked king. He left[1] the splendour of the court, and openly declared himself a friend[2] of the Israelites. He even slew an Egyptian when he saw him illtreating a Hebrew.

The king, hearing this, sought to kill him; but Moses fled to the land of Madian[3]. On his way he sat down by a well, and behold, the seven daughters of Jethro, a priest, came to draw water for their flocks. But when the sheep stood near the troughs, some shepherds rushed in and rudely drove away the flocks. Thereupon Moses arose, defended the maidens, and watered their sheep.

Then the sisters went home, and their father asked: "Why have ye returned sooner than usual?" They answered: "A man of Egypt drove away the shepherds, and gave our sheep to drink." Jethro asked again: "Where is he? Call him that he may eat bread." So Moses entered the house and swore to dwell with Jethro to keep his sheep, and remained for forty years[4], and married Sephora, one of the daughters of Jethro.

---

[1] *He left.* He left the king's court when he was forty years old.

[2] *A friend.* And did what he could to defend them against the oppression of the Egyptians.

[3] *Madian.* This land was in the neighbourhood of Mount Sinai. The inhabitants of this district were descended from Abraham, and had kept their faith in the true God. It is well to distinguish between them and the heathen Madianites, who lived further east.

[4] *Forty years.* During that time Moses lived a simple and solitary life. He prayed fervently to God, especially for the deliverance of his people; he practised humility and self-denial, and learnt the ways of the wilderness, thus preparing himself for his calling.

COMMENTARY.

Steadfast faith. Moses, while living at home with his parents, had been taught to believe in the true God and the promised Redeemer. When he left home, he went to live at the king's court, and was surrounded on all sides by pagans. Still he preserved the true faith taught to him as a boy, and remained firm in the worship of the one true God. When he was a man, he preferred to be poor and persecuted, rather than rich and honoured, and unable to help his brethren in the faith. He therefore left the pagan court, and joined his oppressed countrymen.

The blessings of solitude. It was in his solitude that God appeared to Moses. God is to be found, not in the turmoil of the world, but in solitude. There He speaks to our hearts, and there we can speak to Him. He who is always in society, must be distracted, and cannot pray well. All the Saints loved solitude, and sought it out, so that they might be alone with God. St. Bernard praised it in these words: "O blessed solitude! O solitary blessedness!"

Moses a type of Christ. Moses, despising the splendour of Egypt in order to comfort the Jews, is a figure of the Son of God, who came down from heaven, was born in a stable, and laid in a manger, to redeem us from the flames of hell.

———

APPLICATION. O, may you, when you grow up, be as steadfast in faith as Moses was, and never forget or deny that Christian teaching, which you are now receiving in your youth. Pray for steadfastness and perseverance in the holy Catholic faith!

Cannot you sometimes contrive to be alone for a few minutes, imitating in this St. Aloysius, who used to retire into some corner of his father's house, so as to be able to pray undisturbed?

CHAPTER XXXI.

THE BURNING BUSH AND CALL OF MOSES.

[Ex. 2, 23 to 4, 31.]

NOW Moses fed the sheep of Jethro, his father-in-law. One day he drove his flock into the desert[1], and came as far as Mount Horeb[2]. There the Lord appeared to him in a flame of fire, which issued from the midst of a bush. Moses saw that

———

[1] *The desert.* An uninhabited and sterile country, stony and sandy, in which grass and shrubs grew only here and there.

[2] *Horeb.* Which was part of Mount Sinai.

the bush was on fire and was not burnt[1]. He said: "I will go near to see why the bush is not burnt." As Moses drew near, the Lord cried out to him from the burning bush: "Moses, Moses!" And he answered: "Here I am." And God said: "Come not nigh hither. Put off the shoes[2] from thy feet; for the place whereon thou standest is holy ground[3]. I am the God of thy father, the God of Abraham, the God of Isaac, and the God of Jacob."

Moses, in awful reverence, hid[4] his face, and dared not look at God. The Lord said to him: "I have seen[5] the affliction of my people in Egypt, and I am come to deliver them out of the hands of the Egyptians, and to bring them out of that land into a land flowing with milk[6] and honey." The Lord further told Moses that he should go to Pharao to demand the liberation of the children of Israel. Moses answered: "Who am I[7] that I should go to Pharao, and should bring forth the children of Israel out of Egypt?" The Lord said: "I will be with thee."[8]

Moses objected that the people would not believe him, but would ask who[9] sent him. Then God said to Moses: "*I am who am*[10]. Thus shalt thou say to the children of Israel: *He who is*, hath sent me to you." Moses answered and said: "They will not believe me, nor hear my voice; but they will say: The Lord hath not appeared[11] to thee." Then God asked Moses: "What is it that thou holdest in thy hand?" Moses answered: "A rod."[12] The Lord then told Moses to cast his rod upon the

---

[1] *Not burnt.* The fire was a supernatural, not a natural phenomenon.

[2] *Put off the shoes.* The removal of shoes or sandals was a mark of reverence. The Jewish priests had to be bare-footed, when serving in the sanctuary.

[3] *Holy ground.* Because of the presence of God manifesting Himself to Moses.

[4] *Hid.* Or covered it.

[5] *Seen.* And heard their cry for help and deliverance.

[6] *Flowing with milk and honey.* Such a rich, fertile land that it produces milk and honey in plenty.

[7] *Who am I.* How can I, a poor shepherd, undertake such a great work?

[8] *Be with thee.* "I will protect you and stand by you."

[9] *Who.* Why would they ask this? In order to prove whether it were the true God, who had appeared to him.

[10] *I am who am.* I am He who exists of Himself; He who is. This is the proper Name of God, and the meaning of the word 'Jehova'.

[11] *Hath not appeared.* This is the third time that Moses raised an objection.

[12] *A rod.* His shepherd's staff. This staff, consecrated by these miracles, was to be the sign of Moses' leadership of the people.

ground. He threw it upon the ground, and the rod was turned into a serpent, so that Moses fled from it in terror.

But the Lord called him back, saying: "Take it by the tail." Moses did so, and the serpent became again a rod. The Lord told Moses to work this and some other signs before the Israelites, and they would believe. But Moses still objected[1], saying that he was not eloquent[2], but that his speech was slow and hesitating.

Then the Lord said to him: "Who made[3] man's mouth? Or, who made the dumb and the deaf, the seeing and the blind? Did not I? Go, therefore, and I will teach thee, what thou shalt speak." Moses answered[4]: "I beseech Thee, Lord, send whom Thou wilt send."[5] The Lord, being angry with Moses, said: "Aaron, thy brother, is eloquent; speak to him, and put My words[6] into his mouth; he shall speak, in thy stead, to the people." So Moses returned to Egypt; and Aaron, his brother, inspired by the Lord, came forth to meet him.

Moses repeated to his brother all the words of the Lord. Then they went together to assemble the children of Israel; and Aaron spoke to them that the Lord had looked upon their affliction. And Moses wrought the sign of the rod and other miracles, whereupon the people believed[7]; and falling down, they adored[8] the Lord.

COMMENTARY.

The Attributes of God. This story reveals God to us in a wonderful way. It shows us that:

1. God is *eternal.* "I am Who am!" God exists of Himself. He has His being of Himself. He is Who is, and was, and is to be.

---

[1] *Objected.* For the fourth time.

[2] *Not eloquent.* And he would be unable to act as spokesman.

[3] *Who made.* Am I not He who gave the gift of speech to man? Cannot I make thee eloquent?

[4] *Answered.* Although the Lord had answered his four previous objections, Moses still could not resign himself completely to the will of God, and made a fifth objection.

[5] *Whom Thou wilt send.* Send the Redeemer! Send Him at once that He may deliver Thy people! (See Gen. 49, 10.)

[6] *Put My words.* Tell him all that I have said, and he will tell it to the people.

[7] *Believed.* That Moses was sent by God.

[8] *They adored.* Had they not prayed to God before? Yes, indeed; but now they thanked Him for having mercy on them, and for sending a liberator to them.

He alone is eternal. All else has been made by Him and has a beginning.

2. God is *unchanging*. His command: Thou shalt bring My people out of Egypt, could not be altered by any hesitations or objections on the part of Moses.

3. God is *omniscient*. "I have seen the affliction of My people, and heard their cry." — "Do these signs, and they will believe."

4. God is *almighty*. "Who made the dumb and the deaf; the seeing and the blind? Did not I?" God's power was also proved by the miracles of the rod &c.

5. God is *holy*. "The Lord was angry with Moses", i. e. He showed His displeasure with Moses for having so little confidence, and for making so many objections.

6. God is *merciful*. "I will deliver them out of the hands of the Egyptians."

7. God is *faithful*. He fulfilled that which He promised to Jacob: "I will bring thee and thy seed back from Egypt."

The object of miracles. Moses was the first of those sent by God, who received the power of working miracles; and, as we are told, the object of these miracles was that the children of Israel might believe. How much more, then, ought we to believe in Jesus Christ, who worked so many more, and much greater miracles, than Moses! The difference between our Lord's miracles and those of Moses is this that Moses wrought them by the power of God, and our Lord by His own power.

Humility and confidence in God. One of Moses' most prominent virtues was a sincere humility. He held himself to be neither capable nor worthy of the great task allotted to him by God. But it was just on account of his humility that God chose him to be the leader of His chosen people, for He "exalteth the humble, and abaseth the proud". Moses, however, failed, by giving way to so many hesitations. After God had said: "I will be with thee", he ought to have said, as St. Paul did: "I can do all things in Him who strengtheneth me" (Phil. 4, 13). Instead of that, he made more and more objections, and on account of this Almighty God reproached and blamed him. At last, however, he obeyed God's commands, and full of confidence he accomplished his appointed task splendidly. True humility distrusts itself, but trusts all the more in God.

APPLICATION. You are not called on to take off your shoes when you enter a church; but you are called on to leave all worldly thoughts outside. You are not obliged to cover your eyes, but you ought to hold them in check, and be recollected, and not look about you curiously.

CHAPTER XXXII.

THE TEN PLAGUES OF EGYPT.

[Ex. 5—10.]

MOSES and Aaron went to Pharao (Fig. 21) and demanded, in the name of God, that he should allow the people of Israel to go out into the desert to offer sacrifice to the Lord. Pharao proudly answered: "Who is the Lord[1] that I should hear His voice, and let the people go? I know not the Lord, neither will I let Israel go." And from that day forth, he ordered the overseers and taskmasters to oppress the Israelites more and more, by putting them to still harder work.

Fig. 21. Head of Pharao (Menephtah I.).
Old Egyptian sculpture.

The Lord told Moses and Aaron to appear again before Pharao. They did as the Lord commanded, and Aaron cast his rod before Pharao, and it was changed into a serpent. Pharao called the magicians[2], and they, by enchantments and certain secrets, also turned their rods into serpents; but Aaron's rod devoured their rods. Yet the heart of Pharao remained hardened[3], and he would not let the people go. Then the Lord began to send ten plagues[4] upon the Egyptians.

Next morning, by the command of God, Aaron went to the bank of the Nile, and struck the river with his rod, and instantly

---

[1] *Who is the Lord.* i. e. I do not know your God, and will not be commanded by Him. Pharao, in his pride, would not acknowledge God to be the Lord. Therefore God sent the ten plagues, to compel Pharao and his people to admit that He is Lord over the whole earth.

[2] *The magicians.* They worked apparent miracles by arts known only to themselves, and by the help of the devil.

[3] *Hardened.* He was stubborn like the firmly rooted trunk or stump of a tree.

[4] *Ten plagues.* The plagues were sent through the medium of Moses and Aaron, who, in God's name, commanded the very elements and powers of nature, and they obeyed.

it was turned into blood. Thereupon the fish died, the water was corrupted, and the water of all the streams and ponds in Egypt was turned into blood. And the Egyptians dug new wells round about the river; for they could not drink the water of the river. Even then the heart of Pharao did not relent. (First plague.)

After seven days, Aaron stretched forth his hand over the rivers and streams and pools of Egypt, and inmediately a multitude of frogs came forth from the waters, and covered the whole land of Egypt. They entered the houses and the ovens, and covered the tables and the beds, and spared neither the hut of the peasant nor the palace of the king. Then Pharao, being frightened, called for Moses and Aaron, and said to them: "Pray ye the Lord to take away the frogs from me, and from my people, and I will let the people go to sacrifice to the Lord." Moses did as the king desired, and the frogs disappeared. (Second plague.)

But when Pharao saw that the frogs were gone, he hardened his heart again. Then Aaron was commanded by God to strike with his rod the dust of the earth; and instantly myriads of gnats arose, and tormented both men and beasts throughout all Egypt. All the dust of the earth was turned into gnats. But Pharao's heart remained obdurate. (Third plague.)

Then the Lord sent a very grievous swarm of flies into the houses of Pharao and his servants, and the whole land was corrupted by them. Then Pharao's heart began to fail, and he said to Moses and Aaron: "I will let you go to sacrifice to the Lord your God in the wilderness; but go no further. Pray for me." But when God, at the prayer of Moses, had banished the flies, Pharao's heart grew hard again, and he refused to let the people go. (Fourth plague.)

Then God sent a murrain among the cattle, which destroyed the best part of the flocks and herds of the Egyptians, but spared those of the Israelites. Still Pharao would not submit. (Fifth plague.)

Then the Lord ordered Moses and Aaron to sprinkle ashes in the air in presence of Pharao, and there came boils with swelling blains in men and beasts. (Sixth plague.)

Then again Moses stretched forth his rod towards heaven, and the Lord sent down thunder and hail and lightning running along the ground; and the hail, mixed with fire, smote every herb of the field and every tree of the country, and killed every

man and beast that were in the open fields. None of it fell,
however, in the land of Gessen, where the children of Israel dwelt.
Pharao called Moses and Aaron, and said: "I have sinned this
time also. Pray ye the Lord that the thunder may cease, and
that I may let you go." But when, at the prayer of Moses, the
hail had ceased, the king broke his promise, and his heart became
exceedingly hard. (Seventh plague.)

Then the Lord sent a burning wind, which blew all that day
and night; and in the morning, the locusts[1] came, and they
covered the whole face of the earth and wasted all things, devouring the grass of the earth, and whatever fruits the hail had
left; and there remained not anything that was green, either on
the trees, or in the herbs in all Egypt. Therefore Pharao in haste
called Moses and Aaron, saying: "Forgive me my sin this time
also, and pray to the Lord your God that He take away from

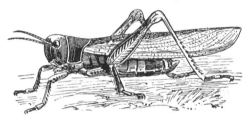

Fig. 22. Locust.

me this death." Moses
prayed to the Lord, and
the Lord sent a very strong
wind from the west which
took the locusts and threw
them into the Red Sea. This
time, again, Pharao hardened
his heart. (Eighth plague.)

Then Moses stretched forth his hand towards heaven, and
there came a horrible darkness[2] in all the land of Egypt for three
days. No man saw his brother, nor moved himself out of the
place where he was. But where the children of Israel dwelt,
there was light. Then Pharao called Moses and Aaron, saying:

---

[1] *The locusts* (Fig. 22). A horribly dense swarm of creatures, something
like grasshoppers, but three or four inches long, passed over the land, devouring
everything green, on which they settled.

[2] *Darkness.* In the Book of Wisdom (17, 2 &c.) this terrible darkness is
thus described: "For while the wicked (Egyptians) thought to have dominion over
the holy nation, Thou didst fetter them with the bonds of darkness and a long
night, shut up in their own houses. No power of fire could give them light,
neither could the bright flames of the stars enlighten that horrible night. For if
anyone were a husbandman, or a shepherd, or a labourer in the field, and was
suddenly overtaken, he endured a necessity from which he could not fly. For
they were all bound together in one chain of darkness." The darkness, being the
effect of a miracle, and meant to serve as a plague, was more dense than the
darkest night.

"Go, sacrifice to the Lord — let your sheep only and your herds remain." Moses answered: "All the flocks shall go with us." Thereupon the king hardened his heart again, and would not let the people go. Moreover he said to Moses: "Get thee from me. In what day soever thou shalt come into my sight, thou shalt die." Moses replied: "I will not see thy face any more." (Ninth plague.)

The Lord spoke again to Moses: "Yet one plague more will I bring upon Pharao and Egypt, and after that he will let you go and thrust you out." Now Moses was a very great man in the land of Egypt in the sight of Pharao's servants and of all the people.

Moses, therefore, spoke to all the people: "Thus saith the Lord: 'At midnight I will enter into Egypt; and every first-born in the land of Egypt shall die, from the first-born of Pharao, who sitteth on his throne, even to the first-born of the hand-maid that is at the mill, and all the first-born of the beasts; and there shall be a great cry in all the land of Egypt, such as neither hath been before, nor shall be hereafter. But with all the children of Israel there shall be no death, nor mourning, that you may know how wonderful a difference the Lord maketh between the Egyptians and Israel. And all these thy servants shall come down to me, saying: Go forth, thou and all the people that is under thee. After that we will go out.' " (Tenth plague.)

COMMENTARY.

The object of the plagues, with which God visited the Egyptians, was manifold. The plagues, which devastated Egypt, while they did not touch the land of Gessen, were sent, firstly, to teach Pharao and his people that the God of Israel was also Lord over Egypt, and the one True and Almighty God. Secondly, to convert the haughty king and force him to obey the commandments of God. Thirdly, to punish Pharao and his people for their unreasonable idolatry and their cruel oppression of the people of God. The Egyptians worshipped the Nile as a god, and now destruction was brought upon them by means of it. Disease killed the cattle which were objects of their worship; and lower creatures, such as gnats, flies and locusts, inflicted torments on them. Thus they were punished by the very things through which they sinned. Fourthly, the plagues were sent to teach the pagans that the gods whom they worshipped were vain and powerless; however earnestly they appealed to them, they could obtain no help from them.

Fifthly, they were intended to confirm the Israelites in their belief in the one true God and in confidence in Him who protected them in such a wonderful way; and to fill their hearts with gratitude towards Him.

The Justice and Patience of God. By these plagues, Almighty God not only manifested His terrible justice, but also His merciful patience. He sent the first plague only after the miracles worked before Pharao had produced no effect. The plagues gradually succeeded each other, beginning with the least; and when these availed nothing, they became more and more dreadful. Moreover, they did not follow each other day after day, but between the several plagues there was an interval of days, sometimes of weeks.

Impenitence. Pharao is a warning example of impenitence and obduracy. God did not warn him only outwardly, by Moses' words and by the ten plagues, but also inwardly, by His grace. But Pharao would neither listen to the admonitions of God, nor obey the movements of divine grace, and thus, by rendering himself unworthy of further graces, he at last became quite hardened. Once or twice he made good resolutions about letting God's people go, but as soon as the pressure of necessity was removed he did not keep them. God foretold to him the last and worst plague some fourteen days before it was sent, and would, in His mercy, have spared Pharao and his people this last terrible visitation, if only he would have consented to let the Israelites go. Pharao, however, despised the divine warning as an empty threat, and remained hardened. He is the type of a defiant sinner who will not listen to any exhortations, does not carry out good resolutions, perseveres in sin, and finally becomes quite hardened.

APPLICATION. Are you at all like Pharao? Do you pay attention to the admonitions of your parents, confessor &c.? Have you made good resolutions with your lips only, or have you taken real pains to give up your bad habits? Have you ever made a bad confession, and concealed your sins? All this would be the beginning of impenitence, and would lead you to obduracy and the loss of your soul. Pay heed, then, to the warnings of those set over you; listen to the inspirations of divine grace, and the voice of your conscience, so that your heart may not grow obstinate and hard. St. Paul is urgent in his warnings against obduracy: "According to thy hardness and impenitent heart thou treasurest up to thyself wrath against the day of wrath and revelation of the just judgment of God" (Rom. 2, 5).

CHAPTER XXXIII.

THE PASCHAL LAMB.—DEPARTURE FROM EGYPT.

[Ex. 12—13, 16]

AFTER this Moses and Aaron spoke to the children of Israel, telling them of the Lord's command to make this month [1] henceforth the first of the year, and to kill in every family a lamb without blemish, on the fourteenth day of the month, and to sprinkle the door-posts with the blood of the lamb [2]. The Lord also commanded that, on the same night, they should eat the flesh of the lamb with unleavened bread [3] and wild lettuce [4]. They should, moreover, have their loins girt [5], and shoes on their feet and staves [6] in their hand; for that it was the passing [7] of the Lord, and that, on that night, His angel would slay every first-born of the Egyptians.

The Israelites did as they were commanded, and at midnight, the fourteenth day of the month, the destroying angel visited every house in Egypt and slew every first-born, from the king's own to the first-born of the captive woman in prison. But the houses of the Jews he did not enter; for the doors thereof were sprinkled with the blood of the lamb. And a fearful cry [8]

---

[1] *This month.* When Moses announced the institution of the Pasch, they were in the seventh month of the year, which had hitherto begun at the autumnal equinox, or about the middle of September. Henceforward this seventh month, in which fell the vernal equinox, was to be the beginning of the year.

[2] *The lamb.* The lamb was to be one year old, and without blemish, i. e. fine and healthy. The paschal lamb was to be a burnt offering, and everything that was offered to God, had to be of the best.

[3] *Unleavened bread.* Bread baked without leaven or yeast. Baked cakes were used, made of flour and water, such as the Jews still use at paschal time. As the fermentation caused by leaven is a form of corruption, the absence of leaven was a type of incorruption.

[4] *Lettuce.* A herb with a bitter taste.

[5] *Girt.* They were to fasten up their robes by a girdle round their hips, so that they might be ready to start on their journey at a moment's notice.

[6] *Staves.* Therefore, actually ready to start.

[7] *Passing.* The day was called the Pasch, or passing of the Lord, because the angel of God, who killed the first-born of the Egyptians, passed over the houses of the Israelites, the doors of which were sprinkled with the blood of the lamb.

[8] *Fearful cry.* Because it was the eldest sons, the hope and prop of their parents, who lay dead.

arose from all the land of Egypt, because there was death in every house.

And Pharao arose in the night, and, struck with terror, he besought Moses and Aaron to go with the Israelites, and take with them their herds and all they possessed. "Go", he said, "and, departing, bless me." The Egyptians themselves pressed[1] the people to go forth speedily, saying: "We shall all die." Then the people of God rose up in haste, while it was yet night, and began their journey, taking the unleavened bread with them. Moses also carried the bones of Joseph[2] with him.

The descendants of Jacob had lived in Egypt four hundred and thirty years. Leaving Egypt, they numbered six hundred thousand men[3], besides women and children. Moses commanded the people, saying: "Remember this day, in which, with a strong hand[4], the Lord brought you forth out of this place, that you eat none but unleavened bread." He also told them to sanctify[5] unto the Lord every first-born, because the Lord had spared their first-born children on the night on which He slew every first-born of the Egyptians.

COMMENTARY.

The Paschal Lamb was a figure of Jesus, who died on the Cross for the sins of men. As the destroying angel dared not enter the houses of the Jews that were sprinkled with the blood of the lamb, so the devil has no power over those Christians who receive worthily the Body and Blood of our Lord in Holy Communion. In Pharao we behold a sad picture of a man grown old in sin. When oppressed by calamity he seemed to repent, but as soon as the danger was past, he fell back into his pride and hardness of heart.

---

[1] *Pressed.* Forced them to go.

[2] *The bones of Joseph.* In fulfilment of Joseph's dying wish (Chapt. XXVII).

[3] *Six hundred thousand men.* Such men as were capable of fighting in time of war. The whole number of living souls was over two millions.

[4] *With a strong hand.* With great might, by which he overcame the stubbornness of Pharao.

[5] *Sanctify.* All the first-born of clean beasts had to be sacrificed to the Lord. The first-born of those which were unclean had to be redeemed with money. All first-born sons were consecrated to God, to be the priests of the family. Soon after this, however, the tribe of Levi was substituted for the first-born (Chapt. XXXIX), and thenceforward the first-born sons had to be redeemed with money from the special service of God. Almighty God, to whom everything belongs, laid a special claim to the first-born of the Israelites, because He had spared their first-born in Egypt.

The avenging Justice of God. The slaying of the first-born in Egypt was a punishment sent by God on account of the obstinate unbelief of Pharao and his people. This shows the justice of God. If Pharao had been converted by the lesser plagues, he would have been spared this last terrible one. Many sinners, who care nothing about God, can only be converted by means of some severe visitation. No one can resist God, because He is almighty. They who defy Him, must and will feel the weight of His avenging justice either in this world or in the next. "Thou art Lord of all, and there is none that can resist Thy majesty" (Esth. 13, 11).

The Faithfulness of God. All those promises which God made about increasing the people of Israel, and delivering them from Egypt, were faithfully fulfilled.

God is Lord over life and death. By the first plagues God proved that He was Lord of all nature. By the last and worst plague, He showed that He was Lord over life and death, because in one night He slew the first-born in every Egyptian house, while not one of the Israelites was touched.

The Paschal Lamb, a type of Jesus Christ. The paschal lamb was a sacrifice, for it is expressly said (Ex. 12, 27) that it was "the victim of the passage of the Lord". As such, it was pre-eminently a type of our Lord, and principally in the following ways. The paschal lamb was to be without blemish: Jesus Christ is the Most Pure, the Most Holy, "a lamb unspotted and undefiled" (1 Petr. 1, 19). The paschal lamb was killed, and its blood spilt: Jesus Christ was slain for us on the altar of the Cross, and shed all His Blood for us. Of the paschal lamb "no bone was to be broken": contrary to the usual custom with those crucified, not one of our Lord's bones was broken. Through the blood of the paschal lamb the Israelites were saved from temporal death: through the Precious Blood of Jesus Christ we are saved from the spiritual death of sin, and the eternal death of hell. The paschal lamb, therefore, foretold that the future Saviour would be unspotted; that He would sacrifice Himself for us; that He would give His Life and Blood for us; that not one of His bones would be broken; and that we, through His sacrifice, would be saved from death.

There is no salvation, except through Jesus Christ. The blood of the paschal lamb obtained mercy for the Israelites, and saved them from death, only because it was a type of the Redeemer of the world. Its atoning and saving power did not lie in itself, but came from the Blood of Jesus Christ whose sacrifice and death were pre-figured by the death of the lamb. The Israelites, because they sacrificed the paschal lamb and sprinkled their houses with its blood, having faith in the future Redeemer, were spared by reason of that faith. Even in the Old Testament, it was only through faith in the future Redeemer that men could obtain pardon.

The meaning of the Paschal Feast in the Old Law and the New Law. The Jewish Pasch was instituted by God through Moses, in thankful commemoration of the deliverance of the Israelites from their slavery in Egypt, and also as a type of their future deliverance from sin and hell. The Christian Paschal Feast was instituted by God through His Church, in thankful commemoration of the redemption of all mankind from sin and hell by Jesus Christ, of our deliverance by Him from the bondage of Satan, and of His overcoming the death of the body by His glorious resurrection. The former was a reminder of the promise of redemption, the latter a reminder of its fulfilment, of our real redemption by the Lamb of God, who taketh away the sins of the world.

The importance of the Paschal Feast, as a type of our redemption, is shown by the command of God to make it from thenceforth the beginning of a new year.

The Paschal Lamb, a type of Holy Communion. The paschal lamb was not only a sacrifice; it was also a food which had to be partaken of. In Holy Communion our Lord, the true Paschal Lamb, gives Himself to us to be the Food of our souls. This priceless Food, if It is to nourish us, must be partaken of, mingled with the "bitter herb" of penance and a sincere confession of our sins. If we receive It worthily, It strengthens us for our journey through the wilderness of this life, and will enable us to reach the Promised Land of everlasting happiness. "He that eateth this bread", said our Lord, "shall live for ever" (John 6, 59).

The connection between type and fulfilment. It could not be said that the bones of our Lord were not broken, because the bones of the paschal lamb, which was a type of Him, were not broken. The case must be reversed; for a type points to the person typified, and not the person to the type. Because, therefore, God in His omniscience knew that no bone of the crucified Redeemer would be broken, He commanded that no bone should be broken of the paschal lamb, which was intended to be a type of that Redeemer. It is the same with all types. The omniscient God has so disposed them that they point to the Redeemer, to His work and His kingdom.

Persons and things as types. The types about which you have till now learnt (Adam, Abel, Noe, Melchisedech, Isaac, Joseph and Job), were *men*. But the paschal lamb and the slaying of the first-born were *things*. You will come across many other things which were types of our Lord, such as the manna, the brazen serpent &c. &c.

APPLICATION. How the Israelites must have thanked God, when their first-born sons were spared, and when they were delivered from the cruel slavery of Egypt! Thank God daily that

His only-begotten Son has redeemed you, has won pardon for you, and has opened heaven to you. Serve God with a grateful love, for you were dedicated to His service at your Baptism. Above all things, hear Mass willingly and devoutly, and be thankful to the Lamb of God who daily sacrifices Himself for you.

When you obey your evil inclinations and passions, you are still in the bonds of the cruel servitude of Satan and sin. Tear yourself away from this ignominious slavery. Seek out and fight against your besetting sin. Make resolutions against it every morning when you say your prayers, and examine your conscience about it in the evening.

CHAPTER XXXIV.

PASSAGE OF THE RED SEA.

[Ex. 13, 17—27.]

NOW God himself conducted the Israelites in their march, going before them by day in a pillar[1] of cloud, by night in a pillar of fire. They at length reached the shores[2] of the Red Sea, where they pitched their tents[3]. Suddenly Pharao repented[4] of having allowed the Israelites to go, and pursued them with chariots[5] (Fig. 23, p. 146) and horsemen, and with his whole army[6] (Fig. 24, p. 147); and he overtook them at nightfall near the Red Sea.

When the Israelites saw the Egyptians behind them, they were seized with fear[7], and cried to the Lord for help. Moses,

---

[1] *Pillar.* A cloud which raised itself up like a pillar, so that it could be seen by all the people. In this cloud which, later on, rested on the Ark of the Covenant (Chapter XXXVIII), God was present in an especial manner, to prove to the Israelites that He was their leader and protector.

[2] *Shores.* The track followed by the Israelites is marked by a blue line on Map I.

[3] *Pitched their tents.* They encamped to rest for the night.

[4] *Repented.* His first terror, caused by the slaying of the first-born, was passed, and his old spirit of defiance had returned. He and his people wished to revenge themselves on the Israelites for the death of their sons, and seize them to reduce them once more to slavery.

[5] *Chariots.* Cars full of soldiers who, from these chariots, attacked the enemy with arrows, spears and swords.

[6] *His whole army.* Which was more than 200,000 strong.

[7] *With fear.* The Israelites really were in a terrible position. Before them lay the deep sea, behind them Pharao's host; to right and left of them were high mountains! They could not possibly have escaped, if God had not helped them. But

however, calmed and encouraged them, saying: "The Lord will fight for you." At the same time the pillar of cloud, which had gone before them, went back and stood between their camp and the army of the Egyptians. Moreover the cloud gave light to the Israelites, but it made the night darker for the Egyptians, so that they could not see nor stir for the rest of the night. Then Moses, commanded by God, stretched his rod over the sea, and inmediately the waters divided and stood like a wall on either side, leaving a dry road between for the children of Israel to pass over. And the children of Israel went in through the midst of the sea.

Fig. 23. Egyptian King (Ramses II.) on his chariot, taking a hostile fortress. Painted sculpture from Abydos.

At the dawn of day the Egyptians pursued them into the midst of the sea. But suddenly a great tempest[1] arose, and overthrew their chariots and horsemen. And the Lord said to Moses: "Stretch thy hand over the sea"; and behold! the divided waters came together again, swallowing up Pharao and his whole army, so that not one of the Egyptians escaped.

the Lord, in order to strengthen His people's faith, worked a mighty miracle, and made the water cease flowing, and rear itself up like two walls, letting the people of Israel pass between them to the other side.

[1] *A great tempest.* Thunder and lightning burst from the cloud, and the whole army of Pharao fell into disorder.

Thus did the Lord, by a splendid miracle, deliver the Hebrews that day from the Egyptians. And the people feared the Lord, and believed in Him[1], and in Moses, His servant. "And the children of Israel came into Elim, where there were twelve fountains of waters and seventy palm-trees, and they encamped by the waters."

COMMENTARY.

The almighty Power of God divided the waters, held them up as walls on either side, made the burning wind to blow, and the lightning to strike the Egyptians.

God's Goodness to His people is shown throughout the whole story. First, He led His people by a visible means, the pillar of cloud. Then He worked a great miracle, and saved them, for good and all, from the power of the Egyptians. By the destruction of their army the Egyptians were so weakened, and the damage done to them so lasting, that they were unable to molest the Israelites, the whole time they were wandering in the wilderness.

Fig. 24. Egyptian soldiers. Old Egyptian painting.

The retributive Justice of God. Pharao's terrible end was a punishment for his impenitence and obstinate resistance to God's grace. His people were punished also, and perished with him. The Egyptians drowned the Israelite babes in the Nile, and, in punishment for this, their sons were drowned in the sea. How terrible is God's justice!

Confidence in God. While the Israelites, filled with fear, called upon the Lord for help, Moses remained perfectly calm. Full of confidence in God, he said to the people: "Fear nothing! The Lord will fight for you": and his confidence was justified and rewarded; for God, to whom nature is subject, sent thunder and lightning, wind and rain

---

[1] *Believed in Him.* They believed that God indeed had sent Moses to deliver them out of Egypt and make them into a people of God.

to their aid. God can help us, when all other help is useless. The greater the need, the nearer is God!

Apparent conversion. Pharao was not really converted. The death of the first-born so frightened and staggered him that he let the Israelites go. But when the first terror was over he returned to his former obduracy, and again defied God. He wished to overcome God's will, and bring back His people by force of arms. But at last the measure of his sins was full. He had despised the warnings of God's mercy, so now God's justice overtook him, and he died a miserable death. He was like those sinners who in times of tribulation, such as sickness or misfortune, promise to amend their ways, but who, when the trial is removed, do not keep their promise, and fall back into their old habits and forgetfulness of God. — Such sinners will die an impenitent death, as Pharao did, and be lost eternally. "Hell is paved with good intentions."

The object of miracles. The people feared God, because they saw His power and justice with their own eyes; and they believed that Moses was sent by God, because it was through him that His great miracles were wrought.

The Passage of the Red Sea, a type of Baptism. The passage of the Red Sea was (according to 1 Cor. 10, 1) a type of holy Baptism. As the Israelites had to pass through the Red Sea in order to escape from the slavery of Pharao, and reach the Promised Land, so must we pass through the waters of Baptism in order to be freed from the slavery of sin and Satan, and finally attain to heaven.

Faith, our guide. We also want a guide on our way through life. Who will be our guide? God leads us through the wilderness of this life to the promised land of heaven, by His holy faith, which Jesus Christ, the Light of the world, taught and deposited in His Church. If we follow the light of faith, that is, if we live up to our faith, we are sure to arrive at our heavenly home. "I am the Light of the world: he that followeth Me, walketh not in darkness, but shall have the light of life" (John 8, 12).

APPLICATION. Moses and the children of Israel sang a canticle of praise in thanksgiving for their wonderful deliverance. It began by the words: "Let us sing to the Lord, for He is gloriously magnified: the horse and the rider He hath thrown into the sea."

You too should thank the Lord God frequently for your creation, preservation and redemption. Thank Him daily for your Baptism, and for the holy Catholic faith.

CHAPTER XXXV.

THE MIRACLES WROUGHT IN THE DESERT.

[Ex. 16—18.]

MOSES ordered them to depart from Elim and go on to-wards the wilderness. They marched three days through the wilderness, and found no water. Finding some at last they could not drink it, because it was bitter [1]. The people murmured against Moses, saying: "What shall we drink?" Moses prayed, and the Lord showed him a tree, the wood of which, when cast into the water, rendered it sweet [2].

And when they had gone far [3] into the wilderness, the people began to murmur still more, seeing that there was no food, and they wished that they had remained and died in Egypt, asking Moses why he had brought them out into the wilderness to die. Instead of punishing them for their want of confidence, God, full of mercy and goodness, promised to give them food in abundance.

He sent them, accordingly, every evening quails in vast numbers, sufficient for all the children of Israel to eat; and, in the morning, a delicious white food which fell from heaven. When the Israelites saw the bread, which looked like hoar-frost, they exclaimed "Manhu", which signifies: "What is this?" Moses informed them that it was the bread which the Lord [4] gave them. He then told every one to gather of it, as much as he needed.

They did so, and found it pleasant to eat, tasting like flour mixed with honey. On the day before the Sabbath they gathered a double quantity, as none fell on the Sabbath. This Manna [5] was their food for forty years, until they reached the confines of Chanaan.

---

[1] *Bitter*. Whence the name *Mara* (see Map). The water was briny and not fit for drinking.

[2] *Sweet*. Drinkable water is known as fresh or sweet water, in opposition to sea water or salt water.

[3] *Gone far*. They had now been four weeks in the wilderness, and had exhausted the provisions which they had brought with them from Egypt.

[4] *The Lord*. Without any intervention on the part of man.

[5] *Manna*. This is the same word as "Manhu", and means the same thing. The fall of Manna went on, and was renewed, every day except Saturday, for forty years.

Some time after these events, they encamped in another part of the desert, where again there was no water. Here also they murmured against Moses, and with great anger upbraided him for having brought them out of Egypt. Then Moses reproved them for their want of confidence in God; and, addressing the Lord in prayer, he said: "What shall I do with this people? Yet a little more, and they will stone me." The Lord commanded him to strike a rock[1] on the side of Mount Horeb with his rod. Moses did so, and a stream of pure water burst forth from the rock, so that all the people and the cattle could quench their thirst at will.

At this time the Amalekites[2] marched against the chosen people. Moses sent Josue with a number of picked men against them. During the battle Moses prayed on the top of the hill. As long as his hands were uplifted[3], the Israelites remained victorious; but when, through fatigue, he let them sink, they lost. Hence Aaron and Hur[4] upheld his hands, until the enemy was put to flight.

While Moses and the Israelites were near the mountain of God (Horeb), Jethro, having heard all the wonderful things, came with the wife and the two sons of Moses (Gersam and Eliezer) to pay a visit to Moses. He offered holocausts and sacrifices to God in thanksgiving and counselled Moses to institute seventy ancients as judges to help him in judging the people. (Ex. 18.)

COMMENTARY.

The wood thrown into the bitter well by God's command possessed no natural properties, by which to make the water sweet; therefore the miracle worked was simply the effect of God's almighty power. In the same way, the stroke dealt by Moses' rod did not of itself bring water from the rock: it was the omnipotence of God, which caused that abundant spring to pour from the dry stone. To show that the power came from Him, the Lord God, present in the pillar of cloud,

---

[1] *Strike a rock.* Which He would show to him, saying: "I will stand there before thee on the rock Horeb" (Ex. 17, 6).

[2] *The Amalekites.* They were descendants of Esau, and a wild, marauding, pagan people, who lived in the country between Chanaan and the Red Sea, in the peninsula of Sinai. They desired to hinder the Israelites on their way to the Promised Land, and, as far as they could, to destroy all worshippers of the true God.

[3] *Uplifted.* In intercessory prayer.

[4] *Hur.* A leading representative of the tribe of Juda.

rested on the rock. It was also His almighty will which summoned the flock of quails, and which rained the Manna from heaven every day (except the Sabbath), during forty years, so that His chosen people might be able to exist in the barren desert.

Goodness and Patience of God. Almighty God was marvellously good and patient with the unbelieving Israelites. He dwelt in their midst in a visible way; He protected them from the heat of the sun by the pillar of cloud; He forgave them their repeated murmurings; He was always showering fresh benefits on them, and defending them against their enemies.

Sins against religion. The Israelites were an ungrateful, carnal people. They cared more for good food and drink than for their liberty and the Promised Land. Though Almighty God worked such great miracles for them, and dwelt in their midst in the pillar of cloud, they were always murmuring against Moses and reproaching him. Their reproaches and ingratitude were, indirectly, offences against God, for Moses was but carrying out His commands. The Israelites sinned against the First Commandment by their ingratitude, want of confidence, and murmurings against the decrees of God.

The power of prayer. Moses raised, not only his hands, but also his heart to God. "The continual prayer of a just man availeth much" (James 5, 16). It was not only Josue's valour, but Moses' prayers, which overcame the enemy. Raise your heart with your hands to heaven, when you pray. Like Moses, the priest at the altar prays with outstretched, upraised hands.

Helping ourselves. The Israelites did not depend only on the prayers of Moses; they exerted themselves, and defended themselves as best they could. In all our times of danger and necessity, we ought to do the same: do what we can for ourselves, and pray to God.

Unappreciated gifts of God. Daily bread to eat, and good water to drink are very great boons. We only learn to prize them when we have to go without them.

The wood, which made the waters sweet, is a type of the Cross of Jesus Christ. His Cross makes sweet to us all that is bitter and distasteful. Firstly, it gives us the grace to be patient, and, secondly, it teaches us to bear all sufferings cheerfully, for love of Him who suffered so much for us.

The Manna is, as our Lord Himself declared (New Test. XXXIV), a type of the Blessed Sacrament. It came daily from heaven to give strength to the Israelites for their journey, and was sweet to the taste. Our Lord, in the Blessed Sacrament, comes from heaven, and gives Himself to us to nourish our souls on their journey to heaven, through the wilderness of this life; and He is a sweet and life-giving food to those who love Him. The Church sings at the Benediction of the Blessed

Sacrament: "Thou hast given them bread from heaven, containing in itself all sweetness."

The water flowing from the rock is (according to 1 Cor. 10, 24) a type of the stream of divine grace, which, proceeding from our Saviour who was pierced for us, flows down on the languishing souls of men (compare what our Lord says about the living water, New Test XVI). "If any man thirst, let him come to Me and drink", said our Divine Saviour (John 7, 37).

Moses praying on the mountain with outstretched arms is a type of our Lord, who was nailed with outstretched arms to the Cross on Calvary, and prayed for the salvation of the world.

The victory of God's chosen people over the heathen Amalekites is a type of the victory of the Church militant over her enemies — a victory won by the spiritual weapons of virtue and prayer.

APPLICATION. He who wishes to reach the promised land of heaven must suffer and deny himself. He must renounce his bad desires, and patiently bear trials for love of God. He must fight against the enemies of his soul, and all temptations to evil. We must fight, endure and suffer in this world, and we must do so from our youth upwards. Ask yourself, what you have done hitherto. Deny yourself voluntarily something in the way of food and drink. Do not complain, if anything hurts you, but rather suffer it in silence, and offer your pain to your crucified Saviour. Suppress at once all movements of anger, pride, envy, or sinful curiosity.

We must not only fight: we must also pray, to be enabled to overcome the enemy of our souls. Say to-day a prayer in honour of the Five Wounds of our Lord, or say a decade of the sorrowful mysteries of the rosary, to obtain the grace to overcome yourself.

CHAPTER XXXVI.

GOD GIVES THE TEN COMMANDMENTS ON MOUNT SINAI.

[Ex. 19—24.]

IN the third month [1] after their departure from Egypt, the Israelites came to Mount Sinai [2], where they rested and pitched their tents. Moses ascended the mountain, and God appeared to

----

[1] *Third month.* They had left Egypt on the fifteenth day of the first month; and now it was the third day of the third month, or forty-eight days since their departure.

[2] *Mount Sinai* (see Map). A distinction must be drawn between Sinai in its larger sense, and Sinai in its particular sense: for all the mountains in that

him there, and said: "Thus shalt thou say to the house of Jacob and tell the children of Israel: You have seen what I have done to the Egyptians and how I have carried you upon the wings of eagles and have taken you to Myself. If, therefore, you will hear My voice and keep My covenant[1], you shall be *My peculiar possession* above all peoples, and you shall be to Me *a priestly Kingdom* and a *holy Nation.*"

Moses went down from the mountain, and related to the people what God had said. They all cried out with one voice: "All that the Lord hath spoken we will do." Then Moses went up again to the mountain, and the Lord told him that all the

Fig. 25. Mount Sinai with St. Catherine's Convent in the foreground.

people should sanctify and purify[2] themselves from all defilement that might render them unfit to appear in His presence, and to

part of Arabia are, in the wider sense, known as Sinai. In this chain there are two peaks; one is Horeb, and the other is known as Sinai in the more particular sense of the word (Fig. 25). It was in front of this latter mountain that the Israelites encamped. It is 7363 feet high, and rises perpendicularly from a large plateau to a height of 2000 feet. From this plateau the Israelites could see everything which took place on the mountain.

[1] *My covenant.* God renewed with all the people the covenant which He had made with their forefather Abraham (Chapter IX).

[2] *Purify.* They were to purify themselves inwardly by penance, as well as outwardly by ablutions, because the Most Holy was going to manifest Himself to them.

come, on the third day, to the mountain; but that barriers[1] must be placed around it, so that they might not approach too near and die.

The third morning being come, there was thunder and lightning around the mountain, and a thick cloud covered its top. Smoke mixed with fire[2] was seen to ascend, the mountain rocked and trembled[3], while a trumpet sounded very loud, and the people below on the plain feared exceedingly. Then was heard the voice of the Lord, speaking from the cloud that covered the mountain, saying:

I. I am the Lord thy God. Thou shalt not have strange gods before Me. Thou shalt not make to thyself a graven thing; nor the likeness of anything; thou shalt not adore them, nor serve them.

II. Thou shalt not take the name of the Lord thy God in vain.

III. Remember that thou keep holy the Sabbath-day.

IV. Honour thy father and thy mother, that thou mayest be long-lived upon the land which the Lord thy God will give thee.

V. Thou shalt not kill.

VI. Thou shalt not commit adultery.

VII. Thou shalt not steal.

VIII. Thou shalt not bear false witness against thy neighbour.

IX. Thou shalt not covet thy neighbour's wife.

X. Thou shalt not covet thy neighbour's goods.

The people, trembling and afraid at the foot of the mountain, cried out to Moses: "Speak thou to us, and we will hear; let not the Lord speak to us, lest we die." Moses told them that the Lord had come down to instil fear into their hearts, that they might not sin.

---

[1] *Barriers.* Or boundaries, probably marked by stakes, which were not to be passed.

[2] *With fire.* When God spoke to Moses the first time, He appeared to him in the midst of flames, in the burning bush.

[3] *Trembled.* There was an earthquake.

And the people stood afar off, but Moses went into the dark cloud[1], and the Lord gave him further laws[2] which he wrote down and explained to the people. They answered with one voice: "We will do all the words of the Lord, which He hath spoken." Moses raised an altar at the foot of the mountain, and offered a holocaust to the Lord. And taking the blood of the victim he sprinkled the people with it, saying: "This is the blood[3] of the covenant, which the Lord hath made with you, concerning all these words."

COMMENTARY.

The Holiness of God. God, who wills what is good, and abhors what is evil, revealed His will to the children of Israel by His holy Commandments, so that they might avoid what was evil, and do what was right. And because He is holy, He desired them to sanctify and prepare themselves by penance for His Revelation.

The fearful Majesty of God. The tremendous signs, under which God manifested Himself, were intended to convince the people of His greatness and majesty, and inspire them with a wholesome fear of breaking His Commandments. Therefore Moses said to them: "The Lord is come that you may fear Him and not sin." These tokens of the presence of God are typical of His attributes. The cloud and the smoke signified that God is invisible, and cannot be gazed at by mortal eyes. The crashing of the thunder and the terrible blast of the trumpets revealed God's might and majesty. The lightning and the flames pointed to God's holiness and avenging justice. The quaking of the mountain signified the fearful and unapproachable majesty of God, before which the very angels tremble. No wonder that these tokens of the presence of God filled the Israelites with fear and awe. When the Lord God Himself spoke the Ten Commandments, they were filled with such consuming fear that they nearly fainted away, and said to Moses: "Speak thou to us &c." They felt that they must die if God spoke to them in that way. How terrible is the majesty of God! The Israelites did not see Him; they only saw the signs of His presence, and heard His voice, and yet they nearly died of terror. Fear the just God, and keep His Commandments.

---

[1] *The dark cloud.* In which God was (Ex. 20, 21).

[2] *Further laws.* Laws, relating partly to the civil and partly to the moral life of the people, in further explanation of the Ten Commandments. Moses, in the name of God, formally and solemnly ratified His covenant with the people, after they had promised obedience to His law, and sealed it with the blood of a sacrifice.

[3] *This is the blood.* i. e. This blood is for the ratification and sealing of the covenant.

The Ten Commandments and the Natural Law. The Ten Commandments were but the expression of that natural law, which God has written in every man's heart, and which every man can know if he listens to the voice of reason and conscience. Therefore the Ten Commandments apply to all men and all times: and, for this reason, God wrote them on stone to signify that they are as durable as stone, and are to last for all ages. We Christians ought to observe the Commandments even more perfectly than was expected of the Israelites; for our Lord has said: "Think not that I am come to destroy the law or the prophets. I am not come to destroy, but to fulfil" (New Test. XXI).

The contents of the Ten Commandments are fully explained in the catechism, so I will only draw your attention here to their connexion with each other, and to their general tenor. The first three say to us: 'Thou shalt worship God; thou shalt honour and keep holy His name; thou shalt respect and keep holy His day." The fourth Commandment is a transition from one division to the other. The next four protect our most valuable possessions, and forbid any injury to life, innocence, property and honour. The last two forbid evil desires, because they corrupt the heart and lead to evil deeds.

The Ten Commandments are a benefit to mankind. God gave them to us out of love and for our good, or, in other words, for our temporal welfare and our eternal salvation. How would the world fare, if murder, rapine, robbery and defamation of character were not forbidden! Nobody would be sure of either life or property. There would be an end to all order and obedience in family life; evil and lawlessness would reign triumphantly; men would live like wild beasts in accordance with their savage lusts, and hunt down and devour each other. The Ten Commandments were, therefore, given to us for our good; that peace and order might reign among men, in family, society and state, and that we might attain to everlasting happiness. For this reason, he who does not observe the Ten Commandments is not only an enemy to God, but an enemy to mankind and to his own self.

The Old Covenant and the New. The Old Covenant was made through Moses, the New through Jesus Christ. The Old Covenant was made with only one nation; the New with all mankind. The Old Covenant was made to last for a limited time; the New will last to the end of time. The Old Covenant was sealed with the blood of victims; the New with the Blood of God made Man ("This is My Blood of the New Testament"; New Test. LXV). In the Old Testament, severe laws were made, but the power of observing them was not given. The New Testament has not only its own holy laws, but abundant grace is given by which to observe them; and the New Covenant is therefore called the Covenant of grace.

The Ten Commandments and the other laws of the Old Testament were a preparation for Jesus Christ (Gal. 3, 24). The Jews could not perfectly observe those laws which forbade even evil desires; and, feeling this, they came to know their own weakness and sinfulness. They saw that they required divine help to do that which they ought to do, and to be just in the eyes of God. They longed, therefore, for the promised Saviour. But we Christians can, by God's grace, keep all the Commandments, if only we desire to do so, and use the means of grace.

Pentecost. God gave the Ten Commandments fifty days after the departure from Egypt. In commemoration of this, the Jews always kept the feast of Pentecost fifty days after the Pasch (Old Test. XXXIX). The Christian Pentecost is also kept fifty days after Easter, because, on that day, God the Holy Ghost descended from heaven, and inscribed the law of love on the hearts of the faithful.

The first day of Pentecost in the Old Testament is a type of the first day of Pentecost in the New Testament. On the former, the mountain shook; on the latter, the house in which the apostles were. There the thunder and storm; here, the rushing as of a mighty wind. There, flames appeared; here, tongues of fire. There, God came down to give the Commandments; here, God the Holy Ghost came down to fill the hearts of the faithful with love of the Commandments.

No more barriers. The boundaries, set round the mountain, were meant to say to the Israelites: "You are not worthy on account of your sins to approach the Lord." Now, the barriers which separate man from God are removed by Jesus Christ. We dare now approach God. We dare receive Him into our very hearts, and unite ourselves to Him in the closest manner.

———————

APPLICATION. Thank God that, by the Ten Commandments, He has shown you the road to heaven. Take the trouble to learn the meaning of the Commandments thoroughly. Ask yourself, which Commandment you have most sinned against, and pray to the Holy Ghost for the gift of holy fear. "If thou will enter into life, keep the Commandments", says our Lord (see Deut. 5, 29).

The Israelites had to prepare themselves for the hearing of God's voice, by the sanctification of their hearts. How much more ought we to prepare ourselves for receiving God into our hearts in Holy Communion.

CHAPTER XXXVII.

THE GOLDEN CALF.

[Ex. 32.]

MOSES again ascended the mountain, and remained there forty days[1] and forty nights conversing with God. And when God had finished speaking with Moses, He gave him two tables[2] of stone, on which were written the Ten Commandments. Now the people, seeing that Moses tarried[3] in coming down from the mountain, rose up against Aaron and besought him, saying: "Make us gods that may go before us. For, as to this Moses, the man that brought us out of the land of Egypt, we know not what has befallen him."

Hoping to dissuade them from their impious project, Aaron replied: "Take the golden ear-rings from the ears of your wives, and your sons and daughters, and bring them to me." Contrary to his expectation[4], they brought their rings to Aaron who, fearing to offer resistance, accepted them, and made a molten calf[5], and built an altar. And the people exclaimed: "These are thy gods, O Israel, that have brought thee out of the land of Egypt." Next morning they offered holocausts and peace-victims, and began to eat and drink and to dance, after the manner of the Egyptians.

Meanwhile Moses came down from the mountain with the two tables of stone, whereon God Himself had written His Command-

---

[1] *Forty days.* Moses passed the forty days and forty nights without food, and in prayer and contemplation, and was instructed by God about the making of the Tabernacle and the worship of God.

[2] *Two tables.* The tables of the Commandments were the document of the Covenant. On the first table were written the first three Commandments, which teach us our duty towards God. On the second were the seven others which relate to our duty towards our neighbour.

[3] *Tarried.* They believed that some misfortune had befallen Moses, and that God would now no longer be with them. This, however, was not the real cause of their idolatry, the plea of his absence was only an excuse. The real causes were the weakness of their faith and their sensuality, which made them crave for the low and dissolute pleasures of idolatry.

[4] *Contrary to his expectation.* Aaron had reckoned that they would rather give up their project than sacrifice their ornaments and treasures. However, their craving for idolatry proved stronger than their vanity or avarice.

[5] *A molten calf.* They insisted on a calf being made in imitation of the Egyptian worship of Apis (Fig. 26). The gold was melted on the fire, and then cast into a mould.

ments. When he heard the shouts of the people, and saw them dance before the golden calf, he dashed the tables to the ground and broke them [1] at the foot of the mount. Then, laying hold of the calf, he burnt it and beat it to powder [2].

He severely rebuked Aaron for yielding to the wicked desires of the people. Then, standing in the gate of the camp, he said: "If any man be on the Lord's side, let him join with me." And all the sons of Levi [3] gathered around him. Then Moses ordered them to take their swords, go through the camp, and slay every man whom they found practising idolatry. They did as they were commanded, and about twenty-three thousand men were put to death that day.

Fig. 26. Apis.
Egyptian Sculpture.

Next day Moses again ascended the mountain, and earnestly entreated the Lord for His ungrateful people. But the Lord said: "Let me alone that I may destroy them." Still Moses insisted, saying: "I beseech Thee, this people hath sinned: either forgive them this trespass, or, if Thou do not, strike me out of the book [4] that Thou hast written."

The Lord heard his prayer, and ordered him to cut two other tables of stone. Moses obeyed, and on those tables the Lord again wrote the Ten Commandments. But when Moses came down from the mountain with the tables in his hands, his face was so radiant [5] with glory that the Israelites were afraid to come near; hence he veiled his face whenever he spoke to the people.

---

[1] *Broke them.* The people having broken their covenant with God, Moses broke the words of the covenant. He meant also to show by this action that the people had proved themselves unworthy of the benefits of the law.

[2] *To powder.* He ground it into gold dust. He did this to make the people understand the utter nothingness of idols, and the folly of worshipping them.

[3] *The sons of Levi.* The descendants of Jacob's son Levi. Most of the tribe of Levi had refrained from the worship of the golden calf.

[4] *The book.* The book in which are written the names of the just and heirs to heaven. By this forcible language Moses wished to say: "I (if I could do so without sin) would renounce eternal life rather than that this whole people should perish."

[5] *Radiant.* With a wonderful, supernatural light. Therefore Moses is always drawn with two rays of light on his brow.

COMMENTARY.

The Mercy of God. The people of Israel had sinned horribly against God by their idolatry, and yet, at Moses' intercession, He forgave them.

Idolatry. The weak people were most ungrateful and faithless to God. The Lord had done such great things for them! Only forty days before, full of holy fear, they had heard His voice and had repeatedly promised obedience to His Commandments; and now they transgressed the first and most important of them, and forsook God to worship idols. St. Paul calls lust and covetousness idolatry. Whenever a man loves anything more than he loves God, he is guilty of idolatry.

Pleasure-seeking and sensuality lead to many sins, and finally to unbelief and impiety.

Fear of man. Aaron sinned grievously. It was from fear of man, fear for his life, that he sinned. He ought to have died rather than assist the people in their terrible sin.

Righteous anger. The anger of Moses was not sinful anger; it was, rather, a holy zeal for God's honour and the good of the people. He who loves God cannot feel indifferent when he sees Him being offended; and he who really loves his neighbour must be pained when he sees him walking on the road to hell. We ought therefore to prevent sin, whenever we can; punish it, when we have the right to do so; and pray zealously for the conversion of sinners.

Intercession for sinners is pleasing to God. We can see this by the way in which God forgave the people their great sin, when Moses interceded for them; and we can also see how great a power is the intercession of Saints for sinners.

Love of our neighbour. Moses' love for his people was truly wonderful. He even offered to sacrifice himself that they might be spared and not cast off by God. He sought neither his own honour nor advantage, but only the good of his people.

Moses, the eighth type of Jesus Christ. Through Moses God instituted the Old Law, on which account he is called the mediator of the Old Law. As such, Moses was a striking type of Jesus Christ, who instituted the New Law. Moses, as a child, was condemned to death by a cruel king, and was saved in a wonderful way; Jesus Christ was condemned by Herod, and also wonderfully saved. Moses forsook the king's court so as to help his persecuted brethren; the Son of God left the glory of heaven to save us sinners. Moses prepared himself in the desert for his vocation, freed his people from slavery, and proved his divine mission by great miracles; Jesus Christ proved by still greater miracles that He was the only begotten Son of God. Moses was the advocate of his people; Jesus was our advocate with His Father on the Cross, and is eternally so in heaven. Moses was the law-giver of his people and announced to them the word of God: Jesus Christ is the supreme law-giver, and not only announced God's word, but is Himself the Eternal Word made flesh. Moses was the leader of the people to the Promised Land: Jesus is our leader on our journey to heaven.

The fruits of prayer. After Moses had fasted and prayed a second forty days on the mountain, his countenance was glorified, and heavenly rays shone forth from it. This shows us that fervent prayer and communion with God ennoble a man, purify his heart and mind, and make him heavenly-minded. The Saints of the Old and the New Testament became holy by dint of fervent prayer and contemplation.

APPLICATION. I am sure you detest the ingratitude and faithlessness of the Israelites. But look into your own heart and search your own conscience to see whether you too have not been ungrateful and faithless. What did you promise when you were baptized, and when you renewed your baptismal vows, and every time that you have been to confession? Have you kept your promises? Have you never committed a mortal sin? Do you not know that mortal sin is an execrable ingratitude towards your loving Redeemer? Just think how weak and wavering you are! So do not trust in yourself, but pray humbly for God's grace, and especially for the grace of perseverance.

Moses spent forty days in prayer, and yet was not weary, for prayer was his joy, his comfort and his strength. All the Saints of both the Old and New Testament have prayed willingly. How is it with you? We can learn to pray only by means of prayer. In this, as in other things, "practice makes perfect". Never neglect your prayers, and try to be very recollected and devout during divine service. Put yourself in the presence of God several times each day, and thus you will learn how to pray well, and to find delight in prayer.

CHAPTER XXXVIII.

THE MAKING OF THE TABERNACLE.

[Ex. 25—27.]

HITHERTO the Israelites had no fixed place of worship nor, properly speaking, any priesthood. Their patriarchs had offered sacrifice to God; now in one place, now in another. In later times, the heads of families had exercised the priestly functions; but this state of things was no longer to exist. Moses, while conversing with the Lord on the mountain, had received from Him the clearest and most definite directions [1] regarding divine worship, with all the ceremonies that were to accompany it.

Moses, therefore, built a shrine or Tabernacle (Fig. 27) that could be taken to pieces and carried from place to place. It was a portable [2] Tabernacle, or church, as we should call it, and well suited to the wandering life of the children of Israel. It was made of the most precious wood. Its length was thirty, its breadth ten, and its height also ten cubits. The boards were overlaid with plates of gold, and furnished with sockets of silver. It was divided into two parts: the fore part, which was the larger, was called the Sanctuary; the smaller part was called the Holy of

Fig. 27. The Tabernacle in the desert.

Holies. Each part was separated from the other by a curtain worked with great art. Outside and around was a covered court for the people.

---

[1] *Directions.* God said to him: "They shall make me a sanctuary, and I will dwell in the midst of them. According to all the likeness of the Tabernacle which I will shew thee and of all the vessels for the service thereof" (Ex. 25, 8—10). The people were to furnish the materials for it. Accordingly they brought Moses gold, silver, precious stones, and costly stuffs, with which to make the Tabernacle, sacred vessels &c. &c. They brought so much to him that, at last, Moses had to announce to them that he could receive no further gifts. They wished, by this generosity, to make reparation for their act of idolatry, and show their gratitude for the benefits they had received.

[2] *Portable.* It could be partially taken to pieces, and carried. This had to be done, because the Israelites had no fixed dwelling-place, and were always wandering about.

On the inside the roof and the walls were covered with rich tapestry, and on the outside with skins and furs. Moreover, on the ceiling of the Sanctuary as also on its inner walls, was fastened a most precious weaving in very brilliant colours, adorned with an embroidery of cherubim and palms and flowers.

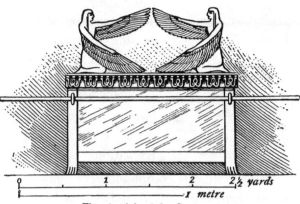

Fig. 28. Ark of the Covenant.

In the Holy of Holies he placed the Ark of the Covenant (Fig. 28) which was covered with gold within and without. At its four corners, on the outside, were attached rings of gold, through which bars, overlaid with gold, were passed, whereby to carry the Ark. In the Ark he put the tables of the Law. As these tables, on which the Ten Commandments were written, contained the chief heads of the Old Covenant, the Ark itself was called the Ark of the Covenant. Later on, there was also placed in the Ark a vase filled with Manna, and the rod of Aaron. He then placed over the Ark a cover or lid of the purest gold, called the Propitiatory, at the ends of which stood two cherubim of beaten gold, looking at each other, and spreading their wings so as to overshadow the Propitiatory.

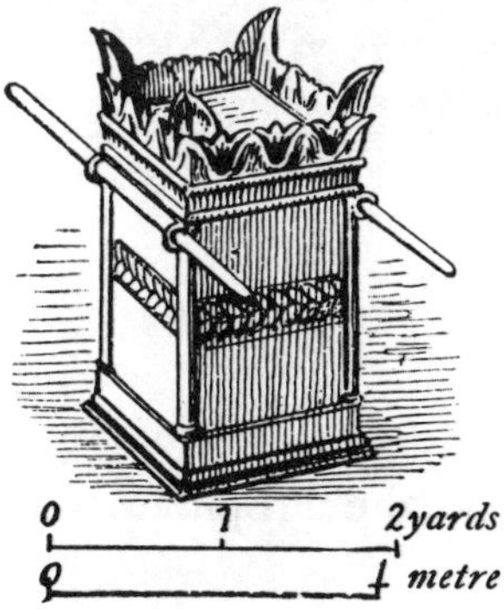

Fig. 30. Seven-branched Candlestick.

In the Holy were three principal sacred objects: 1. the altar of incense (Fig. 29) made of acacia wood and overlaid with the purest gold. On this altar was offered the daily sacrifice of incense. 2. The seven-branched

Fig. 29. Altar of incense.

candlestick wrought of the finest gold, on which seven lamps were burning perpetually (Fig. 30). 3. The table of the twelve loaves of proposition, or shew-breads, likewise overlaid with the finest gold (Fig. 31). These loaves were unleavened bread made of the finest flour and had to be renewed every Sabbath. By the side of the table stood a golden vial filled with wine. In the

Fig. 31. Table of the loaves of proposition.

outer court stood the brazen altar on which the holocausts were burnt (Fig. 32), and by its side a brazen laver for the use of the priests. The people had to remain in the outer court. Only the priests were allowed to enter the Holy, and into the Holy of Holies no one but the High Priest could enter, once a year (on the great day of Expiation).

When all was completed according to God's command, Moses poured sacred oil on the Tabernacle, and on all it contained; and then the cloud[1] covered the Ark of the Covenant, and the glory of the Lord filled the Tabernacle, and rested between the

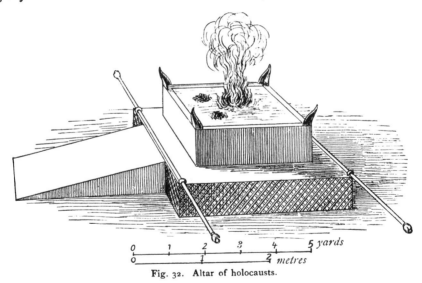

Fig. 32. Altar of holocausts.

two cherubim. As often as Moses had occasion to consult[2] the Lord, he received an answer of Him from the Propitiatory of the Holy of Holies.

---

[1] *The cloud.* i. e. the cloud, in which God was present, descended upon the Propitiatory between the two Cherubim.

[2] *To consult.* Moses was privileged to enter the Holy of Holies in order to consult the Lord. After him only the High Priest could enter, once a year.

COMMENTARY.

The immediate meaning of the building of the Tabernacle. The Ark of the Covenant, in which were kept the two tables of the law, was more costly than anything else in the Tabernacle. By it the Israelites were to be constantly reminded of the covenant .nade with God as to the strict observance of the Commandments. The Manna, which was also deposited in the Ark, was to remind them of God's loving guidance and preservation of them, and move them to love and trust Him. As cherubim kept guard over Paradise, so they now watched over the Ark of the Covenant; and, at the same time, they reminded the people that they should worship God, and serve Him as willingly as do the angels in heaven. The golden candlestick with its lights always burning was an emblem of faith in the true God, and admonished the Israelites to live according to that faith, to avoid the works of darkness, and walk in God's presence. The laver and the strict laws regarding ablutions were to remind the priests that they ought to approach the holy service of God with clean hearts. The never-ceasing smoke, ascending from the altar of incense, bade the people to lift up their hearts to God, and send up constant prayers, like incense, to heaven. The loaves of the proposition were a perpetual exhortation to be grateful to God, from whom come all good gifts for our souls as well as our bodies. The curtain, which shut off the Holy of Holies, and through which even the High Priest dared pass only once a year, signified "that the way into the holies was not yet made manifest" (Hebr. 9, 8). As God was present in the pillar of cloud, resting on the Ark, so the Tabernacle was God's dwelling in the midst of His people.

Its typical meaning. "The Tabernacle is a parable of the time present" (i. e. the Christian era), writes St. Paul. It foreshadowed the Church of the New Testament and its houses of God. As there was only one Tabernacle and one divine worship instituted by God Himself, so there is only one Church and one true worship of Christ in the world instituted by Himself. In every Catholic church or chapel you will find the same divine worship regulated by one supreme authority, the Vicar of Christ. The different rites (Latin, Greek, Coptic, Syrian, Slavonic &c.) differ only in accidentals and are one even in their difference, because approved by one and the same authority. As there was a real but mysterious and hidden presence of God in the Tabernacle (in the cloud over the ark), so there is the real presence of Jesus Christ in the Sacrament of the Altar. He is both the cloud and the living bread (Manna) that has come down from heaven to give life to the world.

As there was an altar of holocausts and bloody sacrifices and an altar of shew-breads, so there is in the New Testament one and the same altar ever representing the bloody sacrifice of the cross and ever offering up the "living bread that descended from heaven". The seven lights are the seven Sacraments which are here dispensed, and the laver is the baptismal font and the confessional, where we are cleansed from our sins — or even the stoup of holy water, by the devout use of which venial sins are remitted. You can see, therefore, that in many respects the Tabernacle was a type, which finds its perfect fulfilment in our churches; and that even the poorest village-chapel is holier than was the Tabernacle of the Old Covenant. As the Tabernacle was divided into two parts, so our churches have two parts: one for the priests, called the sanctuary, and another for the faithful, called the body of the church. Hence the Tabernacle was a pattern for our Christian churches.

God's Goodness to the Israelites was exceedingly great; for He deigned to dwell in their midst in a visible way, in the pillar of cloud. But immeasurably greater is God's love and condescension to us; for His Divine Son made Man dwells with us not only in one place, but in thousands of different churches and chapels, under the appearance of bread, blesses us, offers Himself up for us, and feeds our souls with the bread from heaven, that contains within itself all sweetness.

The veneration of images. By God's command Moses had figures of cherubim embroidered on the hangings of the Sanctuary, and placed golden cherubim on the Ark of the Covenant. These images served for the glory of God and the edification of the Israelites. It is evident, therefore, that it is pleasing to God that we should venerate the images of the angels and saints.

Ark of the Covenant. Mary is called, in the Litany of Loretto, *the Ark of the Covenant,* because she is the Mother of Jesus Christ, who instituted the New Covenant.

APPLICATION. We should be zealous for the beauty of the house of God. "I have loved, O Lord, the beauty of Thy house, and the place where Thy glory dwelleth" (Ps. 25, 8). Gladly visit the church; and beware of desecrating it. Be careful how you behave in it, and how you use holy water &c.

CHAPTER XXXIX.

LAWS REGULATING DIVINE WORSHIP.

[Ex. 28—40. Lev. 1—10; 16; 21; 23; 25. Numb. 3; 4; 28; 29. Deut. 16—27.]

BY God's command Moses now prescribed what sacrifices were to be offered, together with the manner of offering them, and the times when they were to be offered. Some of these sacrifices were bloody [1], others unbloody [2]. The former consisted of sheep, goats and oxen without blemish; the latter of flour, fruits, oil and wine. When the thing offered was wholly consumed on the altar, it was called a holocaust [3] or whole-burnt offering, and represented the highest act of adoration. But when only the fat, as the most delicate part, was burned, and the rest eaten, it was called either a sacrifice of thanksgiving for benefits received, or a sacrifice of expiation for sins committed. The latter is also called a sin-offering [4] or simply a sin.

Moses also instituted the feasts of the Lord; for the Lord had told him to establish, first, the Feast of the Pasch or Passover, in memory of the paschal lamb, eaten by the children of Israel on the night when the first-born of the Egyptians were slain, and also in memory of their deliverance from Egyptian bondage. For seven days they were to eat unleavened bread [5] while celebrating that feast.

Secondly, they were to keep holy, seven weeks after, the Feast of Pentecost, in remembrance of the law given them on Mount Sinai. On that day they were to bring the first-fruits of their harvest [6] as an offering to the Lord. Thirdly, when the harvest was all gathered in, they were to solemnize the Feast of Tabernacles, during which they were to take branches of trees and build tents, and dwell in them, so that their descendants might learn how the

---

[1] *Bloody.* He who offered the sacrifice laid his hand on the head of the victim, while the priest killed it and poured the blood on the altar, or sprinkled the people with it. This pouring of the blood on the altar was the most important part of the sacrifice, for by the shedding of its blood the life of the victim was offered.

[2] *Unbloody.* For this reason they were called meat-offerings. All these offerings, even the incense, were sprinkled with salt which, being a preservative against corruption, is a type of purity. It was also a token of friendship and in this case of friendship with God; wherefore it was called the salt of the covenant. Neither leaven nor honey might be presented on the altar, for they, being conducive to fermentation or corruption, were regarded as figures of sin.

[3] *Holocaust.* Every morning and every evening a one-year old lamb was offered as a holocaust. This was called the perpetual sacrifice.

[4] *Sin-offering.* In conjunction with these sacrifices, there was obligatory at least a general confession of the sins committed. For particular sins special sin-offerings were commanded and, before such could be offered, the offender had to confess the sin explicitly to the priest. No Israelite who had transgressed the law in a grave matter was allowed, under pain of death, to offer either a burnt offering or a peace-offering, unless he had first made a sin-offering and confessed his sin.

[5] *Unleavened bread.* It was therefore also called the Feast of unleavened bread (Chapter XXXIII).

[6] *Harvest.* The harvest is much earlier in those countries than it is with us.

Lord had made their fathers dwell in tents[1] in the deserts.   All the men[2] of Israel were to appear on these three festivals[3] before the Lord in the Tabernacle, and later on in the Temple.

There was also to be a day of expiation[4], kept as a most solemn fast[5].   On that day the High Priest was to sacrifice a calf in atonement for his own sins, and a he-goat for the sins of the people. After the sacrifice he was to raise the veil, and enter into[6] the Holy of Holies, taking with him the blood of the victim and the golden censer; he was then to incense the Propitiatory, or cover of the Ark, and to sprinkle it and the front of the Ark with the blood[7].

Finally, Moses consecrated Aaron as High Priest, his sons as priests, and the other men of the tribe of Levi as ministers[8] of

---

[1] *Tents* or Tabernacles.   Hence the name of Feast of Tabernacles.

[2] *All the men.*   From twelve years old and upward.   Old men, women and children were not bound to appear, but they might take part in the pilgrimage, if they chose.

[3] *On these three festivals.*   Besides these annual feasts, every seventh year was set apart as a year of Sabbath or of rest, and every fiftieth year as a year of Jubilee.   In the year of rest, no work of cultivation of the earth was allowed, and everything that grew naturally on it was common property; nor could any debts be claimed during the year.   The Jubilee-year was also a year of rest from labour, and of exemption for debtors.   In that year, moreover, all slaves received their freedom; and possessions that had been sold reverted to their first owner without purchase, the reason for this being given by God in these words: "The land shall not be sold for ever: because it is mine, and you are strangers and sojourners with me."   By this decree, the impoverishment of individual families and tribes was prevented.

[4] *Day of expiation.*   Kept five days before the Feast of Tabernacles.

[5] *Solemn fast.*   Every person, with the exception of the sick and children, was bound to observe a strict fast, touching no food till after sunset.   They also had to pray, confess their sins, and implore God's mercy.

[6] *Enter into.*   This was the only day in the year on which he entered it.

[7] *Sprinkle with the blood.*   After his return from the Holy of Holies, he took another goat and, having laid his hands on its head, he confessed the sins of the whole people, and then drove the goat away into the wilderness, laden with the people's sins.   This was a typical ceremony, and was meant to indicate that the sins of the people were taken away and lost in the infinitude of God's mercy.

[8] *Ministers.*   Hitherto the first-born son had been set apart for the service of God, but from henceforward the tribe of Levi was chosen for the priestly office and the service of the Tabernacle.   In other words, hitherto priests had been taken from all tribes and all families, but now a peculiar priesthood was instituted.   The priestly office was hereditary in Aaron's family.   The first-born of this family was always to be High Priest, and the other male descendants priests.   The other men of the tribe of Levi were to assist the priests in the service of God, and were known by the name of Levites.

the Sanctuary. He purified [1] Aaron with water, and clothed him with divers sacred vestments [2], chief of which was the ephod, a marvellous work of gold and purple and fine linen, the edges of which were ornamented with rich embroidery of gold.

He suspended from his neck the rational, on which were twelve stones, each bearing the name of one of the twelve tribes (Fig. 33); he placed upon his head the mitre, in the middle of which, in front, was a gold plate, with the inscription: "Holy to the Lord." Finally, he poured oil upon his head, and consecrated him. After his sons and the Levites had also been consecrated, Aaron advanced to the

Fig. 33. Breast-Plate (Rational) of the High Priest.

altar, and, having offered a victim, stretched his hand over the people, and blessed them.

And behold! a fire came forth from the pillar of cloud and consumed the holocaust. Seeing this, the people fell prostrate on the ground, praising the Lord.

COMMENTARY.

Sacrifice is the highest and most perfect form of worship; therefore, God ordained sacrifices to be the centre of divine worship under the Old Law. What was sacrificed, was given to God, and had to be wholly consumed in His honour. Thus victims were killed and burnt, wine was poured out, and incense was burnt. These actions were meant to express on the part of him who made the offering some such thought as this: "Thou, O Lord, hast created all things! Everything

---

[1] *Purified.* In the brass laver in the outer court.

[2] *Vestments.* The vestments common to all priests were 1) a long white linen robe with a tesselated or diaper pattern (something like our alb) reaching down to the ankles; 2) a girdle of linen; 3) a bonnet or turban of linen (Fig. 34, p. 170). Besides these the High Priest (Fig. 35, p. 171) had the following special vestments: 1) a mitre of blue with a gold plate engraved with the words: "Holy to the Lord", and worn on the forehead of the High Priest; 2) the tunic or robe of blue and of woven work, forming part of the ephod, and having trimmings of pomegranates in blue, red and crimson, with golden bells between them, tinkling at every movement of the High Priest; 3) the ephod consisting of two parts, one covering the back, the other the front, clasped together on the shoulder with two large onyx stones, each having engraved on it six names of the tribes of Israel, and fastened by a girdle of gold, blue, purple and scarlet; 4) the breast-plate or rational suspended from the neck. One part of the sacerdotal dress was the Urim and Thummim, but it is difficult to say which.

comes from Thee. To Thee I owe my life and all that I possess! I have, indeed, deserved death at Thy hands, but as Thou dost not require of me my life, I offer to Thee instead the life of this lamb." The bloody sacrifices were sacrifices of vicarious expiation, and for this reason the person who offered it laid his hand on the head of the victim, as a token that he laid his sins on it, and sacrificed it as a substitute for himself. Therefore the only animals which could be offered up were the domestic animals which are useful and valuable to man.

The ends of sacrifice. By sacrifices men were 1. taught that they depended absolutely on God, and owed Him worship and thanksgiving as their supreme Lord; 2. they were roused to a consciousness that they were sinners before God, and owed satisfaction to the divine justice; 3. they were shown that they, of themselves, could not make satisfaction, but required a mediator.

Fig. 34. Priest.

In what lay the efficacy of sacrifice? Could pardon and inward sanctification be obtained through the blood of beasts which themselves were not clean, but lay under the curse which Adam's sin had brought on the earth? No! these sacrifices could only effect an outward justice, and a legal purification by which those who offered the sacrifice were made clean in the eyes of the law, and were enabled once more to take part in the public worship of God. But in so far as these sacrifices were types of the one atoning Sacrifice of Jesus Christ, and pointed to this only source of grace and pardon, they could effect sanctification and pardon, provided he who offered the sacrifice believed in the future Saviour, and repented of his sins. This faith, this hope, and this repentance were expressed and stimulated by sacrifice; and, in virtue of this intention, he who offered it received pardon and grace.

The chief significance of the Old Testament sacrifices lay in their being types of the most holy and world-redeeming Sacrifice of Jesus Christ. The bloody sacrifices were typical of His bloody Sacrifice on the Cross; the unbloody sacrifices were typical of the holy Sacrifice of the Mass; and the meat-offerings, of Holy Communion. All the sacrifices of the Old Law· found their fulfilment in the Sacrifice of our Lord, because, firstly, His was a real vicarious sacrifice, and, secondly, it had infinite efficacy to blot out all sin, and win grace for all men. It was a real vicarious sacrifice, for Jesus Christ is truly man, and took the sins of His brethren upon Him. It had infinite efficacy, because Jesus

Christ is also true God, and so able to make infinite satisfaction to the divine justice. The Sacrifice of Christ was a true holocaust, because He shed all His Blood, and was consumed by the fire of infinite love in honour of His heavenly Father. It was a sin-offering, in the highest sense of the word, because it took away the sins of the world, and cancelled the debt of man. It was the greatest of peace-offerings, because it reconciled heaven to earth, and brought peace to the world. Since our Lord offered Himself as a Sacrifice, the typical sacrifices of the Old Law have lost all efficacy and all legitimate existence.

The confession of sins required for sin-offerings is typical of the holy Sacrament of Penance, without recourse to which no sinner dare partake of the "meat-offering" of Holy Communion.

Two significant facts. The entrance of the High Priest into the Holy of Holies, and his blood-offering there on the Day of Atonement, signified that reconciliation with God can only proceed from His throne; and that one day the Redeemer would rend asunder the veil of separation and open the way into the Holy of Holies. Secondly, it was foreshown that even as the goat which was the sin-offering of the people had to be burnt outside the camp, so Jesus Christ, the Lamb of God, laden with the sins of the whole world, would be crucified outside the city. He is the great, the true atoning Sacrifice to whom all the ceremonies of the Day of Atonement pointed.

Fig. 35. High Priest.

The immediate meaning of the Jewish feasts. The religious feasts of the Jewish people had a double meaning, a retrospective and a prospective or prophetical. The feasts served immediately to remind the people of the wonderful graces and benefits which they had received from God. The Christian feasts are also intended to remind us of, and make us grateful for the grace of sanctification and redemption.

The typical meaning of the Jewish feasts. Their significance lies in this, that they were types of the Christian feasts, and pointed towards that manifestation of grace which is the foundation of these last. You learnt in chapters XXXIII and XXXVI the connexion between the Jewish feasts of the Pasch and Pentecost and our Easter and Pentecost. The Feast of Tabernacles corresponds with our Corpus Christi, which is solemnized in the open air, and is a Feast of thanksgiving to God, that Jesus Christ, God made Man, has given Himself to be our Leader through the wilderness of this life, feeding our souls with the true

Bread from heaven. Our great day of expiation is Good Friday, on which day Jesus Christ was crucified outside the walls for the sins of the world. Even as the Jewish High Priest went into the Holy of Holies on the Day of Atonement, to carry there the blood of the sacrifice, so Christ, "being come an High Priest of the good things to come, by a greater and more perfect tabernacle (j. e. heaven), not made with hand, that is, not of this creation, neither by the blood of goats and of calves, but by His own blood, entered once into the Holies, having obtained eternal redemption" (Hebr. 9, 11. 12). This means that Jesus Christ, having won for us by His death on Good Friday justification, sanctification, and salvation, entered into heaven, where He continually offers the merits of His Passion and Death to His heavenly Father. The great year of Jubilee, which began with the Day of Atonement, is a beautiful type of the Christian era, which will last till the end of times, and in which man, by the atoning Death of Jesus Christ, is freed from the slavery of sin and Satan, and is once more made heir of the kingdom of heaven. — The recurring years of Rest and Jubilee correspond with our years of jubilee, in which the Church throws open her treasuries of grace and offers to us indulgences, i. e. remission of the temporal punishment of sin, so that we may be cleansed from all guilt and made partakers of the heavenly inheritance. Thus we see that all these types find their fulfilment in the Catholic Church, and in her alone; for she alone has priest and High Priest, altar and sacrifice. It follows then that the Catholic Church alone is the true Church, founded by God, and foreshadowed in the Old Testament.

The festal assemblies and pilgrimages of the people of Israel had a very beneficial effect. They served, firstly, to preserve and increase the belief in the true God, and thus to keep the people from idolatry. Secondly, they served to foster unity and a common feeling among the people, who came to look upon themselves as all members of one body, confessors of the same faith, and heirs of the same promises.

Reward of faithfulness. The tribe of Levi was smaller than the others, but it had become less infected with idolatry; and on account of its faithfulness, God chose it for His special service.

The High Priest was the spiritual head of the people, the visible representative of God, and the mediator between God and the people. He had the privilege of entering the Holy of Holies once a year; and, later on, of anointing the kings.

The Priests had the right and the duty to offer sacrifice, to enter the Sanctuary, to keep burning the lights of the seven-branched candlestick and the sacred fire for the burnt-offerings, to bless the people and pray for them, and instruct them in the law.

The Levites were the assistants of the priest. They might not enter the Sanctuary, but had to guard the Tabernacle, and, later on, the Temple. They assisted with the sacrifices, sacred canticles, and the instruction of the people, and purified the sacred vessels.

The Priests were to be holy. "Let them, therefore, be holy, because I am holy", said the Lord (Lev. 21, 8). Whenever they had any service to perform in the Sanctuary, they had, under pain of death, to keep away from their wives, guard against all defilement, and abstain from all intoxicating drink. This purity of life was signified by their white tunic; and purity of intention by the white turban or tiara.

The High Priest was to be most holy. The inscription on the gold plate on his mitre meant that he belonged entirely to God, and that his thoughts were to be constantly fixed on Him. The breast-plate, on which were inscribed the names of the twelve tribes, implied that he was to bear the people lovingly in his heart, and be careful for their welfare. The bells on his upper tunic, which sounded at each step he took, reminded him that, by word and deed, he had to be a witness to the true faith.

Jesus, the Anointed. It was only when the priesthood was first instituted that priests were anointed; later on, this was not done. But every High Priest was anointed when he entered on his office, and every High Priest was called the Anointed. Jesus Christ, being the great and eternal High Priest who always liveth to make intercession for us (Hebr. 7, 25), is especially called "Christ", or the Anointed.

The priesthood of the Old Covenant, a type of the priesthood of the New Covenant. As there was a gradation in the former, so is there in the latter. The gradation in the Church of Christ is twofold: one of order (Bishops or High Priests, Priests and Deacons or Ministers), and one of jurisdiction, i. e. power of ruling (Pope, Patriarchs, Archbishops or Metropolitans, Bishops and Priests). As in the Old Testament there was only one High Priest, so the Christian Church considered as a whole has only one High Priest (Bishop of bishops), the Pope, who is the visible representative of our invisible High Priest, Jesus Christ. And even as the High Priest of the Old Testament was called "Holy of the Lord", so do we call the Pope "Holy Father", because he fills the holiest office on earth.

The Christian priesthood is far higher than the Jewish priesthood. The latter was propagated by natural descent, the former is perpetuated by a spiritual descent, i. e. by means of Holy Orders, which is one of the seven sacraments. The Jewish priests could only offer typical sacrifices; Christian priests offer up the true Lamb of God who taketh away the sins of the world. The former partook of earthly meat-offerings; the latter receive the priceless Flesh and Blood of the Divine Saviour. The Jewish priests prayed for the people; Christian priests remember them daily in the holy Sacrifice of the Mass, and also, except in Masses for the dead, give their blessing to the faithful.

Holy virgins, as well as the Levites, were employed in the service of the Tabernacle and, later on, of the Temple. They attended to the linen &c., and served the Lord with prayer and fasting. Tradition tells us that Mary, the Mother of God, was dedicated to the service of the Temple at a very early age.

APPLICATION. Thank God for the holy Sacrifice of the Mass, and assist regularly and devoutly at it. There you can receive priceless gifts, for the Sacrifice of Jesus Christ is the source of all grace.

Keep the Feasts of the Church, devoutly contemplating the sacred mysteries of our redemption, and avoid extravagant amusements on those days: "Rejoice in the Lord" (Phil. 4, 4).

Have great reverence for the priesthood. Priests are the "ministers of Christ and the dispensers of the mysteries of God" (1 Cor. 4, 1). We should always pray that there may be good priests in the Church.

CHAPTER XL.

THE SPIES.

[Numb. 13.]

IN the second year after their departure from Egypt, the Israelites set out[1] from Mount Sinai, and pursued their march[2] to the desert of Pharan. Thence Moses sent twelve men, one of every tribe, to explore the Land of Chanaan. He said to them: "Go and view the land, whether it be good or bad; and the people, whether they be strong or weak; and the cities, whether they be walled or without walls." So the men went out and viewed the land, entering at the south side and arriving at Hebron. Thence they proceeded as far as the torrent of the cluster of grapes. Here they cut off a branch with its cluster of grapes, and the men carried it upon a pole[3]. After forty days they returned bringing

---

[1] *Set out.* After they had passed a year in the neighbourhood of Mount Sinai.

[2] *Their march.* The pillar of cloud moved on, and the Israelites followed it. They stopped at Cades (see Map). They could now have marched straight into Chanaan, but as the people were so timid, and trusted so little in God, it was first necessary to send some spies to find out whether the inhabitants were strong and numerous, and whether the cities were fortified &c. Moses chose a leading man out of each tribe; therefore, twelve in all, and sent them into Chanaan.

[3] *Upon a pole.* At this present time there grow bunches of grapes in those parts 24 inches long and weighing 12 lbs.

with them figs, grapes, and other rich fruits, as specimens of what the land produced.

They told Moses and all the people that the Land of Chanaan was good, flowing with milk and honey, as might be seen by these fruits; but that it would be very difficult to conquer the country, as the men were big and strong, and the cities surrounded by walls. They added: "There we saw certain monsters of the sons of Enac, of the giant kind, in comparison to whom we seemed like locusts." [1] Then the people, losing courage [2] and confidence in God, began to murmur against Moses and Aaron, wishing that they had died in Egypt, or in the desert. They exclaimed: "Let us appoint a captain and return to Egypt!"

In vain did Caleb and Josue, who were of the number of the spies, or explorers, endeavour to appease the anger of the multitude, saying that the Land of Chanaan was very good, and that, if the men of that country were strong, the Lord would fight for the children of Israel. But the people would not listen to reason. They threatened [3] to put Josue and Caleb to death.

Then the glory of the Lord appeared over the Ark, and God said to Moses: "How long will this people detract Me? [4] How long will they not believe Me for all the signs that I have wrought before them? I will strike them, therefore, with pestilence, and consume them." Moses interceded for the people, saying: "Forgive, I beseech Thee, the sin of the people, according to the greatness of Thy mercy."

The Lord answered: "I have forgiven, according to thy word. But yet, all the men that have seen the signs that I have done in Egypt and in the wilderness, and have tempted Me now ten times, shall not see the land. You shall wander forty years [5] in

---

[1] *Like locusts.* This was evidently an exaggeration, in which Josue and Caleb took no part.

[2] *Losing courage.* Feeling quite convinced that they would never be able to conquer the country.

[3] *Threatened.* To stone them. They wished to choose another leader instead of Moses, who would take them back to Egypt.

[4] *Detract Me.* Because they will not believe My promises, and will not trust in My omnipotence.

[5] *Forty years.* Counting from the time they left Egypt.

the desert, and faint away and die in the desert; but your children [1]
shall possess the land."

After pronouncing this sentence on the rebellious Israelites,
the Lord struck dead [2] the ten spies who had excited them [3] to
sedition. But Josue and Caleb were spared and blessed. In spite
of the divine sentence "that they should not see the land", the
rebellious Israelites determined to enter at once. Moses warned
them, saying: "Go not up, for the Lord is not with you; it shall
not succeed prosperously with you"; and he remained with the
ark in the camp, while they in their blindness [4] set out and were
routed by the Amalekites and Chanaanites. After this the Israelites
returned once more into the interior of the desert towards the
Red Sea.

COMMENTARY.

The Justice, Mercy, and Wisdom of God. Almighty God had borne
for a long time with the murmuring, refractory Israelites; but at last
His divine patience was exhausted, and His justice demanded that they
should be punished. The people of Israel were condemned to wander
about the desert for forty years, and of the 600,000 fighting men who
left Egypt, only two entered the Promised Land. But even while
He punished, God showed mercy; for at the request of Moses He so
far forgave the people that He did not destroy them. He excluded all
those who were grown up from the Promised Land, which, however,
He explicitly promised anew to the younger generation. By the wisdom
of Divine Providence the forty years of wandering served this end, that
the Israelites put aside all the heathen ideas and customs which they
had imbibed in Egypt, and grew accustomed to the observance of the
law of God and obedience to those whom He had placed over them,
and were trained to be a valiant, warlike people.

The sins of the Israelites. In the story you have just heard the
Israelites sinned against the First Commandment by their want of faith,
hope, and charity. They sinned against the Second Commandment by

---

[1] *Your children.* God said explicitly that all those over twenty years of age
(with the exception of Josue and Caleb) should die in the wilderness, and that
only those who at this time were under twenty, should enter the Promised Land.

[2] *Struck dead.* They died a sudden and unforeseen death.

[3] *Excited them.* To believe that the land of Chanaan could not be conquered.

[4] *Their blindness.* It was against the command of God that the Israelites
went into Chanaan to attack its inhabitants. They had refused to put their trust
in God, and now they presumptuously trusted in their own strength and numbers,
and acted as if they could very well dispense with the divine assistance. This
was a formal defiance of God. The Chanaanites fell upon them and utterly defeated them.

cursing and blaspheming, and speaking and acting as if God were not the one, true, almighty Lord. These sins were all the more grievous, because God was ever before their eyes, and was constantly working wonderful miracles for their benefit. They sinned against the Fourth Commandment, by rising against Moses, the servant of God; and also against the Fifth Commandment, by trying to kill the true and faithful spies, Josue and Caleb.

Cursing. The people called a curse on themselves: "Would to God that we might die in the wilderness!" Their sinful wish was granted for their punishment: they were condemned to die in the wilderness, and never entered the Land of Chanaan. This should be a warning to us to avoid all kind of imprecations. The cry of the unbelieving Jews in the time of our Lord: "His Blood be upon us and upon our children" (New Test. LXXII), is another terrible instance of an imprecation being fulfilled.

The power of intercession. Because Moses, the just servant of God, prayed earnestly for his people, God forgave them their many and grievous sins.

Temporal punishment. God told Moses explicitly that He forgave the people their sin on account of his intercession. Nevertheless He visited them with a temporal punishment.

Lies and scandal. By a lying exaggeration of the strength of the Chanaanites, the spies (with the exception of Josue and Caleb) induced the Israelites to murmur against God. "Thou wilt destroy all that speak a lie" (Ps. 5, 7).

Sudden death is the worst punishment that can befall a sinner, because he has no time given him to do penance. Therefore, in the Litany of the Saints, the Church prays thus: "From sudden and unprovided death, O Lord, deliver us!"

God's blessing is everything. The Israelites were completely routed by the Chanaanites and Amalekites, over whom they had previously obtained a victory (chapter XXXV). This was because God neither blessed nor helped them. Our help comes from the Lord: without Him we can do nothing.

The kingdom of heaven suffereth violence. The grown-up Israelites did not enter the Promised Land, because they shrank from the burdens involved in the journey. For the same reason many Christians do not reach heaven, because they do not correspond with God's grace, and will not fight against the enemies of their souls. "The kingdom of heaven suffereth violence, and the violent bear it away" (Mat. 11, 12).

APPLICATION. Are you inclined to tell lies and to exaggerate? It was on account of a lie that God punished the ten spies with sudden death. Learn from this how much God, who is truth itself, abhors lies. "Putting away lying, speak ye the truth every man with his neighbour" (Eph. 4, 25).

Have you the evil habit of uttering curses or imprecations?

CHAPTER XLI.

THE REVOLT OF CORE AND HIS ADHERENTS.

[Numb. 16—17.]

ONE day, whilst the children of Israel were in the wilderness, they found a man gathering wood on the Sabbath-day, and they brought him to Moses and Aaron, who put him in prison, to see how he should be punished. But the Lord said to Moses: "Let that man die; let all the multitude stone him without the camp." So it was done.

Some time after, two hundred and fifty men, belonging partly to the tribe of Reuben, and partly to the tribe of Levi, and having for leaders Core[1], a Levite, and Dathan and Abiron[2], both of the tribe of Reuben—all these rose up against Moses and Aaron. They were envious of the high position of Moses and Aaron, and accused them of tyranny and ambition. They said: "All the people are holy[3]; why do ye raise yourselves above the people of God?" Moses, hearing this, and knowing that it was a revolt against God Himself, was much afflicted, and fell flat on his face.

He afterwards spoke to the rebellious Levites, saying: "Is it because God has chosen you to serve near the Tabernacle, that you wish to usurp the dignity of the priesthood also? To-morrow

---

[1] *Core.* Core's father was brother to Moses' mother. Core, Moses and Aaron were, therefore, first cousins.

[2] *Dathan and Abiron.* As Reuben was Jacob's eldest son, these men felt themselves aggrieved that the descendants of Levi should have privileges, which they themselves had not.

[3] *Are holy.* They meant to say: "All men are called to the service of the Lord. We want no peculiar priesthood; and you (Moses and Aaron) are no better than we are." It was, in their opinion, presumption on Moses' part to assume the leadership, and on Aaron's part to set himself up as High Priest of the people. We have here the first example of schism and heresy introduced into a divinely constituted Church. It was schism to rebel against the lawful authority of Moses and Aaron; and it was heresy to deny that God had given jurisdiction and the priesthood to Moses and Aaron.

the Lord will make known who they are that belong to Him. Prepare, then, and stand each with his censer on one side, and Aaron will stand on the other."

On the following day, when the two hundred and fifty men were to appear before the Lord with their censers, Moses ordered the leaders of the revolt to come forth from their tents. But they impudently replied: "We will not come." Then Moses went himself to their tents, accompanied by Aaron, and told the people to separate themselves from those wicked men, lest they should perish with them. Moses said: "If these men die the common death of men, the Lord did not send me; but if the earth, opening her mouth, swallow them down, and they go down alive into hell, you shall know that they have blasphemed the Lord."

Hardly had Moses ended these words, when lo! the earth opened under the feet of these hardened sinners, and swallowed them up, with their tents, and all that belonged to them, and they went down alive into hell. At the same time fire came down [1] from heaven and destroyed the two hundred and fifty men who had taken sides with Core, Dathan and Abiron.

After this, the Lord spoke to Moses, saying: "Speak to the children of Israel, and take of every one of them a rod, by their kindreds, of all the princes of the tribes, twelve rods [2], and write the name of every man upon his rod; and lay them up in the Tabernacle of the Covenant. Whomsoever of these I shall choose, his rod shall blossom." Moses did as the Lord had commanded.

Next day, when Moses entered into the Tabernacle, he found that the rod of Aaron had budded and blossomed. He then brought out all the rods of the children of Israel, and each one received back his own rod. But the rod of Aaron he placed in the Ark [3] of the Covenant.

---

[1] *Fire came down.* The fire proceeded from the pillar of cloud and killed the 250 men who, with Core, had assumed the priestly office of offering incense in the Tabernacle.

[2] *Rods.* They were sticks cut from almond-trees.

[3] *In the Ark.* In the Ark of the Covenant, to be a lasting witness to the divine vocation of Aaron and his sons.

COMMENTARY.

The Justice of God was shown by the punishment of the Sabbath-breaker, as well as by that of Core and his adherents.

God's omnipotence worked a great miracle in connexion with Aaron's rod, which, in one night, brought forth not only leaves, buds and flowers, but also ripe almonds.

Sabbath-breaking. The severe punishment of the Sabbath-breaker teaches us that the profanation of the Sabbath is a great sin. This sin often calls down temporal punishment, and it will certainly bring eternal punishment. "Remember", i. e. do not forget "to keep the Sabbath-day holy."

The divine institution of the Priesthood. By the terrible punishment of the rebels, and the blossoming of Aaron's rod, God again declared that the priesthood of the Old Testament was instituted by Him.

Rebellion against authority. The rising of Core and his adherents was a rebellion against both spiritual and temporal authority, against throne and altar, for they refused to acknowledge that God had ordained Moses to be their leader, and Aaron to be their High Priest. The rebellion was, therefore, really against God, who had called Moses and Aaron, and who had attested their divine vocation by so many miracles. Hence Moses was right in saying: "Why do you stand against the Lord?" The terrible punishment of Core and those with him shows us how great a sin it is to rebel against those whom God has put in authority over us. "He that resisteth the power, resisteth the ordinance of God. And they that resist, purchase to themselves damnation" (Rom. 13, 2).

Pride is a capital sin. Core, being proud, was offended at the idea that he was only a Levite, while Aaron and his sons were priests; and the family pride and ambition of Dathan and Abiron were injured by the fact that men of the small tribe of Levi were the representatives before God of the whole people. Their pride developed into envy, and this again developed into rebellion against the authorities ordained by God.

Aaron's rod, a type of the Cross. Aaron's rod, which blossomed and bore fruit, is a type of the holy Cross, which by the Blood of Christ has brought forth such wonderful fruits of grace and virtue.

The Priesthood of the New Testament. We Christians are all called to be holy, and were all sanctified in baptism; but all Christians are not priests, for Jesus Christ has instituted a special priesthood in His Church, for the sanctification of all the faithful. If, even in the Old Testament, a special priesthood was necessary for the care of the things of God, how much more necessary is it that there should be a priesthood in the New Testament to look after the sacred mysteries of the Church! "Honour God with all thy soul, and give honour to the priests" (Ecclus. 7, 33).

Union of temporal and spiritual authority. God, by entrusting the highest spiritual and the highest temporal authority to the two brothers, Aaron and Moses, gave it to be understood that in all ages spiritual and temporal authority, Church and State, ought to work together for the good of mankind.

APPLICATION. Do you show reverence for your spiritual and temporal superiors, your priests and teachers? Are you unruly or obstinate? Do you ever pray for them?

CHAPTER XLII.

THE DOUBT OF MOSES.—THE BRAZEN SERPENT.

[Numb. 10—11.]

IN the beginning of the fortieth year of their wanderings[1], the Israelites—the children of those that had died in the desert—suffered from the want of water, and began to murmur against the Lord. Then the Lord appeared in glory, and said to Moses: "Speak[2] to the rock, and it shall yield waters." Then Moses, taking the rod[3] from the Tabernacle, assembled the people before the rock, which he was about to strike. Then he raised the rod and struck; but doubting[4] a little he struck a second time.

That momentary diffidence, which was only a venial sin, and which made Moses strike the rock a second time, was displeasing to the Lord, and He told Moses and Aaron: "Because you have not believed[5] Me, you shall not bring these people into the land which I will give them."

Thence the Israelites removed their camp and came to Mount Hor[6], where Aaron died[7], and Eleazar, his son, became High

---

[1] *Their wanderings.* The Israelites were now back again at Cades on the borders of Chanaan.

[2] *Speak.* "Command it to bring forth water."

[3] *The rod.* The miraculous rod, kept in the Tabernacle.

[4] *Doubting.* He doubted whether God would work another great miracle for this refractory people.

[5] *Not believed.* Not believed quite firmly enough. If Moses had not believed at all, he would not have assembled the people before the rock.

[6] *Mount Hor.* As it was not easy to enter Chanaan on the south side, Moses wished to enter it from the east. He went round to the south-east and came to Mount Hor (see Map).

[7] *Died.* On Mount Hor God called Aaron to Himself at the age of a hundred and twenty-three years; for he, equally with Moses, was not allowed to enter the Promised Land.

Priest. Some time later, the Israelites, tired[1] of their incessant wanderings in the desert, began to murmur against the Lord and Moses. Wherefore fiery serpents[2] were sent amongst them, by whose deadly bite a great number were killed[3].

Then the people, knowing that the serpents had been sent in punishment of their sins, came to Moses and said: "We have sinned, because we have spoken against the Lord and thee: pray that He may take away these serpents from us." And Moses prayed for the people. Whereupon the Lord said to him: "Make a brazen serpent, and set it up[4] for a sign: whosoever, being struck, shall look on it, shall live." Moses, therefore, made a brazen serpent, and set it up for a sign[5] which healed all those that looked upon it.

COMMENTARY.

The Justice, Mercy and Omnipotence of God are all shown in this story.—God punished both the doubt of Moses and the murmuring of the people: but He gave the ungrateful Israelites water, listened to Moses' prayer for them, and healed them from the bites of the snakes. By His almighty power He called forth the water from the rock; and, through one glance cast at the brazen serpent, He restored the dying to life and health.

Murmuring against God is a great sin, as we can learn by the severe punishment which it brought on the murmuring Israelites. We must submit humbly to the will of our God and Creator, and never resist or murmur against Him and His divine decrees.

The use of sufferings. Whenever God visited the Israelites with sufferings, they acknowledged their grievous sins and repented.

Temperance. The sensuality of the Israelites was the cause of all their grumbling. They craved for other food than that which God fed them on, and refused to put up with any hardship. Instead of subduing

---

[1] *Tired.* To avoid the territory of the Edomites, the children of Israel had to turn towards the south, and then again return northwards along the eastern side of Edom (see Map). All this time they had nothing to eat except manna, and they craved for other food.

[2] *Fiery serpents.* These were poisonous snakes. They were covered with fiery red spots and stripes, and the wound of their bite burnt like fire, and caused a deadly inflammation.

[3] *Killed.* The poisonous reptiles lurked round the camp and crept into the tents. The whole camp resounded with the cries of the sick, and the moans of the dying. The people now saw how much they had sinned.

[4] *Set it up.* On a pole.

[5] *A sign.* Of salvation.

their appetites and submitting themselves to God's will, they were discontented, and were always complaining and murmuring. They did not possess the virtue of temperance.

Doubts about faith. Moses and Aaron did not doubt Almighty God's power, but, for one moment, they doubted His mercy. They were righteously angry when they perceived that the new generation of Israelites, who from their youth up had witnessed the miracles of God, and who had been daily fed with manna, should be as wavering and refractory as their fathers had been before them. They felt that these thankless people were not worthy that God should again perform a miracle for their benefit. But God's thoughts are not our thoughts, and His mercy is infinitely great. God, who is the very truth, had said: "Speak to the rock and it shall yield waters"; so they ought to have believed unconditionally and not doubted for a single moment. Anyhow, their doubt was a sin.

Venial sins. Wilful unbelief is a grievous sin. But as the doubt of Moses and Aaron was only a passing one, and as they did not give their full consent to it, but, in spite of it, obeyed God's command by going to the rock &c., their sin was not mortal, but only venial: nevertheless they were severely punished for it. If a person has laboured for a long time to attain a certain object and has nearly reached it, it would be a very severe trial to him to be told that he must renounce it. Moses and Aaron had during forty years trained the Israelites and prepared them for their entrance into the Promised Land; they longed to complete their work and return to the land of their forefathers. But now, at the end of their labour, care and toil, they were told that they must die without setting foot in the long wished for country! It was indeed a severe punishment! But they humbly submitted to God's will, and preferred to expiate their sin in this world rather than in the next. This severe punishment of one venial sin teaches us to know and fear God's justice, and shows us that even venial sin is a great evil, and must be expiated either here or in the world to come.

The intercession of the Saints. The sinful people knew well that they did not deserve that their petition should be heard by God; therefore they begged His faithful servant, Moses, to intercede for them, and to him God hearkened. For this same reason we call on the Saints in heaven, the friends of God, to intercede for us.

The brazen serpent, a type of our crucified Lord. The brazen serpent set up on a pole is a type of our Divine Saviour. He Himself, in His discourse with Nicodemus, told him that it was so (New Test. XV): "As Moses lifted up the serpent in the desert, so must the Son of Man be lifted up, that whosoever believeth in Him may not perish, but may have life everlasting." As the brazen serpent was raised up on high, so Jesus Christ (who, by the mouth of David, said of Himself: "I am a worm and no man"; Ps. 21, 6) was raised up on the Cross. Whoever was bitten by a poisonous snake was cured by turning his eyes in faith to the brazen serpent. So we, when our souls are wounded by the infernal serpent, shall be healed of our sins, if we, being full of faith, turn our eyes to our crucified Saviour.

The Israelites bitten by the fiery snakes were a type of mankind. The infernal serpent has wounded all men, and has kindled in them the flame of sinful passions, and caused them to be subject to everlasting death. It is of great significance that He who redeemed us from sin and death should be typified by a (brazen) serpent. How is it that the serpent, the very type of sin, should also be a type of the Redeemer, and a means of salvation? Because the brazen serpent, hanging on the tree, was not poisonous, even though it had the form of a poisonous snake. Thus Jesus Christ, though free from the poison of sin, being "holy, innocent, undefiled" (Hebr. 7, 26), took the form of sinful man, loaded Himself with the sins of the world, and suffered Himself to be raised on and nailed to the Cross in order to save all men from sin and eternal death. The brazen serpent, therefore, foreshadowed the fact that the Redeemer would appear in the form of sinful man, would be raised on and nailed to a Cross, and by this very means would redeem man from the death of sin, and from eternal loss.

Jesus Christ, the source of salvation. The brazen serpent being a type of the Saviour of the world, God promised that "whosoever should look on it should be saved". The wonderful healing power of the lifeless serpent did not lie in itself, but in the crucified Saviour, of whom it was a type.

The necessity of faith. Even as none of the mortally stricken Israelites could be cured unless, full of faith, they looked at the brazen serpent, which was set up as a sign of salvation, so no man can be saved unless, full of faith, he turns to the crucified God made Man. Only they who believe in Him will have life everlasting.

Christ the Rock. The waters which flowed from the rock in the wilderness to refresh the Israelites and slake their thirst, were emblematic of the divine graces, which flow to mankind through the Sacraments of the Church of Jesus Christ. "And all drank the same spiritual drink, and they drank of the spiritual rock that followed them, and the rock was Christ" (1 Cor. 10, 4).

———

APPLICATION. You have often done wrong, and said to yourself: "Oh, it is only a venial sin!" But think, even a venial sin is an offence against God, and is deserving of punishment. Ask yourself to which sin you are most prone, whether anger, lying, greediness, or so forth, and firmly resolve to overcome it.

CHAPTER XLIII.

THE PROPHECY OF BALAAM.

[Numb. 22—24.]

AS the Israelites were nearing the Promised Land, they came to the confines of Moab[1]. Balak, the king of that country, being in very great fear[2], sent the elders and the nobles of his kingdom with rich presents to Balaam[3], that he might come and curse his enemies. This Balaam believed in the true God; but, at the same time, he practised soothsaying and divination.

When the messengers had arrived with their presents, Balaam said: "Tarry here this night, and I will answer whatsoever the Lord shall say to me." And God told him: "Thou shalt not go, neither shalt thou curse the people." So the princes returned to the king. But Balak sent a greater number of nobles and richer presents than the first time. Balaam told the messengers again to stay for one night. In that night God came to Balaam and said: "Arise and go; yet so, that thou do what I shall command thee."

Then Balaam arose and went to the land of Moab. The king took him to three different mountains, whence he could behold the Israelites in the valley, and ordered him to curse them. But Balaam, being each time prevented by God from cursing, blessed[4] them, saying: "How beautiful are thy tabernacles, O Jacob, and thy tents, O Israel! He that blesseth thee shall also himself be blessed, and he that curseth thee shall be reckoned accursed."

Then Balak grew angry, and exclaimed: "I had intended to honour thee, but the Lord hath deprived thee of the honour; for I called thee to curse my enemies, and thou, on the contrary,

---

[1] *Moab.* This country lay to the east of the Dead Sea (see Map).

[2] *Great fear.* That Israel would conquer his country; for the chosen people had already overcome several neighbouring kings at the point of the sword.

[3] *Balaam.* He was a heathen soothsayer of Mesopotamia, the country which lay between the Euphrates and Tigris, but he had heard of the wonderful things which God had done for the Israelites, and had learnt thereby to know the true God. The Lord revealed future things to him, in order that through him the heathen nations also might learn to look for the Redeemer. Balak, the superstitious king of Moab, wanted Balaam to curse God's people, hoping, if this were done, to be able to overcome them.

[4] *Blessed.* By this God revealed His omnipotence to the heathen.

hast blessed them three times." So he ordered him to return to his country. Thereupon the eyes of Balaam were opened and he saw a vision[1], and his lips were opened, and he prophesied: "I shall see him, but not now[2]; I shall behold him, but not near[3]. A star shall rise out of Jacob, and a sceptre[4] shall spring up from Israel[5], and shall strike the chiefs of Moab[6] and shall smite the children of Seth." And having prophesied also of the fate of the nations he returned to his country.

COMMENTARY.

God's Omnipotence is shown by His forcing Balaam to bless the Israelites against his will.

God's Omniscience is shown by His revealing to Balaam what would happen in the far future.

The sixth promise of the Messias. The prophecy of Balaam points to the Divine Redeemer, and reveals, firstly, that He would not come for a long time; secondly, that He would be one of the children of Israel; thirdly, that He would come, like a star, from above, shedding light around Him; fourthly, that He would be a king; and fifthly, that He would overcome the enemies of His kingdom. Let us see how this prophecy has been fulfilled. Firstly, the Redeemer did not come till 1450 years after Balaam spoke; secondly, He was, as Man, descended from Jacob, and was born in Judea; thirdly, He came down from Heaven to be the Light of the world; fourthly, He has founded the Church, the kingdom of God, which, fifthly, overcomes all His enemies, and will last till the end of time. The brazen serpent foreshadowed our Lord's humiliation; the prophecy of Balaam foreshadowed His majesty.

Faith in God's word. Balaam said to Balak that he could not alter the word of the Lord; and this rule applies to every word of God revealed to us. Nobody can or dare alter God's word, either by adding to it or by taking away from it. We must believe and accept revelation just as it is.

Superstition. Balak did not believe in the true God, but he cherished the foolish, superstitious idea that Balaam's curse could injure the people of God.

The star out of Jacob and the three kings from the East. Balaam's home was in the east, that is, east of the Promised Land. There, the

---

[1] *Vision.* In which God revealed the future to him.

[2] *Not now.* i. e. not now, but later.

[3] *Not near.* i. e. but in the far future.

[4] *Sceptre.* A ruler.

[5] *From Israel.* One who should belong to the chosen people and be descended from Jacob, or Israel.

[6] *Chiefs of Moab.* The heathen powers.

prophecy of Balaam was well known, and during the hundreds of years which elapsed before our Lord's Incarnation, the tradition of this prophecy was preserved, and there existed a living expectation of the rising of a wonderful star, and at the same time of a sceptre, i. e. a king who should spring up out of Israel. Therefore, the three kings from the east, as soon as they had seen the wonderful star, went straight to Judea, to look for Him, the new-born king, whose birth was heralded by the star.

APPLICATION. Do not curse! Say to yourselves: "There is a God, who cannot be mocked."

CHAPTER XLIV.

PARTING ADVICE OF MOSES.—HIS DEATH.

[Deut. 1—34. Numb. 27.]

THE hour[1] had come at last when Moses was to be taken away from his people. Before he died, God commanded him to lay his hands[2] upon Josue, in the presence of all the people, so that they might obey him as their ruler. For God had said to Moses: "Thou shalt not pass over this Jordan; but Josue shall bring the people into the land which I swore I would give to their fathers."·

Then Moses made his farewell discourse[3] to the people in the most touching manner: "Hear, O ye heavens, the things I speak; let the earth give ear to the words of my mouth. Hear, O Israel, the Lord our God is one Lord. Thou shalt love the Lord thy God[4] with thy whole heart, and with thy whole soul, and with thy whole strength. Let none be found among you that consult soothsayers, or observe dreams and omens. These things the Gentiles do; but thou art otherwise instructed. The Lord thy

---

[1] *The hour*. The forty years of wandering were drawing to a close, and the time had come for the Israelites to enter the Promised Land. Moses, however, was not to lead them in (chapter XLII).

[2] *To lay his hands*. From henceforward Josue was to be God's chosen leader of His people, instead of Moses. Therefore Moses had to lay his hand upon him in the presence of all the Israelites, that they might know that he was their appointed leader. You have already heard about Josue in chapters XXXV and XL.

[3] *His farewell discourse*. Pay particular attention to these parting words of Moses.

[4] *Thy God*. Who has done such great things for you, and has made you His chosen people.

God will raise up to thee a prophet of thy nation, and of thy brethren, like unto me. Him thou shalt hear."

He reminded them of all the wonders which God had wrought in their behalf. He promised them that, if they were faithful in observing the commandments of God, they should be blessed in their houses, blessed in their fields, blessed in the fruits of the land, blessed in their cattle, blessed when they came in and when they went out. Then he warned [1] them that, if they did not hear

Fig 36. Mount Nebo. (Phot. Bonfils.)

the voice of the Lord and keep His commandments, curses should come upon them and all they possessed.

Then, having at the order of God composed a great hymn [canticle of Moses] for the people, he blessed the people, and went up from the plains of Moab to Mount Nebo (Fig. 36) [2]. From that place the Lord showed him, from afar off, the Land of Chanaan,

---

[1] *He warned.* The choice of serving God or not was given to them. As a dying father exhorts his children, so did Moses, in the most moving way, exhort his beloved people to choose what was right.

[2] *Mount Nebo.* East of the Dead Sea (see Map).

which He had promised to his fathers, Abraham, Isaac and Jacob.

There Moses died[1], at the age of one hundred and twenty years; and all Israel mourned him for thirty days[2].

COMMENTARY.

The Justice and Faithfulness of God are shown to us in a very awe-inspiring manner in this story. Moses was a very holy servant of God, distinguished for his virtues and services. But, in company with his brother Aaron, he, for one short moment, doubted God's mercy, and for their sin God pronounced on both of them this sentence: "You shall not bring these people into the land which I will give them." Soon after this Aaron died on Mount Hor. At last the Israelites arrived at the borders of Chanaan, and the time had come for them to cross the Jordan and take possession of the Promised Land; but Moses was not allowed to go further. From the top of Mount Nebo, Almighty God showed him the beautiful Land of Promise, and then he had to die; for God always does that which He says He will do. If the Lord God punished Moses so severely for one venial sin, how much ought we to fear His justice, and avoid everything that is wrong!

In Moses' parting discourse he exhorted the Israelites as follows:

1. *They were never to forget the Covenant* sealed with God, but were always to keep it faithfully. His exhortation applies to us also, who ought never to prove unfaithful to our baptismal vows.

2. *They were to worship God only,* and love Him with their whole hearts. Our Lord tells us that this commandment is the first and greatest commandment, for it contains all the others.

3. *They were to bring up their children in the fear and love of God,* and relate to them all God's wonderful works and the benefits which He had showered on them, so that they might be moved to be grateful and to love Him. It is a sacred duty of parents to bring up their children in the fear of God; for He has done far more for us Christians than He ever did for the Israelites.

4. If the Israelites kept the Commandments, *God promised them rich earthly blessings;* for, as the people were sensual and earthly, sensible and earthly rewards were held out to them. It is true in all times

---

[1] *Died.* Holy Scripture says that "his eye was not dim, neither were his teeth moved". This means that he was not feeble from old age, and might, humanly speaking, have lived some time longer, if God had not called him away.

[2] *Thirty days.* And quite rightly too; for, after God, he was the greatest benefactor of his people. Through him God had instituted the Covenant and worked great miracles, and had spoken face to face with him.

that only he who fears God can have any true happiness on earth, and for this reason St. Paul says: "Glory and honour and peace to every one that worketh good" (Rom. 2, 10); but all the same we Christians ought not to serve God for earthly rewards, but for those which are imperishable and eternal. We ought to love God for His own sake (independently of all rewards and punishments), because He is infinitely worthy of love. The law of the New Testament is more perfect than the law of the Old Testament. Moses pointed to the New Covenant, for, in his parting discourse, he gave utterance to

5. *The seventh promise of the Messias.* He foretold to his people that one day another prophet should rise in their midst, who also would institute a Covenant: "The Lord will raise up to thee a prophet of thy nation, and of thy brethren, like unto me. Him thou shalt hear." Who is this prophet? Jesus Christ, who was a Prophet like to Moses; for, firstly, He instituted the New Covenant as Moses had instituted the Old; and secondly, He foretold the future as Moses did, proclaiming the divine law. (See chapter XXXVII, in what way Moses was a type of our Lord, and also New Testament, chapter XXXVII, where Moses appears at the Transfiguration.)

The threefold office of Christ. Moses' prophecy about the Redeemer points to the prophetical office of our Lord. Balaam's prophecy points to His kingly office: and the typical brazen serpent pointed to His priestly office, by foreshowing that the Divine Saviour would be sacrificed on the Cross, and would heal our sins.

Look back at Moses' great virtues, his living faith, his firm confidence in God, his burning zeal for God's honour, his patience, humility, piety, gentleness, fortitude, and love of his people. Think of his blessed death at the end of his laborious life spent in the service of God. He is now great in heaven, and we on earth venerate him as one of the best and noblest of men.

Our pilgrimage to heaven. The forty years' wandering of the Israelites in the desert is a sensible type of our pilgrimage to the promised land of heaven. The passage of the Red Sea delivered the Israelites from the bondage of Egypt: we must pass through the waters of Baptism to be freed from the bondage of sin. The Israelites wended their weary and perilous way through the desert to the Promised Land: our road to heaven is also wearisome, and many are the enemies that we meet on the way ("Narrow is the gate, and strait is the way which leadeth to life." New Test. XXI). The Lord God Himself, going before them, showed the Israelites the way: Jesus has gone before us and has, by word and example, shown us the way to heaven. God fed them with manna: Jesus feeds and strengthens our souls with the true Bread from heaven, His Sacred Body and Blood. The Israelites strove and fought and conquered only by the help and protection of God: we too, in our fight against the enemies of our salvation, must seek God's grace, without which we can do nothing. The children of Israel received, as the reward of their labours, the safe possession of the land of Chanaan: we shall receive, as our reward, the eternal possession of the kingdom of heaven.

APPLICATION. You should seek to know what God has done, and is still doing for you, and what He requires of you. You can learn this by your instructions in the Catechism and Bible History. But are you not lazy and negligent about such instruction? Do you always learn the lesson set you? Do you always pay great attention to what you are taught?

III. EPOCH:

JOSUE AND THE JUDGES.
(About 1450—1095 B. C.)

CHAPTER XLV.

ENTRANCE OF THE ISRAELITES INTO THE PROMISED LAND.

[Jos. 1—24.]

AFTER the death of Moses, the Lord spoke to Josue: "My servant Moses is dead; arise and pass over this Jordan [1], thou and the people with thee. I will deliver to thee every place which the sole of your foot shall tread upon. No man shall be able to resist thee all the days of thy life." Encouraged by these promises the people advanced towards the Jordan. When they reached its banks [2], Josue ordered the priests to take the Ark of the Lord, and go before the people. As soon as the priests, carrying the Ark, stepped into the Jordan, and their feet touched the water at the bank, the waves that came from above stood heaped together, and swelling up like a mountain, were seen afar off; but the floods, which were beneath, ran down into the sea,

---

[1] *This Jordan*. This river is very rapid, because between the Sea of Galilee and the Dead Sea it has a fall of nearly 666 feet: its breadth is from 66—100 feet, and its mean depth 10 feet.

[2] *Its banks*. The Jordan was swollen. It was a short time before the Pasch, and the snow on the mountains was melting.

until they wholly failed. Then all the people passed over through the channel that was dried up. They pitched their tents before Jericho. On the following day they celebrated the Pasch, and having eaten of the fruits of the earth, the manna ceased to fall[1].

Jericho (Fig. 37)[2] was a strongly fortified city, capable of offering a long resistance. The children of Israel wished to take it, but they lost courage when they saw the height and strength of the ramparts. But the Lord, seeing their want of confidence, ordered Josue to bring together all the fighting men of Israel, and to march in deep silence around the city[3] once a day for six days,

Fig. 37. Ruins of Jericho. (Phot. Bonfils.)

and on the seventh day go around the city seven times; and at the last time, all the people, on hearing the priests that

---

[1] *Ceased to fall.* Because the Israelites had reached the end of their wanderings in the desert, and would be able from henceforth to find sufficient food in the fruitful land of Chanaan.

[2] *Jericho.* Jericho was a strongly fortified town, and there were many fighting men inside to defend it. The Israelites were not provided with battering-rams, or any other implements for breaking down the walls, and were not accustomed to that kind of warfare. They did not, therefore, think it possible that they would be able to take a fortified city.

[3] *Around the city.* The repeated marching round Jericho convinced the Israelites both of the strength of the city and of the necessity of divine assistance.

were before the Ark sound the trumpets, were to shout together with a great shout. So it was done. When the seventh day came, they marched silently six times around the city; but at the seventh turn, when the priests sounded the trumpets, all the people shouted, and instantly the walls fell[1] down. Every man went up by the place that was against him; and they took the city.

After many hard-fought battles, Josue at length made himself master of all the land of Chanaan. During this period he several times experienced the especial assistance of God. On one occasion he waged war against the five kings of the Amorrhites. The Israelites conquered and pursued their enemies. But night coming on would soon have put an end to the victory. Then Josue spoke to the Lord, in the sight of all the people: "Move not[2], O sun, toward Gabaon; nor thou, O moon, toward the valley of Ajalon." So the sun stood still[3] in the midst of heaven. There was not, before nor after, so long a day.

Chanaan was divided[4] among the twelve tribes of Israel. The tribe of Levi[5] alone received no portion, as they lived on the tithes and sacrifices; but they received forty-eight cities in different parts of the country. The descendants of the two sons of Joseph, Ephraim and Manasses, received each a portion of the land. Thus the country was divided among the twelve tribes[6]:

---

[1] *The walls fell.* Of course this was not the effect of the noise of the trumpets and shouting, but of the divine omnipotence.

[2] *Move not.* Josue, and Scripture generally, speaks here, as we do still, according to appearances; for, judging by what we see, it seems as if the sun moved round the earth.

[3] *Stood still.* God, in a wonderful way, prolonged the daylight, so that the Israelites were able to profit by their victory, and follow it up. The opposite miracle to this took place at our Lord's crucifixion, when the sun was darkened for three hours.

[4] *Divided.* Both east and west of the Jordan. Two tribes and a half, those of Reuben, Gad and half Manasses, lived to the east of the Jordan, the other nine tribes and a half to the west. The Tabernacle was set up at Silo, between Jerusalem and Sichem, and remained there for 300 years.

[5] *Tribe of Levi.* The priests and Levites received no land, for they were entirely devoted to God's service, and were not to trouble themselves about agriculture &c. They received the tenth part of all wheat, fruits and clean beasts, and a certain portion of the sacrifices.

[6] *Twelve tribes.* As the tribe of Levi fell out in the division of the Promised Land, the number of twelve was restored by dividing the tribe of Joseph into

Reuben, Simeon, Juda, Zabulon, Issachar, Dan, Gad, Aser, Nephtali, Benjamin, Ephraim and Manasses. Thus were the promises fulfilled which God had made to the patriarchs. When Josue was old, he assembled the people and admonished them to observe the law[1], and to avoid intercourse and marriage with the heathen. Josue died at the age of one hundred and ten years.

COMMENTARY.

The Omnipotence of God. By God's will the running waters of the Jordan rose up like rocks; at His bidding the strong walls of Jericho fell down; and by His command the light of day was prolonged. Nothing can resist God's omnipotence, nothing can hinder the workings of Divine Providence.

The Faithfulness of God. The promise which God had made to Abraham six hundred and fifty years before was now fulfilled, and by His wonderful guidance, Abraham's descendants were now given possession of the Promised Land. God also fulfils what He threatens. Not one of those men who departed from Egypt, except Josue and Caleb, entered the Promised Land. They all died in the desert, as God said they should die. God has promised us everlasting happiness if we keep our baptismal vows, that is, if we stand fast in faith, keep the commandments, and use the means of grace given to us: if we neglect to do this, we shall not go to heaven, but to hell.

The object of miracles. During the journey of the Israelites to the Promised Land God worked great miracles for His people. Now that it was a case of completing the great work, and putting His people in possession of the Promised Land, He worked still greater miracles. By doing this the Lord wished to confirm His people's faith in His omnipotence, and their confidence in His loving care. He wished them also to learn that they could do nothing by their own strength and numbers, and that it was only by His help they could attain to the Promised Land, and that they therefore owed Him an everlasting debt of gratitude. Neither can we reach the promised land of heaven by our own strength, but only by the help of God's grace.

The folly of idolatry was proved to the Chanaanites by the miracle which made the sun to shine on the earth for a longer time than was its wont, and this for the purpose of bringing defeat upon them. The Chanaanites worshipped the sun and moon as gods, and the fact that

---

two tribes. A counterpart to this is seen in the New Testament. When Peter was made the Chief Shepherd and Vicar of Christ on earth, St. Paul was called by God to fill up the number of the twelve Apostles.

[1] *The law.* Moses had written down the revelation of God from the beginning, and had, in five books, recorded all the laws of God.

these heavenly bodies obeyed the command of Josue, the servant of God, ought to have proved to them that the God of Israel was infinitely more powerful than their self-made deities which, far from being able to help them, were compelled to help their enemies.

The power of prayer. Full of faith, Josue prayed, and at his prayer the day was prolonged.

The power of faith. "By faith the walls of Jericho fell down" (Hebr. 11, 30). The Israelites knew very well that their marching round the town, the blowing of the trumpets and the shouting of the multitude could not, of themselves, overthrow the walls; but full of faithful confidence in God, they did exactly everything that He commanded, and through their faithful obedience God worked the miracle.

Josue, the ninth type of Jesus Christ. He was this, inasmuch as he led the Israelites into the Land of Promise, and triumphantly conquered it. Jesus Christ, by His Death and Resurrection, has overcome sin, Satan and death, and has opened to us the kingdom of heaven. He leads us there by His doctrine, His example and His grace, and especially by holy Baptism.

The passage of the Jordan (as well as that of the Red Sea) *is a type of Baptism,* by which we enter the kingdom of God upon earth, i. e. the holy Church, and acquire a claim to those priceless means of grace which Jesus Christ bequeathed to His Church.

The Promised Land was a figure of heaven. As the Israelites did not obtain possession of Chanaan till they had toiled, fought, and suffered much, so Christians cannot enter heaven, the true land of promise, unless they contend bravely against the enemies of their salvation.

Processions. By God's command the Israelites went in procession round Jericho thirteen times. These were religious processions, in which the Ark of the Covenant was carried.

APPLICATION. After crossing the Jordan the Israelites had to fight for a long time before they acquired the Promised Land. Thus we, after our holy Baptism, must fight against the enemies of our souls, especially against evil inclinations and passions. "Labour as a good soldier of Christ Jesus . . . He also that striveth for the mastery is not crowned except he strive lawfully" (2 Tim. 2, 3. 5). As a reward, we shall receive the everlasting possesion of heaven. Fight especially against your besetting sin. Make a good resolution to overcome it every day, and let it be the object of your particular examination of conscience.

CHAPTER XLVI.

THE JUDGES.—GEDEON.—SAMSON.

[Judg. 6—8; 13—16.]

SO long as that generation of the Israelites lived who had eaten of the manna in the desert, and who had seen the wonders of the Lord wrought for them, both in the wilderness and in the taking of Chanaan, they did not depart from the way of the Lord; but their children, having intermarried[1] with the pagan nations around them, contrary to the express command of God, began to adore the idols which their wives worshipped. Then the Lord delivered them[2] into the hands of their enemies.

They afterwards repented and turned again to the Lord their God. In this manner, falling into idolatry and returning again to the worship of the true God, they went on for several generations. Whenever they humbled themselves before God, and showed signs of true repentance, the Lord hastened to their relief. From time to time He raised up among them brave and pious men[3], who smote the enemy with a strong hand. These men were called Judges[4]. Amongst them were Barac, Jephte, Samson—who was famous for his great strength—and the pious Samuel.

But the most renowned of all the Judges was Gedeon, the son of a common Israelite, who lived at the time when God had

---

[1] *Intermarried.* Josue had expressly warned them (Josue 23, 12—13) to avoid intermarriage with heathens as a sure means of their ruin. The heathen nations were not rooted out; for God suffered them to exist in order to prove whether His people were steadfast in faith, and would resist the allurements of the heathen.

[2] *Delivered them.* God's will was that the idolaters should be exterminated, that they might be punished for the enormities (such as human sacrifices) of their idolatry. This judgment ought to have been executed by the Israelites, but they proved slothful, and even formed friendships with the heathens, though Josue had expressly warned them not to do so. Then God was angry with His people, and allowed the heathen nations to have dominion over them. They fell in turn under the power of the Moabites who lived to the east of the Dead Sea; of the Madianites who lived in Arabia near the Moabites; and of the Philistines who lived on the coast of the Mediterranean (Fig. 38).

[3] *Pious men.* Full of the Spirit of God and strong in faith.

[4] *Judges.* They were so called, firstly, because they executed God's judgments on the heathens, and secondly, because they governed and judged the Israelites according to the law of God. Fifteen Judges, in all, were raised up during the space of three hundred years.

delivered the children of Israel into the hands of the Madianites [1] on account of their sins [2].

The Lord sent an angel to Gedeon, as he was threshing and winnowing wheat at his father's house [3]. The angel said to him: "The Lord is with thee, O most valiant of men. Go in this thy strength, and thou shalt deliver Israel out of the hands of the Madianites." Gedeon asked how he could deliver Israel, seeing that his family was the lowest in the tribe of Manasses, and that he himself was the least in his father's house. The angel assured him that God would be with him, and that the Madianites should be cut off to a man.

Soon after this the Madianites crossed the Jordan with a large army, and encamped in the valley of Jezrael. But the Spirit of the Lord [4] came upon Gedeon, and he sounded the trumpet, and calling together the Israelites, formed an army of thirty-two thousand men and drew them up in battle array. Before commencing the attack Gedeon said to God: "If Thou wilt save Israel by my hand, I will put this fleece [5] of wool on the floor [6]; if there be dew on the fleece only, and it be dry on all the ground beside, I shall know [7] that by my hand, as Thou hast said, Thou wilt deliver Israel." And it was so.

Fig. 38. Type of Philistine (ulasati). Egyptian Sculpture. (After Maspero.)

The next day he asked God that the fleece might be dry and the ground wet with dew. And God did as Gedeon requested.

---

[1] *Madianites.* Who, with Amalekites, and other people, lived south-east of the Jordan, and "like locusts filled all places" (Judg. 6, 5).

[2] *Their sins.* Especially for having adopted the worship of the false god, Baal, and built altars to him, though they worshipped the true God as well.

[3] *His father's house.* In order to conceal it from the enemy. He did not dare do it on a threshing-floor in the open field, for fear of being seen.

[4] *The Spirit of the Lord.* Filling him with a great courage and confidence, and a burning zeal for God's honour.

[5] *This fleece.* The skin of a lamb.

[6] *The floor.* The Israelites, like all Eastern nations, had their threshing-floors in the open field, and without a roof.

[7] *I shall know.* Gedeon asked for a sign from God not only for his own sake, but in order to give courage to the thirty-two thousand Israelites with him.

But the Lord spoke to Gedeon and told him that his army was too great, and that the Madianites should not thus be delivered into his hands, lest the children of Israel should glory, and say that they conquered by their own strength.

And the Lord commanded Gedeon to speak to the people and proclaim in the hearing of all that whosoever was fearsome or timorous should return home. And the army hearing this, twenty-two thousand men retired from the field, leaving only ten thousand to meet the enemy. The Lord spoke again to Gedeon, telling him that there were still too many soldiers. "Bring them to the waters", He said, "and there I will try them."

He then told Gedeon to observe how the men would drink when they came to the water. "They that shall lap the water with their tongues, as dogs are wont to lap, thou shalt set apart by themselves; but they that shall drink, bowing down their knees, shall be on the other side." The number of those who had lapped the water from the hollow of their hand, in order to save time, was three hundred men[1]; all the rest of the multitude had knelt down to drink at their ease.

Gedeon kept with him only the three hundred who drank the water from the hollow of their hand: the rest he sent to their homes. He then divided the three hundred men into three companies, and gave them trumpets in their hands, and empty pitchers, and lamps within the pitchers. And he said to them: "What you shall see me do, do you the same; I will go into one part of the camp, and do you as I shall do."

Gedeon and the three hundred men who were with him approached the enemy's camp at the midnight-watch, and entering in, began to sound their trumpets and to strike the pitchers one against the other, dazzling the bewildered enemy with the sudden light of the concealed lamps. At the same time the Israelites cried out with a loud voice: "The sword of the Lord[2] and of Gedeon."

---

[1] *Three hundred men.* These three hundred were temperate men, who had their desire to quench their thirst under control, whereas the remainder threw themselves on the ground so as to drink as speedily and copiously as possible.

[2] *The sword of the Lord.* Has come upon you and will overcome you. The sword of Gedeon was at the same time the sword of the Lord, because God was with Gedeon and would through him overcome the enemy. The night-attack caused

The sudden alarm and the fierce attack of Gedeon's men threw the Madianites into such confusion that they turned their swords against each other and fled in all directions. Then all the tribes of Israel, seeing that victory was on their side, rose up and pursued the Madianites, cutting off their retreat on every side, so that of the whole army of one hundred and thirty-five thousand men, only fifteen thousand returned alive to their own country. Israel had peace for forty years.

The Israelites fell again into idolatry, and were persecuted by the Philistines[1]. But an angel appeared to the wife of Manue[2], of the tribe of Dan, and said: "Thou shalt bear a son; no razor shall touch his head, for he shall be a Nazarite of God from his infancy, and he shall begin to deliver Israel from the hands of the Philistines." When the child was born, he was called Samson[3].

Going to the city of the Philistines, he met a young lion; but the Spirit of the Lord[4] came upon Samson, and he tore the lion to pieces. Being delivered[5] into the hands of the Philistines, he tore the cords with which he was bound, and finding the jaw-bone of an ass, he slew with it a thousand men. Remaining over night in Gaza[6], the Philistines bolted the gates of the city to prevent his escape. But Samson arose at midnight, took the gates with their posts and bolts, and carried them to the top of a hill[7].

---

such confusion among the Madianites that in the dark they turned one against the other. In their flight they were cut down by the Israelites who, by Gedeon's orders, had taken possession of the banks of the river.

[1] *The Philistines.* The Israelites were oppressed by the Philistines for forty years on account of their idolatry.

[2] *Manue.* Manue and his wife, being well advanced in years, had given up all hope of having children.

[3] *Samson.* Samson was given miraculously to his parents, and was consecrated to God, first by their vow, and later by his own. God blessed him, because from his youth up he remained faithful to his vow, refraining from intoxicating drinks, and never cutting his hair.

[4] *The Spirit of the Lord.* Giving him a superhuman strength.

[5] *Delivered.* So low had the Israelites sunk that they delivered over to the enemy him whom God favoured, instead of joining him, and, under his leadership, casting off the yoke of the Philistines.

[6] *In Gaza.* One of the chief towns of the Philistines (see Map).

[7] *The top of a hill.* So that in the morning the Philistines, to their humiliation and warning, could see the city gates set up on the top of the hill.

Dalila, a Philistine woman, after many pleadings[1], extracted from him the secret of his strength. "The razor hath never come upon my head, for I am a Nazarite: that is to say, consecrated to God. If my head be shaven[2] my strength will depart, and I shall be like other men." During his sleep Dalila cut off his hair,

Fig. 39. Dagon. Relief.
Paris, Louvre.

called the Philistines, who captured him, put out his eyes, and cast him into prison[3]. Some time after, a great feast was celebrated in honour of the idol Dagon (Fig. 39)[4], when more than three thousand Philistines were assembled in the house. Blind Samson, whose hair had grown again, was brought out that he might amuse them by feats[5] of his strength. He told the boy who led him to bring him to the pillars upon which the whole house rested. Then he prayed: "O Lord God, remember me and restore to me my former strength." Then grasping the pillars, he shook them so strongly that the whole house rocked and fell upon himself and all the people. In this manner he killed many more enemies of God at his death[6] than he had killed during life.

COMMENTARY.

Justice, Patience, and Mercy of God. The Chanaanites, if they had had a right will, could have learnt to know the true God by means of the wonders which He wrought before their very eyes. As, however, in spite of this, they persevered in impiety and immorality, the judgments of God overtook them, and they were rooted out by the Israelites.

---

[1] *Many pleadings.* Because the princes of the Philistines had promised her much money if she would extract Samson's secret from him.

[2] *Shaven.* By shaving his head Samson would break his vow and would no longer be consecrated to God.

[3] *Into prison.* They treated him as a slave and set him to the most servile works. How, in his misery, Samson must have repented of his folly, and prayed to God for pardon!

[4] *Dagon.* A fish-god. They said: "Our god (Dagon) hath delivered our enemy Samson into our hands" (Judg. 16, 23). The feast was, therefore, held to celebrate the triumph of the idol Dagon over the God of Samson.

[5] *By feats.* And by singing and dancing. They wished to make sport of him whom God had chosen to be judge over His people! What a humiliation for Samson!

[6] *At his death.* He sacrificed his own life, so as to destroy the despisers of God and the oppressors of his people.

God's justice was also manifested to the Israelites on account of their faithlessness, when He allowed them to be overcome and oppressed by the pagans. But He also showed mercy to them, for as often as they acknowledged their sin and turned to Him, He forgave them and delivered them from their oppressors. Even when they again forsook Him, He did not give them up, but bore patiently with them, and visited them with tribulations, whereby they might be once more converted to Him. Indeed, "O Lord, Thou art a God of compassion and merciful, patient and of much mercy" (Ps. 85, 15).

Why God permits evil. God permitted some of the heathen nations to remain in Chanaan, so that His chosen people might be proved. Thus it is that God still suffers faithless and bad people to exist, both in order to give them time for repentance, and to prove the virtuous and faithful, so that their virtue and fidelity may be more meritorious.

Bad company. Man, being inclined to evil, ought, as far as is possible, to avoid associating with bad people. Evil communications corrupt good manners.

The misery of sin. He who forsakes God will be forsaken by God. "Sin maketh nations miserable" (Prov. 14, 34), and not only nations, but individuals also, "Many are the scourges of the sinner" (Ps. 31, 10). Just think what a scourge a bad conscience is! "There is no peace to the wicked" (Is. 48, 32).

The use of trials. In their misery the Israelites turned to God. God sends trials to sinners in order to convert them.

Original sin. By these repeated falls of the Israelites we can see how corrupt and prone to evil the human heart is. This natural inclination to evil is an effect of original sin, and can only be overcome by the grace which Jesus Christ has obtained for us.

The necessity of self-denial. Even after we have been cleansed from original sin and made children of God by holy Baptism, there still remain the sinful inclinations and passions. We must unceasingly fight against these by steadily denying ourselves, or else we shall be overcome by them and be made the slaves of sin. The grace necessary for this holy warfare is given to us in the Sacrament of Confirmation.

Mixed marriages. Holy Scripture especially reproaches the Israelites for contracting marriages with unbelievers, and for becoming thereby indifferent about their faith, and even being led into apostasy. Mixed marriages are always dangerous to faith, and they easily lead to spiritual indifference and even to apostasy. For this reason marriages between Catholics and those who are not Christians are absolutely forbidden, and are null. Even marriages between Catholics and non-Catholic Christians are dangerous, and are therefore forbidden, being only allowed by dispensation when security is given against the danger of apostasy, and for the Catholic education of the children of the marriage.

A mixed marriage, it has been most truly said, begins by a spiritual divorce; for, from the beginning, those who are married are separated on the most important point, namely religion.

God governs the world. God gave the Israelites into the hands of the Madianites, for these could never have overcome them except by His permission; and when in their misery they turned to Him, He delivered them through Gedeon and gave them peace for many years. But that Israel might know that it was to God it owed the victory, He told them that if 32,000 men went out to fight, they would not conquer the enemy, but that if only three hundred fought, then the victory would be theirs. God directs the lives of nations, as of individuals, with power, wisdom, and mercy. He is Lord also over nature, and turns its powers which way soever He will, as He showed by the twofold miracle of the fleece.

Prayer obtains help in time of need. When neither life nor property was safe, and the Israelites were hunted from their homes, they turned to God and cried for help. And God heard their prayer and raised up Gedeon to be the saviour of his people.

Humility. Gedeon was humble of heart. He considered himself to be the lowest of the low, and did not trust to his own skill or strength, but only in God's help. As soon as the twofold miracle of the fleece had convinced him that God was favourable to the Israelites, and had chosen him to save them, he confidently attacked the overwhelming host of the enemy with a mere handful of fighting men, and put it to flight. God exalteth the humble. "He that exalteth himself shall be humbled, and he that humbleth himself shall be exalted", says our Lord. Gedeon considered himself to be small and weak, but he did great things by the help of God. "The weak things of the world hath God chosen that He may confound the strong, that no flesh should glory in His sight" (1 Cor. 1, 27).

The confidence in God shown by the three hundred. They might easily have felt disheartened, and might have said: "How can we conquer an enemy who outnumbers us by four hundred and fifty to one!" But they trusted in God's help, followed the example of their valiant leader, and thus gained a glorious victory, in spite of overwhelming odds against them. We too, in our fight against the enemies of our salvation, ought not to lose courage, but should trust in God and say with the holy apostle: "I can do all things in Him, who strengtheneth me" (Phil. 4, 13).

Temperance. Gedeon was to know those whom God had chosen for the battle by their self-control and temperance. For the service of God temperance and self-denial are absolutely necessary, · since without these there can be no true virtue. He who does not govern himself is a slave to his evil inclinations and passions: "Better is he that ruleth his spirit than he that taketh cities."

Gedeon, the tenth type of Jesus Christ. Gedeon, as saviour of his people, is a type of Jesus Christ, the Saviour of the whole world. Like Gedeon, our Lord during His early years led a humble, hidden life. As Gedeon overcame his numerous enemies with a few soldiers, so did our Lord overcome the pagan world by His few apostles and disciples, whose only weapons were the trumpet (preaching) of the Gospel, and the torches (the light) of good works.

The fleece wet with dew is, according to the holy fathers of the Church, a type of the Incarnation of the Son of God. His human nature taken from the purest of creatures is the white fleece; the Divine Person of the Son of God descending and uniting himself to it, is the dew. Thus it is said (Ps. 71, 6): "He (God) shall come down like rain upon the fleece."

The fleece left dry is a type of the Immaculate Conception of our Lady. Even as this fleece remained dry when all the ground around was wet, so was Mary alone preserved from the stain of original sin, which adheres to everyone else.

The Goodness of God. God chose Samson before his birth, and therefore without any merit on his part, and gifted him with many graces, especially that of superhuman strength, in order that by him the enemies of Israel might be punished and humbled. This God did when Israel had not repented and was still persisting in idolatry. With preventing care He showed the Israelites by the call of Samson, that though they were unfaithful to Him, He had not forsaken them, but could and would free them from their degradation if only they would turn to Him.

The Mercy of God is shown by this, that God forgave Samson his sin when he repented of it in captivity and misery, and restored to him the gift of supernatural strength, which he had lost by his own fault. God not only forgives the repentant sinner his sin, but restores to him the lost grace of justification, and revives all his merits.

Self-denial. During all his life Samson practised self-denial, for he abstained from wine and all intoxicating drinks. But one irregular desire brought the hero Samson to his fall. This should warn us to suppress promptly every sinful movement. St. Ambrose says: "The strong and powerful Samson strangled a lion, but he could not strangle his own passions. He broke the bonds of his captors, but he could not break the bonds of his own lusts." If such a strong hero could be so weak, how great care ought we to take not to allow our passions to obtain a mastery over us. Our Lord Himself warns us: "Watch ye and pray, that ye enter not into temptation. The spirit indeed is willing, but the flesh is weak" (New Test. LXIX).

Samson, the eleventh type of Jesus Christ. The rough, warlike period of the Judges possessed its types by which the future Saviour of Israel and the whole world was foreshadowed. Samson and Gedeon were both types of our Lord. St. Augustine says of Samson: "He acted like a strong man, and suffered like a weak man. I see in him both the strength of the Son of God and the weakness of man. In those great and wonderful things which he did he was a type of Christ." His birth was announced by an angel: so also was the Birth of Jesus Christ. He overcame a lion: Jesus Christ has overcome the infernal lion. He fought and conquered, all alone, and with an ignoble weapon: Jesus Christ fought and conquered, all alone, by the despised Cross. He was betrayed for money, was given up to the enemy by the men of his own tribe, and was bound and mocked: thus was it with Jesus. Samson gave his life for his people, doing his enemy much injury by his death: Jesus offered Himself up of His own will, and by His death overcame sin and Satan. Samson lifted up and carried away the gates and bolts of Gaza: Jesus Christ, by His resurrection, threw open the gates and burst asunder the bolts of the grave.

Consequences of mortal sin. Samson, from his youth up, led an austere life, consecrated to God. He was a soldier of God, a hero of the faith, and a saviour of his people, as long as he remained true to his holy state and corresponded with grace; but when he formed a friendship with a heathen woman, and by so doing forsook God, he in his turn was forsaken by God, and fell into the hands of his enemies, who oppressed and degraded him, and made him a slave. Thus it is with those Christians, consecrated to God by Baptism, who yet obey their sinful passions and separate themselves from God by mortal sin. There falls on them the sleep of spiritual sloth, they are bound with the bonds of sin, they lose all their strength, i. e. the grace of God, they become spiritually blind, and fall into the slavery of sin and bad habits.

APPLICATION. I dare say you think it horrible and inconceivable that the Israelites, in spite of all God's benefits, visitations and warnings, should have proved faithless to Him and have broken the covenant sealed with Him! But give a glance at your own life. Have you never been faithless to God? Have you never fallen back into your former sins? Have you always kept the promises you made to God, and acted up to your resolutions? You will often fall from weakness, but try not to offend wilfully and intentionally.

In your Confirmation you were consecrated and fortified to be a soldier of Christ. You must therefore fight courageously against the enemies of your salvation. Practise self-control, and pray humbly for God's help, and you will conquer them.

Let Samson's story teach you this: "He that thinketh himself to stand, let him take heed lest he fall" (1 Cor. 10, 12).

CHAPTER XLVII.

RUTH'S AFFECTION FOR HER MOTHER-IN-LAW.

[Ruth 1—4.]

IN the days when the Judges ruled in Israel there was a famine in the land. And a certain man of Bethlehem [1], with his wife and two sons, went to sojourn in the land of Moab [2]. His name was Elimelech and his wife's Noemi. After having lived many years in Moab Elimelech died, and his two sons, who had taken wives from amongst the daughters of Moab, also died ten years after their father's death.

Noemi being now left alone, and full of sorrow for the loss of her husband and two sons, arose to return to her own country [3]. Her two daughters-in-law [4], Orpha and Ruth, went forth with her. As they journeyed on towards the land of Juda, Noemi spoke to Orpha and Ruth: "Go ye home to your mothers. The Lord deal mercifully [5] with you as you have dealt with the dead and me." And she kissed them. But they lifted up their voice and wept, and said: "We will go on with thee to thy people."

Noemi answered: "Do not so, my daughters; for I am grieved the more for your distress; and the hand of the Lord is gone out against me." Then Orpha kissed her mother-in-law and returned. Ruth, however, would not depart. Noemi spoke again: "Behold, thy kinswoman is returned to her people; go thou with her."

Thereupon Ruth replied: "Be not against me, for whithersoever thou shalt go, I will go, and where thou shalt dwell, I also will dwell. Thy people shall be my people and thy God my God [6]. The land that shall receive thee dying, in the same will

---

[1] *Man of Bethlehem.* Of the tribe of Juda.

[2] *The land of Moab.* East of the Dead Sea. There was no famine in that country.

[3] *Her own country.* She had learnt that the famine had ceased in Chanaan, and she longed to be back in her own country.

[4] *Daughters-in-law.* The two Moabite women, widows of her dead sons.

[5] *Deal mercifully.* May God be merciful to you and prosper you, because you were merciful to my sons, nursing them in their sickness &c., and have been full of love for me, a poor forsaken widow.

[6] *Thy God my God.* We can see by this that Ruth had renounced idolatry, and had received the true faith.

I die, and there will I be buried." Then Noemi, seeing that Ruth was steadfast, would not urge her any more to return to her friends.

So they journeyed on together, and came to Bethlehem, where the report was quickly spread, and the women said: "This is that Noemi."

It was the beginning of the barley-harvest, and Ruth asked Noemi: "If thou wilt, I will go into the fields and glean the ears[1] of corn that escape the hands of the reapers." And Noemi said: "Go, my daughter." Now it so happened that the field in which

Fig. 40. So-called field of Booz near Bethlehem.

Ruth went to glean belonged to a kinsman of Elimelech, named Booz, who was very rich. And behold, Booz came out to see the reapers, and said: "The Lord be with you." They answered: "The Lord bless thee."

And having observed Ruth gleaning in the barley-field (Fig. 40), he asked the overseer: "Whose maid is this?" The

---

[1] *Glean the ears.* It was her own impulse to go and glean ears of corn for her mother-in-law, as was the custom among the poor; but she first modestly asked Noemi's consent.

overseer replied: "This is Ruth who came with Noemi from the land of Moab; and she desires leave to glean the ears of corn that remain, following the steps of the reapers. She hath been in the field from morning till now[1], and hath not gone home for a moment."

Then Booz addressed Ruth very kindly, and said: "Hear me, daughter: Keep with my maids and follow where they reap. I have charged my young men not to molest thee, and if thou art thirsty, go to the vessels and drink of the waters whereof the servants drink, and dip thy morsel in the vinegar." Full of gratitude for these kind words, Ruth bent down before Booz, and asked how it came that she, a woman of another country, should find favour in his sight.

Booz told her that all she had done for her mother-in-law since the death of her husband had been related to him. He prayed: "Mayest thou receive a full reward of the Lord, under whose wings thou art fled." He then privately told the reapers: "Let fall some of your handfuls of purpose, that she may gather them without shame." She gleaned therefore in the field till evening, and then beat out with a rod what she had gleaned, which was an ephi: that is three bushels. Grateful for the kindness shown her, she returned to her mother-in-law, carrying with her the barley she had threshed, and the leavings of the meal that had been given her. Noemi was astonished and asked: "Where hast thou gleaned to-day, and what hast thou wrought? Blessed be he that hath had pity on thee." Ruth told the man's name, that he was called Booz.

Next day she returned to the field of Booz and continued to glean after the reapers, till all the barley was laid up in the barns. Some time after Booz said to Ruth: "My daughter, all the people that dwell within the gates of my city know that thou art a virtuous woman." So he married her. Then the ancients came and said to Booz: "May this woman be an example of virtue in Ephrata, and may she have a famous name in Bethlehem." The Lord blessed their union and gave them a son whom they called Obed. Then Noemi, full of joy, taking the child, laid it

---

[1] *From morning till now.* She was, therefore, very industrious. This pleased Booz, and made him speak to her as he did.

in her bosom; and she carried it and was a nurse to it. Now
Obed was the father of Isai, whose son was David, of whose race
Christ was born[1].

COMMENTARY.

Divine Providence. Was it by chance that Ruth went to the field
of Booz? No, she went there by the guidance of a good and wise
Providence. God ordained that Booz should get to know the virtuous
Ruth, and should, though she was poor, take her as his wife. This
was so ordained in order that Ruth and Noemi should be rewarded
for their virtues. Noemi was now above want, and could serve God
without anxiety about her maintenance. Nothing happens by chance.

Several beautiful examples of virtue are put before us in this story.

Noemi left her home only from necessity, and kept her faith
untarnished in the midst of a heathen society; and as soon as the
famine was over, she returned to her own country and fellow-believers.
She unselfishly allowed her daughters-in-law to remain in Moab, and
asked God to bless them: she did not wish them to share her poverty
or help to support her. There is one point to which I wish to draw
your attention, as it might not strike you of yourselves. By her living
faith, her real piety and sincere love, in a word, by her good example,
Noemi converted her daughter-in-law Ruth to the true faith, so that the
latter was able to say: "Thy God is my God." Oh, if only all Catholics
would act as she did; if they would only act up to their holy faith and
practise the virtues which it teaches, then the whole world would be
convinced of the truth and excellence of the Catholic faith! Our Divine
Lord said: "Let your light shine before men that they may see your
good works, and glorify your Father who is in heaven."

Ruth left her home and friends both out of attachment to her
mother-in-law and fidelity to her faith. Once she had got to know the
true God, she wished to dwell with the people of God; and so firm
was she in her resolution that neither the persuasions of Noemi nor the
example of Orpha could move her from it. She was, therefore, steadfast
in faith, and gave up everything rather than live with unbelievers, and
place her soul in danger. She was, furthermore, distinguished for her
humility, obedience, and diligence. She asked Noemi's permission to
glean; she was not ashamed of her poverty; she was indefatigable in
her labour of gleaning, and saved some of her dinner for Noemi: thus
she perfectly fulfilled the Fourth Commandment. Would that all children
had as great a love for their own parents as Ruth had for her mother-
in-law! You see how Holy Scripture praises Ruth's diligence. Diligence
is a virtue and does honour to those who practise it. Sloth is a vice

---

[1] *Christ was born.* David, therefore, was grandson to Obed, and great-grandson
to Booz and Ruth.

and a capital sin, and brings shame and disgrace in its train. Ruth was also retiring, modest and pure; the whole town testified to her being a virtuous woman. God rewarded her virtue by giving her a good and wealthy husband, and by making her the great-grandmother of king David and (because Christ was of the family of David) one of the ancestors of the Divine Redeemer.

Booz loved his neighbour, and had compassion on the poor. He behaved very nobly in taking Ruth as his wife in spite of her poverty: he very rightly valued Ruth's virtues more highly than gold and riches. God rewarded him, for He gave him a most virtuous wife, and blessed his marriage, so that he became one of the forefathers of the Messias.

Ruth is a type of the Church of the Gentiles. Though born a heathen she obtained by her conversion a share in the blessings of Israel, and was even chosen to be an ancestress of the Redeemer. By this God signified that the heathen, if they would believe and be converted, should have a share in the salvation which was to spring from Israel.

APPLICATION. Ruth brought joy and honour to her mother-in-law. Do you cause joy to your parents? Have you never brought shame on them or caused them grief?

Be kind and generous to the poor. Do not look down on poor children. Do you not give preference among your friends to the children of rich parents? A man's worth does not consist in what he has, but in what he is. Virtues such as faith, charity, diligence, modesty, truth and humility are the greatest of riches: everything perishes except virtue. God looks to the heart, not to the outward appearance or wealth. He who is without faith is the poorest of men, never mind how much money he may possess. Are these your sentiments? Do you like associating with good children?

Are you diligent from morning till night, as Ruth was?

CHAPTER XLVIII.

SAMUEL.—IMPIETY OF THE SONS OF HELI.

[1 Kings 1—7.]

IN the days when Heli[1], the High Priest, was Judge in Israel, there lived at Mount Ephraim a virtuous man, called Elcana, and the name of his wife was Anna. Now Anna had no children. She therefore multiplied her prayers before the Lord that He

---

[1] *Heli.* Heli, of the family of Aaron, was High Priest, and was also at this time Judge. He, therefore, combined in his person the highest spiritual and the highest temporal authority.

would deign to give her children. So one day she went to Silo to pray in the Tabernacle of the Lord. There, before the door of the Tabernacle, she shed many tears and prayed, and made a vow saying: "O Lord of Hosts [1], if Thou wilt be mindful of me and give me a man-child, I will give him to the Lord all the days of his life."

The Lord heard her prayer, and gave her a son, whom she called Samuel, which means "heard of God", or also "asked of God". Now when three years were passed, and the child was yet very young, Anna took three calves, three bushels of flour, and a bottle of wine, and carrying the boy with her she went to the House of the Lord. There she offered her son to Heli the High Priest, saying: "The Lord has granted my petition, therefore I also have lent my child to the Lord all the days of his life." And the child ministered in the sight of the Lord before the face of Heli. Now the two sons of Heli, Ophni and Phinees, were wicked [2] and had no fear of God, for when the people came to offer sacrifices, Ophni and Phinees carried the flesh of the victims away by force. So their sin was very great, because they withdrew men from the sacrifice of the Lord.

Heli knew all this; he knew what wicked things his sons did in the Sanctuary, and he mildly rebuked them, saying: "It is no good report that I hear, that you make the people of the Lord to transgress." But, being very old, he took no severe measures to punish them, or prevent their evil deeds.

It came to pass that one night, before the lamp of the Lord had gone out, Heli slept on a couch near the Tabernacle, and Samuel hard by [3]. The Lord called Samuel. He answered: "Here am I", and went to Heli and asked: "Why hast thou

---

[1] *Of Hosts.* i. e. of angels in heaven.

[2] *Wicked.* Holy Scripture calls them children of Belial, or of the devil, because of their wickedness. Whilst the sacrifice (sin- or peace offering) was seething in the caldron, they used to thrust in a flesh-hook and take the best of the flesh for themselves. They also took for themselves of the flesh of the whole-burnt offerings, in which the victims ought to have been entirely consumed by fire. This made the people very angry, and they were unwilling to offer sacrifices. If the sons of the High Priest violated the sacrificial laws so grossly, it was only natural that the people should lose their respect for the sacrifices.

[3] *Hard by.* Where cells, or little rooms, were built for those priests who had to attend to the service of the Tabernacle.

called me?" But Heli replied: "I did not call thee, my son: return and sleep."

So he returned and slept again. But the Lord called him a second time, and Samuel acted as before. Heli said: "I did not call thee, my son: return and sleep." Then the Lord called Samuel a third time. And Samuel, rising up, went again to Heli, saying: "Here am I, for thou didst call me." Heli now understood that the Lord had called the boy.

And he said to Samuel: "Go and sleep, and if He shall call thee any more, thou shalt say: 'Speak, Lord, for Thy servant heareth!'" So Samuel went and slept in his place. Then the Lord came and stood, and called: "Samuel, Samuel." He answered: "Speak, Lord, for Thy servant heareth." The Lord spoke: "Behold, I will do a thing in Israel, and whosoever shall hear it, both his ears shall tingle. In that day I will raise up against Heli all the things that I have spoken. I will begin and I will make an end, because he knew that his sons did wickedly, and he would not chastise them."

Next morning, Heli asked the boy to tell him [1] what the Lord had said. But Samuel was afraid. Heli, however, insisted, and Samuel at length told the vision. Thereupon Heli humbly replied: "It is the Lord: let Him do what is good in His sight."

And swiftly the judgment of God overtook the house of Heli. For it soon came to pass that the Philistines waged war against Israel, and when they joined battle the Israelites were defeated, and lost about four thousand men. After the people had returned to the camp, the ancients of Israel said: "Let us fetch the Ark [2] of the Covenant from Silo, that it may save us from the hands of our enemies." They sent therefore to Silo, and the two sons of Heli, Ophni and Phinees, accompanied the Ark to the camp. The people, on beholding the Ark in their midst, set up a great shout, and the earth rang with their shouting.

---

[1] *Tell him.* He suspected that the revelation contained nothing that portended good to himself.

[2] *Fetch the Ark.* They wished to have the Ark of the Covenant with them, because they remembered the miracles which God had worked by means of it, both at the passage of the Jordan, and at the siege of Jericho, and they hoped that its sacred presence would now procure a victory for them.

The Philistines, however, made a new attack, and the Israelites were again defeated, with great slaughter; thirty thousand were slain, and the rest put to flight. And a messenger came to Heli, saying: "Thy two sons, Ophni and Phinees, are dead, and the Ark of the Lord is taken." Now Heli, who was far advanced in years, on hearing that the Ark was taken, fell from his chair[1] backwards by the door, and broke his neck and died. The Philistines took the Ark of the Lord, and placed it in the temple of Dagon[2], their false god.

Next morning, when they went into the temple, they found the idol lying prostrate on the ground before the Ark. Besides, the Lord afflicted them with many evils on account of the Ark. Many persons died, and from the fields there came forth a multitude of mice, and there was great confusion in the country.

Perceiving this, the Philistines resolved that the Ark of God should no longer remain amongst them. Then they took the Ark and laid it upon a cart, and taking two kine, or young cows, they yoked them to the cart. The cows took the way that led to Bethsames, and thus the Ark was brought again into the country of the Israelites.

Meanwhile, after the death of Heli, Samuel had become Judge in Israel. He assembled the people, reproached them for their evil doings, and then said: "If you turn to the Lord with all your heart, and put away the strange gods from among you, and prepare your hearts unto the Lord, and serve Him only[3], He will deliver you out of the hands of the Philistines."

So they humbled themselves before God in prayer and fasting, Samuel interceding and offering sacrifice for them. And the Lord

---

[1] *Fell from his chair.* The good old High Priest did not fall backwards when he heard that his sons had perished, but only when the messenger told him that the Ark had been taken. This last news struck him with more horror than the first, for he believed that it meant that God's covenant with His people was now broken, and that Israel would be destroyed.

[2] *In the temple of Dagon.* This was not in order to pay honour to the Ark, but so as to make an offering of it to their god Dagon, to whom they believed they owed their victory. God, however, proved to them that their idol was worth nothing, and could do nothing.

[3] *Him only.* For they worshipped idols at the same time that they were worshipping the Lord God.

took pity upon them, and gave them such a victory[1] over the Philistines, that for many years after the latter did not dare to approach the frontiers of Israel.

COMMENTARY.

The Justice of God. This story teaches us above all things to know, fear, and love God. He rewarded the virtuous Samuel by revealing Himself to him, by calling him to be Judge, and by freeing and converting His people through him. On the other hand God punished Heli, his sons, and the impenitent Israelites by their defeat, and the loss of the Ark. He also punished the idolatrous Philistines by means of various plagues, and finally by their complete overthrow.

The Goodness and Mercy of God. He graciously heard Anna's prayer, and sent her a son. He called Samuel from his earliest infancy to serve Him in the Tabernacle, loaded him with favours, preserved him from being contaminated by Heli's sons, and made him judge and saviour of his people. God forgave the repentant people their faithlessness, and gave them a great victory over those who had oppressed them.

The Faithfulness of God. Samuel, in God's name, said to the Israelites: "If you turn to the Lord with all your heart, He will deliver you." God kept this promise, as He also fulfilled His threat against Heli and his sons.

God is Lord over nature. It was God who overthrew the image of Dagon; it was He who sent the mice to devastate the land of the Philistines, the pestilence which swept away the idolaters, and the storm which threw their army into confusion.

Prayer in time of trouble. Anna's example teaches us that we ought to have recourse to fervent prayer when we are suffering, or in any sort of trouble; for God is the great Consoler and Helper, being holy and all powerful. "Is any of you sad, let him pray" (James 5, 13).

The power of prayer. By prayer Anna obtained a son; and by prayer Samuel obtained help for his people. "Samuel cried to the Lord for Israel, and the Lord heard him" (1 Kings 7, 9). Why, therefore, should not God hearken to the intercession of the Saints in heaven?

Keeping vows (see Old Test. XVII). Anna kept her vow faithfully. She most certainly wished to keep her beloved child with her, but, all the same, she "lent him to the Lord".

Fasting and confession of sins are penances well-pleasing to God, and obtain pardon from Him. The Israelites bewailed and confessed their sins, formed good resolutions, and made satisfaction by fasting.

---

[1] *A victory.* God sent a terrible storm of thunder and lightning which threw the Philistine army into confusion, and made its defeat easy.

Piety, obedience, and truthfulness. Young Samuel did not let himself be led away by the bad example of Heli's sons, but rather imitated the piety of the aged High Priest, and was zealous in the performance of the work given him to do for God. He was obedient to Heli, whose own sons had renounced the obedience due to him. Each time during the night that he heard his name called he sprang from his bed, and ran to Heli, saying: "Here am I!" Thus promptly and cheerfully should all children obey their parents and those set over them. Samuel showed his truthfulness when Heli asked him what the Lord had revealed to him. It pained him to say anything disagreeable to the kind old High Priest, but, being asked, he told him everything. Thus you, too, should always speak the truth when questioned by those set over you.

Sacrilege. Reverence in the House of God. Heli's sons were impious and dissolute. They dishonoured the Sanctuary, and brought sacrifices into disrepute. If the desecration of the Tabernacle of the Old Covenant was such a great sin, how much more ought we to guard against any desecration of our churches! If any wrong conduct relating to the typical sacrifices of the Old Testament was so severely punished, how sinful and criminal must it be for Christians to behave irreverently during the Holy Sacrifice of the Mass, and even talk, laugh &c.!

Punishment of disobedient children. If the sons of Heli had hearkened to and obeyed the injunctions of their good father, they would not have been punished by God. But as they would not listen to his warnings, they died a violent death, and their names have ever since been associated with ignominy.

Sharing in the guilt of others. Heli was a virtuous, God-fearing man. He was so anxious about the Ark of the Covenant that the news of its capture affected him more than the news of the death of his sons. Moreover, he was entirely resigned to God's will, when Samuel announced to him his approaching punishment. "It is the Lord; let Him do what is good in His sight!" Why, then, was this virtuous servant of God punished by sudden death? God Himself said that it was because he did not correct his sons. He was too good-natured and weak towards them. He ought to have been strict with them when they were young, and to have punished them severely when they would not listen to his injunctions. "He who will not hear must feel." He was too indulgent; he said to himself that they would be more reasonable and would improve as they grew older. Instead of this they grew up quite beyond control, became accustomed to evil, and no more consulted their father about anything. Now I ask you: Was it for the good of these men that their father should be so indulgent towards them, and should never correct them? How much sorrow and suffering would Heli have spared himself, how much trouble would he have avoided, if he had corrected his sons betimes! As he did not do so, he shared in their guilt, and was punished by God. Children, if they take advantage of their parents' kindness, bring unhappiness and even eternal ruin both on themselves and on their parents. It is a strict duty of parents to punish the wrong-doings of their children. It is a false love, and a great misfortune for children when parents are weak and over indulgent. Holy Scripture says: "He that spareth the rod hateth his son: but he that loveth him correcteth him betimes" (Prov. 13, 24).

Grace cannot be obtained without repentance. The Israelites thought that if they had the Ark with them, God would be sure to protect them and give them the victory. But how could the tables of the law inside the Ark avail them, if they no longer carried the law of God in their hearts? They ought first to have sincerely repented, and then God would have been gracious to them. Nothing holy, not even the Sacraments, can help us, if we do not first turn to God and cast away strange gods, i. e. sinful habits and passions.

Resistance to God's grace. Samuel, the "asked or heard of God", was, as his very name signifies, a child of grace. He did, in fact, receive many graces from God; but then he faithfully co-operated with them, and thus became in time the reformer and saviour of his people when they were in adversity. Heli's sons were also highly favoured by God. They were called to the priesthood by right of their birth; they grew up in the Tabernacle, and had the good example of their father before their eyes from their youth up; but they resisted God's grace, lightly rejected their father's warnings, and drew on themselves the displeasure of the best among the people. By their misuse of grace their hearts grew harder and harder. Once more God tried to move them, by letting them know through Samuel that the day was not far off when He would punish them and their father, but they would not profit by this grace. Still hardened in sin, they went out to fight, and died an impenitent death at the hands of the enemy.

Hearkening to the word of God. Whenever we hear the word of God (whether in sermons, or instructions &c.), we should say with Samuel: "Speak, Lord, for Thy servant heareth." We should listen eagerly to the word of God which He speaks to us through the mouths of His priests. "He that heareth you, heareth Me", said our Lord (Luke 10, 16).

Worthy and unworthy Communion. The Ark brought blessing and divine protection to the Israelites as long as they feared God, but when they forgot Him and would not repent, it brought them misfortune and defeat, and even brought plagues and pestilence on the Philistine idolaters. Thus it is with the Most Holy of the New Covenant. Holy Communion brings priceless blessings to the penitent, but a curse and eternal damnation to the impenitent.

APPLICATION. Do you promptly obey the commands of your parents and those who are set over you? Do you go to them as soon as you are called? Do you rise in the morning as soon as you are called? Do you take to heart their injunctions and exhortations? Are you more like Samuel, or the sons of Heli?

How do you behave during the services of the Church? Do you like to hear the word of God, or do you feel an aversion to sermons and try to escape them by merely hearing a Mass? Do you assist at the afternoon or evening services?

IV. EPOCH:

THE KINGS.

(About 1095—588 B. C.)

CHAPTER XLIX.

SAUL ELECTED KING.

[1 Kings 8—15.]

SAMUEL having grown old appointed his two sons as Judges over Israel. They, however, were not just and God-fearing like their father, but took bribes and perverted judgment. So the ancients came to Samuel and said: "Thy sons walk not in thy ways; therefore give us a king[1] to judge us, as all nations have." This word was displeasing to Samuel, for he knew that the Lord was their king, and none other. Still the Lord told him to hearken to the voice of the people, and to give them a king for their punishment. Moreover, he added, the king would rule over them with a heavy hand[2], and they would cry out and lament, but the Lord would not hear them, because they had desired for themselves a king.

Now there was a man of the tribe of Benjamin who lost his asses, and he said to Saul, his son: "Take one of the servants with thee, and arise, go, and seek the asses." So they both started out, seeking the asses; and not being able to find them anywhere,

---

[1] *A king.* This desire to have an earthly king seemed to him to be, on the people's part, a renunciation of the divine government of God.

[2] *A heavy hand.* Imposing burdens and taxes on them. He foretold them this so that later, when they felt the hand of the king to press heavily on them, they might not complain.

they resolved to go to the city of Suph in order to consult Samuel, the seer, about them. Now the day before Saul's arrival, the Lord had spoken to Samuel: "To-morrow, about this same hour, I will send to thee a man, whom thou shalt anoint king over my people Israel." It so happened that Samuel met Saul in the midst of the city. And Samuel said: "Go up before me, that you may eat with me to-day, and that I may let you go in the morning; and as for the asses, be not solicitous, for they are found."[1] Next morning, when the day began to dawn, Samuel took a little vial of oil[2], and poured it on the head of Saul, and kissed[3] him, and said: "Behold, the Lord has anointed thee to be prince over His inheritance."

Thereupon Samuel assembled the people, and Saul stood in their midst; and he was a choice man, being taller than any one else from his shoulders and upwards. Then Samuel said: "Behold him whom the Lord has chosen." And the people cried out: "God save the king!"[4]

Now the people of Amalec were very bad, and the measure of their iniquity was full. God, in His wrath, sent Samuel to Saul, saying: "Go and smite Amalec and all that he hath. Spare him not, nor covet anything that is his, but slay both man and woman and child, ox and sheep and camel."

Saul, therefore, waged war against Amalec, and defeated them along the line from Hevila till Sur. The common people he slew with the edge of the sword; but, contrary to the command of God, he spared Agag the king. The flocks and herds of little value he also destroyed, but spared the best flocks and the best herds. Moreover, filled with pride, and forgetting that success comes from God, he erected an arch of triumph[5] in memory of his victory.

---

[1] *They are found.* Samuel knew this, because God had revealed it to him.

[2] *Oil.* For the typical signification of oil see chapter XVI. The anointing of Saul was a sign that God had chosen him to be king; and at that moment the Lord gave to His anointed the gifts necessary for his high calling, i. e. wisdom, strength, justice.

[3] *Kissed him.* As a sign of homage.

[4] *God save the king!* By these words they acknowledged him as their king, and paid him homage.

[5] *An arch of triumph.* As if he owed the glory of his victory to himself and not to God.

When Samuel had come to the camp of Israel, Saul said to him: "I have fulfilled the word of the Lord." Samuel answered: "What meaneth, then, the bleating of the flocks, and the lowing of the herds which I hear?" Saul tried to excuse himself, saying that the people had spared the best flocks and herds, to sacrifice [1] them to the Lord. Samuel, being angry, spoke to him in the name of the Lord: "Doth the Lord desire holocausts and victims, and not rather that the voice of the Lord should be obeyed? For obedience is better than sacrifices; and to hearken better than to offer the fat of rams. For as much, therefore, as thou hast rejected the word of the Lord, the Lord hath also rejected thee [2] from being king over Israel. The Lord hath rent the kingdom from thee this day, and has given it to one who is better." Then Samuel departed, and beheld Saul no more till the day of his death.

COMMENTARY.

God's Providence directed that the asses should be lost and that Saul, while seeking them, should meet Samuel. By God's command Samuel anointed Saul king, and presented him as such to the people. God commands and directs everything as He wills.

God's Goodness to the Israelites is shown by His granting their request to have a king. It was Saul, however, whom he especially loaded with proofs of His love. Saul acknowledged his unworthiness in the words which he used to Samuel: "I am of the least tribe of Israel, and my kindred the least among all the families of the tribe of Benjamin!" And yet God chose him to be king over His people, turned the hearts of the Israelites towards him, and gave him the victory over all his enemies. — What more could God have done to ensure Saul's unbounded gratitude and willing obedience?

The Justice of God. Saul was ungrateful and disobedient to God, and therefore the punishment of divine justice fell on him. He was rejected by God; God's blessing left him; and his throne passed, not to his son, but to David.

Pride. Saul's misfortunes sprang from pride. He became proud on account of his high dignity, and on account of the victories which

---

[1] *To sacrifice.* He thus told an untruth and aggravated it by feigning a pious motive.

[2] *Rejected thee.* God's rejection of Saul consisted in this: firstly, that the kingdom would not remain in Saul's family; and, secondly, that the crown was snatched from Saul himself by a premature death, and given to David, who, even in Saul's lifetime, was anointed to be his successor.

God gave him, so that he began to trust in himself and did not give glory to God. Being proud and arrogant, he no longer obeyed God's commands, but kept back the best of the flocks of the Amalekites. Pride leads to disobedience. When Saul, by his grievous sin, had forsaken God, then God forsook him. "God resisteth the proud, and giveth grace to the humble" (James 4, 6).

Obedience to God. To Saul's excuse that the flocks and herds had been kept to offer as sacrifices, Samuel, filled with the Holy Ghost, replied: "Obedience is better than sacrifice", i. e. sacrifices of beasts are good and pleasing to God if they are offered with a right intention; but still better and more pleasing to God is obedience, whereby a man offers to God the spiritual sacrifice of his own will, on the altar of his heart. By sacrifices man gives to God something which he possesses; by obedience he offers himself, and his free will, the noblest of all his possessions. He who loves God will love and do His holy will.

Jesus Christ or the Anointed. In the Old Testament kings, as well as High Priests, were the anointed of the Lord. In the New Testament Jesus, being both High Priest and King, is indeed the Christ, i. e. the Anointed.

The kingdom of Israel belonged to God. It was a theocracy which means that hitherto the Lord God had been the immediate King, Lawgiver and Leader of His people. Now it was His will to give them an earthly king to be His representative, and to govern them in His name, and according to His laws. He did not let them choose their own king, but set over them one whom He chose, in order to show the Israelites that He Himself still remained their supreme King and Lord. He established the kingdom of Israel in order, firstly, to bind the twelve tribes into a closer unity than had existed under the Judges; secondly, to show the people that even under kings they could prosper only if they observed the laws of God; and thirdly, to foreshadow the kingdom of the Messias. Kings, princes, and all heads of States reign "by the grace of God": because they receive the power from Him and govern in His name; therefore their subjects ought to honour, love and obey them, as the representatives of God. "Fear God; honour the king" (1 Petr. 2, 17).

APPLICATION. Ask yourself whether you are proud or self-willed? Do you give glory to God when you succeed in anything? Do you boast? Are you fond of talking about yourself? Do you take pleasure in praising others, or is it more pleasing to you to find fault with them? No other virtue is of any value in God's sight, without humility. You owe to God everything that you are, or have, or can do; therefore, thank God and do not offend Him by pride. Be very careful to-day to utter no word in self-praise. Do not tell an untruth nor feign piety as Saul did.

CHAPTER L.

DAVID, THE YOUNG SHEPHERD.

[1 Kings 16.]

SAMUEL loved Saul, and mourned for him because the Lord had rejected him. One day the Lord said to Samuel: "How long wilt thou mourn for Saul whom I have rejected? Fill thy horn with oil, and come that I may send thee to Isai, the Bethlehemite; for I have provided me a king among his sons."

So Samuel went to Bethlehem[1], and took with him a victim, and called Isai and his sons to partake[2] of the sacrifice. Now when Eliab, the eldest son, had come forward, who was of a high stature, the Lord said to Samuel: "Look not on his countenance; for man seeth those things that appear, but the Lord seeth the heart." [3]

Isai then called in his other sons, one by one, six in number. When Samuel had seen them all, he said: "The Lord has not chosen any of these. Are these all thy sons?" Isai replied: "There remaineth yet a young one who keepeth the sheep." Samuel hastened to answer: "Send and fetch him, for we will not sit down till he come hither."

Now when David came in, he was beautiful to behold, and of a comely face; and the Lord said: "Arise, and anoint him, for this is he." Then Samuel, taking the horn of oil, anointed him in the midst of his brethren. Immediately the Spirit of the Lord came upon David, and remained with him.

But the Spirit of the Lord departed from Saul, and an evil spirit[4] troubled him. Wherefore the servants of Saul said to him: "Let our lord give orders, and we will seek out a man skilful in playing on the harp, that when the evil spirit is upon thee he may play with his hand, and thou mayest bear it more easily."

---

[1] *Bethlehem.* This little town lay in the territory of the tribe of Juda.

[2] *To partake.* To assist at the offering of the sacrifice and also to partake of it.

[3] *The heart.* i. e. the qualities of the heart, whether a man be God-fearing, humble &c.

[4] *An evil spirit.* The consciousness that, through his own fault, he was forsaken by God, oppressed him. As he did not turn to God by prayer and penance, an infernal spirit gained influence over him, and kindled in him an unnatural melancholy so that his soul became a prey to the evil passions of envy, hatred and blood-thirstiness, till at last he was driven to despair and suicide.

When the servants saw that this counsel was pleasing in the eyes of Saul, one of them added: "Behold, I have seen the son of Isai, a skilful player, and a man fit for war, and prudent in his words, and a comely person." Thereupon David was sent for, and Saul made him his armour-bearer. And whenever the evil spirit was upon Saul, David took his harp and played with his hand, and Saul was refreshed and better, for the evil spirit departed [1] from him.

COMMENTARY.

The Omniscience of God. He knows the mind and feelings of man. He knew David better than his own father knew him.

The Wisdom of God. It was by the guidance of Divine Providence that, on account of his musical talents, David was summoned to the court of the king, who naturally had no suspicion that the young shepherd was destined to be his successor. The simple youth, who was then about twenty years old, learnt at court the art of government and the duties of a king, and was thus prepared for his future position.

The Faithfulness of God. Almighty God, by choosing David of the tribe of Juda to be king, fulfilled that which He promised by the mouth of the dying Jacob, i. e. that there should be a sceptre in Juda, which should not depart from him till the Messias Himself came.

Obedience. Samuel was obedient to God, for though he was very sorry that Saul was rejected, he obeyed when commanded to anoint another king. David was obedient to his father. He did not murmur at the humble task set him by his father of guarding and feeding the flocks in the fields of Bethlehem.

The value of virtue. God rejected the proud Saul and chose the young and humble David to be his successor. Even David's father, to whom Samuel had confided that one of his sons was chosen to be king, had not the remotest idea that David, the shepherd-boy, could be the chosen one. He had not even thought it worth while to mention his youngest son to the prophet, when he asked to see his sons. He said to himself: "God will be sure to have chosen one of my elder, fine, warlike sons." But the eyes of God were fixed on the young, modest David, for He does not look to the appearance, but to the heart. David was pious, humble, steadfast, and pure; therefore God loved him, and chose him to be the shepherd of His people. Beauty, fine clothes, riches are nothing in the eyes of God; the only thing that is of value

---

[1] *Departed.* David, to the accompaniment of his harp, sang holy Psalms composed by himself. As Saul had not as yet entirely given himself over to the influence of the evil spirit, his mind was calmed and cheered by David's sacred music and the consoling words of his songs and psalms.

in His sight is a virtuous heart. He who wishes to be well-pleasing to God must strive to be virtuous.

The pious shepherd-boy. David did not waste his time while he was watching his sheep. He prayed and meditated on the attributes of God, which were revealed to his holy mind in the works of creation; and in the joy of his heart he composed and sang holy psalms and canticles. The stars of heaven, the flowers of the field, the songs of the birds, all raised his heart to God, and so he lived constantly in God's presence, having God before his eyes and in his heart. By his holy and innocent youth this humble, though highly gifted boy was prepared to be God's chosen instrument.

The pain of a bad conscience. Woe to the man who forsakes God, and who is too proud to do penance for his sins, and return contritely to God! For such cannot be happy either now or hereafter. We see this in the case of the God-forsaken Saul. Neither his high position nor his riches could make him happy, because he had no peace in his heart. His bad conscience gave him no rest; it drove all cheerfulness from his mind, so that he grew discontented and melancholy. "There is no peace for the wicked" (Is. 48, 22). "Tribulation and anguish upon every soul of man that worketh evil" (Rom. 2, 9). Man can find true happiness in God alone, i. e. in the love of God and in doing His will.

APPLICATION. Do you like thinking about God? Do you pray and work as David did? Do you like to sing sacred canticles? The Psalms which we sing at Vespers were mostly written by David. Assist when you can at Vespers, and sing the Psalms devoutly, as David used to sing them, in honour of God. Never degrade the noble gift of music by singing bad, low songs.

CHAPTER LI.

DAVID SLAYS GOLIATH.

[1 Kings 17.]

THE Philistines again took the field against the Israelites and posted themselves on one mountain, while the Israelites occupied another. And behold, there was in the camp of the Philistines a giant named Goliath. He was not only taller[1] than any other man, but his strength was in proportion to his size. He had a brazen helmet on his head and was clothed in scaly armour of enormous weight.

---

[1] *Taller.* He was six cubits and a span, or, in other words, nearly ten feet high.

He had greaves[1] of brass on his legs, and a brazen shield on his shoulder, and the staff[2] of his spear was like a weaver's beam. This giant, clad in armour from head to foot, came daily out, morning and evening, from the Philistine camp, and challenged any one of the Israelites to meet him in single combat, saying: "Give me a man, and let him fight with me hand to hand. If he be able to kill me, we will be servants to you; but if I prevail and kill him, you shall serve us."

This went on for forty days, and there was no one found in all Israel to accept the challenge of Goliath. Hence Saul and the Israelites were in great terror and confusion, because of Goliath and of his proud boasting that they could find no man in Israel to fight him.

When David's three eldest brothers had gone out with Saul to battle, his father told him to take bread and go to the camp, and see how it fared with his brothers. Whilst David was conversing with the people, Goliath came out, as usual, from the Philistine camp and repeated his insulting and contemptuous challenge. Full of surprise David asked: "What shall be given to the man that slayeth the Philistine who defieth the army of the living God?"[3] Now when Eliab, his eldest brother, heard that David was asking such questions of the soldiers, he grew angry and said: "Why camest thou hither? Why didst thou leave those few sheep in the desert? I know thy pride and that thou camest down to see the battle."

However, these words were repeated to Saul, who sent for David and said to him: "Thou art not able to withstand this Philistine, for thou art but a boy, and he is a warrior." But David said: "Let no man be dismayed; I, thy servant, will go and fight against the Philistine. For thy servant kept his father's sheep, and there came a lion and a bear and took a ram out of the midst of the flock. And I pursued after them and struck them; and they rose up against me, and I caught them by the throat, and I

---

[1] *Greaves.* The giant was protected from head to foot. His armour was made of leather, covered with brazen scales, through which no spear or arrow-point could pierce.

[2] *The staff.* The wooden shaft of the spear, to which the point was fastened.

[3] *The living God.* He is called the living God in contradistinction to the gods of the heathen, which were nothing but dead idols made of wood, brass &c. He is the living God because He has life in Himself, and is the Author of all life.

strangled and killed them. I will go now and take away the reproach of the people. The Lord, who delivered me out of the paw of the lion and the bear, will deliver me out of the hand of this Philistine."

At last Saul consented and said: "Go, and the Lord be with thee." Saul then clothed David with his own armour or coat of mail, and put a helmet of brass on his head. But David, unused to wear armour, could not move freely under its weight, and therefore he laid it aside.

Then he took his staff which he had always in his hands, and chose five smooth stones [1] from the brook and put them in the shepherd's scrip which he had with him; and taking a sling in his hand he went forth to meet the Philistine.

When Goliath drew near and beheld David coming on, he despised him and said: "Am I a dog that thou comest to me with a staff?" Then cursing David by his gods he said: "Come to me, and I will give thy flesh to the birds of the air, and to the beasts of the earth." David answered: "Thou comest to me with a sword, and with a spear, and with a shield; but I come to thee in the name of the Lord [2] of Hosts whom thou hast defied [3]. I will slay thee and take away thy head from thee, that all may know that there is a God in Israel."

Meanwhile the Philistine arose, advanced and made ready for the fight; David, on his part, making haste ran up to meet the giant. While running he quickly took a stone from his scrip, laid it in his sling, and swinging [4] it swiftly he aimed and struck Goliath so violently on the forehead that he reeled and fell on his face upon the earth. Then David, rushing up and taking Goliath's sword from its scabbard, cut off his head.

---

[1] *Smooth stones.* They had to be smooth so as to slide easily from the sling.

[2] *In the name of the Lord.* i. e. you rely on material weapons and human strength, while I rely on spiritual arms, faith and trust in the power of the true God who is the Lord of invisible (heavenly) armies.

[3] *Defied.* Goliath, by mocking the Israelites and treating them as if God were powerless to help them, was really defying God.

[4] *Swinging.* By swinging the sling, such velocity was given to the stone cast by it that even the skull of the giant could not resist it. But to take aim well and sling truly, great skill and practice are required. David possessed both, and God now gave him the grace not to lose courage or presence of mind, without which he could not have taken a cool and sure aim.

The Philistines, seeing that their champion was dead, were seized with fear and fled. But the Israelites, following after, slew a great number of them, and took possession of their camp.

COMMENTARY.

Pride. Goliath was arrogant and trusted in his own strength and mighty weapons. He boasted, sought the single combat for his own glory and scorned the people of God. This pride was the cause of his fall. "Pride comes before a fall", and "humiliation followeth the proud, and glory shall uphold the humble of spirit" (Prov. 29, 23).

Humility and confidence in God. David was humble. It was no thought of renown which impelled him to fight the giant, but only zeal for God's glory and the good of his people. He trusted in God's help and not in his own powers or skill, and went forth to the unequal combat, full of the confidence that God would overthrow the Philistine by his means, and would thus manifest His power to the heathen. "The Lord who delivered me out of the paw of the lion and out of the paw of the bear, He will deliver me out of the hand of this Philistine" (1 Kings 17, 37). God rewarded the humility and confidence of His servant by giving him a splendid victory over the terrible giant. God wished, by this victory of David, to draw the eyes of the Israelites to his virtues, and to awaken in them a feeling of gratitude towards him who was to be their future king.

APPLICATION. Do you boast? Are you proud of your fine figure, of your strength, or of your understanding, memory &c.? Make a resolution to subdue promptly all such thoughts of self-complacency.

You, too, have a Goliath to overcome, namely your besetting sin. Ask yourself which is your besetting sin, whether anger, envy, pride, sloth &c. Against this sin you must fight, not once, but every day of your life, if you hope to overcome it. Your weapons must be prayer and watchfulness. Pray for the virtue opposed to your besetting sin, and take care to subdue its movements when it first appears.

CHAPTER LII.

FRIENDSHIP OF JONATHAN AND DAVID.

[1 Kings 18.]

WHEN David returned from the slaying of the Philistine, Saul called for him and asked: "Young man, of what family art thou?" Then David related all about his family and about himself. Now Jonathan, the eldest son of Saul, was standing by and listened to the words of David; and when David had made an end of speaking, Jonathan began to love him as his own soul. There was a custom for friends to exchange garments; so Jonathan took his coat and gave it to David. He took his sword, and his bow, and his girdle, and gave them also to David.

Now when David returned home with Saul, after having slain Goliath, the women came out of all the cities of Israel, with flutes and cymbals, and they sang: "Saul slew his thousands, and David his ten thousands." Hearing this Saul was angry, and ever after regarded David as his rival. Next day Saul was again troubled by the evil spirit, and whilst David played the harp before him, the king threw a spear at him hoping to nail him to the wall.

David, however, stepped aside and avoided the blow. Some time after David was appointed by Saul captain over a thousand men. He was moreover promised Michol, the king's daughter, in marriage, if he killed a hundred Philistines. By this proposal Saul hoped to get rid of David, thinking that he would never be able to fulfil the conditions,. but that he would be slain by the Philistines. Saul, however, was disappointed, for David slew two hundred of the enemy, and thereby gained the affection of the whole people. This unexpected success of David enraged Saul more than ever.

Blinded by passion, Saul ordered Jonathan[1], his son, to kill David. But Jonathan, knowing David's innocence and virtue and loving him exceedingly, gave warning to him and said: "My father seeketh to kill thee; wherefore look to thyself, and abide in a secret place, and thou shalt be hid." David listened to his advice and remained hidden[2] in the fields.

One day, however, when Saul was in a better humour than usual, Jonathan said to him: "Sin not, O king! against thy servant David, because he has not sinned against thee, and his works are very good towards thee. Why, therefore, wilt thou sin against innocent blood?"

---

[1] *Jonathan.* Constantly spoke to his father in defence of his friend and, whenever he could, warned the latter of his danger.

[2] *Hidden.* David had from henceforth to live as a fugitive in the mountains, hiding in holes and caves, for nowhere was his life safe.

Saul was appeased by these words of Jonathan, and swore that David should not be slain. And Jonathan brought David again into his father's presence, and Saul was gracious to him as he had been before. At this time, however, war was renewed against the Philistines, and David went out against them and defeated them with great slaughter.

Then the evil spirit came back upon Saul, who tried to pierce David with his spear as he played upon the harp; but David warded off the blow and fled. Jonathan, however, took occasion once again to speak to his father in behalf of David. But Saul was angry and blamed his son for his affection for the son of Isai, who was supplanting him with the people.

He told Jonathan that so long as David lived, he could have no hope of ascending the throne. "Therefore now presently send and fetch him to me, for he is the son of death." Jonathan asked: "Why shall he die? What hath he done?" And Saul, being enraged at Jonathan, took his spear to strike him. But Jonathan escaped and fled to David's hiding-place, in order to warn him against returning to the court. The two friends then embraced each other, wept together, and before parting, renewed their vow of friendship in the name of God.

COMMENTARY.

Envy. Saul was avowedly the tallest man in Israel, but he had not the courage to face Goliath, because he had no confidence in God. He ought to have been all the more grateful to David for freeing him and all Israel from this proud and overbearing enemy. But because the people praised David more than they praised himself, he allowed a hateful envy to take possession of his heart. From this time he disliked him, and was suspicious and distrustful of the noble-minded David. See how ungrateful and unjust envy makes a man!

True friendship. David and Jonathan were knit together by a real, true, noble friendship. Jonathan loved David for his good qualities, his piety, courage, modesty &c. He loved him "as his own soul", though he knew that David, and not he, was destined to succeed Saul as king. He remained true to his friend in his adversity, and did everything that he could to help him. David responded with all his heart to the love of the king's son. When Jonathan died, David tore his clothes for grief, wept bitterly and expressed his sorrow in the most moving words. A true and noble friend is a great treasure; therefore Holy Scripture says: "Nothing can be compared to a faithful friend, and they that fear the Lord shall find him" (Ecclus. 6, 15. 16). True friendship can only exist between good people. He who is not faithful to God and does not love and fear Him, will only be faithful to his friend as long as he hopes to gain something by his friendship. Friendship and intercourse with the good exercise an ennobling and elevating influence, but intercourse with the wicked is a great source of danger both to faith and morals. "Evil communications corrupt good manners."

APPLICATION. You should be *friendly* with all your school-fellows, but *make friends* of the good only. How has it been with you hitherto? Have you taken pleasure in being with bad companions? Many a good child has been corrupted and led into committing grievous sins by associating and making friends with bad children. Therefore, form friendships with only good and well-behaved children, and avoid anything like intimacy with bad children.

CHAPTER LIII.

DAVID'S NOBLE CONDUCT TOWARDS SAUL.

[1 Kings 23—26; 31; 2 Kings 1.]

DAVID seeing that he could no longer live in safety near Saul, fled to the mountains of Juda. Even there death threatened him on every side, but his courage never forsook him. He consoled himself with the thought that he who places himself under the protection of God, is in safety everywhere, and has nothing to fear. His trust in God was rewarded.

Now the men of Ziph came to Saul and said: "Behold, David is hid in the hill which is over against the wilderness." Immediately Saul arose, having with him three thousand chosen men, and encamped in the way of the wilderness. As soon as David had heard that Saul had come after him, he sent out spies to see where the king had pitched his tents. David, on learning where Saul was, arose and came secretly to the camp of his enemy.

And David said to his followers: "Who will go down with me into the camp of Saul?" Abisai answered: "I will go with thee." So David and Abisai came upon the tents by night, and found Saul sleeping on his couch, and his spear fixed in the ground near his head. Moreover all the soldiers were sleeping about. And Abisai said to David: "Now then, I will run thy enemy through with my spear, and there shall be no need of a second time." But David answered: "Kill him not; for who shall[1] put forth his hand against the Lord's anointed, and remain guiltless? But now take the spear[2] which is at his head, and the cup of water, and let us go."

So they took the spear and the cup of water and went away. And no man knew it, or saw it, or awoke; for a deep sleep from the Lord was fallen upon them. They both went on till they came to the other side, and stood on a hill afar off. Then David called aloud to Abner, the captain of Saul's army, and said: "Wilt thou not answer, Abner? Art thou not a man? Why then hast thou not kept thy lord the king? And now where is the king's spear, and the cup of water which was at his head?"

At these words Saul awoke from his sleep and cried out: "Is this thy voice, my son David?" And David answered: "It is my voice, my lord the king. Wherefore doth my lord persecute his servant? What have I done?" Saul, feeling his own injustice, exclaimed: "I have sinned; return, my son David, for I will no more do thee harm, because my life has been precious in thy eyes this day. Blessed art thou, my son David." Then they parted in peace.

A short time after this there was a battle fought between the Israelites and the Philistines on Mount Gelboe[3]. A great number of the Israelites were slain, and amongst them the three sons of Saul. At last the whole weight of the fight turned upon Saul; the archers overtook him and grievously wounded him.

Seeing himself surrounded by the enemy, who wished to take him alive, he drew his sword and fell upon it[4]. David was thus delivered from his mortal enemy; yet so far from rejoicing at his

---

[1] *Who shall.* He meant that nobody could kill the king, the anointed of the Lord, without committing a grievous sin.

[2] *Take the spear.* David took them with him, so as to prove to the king that he had been inside his tent and could have killed him, had he wished to do so. When Saul had acknowledged his injustice, David sent him back the spear and cup.

[3] *Mount Gelboe.* The mountain in which the brook Kison takes its rise. It is south of Naim (see Map).

[4] *Fell upon it.* So that it pierced his body, and he died in a few moments. The Philistines found his corpse and cut off his head, which they sent, with his weapons, to their country. The head of the king was set up by his enemies as a token of their victory. How humiliating was the end of Saul!

death, when he heard the sad news he wept, and forgetting all the injuries he had received, he remembered only the good qualities of the king.

Filled with sorrow, he even rent his garments and wept, and cursed[1] the mountain of Gelboe whereon the king and his three sons had met their death. Then he lamented and made a dirge over Saul and Jonathan: "How are the valiant fallen! Tell it not in Geth; publish it not in the streets of Ascalon. They were swifter than eagles, stronger than lions. I grieve for thee, my brother Jonathan, exceeding amiable. As the mother loveth her only son, so I did love thee."

COMMENTARY.

The Justice of God. God protected the innocent David and enabled him to escape from the snares of the bloodthirsty king. But He humbled the sin-laden Saul by subjecting him to a humiliating defeat and a premature and dishonourable death.

The Wisdom of God decreed that many troubles should overtake David, in order that he might be exercised in virtue and prepared for his high position. By the persecutions and privations to which he was subjected, David was confirmed in humility and confidence in God, and experienced for himself how much harm is caused by evil-doing. He saw from which faults a ruler should be free, and was thus fitted for the high dignity for which God had destined him.

The Fifth Commandment. The story we have just heard is well suited to explain and impress upon us the precepts taught by the fifth Commandment. David observed this Commandment most conscientiously when he would not allow his mortal enemy, Saul, to be killed, although he was in his power. The armour-bearer, Abisai, on the other hand, did sin against the fifth Commandment, because he had the desire to murder Saul in his sleep, and would have carried out his wicked project, had David given his consent. By this sinful intention Abisai also sinned against the fourth Commandment; for Saul, the anointed of the Lord, was the representative of God. But it was Saul who sinned most grievously against the fifth Commandment. He allowed his anger against David to grow till it turned to hatred, and from this to bloodthirstiness, which passion Saul cherished in his heart for a long time, and tried to satisfy by his untiring persecution of David. Each fresh desire to get rid of David, and each new pursuit of him for that object was a grievous sin.

---

[1] *Cursed.* "Ye mountains of Gelboe", said he, "let neither dew nor rain come upon you, nor let there be in you fields of first fruits." Their infertility was a token of mourning.

Suicide was Saul's crowning sin. He saw that the enemy was pressing on him in overwhelming numbers, and that he could not escape; therefore, so as not to fall into the hands of the Philistines, he killed himself. This was a terrible sin, for on no account may a man take away his own life, as he did not give it to himself. God is Lord of life and death, and he who kills himself robs the divine Majesty of His rights. But it might be argued, Saul could not anyhow have had long to live, for most likely the Philistines would have killed him on the field of battle. True, but if Saul had, by God's permission, been killed by his enemies, he would have died the death of a hero, in defence of his religion, his people and his country. Very likely, however, the Philistines would not have killed him at once, but would have taken him prisoner, and would later have put him to death. Saul would in this way have had to endure humiliations and tortures, but he would have had time to repent of his many sins, and if he had offered his sufferings to God in the spirit of true penance, his soul would have been saved, and he would have died the death of a martyr to faith in the one true God. By his suicide he not only killed his body, but also his soul; for his last act on earth was one of mortal sin, and the very nature of the act made repentance impossible. Every voluntary suicide is a suicide of the soul which can in no way be expiated; and it is in this that lies the horror of this sin. Cowardice, moreover, lies at the root of every suicide, as we have seen was the case with Saul. He shrank from humiliation and degradation, and to avoid them put an end to his life. The suicide is too cowardly to endure such temporal evils as poverty, sickness, or shame, and therefore puts an end to his life, never considering that he thereby subjects himself to the everlasting torments of hell. Suicide is the most foolish of all sins and crimes; for in order to escape a passing evil he who commits it exposes himself to eternal suffering.

Humility and love of our enemies. There are many beautiful virtues to admire in David. He remained humble in spite of the adulation of the world; he did not glory in being chosen by God to be king; he bore no grudge in his heart against the unjust, ungrateful Saul; he did not rise up against him, but honoured him as "his lord and king", called himself his servant, forgave him from his heart, and spared his life when the opportunity of revenge was given him. David had a most noble and magnanimous heart; he did not return evil for evil, but really loved his mortal enemy, and bitterly bewailed his sad end. Thus David gives us a splendid example of love of our enemies, which teaches us that we should never take vengeance on them. St. Paul writes (Rom. 12, 19): "Do not revenge yourselves, but give place unto wrath (i. e. leave vengeance to God), for it is written: 'Revenge to me, I will repay, saith the Lord.'" By this noble virtue of love of his enemy David won a victory over himself (over anger and the desire of revenge) which was far greater and more worthy of renown than his victory over Goliath. St. Chrysostom says of him: "Women did not come to meet him, singing the praises of this victory, but the choirs of angels, full of admiration, sang the praises of his magnanimity." Learn then how beautiful and praiseworthy it is to overcome yourself and forgive those who have injured you.

Love until death. David loved Saul and Jonathan till they died, and bitterly mourned their death. True love lasts beyond the grave, and we should preserve our love for those dear unto us after they are dead. You should pray for the souls of your departed parents, friends and relations.

Resistance to grace. Learn from the case of Saul how low a man can fall when he forsakes God, resists grace and gives himself over to his passions. If you give the devil one finger, he will want to have your whole hand and your whole self. Saul was originally humble, and God was with him and gave him many graces; but his victories made him proud and disobedient to God. His pride could not endure that David should be so highly honoured and esteemed, and therefore he was envious and jealous of him. Envy embittered his life and made him ungrateful towards David, and this led further to hatred of him and desire for his death. Thus Saul became more and more unworthy of the divine assistance. Quite forsaken by God, he was defeated by the Philistines in spite of his valour, and ended his life by suicide. What a sad end for a man chosen out by God from among all men!

APPLICATION. What do you do when anyone injures you by word or deed? Do you cherish a grudge against him in your heart? Do you wish evil to any of your companions? Do you speak evil of him to others? "Forgive and forget!"

CHAPTER LIV.

DAVID'S PIETY.—HIS ZEAL FOR GOD'S GLORY.

[2 Kings 5—6.]

AFTER the death of Saul David was chosen king. He established his court in Jerusalem[1], where he became renowned for his great valour. He defeated the Philistines and many other

---

[1] *Jerusalem.* This, the House of Peace, is the Salem of earlier times, of which in the days of Abraham Melchisedech was king. The town was divided into two parts, the upper town and the lower town. The lower town had been for some time in the possession of the Israelites, but the upper town, which was built on Mount Sion, still belonged to the heathen Jebusites, who had fortified it so strongly that hitherto no one had been able to conquer it. David now took possession of it and fortified it even more strongly than it had been before. He built himself a palace there and called it the City of David. From henceforward Jerusalem was the capital of the kingdom (Fig. 41).

nations[1]. His reign was glorious, because he governed his people with justice and clemency. As he feared God, he was a just ruler[2], and never imposed on his people any but just and righteous laws.

The counsellors whom he chose to aid him in the government of his kingdom were not flatterers, but men of wisdom and virtue, whose advice was always founded on reason and justice. The promotion of God's glory was the primary object of all their plans and views.

Fig. 41. David's Tower at Jerusalem. (Phot. Bonfils.)

Near Jerusalem was Mount Sion, on which David erected a splendid tabernacle[3] for the Ark of the Covenant. When the tabernacle was completed, he caused the Ark to be carried in

---

[1] *Many other nations.* Such as the Moabites, Syrians &c. David extended his kingdom on the west as far as the Mediterranean, on the south to the Red Sea, on the east to the deserts of Arabia and Syria, and on the north to the Euphrates.

[2] *Just ruler.* He settled the principal matters of dispute himself. Besides this he appointed six thousand Levites to be judges.

[3] *Tabernacle.* The new tabernacle was made on the model of the old one constructed under the direction of Moses, but which was worn out on account of its great age.

triumph to Mount Sion. The procession was very grand, comprising all the princes [1] of Israel in purple robes, the priests in their rich vestments, and thirty thousand armed men. The sound of all manner of musical instruments [2] made the procession still more imposing. David himself went before the Ark playing on the harp and singing: "Lord, who shall dwell in Thy tabernacle, and who shall rest in Thy holy hill?"

At every few paces taken by the Levites who carried the Ark, an ox and a ram were sacrificed to the Lord. And when the Ark had been placed in its destined position, a great number of victims were offered. David then divided the priests into 24 classes,

Fig. 42. Musical Instruments of old Egypt (harp, flute, lute, lyre, little drum).
Egyptian wall-painting. (After Champollion.)

who were in turn to officiate in the divine worship. He established a like order amongst the Levites, four thousand of whom were chosen to sing the praises of the Most High.

COMMENTARY.

Religion, the foundation of all government. David was, therefore, a wise as well as a holy ruler. He knew that a nation cannot be happy and contented, nor rights and laws be respected, unless religion be observed, and God feared. Hence, as far as lay in his power, he furthered religion. He arranged the solemn services of God, and he kindled the hearts of the people and awakened their religious sense by his sacred music and Psalms. Above all, he himself gave them the example of piety and reverence. He did not shrink from openly

[1] *All the princes.* The ancients of the tribes and the leaders of the army.

[2] *Musical instruments.* Some blew trumpets, others beat little drums with their hands, others clashed cymbals, some played on metal triangles, while others played on stringed instruments, such as harps and lutes (Fig. 42 and 43).

confessing his faith; he publicly humbled himself before God and danced in front of the Ark of the Covenant, singing and playing on the harp. In reward for David's care and zeal for His glory God gave him the victory over all his enemies, increased his kingdom and promised him that the Redeemer should be born of his race, and should found and possess an everlasting kingdom.

The First Commandment. David was a shining example to high and low by his zeal for God's glory. His heart was holy, he had a living faith, firm confidence in God, an interior love for Him, and he expressed all these holy dispositions in his wonderful Psalms. By these Psalms (some of which are sung at Vespers) he not only edified the Israelites of his own time, but he has edified all the faithful for 3000 years, moving them to worship God.

Religious Processions which the Church has instituted, give us an opportunity of outwardly confessing our faith and of honouring God.

Fig 43. Musical Instruments of the Assyrians. Sculpture from Koyoundjik. London, British Museum. (After Layard.)

In the procession formed by David the Ark of the Covenant, held most sacred by the Israelites, was carried. We have far more holy processions, in which the Lawgiver of the New Testament, Jesus Christ Himself, present in the Blessed Sacrament, is carried about for our veneration and adoration.

Religious Music. Its purpose is to glorify God and to edify the faithful. As to its necessary qualities, St. Bernard remarks that it must be earnest and grave and dignified, not effeminate, light or worldly. It should please the ear, but also move the heart; it should not obscure the words, but help to make them clear and bright and impressive. While the soft sweet sounds flow into the ear, says St. Augustine, divine truth should gently steal into our hearts. If the Old Testament, which was material and earthly, admitted of noisy instruments, it does not follow that the Church of Christ with its spiritual worship should do the same, or to the same extent. Church music is not a mere matter of musical taste, but of fitness and appropriateness to the divine worship of the New Testament Church. It is both a duty and a great privilege for any one to be a member of the choir or to promote good music in the Church.

Importance of the City of Jerusalem. Divine Providence brought it about that David should choose this old and naturally fortified city of the Jebusites as the capital of his kingdom, the centre of the Jewish religion, and the cradle of the Christian religion. Here it was that Melchisedech exercised his royal priesthood, and here it was that the great High Priest according to the order of Melchisedech offered and instituted His Eucharistic Sacrifice and Sacrament of love. Here on Mount Moria Abraham offered his son Isaac, and here the eternal Father offered His only-begotten Son for the sins of the world. Here David, the shepherd-boy of Bethlehem, entered as the meek, gentle, God-fearing king, and established the divine worship of Moses in its fullest splendour; and here the Son of David, the Son of man born in Bethlehem entered, riding on an ass and acclaimed by the Hosannas of the children of Israel. Here he died and rose, ascended into heaven, and poured out the Spirit of God on the day of Pentecost. Here He gave life to the Church of the Redeemed, and from here She began her world-wide work and mission. For these reasons Jerusalem is and remains the holiest city on earth, and is a type of the everlasting city of peace and happiness of heaven.

Joy in the House of God. David rejoiced and exulted that now the Ark would be close to his dwelling on Mount Sion, and that he would be able to assist at the sacrifices. How much more ought we to rejoice and thank God that in our midst are real houses of God, where we can visit our Divine Lord, and assist at the Holy Sacrifice of the Mass.

APPLICATION. Do you like going to Mass? Do you take pleasure in the services of God? How do you behave in Church and during processions? Do you give a good example to others, or do you disturb them in their devotions?

CHAPTER LV.

THE PROPHECIES OF DAVID.

[2 Kings 7. Ps. 2; 21; 109.]

DAVID, as he had done when only a simple shepherd-boy, composed Psalms[1] and Canticles in honour of the Most High, and conducted himself in all things according to the holy

------

[1] *Psalms.* These were written by the inspiration of the Holy Ghost, who also revealed to the Royal Prophet the future of the kingdom of God. There are

will of God. Wherefore the Lord blessed him and not only favoured all his undertakings, but promised him that one of his descendants should rule the whole world and sit upon a throne more lasting than the heavens.

He furthermore endowed him with the gift of prophecy. David expresses in lofty and sublime language the eternal relationship existing between the Father and the Son: "Thou art my Son, this day have I begotten Thee." He foreshadows the boundless dominion which was to be the inheritance of the Redeemer, and the peaceful character of his reign. "I will give Thee the Gentiles for Thy inheritance, and the utmost parts of the earth for Thy possession. In His days shall justice spring up, and the abundance of peace." [1]

He sees in his prophetic visions the Ethiopians falling down before the great Ruler, the Prince of Peace, and beholds His enemies prostrate at His feet. He sees the kings of Tharsis and of the Islands offering Him presents; the kings of the Arabians and of Saba bringing Him gifts. (Ps. 71.)

He foretells the future crucifixion with all its sorrowful scenes and circumstances. "They have pierced my hands [2] and my feet, they have numbered all my bones." The gall and vinegar that were presented to the Divine Victim suffering and dying on the Cross; the lance that pierced His most Sacred Heart; the nails that held Him fast to the Cross; all these are mentioned by David in his Psalms. (Ps. 21; 68.)

Death overcome, the grave robbed of its prey, the earthquake that rent the rocks of Calvary, and the glory of the

---

in all one hundred and fifty Psalms, which form one of the books of Holy Scripture. Most of the Psalms are songs of praise; some are petitions; and seven are called the penitential Psalms.

[1] *Abundance of peace.* i. e. virtue and holiness will flourish and, in consequence, men will live in perfect peace both with God and with their neighbours. The Psalmist goes on to say: "And He shall rule from sea to sea. And all the kings of the earth shall adore Him, all nations shall serve Him." (Ps. 2 and 109.)

[2] *My hands.* It is as if the Psalmist heard the Divine Redeemer utter these and the other words: "I am a worm and no man (i. e. down-trodden and despised like a worm), the reproach of men and the outcast of the people. All they that saw me have laughed me to scorn, they have spoken with the lips and wagged their heads (in token of their scorn). They have pierced my hands and my feet. They parted my garments among them, and upon my vesture they cast lots."

Resurrection were all and each familiar[1] to the mind of the royal prophet. (Ps. 15.)

He sees in the distant future the brightness of the Ascension[2]. He calls upon the eternal gates to be lifted up, that the triumphant Conqueror of sin and death may take possession of His everlasting throne in heaven. David, the progenitor or forefather of Jesus Christ, who is Himself called the Son of David[3], was a figure of the Redeemer by the place of his birth, Bethlehem, by the obscurity and lowliness of his early years, by the victories he obtained over the enemies of the people of God, and also by his twofold character of king and prophet.

COMMENTARY.

The eighth promise of the Messias. David lived more than a thousand years before our Lord's birth. (He reigned from 1055 to 1015 B. C.) But the Spirit of God, to whom a thousand years are but as one day, inspired his spirit and enabled him to look forward over centuries, and contemplate the sufferings and glory of the Redeemer.

The prophecies about our Lord's sufferings have been very literally fulfilled (New Test. LXXV and LXXVI). It amazes us that the prophet, writing 1000 years before our Lord suffered, should have described such details as the piercing of His Hands and Feet, the division of His garments, the casting lots for the seamless robe, the scoffing and wagging of the head on the part of the bystanders! This foretelling of future events was only possible by means of divine revelation.

About the Resurrection David prophesied that our Lord's soul would descend to Limbo, but would not stay there; and that His body would rest in the grave, but would not know corruption ("He descended into hell; the third day He rose again from the dead").

---

[1] *Familiar.* "My flesh also shall rest in hope (in the grave); because Thou wilt not leave my soul in hell (i. e. in Limbo), nor wilt Thou give Thy Holy One (He who is anointed by Thee) to see corruption (to experience it in His own body)."

[2] *The Ascension.* "The Lord said to my Lord (to David's Lord, the Messias): 'Sit Thou at my right hand until I make thine enemies Thy footstool (till all Thine enemies are overthrown).' The Lord hath sworn and He will not repent: 'Thou art a priest for ever according to the order of Melchisedech (who was both priest and king and offered an unbloody sacrifice of bread and wine).'" (Ps. 109.)

[3] *The Son of David.* God said to David: "I will raise up thy seed after thee, and I will establish the throne of His kingdom for ever (to last for all eternity). I will be to Him a Father, and He shall be to me a Son." (2 Kings 7, 14.)

Alluding *to our Lord's glory in heaven* and His kingdom the Psalmist says that He will sit at the right hand of God ("He ascended into heaven, sitteth at the right hand of God the Father Almighty").

His enemies will be overcome: the doctrines of Christianity have overcome paganism.

He will remain for ever a King and Priest: Jesus Christ is King of that kingdom which He founded, and He offers Himself in an unbloody manner in the Holy Sacrifice of the Mass.

He will rule over the whole earth: Jesus Christ's kingdom, i. e. His Church, is spread over the whole world, and is ever being spread further and further.

His reign will bring justice and peace: Jesus Christ has justified us and reconciled us to God by the grace which He has won for us; at His birth the angels proclaimed peace to men.

Finally the Psalmist says that *the Redeemer will be of the seed of David,* and that He will be likewise the Son of God and will rule for ever: therefore David calls Him his Lord. Jesus Christ is the Son of God from all eternity, and in time He took our human nature on Him. According to His human nature He was descended from David, for His holy Mother was of the race and house of David. (Compare what the Angel Gabriel said at the Annunciation. New Test. II.)

APPLICATION. David's example teaches us to worship God from our hearts; to assist at the services of God with holy joy, and, according to our capabilities, to work for their adornment by singing &c.

CHAPTER LVI.

DAVID'S FALL AND PENANCE.—REVOLT AND PUNISHMENT OF ABSALOM.

[2 Kings 15—18.]

DAVID was a great and glorious king and a man according to the heart of God. But perhaps his very glory and success were calculated to blind him with regard to the true source of all his greatness, which came from God alone. Hence God allowed him to fall into the most grievous sins of adultery and murder. Being idle one day and looking from the roof of his house down upon people, he saw Bethsabee, the wife of Urias[1], one of his captains in the army, and being seized with a guilty passion he

---

[1] *Urias.* This valiant captain in the army was very devoted to the king's service.

caused her to be unfaithful to her lawful husband. Then, in order to conceal his sin and to marry Bethsabee, he wrote to the general of the army to put Urias in the front of the next battle, so that he would surely be slain. Joab, the general, did as his Lord and master commanded. Urias fell in battle, and David took Bethsabee for his wife. Then came the prophet Nathan [1] to him, and told him how a rich man with many sheep had robbed a poor man of his one ewe-lamb in order to entertain a guest, and when David in great indignation at such heartless conduct inquired after the name of the man, saying "He shall die", the prophet answered: "Thou art the man." David was thunderstruck by this retort, and confessed his fault and asked pardon of the Lord. He then composed the seven penitential Psalms, which ever since have been the consolation of all truly penitent sinners.

The Lord, seeing the sorrow of David, ordered Nathan to tell him that his sin was forgiven, but that nevertheless he must undergo many temporal punishments [2], and that the child that was about to be born to him should die. David, humbling himself before God, willingly accepted this and many other punishments inflicted upon him, and added, on his own part, the most severe penance in expiation of his sin.

The most terrible chastisement inflicted on David was the ingratitude of his son Absalom. Now Absalom was endowed with rare beauty of person, so that from the top of his head to the sole of his foot there was no blemish in him. His hair was long and beautiful. And David gave Absalom a princely retinue of chariots and horsemen, and a guard of young men to accompany him everywhere.

Absalom was wont to rise early in the morning and stand at the gate of the palace, and when any man presented himself to ask justice of the king, he kindly inquired what complaint he had to make, and on hearing it always replied: "Thy words seem good and just to me; but there is no one appointed by the king to hear thy cause." In this manner he made friends for himself among the people by wrongfully blaming his father.

---

[1] *Nathan.* Nathan recalled to the king's mind all the benefits which God had bestowed upon him, in order to lead him to perceive and confess his shameful ingratitude towards God.

[2] *Temporal punishments.* Chiefly at the hands of his own children.

Sometimes he would exclaim in the hearing of these people: "O that they would make me judge over the land, that all who have business might come to me, that I might do them justice!" Moreover when any man came to salute him, he put forth his hand and took him and kissed him. Thus he enticed the hearts[1] of the men of Israel.

When he thought he had gained over all the men of Israel to his side, he asked his father to let him go to Hebron in fulfilment of a vow. David, suspecting no evil, allowed his son to depart. And when Absalom had reached Hebron, he sent messengers to all the tribes of Israel, telling them that when they heard the sound of a trumpet, they should say: "Absalom reigneth in Hebron." And it came to pass that many of the people, not knowing his treachery[2], followed Absalom.

When David heard of Absalom's revolt, he determined to leave the city, lest the citizens should suffer on his account. And having left the city with his attendants he came to the brook Cedron[3], his feet bare and his head veiled. And crossing the brook he came to Mount Olivet, where he wept for the guilt of his unnatural son and for his own sins. On the side of Mount Olivet he was met by a man named Semei, of the family of Saul, who threw stones and earth at David and cursed him: "Come out, come out, thou man of blood." Abisai, full of wrath, cried out: "Why should this dead dog curse my lord the king? I will go and cut off his head." But David answered: "Behold, my own son seeketh my life; how much more one of the house of Saul! Perhaps the Lord may look upon my affliction and render me good for the cursing of this day." He saw the hand of God in this new trial.

---

[1] *Enticed the hearts.* By flattering the people and making himself familiar with them he won their hearts, and gave it to be understood that if he were king, it would be all the better for them. Thus by degrees he gathered round him a large number of adherents.

[2] *His treachery.* i. e. the design to march on Jerusalem and take it, in order to seize the person of his father and take possession of the throne.

[3] *Cedron.* Which flowed in a deep valley to the east of the town, between it and the Mount of Olives, being crossed by a bridge. Picture to yourselves the aged king ascending the Mount of Olives, barefoot, weeping and with his head covered, a fugitive before his own son. How grieved he must have felt at the faithlessness of his people and the unnatural conduct of his son! How weary the way must have been to him!

Absalom, having resolved to destroy David and his army, went in pursuit of them. David however reviewed his men and placed brave captains in command, and said that he would himself march at their head. But this his men would not permit, saying that if ten thousand of them fell in battle, they would not despair; but that if he perished, all was lost. The king therefore remained in the city of Mahanaim, but he commanded Joab and his other officers, saying: "Spare me [1] the boy Absalom."

Fig. 44. Valley of Josaphat with Absalom's Tomb. (To the right the Tombs of St. James and Zacharias.)
(Phot. Bonfils.)

The battle was fought in the midst of a great wood, and Absalom's army [2] was cut to pieces. He himself fled, but he could not escape from divine justice, which pursues the wicked wherever they go. Having mounted a mule, he endeavoured to escape through the forest; but his long hair having become entangled in a tree, he remained hanging from a branch, while his mule passed on.

---

[1] *Spare me.* "Spare his life: do not kill him."
[2] *Absalom's army.* About 20,000 of his adherents perished.

And word was brought to Joab, the general of the king's army. Joab taking three javelins went to the place where Absalom was hanging from the tree, and with his javelins pierced the ungrateful, unnatural heart of the king's son. Absalom still breathed and struggled for life, when some of Joab's soldiers running up slew him with their swords. They then took Absalom's body, and casting it into a deep pit in the forest piled over it a large heap of stones [1].

A herald was sent to David with news of Absalom's defeat. David with the anxiety of a loving father asked: "Is Absalom safe?" When told that Absalom was dead, the king refused all comfort, and going up into a high chamber mourned his ungrateful son for many days. "Absalom, my son", he cried, "my son Absalom, who would grant me that I might die for thee, Absalom, my son, my son Absalom!"

The people of Jerusalem, hearing of David's victory, went out to meet him and carried him in triumph into the city.

COMMENTARY.

The Omniscience of God. God knew of David's secret adultery, and He knew that he was guilty of the death of Urias. For He sent Nathan to David, saying: "Thus saith the Lord: Why hast thou done evil in my sight?"

God is Good. Therefore the prophet said to the king: "The Lord has done good to thee."

God is Merciful. For He forgave David his grievous sin: "The Lord has taken away thy sin."

God is Holy. Therefore David's sin was "displeasing to the Lord"

God is Just. The sentence which God pronounced on David through Nathan was this: "I will raise up evil against thee out of thy own house", and "The child that is born to thee shall surely die." Both sentences were executed, and David suffered anguish of soul.

The Sixth and Ninth Commandments. When David looked on the wife of Urias, instead of at once turning his eyes from her and thinking of God's Commandment: "Thou shalt not covet thy neighbour's wife", he allowed an evil desire to grow in his heart. Then, instead of resisting this sinful desire and calling on God for help against the temptation, he consented to it, and sending for the woman induced

---

[1] *Heap of stones* (Fig. 44). As a monument of his infamy this memorial might well have had written over it: "Here lies one worthy of being stoned!"

her to be unfaithful to her husband. He thus sinned against the ninth and sixth Commandments; and also against the fifth, by leading the woman to do what was wrong. Even this was not all, for his adultery led him to commit the further sin of murder. But did David kill Urias? Not directly, but his urgent command was the cause of his death, so that he really killed him by the hands of the Amorrhites, as much as the Jews really crucified our Lord by the hands of the pagan soldiers.

Tepidity. How did it happen that the royal prophet fell into this grievous sin? He had become tepid in prayer and was living an idle and comfortable life at home, while he sent his captains out to fight against the unbelievers. His fall gives us a useful lesson against laxity in the spiritual life, and teaches us that we should keep a careful watch over our eyes and turn them away from anything that awakes evil desires in our hearts: "Watch ye (over your senses and the movements of your hearts) and pray that ye enter not into temptation (New Test. LXIX)." "He that thinketh himself to stand (firm in what is right), let him take heed lest he fall" (1 Cor. 10, 12).

The evil of mortal sin. In order that David might see the enormity of his sin, Nathan put before him: 1. that he had sinned in the sight of God, and 2. that he had repaid with the basest ingratitude all the benefits which God had showered upon him.

True penance. David was not a hardened, obstinate sinner. He opened his heart to God's grace and listened to the voice of his conscience, which day and night reproached him for his sin. He thus speaks in Psalm 30: "Day and night Thy hand was heavy upon me. I am turned in my anguish, whilst the thorn is fastened." Then, by God's merciful command, the prophet Nathan went to the powerful king and reminded him of God's great benefits, candidly pointing out to him his grievous and twofold sin. David, quite crushed, fell upon his knees, penitently confessed his sin, without excusing himself as Saul did, and prayed for pardon. He did public penance, bewailed his sin (Ps. 6, 7: "Every night I water my couch with my tears"), fasted and grieved, so that his sight failed him. During this period of contrite conversion he composed the penitential Psalms, in which he expressed his repentance in moving words, and humbly asked for pardon. Then Nathan went to him again and told him that God had forgiven him, though he would still have to suffer temporal punishment. From that time forward David met with many sufferings and misfortunes, which he bore patiently in expiation of his sin. Contrition, confession and satisfaction are the principal parts of penance and the necessary conditions of absolution.

Temporal punishment. Although the sin and its eternal punishment were remitted, David had still to suffer temporal punishment.

The Fourth Commandment. Absalom sinned grievously against this Commandment, by violating the laws of obedience and reverence which he owed David, as a son to his father and as a subject to his king. For firstly he spoke evil of his father, deeply grieved him and caused him to shed tears of anguish, and not only disobeyed him, but set himself up actively against him. Secondly, he wantonly blamed the king's mode of government and, arms in hand, rebelled against the anointed of the Lord. He also sinned against the fifth Commandment by inducing a number of the people to revolt against their lawful sovereign.

The punishment for breaking the Fourth Commandment. Absalom's unnatural and detestable conduct towards a father so worthy of love met with the punishment which it deserved. A terrible fate awaited Absalom. He did not perish in battle, for very early in the day he thought of saving his own life and took to flight. He believed he could escape from his pursuers; but, by God's Providence, his head caught in a tree and there he hung in mid-air till Joab came and pierced his ungrateful, disobedient heart. He had hoped to be raised to the throne, but he met with the death of a criminal. His hair, of which he was so proud and which he had hoped to adorn with a royal crown, caught in the branch of a tree and brought him to his ruin. Instead of the sceptre which he had tried to grasp, three spears transfixed his treacherous heart. Instead of being crowned with the honour and renown he had coveted, he was buried in a dishonourable grave and his memory laden with infamy. In him God fulfilled His words: "Cursed be he who honoureth not his father and mother"; and this curse will fall on all those children who despise and neglect their parents, or cause them anguish of heart by their defiance and disobedience. How will it have fared with Absalom in the next world? For not only his father's tears, but the blood of the 20,000 slain whom he induced to sin by his flatteries and promises will have accused him before God and cried out for vengeance.

The love of parents for their children. David's love for his thankless son never changed. "O, that I had died for thee!" he cried. Parents often love their children much more than they deserve, therefore it is all the more heartless and ungrateful of children to offend their parents.

Gentleness and patience under suffering. It grieved David deeply that his own son should come out against him as a mortal enemy. His heart bled, and he shed bitter tears when he thought of the ingratitude and impiety of his child, the faithlessness of his people, and the misery which this civil war kindled by Absalom would bring on his country. Yet he neither complained nor murmured, nor did he curse his wicked son; but he bore all the suffering and injustice with patience and gentleness, saying to himself: "I have deserved all these misfortunes, for I have grievously sinned against God." Thus we too ought to do penance for our sins, by patience under suffering.

Love of our enemies. Even as God forgave David his sin, so did David forgive those who sinned and rebelled against him. "Forgive us our trespasses, as we forgive them that trespass against us." He who forgives from his heart is like unto the merciful God. There is something noble, nay, something divine, in forgiving and forgetting.

Pride, the source of many sins. The great sins of which Absalom was guilty sprang from pride. The beauty of his person and especially of his hair made him vain and conceited. Being the most beautiful he wished also to be the first man in the kingdom. He therefore rebelled against his royal father, and led his people into a revolt which cost many thousand lives.

The value of virtue. Do you like Absalom? No? and why not? He was a handsome young man, behaved very politely and courteously to the people, and knew perfectly how to say nice and pleasant things; so why do you not like him? Because he had a false, bad heart, and was a flatterer and a hypocrite. So you see that however handsome and pleasant a man may be, if he has a proud, bad heart, he is neither loveable nor worthy of respect, but on the contrary hateful and despicable in the eyes of God and man. It is only virtue which can give real worth to a man.

David, in crossing the brook Cedron in sorrow and tribulation, in his ascent of Mount Olivet, in his patient forbearance when outraged and insulted by Semei, and his triumphant entry into Jerusalem, presents a very striking figure of Christ.

APPLICATION. David is the model of a truly penitent man. Though he was a king, he humbly accepted Nathan's reproaches and contritely confessed his sin. Are you ashamed to make a sincere confession of your sins? He, an Israelite, bitterly repented and bewailed his sin: you are a Christian, but where are your tears of repentance? This very day say one of the penitential Psalms as a prayer!

Keep a guard on your eyes; they are the windows of your soul. Drive any bad thought from your heart at once. Say: "Away with it!" and pray for help. Nathan's words to David: "The Lord has done good to you: why have you done evil in His sight?" apply to you as well as to David.

Has your mother ever shed tears on your account? Have you ever injured or grieved or seriously irritated your father? In what way do you most grieve your parents? Have you truly repented of all sins committed against the fourth Commandment? Has your conduct towards your parents improved? Do you obey them at once and without arguing; or is it only when they scold and are angry, that you obey? Children, I wish for everything that is most good for you; that everything may be well with you on earth, and that you may be eternally happy in heaven. Therefore, because I wish this, I say most earnestly to you: "Honour and love your parents and obey them, or else you will know no happiness on earth and never get to heaven." Woe to those children who do not observe the fourth Commandment!

CHAPTER LVII.

DAVID'S LAST WORDS.—HIS DEATH.

[2 Kings 23. 3 Kings 1—2.]

DAVID was thirty years old when he ascended the throne of Israel, and he reigned forty years in honour and glory. When the time of his death drew near, he gathered together the princes of Israel, and told them that he had intended to build a house to the Lord, and had prepared all the materials for a new Temple; but that the Lord had not allowed him to carry out his plan, because he had shed much blood in his many battles.

The building of the Temple was reserved for Solomon[1], his son, whose kingdom should be great and powerful if he would be faithful to the Commandments of God. David therefore exhorted his son to serve God with a good will, because the Lord sounds the depths of hearts and penetrates the thoughts of men. "If thou seek Him", said David, "thou shalt find Him; but if thou forsake Him, He will cast thee off for ever."

David then gave his son gold and silver[2] for the vessels of the Sanctuary, together with the plan of the Temple and its precincts, and said to him: "All these things came to me written by the hand of the Lord[3]. Act like a man, take courage and fear not; for the Lord my God will be with thee nor forsake thee till thou hast finished the House of the Lord."

---

[1] *Solomon.* Solomon was decreed by God Himself to be David's successor. His name signifies Prince of Peace.

[2] *Gold and silver.* Which he had saved from the booty taken in war and from the income of his own possessions. There were 3000 talents of gold and 7000 talents of silver.

[3] *By the hand of the Lord.* "God has put it into my mind." As on a former occasion God gave Moses instructions as to the making of the Tabernacle (chapter XXXVIII), so now He made known to David the plan on which He desired the Temple to be built, because the Temple was to be the type of the Church of the New Testament.

Then addressing the assembled princes David said: "The work[1] is great; for a house is prepared not for man, but for God. Now, if any man is willing to offer, let him fill his hand to-day, and offer what he pleaseth to the Lord." And the princes and the people joyfully brought their gifts[2] for the Temple of the Lord.

And David rejoicing exclaimed: "Blessed art Thou, O Lord, the God of Israel, our Father from eternity to eternity. All things are Thine, and we have given Thee what we received of Thy hand. O Lord, keep for ever this will of their heart and let this mind remain always for the worship of Thee; and give to Solomon, my son, a perfect heart, that he may keep Thy Commandments." Having thus spoken, David slept in peace. He was buried in Sion (Fig. 45)[3].

COMMENTARY.

God's Omniscience. David said to Solomon: "Serve God with a perfect heart; for the Lord searcheth all hearts and thoughts of the soul."

God's Holiness. God indeed forgave David his sin, but all the same He told him that he should not build Him a Temple, because he was a man of blood.

God's Justice. "If thou forsake God", said David to Solomon, "He will cast thee off for ever."

The end of David's life. The last days of the royal prophet's life were beautiful and edifying. His only care was that a fitting Temple should be raised to the Lord, and he urged his son most earnestly to be faithful and obedient to God. And then he slept "in the Lord", i. e. in the grace of the Lord. He was able to gaze back on his active and eventful life, and leave it with the thought that he had finished his task. The task which God had given the former shepherd to do was very great and important for the development of God's kingdom upon earth. David had secured to the chosen people their possession of the Promised Land, he had disabled his enemies for a long time to come, he had strengthened the unity of the people, ordered the government of the country according to God's laws, extirpated the

---

[1] *The work.* The work of building the House of God.

[2] *Their gifts.* As formerly their forefathers had eagerly brought of their wealth for the making of the Tabernacle (chapter XXXVIII), so now did they joyfully bring splendid offerings with which to build a worthy Temple for the Lord.

[3] *Buried in Sion.* St. Peter in his first sermon on the day of Pentecost (Acts 2, 29) alludes to the fact, saying: "Ye men brethren, let me freely speak to you of the Patriarch David, that he died and was buried, *and his sepulchre is with us to this present day.*"

remnants of idolatry and advanced the worship of God by his regulations concerning it, by his example and his ever-beautiful Psalms. His prophecies concerning the Messias had quickened the spiritual life of the people, and turned their thoughts to the source of grace. He was a chosen instrument of God and, with the exception of his fall, of which he deeply repented, he lived a life well-pleasing to Him. God therefore gave him the grace of perseverance and of a happy death.

A retrospect of David's virtues: humility, confidence in God, piety, zeal for God's glory, patience, love of his enemies, justice, generosity and fatherly care of his subjects. The Holy Ghost says about him (Ecclus. 47, 10): "With his whole heart he praised the Lord and loved

Fig 45. Sepulchre of David in Sion at Jerusalem.

the God who made him." He is rightly counted among the Saints of the Old Testament and is still venerated by the Church.

David, the twelfth type of Jesus Christ. David not only foretold the sufferings and glory of the Redeemer, but was himself a type of Him. He was born at Bethlehem; he led a hidden life during his youth, and conquered Goliath with a contemptible weapon (Jesus overcame Satan by means of the despised Cross). He was persecuted by Saul, to whom he had done nothing but good; he was patient and full of love towards his enemies. He was both prophet and king; he ascended the Mount of Olives, crossing the brook Cedron, bowed down with grief; and returned triumphantly to Jerusalem (the type of the

Ascension), having gained the victory over his enemies ("sitteth at the right hand of God").

The end of man. When Solomon was anointed king, in his father's lifetime, David said to him: "Serve God with a perfect heart and willing mind." When he was dying, he thus exhorted him: "Keep the charge of the Lord thy God to walk in His ways, as is written in the law of Moses." All men, whatever their age or position may be, have one end to live for, namely to love God and serve Him by a faithful observance of His law.

The four last things. The journey of life leads to death. High and low, rich and poor, we must all die. And after death come the judgment and an eternity, either of joy in heaven or of misery in hell.

Offerings for the House of God. In Psalm 25 David says: "I have loved, O Lord, the beauty of Thy house and the place where Thy glory dwelleth." He made rich offerings to the Temple which was to be built to the Lord, and his example fired the people to make generous gifts for the same purpose. He who loves God, will gladly make offerings to Him for the building and decorating of His churches and for the splendour of His worship. What we give for such an object, is given to God. "Give to the Lord", said David when he asked for stones wherewith to build the Temple.

APPLICATION. Take to heart David's exhortations to Solomon, as much as if they had been made to yourself. Be steadfast! Hitherto you have been very inconstant. Observe everything which the Lord has commanded. On what point do you generally and chiefly transgress God's law? Pray to-day for the grace of steadfastness!

CHAPTER LVIII.

SOLOMON'S PRAYER.—HIS WISDOM.

[3 Kings 3—4.]

AFTER the death of David Solomon ascended [1] the throne. He loved the Lord, and walked in the ways of David, his father. The Lord appeared to him in a dream by night and told him to ask any favour he wished, and that it would be granted. Solomon answered: "O Lord God, Thou hast made Thy servant king instead of David, my father, and I am but a child [2]. Give therefore

---

[1] *Ascended.* He now began to govern as king, having been anointed during his father's lifetime.

[2] *A child.* Solomon, when he began to reign, was only twenty years old.

to Thy servant an understanding heart to judge Thy people and to discern between good and evil."

The Lord was pleased with his petition, and He said to him: "Because thou hast asked this thing and hast not asked for thyself long life nor riches nor the lives of thy enemies, but hast asked for thyself wisdom to discern judgment, behold, I have done for thee according to thy words and have given thee a wise and understanding heart, insomuch that there hath been no one like thee before thee, nor shall arise after thee. Yea, and the things also which thou didst not ask, I have given thee: riches and glory, so that no one hath been like thee among the kings in all days heretofore. And if thou wilt walk in my ways and keep my precepts and commandments, as thy father walked, I will lengthen thy days." And Solomon became renowned for wisdom and for power and glory.

On one occasion two women came to Solomon, asking him to decide their dispute. The first woman said: "We were living alone in a house, only we two. Now I had a child, and she had a child; and in the night when she was asleep, she overlaid her child, and it died. And rising in the dead of the night she took my child, while I, thy handmaid, was asleep, and laid her dead child in my bosom. When I arose in the morning, behold, my child was dead; but considering him more diligently when it was clear day, I found that it was not mine." Then the second woman answered: "It is not so as thou sayest, but thy child is dead and mine is alive."

But the first woman insisted that the living child was hers, and so they disputed[1] before the king. Then Solomon ordered a sword[2] to be brought to him, and when it was brought he said: "Divide the living child in two and give half to the one and half to the other." Hearing this, the woman whose child was alive, being moved to pity, cried out in terror: "I beseech thee, my lord, give her the child alive, and do not kill it."

---

[1] *Disputea.* The dispute between the women was hard to decide, because no witnesses could be called.

[2] *A sword.* The king gave this command, because he had the foresight to know that by it he would find out the true mother, and that there would be no question of its being really carried out. He rightly judged that the maternal heart of the woman would move her rather to give up her child than see it killed.

But the other said: "Let it be neither mine nor thine, but divide it."[1]

Then the king commanded the child to be given to her who would rather give it up to another than have it killed, knowing that she must be its mother. The report of this judgment having gone abroad, the people all feared the king and knew that the wisdom of God[2] was in him. How necessary it is that kings and rulers should examine in the spirit of justice and wisdom all cases brought before them!

COMMENTARY.

God's Goodness to Solomon was wonderful. What gifts did He bestow and what promises did He make the young king?

Love of God and our neighbour. Solomon, by his great virtues, had made himself worthy of God's gifts and graces. He loved God above everything and served Him with a willing heart. Moreover he loved his people and was full of zeal for their good. He therefore prayed to God to give him the gift of wisdom to enable him to govern his people well and provide for their spiritual and temporal welfare.

His humility was most pleasing to God. He showed it by his words: "Thou hast made Thy servant king, who am but a child." In him were fulfilled the words: "To the meek God will give grace" (Prov. 3, 34).

Prayer for spiritual gifts. Solomon's prayer was pleasing to God, because firstly he made it with a humble heart; and secondly because he did not pray for riches or long life, but for far higher gifts. This shows us that we must not pray only for temporal blessings, such as health or a good harvest or peace and so forth, but above all for higher and more precious gifts, such as the forgiveness of sins, virtue, and especially for the grace to do our duty in our own state of life. In the "Our Father", the model-prayer taught us by our Lord, there are five petitions for spiritual gifts, and only two for temporal gifts, the fourth and the seventh, even these two being combined with spiritual petitions. Bear in mind our Lord's exhortation and promise: "Seek ye, therefore, first the kingdom of God and His justice, and all these things shall be added unto you" (New Test. XXI).

---

[1] *Divide it.* By this hard-hearted speech Solomon knew at once that the speaker was not the mother of the living child.

[2] *The Wisdom of God.* i. e. they knew that the young king had not settled the difficult question thus skilfully and decisively by his own natural ability, but by a supernatural inspiration of God. Without this inspiration it would not have occurred to Solomon to find out the true mother in such a peculiar way.

Envy. The woman who accidentally smothered her baby, was a bad woman with no conscience. She envied the happiness of the other woman whose child was living, and would have liked the innocent baby to be killed in order that the other woman might be childless as well as herself. This shows what a cruel and hateful sin envy is.

Lies. The envious woman told the most barefaced lies in order to gain possession of the living child.

Mortal sin. The envious woman lied about a serious matter; for her object was to rob a mother of her child; and therefore her lie was a mortal sin. She sinned not only against the eighth Commandment, but also against the tenth and fifth Commandments; for in the first place she coveted the child which was its mother's dearest earthly possession, and then desired its death. All these sins proceeded from the hateful sin of envy.

The gift of wisdom. The first and highest of the gifts of the Holy Ghost, and the crown of all the others, is the gift of wisdom. God gave Solomon this gift in an extraordinary measure. Not only did he possess a knowledge of divine things, but he was versed in all human sciences, knowing the secrets of nature, the course of the stars, and the properties of beasts, plants &c. Moreover, he was gifted with the art of government; and the renown of his wisdom spread far and wide, as you will see in chapter LX.

APPLICATION. Do you pray mostly for spiritual or temporal gifts? In future pray more diligently for God's grace and especially for the seven gifts of the Holy Ghost. Pray also for the gift of the virtue most opposed to your besetting sin.

CHAPTER LIX.

THE BUILDING AND CONSECRATION OF THE TEMPLE.

[3 Kings 6—8. 2 Paralip. 5.]

IN the fourth year of his reign Solomon began to build the Temple of the Lord on Mount Moria[1] in Jerusalem. He had ten thousand men employed cutting cedars[2] on Mount Lebanon

---

[1] *Mount Moria.* On which mountain Abraham had built an altar and prepared to sacrifice his son (chapter XIII). It is situated to the north-east of Mount Sion, being separated from it by a valley.

[2] *Cedars.* The cedar is the king of the pine-tribe; its wood is durable, sweet smelling and does not get worm-eaten. The great stones which were necessary for the building of the Temple also came from Lebanon. The materials for building were taken to the sea-coast, at either Tyre or Sidon, there put on vessels or rafts, and taken to Joppe and thence to Jerusalem.

(Fig. 46). Seventy thousand were engaged in carrying the materials to the site of the Temple. Eighty thousand were hewing stones, while three thousand three hundred were employed as overseers of the work.

The vast number of persons employed corresponded with the grandeur and magnificence of the house of God, the general plan of which was that of the Tabernacle[1]. In other respects, however, the Tabernacle could not be compared with the Temple, which was sixty cubits long, twenty cubits wide, and thirty cubits

Fig. 46. Cedars on Mount Lebanon. (Phot. Bonfils.)

high. The house was built of stones hewed and made ready, so that when it was in building, neither hammer nor any iron tool was heard. Then there were besides porches and galleries running all around it, and two large courts[2] for the priests and the people.

---

[1] *The Tabernacle.* Which is described in chapter XXXVIII.

[2] *Two large courts.* The inner one for the priests, and the outer one for the people. The outer court was surrounded by high walls, on the inner side of which were built houses, several stories high, to serve as dwellings for the Priests

The porch before the Temple was twenty cubits in length, and ten cubits in breadth. The inner walls were lined with planks of cedar, on which were carved cherubim and palm-trees and divers flowers, all standing out, as it were, from the wall, so skilfully were they carved. All the furniture [1] was of the purest gold. The walls and floor of the Holy of Holies were covered with plates of fine gold, fastened by nails of gold.

When, after seven years, Solomon had finished the Temple, he assembled all the ancients of Israel with the princes of the tribes, to carry the Ark of the Covenant in triumph to the Temple. And all the people marched before the Ark in an ecstasy of joy and religious fervour, making peace-offerings to the Lord at every step they took. The Levites played on the harp and cymbal and many other instruments of music, while a hundred and twenty priests sounded the trumpet.

And the multitude sang in one grand chorus: "Praise the Lord, for He is good, and His mercy endureth for ever." Then the Ark having arrived at the gates of the Temple, only the priests who carried it entered in, and they brought it to the Holy of Holies, and the cherubim shaded it with their wings. And the majesty of God in the form of a cloud [2] filled the Temple, so that the priest could not stand to minister, because of the dazzling glory thereof.

Then Solomon, arrayed in his richest robes, fell on his face before the altar of holocausts, and stretching out his hands he said: "Lord God of Israel, there is no God like Thee in heaven or on earth. If heaven and the heaven of heavens cannot contain Thee, how much less this house which I have built! O Lord my God, hear the hymn and the prayer which Thy servant prayeth before Thee this day, that Thy eyes may be open upon this house night and day, that Thou mayest hearken to the prayer which Thy servant prayeth in this place to Thee. Mayest Thou hearken to Thy people when they pray in this place. Mayest Thou hear them and show them mercy."

---

and Levites. In the inner or priests' court were the altar of holocausts, and the great laver which on account of its enormous size was called the "molten sea". It measured ten cubits across and contained 10,000 gallons of water.

[1] *The furniture.* Such as the table of proposition, the seven-branched candlestick, cans, and thuribles.

[2] *A cloud.* In which the glory of the Lord was present (chapter XXXVIII).

Solomon's prayer being ended, fire fell from heaven und consumed[1] the holocaust. Seeing this, the Israelites fell prostrate on the ground and adored the great God of heaven, who wrought such wonders before them, and they went away praising His awful name. The Lord appeared a second time[2] to Solomon and said: "I have heard thy prayer, and I have sanctified[3] this house which thou hast built; and My eyes and My heart shall be always there."

COMMENTARY. (Compare with chapter XXXVIII.)

God is infinitely Great or Immense and is not subject to the limits of space or time, for both were created by Him. He is present everywhere in heaven and on earth, but neither heaven nor earth can contain Him who is infinite and immeasurable.

God is Good and Merciful. The Levites sang: "Praise the Lord, for He is good, and His mercy endureth for ever." The story we have just read shows forth His goodness. He came in the cloud and took possession of the Temple, to dwell there in an especial manner. He was pleased with Solomon's prayer and sacrifice. He appeared to Solomon, and promised Him that the Temple should be a holy place, and that He would hearken to those who prayed therein.

Exterior worship. Our worship of God must have an outward expression; for everything which moves our hearts (as, for instance, anger) shows itself outwardly. The Israelites expressed their worship of God by solemn processions, by canticles, by praying aloud, by genuflections, by uplifting of the hands and by sacrifices. And God was pleased with these outward expressions of worship, because they came from the heart.

The necessity of places of worship. God needs no house nor church, but *we* must have places where we can worship Him in common and praise Him and ask for blessings; so that it is on our account that God requires places of worship. For this cause He Himself designed the Tabernacle and later on the Temple. The Israelites could worship God everywhere; but in the Temple He was present in an especial manner, to listen to prayers and grant graces, and they were therefore commanded to visit the Temple. By the second Commandment of the Church, visiting churches is imposed on us as a duty.

---

[1] *Consumed.* This was a sign that God was well-pleased with the sacrifices and the prayer.

[2] *A second time.* For an account of the first time God appeared to Solomon see chapter LVIII.

[3] *Sanctified.* By My presence.

The Sanctity of Catholic churches. The Israelites had only one Temple: we have many churches. Although the Temple at Jerusalem was exceptionally beautiful and costly, the poorest Catholic chapel is far holier and richer, because in our churches the holy Sacraments are dispensed, and because, above all other reasons, our Lord Jesus Christ, with His Divinity and Humanity, is there present and, in the Mass, offers Himself for us to His Heavenly Father. As St. Chrysostom beautifully says: "If we could open the heaven of heavens, we should find nothing greater or more holy than that which reposes on our altars." We ought to have the utmost veneration for our churches, and visit them diligently and devoutly. King Solomon threw himself on his knees in the outer court of the Temple and raised his arms to God in prayer; and shall we be ashamed to kneel down before the Blessed Sacrament and devoutly clasp our hands?

The Consecration of churches. Our churches are solemnly consecrated. Thereby they are sanctified to be the property and dwelling-place of God and the abode of grace. In memory of its consecration or dedication, and as a thanksgiving for the benefits it has brought to us, it is usual to keep every year the feast of the dedication of a church. On that anniversary we have more cause than had the Israelites to say: "Praise the Lord, for He is good, and His mercy endureth for ever."

The Presence of Jesus Christ in the Blessed Sacrament. God was present to the Israelites in a visible cloud in the Temple; and therefore the Temple was in very deed "a dwelling-place of God among men". Now, after God had become Man, would He have removed Himself further from us than He was from the Israelites? Are we to have no dwelling-place of God in our midst? Is nothing to be left to us Christians but the bare memory of God made Man? No! It would be inconceivable that God, after His Incarnation, should be less approachable than He was before it! Jesus Christ would not leave us orphans; therefore He has remained with us, being present on our altars under the visible appearances of bread and wine in the Blessed Sacrament. There He is in the Tabernacle, His Eyes and His Heart beholding those who come to adore Him. If Jesus were not present in the Most Holy Sacrament, then those who lived under the Old Testament would have been better off than we who are living under the New Testament, and we should, perforce, envy the Israelites with whom God was present in at least one Temple.

APPLICATION. Visit your Divine Saviour present in the church. Visit Him this very day. Pray to Him with devotion and faith, and thank Him for the love which makes Him dwell with us, offer Himself up for us, and give Himself to us as the food of our souls.

CHAPTER LX.

SOLOMON'S MAGNIFICENCE.—HIS APOSTASY
AND ITS PUNISHMENT.

[3 Kings 9—11. 2 Paralip. 9.]

BESIDES the Temple which he erected to the Lord, Solomon built for himself a palace[1] of wonderful magnificence. His throne was of ivory, overlaid with the finest gold. It had six steps, and at the two ends of each step there stood a lion: six to the right and six to the left—in all twelve lions. But the top of the throne was round and had a large lion, well made, on either side. And Solomon made two hundred shields of the purest gold and hung them in his palace.

All the vessels out of which the king drank were of gold, and all the furniture of his house was likewise of gold. In the days of Solomon there was no silver; no account was made of it, because the royal fleet brought from foreign countries[2] riches of all kinds and precious metals in abundance. Solomon built several new cities; he beautified and strengthened Jerusalem, so that, with few exceptions, it surpassed all the cities of that time in beauty and splendour.

And Solomon reigned from the Euphrates to the confines of Egypt, and he was at peace with his neighbours on every side, and each man rested without fear under his own vine and fig-tree. Kings from far and near showed Solomon respect[3] and sent him presents. The queen of Saba[4] came herself from her far distant land to behold his magnificence and hear the words of his wisdom. When she had seen and heard, her spirit failed and she said to the king: "The report is true which I heard in my own country, but I would not believe. Blessed are thy servants who stand before thee and hear thy wisdom." Thus did Solomon exceed all the kings of the earth in riches and in wisdom[5].

---

[1] *Palace.* Or castle.

[2] *Foreign countries.* Especially from India and Spain.

[3] *Respect.* And desired to see him.

[4] *Saba.* In Arabia.

[5] *Wisdom.* Solomon's wisdom is shown forth in his written books, namely the Book of Proverbs, Ecclesiastes or the Preacher, and the Canticle of Canticles. These were written under the inspiration of the Holy Ghost and form part of the

But glorious as was the beginning of Solomon's reign, his end was deplorable. Solomon was far advanced in life when his heart was corrupted by pagan women; and that king, hitherto so wise, became so blind and depraved that, in order to please these women, he offered incense to false gods and built temples to them.

The Lord being angry said to Solomon: "Because[1] thou hast done this and hast not kept My covenant and My precepts, which I have commanded thee, I will divide and rend thy kingdom. Nevertheless in thy days I will not do it for David, thy father's, sake; neither will I take away the whole kingdom, but I will give one tribe to thy son, for the sake of David, my servant, and for the sake of Jerusalem, which I have chosen."

Then secret revolt and sedition arose among the people, because Solomon, blinded as he was, had over-taxed and oppressed the people, to build palaces for the heathen women who had turned him away from God. Things were in this unhappy state[2] when Solomon died, having reigned forty years; and he, who had been a great and powerful king while he walked in the ways of David his father, died without honour.

COMMENTARY.

The First Commandment: Sins against faith. It causes real pain to read that a man so gifted with grace as Solomon could have fallen so low. Look back and think what he was at the dedication of the Temple, and how he cast himself on his knees and prayed so beautifully to the ever present God; and then think of his becoming indifferent about the worship of the true God, of his building temples to the false gods of his wives, and of his tolerating idolatry! It is impossible for us to conceive that Solomon ever believed in and worshipped idols himself; but it is certain that, for the sake of his heathen wives and against his own convictions, he sanctioned idolatry and even enforced it! By so doing he denied his faith and offended his people. Thus

Canon of Holy Scripture. The first of the three contains wise sayings and rules of life; the second preaches the vanity of all earthly things; and the third sings of the love of God for His spouse the Church.

[1] *Because.* The reason why the great and glorious monarchy was divided into two kingdoms (Israel and Juda) was the sin of apostasy on the part of Solomon. His rebellion against God brought about the rebellion of his people against himself.

[2] *State.* His kingdom was crumbling to pieces, for the other tribes of Israel were jealous of Juda; and moreover several subjected nations were in a state of rebellion.

he sinned both by being indifferent about the true faith and by denying it.

Worldliness and pride lead to religious indifference. But how was it possible that the wise and devout Solomon could offend God so grievously? He gave himself over to worldliness, led a sensual, luxurious life, and set his affections on the earthly riches with which God had endowed him. His love for God grew cold, his zeal for prayer and the service of God grew weak, and he became lax and indifferent about religion. Intercourse and friendship with the pagan kings of Tyre and Sidon and his unlawful intermarriage with pagan wives increased his religious indifference; and besides this the universal admiration of which he was the object made him proud, so that he became less and less worthy of divine grace. He lost the grace necessary for perseverance in good and sank so low that he denied the true faith and upheld idolatry!

Happiness and riches are dangerous. Trials are wholesome. Solomon's sad fall shows us how difficult it is to fear God and persevere in good in the midst of happiness, riches, honours and pleasures. Those with whom everything goes well love the world and earthly possessions, forget the end for which they were made, cease to love God and often lose belief in Him and His revelation. This is why God, in His merciful wisdom, sends us sufferings, so as to prevent our being arrogant and forgetful of God and His holy Commandments. These sufferings sent are real benefits to us and are a proof of the love which God has for our immortal souls, and of the desire He has to draw us to heaven. "Whom the Lord loveth He chasteneth" (Hebr. 12, 6).

Solomon, the thirteenth type of Jesus Christ. Solomon was also a type of Jesus Christ, but in a different way from the preceding ones. While for instance Abel, Noe, Isaac, Joseph, Job, Moses and David were typical of the suffering Redeemer, in Solomon we find a type of the glorified Redeemer. His very name, signifying peace, presents him to us as a type of Him who is the true Prince of Peace. By his wonderful wisdom Solomon was a faint type of Him "in whom are hid all the treasures of wisdom and knowledge" (Col. 2, 3). Likewise the riches of Solomon point to the immeasurable riches of grace of our Lord Jesus Christ. Solomon built the Temple of strong and well-hewn stones: Jesus Christ founded the spiritual temple, the Church, on the rock of Peter and on the Apostles, making it one united whole. The queen of Saba came to Solomon, to testify her reverence for him, and load him with presents: to our Lord came the three Magi from the East to adore Him and offer Him costly gifts. Solomon, seated in majesty on his lofty and magnificent throne, ruled over many nations. Jesus Christ, raised on the throne of heaven and sitting at the right hand of God the Father, rules with divine majesty over all the nations of the earth and over the whole host of heaven.

The conversion of Solomon. Most of the Fathers of the Church are of opinion that, when troubles overtook him towards the close of his life, Solomon was converted and did penance, and thus was not eternally lost.

True happiness. Towards the end of his life Solomon wrote these words in the Book of Ecclesiastes: "Vanity of vanities, all is vanity. I made me great works, I built me houses and planted vineyards. I made gardens and orchards and set them with trees of all kinds. I heaped together for myself silver and gold. I made me singing men and singing women. I surpassed in riches all that were before me in Jerusalem; my wisdom also remained with me. Whatsoever my eyes desired, I refused them not; and I withheld not my heart from enjoying every pleasure. I saw in all things vanity and vexation of mind. Fear God and keep His Commandments, for this is all man." By these words he meant to say: "All earthly possessions and joys are passing and cannot make a man really happy. Only the fear and love of God can bring happiness on earth and joy in eternity." We should not therefore set our hearts on the good things of this earth, but should strive with all our hearts after those which are eternal.

Means of perseverance. He who desires to avoid grievous sin and to persevere to the end in what is right must, firstly, refrain from pleasure-seeking and laxity; secondly, he must avoid all intercourse with bad companions; thirdly, he must be humble and pray to God for the grace of final perseverance; for this most important of all graces can be obtained only by prayer.

APPLICATION. Solomon served God for many years and received the gift of wisdom from Him; and yet how deeply he fell!

Do you desire to stand fast in what is right? Then distrust yourself and be watchful. "Watch and pray that you enter not into temptation." Pray often for the grace of perseverance.

CHAPTER LXI.

DIVISION OF THE KINGDOM.

[3 Kings 12. 2 Paralip. 10.]

AFTER the death of Solomon all the people[1] of Israel came to Roboam, his son, and said: "Thy father laid a grievous yoke[2] upon us, do thou take off a little of his most heavy yoke,

---

[1] *All the people.* The representatives of all Israel. They had assembled themselves at Sichem, where Roboam went to receive their homage.

[2] *Yoke.* Heavy taxes.

and we will serve thee." Roboam told them to come back on the third day, and he would give them his answer. He then took counsel with the ancients of the people who had stood before Solomon, his father, as to what course he should pursue. The ancients advised the king, saying: "If thou wilt yield to this people and speak gentle words to them, they will be thy servants[1] always." Roboam, not satisfied with this advice of the old men, betook himself to the young men who were his own companions, and asked what they would counsel him to do. The young men who had been brought up with him said: "Thus shalt thou speak to this people: My father put a heavy yoke upon you, but I will add to your yoke; my father beat you with whips, but I will beat you with scorpions."[2] When the people had returned on the third day for an answer, Roboam spoke to them as the young men had advised. Then, seeing that they had nothing to expect from their new king, ten of the tribes threw off his authority and chose for their king Jeroboam, who had been a servant[3] of Solomon. Only the two tribes of Juda and Benjamin[4] remained with Roboam. From that day forth the people of Israel were divided into two kingdoms, that of Juda and that of Israel[5].

Jerusalem continued to be the capital of Juda, while Samaria became the capital of Israel. But the effects of the separation went still further; for Jeroboam, king of Israel, thought within himself, that if the people continued to go up to Jerusalem to offer sacrifice to the Lord in His Temple, their hearts would turn

---

[1] *Thy servants.* They will obey you as loyal subjects.

[2] *With scorpions.* The scourges generally used were made of leather, but sometimes, to inflict a more severe punishment, thorns and spikes were twisted in with the leather, and such spiked scourges were known by the name of scorpions. Roboam wished to say: "I will be even harsher to you than my father was." The arrogant young king wished to bend and intimidate his subjects by this senseless threat.

[3] *A servant.* Appointed by Solomon to be tax-gatherer of the tribe of Ephraim.

[4] *Juda and Benjamin.* To these two tribes the Levites joined themselves, as also many members of the other tribes who adhered to the worship of the true God at Jerusalem. The two kingdoms were about equal in strength, for Juda (to which was attached the tribe of Benjamin) was the most numerous and powerful of all the tribes; though, as far as extent of territory went, the northern kingdom, Israel, was superior to the southern kingdom of Juda.

[5] *Israel.* The whole united kingdom had hitherto been known by the name of Israel, but from henceforward only the ten tribes are to be understood by the name.

again to Roboam, and the kingdom of Israel would surely return to the house of David.

To avoid this danger he made two golden calves, which he placed at the two extremities of his kingdom, one at Dan[1], and the other at Bethel[2], and told the people that they should not go up to Jerusalem to worship, for that these were the gods which had brought them out of Egypt. In this way[3] he led the people into idolatry, for they repaired to the places pointed out to them by their king, and worshipped the golden calves.

On the other hand Roboam, king of Juda, who had seen with grief the defection of the ten tribes, was all his life making war on Jeroboam. This state of continued warfare was kept up by their successors on both sides, and more than once the aid of foreign nations was called in by one or the other. In this way did these wicked kings cause much sin and misery among their people.

Even the kings of Juda soon fell into idolatry, and the people, following their example, forgot the worship of the true God and gave themselves up to all manner of wickedness. Thus it went on till destruction overtook both kingdoms[4].

COMMENTARY.

The Faithfulness of God. See how the punishment threatened in chapter LX was now brought to pass! Roboam's arrogance led to the accomplishment of God's designs, by alienating the ten tribes. It was not that God *willed* the sin, but that He *permitted* it, in order that Solomon's faithlessness should be punished as He had said.

Arrogance and flattery. Roboam's conduct towards his subjects was very unwise; for it was his harsh answer to their appeal which drove them into rebellion. How could Roboam, the son of the wise Solomon, commit such a folly? He spoke and acted thus foolishly,

---

[1] *Dan.* See Map, east of Tyre.

[2] *Bethel.* See Map, north of Jerusalem.

[3] *In this way.* i. e. by this false policy, arguing that if the people went up to Jerusalem to offer sacrifice in the Temple and thus maintained a spiritual union with Juda, they would before long be wishing for a national union and separate themselves from him.

[4] *Both kingdoms.* The kingdom of Israel lasted for 253 years (from 975 (?) to 722 B. C.), and during that time it had nineteen kings, belonging to ten different families, who all did evil in the sight of God.

The kingdom of Juda lasted 387 years, till the year 588 B. C. It had twenty kings, all of the family of David, of whom the greater number were wicked.

firstly, because he was blinded by pride; secondly, because he would not take the advice of the wise, but followed instead that of his young companions, who took care to flatter his pride. You can see by this how passion makes a man blind, and how disastrous it is to listen to the voice of unscrupulous flatterers. "He that walketh with the wise, shall be wise: a friend of fools shall become like them" (Prov. 13, 20).

Gentleness. If Roboam had returned a kind, friendly answer to the people, he would have conciliated them, and all the twelve tribes would have acknowledged him as their king. "A mild answer breaketh wrath: but a harsh word stirreth up fury" (Prov. 15, 1). "Blessed are the meek."

Schism. The ten tribes sinned by rebelling against the throne of David, and their sin was all the greater, because their defection from the house of David implied a defection from the future Messias and a renunciation of the promises of God.

Partaking in the guilt of others. His young advisers shared in the guilt of Roboam's sin and in its evil consequences, by urging him to a hard and cruel course of action. Jeroboam committed a terrible sin when he incited the people to idolatry and induced them to apostatize from the true God. God punished him by the overthrow of his whole family. Jeroboam's son, Nadab, only reigned two years. Then a rebellion against him broke out, and the whole house of Jeroboam was destroyed.

APPLICATION. Are you fond of being with giddy companions? Do you follow their advice in preference to the injunctions and exhortations of older and more prudent persons? Do you listen to the voice of your passions rather than to that of your conscience? Roboam lost the larger part of his kingdom, because he listened to the unprincipled advice of flatterers. So, if you like the company of those who are unprincipled, you will lose both faith and innocence, which are more valuable than a whole kingdom. Therefore avoid bad companions.

CHAPTER LXII.

GOD RAISES UP PROPHETS.—MISSION OF THE PROPHET ELIAS.

[3 Kings 17.]

IN order to bring back the kings and the people to better sentiments, God raised up, at different times, holy persons who are known as prophets[1]. These prophets preached penance in a

---

[1] *Prophets.* (A Greek word meaning "one who speaks out" to people in the name of God.) They were men of God who led a life of penance, wore coarse

very impressive manner, and they proved the truth of their divine mission by working great miracles.

God revealed to them many future events. They predicted the principal circumstances of the birth, life, passion, death and glory of the Messias. One of the most celebrated of the prophets was Elias. He lived in the reign of Achab [1], king of Israel. This king was very wicked. None of his predecessors had committed so many crimes as he.

Fig. 47. God Moloch.
Terracotta bust, found in Palestine.
(After Vincent.)

He had married a Gentile woman named Jezabel; and he had built a temple to Baal and had consecrated to the service of that false god four hundred and fifty priests, whilst he had caused the priests of the Lord to be put to death. In a word, his intention seemed to be to destroy the true religion entirely among the ten tribes.

Elias, clad in a rough sheep's skin and with a staff in his hand, presented himself before Achab and said: "As the Lord liveth, the God of Israel, in whose sight I stand, there shall not be dew nor rain these three years, but according to the words of my mouth." Achab was very angry to hear these words of the prophet, and secretly resolved to put Elias to death.

Then the Lord, knowing the evil intention of the king, commanded Elias to go and conceal himself near the brook Carith [2],

---

clothing, prayed and fasted. They were sent by God to maintain the true faith and the observance of His Commandments, and to bring back the people to Him. They announced the judgments which would fall on king and people if they were not converted, and they pointed onwards to the hope of Israel, the Redeemer, foretelling many things about Him. It was chiefly on account of these prophecies that they were called prophets.

[1] *Achab.* Achab, the 7th king of Israel, reigned from 923 to 902 (?) B.C. Jezabel was daughter to the king of Sidon. At her request Achab built in Samaria a temple to the sun-god Baal and, besides the worship of calves, introduced the horrible worship of Baal and of Moloch (Fig. 47), to whom children were offered up in sacrifice. Added to this he killed the priests of God. Thus there was every fear that the true faith would be entirely eradicated. For this cause God raised up the prophet Elias, that through him the true faith might be preserved in Israel.

[2] *The brook Carith.* This brook flows into the Jordan from the east, through a country full of forests and caverns. Here Elias could easily hide himself, even if the king searched the whole country through for him.

in the vicinity of the Jordan. The prophet obeyed, and behold, the ravens[1] brought him bread or flesh every morning and every evening for many days: and he drank of the torrent.

Some time after the brook ran dry[2], and the Lord commanded Elias to go to Sarepta (Fig. 48)[3], a city of Sidon. Elias went accordingly, and when he drew near the gate of the city he saw a woman gathering sticks[4], and he called her and said: "Give me a little water in a vessel that I may drink."

Fig. 48. Place where ancient Sarepta stood. (Phot. Bonfils.)

As the woman was going to fetch it he called after her: "Bring me also a morsel of bread." She answered: "As the Lord thy God[5] liveth, I have no bread, but only a handful of meal in a pot and a little oil in a cruse; I am gathering two sticks that

---

[1] *The ravens.* From whence did they get this food? The Lord who commanded them to bring it provided for that (St. Augustine).

[2] *Ran dry.* Because no rain had fallen for a long time.

[3] *Sarepta.* See Map: between Tyre and Sidon.

[4] *Sticks.* To make a fire.

[5] *Thy God.* She recognised Elias to be an Israelite, and swore by the living God; for she believed in Him, though she was living in the midst of the pagan Sidonians.

I may go and dress it for me and my son, that we may eat it and die." [1]

The prophet assured her saying: "Fear not, but go and do as thou hast said; but first make for me [2] of the same meal a little hearth-cake. For thus saith the Lord: 'The pot of meal shall not waste nor the cruse of oil be diminished until the day wherein the Lord will give rain upon the earth.'"

The woman did as Elias had told her, and from that day forth she had meal in her pot and oil in her cruse and knew no want, neither Elias nor she nor her son. Now it happened some time after that the son of this poor woman of Sarepta fell sick and died. She said to the prophet: "What have I done to thee, thou man of God? Hast thou come to me that my iniquities should be remembered?" Thereupon Elias took the child and went into the upper chamber, and laid it upon his own bed. Then he cried [3] to the Lord: "O Lord, hast Thou also afflicted the widow with whom I am after a sort maintained?" Then he stretched himself and measured himself three times upon the child; and the soul of the boy returned and he revived.

Elias took the child and brought him down to his mother and said: "Behold, thy son liveth." Full of joy and gratitude the woman exclaimed: "Now by this I know that thou art a man of God, and the word of the Lord in thy mouth is true."

COMMENTARY.

The Mercy of God. Of His mercy He did not entirely reject the faithless Israelites, but sent His prophets to them from time to time to give them a chance of repentance and pardon.

The Omniscience of God. The prophets were inspired by God, or else they would not have been able to foretell the future. The future is known only to God, with whom times and seasons are as nothing.

The Omnipresence of God. "As the Lord liveth in whose sight I stand", said Elias to Achab. Wherever we are or go, God is with us. Elias lived in the constant recollection of God's presence, and this it was that gave him courage and consolation under persecution and when in danger of death. He did not feel himself deserted even in the cave of Carith, because God was with him.

---

[1] *Die.* Of hunger.

[2] *Make for me.* By acting thus Elias put the faith and charity of the widow to a very severe test.

[3] *Cried.* i. e. prayed aloud and fervently.

The Omnipotence of God. Winds and clouds, dew and rain obey Him, and by His command a terrible drought pervaded Israel for three years and a half. The unreasoning ravens did His will, and twice each day brought food to the prophet of God. "The most ravenous of birds", says St. Basil, "were compelled to supply the prophet with food; and they, whose nature it was to seize the food of others, waited on the man of God. Completely forgetful of their nature, they obeyed the divine behest." It was by God's almighty will that the meal in the widow's pot and the oil in her cruse remained undiminished. And He who is Lord of life and death called the widow's son back to life, commanding his soul to return to his dead body.

The Goodness of God. God lovingly provided for the safety of His persecuted servant, hid him from Achab's bloodthirsty emissaries, and fed him by a continuous miracle in the desert. He protected him on his perilous journey to Sarepta, increased the meal and oil by a miracle for the sustenance of himself and the widow, and called the poor woman's dead son back to life.

Justice and Mercy. The long drought which was sent by God at the prayer of Elias (James 5, 17 &c.), was a miracle both of divine justice and of divine mercy. On the one hand it most justly punished the idolatrous king and people; on the other hand it proved to the Israelites that the fruits of the earth did not come from Baal, but from God, who is the Lord of heaven and earth. The famine was sent to them as a means of inducing them to return to the true faith.

Confidence in God. Elias showed admirable courage by fearlessly announcing the impending judgment. The prophet drew his courage from his great confidence in God, giving himself over entirely to His gracious guidance. When the brook dried up, he gave way neither to fear nor lamentation. He did not say: "Now I must die of thirst", but on the contrary he said to himself: "God will help me." When he was sent to the poor widow of Sarepta, a town in the kingdom of Sidon, he might naturally have thought: "Why am I to go among Jezabel's people? Are they not sure to kill me? And why am I to go to a poor widow? How can she support me? Why should I not seek hospitality of some rich person?" But the holy man of God gave ear to no such doubts and obeyed God's commands with simplicity and confidence. It is in this way that we ought always to trust in God.

Faith. Achab and his people would not believe Elias when he foretold the coming drought. On the other hand the Gentile woman did believe the promise which he made to her in God's name. To find faith the prophet of God had to go into a heathen country. It was hard for the widow, herself dying of hunger, to be told to divide her last morsel of food with the prophet; but she did so, because she believed and obeyed a secret inspiration of God; and God rewarded her faith and charity by miraculously increasing her meal and oil, by restoring her dead son to life, and by confirming her in the true faith. Works of mercy dráw down on us the grace of God.

The power of prayer. At Elias's prayer the heavens were shut, so that no rain fell for a long time. By prayer he raised the dead boy to life. At the brook Carith he spent his days in prayer and contemplation. His prayer was efficacious, firstly, because he prayed with devotion, humility and confidence; and secondly because he was a just man, lived in the grace of God, and avoided sin.

The soul is the life of the body (chapter III). As soon as the soul is separated from the body, the latter dies; and if the dead body is to be restored to life, the soul must return to it. It was thus therefore that Elias prayed: "Let the soul &c."

The raising of the widow's son by Elias is, according to St. Augustine, a type of the spiritual resurrection of the sinful world through Christ. The world lay dead in sin; but Jesus Christ has restored it to life by stretching Himself on the cross.

As Elias stretched himself three times on the body of the boy, breathing on his face, so, when administering holy Baptism, the priest bows himself three times over the person to be baptized and breathes upon him, as a sign that by sanctifying grace the soul is raised to a supernatural state of life.

APPLICATION. Do you pray willingly and devoutly? He who wishes to pray well, must accustom himself to pray diligently. Each time you pray, place yourself in the presence of God and say: "Lord, help me to pray."

Could you not sometimes give an alms or do some service of love to your fellow-men, either to your comrades or to some sick or poor person? Make a resolution to do something of the sort to-day.

CHAPTER LXIII.

THE SACRIFICE OF ELIAS.

[3 Kings 18.]

AFTER the earth had remained three years[1] and six months without rain or dew, the Lord spoke to Elias: "Go and show thyself to Achab that I may give rain upon the face of

---

[1] *Three years.* During these three years and a half nothing could grow, so that both men and beasts were in a state of great want. Many died, for the necessaries of life, brought in from other countries, cost a great deal. In the third year of the famine Achab said to the governor of his house: "Go into the land unto all fountains of water and into all valleys, to see if we can find grass and

the earth." The prophet obeyed. When Achab saw him, he said: "Art thou he that troublest Israel?" The prophet answered: "I have not troubled Israel, but thou and thy father's house, who have forsaken the Commandments of the Lord and followed Baalim. Nevertheless send now and gather unto me all Israel unto Mount Carmel (Fig. 49)[1], and the prophets of Baal, four hundred and fifty, and the prophets of the groves, four hundred."

Fig. 49. Mount Carmel. (Phot. Bonfils.)

Achab obeyed[2], being afraid to do otherwise, on account of the famine that was everywhere, and he went himself to the mountain. Then Elias spoke to the people of Israel saying: "How

save the horses and mules, that the beasts may not utterly perish" (3 Kings 18, 5). By this we can see how great the want was. Trees were withered, meadows burnt up, gardens and fields bare. Nothing green was to be seen, and the parched earth cried out for life-giving rain.

    [1] *Mount Carmel.* Mount Carmel is situated to the north of Samaria, projecting into the Mediterranean, where it terminates in Cape Carmel (see Map). The sacrifice of Elias took place on one of the heights of the chain. There stands, not far from the sea, a famous Carmelite Monastery.

    [2] *Obeyed.* He accepted the proposal of the man of God, being forced thereto by the need of his subjects.

long do you halt between two sides[1]? If the Lord[2] be God, follow Him; but if Baal, then follow him."

The people, feeling the justice of his reproach, made no answer[3]. They were ashamed and afraid. Elias then added: "I only remain a prophet of the Lord, but the prophets of Baal are four hundred and fifty men. Let two bullocks be given us; and let them choose one bullock for themselves, and cut it in pieces, but put no fire under; and I will dress the other bullock, and lay it on wood, and put no fire under it. Call ye on the names of your gods, and I will call on the name of my Lord; and the God that shall answer by fire, let him be the God." All the people answered: "A very good proposal".

Then the priests of Baal, clad in their richest garments and crowned with laurel, took an ox and slew him. They erected an altar, placed the dead ox upon it, and danced around it crying out: "Baal, hear us." This they did from morning until noon, but no fire came to consume their sacrifice. Then Elias, mocking them, called out: "Cry with a louder voice: for he is a god, and perhaps he is talking with some one, or on a journey, or he is asleep and must be awaked."

Then they began to cry louder[4] than ever, hacking their bodies with knives[5], as they were accustomed to do, until they were covered with blood. This they kept up till evening, but all in vain[6]. Then Elias told the people to come to him. And he erected an altar to the Lord; took twelve stones[7] and laid the wood in order upon them, then placed the ox which had been cut in pieces on the wood.

---

[1] *Two sides.* i. e. why do you waver to and fro between God and Baal? They wished to serve two masters, God and Baal; and for this reason Elias bade them come to a decision.

[2] *Lord.* i. e. Jehova, whom your fathers worshipped.

[3] *No answer.* Because on the one hand they could not excuse themselves, and on the other they did not wish to sever themselves from the worship of Baal and the pleasures accompanying it.

[4] *Louder.* They did not notice the scorn contained in the words of Elias, for they really believed that their god slept and travelled like a man.

[5] *With knives.* They cut themselves till the blood flowed, in the hope that this would move Baal to listen to them.

[6] *In vain.* Why? Because Baal was the creation of their fancy. The absurdity of idolatry was now made manifest.

[7] *Twelve stones.* Why twelve? Because they represented the twelve tribes of which the chosen people consisted.

He then poured water[1] upon the victim till it ran down on every side and filled the trench around the altar. This being done, he said: "O Lord God, show this day that Thou art the God of Israel, and I Thy servant, and that according to Thy commandment I have done all these things. Hear me, O Lord, hear me; that this Thy people may learn that Thou art the Lord God, and that Thou hast turned their hearts again."[2]

That instant fire came down[3] from heaven and consumed the holocaust, the wood, the stones and the water in the trench. The people, having witnessed this prodigy, fell on their faces[4], exclaiming: "The Lord He is God! The Lord He is God!" And the prophet, retiring from the multitude, went up alone to the top of the mountain where he prostrated himself before the Lord in praise and thanksgiving.

Then he besought the Lord to refresh the earth with water. And behold, a little cloud arose from the sea, no bigger than the foot of a man, and it spread itself gradually over the heavens, and rain fell in abundance.

COMMENTARY.

The object of miracles. The extraordinary drought, lasting for three years and a half, was the effect of God's interrupting by miracle the law which He Himself gave to nature. The drought was sent both as a punishment to Achab and the people for their idolatry, and as a means of their conversion. The silence however of the people, when Elias demanded of them a confession of faith, shows that pagan opinions were still dominant among them. The priests of the true God had been killed, so that there was no one to teach the truth to the poor people; and the priests of Baal, whom the king upheld, taught them that the famine had been sent by Baal as a punishment for their lack of staunchness in the pagan belief. But God in His mercy worked new and startling miracles to convince the deluded people of the folly of idolatry and to help them to return to the true faith. It was in

---

[1] *Poured water.* He did this to prove that the fire was due to no natural causes.

[2] *Turned their hearts again.* The object of his prayer is that the bystanders and all the people should be converted and come back to the true God.

[3] *Fire came down.* It fell from a cloudless sky, for not even the smallest cloud was to be seen, as we know by the conclusion of the story.

[4] *Fell on their faces.* They were now convinced of the impotence of Baal and of the omnipotence of God. Therefore they fell on their faces and worshipped Jehova.

the presence of them all that He rained down this wonderful fire from a cloudless sky, which consumed even the wet stones of the altar. As soon as the people, overwhelmed by the stupendous miracle, fell on their faces and adored Him, confessing aloud their faith in Him, by another miracle He sent the wished-for rain, so that all men might know that the drought had come from Him, and that from Him came help and salvation. But it was also for our benefit and instruction that this great miracle was wrought, in order that none of us may waver in our faith in the merciful, just and almighty God. It teaches us that God is the Lord of all the universe, that all the powers of nature, rain and drought, dews and clouds, obey Him. We may sow and plant, but the increase comes from God.

Firm faith. Like a very rock of faith and confidence Elias confronted the wavering multitude, the unbelieving king, and the frantic idolatrous priests. He reproached the people for their indecision; he mocked the insane superstitions and vain efforts of the priests of Baal, and never doubted for one instant that God would hear his prayer and confound his enemies.

Fortitude. Achab hated Elias, and his hatred was increased by the long drought which he attributed to the prophet. Elias knew of the hatred borne him by the king; nevertheless, at the Lord's bidding, he fearlessly confronted him. He showed equal fortitude when he challenged the priests of Baal in the face of all the people. If God had not heard his prayer and sent fire from heaven, he would most certainly have been killed; but his ardent faith and zeal for God's glory induced him to risk his life in the hope of bringing back the people from their sad defection.

The power of prayer. It was at the prayer of Elias that God worked the wonderful miracle which has been described. For this reason St. James cites the prayer of Elias as an example of efficacious prayer. He says (5, 16, 18): "The continual prayer of a just man availeth much. Elias was a man passible like unto us: and with prayer he prayed that it might not rain upon the earth, and it rained not for three years and six months. And he prayed again: and the heaven gave rain, and the earth brought forth her fruit."

Half-heartedness and indecision. The reproach made by Elias to the people for their wavering and indecision applies equally to many Christians who hesitate between virtue and vice, the spirit of Christ and the spirit of the world, the service of God and the service of the devil, although in holy Baptism they renounced Satan and all his works, and promised to be faithful to God. Our Lord warns us thus: "No man can serve two masters (who give opposite commands); for either he will hate the one, and love the other: or he will sustain the one, and despise the other. You cannot serve God and mammon", i. e. the riches &c. of this world (Mat. 6, 24).

The want of priests. The people of the kingdom of Israel sank deeper and deeper into idolatry and crime, because the priests who taught them the true religion and the practice of it, were killed. It is a great misfortune for Christian countries when there is a lack of good priests; for in that case faith grows weak, morals become lax, and many souls are lost (New Test. XXXII).

Figures and Types. The land of Israel, suffering from the long drought, was a figure of the great spiritual drought from which the whole world suffered before the coming of Christ. Elias bidding the heavens to rain was a figure of Christ opening the fountains of grace to a perishing world. The rain itself, which gave a new life to the earth, is a type of the grace of God, which renews the soul of the converted sinner.

APPLICATION. Do you halt between two sides? Do you hesitate between good and evil, between the commands of God and the promptings of your own evil passions? To-day perhaps you have promised to serve God, and to-morrow you will follow some evil desire. This wavering between good and evil is a grave danger to the salvation of your soul; for you are really wavering between heaven and hell. Away then with indecision! Love God with your whole heart and be true to Him till death. Renew this day your baptismal vows.

CHAPTER LXIV.

WICKEDNESS OF ACHAB AND JEZABEL. THEIR PUNISHMENT.

[3 Kings 21—22. 4 Kings 9.]

ACHAB had a palace at Jezrahel[1], and near it was a vineyard owned by a man named Naboth. Achab, coveting the vineyard, said one day to Naboth: "Give me thy vineyard, that I may make me a garden, and I will give thee a better vineyard, or I will give thee the worth of it in money." Naboth answered him: "The Lord be merciful to me and not let me give thee the inheritance[2] of my fathers." For the law of Moses forbade the son to sell the property which he had inherited from his forefathers.

---

[1] *Jezrahel.* Achab generally lived in Samaria, but he had also a summer-palace at Jezrahel, where Naboth's vineyard was.

[2] *The inheritance.* It was expressly forbidden by the Law to sell a family heritage; though in cases of necessity it could be mortgaged until the next jubilee-year. It was therefore out of fear of God that Naboth refused to sell his vineyard.

The king was so troubled [1] because he could not have the vineyard, that he could neither eat nor sleep. Jezabel, his queen, perceiving this, inquired the cause of his sadness and fretting. The king having explained the cause, Jezabel mockingly said: "Thou art of great authority indeed and governest well the kingdom of Israel! Arise and eat bread and be of good cheer: I will give thee the vineyard of Naboth the Jezrahelite."

She then wrote letters in the king's name to the chief men [2] of the city, whom she knew to be wicked like herself, requesting them to find some men who would wrongfully accuse Naboth. These men were easily found, and they bore false witness against Naboth, saying that he had blasphemed [3] God and the king. And on their testimony Naboth was condemned, taken out of the city and stoned to death.

Jezabel being informed of Naboth's death, went and told her husband that he might now take the vineyard, as Naboth was dead. And Achab took the vineyard. Then the Lord commanded Elias to go to Achab, to reproach him with his crime and to tell him that the dogs would lick up his own blood on the very spot on which Naboth was slain, and that the queen would be devoured by dogs in the same field. This prediction was literally fulfilled.

Three years after, Achab was mortally wounded [4] in a battle with the Syrians; and when the chariot in which he received the fatal wound was being washed after his death, the dogs came and licked up [5] his blood.

Some time after, when Jehu was king, he went to Jezrahel. And when Jezabel heard of his coming, she dressed herself in her richest apparel. She painted her face and adorned her head and

---

[1] *Troubled.* Like a spoilt child who cannot have his own way.

[2] *The chief men.* i. e. men of position, power and influence. Holy Scripture calls these men sons of Belial or of the devil, because they bore false witness against Naboth, thus causing his death. How great must have been the corruption of the whole people, if even their chief men and the witnesses called by them were so wicked!

[3] *Blasphemed.* Death by stoning was the punishment decreed for blasphemy. The wicked Jezabel, who did not herself believe in God, caused an innocent man to be put to death on the charge of blasphemy against Him!

[4] *Wounded.* An arrow, which pierced a joint of his coat of mail, wounded him so seriously that he died soon after.

[5] *Licked up.* As his bloody corpse was being washed in the pool of Samaria.

stood at the window of her palace. Jehu [1], seeing her at the window, ordered her servants to cast her down. They did so, and the walls were sprinkled with her blood, and the hoofs of the horses trod upon her, and the dogs came and ate her flesh, so that only her skull, feet and hands remained for burial.

COMMENTARY

The Omniscience of God. God knew and revealed to Elias that Naboth was innocent, and that Achab had seized his vineyard by unjust means.

The Justice of God. Achab and his wicked wife were not able to enjoy for long their ill-gotten possession. The measure of their sins was full, and God punished them by a terrible and unexpected death. Jezabel's body was trampled on by horses and devoured by dogs in Jezrahel, where she had murdered Naboth. Such was the terrible end of this imperious and arrogant woman! "Treasures of wickedness shall profit nothing" (Prov. 10, 2).

The Faithfulness of God. The punishment with which Almighty God threatened Achab and Jezabel came to pass. When Achab went out to fight against the Syrians, he disguised himself so that he might not be recognised as king and attacked. But "a certain man (of the Syrians) bent his bow, shooting at a venture, and chanced to strike the king of Israel between the lungs and the stomach. And the blood ran out of the wound in the midst of the chariot, and he died in the evening. And they washed his chariot in the pool of Samaria, and the dogs licked up his blood" (3 Kings 22, 34 &c.). Now was it by chance that the arrow hit the disguised king? that his blood flowed into the chariot? and that the dogs licked it up? No, all this occurred under the Providence of the just and true God, who moulded circumstances so as to bring that to pass which He had threatened.

The eighth Commandment. The witnesses against Naboth sinned grievously; for they bore false witness in a court of justice, as to a serious matter that involved life and death. They were rightly called children of the devil, because it requires a devilish malice to commit such a sin.

The tenth Commandment. Achab sinned grievously against this Commandment by coveting the inheritance of Naboth.

The seventh Commandment. He also sinned grievously against this Commandment by taking for himself the property of the murdered man.

Sharing in the guilt of others. The prophet said to Achab: "*Thou hast slain &c.*" But how could Achab be Naboth's murderer? He had

---

[1] *Jehu.* Jehu had all Achab's children and relatives put to death, so that the whole race of the impious king was destroyed.

not accused him or sentenced him to death! No, but Achab knew perfectly well that his wicked wife would use unlawful means to gain possession of the vineyard, and yet not only did he utter no word of protest, but consented to Jezabel's writing a letter in his name and sealed it with his royal seal! Thus, by his silence, he consented to his wife's wicked project. Neither did Jezabel kill Naboth with her own hands; but she commanded the ancients of the city to have him falsely accused and put to death. In this way she shared in the guilt of others by command and was guilty of murder.

Unlawful obedience. The ancients of the city ought not to have obeyed the royal command.

Covetousness. The source or root of all these sins we have been hearing about was covetousness. Achab's desire to possess Naboth's vineyard led to anger, bribery, injustice, murder and robbery. Covetousness or avarice is therefore one of the capital sins.

Inordinate desires make men unhappy, peevish and ill-tempered. Achab, not being able to gratify his longing for the vineyard, became sad and angry, and his very life was, as it were, darkened. Was not that silly and ridiculous?

APPLICATION. Have you ever taken anything that does not belong to you, such as fruit &c.? Are you contented with what you have got? If the desire to have that which is unlawful seizes you, overcome it at once and think of the just God who hates and punishes injustice. He who is contented is happy, but he who is discontented lives a life of disquiet and is in great danger of sin and eternal damnation.

CHAPTER LXV.

ELIAS TAKEN UP TO HEAVEN.—THE PROPHET ELISEUS CHOSEN TO SUCCEED HIM.

[3 Kings 19. 4 Kings 1—12.]

AT one time Elias, being persecuted by Jezabel[1], fled into the desert[2]. He was very sad[3] and desired to die[4], for he thought all the Israelites had fallen into idolatry. Being fatigued,

---

[1] *By Jezabel.* Ever since the great miracle on Mount Carmel, Achab had not ventured to persecute the prophet of God; but Jezabel's hatred of him had been intensified by the overthrow of the priests of Baal, and she now did all she could to seize the prophet and put him to death.

[2] *The desert.* To Bersabee, south of the kingdom of Juda.

[3] *Sad.* Because impiety had gained the upper hand, and the true religion was oppressed and persecuted.

[4] *Die.* So that he might no longer have to behold the triumph of vice and unbelief.

he cast himself down and slept in the shadow of a juniper-tree; and behold, an angel of the Lord touched him and said: "Arise, eat; for thou hast yet a great way to go." Elias looked and saw at his head a hearth-cake and a vessel of water. He arose, ate and drank, and walked in the strength[1] of that food forty days and forty nights, until he came to the mount of God[2], Horeb.

Then the Lord appeared to him amidst the breezes of a gentle wind, consoled him and said: "Return and anoint Eliseus to be prophet in thy room, and I will leave Me[3] seven thousand men whose knees have not bowed before Baal." Elias departed and found Eliseus[4] ploughing with oxen. He cast his mantle[5] upon him, and Eliseus forthwith left the oxen and the plough, followed Elias and ministered to him.

But the time came when the Lord wished to take Elias from the earth. The Spirit of God led him[6] to the Jordan, and Eliseus accompanied him. Elias took his mantle, folded it together and struck the waters; the waters divided, and both passed over on dry ground. As they walked on, there appeared a fiery chariot[7] with horses. Elias was taken up alive to heaven[8]. Eliseus saw him

---

[1] *In the strength.* He was so strengthened by this food that he was able to travel fasting for forty days and forty nights, as far as Horeb, one of the mountains of Sinai.

[2] *The mount of God.* So called, because God Himself had appeared there to Moses (chapter XXXI). It was only two hundred miles from Bersabee to Sinai; and if Elias had not made a circuit he might have reached the holy mountain much sooner than he did. Probably he visited on the way some of the places sanctified by the miracles wrought by God during the Israelites' passage through the wilderness. By his pilgrimage to the mountain, consecrated by the giving of the Law, and to other places full of mighty associations, Elias hoped to gain strength, courage and consolation for the further pursuit of his high calling.

[3] *Will leave me.* i. e. "you must not believe that idolatry is universal in Israel. There are several thousand who have not bowed the knee to Baal, or who in other words have not succumbed to idolatry".

[4] *Found Eliseus.* In the plain to the south of the Sea of Galilee. Eliseus and his servants were ploughing with twelve yoke of oxen, by which we can see that he was a man of means.

[5] *His mantle.* As a sign that Eliseus was to be his successor in the prophetical office.

[6] *Led him.* The Spirit of God had revealed to Elias his approaching translation from this earth, and had inspired him to go to the Jordan.

[7] *A fiery chariot.* Angels snatched up Elias from the earth by means of a fiery apparition having the semblance of a chariot and horses.

[8] *To heaven.* Or rather heavenwards. He could not be taken *into* heaven. Like Henoch, he was translated without tasting death, and was taken to a

and cried: "My father! my father! The chariot of Israel and the driver thereof!" When he saw Elias no longer, he rent his garments in grief; then taking the mantle which Elias had dropped, he went back and struck with it the waters of the Jordan. They were divided, and Eliseus passed over. The other disciples[1] of Elias seeing this said: "The spirit of Elias hath rested upon Eliseus."[2] And coming to meet him, they worshipped him, falling to the ground.

After Elias had been taken up into heaven, Eliseus arose and exhorted the Israelites to remain faithful to the Lord. God also favoured him with the gift of miracles[3]. When he came to Jericho, the men of the city said to him: "The situation of this city is very good, but the waters are very bad." Eliseus answered: "Bring me a new vessel and put salt into it." When they had brought it, he went out to the spring (Fig. 50, p. 280)[4], cast the salt into it, and the waters were healed.

One day when Eliseus was going up to Bethel[5], where the golden calf was worshipped, some boys came out of the city and mocked him, saying: "Go up, thou bald head." Eliseus, knowing that in dishonouring him they dishonoured God, turned back and cursed them[6] in the name of the Lord. Immediately two bears came out of the wood that was near by, and killed forty-two of the boys.

---

mysterious abode of peace and consolation. Before our Lord's second coming to judge the world, Elias will come again to this earth to preach penance (Mat. 17, 11).

[1] *Other disciples.* Elias' disciples had stayed on the other side of the Jordan, and from thence had seen his marvellous translation.

[2] *Upon Eliseus.* They knew by the testimony of this great miracle that the gifts of prophecy and working miracles had passed from Elias to Eliseus.

[3] *The gift of miracles.* God worked a great many miracles through him, in order that the people might believe that God had sent him.

[4] *The spring.* To the well outside the town from which the water was conducted to the city. This well, like all those in the neighbourhood of the Dead Sea, had a briny taste. Therefore when Eliseus threw salt into it, it was not by the salt itself that the water was turned sweet, but by the power of God, invoked by Eliseus. The spring is still running: it is known by the name of the Sultan's spring or Eliseus' spring, and its water is very good.

[5] *Bethel.* Bethel was the head centre of idolatry. It is probable that the boys were set on to mock Eliseus by their impious parents, who very likely recognised him by the mantle of Elias.

[6] *Cursed them.* He foretold to them as well as to their wicked parents that God would punish them, which He did by means of the two bears.

Some time after Eliseus cured of leprosy, in a miraculous manner, Naaman[1], general of the Syrian army, a rich and valiant man. The wife of Naaman had in her service a young Israelite girl who had been carried off into Syria by robbers. This maiden then said one day to her mistress: "I wish my master had been with the prophet that is in Samaria. He would certainly have healed him of the leprosy." When Naaman heard this he set out for Samaria with horses and chariots.

Fig. 50. Eliseus' spring near Jericho. (Phot. Bonfils.)

When Naaman reached the prophet's dwelling he sent a messenger to let him know of his coming, and why he had come. Eliseus sent him word by his servant Giezi to bathe seven times in the Jordan, and he would be healed. Naaman was angry[2] and went away, saying: "I thought he would have come

---

[1] *Naaman.* Syria with its capital Damascus is situated to the north-east of Israel. Naaman was the king's general, a rich and valiant man. He travelled into Israel with horses and chariots, taking much gold with him.

[2] *Angry.* Naaman was neither pleased with his reception, which he thought disrespectful, nor with the remedy proposed, which did not commend itself to his

out to me and standing would have invoked the name of the
Lord his God, and touched with his hand the place of the leprosy
and healed me. Are not the rivers of Damascus better than all
the waters of Israel?"

As he was thus turning angrily away, his servants[1] said to
him: "Father, if the prophet had bidden thee to do some great
thing, surely thou wouldst have done it; how much more what
he now hath said to thee: 'Wash, and thou shalt be clean.'"
And Naaman, seeing that what they said was just, alighted
from his chariot, bathed seven times in the Jordan and was
made clean. He returned to the man of God and told him
that now he knew for certain that there was no God but the
God of Israel[2]; and he offered him presents, but Eliseus refused
to receive anything.

Hardly had Naaman gone a little way when Giezi, the servant
of Eliseus, went after him and said: "My master hath sent me to
thee saying: 'Just now there are come to me from Mount Ephraim
two young men, sons of the prophets[3]; give them a talent of
silver and two changes of garments.'"[4]

Naaman gladly gave him two talents of silver and two changes
of garments. Giezi returned with the presents, and having hidden
them, he stood before Eliseus. The prophet asked him where
he had been, and Giezi answered that he had been nowhere.

Eliseus being angry said: "Was not my heart present[5] when
the man turned back from his chariot? Now thou hast money to
buy oliveyards and vineyards and sheep and oxen and men-
servants and maid-servants; but the leprosy of Naaman shall stick

---

natural reason. "If that be all", he thought, "I might as well have stayed at
home, and as for bathing in the dirty waters of the Jordan, the river of Damascus
is far preferable and better."

[1] *His servants*. They called Naaman 'Father', which shows that he was
good to them. On their side they were very loyal to him and affectionately
counselled him to obey the prophet.

[2] *The God of Israel*. Naaman was converted to faith in the true God by
his wonderful cure. He had become so humble that he called himself the servant
of the prophet.

[3] *Sons of the prophets*. The disciples of the prophets led a retired community life of poverty, prayer and contemplation. They were, so to speak, the
monks of the Old Testament.

[4] *Garments*. Fine clothes, such as would be worn on great days and festivals.

[5] *Present*. God had enabled the prophet to know in the spirit exactly what
had occurred.

to thee for ever." And Giezi went out a leper, as white as snow [1]. Eliseus wrought other great miracles [2].

One great miracle the prophet wrought even after his death [3]. It happened in this manner: On one occasion a number of men were carrying a corpse to the cemetery for burial. As they were making the grave, behold, robbers from Moab rushed in upon them. They in their fright cast the corpse into the sepulchre of Eliseus [4]. No sooner had the dead man touched the bones of the prophet than he was instantly restored to life and came forth from the tomb.

COMMENTARY.

The Goodness of God towards His holy and zealous servant Elias was very great. He revived and strengthened him with a miraculous food, appeared to him most lovingly so as to comfort him, and finally took him from earth in a glorious manner, without letting him taste of the bitterness and humiliation of death.

The Omnipotence of God was shown by the supernatural power of the bread, in the strength of which Elias fasted forty days; and also by the twice-repeated division of the waters of the Jordan. It was God's omnipotence which purified the well at Jericho by a means which, in the natural order of things, would have made the briny water more unpalatable than it was before. He cured the leprosy of Naaman and raised the dead man to life by contact with the bones of Eliseus.

Sadness which is pleasing to God. The sadness of Elias was not sinful, but on the contrary praiseworthy, for it sprang from love of God and zeal for His glory; and his heart, all aglow with divine love, was sad even unto death, when he contemplated the idolatry and impiety of the Israelites. We too ought to grieve when we see how much God is forgotten and offended, and how unbelief and hatred of the Church of God and her laws are ever increasing. It is to such sorrow as this that our Lord's words apply: "Blessed are they that mourn, for they shall be comforted."

A holy desire for death. We may not wish for our own death or for that of others, from reasons of impatience or despair. Elias' desire for death arose not from a spirit of fretfulness, but from love of God,

---

[1] *As white as snow.* He was afflicted, as it were, with leprosy upon leprosy, so that there was no part of his body which was not covered with it.

[2] *Other great miracles.* So for instance he raised to life the dead son of a woman of Sunam.

[3] *His death.* He died at an advanced age, having filled the prophetical office for over fifty years.

[4] *Of Eliseus.* Into the grave which had been dug for Eliseus, from which they quickly rolled the stone, and cast the corpse into it.

as he was loth to witness any more offences committed against Him. Moreover he longed to go to God. It was in this spirit that St. Paul wrote: "I have a desire to be dissolved and be with Christ" (Phil. 1, 23).

Gentleness. The gentle sighing of the wind when Almighty God appeared to Elias was meant to indicate His goodness, mercy and patience, and to warn the fiery prophet that he too must work with patience and long-suffering. We can, as a rule, do far more for God's glory and the salvation of souls by patience and gentleness than by violence and severity. St. Francis of Sales says: "You can catch more flies with a spoonful of honey than with a cask of vinegar." "Blessed are the meek."

The virtues and works of Elias. After Moses Elias was the greatest of the prophets. Firstly, he was great by his virtues. He led a severe life of penance, not loving the world, but loving only solitude, prayer and the contemplation of divine things. He was devoured by a holy zeal for God's glory and the salvation of his people. He was intrepid, patient and strong under suffering and persecution, and was possessed of the most unshaken confidence in God. Secondly, he was great by his divine calling and his influence on the world. He preserved the true faith in Israel, he worked wonderful miracles, such as raising the dead, and was translated from earth in a marvellous manner. He is therefore venerated as a great Saint by both Christians and Jews.

Elias, the fourteenth type of Jesus Christ. Elias was in several respects a type of our Lord. He was sent by God, was a prophet and a worker of miracles. He raised to life the son of the widow of Sarepta: our Lord raised to life the son of the widow of Naim. He multiplied the meal and oil: our Lord multiplied the loaves and fishes. Moreover Elias fasted forty days in the wilderness, was hated and persecuted by the ungodly, was sorrowful even unto death, was strengthened by an angel, was translated to heaven in the sight of his disciples, and will come again at the end of the world.

Faithful correspondence with grace. Eliseus was a God-fearing husbandman, and was called from the plough to be the follower of the great prophet. He obeyed the call of God instantly, corresponded with grace, left his home and possessions and served Elias. He was poor in spirit and obedient to the will of God, therefore he was singled out by God to be the recipient of special graces. "Blessed are the poor in spirit."

The fourth Commandment. Eliseus and the disciples of Elias show us by their example in what way we should love and revere teachers sent to us by God. Eliseus loved Elias as his spiritual father ("My father! my father", he cried), and when he was parted from him, he rent his garments in grief. The disciples of Elias received Eliseus with the deepest reverence as soon as they recognised him to be the spiritual heir to Elias and a prophet chosen by God.

The relics of Saints. The cloak which Elias left behind him when he was translated was a relic of the holy prophet. By means of this relic and for the sake of the prayers and merits of Elias God worked great miracles. By means of the relics (i. e. the bones) of Eliseus also a great miracle was wrought. If therefore God glorifies the relics of his Saints by working miracles through them, it is certainly reasonable and pleasing to God that we should value· and honour them; and the Church teaches that we ought to venerate them. She places them under the altars on which the holy Sacrifice of the Mass is offered, and exposes them for our veneration.

A type of Holy Communion. The wonderful food brought to Elias by an angel was an evident type of Holy Communion. We have before us a long and dangerous journey through the desert of this life, before we can reach heaven. During this pilgrimage God strengthens us by the most holy Sacrament, the bread of angels, in the power of which we may rise from virtue to virtue and finally scale the holy Mount of God, heaven.

At our Lord's *Transfiguration* on Mount Tabor Moses and Elias, on account of their high place in the kingdom of God, were allowed to speak with the Saviour of the world, the former as the representative and founder of the Law, the latter as the representative of the prophets (New Test. XXXVII).

God's Justice was manifested in the punishment of the impious children of Bethel and the chastisement of the covetous servant Giezi.

God's Mercy sent the erring and deceived Israelites another prophet (Eliseus) in the place of Elias, and gave him the power of working mighty miracles, in order to induce the people to do penance and escape the coming judgment. How wonderfully did God's mercy reveal itself in the case of the pagan Naaman! According to human ideas the carrying off by robbers of the Israelite maiden was an unlucky accident, but by divine Providence it became the means by which the chiefs of the Syrians were made acquainted with the miracles which Eliseus worked in God's name. It was also the cause of the conversion of Naaman to the true faith. God ordained that this little maid should be taken into the service of Naaman's wife, should relate the wonderful things done by Eliseus, and should awaken in Naaman's breast the hope that the prophet might heal him of his terrible disease.

The object of miracles. Leprosy could indeed be cured, except in such aggravated cases as those of Job and Giezi, but the cure was a very slow one. Naaman's sudden recovery was therefore clearly a miracle, for it was not the water of the Jordan which cured him, but the almighty power of God. God performed this miracle on the distinguished Gentile in order that he might be converted, and that the name of God should be glorified even among the heathen. Naaman was healed in soul as well as in body.

Reverence for old age and for the servants of God. The sin committed by the boys of Bethel was great, because the person they mocked was both an old man and a prophet. They proved themselves to be bad, vicious children, full of hatred of God and His servants. Their severe punishment was sent, firstly, to prevent their reaching a mature stage of wickedness; secondly, to teach the inhabitants of Bethel to fear God and honour His prophets; and thirdly, to serve as a warning for all time that old age is to be honoured, and all those sent by God are to be revered. "Rise up before the hoary head, and honour the person of the aged man" (Lev. 19, 32). Our Lord said, referring to the apostles and their successors: "He that heareth you, heareth Me: and he that despiseth you, despiseth Me: and he that despiseth Me, despiseth Him that sent Me" (Luke 10, 16).

Humility. Naaman's story shows us that only the humble can find favour with God. The narrative of the little maid had inspired the Syrian general with a great confidence in the power of God and the prayers of Eliseus. But when he arrived, and the prophet did not come out to meet him, to touch him and pray over him, and still more when he was told to bathe in the Jordan, his pride was aroused. He said to himself: "What, am I not even good enough for the prophet to speak to? What good can the water of the Jordan do me?" It was only when his servants reasoned with him, that he overcame his pride and humbly obeyed the directions of the man of God. Had he not become humble and obedient, he would not have been healed either in body or soul.

Consider the *gratitude* of Naaman.

Disinterestedness of Eliseus. As he did not care for his own interests, but only for the glory of God, Eliseus found his full reward in the conversion of the pagan Syrian, and thanked God for it.

Covetousness. Giezi, like Judas Iscariot, was a covetous man, though he had constantly before him the example of his poverty-loving master. In order to enrich himself he lied first to the Syrian and then to Eliseus, exposing the latter to a charge of avarice and perjury, for the prophet had said to Naaman: "As the Lord liveth I will take nothing." This story shows us that covetousness is a capital sin, leading to many other sins, especially to lies and deceit.

Ill-gotten gains profit nothing. The rich presents received by Giezi from Naaman were ill-gotten, for he told lies to obtain them. These ill-gotten goods brought him no blessing. Covered with an incurable leprosy, he could enjoy neither riches nor life. He must very often have cursed his avarice and deceit, for health is of more value than gold. Many a rich invalid would give all he possesses, could he thereby regain his health!

Justification of the sinner. Naaman's wonderful cure from leprosy is, according to the Fathers of the Church, a type of the sinner's justification by the Sacraments of Baptism and Penance. Leprosy represents sin, and the waters of Jordan both the baptismal waters and tears of contrition in the Sacrament of Penance. In Naaman's case his flesh became as the flesh of a little child: even so is ·the soul washed from all its sins by Baptism and Penance. But to obtain this inward purity, the sinner must, like Naaman, humble himself and fulfil the exact conditions of forgiveness.

Holy water. The blessing of the water of Jericho by Eliseus was a type of the blessing of holy water by the Church; and at the blessing of it the miracle of Eliseus is expressly referred to. Have you ever seen how holy water is blessed, and what the priest throws into it? He throws in blessed salt and prays in the name of the Church that the water may be freed from the influence of the evil one, and be salutary to all who use it devoutly.

Good and pious servants bring a blessing on their employers. Naaman's Israelite slave remained true to her faith though she lived among heathens, and her pious narration was the cause of Naaman being cured of his leprosy and converted to the true faith.

The free gift of grace. "There were many lepers in Israel in the time of Eliseus the prophet, yet none of them were cleansed but Naaman the Syrian" (New Test. XVII). Thus spoke our Lord at Nazareth, to prove by this example that "election" was not hereditary in the family of Abraham.

———

APPLICATION. If you want to know yourself (and without self-knowledge there can be no amendment of life), ask yourself what it is that most easily disturbs you. Do you feel sad when others are praised or rewarded? Do you feel glad when they are blamed or punished? If so, you are full of selfishness and envy. Are you put out when you cannot have your own way, or if leave is refused you to do something you wish? If so, you are self-willed and disobedient.

Never laugh about the sins of others. Remember the offence against God, and pray for the conversion of those who have sinned.

Have you ever derided old or infirm people? Do you mock at your comrades for their physical infirmities? Just think how unkind, how rude, how unjust it is to do so, for they are not responsible for their physical defects!

Examine your conscience on the subject of lies. Even if your lies do no harm to other people, they do harm to your own soul, because every lie is a sin. For the future say an "Our Father" whenever you tell a lie, and then you will keep a better watch over yourself, and will cure yourself of this detestable habit.

CHAPTER LXVI.

THE PROPHET JONAS.

[4 Kings 14, 25. Jonas 1—4.]

AFTER the death[1] of Eliseus, the Lord wishing to show mercy to the Gentiles, raised up the prophet Jonas that he might go to Ninive[2], and preach penance to the inhabitants of that city. The wickedness of the pagan Ninivites had provoked the anger of God, and He had said to Jonas: "Arise, and go to Ninive and preach in it, for the wickedness thereof is come up before Me."[3]

Jonas, however, knew that the Lord easily forgives; hence he was afraid that if he preached to the people of Ninive they would do penance, and that consequently the Lord would spare them, while he himself would be looked upon as a false prophet. So Jonas rose up to flee from the face[4] of the Lord, and he embarked on board a ship which sailed for Tharsis. But the Lord sent a great storm, and the sea heaved and swelled, and the ship threatened to sink[5].

Then the sailors, being frightened, threw into the sea all the merchandise that was on board, in order to lighten the vessel. And each one began praying to his own god for help. But Jonas was below, fast asleep, and the shipmaster went to him and said:

---

[1] *The death.* Under the reign of king Joas.

[2] *Ninive.* The capital of the kingdom of Assyria, situated to the east of Syria. This was the greatest empire of those days, and embraced all the country between the Euphrates and the Tigris (Mesopotamia), and a large tract to the north and south of it (Media, Elam and Babylonia). Ninive, the greatest city of antiquity, was on the Tigris, and was twenty-four leagues in circumference, its houses being surrounded by gardens and vineyards. The inhabitants, who numbered about 700,000, were proud and immoral.

[3] *Before Me.* i. e. their wickedness constrains Me to punish them if they will not do penance. Jonas suspected that if the Ninivites repented, God would spare them and abandon the Israelites. He wished Ninive to be destroyed, so that the Assyrians should be rendered incapable of overpowering Israel; he did not wish to preach penance to the city, through fear that God might find reason to spare it.

[4] *From the face.* He wished to avoid the mission with which God had charged him, and therefore embarked on a ship bound for Spain. The prophet knew very well that he could not escape from the omnipresent God.

[5] *To sink.* And break in pieces.

"Why art thou asleep? Rise up, call upon thy God, if so be that God will think of us, that we may not perish!"

But the sailors, seeing that the violence of the storm continued to increase, proposed to cast lots that they might know why this evil[1] had come upon them. And they cast lots, and the lot fell upon Jonas[2]. Then Jonas confessed his sin and said: "Take me up, and cast me into the sea, and the sea shall be calm to you."

The sailors, unwilling to throw Jonas overboard, rowed very hard to gain the shore, where they might leave him in safety. But they were not able; for the sea swelled and tossed higher than ever. At last they took Jonas and cast him into the sea, and immediately the storm ceased, and the sea was calm.

At the same moment the Lord sent a great fish[3], a whale, which opened its jaws and swallowed Jonas. And he remained

Fig. 51. Shark.

three days and three nights in the belly of the whale, continually calling on God to save him, saying: "I am cast away, out of the sight of Thy eyes; but yet I shall see Thy holy temple again."

His prayer was heard, and on the third day the fish threw Jonas out of its mouth on the dry land.

And the Lord spoke a second time to Jonas and told him to go to Ninive, the great city, and preach penance. Jonas went without delay, and entering into the city, he walked a whole day through the streets, calling out as he went: "Yet forty days, and Ninive shall be destroyed." The people of Ninive were struck with terror, knowing how guilty they were, and a general fast was proclaimed throughout the whole city, both for man and beast.

---

[1] *Why this evil.* They were convinced that some one on board must have secretly committed a great sin, and that an angry divinity had sent this terrible storm as a punishment. Even the heathens believed in divine retribution.

[2] *Upon Jonas.* By God's Providence.

[3] *A great fish.* Probably a shark (Fig. 51). This fish has been known to be as much as thirty feet long, and has such enormous jaws that it could easily swallow a man whole. That Jonas remained alive inside the fish and was thrown up by it on dry land, was a miracle of God's omnipotence.

The king himself put on sackcloth and sat in ashes, and he and all his people, from the greatest to the least, fasted and did penance, in order to appease the anger of God. And because of their repentance God had mercy on the people of Ninive, and spared their city. Meanwhile, Jonas had gone out of the city, and sat down at some distance, towards the east, to see what would happen. And finding that God had spared Ninive, he was angry [1] and much troubled lest he should pass for a false prophet.

God, however, wishing to show his prophet the unreasonableness of his anger, caused to spring up, during the night, a large vine [2], which sheltered him next day from the scorching rays of the sun. But on the following morning God sent a worm which ate up the root of the plant, and it withered away.

Now, when the sun had risen, God sent a hot and burning wind; and the sun struck full on the head of Jonas, and he broiled with the heat to such a degree that he desired to die. Then the Lord said to him: "Thou art grieved for the ivy for which thou hast not laboured, and shall not I spare Ninive, in which there are more than a hundred and twenty thousand persons that know not how to distinguish [3] between their right hand and their left, and many beasts?"

COMMENTARY.

God never changes. What! did He not change His intention towards Ninive? It may appear so; for first He made Jonas proclaim that the city would be destroyed in forty days, and yet after all He spared it. To this St. Jerome replies: "God did not change His purpose, but man changed his actions! From the first it was God's intention to be merciful, and He proclaimed the punishment in order that He might be able to show mercy." As God is ever ready to be merciful if only man will be converted, we must add to the words 'Ninive shall be destroyed' this reservation: 'unless it do penance'. God threatened to punish the Ninivites for the express purpose of bringing them to repentance, so that, of His mercy, He might remit the punishment with which His justice had threatened them.

---

[1] *Angry.* Because he feared that Ninive's salvation would be Israel's destruction.

[2] *A large vine.* Over his unprotected head.

[3] *How to distinguish.* Whom did the Lord God mean by those who knew not their right hand from their left? Little children under seven. It was, therefore, as if He had said: "Shall I not have compassion on this great city, in which are 120,000 innocent children, who have not as yet committed any actual sin?"

The Omnipotence of God stirred up the storm at sea, and instantly calmed it; made the lot to fall on Jonas, sent the fish to swallow him, kept him alive inside it, made it cast him up on dry land, and caused the rapid growth and as rapid decay of the plant which gave shelter to the prophet. Everything is in the hands of Almighty God; the elements obey Him, and the animals do His will.

The Goodness and Holiness of God. God loves little children, because they are innocent, and have not committed any actual sin; and for the sake of them He had mercy on the whole city.

The Justice of God. God punished the disobedience of Jonas by stirring up the storm on his account, by letting him be devoured by the fish and keeping him shut up inside it in a state of mortal fear.

The Mercy of God. He showed His mercy to Jonas first; and then to the Ninivites. "As I live, saith the Lord God, I desire not the death of the wicked, but that the wicked turn from his way and live" (Ez. 33, 11).

The faith and repentance of the Ninivites was very edifying. In spite of the wonderful words and deeds of Elias, most of the Israelites had remained impenitent. Then God turned to the Gentiles, who showed more good-will and faith than the chosen people. The Ninivites believed the word of the Lord as soon as the prophet announced it to them; and they practised penance with prayer and fasting when he quoted his own miraculous deliverance as a sign that God had sent him (Luke 11, 30). Our Lord Himself held up the Ninivites as an example to the hard-hearted Israelites, when He said: "The men of Ninive shall rise in judgment with this generation and shall condemn it, because they did penance at the preaching of Jonas; and behold a greater than Jonas is here" (New Test. XXVII). How disgraceful would it be for Christians if they allowed themselves to be outdone in faith and penance by the Ninivites!

True conversion. Jonas sinned by refusing to obey God's command. But he saw, confessed and repented of his sin, and in his repentance declared himself willing to suffer death by drowning. His conversion was sincere; for immediately after his miraculous deliverance he set off for Ninive to execute God's commission. The surest proof of conversion is to be willing to do God's will, no matter how hard it may be.

Fasting is, as we can see by this story, a work of penance well-pleasing to God. Therefore the Church, in order to kindle and increase our ardour for penance, has prescribed fixed fasting days.

The good works of sinners. The Ninivites were not in a state of grace when they performed their good works of prayer, fasting &c., for they were great sinners. Nevertheless, these good works were not useless, for they availed to avert the threatened judgment, and to win for many of the inhabitants the grace of conversion.

Jonas, the fifteenth type of Jesus Christ. Jonas was a type of the Divine Redeemer. Our Lord Himself teaches us this when He says (New Test. XXVII): "An adulterous generation seeketh after a sign, and a sign shall not be given it but the sign of Jonas the prophet. For as Jonas was in the whale's belly three days and three nights, so shall the Son of man be in the heart of the earth three days and three nights." Jonas is also a type of our Lord in other ways. He was sent not only to the Jews, but also to the Gentiles: our Lord came and died for both Jews and Gentiles. Jonas offered himself up to die of his own free-will, to appease God's anger, and save his fellow-passengers. Our Lord went willingly to death in order to satisfy the divine justice and save us, His brethren, from eternal death.

Revelation to the Gentiles. God showed mercy to the Gentiles and manifested Himself to them. The sojourn of Jacob and his descendants in Egypt, as also Moses' great miracles in the desert, had served to make God more or less known among the Gentiles. Elias was sent to Sarepta, and there worked miracles in God's name among the heathen. Eliseus cured the Syrian Naaman, and thereby made known God's almighty power to the pagan Syrians. Jonas was sent by God to the greatest city of the pagan world, to preach penance to its inhabitants, and make known to them the Omnipotence, Justice, and Mercy of the true God.

Relapse into sin. Two hundred years after, when the Ninivites had returned to their former state of wickedness and, this time, remained impenitent, God's threatened judgment fell on them. The abominable city was entirely destroyed and levelled to the ground, 606 B.C. This shows us how dangerous it is to fall back into sin.

Cruelty to animals. God showed mercy even to the beasts in Ninive, for they too are his creatures. How good it would be if men would take pity on beasts and refrain from ill-treating them.

APPLICATION. Do you take compassion on your unfortunate fellow-creatures? Do you do your best to comfort them and help them? Or do you rejoice when any evil or punishment overtakes them? Are you ever cruel to animals?

Are you sorry for your sins? What have you done to make satisfaction for them? You could very well forego some pleasure at times, or deny yourself in eating, and offer these acts of self-denial to God as a penance for your sins. Try every day to arouse feelings of compunction in your heart!

CHAPTER LXVII.

FALL OF THE KINGDOM OF ISRAEL.—ASSYRIAN CAPTIVITY. TOBIAS.

[4 Kings 17—18. Tobias 1—3.]

THE Lord ceased not to send to the Israelites holy prophets[1] who preached penance to them both by word and example. But the Israelites would not be converted, and their wickedness[2] increased to such an extent that the Almighty resolved to punish them in His wrath, and utterly to destroy them. He therefore caused Salmanazar, king of Assyria, to come against them with a mighty army. He laid siege[3] to the strong city of Samaria, and after three years took it and carried off most of its inhabitants captives[4]; and thus the kingdom of Israel ceased[5] to exist. Thus the prophecy of Amos (9, 8) was fulfilled: "Behold, the eyes of the Lord God [are] upon the sinful kingdom, and I will destroy it from the face of the earth: but yet I will not utterly destroy the house of Jacob."

The Israelites having been slain or carried off into captivity, their land had become almost a wilderness[6], and the Assyrian king, in order to people it again, sent thither thousands of his pagan subjects who, settling amongst the scattered remains of the ten tribes, were soon so mixed up with them that they became, as it were, a new nation, and scarcely a trace remained of the people of Israel.

---

[1] *Prophets.* Among these prophets were Osee and Amos, who announced the judgments of God which were to come.

[2] *Wickedness.* The prophet Osee (4, 2 and 11) thus describes the moral condition of the people: "Cursing, and lying, and killing, and theft, and adultery have overflowed. Wine and drunkenness take away the understanding." Sedition, regicide and civil war became more and more common.

[3] *Siege.* He encamped all round the town so that no necessaries of life could be brought to it.

[4] *Captives.* Imagine to yourselves with what tears and aching hearts they must have left their homes. Now, no doubt, they repented of their sins and deplored their blindness; but it was too late. The Israelites were divided among the towns in Northern Assyria and were much hampered in the free practice of their religion.

[5] *Ceased.* Being merged in the Assyrian Empire in the year 721 B. C.

[6] *A wilderness.* Because its inhabitants were very few, and the land only partially cultivated.

The religion[1] of the Samaritans was a mixture of Judaism and Paganism; hence they hated the two tribes of Juda and Benjamin, who had remained true to the old religion.

Those who were taken captive to Assyria never returned to their own country. Still God did not fail to give numerous proofs of His watchful care over those unhappy exiles. One of the most remarkable of these instances is found in the history of the good Tobias[2]. When he was in his own country and in his earliest years, Tobias never associated with the wicked; never went to adore the golden calf[3], but kept the law of the Lord exactly.

Hence God protected him in the land of captivity, and caused him to find favour in the sight of Salmanazar, who allowed him to go wherever he wished. He went accordingly to all his fellow-captives, consoling and encouraging them. He shared with them all he possessed, fed them when they were hungry, and clothed them when naked. His life was spent in such works of charity.

Fig. 52.
Sennacherib on his throne.
Assyrian Sculpture.
London, British Museum.

King Salmanazar being dead, Sennacherib (Fig. 52)[4], his son, who succeeded him on the throne, was not so favourable to Tobias and put many of the Israelites to death. But Tobias, fearing God more than the king, hid the bodies of his brethren in his house, and buried them by night. The king, having heard this, sentenced Tobias to death, and took away all his property.

Tobias fled with his wife and son, and remained concealed in a place of safety, till the death of the wicked king, who forty

---

[1] *The religion.* They worshipped false gods at the same time that they worshipped the Almighty. It was only later that they abandoned idolatry and built a temple to the Lord on Mount Garizim, near Sichar.

[2] *Tobias.* He lived in Ninive, the capital of Assyria.

[3] *Golden calf.* Although he lived in Israel, and not in Juda, he did not go to Bethel to worship the golden calf, as did most of his fellow-countrymen. He faithfully observed all the rules laid down for the worship of God and for the offering of sacrifices.

[4] *Sennacherib.* In revenge for a great defeat he had suffered before Jerusalem (as will be told in chapter LXXIII). When Sennacherib learnt that Tobias buried the dead, he gave orders for him to be put to death. Tobias, however, hid himself and continued to bury the dead.

days later was killed by his own sons. Then Tobias returned, and all his property was restored to him. But the persecution against the Israelites was still raging, so Tobias resumed his former works of charity, relieving the distressed, and burying the dead.

Coming home one day very much fatigued, he lay down near the wall and fell asleep. While he was sleeping the droppings from a swallow's nest fell on his eyes and made him blind [1]. This was a great affliction, but it did not prevent Tobias from fearing and blessing God and thanking Him for all his mercies, even for this new trial. Now Anna, his wife, was his only support. She went out every day to work, and by her hard earnings kept her husband from want. On one occasion, Anna received a young kid for the labour of her hands, and she brought it home. Now Tobias, hearing it bleat, was afraid and said: "Take heed, lest perhaps it be stolen [2]; restore it to its owner." He questioned Anna as to how she got the kid. Now Anna was a good and virtuous woman, but this suspicion of her husband roused her to anger. She replied very sharply and made use of words that were aggravating [3] to her husband. Tobias, however, only sighed and began to pray.

COMMENTARY.

The Patience and Justice of God. God was very patient with His ungrateful people. He continued to send prophets who, in stirring language, pointed out to the people their ingratitude and faithlessness towards God, and graphically described the judgments which would overtake them. For two hundred years and more God visited them with famines and other tribulations in the hope of bringing them back to Him, but all in vain! Ninive did penance, but Israel remained impenitent! At last Almighty God's patience was exhausted, His judgment fell, and the faithless kingdom of Israel came to an end! "Justice exalteth a nation: but sin maketh nations miserable" (Prov. 14, 34).

God's Mercy and Wisdom. Even in His punishments God showed mercy. As a nation Israel was overthrown, but the punishment served

---

[1] *Blind.* Inflammation set in and blindness ensued. This was a severe trial for Tobias; however, he did not complain, but, like Job, daily thanked God even for the sufferings sent to him.

[2] *Stolen.* He may have had reasons for doubting the honesty of the giver of the kid.

[3] *Aggravating.* Reproaching him for having given away all his substance.

for the conversion of individuals. The Israelites had been driven from the land of their fathers, they were scattered and homeless, living among strangers and earning a livelihood by hard work, being all the while sorely oppressed. In their necessity many turned contritely to God, acknowledged His just judgments and found all their consolation in the hope of the promised Redeemer. In them were fulfilled the words of the prophet Jeremias (2, 19): "Know thou and see that it is an evil and a bitter thing for thee to have left the Lord thy God." For the kingdom of Assyria also the dispersion of Israel was a great blessing. Through the Israelites living in their midst the pagans learnt to know the true and unseen God and the promised Redeemer, for whose coming they were, therefore, prepared. Thus, by God's Providence, even the sin of Israel and its punishment served for a good end.

The Faithfulness of God. That which God had threatened a hundred years before was brought to pass. The impenitent kingdom of Israel was merged in the great Assyrian empire, and ceased to be an independent state.

The fall of him who resists grace. The history of Israel is the counterpart of the history of every impenitent sinner. What happened to the people of Israel when they broke their covenant with God, is repeated in the case of very many Christians, who do not keep their baptismal vows. By the mouth of His priests, and by the voice of their own consciences, God exhorts sinners to be converted and do penance. He reminds them of the terrors of the judgment and the torments of hell. But, alas, many sinners will not believe, and take these solemn truths of faith for empty threats. Often God visits sinners with sickness or misfortunes, but the amendment of life which these may produce lasts but a short time. Hardly is the trouble removed before the sinner turns away again from God and commits fresh sins. God will bear with him for a long time, seeking to bring him back to Him, but at last His patience is exhausted, the time of grace is past, and God calls the impenitent sinner before His judgment-seat, and gives him over to the power of the enemy. The sinful soul is damned, and thrust for ever out of its heavenly home, to suffer hopelessly, in captivity, the unbearable torments of hell. There, indeed, he at last recognizes his folly and blindness, and bitterly rues his sin and impenitence. But it is too late!

The Virtues of Tobias. 1. His *piety.* He loved God from his youth up, prayed willingly, and faithfully fulfilled all his religious duties. The foundations of piety are laid in youth.

2. *His brotherly love.* His love was *universal,* for he did not show it towards his friends only, but towards all who were in want, especially Israelites. His love was *practical,* for he sought out the needy, even sacrificing health and fortune in order to help them. He consoled, instructed, and supported all whom he could, and practised works of

mercy towards the living and the dead. Finally, it was *disinterested.* He did everything in secret, and sought his own glory in nothing. He asked for no reward from man, for no thanks, no honours. This proves that his love was *sincere* and *disinterested.*

3. *His fortitude.* He did not shrink from the perils and labour of long journeys, nor did he fear the anger of the king. He exposed himself to every danger to help the needy and bury the dead.

4. *His justice.* He conscientiously performed his duty towards God and man. This rudimentary virtue of justice proceeded from his uprightness, which made him, though poor, refuse any reward which he had not justly earned. He said to himself: "If the person who gave us this kid, stole it, it is not his property, and he has no right to give it; and as for me, I may neither buy nor receive as a gift any stolen goods."

5. *His patience in suffering.* This was the fruit of faith and hope. Tobias was specially distinguished for his great patience and resignation under suffering. He did not murmur against God, or say to himself: "What have I done to deserve these trials? Have I not feared God from my youth up?" No, he accepted his trials humbly, as a punishment for his own sins and those of his people (Tob. 3, 2 f); he thanked God for them, and set all his hopes on a future life. "For we are the children of the Saints", said he, "and look for that life which God will give to those that never change their faith in Him" (Tob. 2, 18). The belief in a future reward comforted him and supported him in the midst of his tribulations. Faith makes people patient and contented under suffering; but a man without faith is without comfort in tribulation, and without hope in death. Poor, unfortunate man!

The object of suffering. Why did God permit so many troubles to overtake the holy, faithful Tobias? The angel Raphael explained the reason when he said to him: "Because thou wast acceptable to God, it was necessary that temptation should prove thee" (Tob. 12, 13). Suffering, therefore, was intended to serve as a probation of Tobias, and to give him the opportunity of practising patience, and gaining more merit. Holy Scripture offers a further explanation of the reason for this holy man's tribulations in the following passage: "Now this trial (of blindness) the Lord therefore permitted to happen to him that an example might be given to posterity of his patience, as in the case of holy Job" (Tob. 2, 12).

The bodies of the dead are worthy of reverence. Why did Tobias expose himself to such great danger in order to bury mere dead bodies? He knew and believed that man is an image of God, so he could not endure the thought that men's bodies should lie uncared for, to be devoured by wild beasts. The bodies of Christians, furthermore, are the temples of the Holy Ghost, and sanctified by the reception of the holy Sacraments. For this reason they are buried in consecrated ground.

Lawful obedience. Was it not wrong of Tobias to continue to bury the dead after Sennacherib had forbidden it? No, it was rather Sennacherib who did wrong in ordering the dead bodies to be left unburied, for God had commanded, writing it on men's hearts, that the bodies of the dead should be treated reverently, and buried.

APPLICATION. Dear children, none of you would wish to suffer eternally, to be shut out for ever from the presence of God, and banished from heaven. Lay to heart, therefore, the teaching and holy exhortations which you receive, obey God's grace, avoid sin, and do heartfelt penance for the sins you have heretofore committed.

Do you think any one will ever be able to say of you: "He has from his youth up observed the commandments of God, and avoided the society of the wicked"?

Do you possess any ill-gotten goods? Have you ever taken anything, even a trifle such as a picture, a pen, or an apple, from any one? Give it back at once, or if you no longer possess it, make compensation for it. Do you ever take things from your parents' stores? What a shame for a child to steal from his own parents!

Even you could practise many works of mercy. Do you look after your sick companions? Do you pray for the holy souls? You could prevent many a sin by gently appealing to the consciences of your comrades, or brothers and sisters, showing them what they ought to do.

CHAPTER LXVIII.

PARTING ADVICE OF TOBIAS TO HIS SON.—DEPARTURE OF YOUNG TOBIAS.

[Tob. 4—9.]

TOBIAS, seeing himself surrounded by so many miseries, thought he could not live much longer. He, therefore, called his son and said: "My son, when God shall take my soul, thou shalt bury my body; and thou shalt honour thy mother all the days of her life; for thou must be mindful what and how great perils she has suffered[1] for thee. And when she also shall have ended the time of her life, bury her by me.

---

[1] *She has suffered.* Peril to life and health. A child comes helpless into the world, and for many years requires much care on the part of its mother. A mother has to endure much for the sake of her children: pain, sleepless nights, anxiety, care, labour and fatigue.

"And all the days of thy life have God in thy mind [1], and take heed thou never consent to sin [2], nor transgress the commandments of the Lord our God. Give alms out of thy substance, and turn not thy face away from any poor person. If thou hast much, give abundantly; if thou hast little, take care even so to bestow willingly a little. For alms deliver from sin and death, and will not suffer the soul to go into darkness. Take heed to keep thyself, my son, from all fornication.

"Never suffer pride to reign in thy mind, nor in thy word, for from it all perdition took its beginning [3]. If any man has done work for thee, pay him his hire. See thou never do to another what thou wouldst hate to have done to thee by another. Bless God at all times [4], and desire of him to direct thy ways [5] and that all thy counsels may abide in Him. Fear not, my son, we lead indeed a poor life; but we shall have many good things (grace and consolations on earth and eternal glory in heaven), if we fear God and depart from all sin, and do that which is good."

Then the son answered, saying: "I will do all these things, father, which thou hast commanded me."

Tobias, having thus advised his son, sent him to Rages [6], a distant city, to collect a debt [7] of long standing. And the young Tobias, not knowing the road, went out to seek a guide who would show him the way.

He had not gone far when he met a beautiful young man, standing ready girt as for a journey. It was the Archangel Raphael [8]. Tobias did not know who the young man was, but he addressed him, saying: "Good young man, knowest thou the way that leadeth to the country of the Medes?" The Angel

---

[1] *In thy mind.* Fearing Him and loving Him.

[2] *To sin.* i. e. to sin wilfully.

[3] *Its beginning.* Both the fallen angels and our first parents sinned through pride.

[4] *At all times.* In health and in sickness, in prosperity and adversity.

[5] *Thy ways.* "That His Providence may watch over you, and may keep you in the ways of His commandments."

[6] *Rages.* This town lay several hundred miles east of Ninive.

[7] *A debt.* When Tobias was rich he had lent a considerable sum of money to a poor Israelite, without charging any interest.

[8] *The Archangel Raphael.* Who had assumed the form of a noble-looking youth.

answered: "I know it." Then the young Tobias introduced him to his father, who asked him: "Canst thou conduct my son to Gabelus, at Rages?"

The young man replied: "I will conduct him thither, and bring him back to thee." Then Tobias blessed the two young men, praying: "May you have a good journey; may God be with you on your way, and may His Angel[1] accompany you." Then they both set out on their journey, and the dog followed them. But his mother wept and said to her husband: "Thou hast taken the staff of our old age, and hast sent him away."

On the evening of the first day the travellers reached the banks of the river Tigris. Tobias, heated and warm, sat down on the bank and put his feet[2] into the water. Suddenly an enormous fish came up to devour him[3]. Tobias cried out to the Angel: "Sir, he cometh upon me!" The Angel, seeing his terror, exclaimed: "Take him by the gill and draw him to thee." He did so, and when the fish lay panting before his feet, the Angel said: "Take out his heart, his gall and his liver, for these are useful medicines." Then, making a fire, Tobias broiled some of the fish, which furnished a repast; then he salted a portion of what remained, to serve as provision for the journey.

When they came to a certain city, Tobias said to his guide: "Where wilt thou that we lodge?" The Angel answered: "There is here a man named Raguel, a kinsman of thy tribe, who has a daughter named Sara: and thou must take her to wife." Tobias replied: "I hear that she hath been given to seven husbands, and they all died, and a devil killed each of them on the night of his wedding."

Tobias said this, because he was the only son of his aged parents, and if such a misfortune should befall him, it would bring down their old age with sorrow to the grave. The Angel answered that the devil had such power over those who in their marriage banish God from their heart, and think only of gratifying

---

[1] *His Angel.* The idea of a guardian angel was quite familiar to the good Israelites from the days of the Patriarchs and of their deliverance from Egypt. But Tobias had no suspicion that his pious prayer had been answered even before it was uttered.

[2] *His feet.* To wash off the dust and take away the fatigue.

[3] *To devour him.* It opened wide its jaws, as if it were going to devour Tobias.

their passions. "But thou", he continued, "when thou shalt take her, give thyself for three days to nothing else but prayers with her; then the devil shall be driven away, and you shall obtain a blessing."

Having entered into the house of Raguel, Tobias made himself known, and was warmly received by Raguel, as the son of an old friend and of a most worthy man. At the same time Anna, the wife of Raguel, and Sara, his daughter, wept for joy. They then prepared a repast for the travellers, and Raguel prayed them to sit down to eat. Tobias told him that he would neither eat nor drink till he promised to give him Sara, his daughter, in marriage.

Raguel seemed to hesitate, but the Angel told him not to be afraid to give his daughter to the young man, for that he feared the Lord. Then Raguel consented, and taking his daughter's right hand, placed it in that of Tobias, saying: "The God of Abraham, the God of Isaac, and the God of Jacob be with you: may He join you together, and fulfil His blessing in you."

Then they sat down to eat. And Tobias and Sara spent three days in prayer, after which the devil had no power to harm them. Then, at the request of Tobias, the Angel took the note of hand, went to the country of the Medes, collected the money from Gabelus, and returned with Gabelus to be present at the wedding.

Gabelus came with great joy, and when he saw the young husband he wept and embraced him, saying: "The God of Israel bless thee, because thou art the son of a very good and just man, who feareth God, and doeth alms-deeds. And may a blessing come upon thy wife."

COMMENTARY.

The elder Tobias is the model of a good father. By word and example he brought up his son from his earliest youth in the fear of God. When the time came that he expected to die, he forcibly re-iterated the most important points of his teaching, and his exhortations must have made all the greater impression on the son, because the father preached nothing that he had not himself constantly practised. Tobias cared for the salvation of his son's soul more than anything, and therefore he admonished him above all things to avoid sin and especially to cultivate the virtues of filial piety, the fear of God, justice, brotherly love, gentleness and a great confidence in God.

The younger Tobias is the model of a good son. He listened eagerly to his father's beautiful exhortations, and made this promise: "I will do all these things, father, which thou hast commanded me." He kept this promise most faithfully, as you will see by what follows. If a child does not receive his parents' advice willingly, he sins against that obedience which he owes them.

The connexion between the First and Fourth Commandment. Tobias' exhortation shows us how very important the observance of the Fourth Commandment is for children. Does it not strike you as strange that his first exhortation should be: "Honour thy mother &c." and that he should only say afterwards: "Have God in thy mind &c.?" There is a reason for this, because reverence for parents is, so to speak, at the root of religion and of the fear of God. He who does not love and honour his parents, who are his visible benefactors, will not love and honour God, who is his invisible Father and Benefactor. The son who does not observe the Fourth Commandment is ungrateful and irreligious.

Defrauding of wages. Among his other exhortations Tobias said to his son: "If any man has done work for thee, pay him his hire." This is a duty of justice. He who does not give his promised wages to the labourer, that lives by the work of his hands, commits one of the four sins which cry to heaven for vengeance.

Death is the separation of soul and body. Tobias said to his son: "When God shall take my soul, thou shalt bury my body." By death the soul is parted from the body, and God calls it before Him to be judged. The body, meanwhile, returns to the earth, until God shall raise it up at the last day, and re-unite it for ever to the soul.

The enemies of our souls are all those things which lead to mortal sin. They who commit grievous sins are enemies not only of God and their neighbour, but also of their own soul; because they rob it of God's grace, and plunge it into everlasting ruin.

The married state. We learn some good lessons from this history of Tobias. The Angel advised him to enter into the married state. Therefore that state is good and pleasing to God, and persons who intend to marry should not do so without consulting God by earnest prayer. We also learn that some marriages are bad and full of danger, like those of Sara with her previous seven husbands, who had no religion and no fear of God and no pure motives in their action. It is therefore necessary to prepare oneself by prayer and to purify one's intention by the highest motives, both before and at the beginning of that holy and difficult state. These lessons have double force in the New Testament, where marriage has been raised by our Lord to the dignity of a Sacrament.

APPLICATION. Lay to heart the exhortations of old Tobias, just as if your own father had spoken them to you on his death-bed. Ask yourself every day whether you have acted up to his teaching.

Have you always gladly followed the advice of your father and mother? Are your parents obliged to find fault with you very often? Have you ever grieved or angered them? You cannot be a child of God if you do not honour and obey your parents. Whenever they bid you do anything, say to yourself, in the words of the young Tobias: "I will do all these things, father (or mother), which thou hast commanded me."

CHAPTER LXIX.

TOBIAS RETURNS HOME AND CURES HIS FATHER.

[Tob. 10—12.]

FOURTEEN days had passed since the marriage of Tobias, and his parents at home began to be exceedingly sad, and they wept together, because their son did not return. But his mother was quite disconsolate, and she groaned and sighed: "Woe, woe is me, my son, why did we send thee to a strange country; the light of our eyes, the staff of our old age, the comfort of our life, the hope of our posterity!" Then Tobias said to her: "Hold thy peace, our son is safe." Yet she would not be comforted, but went out into all the ways that she might see him coming afar off.

Now Tobias the younger said to Raguel: "I know that my parents count the days, and their spirit is afflicted within them." However, Raguel pressed him to stay a little longer, but in vain. He then gave him Sara his wife, and the half of all he possessed, saying: "May the holy Angel of the Lord be with you in your journey, and bring you through safely, and may you find all things well about your parents."

When the travellers had made half the journey homeward, the Angel said to Tobias: "Let us go before and let the family softly follow [1] after us." They did so, and Raphael told Tobias

---

[1] *Softly follow.* Tobias hastened on to relieve his parents' anxiety as soon as possible, while Sara travelled after him more leisurely, with the servants, camels, flocks and herds which her father had given her.

to take with him the gall of the fish, because it would be very useful.

Meanwhile Anna sat daily beside the way on the hill-top; and while she watched, she saw him coming far off. When she was sure that it was her son coming, she ran to tell her husband. She had scarcely done so when the dog which had accompanied her son on the journey, running before, reached the house, wagging his tail and jumping for joy, as if he had brought the news. Thereupon, the elder Tobias, blind as he was, groped his way and went out to meet his son. And they all wept for joy.

Young Tobias then rubbed his father's eyes with the gall of the fish, and he saw[1]; and the old man exclaimed: "I bless Thee, O Lord God of Israel, because Thou hast chastised me, and Thou hast saved me, and, behold, I see Tobias, my son!" Seven days after, Sara and her retinue arrived, and completed the joy of that favoured and happy household.

Then the son related to his parents all the benefits he had received from the young man, his guide. He said they could never repay him for all he had done for him, but asked his father's permission to give him one half of the money he had received from Gabelus.

The father willingly consented, and they pressed the young man to accept the money. But the heavenly messenger said to them: "Bless ye the God of heaven, and give glory to Him in the sight of all that live; because He hath shown His mercy to you. Prayer is good with fasting and alms, more than to lay up treasures of gold. When thou didst pray with tears, and didst bury the dead, I offered thy prayer to the Lord. And because thou wast acceptable to God, it was necessary that temptation should prove thee. The Lord hath sent me to heal thee, and to deliver Sara, thy son's wife, from the devil. For I am the Angel Raphael[2], one of the seven who stand before the throne of God." Hearing this, they were seized with fear[3], and all fell prostrate

---

[1] *And he saw.* This cure was miraculous, because it followed immediately after the application of the remedy, and because this remedy was unknown before, and is so still.

[2] *Angel Raphael.* Michael, Gabriel and Raphael are Archangels.

[3] *With fear.* The thought that one of God's great Angels should have visited them, filled them with a holy awe.

on the ground. Still the Angel told them not to fear, but to bless and thank the Lord, who had sent him to do His holy will in their regard.

Having spoken thus, he vanished from their sight, leaving the little family lost in wonder[1] and gratitude to God. The elder Tobias lived forty-two years after these events to share in the happiness of his family, and died at the age of one hundred and two years. Tobias, his son, lived to be very old; he saw the children of his children, who remained faithful, and were beloved by God and man.

COMMENTARY.

The Goodness of God. This story of Tobias shows us most clearly how good God is to His servants. He gave old Tobias a good son; He sent His Angel in the form of a man to guide him; He gave the son a rich and virtuous wife; He cured the father, granted him a happy old age in the midst of God-fearing children and grand-children, and blessed his family for many generations. God changed Tobias' suffering to great joy; for who could describe the father's happiness when, after four years of blindness, he once more saw standing before him his beloved son, on whose account he had endured so much anxiety? The sufferings he had gone through made his present joy all the greater. God sends tribulations to the just, in order that He may reward their patience with great joys, often given in this world, but always in heaven.

The blessings brought by piety. St. Paul (1 Tim. 4, 8) writes thus: "Godliness is profitable in all things, having the promise of the life that now is, and of that which is to come." Piety made old Tobias a good father, training his son in virtue; it kept him from sin, and urged him to the ceaseless practice of good works; it won for him the favour of King Salmanazar, and gave him patience under his sufferings, filling him with consolation. Piety made the young Tobias an affectionate and dutiful son, a virtuous youth and a holy man, the joy and support of his parents. It drew down on both father and son God's protection and blessing on earth, and untold glory in heaven. True interior piety cannot be too highly valued.

The love of parents for their children is fully illustrated by this story.

The filial love of children for their parents. In young Tobias was fulfilled the promise attached to the observance of the Fourth Commandment: "that thy days may be long in the land &c."

---

[1] *Lost in wonder.* After the Angel's disappearance they remained on their faces for three hours, praising God.

Guardian Angels. This story fully confirms the Catholic doctrine about guardian Angels. Tobias' parting words to his son: "May God's Angel accompany you", plainly show that he believed in the protection of guardian Angels. By Raphael's actions we can see what it is that our guardian Angels do for us, since they do for us in an invisible manner just what he did, visibly, for young Tobias. He guided him, protected him on his long and perilous journey, showed him what was the right thing to do, and prayed for him and his father. This is what our guardian Angels do for us. The Angel's words: "When thou didst pray with tears, and bury the dead, I offered thy prayer to the Lord", show us plainly that the holy Angels know all about our prayers, sufferings and labours, and carry our prayers and good works before the throne of God, uniting their prayers to ours, and interceding for us. The example of Tobias shows us how we ought to conduct our selves towards our holy guardian. Tobias reverenced the holy Angel, obeyed his directions, executed his commands, called on him in the hour of danger, and showed him the most heartfelt gratitude.

Humility of the holy Archangel Raphael. He gave all the glory to God.

Gratitude shown by the old and the young Tobias towards their benefactor. They wished to give him half of what they possessed. Gratitude is pleasing, whereas everybody detests ingratitude.

Good works. The Angel of God praised Tobias on account of his prayers, fasting and alms-deeds, thereby putting such works before us as excellent, and pleasing to God. Under the head of "prayer" we are to understand all acts of worship both interior and exterior: for Tobias did not merely pray, but offered sacrifice, and observed the great feasts of God. Under the head of "fasting" are included all acts of mortification. Tobias observed all the laws regarding abstinence from certain food: he shortened his night's rest to bury the dead, and bore all his sufferings with patience and resignation. Under the head of "alms-deeds" we are to understand all the works of mercy which Tobias practised in such a high degree, comforting the afflicted, feeding the hungry, and burying the dead. Now, why are these good works enjoined on us? Firstly, because by prayer we prove our love of God, by fasting our love of ourselves, and by alms-deeds our love of our neighbour. Secondly, because these three good works united represent the most perfect offering which we can make to God, for by prayer we offer Him our soul, by fasting our body, and by alms all we possess. Thirdly, because these three good works are the best weapons against our three enemies: by prayer we can fight against pride, by fasting against the lust of the flesh, and by alms-deeds against the lust of the eyes.

Imperishable treasures. Why is "prayer, with fasting and alms, better than laying up treasures of gold"? Because gold and earthly treasures can be taken away from us, and must inevitably be taken away by death, whereas our prayers and other meritorious works are real treasures which no one can take away, but which will go into eternity with us, and obtain for us a favourable judgment. Earthly treasures make it difficult to die, but heavenly treasures make it easy. Therefore our Divine Saviour says: "Lay up for yourselves treasures in heaven" (New Test. XXI).

The prayer of praise and thanksgiving. A great many men err by offering up only prayers of petition, quite neglecting either to praise or thank Almighty God. The Angel expressly urged Tobias to offer up prayers of praise and thanksgiving, and Tobias was in the habit of doing so.

The wings of prayer. Our prayers should be joined to fasting and alms-deeds, or in other words to works of self-denial and charity. By this means they have greater power, are more pleasing to God, and are more surely heard. The holy Fathers say therefore: "Fasting and alms are the two wings with which our prayers fly to heaven."

The sufferings of the just serve the double purpose of proving them and of increasing their merits. "Because thou wast acceptable to God, it was necessary that temptation should prove thee", said the Angel to Tobias.

Great awe and veneration were experienced by both father and son when they discovered that an Angel of the Most High had appeared to them in the form of a man. "Being seized with fear they fell upon their faces on the ground." How much more reverence ought we to feel each time we are in the presence of the most holy Sacrament, in which our Lord is really and personally present with His Divinity and sacred Humanity.

A good education produces good fruit for several generations. Tobias the younger, having received a good education from his father, brought up his own children in the fear of the Lord; and they too, in turn, brought up their children well. So it happened that the descendants of Tobias "continued in good life and in holy conversation, and thus were acceptable both to God and man".

APPLICATION. Do you keep in mind that your holy guardian Angel is always with you? Do you commend yourself to his care, and obey his inspirations?

Do you take pains, like young Tobias, to be a joy to your parents, and to spare them anxiety and vexation? Do you return home as soon as you can, when you are sent out by them on an errand?

CHAPTER LXX.

DECLINE OF THE KINGDOM OF JUDA.—THE PROPHETS JOEL AND MICHEAS. (790—730 B. C.)

[4 Kings 14→18. Joel. Micheas.]

GOD also sent to the inhabitants of the kingdom of Juda a great number of prophets, whose powerful voice was heard throughout the land calling them to repentance, by proclaiming and foretelling the judgments of God. Many times did their words produce the desired effect, and bring the people to repentance, and for a while they served God with fidelity and sincerity.

Unhappily these returns to virtue and religion were of short duration[1]. Then it was that the prophets, with sorrowful hearts, began to announce to the rebellious people the gradual downfall[2] of their country, and the only consolation left to the prophets was the thought of the Messias, whose coming they saw more clearly as time went on.

The prophet Joel spoke to the people in these terms: "Hear this, ye old men, and give ear, all ye inhabitants of the land. Blow the trumpet in Sion, sound an alarm in my holy mountain; because the day of the Lord comes; because it is nigh at hand. A day of darkness and of gloom; a day of clouds and whirlwinds; a numerous people and a strong people, as the morning spread upon the mountains. Before the face thereof a devouring fire and behind it a burning flame. Sacrifices and oblations have ceased to be offered in the house of the Lord. Rend your hearts and not your garments, and turn to the Lord your God. Between the porch and the altar, the priests,

---

[1] *Of short duration.* Terrible impurity, sorcery, and superstitions of all kinds reigned among the chosen people. Of the twenty kings who ruled over Juda the greater number shamelessly served idols. Achaz and Manasses even offered up their own children in sacrifice to the false god, Moloch. Achaz closed the Temple; Manasses set up altars to the false gods in the outer court of it.

[2] *The gradual downfall.* Foretelling such punishments as invasions of the enemy, despoiling of cities, devastation of the country &c. &c. Manasses was cast into prison, loaded with chains, and carried off to Babylon; and many kings were murdered by conspirators.

the Lord's ministers, shall weep and shall say: "Spare, O Lord, spare Thy people."

The prophet Micheas is not less terrible in his warning: "Hear, all ye peoples", he cries out, "and let the earth give ear. I will make Samaria as a heap of stones! I will bring down the stones thereof into the valley, and will lay her foundations bare. Hear this, ye princes of the house of Jacob; you that abhor judgment, and pervert all that is right; you who build up Sion with blood, and Jerusalem with iniquity. Therefore, on account of you, Sion shall be ploughed as a field, and Jerusalem shall be as a heap of stones; and the mountain of the Temple as the high places of the forests. And [= but] thou, Bethlehem Ephrata, art a little one among the thousands of Juda; out of thee shall He come forth unto me that is to be the Ruler in Israel; and His going forth is from the beginning, from the days of eternity."

These prophecies have all been literally fulfilled. The prophecy about Bethlehem refers to the Saviour, so that the Jews might know that the Redeemer promised to Adam, to Abraham, Isaac and Jacob, to Juda, and to David would be born in Bethlehem.

COMMENTARY.

Evil passions are at the root of unbelief. It seems almost incredible that, although God had made Himself known to them in such marvellous ways, so many of the kings of Israel and of Juda should have fallen away from Him. Their apostasy shows us the enormous power of those human passions which obscure the reason. The idolatrous kings knew the true God, but they refused to acknowledge Him, because His commandments put a curb on their passions. The worship of false gods, which encouraged sensuality, and was not opposed to despotism or extravagance, was preferable to them, for while practising it they were free to live according to their lusts. Therefore, they turned their hearts from God and set up a senseless idolatry which permitted them to do exactly as they wished.

APPLICATION. Bear in mind that the evil passions of the heart are to-day, as they were in the days of the kings of Juda, the principal cause of unbelief in the eternal and true God.

CHAPTER LXXI.

KING OZIAS, WISHING TO USURP THE PRIESTLY FUNCTIONS, IS STRICKEN WITH LEPROSY.

[2 Paralip. 26. 4 Kings 15.]

OZIAS[1] was one of the few faithful kings who reigned in Juda. He reigned fifty-two years, and did that which was right in the sight of the Lord. And God directed him in all things. Unhappily prosperity made him proud, and he carried his audacity so far as to usurp the priestly office[2]. One day, going into the Temple[3], he went to burn incense upon the altar. Eighty priests, with Azarias, the High Priest, at their head, opposed the king, and prevented him from burning incense.

Ozias, being very angry, threatened to strike the priests with the censer which he held in his hand. No sooner had he raised his hand than he himself was stricken with leprosy[4], which appeared on his forehead before all the priests. And they, seized with horror at this sudden and awful punishment, took hold of the king and put him out of the Temple.

The king was terrified, and feeling the leprosy spread all over his body hastened away from the Temple to shut himself up in a palace apart from all others. He remained a leper till the day of his death. Such was the fearful punishment which God inflicted on an otherwise faithful king, because of his sacrilegious attempt to perform an office that belonged only to priests.

COMMENTARY.

After pride comes a fall. The case of Ozias, like that of Saul, shows us that it is easy for a man to be made proud by prosperity, power or riches. To be king, no longer satisfied him; he must be

---

[1] *Ozias.* Ozias, also called Azarias, overcame the enemies of Juda, and brought his kingdom to a state of great prosperity.

[2] *Priestly office.* He wished to be both priest and king as the heathens were; and to be, therefore, not only the temporal head, but also the spiritual head of his people.

[3] *The Temple.* Into the Sanctuary, which, according to the Law, only the priests might enter.

[4] *Leprosy.* On account of the contagion, the king had till his death to live in a house apart, and might not even enter the outer court of the Temple. The throne passed to his son, Joatham.

priest as well! This led him to sin grievously against the law of God, and as a punishment for his pride he lost even his royal position, and led a sad and solitary life. No doubt, in his solitude, he renounced his pride, and heartily repented of his crime. "Everyone that exalteth himself shall be humbled" (Luke 14, 11).

Temporal and spiritual authority. Even in the Old Testament God, in His wisdom, separated the spiritual or priestly from the temporal or royal authority, perpetuating it in Aaron and his descendants. In the New Testament our Lord instituted a special priesthood, entrusting its authority to the apostles and their successors. Both Church and State represent God's authority, and they ought mutually to respect each other, and work together for the good of the people, but neither of them ought to usurp the prerogatives of the other. The severe punishment which followed the crime of Ozias ought to serve as a warning to temporal rulers in all ages not to encroach on the rights of the Church; and it ought to show all men that it is a sin not to respect the spiritual authority instituted by God, to set themselves up against it, or blame or abuse its decrees.

Lawful obedience. The High Priest did his duty in undauntedly opposing the king in his sinful purpose. This was a case when it would have been wrong for him to obey the king, for he commanded a thing which God had forbidden.

APPLICATION. Remind yourselves of the cases in which you are not bound to obey your parents and those set in authority over you.

CHAPTER LXXII.

THE PROPHECIES OF ISAIAS. (700 B. C.)

[Isaias.]

DURING the reign of Ozias, Joatham, and especially Achaz, the people of Juda were guilty of many acts of idolatry. Wherefore God sent them the great prophet Isaias[1]. In sublime and terrific language he warned them of many fearful calamities that were to come upon their country, unless they did penance. Isaias was the great preacher of penance and of forgiveness of sins. "Hear the word of the Lord", he wrote: "Wash yourselves,

---

[1] *Isaias.* He lived from about 750 to 700 B. C. He was the chief among the prophets of that time, being remarkable not only for what he did, but still more on account of his wonderful prophecies. Holy Scripture itself calls him "the great prophet, faithful in the sight of God" (Ecclus. 48, 25).

be clean, take away the evil of your devices from my eyes: cease to do perversely[1]. Learn to do well: seek judgment. Then come and accuse me, saith the Lord. If your sins be as scarlet, they shall be made as white as snow: if they be red as crimson, they shall be as white as wool. But if you will provoke me to wrath, the sword shall devour you."

To this prophet also the Lord revealed so many particulars[2] relating to the Saviour of the world that, reading his prophecies, one would suppose Isaias had lived at the same time as our Divine Lord, instead of living seven hundred years before. A few of these prophecies will show how clearly this greatest of all the prophets foresaw the Birth, Passion and Death of the Redeemer.

Speaking of the Mother of the Messias, as well as of the Messias Himself, he said: "Behold, a virgin shall conceive and bear a son, and His name shall be called Emmanuel, that is, God with us."—"And there shall come forth a rod out of the root of Jesse, and a flower shall rise up out of his root. And the Spirit of the Lord shall rest upon Him, the spirit of wisdom and understanding, the spirit of counsel and of fortitude, the spirit of knowledge and of godliness. And He shall be filled with the spirit of the fear of the Lord."

"A Child is born to us, a Son is given to us, and the government is upon His shoulder. His name shall be called Wonderful, Counsellor, God the mighty, the Father of the world to come, the Prince of Peace." "God Himself will come and save you; then[3] shall the eyes of the blind be opened and the ears of the deaf shall be unstopped."

Concerning the Passion of our Lord he prophesied: "There is no beauty[4] in Him, nor comeliness. Despised, and the most abject of men, a man of[5] sorrows. He has borne our infirmities;

---

[1] *Cease to do perversely.* The Lord thus reminds the inhabitants of Juda that they were not only to worship Him outwardly, but to serve Him by thought, word and deed. If they were converted, He would take away their sins, however grievous or numerous they might be.

[2] *Particulars.* Isaias described much of our Lord's Life as accurately as if he had been one of the evangelists, who wrote and described what they had themselves seen. Only a few among the many prophecies of Isaias are quoted above.

[3] *Then.* That is when the Redeemer shall have come.

[4] *No beauty.* i. e. He, the Redeemer, is quite disfigured and marred by the treatment He has received.

[5] *A man of.* i. e. a man full of suffering—only there for the purpose of suffering.

He was wounded for our iniquities; He was bruised for our sins, and by His bruises we are healed[1]. The Lord hath laid on Him the iniquity of us all. He was offered because it was His own will, and He opened not His mouth[2]. He shall be led as a sheep to the slaughter, and shall be dumb as a lamb[3] before his shearer." Regarding His future glory, the prophet says: "The Gentiles shall beseech Him, and His sepulchre shall be glorious." Isaias was prophesying for about fifty years. It is said that he, while yet alive, was sawn in two by order of the impious king Manasses.

COMMENTARY.

The Omniscience of God. God sees the future as if it were actually present, and He revealed the life of the Redeemer so clearly to Isaias, that the prophet was able to describe it as if he had seen it in person.

The Holiness of God. He loves only that which is good, and detests evil. He wishes man to be good in thought, word and deed. "Wash yourselves, be clean, take away the evil of your devices from my eyes; cease to do perversely."

The Mercy of God. He is quite ready to pardon if only the sinner will be converted. "Then (when you are converted), come and accuse me. If your sins be as scarlet, they shall be made as white as snow &c."

True conversion consists, as the words of Isaias show, in a complete change of heart and life. The sinner must renounce all bad thoughts and sinful deeds, and must do what is right. He must hate the sins which he has hitherto loved, and must worship the God whom he has hitherto despised and offended.

Even the most grievous sins can be remitted, if only the sinner be truly penitent. "If your sins be as scarlet, they shall be made as white as snow; and if they be red as crimson, they shall be as white as wool." Therefore, not even the greatest of sinners should despair of God's mercy. If he does, he sins against the Holy Ghost, and is in danger of being lost eternally.

The testimony of the prophets helps and confirms our faith. The prophecies of Isaias and the other prophets were written by the in-spiration of God, and have to his day been preserved in the Holy

---

[1] *Are healed.* His wounds obtain for us pardon and grace.

[2] *His mouth.* To complain.

[3] *As a lamb.* This was fulfilled to the letter. When asked to answer to all the accusations brought against Him before the High Priest and Pilate, Jesus was silent. The beautiful expression *"Lamb of God"* was taken up by John the Baptist and has remained in the Church ever since.

Scriptures in order to strengthen our faith. Our Saviour says: "Search the Scriptures, the same are they that give testimony of Me" (John 5, 39). It must, indeed, confirm our faith to see that the very things which the Church teaches us about the Person and Life of the Redeemer, were foretold by the prophets hundreds of years before His Birth.

The prophecies of Isaias constitute *the ninth promise of the Messias,* and contain the following important doctrines of faith:

a) That the Redeemer is God; for Isaias writes: "God Himself will come and will save you", and he calls Him "Emmanuel, or God with us". Jesus Christ is indeed the true God with us, for He is the Son of God, made Man.

b) That the Divine Redeemer would be conceived and born of a virgin: "Conceived of the Holy Ghost, born of the Virgin Mary".

c) That He would suffer sorrow and pain, that He would be wounded, sacrificed and slain (New Test. LXXIV).

d) That like a lamb He would suffer and die patiently and willingly. "He was offered because it was His own will, and He opened not His mouth. He shall be led as a sheep to the slaughter, and shall be dumb as a lamb before his shearer."

e) Isaias foretells in plain words that it was on account of the sins of men that the Redeemer would suffer and die, in order to win pardon and salvation for them. Thus he teaches the doctrine of the Vicarious satisfaction or Atonement made by the Redeemer of the world.

f) Finally, the prophet glances at the glory of the Divine Saviour, saying that His sepulchre would be glorious, and that the nations (Jews and Gentiles) would adore Him. The grave of our Lord was made glorious by His Resurrection; and the nations could not adore Him, were He not still in heaven our God and Mediator. Thus the prophecy foretells that, as Saviour of His people, He would rise from the dead, and sit on His throne in heaven: "He rose again from the dead, ascended into heaven, and sitteth at the right hand of God the Father Almighty."

Isaias also describes in glowing terms the beauty, grandeur and universality of the Church of Christ under the names of the new Israel, new Jerusalem, new Sion.

Isaias was a great Saint of the Old Testament. He is venerated by the Church as a great preacher of penance, zealous for the glory of God and the salvation of souls, and also as a highly inspired prophet and martyr. When you recite the Litany of the Saints, and say, "All ye holy patriarchs and prophets, pray for us", you can think especially of God's holy prophet, Isaias.

APPLICATION. Is your piety only exterior? Does the holy fear of God reign within you? Do you love God with all your heart, and detest sin? Do you ever allow envious, malicious, revengeful, impure, or proud thoughts to enter your mind? Have you tried to amend your life since your last confession?

CHAPTER LXXIII.

THE PIOUS KING EZECHIAS. (723—694 B. C.)

[2 Paralip. 29—32.]

DURING the reign of Achaz the people of Juda were visited with a terrible calamity. That unhappy king had sacrificed his own children to the idol Moloch, one of the chief gods of the Gentiles. He had closed the gates of the Temple, and broken the sacred vessels. The Lord therefore delivered him into the hands of the king of Syria, who slew in one day a hundred and twenty thousand men of Juda, while two hundred thousand women and children were carried into captivity.

Achaz having died a short time after, his son Ezechias ascended the throne. This pious prince immediately cast down the altars which his unhappy father had everywhere raised to the pagan gods; he threw open again the gates of the Temple, and exhorted the Levites to purify it from the profanations that had taken place there; saying that it was because of the sins of the people, and, above all, because of their idolatry, that so many misfortunes had come upon them.

And God blessed Ezechias and was with him in all he did; so that in his days the kingdom of Juda regained all its former prosperity. Nevertheless it came to pass that after some years, Sennacherib, king of Assyria, came with a mighty army, and besieged Jerusalem.

Then Ezechias went to the Temple and prayed. He also sent priests, clothed in sackcloth, to the prophet Isaias, to ask him to intercede with God on behalf of him and his people. The prophet sent word to Ezechias not to fear, for that God had heard his prayer, and would destroy the Assyrians, and that their king, returning to his own country, should perish by the sword.

That same night the angel of the Lord went to the camp of the Assyrians, and killed one hundred and eighty-five thousand warriors. Thus Sennacherib was obliged to return in disgrace to his own country. There he went to the temple of his god, and his own sons slew him with the sword. Thus was fulfilled the prophecy of Isaias.

Ezechias, some time after, fell sick and lay at the point of death. The prophet Isaias was sent to tell him to put his house in order, for that he must die. The king, terrified at the thought of death, turned his face towards the Temple, and prayed with tears that God might prolong his life. God heard his prayer, and sent the prophet again to tell him that fifteen years should be added to his life. And so it came to pass; and at the end of the fifteen years he died, after a happy and prosperous reign, the reward of his fidelity to God.

COMMENTARY.

The Justice of God. The holy king Ezechias was blessed by God, and saved from a great danger in the most wonderful way. On the other hand, the pride of Ozias was punished by a life-long illness; and all the other kings of Juda who were unfaithful to God were punished by Him in different ways.

In the hour of danger we ought to do as the pious king Ezechias did. He took every possible human precaution to defend Jerusalem, and then, full of confidence, humbly asked God's protection. In the hour of need we, in the same way, ought to do all we can ourselves, though we must not depend on our own efforts for success, but humbly pray to God for help and deliverance. "Our help cometh from the Lord!"

The power of prayer. The marvellous help which was sent to Ezechias ought to prove to us the power and efficacy of fervent prayer.

APPLICATION. Have you always prayed with confidence? Very likely you have prayed for many things, and have not received them because you lacked confidence. Have more faith, for the future, when you pray, especially in times of trouble and spiritual need; and then you will certainly be heard.

CHAPTER LXXIV.

THE HEROIC JUDITH.

[Judith.]

AFTER a brief season of repentance and of penance, the people of Juda again forgot the Lord. Then[1] God, in His anger, sent them a new and terrible punishment, which would have ended in the total destruction of their nation, had it not been for the heroic courage of a certain holy woman. At that

---

[1] *Then.* This was about the year 690, during the minority of Manasses.

time Holofernes, general-in-chief of the Assyrian forces, came at the head of a mighty army[1] to overthrow the kingdom of Juda, as he had overthrown many other kingdoms.

Having taken all the cities and strongholds of the country, and treated their inhabitants with savage cruelty, he came to lay siege to Bethulia (Fig. 53)[2]. He cut off the aqueducts which supplied the city with water, and thereby reduced the citizens to such an extremity that the elders resolved to give up the city[3] in five days, unless they were relieved before that time. Mean-

Fig. 53. Bethulia (Sanur). (Phot. Bonfils.)

while they prayed fervently to God, humbled themselves before Him, and strewed ashes on their heads.

---

[1] *A mighty army.* Of 120,000 men on foot, and 22,000 horsemen.

[2] *To Bethulia.* This was a mountain fortress on the northern side of Mount Gelboe, in which the brook Kishon takes its rise, and to the south of Naim.

[3] *Give up the city.* The army of Holofernes was quite twenty times as strong as that of Bethulia, and, humanly speaking, there was no salvation to be looked for, especially after he had turned off the water-supply. The Assyrian general did not attempt to storm Bethulia, for he reckoned confidently that the people of the town, dying of thirst, would very soon surrender; and he quietly awaited the result of the want of water.

Now there was in the city a woman named Judith, of rare beauty and of great wealth, who, being a widow, lived retired in her own house, and spent her days in prayer[1] and good works. Being touched with compassion for the sad condition of her people, she presented herself before the ancients of the city and said: "What is this word by which you have consented to give up the city within five days? You have set a time for the mercy of the Lord according to your pleasure. This is not a word that may draw down mercy, but rather indignation. Let us therefore be penitent for this same thing, and remember that all the Saints were tempted and remained faithful; but that those who rejected the trials of the Lord were destroyed. And let us believe that these scourges have happened for our amendment and not for our destruction."

The ancients, inspired by these noble words, begged her to pray for the people. She consented, and retiring to her oratory, clothed herself in hair-cloth[2], put ashes on her head, and falling prostrate before the Lord, she besought Him to humble the enemies of her nation. While she thus prayed, Almighty God inspired her with the thought that she should go into the camp of the enemy and cut off the head of the Assyrian general Holofernes.

Then, putting off the hair-cloth, she immediately arrayed herself in her richest garments, perfumed herself with the best ointments, plaited her hair, and adorned herself with bracelets, earlets, and rings. And the Lord increased ·her beauty, because all her dressing up did not proceed from vanity. Then she took a servant-maid with her and set out for the camp of Holofernes.

Being brought before Holofernes, the tyrant was charmed with her majestic beauty, and supposing that she had fled from her own people, ordered her to receive every attention, and to be allowed to go and come as she pleased. On the fourth day Holofernes gave a grand banquet to the officers of his army. He and they overcharged themselves with wine, and when they lay

---

[1] *In prayer.* And fasting; Judith took only one meal a day, and that one in the evening.

[2] *In hair-cloth.* A rough garment worn under the other clothes, for the purpose of inflicting penance on the body.

down on their couches, they fell into a death-like sleep. Then
Judith resolved to strike the decisive blow that was to save her
country and her people.

She besought God, saying: "Strengthen me, O Lord God of
Israel, and in this hour look upon the works of my hands, that I
may bring to pass that which I have purposed, having a belief
that it might be done by Thee." Then she moved softly towards
the tent of Holofernes. And taking his sword, which hung from
a pillar near by, she drew it from its scabbard, raised it aloft,
and, at the second stroke, cut off the head of the sleeping tyrant.
She then gave the head to her maid, who waited without, and
bade her put it into her wallet[1].

Departing from the camp, she returned with her servant to
Bethulia, and having assembled the people, showed them the head
of Holofernes, saying: "Praise ye the Lord our God, who hath
killed the enemy of His people by my hand. His angel hath been
my keeper and hath brought me back to you." Then Ozias, the
prince[2] of the people of Israel, said to her: "Blessed art thou,
O daughter of the Lord, the Most High God, above all the women
upon the earth." Then the people, praising God, rushed towards
the camp of the Assyrians. The guards, terrified and confused,
made a great noise at the door of their general's tent in order
to awaken him.

But finding their efforts useless they at length ventured to
enter the tent, and seeing the headless body of their mighty general
weltering in blood, they were seized with fear and fled in haste[3],
crying out that Holofernes was slain. A great confusion ensued,
and the people of Bethulia had only to complete the work commenced by Judith, and take possession of the Assyrian camp with
its rich spoils.

Then the Jewish people, turning to Judith, sang with one
accord: "Thou art the glory of Jerusalem; thou art the joy of
Israel; thou art the honour of our people." The rejoicings following

---

[1] *Wallet.* In which she had brought food from Bethulia.

[2] *The prince.* The chief man of the town.

[3] *Fled in haste.* Many were killed in their flight, and the whole camp was
plundered by the people of Bethulia. What joy and gratitude to God must they
have felt at being delivered from so great a danger!

on this splendid victory were kept up for three months. And Judith became great throughout all Israel. She died at an advanced age[1], and was mourned by all the people.

COMMENTARY.

The Goodness of God to His people. The attack of the powerful Holofernes reduced the kingdom of Juda to a state of the greatest danger. He had already taken several places, and if the strong fortress of Bethulia had fallen, the way to Jerusalem itself would have been open to him. The Temple would then have been destroyed, and the whole country conquered. Humanly speaking all this must have happened, for Bethulia was suffering from want of water and could not hold out beyond a few days. But once more God spared for a time the faithless kingdom of Juda; and brought to nought the plots of the wicked Holofernes, through the instrumentality of a weak woman. God put it into the heart of Judith to slay the enemy of her people, and enlightened and strengthened her to carry out her dangerous undertaking. He, moreover, produced such a panic in the Assyrian army and its leaders, after the death of their general, that they completely lost their heads, abandoned their camp in their confusion, and took to flight before a mere handful of Bethulians. In this instance, as in that of Goliath, God chose the weak things of the world to confound the strong (1 Cor. 1, 27).

Resignation to God's will. The people of Bethulia believed in the true God, and had not been led away to serve idols (Judith 8, 18); still their faith was not sufficiently enlightened, and their wills not sufficiently resigned. They "tempted" God, or dictated to Him, by saying: "If Thou wilt help, help soon; if Thy help does not come in five days, we shall despair of Thine assistance and surrender." Judith was right to blame them, for it is not for us, blind, wretched men, to dictate to the great God as to when and how He shall help us. Probably the Bethulians expected that by sending rain He would put an end to the want of water; but God had decided on saving them in another way, for His thoughts are not our thoughts. Let us beware of dictating to God as to what way He is to help us. We must leave the time and mode of help entirely to Him.

The virtues of Judith. She was a very virtuous and a very holy woman. Let us see what virtues she especially displayed in this story.

a) *Piety.* She prayed often and devoutly. By constant communion with God she learnt to know Him, and obtained great confidence in Him. It was in prayer that her great thoughts and resolutions came to her, as also the wisdom to carry them out.

---

[1] *Advanced age.* At the age of a hundred and five years.

b) *Mortification and self-denial.* Her husband left her great riches, many servants, and flocks and herds. But although she had such great possessions, and might have led a luxurious and brilliant life, she lived quite retired from the world, in a state of voluntary poverty and chastity, and practised severe penances, wearing hair-cloth, and fasting every day. "Blessed are the poor in spirit!" It was this life of mortification that made Judith a heroine.

c) *Heroism,* which enabled her to save her people. The more we deny ourselves and resist our natural desires, the more holy and strong will be our wills, and the less shall we shrink from any burden or danger which could advance God's glory and the good of our neighbour. The High Priest was right when he said to Judith: "Thou hast done manfully, because thou hast loved chastity" (Judith 15, 11).

d) *Love of her country.* Judith knew that the Temple and her country were in extreme danger, and it was to save them that she went unprotected into the enemy's camp, and placed herself in what was, apparently, imminent danger of death. She was willing to sacrifice herself for them, out of love for God and His holy Law.

e) Her *humility* is especially worthy of admiration. She was proud neither of beauty nor riches, and was truly humble of heart. "Let us be penitent, and humble our souls before God", said she to the elders. After her heroic action she gave all the glory to God. "Praise ye the Lord our God", said she, "who hath killed the enemies of His people by my hand."

Type of the Blessed Virgin Mary. Even as the chaste Judith cut off the head of Holofernes, thereby saving her people from captivity and slavery, so did Mary, the Immaculate Mother, through her Divine Son, trample on the head of the infernal Holofernes, and free all mankind from his power. Even as Judith was lauded as "blessed above all women on earth", so did St. Elizabeth and the angel Gabriel both say to our Lady: "Blessed art thou among women." Judith gave all the glory to God, as did Mary in the Magnificat (New Test. IV). Judith was devout: Mary is the vessel of singular devotion. Judith was a holy woman: Mary is the Virgin Most Holy, and the Mirror of justice in which all virtues are reflected. Judith was heroic: Mary was the most heroic of women, and the Queen of martyrs. Judith was the glory of Jerusalem: Mary is the Queen of all Saints, the glory of the heavenly Jerusalem, the joy of the elect, and the honour of the whole Church.

The invocation of the Saints. The people of Bethulia recommended themselves to the intercession of Judith, because she was a holy woman, and because on that account her prayers would have great power with God. It is for the same reason that we recommend ourselves to the intercession of the Saints.

Belief in guardian angels. "God's angel hath been my keeper", said Judith; and her words show us that she believed that she had a guardian angel. The Catholic doctrine about guardian angels is thoroughly founded on Holy Scripture.

APPLICATION. Do you always give glory to God, or do you cherish vain thoughts, and boast of your own attainments? Are you fond of talking about yourself? Do you try to depreciate others in order to exalt yourself? Renounce pride! Be ashamed of your silly vanity and boasting! Each day direct all your intentions to the greater glory of God, for this is an excellent way to put down pride and to obtain merit in the sight of God.

V. EPOCH:

THE BABYLONIAN CAPTIVITY.

(606—536 B. C.)

CHAPTER LXXV.

FALL OF THE KINGDOM OF JUDA.—THE BABYLONIAN CAPTIVITY (588 B. C.).

[4 Kings 24—25. Jerem. Baruch. Ezech. Daniel.]

AT last the people of Juda became so hardened in sin that the divine chastisements had no longer any effect upon their hearts. They gave themselves wholly up to the vile practices of idolatry, and persecuted the prophets of God, several of whom they put to death. In vain did the great prophet, Jeremias[1], who lived at that time, endeavour to recall them to repentance. Finally, the patience of the merciful God was exhausted, and the ruin so often foretold by the prophet Isaias fell heavily on the people.

---

[1] *Jeremias* tried to convert the people and avert the threatened punishment by his own penances. He put on himself an iron yoke (i. e. the strong bar which fastens two oxen together), and thus preached penance to the people. He did this in order to bring home to them into how degrading a servitude they had fallen. But they scourged him and threw him into a dungeon, from which he was delivered by Nabuchodonozor when he conquered Jerusalem.

In the year 606 B. C., Nabuchodonozor (Fig. 54)[1], king of Babylon, placed himself at the head of an immense army, marched

Fig. 54.
Cameo with inscription of Nabuchodonozor.
Berlin Museum.
(From *Jeremias*, Das Alte Testament, 2. ed.)

against Jerusalem[2], and, having taken it, carried away the king and the principal inhabitants as captives[3]. Sixteen years later, those who were left in Jerusalem revolted once more against Nabuchodonozor, and the latter returned with a still greater army, and after a siege of eighteen months, he took Jerusalem by storm (588 B. C.).

Then the whole city was given up to fire and pillage[4]. The Temple itself was consumed by fire, and the sacred vessels were carried off. All the people[5] that escaped the sword were led into captivity in Babylon, and the splendid city of Jerusalem was reduced to a heap of ruins.

Jeremias[6] remained in Jerusalem (Fig. 55), and, sitting on the ruins of the desolate city, he lamented in the most pathetic manner the miseries of his people, and the destruction of Jerusalem. "How doth the city sit solitary that was full of people; how is the mistress of nations become as a widow[7]; the princess of provinces

---

[1] *Nabuchodonozor.* About 610 B. C., he and his father had destroyed Ninive and the Assyrian empire (to which Babylon belonged), and set up a new Babylonian empire, and subjected half Asia.

[2] *Against Jerusalem.* It appears that between 606—588 Nabuchodonozor had to march several times against Jerusalem to quell revolts, before it was finally destroyed.

[3] *Captives.* 10,000 men.

[4] *Pillage.* The famine during this siege was so terrible that mothers cooked and ate their children who had perished from starvation. A pestilence, moreover, broke out and swept off many of the inhabitants. When, at last, the city was stormed, thousands were killed, and the streets literally ran with blood. The city was sacked, the beautiful Temple destroyed, the houses burnt, and the walls overthrown.

[5] *All the people.* Only the very poor were left behind to cultivate the fields and vineyards. The king Sedecias was carried off, his eyes were put out, and he was kept in prison till he died.

[6] *Jeremias* was given the choice of either remaining in Juda, or of filling an honourable post in Babylon. He chose to remain among the ruins of the Temple to comfort the Jews who were left behind.

[7] *As a widow.* Jerusalem, formerly the mistress of many nations, now robbed of her king and her inhabitants.

made tributary[1]. The ways[2] of Sion mourn, because there are none that come to the solemn feast. O all ye that pass by the way, attend, and see if there be any sorrow like to my sorrow[3]. To what shall I compare thee, or to what shall I liken thee? Great as the sea is thy destruction. Who shall heal thee? Convert us[4], O Lord, to Thee, and we shall be converted, renew[5] our days, as from the beginning."

Jeremias, however, was not without consolation. He knew[6] that Israel would be restored, and that God would make a new

Fig. 55. Jeremias' Grotto near Jerusalem. (Phot. Bonfils.)

covenant with His people. "The days shall come, saith the Lord, and I will make a new covenant with the house of Israel[7] and

---

[1] *Tributary.* Subject to Babylon, and forced to pay tribute to her.

[2] *The ways.* The road to Sion, formerly thronged with pilgrims.

[3] *My sorrow.* This is supposed to be spoken by Jerusalem.

[4] *Convert us.* We have sinned, therefore we are punished. We cannot be converted of ourselves: convert us, and then our conversion will be sincere.

[5] *Renew.* Bring back the former happy days.

[6] *He knew.* And foretold that the Jews would return after a captivity of seventy years (chapter LXXX).

[7] *With the house of Israel.* i. e. with the spiritual Israel of the New Testament, and with the house of Juda, i. e. with the disciples of Christ.

with the house of Juda. Not according to the covenants which I
made with their fathers, which they made void. But this shall be
the covenant that I will make with the house of Israel after those
days. I will give my law and will write it on their hearts[1], and
I will be their God, and they shall be my people. I will forgive
their iniquity and I will remember their sin no more."

The captive Jews[2] were treated with kindness by the king
of Babylon, but they longed for the land of their fathers and for
the city of Jerusalem. This longing of their hearts is beautifully
expressed in one of the Psalms: "Upon the rivers of Babylon,
there we sat and wept, when we remembered Sion. On the willows[3]
in the midst thereof we hung[4] up our instruments, for there they
that led us into captivity required of us the words of songs[5]. How
shall we sing the song of the Lord in a strange land?[6] If I[7]
forget thee, O Jerusalem, let my right hand be forgotten. Let
my tongue cleave to my jaws, if I do not remember thee, if I
make not Jerusalem the beginning of my joys."

During the captivity God did not abandon His people, but
sent the prophet Ezechiel, who admonished and instructed them.
He also consoled them by telling them of a divine vision which
foreshadowed the deliverance of the people from their captivity.
The spirit of the Lord brought Ezechiel to a plain filled with
bones of dead men. Being told by God, he commanded the bones
to come together, which was done, and they were covered with
flesh and skin, but there was no spirit in them. And the Lord
told Ezechiel to say to the spirit: "Come, spirit, and let them
live again." The spirit entered into them, and they lived; they
stood upon their feet, an exceeding great army. Then the Lord
said: "These bones are the house of Israel; they say that our

---

[1] *On their hearts.* This new covenant will be an inward covenant of grace.

[2] *The captive Jews.* As also the scattered Israelites, who from this time were
usually termed Jews.

[3] *Willows.* The species known as weeping willow.

[4] *Hung up.* As a sign of grief, for it was impossible for them to make
music, or sing joyful songs.

[5] *Songs.* i. e. sacred songs of joy which were sung to the accompaniment
of music, which was not the case with songs of mourning.

[6] *A strange land.* They regarded it as an act of desecration to sing divine
canticles in a heathen land, for the entertainment of their captors.

[7] *If I.* These words express a kind of oath. They mean, I would rather
be maimed or dead than cease to be a Jew, a lover of Sion.

bones[1] are dried up and our hope is lost, but say to them: Thus saith the Lord God: Behold, I will open your graves, and bring you into the land of Israel, and you shall know that I am the Lord, O my people."

Amongst the captives were several young men of high rank, belonging to the first families. The king ordered the most distinguished of these to be brought up in his own palace[2], clothed in kingly apparel, and fed with meats from his own table. Amongst these young men were Daniel[3], Ananias, Misael and Azarias.

They resolved not to eat the meats from the king's table, because the Jewish law forbade the use of certain meats[4], and they begged the chief steward to allow them to eat only vegetables, and to drink only water. The steward was disposed to comply with their request, but he told them that if they lived on such diet, they would become so lean that the king would blame him, and perhaps punish him severely.

Daniel besought the steward to try them for ten days with the food and drink they desired to have. The steward consented, and at the end of ten days the faces of these young men were fresher and more comely than those of the other young men of the court.

After this the steward gave them only vegetables and water; but God gave them wisdom[5] and science. When the time came for them to be presented to the king, he was so charmed with their beauty and wisdom that he retained them in his service.

---

[1] *Our bones.* The Jews, in their banishment, considered themselves to be like unto those who are dead and buried.

[2] *Palace.* To be educated and to fill places about the court. They were therefore instructed in the language, writings and sciences of the Babylonians or Chaldees.

[3] *Daniel.* Who was then about fourteen years old.

[4] *Certain meats.* Such as the flesh of unclean beasts, blood, and flesh full of blood. Moreover, certain portions of the flesh of oxen, sheep and goats, as well as wine, were offered to idols, and after they had been thus offered were sold in the markets, so that the Jews could never be sure that, when eating at pagan tables, some food might not be placed before them which it was unlawful for them to eat. In order to be on the safe side, Daniel and his companions wished to refrain from all the flesh and wine sent to them by the king.

[5] *Gave them wisdom.* As a reward for their conscientiousness and self-restraint, God gave them an extraordinary and supernatural understanding and wisdom, so that they not only excelled the other youths, but even the wise men of the kingdom (Dan. 1, 20). To Daniel God gave the gifts of prophecy and interpretation of dreams.

COMMENTARY.

The Long-suffering Justice and Faithfulness of God. He was very patient and long suffering with Juda. Up to the very moment of its overthrow He held out, through Jeremias, hope of pardon and the averting of punishment, if only the people would be converted. And was not the fate of the kingdom of Israel itself an impressive warning? However, neither king nor people would give heed to this, or to the warnings of the prophets sent by God, but listened rather to false prophets, resisted grace, and persisted in their impenitence. At last the measure of their sins was full, the justice of God manifested itself, and the long-threatened punishment overtook Juda.

The Goodness and Mercy of God. The Lord did not leave His miserable people without comfort, but gave them through Jeremias the assurance that He had not finally rejected them, but would restore them to His favour, and institute a new and higher covenant with them.

The uses of suffering. Their captivity served for the salvation of many of the Jews. They turned to God with their whole hearts, for they felt that all their hopes of liberty rested in Him. At last they abhorred idolatry, and were so completely cured of their inclination towards it, that they never relapsed into it, even after their return to the Promised Land.

The love of Jeremias for his people. Even though he was misunderstood and persecuted by them, he felt no malicious satisfaction when the judgment foretold by him really overtook them. No, he bewailed the hard fate of his people, and gave utterance to the deep grief of his noble soul in the "Lamentations".

The necessity of grace. This is taught by the words: "Convert us to Thee, O Lord, and we shall be converted." The sinner cannot be converted without the assistance of grace.—In their captivity the Jews acknowledged themselves to be religiously and politically dead, and had no hope of ending their banishment by their own efforts, or of returning to their country and becoming once more an independent nation: "Our bones are dried up, and our hope is lost." It was only by God's Spirit that the dead and captive people could be raised to a new political and religious existence; and only by the help of God that they could be freed and restored to their own country. This applies to nations and individuals of all ages. A fallen nation can be restored and renewed only by religion and the Spirit of God. And no individual who has succumbed to the death of sin can raise himself up by his own strength, but only by the help of God, who by His grace can restore a dead soul to life. "I will forgive their iniquity and I will remember their sin no more."

The tenth promise of the Messias. The New Covenant foretold by Jeremias was instituted by our Lord Jesus Christ. The Old Covenant was an external law, written on stone tables, observed out of fear, which could effect no inner justification or sanctification. The law of the New Covenant was written in men's hearts by the Holy Ghost, so that it is a law kept out of love, which changes man inwardly, cleanses and heals him from sin. For this reason the Holy Ghost came down on Whitsunday, and wrote the law of Christ on the hearts of the apostles, illuminating them, and kindling in them the fire of love. The law of the New Covenant is engraved in the hearts of individuals in holy Baptism.

The Lamentations of Jeremias are very impressive, and full of deep meaning. They refer literally to the destruction of Jerusalem, and the captivity which the Jewish people had brought upon themselves; but they bear (as the Church has always taught) a deeper meaning, and contain allusions both to the sufferings of the Divine Redeemer, and to the sad condition of man when he is separated from God.

1. The Church applies the passages: "O all ye that pass by the way, attend and see if there be any sorrow like unto my sorrow", and "Great as the sea is thy destruction. Who shall heal thee?" to our Lord, suffering and dying, and also to His sorrowful Mother (see the Lamentations sung in the office of the last three days of Holy Week).

2. The passages relating to the desolation of Jerusalem and the Temple are applied by the Church to the sad condition to which man is brought by sin and its consequences, and to the desolation which mortal sin entails on the individual, whose soul is the temple of God. Of a soul which is in a state of mortal sin, we can truly say: "O how desolate is that soul, which was formerly so rich in virtues and merits. She was the mistress over the powers of human nature, and now, behold, she is the slave of sin and Satan! Once she was beautiful, now she is defaced, and full of sorrow, unrest, and remorse of conscience."

Comfort in suffering. Almighty God did not quite forsake His people. Even during their captivity he raised up prophets among them, to urge them to do penance, to strengthen their faith, to warn them against idolatry, to comfort them and give them hope both of deliverance from their present captivity, and of the coming of a future Saviour. We too, in our troubles and adversity, ought to draw comfort from the thought of our Divine Saviour, who endured unspeakable sufferings for our sake. We should also draw comfort and courage from the thoughts of eternal life. St. Paul writes: "The sufferings of this world are not worthy to be compared with the glory to come, that shall be revealed in us" (Rom. 8, 18).

The eleventh promise of the Messias. The vision of Ezechiel is, primarily, prophetical of the resurrection of the body, in which all the Jews believed, even as patient Job believed in it. Thus the vision presupposes and describes this belief, and then employs it to convey further teaching. By it God wished to say thus to the Jews: "You are now dispersed, and, as it were, dead; but I, your God, will not forsake you, I will gather you together again, and take you back to your own country." This promise was immediately and literally fulfilled by the return of the Jews from captivity (chapter LXXX), by which they became once more a nation; but it was more perfectly and gloriously fulfilled by the New Covenant, by which God poured out His Holy Spirit on all nations, and raised up a greater and more perfect Israel.

Longing for home. The Jews loved their country, their Temple and their worship, so that even though they experienced no want in Babylon, they pined to return to their own home. The more pious among them longed to celebrate once more the feasts of the Lord, to offer sacrifice and sing canticles of praise. We too are living in banishment "in this vale of tears"; for heaven is our one, eternal home. We ought to pine for the heavenly Jerusalem, and do all we can to deserve admittance thereto.

Conscientiousness. Daniel and his three companions offer us a noble example of conscientious fidelity in the observance of God's laws. The inducement to partake of the meats and wine sent from the king's table was very great; but the four youths practised self-denial, and contented themselves with the poorest and most simple of fares, rather than expose themselves to the danger of sin. They acted thus, because they were possessed by the holy fear of God, and dreaded anything that might offend Him.

Fortitude and temperance. Furthermore, they offer us a noble example of fortitude. Their temptations to unbelief and sin in the luxurious court of the pagan king were numerous and powerful, but Daniel and his companions remained firm in faith and in the observance of the divine law. They practised the greatest abstemiousness, and did not let themselves be led away by the example of the other youths in the palace who did partake of the king's dishes. Ought this not to put those Christians to shame who have not the courage to confess their faith before those who are unbelievers or non-Catholics, and who have not even the fortitude or self-denial to abstain from meat on Fridays? Does not this show great weakness, cowardice, and want of character?

The fruits of temperance. The abstemiousness practised by the four youths had a good effect on their bodies as well as their souls. These boys, who were content with simple fare, and who did not taste wine, were more healthy, fresh and comely than those who ate and drank from the king's table. Moderation in eating and drinking preserves health, while the contrary course spoils it and leads to many diseases. "By surfeiting many have perished, but he that is temperate shall prolong life" (Ecclus. 37, 34). A man should eat to live, and not live to eat. The minds of these youths were also strengthened by their abstemiousness. They learnt with ease, and made great progress in knowledge. They knew how to govern themselves, and advanced in every virtue. Moreover, by reason of their temperance they received supernatural gifts from God, especially the gift of wisdom; and to Daniel was given that of prophecy. Temperance, practised for love of God, is meritorious and wins many graces for us.

Good example. Daniel was especially favoured by God; and why? Because he showed a good example to his companions. Even as it is a terrible sin to lead others to do evil, so is it meritorious to show to others a good example, and lead them to do what is right.

The greatest of honours. It was a great honour for the four youths to be chosen by king Nabuchodonozor to be in his court; but it is a far greater honour to be chosen to be the servants of God; for God is the Most High, who rewards His faithful servants with eternal glory and happiness.

Conscientiousness and fortitude win respect even from the unbelieving. We see this in the case of Daniel and his companions. Their faithful observance of their religion, and their abstemiousness clearly pleased the chief steward; otherwise he would not have agreed to their proposal. He had a greater respect for these four than for the other Jewish youths, who ate without demur of the heathen dishes. In their hearts even the vicious pay tribute to virtue.

APPLICATION. Do you take to heart the admonitions and warnings of your parents and teachers, or do you, by preference, listen to bad companions? Do you follow the example of those who make no account of sin? Just think how terrible it is for a young heart to be hard and impenitent! If you have not amended your life since your last confession, begin at once. Make good resolutions every morning, and pray for grace to carry them out!

Think what terrible havoc mortal sin makes in the soul. Conceive a great horror of mortal sin, and resolve rather to die than commit one.

Does the Holy Ghost dwell within you; in other words, are you in a state of grace? Do not grieve the Holy Ghost who is within you by venial sin, and do not drive Him from you by mortal sin.

Had you been in Daniel's place, would you have acted as he did? Do you care more for good eating and drinking than for anything else? Are you sometimes discontented with the food which is set before you? Have you ever sinned by greediness? Are you fond of strong drinks? From henceforward practise abstemiousness. Choose the worst rather than the best of what is offered to you. Faithfully observe all the laws relating to abstinence.

CHAPTER LXXVI.

DANIEL SAVES SUSANNA.

[Daniel 13.]

AMONG the captive Jews in Babylon[1] there was a man named Joakim, whose wife, Susanna, was very beautiful, and feared God. Now Joakim being very rich and influential, it happened that many of his countrymen resorted to his house. Among these were two of the ancients who had been appointed judges[2] for that year. The two old men were considered by the people as wise and virtuous, but in reality they were very wicked.

Now the visitors that came to Joakim generally left at noon, and then Susanna would walk forth into the orchard[3] near by to refresh herself in the shade. The two old men knew this, and one day they went into the orchard and hid themselves behind the trees. A little later Susanna came in and fastened the gate, believing herself alone. Then the wicked old men came forth from their hiding-place and tried to make her commit sin[4].

Susanna was horrified at their proposal; but they said that if she did not consent to their wishes, they would publicly accuse her[5] of a great crime. Then Susanna raised her pure and beautiful eyes to heaven, sighed and said: "I am straitened on every side, for if I do this thing it is death to me[6], and if I do it not I shall not escape your hands[7]. But it is better for me to

---

[1] *Babylon.* This city had been made by Nabuchodonozor the capital of his kingdom, and he had enlarged it to such an extent that it measured fifty-four miles in circumference, and was surrounded by an enormous wall, flanked by two hundred and fifty towers.

[2] *Judges.* Being esteemed by the people as righteous men. Nabuchodonozor had allowed the Jews to govern themselves and live in accordance with their own laws. The court of justice was held in the house of Joakim, on account of his position among the Jews.

[3] *The orchard.* Large gardens and pleasure-grounds were attached to the houses of the luxurious city of Babylon.

[4] *Sin.* The sin of adultery and unfaithfulness to her husband.

[5] *Publicly accuse her.* So as to expose her to the danger of loss of life and honour.

[6] *Death to me.* i. e. death to my soul and my body, as adulterers were to be stoned.

[7] *Your hands.* "If I do not commit it, you, by false witness, will cause my bodily death." Thus Susanna was in danger of death on both sides; but she did not even hesitate in her choice, saying that she would rather die innocent than commit sin.

fall into your hands, without doing it, than to sin in the sight of the Lord."

She then cried out with a loud voice; but the elders cried out against her. One of them ran to the orchard-gate, and opened it that the people might enter.

Then he and his companion falsely accused Susanna of the very crime they had proposed to her. Next day, accompanied by her parents and children, and other relatives, Susanna was brought before the tribunal of justice, where she was condemned and sentenced to death. But she, weeping, looked up to heaven, for her heart had confidence in God.

And the Lord heard her prayer. As she was led out to death[1], Daniel, inspired from above, exclaimed: "I am clean from the blood of this woman." Then all the people began to ask him: "What meaneth this word that thou hast spoken?" He told them to return to judgment, because the elders had borne false witness against Susanna. Then the people went back in haste. But Daniel ordered the two accusers to be brought in separately.

This being done, he said to the first that came: "O thou that art grown old in evil days, now are thy sins come out. Tell me, under what tree thou sawest them conversing together?" He said: "Under a mastic-tree."[2] Daniel replied: "Thou hast lied against thy own head."[3] Then he sent him away, and had the other brought in, whom he asked: "Tell me, under what tree didst thou take them conversing together?" He answered: "Under a holm-tree." Daniel replied: "Thou hast lied against thy own head."

The people saw by the contrary statements of the old men that their testimony was false, and rising up against them, they put them both to death. Susanna was restored to her joyful husband and children, and they and all the people blessed God, who always saves and protects those who place their hopes in Him. Whereupon Daniel became great[4] in the sight of the people.

---

[1] *Death.* By stoning.

[2] *Mastic-tree.* This tree does not grow in Europe. It has a sweet smelling sap, from which incense is made.

[3] *Thy own head.* To your own ruin.

[4] *Became great.* He was honoured and respected, because the people recognised that God's Spirit dwelt within him.

COMMENTARY.

The Omnipresence of God. The old sinners "perverted their own mind and turned away their eyes that they might not look into heaven, nor remember just judgments" (Dan. 13, 9). They intentionally banished all thought of the ever present and most just God, and said to Susanna: "No one seeth us." But on the other hand the holy woman did remember Him, and said: "It is better for me to fall into your hands without sinning, than to sin in the sight of the Lord."

The Omniscience of the Eternal God. "O Eternal God, who knowest hidden things, who knowest all things before they come to pass, Thou knowest that they have borne false witness against me." God knows everything that is hidden, what is past, and what is still to be. He revealed to Daniel that the two elders had borne false witness against Susanna; and it was the thought of God's omniscience that gave Susanna courage and comfort in her hour of peril.

The Justice of God. He brought to light the innocence of Susanna, and the guilt of her accusers, in the most wonderful manner, in order that she might be rewarded, and they punished. God often manifests His justice in this way, even upon earth.

Fortitude. Susanna was a valiant woman, a very heroine of virtue. She preferred to die rather than sin. St. Chrysostom says of her: "Susanna stood as a lamb between two wolves. She was left alone between these two beasts, with no one to help her but God alone. He looked down from heaven, and suffered the dispute to make clear both the chastity of Susanna, and the wickedness of the elders; so that she might become a glorious example to women of all times. Susanna endured a severe fight, more severe than that of Joseph. He, a man, contended with one woman; but Susanna, a weak woman, had to contend with two men, and was a spectacle to men and to angels. The slander against her fidelity to her marriage-vow, the fear of death, her condemnation by all the people, the abhorrence of her husband and relations, the tears of her servants, the grief of all her household, she foresaw all this, and yet nothing could shake her fortitude."

The way to preserve chastity. Susanna's example shows us how we ought to act when tempted to sin against holy purity. She not only reminded herself of the Presence of the Just and Holy God, but she called loudly for help to drive away the two wicked tempters. Thus, if we were to find ourselves in a similar position, we ought to think of God and crave His help, and besides this (if we cannot flee, as Joseph did in the house of Putiphar), we should seek the help of others.

Consequences of want of chastity. The two elders committed sin upon sin. They coveted their neighbour's wife; they intentionally sought her out, and by threats tried to drive her to sin; they calumniated her to her maids; they bore false witness against her in the court of justice; and, finally, by their wicked lies, caused her to be condemned to death. The source of all these sins was want of chastity. They allowed impure desires to rise in their hearts, and these unresisted desires drove them to further sins. Their sin was all the more grievous, because both these men were judges, and therefore bound to give a good example, to protect virtue, and to punish vice and crime. See, then, what evil consequences follow on impure desires! They lead to many sins, to deadness of conscience, injustice, and even to murder.

The beauty of virtue. In the same way that we detest the hateful crime of the elders, we love Susanna for the beautiful and honourable virtues which she exhibited. Her body was beautiful, but her soul was a thousand times more so. She was chaste and faithful, because she feared God. She dreaded sin as the greatest of all evils, and preferred dishonour in the eyes of the world, and loss of life, to the committing of a grievous sin. She has therefore been praised and honoured for centuries as a model of holy fear, fortitude, fidelity and chastity. We can apply to her the words of the Holy Ghost: "O how beautiful is the chaste generation with glory: for the memory thereof is immortal, because it is known both with God and with men" (Wisd. 4, 1).

The prayer full of confidence offered up by Susanna was heard, and God made known her innocence.

To set prisoners free is a work of mercy. Daniel did this, for, by the inspiration of God, he obtained the liberty of Susanna, who had been unjustly put in prison and condemned to death.

The shame of sinners at the Last Judgment. What shame and terror must those two old sinners have felt when their lies and wickedness were revealed before all the people, who had hitherto esteemed them to be just men! Such will be the experience of many Christians who have succeeded in hiding their secret sins and evil doings from men, when, at the Last Day, they find their hypocrisy unmasked before the eyes of the whole world, and they themselves covered with confusion and ignominy, and sentenced to everlasting death!

APPLICATION. Is your holy fear of God strong enough to enable you to stand firm as Susanna did, in the midst of severe temptations? Do not suffer either flattery or threats to lead you into sin. Pray for the gift of holy fear.

Resist the beginnings of evil. Do not let any impure thought or dishonourable desire take hold of you. Recollect immediately the Presence of God, and commend yourself to the protection of the most pure Virgin-Mother of God.

CHAPTER LXXVII.

THE PROPHET DANIEL.—THE THREE YOUNG MEN IN THE FIERY FURNACE.

[Dan. 2—3.]

NABUCHODONOZOR had a dream[1] which terrified[2] him greatly. He saw a large statue[3]; the head was of gold, the breast and arms of silver, the belly and thighs of brass, the legs of iron, and the feet part iron and part clay. Then he noticed a stone rolling[4] from the mountain, which struck the statue on the feet and shattered it; and behold, the stone became a great mountain and filled the whole earth. None of the wise men[5] could interpret the dream[6]. Whereupon the king passed sentence of death upon all the wise men. Then Daniel came to the executioner, saying: Do not kill the wise men, but bring me before the king, and I will tell him the solution of the dream. Daniel first told the king that no one but the God of heaven and earth revealeth mysteries, and then proceeded to explain the dream.

The whole statue signified the great empires of the world that would succeed each other. The head of gold betokened the reign of Nabuchodonozor himself, most glorious among kings; the breast and the arms of silver represented the next empire, that of the Medes and Persians; the belly and the thighs of brass prefigured the dominion of Alexander the Great; the legs and

---

[1] *Dream.* A vision shown to him in the night.

[2] *Terrified.* When he awoke he knew that he had had a dream which had filled him with fear, but he could not remember what it was. The cause of his fear is fully explained by Daniel's description, for the crashing fall of the huge statue must have been terrible.

[3] *Statue.* The parts of the statue were made of different materials: the lower the part, the less costly the material.

[4] *A stone rolling.* Without the intervention of man.

[5] *The wise men.* They were required not only to interpret the dream, but to recall to the king's mind what the dream was. This was asking a great deal; but the king made the demand, because these wise men gave out that there was nothing they did not know; so that he thought he was requiring nothing unreasonable.

[6] *The dream.* Because of their failure to interpret the dream, all the wise men were condemned to death. Daniel and his friends were included in the condemnation, for they came under the category of 'wise men'.

feet of iron signified the great Roman empire which conquered all the others. The stone[1] that fell from the mountain typified a new kingdom that God Himself would found on earth, and which, from a small beginning, would gradually grow strong and overcome all other kingdoms, and would last for ever. The king, hearing the interpretation, said to Daniel: "Verily your God is the God of gods[2], and Lord of kings, and a revealer of hidden things." He raised Daniel to a high station[3] and bestowed on him many gifts.

Fig. 56. Bel with lion.
Assyrian sculpture.

About this time king Nabuchodonozor made a great statue[4] of gold, which he placed on a pillar in the plain of Babylon. All the princes and nobles of his kingdom were invited to assist at the dedication[5] of this statue. Heralds were sent out everywhere to announce to all the people that when they heard the sound of the trumpets and flutes and other instruments of music, they should fall down and adore the golden statue. And it came to pass that no one disobeyed this order except Ananias, Azarias and Misael[6].

It was announced to the king that the three young men had refused to worship the golden statue. Then Nabuchodonozor, full of rage, said to them: "Who is the god[7] that shall deliver you out of my hand?" They answered: "Our God, whom we worship,

---

[1] *The stone*. 'Cut out without hands'.

[2] *The God of gods*. The greatest among the gods. The king acknowledged that the God of Daniel was greater than the pagan gods, because He alone had revealed the meaning of the dream.

[3] *High station*. Of governor of the province of Babylon.

[4] *A great statue*. The image probably represented Bel, the chief god of the Babylonians, in whose person light and fire were idolatrously worshipped (Fig. 56).

[5] *Dedication*. i. e. the first time of its being publicly worshipped.

[6] *Ananias, Azarias* and *Misael*. These three were among the principal men of the kingdom, for, at Daniel's proposal, they had been made deputy-governors, under him, of the province of Babylon. For some reason not recorded Daniel himself was not present at this dedication of the image.

[7] *Who is the god?* The king meant to say: "No god can save you from my power." Evidently, the impression made on Nabuchodonozor's mind by the wonderful dream and its interpretation had faded from his memory, for several years had elapsed sine then.

is able to save us from the furnace of burning fire; but if He will not, we will not[1] worship thy god, nor adore the golden statue." The king then ordered that a furnace should be heated seven times more than ordinarily, and that three of the strongest soldiers of his army should bind the young men and cast them, clothed as they were, into the furnace.

The order was instantly executed. But the angel of the Lord went down with the three holy youths into the furnace, and behold, inside the flames were extinguished, but outside the fires burned and flashed and destroyed the men who had executed the king's cruel order. They were instantly consumed by the raging fire.

Within the furnace the air was cool and fresh, like to the breeze when the dew is falling. And the three young men, seeing themselves so wonderfully preserved, sang a glorious canticle[2] of praise and thanksgiving, which the Church of God still sings in her divine service.

The king, astonished to hear voices in the furnace singing, rose up and said to his nobles: "Did we not cast three men, bound, into the midst of the fire? I see four men, loose, and walking in the midst of the fire, and the form of the fourth is like the Son of God."[3]

Then going to the door of the furnace, he said: "Ye servants of the Most High God, go ye forth and come." Thereupon the young men came forth safe and sound: not so much as a hair of their head was burned, nor was the smell of fire on their garments. Seeing this prodigy[4], Nabuchodonozor blessed God, saying: "Blessed be the God of Ananias, Misael and Azarias, who has sent His angel, and delivered His servants that believed in Him."

He then decreed that whosoever, in all his kingdom, blasphemed the God whom these young men adored should be put

---

[1] *We will not.* By this beautiful answer the young men conveyed their belief that God could save them if He would, but that they would not dare demand that He should do so, for they did not think themselves worthy that a miracle should be worked on their behalf. "Anyhow", said they, "we will not worship the image!"

[2] *Canticle.* "All ye works of the Lord, bless the Lord" &c.

[3] *Son of God.* Like a higher and supernatural being.

[4] *This prodigy.* This great miracle again convinced Nabuchodonozor that the God whom the young men served was the Most High God.

to death, for that there was no other God who had power to save. The three young men were raised to high dignities in Babylon.

COMMENTARY.

The object of the revelation made to Nabuchodonozor. Only an obscure revelation was made directly to the heathen king. This filled him with fear, and made him anxious and ready for its further inter-pretation, which was to be given by a chosen prophet of God. The object of this revelation was manifold. Its first object was to make known to the king and wise men the greatness and wisdom of God. This object was so far gained that Nabuchodonozor professed himself to be convinced that the God of the Jews was greater and more powerful than the gods of the heathen. Secondly, it was to make known to the proud king, for his humiliation, that his great kingdom would not last for ever, but would fall after his death. Thirdly, it was meant to turn the eyes of the whole world to the Messias, and the everlasting kingdom which He was to found. Such were the chief objects of the revelation made to Daniel. It is essentially a promise of the Messias.

This twelfth promise of the Messias treats of the kingdom of God (i. e. of the Messias) in contradistinction to the kingdoms of this world. The first part of the vision foretold that three great kingdoms would in succession follow Nabuchodonozor's Babylonian empire. This came to pass. The Medo-Persian empire followed that of Babylon; to that succeeded the Macedonian empire, and to that again the Roman empire. This last was an iron empire, being kept together by the power of the sword; its feet, or foundation, were of iron mixed with earth, and on account of this weakness it fell, first into two separate empires, and finally into many separate states. It would be at this stage of the world's history, God said, that He Himself would found another kingdom, which would overthrow paganism, and itself remain standing for ever; this kingdom being the kingdom of the Messias. The stone which, without any intervention on the part of man, rolled down the mountain, signifies the Son of God, who came down from heaven, and by the operation of the Holy Ghost became Man. He founded a spiritual kingdom which fills the whole earth, and which will last for ever, namely the Catholic Church. Our Lord calls Himself a stone (Mat. 21, 42), and St. Peter calls Him the "stone which is become the head of the corner" (Acts 4, 11).

The Church is Catholic. According to Daniel's prophecy, the kingdom of the Messias, which was to overcome its worldly enemies and last for ever, was to be universal as to time and place, or, in other words, Catholic. The prophecy finds its fulfilment only in the Roman Catholic Church. For she was originally small, but afterwards spread gradually over the whole world, and, in spite of all her enemies, has endured to this day. It follows, therefore, that the Roman Catholic Church is the true Church, the kingdom of God, having its origin in heaven, and promised by God through His prophet Daniel.

God governs the world. This prophecy revealed Almighty God to Nabuchodonozor as the "Lord of kings", or, in other words, as the Lord and ruler of the world, from whom all power comes ("The God of heaven hath given thee a kingdom, and strength and power and glory", said Daniel); by whom nations are overthrown, and raised up again.

The power of prayer said in common. It was only after Daniel and his three friends had prayed together fervently and confidently that the interpretation of the dream was revealed, and that, thereby, not only Daniel and his friends, but all the other wise men and soothsayers were saved from death. Our Lord has encouraged us to pray in common by giving us the promise: "If two of you shall consent upon earth concerning anything whatsoever they shall ask, it shall be done to them by my Father who is in heaven" (Mat. 18, 19).

Humility. Daniel was humble. He gave the glory to God, declaring to the king that it was from Him that the interpretation came. And because he was humble, God exalted him.

Anger, a capital sin. What induced Nabuchodonozor to issue the cruel edict that all the wise men and diviners in the kingdom were to be killed? He was angry at their not being able to do what he wished, and, in his violent anger, he gave the cruel order.

Despotism and cruelty of pagan kings. The command to kill all the diviners and wise men was unjust and cruel. It shows how despotically pagan kings governed, and how little regard they had for the lives of their subjects. Christianity put an end to that kind of cruelty, for it teaches that all men are equally made to the image of God, and that if kings do not govern according to the law of God, they will have to render an account to Him.

The Power and Mercy of God. The mighty miracle which God wrought in order to save His faithful servants, was a great act of mercy towards the heathen. He thereby revealed His power to the king, and to all the great men of the country, and showed that the very elements obey Him. Everybody could see that Bel, whom the young men despised, was powerless to hurt them, and that the God whom they worshipped was alone Almighty. The king confessed this when he issued the decree that the God of the three youths was the "Most High God, and more mighty than any other god". He was seized by so great a fear of God, that he forbade any blasphemy against Him, under pain of death.

Fortitude. It is impossible not to admire the fortitude of the three young men, whereby they remained true to their faith, and refused to worship idols in spite of the king's terrible threats. If they had bowed down before the golden image they would have denied their faith in the true God, and have been guilty of idolatry. But they feared God more than the king, and loved Him more than aught else; so they preferred to be burnt to death rather than offend Him grievously. The abstinence which these noble youths had for so long practised enabled them to attain to heroic fortitude. Their unfailing temperance confirmed them in the fear and love of God, and prepared them for the grace of martyrdom. Finally, their fortitude was rewarded by God saving them from death in a wonderful way.

Resignation to God's will. The example of the three young men shows us that real confidence in God must be united with an entire resignation to His will. They trusted firmly: "God can save us if He will", said they, and they also prayed to be saved; but they left it entirely to God whether He would save them or not, and declared that in no case would they worship the idol.

Prayer of praise and thanksgiving. When God saved the three youths from death by means of His angel, they began with a loud voice to praise and thank God. We too ought always to praise and thank Him when we receive benefits, or are saved from danger.

The three theological virtues of faith, hope and charity were most perfectly practised by the three youths.

Denial of faith. In conclusion I will put to you one question: Ought not the three young men to have obeyed the king's command? Ought they not to have said to themselves: "It would not be right to offend the king, who has been so good to us, and who has entrusted us with important posts. We will, therefore, outwardly conform to his wishes, and prostrate ourselves; but in our hearts we will despise the idol, and worship the true God?" Ought they not to have acted thus? No! for they would have outwardly denied their faith, and have led the pagans to think that they believed in Bel.

APPLICATION. Pray to the Almighty and All-wise God with the deepest reverence. Give yourself confidently over to His wise and good Providence, for He governs the lives of individuals and of nations as He will. Say with St. Paul (Rom. 11, 33—36): "O the depth of the riches of the wisdom and of the knowledge of God! How incomprehensible are His judgments and how unsearchable His ways . . . For of Him and by Him and in Him are all things; to Him be glory for ever!"

Are you as ready as were Ananias, Misael and Azarias to suffer death rather than offend God? If you are not so decided, then you do not love God above all things. Say to-day three Hail Maries for the increase of your faith, the confirmation of your hope, and the kindling of your love.

CHAPTER LXXVIII.

KING BALTASSAR.—THE GOD BEL.

[Dan. 5 and 14.]

AFTER the death of Nabuchodonozor, Baltassar, his grand-son, ascended the throne. One day Baltassar gave a great banquet [1] to the nobles of his kingdom, and ordered the golden cups, which his grandfather had taken from the Temple of Jerusalem, to be brought forth and used at the banquet.

The sacred vessels were brought, and the king and his wives and his officers drank from them, and they praised their gods of gold and of silver and of stone. At that moment a hand appeared, and fingers were seen writing three words upon the wall over against the king. Baltassar grew pale [2] and trembled, for the joints of that hand were moving and wrote: *Mane, Thecel, Phares* [3]. He called for his wise men, that they might interpret the writing. But none of them could do so. Then Daniel, who had received from God the gift of prophecy, together with that of explaining hidden things, came forth and spoke to the king:

"Thou hast lifted up thyself against the Lord of heaven. Thou hast praised thy gods of gold and silver; but the Lord of heaven, who hath thy breath in His hands, thou hast not glorified. Thou knowest that thy grandfather was punished for his pride; that he was driven away from the sons of men, and that he ate grass in the field with the ox and the ass, and yet thou hast not humbled thy heart.

---

[1] *A great banquet.* This was on a day when, every year, the Babylonians celebrated a great feast in honour of their gods. It was a great sacrilege to use the sacred vessels of the Temple in honour of their gods. "While they drank, they praised their gods of gold and of silver, of brass, of iron and of wood and of stones" (Dan. 5, 4); and by so doing they treated with contempt the true God to whom the vessels were consecrated.

[2] *Grew pale.* He was pale from fear, for his guilty conscience told him that the apparition could foretell nothing favourable to him.

[3] *Mane, Thecel, Phares.* These are Chaldaic words and mean: *Numbered, Weighed, Divided.*

"Wherefore God hath sent the fingers of the hand to write, and this is the writing, and this is the interpretation thereof: *Mane:* God hath numbered[1] thy kingdom, and hath finished it. *Thecel:* Thou art weighed[2] in the balance and found wanting. *Phares:* Thy kingdom is divided, and is given to the Medes and Persians." That very night Baltassar was slain[3] and the prophecy of Daniel was thus fulfilled. Some time after, the army of the Medes and Persians, under Darius, their great leader, took the city of Babylon, and divided[4] the kingdom.

But Cyrus (Fig. 57), king of Persia, and successor of Darius, soon took possession of all the Assyrian empire, of which Babylon was the capital. He treated Daniel with marked respect, and made him sit down at his own table. At this time the god Bel was worshipped in Babylon as the supreme deity. There were spent upon him every day twelve large measures of flour, forty sheep and sixty vessels of wine.

The king went every day to adore this god Bel.

Fig. 57. Monument of Cyrus at Murghab.

But Daniel adored the true God. Then the king asked him why he did not adore Bel. Daniel replied that he adored the true and living God, who created earth and heaven, and whose power

---

[1] *Hath numbered.* The days of your rule have come to an end.

[2] *Weighed.* You are found unworthy either to live or reign any longer.

[3] *Was slain.* By his brother-in-law.

[4] *Divided.* The northern part fell to the share of the Medes, and the southern part was possessed by the Persians. When, soon after, the king of the Medes died, leaving no children, both Babylon and Media fell into the hands of the Persian king Cyrus.

extends over all things. The king, much surprised, asked Daniel if he did not believe that Bel was a living god, seeing how much he consumed every day.

Daniel smiled and said: "O king, be not deceived, for this Bel is clay within and brass without, neither hath he eaten at any time." The king, being angry, called for the priests of the god, and said to them: "If ye tell me not who it is that eats up these provisions, ye shall die. But if ye can show that Bel eateth these things, Daniel shall die, because he hath blasphemed against Bel." Daniel agreed to the king's proposal.

Then the king, accompanied by Daniel, went to the temple of Bel. And the priests of Bel said to the king. "Behold, we go out, and do thou, O king, set on the meats, and make ready the wine, and shut the door fast, and seal it with thy own ring; and when thou comest in the morning, if thou find not that Bel hath eaten up all, we will suffer death, or else Daniel who hath lied against us."

They were not afraid, because they had a secret door under the altar, whereby they entered and consumed the meats. The priests having gone out, the king caused the meats and the wine to be placed before Bel. This being done, the servants of Daniel brought ashes, and he sifted them[1] all over the temple, in the presence of the king. Then they all left the temple, the door of which was sealed with the royal seal.

But the priests went in by night with their wives and children, as they were accustomed to do, and they ate and drank all that had been placed before the idol. The king arose early in the morning, and went to the temple with Daniel. They found the seal unbroken, and, opening the door, went in. The king looked at the table, and, seeing that all the provisions had disappeared, cried out: "Great art thou, O Bel, and there is not any deceit with thee."

Daniel laughed[2], and pointing to the floor, said: "Mark, whose footsteps these are!" The king, much amazed, said: "I see the footsteps of men, women and children." Then, examining

---

[1] *Sifted them.* The ashes were sifted so fine that the priests of Bel could not have remarked them.

[2] *Laughed.* And held back the king, so that he should not enter and obliterate the footsteps.

more closely, he found the secret door[1], by which the priests were wont to go in and out. Thereupon the king, being enraged against the priests of Bel, ordered them all to be put to death. And he gave Bel up to Daniel, who destroyed him and his temple.

COMMENTARY.

The Justice and Faithfulness of God. Baltassar's sudden death was in punishment of the wanton sacrilege which filled up the measure of his sins. His day of grace was past, and God summoned him before His judgment-seat. His overthrow fulfilled Daniel's prophecy to Nabuchodonozor (chapter LXXVII), namely that the Babylonian kingdom would come to an end, and that another kingdom would rise up in its place.

Sacrilege. The sacred vessels of the Temple were consecrated to God, and might be used by the priests alone for the divine worship. Therefore Baltassar's was a threefold sacrilege. Firstly, those who were not priests and even women, used them. Secondly, they were used for the purpose of intoxication. Thirdly, in drinking from them, the false gods were honoured and glorified.

Intemperance in drink. It was drunkenness which led the king to commit sacrilege. Drunkenness deprives men, either partially or entirely, of the use of their reason. They no longer consider what they say or do, and bad passions are awakened in their hearts. Such are the consequences of gluttony or intemperance, which is one of the seven capital sins, or sins which are the source of other sins. Drunkenness debases man and makes him like the lower animals. Our Lord Himself thus warns us: "Take heed to yourselves, lest perhaps your hearts be overcharged with surfeiting and drunkenness and the cares of this life: and that day (of judgment) come upon you suddenly" (Luke 21, 34).

Our days are numbered; and as a rule the end comes sooner than we expect. Then comes the judgment, at which all our thoughts, words and actions will be weighed and proved according to their merit before God. All our possessions will be divided, and will pass into other hands after our death.

Zeal for God's Glory. We should admire Daniel's zeal for God's honour and glory. It grieved him to think that so many millions of men should be victims to the folly of idolatry, and be ignorant of the true God. Therefore he laboured to convince them of the nothingness of idols, and to convert them to a belief in God. He knew very well that the obstinate worshippers of false gods, and especially the priests, would hate and persecute him; but in spite of this, and with great

---

[1] *The secret door.* Under the altar.

skill, he showed up the deception of the priests of Bel, destroyed his image, and also killed a dragon which was worshipped as a god. Daniel was a valiant servant of God, and quite ready to suffer death on account of his faith.

APPLICATION. If God punished the desecration of the sacred vessels of the Old Law so severely, how much more heavily will he punish any want of reverence towards the sacraments and holy things of the New Law! Have you ever made a sacrilegious confession? Resolve to pay more reverence to God's holy Sacraments than you have hitherto done, and make a better preparation before receiving them.

CHAPTER LXXIX.

DANIEL IN THE LIONS' DEN.

[Dan. 6 and 14.]

THE people of Babylon worshipped also a great dragon[1]. One day the king said to Daniel: "Behold, thou canst not say now that this is not a living god; adore him, therefore." Daniel replied: "Give me leave, O king, and I will kill this dragon without sword or club." The king replied: "I give thee leave." Then Daniel took pitch, fat and hair, and boiling them together, he made lumps and put them into the dragon's mouth.

The monster, swallowing the lumps, very soon burst asunder, and Daniel said to the king: "Behold him whom you worshipped!" The Babylonians hearing this, assembled in crowds, and said that the king had become a Jew, had destroyed Bel, killed the dragon, and put the priests to death. They came, therefore, to the king, threatening and saying: "Deliver Daniel to us, or else we will destroy thee and thy house."

Although the king loved Daniel, he was forced[2] through the violence of the people to give him up to their fury. Immediately they[3] cast him into a den of lions[4]. There were seven lions in

---

[1] *Dragon.* A great serpent.

[2] *Forced.* In order to avert the outbreak of a revolution.

[3] *They.* There are two apparently different occasions on which Daniel was cast into the lions' den. One is recorded in chapter VI and the other in chapter XIV. In the latter the people cast him into the den, in the former the king. Nevertheless both may refer to the same incident.

[4] *A den of lions.* Which was underground and walled in.

the den, to whom they gave two carcasses every day, and two sheep; but now nothing was given them, that they might devour Daniel. Yet Daniel remained unhurt.

Daniel having been for some time in the lions' den, needed food. Now there was at that time in Judæa a prophet named Habacuc, who carried food to the field for the reapers. The angel of the Lord appeared to him and said: "Carry thy dinner to Daniel who is in the lions' den at Babylon."

Habacuc replied: "Lord, I never saw Babylon, nor do I know the den." Then the angel took him by the hair of his head, carried him in an instant[1] to Babylon, and placed him over the den of lions. And Habacuc called to Daniel[2]: "Thou servant of God, take the dinner that God has sent thee!" Daniel exclaimed: "Thou hast remembered me, O God, and Thou hast not forsaken them that love Thee." Then he arose and ate.

But the angel of the Lord carried Habacuc back to his own place. On the seventh day the king came to bewail[3] Daniel. And standing near the den he looked in and saw Daniel sitting amongst the lions, and he cried with a loud voice: "Great art Thou, O Lord, the God of Daniel!"

Immediately he drew Daniel out of the den, but those who had desired the prophet's death he threw in, and they were devoured by the lions in a moment. Then the king said: "Let all the inhabitants of the whole earth fear the God of Daniel, for He is the Saviour, working signs and wonders."

COMMENTARY.

The Goodness of God. Not only did the Lord God protect His faithful servant from the fury of the hungry lions, but he fed him during his captivity in the den in the most wonderful way, sending him food by Habacuc. Full of thankfulness, Daniel exclaimed: "Thou hast remembered me, O God, and Thou hast not forsaken them that love Thee."

The Omnipotence of God worked two miracles on behalf of Daniel. It was miraculous that the wild beasts should remain ravenously hungry rather than devour Daniel. It was also miraculous that Habacuc should in one moment be translated from Judæa to Babylon, and back again.

---

[1] *In an instant.* As swiftly as the spirit can transfer itself from one place to another. You can, in thought, convey yourself in an instant to any distant city.

[2] *Daniel.* Had been six days in the den, and was very hungry.

[3] *To bewail.* He took for granted that Daniel had been devoured by the lions.

The object of miracles. God worked these miracles, firstly, in order to protect His faithful servant, Daniel; secondly, to manifest Himself to the pagans, and especially to king Cyrus, as the one true and Almighty God and Lord, and the Saviour working signs and wonders on the earth; and thirdly, so as to move the king to send the people of God back to their own country, and let them rebuild the Temple.

Grace at meals. Before Daniel partook of the food miraculously sent to him, he gratefully remembered the goodness of God, who had provided him with it. We ought always to thank God for the food which we receive. We say before meals: "Bless us, O Lord, and these Thy gifts which we are going to receive of Thy bounty", and after our meals we thank Him for having fed us, unworthy creatures, and made us participate in His gifts.

The power of pagan superstition and the wonderful victory of Christianity. This story shows us how deep a root the follies of idolatry had taken among pagan nations. Although Daniel had proved the utter powerlessness of their idols, and although God had manifested His own Omnipotence by the most wonderful miracles, they would not abandon idolatry; and even the king could not save Daniel from their fury. If we consider all this it makes us realise how wonderful was the complete triumph of Christianity over paganism. It is a noble work both for God and our neighbour to support Catholic missionaries, who preach the religion of the cross to the heathen at the peril of their own lives.

APPLICATION. Have you always said your grace devoutly? Even the beasts without reason are grateful to those who feed them; so how can reasonable men not be grateful to their Lord and Creator, who gives them life and health, food and drink?

We were all created for the glory of God. What have you done hitherto for His glory? Could you not prevent many sins among your comrades? Could you not offer your daily labours and burdens to God? Do not forget to frame your intention thus every day: "O my God, I will do everything for Thy glory."

VI. EPOCH:

JUDÆA AFTER THE BABYLONIAN CAPTIVITY.

(From 536 B. C. until the Birth of Christ.)

CHAPTER LXXX.

RETURN OF THE JEWS FROM BABYLON. (536 B. C.)

[1 Esdr. 1.]

THE prophet Jeremias had foretold that the captivity[1] of Babylon would not last longer than seventy years[2], and that the Jews would then return to their own country. Daniel had renewed this consoling promise, and had added another prophecy of greater importance; namely, that from the day on which the order should be given to rebuild Jerusalem till the death of the Messias, there would remain only seventy weeks of years; that is, 490 years[3], so that the Jews knew not only the family from which the Saviour would spring, but also the city where He would be born, and the year in which He would die.

The severe sufferings of the captivity in Babylon, together with the exhortations of the prophets, particularly those of Daniel and Ezechiel, had brought the Jewish people to a sense of their duty. Wherefore it happened that in the seventieth[4] year of their sad captivity, Cyrus, king of Persia, by a divine inspiration, issued an edict[5] that all the Jews who were in his kingdom should go back to Jerusalem and rebuild the Temple of the Lord.

---

[1] *The captivity.* Which began in 606 B. C.

[2] *Seventy years.* "When", said the Lord by the mouth of the prophet Jeremias, "the seventy years shall be accomplished, I will bring you again to the place, for I think towards you thoughts of peace and not of affliction." It is as if He said: "Though I have given you over to captivity, I have no intention of giving you over for ever to affliction, but I mean to lead you to repentance by suffering, and when you have repented, I will be gracious to you again" (Jerem. 25, 12).

[3] *490 years.* The walls of Jerusalem were built up in 453 B. C. From that time to the beginning of the public life of our Lord were 69 weeks, or 483 years. Thus we have 453 + 30 = 483. 483 years are 69 weeks, and the three years of public life are half the seventieth week. In the middle (i. e. after 3 years) of the seventieth 'week of years' our Lord Jesus Christ died upon the cross.

[4] *In the seventieth year.* Counting from the first carrying off of the people into captivity, to the year 536 (from 606—70 = 536).

[5] *An edict.* This was not a command, only a permission.

He also restored[1] to them the sacred vessels which Nabucho-donozor had carried away. Thereupon more than forty thousand Israelites, under the leadership of Prince Zorobabel and of the High Priest Josue, returned to Judæa, the name thenceforward given to the ancient kingdom of Juda, together with the remnants of the other ten tribes, which had joined themselves to Juda and Benjamin before the downfall of Israel. They immediately built an altar[2], and offered sacrifice every morning and evening.

One year after the return from captivity, the foundations of the new Temple were laid in Jerusalem. The priests and the Levites were there with their trumpets and cymbals, as of old, singing to the Lord canticles of praise and thanksgiving, while the people all rejoiced with exceeding great joy. And when, after many years, the Temple was completed, it was consecrated and dedicated with great solemnity.

Many of the old people who remembered the former Temple, wept to see that the new one did not equal the old in magnificence.

But the prophet Aggeus[3] consoled them with the assurance that the second Temple would be more glorious than the first, because the Messias, the Desired of all nations, would be seen in it, and would honour it with His presence. The same prediction was made by the prophet Zacharias[4].

About eighty years after their return from captivity, the Jews, by command of the king of Persia, commenced to rebuild the walls of Jerusalem. The Samaritans opposed them and tried even by violence to prevent the people from rebuilding their city. But the Jews prayed to God to assist them, and in order to

---

[1] *Restored.* Cyrus gave back 5,400 vessels of gold and silver which had belonged to the Temple.

[2] *Built an altar.* On the same spot where the altar of holocausts used to stand.

[3] *Aggeus.* "Yet one little while", said Aggeus, "and the Desired of all nations shall come (the Messias, whom, as Jacob [chapter XXVII] had already prophesied, all nations should expect), and great shall be the glory of this house more than of the first" (Agg. 2, 7—10).

[4] *Zacharias.* "Rejoice greatly", said he, "daughter of Jerusalem. Behold, thy king will come to thee, the Just, the Saviour. He is poor, and riding on the foal of an ass", i. e. on a young ass never yet ridden, not on a proud horse such as the kings of this earth ride on (Zach. 9, 9).

prevent surprise from the Samaritans, divided themselves into two great bodies[1].

Those who were most brave and courageous they placed on the outposts of the city, well armed, in order to keep off the enemy, while those who were skilled in masonry and other mechanical arts carried on the work. At the end of fifty-two days all the walls and ramparts were completed. The Samaritans, seeing that the hand of God was there, ceased to trouble their neighbours.

The Jews, understanding that they had been successful in rebuilding the Temple and walls of Jerusalem in spite of so many obstacles, returned sincere thanks to God. And Esdras, the High Priest, having publicly read the law of the Lord, they all promised[2], with tears, to be faithful to it. For they had received a new and strong proof that God had forgiven their own sins and the ingratitude of their fathers.

COMMENTARY.

God's Mercy to the people of Israel was very great. This faithless people had broken the covenant made with God, and had given themselves over to idolatry and a pagan way of living. God sent prophet after prophet to move them to repent, but the prophets were despised and persecuted, and Israel remained impenitent. At last the judgments threatened by God overtook His people. He punished them by letting them be carried off into captivity, but He punished them only for the purpose of converting them. When the Jews, full of mourning and sorrow, left their home, God gave them the comforting assurance: "When seventy years shall be accomplished, I will bring you again to this place. I think towards you thoughts of peace and not of affliction." And after the Jews were converted to Him, and had renounced idolatry

---

[1] *Two great bodies.* At first the Samaritans wished to help with the building of the Temple, but Josue and Zorobabel rejected their help, fearing that the Jews who believed what was true might be infected by their heathen practices. Then the Samaritans were offended, and tried to hinder the work of rebuilding; but so long as an attack from them was to be feared, Nehemias, the leader of the Jews, commanded that a portion of the people should carry arms while working at the building, so as to be ready to repel the enemy. Nehemias had been cup-bearer to Artaxerxes, king of Persia, and he it was who had obtained permission to build up the walls of Jerusalem. He was appointed governor of Judæa.

[2] *All promised.* But the Jews soon got lax in their observance of the Law, and did things forbidden by it, such as marrying with Gentiles, neglecting to pay tithes, or to make offerings to the Temple. Moreover they offered sacrifices of blind, lame, or blemished beasts, as we learn from the prophet Malachias (1, 7—9).

for good and all, He restored everything to them, their country, their temple, their worship, and their hope in the coming of the Messias. The whole history of the people of Israel is one continuous proof of God's infinite goodness and mercy, one long chain of divine favours bestowed on a sinful nation, one long fight between divine mercy and human obduracy.

The Faithfulness of God is the ground of all our hope. He promised, through Jeremias, that His people should return to Jerusalem after a captivity of seventy years, and this promise was most literally fulfilled; for by a miracle God inclined the heart of king Cyrus towards the Jews, filling him with the fear of God, so that he issued an edict for the return of the Jews and the rebuilding of the Temple. This instance of the faithful fulfilment of God's promises ought to give us a great confidence that He will perform everything that He has said.

The thirteenth promise of the Messias (through Aggeus) foretells the speedy coming of the Desired of all nations, and gives the assurance that on account of His Presence in it, the new Temple would be made more glorious than the splendid Temple of Solomon. Jesus Christ, God made Man, was presented in that Temple as a Child, stayed behind in it as a Boy of twelve years; and as a Man, He prayed and taught and worked miracles therein.

The fourteenth promise of the Messias. It might have been gathered from the prophecy of Aggeus about the glory which the Messias would shed on the Temple, that He would come with great majesty and pomp; but the prophecy of Zacharias made it plain, that, though the long-desired One would indeed be a king, He would not wield an earthly power, but would enter Jerusalem in poverty and simplicity (New Test. LX).

The fifteenth and last promise of the Messias is that of Malachias (2, 11), where he prophesies that Christ shall be offered as a sacrifice and a clean oblation among the Gentiles in every place of the earth.

Unity is strength. The number of Jews who at first returned from Babylon was not very great, but they held faithfully together, and accomplished the rebuilding of the Temple and of the walls of Jerusalem.

APPLICATION. Are you not ungrateful to God, and very often lukewarm in His service, and negligent in prayer and in the receiving of the holy Sacraments? In truth you owe God much more gratitude than did the Jews!

CHAPTER LXXXI.

ESTHER.

[Book of Esther.]

AS the government of the kings of Persia was exceedingly mild, many of the Jews remained in the kingdom of Babylon. God permitted this for the spiritual good of the Gentiles, so that the latter, being brought into daily contact with the Jews, might more easily arrive at the knowledge of the true God, and be instructed in the promises made concerning a Saviour to come.

It happened, by a special dispensation of God, that many of the Jews, like Daniel and his companions in former years, were in high favour with the kings of Persia, and made use of their influence to protect their countrymen and to propagate the true faith. At a certain time it pleased Divine Providence to employ in this way a pious Jewess, named Esther.

She lived in the reign of Assuerus, in the house of Mardochai[1], her uncle, who had brought her up from her infancy. Assuerus, having seen her, was pleased with her beauty and virtue, placed the crown upon her head, and made her his queen. But she, by Mardochai's advice, left the king in ignorance concerning her nation. And Mardochai who loved Esther as his own child, came every day and sat at the gate[2] of the palace (Fig. 58, p. 352).

Now it came to pass that two officials of the palace had conspired together to kill the king. Mardochai, having discovered the plot, revealed it to Esther, who immediately told the king. The affair being examined, Mardochai's statement was found to be true. The two conspirators were hanged, and the facts recorded in the annals of the kingdom.

Some time after, Assuerus raised a certain Aman[3] to the highest dignity in the empire. All the king's servants bent the

---

[1] *Mardochai.* She had been left an orphan in early life, and her uncle, Mardochai, who lived at Susa, the Persian capital, adopted her and brought her up. On account of her beauty, modesty and innocence, Assuerus chose her to be his queen, out of all the maidens presented to him for choice. Assuerus is known in profane history as Xerxes I., the celebrated king of Persia, who reigned from 485—465 B. C.

[2] *At the gate.* He held an office about the court.

[3] *Aman.* He was a Mede, and was raised by the king to the post of Grand-Vizier, which was the highest in the kingdom after the king.

knee before Aman and worshipped him. Mardochai alone did not bend the knee[1] before Aman, as he would not give to man the honour due to God alone. Aman, perceiving this, and learning

that Mardochai was a Jew, became very angry. To be revenged on Mardochai, he told Assuerus that the Jews were planning a revolt, and prevailed upon the king to publish an edict[2] commanding all the Jews in his empire to be put to death, and their property to be taken away.

The Jews were terrified and began to weep and lament. But Mardochai told Esther of the edict, so that she might intercede with the king for her own people.

Then Esther said: "All the provinces know that whosoever cometh

Fig. 58. Ruins of the Palace of Assuerus (Xerxes I.) at Persepolis.

into the king's inner court, who is not called for, is immediately put to death. How then can I go in to the king, not being called?" To these words Mardochai replied: "Who knoweth whether thou art not therefore come to the kingdom that thou

---

[1] *Bend the knee.* It was not, therefore, pride which made him refuse to bow the knee before Aman, but a religious sense of duty, which forbade him to render divine homage to any man.

[2] *An edict.* The edict was issued in April, 474 B. C., that on a certain day in March, 473, every Jew was to be massacred. The day of this general massacre was decided by lot, and the order was made known by messengers throughout the length and breadth of the kingdom. What terror must have seized all the Jews! It is written in the Book of Esther (chapter 4): " In all the provinces, towns and places to which the king's cruel edict was come, there was great mourning among the Jews, with fasting, wailing and weeping, many using sackcloth and ashes for their bed." They tried by these severe penances to avert the calamity.

mightest be ready for such a time as this?" Esther, therefore, praying fervently, and abstaining from food and drink for three days, resolved against the law, to go in to the king without being called, and thus expose herself to the danger of death.

On the third day she put on her glorious apparel and wore her glittering robes, and passed through the door with a smiling countenance which hid a mind full of anguish and exceeding great fear. But when the king had lifted up his face, and with burning eyes had shown the wrath of his heart, Esther sank down and rested her head upon her handmaid. Then the king was seized with pity. He leaped from his throne, upheld her in his arms and said: "What is the matter, Esther? I am thy brother, fear not! Thou shalt not die, for this law is not made for thee, but for all others. What wilt thou, queen Esther?" She, recovering herself, answered: "If it please the king, I beseech thee to come to me this day, and Aman with thee, to the banquet[1] which I have prepared."

The king acceded to her wish; and during the repast he desired to know her request. She answered: "If it please the king to give me what I ask, and to fulfil my petition, let the king and Aman come again to the banquet which I have prepared them, and to-morrow I will open my mind to the king." The king promised to do so, and Aman left the palace with a joyful heart[2]. But in going out he saw Mardochai sitting at the door of the palace. And because Mardochai would not bow down before him like the others, he was filled with rage; and going home to his house, ordered a gallows fifty cubits high to be erected whereon to hang Mardochai on the following morning.

Now it happened that the king could not sleep that night, and to divert his mind he ordered the annals of his reign to be read to him. When the reader came to the place which related how Mardochai had discovered the plot against the king's life, Assuerus suddenly asked what reward Mardochai had received for

---

[1] *The banquet.* Because she had approached the throne without being summoned. With great prudence she abstained from at once presenting her chief petition, and only invited the king to sup with her. The king would probably have been angry when he discovered that she had concealed her nationality from him.

[2] *A joyful heart.* For it was an extraordinary honour for him to be invited alone to supper with the king.

this important service. He was told that the man had never received any reward. Then the king called for Aman, whom he asked what ought to be done to honour the man whom the king desired to honour.

Aman, supposing that there was question of himself, said that the man whom the king desired to honour ought to be clothed with the king's apparel, and be set upon the king's horse, and have the royal crown put upon his head, and that the first of the king's princes and nobles should hold his horse, and, going through the streets of the city, they should proclaim before him: "Thus shall he be honoured, whom the king hath a mind to honour!"

Then the king said to him: "Make haste and take the robe and the horse, and do as thou hast spoken to Mardochai[1], the Jew, who sitteth before the gate of the palace."

Aman was surprised and enraged to hear these words, but he dared not to disobey the word of the king. He went, therefore, and did as he was ordered. Meanwhile the hour came for the queen's banquet, and Aman went thither in all haste.

While they sat at the table the king said again to the queen: "What is thy petition, Esther, that it may be granted thee? Although thou ask the half of my kingdom thou shalt have it." Esther replied: "If I have found favour in thy sight, O king, give me my life, for which I ask, and my people for which I request. For we are given up, I and my people[2], to be destroyed, to be slain, and to perish."

The king, in surprise, asked: "Who is this, and of what power, that he should dare to do these things?" Esther answered: "It is Aman that is our most wicked enemy." But Aman, hearing what the queen said, was seized with terror. The king arose from the table in great wrath. Being told by one of the attendants that Aman had prepared a gibbet fifty cubits high whereon to hang Mardochai, he ordered Aman himself to be hanged upon it.

---

[1] *Do to Mardochai.* This was a great humiliation for the proud man who had hitherto been the king's favourite. He had reckoned on the certainty that the king would give him permission to hang Mardochai on the gallows he had already set up; and instead of this he was now forced to pay the utmost honour to the detested Jew!

[2] *I and my people.* By these words Esther revealed that she was a Jewess.

The same day king Assuerus raised Mardochai to the high dignity which Aman had held, and the edict against the Jews was immediately revoked. The Jews rejoiced[1] beyond measure at their unexpected deliverance, and many of the Gentiles, seeing how wonderfully God protected them, embraced their religion.

COMMENTARY.

The Goodness and Providence of God extended itself not only to the Jews who returned to Judæa, but also to those who remained behind in the pagan country. He protected them, and rescued them completely from the destruction planned against them by Aman. Their deliverance was really wonderful; for Divine Providence so adapted circumstances that the projected plan of massacre was simply brought to nought. By God's Providence Esther was raised to be queen. Again, it was by His Providence that Mardochai discovered the conspirators' plot; and also that the annals of the reign were read to the king that night when he could not sleep, the name of Mardochai being thus recalled to him. By His grace God changed the anger of the king to gentleness, and moved him to grant Esther's petition. So also it was God who turned the plans of wicked Aman to his own shame, saved His people from destruction, and made His name glorious among the Gentiles.

Pride is, firstly, a capital sin which leads to many other sins. See what a number of sins Aman's pride led him to commit. It made him hate Mardochai, and extend his hatred to all the Jews. He calumniated them to the king, and obtained thereby an unjust edict for their massacre. His blind hatred grew to such an extent that he could not even wait for the day of the general massacre of the Jews, but wished to have Mardochai hanged at once.

Pride, moreover, makes men unhappy and discontented. Aman possessed riches, power and honours, and was held to be the most fortunate of men. But this highly-favoured man was discontented, and thought himself ill-used, because one individual Jew refused to pay him the homage that was paid to him by others. His injured pride embittered his life, and gave him sleepless nights.

Pride, thirdly, leads to humiliation and downfall. In Aman were fulfilled the words of Scripture: "Pride goeth before destruction, and the spirit is lifted up before a fall" (Prov. 16, 18). His pride paved the way to his utter abasement. Imagining that he himself must be the man whom the king wished most to honour, he obtained really royal honours for his enemy, and had to pay this honour himself to the hated Mardochai, and proclaim his glory to the whole city. His

---

[1] *Rejoiced.* The Jews celebrated a great feast in honour of their deliverance, the anniversary of which has been kept ever since. It is called the feast of Purim.

injured pride made him desire the destruction of the Jews; but this bloodthirsty project led to his downfall and ignominious death.

The four cardinal virtues. This story affords a shining example of each of these virtues.

1. *Prudence.* Mardochai, Esther and all the Jews acted very prudently, because in their hour of need and peril they had recourse to prayer and fasting. They were convinced that these good works were pleasing to God, and that they would thereby obtain help and deliverance at the hands of the Almighty. They also used every human means of help which prudence suggested.

2. *Justice.* The king fulfilled a duty imposed by justice when he rewarded Mardochai who had saved his life, and punished Aman who had induced him to issue a cruel and murderous edict. It was also an act of justice on his part, when, having assured himself of the innocence of the Jews, he recalled and annulled the edict.

3. *Temperance.* Assuerus practised this virtue when, obedient to divine grace, he subdued his rising anger against Esther and listened favourably to her petition. But Aman, on the other hand, sinned against this virtue, when he let himself be carried away by his anger against Mardochai, and conceived the atrocious project of having every Jew in the kingdom massacred.

4. *Fortitude.* Esther, though raised to be queen, remained humble, pious, and full of confidence in God. This made her valiantly risk her life in order to save her people. She knew that the passionate king would be in a violent rage when she appeared, unsummoned, in his presence, but she prayed, and hoped that God would soften the king's heart; nor was her trust misplaced. Confidence in God gives fortitude.

Esther is a type of the ever Blessed Virgin Mary. Esther, on account of her beauty, was raised from her low estate to be queen: Mary, on account of the beauty of her pure and humble heart, was raised to be the Mother of the Redeemer, and afterwards, Queen of Heaven. Esther alone was exempted from the king's severe law: Mary alone is exempted from the curse of original sin. Esther, adorned in splendid garments, went before the king, prayed for her people, and was heard: Mary, the Queen of Heaven, radiant with virtues and merits, goes before the throne of God to intercede for her people.

Concealing sin. Was it right of Mardochai to reveal the conspiracy against the king's life which he had discovered? He was doubly bound to do so, both as a servant of God and as a servant of the king. To conceal the sin of others, when you can prevent it by revealing it, is one of the nine ways of sharing in the guilt of others.

APPLICATION.   Are you easily moved to anger? Have you in anger insulted, struck, or wished ill to others? Just observe the words and actions of an angry man, and you will see what a hateful passion anger is. Do not allow yourself to be ever carried away by it, but suppress its very first movements. If the angry impulse comes, be silent, and say within yourself: O gentle Jesus, have mercy on me and help me to overcome anger.

CHAPTER LXXXII.

TRANSLATION OF THE OLD TESTAMENT INTO GREEK. (285 B. C.)—WISE SAYINGS OF JESUS, THE SON OF SIRACH.

[Book of Ecclesiasticus.]

THE Jews, who had returned to their country, lived in peace for two hundred years under the dominion of the successors of Cyrus. This peace was not disturbed even when Alexander the Great, king of Macedonia, destroyed the Persian empire. Whilst Alexander lived, he treated the Jews with great kindness; but when, at his death, the Macedonian empire was divided, evil times came upon Judæa.

That province formed the object of dispute between the kings of Syria and those of Egypt, who made it the battle-ground for their contending armies, so that it was turned almost into a desert. As a natural consequence of these protracted wars, ignorance, corruption and vice struck daily deeper root among the Jewish people. This was one of the darkest periods of their history, all the more so as the succession of prophets[1] seemed to have ceased.

While the Jews were under the sceptre of the king of Egypt, it happened that the king desired a Greek translation of the sacred books[2] of the Jews. He therefore expressed his desire to the

---

[1] *Succession of prophets.* After about 400 B. C. God sent no more prophets to His people. The last of the prophets, Malachias, was raised up to upbraid the people for their falling away from the correct observance of the Law. Regarding the priests we read: "I have no pleasure in you, saith the Lord of hosts: and I will not receive a gift of your hand. For from the rising of the sun even to the going down, my name is great among the Gentiles, and in every place there is sacrifice, and there is offered to My name a clean oblation." Inspired writers, however, did not cease to exist.

[2] *The sacred books.* The Holy Scriptures of the Old Testament consist of twenty-one historical books, seven moral books, and seventeen prophetical books

High Priest at Jerusalem, who granted the request and sent to Alexandria, the capital of Egypt, seventy-two wise men well versed both in Greek and in Hebrew. These men were kindly received by the king, and made a correct translation for him called for that reason the *Septuagint*. At that time educated men among the heathen nations knew and spoke the Greek language. Hence this translation of the Scriptures began to be read by the pagans, who thereby came to the knowledge of the true God, and to the belief in the Messias. Thus do we see the hand of Divine Providence, in His design to prepare the Gentiles for the coming of the Saviour.

Almighty God also inspired a pious Jew, called Jesus, the son of Sirach, to write a work on religious and moral instruction, which forms one of the books of the Catholic Bible, and is called *Ecclesiasticus*[1]. The following beautiful maxims taken from it deserve careful study. "The fear of the Lord is the beginning and crown of wisdom. The word of God is the fountain of wisdom, and her ways are everlasting commandments. The fear of the Lord shall delight the heart, and shall give joy, and gladness, and length of days. It shall go well with him that feareth the Lord, and in the days of his end he shall be blessed. My son, from thy youth up receive instruction, and even to thy grey hairs thou shalt find wisdom."

"Come to her as one that plougheth and soweth, and wait for her good fruits. For in working about her thou shalt labour a little, and shalt quickly eat of her fruits. Take all that shall be brought upon thee, and keep patience, for gold and silver are tried in the fire, but acceptable men in the furnace of humiliation. Hear the judgment of your father and grieve him not in his life.

The historical books are: the five Books of Moses, the Book of Josue, the Judges, Ruth, the four Books of Kings, two Paralipomena, two of Esdras, Esther, Tobias, Judith, and two of Machabees. The moral books are: Job, the Psalms, Proverbs, the Preacher, the Song of Solomon, Wisdom and Ecclesiasticus. The prophetical books are: Isaias, Jeremias with the Lamentations, Ezechiel, Daniel, Osee, Joel, Amos, Abdias, Jonas, Baruch, Micheas, Nahum, Habacuc, Sophonias, Aggeus, Zacharias and Malachias. These 45 books form the Catholic Bible of the Old Testament. The Protestant Bible excludes 7 books, viz. Wisdom, Ecclesiasticus, Tobias, Judith, Baruch and the two books of Machabees, which it calls "apocrypha".

[1] *Ecclesiasticus.* This book contains maxims, sayings and lessons, and praises of the great men of Israel. It was written about 180 B. C.

The father's blessing establisheth the houses of the children, but the mother's curse rooteth up the foundation."

"Despise not a man in his old age, for we also shall become old. Despise not the discourse of them that are ancient and wise; but acquaint thyself with their proverbs. Praise not a man for his beauty, neither despise a man for his look. The bee is small among flying things, but her fruit hath the chiefest sweetness. Be in peace with many, but let one of a thousand be thy counsellor."

"Nothing can be compared to a faithful friend, and no weight of gold and silver is able to countervail the goodness of his fidelity. If thou wouldst get a friend, try him before thou takest him, and do not credit him easily. For there is a friend for his own occasion, and he will not abide in the day of thy trouble. A lie is a foul blot in a man. In nowise speak against the truth, but be ashamed of the lie in thy ignorance."

"Let not the naming of God be usual in thy mouth, and meddle not with the names of Saints. A man that sweareth much shall be filled with iniquity, and a scourge shall not depart from his house. Before thou hear, answer not a word, and interrupt not others in the midst of their discourse. Hast thou heard a word against thy neighbour, let it die within thee, trusting that it will not burst thee. Hedge in thy ears with thorns; hear not a wicked tongue; and make doors and bars to thy mouth."

"Melt down thy gold and silver, and make a balance for thy words. Flee from sin as from the face of a serpent. All iniquity is like a two-edged sword; there is no remedy for the wound thereof. Observe the time and fly from evil. He that loveth danger shall perish therein, and he that toucheth pitch shall be defiled with it. In every work of thine regard thy soul in faith, for this is the keeping of the commandments. In all thy works remember thy last end, and thou shalt never sin."

COMMENTARY.

The fifteenth promise of the Messias (through Malachias) is of great importance for the Catholic faith, since, as the Council of Trent in union with the Fathers of the Church teaches, it contains a most clear prophecy of the unbloody Sacrifice of the New Testament, or, in other words, of the most holy Sacrifice of the Mass. Let us examine what it is that God promised by the mouth of the prophet Malachias.

By the words "From the rising of the sun—for my name is great among the Gentiles" God announced that many nations instead of only one would worship Him. Then He further foretold: a) that a sacrifice would be offered to Him, not in one place only as with the Jews, but in all places; b) that this sacrifice would be a clean oblation or offering, c) and a meat-offering or, in other words, an unbloody sacrifice; d) and that it would be a perfect sacrifice, and take the place of the Jewish sacrifices. Now, in what way does the holy Sacrifice of the Mass correspond with and fulfil this prophecy? a) The holy Sacrifice of the Mass was instituted at the Last Supper, and is offered up in every Catholic church all over the world. b) It is a clean oblation, nay, the most clean, the most holy oblation that can be, for in it is offered up Jesus Christ, the All-holy Son of God. c) It is an unbloody Sacrifice, and at the same time it is a meat-offering, for in it Jesus Christ offers Himself in an unbloody manner in the holy Mass, under the form of bread and wine, and gives Himself in Holy Communion to be the Food of both priest and people. d) It replaces the sacrifices of the Old Testament, which were only types of this, the spotless Sacrifice of the New Testament, and which are fulfilled by it.

APPLICATION. Thank God in an especial manner for the most holy Sacrifice of the Mass, and resolve that you will assist at it frequently and with devotion.

CHAPTER LXXXIII.

THE MARTYRDOM OF ELEAZAR (168 B. C.).

[2 Mach. 6.]

THE most terrible trial which the Jews had to undergo was that which came upon them at the time when they were made subject to the proud and cruel Antiochus[1], king of Syria.

---

[1] *Antiochus.* The Jews lived under the Persian supremacy in peace and quiet. This lasted till 329 B. C. In that year, Alexander the Great, who had conquered the Persian empire, took possession of Judæa and Jerusalem; but he was favourable to the Jews and allowed them to practise their religion, for which he had a great respect. When Alexander died (323 B. C.), his four principal generals divided his vast empire; and the Jews lived for a hundred years under the Egyptian rule, which was in no way oppressive. But in the year 200 Judæa fell under the dominion of the kings of Syria. The worst of these kings was Antiochus IV., of whom we read in this story. He fell upon Jerusalem with a large army in the year 169, killed 40,000 inhabitants, and plundered the Temple. He proclaimed Greek paganism to be the religion of the state, and, in 167 B. C., having desecrated the Temple in all sorts of ways, he set up in it the image of the Greek god

The king ordered the Holy Books to be torn and burnt; he profaned the Temple, and forbade the observance of the divine laws under the penalty of death.

Unhappily, many of the Jews, yielding to a guilty fear, obeyed the king's order; but many more refused to comply with the impious mandate, and chose to die rather than violate the holy precept of God. Among these was an old man named Eleazar, ninety-nine years of age, who was renowned as a doctor of the law.

When Eleazar refused to eat swine's flesh, the use of which was forbidden by the law of Moses, they opened his mouth by force to compel him to eat. But he still refused, and declared that he would undergo any torment that might be inflicted on him, rather than stain his soul with sin by a violation of the commandment of God. Then some of those who stood by, pitying the good old man, advised him to eat of other meat which was not forbidden, so as to feign compliance with the king's command.

Fig. 59. Zeus (Jupiter). Old Roman painting. Naples Museum.

Eleazar replied: "It does not become our age to dissemble[1]." He then explained to these false friends that even if he made a mere show of complying with the king's orders in this matter, the young men of his nation might be tempted to follow his example, saying: "The aged Eleazar has become a pagan, why may not we do the same?" Moreover, he exclaimed: "Though for the present time I should be delivered from the punishment of men, yet should I not escape the hand of the Almighty, neither alive nor dead."

Having thus spoken, the holy old man was dragged to the place of execution, where he suffered a glorious death. In the

---

Zeus (Fig. 59). All the Jews were forbidden under pain of death to practise any religion but that of the state. They did not dare to circumcise their male children, or observe their sabbaths and festivals, or offer sacrifice to the true God.

[1] *To dissemble.* But why did Eleazar refuse to eat meat which he was allowed to eat? Firstly, because he would have thereby dissembled and acted as if he had apostatised from the true faith. Secondly, because by this seeming apostasy he would have given a bad example and scandal to the Jewish young men.

midst of his torments he cried out: "Lord, Thou knowest I suffer grievous pains, but I am well content to suffer these things, because I fear Thee."

COMMENTARY.

Firm faith. Eleazar was strong and steadfast in faith, preferring to die under torture rather than deny his faith by eating the forbidden meat.

The fear of God. The fortitude with which Eleazar endured his torture proceeded from the holy fear of God, to whom he said in presence of the bystanders: "I am well content to suffer, because I fear Thee"; being persuaded within himself: "If I escape from this torture by a miserable hypocrisy, I could not escape the punishment of God." It is thus we ought to reason when tempted either to do what is wrong, or to neglect what is right. Our Lord has spoken these warning words: 'Fear not them that kill the body, and are not able to kill the soul: but rather fear Him that can destroy both soul and body in hell" (Mat. 10, 28).

Bad example. Eleazar wished to avoid even the appearance of sin, and therefore refused to adopt the suggestion made to him of secretly eating meat which was allowed, though he seemed to be eating swine's flesh. Every one would have thought that he had eaten forbidden meat, and, as he himself said, he would thus have given a bad example to all the Jews, and especially to the young. This act would also have drawn others into transgressing the law and denying their faith. Those who are the occasion of sin in other persons give scandal, and sin against the Fifth Commandment.

Counselling sin. Did those who advised Eleazar to act as if he had eaten the forbidden meat commit sin? Yes, for though it is true that they felt full of compassion for the poor, weak, aged man, they felt no compassion for his soul; and it was, after all, a very erroneous sort of compassion which made them counsel him to commit a sin.

The shameful faithlessness of many Christians. Our Lord Jesus Christ had not yet died for Eleazar. He had not received the teaching and graces of Christianity, nor was heaven open to him; and yet he gave a splendid example of fortitude. How much more shameful would it be for Christians to deny their faith, having before them, in very truth, the example of our Lord, of the holy apostles, and of 13,000,000 martyrs of the Catholic Church, and receiving, as they do, so many graces from God!

APPLICATION. Are you ready to suffer a painful death rather than deny the holy Catholic faith, or commit any other grievous sin? Do you pray for the gift of fortitude?

If a Catholic eats meat on Friday, he acts as if he were not a Catholic, and refuses obedience to the Church of God. Do you always observe the days of abstinence?

CHAPTER LXXXIV.

THE MARTYRDOM OF THE SEVEN MACHABEES.

[2 Mach. 7.]

ANTIOCHUS[1] commanded that a certain widow, with her seven sons[2], should be brought into his presence, and should be forced to eat of the forbidden flesh. They all told him that, as their law did not allow them the use of such meat, they could not obey his command. He immediately had them scourged with whips.

The eldest of the brothers told the king that they were ready to die rather than transgress the law of their God. Then the king, enraged at the young man's boldness, ordered his tongue to be plucked out, the skin of his head to be torn off, his hands and feet to be cut off, and finally that he should be burnt alive before his mother and brothers. While he was suffering[3] these cruel torments, his mother and his brothers exhorted him to die courageously.

The first brother being dead, they seized the second, and, having torn the skin from off his head, they asked him if he would eat rather than undergo the rest of the torments. But he, refusing not less firmly and courageously than his elder brother, was tortured in the same way till he expired. When he was about to die he exclaimed: "Thou, O most wicked man, destroyest us out of this present life, but the King of the

---

[1] *Antiochus.* See preceding chapter.

[2] *Seven sons.* These brothers are called the seven Machabees, because their heroic sufferings are related in the second Book of Machabees. It is generally believed that the seven brothers and their mother were martyred in the year 166 B. C. at Antioch, the city where the king resided, situated not far from the sea, to the north-east of the island of Cyprus.

[3] *Suffering.* According to 2 Mach. 7, 5. his martyrdom lasted a long time. Picture to yourself the horrors of this prolonged torture. The king hoped that the cruel torments of the eldest brother would frighten the younger ones into submission; but instead of this, they encouraged each other to follow his example.

world[1] will raise up us who die for His laws, in the resurrection of eternal life."

The third brother offered his hands and feet to be cut off, saying: "These I have from heaven, but for the law of God I now despise them, because I hope to receive them again from Him." Some minutes before his death he declared aloud his willingness to die for God, as his brothers had already done. When he was dead, the fourth brother, the fifth, and the sixth were all three subjected to the same torments as their elder brothers, but each one died in the same manner, having the same spirit. They made no account of pain and death, because they suffered all for God.

The king and his courtiers were amazed at the constancy of these young men, so that when the seventh, a mere youth, was brought forward, the king told him, with an oath, that he would make him rich and happy[2] if he would obey his command. Seeing that his words had no effect on the courageous boy, Antiochus called on the mother to advise her son for his own good.

The mother agreed to do so. Then, addressing her son[3], she said with all a mother's tender affection: "My son, look upon heaven and earth, and all that is in them; and consider that God made them out of nothing, and mankind also; so thou shalt not fear this tormentor, but, being made a worthy partner[4] with thy brethren, receive death, that in that mercy I may receive thee again with thy brethren."[5]

While she was yet speaking, the boy said[6]: "For whom do you stay? I will not obey the commandment of the king, but

---

[1] *The King of the world.* The expression has much force and beauty. It reminded the tyrannical king that there was a King of the whole world to whom also the kings of earth are subject, and that obedience to this King was true loyalty.

[2] *Rich and happy.* The king thought that by fair promises he would be able to induce the boy, as he was young and weak, to apostatise.

[3] *Addressing her son.* She spoke to him in her native Jewish tongue. She purposely made use of a language which the king could not understand, for, had he taken in what she was saying, he would not have suffered her to speak any more to him.

[4] *Worthy partner.* "Prove that you have as much fortitude and as great a fear of God as had your brothers!"

[5] *With thy brethren.* "For if you turn from your faith you will not attain to eternal life."

[6] *The boy said.* "We suffer thus for our sins", he also said, "and though the Lord our God is angry with us a little while, yet He will be reconciled again

the commandment of the law which was given us by Moses."
Then, turning to the king: "Thou", said he, "thou that hast
been the author of all mischief against the Hebrews, shalt not
escape the hand of God." But the king, inflamed with rage, tortured him most cruelly till he yielded up his soul. Last of all
the mother herself was put to death.

COMMENTARY.

Fortitude. It is impossible to extol and admire sufficiently the
unshaken fortitude of the seven brothers. It was comparatively easy
for the aged Eleazar to give up his life, for under no circumstances
could he have had much longer to live, and the world could not offer
him anything worth having. But the Machabean brothers were young,
they could look forward to many years of life, and the world offered
them many pleasures and enjoyments. Nevertheless, they freely and
valiantly gave up their lives, refusing to be turned from their allegiance
to God, either by flattering promises or horrible tortures.

The mother's heroism is even more to be admired. She had most
to suffer, for in her heart she suffered all her sons' tortures. She was,
in fact, an eightfold martyr, for she shared in the sufferings of each
of her sons, and finally offered up her own life. In truth, the courage
of the most valiant of soldiers cannot be compared with the heroism
of this woman!

What gives fortitude? What made this mother and her sons so
heroically resolved to give up their lives for God's sake? What enabled
them to endure such horrible tortures?

1. *Their firm faith* in God and His reward. They believed and
confessed that

a) God is the Almighty Lord and Creator of the world: "These
hands I have from heaven" — "The King of this world will raise us
up" — "God made all these things out of nothing."

b) That God is just, rewarding the good and punishing the wicked:
"We suffer thus for our sins" — "Thou, O most wicked of men, shalt
not escape the judgment of Almighty God" — "Receive death, that in
that mercy I may receive thee again."

c) That there is an eternal life, a resurrection of the body, and a
meeting again in another world: "The King of this world will raise
us up in the resurrection of eternal life" — "These hands I have from

---

to His servants" (2 Mach. 7, 32 33). He was not alluding to their own particular
sins, but to the sins of the Jews in general, on account of which God had subjected
them to this long persecution. The brothers looked on their death as a sacrifice
for the sins of the people, and hoped that it would turn God's anger from the
Jews, and that He would be gracious to them, and put an end to this persecution.

heaven ... I hope to receive them again from Him" — "That I may receive thee again with thy brethren." They raised their eyes beyond the perishable things of this earth, to those things which are heavenly and eternal; and they looked to being rewarded by God in another world. They gave up their earthly life, in order to gain eternal life.

From their firm faith proceeded a great fear and love of God: "We are ready to die rather than transgress the laws of God."

2. *Their firm hope* in the promises of God. They believed in the future Redeemer; and, on account of this faith, God assisted them by His grace, without which no one can keep the commandments.

Unlawful obedience. The example of these holy martyrs teaches us that we must not obey our superiors when they command us to do anything which God has forbidden, or when they forbid anything which God has commanded. In such cases we must say, as did the Machabean brothers: "The law of God forbids it; we will not do it."

The commandment of abstinence. The seven Machabees died martyrs of obedience to God's commandments. They preferred to suffer the most cruel tortures rather than transgress the commandment not to touch swine's flesh. Jesus Christ, through his Church, has given us a similar law in the Third Commandment of the Church.

The duty of parents in the education of their children. Parents should learn from the mother of the Machabees to bring up their children in the fear and love of God, and to care for their souls more than for anything else, so that they may look to meet them again in eternal life. "What doth it profit a man if he gain the whole world and suffer the loss of his own soul!"

Commemoration of the holy Machabees. The Church commemorates these martyrs on August 1st: "For", says St. Gregory Nazianzen, "what would not these men, who suffered martyrdom before Christ suffered, have endured if they had been called to suffer persecution after His Incarnation, and had present before their eyes the Death which He suffered for our salvation! Yes, I think I may assume, in union with all friends of God, that there was a certain mysterious communion between the martyrs of the Old Testament and Jesus Christ, without belief in whom none of those martyrs before the Incarnation could have attained to such a glorious end."

APPLICATION. Put yourself in the place of the youngest brother, and imagine the king speaking to you, making you splendid promises on the one hand, and, on the other, threatening you with death by torture. Would you remain firm, and suffer a lingering martyrdom rather than offend God by committing a grievous sin? "We will rather die than transgress God's law" had been the maxim of these brothers' lives from their earliest youth, so that, when they found themselves assailed by a severe temptation, they remained firm. Let the same maxim be stamped on your heart! Abide by this principle in little things, and then, by God's grace, you will stand firm in the hour of trial. "Lead us not into temptation!"

CHAPTER LXXXV.

VALIANT EXPLOITS OF JUDAS MACHABEUS (160 B. C.).

[1 Mach. 1—10. 2 Mach. 8—15.]

AT the time when Antiochus was thus cruelly persecuting the Jews, there was in Judæa a priest named Mathathias, who had five sons. This zealous priest, having learnt that Antiochus had profaned the Temple and nearly destroyed the worship of the true God, was filled with the deepest sorrow. He knew that the wicked king would soon succeed in his impious designs, if the Jews did not offer a vigorous resistance[1].

He, therefore, called upon all who had any zeal for the laws of God to rise up with him, in defence of their sacred rights. Then he and his sons fled to the mountains, where they were soon joined by the valiant men of Israel, and quickly formed a powerful army. They destroyed the altars[2] of the false gods, bravely defended the law of the Lord, and compelled the apostate Jews to leave the country.

After the death[3] of Mathathias, Judas, surnamed Machabeus[4], or the Hammerer, on account of his invincible courage and great valour, assumed the command of the Jewish army. In battle he showed himself brave as a lion—had several engagements with the Syrian generals, and recovered Jerusalem and the Temple. With a sorrowful heart he saw the Temple in its desecrated and desolate state, the altar profaned, and the grass growing in the deserted courts.

---

[1] *Resistance.* The severe test of conscience put by Antiochus forced the faithful Jews into resistance. The priest Mathathias and his sons placed themselves at the head of those who were resolved to fight for their religion.

[2] *The altars.* Which Antiochus had set up all over the country.

[3] *After the death.* 166 B. C.

[4] *Machabeus.* Because he overcame or, so to speak, hammered down the enemies of the Jews.

He then purified[1] the Temple, celebrated his victory by a grand festival, and dedicated the altar anew, with the sound of harps, and lutes, and cymbals, and hymns of joy, in the sight of the wondering multitude.

Antiochus, hearing of the splendid victories of Judas Machabeus, was roused to fury, and, hastening to assume the command of his army, set out[2] at once for Jerusalem. But driving at full speed in his war-chariot, he was thrown[3] to the ground and grievously wounded. Soon worms came forth from the body of that impious king; the flesh rotted on his bones, and he became an object of horror and disgust, so that no one could approach him. He who so lately thought that the very stars of heaven should obey Him, was deserted even by his slaves.

Then, seeing the folly and wickedness of his pride, he began to humble himself[4] before the Lord, promising[5] to repair all the evil he had done and to proclaim throughout the whole earth that there was no god but the great God whom the Jews adored. But inasmuch as his repentance proceeded only from the fear of death and the dread of temporal punishment, it was of no avail before God. His sufferings continued unabated, and at last the wicked king, the blasphemer of God, the oppressor of His people,

---

[1] *Purified.* It had been polluted, made desolate, and desecrated by the erecting in it of altars to the false gods (chapter LXXXIII). The purification consisted in the removing of everything unholy and pagan which had served for the worship of false gods.

[2] *Set out.* It was after he had suffered a defeat in Persia, that he learnt that the Jews had gathered together to fight for the exercise of their religion. He determined to vent the anger he felt at his defeat in Persia on the little Jewish state. He intended to attack Jerusalem and 'make it a common burying-place of the Jews', i. e. destroy the city and bury its inhabitants under its ruins.

[3] *Thrown.* So that he had to be carried in a litter, and could advance but slowly.

[4] *To humble himself.* Holy Scripture says (2 Mach. 9, 12): "When he could not abide his own stench, he spoke thus: 'It is just to be subject to God, and that a mortal man should not equal himself to God.'" His pride had been so great that he would acknowledge no God, and, out of hatred for Him, inhumanly oppressed His people.

[5] *Promising.* He promised to guarantee freedom of worship to the Jews; even to become a Jew himself, and wander through the world proclaiming God's power (2 Mach. 9, 17). He promised a great deal, as is the way with those whose word is not to be depended on; but God, who sees the heart, would not hearken to him, because his promises were not sincere, and because God foreknew that he would not keep them.

died in torment, the death of a reprobate, as the seven Machabean brothers had foretold [1] him.

The son and successor of Antiochus sent his ablest generals with mighty armies [2] to take Judæa and Jerusalem again. Judas Machabeus and his small army, seeing the hosts [3] that were marching against them, had recourse to God in humble prayer. Then they took up their arms and advanced to meet the enemy, trusting in God alone.

In the midst of the combat five horsemen, in shining armour [4], were seen by the enemy in the air above, fighting for the Jews. Two of these heavenly warriors were with Judas Machabeus, as it were shielding him from danger, while the other three cast darts from on high against the Syrian host [5]. Seeing this strange sight the enemy were seized with terror, and fled in confusion, leaving twenty thousand of their number dead on the field.

Thus favoured by divine assistance, Judas Machabeus defeated the Syrians in many other bloody engagements. But it happened in one of these that some of the Jews were slain, and on the following day, when Judas and his soldiers came to bury them, they found under their tunics certain heathen charms, or amulets [6], which it was not allowable even to touch.

---

[1] *Foretold.* The punishment foretold to their cruel persecutor by the Machabean brothers had not failed to overtake him. In the story as narrated in the last chapter, only the threat of the youngest brother is related; but the fourth, fifth, and sixth brothers had also foretold the judgments of God. The fourth brother had said: "As to thee, thou shalt have no resurrection to life." The fifth had said: "Thou shalt see God's great power, in what manner He will torment thee and thy seed." And the sixth, when dying, had cried out: "Do not think that thou shalt escape punishment, for that thou hast attempted to fight against God."

[2] *Mighty armies.* The Syrian kings had allied themselves to several neighbouring people, namely the Edomites or Idumæans, who had taken possession of the southern portion of Judæa; the Ammonites on the east, who had increased in power since the fall of the kingdom of Israel; and the Arabs on the south-east.

[3] *The hosts.* Gathered together by the Ammonite general Timotheus (2 Mach. 10, 24): "Timotheus having called together a multitude of foreign troops, and assembled horsemen out of Asia." Before Judas and his soldiers went to meet the Syrian army, they clothed themselves in sackcloth, threw themselves down before the altar of the Lord, and prayed for help (2 Mach. 10, 25 &c.).

[4] *In shining armour.* Angels in the form of horsemen.

[5] *The Syrian host.* These were so dazzled and terrified that they took to flight. More than 20,000 men were killed.

[6] *Amulets.* They had kept back from the booty some charms of the false gods, though the law (Deut. 7, 25) commanded the destruction of everything that had served for the worship of idols.

It became manifest to all that it was because of the amulets that these men had been killed; and, praising the justice of God, they besought Him to pardon the sins of the unhappy dead. And Judas collected a sum of twelve thousand drachms of silver, and sent it to Jerusalem to have sacrifices offered for his soldiers who had thus fallen in battle. "It is, therefore", says the Scripture, "a holy and a wholesome thought to pray for the dead, that they may be loosed from their sins."

Before one of the many battles which Judas fought, he had a vision. He saw the deceased High Priest, Onias[1], holding up his hands, and praying for the Jewish people. After this another man appeared, surrounded with great glory. Onias said: "This is he that prayeth much for the people, and for all the holy city, Jeremias, the prophet of God." Then Jeremias gave Judas a sword of gold, saying: "Take this holy sword, a gift from God, wherewith thou shalt overcome the adversaries of My people Israel."

Judas, encouraged by these heavenly favours, gained many battles. At last it happened that he engaged the enemy with very unequal numbers[2]. In this battle he was vanquished and slain[3]. Then all the people mourned him for many days, saying: "How is the mighty man fallen that saved the people of Israel!"

COMMENTARY.

The Justice of God is very clearly revealed in the account of the death of Antiochus. The wicked king had deliberately prepared tortures for the Jewish martyrs, and now he himself was slowly tortured to death. His body while still alive became corrupt, and he was unbearable both to himself and to those about him. In his arrogance he had despised God and forbidden His worship; now he had to bow down under the hand of the Almighty, and acknowledge that his terrible sufferings were but the just punishment of his pride and cruelty to God's servants. He even prayed and made vows to God, knowing that it was only from Him that help could come; but his prayer was not heard, and he died

---

[1] *Onias*. This faithful servant of God had been killed by an assassin, 170 B. C. Judas had personally known the zealous High Priest.

[2] *Unequal numbers*. Bacchides, the Syrian general, was at the head of an army of 25,000 men, which Judas opposed with only 800. His followers urged him to retreat, but he replied: "God forbid we should do this thing and flee away from them. But if our time (i. e. the hour of our death) be come, let us die manfully for our brethren, and let us not stain our glory."

[3] *Slain*. He died for the cause of liberty and the free exercise of religion.

a miserable death in unendurable agony. Contemplate the once proud king on his death-bed. His flatterers have forsaken him; his servants cannot endure to be near him. Day and night he is tormented; day and night he complains and laments—but there is no help for him! In the days of his health he had tormented many, and now he himself is tormented by bodily pain and remorse of conscience, "and indeed very justly, seeing he had tormented the bowels of others with many and new torments". Let this story teach you to know and fear the justice of God. "It is a fearful thing to fall into the hands of the living God" (Hebr. 10, 31). Another instance of God's justice is given in the death of the Jewish soldiers. Judas Machabeus was convinced that the reason of their death lay in their secreting the idolatrous amulets; for he believed that God, on account of their sin, had withdrawn His protection from them, and punished them by death.

Repentance must be supernatural. Why did not Antiochus obtain mercy? Because he was not truly penitent. It is true that he did repent of his offences against God's people, but his repentance was natural, not supernatural, and sprang not from fear or love of God, but from horror of his temporal punishment (i. e. his fearful disease), and from terror of approaching death. He wished to be well again, and to live and reign longer; this was the only reason why he repented of his cruelty. Such is not supernatural repentance. It is true that he also made good resolutions, but these were of no value in the sight of God, for they were as little supernatural as his repentance. It is only supernatural repentance, and supernatural purpose of amendment which make a man truly penitent; and, not possessing these, Antiochus failed to obtain pardon, and died impenitent. As he lived, so he died. "The death of the wicked is very evil" (Ps. 33, 22).

Death-bed conversions. For the same reasons that the conversion of Antiochus was not real or sincere, most death-bed conversions are very doubtful and untrustworthy, since, as a rule, they do not proceed from supernatural motives, but only from fear of death. Therefore sinners should never put off repentance till they are near death; because, firstly, they might be called away suddenly without any preparatory illness; and, secondly, it is very difficult for a sinner to be sincerely converted on his death-bed after a long life spent in resisting grace, and heaping sin upon sin. "Delay not to be converted to the Lord, and defer it not from day to day. For His wrath shall come on a sudden, and in the time of vengeance He will destroy thee" (Ecclus. 5, 7. 8).

The immortality of the soul. Judas and his companions believed that the souls of those who had died still lived, and therefore they prayed for them.

Purgatory. The Machabees and their followers believed that those who fell were not eternally lost in hell, seeing that they had fought and died for God's honour. But, on the other hand, they did not believe that their fallen brethren were with the blessed in Limbo, for otherwise their sin-offerings for them would have had no meaning. No, they believed: a) that those who had been slain were in a middle state between that of the blessed and that of the damned; b) that they had to make satisfaction for venial sin; and c) that the survivors could help them by prayers and sacrifices, and thus make satisfaction for them to the divine justice, so that they might be delivered from their present state. Holy Scripture testifies that this belief is a correct one, since it praises Judas for offering up these prayers and sacrifices, saying explicitly: "It is a holy and wholesome thought to pray for the dead." This completely corroborates the Catholic doctrine of purgatory, and of prayers for the dead.

Prayers for the dead. It is a "holy" thought to pray for the dead, because it proceeds from a living faith and a sincere brotherly love. It is also a "wholesome" thought, for these prayers help the holy souls as well as ourselves. They procure for them admission to heaven, and they increase our merits and, moreover, bind the delivered souls, out of gratitude, to intercede for us before the throne of God. This leads us on to another Catholic doctrine, also confirmed by this story, namely:

The intercession of the Saints. In Judas' vision not only did Onias pray for the Jews, but he said that Jeremias also prayed for them ("This is he that prayeth much for the people, and for all the holy city, Jeremias, the prophet of God"). The Saints, therefore, know about us and care for us, for our sufferings, struggles and necessities; and seek to help us by their intercession. Jeremias appeared as the special guardian and patron of Jerusalem. In the same way we believe that those Saints who have been chosen and devoutly venerated, as the special patrons of individual Christians, or of churches, villages, towns, parishes or estates, intercede especially for those who have been committed to their care.

The virtues of the Machabees. Mathathias and his sons fought a noble fight. They did not take up arms out of ambition or thirst for renown, but simply out of holy zeal for God's honour, for liberty of conscience and the welfare of their country. They said: "It is better for us to die in battle, than to see the evils of our nation and of the holies." They were ready to bleed and die for God and for their country. They carried on the war with heroic courage and endurance, and their heroism proceeded from their unshaken confidence in God. They fought not only *for* God, but *with* Him. They knew that they could not overcome without His help, so before the battle, and in the battle, they called on Him, and after it they humbly gave Him the glory, and thanked Him who had given them the victory.

The power of prayer. The wonderful assistance which was so repeatedly granted to Judas shows us the power of fervent and trustful prayer, and should encourage us to turn to God in all our necessities. Almighty God gave the victory to the faithful Jews, because "they fought with their hands, and prayed in their hearts".

The soldiers of Christ. We all have a holy war to wage for God's glory and the salvation of our souls, namely, the war against our own passions and inclinations, as also against temptations from without, from unbelieving and wicked men, and from the evil spirits. In this war our weapons are the sword of God's word, the shield of faith, and the lance of prayer. Our companions in arms are our holy guardian angels, who invisibly help us during the strife in the same way that they visibly helped Judas. We are consecrated to, and strengthened for this war by the Sacrament of Confirmation.

APPLICATION. Of what kind is your repentance and your purpose of amendment? Have you always carried out your good resolutions? In order to have a hatred of sin you ought every evening to try to excite in yourself a feeling of contrition.

Do you properly venerate your guardian angel and your patron Saint? Have you read your Saint's life? Do you commend yourself every day to his care, and try to imitate his virtues?

Do you pray diligently for the dead, especially for your relations and benefactors? Never neglect to do this, for it is a duty of love, and obtains merit for yourself. Especially remember the holy souls at Mass, after the Elevation. If even the sacrifices of the Old Testament, which were only shadows and types, could help the dead, how much greater must be the help which is afforded to them by the Most Holy Sacrifice of the New Testament.

CHAPTER LXXXVI.

THE FULNESS OF TIME.

[1 Mach. 10—16]

AFTER the death of Judas Machabeus, his brothers, Jonathan and Simon [1], successively placed themselves at the head of the Jewish people, and performed wonderful exploits. Their successors, however, fell away from God, and brought the people,

---

[1] *Jonathan and Simon.* Jonathan was treacherously murdered by the Syrians, 143 B. C. After his death his brother Simon was chosen to be both High Priest and leader of the people. He succeeded in entirely freeing the Jewish state from the dominion of the Syrian king, Demetrius, 142 B. C. (Fig. 60, p. 374). Out of gratitude, the Jews made the dignities of prince and High Priest hereditary in the family of Simon.

always unsteady and prone to evil, into a multitude of sins and vices. They, indeed, still worshipped the true God[1]; but it was only with their lips, and their hearts were far from Him.

Fig. 60. Coin of Simon Machabeus (silver shekel).

Their chief care consisted in the outward observance of the law; the inward disposition and purity of heart[2] they neglected. Whatever good there might be among the Jews was stifled by the sect of the hypocritical Pharisees, or of the unbelieving Sadducees[3]; and these two sects, although mortal enemies of each other, exercised a great power over the people. Throughout the rest of the world[4] idolatry reigned supreme, and all the nations of the earth were sunk in misery and corruption.

The few just men who were scattered[5] here and there among the different races sighed for the coming of the promised

---

[1] *The true God.* They had done so ever since their return from the captivity, and had been further confirmed in the true worship since the days of Judas Machabeus.

[2] *Purity of heart.* They had no fear or love of God in their hearts. In consequence, immorality gained such ground, that a Jewish writer, Flavius Josephus, has called Jerusalem a second Sodom.

[3] *Pharisees and Sadducees.* The Pharisees introduced many human doctrines and precepts, and attached almost more importance to these than to the law of God. They sought justice in such outward observances as the washing of hands and of vessels, and the repetition of prayers, and they neglected purity of heart. They were, for the most part, full of pride, avarice, envy and hypocrisy. The Sadducees were freethinkers and materialists. They did not believe in the immortality of the soul or in the resurrection of the body, so that they had no thought of eternal life, but sought their heaven in this world. They led a bad and dissolute life, having no fear of God. This sect found most of its adherents among the rich (see "The rich man" New Test. XLVI).

[4] *The rest of the world.* Pagan Rome had by degrees subjected to her rule nearly all the then known world, so that the nations of the world formed one vast empire, of which Rome was the capital, and the Roman emperor the sovereign. At the time of our Lord's Incarnation all manner of idolatry, unbelief, superstition, and an unbounded immorality reigned throughout this pagan empire. Rome alone possessed 30,000 deities, many of whom were honoured solely on account of their immorality. The largest portion of the population groaned in a miserable state of slavery. Corruption was so universal that all thinking men felt there was no deliverance from it possible, unless help were sent from heaven.

[5] *Scattered.* By means of the captivity of Babylon many Jewish colonies had been formed in the midst of the pagans, which continued to exist in the Christian era. After the division of the empire of Alexander the Great these colonies spread

Redeemer, the only hope of fallen man. They prayed that the clouds might rain down the Just One, and that the earth might bud forth the Saviour.

All was in readiness for the coming of our Lord, which event, according to signs and prophecies, must be near at hand. Four hundred years before the Birth of Christ, Malachias, the last of the prophets, could not restrain his joy at the near approach of the Messias. He told the Jewish priests that the Temple should soon be closed for ever, and the fires on their altars extinguished, for that their offerings had ceased to be pleasing to the Lord of Hosts. He said: "I have no pleasure in you, saith the Lord of Hosts, and I will not receive a gift at your hand. For from the rising of the sun even to the going down, My name is great among the Gentiles, and in every place there is sacrifice, and there is offered to My name a clean oblation. For My name is great among the Gentiles, saith the Lord of Hosts."

Nothing remained to be accomplished, save the prophecy of Jacob[1] to his son Juda. This last sign was not delayed. The Jewish people, torn and weakened by continual dissensions among themselves, called in the Romans to decide their quarrels, and the Romans, a great and powerful nation, settled the dispute by taking possession[2] of all Judæa, and placing on its throne Herod, a stranger[3], a satellite of the Roman emperor. Thus was the sceptre departed[4] from Juda, and that event ushered in the Redeemer of the world, the desired[5] of the nations. Herod reigned

---

themselves into Egypt, Asia Minor and Greece, and by force of the Jewish spirit of commercial enterprise gradually extended themselves over the whole Roman empire, as far as Spain and the south of France. There was a very large colony of Jews at Rome at the time of the Incarnation, for we hear of the emperor Augustus receiving a deputation of eight thousand of them. Wherever they settled down, these Jews built synagogues and houses of prayer, and through them the pagans got to know the Unseen and Living God, and the prophecies about the Messias; and many of them even adopted the Jewish religion.

[1] *Prophecy of Jacob.* See chapter XXVII.

[2] *Taking possession.* Under Pompey.

[3] *A stranger.* An Idumæan, who, in order to assure himself of the government, slew all the descendants of the Machabees, among others his own wife Mariamne and the two sons whom he had by her. Moreover, he oppressed the Jews with heavy taxes.

[4] *Departed.* Though the Jews had a ruler, he was a foreigner, and therefore the time had now come for the Advent of the Saviour, the "Expected of all nations".

[5] *Desired.* The prophet Isaias thus expressed the longing of Israel for the Redeemer: "Drop down dew, ye heavens, from above, and let the clouds rain the

in Judæa when the Messias, so long promised, appeared on earth in human form, even Christ the Lord, to whom be honour and glory for ever and ever.

COMMENTARY.

A retrospect by which we can recognise God's wisdom in the guidance of mankind:

1. Even in Paradise God revealed Himself to man, and promised a Redeemer. But the greater number of Adam's descendants turned away from God, and sank so low that their reason was obscured and they lost all power of understanding even that natural religion which was taught to them by the visible creation, and the voice of their own consciences. Nevertheless, in all pagan religions, there were preserved some remains of the original revelation, such as the memory of a former and happier state, the consciousness of the debt of sin hanging over the human race, the sense of the necessity of reconciliation with an offended God, the dim expectation of a Redeemer, and of a future and better state.

2. God revealed Himself supernaturally to the people of Israel, in order to preserve in them belief in the true God and in the future Redeemer, and through them to spread abroad this belief among the Gentiles. However, the inclination towards idolatry was so strong in the chosen people that it was many centuries before God, by repeated revelations and visitations, could wean them from it. Man is very ready to make his own god, that is, to make out God to be such as his own inclinations lead him to wish Him to be. Instead of moulding his own inclinations, will and actions to accord with God's almighty will, he seeks to accommodate God and His attributes to his own desires. It was not until paganism was eradicated from the religious belief of the

---

Just; let the earth be opened, and bud forth a Saviour", i. e. "as the dew falls from heaven, so may the Most Just (the Redeemer) descend from heaven; and as the earth brings forth plants, so in like manner may the Saviour be brought forth " The hope and longing for the Redeemer was expressed by the Jews in the daily prayers recited in the synagogues, in which was found the following petition: "Build up Jerusalem for ever, and raise up David's throne in the midst. Let the seed of David, Thy servant, bud forth speedily, for we hope continuously for Thy redemption." We can see in the case of Simeon, Anna, and those like them (New Test. VII), how very keen had become the expectation of the Messias in the fulness of time. The conjecture of the Jews that John the Baptist might be the Messias (New Test. XI) points in the same direction, as also do the words of the woman of Samaria at Jacob's well (New Test. XVI). We know, therefore, that the longing for the Redeemer was very general by the time that He came. However, only very few of the Jews thought of the Messias as being a Redeemer from sin, and a bringer of grace and truth; they expected, rather, that He would come to deliver them from the dominion of Rome and the tyranny of Herod, to set up the earthly throne of David, enlarge the borders of Judæa, and subject all

Jews, and the Old Testament revelation had become an essential part of their existence, that they were ready for a further and more perfect revelation. Then, and not till then, the world was prepared for the coming of the Only-Begotten of the Father to be its Redeemer.

3. As time went on, the promises concerning the Redeemer became more and more explicit. These promises were conveyed partly in prophecies, partly by types. Let us then recall the prophecies which have been mentioned: 1) that made to Adam and Eve after the Fall, 2) and 3) made to Abraham, 4) and 5) made through Jacob, 6) through Balaam, 7) through the dying Moses, 8) through David, 9) through Isaias, 10) through Jeremias, 11) through Ezechiel, 12) through Daniel, 13) through Aggeus, 14) through Zacharias, and 15) through Malachias. The *people* whom we have studied as types of the Messias are: 1) Adam, 2) Abel, 3) Noe, 4) Melchisedech, 5) Isaac, 6) Joseph, 7) Job, 8) Moses, 9) Josue, 10) Gedeon, 11) Samson, 12) David, 13) Solomon, 14) Elias, and 15) Jonas. The *objects* to which our attention has been directed as types are: the Tree of Life; the sacrifice of Melchisedech; the paschal lamb; the manna; the sacrifices of the Old Law; the brazen serpent &c. The prophecy uttered by Malachias was the last one vouchsafed, because from that time forward the Jews, being confirmed in their own faith, were employed by God to spread His revelation among the Gentiles.

4. The pagan world was on the brink of an abyss. It had learnt by its own experience what man comes to, when he has forsaken God. The ancient world had made great progress in the arts and sciences, but it found no satisfaction in them, because its moral and social condition was deplorable. The truth, which raises man, and delivers him from all uncertainty, was lacking to this world which had cast off its God. Its best and most learned men were fully aware of the folly of paganism, but this conviction only led them to doubt everything; as we can see, for example, by Pilate's question: "What is truth?" This state of doubt did not help them to arrive at truth, for truth can only be found in God. Moreover, grace was wanting to them,—that grace which enables man to will and to do what is right, which puts an end to the disorders of human nature, and brings peace to the restless heart of man. When the pagan world at length saw what was lacking to it, and that no help could come to it except from heaven, then it was that God dispersed the Jews into all parts of the world, and by their means spread abroad the knowledge of the living and true God, and the hope of the Redeemer. Thus, four thousand years after the

---

nations to her rule. Even the influential Pharisees regarded a more complete revelation of God as impossible. That the Messias should be a Saviour of all men, Gentiles as well as Jews, was an idea quite inconceivable to their narrow-minded selfishness.

Fall, a large portion of the pagan world had begun to long for the Saviour who was expected in Judæa.

Now, "when the fulness of time was come, God sent His Son that we might receive the adoption of sons" (Gal. 4, 4). "The Word was made flesh and dwelt among us, and we saw His glory, the glory as it were of the Only-Begotten of the Father, full of grace and truth" (John 1, 14).

The signification of Advent. This season ought to make us think of the sad condition of the world before our Lord's Incarnation, and prepare ourselves, by penance and a longing desire, for the Birth of Christ in our hearts.

The two natures of the Redeemer. The passage: "Drop down dew, ye heavens, from above, and let the clouds rain the Just; let the earth be opened, and bud forth a Saviour", which occurs in Isaias 45, 8, clearly foretells the twofold nature of God made Man. The Divine nature is signified by the prophecy that the Saviour shall come down from heaven (in another passage Isaias cries out: "O that Thou wouldst rend the heavens, and wouldst come down!"); and His Human nature is shown by the prophecy that the earth shall bring Him forth. As God, Jesus Christ came down from heaven, and took His Human nature on earth in the womb of the Immaculate Virgin Mary. Heaven and earth worked together to bring forth the God made Man, through whom earth has been reconciled to heaven.

APPLICATION. Have you a great desire for the truth which has been revealed to us through Jesus Christ? Do you take great pains to learn all you can about the true doctrines of Christianity? Do you take pleasure in your religious instruction?

Have you a desire that Jesus Christ should come and reign in your heart and dwell therein; or do you look forward to the hour of your first Communion for any less worthy reasons? When you are hearing Mass, make a spiritual Communion, and excite in yourself a longing desire to receive your Divine Saviour. Be sorry for your sins, and pray our Lord to come and dwell spiritually in your heart!

SECOND PART

THE NEW TESTAMENT

FIRST SECTION.

HISTORY OF JESUS CHRIST.

His Birth and Infancy.

CHAPTER I.

ANNOUNCEMENT OF THE BIRTH OF JOHN THE BAPTIST.

[Luke 1, 5—23.]

AT the time when Herod[1] was king in Judæa[2], there lived, in a small city in the hill-country, a priest named Zachary, whose wife was called Elizabeth. They were both just before God, and walked blamelessly[3] in all the commandments of the Lord. They had no children[4]; this was a cause of great affliction to them. They often prayed that God would give them a son; but their prayer seemed to remain unanswered, as they were both now advanced[5] in years.

It so happened that Zachary went to Jerusalem, when his turn came to perform the priestly office[6]. He entered the

---

[1] *Herod.* This king, who was referred to in chapter LXXXVI, Old Test., reigned from the year 40 B. C. to A. D. 3.

[2] *Judæa.* This was the name given to the southern portion of Palestine. The centre was called Samaria, and the north, Galilee. The country east of the Jordan was called Peræa (see Map).

[3] *Walked blamelessly.* i. e. they were not in a state of sin, and carefully observed all the commandments of God.

[4] *No children.* They grieved over this, for the Jews rightly looked upon children as a precious gift of God.

[5] *Advanced.* They were very old, and therefore entertained, humanly speaking, no hope of having a child. However, they had great faith in the power and goodness of God, with whom nothing is impossible, and who before this had given a son to Sara in her old age and to Anna who was childless.

[6] *Priestly office.* The priests were distributed into twenty-four classes or families or courses; and each class had to attend to the service of the Temple for

Sanctuary to offer incense on the altar, while the people prayed without [1]; and, behold, an angel of the Lord appeared to him, standing at the right hand of the altar of incense.

Zachary was troubled at the sight of the angel; but the angel said to him: "Fear not, Zachary, for thy prayer [2] is heard. Thy wife Elizabeth shall bear thee a son, and thou shalt call his name John. Thou shalt have joy and gladness, and many shall rejoice at his birth; for he shall be great before the Lord, and shall drink no wine nor strong drink, and he shall be filled [3] with the Holy Ghost even from his mother's womb. He shall convert many [4] of the children of Israel to the Lord their God. He shall go before Him [5] in the spirit and power of Elias [6], to prepare for the Lord a perfect people."

Zachary said to the angel: "Whereby [7] shall I know this? For I am an old man, and my wife is advanced in years." The angel replied: "I am Gabriel, who stand before God, and am sent to speak to thee, and to bring thee these good tidings. Behold, thou shalt be dumb, and shalt not be able to speak until the day in which these things shall come to pass, because thou hast not believed my words." Having spoken thus he disappeared.

---

eight days (Old Test. LIV). When Zachary's turn came round, he went to Jerusalem. The various services of the Temple, such as the offering of the daily sacrifice and incense, the care of the sacred fire and the lamps of the seven-branched candlestick, changing the loaves of proposition &c., were apportioned to the various priests by lot. This time the lot of offering incense in the Sanctuary had fallen to Zachary.

[1] *Without.* For only the priests were allowed to enter the Sanctuary.

[2] *Thy prayer.* The prayer for the coming of the Saviour of Israel.

[3] *Be filled.* And thereby cleansed from original sin.

[4] *Many.* That many of these required conversion, may be seen by chapter LXXXVI, Old Test.

[5] *Before Him.* Before the Lord God, i. e. the Divine Saviour. He would go before the Redeemer (who, therefore, would come after him), to bring the people to do penance and sanctify themselves in preparation for the coming of the Saviour.

[6] *Of Elias.* i. e. with the same dispositions and the same zeal, speaking out with courage even against the evil doings of kings, as the great prophet Elias had preached penance of old (Old Test. LXII, LXIII, LXIV).

[7] *Whereby.* The angel told Zachary that not only he should have a son, but that this son should be the precursor of the Redeemer. The news was too great for Zachary, being more than he had dared to ask for. Not feeling able to believe it, he asked for a sign, by which he might be certain that this thing would be as the angel had said.

Meanwhile the people without in the Temple were expecting [1] Zachary, and wondered at his long delay [2].   When he at length appeared, he could not speak to them, except by signs; and the people knew [3] that he had seen a vision in the Temple.   After the days of his ministry were accomplished, Zachary departed to his own house.

COMMENTARY.

The promise of the Redeemer.   By announcing to Zachary that his holy son should precede the Redeemer, the angel foretold the speedy advent of the Messias.

The Divinity of Jesus Christ.   The words of the angel testified that the Redeemer was God: "He shall", said Gabriel, alluding to the son of Zachary, "convert many of the children of Israel to the Lord their God, and he shall go before Him."   Now, who is meant by "Him"? The Lord God is meant; and therefore the Redeemer, before whom John was to go, must be the Lord God Himself.

The power of persevering prayer.   Zachary and Elizabeth had probably prayed for many years that they might have a son.   Their prayers seemed to be offered up in vain, but nevertheless they persevered in laying the great desire of their hearts before God.   At last they were heard, and received from God much more than they had asked for.   They had asked for a son who might succeed his father in the priestly office, and they received a son who was to become a great Saint, a prophet of God, and the precursor of the Divine Redeemer. This was the rich reward of their perseverance in prayer.

Steadfastness.   Zachary and Elizabeth are models of steadfastness in what is right.   They lived in an evil time when most of the Israelites, and even most of the priests, had grown lax in the service of God, and no longer worshipped Him in their hearts.   But in spite of the evil example of those around them, Zachary and Elizabeth remained true to God, and faithfully observed His commandments.

True justice.   Zachary and Elizabeth were not only just in the eyes of men, as were the hypocritical Pharisees, but were "just before God". Many people think it is enough to appear righteous in the eyes of the world.   This may be sufficient to save us from being put into prison, but it will not prove enough to obtain for us an entrance into heaven.

---

[1] *Expecting.*   Because the priest, after offering incense, solemnly blessed the people.

[2] *Delay.*   Longer than was necessary for doing what he had to do.   It was considered a mark of irreverence to remain longer than necessary in the Sanctuary.

[3] *Knew.*   They knew this, first, because he was dumb, and secondly, because his countenance was illuminated with a holy joy.

He who wishes to be just before God, and to dwell with Him one day in heaven, must observe all God's commandments, and must do His will in all things as Zachary and Elizabeth did.

Abstinence from strong drink. St. John the Baptist abstained from wine and strong drinks throughout his whole life. You ought, while you are young, to abstain from all strong drinks, and especially from spirits. Such drinks ruin the health of both the soul and body of the young.

The doubt of Zachary; the sign given to him. The angel said to Zachary: "Thy prayer is heard." Zachary ought to have known by these words that the speaker was a messenger sent by God, for God alone can see the heart, and it was from Him alone that the angel could have known what Zachary had prayed for. Nevertheless, Zachary would not fully believe the good tidings. He and his wife being old, it was so unlikely they should have a son that he asked for a sign. His request was granted. At that very moment he lost both speech and hearing, becoming (according to St. Ambrose, Maldonatus and others) deaf as well as dumb. We shall see in chapter IV that his friends had to make signs to him, because he could not hear them. This deafness and dumbness were meant to serve a threefold purpose: 1. They were to be a sign by which Zachary should know that the angel's message had come from God, and would surely be accomplished; 2. they were a punishment of the holy man's passing doubt, for a wilful doubt is a sin. However, we may assume that Zachary's doubt was not quite wilful, but rather the result of surprise and want of consideration, and that therefore his sin was only venial; 3. this particular mode of punishment was to be the means of keeping secret the revelation made to Zachary. It had been revealed to him that his son should go before the Redeemer, and that therefore the Redeemer would soon come. Zachary's impulse, in the joy of his heart, would have been to announce to all pious Israelites the good news that the day for which they all longed and the hour of salvation were at hand. Now, however, he was struck dumb, and, according to the decrees of God's wisdom, the great secret could not just yet be disclosed to the world.

APPLICATION. You would have received many more graces from God, if you had prayed more fervently and persistently. You ought to have great confidence in the power of prayer, and excite in your heart a greater love for it. From this day forward make a point of saying all the prayers you have to say with greater faithfulness and devotion.

CHAPTER II.

ANNUNCIATION OF THE BIRTH OF CHRIST.

[Luke 1, 26—38. Mat. 1, 18—25.]

SIX months later, the angel Gabriel was sent from God to a virgin living in a city of Galilee, called Nazareth[1] (Fig. 61, p. 386). The virgin's name was Mary[2], and she was espoused to a man called Joseph, and they both belonged to the house of David. The angel being come in[3], said to her: "Hail, full of grace[4], the Lord is with thee[5]; blessed art thou among women."[6]

Mary, hearing these words, was disturbed and troubled, wondering what this strange salutation meant[7]. But the angel spoke again: "Fear not, Mary, for thou hast found grace with God[8]. Behold, thou shalt conceive in thy womb, and bring forth a son, and thou shalt call His name Jesus[9]. He shall be great, and shall

---

[1] *Nazareth.* See Map.

[2] *Mary.* She was the only child of St. Joachim and St. Anne, and, according to tradition, was presented in the Temple at the age of three years, to be one of the holy virgins who served God there. She, like St. Joseph, was of the family of David. She was brought up and instructed in the Temple, and spent her youth there in prayer, spiritual reading, and manual work; and, later, she was espoused to St. Joseph. Most likely Mary was rapt in devotion, when the angel came to her. That she often and earnestly prayed to God to send the promised Saviour cannot be doubted.

[3] *Come in.* Into her room.

[4] *Grace.* Full of sanctifying grace, and therefore so holy that there is no sin in thee. According to the holy Fathers Mary received as much grace as human nature is capable of receiving.

[5] *With thee.* Because thou art full of grace, the Lord is in a special manner with thee and in thee.

[6] *Among women.* Thou art the most blessed of all women. She was, indeed, the woman chosen to tread on and crush the head of the infernal serpent.

[7] *Strange salutation meant.* Mary was not only troubled at the appearance of the angel, as Zachary had been, but also at the manner of his salutation. This salutation must indeed have been startling, for never before and never since has a human being been thus greeted by an angel. The great angel of God saluted the simple virgin as a servant might salute his mistress, or a subject his sovereign. This homage troubled her, and she asked herself what it could mean, and whether the words were really a message from God, or a deception of the devil [as in the case of Eve].

[8] *Found grace with God.* Namely, the quite singular grace of being, while yet a virgin, the Mother of the Redeemer, for whose coming thou hast so often prayed. Mary had, therefore, sought and found grace not only for herself, but for all mankind.

[9] *Jesus.* i. e. Saviour or Redeemer.

be called the Son of the Most High, and the Lord God shall give Him the throne of David His father [1]; and He shall reign in the house of Jacob for ever, and of His kingdom there shall be no end." [2]

Fig. 61. Church of the Annunciation at Nazareth. (Phot. Dr. Trenkler & Co., Leipzig.)

Mary asked how this could be, seeing that she was a virgin [3]. The angel answered: "The Holy Ghost shall come upon thee, and the power of the Most High [4] shall overshadow thee [5]. And

---

[1] *His father*. His mother being descended from David, her Divine Son was also, as far as His human nature went, a descendant of David, or, in other words, king David was a forefather of our Lord.

[2] *No end*. His kingdom will not come to an end as earthly kingdoms do, but will be an eternal and supernatural kingdom.

[3] *A virgin*. Mary did not, like Zachary, doubt that what the angel announced would come to pass, but she wondered how it could be brought about, for she had vowed to remain ever a virgin. Now, however, the angel explained to this chaste Virgin that she would become a mother and bear a son in a supernatural manner, by the operation of the Holy Ghost.

[4] *The Most High*. i. e. the Holy Ghost.

[5] *Overshadow thee*. As once the Ark of the Covenant was overshadowed by the pillar of cloud, so will you now be overshadowed by the Holy Ghost.

therefore[1] also, the Holy which shall be born of thee shall be called the Son of God. And behold, thy cousin Elizabeth, she also hath conceived a son in her old age, because no word shall be impossible with God."[2]

Then Mary said: "Behold the handmaid of the Lord; be it done to me according to thy word!"[3] The angel, having thus delivered his message, and having obtained the consent of Mary, departed from her[4].

Joseph knew not yet that Mary was the chosen Mother of the Saviour, but an angel of the Lord appeared to him also in his sleep, and said: "Joseph, son of David, fear not to take unto thee Mary, thy wife, for That which is conceived in her, is of the Holy Ghost. And thou shalt call His name Jesus[5], for He shall save His people from their sins."

COMMENTARY.

The Incarnation of the Son of God (the third article of the Creed). The Son of God, who is also called "the Word", became incarnate, i. e. flesh or man by the power of the Holy Ghost, being "conceived of the Holy Ghost", i. e. having no human father—St. Joseph being only his foster-father or legal father [in the eyes of the law]—, and "born of Mary the most pure Virgin". St. John (1, 18) says: "The Word was made flesh and dwelt among us." When the Son of God became man, He did not cease to be God, for that would have been quite impossible, but He assumed the human nature unto His Divine

---

[1] *And therefore.* Because by the overshadowing the Son of God descends into the virgin's womb, therefore he, who is born of her, is the true Son of God, and must be called the Son of God as well as the Son of Mary.

[2] *Impossible with God.* In order to strengthen Mary's faith in the great mystery which he had just revealed to her, the angel announced to her that her cousin Elizabeth was likewise miraculously bearing a son in her old age. Therefore all things are possible with God.

[3] *According to thy word.* Mary believed and, full of faithful obedience, said: "God is the Lord. I am His handmaid and will do His will in all things. If it is, therefore, God's will that I should have a son, I submit myself to His will. Be it done unto me according to thy word, that I shall have a son by the operation of the Holy Ghost!" By these words Mary gave her consent to be the Mother of the Redeemer.

[4] *Departed from her.* He disappeared, full of joy, for he had received an answer well-pleasing to God.

[5] *Jesus.* The name of Jesus was to be given to the Child, because He was, in truth, the Saviour and Redeemer. Joseph obeyed the divine command, and full of reverence took to himself the pure Virgin who was chosen to be the Mother of the Redeemer.

Person. There are, therefore, two natures in Jesus Christ, the divine nature and the human nature, but there is only one person in Him, the person of God the Son. Jesus Christ is therefore God and Man, the Son of God and the Son of David, the true Emmanuel, i. e. God with us.

Proof of our Lord's Divinity taken from the angel's words. Firstly, Gabriel said that Jesus was the "Son of the Most High" and the "Son of God". Secondly, he said that Jesus should "save His people from their sins". Now, God alone can redeem from sin; therefore Jesus must be God.

Fulfilment of the prophecies. This chapter relates how those prophecies were fulfilled which foretold, firstly, that the Redeemer would be born of a virgin; and secondly, that He would be a descendant of David.

Mary co-operated in our salvation by giving her consent to become the Mother of the Saviour. The angel of the Lord was sent to Mary in order to procure this consent. The time had arrived, and the Son of God was ready to descend from heaven and become Man. It only remained for her, whom God the Father had chosen to be the Mother of His Son, to give her consent to be so. The angel of God therefore explained this great mystery, and waited for her answer, on which depended the salvation of the world. While meditating upon that decisive moment, St. Bernard uttered this prayer to Mary: "Now, O Virgin, thou hast heard what is to be, and how it is to be. Both mysteries are exceeding joyous and wonderful. But the angel awaits thine answer, for it is time for him to return to God who sent him. We too, O Mary, our Queen, we who are weighed down by the divine sentence, we wait for thy speech, thy words of mercy. For behold, the price of our redemption is offered to thee; and as soon as thou dost accept it, we shall be saved. We were all created by the eternal word of God, and yet, behold, we die! But if thou wilt speak one little word, we shall live! Speak then, Oh, speak that decisive word. Adam and his unhappy children, banished from Paradise, beseech this of thee! David and all our holy fathers—thy fathers too—beseech thee! The whole world, prostrate before thee, looks to thee and beseeches! On thy words depend the comfort of the afflicted, the deliverance of the condemned, the salvation of the children of Adam! Hesitate not, O Virgin! Speak, O Mary, that sweet word of consent, which we who are on the earth, and under the earth, now wait for!" Mary, as you know, did utter that decisive word of compliance: "Behold the handmaid of the Lord, be it done to me according to thy word!" By these glorious and precious words she pronounced the longed-for consent. Our Redemption began from the moment in which Mary acknowledged herself to be the handmaid of the Lord, and became the Mother of God! It is therefore reasonable, just, and right that all Christians should honour Mary as the "cause of our joy", in the words of her Litany, and should venerate her as the "Mother most pure", through whom our Redeemer was given to us. The Feast of her Annunciation is kept on March 25th.

The Angelical Salutation (the Hail Mary). A pious writer (Ludolphus) says about this salutation: "Mark well: God the Father entrusted the angel with this salutation, sending it by him to the Virgin. Therefore, never can she be addressed in words more honourable, more pleasing, or more agreeable to her."

The Angelus. Besides the Hail Mary, thrice repeated, the Angelus contains: 1. the message of the angel; 2. the consent of Mary; 3. the result of her consent, namely, the Incarnation of the Son of God. It therefore reminds us of the beginning of our Redemption and of the part Mary had in it. The words which it contains and which are repeated by us three times every day, are more important, more significant and more precious than any other words that human lips can utter, with the exception of the "Our Father".

The virtues of Mary. The story we have just heard shows forth especially Mary's faith, chastity, and humility. Firstly, the angel announced to her something stupendous, namely, that God was about to become Man, and that she, without losing her virginity, was to be His Mother: and Mary confidently believed what was told her. Secondly, she had made a vow of virginity, in the full persuasion that the state of virginity was a far higher one and far more pleasing to God than that of maternity. This being perfectly true, God combined the two in her case and gave her the glory of both states. Lastly, her humility has been shown forth. She was troubled by the angel's respectful manner of salutation, and, in spite of all he had said, she still called herself the handmaid of the Lord. "God resisteth the proud and giveth grace to the humble." (James 4, 6.) Mary, in real humility, abased herself; therefore God raised her to the highest dignity.

Comparison between Eve and Mary. Eve was the mother of all mankind, according to the flesh: Mary is the spiritual mother of all the faithful. Both entered life without the stain of sin, and in a state of grace; but Eve lost grace, while Mary, on the contrary, preserved it and increased it by corresponding with it. Eve thoughtlessly allowed herself to be deceived by the devil, without asking herself whether it were a good or an evil spirit who spoke through the serpent; but Mary pondered, and asked herself whether the salutation of the angel came from God or not. Eve conversed with the devil, for the ruin of man: Mary with Gabriel, for the salvation of man. Eve sinned by unbelief: while Mary believed the wonderful message which God sent. Eve sinned by pride, wishing to be as God: Mary was humble, calling herself the handmaid of the Lord. Eve was disobedient to God: Mary gave herself over entirely to His will. Eve consented to sin: Mary to God's will. Eve, by her pride, degraded herself, and brought sin and death on all

mankind: Mary, by her humility, was herself exalted, and through her
Divine Son gave grace and life to the world. As far as she could,
Mary paid the debt owed by Eve to the human race. Eve was the
mother of the curse: Mary of the blessing. She is the true mother of
the living, the new and better Eve. These striking contrasts are, of
course, the result not of accident, but of the action of the mysterious
wisdom and counsel of God, and they teach us to value God's merciful
Providence.

APPLICATION. Do you say the Angelus regularly three times
a day? Do you uncover your head when you hear the Angelus-
bell ring? Always repeat the Hail Mary very devoutly. Salute
our Lady with as much reverence as did the holy angel. And
while you are saying the Angelus, meditate on Mary's humility,
and on the love of the Son of God who became Man for
love of us.

CHAPTER III.

THE VISITATION.

[Luke 1, 39—56.]

MARY, rising up in those days [1], went with haste into the
hill-country [2] to visit and congratulate her cousin Elizabeth.
No sooner did Mary enter the house [3] than Elizabeth, filled with
the Holy Ghost [4], cried out [5]: "Blessed art thou among women,
and blessed is the fruit of thy womb [6]. And whence is this to

---

[1] *Those days.* Soon after the angel had delivered his message to her.

[2] *Hill-country.* According to tradition, the little town where Zachary and
Elizabeth dwelt lay six miles to the west of Jerusalem. It still exists and is called
"St. John in the Mountains" (Fig. 62), because St. John the Baptist was born there.
The journey thither from Nazareth is one of seventy miles. The road crosses hills
and valleys, and it was a difficult journey for our Lady, the rainy season being just
over when she made it. According to tradition the Annunciation of the Birth of
our Lord was on March 25th, so that Mary's journey was made during the last
days of March.

[3] *Enter the house.* Greeting her with the usual salutation: "Peace be
with thee."

[4] *Holy Ghost.* She already possessed the grace of the Holy Ghost, being,
as we read in the first chapter, "just before God". But at the salutation of the
Blessed Mother of God, Elizabeth received from the Holy Ghost the gift of prophecy, or of supernatural illumination.

[5] *Cried out.* Impelled by a holy joy.

[6] *The fruit of thy womb.* Namely Jesus, the Divine Child.

me, that the Mother of my Lord should come to me?[1] Blessed art thou that hast believed, because those things shall be accomplished that were spoken to thee by the Lord."

Fig. 62. St. John in the Mountains. (Phot. Bonfils.)

Whereupon Mary exclaimed[2]: "My soul doth magnify the Lord, and my spirit hath rejoiced in God my Saviour. Because He hath regarded[3] the humility of His handmaid; for behold, from henceforth all generations shall call me blessed. For He

[1] *To me.* "Why does this high honour come to me? How have I deserved this extraordinary grace that the Mother of God should visit me? I ought to go to you, and serve you, and yet you come to me!" Elizabeth, by the inspiration of the Holy Ghost, knew what the angel had announced to Mary, and what she had answered. She therefore congratulated the Blessed Virgin on having believed the message of God. At the same time the Holy Ghost, by the mouth of Elizabeth, gave the assurance that everything which God had announced by the angel would come to pass: Mary would bear a son by the operation of the Holy Ghost, and this son would be the Son of God, and would save His people from their sins.

[2] *Exclaimed.* Mary knew by the words of Elizabeth that God had revealed to her cousin His choice of her to be the Mother of His Son, and the speedy advent of the Redeemer. She could therefore no longer keep silence about the great joy that had come to her, and burst out into the "Magnificat".

[3] *Regarded.* He has taken pity on my humility, and chosen me to be the Mother of His Son.

that is mighty hath done great things to me, and holy is His
name[1]. And His mercy is from generation unto generation, to
them that fear Him. He hath shown might with His arm: He
hath scattered the proud in the imagination of their heart[2]. He
hath put down the mighty from their seat, and hath exalted the
humble[3]. He hath filled the hungry with good things; and the
rich he hath sent empty away. He hath upholden Israel[4] His
servant, being mindful[5] of His mercy. As He spoke to our fathers,
Abraham and his seed for ever." Mary abode with her cousin
about three months; then she returned to Nazareth.

COMMENTARY.

The Divinity of Jesus Christ. Elizabeth, inspired by the Holy
Ghost, testified to the Divinity of Jesus when she called Mary the Mother
of God; for, if Mary is the Mother of God, her Son must be God.

Mary is the Mother of God. The Holy Ghost has called her so
by the mouth of Elizabeth.

The dignity of the Mother of God is inconceivably high, for, as
Mother of God, Mary is nearer than any other creature, nearer even
than the highest angel, to the Blessed Trinity. Mary, being nearest of
all creatures to God, who is the source of all dignity and grace, holds
the highest place amongst all creatures in the kingdom of God, and is
the Queen of all Saints.

Veneration of the Mother of God. In the Magnificat Mary said
prophetically: "From henceforth all generations shall call me blessed."
This prophecy has been fulfilled in the Catholic Church, for our holy
Church honours our Lady by special feasts and special devotions. How
would it be possible not to pay honour to her whom God raised to
such a high dignity, and praised in such a manner by the mouths of
Gabriel and Elizabeth! Our veneration of the holy Mother of God is
well founded both on Holy Scripture and on reason.

It is on account of her Divine Son that we honour Mary. When
the Holy Ghost, by the mouth of Elizabeth, said: "Blessed art thou
among women, and blessed is the fruit of thy womb (Jesus)", He testified to the close connexion that lies between the veneration of the

---

[1] *His name.* i. e. His Being and Nature is holiness itself. The All-powerful
and All-holy God has done great things to me.

[2] *Their heart.* Brought to nought their proud plans.

[3] *The humble.* Remember proud Saul and humble David, and what befell them!

[4] *Israel.* i. e. the people of Israel.

[5] *Mindful.* Mindful of the gracious promises which He made to Abraham
and to all his children for ever, namely, that the Redeemer would come and bring
grace and blessing to all men.

Mother and the worship of the Son. It is because Mary is the Mother of God that she is so full of grace, and entitled to the love and veneration of all who love and worship Jesus; and all the honour which we pay to her, returns to her Divine Son. On the other hand, those who despise and depreciate Mary depreciate thereby our Lord Jesus Christ. The Church has added St. Elizabeth's words (Blessed is the fruit of thy womb) to the Angelical Salutation, to prove that the veneration of Mary is inseparable from the veneration and worship of Jesus Christ.

Mary, a pattern of charity. Why did Mary hasten to visit her cousin? She loved retirement, communion with God, and solitude; so it must have been a grave reason which made her leave her retired home and undertake a long journey. What were her reasons? Firstly, the angel had referred her to Elizabeth, although she had believed his words without asking for a sign. She therefore believed it to be God's will that she should visit her cousin, and convince herself of the truth of the sign given her, i. e. that Elizabeth was about to have a son. Secondly, Mary knew well that her cousin had grieved for many years on account of being childless, and she knew how happy she must be now that the cause of her grief was removed. Mary's loving heart sympathised with the happiness of her cousin; she desired to wish her joy, rejoice with her, and join her in praising God's mercy. He who really loves his neighbour has a loving sympathy with his joys and sorrows. Thirdly, Mary, as the holy Fathers teach, wished to minister to her cousin, and help her in her household affairs.

Prompt service. Mary went to Elizabeth in haste, because her loving sympathy and desire to be of assistance impelled her to go to her cousin with as little delay as possible. Her example teaches us that we should never be dilatory in the performance of any good work. Let us never put off till to-morrow what we can do to-day.

The humility of Mary. Although Mary was the Mother of God, she hastened to visit her cousin, to congratulate her and minister to her. And when Elizabeth received her so reverently, and praised her as the Mother of God, Mary called herself God's handmaid, and gave all the glory to Him, magnifying His power, His mercy and His truth.

The Magnificat. Our Lady's canticle of praise is called the "Magnificat", because in Latin it begins with that word. This canticle of praise is always sung at Vespers, and we ought to join in it with devotion and joy, in thanksgiving to God for the gift of His Son, and for all the great graces of Redemption.

Humility in receiving Holy Communion. Elizabeth was quite right to consider it a great and undeserved honour that the Mother of her Lord should enter her house. How much greater and more undeserved is the grace which is given to us of receiving our Lord Himself into our hearts in Holy Communion! Then, indeed, we ought to think and say: "Whence is this that my Lord and my God should come to me!"

APPLICATION. Cherish a filial love and veneration for the most Blessed Mary, Virgin and Mother of God. Say devoutly in her honour such prayers as the Litany of Loreto &c, and frequent all devotions practised in her honour.

CHAPTER IV.

BIRTH OF JOHN THE BAPTIST.

[Luke 1, 56—80.]

THE time[1] of her delivery being come, Elizabeth brought forth a son, according to the promise[2] of the Angel. All her neighbours and her kinsfolk rejoiced with her. Eight days after his birth the child was circumcised. The relatives and friends thought the child should be called Zachary like his father. But Elizabeth answered: "Not so, he shall be called John."[3] Upon this they reminded her that there was no one in the family who bore that name.

Then they made signs[4] to his father, how he would have him called. But he, being still dumb, made signs, and demanding a tablet[5] wrote on it: "John is his name." At the same moment

---

[1] *The time.* The time appointed by God.

[2] *The promise.* See chapter I.

[3] *John.* The law ordered that a child should be circumcised on the eighth day after his birth, he being thereby admitted to the covenant of God and the communion of the faithful (Old Test. XI). At his circumcision a name was given to the child. Now, how did Elizabeth know that her child was to be called John? She knew it by the inspiration of the Holy Ghost, with whom she had been filled ever since the visit of the Mother of God. It was customary to give a child at his circumcision the name of some relative, and as none of Zachary's family had the name of John, there was some hesitation about complying with Elizabeth's wishes, without first learning the opinion of her husband.

[4] *Signs.* Zachary being deaf and dumb, they had to inquire of him by signs what name he wished to be given to his son.

[5] *Tablet.* Why did he write, "John is his name"? Because this was the name which God, by His angel, had already given to the child. The name of John signifies "Jehovah has had mercy". What the angel foretold to Zachary had now come to pass; the child was born, had been circumcised, and had received the name ordained by God; so now the sign was no longer required, and Zachary was able to speak and hear again.

his tongue was loosened, and he spoke. And all those who were present were amazed[1], saying one to another: "What think ye this child shall be? for the hand of the Lord[2] is with him.

Zachary, filled with the Holy Ghost and in an ecstasy of joy and gratitude, began to prophesy and bless God in the canticle[3] which still bears his name:

"Blessed be the Lord God of Israel; because He hath visited[4] and wrought the redemption of His people,

"And hath raised up a horn of salvation to us, in the house of David His servant,

"As He spoke by the mouth of His holy prophets, who are from the beginning:

"Salvation from our enemies, and from the hand of all that hate us,

"To perform mercy to our fathers, and to remember His holy testament:

"The oath which He swore to our father Abraham, that He would grant to us,

"That, being delivered from the hand of our enemies, we may serve Him without fear,

"In holiness and justice before Him, all our days.

"And thou[5], child, shalt be called the prophet[6] of the Highest: for thou shalt go before the Lord to prepare[7] His ways,

"To give knowledge of salvation to His people, unto the remission of their sins.

---

[1] *Amazed.* Why? First, because such an unusual name had been given to the child, and secondly because, after naming him, Zachary had been instantaneously cured of his malady.

[2] *The hand of the Lord.* They recognised that God had shown His might in the child because he had been given in a wonderful way to his aged parents, and because Zachary was suddenly cured at his circumcision. They felt that God destined this child for something great.

[3] *The canticle.* Canticle of Zachary, in which he first thanks God for giving him a son, chosen to be the immediate precursor of the Redeemer, and secondly for giving redemption to His people, by the speedy coming of the Saviour.

[4] *Visited.* Visited by his personal appearance on earth.

[5] *Thou.* His own son, John.

[6] *Prophet.* St. John the Baptist was the last of the prophets, for he proclaimed the immediate approach of the Redeemer, as you will learn in chapters XI and XIII.

[7] *Prepare.* By instructing the minds and disposing the hearts of the Jews to receive the Divine Saviour, as is explained in the next verse.

"Through the bowels of the mercy of our God: in which the Orient from on high hath visited us,

"To enlighten them that sit in darkness, and in the shadow of death; to direct our feet into the way of peace."

And the child grew and was strengthened in spirit[1]; and was in the desert[2] until the day of his manifestation to Israel.

COMMENTARY.

The Faithfulness of God. His promise to Zachary: "Thy wife shall bear thee a son", was faithfully kept. The punishment of dumbness pronounced on Zachary, because of his doubt, was accompanied by the promise that his dumbness should cease on the day when all that the angel had foretold came to pass. This promise also was exactly fulfilled, for the moment Zachary asserted that the child's name was John, his tongue was loosed, and he was able once more to speak. The instant that he obediently executed the angel's command: "Thou shalt call his name John", speech was restored to him.

The Divinity of Jesus Christ. Inspired by the Holy Ghost, Zachary in his canticle of praise and thanksgiving testifies to the divine nature of the Redeemer. If John was to be the prophet of the "Highest", and to go before the face of the "Lord", then is the Saviour of whom this was foretold both Lord and Highest, or, in other words, God.

The friendly sympathy of their neighbours and relatives with the joy of the aged couple is worthy of praise. Zachary and Elizabeth rejoiced that God had heard their prayer and had given them a son; and their friends really and sincerely shared their joy. He who possesses true brotherly love rejoices at the happiness of his fellow creatures. Those who are envious do not know what love means, being full of nothing but selfishness.

Holy youth. John spent his youth leading a hermit's life in the desert, till he was thirty years old. Far from the turmoil of the world, he served God with prayer, fasting and contemplation, and grew daily in grace and virtue. Great fortitude was required to lead such a severe and self-denying life for so many years, and therefore the Evangelist says about him that he was "strengthened in spirit". His angelic and innocent youth prepared John for being a worthy preacher of penance and precursor of the Redeemer. O, how lovely a thing is youth passed in innocence!

---

[1] *In spirit.* Taught by the Holy Ghost, he led a truly supernatural life, renouncing the world and its possessions, and resolutely denying himself.

[2] *The desert.* In the stony, barren, and, for the most part, uninhabited country on the western shores of the Dead Sea.

The Benedictus is the name given to Zachary's canticle of praise. It is a splendid song of thanksgiving for the blessing of redemption, and is therefore daily recited by the priests of the Church in their office at Lauds. In this prayer Zachary exhibits a truly priestly mind. He does not think of himself or of his own happiness, or of the honour which was brought to him by the birth of such a son. His thoughts are occupied by the salvation which God had prepared for the whole world; and he regards his son only in the light of the prophet and precursor, whose birth heralded the near approach of the Saviour.

Birthdays and feast-days. The Church celebrates the nativity of St. John the Baptist on June 24th. In the case of other Saints it is not the day of their birth, but the day of their death which is solemnized, this last being the day of their entry into the glory of heaven. The nativity of only two Saints is celebrated, namely, that of our Lady (Sept. 8th), because she was conceived without the stain of sin, and that of St. John the Baptist, because he was filled with the Holy Ghost before his birth, and was thereby cleansed from original sin. We all come into the world the children of wrath, infected by the taint of original sin, and for this reason Catholics do not celebrate their natural birthday so much as the day of their supernatural birth, or their feast-day, i. e. the feast of the Saint whose name they received in Baptism. On our feast-day we should thank God not only for having given to us and preserved the life of our body, but also for that supernatural and eternal life to which we were born again in holy Baptism, being hereby made members of His holy Church and heirs of heaven. The name of a Saint was given to us in Baptism, in order that he whose name we bear may intercede for us with God, and that we may have a model before us to imitate.

APPLICATION. John came into the world in a state of grace, and grew daily in grace and virtue. You, indeed, came into the world in a state of original sin, but by Baptism this sin was taken from you, and you received sanctifying grace. But have you never lost that grace by mortal sin? Have you spent the years of your youth in piety and the fear of God, or in thoughtlessness and forgetfulness of God? Oh, do not desecrate the beautiful years of your youth by sin and folly, or you will bitterly repent it some day, and, full of sorrow, will exclaim: "Give back to me my youth. Oh, would that I had better employed the years of my youth!" "Remember thy Creator in the days of thy youth" (Eccles. 12, 1).

CHAPTER V.

BIRTH OF JESUS CHRIST.

[Luke 2, 1—7.]

IN those days a decree went forth from the Roman emperor, Caesar Augustus [1], commanding that all the people of the empire should be enrolled. Each one had to give in his name "in his own city," [2] i. e. in the tribe and city to which he belonged. So

Fig. 63. Bethlehem. (Phot. Bruno Hentschel, Leipzig.)

Joseph and Mary went to Bethlehem [3] (Fig. 63), the city of David, because they were of the family of that king.

---

[1] *Augustus.* He was ruler of the vast empire to which Judæa now belonged (Old Test. LXXXVI). Herod was not an independent sovereign, but governed in the name of the Roman emperor, to whom he had to pay part of the taxes as tribute. The enrolment of the subjects of the empire had, therefore, to take place in Judæa as well as elsewhere; and, according to the Jewish custom, it was made by tribes and families.

[2] *In his own city.* i. e. the town where his family originated, and in which the public register was kept.

[3] *Bethlehem.* Bethlehem was the town to which David had belonged (Old Test. L), and as Mary and Joseph were descended from him, their names had to

Fig. 64. Church of the Nativity and Convent at Bethlehem.

But the city being crowded with strangers who had come for the enrolment, they could not obtain lodging in the inn, and were forced to seek shelter in a stable[1] outside the city. "And it came to pass that, when they were there, Mary brought forth her first-born Son, and wrapped Him up in swaddling clothes,

---

be inscribed at Bethlehem. This town lay about five miles to the south of Jerusalem (see Map). The journey from Nazareth to Bethlehem was one of seventy miles, and full of difficulties. The town of Bethlehem stood on the ridge of a hill a little higher than Mount Sion, which was the highest part of ancient Jerusalem, and about 2300 feet high. It still exists, and is chiefly inhabited by Christians to the number of between three and four thousand, though in all the other towns of the Holy Land the Turks, in whose possession Palestine is, outnumber all other creeds.

[1] *A stable.* When Mary and Joseph arrived at Bethlehem, the only public inn in the place was quite full; so they went to a cave or grotto outside the town, which in bad weather was used as a stable by shepherds, and which was therefore fitted with a manger. The emperor Constantine and his mother, St. Helena, built a splendid church, which still exists (Fig. 64), over the grotto in which our Lord was born. In the grotto of the Nativity (Fig. 65, p. 400) thirty-two lamps are always kept burning.

and laid Him in a manger [1], because there was no room for them in the inn."

COMMENTARY.

Divine Providence. The Prophet Micheas (Old Test. LXX) had foretold that the Saviour would be born at Bethlehem. But how was it likely that this prophecy would be fulfilled, seeing that she who was chosen to be the Mother of the Divine Saviour dwelt at Nazareth? The Providence of God directed that the pagan emperor of Rome should order all his subjects to be enrolled, and that this decree should

Fig 65. Grotto of the Nativity in the Church at Bethlehem.

be executed in Judæa at the very time when the Birth of the Redeemer was at hand. Obedient to authority, Mary and Joseph journeyed to Bethlehem to inscribe their names in the city from which originated their royal race, and thus, unwittingly, the Roman emperor was made to take a part in the fulfilment of the prophecy that the Redeemer would be born in Bethlehem, the city of David.

The Divinity of Jesus Christ. Jesus Christ is true Man, born of the Virgin Mary, the child of Mary, the son or descendant of David. But He is also true God, the Son of the Highest, as was announced to the Blessed Virgin by the angel. He shows Himself to our sight as Man, for in the crib we can see nothing but a little child. But He reveals Himself as God to our hearing, for His angels come and announce that this little Child in the crib is the Saviour, Christ the Lord Himself. Therefore let us fall on our knees before the crib, and adore

---

[1] *A manger.* While Mary was absorbed in prayer the Child was born to her. The Virgin Mother wrapped Him in swaddling clothes with her own hands, and laid Him in the manger belonging to the stable, and, full of faith, adored Him as the Son of the Most High.

the Child there, saying: "I believe in Jesus Christ, His (the Almighty Father's) only Son, our Lord."

The love of God. The Eternal Son of God became Man, and hid His Omnipotence and Majesty under the form of a poor, helpless child. He, the Lord, took the form of a servant, and became like to us in all things, sin only excepted. Why did He become Man? Why did He suffer and die? Why did He wish to redeem us? It was because He loved us with an infinite and divine love. "God so loved the world, as to give His only-begotten Son &c." (John 3, 16). "Let us therefore love God, because God first loved us" (1 John 4, 19).

Christmas. According to tradition our Lord was born in the night between the 24th and 25th of December. Christmas, or the Nativity of our Lord, is therefore kept on the 25th of December, and on this great Feast three Masses may be said by each priest.

The sufferings of Jesus began with His Birth. The Son of God became Man to suffer for us, to make satisfaction for our sins, and to redeem us from sin and hell. All His life He suffered unspeakably for us, and His sufferings began with His Birth. He came into the world in a state of the utmost poverty and humility. For the Son of God to take to Himself human nature at all would have been an infinite humiliation, even had He been born in a royal palace, and laid at His Birth on silken cushions, in a golden cradle. But He wished to humble Himself still more, and therefore was born into the world in a poor stable, and laid in the rudest of cribs. The Lord of the universe, the son of David, of whose kingdom there was to be no end, could find no home in the city of David! Shut out from the dwellings of man, rejected by human society, He was driven to find a refuge among the beasts, and, wrapped in the coarsest of swathing bands, was laid in a manger belonging to the shepherds. "The foxes have holes, and the birds of the air nests, but the Son of Man hath not where to lay His head" (Luke 9, 58). He had no comfortable little bed, no soft, warm pillow. His tender body lay on the hard straw, in a narrow crib, and was exposed to the damp, raw winter-air. A piece of wood at His Birth, and a piece of wood at His Death, that was all that Jesus received from this world! Truly the Divine Infant was poorer than the poorest child! Our Lord chose for Himself this extreme poverty and humility to make satisfaction even from His Birth for our many sins of pride, for our concupiscence of the eyes and of the flesh, and to give to us an example of humility, self-denial and mortification. Man fell by pride, desiring what was impossible, namely to be as God, and his fall was so deep that he fell into the bondage of Satan and the concupiscence of the eyes and of the flesh, and into sins and crimes of the basest description. In order to free us from sin and hell, God the Son became Man, and was like to us in all things, sin only excepted, so that we might become once more the children of God. He humbled Himself that we might be exalted. He became poor that

we might be rich in grace here, and richer still some day in heaven.
Let us thank Him as we kneel before His crib, and renounce all pride,
all avarice, and fleshly desires!

APPLICATION. Jesus, your Saviour, is so humble, poor and
patient, and yet how proud, covetous and impatient you are!

CHAPTER VI.

THE SHEPHERDS AT THE MANGER.

[Luke 2, 8—20.]

THERE were in the same country[1], i. e. in the neighbourhood
of Bethlehem, shepherds watching, and keeping the night-
watches over their flock. Suddenly an angel of the Lord appeared
before them, and the brightness of God[2] shone round about them,
and they were seized with a great fear. But the angel said:
"Fear not, for behold, I bring you good tidings of great joy,
that shall be to all the people; for this day is born to you a
Saviour, who is Christ[3] the Lord, in the city of David. And this
shall be a sign unto you. You shall find the Babe wrapped in
swaddling clothes, and laid in a manger."[4]

Then there was with the angel a multitude of the heavenly
host, praising God and singing: "Glory to God in the highest,
and on earth peace to men of good will!"

------

[1] *In the same country.* In the valley below the town. It was in these
parts that, once upon a time, David, the forefather of the Redeemer, kept his
father's sheep.

[2] *The brightness of God.* Changing the dark night into brightest day. The
light was not only the glory of the angels, but a glimpse of that supernatural,
never-dying light by which God, who cannot be gazed upon by mortal eye, revealed
Himself. The Son of God, who hid His divine glory under the form of a poor
child, desired to reveal His Divinity through the angels, who are clothed with
His glory.

[3] *Christ.* i. e. the Anointed, the promised Messias.

[4] *Laid in a manger.* How marvellous a sign! Christ the Lord a little Infant, lying in a manger, poorer than the poorest child! The shepherds might,
perchance, have doubted such a sign; but immediately another was given to
them. A multitude of the heavenly host, i. e. an innumerable throng of angels,
appeared, singing: "Glory to God in the highest!" The pious shepherds believed
themselves to be translated to heaven. The heavenly splendour, the host of angels,
the enchanting, inspiring song filled them with a holy awe, as well as with unspeakable joy.

When the angels had disappeared, the shepherds said one to another: "Let us go[1] over to Bethlehem, and see the word that has come to pass, which the Lord hath shown us." Going in haste[2], they found[3] Mary and Joseph in the stable, and the new-born Babe lying in the manger.

The shepherds adored Him, and went back to their flocks, praising and glorifying God for the wonders they had seen and heard. All the people that heard these things from the shepherds were astonished. But Mary kept all these things, pondering them[4] in her heart.

And after eight days the Child was circumcised, and His name was called Jesus, that is, Saviour, as the angel had commanded.

COMMENTARY.

Glory to God in the highest. Our redemption began at the Birth of Jesus Christ. For this reason the angels rejoiced and sang: "Glory to God!" The unbelief and disobedience of man had robbed God of the honour due to Him. Jesus Christ restored the honour of God by being obedient to His heavenly Father, even unto death on the cross, and by teaching the one true faith in God and the one true worship of God.

Peace to men of good will. Our Lord Jesus Christ has brought peace to man by reconciling earth to heaven, and winning pardon and grace for us. This peace on earth, which leads to the eternal peace of heaven, can only be obtained by those men who are of good will, i. e. by those who are willing to believe the doctrines of Christ, and who correspond with His grace. The shepherds were men of good will; they believed the angel, and hastened to obey his injunctions. It is

---

[1] *Let us go.* All doubt on the part of the shepherds had fled. They believed that "the Lord" had sent them the message, and but one thought filled them: "Let us go and see."

[2] *In haste.* Impelled by an eager desire to see the Child who, according to what the angels had said, was come to be their Saviour.

[3] *They found.* Finding the Babe exactly as the angel had described, they believed all the rest which had been told them about the Child, namely, that He was Christ the Lord; and they fell on their knees before the manger and adored. With their hearts full of the glad news they had received, they related all they had seen and heard, first of all to the holy Mother of God and to St. Joseph, and then to all their friends and acquaintances.

[4] *Pondering them.* She treasured up every word of what the shepherds had seen and heard. She compared every word they had told her with the promises of the Messias contained in the prophets, and with what Gabriel had announced to herself; and on all sides she discovered a confirmation of her own belief that her Child, so wonderfully born of her, was the Son of God.

in this way that we should obey the inward admonitions of grace
to do what is right. If we do this, we shall one day be with Jesus
in heaven.

The Christmas Tree represents Jesus Christ, who is the true tree
of life in the newly restored paradise. He that eateth of this tree shall
live. The burning tapers on the tree are meant to show that Christ is
the light of the world, "full of grace and truth". The various fruits and
sweets hanging on the branches symbolise the rich gifts and blessings
brought by Jesus Christ to the children of men. The latter too are
accustomed to give presents to each other, because on this day God
has given to the world His only Begotten Son and with him
everything else.

The Christian era. As quite a new era began with the Birth of
Jesus Christ, an era of grace and reconciliation, our years are counted
from that time. The year in which our Lord was born was the first
year of the Christian era. On Christmas-Day this year, 1910 years will
have passed since the Birth of Jesus Christ.

Why Jesus subjected Himself to circumcision. Our Lord was without
sin, so He stood in no need of circumcision. But He submitted to
the rite for the following reasons: 1. According to the prophecies the
Redeemer was to be a true Israelite and son of Abraham. To be
such, and to be recognised as such, circumcision was necessary. 2. By
His Incarnation our Lord took upon Himself the sins of mankind,
so as to make satisfaction for them. For this purpose He shed
His Precious Blood for the first time in His circumcision, and showed
us thereby that He was come to redeem us by His Blood. Therefore
the name of Jesus, or Saviour, was given to Him at His circumcision.
3. By voluntarily obeying the law and submitting Himself to the rite
of circumcision, He wished to give us an example of obedience to the
divine law.

The Name of Jesus is the sweetest of all names; for if that blessed
name did not exist, neither would there exist for us pardon, or grace
or eternal happiness. It is the object of our faith, our hope and our
love. Moreover the name of Jesus testifies to the divine nature of the
Redeemer; it not only means Saviour, but Divine Saviour, and says
to us: "Jehovah, God, is our salvation and deliverance!" Thus St. Paul
writes: "In the name of Jesus every knee shall bow, of those that are
in heaven, on earth, or under the earth" (Phil. 2, 10).

APPLICATION. Are you of good will as the shepherds were?
Do you listen to the admonitions of your guardian angel, of your
parents and superiors? From henceforward try, for love of Jesus,
to be very obedient.

CHAPTER VII.

THE PRESENTATION IN THE TEMPLE [1].

[Luke 2, 22—38.]

FORTY days after His birth, Mary and Joseph brought Jesus to the Temple of Jerusalem to present Him to the Lord,

---

[1] *The Temple*, which was rebuilt under the direction of Zorobabel (Old Test. LXXX), had several additions made to it by king Herod, which he undertook for the purpose both of gaining renown for himself, and of ingratiating himself with the Jewish people. The work was begun in the year 16 B. C., and was nearly completed at the time of our Lord's Presentation (Fig. 66, p. 407). By means of enormous supports, the court of the Temple was increased to a width of a thousand feet and a length of nearly one thousand seven hundred feet. This great space was enclosed by a high wall, inside which were two beautiful porticoes, 74 feet wide, supported by columns of white marble, and with flat ceilings of cedar-wood. On the south side of the enclosure were three similar halls, supported by pillars, the centre one of the three being 150 feet high. These halls with columns belonged to the first or outer court of the Temple, which was also called the court of the Gentiles, because even Gentiles were allowed to enter it. This outer court, which was very large, contained a synagogue, and cells for the Levites. It was also a market, fitted with the tables and booths of the money-changers, and of the cattle-merchants who sold beasts for the sacrifices. Inside this outer court, and surrounded by it on all sides, was the Temple proper, into which neither Gentiles nor unclean Israelites might enter, under pain of death. The Temple, to which access was obtained by ascending twenty steps, was surrounded by a wall that, on the inside, stood 33 feet high. Nine gates, four on the north, four on the south, and one on the eastern side, led into the Temple. The principal gateway was the one on the eastern side: it was made of brass, richly ornamented with gold and silver, and was 73 feet high by 60 broad It required the united strength of twenty men to close the gate in the evening. At this gate took place the purification of lepers, and of women after childbirth. Through this principal gate the court of the women was entered, in which stood a chest for offerings with thirteen trumpet-shaped openings. This court was surrounded with porticoes and galleries into which the women passed, while the men remained below. Through the court of the women and up fifteen steps was the entrance to the outer court of the Israelites, or of the men. From this was reached the outer court of the priests and Levites, and there stood the colossal altar of holocausts, and the brazen sea or laver (Old Test. LIX). From the outer court, twelve steps led to the porch of the Temple itself. Immediately after passing through the porch was an outer hall 150 feet broad and 150 feet high, and next to it the actual Temple, which was 150 feet broad and 83 high. The Temple, as well as the outer hall, was built of great blocks of white marble and richly overlaid with gold, both inside and out. Two-thirds of the Temple proper formed the Sanctuary, and the remaining third, which was at the western end, formed the Holy of Holies. This latter, which was quite empty, was separated from the other part by a costly curtain. In the Sanctuary stood the seven-branched candlestick, made of gold, the golden table of proposition, and the golden altar of incense. The ceiling of the Temple was overlaid with plates

as the law of Moses[1] prescribed. They carried with them the usual offering of the poor, a pair of turtle-doves[2].

There was at that time in Jerusalem a just and God-fearing man named Simeon[3]. He was looking anxiously for the coming

---

of gold. The whole building, raised up on high with its terraces, white marble columns and blocks, and golden decorations, must have presented a very majestic appearance, as it stood glittering in the sun.

[1] *The law of Moses.* See Old Test. XXXIII.

[2] *Turtle-doves.* According to the law a mother was considered unclean for forty days after the birth of a son, and during that time might not appear before the Lord in the Temple. On the fortieth day she had to offer a sacrifice of purification, namely a lamb and a young pigeon; or, if she were poor, she made the offering of the poor, namely two young pigeons, one to be a sin-offering, and the other a burnt offering.— Let us accompany the holy Mother with her Divine Child to the Temple. Standing at the great gate on the eastern side, which led to the outer court of the women, Mary handed to the priest the two pigeons, the offering of her poverty. The priest then went into the outer court of the temple, sprinkled the blood of one pigeon on the side of the altar as a sin-offering, and burnt the other in the fire as a thank-offering. Mary had to stay at the gate, but in spirit she accompanied the priest to the altar and thanked God from her heart that He had chosen her to be the Mother of God. Truly, the offering of the most pure Virgin was more pleasing to God than the sacrifice of either Abel or Melchisedech. After this, she presented the Divine Child as an offering to the Lord. She handed Him to the priest, and, having paid the five shekels (about thirteen shillings) redemption-money, received Him back again. We can imagine how wholly she gave her Child to the Lord, to belong entirely to Him and fulfil His holy will! Her heart, indeed, was full of anxious forebodings, for she knew that her Son was the Redeemer, and that, according to the words of the prophets, He would suffer and die a violent death. But she gave herself over entirely to the will of God. "Take Him, O Lord", she said, "for He is Thy Son. I will bring Him up for Thee. Do what Thou wilt, and if so be I must see Him die for the salvation of men—Thy will be done!"

[3] *Simeon.* Mary's forebodings were soon to be confirmed by Simeon. As Mary passed through the crowded outer court with her Divine Child, she was un-observed: the crowd had no suspicion that the Messias, whom all the sacrifices in the Temple typified, had just entered His Father's House for the first time. One man alone, the aged Simeon, recognised his Saviour in this Child. Scripture calls him a "just" man, for he had observed the law of the Lord from his youth up. His longing for the Redeemer was a holy and religious longing, unlike that usually entertained by the Jews, who looked for a merely earthly Messias. He hoped for One who should bring redemption, grace and truth; and as he saw the corruption of his people increasing, he prayed the more fervently to God to send the promised Saviour. God heard his prayer, and the Holy Ghost gave him the assurance that, before he died, he should behold the Christ. For this reason Simeon went daily to the Temple where the Messias was to manifest Himself to him. As Mary entered with her Child, an inward illumination of the Holy Spirit made known to him that this Babe was He whom he expected. Full of a holy joy he took the Child in his arms, and raising his eyes to heaven, sang his canticle "Nunc dimittis".

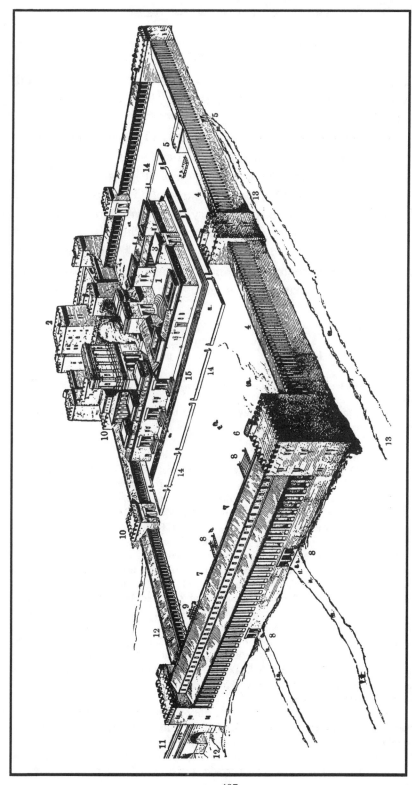

Fig. 66. The Temple of Herod.

1. Temple. 2. Fort Antonia. 3. Gate of Nicanor. 4. Hall of Solomon. 5. The Golden Gate. 6. Outer Pinnacle. 7. Royal Hall. 8. Hulda Gates. 9. Subterranean Passage to the Lower City. 10. Gate for Suburb. 11. Bridge to Upper City. 12. Valley of Tyropœon. 13. Valley of Cedron. 14. Stone Palings with Inscriptions. 15. Steps to the Forcer.

of the Messias, the Holy Spirit having revealed to him that he should not die till he had seen the Christ of the Lord. Led by the Spirit, he came that day to the Temple, and seeing the Child brought in by Mary and Joseph, he took Him in his arms, and blessed God, saying:

"Now Thou dost dismiss Thy servant [1], O Lord, according to Thy word [2], in peace [3]: because my eyes have seen Thy salvation [4], which Thou hast prepared before the face of all peoples; a light to the revelation [5] of the Gentiles and the glory of Thy people Israel." [6]

He then blessed [7] Joseph and Mary, who wondered [8] at these things, and to Mary he said: "Behold, this Child is set for the fall and for the resurrection of many in Israel [9], and for a sign which shall be contradicted [10]. And thy own soul a sword shall pierce [11], that out of many hearts thoughts may be revealed."

---

[1] *Thy servant.* i. e. me.

[2] *Thy word.* i. e. according to Thy promise.

[3] *In peace.* Now I can leave this world in peace, I can die contentedly and joyfully.

[4] *Thy salvation.* The Saviour promised by Thee, whom Thou hast sent for all nations.

[5] *The revelation.* That He may, by His divine teaching, enlighten the heathen who are living in the darkness of unbelief.

[6] *Israel.* Being the people of whose race the Redeemer was born, and the place where He worked miracles and founded His Church.

[7] *Blessed.* Or congratulated them on having received the Divine Child. Then the inspired old man turned especially to Mary, the Mother of the Child, and foretold how much she would have to suffer on His account.

[8] *Wondered.* Joseph and Mary had indeed been taught by the angel that the Child was the Son of the Highest, and the promised Redeemer, but it filled them with astonishment that God should have revealed to Simeon the secret He had confided to them, and revealed it just at the moment when Jesus had been presented in the Temple and redeemed with money like an ordinary Israelite child. It astonished them, also, that Simeon should extol Him not only as the glory of Israel, but also as the light for the revelation of the Gentiles. The words which Simeon uttered by the inspiration of the Holy Ghost gave Mary and Joseph a deeper insight into the plan of Redemption than they had before possessed.

[9] *Many in Israel.* The people of Israel would be forced to come to a decision about our Lord. Those who rejected Him and refused to believe in Him would fall by reason of their unbelief, as did most of the Pharisees. But, on the other hand, those who did believe in Him would receive salvation, as did, for instance, the apostles, Nicodemus &c.

[10] *Contradicted.* He will be the mark against which will be levelled the hatred and persecution of the enemies of God, and of truth and virtue. How far this hatred would be carried is hinted in Simeon's next words.

[11] *Pierce.* This word is not to be understood in a literal sense; the term rather signifies the violent pain which would pierce Mary's heart like a dagger.

There was also in Jerusalem a prophetess[1] named Anna—a woman far advanced in years, who departed not from the Temple —by prayer and fasting serving the Lord night and day. She also coming in, and seeing the Child, gave praise to the Lord, and spoke of Him to all who were looking[2] for the Redemption of Israel. And when these things were accomplished in obedience to the law of God, Mary and Joseph, with the Divine Babe, returned to Galilee[3], to their own city of Nazareth, and dwelt there in peace.

COMMENTARY.

The Faithfulness of God. By the Presentation of Jesus in the Temple, the prophecy of Aggeus (Old Test. LXXX) was fulfilled.

Jesus is the Messias. The Holy Ghost revealed Him as such to Simeon, who, full of joy, greeted Him as the Saviour of all men, and the Light of revelation to the Gentiles.

Jesus is God. Anna, by the inspiration of the Holy Ghost, testified to this, when she extolled the Child as "the Lord", and joyfully announced that in this Child God had revealed Himself as the Redeemer.

Faith is a gift of God. It was only by the help of the Holy Ghost that Simeon and Anna were enabled to recognise in the Child Jesus the Divine Saviour of the whole world, of Gentiles as well as Jews.

Good works. Simeon and Anna obtained the great grace of faith in our Lord's Divinity by a faithful observance of the law, by fasting and prayer, and a great inward desire for His coming.

Belief in Jesus Christ drives away all fear of death. Simeon now rejoiced at the prospect of death. Such a sensation was hitherto unknown in Israel. "Pious Israelites closed their eyes in death, weary of life and submissive to God's will; not altogether hopeless, but full of horror of the future. Death was a thing to be feared, and each new day of life which was granted was looked on as a gain" (Grimm). But

---

This pain was suffered by Mary at the foot of the Cross. There the love of three hearts (thoughts of many hearts) was revealed: the love of God and man in the Heart of Jesus and the love of Mary, His and our mother.

[1] *A prophetess.* A person endowed by God with the gift of prophecy, and known as such to all the people. Therefore her testimony had greater weight with them than that of Simeon. Moreover, Anna was a woman of extraordinary virtue, her life being one of exceptional holiness and mortification.

[2] *All who were looking.* We can see by these words that many of the Jews were expecting the speedy advent of the Redeemer.

[3] *Returned to Galilee.* This does not mean that they returned at once; for a number of other events which St. Luke passes over come between, as the adoration of the Magi and the flight into Egypt mentioned by St. Matthew.

all at once every thing was changed. Holy Simeon had seen the Saviour, and was now ready to die joyfully. In fact, he did die very soon after; a pious tradition even goes so far as to say that he died before he left the Temple. He was thus the first to take the joyful news to Limbo that the Saviour was born and the day of salvation at hand.

Humility and obedience of Mary. Mary was without sin, therefore she needed no purification. Nevertheless she remained excluded from the Temple for forty days just as if she were an ordinary, sinful mother, and submitted to the law of purification which in no way applied to the most pure Mother of God. Her humility made her wish to appear in the eyes of the world as an ordinary, sinful woman. She wished, moreover, to give an example of obedience to the precepts of the law, her love of her fellow-creatures making her shrink from being a cause of offence and giving scandal by any neglect of the legal purification.

The Feast of our Lady's Purification, or Candlemas. We keep a feast on the 2nd of February, forty days after Christmas, in memory of our Lord's Presentation in the Temple. This feast has several names. First, it is known as the Feast of the Presentation of our Lord Jesus. Secondly, it is called the Feast of the Purification of the Blessed Virgin Mary. But the usual and popular name for this Feast is Candlemas-day, because on this day candles are blessed before Mass, and there takes place a procession with lighted candles. Candles are blessed and lighted on this particular feast, because on it Simeon acknowledged and confessed Christ to be "the Light of the world".

The dolours of Mary. Mary is, as the Holy Ghost foretold by the mouth of Simeon, the Mother of sorrows, feeling in her own heart all the sufferings of her Divine Son. The dolours of Mary are usually enumerated as follows: 1. the prophecy of Simeon, 2. the flight into Egypt, 3. the loss of the Child Jesus for three days when He was twelve years old, 4. the meeting with Jesus, carrying His Cross, 5. the Crucifixion and death of Jesus, 6. the taking down from the Cross, 7. the Burial of Jesus. Mary suffered for a longer time and more acutely than any of the holy martyrs, and therefore she is called the Queen of martyrs.

The "Contradiction" of Jesus. In what way has Simeon's prophecy that our Lord should be a "sign of contradiction" been fulfilled? Even when He was an Infant, He was persecuted by Herod, and had to flee. When He began His public life, He met with the greatest opposition, especially from the Pharisees and Sadducees. The inhabitants of Nazareth thrust Him out of their city (chapter XVII). The Pharisees slandered Him and said He was in league with the devil (chapter XXVII); and, on the Feast of the Dedication of the Temple, the Jews wished to stone Him as a blasphemer (chapter LIII). He was accused before Pilate of being a seducer of the people &c.; and His enemies never rested till He was nailed upon the Cross. Even after His Resurrection the opposition to His doctrine and His Church continued. "Christ crucified, unto the Jews indeed a stumbling-block, and unto the Gentiles foolishness, but unto them that are called, Christ the power of God and the wisdom of God" (1 Cor. 1, 23. 24). And this contradiction on the part of the unbelieving will continue till Christ comes again to judge the world.

The testimony of the Holy Ghost. There had been no prophets in Israel since Malachias; but as soon as the Messias had appeared, the gift of prophecy was richly bestowed on those who believed. Zachary, Elizabeth, Mary, Simeon and Anna, all proclaimed the goodness of God, who had given His only begotten Son for the salvation of the world. "For four hundred years the spirit of prophecy had been dumb in Israel: it was a long and dreary winter, but it was followed by the most glorious spring-tide! Song filled the air; for He had come whose name was Wonderful! The angel Gabriel, Mary, Zachary, Elizabeth, the angel who spoke to the shepherds, Simeon, and Anna basked in the ray of salvation which streamed down from heaven. Heaven itself streamed down with it; and the sons of the earth lifted up their heads with a feeling of rapture, for the Prince of peace had come and reconciled earth to heaven! The great God, the 'Father of the world to come' (Is. 9, 6) lay a little Babe in Mary's arms" (Stolberg). Thus was the advent of Jesus Christ, the Divine Redeemer, borne witness to in various ways.

APPLICATION. Have you, like Mary, always observed the commandments of God with exactitude? Against which of the commandments have you most often sinned? You too were presented to God in your Baptism, and you ought to belong to Him, to love Him and serve Him. Say thus to yourself: "I will keep God's commandments all the days of my life."

Simeon thanked God with a full heart for having sent the Saviour. In what way do you thank Him for the unspeakable grace of Redemption? You should thank Him every day of your life for the great gift of the Christian, Catholic faith.

CHAPTER VIII.

ADORATION OF THE MAGI.

[Mat. 2, 1—12.]

NOW when Jesus was born in Bethlehem in the days of king Herod, behold, there came three wise men[1], or Magi, from the East[2] to Jerusalem, saying: "Where is He that is born king

---

[1] *Wise men.* Men especially learned in the science of the stars. According to tradition, the three wise men were of high rank, and that is why they are often called the three kings.

[2] *The East.* From the land which lies towards where the sun rises. Probably they came from Babylon. In that part there was still preserved the memory of

of the Jews? For we have seen His star[1] in the East, and are come to adore Him."[2] Herod, hearing this, was troubled[3], and all Jerusalem[4] with him. And having assembled all the chief priests[5] and scribes[6], and the ancients of the people, he inquired of them where Christ (the promised Messias) should be born[7].

Balaam's prophecy (Old Test. XLIII), that one day a star would rise in Judæa and that then the Redeemer, the heavenly king, would appear. This belief in a future Saviour had been rekindled in Babylon by the prophet Daniel, who was one of the wise men of his day.

[1] *His star.* This star which the Magi, before they left their home, had seen rising in the direction of Judæa, and therefore in the west, was no ordinary star, for it "went before them" from Jerusalem to Bethlehem, and there stopped over the house where the Child Jesus dwelt. It was, we may suppose, a sort of meteor, an appearance of light in the form of a star, of an extraordinary and brilliant description. The holy bishop of Antioch, Ignatius, a disciple of the apostle St. John, thus writes about it in his epistle to the Ephesians: "A star appeared in the heavens which eclipsed all the other stars; its light was indescribable, and its novelty caused astonishment." The holy kings who, full of faith, were waiting for the promised Saviour, by divine inspiration recognised this star to be the sign which was to herald the Birth of the Messias; therefore they called it His star.

[2] *Adore Him.* The star had only directed the wise men generally towards Judæa and had then temporarily vanished. They were so firmly convinced that the Messias was born that they never thought of inquiring *if* He were born—but only *where* He was to be found. They hoped to be able to learn this at the capital of Judæa, so they travelled straight to Jerusalem. The appearance of these strangers with their servants and camels naturally caused a great sensation in Jerusalem, which was changed to a state of painful excitement, when the strangers asserted that the Messias was already born.

[3] *Troubled.* He feared, being hated as he was for his cruelty, that, if the Messias were really come, the Jews would turn against himself and dethrone him.

[4] *All Jerusalem.* The inhabitants of Jerusalem said thus to themselves: "How? The Messias born, and we know nothing about it! God has revealed it to these strangers and not to us! What does it mean?" And when they found out that the king was troubled by the news, they, with reason, dreaded new acts of cruelty on his part.

[5] *Chief priests.* Namely, the actual High Priest and those who had on former occasions held the office. In violation of the law, the High Priest was often deposed by the temporal authority, and consequently there were several High Priests at once, the actual and the former ones.

[6] *Scribes.* Since there had been no more prophets, these scribes were the authorized expounders and interpreters of Holy Scripture.

[7] *Where Christ should be born.* The wise men had inquired for the "new-born king of the Jews". Herod quite understood whom this expression meant, for he asked the chief priests where the Messias, or Christ, was to be born. Herod was more of a pagan than a Jew, and was not well acquainted with the prophecies about the Messias. Therefore he sent for the appointed interpreters of Scripture, to inquire of them the place where the Redeemer should be born.

They said to him: "In Bethlehem of Juda, for so it is written by the prophet."[1]

Then Herod privately questioned[2] the three Magi as to the exact time[3] when the star appeared to them. When they had told him, he said: "Go, and search after the Child, and when you have found him, bring me word again, that I also may come and adore Him."[4]

The Magi set out for Bethlehem, and no sooner had they left the palace of Herod than the star, which they had not seen since their entrance into Jerusalem, again appeared[5] in the heavens; and, following its guidance, they came to the place[6] where the Divine Infant was, with Mary His Mother and St. Joseph.

Fig. 67. Myrrh.

And entering in, they adored the Child[7], and opening their treasures they offered[8] him gifts—gold, frankincense and myrrh[9] (Fig. 67).

That night God appeared to the kings in a dream and commanded them not to return to Herod[10]. So they went back by

---

[1] *The prophet.* Micheas: "And thou Bethlehem, the land of Juda, art not the least among the princes of Juda: for out of thee shall come forth the captain that shall rule my people Israel."

[2] *Questioned.* He called them secretly, for he had formed a dark and murderous plan which he did not wish to be known. He feared that the Jews would put the Child in a place of safety, if they found out what close inquiries he was making about Him.

[3] *Exact time.* He judged rightly that the star must have appeared at the time of the Child's Birth, so he wished, by these inquiries, to find out how old our Lord was.

[4] *Adore Him.* The guileless Magi quite believed that the king wished to adore the Child, though no Jew would have trusted the hypocritical monarch.

[5] *Again appeared.* It had disappeared for some time from their sight, so that they were all the more glad to see it once more.

[6] *The place.* Or house (see Mat. 2, 11). As soon as the strangers who had flocked to Bethlehem for the prescribed enrolment had gone away again, Mary and Joseph had moved with the Divine Child to a human dwelling-place. What joy must have filled the hearts of the Magi! If they rejoiced as they did at the appearance of the star, their happiness must have been quite unspeakable when, at last, they found the Child on whose account they had undertaken their long and difficult journey.

[7] *They adored the Child.* Because, by the inspiration of divine grace, they recognised the Son of God in this Child.

[8] *Offered.* What we give to God is called an offering.

[9] *Myrrh.* This is a bitter though sweet-smelling resin which is laid on the bodies of the dead to preserve them from corruption.

[10] *Not to return to Herod.* God gave them this command in order to prevent Herod from finding out the abode of the Child.

another way[1] to their own country. Thus was the wicked king disappointed in his expectation of finding out, by means of these strangers, the place where the Child was.

COMMENTARY.

The Omniscience of God. He knew exactly the thoughts both of Herod and of the wise men. He knew that the latter, in their guilelessness, would show Herod the place where the Child lived, and He knew that Herod was resolved on the death of the Child. Therefore He bade the wise men return home another way.

Faithfulness of God. He caused the prophecy uttered by Micheas to be fulfilled, and, by a wonderful chain of circumstances, carried out His design that the Redeemer should be born at Bethlehem.

Jesus Christ is God and the Redeemer of all mankind, of Jews as well as Gentiles. He proved Himself to be such by revealing Himself after His Birth, first to the Jewish shepherds by means of His angel, and then to the Gentile Magi by means of His star. He manifested Himself as the Omnipotent God, and the Lord of hosts (of the angels and of the stars).

The properties of Faith. It is impossible not to admire the strong and living faith of the three wise men. They believed in the prophecy, from which they knew that the Redeemer would appear in Judæa, and that His advent would be heralded by a star. As soon, therefore, as they perceived the wonderful star, they set off on the road to Judæa. Full of a holy desire to behold and worship the Saviour, they did not shrink from the dangers or difficulties of the long journey. Nor did they despond when the star disappeared, but travelled on courageously, and sought in Jerusalem further information as to the place where the Saviour was to be born. Here, however, their faith was severely tried; for nobody in Jerusalem knew anything about the Redeemer's Birth. It was they who first brought the tidings of it to the city, and the tidings did not awaken feelings of joy, but of trouble. This might easily have aroused within them doubts as to whether the sign in the heavens had deceived them; but they gave no place to such doubts, remaining firm in faith and unshaken by the opinion of others. They believed the prophecy of Micheas and the interpretation of it given by the chief priests and scribes, and, while it was still night, started for Bethlehem. No one from Jerusalem accompanied them; they travelled all alone to the city of David. One might have thought that all Jerusalem would have flocked with them to seek the Messias; but no! even the priests, doubtful or sceptical, remained behind, and left it to the Gentile

---

[1] *Another way.* Round by the south, by a road which did not pass Jerusalem. They either crossed the Jordan at Jericho, or else went round the Dead Sea.

kings to discover the new-born Saviour. This was by no means encouraging for the wise men, but they remained steadfast, and did not suffer their firm faith to be shaken. As a reward for their constancy, the wonderful star re-appeared, and led them to the house where the Child Jesus and His Mother had found a lodging. There, in a poor dwelling, they beheld a little Child with His poor and humble Maiden-Mother; and inspired by divine grace they threw themselves on their knees and, full of a living faith, worshipped this infant as their God and Saviour. "Would they have done this", asks St. Augustine, "if they had not recognised Him as the Eternal King?"

True correspondence with grace. When our Lord was born, the angels sang: "Peace on earth to men of good will!" Now the Magi were men of good will. They co-operated with grace, and therefore obtained peace and salvation. How did the three wise men correspond with grace? It was grace which made them see the star and understand its meaning. No doubt many other wise men in the East understood that the star indicated the Birth of the Messias; but they did not stir to obey its divine invitation to seek for the Messias. But these three did obey the invitation of grace, and, leaving home and friends, undertook the far journey to Judæa. By corresponding faithfully with this first grace, they obtained the further one of learning in Jerusalem the place where the Messias was born. And because they believed the prophecy of Micheas and went to Bethlehem, God not only showed them the way to the Child's abode, but illuminated them interiorly, so that they understood the mystery of the Incarnation, and worshipped the Child Jesus with divine worship. They so faithfully preserved this faith in the Divine Saviour that, according to a trustworthy tradition, they were counted worthy to suffer martyrdom for their faith, and are venerated as Saints by the Church. All this should impress upon us the important doctrine that the more a man co-operates with the grace given to him, the more worthy will he be to receive further and greater graces from God.

The indifference shown by the chief priests and scribes is almost inconceivable. They received through the wise men certain tidings of the wonderful star, and they knew accurately the prophecies about the Redeemer; but they did not co-operate with the grace received, and did not stir a foot to seek the Messias. They showed the wise men where the Messias was to be found, but they themselves remained at home. They waited for the Saviour to come to them; and when, later on, He did come to them, they would not receive Him, because He was poor and humble, but persecuted Him and nailed Him to the Cross!

Pride is a capital sin. Herod formed the cruel resolve to kill the Messias; and it was his pride, ambition and envy which led to this horrible design. In order to attain more surely his evil end, he dissembled and lied to the wise men, saying that he also wished to worship the Child. Lies and hypocrisy have been from the beginning the weapons used against Christ and His Church.

The Feast of the Three Magi, or the Feast of the Epiphany (Jan. 6th). The three wise men were the first Gentiles to whom our Lord manifested Himself as the Saviour of mankind; and as the representatives of the pagan world, which was sighing for its Redeemer, they offered their adoration to Him. We ought therefore, especially on this Feast, to thank God for the Christian faith, because our forefathers too were pagans; and we ought to praise the infinite love of God, who gave His only-begotten Son for the salvation of man.

The signification of the gifts of the wise men. The gifts offered to the Child Jesus by the wise men are full of deep significance. "In Israel incense could be offered to God alone, and could be burnt only before Jehovah! Any human king of Israel to whom incense was offered was an abomination in the sight of God" (Grimm). So by offering incense to the Child Jesus the Magi wished to express their worship of God hidden under the lowly form of a child. By the offering of gold they acknowledged Him as king. By the myrrh they desired to testify their veneration for the human nature of Jesus, which was destined to suffering, death and burial. They therefore offered gold to the king, incense to God, and myrrh to the man.

Worship of the Blessed Sacrament. It is the same Son of God whom the wise men worshipped under the form of a child, whom we, full of faith and reverence, worship in the most holy Sacrament of the Altar.

APPLICATION. You have received so many and such great graces from God. Have you always faithfully corresponded to them? Have you never actually resisted God's grace? "We exhort you that you receive not the grace of God in vain!" (2 Cor. 6, 1.)

You too can offer gifts to our Lord Jesus: the gold of love, the incense of worship, and the myrrh of patience in suffering.

CHAPTER IX.

THE FLIGHT INTO EGYPT.

[Mat. 12, 13—23.]

HEROD awaited with anxiety the return of the Magi. At last, perceiving that he waited in vain, he became furious, and gave orders that all the male children of two years old and under, in Bethlehem and in all the confines thereof, should be slain [1].

---

[1] *Slain.* Herod had cunningly hidden his wicked project from the wise men, and deceived them by an appearance of holiness, believing that the Child Jesus could not escape him. But when the Magi did not return, he saw that his wicked

He thought that, in this way, the Child Jesus would certainly perish.

But the angel of the Lord appeared at the same time [1] by night to Joseph, and said: "Arise, and take the Child and His Mother, and fly into Egypt [2] and be there until I shall tell thee; for Herod seeks the Child, to destroy Him." Then Joseph arose [3], took the Child and His Mother by night, and retired into Egypt.

Hardly had the Holy Family departed from Bethlehem, when the men of blood whom Herod had chosen to execute his cruel order, suddenly rushed into the city, dragged the infants from the arms of their mothers, and massacred them all. Then was heard throughout the city of David the piteous cry of the bereaved mothers, mourning and bewailing the innocent babes that were so cruelly put to death by the tyrant.

---

plans were frustrated. The kings did not purposely deceive him, for they had intended to keep their promise of returning to him, had not God forbidden them. But Herod believed that they had designedly misled him, and was therefore doubly angry. The dread of this new-born king of the Jews aroused all his evil passions, and he did not shrink from crowning his many acts of murder by a massacre of innocent children. He did not know whereabouts in Bethlehem the Messias was to be found, so, to be on the safe side, he had all the baby boys there and in the neighbourhood killed. Nor did he know the day of the Birth of the Child Jesus, but he had ascertained from the wise men the exact time of the star's first appearance, and felt confident that anyhow the Child could not be more than two years old; and therefore ordered the massacre of all the little boys of two years old and under. The number of these children must have been about 50.

[1] *The same time.* Soon after the Magi had adored the Child Jesus and had returned to their home.

[2] *Egypt.* There Herod could not touch the Child. Egypt was indeed a pagan land, but there were some Jews living in it who were able to observe, unhindered, their own law.

[3] *Arose.* How horrified St. Joseph must have been when he learnt Herod's wicked intention. The Divine Child—all that he treasured most—in danger of death! He did not hesitate a moment, but rose up at once, in the middle of the night, and, fetching an ass, placed upon it the amazed Mother with her Child, and hastened off, walking by their side, so as to get as soon as possible out of the territory of Herod. They travelled through the Arabian desert as far as the land of Gessen where, once upon a time, the patriarchs of their people, Jacob and his sons, had dwelt. The journey was one of two hundred miles, and was full of difficulties and dangers, arising from want of water and from the attacks of robbers and wild beasts. In their love of Jesus, however, Mary and Joseph thought but little of their difficulties and deprivations, and went on their way, full of patience and submission to God's will; until, at length, after enduring the hardships of a journey that lasted about ten days, they reached Gessen.

The punishment of this dreadful crime was not long delayed. A few years after the bloody deed, Herod was stricken with a most loathsome disease[1] and died in fearful torments. Then the angel of the Lord appeared again unto Joseph in Egypt during his sleep, and said: "Arise, take the Child and His Mother, and go into the land of Israel; for they are dead that sought the life of the Child."

Joseph, therefore, taking Mary and the Child, went back to the land of Israel, and retired into the parts of Galilee[2]. And He dwelt in Nazareth[3], that the word of the prophet might be fulfilled: "He shall be called a Nazarene." In the peaceful retirement of that town the Child Jesus grew in wisdom and in grace before God and men. What a heaven on earth was that thrice-hallowed, though humble home in Nazareth!

COMMENTARY.

The Omniscience of God. God knew that in the morning Herod would send soldiers to Bethlehem, to slay the little boys under two years old; therefore He ordered St. Joseph to flee in the middle of the night. The Lord God knew also the moment of Herod's death, as well as the evil disposition of his son and successor, Archelaus. He therefore warned St. Joseph not to return to Judæa, but to take up his abode at Nazareth in Galilee.

The Justice of God. Herod's horrible disease and miserable death were evidently a punishment for his cruelty, and especially for his desire to kill the Child Jesus. And as Herod, in spite of his sufferings, persevered to the end in evil and impenitence, the torments of his illness were but a prelude to the eternal torments which awaited him.

---

[1] *Disease.* When he knew that he must die, Herod flew into a terrible rage. He gave orders that, after his death, the principal men of the land should be executed, so that the people might have cause to regret his loss. Tormented by unbearable pain, he would, in his despair, have plunged a knife into his breast, had it not been snatched from him. Five days before he died, he had his eldest son, Antipater, executed. At last he died a miserable death, cursed by all the people.

[2] *Galilee.* He was "warned in sleep" not to go back to Bethlehem of Judæa, but to go instead to Nazareth of Galilee; for in Judæa and Samaria there now reigned Archelaus, a son of Herod, who was nearly as wicked as his father.

[3] *Nazareth.* Nazareth, situated six miles to the west of Mount Tabor, was and is a little town planted on the edge of a mountain. Not having taken any important part in the history of Israel, and not being even mentioned in the Old Testament, it was despised by the Jews. Here the Child Jesus found a safe retreat, for no one would dream of seeking the King of the Jews in such an insignificant place.

The Providence of God. Jesus was not to die before the appointed time; therefore God's Providence watched over Him and saved Him from the snares of His enemies Herod and Archelaus, making use of His holy angels for that purpose. God's Providence watches over us also, and, without His leave, not a hair of our head can fall. Moreover, His holy angel keeps guard over us.

The Foster-father of our Lord Jesus. The angel said to St. Joseph: "Take *the* Child and His Mother." He did not say: "Take *thy* Child", for St. Joseph was not the father, but only the foster-father of our Lord. The angel, moreover, placed the name of the Child before that of the Mother, He being the only-begotten Son of God.

St. Joseph's high place in the kingdom of God comes from this, that God chose him to be the guardian and protector of His Son, entrusting him with what was greatest and dearest to Himself, singling him out and especially blessing him for this office. The Church celebrates a Feast in honour of St. Joseph on March 19th, and desires that all the faithful should honour him, ask for his intercession, and imitate his virtues. St. Joseph is the especial patron of the Church. Even as he was the protector of the Child Jesus on earth, so, we believe, is he now the protector of the mystical Body of Jesus, His holy Church. We also especially seek his intercession for a good death, because, having died so blessedly, in the presence and with the assistance of Jesus and Mary, he should be supplicated to obtain for us from Jesus the grace of a happy death.

The virtues of St. Joseph corresponded to his high calling. He gives us a splendid example of a firm and living faith, of great confidence in God, resignation, obedience, humility, chastity and industry.

The faith and obedience of Mary and Joseph. Many thoughts might have occurred to them when commanded to flee into Egypt. "If", they might have said to themselves, "the Child is the Son of God, why is He so helpless? Why should the Son of the Almighty flee before the wicked king? Why did not the angel say how long we were to remain in the pagan country? How can we undertake such a long and dangerous journey without any preparation?" However, they gave no ear to any such thoughts, but obeyed the divine commands precisely and promptly, and started forth, filled with confidence in God and submission to His holy will. They knew very well that God could have taken care of the Child in some other way, if He had so willed it; but as it was His will that the Child should be saved by flight, they consented willingly, although it was very painful to them to leave their own country, the Promised Land, and to expose the Child to so many privations.

Anger is a capital sin. It led Herod to murder a number of innocent children, and to commit a sin crying to heaven for vengeance. He committed as many sins of this description as there were children!

Evil desires. But did Herod actually and grievously sin against the Child Jesus? For after all he did not really kill Him! No, but he had the will to do so, and in this way sinned against Him.

The Holy Innocents gave their lives for Jesus, because Herod put them to death, thinking to reach Jesus through them. They were, so to speak, cleansed from original sin by the Baptism of blood, and taken by Jesus to heaven, seeing that they lost their lives for His sake. The Church venerates them as martyrs and commemorates them on Dec. 28th.

_____

APPLICATION. Have you never murmured against the decrees of Divine Providence when evil has befallen you? You ought to give yourself over to God in all things, and say: "Thy will be done!"

Think what Jesus suffered for you during His flight into Egypt. It was still winter; the weather was cold, wet and stormy; and often He had no shelter over His head at night. Bear all sufferings patiently for love of Jesus; and, above all things, learn to bear and forbear.

CHAPTER X.

JESUS AT THE AGE OF TWELVE YEARS GOES TO THE TEMPLE.

[Luke 2, 40—52.]

NOW Mary and Joseph went every year [1] to Jerusalem to celebrate the Pasch. When Jesus was twelve years old, He accompanied His parents to the holy city.

The festival days [2] being over, Mary and Joseph set out for their distant home; but the Child Jesus remained [3] in Jerusalem, and His parents knew it not [4]. They thought, at first, that He was in the company of some of their relatives, and so they jour-

_____

[1] *Every year.* It was commanded by the law that every male Israelite should go to Jerusalem each year, for the three principal feasts (Old Test. XXXIX). This was not obligatory on the women, but pious women and maidens liked to take part in the pilgrimage, and Mary did not shrink from the severities of the long journey from Nazareth to Jerusalem which enabled her to visit the Sanctuary of the Lord. Boys above the age of twelve were bound to fast, to go to Jerusalem for the three feasts, and in all things to observe the law.

[2] *Festival days.* Which lasted a week.   [3] *Remained.* Intentionally.

[4] *Knew it not.* Owing to the great throng of about 500,000 pilgrims pressing through the gate, they lost sight of the relatives and acquaintances who accompanied them from Nazareth.

neyed a whole day without noticing His absence. But when evening came, they looked for Him, and, not finding Him[1], were overwhelmed with grief.

They returned immediately to Jerusalem, and during three days sought Him[2] through the city, but in vain; no one had seen the Child. At length, on the third day, they went to the Temple, and there they found Him[3], sitting in the midst of the doctors of the law, hearing them and asking them questions. All the doctors were astonished[4] at His wisdom and His answers.

Mary and Joseph were filled with wonder[5] and joy at seeing Him again, and His Mother said to Him: "Son, why hast Thou done so[6] to us? Behold, Thy father and I have sought Thee sorrowing." But He answered: "How is it that you sought me? Did you not know that I must be about My Father's business?"[7] But "they understood not[8] the word that He spoke to them."

---

[1] *Not finding Him.* What anxiety must they not have felt when they lost Jesus, who had been entrusted to their charge by God! Was He lying in prison— or killed? Had His sufferings already begun? Such thoughts filled their hearts with the keenest pain, and they could neither rest nor sleep till they had once more found the Divine Child.

[2] *Sought Him.* They sought Him on the way back, inquiring about Him from all the pilgrims behind them, and at all the places through which they had passed; but nobody could give them tidings of Him. With growing anxiety they arrived at Jerusalem, and vainly searched the streets of the city.

[3] *They found Him.* In a hall in the outer court of the Temple, where the doctors met to expound the law, and to answer questions and objections. To these assemblages there came both the earnest inquirers and the curious, all of whom sat at the feet of the doctors on low stools, placed on the ground. Jesus however was not sitting among the inquirers, but among the doctors, who were held by the people in the highest esteem! He listened to them, put questions to them, and answered their questions, so as to lead them to a knowledge of the truth. Most likely the discourse was about the prophecies.

[4] *Astonished.* Because such questions were unheard-of as coming from a boy of twelve years old. They suspected that they were in presence of some super-natural manifestation.

[5] *Wonder.* They "wondered" at seeing Jesus seated among the doctors, and the gaze of every bystander turned on Him with astonishment and veneration.

[6] *Done so.* Remaining behind without our knowledge. These words are the expression of the great love and anxiety of soul which Mary had experienced on account of her beloved Child.

[7] *My Father's business.* You should not have sought me, nor have feared for me, for you ought to have remembered that I leave you only to do the work which my Heavenly Father has given me to do.

[8] *Understood not.* They understood, indeed, the literal meaning of what He said, but not its deeper sense. They knew that Jesus was the Son of God, the

And rising, He went with his mother (who "kept all these words in her heart"[1]) and His foster-father[2] to Nazareth, and was subject to them. And Jesus increased[3] in wisdom, and age, and grace with God and men.

COMMENTARY.

The Two Natures in Jesus Christ. Our Lord is at once true God and true Man. The foregoing story manifests both His natures to us. As Man, Jesus was the Child of Mary; as Man, He increased in age, and with time developed into boyhood, youth and manhood. Each of the foregoing chapters testify also to Jesus being *true God*, though we have hitherto seen the Incarnate Son of God in a state of humility, poverty, and persecution, and have heard no word proceed from His mouth. In this last chapter we hear Jesus speak for the first time, and His words are words of superhuman wisdom, and bear most clear testimony to His divine nature. As soon as Jesus had completed His twelfth year, He was an adult in spiritual matters, so now, for a time, He withdrew Himself from the protection of His parents, and came forward, according to the will of His Father, as a teacher of the law, and allowed a few gleams of His divine wisdom to escape Him, thus preparing the way for His future public appearance as fulfiller of the law and prophets. He Himself refers directly to His divine nature by the words: "Did you not know that I must be about My Father's business?" He calls God His Father, and thus proclaims Himself to be the Son of God. This was our Lord's first declaration of His Divinity.

Redeemer from sin, and the Light of the Gentiles, but they did not understand in what way He would accomplish the great work of Redemption, and how His remaining behind in the Temple could be connected with it.

[1] *In her heart.* She pondered over them and compared them with what she had heard from the angel, from the wise men, from Simeon &c., and thus she entered more and more deeply into the mystery of Redemption.

[2] *Foster-father.* Our Lord passed among the people for the son of Joseph the carpenter, though He was the Son of God, and St. Joseph was only His foster-father.

[3] *Increased.* Shortly before (Luke 2, 40), the Gospel says: "The Child was full of wisdom", and yet now (Luke 2, 52) it says: "He advanced in wisdom and grace." How then is this increase of wisdom to be understood? In a literal sense, Jesus could neither increase nor decrease in wisdom and grace, for from the first moment of His Incarnation He was full of grace and truth (John 1, 14), but He appeared in the eyes of men to increase in wisdom and grace as He advanced in age, by revealing, with increasing years, more and more of the hidden fulness of wisdom and grace which were within Him. Jesus increased in favour with men, because, the more they came in contact with Him, the more they loved and appreciated Him; and in favour with God, because, the more Jesus did for the glory of God, the more His eternal Father was pleased with Him.

Obedience (4th Commandment). Until He was thirty years old, Jesus practised the most complete obedience towards His Mother and foster-father. He did as they bade Him; He helped His Mother in her household work, and served Joseph as an apprentice in his laborious trade of carpenter. Meditate well on this: *Who* was obedient, and *to whom?* The Creator to the creature, the Lord to the servant, the Son of God to man! And *in what* was He obedient? In everything. For *how long?* For as long as He dwelt with Mary and Joseph, namely thirty years. And *why* did Jesus, the Eternal Son of God, practise such obedience? 1. That through His perfect obedience He might make satisfaction for the disobedience of sinful man. 2. In order to give a great example of obedience to all children and inferiors.

Piety. The example of Jesus, who went to the Feast at Jerusalem and remained for three days in the Temple, shows us that we ought to like to be in the house of God, to listen attentively to His word and the expounding of it, to busy ourselves with the things of God and to avoid all distractions.

Industry. Jesus worked, and has thereby made work holy, and taught us to work willingly, each one at his own business, and to be ashamed of no kind of labour. Industry is a virtue, and sloth one of the deadly sins.

Growth in holiness. Finally, Jesus, by His hidden life at Nazareth, teaches us that, as we advance in years, so also ought we to advance in wisdom and grace with God and man. We grow in wisdom if we get to know God and His holy will better, by means of religious instruction, sermons and spiritual reading. We grow in grace or favour with God by good works, and especially by prayer and a worthy reception of the holy Sacraments. Grace or favour with men we gain by brotherly love, friendliness, gentleness and unselfishness.

Zeal for God's Glory. Mary and Joseph went every year to the Temple at Jerusalem. Mary was not bound to do so, but she did it, because it was a work pleasing to God. The example of Mary and Joseph ought to teach us to be obedient to the law of God and zealous for His glory. God still imposes commands on us through His holy Church—to hear Mass on Sundays and Holydays &c. &c.

The Holy Family (Jesus, Mary and Joseph) in the house at Nazareth is a model held up for the imitation of all families. Love, unity and peace reigned there; no sound of discord, no evil word could be heard. The days passed by in work and prayer, and while the members of this Holy Family were occupied with their labour, they raised their hearts to God. Towards their neighbours they were modest, friendly and helpful, taking every opportunity of doing good to others.

The loss of Jesus. Mary lost Jesus through no fault of her own; but with what sorrow she sought Him, with what joy she found Him!

We lose Jesus through our own fault when we separate ourselves from Him by mortal sin. This is the greatest of all misfortunes, for he who has lost Jesus, has lost all, and can never be happy without Him. He to whom this misfortune has happened must seek Jesus with sorrow and tears of penance, and he will find Him again in the Temple (His Church), if he will reconcile himself to God by a good and contrite confession.

APPLICATION. Do you like going to the house of God? Have you never, of your own fault, neglected the services of God? And how do you behave in church when you are there, and how do you listen to the sermon?

As a Christian child you ought to follow the example of Jesus Christ. But how can you be a follower of Him, if you are not obedient to your parents and superiors? Obedience is for you the first and most necessary virtue; and if you will not obey those who stand to you in the place of God, you are not worthy of the name of Christian. How has it been with you hitherto in this respect? Have you always obeyed your parents and superiors both exactly and promptly? If on any future occasion you are told to do something which is distasteful to you, say to yourself: "Jesus, I will do this for love of Thee."

CHAPTER XI.

JOHN THE BAPTIST, THE PRECURSOR OF CHRIST.

[Mat. 3, 1—12. Mark 1, 1—8. Luke 3, 1—18. John 1, 19—27]

THE time was approaching when Jesus would show Himself publicly as the Redeemer of the world. Wherefore the word of the Lord[1] came to John, the son of Zachary, in the desert. Obedient to the divine will, John repaired to the country about the Jordan[2]. He was clothed in camel's hair[3], with a leathern girdle round his loins, and his food was wild honey[4] and locusts[5].

---

[1] *The word of the Lord.* God commanded John, who, as you know, lived the life of a hermit in the desert, to leave his solitude, and enter upon his office of Precursor.

[2] *About the Jordan.* That is, at the southern end of the Jordan, in the neighbourhood of the Dead Sea, about twenty-five miles from Jerusalem.

[3] *Camel's hair.* A dark brown garment shaped like a sack, made of a rough material woven from camel's hair. Instead of sleeves there were two holes for the arms, and the garment was kept together by a leather band round the loins.

[4] *Wild honey.* The honey made by the wild bees which make their hives in the hollows of trees, or in holes in the rocks.

[5] *Locusts.* Which (like crayfish) are either boiled or roasted.

He cried aloud to all the people: "Do penance[1], for the kingdom of heaven is at hand!"[2] In order to excite his hearers more efficaciously to repentance, as also to prepare them for Christian Baptism, he baptized those who were sorry for their sins, in the waters of the Jordan. Then the multitudes came to him from Jerusalem and Judæa to listen to his preaching; and many people of all conditions, after hearing him, confessed their sins and were baptized.

Some of the Sadducees and Pharisees[3] being present among the crowd, John addressed them sternly, saying: "Ye brood of vipers[4], who hath shewed you to flee from the wrath to come?[5] Bring forth, therefore, fruit worthy of penance[6], and think not to say: 'We have Abraham for our father', for I tell you that God is able of these stones to raise up children to Abraham[7]. For now the axe is laid to the root of the trees. Every tree, therefore, that yieldeth not good fruit, shall be cut down and cast into the fire."[8]

---

[1] *Do penance.* Repent of and confess your sins, and amend your ways.

[2] *At hand.* The time has nearly arrived when the Messias will appear from heaven and will found His kingdom.

[3] *Sadducees and Pharisees.* For more details about these sects see Old Test. LXXXVI.

[4] *Vipers.* John called them by this name, because they were as full of evil as are poisonous snakes. They were, as a matter of fact, those very children of the infernal serpent, about whom, after the Fall, God foretold that there should be enmity between them and the Redeemer.

[5] *The wrath to come.* Do not think that you can escape future condemnation, if you come here and are baptized for the sole purpose of winning praise from men.

[6] *Fruit worthy of penance.* Namely, works corresponding with a real conversion. In other words St. John meant: "Repent really, and do not perform only outward, or seeming penance."

[7] *Children to Abraham.* Do not think that penance is unnecessary for you, because you are descended from Abraham, and belong, therefore, to the chosen people; for, if you prove unworthy of divine grace, God will reject you in spite of your descent from Abraham, and He will call others (the Gentiles) to His kingdom, who by their faith will become the spiritual children of Abraham. All those who, like Abraham, live by faith, are the spiritual children of him who is called the father of the faithful. If He so willed it, God could create men from stones, as He first created Adam and Eve of earth and make of them children of Abraham.

[8] *The fire.* Men are signified by the trees; the tree which bears no fruit being the impenitent sinner. John meant to say: "Do not put off your conversion, for the hour has almost come when it will be decided whether you are to have a place in the kingdom of God, or not. He who does not do penance will be shut out from the kingdom of the Messias, and cast into the everlasting fire of hell."

And the people[1] asked him: "What then[2] shall we do?" He answered: "He that hath two coats, let him give to him that hath none; and he that hath meat, let him do in like manner." The soldiers[3] also asked what they should do, and John said to them: "Do violence to no man, neither calumniate any man; and be content with your pay." The Publicans[4] too asked what they were to do, and he answered: "Do nothing more than that which is appointed you."

Now the austere appearance of the Baptist and his startling exhortation led the people to believe that he was the Messias[5]. John, perceiving this, told them that he was not the Messias, but that there was One coming, mightier than he, the latchet of whose shoes he was not worthy to loose[6].

He told them, moreover, that he, indeed, baptized with water[7], but that the Saviour who was to come after him, would baptize with the Holy Ghost and with fire[8]. "Whose fan is in His hand,

---

[1] *The people.* The rich and proud Pharisees and Sadducees were not at all moved by St. John's severe words; but the common people were deeply moved, and ready to obey the precepts of the holy prophet.

[2] *What then.* Why did they say "then"? They meant: "If the case stands as you say it does, and the moment has arrived when we must decide what to do, so as not to be cast into hell, what are we to do?"

[3] *The soldiers.* The soldiers were principally pagans, for the Jews were exempt from military service. As the soldiers, in time of peace, were employed as police, and supported the publicans in their collection of taxes, they had many opportunities of being oppressive and violent.

[4] *The Publicans.* These were collectors who gathered the taxes claimed by the Roman rulers. They were for the most part pagans, and were hated and despised by the Jews, partly because they were dishonest and demanded more than was due, and partly because all taxes paid to the Roman emperors were detestable in the eyes of the Jews. In reply to their inquiry, St. John told them to demand no more money than was required, the amount of the taxes being exactly and precisely laid down.

[5] *The Messias.* The Messias was at this time generally looked for. The deep impression made by John's power and holiness, which indicated him to be a prophet of God, very naturally gave rise to the thought that he might perhaps be the expected Messias.

[6] *To loose.* To loosen the straps of his master's sandals was the duty of a servant; therefore John meant to say: The Messias who will come after me is so high above me that I am not worthy to be even His servant.

[7] *With water.* That is, washing outwardly with water only, in token of internal penance.

[8] *With fire.* He will purify you inwardly, even as fire purifies metal, and He will sanctify you by the Holy Ghost.

and He will thoroughly cleanse His floor [1], and gather the wheat into His barn, but the chaff He will burn with unquenchable fire."

Then the High Priest and the Council sent priests and Levites from Jerusalem to ask John: "Who art thou?" He answered: "I am not the Christ." They continued: "Art thou Elias?" He replied: "I am not." They spoke again: "Art thou the great prophet?" He said: "No!" At last they exclaimed: "Why, then, dost thou baptize, if thou be not Christ, nor Elias, nor the prophet?" John answered that he was the forerunner ['a voice crying in the wilderness, prepare ye the way of the Lord'] of the Messias who would soon appear in their midst, preaching penance and announcing the good tidings of salvation.

COMMENTARY.

The virtues of St. John the Baptist.

1. *His self-denial.* He lived far from the world in the solitude of the desert, wearing one single, coarse, rough garment, and his food was of the poorest description.

2. *His obedience.* It was a hard task to preach penance to the sensual and worldly-minded Jews, but John promptly undertook the task, because God commanded it.

3. *His courage.* He did not hesitate to speak out the truth boldly to the Pharisees and Sadducees, although he knew that they would hate him for it.

4. *His humility.* "I am not the Christ. I am not worthy to loose the latchet of His shoes."

John's mission was twofold: 1. to preach penance to the Jews by word and example, and thus make them ready to receive the grace of Redemption; 2. to herald the Redeemer, and bear testimony to Him. The holy prophet fulfilled both missions most perfectly. His preaching was so persuasive that even the hard-hearted publicans and rude soldiers were moved by it. He especially pointed out:

a) the necessity of good works: "Every tree that bringeth not forth good fruit shall be cut down and cast into the fire"; — "He that hath two coats, let him give to him that hath none; and he that hath meat, let him do in like manner";

---

[1] *Cleanse His floor.* This simile is taken from the manner of threshing corn on open threshing-floors in vogue among the Jews. The grain was cleansed by being thrown up into the air with a shovel; the heavy grain fell back on to the ground, while the light chaff floated away. Thus will the Messias do with the Israelites (and all men): He will gather the good grain into His barn, but the evil and worthless chaff will be thrown into the unquenchable fire of hell.

b) the duty of justice: "Do nothing more than that which is appointed you"; — "Do violence to no man, neither calumniate any man; and be content with your pay".

The testimony to Christ borne by St. John is very striking. He testified that the Messias was much higher and greater than himself; and he testified to His divine nature, for if the Christ could baptize with the Holy Ghost, and had the right to judge and condemn, He must be God.

Confession of sins. Those who were baptized by John openly confessed their sins. They did this, because, being seized with a deep compunction, they hoped to obtain pardon of their sins by a sincere confession. He who is truly contrite, is always willing to confess his sins. In the Old Testament, a confession of sins was an obligatory part of a sin-offering; and in the New Testament, confession is a necessary condition for the Sacrament of Penance.

The Baptism of John was not a Sacrament, and could not effect any purification or sanctification. It was only designed to admonish men that they needed inward purifying from sins, and must prepare themselves for it by true contrition. It was at the same time a type of Christian Baptism, by which men are cleansed and sanctified through the Holy Ghost.

———————

APPLICATION. You too must bring forth fruits worthy of penance. Have you had true contrition and made firm purposes of amendment each time you have been to confession? Have you always confessed your sins sincerely and fully? And do you think you have really improved since your last confession? In what way have you improved?

CHAPTER XII.

JESUS IS BAPTIZED BY JOHN AND TEMPTED BY THE DEVIL.

[Mat. 3, 13 to 4, 11. Mark 1, 9—13. Luke 4, 1—13. John 1, 32—34.]

IN those days when Jesus was about thirty years of age, He went from Nazareth to the Jordan to be baptized by John[1]. But John stayed Him[2], saying; "I ought to be baptized by Thee,

———————

[1] *Baptized by John.* The voice of the prophet crying out to men to prepare by penance for the near approach of the Messias had caused a great movement among the Israelites, who flocked to the Jordan to be baptized by John, not only from Judæa, but also from Galilee in the north of the Holy Land. Among these latter pilgrims came Jesus, who had hitherto lived a hidden and unknown life in Nazareth. But the time had now come when He willed to appear openly as the Messias, and He began His public life by being baptized by John, just as if He were an ordinary Israelite; being at this time thirty years old. John had not as yet seen Jesus, but when our Lord thus humbly approached him to be baptized, a supernatural illumination showed him that this was the Messias.

[2] *Stayed Him.* From stepping down into the water, the ceremony of baptism being one of immersion in the Jordan.

and comest Thou to me?"[1] Jesus answering, said: "Suffer it now, for so it becometh us to fulfil all justice."[2] John obeyed the command, and Jesus was baptized.

Then the heavens were opened; the Holy Ghost descended upon Him in the form of a dove[3], and a voice[4] from heaven exclaimed: "This is My beloved Son, in whom I am well-pleased." Thus did the Eternal Father and the Holy Ghost give testimony that Jesus was the Son of God and the Redeemer of the world.

Before commencing His great work, Jesus was led by the Spirit into the desert[5], where He prayed and fasted forty days[6] and forty nights. Then He was hungry[7], and Satan[8], coming to tempt Him, said: "If Thou be the Son of God[9], command that these stones be made bread." But Jesus answered: "It is written[10]:

---

[1] *Comest Thou to me?* In other words: "Thou, the holy One, dost not require my baptism. Thou canst baptize with the Holy Ghost, whereas I only baptize with water. Thou art mightier than I; why should I baptize Thee"?

[2] *All justice.* Just because I am the Messias, and wish to accomplish the work of Redemption, it behoves me to do everything which God requires of a good Israelite. Thou art called by God to baptize the Israelites, thus preparing them for the New Covenant; therefore, I too desire to be baptized by thee; and it behoves thee to baptize Me, and thus, as it were, to consecrate Me for My public life.

[3] *A dove.* This was no natural dove, but a supernatural vision in the form of a dove, which descended or hovered over His head.

[4] *A voice.* Of God the Father.

[5] *The desert.* Impelled by the Holy Ghost, Jesus went into the desert, namely to a barren ridge of hills, north-west of Jericho, not far from the scene of His baptism, and which is to-day known by the name of Quarantania, or the place of the forty days' fast (Fig. 68, p. 430). This part is full of caves in the rocks.

[6] *Forty days.* Jesus passed the forty days in a state of great mortification, and in the most intimate communion with His Heavenly Father: His dwelling was a cave, His bed the stony ground, and His only society the wild beasts (Mark 1, 13). He neither ate nor drank, His life being miraculously preserved.

[7] *Hungry.* His hunger was intense and painful, and united to great bodily weakness; yet there was no food to be procured in the desert, with which Jesus could satisfy His hunger.

[8] *Satan.* The devil, concealing his real nature under a human form. He had heard the voice from heaven which, at the baptism of Jesus, had said: "This is My beloved Son", but he did not know in what sense Jesus was the Son of God, being ignorant of the mystery of the Incarnation. Yet, at any rate, he suspected that He might be the Messias.

[9] *The Son of God.* If you are really the Son of God, you have only to speak the word, and these stones will become bread, with which you can appease your hunger.

[10] *Written.* In Deut. 8, 3. This passage is taken from Moses' last exhortation to his people, and the whole passage, taken together, runs thus: "He afflicted thee with want and gave thee manna for thy food, which neither thou nor thy fathers

Man liveth not by bread alone, but by every word that proceedeth out of the mouth of God."

Then Satan took Him up into the holy city[1] and set Him on the pinnacle[2] of the Temple, and said: "If Thou be the Son of God, cast Thyself down; for it is written: He hath given His angels charge of Thee[3], and

Fig. 68. So-called Place of Temptation on Mt. Quarantine. (Phot. Bonfils.)

in their hands they shall bear Thee up, lest, perhaps, Thou dash Thy foot against a stone." Jesus said to him: "It is written[4]: Thou shalt not tempt the Lord thy God."

---

knew: to show that not alone in bread doth man live, but in every word that proceedeth from the mouth of God." Jesus quoted the conclusion of this passage, and wished to say: "I suffer hunger willingly; and, as far as concerns My life, mere natural bread is not necessary for Me. God, by His word, can give other food (witness the manna), and His word is powerful enough to sustain man without any food at all."   [1] *The holy city.* To Jerusalem.

[2] *The pinnacle.* On the outer wall of the Temple.

[3] *Charge of Thee.* Jesus having met his first temptation by a passage from Scripture, the devil in his turn quoted a passage from Ps. 90, 11, which contains a promise of God's protection to His servant. Satan wished to say: "If you have such confidence in God as you say you have about your state of hunger, show this same confidence by casting yourself down hence, since He has expressly promised to give His angels charge over you."

[4] *Written.* These words are taken from the last exhortation of Moses (Deut. 6, 16). They mean: "You ought not to put yourself into danger without

But Satan made another attempt. He took our Lord to a very high mountain, and showed Him[1] all the kingdoms of the world, and the glory thereof[2], and said: "All these will I give Thee[3], if, falling down, Thou wilt adore me." Jesus answered: "Begone, Satan[4]; for it is written[5]: The Lord thy God thou shalt adore, and Him only shalt thou serve." Then the devil left Jesus[6]: and, behold, angels came and ministered to Him.

COMMENTARY.

Why Jesus let Himself be baptized by John. 1. He did not require to do penance, because He was without sin; but He had taken our sins upon Him to atone for them; therefore He humbled Himself, placed Himself on a level with sinners, and obediently subjected Himself to be baptized, as He had submitted before to be circumcised, and presented in the Temple. 2. He gave us thereby a lesson in humility and obedience, and has taught us that we too must fulfil all justice, i. e. promptly obey all the ordinances of God. 3. By His baptism He sanctified water, and gave to it the power of purifying and sanctifying the soul of man. In other words, He instituted the Sacrament of Baptism by which, under the outward sign of water, we receive remission of our sins.

The testimony of heaven. The opening of heaven, the appearance of the Holy Ghost, and the voice from above all served to place Jesus before the people as the promised Redeemer, and to give them faith in His divine mission.

The opening of heaven signified that Heaven, which had been closed to man since the Fall, was now once more opened by Jesus. The visible *apparition of the Holy Ghost* proclaimed that in Jesus dwelt the fulness of divine grace and wisdom, and that He it was who would

---

necessity, trusting to miraculous help from God." Thus was the Tempter answered a second time.

[1] *Showed Him.* Pointing them out and describing them.

[2] *Glory thereof.* He described to Him the riches and enjoyments of the world.

[3] *Give Thee.* The proud and lying spirit spoke as if he were lord over the world, whereas he had only a certain power over it, namely, the dominion which Adam had lost through sin.

[4] *Begone, Satan.* Full of horror and indignation, Jesus proved by these words that He well knew who the Tempter was, and showed His authority over him by commanding him.

[5] *Written.* Deut. 6, 13.

[6] *Left Jesus.* Satan now knew who it was with whom he had been striving, and was obliged to obey our Lord's command at once; for, full of spite and rage, he fled before the mighty and holy One who had vanquished him. Then angels appeared and ministered unto Jesus.

baptize with the Holy Ghost (John 1, 33). *The voice of God* the Father proved that this Jesus, who had just received baptism like a sinful son of Adam, was indeed the beloved Son of the Father, in whom, in the days of His humiliation, His Father was well-pleased.

The Mystery of the Blessed Trinity. Even in the Old Testament there were several intimations given that there are more Persons than one in God. "The Spirit of God moved over the waters." Let *us* make man to *our* image and likeness." "I will be to Him a Father, and He will be My Son." Now, in the New Testament, the mystery was fully revealed. The angel Gabriel said: "The Holy which shall be born of thee . . . shall be called the Son of God." This revelation, however, was made to the Blessed Virgin alone. In the story we have just read, the mystery of One God in Three Persons is for the first time proclaimed publicly and solemnly. God the Father speaks from heaven; God the Son, in human form, stands in the Jordan; and God the Holy Ghost, under the form of a dove, hovers over the head of Jesus.

Jesus, the Anointed. The visible descent of the Holy Ghost upon Jesus showed that in Him dwelt the fulness of the Holy Spirit, and that, being the one great Prophet, Priest, and King, He is indeed the Anointed, the Christ. In this way Jesus solemnly entered on His public work of Redemption. The kings and priests of the Old Testament were anointed with oil, and, by this unction, endued with the graces necessary for their state; as, for instance (Old Test. L), you read that the Spirit of the Lord came upon David after Samuel had anointed him: but Jesus was anointed by the Holy Ghost Himself, without the intervention of the outward sign of oil. He is, therefore, the Anointed of the anointed, the Christ.

The effects of Christian Baptism. The wonderful events which followed the baptism of Jesus directly foreshadowed the wonderful effects of Christian Baptism which our Lord then instituted. In the Sacrament of Baptism the Holy Ghost comes down on man, gives him sanctifying grace, and implants in him the three theological virtues of Faith, Hope, and Charity. By the grace of Baptism God adopts man to be His beloved child, and opens for him the way to heaven.

The Prayer of our Lord after His baptism shows that we too ought to pray after receiving the holy Sacraments; that is, we ought to thank God for the grace received, and pray for perseverance in grace and good works.

Humility. St. John showed his humility by the words: "I ought to be baptized by Thee, and comest Thou to me?"

The dove is the type of innocence. The Holy Ghost appeared under the form of a dove to show that Jesus is the Innocent and Beloved One in whom His Father was well-pleased; for the dove is the symbol of innocence, love and gentleness.

The temptations of Jesus came from without, from the devil. No temptation could take hold of Jesus, for though indeed He had two wills, divine and human, His human will was always in complete harmony with His divine will, and could never turn against it and consent to sin. When, therefore, Jesus was tempted, His temptation could only come from without, as was also the case with our first parents in Paradise.

Why our Lord was tempted.

1. Because He came into the world to fight and overcome sin and Satan. The Saviour began His strife with the infernal serpent as soon as He began His public life, by victoriously repulsing Satan's three temptations. He gloriously carried on the strife to the end, crushing the serpent's head by His Death and Resurrection.

2. Because the Son of God wished to do violence to Himself, and abase Himself in order to redeem us. It was a great humiliation to the Son of God that Satan, the essence of all that is evil, should approach Him and dare to try to tempt Him to sin and disobedience against God. O Divine Saviour, how low didst Thou stoop, even to exposing Thyself to the contact and seductions of hell!

3. Because Jesus is the spiritual Father of mankind, and the second Adam. He desired, therefore, to be tempted as was the first Adam, in order to expiate the Fall of our first parents. Compare the temptation of Adam and Eve, and the temptation of Christ. The former took place in the midst of the beauty and abundance of Paradise, the latter in the bare desert, and when our Lord was in a state of painful hunger. Satan tempted our first parents to gluttony, pride and the lust of the eyes; and succeeded. He tried to allure our Lord to the same three lusts; and was overcome. Angels came and drove Adam and Eve from Paradise; whereas angels came and ministered to Jesus.

4. In order to show us how to meet temptations to evil.

5. In order to comfort and encourage us in the many trials and temptations of this life. St. Paul writes thus: "For we have not a High Priest who cannot have compassion on our infirmities: but One tempted in all things like as we are, without sin. Let us go, therefore, with confidence to the throne of grace: that we may obtain mercy and find grace in seasonable aid" (Hebr. 4, 15. 16).

The different kinds of temptation. In the first temptation Satan wished to induce the Saviour, instead of trusting in God and patiently enduring hunger, to create bread by His own power, against His Father's will. He sought, therefore, to make our Lord sin by sensuality and an unlawful desire for food, or in other words by *gluttony*. By the second temptation Satan tried to awaken a *spiritual pride* in Jesus, saying: "Throw yourself down; God will help you and see that no evil befalls you!" The cunning seducer wished thereby to change a humble and submissive confidence in God's mercy into a proud presumption. By the third temptation Satan wished to arouse in Jesus concupiscence *of the eyes*, i. e. a desire for riches, power and pleasure. He had seduced the first man by inciting him to these three evil passions. The words: "Why hath God commanded you that you should not eat of every tree of Paradise?" were an inducement to gluttony, or to the concupiscence of the flesh. The words: "Your eyes shall be opened" were a temptation to pride, while the words: "You shall be as Gods" were an inducement to the concupiscence of the eyes, and a desire for power and glory. Our first parents succumbed to these temptations, because they gave ear to the suggestions of Satan, held intercourse with him, and gazed at the forbidden fruit (Old Test. IV). But Jesus over-came the temptation and conquered Satan.

Means of resisting temptation. As a consequence of the Fall these three evil passions, which are the source of our most dangerous temp-tations, are rife in every man. Besides these passions, our fellow-crea-tures are a source of temptation to us, and the devil, also by God's permission, still tempts us to evil. We are surrounded by temptations, and therefore Jesus has taught us by His example how we are to war against them. Let us then examine closely in what way it was that Jesus obtained a victory over temptation and the Tempter.

1. He did not expose Himself wantonly to temptation, for it was by the impulse of the Holy Spirit that He went into the desert to be tempted. This teaches us not to place ourselves in danger of sin without necessity, but carefully to avoid the occasion of it. "He that loveth danger shall perish in it" (Ecclus. 3, 27).

2. Jesus prepared Himself for temptation by prayer and fasting. We too must pray diligently, and practise self-denial, in order that we may be always ready to fight against the enemy of our salvation. Our Saviour says: "Watch ye and pray that ye enter not into temptation; the spirit, indeed, is willing, but the flesh is weak" (chapter LXVII). He also commands us to pray: "Lead us not into temptation." We shall become strong in spirit and able to resist temptation, if we practise self-denial.

3. During His temptation our Lord remembered the word of God, and finally sent the Tempter away authoritatively and decisively, by the words: "Begone, Satan!" Thus we too, whether the temptation come from within or from without, ought to turn our thoughts at once to God and His holy word, and say to the tempter: "Begone!" Where-fore, "Resist the devil, and he will fly from you" (James 4, 7).

Fasting (the third commandment of the Church). The forty days' fast of Jesus had been typified by that of Moses and of Elias (Old Test. XXXVII. LXV). Mortification being necessary for Christians, the Church has commanded a forty days' fast to be observed each year, in memory of the fast of our Lord.

Satan's efforts. How did Satan in the story we have read prove himself to be a liar? By the words: "All these things will I give you." And how did he at the same time betray that he was the adversary of God, and possessed by a senseless pride? By the condition he made: "If thou wilt fall down and worship me." Thus he demanded divine worship for himself! His whole desire is to oppose what is divine, and to put himself in God's place as lord of creation!

APPLICATION. After you received holy Baptism, you too were a beloved child of God with whom your Heavenly Father was well-pleased. Are you still a holy and innocent child? Is your soul still unstained by sin? Is there anything in you with which God cannot be pleased, such as lies, disobedience, anger or deceitfulness? Oh, remember that by sin you have stained your white robe of innocence; repent of this, detest sin and avoid it for the future.

If you pay attention to yourself, you will find that in the course of the day you are assailed by many temptations. Do you know to what you are most often tempted? Yet temptation is not sin; it only becomes sin when you take pleasure in it and consent to it. As often as you resist and overcome it, you gain in virtue, and merit a reward from God. When you are tempted, turn to God; pray to Jesus and Mary for help, and remember the word of God which warns you against the very sin to which you are tempted. If anger rises within you, say: "Blessed are the meek," or else: "For the anger of man worketh not the justice of God" (James 1, 20). If you are inclined to quarrel or fight, say to yourself: "Blessed are the peace-makers"; or if you are in danger of telling lies, remind yourself of the proverb: "Lying lips are an abomination to the Lord" (Prov. 12, 22).

CHAPTER XIII.

THE FIRST DISCIPLES OF JESUS CHRIST.

[John 1, 28—51.]

JESUS left the desert and returned to the country about the Jordan. As soon as John saw Him, he said to the multitude that surrounded him: "Behold the Lamb of God![1] Behold Him who taketh away the sins of the world! This is He of whom

---

[1] *The Lamb of God.* i. e. this is the true Paschal Lamb, sent and consecrated by God, who will take our iniquities upon Him, and redeem all men from sin, as was foretold by Isaias (Old Test. LXXII).

I said[1]: 'After me cometh a Man, who is preferred before me, because He was before me.'[2] I gave testimony that this is the Son of God."

On the following day, when John was on the banks of the Jordan with two of his disciples[3], he beheld Jesus coming towards him, and he again said: "Behold the Lamb of God!" The two disciples, hearing this, left John and followed Jesus. And Jesus, turning, spoke to them: "What seek you?" They asked Him: "Master, where dwellest Thou"?[4] He said: "Come and see!" They came, and saw where He abode, and they remained with Him all that day.

These two disciples were John and Andrew. The latter had a brother named Simon, who was wishing to see the Messias. Andrew went to seek Simon[5] and said: "We have found the Messias." And he conducted him to Jesus. When Jesus saw Simon, He looked upon him and said: "Thou art Simon, the son of Jona; thou shalt be called Cephas", that is to say, Peter[6], a rock.

The next day Jesus went forth into Galilee, and on the road He met a man named Philip[7], who also longed for the coming

---

[1] *I said.* Compare chapter XI.

[2] *Before me.* As Man, Jesus was half a year younger than John; nevertheless the latter said: "He was before me", for Jesus, as God, is from all eternity.

[3] *His disciples.* The disciples, or pupils, of St. John were a certain number of Israelites who had attached themselves to the holy prophet, to be instructed by him in the religious life. According to Luke 5, 33 they led a severe life of penance, prayer and fasting. John looked upon it as his chief task to prepare these disciples for Jesus.

[4] *Where dwellest Thou?* Full of diffidence and reverence, they did not venture to make known to Him in public their desire to be His disciples, and therefore asked Him where He dwelt. Jesus at once invited them to go with Him, and they spent several precious hours in His company, from four o'clock in the afternoon till the evening. Their personal intercourse with Him completely confirmed their conviction that He was the promised Redeemer; and this belief was such a happiness to them, that they did their best to bring other Israelites of the same mind as themselves to Jesus; as we see in the case of Andrew, who went to fetch his brother, Simon.

[5] *To seek Simon.* Because he knew how great a longing he had for the Messias. Simon believed his brother, and allowed himself to be led to Jesus.

[6] *Peter.* Jesus knew him at once, penetrated into his heart, and destined him to be the rock on which He would found His Church.

[7] *Philip.* He came from Bethsaida, a fishing district in Galilee, on the Lake of Genesareth, close to Capharnaum. Peter and Andrew were also born there (John 1, 44). Philip was likewise a disciple of the Baptist, and of the same mind as his fellow-countrymen, Peter and Andrew, and therefore joyfully accepted our Lord's invitation.

of the Messias. Jesus said to him: "Follow Me!"[1] Now Philip had a friend named Nathanael[2], an upright, God-fearing man. Philip hastened to him and told him: "We[3] have found Him of whom Moses in the law and the prophets did write, Jesus of Nazareth." But Nathanael said to him: "Can anything good come from Nazareth?"[4] Philip answered: "Come and see."[5]

When Jesus saw Nathanael coming, He said: "Behold an Israelite indeed, in whom there is no guile."[6] Nathanael asked in surprise[7]: "Whence knowest Thou me?" Jesus answered and said to Him: "Before that Philip called thee, when thou wast under the fig-tree, I saw thee."

Then Nathanael, filled with wonder and respect, cried out: "Rabbi, Thou art the Son of God[8]: Thou art the King of Israel." Jesus spoke to him: "Because I said to thee: 'I saw thee under the fig-tree,' thou believest; greater things[9] than these shalt thou see. Amen, Amen, I say unto you, you shall see the heaven opened, and the angels of God ascending and descending upon the Son of Man."

COMMENTARY.

John's testimony of Jesus. 1. John testifies to the fact that our Lord will give Himself as a sacrifice for the sins of the whole world, i. e. of all men; for he calls Him 'the Lamb of God that taketh away the sins of the world'. The words of John further imply that our Lord

---

[1] *Follow Me.* Attach yourself to me; be my disciple.

[2] *Nathanael.* Philip was so happy at having found the Messias that he at once sought out his kinsman, Nathanael, to take him also to Jesus. Nathanael was a native of Cana of Galilee, a little town in communication with Nazareth.

[3] *We.* i. e. Andrew, John, Simon and I.

[4] *From Nazareth.* Nathanael understood at once that he meant the Messias. Nazareth being much despised by the Jews, Nathanael thought it very unlikely that the Messias should spring from such a town.

[5] *See.* He was convinced that Nathanael would believe as soon as he had seen and spoken with Jesus.

[6] *No guile.* i. e. he is no deceiver or hypocrite, as were the Pharisees.

[7] *In surprise.* He had heard the words just uttered by Jesus, and was astonished that He should know his heart, although He had never seen him before.

[8] *The Son of God.* Jesus knew, therefore, that Nathanael had been called by Philip, and that, before Philip had found him, he had been under a fig-tree. Jesus could not have known this by any natural means, and therefore Nathanael, full of holy awe, cried out: "Thou art the Son of God!"

[9] *Greater things.* Jesus praised his faith and encouraged him to believe, by promising him that he should see still greater wonders, which would confirm his faith.

would suffer innocently and patiently as foretold by Isaias (chapter LIII); and that in the sacrifice of Christ all other sacrifices find their fulfilment. Hence the Church has put these beautiful words in her Liturgy (Daily Mass, Holy Communion, Litanies).

2. John testifies to our Lord's *Pre-existence* or *Eternity*, saying that though born after him He was before him.

3. Finally, the holy Baptist plainly testifies to Christ's *Divinity:* "I (because I heard the voice which spoke from heaven, when Jesus was baptized), I give testimony that this is the Son of God!"

Jesus Himself made manifest His Divine Nature: 1. by knowing and revealing hidden and distant things. He knew and penetrated the hearts of Simon and Nathanael, and knew that Nathanael had been called by Philip, and that, before then, he had been under a fig-tree; 2. by allowing Nathanael's confession of faith: 'Thou art the Son of God', to pass without protest, and by confirming it with the promise that still greater wonders should justify this faith.

The foundation of the Church. By the calling of His disciples, Jesus laid the foundation of His Church simultaneously with His first appearance in public. These disciples, at first, only remained for a short time with Jesus. Later on, He chose twelve to be His constant followers and disciples.

The rock on which the Church is built. God changes the names of those only whom He calls to accomplish great works. For example, He changed Jacob's name into Israel, which was to be the name of the whole people descended from him, and which indicated his calling. By the change of Simon's name to Peter, our Lord gave it to be understood that He had chosen this disciple to be the foundation-rock of His Church.

Humility. St. John the Baptist did not seek his own glory, but the glory of Jesus Christ, whose precursor God had called him to be. Without any thought of himself, he sent his disciples to our Lord. Even as the morning-star pales and disappears before the light of the rising sun, even so was it John's desire to be extinguished when Jesus came.

Zeal for souls. Andrew and Philip were full of joy at having found the Messias and become His disciples. They showed their thankfulness for the great grace they had received, by their endeavours to impart it to their friends and relatives. All who love Jesus have a zealous desire to make their friends love Him also.

Sincerity also is a great virtue and specially praised by our Lord in the case of Nathanael. We may justly assume that by his sincerity of heart Nathanael obtained the grace of faith and of being called to be a disciple and companion of Christ.

APPLICATION. The disciples rejoiced that they had found Jesus and believed in Him. Do you daily thank God that you are a disciple of Jesus Christ and a member of His holy Church?

Can it be said of you: "Behold a real Christian, in whom there is no guile?" Do you not sometimes dissimulate? Do you always tell the truth?

CHAPTER XIV.

FIRST MIRACLE OF JESUS—HE CHANGES WATER INTO WINE.

[John 2, 1—11.]

THREE days after these events there was a marriage in Cana[1] of Galilee, and the Mother of Jesus was there. Jesus also, together with His disciples[2], was among the guests. While they were at table, the wine failed, and Mary said to Jesus: "They have no wine."[3] He answered: "Woman[4], what is it to me and to thee? My hour[5] is not yet come." But Mary, knowing the goodness of her Divine Son, and convinced that He would not refuse her request, spoke to the waiters: "Whatever He shall say to you, do ye."[6]

---

[1] *Cana.* This little town lay about six miles to the north of Nazareth.

[2] *His disciples.* Jesus travelled back from the Jordan to Nazareth with His five disciples. He did not find His Mother there, as she had gone to the marriage at Cana: probably she was related to the bride or bridegroom. Jesus also went on to Cana, arriving there, perhaps, towards evening. He and His disciples being invited to the marriage-feast, the number of guests was increased by six persons, and, in consequence, the wine came to an end before the feast was over. It is evident that the bride and bridegroom were poor people, and not able to procure more wine. Their embarrassment was great, and they felt their poverty acutely. [It is more probable that Jesus travelled via Lake Tiberias to Bethsaida and thence back to Nazareth via Cana, and was therefore invited to the wedding, as His Mother was there. *Tr.*]

[3] *No wine.* Thus spoke Mary, in the fulness of her compassion for the poor bridegroom. She did not in so many words ask our Lord to help them by a miracle, but He well understood what it was that her compassionate heart desired.

[4] *Woman.* Woman is here a title of honour and equivalent to "Lady". The words "what is it to me and to thee" sound harsh in our language, but not necessarily so in Hebrew. The meaning here is "why should we trouble or interfere"? The words therefore imply no rebuke and no refusal, as the event shows.

[5] *My hour.* The hour for such a public manifestation of My glory. Thus spoke Jesus, because He had intended to reveal Himself and His divine power for the first time at Jerusalem, at the Feast of the Pasch. But Mary's humble confidence could not be shaken, and she prayed the Heavenly Father to hasten "the hour" of His Son, and meanwhile she made preparations for a miracle.

[6] *Do ye.* Even if you do not understand the good of it.

Now there were in the room six water-jars[1] of stone, containing two or three measures[2] apiece. Jesus gave orders to the waiters: "Fill the water-pots with water." They immediately filled them to the brim. He then said to them: "Draw out[3] now, and carry to the chief steward[4] of the feast."

They did so; and the steward, not knowing whence the wine was, said to the bridegroom: "Every man at first sets forth good wine, and later on that which is worse; but thou hast kept the good wine[5] until now." This first miracle Jesus wrought in Cana of Galilee, at the request of His Blessed Mother; and His disciples, seeing His divine power, believed in Him[6].

COMMENTARY.

The object of our Lord's miracles. We can see clearly by this story the reason why our Lord worked miracles. His *first* object was to induce men to believe in the divinity of His mission and in the truth of His doctrine (see the words of Nicodemus, chapter XV: "No man can do these miracles which Thou doest, unless God be with Him"). If God were with Jesus, then everything which He taught must be true, because God is only with what is true. The *second* object of our Lord's miracles was to instruct men not only by words, but by deeds also. The miracle at Cana teaches us that we ought, according to our means, to help our neighbours in their necessities. It is also typical of that great and lasting miracle of divine love, power and wisdom, the changing of bread into the Body of our Lord Jesus, and of wine into His Blood.

---

[1] *Water-jars.* These jars contained water in which the guests washed their hands, and if they came from a distance, their feet also, before eating.

[2] *Three measures.* Or about nine gallons. The six jars together held more than fifty gallons. The carrying of so much water took some time, and aroused general attention. All those present must have said to themselves: "Why is so much water being brought in?"

[3] *Draw out.* The wine was usually transferred from the large vessels into flagons by means of spoons.

[4] *Chief steward.* His duty was to superintend the distribution of the food and drink. Usually a kinsman of the bridegroom filled this post.

[5] *The good wine.* Our Lord had changed the water into wine by His mere will, without speaking a word. We know that this wine must have been exceptionally good, by what the steward said to the bridegroom. We can imagine the bridegroom's reply to the reproach of the chief steward: "This wine is not mine: I do not know whence it comes." Then the waiters were questioned, and related the whole proceeding.

[6] *Believed in Him.* But did not they already believe in Him? Yes, indeed; but hitherto their faith had been mostly based on the testimony of the Baptist; now, however, they acknowledged His glory on account of the great miracle which He had worked, and which mightily confirmed their faith.

Thirdly, our Lord worked miracles in order to help men in their sufferings and necessities. By the miracle at the marriage-feast Jesus desired to deliver the bridegroom from an awkward dilemma, and to restore the festal joy. The help given was so lavish that a quantity of wine remained over after the feast; just as, later on, after the feeding of the five thousand, twelve baskets-full of bread remained over. Let us recognize in all this the goodness of Jesus, and appeal to His Sacred Heart for help in all our necessities, both spiritual and temporal.

The power of Mary's intercession. This first miracle, which confirmed the faith of our Lord's disciples, was wrought at Mary's intercession, for it was by her persuasion that He first manifested His glory by a striking miracle at Cana instead of at Jerusalem. Let us contemplate Mary's compassion on the distress of the poor bride and bridegroom, her living faith in the omnipotence of Jesus, and her confidence in His goodness. Mary is ever willing to help us by her intercession; but then we must obey her exhortation: "Whatever He (Jesus) shall say to you, do ye!"

Matrimony. By His presence at the marriage-feast of Cana Jesus honoured and sanctified marriage, which had already been instituted in Paradise. It was always from the beginning an indissoluble contract sanctioned by God. But now it is to become even more sacred and indissoluble. For Christ is going to make it a Sacrament and a symbol of His own union with the Church. Hence He comes here with the first fruits of His Church to celebrate, so to speak, a double marriage-feast, that of Himself and His Church, and that of the bridegroom and bride.

Lawful pleasures. The fact of our Lord taking part in the marriage-feast teaches us that it is lawful and pleasing to God that we should take part in innocent recreations and harmless pleasures, rejoicing with those who rejoice.

St. Joseph is not mentioned in this story, nor in any part of our Lord's public life, even in His Passion. He had already died a blessed death in the arms of Jesus and in the presence of the Blessed Virgin. Therefore the Church invokes the faithful foster-father of Jesus as the patron of a happy death. We ask him for his intercession, that we, like him, may leave this world, united to Jesus by sanctifying grace, and especially united to Him in Holy Communion.

———

APPLICATION. Are your pleasures always of such a kind that Jesus and Mary might be present at them? Have you never taken part in sinful amusements, or pleasure in improper conversation and actions? Do you always avoid strife and quarrels with your companions? St. Paul says: "Rejoice in the Lord always" (Phil. 4, 4).

CHAPTER XV.

JESUS DRIVES THE SELLERS OUT OF THE TEMPLE.
HIS DISCOURSE WITH NICODEMUS.

[John 2, 13 to 3, 21.]

THE Passover of the Jews being now at hand, Jesus went up to Jerusalem (Fig. 69)[1]. Finding in the court of the Temple men that sold oxen, sheep and doves for sacrifice, together with money-changers[2], He made a whip of small cords and drove them all out of the Temple. He overthrew the money-tables, and said to them that sold doves[3]: "Take these things[4] hence, and make not the house of my Father a house of traffic." Then the disciples remembered that it was written: "The zeal of Thy house hath eaten me up."[5]

---

[1] *Jerusalem.* From Cana Jesus with His disciples went to Capharnaum on the Lake of Genesareth, and from thence He passed on to Jerusalem to keep the Pasch, meaning to come forward there openly as the Messias (John 2, 12).

[2] *Money-changers.* In the great outer court of the Gentiles there were cattle-dealers who sold beasts for the sacrifices, and money-changers who changed Roman and Greek money into Jewish, because offerings for the treasury of the Temple, which every Jew was bound to make, could only be paid in Jewish coin. The beasts defiled the sacred precincts: the haggling and bargaining of the mercenary dealers and dishonest money-changers, the shouts of the cattle-drivers, the lowing of the oxen and the bleating of the sheep, all this caused a great deal of noise, and not only made any worship in the outer court of the Gentiles an impossibility, but even disturbed the worshippers in the other courts. When Jesus saw this unholy traffic going on, He was seized with a righteous indignation, and, making a scourge, He drove the dealers and beasts out of the Temple. No one ventured to resist Him! All, even the stubborn oxen, retreated before Him and obeyed His word of authority. His angry glance exercised a supernatural power. "Heavenly fire gleamed from His eyes, and Divine Majesty shone on His countenance" (St. Jerome).

[3] *Doves.* Jesus treated these more gently, both because their business was less noisy, and because the sellers of doves were poor people, who sold the birds to the poor at a cheap rate.

[4] *These things.* The cages of the doves.

[5] *Eaten me up.* This passage occurs in Ps. 68, 10. The Psalm relates to the Messias and His sufferings. When the disciples saw with what holy zeal Jesus purified the Temple, this passage which speaks of the zeal of the Messias for the house of God came to their memory, and they found in it a fresh proof that Jesus was the Messias.

Fig. 69 Jerusalem seen from Mount Scopus. (Phot. Bonfils.)

443

Now some[1] of the Jews who had remained in the Temple, being angry, asked Him: "What sign[2] dost Thou show us, seeing Thou doest these things?" Jesus, referring to His own Sacred Body, said: "Destroy this temple, and in three days I will raise it up."[3]

The Jews, supposing that He spoke of the material Temple in which He stood, said to Him: "Six and forty years[4] was this Temple in building, and wilt Thou raise it up in three days?" But Jesus spoke of the temple of His Body[5]. Many other signs and wonders did He work in presence of the Jews, many of whom were converted. But many others would not be convinced of His Divinity. Like their fathers of old, they wilfully closed their eyes to the light of truth.

Among those who believed, was Nicodemus, a ruler[6] in Israel. He had a great desire to become a disciple of Jesus, and coming to Him by night[7] for fear of the Jews, he said to Him: "Rabbi, we know that Thou art come a teacher from God, for no man can do these miracles[8] which Thou doest, unless God be with him." Then Jesus explained to him how he was to become a

---

[1] *Some.* These were the priests and elders, who were provoked at this authoritative proceeding on the part of Jesus.

[2] *What sign.* They meant to say: "This market is held in the outer court with our consent. If you take upon yourself to object to it, you must prove by some miracle (sign) that you have received the authority to do so from God Himself."

[3] *Raise it up.* When Jesus perceived their unbelief, He would work no miracle then, but foretold to them his violent death at their hands and the miracle of his Resurrection on the third day.

[4] *Six and forty years.* Herod's additions to the Temple were begun in the year 16 B. C. Jesus was now thirty years old, so that the building had already been going on for forty-six years.

[5] *Temple of His Body.* The Body of Jesus was, in fact, the temple of His Divinity. "For in Him dwelleth all the fulness of the Godhead corporally" (Col. 2, 9).

[6] *A ruler.* A member of the Sanhedrim. This was the highest court of justice among the Jews, and consisted of seventy-one members, priests, scribes, and elders, over whom the High Priest presided.

[7] *By night.* In order not to be seen. He feared to make known to his unbelieving townsfolk his belief in Jesus.

[8] *These miracles.* The miracles which Jesus had wrought in Jerusalem after the purifying of the Temple, had convinced Nicodemus that Jesus was sent by God. But he did not yet believe in His Divinity; he only believed Him to be a prophet. His will, however, was right, and he had an interior desire to be taught by Jesus about the kingdom of the Messias. Our Lord knew that Nicodemus desired to enter into the kingdom of God, and therefore explained to him the conditions of admission.

member of His mystical Body on earth, which is the Church, and told him: "Amen, amen, I say to you, unless a man be born again [1] of water and of the Holy Ghost, he cannot enter into the kingdom of God." These words referred to the Sacrament of Baptism.

He next instructed Nicodemus in the mystery of the Redemption. "As Moses", said He, "lifted up the serpent in the desert, so must the Son of Man be lifted up [2], that whosoever believeth in Him, may not perish, but may have life everlasting. For God so loved the world as to give his only-begotten Son, that whosoever believeth in Him, may not perish, but may have life everlasting. For God sent not His Son into the world to judge [3] the world, but that the world may be saved by Him. He that believeth in Him [4] is not judged [5], but he that doth not believe is already judged." In these words the Saviour taught Nicodemus [6] that He would redeem the world by His Passion and death upon the Cross.

---

[1] *Born again.* Jesus meant to say: "You think that the kingdom of the Messias is to be an earthly one, in which the Jews will reign supreme; but it is a spiritual kingdom, and mere blood-descent from Abraham does not give admission to it. He who wishes to belong to this kingdom, must be created anew spiritually, and become, interiorly, a new man, this new birth being given by the Holy Ghost by means of water, i. e. by Christian Baptism."

[2] *Lifted up.* Our Lord pointed to the raising up of the brazen serpent (Old Test. XLII) as a type of Himself raised up on the Cross. Our Lord calls Himself the "Son of Man" to show that He is a true son of Adam—and that seed of the woman which was one day to crush the head of the infernal serpent. Jesus, therefore, meant to say to Nicodemus: "You think of the Messias as a mighty king, who will make Israel great in the eyes of the world, and free it from the power of Rome: but I say to you that even as Moses lifted up the brazen serpent on the tree, so shall I, the Messias, be lifted up on the Cross and die. And as in the desert all those who, full of faith and confidence, looked up at the brazen serpent, were healed from the deadly bites of the fiery snakes, even so all those who believe in the crucified Messias, shall be saved from the bite of the infernal serpent (i. e. from sin and from eternal death), and made participators of eternal life." But why has faith in the crucified Son of Man such saving power? This Jesus explains in the following part of His discourse.

[3] *To judge.* God might have sent His Son to judge and condemn the sin-laden world; but no! He did not send Him to pass sentence, but that through Him the world might be saved from being condemned, and might be given eternal happiness.

[4] *Him.* The Divine Redeemer.

[5] *Not judged.* The believer is not judged, i. e. condemned, but the unbeliever is judged, because he stands self-condemned by the very fact that he does not believe in the name of the only-begotten Son of God who is truth itself.

[6] *Nicodemus.* We shall see in chapter LXXV that this teaching was not thrown away on Nicodemus.

COMMENTARY.

The Divinity of Jesus Christ is in this chapter proved 1) by His words, 2) by His deeds, and 3) by the prophecy He made.

1. In the Temple and in the presence of many leading Israelites, Jesus distinctly declared Himself to be the Son of God, calling the Temple the house of His Father. If God be His Father, He must be the Son of God.

2. He proved His Divinity by the power and majesty of his indignation when He drove the buyers and sellers from the Temple, quelling in the most wonderful way every sign of resentment or resistance on their part (Origen)

3. He showed His Divinity, or, to speak more exactly, His omniscience, by distinctly foretelling that the Jews would kill Him (destroying the temple of His Body), and that He would raise His dead Body to life again on the third day.

Different ways of receiving grace. Our Lord's miracles served to increase the faith of the disciples, who perceived in His action in the Temple the fulfilment of the prophecy that the Messias would be full of zeal for the house of God. The miracle and our Lord's direct testimony to His own Divinity were likewise a grace for the Jews who happened to be in the outer court of the Temple. The grace of faith was offered to them, and they resisted it: they would not believe, and demanded a fresh miracle in confirmation of the first. God gives His grace to all men. But man has the power of resisting it.

The Body of Christ was the living Temple of God, because in Him dwelt the fulness of the Godhead; He being the Second Person of the Blessed Trinity, with all power, wisdom and holiness. Our bodies, too, become the temples of the Holy Ghost by Baptism and Confirmation, because God the Holy Ghost dwells in us by His grace. "Know you not that ye are the temple of God, and that the Spirit of God dwelleth in you? But if any man violate the temple of God, him shall God destroy. For the temple of God is holy, which you are" (1 Cor. 3, 16 17). This living temple of God is defiled by every mortal sin, especially by those against holy purity.

Behaviour in the House of God. Jesus, full of a holy zeal, reproved and punished the buyers and sellers who were behaving themselves irreverently in the outer court of the Temple. A Catholic church is far more holy than was the Jewish Temple; and Christians who behave without reverence inside, or near it, deserve sharper reproof and heavier punishment than did the sellers in the Temple.

Holy Scripture is not the only source of faith. Scripture, after relating the purifying of the Temple, says that Jesus performed many miracles in Jerusalem and the neighbourhood; but what these miracles were, the holy Evangelists do not tell us. This shows us that not everything which Jesus did and taught is related in Holy Scripture. St. John writes thus at the end of his Gospel (21, 15): "There are also many other things which Jesus did, which if they were written every one, the world itself, I think, would not be able to contain the books that should be written!" Christian revelation is, therefore, only partly contained in Holy Scripture.

In His *Discourse with Nicodemus* our Lord has revealed to us the chief truths of the Christian religion.

1. *The Holy Trinity.* The words of our Lord imply that there are three Persons in God: God the *Father,* who gave His only-begotten *Son,* and the *Holy Ghost,* of whom man must be born again.

2. *The Incarnation.* The only-begotten Son of God, who came into the world, is also the Son of Man, the divine and human natures being in Him united in one Person.

3. *The Sufferings of Christ.* "As Moses lifted up the serpent in the desert, so must the Son of Man be lifted up." Jesus therefore knew definitely from the beginning that He would die on the Cross; and His bitter Passion and Death were ever before Him! To offer Himself on the Cross was the object of His Incarnation!

4. *The Object of His Passion and Death* is also clearly stated in the words: "that the world may be saved by Him", and "that whosoever believeth in Him may not perish, but may have life everlasting". He willed to suffer and die in order to save man from eternal loss, and obtain happiness for him. He died for *all* men, and is therefore the Redeemer of the whole world.

5. *The infinite Love of God.* Why was it the will of the Son of God to redeem us? What was the motive of His Incarnation and Death? It was, in a word, His infinite and divine love for man. "God so loved the world as to give His only-begotten Son!" What! God, the Most Holy, loved the world, laden with sin and a curse! He loved the men who had offended Him and turned against Him millions of times. And He loved them so much as to give for them all that was greatest and dearest, even His only-begotten Son, to suffer for them humility, poverty, persecution, and even a miserable death upon the Cross! O, unfathomable and inconceivable love of God!

6. *The necessity of Baptism.* Only he who is born again of water and of the Holy Ghost has any part in the kingdom of God. By Baptism man becomes a member of God's kingdom upon earth, i. e. the Church of Jesus Christ, and an heir of God's kingdom in heaven. Thus Baptism is absolutely necessary to salvation.[*]

7. *Original sin.* The words of our Lord testify to the existence of original sin. They suppose that by our natural birth we have not that spiritual divine life in our soul which was given to our first parents in Paradise, and consequently that we have lost the principle of that

---

[*] The Church understands this passage of Scripture (that is, *John* 3:5) to mean that the *grace* of Baptism is absolutely necessary for salvation, but that, with regard to the actual Sacrament of Baptism, either the actual Sacrament "or a desire for it" ("*aut eius voto*") is necessary for salvation. (Cf. *Council of Trent,* Session VI, Decree on Justification, Chap. 4 [D 796]; Session VII, Canons on Baptism, Canon 5 [D 861]. Cf. also D 847, 388, 413.) This "desire" includes love for God above all things and desire to do everything necessary for one's salvation. (*Baltimore Catechism,* Official Rev. Ed. No. 2, Q. 323.) —*Publisher,* 2003.

life, sanctifying grace and all that was connected with it. We are born (spiritually) dead. This is the sin of our origin from Adam.

8. *Necessity of faith in the Divine Redeemer.* Our Lord teaches the necessity of such faith by these words: "That whosoever believeth in Him may not perish"; — "He that believeth in Him is not judged, but he that doth not believe is already judged." He who wilfully refuses to believe in the Incarnate Son of God has no part in Redemption. Such an unbeliever refuses to have a Redeemer. He is hopelessly lost, because he refuses to be saved! "The wrath of God abideth in him" (John 3, 36).

APPLICATION. Your body, too, is the temple of the Holy Ghost. Have you ever defiled it by unworthy pursuits? Make a firm resolution to honour your body as the temple of the Holy Ghost, and never to defile it!

Many Christians behave irreverently in church, in the Presence of the Blessed Sacrament. Such people deserve indeed to be driven out of church with scourges! Our Lord does not, it is true, drive them out now, but at the Day of Judgment He will deal more severely with them than He dealt with the buyers and sellers in the Temple at Jerusalem.

Do you thank God every day for your Baptism, and for all the graces which, without any merit of your own, you received with it?

Do you love God, who is so infinitely good, with your whole heart? How do you show your love? Do you pray willingly and devoutly? Do something special to-day, for the love of God.

CHAPTER XVI.

JESUS AT THE WELL OF JACOB.

[John 4, 1—12.]

NOW it came to pass that Herod [1] cast John the Baptist into prison; whereupon the Pharisees, taking courage, began to persecute [2] the Saviour. He therefore left Judæa [3] and returned

---

[1] *Herod.* This was Herod Antipas. He cast John into prison, because the holy prophet reproved him for a grievous sin he had committed (see chapter XXXII). The unbelieving Pharisees in Judæa had delivered up the holy man to his mortal enemy; for they, also, hated John, because all the people ran after him.

[2] *Persecute.* Having got rid of John, they turned all their hatred against Jesus, because He had even more followers than John (4, 1), and they now made attempts against both His liberty and His life, as they had already done by the holy Baptist.

[3] *Left Judæa.* Because the time for Him to suffer and die was not yet come.

again to Galilee. On His way He came to a town called Sichar[1], where there was a well dug by the patriarch Jacob (Fig. 70). Jesus, being weary from the journey, sat down by the well, whilst His disciples went into the city to buy provisions.

Fig. 70. Jacob's well near Sichar to day. (Phot. Bonfils.)

But, behold, a Samaritan woman came to the well to draw water. Jesus said to her: "Give me to drink." The woman, surprised, asked Him: "How dost Thou, being a Jew, ask of me to drink, who am a Samaritan[2] woman!"

---

[1] *Sichar.* It was here that Abraham received a revelation from God, and raised to the Lord the first altar built in the Promised Land (Old Test. IX). Here Jacob dwelt for a long time after his return from Haran. He bought a field and dug a well which exists to this day. It is walled in and is more than eighty feet deep.

[2] *A Samaritan.* In a former chapter (Old Test. LXVII) you learnt that the Samaritans were chiefly of heathen extraction, and did not belong to the chosen people; and again (Old Test. LXXX) that they became hostile to the Jews and wished to hinder the re-building of Jerusalem. This enmity grew with time, till at length it reached such a pitch that the Jews would hold no intercourse at all with the Samaritans. This was why the woman wondered that Jesus should talk to her and ask her for water; for she believed that a Jew would rather endure thirst than ask for water from a Samaritan. She did not meet the request of Jesus in

Jesus said to her: "If thou didst know the gift of God, and who it is that saith to thee, 'Give me to drink,' thou, perhaps, wouldst have asked of Him, and He would have given thee living water."[1] The woman replied: "Sir, Thou hast nothing wherein to draw, and the well is deep; whence then hast Thou living water? Art Thou greater than our father Jacob[2], who gave us the well?"

Jesus answered: "Whosoever drinketh of this water, shall thirst again; but he that shall drink of the water that I shall give[3] him, shall not thirst for ever. The water that I shall give him, shall become in him a fountain of water, springing up into everlasting life." Then the woman spoke again: "Sir, give me this water that I may not thirst, nor come hither[4] to draw."

Thereupon Jesus said: "Go and call thy husband." She answered: "I have no husband." Jesus replied: "Thou hast said well; for thou hast had five husbands, and he whom thou now hast, is not thy husband." The woman exclaimed: "Sir, I perceive that Thou art a prophet."[5]

---

an unfriendly way, and was quite ready to draw the water for Him, but she was astonished that He should ask it of her. As a reward for her kindliness Jesus entered into conversation with her, in order to draw her on little by little to a knowledge of the Messias.

[1] *Living water.* The ordinary meaning of living water is fresh or running water. But our Lord applied the expression to the life-giving grace which flows from Him upon those who believe in Him.

[2] *Our father Jacob.* She thought He must be referring to the actual spring of water at the bottom of the well, so her words meant: "You cannot get the living water from this well, for you have nothing with which you can reach so deep down. Where will you get better water than from this well? Jacob and his sons could find none better in the country. Are you wiser and more powerful than Jacob? Can you, like Moses, procure water miraculously?" She said "our father Jacob", because she erroneously believed that the Samaritans were descended from him.

[3] *The water that I shall give.* Our Lord now gave her to understand that he was speaking of no natural water. The water which He will give is quite different from any natural water, for its effects are eternal. He spoke of the water of divine grace.

[4] *Come hither.* Even now the woman did not yet understand our Lord's words, but thought that the water He referred to would quench bodily thirst for ever. "Sir", she said, "give me of this water." She showed by these words that she quite believed now that Jesus was greater than Jacob, and was able to give water, the effects of which would be miraculously lasting.

[5] *A prophet.* When Jesus saw her readiness to believe, He revealed Himself to her in a different light; and told her that she had hitherto led a dissolute life and had already had several husbands. Ashamed and confounded at this revelation

"Our fathers adored on this mountain[1], and you say that at Jerusalem is the place where men must adore." Jesus said to her: "Woman, believe me, the hour cometh, when you shall neither on this mountain, nor in Jerusalem, adore the Father. The hour cometh[2], and now is, when the true adorers shall adore the Father in spirit and in truth. God is a Spirit, and they that adore Him, must adore Him in spirit and in truth."

The woman answered Him: "I know that the Messias, when He is come, will tell us all things." Jesus replied: "I am He[3] who am speaking with thee."

Rejoiced[4] at this news, the woman left her pitcher, and, going into the city in all haste, she said to the people: "Come out and see a man who has told me all my sins. Is not He the Christ!"[5] Meanwhile the disciples, returning with the food they

---

of her misdeeds, she cried out: "Sir, I perceive that Thou art a prophet!" The fact that Jesus, whom she had never seen before, should know her secret sins and her mode of living, made her say to herself: "This stranger must be a prophet to whom God has revealed hidden things." She did not deny her sin, nor did she excuse it; but acknowledged the truth of what He had said, by the words: "I perceive that Thou art a prophet." As she now believed Him to be a prophet sent by God, she seized the opportunity to put before Him the chief point of dissension between the Jews and Samaritans, or as we should say, to raise the religious question, having full confidence that she would learn the truth from His lips.

[1] *This mountain.* Mount Garizim was near Sichar, and reared itself above the valley to the height of 800 feet. In the year 400 B. C. the Samaritans had built a temple on this mountain, where schismatical Jewish priests offered sacrifice until the year 131, when the temple was destroyed by Hyrcanus Machabeus.

[2] *The hour cometh.* By this answer Jesus revealed to the woman that a new era had dawned, in which the ancient worship would cease, not only on Mount Garizim, but also at Jerusalem, giving place to a better and more perfect worship. The woman did not completely understand Jesus, nor did she comprehend what sort of a worship was to be established, but she believed His assertion that a new era and a new worship would arise. She believed also in the Messias and shared the general expectation that He would soon come, and therefore she said: "When He will come, He will tell us all things."

[3] *I am He.* Jesus now revealed Himself fully to her, saying: "I am He; I am the Messias whom you are expecting."

[4] *Rejoiced.* The woman quite believed what Jesus said, and was speechless with joyful surprise. Just then the disciples returned and spoke with their Master. Then the woman left her pitcher and hastened back to the town. She quite forgot why she had come to the well; she could only think of the joy of having found the Messias, and was full of longing to impart the good news to her townsfolk.

[5] *Is not He the Christ.* She did not say this because she doubted, but because she wished to induce the people of Sichar to come and see and hear Jesus for themselves.

had purchased, pressed Jesus to eat [1]. But He said to them: "I have food to eat that you know not of. My food is to do the will of Him that sent me."

While He was speaking to His apostles, the Samaritans coming out of the city desired that He would stay there. He therefore remained two days [2] teaching and instructing them. Many of that city believed; and they said to the woman: "We now believe not for thy saying, for we ourselves [3] have heard Him, and we know that this is indeed the Saviour of the world."

COMMENTARY.

Jesus is the Messias and Redeemer promised by God. Our Lord made Himself known as such to the Samaritan woman: "I am He who am speaking to thee."

Jesus is God. By revealing to the Samaritan woman the hidden secrets of her conscience, He manifested His omniscience.

Jesus is full of Grace and Truth. The living water which Jesus gives is His divine doctrine and grace. His doctrine and grace give supernatural and eternal life to the soul, which, without grace, is dead and in a state of mortal sin. The human soul thirsts for truth and happiness, and our Lord satisfies this thirst by His doctrine and grace. For he who believes in His teaching and lives in His grace, is at peace with himself and with God, finds joy and calm in the midst of the vicissitudes of this life, and will attain to the inconceivable happiness of heaven.

The Love of Jesus. In spite of His fatigue Jesus seized the op- portunity to save the soul of the sinful woman of Samaria, and to reveal Himself to her and her townsfolk. His zeal for souls, that is, His ardent desire to save souls, made Him forget His hunger and fatigue.

---

[1] *To eat.* The disciples urged Jesus to refresh Himself with food, but He told them that He required no earthly food. He had forgotten His hunger, being possessed by the greater hunger to do the will of His Father, i. e. to fulfil His calling of Messias, and save souls; and this hunger could only be appeased by the conversion of the people of Sichar.

[2] *Remained two days.* They had taken the woman's word that Jesus was the Messias, and He, seeing their good will, remained with them two days and taught them.

[3] *We ourselves.* The teaching of Jesus confirmed their faith, and they were able to say confidently: "We know that this is the Saviour of the world!" The seed which Jesus Himself sowed in Samaria did not prove unfruitful, for we shall see in chapter LXXXVII that the Samaritans were in the time of the apostles the most considerable body of Christians outside Jerusalem.

The Worship of God in Spirit and in Truth. In what does this consist? We must first of all understand that both the question of the woman and our Lord's answer refer to the public and common worship of God by sacrifices and ceremonial. Jews and Samaritans alike knew very well that God can be worshipped everywhere, but as regarded His public worship, laid down in the Law, the Jews affirmed that this could only be offered at Jerusalem, while the Samaritans affirmed the same of Mount Garizim. (In Old Test. XIII, we find the word "worship" used as synonymous with the offering of sacrifice, as when Abraham said to his servants: "When I and the boy have worshipped" &c.). Jesus told the woman that the dispute between the Jews and Samaritans would soon have no meaning, for the time had come when a new worship was to replace the old one. And this new worship was to differ from the old both as to place and kind, for 1. it would be universal, and 2. it would be a worship in spirit and truth. The ancient worship of the Jews was not a worship "in truth" but only "in shadows", i. e. in types and figures of the truth. The truth is to be found only in that Sacrifice ordained by Jesus Christ, even the holy Sacrifice of the Mass, which is the fulfilment of the typical sacrifices. The offering up of the spotless Victim of the New Testament is the highest act of worship possible, and is, indeed, the worship of God in truth. Again, the worship of the Jews was not a worship "in spirit", but "in matter", the sacrifices consisting only in things material which could not cleanse the conscience of the worshipper. In the new worship Jesus says that God will be adored in spirit, i. e. by a truly spiritual sacrifice and victim, the Lamb of God, and that the hearts of men will be cleansed and spiritually united to Him, by faith, hope, charity and contrition, and thus will a worship be offered worthy of Him who receives it. At the same time this new worship will not be limited to one place, but will be spread over the whole face of the earth, and in it will be fulfilled the words which God spoke through Malachias the prophet: "I have no pleasure in you and I will not receive a gift of your hand. For from the rising of the sun even to the going down ... there is sacrifice, and there is offered to My name a clean oblation" (Old Test. LXXXII). All our Lord's discourse on this worship of God in spirit and truth points to the spotless and unbloody Sacrifice of the New Law, in which the typical sacrifices of the Old Law have found their fulfilment. It also contains an exhortation to us to lift up our hearts to God, when we pray, and not to honour God with our lips only (Is. 29, 13).

Correspondence with Grace. We can see by the case of the woman of Samaria, how only those obtain salvation who correspond with grace. The first or prevenient grace which the woman received, consisted in being asked by Jesus to render Him a service of love. She might have refused our Lord's request and said: "You Jews are never civil to us: you hate and despise us!" But she overcame her national antipathy and proffered to our Lord the service He asked for. As a reward for this our

Lord entered into conversation with her, and spoke to her about the wonderful living water. The woman believed that He could give her such water and asked Him for some. She was ashamed and humbled herself, when He reminded her of her sins. She accepted the hard truth, and acknowledged her guilt without excusing it. Then Jesus gave her further grace and revealed Himself to her as the Messias. She believed and with an apostolic spirit tried to spread the faith among her townsfolk.

APPLICATION. Do you honour God merely with your lips? Do you pray with attention? Do you worship God in spirit and truth by hearing Mass, and hearing it with devotion and with a clean conscience in the state of grace? Make a resolution to say all your prayers from this time forward with recollection and devotion.

CHAPTER XVII.

JESUS PREACHES AT NAZARETH.

[John 4, 43—45. Luke 4, 16—30. Mark 6, 1—6. Mat. 13, 54.]

FROM Sichar Jesus returned to Nazareth, in His own country[1], and preached the word of life[2], as He went. Now in Nazareth He entered the synagogue[3], on the Sabbath-day, and stood up[4] to read. They[5] gave Him the book of Isaias[6] the prophet. He unfolded[7] the book and found[8] the place where it was written[9]:

---

[1] *His own country*. Galilee was called thus, because Jesus had hitherto lived there with His foster-father.

[2] *Word of life*. The good news that the reign of the Messias, of redemption and of grace had begun.

[3] *The synagogue*. This was the name given to the house of prayer in every town, in which the Jews assembled in order to pray together and to read the Old Testament Scriptures.

[4] *Stood up*. As a sign that He too wished to read out of the sacred books. The reading was preceded by prayers in which the speedy coming of the Messias was urgently asked for. The holy Scriptures were read standing as an outward token of respect for the word of God.

[5] *They*. i. e. the servers of the synagogue.

[6] *Isaias*. It being the turn for this book.

[7] *Unfolded*. The books of the ancients were written, not printed, and were rolled up, something like a school-map, instead of being laid flat and bound up.

[8] *Found*. Not accidentally, but with a wise purpose.

[9] *Written*. The passage which Jesus read was taken from Isaias 61, 1 2. It was acknowledged by all the Jews to relate to the Messias, who is himself uttering the words quoted.

"The Spirit of the Lord is upon me; wherefore He hath anointed [1] me to preach the gospel to the poor. He hath sent me to heal [2] the contrite of heart, to preach deliverance [3] to the captives [4] and sight to the blind, to set at liberty them that are bruised, to preach the acceptable year [5] of the Lord and the day of reward." [6]

When He had closed the book, He returned it to the minister and sat down [7]. But the eyes of all the synagogue were fixed upon Him. He then told them: "This day is fulfilled [8] this scripture in your ears."

As He thus continued His discourse, all wondered [9] at the words of grace that fell from His lips. Still they did not believe in Him; for they said one to another: "Is not this the son of Joseph?" [10]

But He, answering them, said: "Amen, I say to you that no prophet is accepted [11] in his own country [12]. There were many widows in the days of Elias in Israel, when heaven was shut three years and six months, when there was a great famine throughout

---

[1] *Anointed.* The Lord hath made me God and man; therefore am I His anointed, His Christ.

[2] *To heal.* From their sins.   [3] *Deliverance.* Spiritual.

[4] *The captives.* Of sin and the devil.

[5] *Year.* The jubilee or year of restoration.

[6] *Reward.* Or of judgment.

[7] *Sat down.* As a sign that He wished to expound what He had read, such explanatory discourses being made sitting.

[8] *Fulfilled.* The Messias who is foretold in this passage sits now before you. Thus Jesus explicitly declared that He was the Messias, who had brought grace and truth to all men.

[9] *All wondered.* The words of Jesus were so full of grace, so persuasive and moving, and they flowed from His mouth so easily and sweetly that they made a great impression on His hearers and astounded them. The impression, however, was only a passing one. Soon the doubt occurred to them: Is not this the carpenter's son, whom we have known from his youth? He is of poor parents and is a carpenter (Mark 6, 3); how can this be the Messias? They were offended at His poverty and lowliness, despised His honourable trade, and would not, therefore, believe in Him. Jesus saw with pain the scepticism of His own fellow-citizens and said to them with solemn earnestness: Amen, I say to you &c.

[10] *Joseph.* As if they wished to say that He was of poor parents, and that He had not received a liberal education.

[11] *Accepted.* Well received.

[12] *His own country.* It is with me as it was with the prophets, who found no hearing among their fellow-countrymen, to whom they were sent. Then our Lord quoted the examples of the two prophets, Elias and Eliseus, who worked such great miracles, and who yet found less belief among the Israelites than among the heathen (Old Test. LXII).

all the land. Yet to none of them was Elias sent but to a widow at Sarepta of Sidon. There were also many lepers in Israel in the time of Eliseus the prophet; yet none of them was cleansed but Naaman the Syrian." [1]

Now all those who heard these things in the synagogue were filled with anger [2]. And rising up, they drove Him out of the city, and took Him to the brow of a mountain to cast Him down headlong. But He, striking them with a sudden terror, passed through their midst [3] and went His way.

COMMENTARY.

Jesus is the Messias. He proclaimed Himself to be such, when He said: "What the prophet says about the Messias is fulfilled in and by Me."

Jesus is God. He proved this by the miracle He wrought at Nazareth, passing through the crowd of the furious Nazarenes, who were thirsting for His Blood, without any one among them being able to withstand Him.

Resistance of Grace. In the last chapter we saw how salvation comes to those who correspond with grace. In this chapter we have a terrible example of how salvation is forfeited by resisting grace. The Nazarenes were impressed by the discourse of Jesus, but they did not obey the call of grace which was knocking at their hearts. They resisted it, and *would* not believe.

Causes of unbelief. The Nazarenes had heard of the great miracle which Jesus had worked close to them at Cana. They had also been to Jerusalem for the Pasch and had witnessed the miracles He worked there (chapter XV); and now He came to them and revealed Himself to be the Messias. Still they did not believe in Him, but tried to kill Him. What was the cause of their unbelief? Firstly, their carnal-mindedness. They expected an earthly Messias, who would be a great prince, and would drive away the Romans and make Israel great in

---

[1] *The Syrian.* No Israelite had as much faith as the pagan Naaman (Old Test. LXV).

[2] *With anger.* They felt the severity of our Lord's reproof. The truth, however, irritated them instead of converting them. As they could not refute His words, they tried to kill Him, for falsely (as they said) setting Himself up to be the Messias.

[3] *Their midst.* To the edge of the mountain, where there were several precipices which can still be seen. He allowed them to force Him thither; but once there, He turned round and passed with calm majesty through the crowd of persecutors, who, subdued by a supernatural force, stood there helpless and, as it were, paralysed.

the eyes of the world. The lowliness and poverty of Jesus, therefore, offended them. They wanted their Redeemer to bring them great worldly advantages; they did not care for truth, grace and salvation. Secondly, they despised Jesus, because they had known Him from His childhood; for, as a rule, men do not respect those with whom they are very familiar. Thirdly, a feeling of envy probably arose in them: "Is this man, who is poorer than any of us, to be greater than we are!" The same causes, antipathy to the supernatural, pride &c. &c., are in the present time at the root of much unbelief.

The Sanctification of the Sabbath by frequenting divine services and hearing the word of God. Jesus was in the habit, from His youth up, of going to the synagogue every Sabbath.

Labour honourable. Jesus has sanctified and raised labour and all handicraft to a position of dignity, because, until He began His public life, He followed the trade of a carpenter.

The Sufferings of Jesus. It wounded our Lord's Sacred Heart to be ignored and rejected by His own townsfolk. The Samaritans believed, but the Nazarenes would not believe, and even maltreated Him. Jesus left Nazareth and wandered about without a home, among the very people whom He had come down from heaven to save.

Anger, a capital sin. It was anger which made the Nazarenes attempt to kill Jesus.

Holy Scripture. Jesus, by His reading and subsequent discourse, testified that the prophecies of Isaias were inspired by God. Also, by citing the cases of Elias and Eliseus, He attested that these holy men were indeed sent by God, and that they really worked the miracles which are related of them in Holy Scripture.

———

APPLICATION. You have been accustomed from your childhood to the Presence of Jesus in the most holy Sacrament of the Altar, and to the holy Sacrifice of the Mass. Take care that you do not think lightly of them! "If this most holy Sacrament were only in one place, and consecrated by only one priest in the world, how great a desire would men have to go to that place and to such a priest of God, that they might see the divine mysteries celebrated" (Imit. of Christ 4, 1). Should your reverence and devotion be less, because Jesus of His infinite love is present on so many altars, and is daily offered up? Would not this be a shameful want of gratitude?

CHAPTER XVIII.

MIRACLES OF JESUS AT CAPHARNAUM.

[Luke 4, 31 —44. Mark 1, 21—39. Mat. 4, 13—17 and 8, 13.]

FROM Nazareth Jesus went to Capharnaum[1], and there He taught them on the Sabbath-days. The people were astonished at His doctrine, and at the wonderful force and unction of His preaching. There was, in the synagogue, a man who had an unclean spirit[2], and he[3] cried aloud, saying: "Let us[4] alone, what have we to do with Thee[5], Jesus of Nazareth? Art Thou come to destroy us?[6] I know Thee, who Thou art, the Holy One of God."[7]

Jesus rebuked the spirit, commanding him to be silent[8], and to go out from the man. Then the devil, throwing the man into the midst of the crowd, went out of him, and left him

---

[1] *Capharnaum.* Capharnaum, situated on the north-west shore of the Lake of Genesareth, was a busy commercial town, much frequented by travellers, in which many Gentiles lived. Here Jesus dwelt, not as a house-holder, but merely as a guest in the house of Simon Peter. Simon was a native of Bethsaida, and had probably obtained possession of his house in Capharnaum by his marriage. From this house Jesus went forth on His many journeys for the conversion of sinners; and for this reason Capharnaum is spoken of as "his town".

[2] *Unclean spirit.* A devil had taken possession of this man, governing his senses and bodily organs. A man thus possessed was no longer his own master. His consciousness and free-will were impeded and governed by the evil spirit, under whose despotism he lived.

[3] *He.* The possessed man uttered the words, but it was the devil who really cried out through him. The near presence of Jesus, the Most Holy One, who had overcome the tempter, filled the evil spirit with anguish and terror.

[4] *Us.* He used the plural number, because he felt sure that Jesus had come to destroy the power of all the infernal spirits.

[5] *With Thee.* We wish to have nothing to do with you: leave us in peace.

[6] *Destroy us.* To take from us the dominion of the world, and banish us to hell.

[7] *The Holy One of God.* How did the devil know this? He knew it by the irresistible authority of Jesus, which he was constrained to obey. He knew that the power which rested both in His commands and in the very touch of His Hands, was a divine power.

[8] *To be silent.* Jesus refused to receive testimony to His Godhead from the spirit of lies, who only speaks the truth with an evil intention. According to the plan of divine wisdom our Lord's Divinity was to be revealed little by little. Men were to come to the knowledge of it by degrees, and not by the premature testimony of the devil. Thus Jesus refused to be questioned by this evil spirit, and said to him: "Be still." Hence Spiritism is unlawful.

unharmed[1]. A great fear[2] came upon all who witnessed this miracle, and they said one to another: "What word is this? For with authority and power He commandeth the unclean spirits, and they go out."

From the synagogue Jesus went to the house of Simon Peter. It so happened that the mother-in-law of Peter was grievously sick[3], and Jesus was asked[4] to cure her. He drew near her bed, commanded the fever, and it left her. Immediately[5] she arose, cured of the fever, and waited on them as they sat at table.

When the sun was down[6], the sick and infirm[7] of the city were brought to Jesus, and He laid His hands upon them, and they were healed.

Early next morning He left Capharnaum and retired to a desert place[8]. But the people followed Him in crowds, beseeching Him not to leave them. He said to them: "I must preach the kingdom of God[9] in other places also; for therefore am I sent."

---

[1] *Unharmed.* The devil was obliged to obey the command of Jesus and come out of the man; but, before he did so, he showed his spite against his victim by throwing him to the ground. His rage, however, was futile, for he could not hurt the man, and left him quite restored to himself.

[2] *Great fear.* A holy awe.

[3] *Sick.* Of fever.

[4] *Asked.* It was the disciples Simon and Andrew as well as James and John (these according to Mark 1, 29 being also present), who made this petition. James, the brother of John, had therefore also become a disciple.

[5] *Immediately.* She prepared and served food for them. This shows that she had immediately recovered her full strength, whereas generally a person who has had a fever remains weak and exhausted for a long time.

[6] *The sun was down.* i. e. when the Sabbath was over. The Sabbath of the Jews began at sunset on Friday evening, and ended at sunset on Saturday. The Feasts began and ended in the same way.

[7] *The sick and infirm.* Besides those actually sick there were present those who carried them, as well as many of their friends and relations, who were attracted by curiosity. Picture the scene to yourselves—the sick moaning and crying for help, while those possessed by evil spirits raged and howled; and all present turning their eyes on Jesus, full of expectation and wonder whether He would be able to cure all who were there. Picture Jesus passing from one sick person to another, laying His Hand on each, and behold, each one was cured, whatsoever his malady!

[8] *Desert place.* On a neighbouring mountain.

[9] *The kingdom of God.* i. e. the message of salvation.

He then preached in the synagogues of Galilee: "The time is accomplished, and the kingdom of God is at hand[1]; repent and believe the Gospel." He healed all manner of diseases; and the fame of His power and holiness spread over all the country[2], and people came from far and near to see and hear Him.

COMMENTARY.

The Divinity of our Lord. The astounding miracles which Jesus wrought, in the presence of so many people, are a proof of His Divine Omnipotence. He took the death-stricken mother-in-law of Peter by the hand, and immediately she got up well and strong. He laid His hand on the sick who were brought to Him in front of Peter's house, and at once they were cured. He drove the devils out of those whom they possessed, and imposed silence on them by His word. "What is this?" asked the awe-struck people; "that He commandeth even the unclean spirits and they go out!" This was a proof that Jesus is Lord not only of the visible creation, but of the unseen world of spirits as well.

The Kindness of Jesus was wonderful, for He helped all those who were afflicted by diseases and sickness. "He went about doing good" (Acts 10, 38).

The Prayer of Jesus, when He retired into a desert place, was one of intercession for sinful men. It was also an example to us to pray and not to faint (Luke 18, 1).

The Preaching of Jesus. The gist of our Lord's preaching was: "Repent and believe the Gospel." This is still, and will be for all time, the most important obligation of Christianity and the indispensable condition of salvation. He who wishes to have a part in the kingdom of God, must believe in our Lord and His teaching, and must do penance for his sins.

Dead faith. "The devils also believe and tremble", writes St. James (2, 19). These words are confirmed by the story we have just read, which relates that the devil confessed: "Thou art the Holy One of God." There is a faith which does not avail to salvation — a dead faith, which is not a free act of obedience and love.

The power of intercession. Our Lord yielded to the intercession of His disciples for Peter's mother-in-law. To pray for the living and

---

[1] *At hand.* The time of preparation and of waiting for the Messias is over, for the kingdom of the Messias, i. e. the kingdom which God will found through Him, has begun. Do penance, therefore, and believe the glad tidings.

[2] *All the country.* Throughout Galilee.

the dead is a work of mercy and a duty of brotherly love. "Pray for one another that you may be saved", writes St. James (5, 16).

The hatred and power of the devil. The devil hates and envies man, and does all he can to injure him. Before our Lord came, the devil had obtained a great power over men, especially over idolators; and when our Blessed Redeemer came to conquer Satan, the latter made a last and desperate effort to maintain his supremacy. This is why, during our Lord's sojourn on earth, there were so many cases of possession. They were by the eternal counsel of God permitted, in order that the object of our Lord's mission as well as His power and glory might be made manifest.

Exorcisms. Cases of possession still occur: but the Church, by exorcisms, drives away the evil spirit in the name of Jesus.

The cruelty of the devil. Jesus allowed the devil to throw down the possessed man and rend him, to show us from how cruel an enemy He has delivered us; and to put us on our guard, lest we should allow ourselves to be subjected to his everlasting rage.

Jesus the Physician of our souls. We too are sick of a fever—the fever of anger, ambition, covetousness, gluttony, and all other passions, which incite us to evil and keep us from what is good. Jesus alone can cure us. He can give us grace to overcome our evil inclinations, if only we will ask Him for it; and He will cool the ardour of our passions by His Presence, if we worthily receive Him in Holy Communion.

APPLICATION. Are you prompt in getting up in the morning, or have you to be called several times? Prize the golden hours of the morning.

Do you say your morning prayers devoutly every day? and do you make good resolutions, when you say them? Begin the day with God, and your day will not be spent without Him.

CHAPTER XIX.

THE MIRACULOUS DRAUGHT OF FISH.

[Luke 5, 1—11. Mat. 4, 18—22. Mark 1, 16—20.]

JESUS preached one day near the Lake of Genesareth [1], which is also called the Sea of Galilee. A great crowd came to Him to hear the word of God [2]. He saw moored on the shore two

---

[1] *Lake of Genesareth.* This lake (Fig. 71, p. 462), which is about thirteen miles long and six broad, is oval and surrounded by mountains. To this day it is well stocked with fish. In the time of our Lord, its shores and the plain between it and the foot of the mountains were covered with populous towns and villages.

[2] *The word of God.* The preaching of Jesus, the Son of God.

fishing-boats, one of which belonged to Simon Peter; and, going into Peter's boat, He desired him to put off a little from the shore. Then, seating Himself in the bark, He taught the people.

When he had ceased preaching, He told Peter: "Launch out into the deep[1], and let down your nets for a draught." Peter

Fig. 71. Lake of Genesareth with the Ruins of Tiberias. (Phot. Bonfils.)

answered: "Master, we have laboured all night[2] and have taken nothing, but at Thy word[3] I will let down the nets." Having done so, they caught so great a multitude of fish that their net

---

[1] *The deep.* From the shallow water near the shores into the middle of the lake, where the water was deeper. The words: "Launch out!" were addressed to Peter, he being in command of the little ship, whereas the words: "Let down your nets", were addressed to all those who were assisting, of whom there must have been a good number, for, later on, the Gospel speaks of "all who were with him".

[2] *All night.* "We have already been out in the deep sea, casting our nets, first here, then there." They went out fishing in the night, as fish are more easily caught then than in the day-time.

[3] *At Thy word.* "In obedience to Thee, and confiding in Thy help." He meant to say: "Having caught nothing in the night-time, we cannot naturally expect to catch any thing in the broad day-light; but we have confidence that, if we act in obedience to Thy command, our labour will not be in vain. The miracle which ensued was a reward for this faith and confidence, as well as for the service rendered by the loan of the boat."

was breaking [1]. They beckoned [2] to their partners, James and John, who were in the other bark, to come and assist them. They came, and both barks were so filled with fish that they were in danger of sinking.

Wonder and terror came upon all that were in the ships. But Simon Peter fell down at the feet [3] of Jesus, saying: "Depart [4] from me, for I am a sinful man, O Lord." Jesus said to him: "Fear not, from henceforth thou shalt catch men." [5] Having pushed their ships ashore, they left all things [6] and followed [7] Jesus.

COMMENTARY.

The Divinity of our Lord. Jesus, by the miraculous draught of fish which He procured for His disciples, showed that He was Lord over nature. The fish of the sea obeyed His will and gathered together in the place where the disciples cast in their nets.

The object of this miracle which Jesus worked solely for Peter and the other disciples was twofold: 1. Like all the other miracles it was meant to increase and confirm the faith of the disciples; 2. it was meant to prepare the disciples, and especially St. Peter, for the apostolic office, which was typified by this miracle. Through it Jesus meant to say to His disciples: "Even as just now you put out to sea and cast in your nets, at my bidding, and captured this extraordinary draught, so in the future shall you fish for the souls of men in the sea of this world; and you will have as great a success in that office as you have had just now with your nets, and will bring thousands of souls into the kingdom of God, i. e. the Church." Thus the miraculous draught of fish typifies the apostolic work of the Church of Jesus Christ. The sea is the world; the fish are the men living in the world. The bark is the Church; the helmsman is Peter (and his successors). He steers the bark, and with the help of his companions (the Apostles, and after them the Bishops), casts his net by preaching the doctrine of Christ, and by holy Baptism receives into the Church those who will believe. Our Lord Jesus Christ is in the bark of Peter, i. e in the holy Catholic Church, teaching men,

---

[1] *Breaking.* There were such large holes in the nets that many of the fish escaped, and yet, in spite of this, both little ships were filled with fish.

[2] *Beckoned.* i. e. made signs to them to come and help, because they were too far from the shore for calling.

[3] *At the feet of Jesus.* Who was with him in the boat.

[4] *Depart.* Leave my boat, because I, a sinful man, am not worthy to be so near to Thee.

[5] *Men.* By these words He encouraged Simon, and explained to him the meaning of the miracle He had just wrought.

[6] *Left all things.* That were dear to them, their family, home, and occupation.

[7] *Followed.* As His constant disciples.

and bringing them to salvation through her. The danger of sinking
which threatened Peter's little ship, signifies that the Church will be
beset by many perils and persecutions. The rent in the net, through
which so many of the fish escaped, means that many souls will be lost
to the Church by schism and heresy. The first "draught of fish" (i. e. of
souls) which Peter made on the day of Pentecost, was an extraordinay
one, 3000 being baptized. And after his second discourse, when he
had cured the lame man, the number of those baptized amounted to
5000. The conversion of the world by ignorant fishermen is one of
God's greatest miracles. To this very day the Pope, St. Peter's successor,
keeps sending forth his fishermen into all parts of the world, in as
much as he alone gives real power and jurisdiction to bishops, priests,
and missionaries to teach the truth of Jesus Christ and to sanctify souls
by His Sacraments.

Listening to the word of God. The way that the crowd pressed
round Jesus to hear Him is an example to us of the zeal with which
we should listen to God's word.

Industry. "We have toiled all the night", said St. Peter. Industry
is a virtue, whereas sloth is a sin.

The Blessing of God. In all our occupations we should bear in
mind that nothing can prosper without God's blessing.

St. Peter's virtues, as shown by this story: 1. Faith. He believed
that he would not put out to sea in vain, if he did so at our Lord's
bidding. 2. Obedience. 3. Humility. "Depart from me, for I am a
sinful man, O Lord." Because he humbled himself, our Lord exalted
him, and called him, before the others, to be a fisher of men. 4. Love
of Jesus. He left all and followed Him.

The following of Christ is the way of virtue and perfection. We
need not forsake everything as did the Apostles, but we must follow
the example given to us by our Lord, if we would be with them in
heaven. "Christ also suffered for us, leaving you an example that you
should follow His steps" (1 Pet. 2, 21). He who wishes to be a real
Christian must not only believe in Christ, but must follow Him, i. e.
must imitate His virtues, His love of God and of His neighbour, His
obedience, humility, meekness &c.

APPLICATION. Do you like work? Do you learn your lessons
well and regularly? Do you help without grumbling in the work
about the house given you to do by your parents? Do you work
with a good intention? Whenever you are told to do anything
distasteful to you, say to yourself: "O Jesus, I will do this for
love of Thee!"

CHAPTER XX.

THE CURE OF THE PARALYTIC, AND FORGIVENESS OF SIN.

[Mark 2, 1—12. Mat. 9, 1—8. Luke 5, 17—26.]

JESUS returned to Capharnaum, and, as He was teaching in a private house, a great multitude of people, coming to hear Him, filled the house and crowded round it. But behold, four men brought a paralytic [1] on a bed, and as they could not get near to Jesus on account of the throng [2], they went up on the roof [3] of the house, and making an opening [4], let down the paralytic in his bed.

Jesus, seeing their faith [5], said: "Son, be of good heart, thy sins [6] are forgiven thee."

Now there were among the crowd some Scribes and Pharisees [7], who, hearing these words, thought within themselves: "He blasphemeth. Who can forgive sins but God alone?" Jesus, seeing their thoughts, said to them: "Why do you think evil in your hearts? Which is easier [8], to say: 'Thy sins are forgiven thee?' or to say: 'Rise up, take thy bed and walk?' But that you may know that the Son of Man hath power on earth to forgive sins, I say to thee: 'Arise, take up thy bed, and go into thy house.'"

---

[1] *A paralytic.* i. e. one who was wholly paralysed, so that he could use none of his limbs, but had to be carried about.

[2] *The throng.* The people being packed together as tightly as they could be in the passages and rooms, passing through was quite an impossibility.

[3] *On the roof.* A staircase on the outside of the house led directly to the roof.

[4] *An opening.* By removing a part of the roof, which was at the same time the ceiling of the room below.

[5] *Their faith.* The extraordinary amount of trouble they had taken to convey the sick man to Jesus as speedily as possible, proved both their faith and their desire for help.

[6] *Thy sins.* As the lame man lay before Jesus and raised his eyes to Him, he trembled before the Holy One of God, and, contrite and abashed, cast down his eyes. But Jesus beheld his contrition, and tenderly, addressing him as "Son", comforted him and forgave him his sins.

[7] *Scribes and Pharisees.* Our Lord's miracles and increasing fame in Galilee had stirred up the Pharisees and Scribes throughout the whole land. They came to Capharnaum not only from Galilee, but also from Judæa and Jerusalem to watch Jesus (Luke 5, 17).

[8] *Which is easier?* It is easy enough to say the first, for nobody can look into a man's soul, and see whether he be really cleansed from sin or not. Any deceiver or false prophet could say such words without his deception being proved; but to say to a lame man "Rise up and walk" is a very much harder thing, for it can be proved on the spot whether his words have any power or no.

Immediately the man arose, took up his bed[1] and went forth in the sight of all. And all the people wondered and glorified God[2], saying: "We never saw the like!"

COMMENTARY.

Proofs of our Lord's Divinity. 1. He saw the contrition, faith and hope which were in the soul of the paralysed man, in the same manner as He read the secret thoughts of the Pharisees: therefore He was Omniscient. God alone is Omniscient: therefore Jesus is God. 2. Jesus is Omnipotent; for by His will and word He instantaneously cured the lame man. Even as at the creation He said: "Let things be," so now He said to the palsied man: "Arise!" 3. Jesus, by His own power, absolved the lame man of his sins. This, as the Pharisees very rightly judged, is the prerogative of God, who is offended by sins, and who knows the heart of the sinner: therefore Jesus is God. Had He not been God, He would have been assuming to Himself a divine right and power, and would have been a deceiver and a blasphemer.

Blasphemy. It was the Pharisees who were blasphemers, because, in spite of His miracles and holiness, they despised Jesus and accused Him of blasphemy. Their reason must have told them that God would not be with a blasphemer, and that therefore no blasphemer could work such mighty miracles. But their evil wills and evil hearts obscured their reason, and made them obstinate and defiant. Their unbelief was without excuse.

The dignity of the soul. Jesus first healed the palsied man's soul, and then his body. He desired to teach us by this that He came to cure and save souls, that the soul is worth more than the body, and that the health of the body can only avail those whose soul is healthy. Our love of ourselves ought therefore to be bestowed first of all on our souls.

The necessity of contrition. The sick man possessed real contrition. His sins oppressed and tormented him more than his bodily infirmity;

---

[1] *Took up his bed.* Our Lord, by His word, cured the man so instantaneously that he was able to take up and carry off his bed without help. This should have proved to the Pharisees that our Lord's former words: "Thy sins are forgiven thee," had been equally powerful, and had remitted the man's sins. Jesus had proved that He was no blasphemer; and as his enemies could not deny His power, they remained silent.

[2] *Glorified God.* The people were seized with a holy awe, for they felt that only a divine power could have worked such a miracle: and the Gospel says that "they glorified God who gave such power to men". For as Jesus, the Son of Man, stood before them in a lowly human form, they did not perceive that He was God, and had worked this miracle by His own power, but believed that God had given the power to Him, a man.

and with one beseeching glance he prayed to Jesus for forgiveness. Jesus saw that the state of his soul pained him more than that of his body, and that what he most craved for was pardon and peace; and therefore He said to him: "Son, be of good heart, thy sins are forgiven." If the sick man had had no contrition, he would not have obtained pardon.

The Compassion of Jesus on repentant sinners. He lovingly addressed the sick man as "son", and consoled him.

The object of sufferings. The severe malady of the lame man was perhaps a consequence or a punishment of his sins. God allowed this terrible infirmity to overtake this sinner and torment his body, so that he might learn to repent of his sins, and thus save his soul from everlasting perdition.

Sins of thought. The Pharisees sinned grievously by thought.

The forgiveness of sins by priests. You have just heard that God alone can forgive sins. But does not a priest forgive sins in the Sacrament of Penance? Yes, but he does so not in his own name and by his own authority as Jesus did, but in the name and by the authority received from God—our Lord having left to the apostles and their successors the office of forgiving sins. By the Sacrament of Penance our Lord gave to his Church a really divine power, for the comfort and salvation of sinful men. Let us too, then, "glorify God who has given such power to men".

Indulgences. The palsied man receives first the forgiveness of his sins, then his temporal punishment (the palsy) is removed. This is exactly what is done by indulgences, which are granted for the purpose of removing temporal punishment. Only he who is cleansed from mortal sin and is in a state of grace, can gain an indulgence.

APPLICATION. Do you suppress all bad thoughts—such as envy, pride, impurity, unkindness—as quickly as possible? God sees into your heart. If a bad thought occurs to you, say at once: "Begone!" and turn your thoughts to something that is holy.

Do you make a good act of thanksgiving after you have been to confession?

CHAPTER XXI.

THE SERMON ON THE MOUNT.

[Mat. 5 to 7, 29.]

O N one occasion, when Jesus saw a very great multitude[1] gathered together to hear Him, He went up into a mountain and sat down; and His disciples were with Him. The people

Fig. 72. Mount of the Beatitudes. (Phot. Bonfils.)

placed themselves around, and along the sides of the mountain (Fig. 72), waiting in respectful silence till He commenced to speak. Then He taught them:

---

[1] *Multitude.* The people had gathered together, not only from Judæa and Galilee, but from the countries to the north and east of Galilee, and even from the heathen countries of Tyre and Sidon. They had gathered together and were waiting for Jesus in the plain at the foot of the mountain, where He had spent the night in prayer. In order to be better able to speak to this crowd, He stood on a projection on the slope of the mountain. His apostles and disciples were gathered around and below Him, while on the plain stood or sat the vast multitude.

1. The eight Beatitudes.

"Blessed are the poor in spirit, for theirs is the kingdom of heaven. Blessed are the meek, for they shall possess the land[1]. Blessed are they that mourn, for they shall be comforted. Blessed are they who hunger and thirst[2] after justice, for they shall be filled. Blessed are the merciful[3], for they shall obtain mercy. Blessed are the clean of heart, for they shall see God. Blessed are the peacemakers, for they shall be called the children of God. Blessed are they who suffer persecution for justice' sake, for theirs is the kingdom of heaven. Blessed are you, when men shall revile and persecute you, and shall say all manner of evil against you falsely for My sake; rejoice and be exceeding glad, because your reward is very great in heaven."

COMMENTARY.

The poor in spirit are 1. the humble who know their own misery and sinfulness, and who confess by word and deed that they can do nothing of themselves, but that they have received from God all that is good in them. Examples: Joseph, Moses, Gedeon, David, Judith, John the Baptist, Peter. 2. the unworldly whose heart does not cling to worldly goods and pleasures, and who, be they rich or poor, have no inordinate desire for them. Example: Abraham, Job, Lazarus, the Apostles.

The meek are those who are not made angry or bitter by contradictions, injuries, or abuse. Example: David, in his conduct towards Saul and Absalom.

Mourning which is pleasing to God. There is a great deal of mourning and complaining in this "vale of tears", but all this mourning is not pleasing to God. When, for example, a man grieves, because his pride or his revenge or any other passion is not gratified, his sadness is the result of sin, and can in no way please God. Our sorrow for the dead, or for personal losses or disappointed hopes, is a holy sorrow only so far as it convinces us of the nothingness of the things of this world, and raises our hearts to God in worship and resignation.

---

[1] *The land.* The words "they shall possess the land, be comforted, have their fill, see God &c." are but different expressions of the same idea, i. e. "they will go to heaven".

[2] *Hunger and thirst.* Who crave for faith, virtue and the grace of God as eagerly as a starving man craves for food and drink.

[3] *Merciful.* Those who show mercy to others will find mercy at the judgment-seat of God.

The sorrow most pleasing to God is that of those who renounce the sinful joys of this world, and grieve over their own sins and the sins of others. Examples: Lot, Elias, Jeremias, Judith, John the Baptist.

Hunger after justice.* Men desire and strive after many things, but the best and noblest desire is for virtue and grace. Everything else perishes; only virtue endures. It is not enough for us to keep from mortal sin; we must be ever striving to attain to a higher degree of virtue. Examples: Simeon, Anna, Andrew and John, the Ethiopian Chamberlain.

Mercy is practised by those who, from a real love of their neighbours, are anxious to help them in their spiritual and corporal necessities. Examples: Abraham, Moses, Tobias, the good Samaritan.

Cleanness of heart consists in banishing from our hearts all impure thoughts and desires. This cleanness of heart is also called holy purity; it gives both joy and a taste for the supernatural, increases faith in the soul, and leads to the blessed vision of God. Examples: Joseph in Egypt, Judith, Susanna.

Peacemakers are those who hate discord, love and cherish concord, and try to restore it, when it has been disturbed. Example: Abraham.

Fortitude under persecution. Those suffer persecution for justice' sake who patiently and bravely endure scorn, contempt, neglect, poverty and any other penalty rather than give up either faith or virtue. Examples: Abel, Elias, Jeremias, Daniel and his companions, Eleazar, the Machabean brothers, John the Baptist, Stephen, and all martyrs.

The maxims of Christianity and the maxims of the world. In the Sermon on the Mount, and especially in the Beatitudes, our Lord proclaimed the ruling maxims of His kingdom. It was a discourse—new, utterly unheard-of, and coming straight from heaven! Blessed are the poor, the mourners—the persecuted! This was in direct opposition to the Jews' hopes of an earthly Messias, and showed plainly that His kingdom was not to be of this world, a kingdom of pomp and pleasure, but a kingdom of renouncement and self-denial. These maxims of our Lord's kingdom are in direct contrast to the maxims of the un-Christian world. In the world reign supreme the lust of the eyes, the lust of the flesh, and the pride of life. Its children say, "Come, let us enjoy the pleasures and good things of this earth. Do not deny your senses. Give free scope to your passions and desires. Allow no one to injure you. Take revenge. Have no thought for the needs of others. Let each man look after himself. Eat, drink and be merry, and enjoy to your fill the good things of this earth!" The laws laid down by Christ for His kingdom are very different; and he, therefore, who lives in accordance with the maxims of the world, cannot be a true follower of Christ nor an heir of heaven.

---

* The word "justice" as used in the Sermon on the Mount in the Douay-Rheims Bible means "righteousness" or "holiness" rather than the moral virtue of giving to each what is due to him. (Cf. Attwater, *A Catholic Dictionary*, 1958; TAN, 1997; p. 272.) —*Publisher*, 2003.

APPLICATION. Is your heart still pure and uncorrupted? Have you a horror of everything impure? Guard the innocence and purity of your heart most jealously, for it is your greatest treasure. Avoid the society of bad companions and suppress all sinful curiosity. Pray that you may preserve your innocence.

2. *The Work of Christ's Apostles and Disciples in the world.*

Then, turning to His apostles, He said to them: "You are the salt of the earth [1]. But if the salt lose its savour, wherewith shall it be salted? [2] It is good for nothing any more, but to be cast out, and to be trodden on by men.

"You are the light [3] of the world. A city seated on a mountain cannot be hid [4]; neither do men light a candle and put it under a bushel [5], but upon a candlestick, that it may give light [6] to all who are in the house. So let your light shine before men, that they may see your good works and glorify your Father who is in heaven."

COMMENTARY.

The office of the priesthood. Under the two figures of salt and light our Lord showed the apostles what a high vocation theirs was in the kingdom of God. Under the first figure He described to them the priestly office. "Even as salt gives a savour to food and preserves it from corruption, so must you make sinful man holy and pleasing to God, and keep him from the corruption of sin."

The office of teacher was described to the apostles by our Lord under the figure of the light of the world. They were, He said, to enlighten the world, which was lying in the darkness of sin and unbelief, by their teaching and example, thus showing the way to heaven. They being the vanguard of the Church, all eyes would be directed

---

[1] *Of the earth.* i. e. of men living on the earth.

[2] *Salted.* Salt that has become tasteless, cannot be made salt again: you cannot put salt on salt, and therefore it is of no further use, and is thrown away.

[3] *The light.* What the sun is for the material world, that ought you to be for the spiritual world, i. e. for the souls of men.

[4] *Hid.* Because it is seen from all around. Such, our Lord means, ought to be the case with you.

[5] *Bushel.* A large cask in which wheat was measured.

[6] *Give light.* "You must be placed so that the whole world can see you; otherwise you can shed no light." You must not only give light by your teaching, but by your lives; every one being able to see your good works. In other words you are to teach by your example, so that all men may perceive the effects of the divine grace which is working in you, and be thus constrained to give glory to your Father, Almighty God, who has given you this grace.

to them. Under the same figure our Lord taught them that they could not give light of themselves, but that He would kindle the light in them. Their light was borrowed light, but they must let this light shine through them in such a way as to make themselves models for the whole world by their words and deeds.

Apostolic zeal. By both figures our Lord signified that the apostles must be entirely devoted to their high calling. Even as salt imparts its savour by being itself dissolved, and light can only give light by being consumed, so were the apostles to devote their bodies and souls entirely to their vocation. They were to be consumed, and, if necessary, to give up their lives for the conversion of the world.

APPLICATION. You too ought to be a light to your brothers and sisters and comrades. Do you give them a good example? Do you urge them to do what is right, and warn them against what is evil? Have you ever given scandal?

3. The true justice of the New Law.

Then, addressing the multitude, He said: "Do not think that I am come to destroy the law, or the prophets [1]. I am not come to destroy, but to fulfil [2].

"I tell you that, unless your justice abound more [3] than that of the Scribes and Pharisees, you shall not enter into the kingdom of heaven.

"You have heard that it was said to them of old [4]: Thou shalt not kill; and whosoever shall kill, shall be in danger of the judgment [5]. But I say to you that whosoever is angry with his brother, shall be in danger of the judgment. And whosoever

---

[1] *Prophets.* i. e. the things taught by the law and the prophets.

[2] *To fulfil.* This is to be understood in a twofold manner. Firstly, Jesus, the Institutor of the New Covenant, came to lead men to a perfect observance of the commandments first given by God in the Old Law, and re-impressed on the people by the prophets. Secondly, Jesus fulfilled every type in the Old Law, and every prophecy relating to the Messias which the prophets had uttered.

[3] *Abound more.* The Pharisees and Scribes passed among the Jews for being the most exact observers of the law; but now Jesus said that, if any wished to enter the kingdom of heaven, their justice must be of a much more perfect kind than that of the Scribes and Pharisees. And then our Lord proceeded to give examples in what way their observance of the law was to be more perfect.

[4] *Them of old.* i. e. to the people of the Old Testament.

[5] *Judgment.* He shall be judged by the court of justice of his own district.

shall say to his brother: 'Raca!'[1] shall be in danger of the council[2]. And whosoever shall say: 'Thou fool!'[3] shall be in danger of hell-fire[4]. If, therefore, thou offer thy gift at the altar, and there thou remember that thy brother hath anything against thee[5]; leave there thy offering before the altar, and go first to be reconciled to thy brother: and then, coming, thou shalt offer thy gift."

"You have heard that it was said to them of old: 'Thou shalt not forswear thyself.' But I say to you not to swear at all. Let your speech be yea, yea; no, no: and that which is over and above these[6], is of evil[7].

"You have heard that it hath been said: 'An eye for an eye, and a tooth for a tooth'[8]. But I say to you[9] not to resist evil: but if one strike thee on thy right cheek, turn to him also the other.

"You have heard that it hath been said: 'Thou shalt love thy neighbour[10] and hate thine enemy'. But I say to you: Love your enemies, do good to them that hate you, and pray for them that persecute and calumniate you: that you may be the children of your Father who is in to heaven, who maketh His sun rise upon the good and bad, and raineth upon the just and the unjust.

---

[1] *Raca.* A good-for-nothing.

[2] *The council.* He deserves to be brought before the supreme court at Jerusalem.

[3] *Thou fool.* Or a man rejected by God.

[4] *Hell-fire.* Hitherto you have regarded only the actual and literal taking of life as punishable, but I say to you that he who merely feels anger in his heart against his fellow-men, sins against them, and is worthy of punishment.* He who gives expression to his anger by injurious words, sins still more, and deserves a more severe punishment; but he who really wishes ill to his neighbour, is worthy of the everlasting punishment of hell. God regards our sins against our neighbour as so offensive to Himself, that He will not receive any offering from us, until we have become reconciled to anyone whom we have injured.

[5] *Against thee.* i. e. if he complains of having been offended or injured by you.

[6] *Above these.* Whatever is more than a simple affirmation, such for instance as a declaration on oath.

[7] *Of evil.* Is the result of sin, for, if there were no sins such as lies and deceit, oaths would be quite unnecessary.

[8] *Tooth for tooth.* This is the law of retaliation, which returns injury for injury.

[9] *I say to you.* The perfection consists in this, that you do not retaliate at all, but bear injustice with patience, and subdue all anger against your adversary.

[10] *Thy neighbour.* By the word "neighbour" the Jews understood only those of their own nation, and counted the Samaritans and Gentiles as their enemies.

---

* The phrase "feels anger" is to be understood as meaning "willfully entertains unjust anger," for no sin is committed without consent of the *will.* —*Publisher*, 2003.

For if you love them that love you, what reward shall you have? Do not even the publicans this? And if you salute your brethren only, what do you more? Do not also the heathens this? Be you, therefore, perfect, as also your heavenly Father is perfect[1].

COMMENTARY.

Jesus is the Divine Lawgiver. By the foregoing words our Lord stood forward as the Lawgiver of the New Testament, speaking with divine authority. He put Himself above Moses and the prophets, who spoke in the name of God, saying: "Thus saith the Lord;" for He spoke and commanded in His own name: "I say unto you!"

The moral law of Jesus Christ is a perfect law, because it forbids evil thoughts and words as well as evil deeds. It requires not only an outward observance of commandments, but also an inward amendment, sanctification, and elevation of the soul.

The Fifth Commandment. Our Lord explicitly teaches that the fifth Commandment forbids not merely the actual deed of murder, but every angry thought and injurious word.

Taking an oath is not, according to our Lord's teaching, sinful in itself, for it is a religious and a sacred act; but its abuse is sinful, and therefore no one ought to take an oath without necessity. Our Lord Himself took an oath before the court of the High Priest, when He asserted that He was the Son of God (chapter LXIX).

The command to love our neighbour is applied by Jesus to all men, even to our personal enemies. Our Lord also requires that our love should be of a practical kind.

Christian perfection. Finally, our Lord requires us to strive ceaselessly after *perfection*, placing the perfection of God before us as our model.

The Goodness of God. Our Lord draws special attention to this by reminding us that God does good, and sends rain and sunshine on those who offend Him as well as on those who love Him. He supplies sinners with food and drink, and tries to draw their hearts to Him by gratitude for His benefits.

APPLICATION. Do you ever use bad or injurious words? You have heard how severely our Lord condemns such words; therefore do all you can to cure yourself of this hateful habit. If ever any bad word escapes your lips, say an 'Our Father' as a penance.

---

[1] *Perfect.* You are to strive to become like unto God, who is All-Perfect.

4. Human respect.

"Take heed that you do not your justice before men to be seen by them: otherwise you shall not have a reward of your Father who is in heaven. Therefore when thou dost an alms-deed, sound not a trumpet[1] before thee, as the hypocrites[2] do in the streets, that they may be honoured by men: Amen, I say to you, they have received[3] their reward. But when thou dost alms, let not thy left hand[4] know what thy right hand doth. That thy alms may be in secret, and thy Father who seeth in secret will repay thee.

"And when ye pray, you shall not be as the hypocrites, that love to pray in the synagogues and corners of the streets, that they may be seen by men: Amen, I say to you, they have received their reward. But thou, when thou shalt pray, enter into thy chamber, and, having shut the door, pray to thy Father in secret, and thy Father who seeth in secret will repay thee.

"And when you fast, be not, as the hypocrites, sad. For they disfigure their faces[5] that they may appear unto men to fast: Amen, I say to you, they have received their reward. But thou, when thou fastest, anoint thy head and wash thy face. That thou appear not to men to fast, but to thy Father who is in secret, and thy Father who seeth in secret will repay thee."

COMMENTARY.

God is Omnipresent and Omniscient. He is, as our Lord teaches us, in secret, and sees in secret. He knows all our thoughts and our most hidden intentions.

The Justice of God. He will reward the just, if not in this world, certainly in the next.

---

[1] *Trumpet.* Do not try to make them known.

[2] *Hypocrites.* Thus He styles the Scribes and Pharisees, because they made out that they were seeking God's glory, whereas they were really seeking their own.

[3] *Received.* And have therefore no further reward to hope for. If they do good works to win praise from men and not for God's glory, they must not expect that God will reward them. The praise of men is their object, and must be also their reward.

[4] *Thy left hand.* Keep it hidden even from yourself, not speculating about your good work, even in your own mind.

[5] *Their faces.* They put on a sorrowful face, and neglect to wash and cleanse themselves, so that every one may perceive how hungry they are, and how severe their penance is.

A right intention. Prayer, fasting and alms-deeds are good works, as the angel Raphael told Tobias (Old Test. LXIX). But good works are neither meritorious nor pleasing to God, if our intention in doing them is not good, and not directed to the glory of God. If we seek our own glory when practising good works, we are serving our own self-love and pride, and not God, and therefore we must not expect any reward from Him.

The public worship of God. Our Lord's admonition: "When thou prayest, go to thy chamber &c.", must not be misunderstood. He does not intend to blame the public worship of God in churches, for He Himself went to the Temple, as also did His apostles. The public worship of God in common is necessary and pleasing to Him, but we must frequent it not to seek our own glory, but that of God. But our private devotions ought, if possible, to be made in secret, so that they may not be spoilt and made worthless in the sight of God by a desire for human praise.

APPLICATION. Do you learn your lessons well only in order to win praise? Do you say your prayers in order that you may be thought good? You would be far richer than you are in merits before God, if you always had a right intention in your practice of good works.

5. *How we are to pray.*

"And when you are praying, speak not much as the heathens. For they think that in their much speaking [1] they may be heard. Be not you, therefore, like to them, for your Father knoweth [2] what is needful for you, before you ask Him. Thus therefore shall you pray:

"Our Father who art in heaven, hallowed be Thy name. Thy kingdom come. Thy will be done on earth [3] as it is in heaven. Give us this day our supersubstantial [4] bread. And forgive us our

---

[1] *Much speaking.* The heathen believed that they would be the more surely heard, the more words they used and the louder they cried out (see Old Test. LXIII in the story of the sacrifice of Elias). The Pharisees also believed that the longer and more full of words they made their prayers, the better they were (Mat. 23, 14).

[2] *Your Father knoweth.* It is not therefore necessary to tell Him all the details of your wants.

[3] *On earth.* i. e. by men on earth as it is done by the angels in heaven.

[4] *Supersubstantial.* i. e. heavenly and spiritual food; but it may also mean the same as *daily* or *necessary* food.

debts [1], as we also forgive our debtors. And lead us not into temptation. But deliver us from evil. Amen." [2]

COMMENTARY.

The necessity of Prayer. God does not require our prayers to know what we want, for He is Omniscient, and knows our needs better than we do ourselves. But they are necessary for us, to turn our hearts from the things of this world, and draw us heavenward by a humble sense of our nothingness and by a longing for the gifts of God.

Long prayers. Is it not right then that we should make long prayers? Did not our Lord spend whole nights in prayer? And did not St. Paul, after his conversion, pass three days praying? (chapter LXXXVIII.) Our Lord does not object to the long duration of our prayers, but to empty forms, useless repetition of words, and mere lip-service in prayer, wherein the heart takes no part. In another place He expressly says that men ought always to pray and not to faint (Luke 18, 1), and St. Paul exhorts us to "pray without ceasing" (1 Thess. 5, 17).

The Lord's Prayer. Our Lord has given us the 'Our Father' as a model prayer, and has expressly commanded us to use it. It is the most excellent and comprehensive of prayers: and in it we pray for all that is best, and for deliverance from evil. But, let it be remarked, the good things we ask for are spiritual, and the deliverance we pray for is from spiritual evils. We pray for both a temporal and a spiritual benefit only in the fourth petition, when we ask for the daily necessaries of life. This ought to teach us to pray chiefly for spiritual blessings, such as grace, pardon, virtue &c.; and not only for such temporal benefits as health, a good harvest &c.

6. Confidence in God.

"Lay not up to yourselves treasures on earth [3], where the rust and moth consume, and where thieves break through and steal. But lay up to yourselves treasures in heaven [4], where neither the rust nor moth doth consume, and where thieves do

---

[1] *Our debts.* As God is offended by sin, we owe Him a debt of satisfaction for it. And *Debtors* are those who have injured us.

[2] *Amen.* Means: So be it.

[3] *On earth.* Treasures which have an earthly value, and such things as are perishable. Rust and verdigris eat away metals; moths destroy stuffs and clothes; thieves know where to seek out our treasures, even if they are buried in the ground; and, finally, death, the arch-thief, robs us of all our possessions.

[4] *In heaven.* Such good works as will be rewarded in heaven.

not break through nor steal. For where thy treasure is, there is thy heart [1] also.

"No man can serve two masters [2]; you cannot serve God and mammon [3]. Therefore [4], I say to you, be not solicitous for your life, what you shall eat, nor for your body, what you shall put on. Is not the life more than the meat: and the body more than the raiment? [5] Behold the birds of the air, for they neither sow, nor do they reap, nor gather into barns: and your heavenly Father feedeth them. Are not you [6] of much more value than they? Consider the lilies [7] of the field how they grow: they labour not, neither do they spin. But I say to you that not even Solomon in all his glory was arrayed as one of these. And if the grass of the field, which is to-day and to-morrow is cast into the oven, God doth so clothe: how much more you, O ye of little faith? [8] Be not solicitous, therefore, saying: What shall we eat, or what shall we drink, or wherewith shall we be clothed? For after all these things do the heathens seek. For your Father knoweth that you have need of all these things. Seek you, therefore, first the kingdom of God, and His justice [9], and all these things shall be added [10] unto you."

COMMENTARY.

The Goodness of God. God provides for all His creatures. He feeds the birds of the air and adorns the flowers of the field with beautiful colours. He is the most loving Father to us men, and Him

---

[1] *Thy heart.* If you value your earthly treasures more than anything else, your heart will be set on them and bound up in them. But if you care most for heavenly things, then all your attention will be fixed on them.

[2] *Two masters.* i. e. two whose interests are opposed to each other and who require different services of you.

[3] *Mammon.* i. e. riches.

[4] *Therefore.* That you may not fall into worshipping mammon by reason of an over-anxiety about the needs of this life.

[5] *The raiment.* God, having given you the greater things, such as your body and your life, will surely also provide for such lesser things as food, clothing &c.

[6] *Are not you?* Shall not God provide for you who do sow and reap?

[7] *The lilies.* These grow by the wayside in Palestine, and are of the most brilliant colours.

[8] *O ye of little faith.* Who have so little and such weak faith, and so little confidence in God's Providence.

[9] *His justice.* All that makes you just before God, i. e. grace and virtue.

[10] *Be added.* Whatever is necessary for this earthly life shall be given to you as well.

we have to thank for body and life, food and drink, dwelling and raiment.

Confidence in God. Are we, then, to take no thought for the things of this life, such as food and clothing? Yes; we must, according to our abilities, provide for them, but we are not to be over-anxious, and must trust in the goodness, wisdom and power of God. We must work, but we must also pray; for all our efforts will be quite useless without the blessing of God.

Care for our salvation must be our chief concern as Christians. Before everything else we must try to attain to the kingdom of heaven, i. e. to save our souls, and for this end we must live in the grace of God and strive ceaselessly after His "justice". A true love of ourselves demands this of us, for our soul is more precious than our body, and we ought to seek its interests first.

Covetousness, or the worship of mammon. He who "serves" mammon is the man who fondly considers the gaining and increasing of riches to be the greatest business of life, and neglects the worship of God and the care of his own soul, not even shrinking from such sins as theft, usury and perjury, if they will enable him to add to his wealth.

The right use of worldly possessions consists in using them for God and in the practice of good works. Holy men, such as Abraham, Job and Tobias, possessed great riches, but they were not slaves to them. On the contrary, they made their wealth serve them, and expended it in the service of God and their neighbour.

Good works. All good works, such as works of piety, mortification and brotherly love, are treasures laid up in heaven. When we die, we must leave all earthly things, even our very bodies, behind us: only our good works will go with us, and procure for us a favourable judgment.

APPLICATION. Perform this very day some good work of brotherly love!

7. Charitable judgment about our neighbour.

"Be ye merciful, as [1] your Father also is merciful; give, and it shall be given [2] to you. With the same measure that you shall mete withal, it shall be measured to you again. As you would that men should do to you, do ye also to them.

---

[1] *As.* God being so good and merciful is both the pattern and the motive why you ought to be good and merciful to your fellow-men.

[2] *Shall be given.* i. e. blessings, grace and an eternal reward.

"Judge not[1], and you shall not be judged; condemn not, and you shall not be condemned. Forgive, and you shall be forgiven.

"And why seest thou the mote[2] that is in thy brother's eye, and seest not the beam[3] that is in thy own eye? Or how sayest thou to thy brother: Let me cast the mote out of thy eye, and behold a beam is in thy own eye? Thou hypocrite, cast out first the beam out of thy own eye, and then shalt thou see to cast out the mote out of thy brother's eye!"

COMMENTARY.

The qualities of charity. God being so good and merciful to us, we ought to be full of love and indulgence towards our fellow-men. Since we ought to love our neighbour as we do ourselves, the whole law of brotherly love is summed up in this maxim: "All that you would that men should do to you, do ye also to them," or, to reverse it: All that you do not want men to do to you, be careful not to do to them. Therefore our brotherly love must be:

a) *sincere.* We are to wish our neighbour, in our hearts, quite as much good as we wish ourselves. Further, our love must be

b) *practical.* We must do good to our neighbour according to our means: "Give, and it shall be given unto you." Finally, our love must be

c) *universal.* We must not exclude from our love either our enemies or those who have injured us, but must forgive them from our hearts. "Forgive, and you shall be forgiven."

Sins against brotherly love. Our Lord equally warns us as to all sins against brotherly love, whether they be committed by thought, word, or deed.

a) *Censoriousness and detraction.* He who desires to find fault with others, must make sure that he himself is better than they! And yet, do we not constantly find that those men who have great faults of their own, are the very ones who judge the small faults of their neighbours most severely, not at all remembering their own short-comings? Such men are hypocrites, for they pretend to detest and avoid sin in others, while all the time they are loving and cherishing it in themselves. Furthermore, they sin against brotherly love by preferring to talk about what is bad in their neighbours, rather than about what is good in them, and they are more zealous in exposing their faults than in concealing them.

---

[1] *Judge not.* Do not pass severe judgments on your neighbour.
[2] *The mote.* The very smallest faults of your neighbour.
[3] *The beam.* The great faults which you yourself commit.

b) *False suspicions and rash judgments.* "Judge not!" says our Lord. We cannot judge rightly, not being omniscient and able to search our neighbour's heart. We ought, therefore, to judge others most tenderly and indulgently, and never even *suspect* evil of them without the most conclusive proofs. Still less ought we to *condemn* them, and without sufficient reason to take for granted that the supposed evil is a fact.

Venial sin and mortal sin. By the ·distinction which our Lord draws between "motes" and "beams", He teaches us that there is a great difference between one kind of sin and another.

The reward of heaven is exceeding great. "Good measure pressed down, and shaken together, and running over shall they give unto you" (Luke 6, 38). God will not be sparing, but generous in His rewards.

Degrees of happiness in heaven. The more a man measures, the more will be measured to him, i. e the more good a man does on earth, the higher will be his reward in heaven.

APPLICATION. Do not our Lord's words about the mote and the beam smite your own conscience? You know the faults of others much better than you know your own, and you judge them severely, while you excuse yourself. The Saints did just the contrary: they were severe to themselves, and indulgent to others. Guard against uncharitable judgments and conversations.

8. The narrow gate and the strait way.

Enter ye in at the narrow gate: for wide is the gate, and broad is the way that leadeth to destruction[1], and many there are who go in thereat[2]. How narrow is the gate and strait is the way that leadeth to life[3], and few there are that find it!

COMMENTARY.

The road to heaven and the road to hell. The narrow, up-hill road, entrance to which is gained through a strait gate, signifies walking in the way of God's commandments, which restrain our desires and passions, but which must be obeyed unless we would stray from the road to heaven. It costs much effort, watchfulness and self-denial to observe the commandments and not to stumble in the narrow way, or, if we stray from the road, to return to it by true penance! For this reason our Lord says in another passage: "The kingdom of heaven suffereth

---

[1] *Destruction.* i. e. to everlasting ruin in hell.
[2] *Thereat.* Through the wide gate which leads to destruction.
[3] *To life.* To the everlasting life of heaven.

violence, and the violent take it by force!" On the other hand, the road which leads down-hill to perdition is broad and easy, for unbridled wilfulness and licence reign there, each one going whithersoever his lusts and desires carry him. Very many—the luxurious and the thoughtless—travel on that road to hell, but very few pass through the narrow gate of penance and travel on the road of self-denial to heaven. What a terrible truth this is!

9. A warning against false prophets.

"Beware of false prophets[1] who come to you in the clothing of sheep[2], but inwardly they are ravening wolves[3]. By their fruits you shall know them. Do men gather grapes of thorns, or figs of thistles? Even so every good tree bringeth forth good fruit, and the evil tree bringeth forth evil fruit. Not every one that saith[4] to me: 'Lord, Lord', shall enter into the kingdom of heaven, but he that doth the will of my Father in heaven, he shall enter into the kingdom of heaven."

COMMENTARY.

Faith must be living. We must shape our lives according to the will and teaching of God. Now faith teaches us that God has revealed His will to us by His commandments, so that what we have to do, if we wish to enter the kingdom of heaven, is to keep the commandments. Not every one who says: 'Lord, Lord', shall enter into the kingdom of heaven. Not faith alone, nor a confession of faith by words only, can obtain an entrance there without a faithful observance of God's commandments. The just man must practise good works, and show thereby that the grace, fear and love of God are in him. "Every good tree brings forth good fruit."

False prophets are those who teach things concerning faith or morals contrary to what our Lord and His Church teach, and who therefore, in reality, teach unbelief, and are heresiarchs, seducers, and

---

[1] *False prophets.* i. e. false teachers not sent by God and not filled by His Spirit.

[2] *Clothing of sheep.* Making out that they are as harmless as lambs, and seemingly only wishing you well, like the serpent in Paradise.

[3] *Wolves.* They really have evil intentions towards you. They wish to root out from your hearts all faith in and fear of God, and rob you of His grace and friendship. Our Lord, however, gives a sure rule by which you may know their true character, namely by their fruits, i. e. by their own actions and by the result of their teaching on others.

[4] *That saith.* i. e. faith and pious wishes are not sufficient without the actual observance of God's commandments.

"ravening wolves", who lead others to commit grievous sins, and are the cause of their eternal loss.

APPLICATION. Avoid all companions who are either irreligious or immoral. Do not read any bad or un-Christian books. To read such books is dangerous to both faith and morals, and for this reason it is forbidden by the Church.

10. Conclusion.

"Every one, therefore, that heareth these my words, and doth them, shall be likened to a wise man that built his house upon a rock. And the rain fell, and the winds blew, and beat upon that house, and it fell not, for it was founded upon a rock. And everyone that heareth these my words, and doth them not, shall be like a foolish man that built his house upon the sand. And the rain fell, and the floods came, and the winds blew, and they beat upon that house, and it fell, and great was the fall thereof."

Now it came to pass that, when Jesus had fully ended these words, the people were in admiration at His doctrine. For He taught them as one having power[1], and not as their Scribes and Pharisees[2].

COMMENTARY.

The rock of faith. The magnificent concluding words of the Sermon on the Mount mean this: He who has a living faith in Jesus Christ stands firmly on a rock. He does not totter in time of danger, being assured that, by reason of his aim in life and his good works, his soul is safe. The rock, therefore, which resists all trials and temptations, even the terrors of death and the judgment, is a living faith in Jesus Christ.

Only living faith assures salvation. Once more our Lord reiterates that, in order to be saved, a man must not only *hear*, but also *do* what He says. He who hears and believes our Lord's words, and does not to them, is like the foolish man who built his house on the sand. Faith alone—faith without works—cannot save.

Jesus, the Great Prophet. In Him was fulfilled Moses' prophecy (Old Test. XLIV): "The Lord thy God will raise up to thee a Prophet of thy nation, and of thy brethren, like unto me. Him thou shalt hear." He promulgates by His own authority the Law of the New Testament,

---

[1] *Having power.* Authority to lay down laws, and stir the hearts of men.

[2] *Scribes and Pharisees.* Who were only able to explain the Law literally, and who left the hearts of men unmoved.

which is far greater and more perfect than the Law of the Old Testament given on Mount Sinai.

APPLICATION. Oh, how much better and more beautiful would the world be, if all men would obey the perfect Law which Jesus Christ laid down in the Sermon on the Mount. There would, in that case, be no embittering of one another's lives, no hatred nor enmity, no lies and deceit, no avarice nor hardness of heart, no bad nor uncharitable words. Everywhere we should find peace and happiness. Men would edify one another by their piety and good works, and all would strive together after goodness and salvation. This could be and ought to be; and why is it not? It is because men follow their own passions, instead of the teaching and example of Jesus Christ.

You, dear children, are the hope of the future, and through you things ought to improve. Your village or parish will be the model of all others, if only you will begin at once to live in accordance with your holy faith and obey the glorious lessons of the Sermon on the Mount. Strive earnestly after holiness! Fight against your besetting sins! Correspond faithfully with grace! By so doing you will be happy on earth, and blessed in heaven. What our Lord said will be fulfilled in you: "Blessed are they who hunger and thirst after justice, for they shall be filled."

CHAPTER XXII.

THE CURE OF THE LEPER AND OF THE CENTURION'S SERVANT.

[Mat. 8, 1—13. Mark 1, 40—45. Luke 5, 12—15 and 7, 1—10.]

AS Jesus descended from the mountain, a leper[1] came, who, falling down, adored Him, saying: "Lord, if Thou wilt[2], Thou canst make me clean!" Jesus, stretching forth His hand,

[1] *A leper.* St. Luke (5, 12) calls him a man "full of leprosy"; which would mean that he was afflicted with the malady in its worst form. Even the devil could think of no worse plague than leprosy wherewith to torment Job. In addition to the actual sufferings caused by the malady, we must take into consideration the hard conditions of the Jewish law. The leper was considered unclean, and not allowed to enter the Temple or offer sacrifice, or hold any intercourse with those who were clean. If an Israelite leper was cured of his disease, he had to report himself to a priest at Jerusalem, by whom he was taken to the Mount of Olives and there examined. If he was pronounced clean by the priest, he then had to offer a lamb in the Temple. He was sprinkled with the blood of this lamb mixed with consecrated oil, and was then pronounced once more clean, and restored to the full enjoyment of his rights as a member of the chosen people.

[2] *If Thou wilt.* We can imagine how eagerly the leper must have implored Jesus to help him, for he firmly believed that He could cure him, if He only would do so.

touched him, saying: "I will: be thou made clean." And forth-with[1] his leprosy was cleansed. Then Jesus spoke to him: "See thou tell no man[2]; but go, show thyself to the priest, and offer the gift[3] which Moses commanded as a testimony[4] to them."

After this, Jesus returned to Capharnaum. In this city there lived a centurion[5], a Roman, who was friendly to the Jews, and had built them a synagogue. Now the servant of this man was sick and grievously tormented. The centurion, therefore, knowing that Jesus had come back to Capharnaum, besought some of the Jewish elders[6] to go and ask our Lord to come[7] and cure his servant.

Jesus went with them. But when the centurion saw our Lord coming with the ancients, he said: "Lord, I am not worthy[8] that thou shouldst enter under my roof; but only say the word, and

---

[1] *Forthwith.* How happy the poor man must have been when he both saw and felt that he had been instantaneously cured, and delivered from his horrible sufferings.

[2] *No man.* Take care not to forestall the sentence of the priest, who alone, according to the law, has the right to decide whether you are clean, but go straight to Jerusalem.

[3] *The gift.* A lamb.

[4] *Testimony.* To bear witness, firstly, that I have healed you, and secondly, that I have admonished you to obey the precepts of the law, and that I am, there-fore, no enemy either of the law or of the priests. Jesus sent the man thus mira-culously cured to the unbelieving priest, in order that the latter might be convinced by the man's account of what had occurred that Jesus was the Messias and the Son of God. "The leper who had been cured went his way to the holy city and the Temple, being the latest messenger of grace." (Grimm.) On another occasion Christ healed ten lepers, of whom only one, and he a Samaritan, came to return thanks to God. See Luke 17, 12—19.

[5] *Centurion.* A pagan officer of the garrison of Capharnaum, but one who evidently believed in the unseen God of the Jews, since he had built them a synagogue.

[6] *Elders.* The leading men of the synagogue. He sent them, because he, a pagan, did not dare approach the great miracle-worker of Israel. They pleaded for him, saying: "He is worthy that thou shouldst do this for him."

[7] *Come.* It had not been possible to take the sick man to Jesus. That the centurion had used all human means to cure his servant may be taken for granted.

[8] *I am not worthy.* The centurion had sent to ask Jesus to come; but when he saw from his house that He was really coming, he was seized with a holy diffidence, and hastening to meet our Lord, said: "Lord, I am not worthy that Thou shouldst enter under my roof" (for it is not necessary that Thou shouldst come into my house). "Speak the word (only one word is necessary), and my servant shall be healed."

my servant shall be healed. For I also am a man subject to authority[1], having under me soldiers, and I say to this: Go, and he goeth, and to another: Come, and he cometh, and to my servant: Do this, and he doeth it." Hearing this, Jesus wondered much, and turning to the multitude that followed Him, said: "Amen, I say to you, I have not found so great faith[2] in Israel[3]. And I say unto you that many shall come from the East and the West, and shall sit down[4] with Abraham, Isaac and Jacob in the kingdom of heaven. But the children[5] of the kingdom shall be cast out into exterior darkness[6]; there shall be weeping and gnashing of teeth."[7] Then He said to the centurion: "Go, and as thou hast believed, so be it done to thee." And the servant was healed at the same hour.

COMMENTARY.

The Divinity of our Lord was proved by two astounding miracles. The leper believed in our Lord's Divinity. He did not say to Him: "Pray to God that I may be clean", but he entreated Him as God, and, full of faith, said: "If Thou wilt, Thou canst make me clean", i. e. it only depends on Thy will to cure me, for Thou canst do it, if Thou wilt. And Jesus confirmed his faith by saying: "I will: be thou clean." Our Lord said: "I will!" to show that He could make the sick well by His mere will, or, in other words, that He was Omnipotent. He manifested the same Omnipotence by curing the centurion's servant without even seeing him.

Our Lord's prophecy about the extension of His Church is another proof of His Divinity. The heathen centurion believed, whereas the

---

[1] *Subject to authority.* Means here the same as "placed in authority". The centurion wishes to acknowledge Christ as God. He therefore says: When I command those under me to do anything, it is done at once; how much more will Thy word be obeyed, if Thou commandest disease and approaching death to depart: for Thou art more than man, and art subject to no one.

[2] *So great faith.* As in this man.

[3] *In Israel.* Among Israelites.

[4] *Sit down.* Shall obtain eternal happiness. Heaven is often compared to a banquet, because there man will find peace, joy, and satisfaction.

[5] *The children.* The descendants of Abraham, for whom the kingdom of the Messias was primarily intended.

[6] *Exterior darkness.* The darkness which is outside the kingdom of heaven, or, in other words, hell.

[7] *Gnashing of teeth.* Anguish and rage at the misery they have brought on themselves.

Pharisees and their many adherents would not believe. Our Lord made this the occasion of uttering the significant and striking prophecy that many heathens, all over the world, would believe in Him, becoming thereby the spiritual children of Abraham, and would possess the kingdom of heaven promised to him; whilst, on the other hand, the Israelites, the real descendants of Abraham, who were called into the kingdom of heaven before any one else, would not, as a body, believe and be saved, but would be lost by reason of their unbelief. This prophecy of the spread of His Church among the Gentiles has been completely fulfilled, and proves the Omniscience of our Lord.

The Goodness and Compassion of Jesus. Our Lord did not drive the leper from Him, but "had compassion on him" (Mark 1, 41), and touched him who was counted as unclean. And now also, Jesus drives no sinner from Him, however foul and unclean he may be, if only he will believe and do penance. Our Lord was quite ready to go to visit and help the centurion's sick servant; but in our case He condescends not merely to come into our house, but into our very hearts, in Holy Communion, so as to strengthen us, His feeble servants, and keep us in His grace.

The command of Jesus to submit to God's priests. As Christ would not have cured the leper, if he had refused to show himself to the priest, so now no one obtains forgiveness of his sins, unless he reveals them to the priest in confession.*

The virtues of the centurion:

1. *Compassion.* He had bought this slave with money, and had he died, he could easily have bought another, for he was very rich, or else he could not have built the Jews a synagogue. But he had a kind and compassionate heart, and he was full of pity for his slave, who was suffering such acute pain, and wished to do what he could to help him. His kindness of heart showed to great advantage beside the hardness of heart of the Scribes and Pharisees (Mat. 23, 23). "Blessed are the merciful."

2. *Faith.* The centurion's compassion was the means of his receiving the gift of faith. His compassion made him seek for help from Jesus. He had heard of the miracles which our Lord had already worked, and, by God's grace, what he heard engendered in his heart a firm belief that Jesus was the Messias whom the Jews expected, and that He was able, without even entering his house, to save his servant from certain death.

3. *Humility.* Faith made the centurion humble. The Jewish ancients said about him: "He is worthy that Thou shouldst help him", but he himself said to Jesus: "Lord, I am not worthy" &c. He felt his sinfulness and nothingness acutely in the Presence of Jesus, the Holy and Almighty One, even as Peter felt it at the time of the

---

* "A person in mortal sin can regain the state of grace before receiving the sacrament of Penance by making an act of perfect contrition with the sincere purpose of going to Confession." "Our contrition is perfect when we are sorry for our sins because sin offends God, whom we love above all things for His own sake." (*Baltimore Catechism*, Official Rev. Ed. No. 2, Qs. 403, 399.) —*Publisher*, 2003.

miraculous draught of fish, when he said: "Depart from me, O Lord, for I am a sinful man."

Hell is styled exterior darkness by our Lord, because no ray of divine light or grace can penetrate there. There, says our Lord, is weeping, or wailing, on account of the horrible torment, and gnashing of teeth from despair at its everlasting duration.

Prayers for benefactors. The ancients of the city pleaded the cause of the centurion, because he had built for them a house of prayer. We ought to pray to God for our benefactors, especially for our parents, god-parents, pastors, and teachers.

The power of intercession. The centurion interceded for his servant, and the ancients prayed our Lord to grant the centurion's petition. These prayers were not made in vain, for Jesus yielded to them, and cured the servant.

"Domine, non sum dignus", "Lord, I am not worthy!" The priest says these words at Mass when he receives Holy Communion. He says them also when he administers Communion to the faithful.

Leprosy, a type of sin. Leprosy disfigured the body and made it hideous: mortal sin defaces the soul, which is the image of God, deprives it of sanctifying grace, and makes it foul and horrible in the eyes of God. Leprosy enfeebled the body and made it unfit for work: sin renders man incapable of performing meritorious works. Leprosy caused pain, fear and depression: sin destroys interior peace, creates remorse of conscience and fear of death and judgment. Leprosy was contagious, and, on this account, lepers were avoided by everybody; sin also is contagious, and we ought to avoid the company of sinners and criminals. The leper had to show himself to the priest, exposing to him his breast, face and arms, before he could be pronounced clean and restored to the society of the faithful: the sinner must go to the priest, as the representative of God, and discover to him by a sincere confession his sinful thoughts, words and actions, before he can receive absolution, and be restored to the company of the children of God.

APPLICATION. Have you always made a good confession? Have you a great horror of the leprosy of sin?

CHAPTER XXIII.

JESUS RAISES FROM THE DEAD THE SON OF THE WIDOW OF NAIM.

[Luke 7, 11—17]

NOW it came to pass after this that Jesus went into a city called Naim (Fig. 73)[1], and there went with Him His disciples and a great multitude. As He drew near the gates of the

Fig. 73. Site of ancient Naim. (Phot. Bonfils.)

city, behold, a dead man was carried out[2], the only son of a widow. The poor mother[3], plunged in sorrow, walked after the bier, and a number of friends and relatives accompanied her.

---

[1] *Naim* was a town of some importance about twenty miles south of Capharnaum on the main road.

[2] *Carried out.* It was the custom among the Jews to bury the dead on the day of their death. The body was carried to the grave on a bier, without a cover, the mourners following the bier.

[3] *The poor mother.* She walked behind the bier, bowed down with grief and weeping. Her husband had died many years before, and she had not married

When the Divine Saviour saw the bereaved mother, He was moved with compassion and said to her: "Weep not" [1]. Then coming near He made a sign to the bearers to stop, and touching the bier, He said: "Young man, I say to thee, arise!" Forthwith the young man sat up, and began to speak [2]. Then Jesus gave him [3] to his mother. And all who witnessed this great miracle were afraid, and glorified God, saying: "A great prophet [4] is risen up among us and God hath visited [5] His people."

COMMENTARY.

The Omnipotence of our Lord. In the last chapter we heard how Jesus cured a man who was at the very gates of death. In this chapter,

a second time, so as to be able to live entirely for her son—and now he, her only son, her hope and stay, on whom her whole heart was set, was torn from her by death, in the flower of his youth. The joy of her life was taken from her, and she would gladly have died also. But she was a faithful Israelite, and she knew that the time of the Messias had come. She hoped that she might behold Him before she died; and, next to her natural and maternal grief, the thought that pained her most about the loss of her son, was that now he could never hope to see the Messias. Perhaps she was trying to console herself with the thoughts of Him who was to come, when all at once the bearers of the dead body stood still, and a Voice, solemn, yet full of tenderness, said to her: "Weep not!"

[1] *Weep not.* "What!" she might well have said, "am I, the mother, not to weep, when my only child is being borne to the grave?" It would, indeed, have sounded like irony, if any one else had forbidden a mother to weep under those circumstances, but there was a something that made her pause. He who said to her: "Weep not!" came from the north, accompanied by a great crowd which was gazing on Him with reverence; and there was something in the tone of His Voice which brought comfort to her heart! Could this be the great Prophet of whose miracles at Capharnaum she had heard?

[2] *Began to speak.* A proof that his soul had returned to his body. What did he say? He had awakened, finding himself stretched on a bier! He saw the bearers and the accompanying crowd clad in garments of mourning. All is plain to him now! The funeral procession is his own! He has been dead, and is alive again! In front of him stands a Man of divine dignity, at whom everyone is gazing with wonderment. It must be He who has called him back to life! May we not take it for granted that he threw himself at the feet of Jesus and thanked Him?

[3] *Gave him.* She was speechless with amazement. Her son seemed to be alive again; and yet she knew not if she were dreaming or awake! But Jesus took the risen man, and, leading him up to her, gave him to her. Then tears of joy flowed from her eyes. She pressed her restored son to her heart and could not find words wherewith to thank Him who had given him back to her.

[4] *A great prophet.* The great prophets Elias and Eliseus had restored the dead to life, and therefore, seeing that our Lord called back men from the dead, they judged that He also was a great Prophet.

[5] *Visited.* God hath been gracious to His chosen people by sending among them this great and wonder-working Prophet.

a still greater miracle is related, namely the calling back to life by our Lord of a young man who was actually dead. Elias, too, (Old Test. LXII) raised the dead; not, however, by his own power, but by his prayers; for we are told that he stretched himself three times on the body of the widow's son, and prayed fervently to God, saying: "O Lord, my God, let the soul of this child, I beseech Thee, return into his body." And at the prayer of the holy prophet God called the dead boy back to life. Therefore Elias did not of himself raise the dead, but he prayed to God, and in answer to his prayer God restored the boy to life. The raising up of the young man of Naim was quite different. Our Lord did not pray to God to raise him up, but commanded the dead man, saying: "Young man, I say to thee, arise!" and immediately the youth sat up and spoke. It was by His own Almighty word and power that He raised up this young man, and He showed thereby that He was not only a Prophet, but the Almighty Lord of life and death, or, in other words, that He was God. Elias prayed as a servant; Jesus commanded as God!

The witnesses of this miracle. Jesus performed this stupendous miracle on the public highway, in the presence of many witnesses. Two crowds of people, the one following the body to the grave, and the other accompanying Himself, heard Him command the young man to arise, and beheld the dead man sit up alive and well. Is it not foolish, therefore, of unbelievers to deny the miracles of Jesus?

The Sacred Heart of Jesus. When Jesus saw the deep grief of the mother, the Gospel tells us, He was "moved with compassion", and worked a great miracle to console her. In all the troubles of this life, if we turn to the Sacred Heart of Jesus, we shall find sympathy and consolation. Our Lord's example teaches us that we too ought to comfort the afflicted, especially widows.

A work of mercy. To perform the last services for the dead and to pray for their souls is a spiritual work of mercy.

The love of parents for their children, and of children for their parents. The intensity of the sorrow which overwhelmed the widow of Naim proves how much she had loved her son. The love of parents for their children being as great as it is, children should not repay their love with ingratitude, by vexing and grieving them. The young man of Naim must have been a good son, or the inhabitants of the town would not have followed him to the grave.

The miracle of conversion. The fathers of the Church see in the raising to life of the young man of Naim a type of the conversion of sinners. The raising up of a sinner from the death of mortal sin is a greater miracle of divine power and love than the raising to life of a dead body. "The widowed mother rejoiced, when her son was raised from the dead. Our Mother, the Church, rejoices still more over those who are raised from a spiritual death" (St. Augustine).

APPLICATION. Imagine that you yourself were dead and laid in your coffin, and that our Lord raised you from the dead. How, under such circumstances, you would thank God, and promise faithfully to love Him for ever! But, in fact, each morning of your life, God calls you, as it were, back to life. He has hitherto preserved your life, renewing it to you day by day. Have you thanked Him for this gift? Do you say your prayers every morning? Never again omit to say them! And when you say them, thank God for the new day of life which He has vouchsafed to give you; and make good resolutions, offering to Him all your thoughts, words and actions of the day.

How do you behave, when you follow a body to the grave? When you do so, pray for the soul of the person who is about to be buried, and think of your own death.

CHAPTER XXIV.

JOHN THE BAPTIST SENDS MESSENGERS TO CHRIST.

[Luke 7, 18—35.]

HEROD Antipas, the son of that Herod who had ordered the massacre of the Innocents, was now king of Galilee and Peræa. This Herod was living with Herodias, the wife of his brother Philip, while the latter was still alive. Now John the Baptist said to him: "It is not lawful[1] for thee to have thy brother's wife."

This rebuke provoked the wrath of Herod and Herodias. John was apprehended, bound and put in prison[2]. Herod would

---

[1] *Not lawful.* You were told in chapter XVI that Herod Antipas, Tetrarch of Galilee, had thrown the holy Baptist into prison, the Pharisees having delivered him up to him. In this chapter we are told the reason why Herod persecuted John. He had, in defiance of God's commandment, taken to himself the wife of his half-brother Philip. Gently but solemnly the holy Baptist reminded the light-minded king of God's commandment, and said to him: "It is not lawful for thee to have her."

[2] *In prison.* He was kept shut up in the fortress of Machærus, which stood on a high rock to the east of the Dead Sea. His imprisonment, however, was not a very severe one, for his disciples had access to him, and were able to tell him about the wonderful works of Jesus.

have put him to death, but he feared [1] the people, who considered John a great prophet.

John, being now in prison, and having no other desire than that all should believe in Jesus and follow Him, sent two of his disciples [2], in order that with their own eyes they might see the miracles wrought by Jesus, and with their own ears hear His admirable teaching.

These disciples then presented themselves before Jesus, saying: "Art Thou He who is to come? [3] or look we for another?" Jesus answered: "Go, and relate [4] to John what you have seen and heard. The blind see, the lame walk, the lepers are made clean, the deaf hear, the dead rise again, to the poor the gospel is preached; and blessed is he that shall not be scandalized [5] in me."

---

[1] *He feared.* Herodias hated him, and was only waiting her opportunity to take his life. She was an ambitious and passionate woman, and could not forgive the holy man for his boldness and freedom of speech.

[2] *Sent two of his disciples.* John himself had no doubt whatever, that Jesus was the Messias and Son of God; for this was the burden of his preaching on the banks of the Jordan. But it was different with many of his disciples, especially those who had not seen but only heard of the works of our Lord. In order to confirm their faith, John sends them to Jesus to ask Him directly whether He was the Messias. Our Lord answers them indirectly by referring them to his works. This would confirm the Baptist's own testimony of Jesus.

[3] *Who is to come.* Namely the promised Redeemer. This question shows plainly what it was that John wanted. He asked for no proof, no sign from Jesus, only a brief assertion as to who He was, which would confirm his own testimony of Him. This inquiry of the Baptist is, as it were, his final testimony that Jesus was the Messias, for he thereby declared to the whole world that one simple assertion on our Lord's part was sufficient to command unconditional belief in Him.

[4] *Relate.* St. Luke (7, 21) says: "At that same hour (when John sent his disciples), He (Jesus) cured many of their diseases and hurts, and evil spirits, and to many that were blind He gave sight." Our Lord referred John's disciples for an answer to the works which they saw Him do. "Go", said He, "relate to John" &c. By these words He referred to the prophecy of Isaias (Old Test. LXXII) which foretells that the Redeemer, when He came, would perform such works as these. Therefore the meaning of our Lord's answer is this: "You see with your own eyes that I am doing the works foretold of the Messias by Isaias; therefore you can plainly see that I am the Redeemer who was promised."

[5] *Scandalized.* Who does not take offence at my poverty and lowliness, my sufferings and death. The lowliness and sufferings of Jesus were also foretold by Isaias (Old Test. LXXII); but as the Jews expected a Messias who would appear with pomp and power, and would humble the enemies of Israel, His poverty and humility were the greatest hindrances to faith. The Gospel does not tell us what impression our Lord's message made on St. John, but we can without difficulty conceive that the holy Precursor, who was well versed in the prophecies of Isaias, received our Lord's answer with joy, and that it brought consolation to him in prison, and later on when he suffered a cruel death.

COMMENTARY.

Jesus is the Messias. The miracles of Jesus, so completely coinciding as they do with the prophecies of Isaias, are conclusive evidence that Jesus was the promised Redeemer.

Candour and fortitude of St. John. He exercised his office of preacher of penance not only to the multitude, but to the great and powerful as well.

To admonish sinners is a spiritual work of mercy.

APPLICATION. Do you try, as St. John the Baptist did, to prevent sin as far as you are able? If your brothers or comrades desire to do anything wrong, you too should say: "It is not lawful—it is a sin."

CHAPTER XXV.

THE PENITENT MAGDALEN.

[Luke 7, 37 to 8, 3. Cf. Mat. 26, 7. Maik 14, 3. John 11, 2 and 12, 3.]

IN those days a Pharisee named Simon invited Jesus to a banquet[1] (Fig. 74). Jesus went into the house and sat down to table. Now there was in the city a woman[2] called Mary Magdalen, who, having been a great sinner[3], had recently been converted by the preaching of Jesus. When she heard that our Lord was in the house of Simon, she resolved to honour her Divine Benefactor.

She brought an alabaster-box of precious ointment, entered the house, passed through the dining-room unmindful of the guests, fell down[4] before our Lord without speaking a word, and, breaking the vase, she poured the ointment on His feet. Then, filled with repentance, she began to kiss His feet, and to wash them with her tears, and to wipe them with the hair of her head. And Jesus was pleased.

---

[1] *A banquet.* At which several other guests were present.

[2] *A woman.* It is a tradition that she was called Mary Magdalen, or Mary of Magdala, a city on the Lake of Genesareth.

[3] *A great sinner.* Every person in the town knew that she had led a bad life. She must have been rich, as she had with her, we are told, an alabaster-box of precious ointment.

[4] *Fell down.* She did not speak a word, but performed her work silently and weeping. Her tears betrayed what was in her heart, namely, a deep contrition for her sins.

Now Simon, seeing this, spoke within himself: "This man, if He were a prophet, would surely know[1] who and what kind of woman this is who toucheth Him, that she is a sinner." Jesus, reading his thoughts, said to him: "Simon, I have something to say to thee." But he answered: "Master, say it." Then our Lord said: "A certain creditor had two debtors; one owed him five hundred pence, and the other fifty. And whereas they had not wherewith to pay,

Fig. 74. Roman Banquet. Wall-painting from Pompeii. (After Niccolini.)

he forgave them both. Which, therefore, of the two, loveth his master most?" Simon replied: "I suppose that he to whom he forgave most." Jesus answered: "Thou hast judged rightly."[2]

Then, pointing to the woman, He said: "Dost thou see this woman? I entered into thy house; thou gavest Me no water for My feet; but she hath washed My feet with tears, and dried them with her hair. Thou gavest Me no kiss[3]; but she, since she came

---

[1] *Would surely know.* Being full of self-satisfaction, and hard of heart, the Pharisee despised the poor sinner, and did not think it possible that a prophet of God could accept any service from such a one. And because our Lord did accept the service from her, Simon decided that He could not know she was a sinner, and could not, therefore, be either prophet or Messias. But Jesus now showed him that He was able to see into his heart, and read his most secret thoughts, and that therefore He knew perfectly well what sort of woman she was whose service of love He had accepted: at the same time He wished to show the Pharisee *why* He had thus accepted it.

[2] *Judged rightly.* By the debtor who owed five hundred pence (about £ 17 of our money) is to be understood the poor sinful woman, while our Lord intended the man who owed fifty pence to represent Simon, who considered himself ten times as good as the woman. Simon, not perceiving the gist of the parable, answered at once that that debtor would love his creditor most, to whom most had been forgiven.

[3] *Thou gavest Me no kiss.* In order to understand our Lord's interpretation of the parable, it is necessary to know that among the Jews it was an act of common courtesy to bestow a kiss on guests and give them water to wash their feet. The heads of distinguished guests, to whom it was desirable to show special honour, were anointed with oil. Simon had paid no such honour to Jesus, and

in, hath not ceased to kiss My feet. My head with oil thou didst not anoint; but she with ointment hath anointed My feet. Wherefore, I say to thee, many sins[1] are forgiven her, because she hath loved much. But to whom less is forgiven, he loveth less."[2]

Then turning to Magdalen, He said: "Thy sins are forgiven thee. Thy faith[3] hath made thee safe[4]. Go in peace."[5]

COMMENTARY.

The Divinity of our Lord. In this story our Lord manifested His Divinity in several ways. He showed His Omniscience by His knowledge of Simon's secret thoughts, and of the loving repentance of the poor sinner. He is the creditor to whom all sinners owe a debt, which none of us are able to pay, and from which we can only beg Him to release us. He is the Holy God whom our sins offend, and He forgives us by His own power, which only God can do.

The Compassion of Jesus. He also manifested Himself as the gentle and merciful Redeemer who came not to judge but to save, and who does not thrust sinners from Him, but draws them to Him by His grace, and pardons those who are contrite. He did not reproach the penitent woman; He defended her against the harsh judgment of the Pharisee, praised her works of penance, and by His words of absolution poured balm into her wounded heart.

---

had even neglected the most common duties of hospitality, probably considering, in his pride, that an invitation to his house was, of itself, quite sufficient honour for the poor, low-born Jesus of Nazareth. Then our Lord made plain to the Pharisee his want of courtesy and respect by contrasting it with the very opposite treatment he had received from the woman.—He had withheld ordinary water; she was lavish with the water of her tears. He had bestowed no kiss on his guest's face, but she showered countless kisses on His feet. He did not anoint Jesus' head with even common oil; she poured the most precious ointment over His feet.

[1] *Many sins.* The woman had showed a great love, because her many sins were forgiven her.

[2] *Loveth less.* Like the Pharisee, who, in his self-satisfaction, thought that God had very little to forgive him.

[3] *Thy faith.* In Me, the Redeemer.

[4] *Safe.* Has given you the hope of pardon, and moved you to contrition and penance.

[5] *In peace.* Thus our Lord, for the consolation of this poor woman, pronounced the words of that forgiveness, which her love had already gained for her. At these words of our Lord a heavenly peace took possession of the heart of the penitent sinner. She had obtained that which she had so earnestly desired, viz. pardon and grace. These gracious words none but a God, and a God of infinite mercy and goodness, could have spoken. They have been ever since, and will be to the end of time, a source of hope and consolation to repentant sinners.

A model of penance. Magdalen is a model of a true penitent by her conversion, contrition, confession, satisfaction and perseverance. She was a woman given over to the vanities and pleasures of this world, who led an evil and frivolous life. She heard of our Lord's miracles; and, full of curiosity, she joined the crowd which followed Him, in order to see and hear Him. She saw the wonderful cure of the leper; she gazed on our Lord's countenance, and her heart was touched; she heard His words: "Do penance, for the kingdom of heaven is at hand!" and she opened her heart to His words. She listened to the Sermon on the Mount; she saw what real goodness meant, and she saw the depth of her own wickedness. The reproaches of her conscience became stronger, and her fear of the judgment greater. She believed in Jesus, and she longed for pardon. She had heard how He had forgiven the sins of the palsied man; she knew that He could forgive her sins as well, and she hoped that He would. As she prayed and thought over the words of Jesus, and the miserable condition of her own soul, there grew within her a greater *horror of sin,* and a *love for our Lord* which was *full of hope.* At last, she found the long waited-for opportunity to approach the Holy One, and open her heart to Him. But when she stood before Him, she could utter no word; and then, sobbing, she fell at His Feet and bathed them with her tears. She had loosened her beautiful hair, her cherished adornment, and with it she wiped our Lord's Feet. She broke her vase, and poured the precious ointment over them, to testify her veneration and love. She abased herself as far as she could, and did penance in public, because it was in public that she had sinned. "Her heart was so full of inward shame, that she minded not the outward shame in the eyes of men" (St. Gregory). Her tears were her *confession;* her abasement and service of love were her *satisfaction.* Magdalen was converted and renounced for ever the vanities of the world. We shall find her at the foot of the Cross, and at the feet of the risen Lord. She did severe penance to the end of her life, and is venerated by the Church as a great Saint.

Faith is, as we see in the case of Magdalen, the root of justification. Our Lord therefore said to her: "Thy faith hath made thee safe"; because from her faith had proceeded perfect contrition.

Love and the forgiveness of sin. Many sins were forgiven to this woman, *because* she loved much (for perfect contrition proceeds from perfect love); and after she had received forgiveness of her sins, she loved in proportion to the amount of forgiveness she had received. How could it be otherwise? If anyone wishes to receive pardon of God for the sins which he has committed, the first thing he must do is, by the help of God, to conceive a hatred of his sins, and he must make, at least, an attempt to return to God, or, in other words, to love God. Thus, with even the most imperfect contrition there must be united some spark of the love of God. But it is only when a sinner's heart turns with perfect love to God, that He will impart to him the grace of justification and sanctification. This grace of justification enables man to love God still more. Thus love is, at the same time, the cause and the effect of the forgiveness of sins.

The Pharisee's pride and hardness of heart. It is a great and noble thing to repent of and acknowledge our sins. The proud Pharisee, however, despised the penitent woman, and was unmoved by her tears of contrition. And because Jesus showed Himself to be a true Saviour, and had compassion on the penitent sinner, Simon refused to believe in Him. Thus, even the divine love and compassion of Jesus served as a pretext for unbelief.

———

APPLICATION. Magdalen was not ashamed to do public penance, and in the midst of a joyous banquet to come forward as a penitent sinner. And yet are not you ashamed to own your sins in secret to God's representative, who is bound to silence, and make a good and sincere confession? Where is your contrition? You should say with St. Alphonsus: "Oh that I could weep for ever to think that I could have sinned against Thee, O God—to think that I should be faithless and ungrateful—to think that I should be a traitor!"

CHAPTER XXVI.

JESUS HEALS ON THE SABBATH THE MAN LANGUISHING THIRTY-EIGHT YEARS, AND PROVES HIS EQUALITY WITH THE FATHER.

[John 5. 1—47.]

AT the time of a certain festival Jesus went up again to Jerusalem. Now there was at Jerusalem a pond called Probatica, which in Hebrew is named Bethsaida[1]. It was surrounded by a great building which had five porches, under which lay, at times, a great multitude of the sick, the lame, the blind and the infirm, waiting for the movement of the water. For, at certain times[2], an angel came down into the pond and moved the water; and he who first went down into the pool after the angel's visit, was cured of his disease.

Among the crowd of those who wished to be healed there was a man who had been infirm thirty-eight years. Jesus, seeing

———

[1] *Bethsaida.* i. e. the place of grace. This pond was near the Temple.

[2] *At certain times.* No man knew at what time the angel would come, or else there would have been no necessity for the sick people to wait so long.

him, was moved to pity[1], and said to him: "Wilt thou be made whole?" The infirm man answered: "Sir, I have no one[2], when the water is troubled, to put me into the pond; for, whilst I am coming, another goeth down before me. Jesus said to him: "Arise, take up thy bed and walk!" Immediately the man was healed, and he took up his bed, and went away rejoicing.

This took place on the Sabbath. The Jews[3], therefore, seeing the man carrying his bed, said to him: "It is the Sabbath! It is not lawful[4] for thee to take up thy bed." The man answered: "He who made me whole, He said[5] to me: 'Take up thy bed and walk?'"

But the Jews asked again: "Who is He that said to thee: 'Take up thy bed and walk!'" Now the man was not able to tell them, for Jesus had withdrawn[6] from the multitude. Soon after, Jesus met this same man in the Temple[7], and said to him: "Behold, thou art made whole; sin no more, lest some worse thing[8] happen to thee." The man then went his way, and told[9] the Jews that it was Jesus who had healed him.

The Jews, concealing their envy under the cloak of zeal for the law, persecuted[10] Jesus for curing the man on the Sabbath.

---

[1] *Moved to pity.* This man aroused the compassion of Jesus in an especial manner, and He put this question to him in order to re-kindle in the lame man a desire to be cured, and a hope of relief. His compassionate sympathy inspired the poor man with confidence, and he briefly related his pitiful story.

[2] *No one.* Thus the poor man was utterly forsaken and helpless in his misery. Jesus, however, took an interest in him and cured him instantly by one almighty word: "Arise!" We can picture the joy of the cured man.

[3] *The Jews.* The Scribes and Pharisees.

[4] *Not lawful.* They spoke thus heartlessly, because they expounded the law unspiritually, and beyond God's intention. What did they mean? Did they want the sick man to lie down again on his bed in order not to infringe the Sabbath-rest?

[5] *He said.* "He must know what is allowed to be done on the Sabbath, and He must have had the right to say: 'Take up thy bed and walk.'"

[6] *Withdrawn.* To avoid notice.

[7] *The Temple.* For the cured man had gone straight from his home to the Temple to thank God for his restored health. Now our Lord acted as a spiritual physician to him, by reminding him of the grievous sins of his past life.

[8] *Some worse thing.* It is evident that his thirty-eight years' illness was at once the consequence and the punishment of the sins of his youth. But, what thing could happen to him that would be worse than an infirmity of thirty-eight years' duration? Our Lord meant the eternal punishment of hell.

[9] *And told.* He did this with no evil intention, but in order to bear testimony to Jesus, and to justify his own seeming breach of the Sabbath.

[10] *Persecuted.* They now came forward openly as the enemies of our Lord, calumniating Him and seeking His death.

But Jesus said to them: "My Father worketh until now, and I work."[1] Hearing this, the Jews sought the more to kill Him, because He not only, as they thought, broke the Sabbath, but also said that God was His Father, making Himself equal to God[2].

Jesus then gave them more plainly to understand that He was the Son of God and equal to the Father: "Amen, amen, I say unto you; the Son cannot do anything of Himself, but what He seeth the Father do; for what things soever He doeth, these the Son also doeth in like manner. For the Father loveth the Son, and showeth Him all things which Himself doeth; and greater works than these will He show Him, that you may wonder.

"For as the Father raiseth up the dead, and giveth life, so the Son also giveth life[3] to whom He will. For neither doth the Father judge any man, but hath committed all judgment[4] to the Son, that all men may honour the Son as they honour the Father. Amen, amen, I say unto you, he that heareth My word and believeth Him that sent Me hath everlasting life. Amen, amen, I say unto you, that the hour cometh and now is, when the dead[5] shall hear the voice of the Son of God, and they that hear shall live. Wonder not at this, for the hour cometh, wherein all that are in the graves[6] shall hear the voice of the Son of God. And they that have done good things, shall come forth unto the resurrection of life, but they that have done evil, to the resurrection of judgment."[7]

---

[1] *And I work.* Our Lord meant this: You apply the law about the Sabbath-rest wrongly. It does not apply to God the Father, who is ever active since the days of creation; neither does it apply to me, His Son. The Sabbath is made for man, and applies to human, not divine works; as you can see at the pool of Bethsaida, where my Father works miracles on the Sabbath.

[2] *Equal to God.* They, therefore, quite understood that our Lord called God His Father, making Himself equal to God; but instead of being filled with fear by this declaration, and withdrawing their reproaches about breaking the Sabbath, their rage only increased, and they called our Lord a blasphemer, and sought more eagerly than ever to kill Him.

[3] *Giveth life.* He has the power to raise the dead to life at His pleasure (remember the young man of Naim, the daughter of Jairus, and Lazarus!).

[4] *All judgment.* The judgment of all men.

[5] *The dead.* Here our Lord refers especially to those who are dead spiritually, but who by receiving grace and faith in His teaching are spiritually restored to life.

[6] *In the graves.* Here our Lord speaks of the general resurrection of the dead.

[7] *Judgment.* Damnation.

COMMENTARY.

Our Lord's own testimony to His Divinity. In this chapter our Lord openly and clearly asserts and proves His equality with the Father. He is one with Him in nature, in power, and action. "My Father worketh until now, and I work." He too, like the Father, is Lord of the Sabbath. He, like the Father, has life in Himself and can raise the dead to life. The Jews perfectly understood that He made Himself equal to the Father, and our Lord, far from correcting their interpretation, rather confirmed it in the most solemn manner by an appeal to His works: "Amen, amen, I say unto you &c.", and finally claimed the same honour and worship as the Father.

Jesus the Judge of all men. The Son of God having become Man and redeemed mankind, it is He who will judge men as to the use and misuse of the grace of Redemption.

God's unceasing Action (Old Test. I). About this St. Chrysostom writes thus: "If you observe the rising and the setting of the sun, the movement of the earth, the ponds, springs, rivers, rain, in fact the whole process of nature, whether as seen in plants or in our own bodies and those of the beasts, or in any other thing which the hand of God touches, you will recognize the unceasing work of the Father."

Observance of the Sabbath. "The Son of man is Lord also of the Sabbath" (Luke 6, 5). He permitted the man to prove the completeness of his cure by taking up his bed and carrying it home—therefore it was lawful for the man to do it.

Eternal and Temporal punishment. Grave sin brings on us both eternal and temporal punishment. Our Lord's words: "Sin no more, lest some worse thing happen to thee", are a proof of this.

Relapse into sin. Our Lord warned the cured man not to fall back into sin, because a relapse leads easily to impenitence, and thereby to everlasting damnation.

A type of Baptism. The Pool of Bethsaida was a type of that spring of grace, holy Baptism. As in the one all possible diseases of the body were cured, so in Baptism all possible sins are remitted.

The misery of unredeemed mankind. The condition of the sick man, for so many years miserable and abandoned by all who might have helped him, is, according to St. Augustine, Venerable Bede and others, a striking picture of the misery of unredeemed mankind. Man had turned away from God, and had remained sunk in vice and sin for four thousand years; and there was no one to help him. Then the Son of God had mercy on him and became Man Himself in order to redeem him. He, the Incarnate Son of God, is our helper and comforter!

APPLICATION. Each sin you commit deserves a punishment which you must suffer either here or in Purgatory. Have you ever thought seriously about this? Do you not sometimes say to yourself: "Oh, such and such a sin will hurt no one?" Ah, but it will hurt your own soul, and draw down punishment on you! Do some voluntary penance and guard more carefully against sin for the future.

God works day and night, and every moment, for your good. And you do not thank Him! You do not love Him at all, or, at least, very little!

CHAPTER XXVII.

SIN AGAINST THE HOLY GHOST.—MARY DECLARED BLESSED.

[Mat. 9, 32—34; 12, 22—42. Mark 3, 22—35. Luke 11, 14—32.]

WHEN the days of the Feast were over, Jesus went back again into Galilee preaching, and doing good as He passed along. One day there was brought to Him a man, blind and dumb[1], who was possessed by the devil. Jesus cured him, and the man spoke and saw. The multitude who witnessed this miracle said: "Is not this the son of David?"[2] For never had the like been seen in Israel.

Hearing this, the Pharisees said: "This man casteth out devils by Beelzebub[3], the prince of the devils." But Jesus answered: "How can Satan[4] cast out Satan? If a kingdom be divided against itself, that kingdom cannot stand. But if Satan rise up

---

[1] *Blind and dumb.* Being possessed by the devil, he could neither see nor speak.

[2] *The Son of David.* The promised descendant of David, the Messias (Compare Old Test. LV, and New Test. II: "The Lord God shall give to Him the throne of David His father.") This miracle made a great impression on the people, so much so that it quite inclined them to believe that Jesus was the Messias. This angered the Pharisees, and in order to destroy the people's growing faith, they advanced the theory that it was by the help of the devil himself that He had worked the miracle.

[3] *By Beelzebub.* That Jesus drove out devils they could not deny; but as they absolutely refused to recognize our Lord's divine power, they were forced to maintain that He was in league with the prince of the devils, by whose aid the devils were cast out!

[4] *How can Satan.* Jesus, knowing that they spoke not from conviction, but from sheer malice, proceeds to show: 1) the self-contradiction of their malicious interpretation; 2) that even so they must confess that Satan's kingdom is coming to an end and that the kingdom of God has come upon them.

against himself, he is divided and cannot stand, but hath an end. But if I, by the Spirit of God, cast out devils, then is the kingdom of God come upon you.

"I say to you, whosoever shall speak a word against the Son of Man, it shall be forgiven him; but he that shall speak against the Holy Ghost[1], it shall not be forgiven him, neither in this world, nor in the world to come." *

Then a certain woman from the crowd, hearing what Jesus said, cried out: "Blessed[2] is the womb that bore Thee, and the breasts that gave Thee suck." But Jesus said: "Yea, rather blessed are they who hear the word of God and keep it."

Then some of the Scribes and Pharisees asked Him: "Master, we would see a sign[3] from Thee." Jesus said to them: "An adulterous[4] generation seeketh a sign: and a sign shall not be given[5] to it, but the sign of Jonas the prophet. For as Jonas was in the whale's belly three days and three nights, so shall the Son of Man be in the heart of the earth, three days[6] and three nights. The men of Ninive shall rise in judgment with this generation, and shall condemn it; because they did penance at the preaching of Jonas; and behold, a greater[7] than Jonas is here. The Queen of the south shall rise in judgment[8] with this generation, and

---

[1] *Against the Holy Ghost.* The Pharisees sinned against the Holy Ghost, by ascribing His work to the devil.

[2] *Blessed.* Our Lord's discourse, by which he desired to bring the Pharisees to a knowledge of themselves, made a great impression on the multitude; and, full of admiration, a woman from the crowd cried out: "Blessed is the womb that bore thee &c.", i. e. happy indeed is the Mother who bore Thee and fed Thee at her breast. Jesus confirmed this praise of Mary by responding: "Yea, blessed is My Mother, not merely because she gave me birth and nursed me, but still more because she believed and obeyed the word of God. In like manner you also can become blessed, if you receive and obey My words."

[3] *A sign.* Namely, a sign from heaven (Mark 7, 2). They meant to say: "The healing of the sick and the driving out of devils do not satisfy us, for this might have been done by the powers of hell. Show us some great sign from heaven, such as the raining down of the manna, or of the fire which consumed Elias' sacrifice, and we will believe in you."

[4] *An adulterous.* Our Lord thus styles the unbelieving Jews, because by rejecting the Messias they broke the covenant which wedded them to God.

[5] *Shall not be given.* i. e. no other and greater sign.

[6] *Three days.* The Jews reckoned the beginning of a day and the end of a day, each as a complete day.

[7] *A greater.* Namely, the greatest of prophets, the Son of God.

[8] *Shall rise in judgment.* From Saba (Old Test. LX). This means: "The heathen Ninivites believed the preaching of Jonas, and the queen of Saba believed

---

* There is no sin which God will not forgive if the sinner truly repents; however, some sins, those committed "against the Holy Ghost," so blind the sinner that he does not repent and thus shall not be forgiven.
—*Publisher*, 2003.

shall condemn it; because she came from the end of the earth to hear the wisdom of Solomon, and, behold, a greater than Solomon is here."

COMMENTARY.

Praise of the Mother of God. The pious woman who praised the Mother of Jesus is a figure of the Catholic Church, whose children love, honour and bless the Mother of God. Now, our Lord, in answering this holy person, said that all those are blessed who hear the word of God and keep it. But no one, either among angels or men, ever had a faith so great, or virtues so many, as the Mother of the Redeemer. Hence her throne in heaven is above the thrones of the angels and Saints, and next to that of her Divine Son. By the woman's praise, Mary's own prophetical words, as uttered in the Magnificat, were partially fulfilled: "Behold, all generations shall call me blessed."

The sin against the Holy Ghost was committed by the Pharisees in this manner, that against the dictates of reason they ascribed our Lord's miracles to the power of the devil. They calumniated Him, saying that He was in league with the devil; whereas it was they who, by their persecution of Jesus, were serving the ends of Satan. Being full of the spirit of pride and of envy, they refused to believe in our Lord's divine power. They wilfully and obstinately resisted their reason, which, outwardly convinced by His stupendous miracles, and inwardly illuminated by the grace of the Holy Ghost, urged them to such a belief. Rather than recognize the truth that God was with our Lord, they had recourse to the most foolish evasions and lies. This wilful resistance to God's grace hardened the Pharisees in obstinacy and impenitence, till finally it drove them to deicide. They sinned against the Holy Ghost in a fourfold manner: they envied Jesus on account of His superior wisdom and power of working miracles; they resisted that which they knew to be true; they were obstinate in their opposition to our Lord; and they were hardened into a state of final impenitence.

Impenitence, and prayers for impenitent sinners. Our Lord says of sins against the Holy Ghost that they cannot be forgiven. This means that, when a man continually resists the grace of the Holy Ghost, he falls by degrees into a condition of soul not far removed from that of the fallen angels or devils. The devils are hardened in sin, in resistance to, and hatred of God: their perverted will is incapable of conversion, so that for them redemption is impossible. Now, so long

---

in the supernatural wisdom of Solomon; and yet you will not believe in Me, who am greater than either Jonas or Solomon, and who have worked such mighty miracles before your eyes. The faith of these heathen makes your want of faith all the more reprehensible."

as a man obstinately resists grace, it is obvious that he cannot receive pardon, for the simple reason that he refuses to have anything to do with the grace which would move him to contrition and penance. Such an one is like a drowning man who refuses to take hold of the helping hand which is held out to him. Because, however, the human will can be converted as long as a man remains on earth, God can give a sinner such an extraordinary measure of grace, that his resistance is broken down, and he is saved. We ought, therefore, never to despair of the conversion of a sinner, however obstinate in sin he may appear to be; and the more impenitent he is, the harder we ought to pray for him. In chapter LXXXVI we shall see that, though St. Stephen said to his persecutors: "You resist the Holy Ghost!" he, nevertheless, prayed for them when he was dying.

Calumny. The Pharisees calumniated our Lord most shamefully by saying that He was in league with the prince of devils.

The weapons of unbelief. Lies and calumny were the weapons used by the unbelieving Pharisees against our Lord. They are to this day the weapons with which unbelief and heresy attack the doctrine and Church of Jesus Christ.

Hell. If there are sins which can be forgiven "neither in this world nor in the world to come", there must be a state of everlasting punishment. Therefore it is said in Mark 3, 29: "He that shall blaspheme against the Holy Ghost shall never have forgiveness, but shall be guilty of an everlasting sin."

Purgatory. From our Lord's words that the sins against the Holy Ghost shall be forgiven "neither in this world, nor in the world to come", the Fathers of the Church rightly conclude that certain sins *will* be forgiven in the world to come. Now, there can be no forgiveness of sin in heaven, for nothing sinful can enter there at all. Neither in hell is forgiveness of sins possible, because the damned are incapable of amendment: therefore there must be a middle state between heaven and hell. This middle state is Purgatory, where the soul is cleansed from venial sins, and where satisfaction is made for sins already forgiven.

The General Judgment. Our Lord's words in this chapter indicate that all men of all ages will be gathered together for judgment at the Last Day. "The men of Ninive...the queen of Saba shall rise in judgment with this generation and shall condemn it!"

The Resurrection of our Lord is the miracle of miracles, and the decisive sign which vouches for the divinity of all His other miracles. It was the final test by which the unbelieving Jews were called on to believe and be saved.

Our Lord's prophecy. By referring the Jews to "the sign of Jonas the prophet", our Lord most distinctly foretold His Burial and Resurrection.

Keeping back sins in confession. The unfortunate man who was made dumb by the devil is a type of those sinners whose lips are closed by Satan, so that they do not make a full and sincere confession.

APPLICATION. You see by the case of the Pharisees how detestable and malicious it is to refuse to see the good in other persons, to attribute bad motives to them, and even utter calumnies against them. Have you ever done this?

Do you pray every day for the conversion of sinners? To pray for them is even more necessary than to pray for the holy souls, for these last are certain of heaven, whereas the former are in danger of everlasting damnation.

CHAPTER XXVIII.

JESUS PREACHING ON THE LAKE OF GENESARETH.
PARABLES.

[Mat. 13, 1—53. Mark 4, 1—34. Luke 8, 1—15.]

ONE day when Jesus was near the lake of Genesareth, great crowds came to hear Him; and, sitting down on the shore, He began to teach. But the multitude still increasing, He went into a boat, and thence spoke to the people. And He taught and spoke to them in parables [1].

1. The Parable of the Seed.

"The sower went out to sow his seed. And as he sowed, some fell by the wayside, and it was trodden down, and the fowls of the air devoured it. And some fell upon a rock; and as soon as it was sprung up, it withered away, because it had no moisture. And some fell among thorns, and the thorns growing up with it

---

[1] *Parables.* A parable is the narrative of some event in nature or human life, either true or possible, under the form of which some moral or religious truth is taught. Most of our Lord's parables begin by the words: "The kingdom of heaven is like unto" such and such a thing. Therefore, to understand His parables rightly, we must first know what He meant by "the kingdom of heaven". The meaning was threefold. Firstly, He meant His external and visible kingdom, or, in other words, His Church; secondly, His interior and invisible kingdom, or His reign in the souls of men by His grace and truth; and thirdly, He sometimes meant the eternal happiness of heaven, to which His kingdom upon earth is intended to lead us.

choked it. And some fell upon good ground, and being sprung up, yielded fruit a hundred-fold. He that hath ears to hear, let him hear."[1]

And His disciples asked Him what this parable might be. To whom He said: "To you it is given to know the mystery of the kingdom of God; but to the rest in parables, that seeing they may not see, and hearing they may not understand.

"Now the parable is this: The seed is the word of God. And they by the wayside are they that hear; then the devil cometh, and taketh the word of God out of their heart, lest believing they should be saved. Now they upon the rock[2] are they who, when they hear, receive the word with joy; and these have no roots; who believe for awhile, and in time of temptation fall away[3]. And that which fell among thorns are they who have heard, and going their way are choked with the cares, and riches, and pleasures of this life, and yield no fruit. But that on the good ground are they who in a good and perfect heart, hearing the word, keep it, and bring forth fruit in patience."

COMMENTARY.

The different ways of receiving the word of God. The sower is our Lord Jesus Christ, Who, through the apostles and their successors, proclaims the word of God. The field is the heart of man, for which the divine seed is destined. The chief lesson contained in the parable is that the effect of God's word upon the soul depends entirely on the preparation and disposition of him who hears it, just as the fruitfulness of the natural seed depends on the cultivation and quality of the earth in which it is sown. The three cases mentioned in which the seed brought forth no fruit, point out the chief hindrances which man puts in the way of the efficacy of God's word.

The *first* class are those in whom there is wanting a *good will* to receive God's word with faith. They hear it indeed, but they will not open their hearts to it, because the devil and his human agents have succeeded by scorn, prejudice and false explanations in so setting them against everything supernatural, that they utterly refuse to believe. Take, for instance, the Pharisees in our Lord's time, and also the so-called "enlightened" men of the present day.

---

[1] *Let him hear.* By these words our Lord shows that he treats in this parable of truths which ought to be taken very seriously to heart.

[2] *They upon the rock.* Those in whose case the seed of the divine word falls on stony ground, which does not allow the seed to take root.

[3] *Fall away.* From faith in the doctrines of Christianity.

The *second* class have a good will and are religious-minded people, but they are *shallow* and *weak in character*. They receive the word of God eagerly, but their faith does not penetrate to the depths of their heart and will, and lacks firmness and steadfastness. Therefore they fall away as soon as trials and persecution put their faith to the test. Remember the Israelites in the desert!

The *third* class are those who have faith and hold fast to it, but who *do not live up to it,* being quite absorbed in the things of this world. They give themselves up to the concupiscence of the eyes, the concupiscence of the flesh, and the pride of life, and bring forth no fruits worthy of faith. They have faith, but it is dead.

The three principal enemies of faith and the life of faith are, therefore: 1. the devil and his allies, who seek to deprive men of the willingness to believe, 2. weakness and vacillation of heart and will, 3. the three evil passions which govern the world.

The word of God bears fruit in those only who, besides accepting it willingly, cherish it in a heart purified by faith, and patiently and perseveringly live up to their faith.

Religion and grace are, therefore, affairs, not of reason, but chiefly of the heart and will. A powerful understanding is not necessary or even sufficient for salvation, or to enable us to lead a life according to faith. What is indispensable is a good heart, willing to receive what is great and supernatural.

APPLICATION. You see by this parable how necessary it is that your heart should be well prepared for receiving the word of God. Have you always had a desire to hear God's word? Have you kept what you have heard in your heart, and made corresponding resolutions? Have you thought your religious instruction tedious? To which of the four classes described by our Lord do you think you belong? Pray fervently to the Holy Ghost before you hear any sermon, and listen attentively to it, with the resolve to take to heart and carry out what you hear.

2. *The Parable of the Seed and the Cockle.*

Jesus proposed another parable to them, saying: "The kingdom of heaven[1] is like to a man that sowed good seed in his field. But while men were asleep, his enemy came and sowed

---

[1] *The kingdom of heaven.* It is with the kingdom of God on earth, i. e. the Church, as it is with a man who sowed good seed.

cockle (Fig. 75) [1] among the wheat and went his way. And when the blade was sprung up, and brought forth fruit, then appeared also the cockle. And the servants of the master of the house came, and said to him: 'Master, didst thou not sow good seed in thy field? From whence, then, hath it cockle?' He said to them: 'An enemy hath done this.' The servants said to him: 'Wilt thou that we go and gather it up?' And he said: 'No, lest, while you gather up the cockle, you root up the wheat also together with it. Let both grow until the harvest, and in time of harvest I will say to the reapers: Gather up first the cockle, and bind it in bundles to burn, but the wheat gather ye into my barn.'"

Jesus likewise explained this parable, saying that He who sows the good seed is Himself—the Son of Man. The field is the world. The good seed represents the children of God, and the cockle those of the devil. The enemy who sowed the cockle is the devil. The harvest-time is the end of the world, and the reapers are the angels. As the cockle is plucked up and cast into the fire, so it will happen to the wicked at the end of the world. The Son of Man will send His angels, and take away from His kingdom all scandals; and those who are guilty thereof shall be cast into the everlasting flames of hell. But the just, the faithful servants of God,

Fig. 75. Cockle.

shall be gathered into the eternal granaries of heaven, and they shall shine like the sun in the kingdom of the Father.

COMMENTARY.

Evil in the Church of God. In order that the apostles and other preachers of the Gospel might not lose heart, when, in spite of all their efforts, men would not be converted, our Lord teaches in this parable that it must needs be that evil shall grow up in the Church alongside of the good, and that the complete separation of the evil from the good will only take place at the end of the world.

God suffers evil in His Church, 1. because He gave man a free will; 2. in order that the sinner may have time for conversion; 3. that the just may be proved and gain more merit; that even the wicked

---

[1] *Cockle.* A weed which, until the ear is formed, is exactly like wheat. The cockle, therefore, was only discovered after the ears were formed.

may bring glory to God, His holiness and justice being made manifest in them.

Holiness of the Church. When we say that God suffers evil in His Church, we do not mean in His *Teaching Church,* but in that part of it which is called '*the learning Church*'. The members of the Church, instead of following her teaching, are at times led away by the false maxims of the world. Therefore what is evil in the members of the Church comes from the devil and his allies, not from the Church herself. The Church sows only good seed by her teaching, her commandments and her means of grace; therefore she is holy, and leads to holiness those who obey her voice.

The General Judgment. The Son of Man, Jesus Christ, will come at the end of the world to judge the wicked and the just. (Seventh article of the Creed.)

Hell is the furnace into which the cockle will be cast, and where there shall be weeping and gnashing of teeth.

Heaven. The just will come to the kingdom of their Father, i. e. to heaven, and will be glorified in body and soul, shining like the sun.

3. The Parables of the Grain of Mustard-seed; of the Leaven; of the Treasure hidden in the field; of the Pearl of great price; and of the Net full of fish.

Another parable He proposed unto them, saying: "The kingdom of heaven is like to a grain of mustard-seed [1], which a man took and sowed in his field. Which is the least, indeed, of all seeds; but, when it is grown up, it is greater than all herbs, and becometh a tree, so that the birds of the air come and dwell in the branches thereof."

Another parable He spoke to them: "The kingdom of heaven is like to leaven [2] which a woman took and hid in three measures of meal, until the whole was leavened."

"The kingdom of heaven is like to a treasure [3] hidden in the field, which a man having found, hideth, and, for joy thereof, goeth, and selleth all that he hath and buyeth [4] that field."

---

[1] *Mustard-seed.* This was the smallest seed sown in Palestine. From this seed, however, there sprang a shrub which reached the height of ten feet, and which put forth a great many branches with large leaves.

[2] *Leaven.* Leaven is mixed with dough, to make bread light and palatable.

[3] *A treasure.* By the word "treasure" a large sum of money, or a collection of valuables may be understood.

[4] *Buyeth.* Because he knew the treasure to be buried there. By Jewish law everything found buried in the earth belonged to the owner of the ground.

"Again the kingdom of heaven is like to a merchant seeking good pearls. Who, when he had found one pearl of great price, went his way, and sold all he had and bought it."

"Again the kingdom of heaven is like to a net cast into the sea, and gathering together of all kinds of fishes. Which, when it was filled, they drew out, and sitting by the shore they chose out the good into vessels, but the bad they cast forth. So shall it be at the end of the world. The angels shall go out and shall separate the wicked from among the just; and shall cast them into a furnace of fire: there shall be weeping and gnashing of teeth."

All these things Jesus spoke in parables to the multitudes: and without parables [1] He did not speak to them.

COMMENTARY.

The growth of the Church. The parable of the grain of mustard-seed means this: Even as from a very small grain there springs up a large shrub, so would the Church of God have a small and insignificant beginning, but would grow and grow until she formed a mighty kingdom, embracing all nations in her fold. In this parable, therefore, our Lord foretold the external increase of His Church. She was to be Catholic or world-wide.

The effects of Christianity. By the parable of the leaven our Lord described the manner in which His doctrine and grace would affect the hearts of men. The woman signifies the Church; the leaven, Christian truth and grace; while the meal denotes mankind, both individuals, and the whole race collectively. Even as leaven lays hold of one particle of meal after another, and penetrates everywhere, until the whole is rendered good and palatable, so would Christianity penetrate, purify and sanctify the hearts of men, and govern all their thoughts and aims, until the whole of human society was raised and sanctified by the doctrine and grace of Jesus Christ.

The greatest of treasures. This treasure signifies the graces of Christianity, which far surpass all the riches of this world. He who has found the great treasure of faith and grace is fortunate indeed. He rejoices, and guards his treasure jealously, and is willing to give up everything rather than lose the faith and grace of God.

---

[1] *Without parables.* Jesus preached in parables, because the great mass of the people, together with even their leaders and teachers, were incapable of understanding or receiving the unveiled truth about the kingdom of God. He who has no sense of the supernatural, sees a mere narrative in the parable, without perceiving the hidden and higher teaching which it contains.

The Parable of the Pearl also signifies the great happiness of possessing the true faith and being in a state of grace. He who really and laboriously strives after truth and salvation will obtain them. "There exists, however, only one pearl without price, for there exists only one Truth. And even as the wise merchant who bought this pearl at the cost of all that he possessed, alone knew how rich he had become by the possession of it, so only those who belong to the Church and possess grace know how rich they are. Those who have not the faith are ignorant of its value, and have no conception how rich those are who possess it!" (St. Irenæus.)

The separation at the Last Judgment. The parable of the net full of good and bad fish conveys the same lesson as the parable of the wheat and the cockle. We became members of the Church when we were baptized; but our Baptism by no means ensured our reception into heaven. If we do not keep our baptismal vows and remain in a state of God's grace, we shall be finally rejected, and cast out of the net like the bad fish.

APPLICATION. The grace of God is the greatest of all treasures, and a pearl indeed without price. Have you ever lost it by mortal sin?

You can now understand better than you did before the meaning of the petition: "Thy kingdom come." May the kingdom of God, His holy Church, ever grow, ever put forth boughs and branches, and ever bring unbelievers and heathen into her fold! May the kingdom of God's grace and truth also continually sink into your heart, enlightening, purifying, and sanctifying you, so that you may be able to attain to God's everlasting kingdom in heaven! Say often and devoutly, and in this sense, the prayer: "Thy kingdom come", both for yourself, and for all those dear to you.

CHAPTER XXIX.

CHRIST STILLS THE TEMPEST.

[Mat. 8, 23—27. Mark 4, 35—40. Luke 8, 22—25.]

ONE evening Jesus entered into a boat (Fig. 76)[1], and His disciples followed Him[2]. A great tempest arose in the sea[3], so that the boat was covered with waves, and

---

[1] *Boat.* Being fatigued and wishing to avoid the crowd, and to retire into solitude.

[2] *Him.* They went towards Gadara, a town lying to the south-east of the lake. They must therefore have traversed almost the whole length of the lake.

[3] *Sea.* St. Luke says (8, 23): "There came down a storm of wind upon the lake (that is from the mountains which surround it), and they were filled and were in danger." Violent and sudden storms like the one thus described frequently occur

they were in great danger. But Jesus was asleep[1]. His disciples came to Him, crying out with fear: "Lord, save us, we perish." Jesus arose and said to them: "Why are ye fearful, O ye of little faith?"[2] Then standing, He rebuked the winds and commanded the sea[3], and there came a great calm[4].

But the men[5] wondered, saying:

Fig. 76. Boat on Lake of Genesareth. (Phot. Bruno Hentschel, Leipzig.)

„What manner of man is this, for the winds and the sea obey Him?"

COMMENTARY.

The Divinity of our Lord. "Who is this, that even the wind and the sea obey Him!" exclaimed the witnesses of this wonder. This great miracle was, indeed, a fresh and clear proof of our Lord's divine power. But in order to appreciate the greatness of the miracle you must take

on the Sea of Galilee. The wind blowing from the mountains on one side of the lake is beaten back on to the water from those on the other side, being, as it were, imprisoned in the hollow, and expends all its fury on the surface of the water. As fast as the disciples baled out the water, fresh volumes poured in. At one moment the little ship was raised on the crest of the waves, and the next buried in their depths, till the planks of the boat creaked and threatened to fall asunder.

[1] *Asleep.* As if there were no danger. The disciples watched anxiously whether He would awake; for they believed that He could avert the danger, if only He were awake. But while they hesitated and shrank from disturbing the Holy One, the storm and the danger increased, and in fear for their lives they went to Him and awoke Him.

[2] *Faith.* If your faith were not so weak, you would not be frightened.

[3] *Commanded the sea.* Saying to the sea: "Peace; be still!" (Mark 4, 39.)

[4] *Calm.* The wind abated instantly, the lake became calm, and a great silence succeeded the clamour of the storm.

[5] *Men.* Not only the apostles, but also the men in the other ships; for St. Mark tells us that "there were other ships with him".

into account following circumstances. After a violent storm it is usually many hours before the movement of the waves subsides, and the surface of the sea regains its smoothness. But in this case the calm followed immediately on our Lord's words. Man never feels himself so small, so powerless, so pitiable as when he is in conflict with the uncontrolled powers of nature. Then those who think themselves strongest recognize their weakness and cry out to God for help. But Jesus arises and commands the raging elements, and they obey Him. "O Lord of hosts", cries the Psalmist, "who is like to Thee! Thou rulest the power of the sea, and appeasest the motion of the waves thereof" (Ps. 88, 9).

The Two Natures in Jesus Christ. As Man He was tired and slept; as God He commanded the winds and the waves.

The weak faith of the disciples was shown by their thinking that our Lord, when asleep, was powerless to help them. They forgot that His Godhead cannot sleep, but is ever awake and watchful over His servants.

The object of this miracle was 1. to increase and strengthen the faith of the apostles; 2. to teach the apostles and their successors that they, as fishers of men, would be exposed to many persecutions and afflictions; but that Jesus would always be with them to hush the storm.

The Church Militant, with the successor of St. Peter at the helm, is typified by Peter's little ship threatened with destruction by the storm. The Church has to contend with many adversaries; but our Lord is in her midst, and if at times He seems to slumber, He still knows the sufferings and dangers which threaten His Church, and all at once He will arise, command the storm by His Almighty word, and once more give back peace and liberty to His Church.

The storm of temptation. There arise storms in the lives of individuals also, when sufferings and temptations assail them. Sometimes a person seems in danger of sinking, i. e. of sinning and losing eternal life. But God is near him, with His help, grace and consolation. St. Bernard says about this: "Though the world should rave and Satan rage, though the flesh should rebel, I will still hope in Thee, O my God; for who has ever hoped in Thee and been confounded?"

Storms of life. So it is in all the storms of life. If only we have confidence in God, and ask Him to come to our aid, He will not fail us in the hour of our need. He whom the winds and the seas obey is ever at hand to help those who invoke His name.

APPLICATION. Many storms arise in your heart, as when, for instance, you are moved to anger or jealousy, or are cast down by cowardice. In all such temptations keep Jesus in your heart, and cry out to Him, saying: "Lord, save me, or I perish!"

CHAPTER XXX.

JESUS RAISES TO LIFE THE DAUGHTER OF JAIRUS, AND HEALS THE WOMAN AFFLICTED WITH AN ISSUE OF BLOOD.

[Luke 8, 40—56.]

WHEN Jesus reached the opposite shore [1], a great multitude came to receive Him.   Among the people there was one of the rulers [2] of the synagogue, named Jairus.   This man threw himself at the feet of Jesus and besought Him: "Lord, my daughter is at the point of death; but come [3], lay Thy Hand upon her, and she shall live."   Now this maiden was twelve years old, and the only child of her parents.   Jesus went with Jairus, being followed by His disciples and a great number of people.

Among those who followed Jesus and thronged around Him, there was a woman who had been suffering from an issue of blood for twelve years, and had spent all her fortune in paying doctors; but she could not be healed [4].   She now made her way through the crowd, and came close to Jesus; for she thought within herself: If I shall but touch His garments, I shall be whole. So she walked behind the Saviour, and, stretching out her hand, she touched the hem of His garment, and immediately the issue of her blood stopped [5].

Then Jesus, turning round, asked [6]: "Who hath touched My garment?"   The woman, seeing that she could not hide herself,

---

[1] *Opposite shore.*   At Capharnaum.

[2] *The rulers.*   There were three, and their duty was to superintend the arrangements of the synagogue, and the divine services.

[3] *Come.*   The faith of Jairus was, therefore, not so great as that of the pagan centurion (chapter XXII).   Jairus believed that Jesus could not cure the sick girl unless He went to her, and laid His Hand on her; whereas the centurion believed that it was not necessary for Jesus to visit his sick servant, His word being as mighty to heal at a distance as on the spot.

[4] *Could not be healed.*   Her illness had increased in spite of all remedies, so that not only had she become poor, but also weaker and more infirm.   Reduced to this extremity, she heard of the great miracles wrought by Jesus, and she had the conviction that, if she could but get to Him, He could help her.

[5] *Stopped.*   She felt new health and life coursing through her feeble body.

[6] *Asked.*   Jesus asked this, though He already knew who had touched Him. He desired that the woman should proclaim her wonderful cure in the presence of the multitude, in order that the faith of all present, and especially of Jairus, should be strengthened.

and trembling with fear [1], threw herself at His feet, and confessed for what cause she had touched Him. Jesus mildly said to her: "Daughter [2], thy faith hath made thee whole. Go in peace!"

While [3] He yet spoke, a messenger came from the house of Jairus, saying: "Thy daughter is dead. Do not trouble the Master any further." The father groaned in anguish, but Jesus said to him: "Fear not! Believe only, and she shall be safe." On reaching the house, they saw the mourners [4] weeping and lamenting over the dead girl. But Jesus said: "Why make you this ado and wailing? The damsel is not dead, but sleepeth." [5] And they laughed Him to scorn [6]. Then, going in with the afflicted father and some of the disciples to where the dead girl lay, and taking her by the hand, He said: "Talitha cumi"; that is, "Maid, arise!" Immediately her spirit returned, she rose and walked, and they gave her to eat. The fame of this miracle went abroad through the whole country.

COMMENTARY.

Proofs of our Lord's Divinity: 1. The wonderful cure of the sick woman showed our Lord's Omnipotence; for it could only be a divine

---

[1] *Fear.* At having ventured to touch the Holy One.

[2] *Daughter.* Far from blaming her, our Lord commended her faith, and lovingly called her "Daughter", thus shedding heavenly consolation and peace upon her soul.

[3] *While.* The episode of the infirm woman had somewhat delayed our Lord on His way to the house of Jairus. We can imagine how displeasing this interruption must have been to Jairus; for his daughter lay at the very point of death, and he feared that she might die before Jesus could reach her. On the other hand, his faith must have been strengthened by the miracle which he had witnessed, and he may have said to himself: "If this woman has been made well by the mere touch of Jesus' garment, my daughter will most certainly be cured, when He lays His Hand on her." Thus he stood, wavering between hope and fear, when one of his household brought him the message: "Thy daughter is dead, do not trouble the Master any further—do not press Him to go to thy house, for He can do nothing now." This was indeed a severe trial of Jairus' faith; but our Lord at once spoke words of encouragement to him.

[4] *The mourners.* Namely relations, acquaintances, and mourners who were always summoned by the Jews to lament over the body of the dead.

[5] *Sleepeth.* Jesus said this, because He intended to call the dead maiden back to life.

[6] *To scorn.* They were sure the child was dead, for several among them had actually seen her die. They could not understand our Lord's words "She sleepeth", because they did not believe that He was able to call her back to life. On account of their unbelief they were not worthy to witness the miracle, and Jesus went alone with the child's parents and His three apostles, Peter, James and John, into the chamber of the dead.

power which commanded sickness so imperatively, and restored health
to men: "Virtue went out of Him and healed all" (Luke 6, 19).—
"In Him dwelleth all the fulness of the Godhead corporally" (Col. 2, 9).
2. This cure also showed forth our Lord's Omniscience. Unobserved,
as she supposed, in the midst of the crowd, the poor woman crept up
to Him, and touched the hem of His garment. Jesus, however, knew
that she had touched Him, and knew, moreover, that the touch had
made her whole; but in order that she might not fall into the error
of thinking she had been cured by some strange, mechanical, involuntary
force, He said aloud: "I know that virtue is gone out from Me."
3. The raising to life of the dead maiden showed that Jesus had dominion over life and death, being the Author of life, or, in other words,
being God. Truly, indeed, did He say of Himself (chapter XXVI):
"As the Father raiseth up the dead, and giveth life; so the Son also
giveth life to whom He will." Of the real death of the maiden there
can be no doubt, because 1. all who were in the house knew that
she was dead. 2. Our Lord knew that she was dead, when He said:
"Believe only, and she shall be safe." 3. The Gospel (Luke 8, 55)
says explicitly: "her spirit returned". It is, therefore, an undoubted
fact that the maiden had already departed this life.

The humility of Jairus and the infirm woman. Jairus, the rich
and distinguished ruler of the synagogue, threw himself humbly on the
ground at the feet of the poor Jesus of Nazareth, and begged for help.
As for the woman, she felt herself to be so mean and wretched that
she had not the courage to offer her petition to our Lord; and after
she was healed, she fell trembling at His Feet, and related before the
whole crowd from what misery she had been delivered. The very first
maxim of the kingdom of God is this: "God resisteth the proud, and
giveth grace to the humble" (James 4, 6).

Without faith, neither one nor the other would have obtained help.
Our Lord said to Jairus: "Believe only, and she shall be safe", and
to the woman He said: "Thy faith hath made thee whole." "If thou
hadst not had faith, the touch of My garment would have availed thee
nothing." Without faith there is no cure for the body, no salvation
for the soul.

The prayer of Jairus was heard, because he prayed with confidence and humility.

The hour of death is uncertain. Some die when they are young,
as did the daughter of Jairus and the young man of Naim; others reach
middle age, and some reach old age. We must, therefore, be always
prepared for death and eternity.

Death is a sleep: 1. because the dead "rest from their labours"
(Apoc. 14, 13); 2. because they can work no longer; 3. because the
bodies of the dead shall one day wake up again to life. The church-

yard is "God's acre", where the bodies of the dead are sown like seeds of corn, ready to spring up at the Last Day (1 Cor. 15, 42. 43).

APPLICATION. The sick woman had spent all her fortune, and submitted to painful remedies in order to recover her health. She was not to blame, for health is a great treasure. But the health of the soul is of far more importance than the health of the body. Why do you take so little care of your immortal soul? If ever your soul is sick, i. e. in a state of sin, spare no effort, no labour, by doing penance and making a good confession, to obtain its cure.

CHAPTER XXXI.

JESUS CHOOSES AND SENDS FORTH HIS APOSTLES.

[Mark 3, 13—19. Mat. 10, 1—42. Luke 6, 12 ; 9, 1.]

THE number of followers and admirers of our Lord, even from distant countries, kept increasing as time went on. One day when the multitude were around Jesus, eager to hear His teaching, He had compassion on them, for they were as sheep without a shepherd[1]. He said to His disciples: "The harvest indeed is great, but the labourers are few. Pray ye therefore the Lord of the harvest, that He send forth labourers into His vineyard."

After He had spent the night in prayer[2], and day being come, He called together His disciples[3], and chose from among them twelve, that they should be with Him[4], and that He might send them to preach[5]. Now the twelve whom He called apostles are these: The first, Simon, who is called Peter, and Andrew his brother; James and John the sons of Zebedee; Philip and

---

[1] *Without a shepherd.* For the Jewish priests led them into error, seeking to alienate them from our Lord.

[2] *In prayer.* On a mountain in the neighbourhood of Capharnaum.

[3] *His disciples.* They had followed Him into solitude, and had slept near Him, on the mountain. The Gospel does not tell us what was the number of His disciples. At any rate the number had greatly increased since the call of His first followers (chapter XIII), for, as we shall see (chapter XLI), He chose seventy-two of them, and sent them out to preach.

[4] *Be with Him.* As witnesses of His words and deeds from the day of His Baptism till His Ascension.

[5] *To preach.* Now and hereafter throughout the world.

Bartholomew[1]; Thomas and Matthew[2] the publican; James, son of Alpheus[3], and Thaddeus; Simon called the Zealot[4], and Judas Iscariot[5].

Having chosen His apostles, Jesus commanded them to go to the lost sheep of the house of Israel[6], and announce to them that the kingdom of heaven was at hand. He also gave them power to heal[7] the sick, raise the dead, cleanse lepers, and cast out devils. He told them not to take anything with them on their journey, because the labourer is worthy of his hire.

Jesus spoke: "When you come into a house, say: 'Peace be to this house!' And if that house be worthy[8], your peace shall come upon it; but if it be not worthy, your peace shall return to you. And whosoever shall not receive you, going forth out of that house or city, shake off the dust[9] from your feet. Amen, I say to you, it shall be more tolerable for the land of Sodom and Gomorrha in the day of judgment than for that city.

"Behold, I send you as sheep in the midst of wolves[10]. Be ye, therefore, wise[11] as serpents and harmless[12] as doves. Beware

---

[1] *Bartholomew.* This was the surname of Nathanael, whom Philip brought to Jesus.

[2] *Matthew.* He had been a publican or tax-gatherer. He was sitting at the receipt of custom, when Jesus said to him: "Follow Me", and immediately he arose and joined the other disciples.

[3] *Son of Alpheus.* Or St. James the Less, so called to distinguish him from James the brother of John.

[4] *Zealot.* So called because, before he became our Lord's disciple, he was distinguished for his zealous adherence to all the precepts of the Old Testament, as, later on, was Saul, afterwards St. Paul.

[5] *Iscariot.* An inhabitant of Cariot, a little town of the tribe of Juda. He was the only one of the apostles who came from Judæa, all the others being Galileans.

[6] *The house of Israel.* To the Israelites who were wandering about like sheep without a true shepherd. It was only after our Lord's Resurrection, when He had completed the work of Redemption, that the apostles were commanded to preach to the Gentiles.

[7] *Power to heal.* Our Lord not only gave them power to work miracles, but commanded them to use the power.

[8] *Be worthy.* i. e. if the inhabitants of the house are willing to believe in the Gospel of peace.

[9] *The dust.* As a sign that you will hold no communion with them, but consider them as shut out from the kingdom of heaven.

[10] *Wolves.* Even as wolves lie in wait and attack sheep, so will men persecute you.

[11] *Wise.* Cautious, and on the look-out for danger, so as to avoid it when necessary. [12] *Harmless.* Inoffensive and gentle.

of men; for they will deliver you up in councils, and they will scourge you in their synagogues. And you shall be brought before governors and before kings, for My sake [1]. The disciple is not above his master, nor the servant above his lord [2]. Fear not [3] those that kill the body, and cannot kill the soul; but rather fear Him that can destroy both soul and body in hell.

"Whosoever, therefore, shall confess Me [4] before men, I will also confess him [5] before My Father who is in heaven. But whosoever shall deny Me before men, I will also deny him before My Father who is in heaven. He that loveth father or mother more than Me, is not worthy of Me. And he that loveth son or daughter more than Me, is not worthy of Me. And he that taketh not up his cross and followeth Me, is not worthy of Me. He that findeth his life [6], shall lose it; and he that shall lose his life for My sake, shall find it. He that receiveth you, receiveth Me, and he that receiveth Me, receiveth Him that sent Me. And whosoever shall give to drink to one of these little ones a cup of cold water only in the name of a disciple, Amen, I say to you, he shall not lose his reward."

When our Divine Lord had thus told his apostles what they had to expect from the world, He sent them, two by two, into every city and place, preaching the word of God, and doing the work that He had commanded them to do.

COMMENTARY.

The prayer of Jesus. Why did our Lord pass the night in prayer before choosing His apostles? What was it that He laid before His heavenly Father as He knelt all alone? He was about to take an important step, and to lay the foundation of His Church by this choice of His apostles. He prayed for those whom He was about to choose, and for their successors, as well as for the countless Jews and Gentiles

---

[1] *For My sake.* Because you believe in Me, and preach your belief.

[2] *Above his lord.* You are in no higher position than I, your Master, am; therefore you must not be astonished, if you are hated and persecuted in the same manner as you will see Me persecuted.

[3] *Fear not.* i. e. do not fear men, but fear the Just and Holy God.

[4] *Confess Me.* Acknowledging Me by word and deed as his Lord and Saviour.

[5] *Confess him.* Acknowledging him as My faithful friend and follower.

[6] *Findeth his life.* The meaning of this phrase is that he who loveth the life of this world, shall lose eternal life (See John 12, 25).

who through their preaching would be brought into the Church. "That holy night passed by our Lord in prayer and watching is the Vigil of the Founding of the Catholic and Apostolic Church. On that mysterious night the soul of our Saviour must have been full of the deepest contemplation of His unfathomable work of love, of its results and destiny, as well as of thanksgiving to His Eternal Father for this great and beautiful new creation. He spent the night in prayer, wrestling with God for its welfare and final victory" (Reischl).

The common office of the Apostles. Picture to yourselves the little company of the twelve apostles—twelve plain, unlearned men! Let us see for what object our Lord singled them out. He intended that, when He Himself had ascended into heaven, they should go forth into the world to preach the Gospel. They were to conquer the world for Him, and carry on His work of Redemption by delivering His truth and grace to mankind. What a gigantic task! Therefore, to make them more fit for this great office, our Lord chose them Himself, kept them constantly with Him, prayed for them, and made them His chief care. The whole Church is founded on the apostles, and is therefore called the Apostolic Church.

The miraculous preservation and extension of the Church. The question is, why did our Lord Jesus Christ choose for this stupendous office twelve ignorant men, of a low station in life, and of no importance in the eyes of the world? It was to show to the whole world that the maintenance and spread of the Church and her doctrine were not due to human wisdom and learning, but solely to His grace and protection. "The foolish things of the world hath God chosen that He may confound the wise; and the weak things of the world hath God chosen that He may confound the strong; and the base things of the world, and the things that are contemptible, hath God chosen; and things that are not, that He might bring to nought things that are: that no flesh should glory in His sight" (1 Cor. 1, 27. 28. 29).

The Primacy of Peter. A list of the apostles is given four times, viz. in the Gospels of St. Matthew, St. Mark and St. Luke, and in the Acts of the Apostles. In each, St. Peter's name is put first; and St. Matthew expressly calls him "the first" (Matth. 10, 2). In what way was St. Peter the first of the apostles? He was the third, not the first, to be called (chapter XIII), but all the same he was the first in rank, being ordained by our Lord Jesus Christ to be the chief of the apostles. We have already come across several passages in the New Testament which point to his primacy. When our Lord first called him, He gave him the name of Peter. His mother-in-law was the first of many sick whom Jesus healed. It was Peter's boat from which He chose to preach; and it was to Peter especially that the miraculous draught of fishes was given, as also the promise that henceforth he should be a fisher of men.

The Necessity of Prayer. As Jesus prayed perseveringly and fervently, before He chose His apostles, so ought we to begin every important undertaking by prayer, so as to ensure God's help and blessing.

The Number of the Apostles. Our Lord chose *twelve* apostles, this number having been fore-ordained, and pre-figured in the Old Testament by the twelve patriarchs. The kingdom of the Messias sprang from Israel, the chosen people of God; and even as Israel was descended from the twelve sons of Jacob (or Israel), so does the spiritual Israel or New Covenant of grace, the Church, proceed from the twelve spiritual sons of the true Israel (or Wrestler), Jesus Christ. Whoever was descended from Jacob's twelve sons, belonged to the Old Covenant, and had a share in its promises. In like manner, whoever wishes to belong to the New Covenant, and enjoy its treasures of grace, must be spiritually descended from the twelve apostles, the patriarchs of the Church, or, in other words, must be a member of the One Apostolic Church.

Proofs of our Lord's Divinity. We have already seen with awe the miraculous power of Jesus, by which He showed Himself to be Lord over all creation, even over death and hell, and we saw that this miraculous power was in Himself, and was the result of His Divine Omnipotence. The chapter we have just read makes this even more clear; for we see Him hand over the power of working miracles to His apostles, sending them forth in His name to work miracles, to heal the sick, and cast out devils. How could Jesus have imparted this power to others, if He were not Almighty—if He were not God?

The fear of man and the fear of God. Our Lord told His apostles to fear God more than men, because these last could, at the worst, only deprive them of their mortal life, but that God could cast both their souls and bodies into hell. Christians ought never to do anything, or leave anything undone out of human respect. Daniel, Susanna, the seven Machabees, and the apostles before the council, are splendid examples of how the fear of man is overcome by the fear of God.

Confidence in Divine Providence. Our Lord said to His apostles, when He sent them out: "Not one sparrow shall fall on the ground without your Father. But the very hairs of your head are numbered. Fear not, therefore: better are you than many sparrows."

Necessity and merit of good works. St. Chrysostom writes thus: "So that none might plead poverty as an excuse for not ministering to Christ in the person of His disciples, Jesus cites a cup of cold water as a gift which, though it costs nothing, is a proof of love."

The anointing of the sick with oil. We are told (Mark 6, 13) that the apostles whom our Lord sent out "anointed with oil many that were sick, and healed them". This was not the Sacrament of Extreme Unction, but it was a type of, and a preparation for it. The anointing here mentioned worked visibly and cured the body: Extreme Unction works invisibly, and primarily heals and strengthens the soul.

The high dignity of the Apostles, and their successors and assistants, consists in this, that they are the true representatives of Christ. He who receives them, receives our Lord; he who listens to them, listens to Him; he who ministers to them, ministers to Him.

APPLICATION. Have you ever told lies? or neglected your prayers out of human respect? You ask far too often what such and such people will think, and too little what Almighty God will think. Let your thoughts dwell on hell; and pray for the gift of holy fear.

Pray often, and especially at Mass, for the successors of the Apostles, the Pope and the bishops.

CHAPTER XXXII.

JOHN THE BAPTIST IS PUT TO DEATH.

[Mat. 14, 1—12. Mark 6, 14—29. Luke 9, 7—9.]

HERODIAS was filled with hatred[1] of John the Baptist, and sought to destroy him. But Herod esteemed John, and for a time obeyed him in many things. Moreover Herod was still afraid of the people, who considered John a great prophet.

Now Herod, on his birthday, gave a banquet[2] to the princes[3] and nobles of his kingdom. And the daughter of Herodias, by her former husband, coming in, danced before the guests, and Herod was pleased[4]; whereupon he promised, with an oath, to give her whatsoever she would ask of him, even if it were the half of his kingdom.

But she, being instructed beforehand by her mother, said: "Give me here in a dish[5] the head of John the Baptist." The

---

[1] *With hatred.* The evangelist St. Mark (6, 20) says that Herod heard John willingly, and asked his advice and followed it. This made Herodias fear that, if John preached to him any more, the weak king might end by putting her away from him. She, therefore, knew no rest as long as John was alive.

[2] *A banquet.* In the castle of Machærus, where John was imprisoned.

[3] *Princes.* The chief men about the court of Galilee, who, however, were all Jews.

[4] *Was pleased.* Not only Herod, but also his guests (Mark 6, 21) were pleased by the unseemly dancing and bewitching appearance of the girl, who but too closely resembled her wicked mother.

[5] *In a dish.* The heartless creature, far from being horrified at her mother's request, hastened, without even hesitating, to ask for what she wanted. She demanded that the holy prophet's head should be given to her "forthwith", because

king was grieved on hearing these words, but thinking himself bound to keep the oath which he had sworn before his guests, he sent word to the gaoler, who beheaded John and presented his head on a dish to the wicked daughter of a still more wicked mother. Then the disciples of the holy Baptist took the body of their master, and buried it; and they came to tell Jesus what had happened.

COMMENTARY.

Growth in sin. When Herod persuaded his brother Philip's wife to leave her lawful husband for him, both he and Herodias committed a grievous sin. This sin led them on to commit other sins. Herod threw John into prison, though he "knew him to be a just and holy man". He thus sinned against justice. Herodias hated the holy Baptist, persuaded her daughter to sin, and thus caused the Saint's death.

Oaths. Herod sinned by taking an oath thoughtlessly and without necessity. Now, ought he to have kept his oath when the sinful request for John's head was made to him? No; for an oath to do something sinful is, in itself, invalid. A man sins if he takes such an oath, and he sins again if he keeps it.

Human respect made Herod grant the girl's cruel request. He was ashamed in the presence of his guests to break a promise which obviously could not apply to a gift such as was asked of him. He did not fear to offend God by committing a very grievous sin, but he shrank from the false judgment of men, and thus gave the cruel and murderous order on his birthday—the very day when those in power were accustomed to perform acts of mercy.

Sharing in the guilt of others. Even the guests were not innocent of John's death. They ought to have remonstrated with Herod, and not have passed by his sin in silence.

Virtue alone is beautiful. We all detest the daughter of Herodias. She was beautiful, she wore fine clothes, she danced very cleverly, but she had a vicious heart.

St. John died a martyr to his calling. Having been called by God to be a preacher of penance, he represented Herod's sin to him, and reminded him of the law of God. On this account he died a violent death at the age of thirty-two. To him applies the eighth beatitude: "Blessed are they who suffer persecution, for justice' sake." His soul passed directly into Limbo, where he, like St. Joseph, awaited the

---

she feared that, as soon as he was sober, Herod would refuse her request. Tradition says that Herodias treated the Saint's head with contumely, and pierced his tongue with needles.

arrival of the Messias, and the speedy accomplishment of the work of Redemption. When our Lord ascended into heaven, he was taken up with Him into everlasting happiness. The Church honours him as a great Saint, and on the 24th of June celebrates his nativity, because he was born without original sin.

Dancing is often the occasion of sin, and unseemly dancing is forbidden by the Sixth Commandment.

Intemperance (or gluttony) is a capital sin. Herod would not have been carried away by the sight of the girl's dancing to make a rash and frivolous oath, unless he had been excited by too much wine.

Comparisons to be drawn between St. John and Elias, Herod and Achab, Herodias and Jezabel.

The end of Herod. Later on, Herod was deposed by the Roman emperor and banished to Lyons. Both he and his wife died in misery. The daughter of Herodias perished during a pleasure-party on the ice. The ice broke, she fell into the water, and her head was severed from her body by a piece of broken ice.

APPLICATION. Do you ever swear without necessity, or use the name of God irreverently in your conversation?

CHAPTER XXXIII.

THE MIRACLE OF THE LOAVES AND FISHES AND THE WALKING ON THE WATER.

[Mat. 14, 13—21. Mark 6, 30—44. Luke 9, 10—17. John 6, 1—13.]

THE Feast of the Passover being at hand, the apostles returned to their Divine Master, and gave Him an account of all they had done. But He said to them: "Come ye apart into a desert place, and rest a little." For there were so many coming and going that they had no time to eat. So they sailed across the lake and went into a retired spot[1]. But even there the people followed them in large numbers[2].

Jesus, seeing this great multitude, had compassion on them, and, without giving Himself any rest, went up into a mountain. There He sat with His apostles and disciples, and began to teach

---

[1] *Retired spot.* In an uninhabited neighbourhood.

[2] *Large numbers.* Travelling on foot round the northern side of the Lake (Mark 6, 33).

them many things. When He had finished His discourse, He cured the sick that were brought to Him.

Now the day was already far spent [1], and His disciples came to Him and said: "Send them away, that going into the next villages and towns, they may buy themselves meat to eat, for we are here in a desert place." Jesus said: "They have no need to go. Give you [2] them to eat." He then inquired how much bread they had. Andrew replied that there were only five loaves and two fishes. Jesus said: "Bring them hither to me, and make the men sit down."

When the multitude, numbering five thousand men, besides women and children, had sat down on the grass, Jesus took the loaves [3] and fishes [4], and, looking up to heaven, blessed them [5], and gave to His apostles to distribute [6] among the people.

Now all the people ate and were satisfied. And Jesus ordered His disciples to gather up the fragments, lest they should be lost. They did so, and filled twelve baskets [7] with the remainder of the five loaves and two fishes. The multitude, seeing this wonderful miracle, said among themselves: "This is the Prophet [8] indeed, that is to come into the world."

Jesus knowing their thoughts, and fearing that they would make Him king [9] by force, told his disciples to sail across the water, while He Himself went up into the mountain to pray.

---

[1] *Far spent.* Passed by Jesus in teaching and healing the people.

[2] *Give you.* Jesus wished to remind His disciples that, if only they would have faith, they were themselves quite able to relieve the necessities of the people, for they had already received the great gift of miracles (Origen). However, they did not understand what He meant, neither did it occur to them that our Lord would work a miracle.

[3] *Loaves.* The loaves were about as thick as a finger, and round.

[4] *Fishes.* These were dried or baked.

[5] *Blessed them.* While all eyes were fixed expectantly on our Lord.

[6] *To distribute.* The miraculous multiplication began even while our Lord was dividing the loaves and fishes into pieces, and, by the power of His blessing, it continued in the hands of the apostles, who dealt out the food as they stepped from one group of people to another. The portion of food held by them never grew less, and all who were fed saw with astonishment the wondrous miracle repeated thousands of times under their very eyes.

[7] *Twelve baskets.* More, therefore, was left, than had existed at the commencement.

[8] *The Prophet.* The Prophet foretold by Moses, or, in other words, the Messias.

[9] *Make Him king.* The impression made on the people by this stupendous miracle was very great, and, full of ecstasy, they all acknowledged Jesus to be the

It was dark when the disciples went into the ship. They had rowed about twenty or thirty furlongs in the direction of Capharnaum, and it was now almost the fourth watch of the night, when suddenly a storm[1] arose, and the sea swelled, and the ship was tossed with the waves. But, behold, Jesus came to them walking upon the sea; and drawing near the ship, He was going to pass them by; they knew Him not[2]. They were troubled, and cried out, and thought it was an apparition. Immediately Jesus spoke to them: "Have a good heart; it is I, fear not." Then they were all astonished[3].

But Peter said: "Lord, if it be Thou, bid me come[4] to Thee upon the waters." Jesus said: "Come." Peter left the ship, and walked upon the water, but, seeing the high waves, he feared[5], and began to sink. He cried out: "Lord, save me." Jesus stretched forth his hand, took hold of him and said: "O thou of little faith[6], why didst thou doubt?" They returned to the ship, and the wind ceased. Then those that were in the ship cried out: "Thou art truly the Son of God."[7] Presently the ship was at the place to

promised Messias. But, unfortunately, their hopes of the Messias were 'entirely earthly and political, for they expected that he would come to free them from the yoke of the Romans. They wished, therefore, to proclaim Jesus king of Israel, and make Him march back into Galilee at the head of these five thousand men. Our Lord saw with sorrow how far the people were from faith in Him as a Redeemer from sin, and He went up into the mountain to pray for those who were so miserably blinded.

[1] *A storm.* According to St. John (6, 18), "the sea arose by reason of a great wind that blew". In spite of all their efforts, the apostles could not advance, and their ship was driven about at the mercy of the winds and waves. How ardently they must have longed for Jesus' presence, when they found themselves in such danger.

[2] *Knew Him not.* They were unable to recognise Him on account of the darkness.

[3] *All astonished.* They knew Him by His voice. What a joyful surprise!

[4] *Bid me come.* Peter could not wait until our Lord came up to them. Full of a mighty love for Him and belief in His power, he cried out: "Lord, bid me come to Thee."

[5] *He feared.* Peter was full of courage and determination at first. But when he felt the violence of the wind, and heard the sea roaring under his feet, his courage failed, his faith wavered, and he began to sink. But he knew that Jesus was near, and, trusting in Him, he cried out: "Lord, save me!"

[6] *Of little faith.* If you had had a great and firm faith and had not doubted, you would not have sunk.

[7] *The Son of God.* Overwhelmed by the wonders which they had witnessed during the last twelve hours, they fell at the feet of Jesus and loudly confessed their faith in His Divinity.

which they were going. When they had landed[1], the people brought the sick to Him, and He healed them, and all those who touched His garments[2] were made whole.

COMMENTARY.

Our Lord's Omnipotence. St. Augustine writes thus about the miracle of the loaves and fishes: "Jesus multiplied the bread in His Hands by virtue of the same power wherewith God multiplies a few grains of corn into a waving cornfield. The five loaves were like unto those grains of corn which, when sown, do not lie unfruitful in the ground, but to which increase is immediately given by Him who is the creator of the world." Thus the miraculous multiplication of the loaves showed forth the *creative* Omnipotence of our Lord, proving Him to be the Almighty God who every year multiplies the grains of corn which are sown in the earth.

Figure of the Holy Eucharist. The great miracle of the loaves and fishes is one of the most striking figures of the Blessed Eucharist, in which the Saviour of the world nourishes the souls of countless millions of His faithful people.

The object of the miracle of the loaves. Besides the common object of all our Lord's miracles, viz. the increase of men's faith in Him, this miracle had one special object, viz. to foreshadow, and to prepare men's hearts for the marvellous Food which He gives us in the most holy Sacrament of the altar—the gift which He promised on the following day. Our Lord in the Holy Eucharist feeds the souls of the faithful with the most precious bread from heaven, multiplying His own Body, and distributing It by the hands of His priests. And with this heavenly Food all are satisfied, for it appeases our spiritual hunger by uniting us to our Lord Jesus, the author of all grace.

The Goodness of Jesus. He had compassion on the people, teaching them and healing their sick. He fed the multitude which followed Him with food both for their bodies and their souls; and because they were so eager to hear His word that they forgot to supply themselves with food, He supplied them with it by a wonderful miracle. "Seek first the

---

[1] *Landed.* Without any effort or action on the part of the apostles, the little ship accomplished the rest of the voyage, a distance of at least a mile and a half, in one moment. The whole distance from Capharnaum to the opposite, eastern coast is about six miles. According to John 6, 19, they had rowed 25 or 30 furlongs, or about four miles and a half, before the ship came to a stand-still. Thus the ship was still a mile and a half from the western shore when Jesus entered it.

[2] *Touched His garments.* The cure of the woman with an issue of blood (chapter XXX) had convinced all beholders that the mere touch of our Lord's garments sufficed to cure the sick.

kingdom of God and His justice, and all these things (which are necessary for the life of the body) shall be added unto you.'

Grace at meals. Before multiplying and distributing the bread, Jesus raised His eyes to heaven and prayed. Thus we, before and after our meals, ought to raise our hearts to God, from whom all good things come.

Waste. The words of our Lord bid us also to beware of wastefulness: "Gather up the fragments, lest they be lost." It is wrong to allow the gifts of God to be wasted. What is left over from our food should, if possible, be given to the poor, and, if not, to animals.

The annual multiplication of food. The wonderful miracle of the loaves ought to remind us how every year God gives increase to the seed which we sow. For example, ten grains of wheat sown in the ground produce three or four hundred grains: one small potato produces from ten to twenty potatoes, and so forth with everything. Now, who has given to the seed its power of germinating in the ground, of growing up, and of bearing fruit? Who sends the sunshine, dew and rain, without which no seed can thrive? It is God. The annual increase of food is the work of God's Omnipotence. We do not call it a miracle, for it all happens in what we call the course of nature, and we are so accustomed to it that it makes no impression on us. "The wonderful way in which God governs the world and provides for all His creatures makes no impression on us. His marvels are so constantly occurring that we scarcely observe His wonderful action in every little grain of corn &c. It is on this account that sometimes, in His mercy, God performs wonders out of the course of nature, so that men may realize the marvel (not because it is greater than what is constantly occurring, but only more unusual), since the every-day wonders make no impression on us. The government of creation is really a greater marvel than the feeding of five thousand with five loaves, but whereas no one marvels at the one, all men were astounded at the other, not because it was greater, but because it was more unusual" (St. Augustine).

The Divinity of our Lord. Our Lord wrought four miracles in the early dawn after the miracle of the loaves — miracles of a new kind, which on that account made a great impression on the apostles, and so quickened their faith, that they cried out: "Thou art the Son of God!" 1. Jesus Himself walked on the sea, stepping as easily and firmly over the seething waves as He would have done on dry land. He did not work this miracle on any one else, but by it He manifested Himself as a supernatural Being transcending the ordinary laws of nature. As He trod the dark abyss of water, He stood forth as the Lord of creation, being subject to the otherwise inexorable laws of nature (such as gravitation) only in so far as He pleased. 2. At our Lord's bidding St. Peter walked on the water, and was kept up by an invisible power. 3. When our Lord entered the ship, the storm was immediately quieted, and 4. the ship instantly arrived at its destination.

The object of these miracles. These four miracles, in common with the preceding miracle of the loaves, and the miracle which followed of healing the sick by the very touch of His garments, had the object of quickening and strengthening the apostles' faith and of preparing them for the revelation of the great mystery of faith, the Real Presence of our Lord in the Holy Eucharist. The miracle of our Lord walking on the water was intended to explain to them the attributes of His glorified Body; and the healing of the sick by the touch of His garments fore-shadowed the effects of receiving His Sacred Body, which our Lord described in the next chapter. If the very touch of His garments could heal the sick, surely it is not hard to believe that a soul can obtain everlasting life by receiving His Body and Blood.

The faith and love of St. Peter are remarkable, and show us why our Lord Jesus Christ chose this particular apostle to be the rock on which to build His Church. All the apostles recognised our Lord's Voice, but only to St. Peter did it occur to hasten across the water to meet Him. St. Chrysostom says: "Behold how great were the faith and love of the apostle! His faith made him say: Jesus not only can walk on the water Himself, but He can make others walk with Him! He did not say: 'Lord, teach me to walk on the waves', but: 'Lord, bid me come to Thee!' It was not for display, but for pure love of Jesus, that he demanded this great miracle."

APPLICATION. Do you always say your grace at meals? Do you say it devoutly, or carelessly?

The great miracles you have heard about ought to strengthen your faith in Jesus and His divine word. Say to our Lord joy-fully and with deep conviction: "Truly, Thou art the Son of God!" Pray to Him every day to increase your faith and to keep it from wavering.

CHAPTER XXXIV.

JESUS PROMISES TO GIVE THE BREAD OF LIFE.

[John 6, 24—72.]

MANY of those who had been miraculously fed by our Lord returned next morning to Capharnaum, where they sought and found Him in the synagogue[1]. Here Jesus addressed them,

---

[1] *The synagogue.* When they found Him, they asked: "Rabbi, when camest Thou hither?" They could not understand when and how Jesus, who, as they knew,

saying: "Amen, amen, I say to you: You seek me, not because you have seen miracles, but because you did eat of the loaves and were filled. Labour not for the meat which perisheth[1], but for that which endureth[2] unto everlasting life, which the Son of Man will give you."

Then they said to Him: "Lord, give us always[3] this bread." But He answered: "I am the living bread which came down from heaven. If any man eat of this bread, he shall live for ever. The bread which I will give is my flesh for the life[4] of the world."

Hearing this, the Jews who were in the synagogue began to dispute among themselves, saying: "How can this man[5] give us His flesh to eat?" Jesus, far from putting an end to their dispute, by applying a figurative meaning to His words, repeated[6] with even greater earnestness and solemnity what He had spoken: "Amen, amen, I say unto you, unless you eat the Flesh of the Son of Man, and drink His Blood, you shall not have life in you. He that eateth My Flesh and drinketh My Blood, hath everlasting life, and I will raise him up at the last day. For My Flesh is

---

had not embarked with His disciples, could have come to Capharnaum. He did not answer their questionings, but uttered to them a reproach which proved Him to be a discerner of their hearts.

[1] *Which perisheth.* i. e. earthly food.

[2] *Which endureth.* You seek me so as to obtain food which can sustain your mortal life. I, however, fed you in that wonderful manner in order that, your faith being awakened, you might be prepared to receive that food which will give unto you everlasting life.

[3] *Give us always.* The Jews, being fleshly-minded, could not perceive the meaning of our Lord's words. They thought He was promising them some miraculous earthly food, such as the manna, the receiving of which would take away all necessity of providing for their daily bread. Therefore they exclaimed eagerly: "Lord, give us always this bread!" using words very similar to those used by the woman of Samaria.

[4] *For the life.* Thus our Lord promised 1) to give, i. e. to sacrifice His human Body (His Flesh and Blood) for the life of the world, and 2) to give His Body to be our food. And in this sense the Jews, as we shall see, understood His words.

[5] *How can this man.* The incredulity of the Jews contrasts jarringly with the great promises of our Lord. Setting aside all respect for Him, they spoke of Him as "this man", and loudly disputed with one another, how it was possible for Jesus to give them His flesh to eat and His Blood to drink. Our Lord wished them to believe the *fact,* and leave the *how* to Him.

[6] *Repeated.* Our Lord does three things: 1. He insists that we must eat His flesh and drink His blood. 2. He threatens the unbeliever with loss of eternal life. 3. He comforts the believer with the assurance of eternal life.

meat indeed, and My Blood is drink indeed. As the living Father hath sent Me, and I live by the Father, so he that eateth Me, the same shall also live by Me[1]. This is the bread that came down from heaven. Not as your fathers did eat manna, and died. He that eateth this bread, shall live for ever."

Many of the disciples, hearing these words, did not believe it possible that He could do what He promised; they, therefore, went away[2], saying: "This word is hard[3], and who can hear it?"[4] But Jesus, knowing that they murmured at His teaching, asketh: "Doth this scandalize you? If then[5] you shall see the Son of Man ascend up where He was before? It is the spirit that quickeneth, the flesh profiteth nothing[6]. The words that I have spoken to you are spirit and life[7]. But there are some of you that believe not."[8] But they were scandalized, and many of them walked no more[9] with Him.

---

[1] *Live by Me.* Because His Flesh and Blood are inseparably united to Himself, the Son of God. So intimate is the union with Him of those who receive Him that He compares it to the union between the Father and the Son. God the Father has life in Himself, and I, as God, have life from Him.

[2] *Went away.* Our Lord's promises were by no means favourably received. Not only did the Jews remain incredulous, but even many of His disciples, who had hitherto followed Him, took scandal at His words.

[3] *This word is hard.* Or repulsive.

[4] *Who can hear it?* Or believe it.

[5] *If then.* Our Lord made one more attempt to win them to faith. "Does this offend, or scandalize you?" said He. "But if you see me, the Son of Man, go up to heaven with My glorified Body, will you not then believe that I can give My Body to you to be your Food? Will you even then be so carnally-minded, and receive My words so badly?"

[6] *Profiteth nothing.* Flesh, as flesh, cannot give life; but you must not think of the dead flesh, for it is a question of the Flesh of the Son of Man, in which dwells the Spirit of God, glorifying it and filling it with divine power. My Flesh, united to the Spirit of God, has life-giving power.

[7] *Spirit and life.* For the Flesh which I mean is penetrated by the Spirit and united to the living Godhead.

[8] *Believe not.* In spite of all the miracles which they have seen.

[9] *Walked no more.* They went back to their ordinary way of living and to their various occupations. Their chief object in following our Lord had been the hope which they built on an earthly Messias, and they cared nothing for our Lord's spiritual and supernatural promises. From henceforward they formed a part of the unbelieving mass of Jews. However, besides the twelve apostles, there still remained faithful the seventy-two disciples (whose sending forth by our Lord you will hear about in chapter LXI), as well as some other disciples, and the holy women who followed our Lord. Thus were His disciples sifted. Those whose vocation was real, and whose faith was firm, remained with Jesus; whereas many of the weak and wavering could not stand the test to which their faith was put, and left Him.

Jesus, seeing this, addressed His apostles: "Will you also [1] go away?" Peter answered [2] in the name of all: "Lord, to whom shall we go? Thou hast the words of eternal life. We have believed and have known that Thou art the Christ, the Son of God."

COMMENTARY.

The promises made by our Lord in this discourse. He promised to give us a food, the effects of which would not be passing, but would endure for ever. This Food is Himself: He is the living and life-giving Food which came down from heaven. He promised to give His Flesh for the life of the world, and to offer this His Flesh to be our Food. When the Jews were scandalized at the idea of His giving His Flesh to be eaten, He did not say to them: "You have mis-understood Me." On the contrary, He re-affirmed the very thing which had scandalized them, and asserted repeatedly that His Flesh was meat indeed and His Blood drink indeed, and that those only will have life who eat His Flesh and drink His Blood; though, at the same time, He signified that the Flesh which He would give to be our Food was His glorified Body. When many of His disciples were still offended at the idea of His giving His Flesh to eat, and refused to believe His words, our Lord preferred to let them go, rather than retract or explain away one syllable of the words He had spoken. It is therefore undeniably true that our Lord promised to give His Body, His Flesh and Blood, to be the Food of His servants. Our Lord gave this promise at the time of the third Pasch, kept during His public life, and He fulfilled it a year later when, at the Last Supper, He instituted the most holy Sacrament of the Altar.

Our Lord is entirely present in the most holy Sacrament, under the form of bread, for He says: 1. "I (Myself) am the living bread"; 2. "he that eateth Me", and therefore he who eats His Flesh eats *Him;* 3. "I abide in him" (namely in him who eats My Flesh); 4. "the flesh

---

[1] *Will you also.* Jesus made no further attempt to keep back those who wished to leave Him. On the contrary, He searchingly asked the apostles: "Will you also go away?" He left it to their free-will to forsake Him if they chose, and forced them to make a clear and open declaration of their intentions.

[2] *Peter answered.* Peter, the head and mouthpiece of the Church, made this beautiful answer in the name of the rest: "Lord, to whom shall we go?" (who but Thou canst lead us unto life?) Thou hast the words of eternal life, words of eternal truth which lead men to eternal life. And even if we cannot understand the mysterious words which Thou hast spoken, still we do not doubt them, but believe them, because we have believed and, through faith, have known that Thou art Christ the Son of God. Thus the apostles stood the test splendidly. They remained true to our Lord, openly confessed Him to be the Son of God, and placed themselves in opposition to their unbelieving fellow-countrymen.

profiteth nothing, it is the spirit that quickeneth." His Flesh, therefore, is penetrated by the Spirit, and united to His soul and divinity.

Communion under one kind. It is evident from our Lord's words: "He that eateth this Bread (My Body under the form of bread) will live for ever", that he who receives Holy Communion under one kind, does not receive less than he who receives under both kinds.

The necessity of Communion [the fourth commandment of the Church]. Our Lord makes the attainment of eternal life dependent on the receiving of His Body and Blood. "Except you eat the Flesh of the Son of Man, and drink His Blood, you shall not have life in you." — "He that eateth My Flesh &c., shall live for ever." Since it is the duty of every man to try to save his soul, and Holy Communion is necessary, as of precept, it is the duty of every man to receive Holy Communion, as soon as he is capable of understanding this divine mystery, and as soon as his will is sufficiently formed and enlightened to decide whether or no he desires to partake of this heavenly Food. The Church, therefore, is fulfilling our Lord's command, and providing for the salvation of souls, when she commands all the faithful to receive Holy Communion.

The effects of Holy Communion are rich in blessings. He who receives the Body of our Lord Jesus Christ worthily has, in His own words, everlasting life, and will be raised up by Him at the last day. "He abides in Me, and I in him. He will live in Me!" says our Lord. The Body of Christ is a living bread, which gives us supernatural and everlasting life, and is a pledge to our bodies of a glorious resurrection. Even after the sacred species have disappeared, a nourishing and vivifying strength is left in our souls, which is none other than the divine strength of the Son of God (Grimm). St. Cyril expounds the interior union which exists between our Lord and him who receives Holy Communion by the following simile: "Even as melted wax unites itself to wax, mingling with it, and becoming one with it, so does he who receives the Body of the Redeemer become one with Him, so completely is he united to Him."

The Blessed Sacrament the touch-stone of faith. He who does not believe in the Real Presence of our Lord in the Holy Eucharist, has no part in Him, because he has no firm belief in the Divinity of Christ. The true believer does not ask, as did the Jews: "How can this be?" but believes the words of Christ unconditionally, because he knows that Christ is the Son of God, and that with God all things are possible.

Our Lord's prophecy. In His discourse on the Blessed Sacrament, our Lord, distinctly and without using any figure, foretold the atoning Sacrifice of His death, telling those present that He would give His Flesh for the life of the world. He foretold with equal clearness His Ascension, when He said that the Son of Man (the Incarnate Son of God who came down from heaven) would (as the Son of Man, and therefore with His human nature) return to where He was before His Incarnation.

APPLICATION. These words of our Blessed Lord ought to move all of you who are going to make your First Communion, to prepare yourselves with the utmost care for receiving this Divine Food.

Each time you enter a church where the Blessed Sacrament is preserved, excite in your hearts an act of firm and lively faith in the Real Presence of our Lord Jesus Christ.

CHAPTER XXXV.

THE CURE OF THE DAUGHTER OF THE WOMAN OF CHANAAN AND OF THE DEAF AND DUMB MAN.

[Mat. 15, 21—31. Mark 7, 24—37.]

ON the next Feast of the Passover, Jesus did not go up to Jerusalem because of the snares laid for Him by the Jews, but retired into Galilee. Immediately He was followed by a great crowd of people bringing the sick, the blind, the lame, the deaf, the dumb, whom they laid at His feet, and He cured them all.

Passing one day from Galilee to the confines of Tyre and Sidon, a woman of Chanaan[1] ran after Him, crying out: "Have mercy on me, O Lord, Thou Son of David! my daughter is grievously troubled by a devil." Jesus made no answer[2]. But she continued to beseech Him that he would have mercy on her daughter.

Then the apostles, pitying the woman, and anxious to be rid of her importunity, besought their Divine Master to grant her petition. Jesus replied that He was sent only[3] to the lost sheep of the house of Israel. Hearing this, the woman renewed still more earnestly her supplications, falling at the Saviour's feet, and exclaiming: "Lord, help me."

---

[1] *A woman of Chanaan.* i. e. a descendant of the old idolatrous inhabitants of the land of Chanaan, and evidently a Gentile, though acquainted with the Jewish beliefs, as she calls Jesus Son of David.

[2] *No answer.* In order to try her faith.

[3] *Sent only.* My personal work is due only to the people of Israel. It was after Israel and through Israel (all the apostles being Israelites) that the Gentiles received the grace of salvation.

Jesus, wishing to try her faith still more, said: "It is not good to take the bread of the children, and to cast it to the dogs." [1] But she, nowise discouraged, answered: "Yea, Lord, for the whelps also [2] eat of the crumbs that fall from the table of their master." Jesus was pleased with the humility of her answer, and said: "O woman, great is thy faith. Be it done to thee as thou wilt." At the same moment her daughter was cured.

After this Jesus returned to the Sea of Galilee [3], and they [4] brought to Him a man who was deaf and dumb, and they besought Him that He would lay His hand [5] upon him. He took him aside [6] from the multitude, put His fingers into the man's ears, touched his tongue with spittle, sighed [7], and said: "Ephpheta", that is, "be opened", and immediately he was able to speak [8] and hear. The people cried out: "He hath done all things well [9]. He hath made both the deaf to hear, and the dumb to speak." "And he charged them that they should tell no man. But the more He charged them, so much the more a great deal did they publish it."

---

[1] *The dogs.* The children (of the kingdom) are the Jews, the members of the chosen race. The "dogs" are the heathen, so called on account of their idolatry and impurity. Our Lord's answer appeared to be a refusal, and was a great trial to the poor woman; but she stood the test.

[2] *The whelps also.* She did not protest against our Lord's words. She admitted that Israel must have the preference, and humbly numbered herself among the "dogs". "But", she urged, "even the dogs pick up the crumbs." Thou art so rich in grace, she meant to say, and Thou hast done so much for the children (of Israel) that they are satiated, and will lose nothing if Thou art merciful to me, and showest me only a crumb of Thy power and goodness by answering my prayer.

[3] *The Sea of Galilee.* On the east side of the Lake. The towns in that neighbourhood were heathen.

[4] *And they.* The compassionate relatives of the deaf and dumb man.

[5] *Lay His hand.* They knew that Jesus usually wrought His cures by the imposition of hands, and were quite convinced that this of itself would be enough to restore hearing and speech to the man.

[6] *Aside.* So as to turn the man's attention from the crowd, and fix it entirely on Himself, and on what He was going to do.

[7] *Sighed.* At the misery both spiritual and corporal which sin had brought upon man.

[8] *Able to speak.* He could use his tongue, which had been hitherto, as it were, tied. He could speak fluently and correctly, not like one who was just beginning to learn the use of speech. It was this that most astounded the on-lookers.

[9] *Well.* i. e. excellently, perfectly.

COMMENTARY.

The Omnipotence of our Lord. The first miracle related, i. e. the curing of the woman of Chanaan's daughter, was worked by our Lord at a distance from her who was possessed, and by the sole power of His Almighty will. In the second miracle, the "Ephpheta" and its instantaneous effect remind us of God's great creative words: "Let light be!" and their instantaneous effect: "And light was."

Both miracles were wrought on Gentiles. Our Lord wished to show that, provided they would believe, the Gentiles had a share in the kingdom of the Messias, even if the Israelites, by reason of their election as God's people, had the first claim.

Faith and humility of the woman of Chanaan.

Perseverance in Prayer. This woman did not give way to discouragement, although for a time Jesus would not hearken to her. His sole response to the intercession of His apostles was to say that He was sent only to the Israelites, and His reply to herself sounded very like an absolute refusal. This shows us that we ought never to weary of prayer, even though it seems as if God would not hearken to us.

The meaning of ceremonies. In healing the deaf-mute our Lord made use of several signs and ceremonies wherewith to enable the man to understand what was the matter with him, and to whom it was he owed his cure, inducing him thereby to have faith in Him. 1. The *gazing up* to heaven was meant to show him that God alone could help him. 2. The *sigh* breathed by Jesus was to make him realize what a miserable condition he was in, and to induce him to sigh to heaven for relief. 3. The *touching* and *anointing* of his ears and tongue was intended to show him plainly that he owed his cure to Jesus. In her services and in administering the holy sacraments the Church follows the example of her Divine Lord, and makes use of outward and visible signs, whereby to raise our hearts and minds to the supernatural, and make plain to us the invisible effects of the holy sacraments.

The man deaf and dumb is a type of the unregenerate. He who is unbaptized is deaf to the supernatural truths of religion and dumb to confess his faith and his own sinfulness. By Baptism the theological virtues of faith, hope and charity are implanted in the soul of man; his spiritual ears are opened to the Divine truth, and his tongue is loosened to confess the faith, and to thank the Redeemer for his benefits. In the rite of Baptism the Church imitates the action of our Lord, the priest touching the child's ears and nose with spittle, while he pronounces the word 'Ephpheta': 'Be opened!'

Hearing and speech are gifts of God, and as such should be used rightly. Remember that you have two ears, but only one tongue, doubly enclosed behind lips and teeth! "If any man think himself to be religious, not bridling his tongue, this man's religion is vain" (James 1, 26).

APPLICATION. Jesus forbade any talk about His miracle, and desired to stop all tokens of honour paid to Him. You do just the contrary. If you have done any good work, you let all the town know it. Follow our Lord's example, and say nothing without necessity that tends to your own credit.

CHAPTER XXXVI.

JESUS PROMISES PETER THE KEYS OF THE KINGDOM OF HEAVEN.

[Mat. 16, 13—20. Mark 8, 27—30. Luke 9, 18—21.]

BEING come to the neighbourhood of Cæsarea Philippi (Fig. 77)[1] Jesus asked[2] His apostles, as they went along, who the people said that He was. They replied: "Some[3], John the Baptist, others, Elias, and others, Jeremias, or one of the prophets."[4] Wishing to hear their own opinion, or, rather, to draw from them a profession of faith, He asked: "But whom do you say that I am?"

Simon Peter answered[5]: "Thou art Christ, the Son of the living God." Jesus said to him: "Blessed[6] art thou, Simon Bar-

---

[1] *Cæsarea Philippi.* A heathen city about thirty miles to the north of the Sea of Galilee.

[2] *Asked.* After He had spent some time in prayer (Luke 9, 18), as He was wont to do before He took any important step.

[3] *Some.* Say Thou art &c.

[4] *One of the prophets.* The people quite believed that Jesus was one of the prophets, risen from the dead, and a precursor of the Messias. That He could be the Messias Himself did not occur to them, in spite of His assertions to that effect, supported as they were by miracles; for they utterly refused to admit the idea that the Messias could come in poverty and humility. After the apostles had thus truthfully related the erroneous opinions of the Jews, our Lord startled them by His earnest and significant question: "But whom do you say that I am?"

[5] *Peter answered.* Peter had made a similar confession of faith after the promise of the Blessed Sacrament (chapter XXXIV), as had also the other apostles previously (chapter XXXIII); but on this occasion his confession rang out more distinctly and decidedly: "Thou art Christ, the Son of the living God"; of God, that is, who has life in Himself, and from whom all life proceeds.

[6] *Blessed.* Our Lord called Simon "blessed" in the strongest sense of the word, as it is applied to the blessed in heaven; because faith in Jesus Christ, the

Jona, because flesh and blood hath not revealed it to thee, but My Father who is in heaven. And I say to thee that thou art

Fig. 77. Ruins of Banias (Cæsarea Philippi). (Phot. Bonfils.)

Peter[1], and upon this rock[2] I will build My Church, and the gates of hell shall not prevail against it. And I will give to thee the

---

Son of God, is the source of eternal life. Simon did not obtain this faith by flesh and blood, that is to say through the medium of his human senses, which had seen and recognised our Lord's miracles, nor yet by means of his human reason, but entirely by the grace of God, which had enlarged and enlightened his heart.

[1] *Thou art Peter.* In Greek and Latin the word signifies "rock". The Syro-Chaldaic word used by our Lord is "Cephas", which also means "rock" or "stone".

[2] *This rock.* i. e. on thee, as the rock. Thou hast said that I am Christ, the Son of the living God; therefore I say to thee that thou art that which is signified by the name which I gave thee when I first called thee. Thou art the rock on which I will build My Church, so that it may stand firm for ever. On this occasion our Lord fulfilled the promise which He had made two years before, when He first met Simon and said "Thou shalt be called Cephas (Peter)". A wise man, said He at the end of His Sermon on the Mount, builds his house upon a rock; and therefore our Lord meant to build His Church upon a rock, that rock being Peter. And as a consequence the gates of hell should not prevail against it. Hell would throw open its gates, and let all its powers loose against the Church,

keys[1] of the kingdom of heaven, and whatsoever thou shalt bind upon earth, it shall be bound also in heaven; and whatsoever thou shalt loose[2] upon earth, it shall be loosed also in heaven."

COMMENTARY.

Witnesses for the Divinity of Christ: 1. Peter testified that Jesus was the Son of the living God. 2. Our Lord accepted and ratified this confession of faith, by calling Himself the Son of the Father who is in heaven, and by calling Peter 'blessed' on account of his faith in His Divinity. 3. Our Lord acted and spoke as God, by giving Peter the keys of the kingdom of heaven, and by promising him a continuous power of binding and loosing—a power which, obviously, only God could give.

Faith is a gift of God. The natural reason of the people sufficed to make them understand, from His teaching and miracles, that Jesus was a mighty prophet. But, as our Lord expressly said, supernatural light and grace were necessary to enable them to pierce the veil of His human nature, and recognise in this poor Jesus of Nazareth the Second Person of the Blessed Trinity. St. Leo the Great writes thus: "By divine inspiration Peter's mind soared above that which his senses could perceive, and with the eyes of his spirit he recognised the Son of the living God, and the glory of His Divinity."

The Church of Christ. Our Lord, in this chapter, said that He would found a Church (one only), and that this Church could not be overcome. At the same time He elected Peter to be its foundation, and clearly chose the other apostles to be its pillars. Thus the twelve apostles, with Peter as their chief, were the foundation of the Church, upon which and into which all men, like so many stones, had to be built. The Church of Christ is, therefore, *visible.* She is formed of men, and governed by men, who are armed with the divine power of binding and loosing. The faithful owe obedience to this Church of Christ, and he who refuses to obey her is to be regarded as a heathen, who has no part in the kingdom of heaven (chapter XL).

---

but they would be powerless to overcome or destroy her. By the "gates of hell" are, therefore, to be understood all the powers of evil proceeding from hell, or employed by hell.

[1] *The keys.* By the kingdom of heaven is meant the Church, just compared by our Lord to a building. Now he who possesses the keys of a house has power over that house, and can open and shut it as he will, and can admit or exclude whomsoever he thinks fit, naming the conditions of admission or exclusion. The power of the keys signifies, therefore, the supreme authority over the house and its inhabitants, or, in other words, over the Church and its members.

[2] *Bind and loose.* By binding and loosing is to be understood the exercise of that supreme authority which includes the power of making and unmaking laws (moral ties), and especially of forgiving or retaining sins and punishments for sin.

The duration of the Church. "The gates of hell shall not prevail against it." The Church, therefore, can neither be overcome nor destroyed; it will endure till the end of time.

Peter is the visible head of the Church and the Vicar of Christ upon earth. Our Lord built His Church upon the rock of Peter (on the rock which is Peter), giving to it an invincible strength and stability. Thus Peter, according to the will of the Divine Architect, is the immovable foundation of the Church. On him the visible Church, and all its pillars and stones (or to speak without figure, all its members) must, mediately or immediately, rest, and by this support be kept together. Whatever does not rest on this foundation, does not belong to the Church of Christ. We must, therefore, accept the fact that Peter occupies quite a unique position in the Church; that he is its supreme head, and that his office is to keep all other members in the unity of the faith, and that he is, in fact, the supreme authority in the Church. This is to be understood by the power of the keys, which was given to Peter. The giving up to another of the keys of a house is understood by all to be the token of the surrender to that person of supreme authority over the house and its inhabitants. So, when our Lord Jesus gave to St. Peter the power of the keys, He gave him supreme authority over His Church, that is, the authority to teach, to judge, and to make laws. The promise which our Lord on this occasion made to Peter, He fulfilled after His resurrection, when He gave him the office of Chief Pastor. By this supreme authority Peter became the visible representative of our Lord Jesus Christ upon earth, and this Primacy of St. Peter must needs continue so long as the Church lasts; in other words, there must be successors of Peter.

The Pope. St. Peter became the first Bishop of Rome, and for that reason the Roman Bishop has ever been believed to be the successor of St. Peter in the Primacy. Hence he is called the 'Pope', i. e. the father of all the faithful. The Papacy therefore is of divine institution.

The Infallibility of the Pope. The infernal spirit of lies would overcome the Church, if he could succeed in diverting her from the true faith, and plunging her into error. If, therefore, the Church is to be invincible through Peter (that is, through the Papacy), the Pope must be an infallible teacher. Even as far back as the third century St. Cyprian writes: "To the rock of Peter no error can obtain access."

APPLICATION. How great is the authority of the Church! It is a divine authority. What a great sin it is to disregard it! Do you faithfully observe the Commandments of the Church? Do you love her august head on earth, our Holy Father, the Pope, and pray for him?

CHAPTER XXXVII.

THE TRANSFIGURATION.

[Mat. 17, 1—9. Mark 9, 1—8. Luke 9, 28—36.]

A SHORT time before His Passion, Jesus took with Him Peter, James and John, and went up to a high mountain[1] to pray. And whilst He prayed, He was transfigured[2] before them. His

Fig. 78. Mount Thabor.

face shone like the sun, and His garments became white as snow[3]. And behold, Moses and Elias[4] appeared, discoursing with Him

---

[1] *A high mountain.* Probably Mount Thabor (Fig. 78), which is situated six miles to the south-east of Nazareth, and is 2000 feet high.

[2] *Transfigured.* The shining glory of His Divine nature illuminated His Body and even His raiment.

[3] *As snow.* On which the sun is shining.

[4] *Moses and Elias.* The first, as the representative of the Old Law, and the second, as the representative of the Prophets, came to offer their homage to Jesus and to speak with Him about His accomplishment of the work of Redemption (Luke 9, 31). Elias, who had been translated from this world without tasting of death (Old Test. LXV), appeared in his own body, while the soul of Moses assumed a body, such as the angels assume when they appear visibly.

concerning His Passion and Death, which He was soon to suffer for the redemption of the world.

Transported with joy[1] at the sight, Peter exclaimed: "Lord, it is good[2] for us to be here. If Thou wilt, let us make here three tabernacles; one for Thee, and one for Moses, and one for Elias." As he was yet speaking, a bright cloud[3] over-shadowed them[4], and the Voice of the Eternal Father was heard, saying: "This is My beloved Son, in whom I am well-pleased. Hear ye Him!"

The disciples fell prostrate on the ground, terrified[5] by the heavenly Voice. Then Jesus came to them, and touched them[6], saying: "Arise, and be not afraid!" When they arose, they saw no one but Jesus alone. As they went down from the mountain, Jesus said to the three disciples: "Tell the vision to no one[7] till the Son of Man be risen from the dead."

COMMENTARY.

The Divinity of Christ is proved:

a) by *the testimony of His heavenly Father*, Who, at the time of our Lord's Transfiguration, declared for the second time that Jesus was His beloved Son.

b) by *the teaching of the apostles*, who were eye-witnesses of His divine glory. This glory was visibly manifested at the Transfiguration, and was seen by the three apostles. Therefore St. Peter was able to write in his second epistle (1, 16. 17. 18) thirty-five years later: "For we have not followed cunningly devised fables, when we made known

---

[1] *With joy.* Being quite beside himself with the beauty and glory of his trans-figured Lord, and speaking, according to Luke 9, 33, "not knowing what he said".

[2] *It is good.* "This is so glorious to us that we wish to remain here for ever."

[3] *A bright cloud.* The token of the immediate Presence of God. Compare this cloud with the cloud into which Moses entered on Mount Sinai (Old Test. XXXVI), and with the cloud which rested on the Tabernacle (Old Test. XXXVIII).

[4] *Overshadowed them.* Namely, Jesus, Moses and Elias.

[5] *Terrified.* Because they recognised the Presence of God both in the Voice and in the bright cloud.

[6] *Touched them.* To help them to recover themselves, so amazed and shaken were they by all they had seen and heard.

[7] *Tell no one.* Our Lord gave them this command, because the time for His being glorified was not yet come. St. Chrysostom writes thus: "Silence was im-posed on them, because the greater the things related of the Son of God were, the harder would it be for many to believe, and the greater in consequence would be the scandal of the Cross." It was only by His Resurrection that the stumbling-block of His Death was removed.

to you the power and presence of our Lord Jesus Christ: but having been made eye-witnesses of His majesty. For He received from God the Father honour and glory; this voice coming down to Him from excellent glory: 'This is My beloved Son in whom I have pleased Myself. Hear ye Him!' And this voice we heard brought from heaven, when we were with Him in the holy mount."

c) by *our Lord's own prophecy of His Resurrection*, when He forbade the apostles to tell what they had seen, till after He had risen from the dead.

Jesus is the Messias and Lawgiver of the New Testament. The apparition of Moses and Elias proved Jesus to be the Messias to whom the law and the prophets pointed. They paid homage to Him as their Lord, Who had fulfilled the law and the prophets, and Who by His impending death would release the holy men of the Old Covenant from Limbo, and admit them into heaven. The Voice of the heavenly Father proclaimed Jesus to be the Founder and Lawgiver of the New Covenant, the teaching of which all men are bound to believe, and the commandments of which they are bound to obey. This narrative, therefore, reveals Jesus to us as the Messias, and the Fulfiller of the law and the prophets, the Divine Founder and Lawgiver of the New Covenant, the Redeemer of mankind in all ages, and the centre of the history of the world.

Thabor and Golgotha. This glimpse of glory was meant to make such an impression on the three apostles, as to prevent their losing courage or faith when, ere long, they saw their Lord in the hour of His deep abasement, and in that fearful state of suffering, when "there was no beauty or comeliness in Him" (Old Test. LXXII). In fact, the Transfiguration contrasts with the Crucifixion in every respect. In the one, we perceive Christ in wondrous majesty—on either side of Him two Saints—, the revelation of God, and the disciples in rapture. In the other we see our Lord marred and disfigured—on either side of Him two thieves—, abandoned by God, and with Him His sorrowing Mother, the grief-stricken John, and the weeping women.

The happiness of heaven. If one passing glimpse of their Lord's glory could fill the apostles with such rapture, how unspeakable must be the happiness of heaven, where the blessed see God face to face, and rejoice in the company of the Saints and angels. Truly it will be good to be there!

APPLICATION. While Jesus was praying, He was transfigured. Have you ever been able to watch any one who is praying interiorly and with recollection? You can see devotion on his very countenance, and he is, as it were, transfigured. Prayer raises and ennobles a man, and makes him heavenly-minded, filling him with peace and conformity to God's will. He who prays devoutly feels himself raised and filled with joy. Have you ever prayed thus? Compose yourself carefully before you begin your prayers, and say: "Lord, teach me how to pray!"

CHAPTER XXXVIII.

THE TRIBUTE FOR THE TEMPLE.

[Mat. 17, 23—26 and 23, 13—39.]

JESUS having returned with His disciples to Capharnaum, those who collected the annual tribute for the Temple came to Peter and asked: "Doth not your Master pay the didrachma?" [1] Peter replied: "Yes", and went to tell Jesus.

But when Jesus saw Peter coming, He said to him: "Of whom do the kings of the earth take tribute or custom? Of their own children, or of strangers?" Peter answered: "Of strangers." Jesus continued: "Then the children are free. But, that we may not scandalize them [2], go to the sea and cast in a hook, and the fish which shall first come up, take; and when thou

Fig. 79. Stater from Corinth.

hast opened its mouth, thou shalt find a stater; take that, and give it to them for me and for thee." Peter did as his Master had commanded.

Then Jesus began to upbraid the Pharisees, saying: "Woe to you, scribes and Pharisees, hypocrites, because you tithe mint and anise and cummin, and have left the weightier things of the law, judgment and mercy and faith. These things you ought to have done, and not leave those undone. Blind guides, who strain at a gnat and swallow a camel! Woe to you, scribes and Pharisees, hypocrites, because you are like to whited sepulchres, which

---

[1] *Didrachma.* A didrachma was half a sicle or stater (Fig. 79), that is, about fifteen pence of our money. This was a tax imposed upon every man for the service of the Temple.

[2] *Scandalize them.* Our Lord thus carefully observed every law and precept of the Old Covenant, rather than give scandal; but, on the other hand, He judged with great severity those who thought only of the outward observance of the letter of the law, without having any regard for its spirit.

outwardly appear to men beautiful, but within are full of dead men's bones and of all filthiness. So you also outwardly, indeed, appear to men just, but inwardly you are full of hypocrisy and iniquity!" (See chapter LIX.)

COMMENTARY.

Peter's Superiority. The manner in which Christ associates Peter with Himself in paying the tribute, is most marked and striking. It is a part of the gracious design that our Lord had upon him in the future. [See chapters XXXVI and LXXXII.]

Divinity of Christ. Our Lord claims to be the Son of Him to whom the Temple belongs, that is, God the Father. As the kings of the earth do not exact tribute from their own children, so neither does God from His own Son.

Avoiding of scandal. Our Lord's example shows us that we must avoid even the appearance of giving a bad example. He would have been quite justified in refusing to pay the Temple tax, but He did not refuse lest He should scandalize the weak and ignorant.

That which is most important. Whenever our Lord pronounced a "woe" on anyone, He signified that such an one was worthy of the everlasting punishment of hell, and therefore He wound up His denunciation of the Pharisees (of which only a portion is given above) by these words: "You serpents! How will you flee from the judgment of hell?" (Mat. 23, 33.) But why did our Lord threaten the Pharisees with everlasting punishment? Because they transgressed all the most important precepts of the law without shame and without conscience, and were, all the same, most scrupulous in their minute observance of the less important commandments. Our Lord enumerates the duties of justice, mercy and faith as those which are of most importance, and the Pharisees sinned most glaringly against these by their oppression of widows and orphans, by their unjust extortions, and by their refusal to believe anything that they did not wish to believe.

Hypocrisy. Above all, the Pharisees were hypocrites, because they set themselves up for being outwardly just and God-fearing men, whereas their hearts were full of evil and injustice, and without any true fear of God. Hypocrisy or dissimulation is a lie, and is, therefore, a sin against the eighth Commandment.

APPLICATION. If you want to know yourself (and without self-knowledge there can be no amendment of life), ask yourself what it is that most easily disturbs you. Do you feel sad when others are praised or rewarded? Do you feel glad when they are blamed or punished? If so, you are full of selfishness and envy.

Are you put out when you cannot have your own way, or if leave is refused you to do something you wish? If so, you are self-willed and disobedient.

Never laugh about the sins of others. Remember the offence against God, and pray for the conversion of those who have sinned.

Be compassionate towards the poor, and practise self-denial in order to be able to give them alms. Be kind to those of your companions who are sick or in trouble, and try to comfort and cheer them.

Examine your conscience on the subject of honesty and straightforwardness. Do you never take anything — such as fruit, sweets &c.—that does not belong to you? When you have committed a fault, do you never tell falsehoods in order to excuse yourself and escape punishment?

CHAPTER XXXIX.

JESUS AND THE LITTLE CHILDREN.

1. He blesses them and bids them come to him.

[Mat. 19, 13—15. Mark 10, 13—16. Luke 18, 15—17.]

ON one occasion some pious mothers brought their children to Jesus, that He might impose hands[1] upon them to bless them. But His disciples, thinking that He would not trouble Himself with infants, began to rebuke the mothers[2], and to send them away[3]. However this conduct of His disciples was not pleasing[4] to our Divine Lord, and He said to them: "Suffer little children to come to me, and forbid them not, for of such[5] is the kingdom of heaven." Then, embracing[6] the children, He placed His Hand on their heads and blessed them.

---

[1] *Impose hands.* From the time of the patriarchs, the laying on of hands had signified the imparting of a higher grace or power.

[2] *The mothers.* Some of them were carrying their infants in their arms, while others led them by the hand.

[3] *Away.* Probably they thought Jesus was tired with preaching and working cures, and so wished to shield Him from further importunities.

[4] *Not pleasing.* Because they knew Him and His Divine Heart so little. They ought to have known that Jesus was never tired of doing good, and that showing an interest in innocent children was refreshment to Him rather than labour.

[5] *Of such.* Of those who are childlike in disposition.

[6] *Embracing.* In order to testify His love for them.

2. He commends a childlike disposition and warns us against scandalizing little ones.

[Mat. 18, 1—10. Mark 9, 32—36. Luke 9, 46—48.]

He said to those who stood around[1]: "Amen, I say unto you, unless you become as little children[2], you shall not enter into the kingdom of heaven. He that shall receive[3] one such little child in My name, receiveth Me[4]. But he that shall scandalize[5] one of these little ones that believe in Me, it were better[6] for him that a mill-stone should be hanged about his neck, and that he should be drowned in the depth of the sea. See that you despise not[7] one of these little ones; for I say to you that

---

[1] *To those around.* Returning to Capharnaum the apostles, as they walked along, had disputed among themselves as to who should be the greatest in the kingdom of heaven. Very likely the choice of Peter to be the rock of the Church, and the preference shown to him and to James and John, had given rise to this strife of words. Jesus, knowing their thoughts, had called the twelve to him and said: "If any man desire to be first, he shall be the last of all and the servant of all." Then, calling to Him a little child, He set him in the midst of the apostles, and spoke the words we have just read: "Amen, I say to you, unless you become as little children" &c.

[2] *As little children.* i. e. candid, unassuming, humble. The sight of the little child gave our Lord the opportunity of commending to them all children and childlike people.

[3] *Receive.* Whoever shall minister to the wants of his soul and body.

[4] *Receiveth Me.* It will be counted to him as if he had ministered to Me.

[5] *Scandalize.* Shall rob him of innocence and faith by precept or bad example.

[6] *It were better.* It would have been better for such an one to have died the most miserable death rather than to have drawn on himself everlasting punishment by reason of giving scandal. "Woe to the world because of scandals", our Lord goes on to say, "for it must needs be that scandals come (the world being so corrupt, and man having free will, scandals will never quite cease on earth), but nevertheless woe to that man by whom the scandal cometh. And if thy hand or thy foot scandalize thee, cut it off and cast it from thee. It is better for thee to go into life maimed or lame, than having two hands or two feet to be cast into everlasting fire. And if thy eye scandalize thee, pluck it out and cast it from thee. It is better for thee having one eye to enter into life, than having two eyes to be cast into hell-fire." This means that if anything, be it friendship, pursuit, or amusement, induces you to sin, you are to have nothing more to do with it, never mind how dear it may be to you, or how much the parting from it may cost you. It is better for you to be maimed, i. e. to renounce something dear to you on earth, and reach heaven, than to enjoy everything here and be eternally lost. It stands to reason, however, that there will really be no mutilation in heaven.

[7] *Despise not.* Our Lord returns to the subject of the child. Not only are these little ones not to be scandalized, but they are not even to be despised, as if they were not worth caring for or tending.

their angels[1] in heaven always see the face of My Father who is in heaven."

COMMENTARY.

The love of Jesus for children. How touching is the tender affection shown by our Blessed Lord for little children, the young ones of His flock. What an encouragement, too, for those who seek to guard them from the dangers of the world, and who train their minds in the ways of God! He pressed these little ones to His Heart, and, laying His sacred Hands on them, blessed them. Now, what was His object in blessing them? The mothers begged His blessing for their children, in the hope that it might preserve them from sickness, or early death. But our Lord's object was far higher. He imparted His divine blessing to these little ones, in order that they might remain humble, innocent and pious, and become worthy members of His kingdom. It was because they are simple, humble, believing and innocent that our Lord loved children so much.

Those for whom the kingdom of heaven is intended. Our Lord did not say it was intended literally for children, but for *such* as they—not merely for children in age, but for those who are childlike in heart, simple, believing, and humble.

"Suffer little children to come unto Me." This command was given for all times. Parents, and those who represent them, ought to bring their children to Jesus; they ought to take care that they are, first of all, admitted into the Church by holy Baptism; that they learn to know and love Him by means of a Christian education; and that, as soon as they are capable of receiving it, they are united to Him by Holy Communion, and strengthened in virtue by the imposition of hands and anointing of Confirmation.

Christian teachers. Our Lord's behaviour to children imposes on those who teach them the imperative duty of always loving the children committed to their charge in an especial manner, as the favourites of our Lord; of trying to be a real blessing to these little ones by word and example; and of never being turned from this duty, either by the weariness of the burden, or the ingratitude with which parents may repay their services. To lead children to Jesus is the highest ideal of Christian education.

Our Lord's Omniscience. He knew why His disciples were disputing, and what vain thoughts they were fostering in their hearts.

Humility is a beautiful and necessary virtue. He who wishes to be a follower of Jesus must renounce pride and be humble of heart.

---

[1] *Their angels.* They have angels who are to be their guardians, always gazing on the Vision of God, and always with God; and these angels will rise up and accuse those who scandalize or despise the little ones.

The more humble a man is, the more worthy is he in the sight of God. Mary, Joseph, Peter, and all those to whom such high offices were given, were especially distinguished for their deep humility.

Giving scandal is a terrible sin. He who induces or forces others to sin, acts the part of a very devil, and draws damnation on himself.*

The proximate occasions of sin. Sin is the greatest of all evils. It is a far greater evil than the most miserable death. Therefore a Christian, if he wishes to guard his soul against mortal sin, must carefully avoid the proximate occasions of sin; for no sacrifice on our part can be too great, if it serves to save our souls.

Guardian Angels. In the Old Testament we came across repeated examples which confirm the Catholic doctrine about guardian angels. In the chapter we have just read we learn from our Lord's own lips that children have guardian angels, who are their advocates before God. Although our guardian angels are invisible to our eyes, they themselves are ever gazing on the Face of God. "Whithersoever the angels be sent, and wheresoever they are, they never cease to live in Him who is to be found everywhere, even in God, the Vision of whom makes their heaven and their joy" (S. Thomas Aquinas).

The Value of a Soul. "A human soul is so precious that, as each one enters into being, an angel is given to it to be its guardian" (S. Jerome).

Hell is an everlasting fire.

APPLICATION. What a happiness for those little children to go to Jesus Himself, and be blessed by Him? But how about you? Cannot you also taste of that happiness? Cannot you also go to Jesus Himself? Yes! In the church dwells that same Jesus, present with His Divinity and Manhood in the Blessed Sacrament, and there you can go to Him, worship Him, and speak to Him; and by the hand of His priest receive His blessing, both at Mass and at Benediction. Give your hearts to this Divine Lover of children! Visit Him often in the church; promise Him that you will be holy and humble children, and ask for His help to keep your promise!

Do you ever dispute with your brothers and sisters as to who is the greatest among you? Do you want to be preferred to your comrades? As often as this sort of temptation to pride arises in your heart, say: "I will not be proud! Humble Jesus, I will follow Thee!"

Avoid bad companions!

---

* By the words "draws damnation on himself" is meant: "commits a mortal sin and will go to Hell unless he truly repents." —*Publisher*, 2003.

CHAPTER XL.

FRATERNAL CORRECTION—FORGIVENESS OF INJURIES—THE UNFORGIVING SERVANT.

[Mat. 18, 15—35. Luke 17, 1—4.]

JESUS, continuing His teachings, said: "If thy brother shall offend[1] thee, go[2] and reprove him[3] between thee and him alone[4]. If he shall hear thee[5], thou shalt gain[6] thy brother. But if he will not hear thee, take with thee one or two more. If he will not hear them, tell the Church[7]; and if he will not hear the Church, let him be to thee as a heathen and a publican[8]. Amen I say unto you, whatsoever you shall bind upon earth[9], shall be bound also in heaven; and whatsoever you shall loose on earth, shall be loosed also in heaven."

Peter asked Jesus: "Lord, how often shall my brother[10] offend me and I forgive him? till seven times?" But Jesus answered: "I say not to thee till seven times, but till seventy times seven."[11] Thereupon Jesus related

The Parable of the Unforgiving Servant. The kingdom of heaven is likened[12] to a king who would take an account of his servants. When he had begun to take the account, one was brought to him who owed him ten thousand talents[13]. As he had

---

[1] *Offend.* Or injure you.   [2] *Go.* Do not wait for him to come to you.

[3] *Reprove him.* i. e. show him how he has wronged you.

[4] *Alone.* So as not to put him to shame before others without necessity.

[5] *Hear thee.* If he will listen to and accept your proposals.

[6] *Gain.* For the kingdom of heaven.

[7] *The Church.* The authorities of the Church.

[8] *A publican.* As a man excommunicated from the Church, and having no part in the kingdom of God.

[9] *Bind upon earth.* By these words our Lord explains the reason why a sinner who will not be reconciled is shut out from the kingdom of God; because the sins and punishments which are retained (i. e. not remitted) by the apostles would be equally retained by God. A sentence pronounced by the apostles on earth would hold good before God in heaven. The effect of their judgment would extend from the present to the future, from time to eternity.*

[10] *My brother.* My fellow-creature.

[11] *Seventy times seven.* i. e. there is to be no limit to forgiveness of injuries.

[12] *Is likened.* It happens in the kingdom of God as it happened with a king who was taking an account with his servants.

[13] *Ten thousand talents.* About £ 4,000,000 of our money, therefore an enormous sum—impossible, it may be said, to pay.

---

* It should be noted that this exclusion from the kingdom of God is initiated and caused by the sinner, not by the Apostles. —*Publisher*, 2003.

not wherewith to pay it, his lord commanded that he should be sold[1], and his wife and children and all that he had, and payment to be made."

But that servant, falling down, besought him, saying: "Have patience with me, and I will pay thee all."[2] Now the lord of that servant, being moved with compassion, let him go, and forgave him[3] the debt.

But when that servant was gone out, he found one of his fellow-servants that owed him a hundred pence[4], and laying hold of him he throttled him, saying: "Pay what thou owest!"

Then his fellow-servant, falling down, besought him, saying: "Have patience with me, and I will pay thee all." Yet he would not; but went and cast him into prison till he should pay the debt. Now his fellow-servants, seeing what was done, were very much grieved[5]; and they came and told their lord all that was done.

Then his lord called him and said to him: "Thou wicked servant, I forgave thee all the debt, because thou besoughtest me. Shouldst not thou, then, have had compassion on thy fellow-servant, even as I had compassion on thee?" And his lord, being angry, delivered him to the torturers until he should pay[6] all the debt. So[7] also shall My heavenly Father do to you, if you forgive not everyone his brother from your hearts.

COMMENTARY.

The authority of the apostles. Our Lord gave the power of binding and loosing to the other apostles also; but as He had already made Peter the foundation-rock of the Church and the key-bearer of the kingdom of heaven, it is clear that the other apostles (and their suc-

---

[1] *Sold.* According to the Roman law of that time a creditor was entitled to sell any insolvent debtor, with his family, towards the payment of the debt.

[2] *Pay thee all.* In his terror he promised far more than he was able to perform. His lord knew very well that the debt could never be paid—but as the servant acknowledged the debt, and begged so earnestly, he set him free, and not merely granted him a delay, but entirely forgave him the debt.

[3] *Forgave him.* Just think how this servant must have rejoiced at being freed from the burden which had so long weighed on him.

[4] *A hundred pence.* Equal to not quite £ 3.10.0. of our money.

[5] *Much grieved.* At the hardness and cruelty of their fellow-servant.

[6] *Until he should pay.* In other words, for ever, because such a heavy debt could never be paid by him.

[7] *So.* Even as the king treated that servant who was so unmerciful to his fellow-servant.

cessors) must exercise this power in unity with Peter (the Papal See), and in subjection to him.

To admonish and convert sinners is a spiritual work of mercy; but it should be done without passion, and with the pure intention of converting and saving the sinner. "He who causes a sinner to be converted from the error of his ways, shall save his soul from death, and cover a multitude of sins" (James 5, 20).

The infinite mercy of God to repentant sinners, and the hardness of man towards his neighbour are equally shown in the parable we have just read.

The king is God. The servant who owed ten thousand talents is the sinner. Sin being an injury to the infinite Majesty of God, there rests on the sinner the burden of an infinite debt, which he can never pay of himself, and for which he deserves an eternal punishment. If, however, the sinner confesses his guilt with contrition, and prays to God for pardon, Almighty God, through the merits of Jesus Christ, will remit the whole overwhelming debt of his sin, as well as its eternal punishment—but on the condition that he will equally forgive those who injure him.

The second servant who owed the first a hundred pence is one who has injured his fellow-man. In comparison with the offence against the Majesty of God, any injury towards a fellow-creature is, as far as the fellow-creature is concerned, only a trifle. Now, if the injured man, who is a sinner in the eyes of God, wishes to obtain from the divine mercy pardon of his infinite debt of sin, it is only fair and just that he should himself show mercy to one who has injured him, and forgive what is such a trifling debt. If he will not do so, he proves himself to be unforgiving and revengeful; the just (the angels and saints) will be filled with holy indignation, and accuse him before God; and God will not forgive him his debt, but will thrust him into hell, where he must remain for ever, because he is incapable of ever paying his debt.

The fifth petition of the Our Father is explained by this parable; it being clearly shown that he who does not forgive his fellow-men "from his heart", cannot obtain forgiveness from God, but will be rejected by Him, and banished for ever from His Presence.

The debt of sin. This parable likewise shows that the guilt of sin is inconceivably great in the eyes of God, because by it His infinite Majesty is offended.

Good resolutions. The debtor in the parable made a resolution to pay off his debt if he could. So also we who are sinners should make firm resolutions to offer satisfaction for our sins.

The Divinity of our Lord. His words: "My heavenly Father" contain a direct testimony to His own Divinity.

Slavery. A wretched slavery prevailed throughout all heathendom, men and women being bought and sold like mere goods and chattels. Through Jesus Christ and His Church this slavery has been abolished.

APPLICATION. Think of the number and greatness of your sins. From your early childhood not a day has passed that you have not offended God either by thought, desire, word, deed, or the omission of what you ought to have done. You have wasted and misused grace, and have, perhaps, committed mortal sins. And yet God has borne with you, spared you and forgiven you! Praise Him and love him for what He has done for you.
(Compare Commentary Old Test. XVII.)

CHAPTER XLI.

JESUS SENDS FORTH HIS SEVENTY-TWO DISCIPLES.

[Luke 10, 1—24. Compare Mat. 10, 1—42.]

ON His journey from Galilee to Judæa, Jesus selected from among His followers seventy-two, whom He called disciples[1], that they might assist[2] the twelve apostles in the work of the ministry. He sent them forth two by two, saying: "He that heareth you[3], heareth Me, and He that despiseth you, despiseth Me; and he that despiseth Me, despiseth Him that sent Me."

A short time after, the seventy-two returned to Him, rejoicing, and saying that even the demons were subject to them. Jesus, fearing that they might become vain of the power that was given them, said: "I saw Satan, as lightning, falling from heaven. Rejoice not because the spirits are subject to you, but rejoice in this, that your names are written in the Book of Life."

Then, rejoicing with them, He prayed: "I give thanks to Thee, O Father, Lord of heaven and earth, that Thou hast hid these things from the wise and prudent, and hast revealed them to little ones!"[4]

---

[1] *Disciples.* To distinguish them from the apostles, who held a higher rank and greater power.

[2] *Assist.* Because, as Christ said: "The harvest indeed is great, but the labourers are few. Pray ye therefore the Lord of the harvest, that He send forth labourers into His vineyard."

[3] *Heareth you.* He that listens to and accepts what you say.

[4] *Little ones.* i. e. the lowly, the humble, the unlearned.

COMMENTARY.

The Ecclesiastical Hierarchy. From this chapter we see how our Lord gradually traced the outlines of the Hierarchy of the Church, i. e. of the higher and lower orders of sacred ministers. There we have Peter, the Apostles, the disciples and the faithful; here we have the Pope, the Bishops, the Priests [with Deacons, Subdeacons and four minor orders] and the faithful.

Prayer to God to send more labourers into His vineyard. Jesus, the Lord of the harvest, desires us to pray to Him to send more labourers, i. e. more bishops and priests, and this not only for our own sakes, but for the multitude of our fellow-men, who are still unbelievers. He alone, by His grace, can raise up true apostolic labourers for His vineyard. This prayer is very necessary. Even many Catholic countries are in sad want of priests; but, setting aside this want, the majority of men in this world are either heathens (of whom there are about 700,000,000) or Mahometans (of whom there are about 150,000,000). Only 250,000,000 belong to the One, Holy, Catholic and Apostolic Church; for out of those who claim to be Christians, 80,000,000 belong to the Greek schismatical Church, and about 90,000,000 to the various Protestant sects. The harvest is indeed still great, and the number of Catholic priests and missionaries small in proportion.

Our Lord sent out His disciples two and two 1. so that they could bear witness to the miracles wrought. "In the law it is written that the testimony of two men is true" (John 8, 17), and therefore men would more readily believe the word of two together than of one alone. 2. That they might practise mutual love and unity of spirit, and be thus better able to preach the Gospel of love and peace.

APPLICATION. You ought to pray to God, especially at the four Ember seasons when the ordinations take place, to send forth labourers into His harvest.

Support all Catholic missions according to your means.

CHAPTER XLII.

THE DOCTOR OF THE LAW.—THE GOOD SAMARITAN.

[Luke 10, 25—37. Mat. 22, 35—40. Mark 12, 28—34.]

AGAIN, when Jesus was on His way to Jerusalem, He met a doctor of the law [1], who, hoping to tempt [2] our Lord, asked him, through curiosity: "Master, what must I do to possess eternal

---

[1] *The doctors of the law,* or scribes, were a body of men whose profession it was to preserve the written law, interpret it, and guard it from being falsified

[2] *Tempt.* He hoped to entrap our Lord into teaching some doctrine contrary to the law, or at any rate contrary to its received interpretation. Had he done so, the scribes would have been able to hold Him up as an enemy of the law.

life?" Jesus answered: "What is written in the law? how readest thou?" He replied: "Thou shalt love the Lord thy God with thy whole heart, and with thy whole soul, and with all thy strength, and with all thy mind; and thy neighbour as thyself."

Jesus said to Him: "Thou hast answered right; this do, and thou shalt live." [1] But the doctor, wishing to justify [2] himself, said: "Who is my neighbour?"

Then Jesus replied with the *Parable of the Good Samaritan:*

"A certain man [3] went down from Jerusalem to Jericho, and fell among robbers [4], who also stripped him; and having wounded him, went away, leaving him half-dead [5]. Now it happened that a certain priest went down the same way, and seeing him passed by. In like manner also a Levite [6], when he was near the place, and saw him, passed by. But a certain Samaritan, being on his journey, came near him, and seeing him, was moved with

---

[1] *Thou shalt live.* Or obtain eternal life.

[2] *To justify.* Our Lord told him to love his neighbour as himself. "This do, and thou shalt live." The doctor evidently felt in his own heart that he had not properly and fully practised this command, and therefore he wished to justify himself by saying that it was a disputed point among the Jews as to who was their neighbour.

[3] *A certain man.* Namely a Jew from Jerusalem.

[4] *Robbers.* The road from Jerusalem to Jericho (Fig. 80; see Map) is a very deserted one, and passes through deep defiles which, to this day, are infested by robbers.

[5] *Half-dead.* They surrounded him, took from him all that he had, even his clothes, and because he offered resistance, wounded him so severely that he lay half-dead. He could not stir, and unless help came he must soon die.

[6] *A priest and a Levite.* A Jewish priest, followed by his assistant, a Levite (Old Test. XXXIX). These two were returning from Jerusalem, where they had accomplished the time assigned to them for serving in the Temple, and were now on their way back to Jericho, of which town they were inhabitants. The poor despoiled man lay on the road, the blood pouring from his many wounds. He had become so weak that he could not even cry out for help; but when he heard the sound of approaching footsteps, which told him that help was at hand, hope revived in his heart. The priest heard the poor man's groans, and saw his bleeding condition, but he who was but just returning from the service of the merciful God had no compassion for this poor, dying man, and went on his way. The Levite too, in his turn, passed by, unmoved. Both of them knew and preached the divine law: "Thou shalt love thy neighbour as thyself", but neither of them practised what they taught, or showed love towards their fellow-countryman and fellow-believer. The poor, wounded man had well-nigh given up all hope, when the Good Samaritan rode up.

compassion. And going[1] up to him, he bound up his wounds, pouring in oil and wine; and setting him upon his own beast[2], brought him to an inn and took care of him.

"The next day he took out two pence[3], and gave them to the innkeeper, and said: 'Take care of him, and whatever thou shalt spend over and above, I, at my return, will repay thee.'" Having finished the parable[4], Jesus asked the doctor: "Which of these

Fig. 80. Road from Jerusalem to Jericho. (Phot. P. Dunkel.)

three, in thy opinion, was neighbour to him that fell among the robbers?" The doctor of the law replied: "He that showed mercy to him." Jesus said to him: "Go, and do thou in like manner."[5]

---

[1] *Going.* He was not content with a mere show of compassion, but immediately did all he could to relieve the poor man. He applied the remedies usual in those days for stopping the bleeding and preventing the wounds from festering.

[2] *Beast.* His mule.

[3] *Two pence.* This was sufficient for his keep for two days.

[4] *The parable.* Our Lord had conveyed his teaching in the form of a narrative, so as to compel the scribe to answer his own question for himself.

[5] *In like manner.* Show compassion to all who need it.

COMMENTARY.

Love of our neighbour. He who hopes to be saved must love God with all his heart, and his neighbour as himself. Of the love of God we shall speak in the next chapter: this chapter deals principally with the love of our neighbour, the qualities of which our Lord shows us in His beautiful parable of the Good Samaritan.

The love shown by the Samaritan was, first of all, *real*, for he felt compassion from his heart for the wounded man, and had a real sympathy with him in his misfortunes. He stopped instantly when he perceived the poor man, and went up to him, whereas the priest and the Levite had both passed by regardless of his state. And because his love was real, it was *practical*. He wished to help the poor man, and did all in his power to alleviate his sufferings and save his life; he interrupted his journey, tended the wounded man himself all that day, and when his business called him away for a few days, he left him in charge of the innkeeper, paying for his keep, and promising to return. Lastly, the love he showed was *universal*. He knew that the wounded man was a Jew, the enemy of his people; and he knew that under similar circumstances a Jew would be very unlikely to assist him. All the same he took pity on him, and forgave the enmity shown to the Samaritans by the Jews. In this poor man he saw only a suffering fellow-creature and a brother, and helped him as such.

By this parable, therefore, our Lord teaches us that every man is our neighbour, and that our love ought to be real, practical and universal.

The deeper meaning of the parable. According to the Fathers of the Church the following deeper interpretation can be given to it. Jesus Himself is the Good Samaritan, as proved by His treatment of the robbed and wounded human race. Sin and the devil are the robbers who have despoiled man of his robe of innocence and all supernatural gifts, and grievously wounded him in his natural gifts. Thus man lay, weak, helpless, and half-dead. He still, it is true, possessed his natural life, but he had lost the supernatural life of grace, as well as the prospect of eternal life, and was powerless to raise himself from the misery of sin by any effort of his own. Neither priest nor Levite, i. e. neither sacrifice nor law of the Old Covenant, could help him, or heal his wounds; they only made him realize more fully his helpless condition. Then the Son of God, moved by compassion, came down from heaven to help poor fallen man, living at enmity with God. He healed his wounds with the wine of His Most Precious Blood and the oil of His grace, and took him to the inn, His Church. When He left this earth to return to heaven, He gave to the guardians of His Church the twofold treasure of His doctrine and His grace, and ordered them to tend the still weak man, until He Himself came back to reward every one according to his works. This inconceivable love of the Incarnate Son of God for all men is the great reason why we ought to love our neighbour and even our enemy.

_____

APPLICATION. In the case of the priest and the Levite you can see what a hateful thing is want of compassion. On the other hand, the example of the Samaritan shows you how noble and beautiful is a heart full of pity and a desire to help those in need. Now which heart is yours most like? that of the priest or that of the Samaritan? Do you feel pity for others in their misfortunes? Do you not sometimes feel a wicked joy when evil befalls any one? Do you help the sick or poor as far as you are able? Surely, even if you can give them nothing, you could visit them, show them your sympathy, and pray for them.

CHAPTER XLIII.

MARY AND MARTHA.

[Luke 10, 38—42]

HAVING returned to Judæa and being on His way to Jerusalem, Jesus entered a certain town named Bethania [1], at a short distance from Jerusalem, where he was kindly entertained by two pious sisters, named Martha and Mary [2]. Now Mary sat down at our Saviour's feet, and listened attentively to the words of wisdom which fell from His divine lips. Martha, on the other hand, busied herself with preparing the repast.

Martha, then, seeing that she had to do all the work, complained to our Saviour and said: "Lord, hast Thou no care [3] that my sister has left me alone to serve? Speak to her, therefore, that she help me." But Jesus answered: "Martha! Martha! Thou

_____

[1] _Bethania._ See Map. Bethania was on the eastern slope of the Mount of Olives.

[2] _Martha and Mary._ They lived with their brother, Lazarus. All three believed in and loved our Lord, and therefore He used to stay in their house with His disciples.

[3] _Hast Thou no care?_ Martha's words betray her impatience with our Lord as well as with her sister Mary. In her joy at our Lord's visit she wished everyone to be occupied in providing Him with the best things that could be procured; and it was inconceivable to this busy Martha that her sister could sit quietly at the feet of Jesus, while in her opinion there was more work to be done than could be got through. Her speech sounded very like a reproach to Mary for what she considered to be want of thought.

art careful and troubled about many things! one thing only is necessary. Mary hath chosen the best part[1], which shall not be taken away from her."

COMMENTARY.

The Love of God. The story of the Good Samaritan gave us an example of the love of our neighbour. In Martha and Mary we have a model of the true love of God. Both sisters loved our Divine Lord, but they showed their love in different ways. Mary was all absorbed, listening to and meditating on His words; and, carried out of herself by her love of Him, she forgot everything else. Martha, on the other hand, was taken up with active work in His service, and could only think of how she might most perfectly minister to His wants. Martha spent herself in her efforts to prepare food for our Lord, while Mary was entirely occupied in being fed by Him. We can and we ought to learn lessons from both sisters. Like Martha we ought to do our best to fulfil the duties of our state of life: but we should not, on this account, neglect to hear and meditate on the divine word. "These things you ought to have done, and not leave those undone" (Mat. 23, 23). Pray and work!

Works of mercy. We cannot, as Martha did, minister to the wants of our Lord Himself, but we can and ought to minister to Him in the person of His brethren, the poor and the sick; for whatever we do for these we do for Him (chapter LXIII).

The one thing needful. Men are taken up with a multitude of busy occupations, and yet a great many of these are quite unnecessary. There is, however, one occupation absolutely necessary and indispensable for each one of us, namely, to love God and to care for our salvation. To save our souls and to win heaven is the highest and last end, to which every other object must give way. Christian self-love consists in caring for the salvation of our souls before all things.

Our Lady the perfect Mary and Martha. Mary, the Mother of God, all her life through practised most perfectly those virtues for which

---

[1] *The best part.* By His answer our Lord took Mary's part, and at the same time gently reproved Martha for being too entirely taken up by business. "You are too much occupied with a number of things," He meant to say; "whereas there is only one thing which is worth all this anxiety, for there is only one thing which is absolutely necessary. You are indeed doing a good work by seeking to minister to My wants, but your sister has chosen the better part in listening to My teaching, and feeding her soul with My divine words. Her undivided attention to the things of God shall not be taken away from her, for the contemplation of what is divine and the Vision of God are the eternal inheritance of the Saints in heaven." The one thing necessary, of which our Lord spoke, is the work of salvation. Jesus does not blame Martha for working, but because she worked in a restless and uneasy state of mind.

each of the two sisters was distinguished. From her childhood she had attended to "the one thing needful"; and for thirty years she ministered to our Lord's personal wants, most wonderfully combining the active life with the contemplative life, working with her hands while her heart gazed on God. She was at the same time the Mother who had charge of her Son, and the disciple of that Son, treasuring all His words in her heart and imitating His life. On earth she chose the best part, and in heaven she attained to the best part, being crowned by her Divine Son as the Queen of all Saints. Hence we see why the Church has chosen this portion of Scripture for the Gospel on the *Feast of our Lady's Assumption* into heaven.

APPLICATION. Are you industrious as Martha was, and pious like Mary? Are not your thoughts dissipated all day long? Think often about God in the course of the day, and offer your actions to Him. Do everything with God and for God.

CHAPTER XLIV.

JESUS THE GOOD SHEPHERD.

[John 10, 11—16. Luke 15, 1—10.]

JESUS having come to Jerusalem for the Feast of Tabernacles, went to the Temple and taught there, saying: "I am the Good Shepherd. The Good Shepherd giveth his life[1] for his sheep. But the hireling[2], and he that is not the shepherd, seeth the wolf coming, and fleeth. I am the Good Shepherd, and I know mine, and mine know Me, and I lay down My life for My sheep. And other sheep I have which are not of this fold[3]; them also I must bring[4], and they shall hear My voice, and there shall be one fold and one shepherd."

On another occasion[5] when the proud and conceited Pharisees complained because Jesus dealt kindly with publicans and sinners, He spoke to them this parable[6]: "What man among you that

---

[1] *Giveth his life.* i. e. the sure sign by which a good shepherd can be known is that he is ready to lay down his life for his sheep.

[2] *The hireling.* A man hired for wages to look after the sheep, and to whom, therefore, the sheep do not belong.

[3] *Not of this fold.* Who do not belong to the people of Israel, i. e. the Gentiles.

[4] *I must bring.* Into My fold.

[5] *Another occasion.* Cf. Luke 15, 1—10. Mat. 18, 11—14.

[6] *This parable* was meant to show the love which the Good Shepherd has for individual sheep of his flock who go astray.

hath a hundred sheep, and if he shall lose one of them, doth
not leave the ninety-nine in the desert[1], and go after that which
was lost, until he find it? And when he hath found it, doth he
not lay it on his shoulders, rejoicing?[2] Then, coming home, doth
he not call together his friends and neighbours, saying to them:
'Rejoice with me, because I have found my sheep that was lost.'
I say to you that even so[3] there shall be joy in heaven upon one
sinner that doeth penance, more than upon ninety-nine just that
need not penance."

COMMENTARY.

The Love of Jesus for us. By the simile of the Good Shepherd
our Lord teaches us how great is His compassionate love for all mankind. All men, Jews and Gentiles, are His sheep, and He gave His
life for all, being sacrificed on the Cross to redeem them from sin and
hell. He is therefore the only Good Shepherd, and all others who are
called to the pastoral office are good shepherds only so far as they
imitate Jesus in their love and care of the flock confided to them.
Moreover Jesus knows His own. He knows all about them, their needs,
their weakness, their thoughts, their endeavours; He leads them into
the fold of His Church, He helps them by His grace, He enlightens
them by His doctrine, and nourishes and strengthens them with His
Flesh and Blood in the most Blessed Sacrament. His pastoral love is,
therefore, infinite and divine.

The following doctrines are especially conveyed by this parable:

The Sacrifice and Death of our Lord Jesus Christ. Our Lord distinctly foretells His Sacrifice and Death in the words: "I lay down My
life for My sheep."

Jesus is the Lord and Chief Shepherd of the redeemed. The sheep
belong to Him, because He has bought them with His Precious Blood.

The One, United, Catholic Church. Our Lord foretold that the
Gentiles also would believe in Him, and that all the faithful, both Jews
and Gentiles, would be united in one fold, under one Shepherd. According to our Lord's words there was to be only *one* Church, and this
Church was to be *united*. It was not to be split up into a multitude of
national churches in every part of the world, but was to spread itself

---

[1] *In the desert.* Out on the hills where there were no enclosures, but good
pasturage.

[2] *Rejoicing.* He does not chide or chastise it for having run away, but carries
it back lovingly to the fold.

[3] *Even so.* Our Lord now makes the application of the parable, saying that
it is the same with God, His angels and His Saints.

by degrees over the whole face of the earth, and all nations were to be gathered into its fold. The Church foretold by our Lord was to be a Catholic or universal Church. Now this one, united, and Catholic Church which, according to His good pleasure, our Lord founded, can only be the Roman Catholic Church, in which the faithful of the five parts of the world are joined together in real unity of faith and government under one Chief Shepherd, the Pope.

The Love of Jesus for sinners. The touching parable of the lost sheep shows our Lord's compassionate love for individual sinners. The lost sheep signifies a sinner who, obeying his own evil inclinations and the allurements of sin, has separated himself from Jesus, and is shut out from the number of the faithful. But the Saviour does not withdraw His love from this wanderer. Even as, during His sojourn on earth, He laboured for the conversion of sinners, so does He now go after the sinner. He calls him by His grace, by His priests, and invites him to return once more to the fold, by means of the Sacrament of Penance. And when He has found him, He supports him on the difficult road of penance, and receives him back with joy. Jesus does this not for His own sake, since He does not require this straying sinner: He seeks him out of pure love and compassion for the poor sinner himself, wandering about and in momentary danger of falling into the abyss of hell. And it was because the Good Shepherd and His "friends" were so anxious about the salvation of that sheep which was in danger, that their joy at his return and salvation is greater, and shows itself more outwardly, than their calm joy about the faithful who are walking without wavering on the path of salvation.

Grace. We learn from this parable the important doctrine that it is God who gives the first impulse to the conversion or justification of a sinner, moving him to be converted by His preventing grace (conveyed either by inward inspirations, or by the warning words of parents or pastors, or else by misfortune, sickness &c.), and who then supports him by His grace on the road of penance, until he is once more restored to a state of justification in the holy Sacrament of Penance.

The Communion of Saints. If the blessed inhabitants of heaven rejoice over the conversion of sinners, they must have a knowledge of it. It follows, therefore, that the angels and Saints in heaven know about us, care for us, and pray for us.

APPLICATION. Does not the loving compassion of Jesus, the Good Shepherd of our souls, bind us to love Him with all our hearts, and above all things? How have you loved Him hitherto? He has given His life for you; He has called you into the fold of His one true Church without any merit on your part; He has fed you on the milk of His doctrine, and has showered countless graces on you; and how have you repaid Him? Have you always listened to His Voice, and kept His Commandments? Have you not, on the contrary, offended Him every day of your life? Be sorry for your ingratitude, and try to excite in yourself a greater love for Jesus. Say this prayer: "Kindle in me the fire of Thy love."

CHAPTER XLV.

THE PARABLE OF THE PRODIGAL SON.

[Luke 15, 11—32.]

ON the same occasion Jesus proposed the following parable to the Jews: "A certain man had two sons. And the younger of them said: 'Father, give me the portion of substance that falleth to me.'[1] The father did so. Not many days after, the younger son, gathering all his property, went abroad into a far country[2], and there he spent his substance in riotous living[3].

"After he had spent all, there came a mighty famine in that country, and he began to be in want[4]. Then he went and joined himself to one of the citizens of that country, who sent him into his farm to feed swine[5]. Here he would fain have filled his belly with the husks the swine did eat.

---

[1] *Falleth to me.* According to the Jewish law of inheritance the younger son received only half as much as the eldest, but as long as his father was alive he could count on nothing. The father was therefore in no way bound to give his son his future inheritance during his own life-time; but, rather than force him to stay at home against his will, he gave it to him, though he knew very well that his son would soon squander away his fortune.

[2] *A far country.* He hoped to have more liberty away from his father's house. He chafed under the discipline of his home-life, and his father's supervision. He considered the restraints unnecessary and undignified, and felt sure that he would be happier, if he were his own master and could do just as he liked. The calm happiness of his father's house no longer satisfied him. He thought it monotonous and wearisome, and pined for the licence of noisy pleasures, picturing to himself a happy life in the vortex of the world. His father warned him, but he cast his warnings to the four winds, and defiantly left his home.

[3] *In riotous living.* Joining himself to flatterers and lewd companions, and indulging in drinking, banqueting and unworthy pleasures.

[4] *In want.* For his "friends" quickly forsook him, when they could get nothing more out of him.

[5] *Feed swine.* He had to accept the most degrading situation to save himself from dying of starvation. His labours, however, were so badly paid that often he had not enough to eat, suffered bitter hunger, and even envied the swine their

"But entering into himself[1], he said: 'How many hired servants in my father's house have plenty of bread, and I here perish with hunger! I will arise and will go to my father, and will say to him: Father, I have sinned[2] against heaven[3] and before thee[4]; I am not now worthy[5] to be called thy son; make me as one of thy hired servants!' Then he rose up[6] and went to his father.

"When he was yet a great way off, his father saw him[7] and was moved with compassion, and ran to him and fell on his neck and kissed him. But the son said: 'Father, I have sinned against heaven and before thee; I am not now worthy to be called thy son.' And the father said to his servants: 'Bring forth quickly the first robe[8] and put it on him, and put a ring on his hand, and shoes on his feet. And bring hither the fatted calf and kill

---

food. Poor, unhappy man, how miserable he was! Once the proud and headstrong son of a rich father, he was now clothed in rags, despised, emaciated, and hungry!

[1] *Entering into himself.* What a deep and striking expression! In the same sense it may be said that he had hitherto been out of himself, or beside himself. He had never thought seriously either of himself or of his future; he had been given over to pleasure, and had lived carelessly from day to day. Now bitter necessity forced him to enter into himself, and to ask himself why he was reduced to such a miserable condition, and what was to become of him. He called to mind his happy life in his father's house, and sorrowfully reminded himself that even his father's hired day-labourers were better off than he was now. He recognised that he had only himself to thank for his state of misery, and while repenting of having ever left his home, he made the resolution to return at once to his father, to confess his sin, and humbly beg to be received by him once more.

[2] *I have sinned.* He took all the blame upon himself, and did not try to excuse himself on the score of his youth, or the influence of bad companions.

[3] *Against heaven.* Against God, my heavenly Father.

[4] *Before thee.* Against thee, my earthly father.

[5] *Not now worthy.* How humble had he become who was once so proud! He was now willing to serve his father in the lowest position, and to do any work, if only he would forgive him.

[6] *He rose up.* He carried out his resolution at once. No doubt he said to himself: "What will people say when they see me returning home in such a wretched state!" but he overcame all false shame and was bravely resolved to accept every consequence of his sin—if only he could obtain his father's forgiveness.

[7] *His father saw him.* Every day he went to look out, in the hope that he might see his son returning.

[8] *The first robe, ring and shoes.* The father, seeing his wretched condition, was moved to intense pity, and at once ordered the servants to restore to him all the garments and ornaments befitting a son of the family.

it, and let us eat and be merry[1]; because this my son was dead[2], and is come to life again: he was lost, and is found.'

"Now his elder son was in the field; and when he came and drew nigh to the house, he heard music and dancing. Calling one of the servants, he asked what these things meant. The servant said: 'Thy brother is come, and thy father hath killed the fatted calf, because he hath received him safe.' And he was angry and would not go in. His father, therefore, coming out, began to entreat him[3]. But he[4] answering, said to his father: 'Behold, for so many years do I serve thee, and I have never transgressed thy commandment; and yet thou hast never given me a kid, to make merry with my friends. But as soon as this thy son is come, who hath devoured thy substance, thou hast killed for him the fatted calf.' But the father replied: 'Son, thou art always with me[5], and all that I have is thine. Yet it was fit that we should make merry and be glad: for this thy brother was dead, and is come to life again; he was lost, and is found.'"

COMMENTARY.

By this beautiful parable our Blessed Lord teaches us how willing Almighty God is to receive the penitent sinner, and how rejoiced He is at his return. Our Lord describes: 1. the falling away of a sinner from God; 2. the return of the sinner to God; and 3. God's reception of the penitent sinner.

The father in the parable signifies God; the elder son, the just; and the younger son, the sinner.

1. *Man begins to fall away from God* by allowing unlawful desires to take possession of his heart. In consequence, he will soon come to regard God's commandments as so many fetters, and to long for greater licence. He loses all taste for prayer and the word of God, and imagines that he would be a happier man if he could live according to his

---

[1] *Be merry.* "And they began to be merry." Picture to yourselves the emotion of the son, the heartfelt joy of the father, and the rejoicing of all the servants that their master, whom they all loved and honoured, should no longer have to grieve over his lost child.

[2] *Dead.* To me.

[3] *Entreat him.* To come and take part in the rejoicings.

[4] *But he.* The elder son could not understand his father's treatment of the returned prodigal, and in his vexation made out to himself that his father loved his brother better than himself.

[5] *Art always with me.* "You, therefore, have far more than your brother. Are you not aware of your happiness in never having left me?"

passions. Having thus separated himself inwardly from God, an outward separation speedily follows. He renounces the friendship of good men, neglects the services of the Church and the frequenting of the Sacraments, follows his own way, and shamelessly transgresses God's commandments. He then goes into a strange and distant land, namely further and further from God: The "far country", says St. Augustine, "signifies the forgetfulness of God".

Almighty God lets the sinner go his own way, for He has given to man free-will, and does not want a forced obedience, but an obedience springing from love.

In his forgetfulness of God, the sinner squanders his fortune, i. e. the natural and supernatural gifts which he has received, using his natural gifts, his health, his physical powers, and his reason, to offend God. He acts most unjustly and ungratefully towards his Creator and Benefactor, and loses the grace of God, merit, and the heirship to heaven.

The sinner, having forsaken the service of his God, falls into the servitude of Satan, and becomes the slave of his lowest passions, which are signified by the swine which the prodigal was constrained to feed. But the more he obeys his passions, the more dissatisfied does he become. No pleasure of the senses can give him happiness, and he feels a void and spiritual hunger in his heart which he is powerless to appease. He knows no rest; he only knows that he is miserable, and hateful to himself, and he bitterly tastes the truth of the words of Scripture: "Know thou, and see that it is an evil and a bitter thing for thee to have left the Lord thy God" (Jer. 2, 19).

2. *The sinner's conversion or return to God* begins by a sincere examination of his own heart. Like the prodigal, he must enter into himself, and face the grievousness and number of his sins. He must, by the help of God's grace, confess that his conduct has been wrong, ungrateful, and foolish, and that he is miserable simply because he has forsaken God. He must try to recall the joy and peace which were his, before he fell into sin; and he must gaze into the future, at death, judgment and eternity. Then there will rise within him a longing desire to be at peace with God, and sorrow and repentance for having ever separated himself from Him.

The prodigal son lost a great deal, but he did not lose faith in his father's mercy, and therefore did not despair. Thus a sinner must fan the flame of his faith in God's mercy, and the hope of forgiveness; and this faith and hope will move him to form resolutions of amendment. "I will arise and go to my father", was the resolution made by the prodigal. This resolution was a sincere one, for he determined a) to return home and thus avoid sin and the occasions of sin; b) to humble himself, confess his sin, and obey his father; and c) to do penance by hard, servile work and self-abasement.

The prodigal's contrition was real, interior and supernatural; therefore he hastened to cast himself humbly at his father's feet, confess his sin, and implore his pardon. The confession of sins is the obvious and necessary expression of contrition, and is the indispensable condition of forgiveness.

3. *God's reception of the penitent sinner.* The prodigal son carried out his good resolutions at once. Thus must it be with the sinner: he must not put off his conversion, but must be reconciled to God as soon as possible. And then, even as the father in the parable went to meet his son and received him lovingly, so will God meet the sinner by His merciful grace, forgive him his sins, and give him the kiss of peace. Then, by the hands of His servants (i. e. His priests), He re-clothes him with the robe of innocence, i. e. sanctifying grace, and adorns him again with the supernatural virtues befitting the state of a divine sonship (ring), and enabling him to walk justly before God (shoes). Finally, God prepares a feast for the converted sinner, giving to him the Lamb of God, for the nourishment of his soul, in Holy Communion. The Lord God rejoices and calls on all His Angels and Saints to rejoice with Him, because a man who was dead, who had lost the supernatural life of grace, and who was under the sentence of eternal death, is alive again, and is once more a child of God and an heir of heaven.

Mortal Sin. Our Lord Himself in this parable describes a sinner as one who is dead: therefore we are right in using the term "mortal" sin.

God's incomprehensible love of penitent sinners. Though the sinner has offended Him so grievously and so often, yet He reproaches him not, but forgives him everything, and restores him to his former rights and dignity of sonship. God alone can love in this way, and to us this sort of love is inconceivable. Our Lord portrays this narrow-mindedness of ours in the conclusion of the parable. The elder son cannot understand his father's joy; he murmurs at it, and refuses to take part in it; and even professes to believe that his father prefers the returned prodigal to himself, the faithful, obedient and industrious son. By this behaviour of the elder son our Lord signifies the jealousy of the Pharisees, who considered themselves to be just, and murmured at the deep interest which Jesus took in sinners. By the father's answer in the parable our Lord shows how very unjustifiable any such jealousy would be. The just man ought to think of the great happiness which he has had of being always in the love and grace of God: and if he will try to realize what the infinite love of God is for every soul which He has made, he will rejoice with God as often as a soul which had been lost is found or saved. As the angels rejoice over the return of the prodigal, so ought we to rejoice over the conversion of sinners!

APPLICATION. You too have offended God, though perhaps not so grievously as did the sinner in the parable; and God has forgiven you your sins in the holy Sacrament of Penance. Have you thanked Him for this? You ought to make a devout thanksgiving each time you have been to confession. Do not repay the love of your God with fresh ingratitude.

CHAPTER XLVI.

THE PARABLE OF DIVES AND LAZARUS.

[Luke 16, 19—31.]

JESUS, wishing to show the evil effects of riches, when misused, and the advantage of poverty, when borne with patience, said:

"There was a certain rich man who was clothed in purple and fine linen[1], and feasted sumptuously every day. And there was a certain beggar, named Lazarus, who lay at the rich man's gate, full of sores. He desired to be filled with the crumbs that fell from the rich man's table, but no one did give him. Moreover the dogs came[2] and licked his sores.

"Now it came to pass that the beggar died[3], and he was carried by the angels into Abraham's bosom[4]. But the rich man also died[5], and he was buried in hell. And lifting up his eyes, when he was in torments, he saw Abraham afar off, and Lazarus in his bosom. Then he cried and said: 'Father Abraham, have mercy on me, and send Lazarus that he may dip the tip of his finger in water to cool my tongue, for I am tormented in this flame.'[6] Abraham said to him: 'Son, remember that thou didst

---

[1] *Fine linen.* His upper garments were made of wool, dyed with a costly purple dye, and his under garments were made of fine Egyptian linen.

[2] *The dogs came.* This may mean that the dogs had more pity than the rich man, and that Lazarus had no other friends but the dogs; or it may also mean that he was too helpless to drive away the dogs (unclean animals) that came to lick his wounds.

[3] *Died.* Without regret, for he welcomed death as a deliverer, and had for a long while prepared himself for it.

[4] *Abraham's bosom.* To Limbo, and very near to Abraham.

[5] *The rich man also died.* An unexpected and unwelcome death, for to die was horrible and difficult to him, because he had to leave behind him everything to which his heart clung.

[6] *In this flame.* This is a significant and descriptive expression. As a body which is buried in the earth is surrounded everywhere by earth, so the rich man, when buried in hell, was surrounded everywhere by fire: above, below, to right and to left of him, he was surrounded by flames. On earth there

receive good things in thy lifetime [1], and likewise Lazarus evil things, but now he is comforted [2], and thou art tormented. And besides all this, between us and you there is fixed a great chaos [3], so that they who would pass from hence to you, cannot; nor from thence come hither.'

"Thereupon Dives said: 'Then, father, I beseech thee that thou wouldst send him [4] to my father's house; for I have five brethren, that he may testify to them, lest they also [5] come into this place of torments.' But Abraham said to him: 'They have Moses [6] and the prophets; let them hear them.' But he said: 'No, father Abraham, but if one went to them from the dead, they will do penance!' Abraham said unto him: 'If they hear not Moses and the prophets, neither will they [7] believe, if one rise from the dead.' "

COMMENTARY.

A glimpse of the future state (12th article of the Creed) is vouchsafed to us in this parable, both for our consolation and as a warning. After this life there is, we learn, a future state—a life where everything is quite different from what it is on earth. Lazarus was poor, despised, racked with pain and hunger while he was on earth; but when he died, angels carried his soul to the abode of the just, where he received consolation, and whence, when our Lord ascended into heaven, he would pass to everlasting happiness. On the other hand, the rich man, when on earth, led what was apparently a magnificent life. He was esteemed and honoured, surrounded by flatterers, waited on by a host of servants, clad in costly clothes, and he feasted luxuriously every day. But all this magnificence lasted only a short time. He died and

---

had been a splendid funeral service for him, and half the town had attended it, being anxious to pay him their last tokens of respect—and all the while his soul was in hell!

[1] *In thy lifetime.* You received on earth an ample reward for all the little good you ever did.

[2] *He is comforted.* By the hope of the coming Redeemer, and of his future reception into heaven.

[3] *A great chaos.* A great, insurmountable gap, which means that the separation between the abode of the just and of the wicked is absolute and final.

[4] *Send him.* To tell them how it fares with me.

[5] *They also.* By leading a life such as I led.

[6] *They have Moses.* God has revealed His will to them by Moses and the prophets. If they believe all that they can learn from them, and live accordingly, they will not be damned.

[7] *Neither will they.* The will to believe is wanting to them; they would not believe though one rose from the dead.

was lost for ever, and has been for centuries suffering unspeakable torments.

Limbo. Lazarus joined in Limbo the just souls departed. In their company he rejoiced in unspeakable consolation, and waited in the sure expectation of eternal happiness in heaven. When our Lord ascended into heaven, He took Lazarus with Him into everlasting glory.

Why Lazarus was eternally rewarded. When he was in this world, he was faithful, pious and resigned. He had for many years lived a life of misery, but he bore all his sufferings, poverty, contempt, and pain with the utmost patience and resignation to God's will, making use of them to sanctify his soul. He did not murmur nor complain, but hoped in the Redeemer and the everlasting life to come, and united himself closely to God by a holy love.

Hell. The parable gives us a description of hell. It is a place of torment in which the soul is completely buried. The torment is caused by the flames of a supernatural fire, kindled by the anger of God. There is, therefore, no relief, no hope for the lost soul. It is separated from the abode of the just by a great chaos; it can never get to them, but must remain for ever and without hope in the torment of hell. An unbearable thirst was the principal torment of the lost glutton: his throat and tongue were burnt up with it. He thought that one little drop of water, such as could hang from the tip of a man's finger, would be an alleviation; but he could not get even that. He who had so sinned by gluttony was now consumed by an everlasting thirst. He who had refused to Lazarus even the crumbs which fell from his table, now vainly implored for one little drop of water to cool his burning tongue.

Why Dives was eternally punished. We are not told that he committed any sins which the world would consider to be great ones. On the contrary, he was esteemed as an honourable and generous man. He might quite truly have said to himself: "I have deceived no man, I have never taken any one's life, nor have I sworn falsely. I am no miser; for I circulate my money freely, enjoy the use of it, and am praised by all my friends for my liberality." True! and yet he was damned! Why? Because he was a sensual man, an epicurean, and religion was a matter of no consideration with him. His only thought was how to lead a pleasant life, and he neither troubled himself about the future, nor believed in a coming Redeemer. He led a life without prayer, without fear of hell or desire for heaven, a life without grace and without God. Could such a life as this be rewarded by the everlasting Vision of God? No; its obvious and inevitable sequel could only be found in hell, or in eternal separation from God! He lived his life away from God. He sinned, firstly, by *unbelief.* Neither he nor his brothers believed much, if at all, in the immortality of the soul, or in what God had revealed to man by Moses and the prophets, namely, the necessity of penance and of hope in the promised Redeemer. He sinned, secondly, by *immoderate pride*. It was not avarice which made him refuse his help to poor Lazarus, whom he passed every day of his life, but pride, which made him despise the poor man and refuse to vouchsafe one glance at him. Pride made him hard-hearted and un-loving, and his self-love speedily developed into selfishness. He sinned, thirdly, by *intemperance (gluttony)* in eating and drinking, giving splendid banquets every day, for which reason he is also known as the rich glutton.

The Justice of God. The everlasting reward of Lazarus and the everlasting punishment of the glutton teach us to know the justice of God. But God's justice is also shown by His temporal reward of the rich man, while on earth, for what little good he had done. Perhaps, in his earlier days, Dives had sometimes prayed, or had given an offering to the Temple; and because God, in His Omniscience, knew that this man would remain impenitent to the end, and would go to hell, He gave him his reward on earth. On the other hand, Lazarus had probably committed sins in his youth. But he had heartily repented of them, and by his misery on earth made satisfaction for them, and suffered his temporal punishment in that way; so that when he died he was at once received into the abode of the just. Nothing that is good is left unrewarded, and nothing that is sinful is left unpunished. Thus the fate of Dives ought to serve as a grave warning to the rich not to forget God or the care of their souls, and to make a right use of their riches, especially by alms-deeds. And the everlasting reward of Lazarus ought to bring consolation to the poor and suffering and teach them not to murmur or lose courage, but to endure all in patience and re-signation, fixing their hope on God and His everlasting riches. "Blessed are the poor in spirit, for theirs is the kingdom of heaven."

Unbelief. He who will not believe the teachers appointed by God (Moses and the prophets under the Old Law, and the Church under the New Law), would not believe, even if one rose from the dead and came to preach to him. Lazarus was called back from the grave by our Lord, and Christ Himself rose from the dead, and yet the majority of the Jews refused to believe!

APPLICATION. Whom would you wish to be like, Lazarus or the rich glutton? Would you prefer to spend your short time on earth in eating and drinking, and then suffer the everlasting torments of hell? Or would you rather be poor and humble on earth, and suffer patiently whatever God sends you, and then rejoice for ever in heaven? You must choose: it is a case of heaven or hell! Fear the just God and keep His commandments. Say to-day a prayer to the Holy Ghost for the gift of holy fear.

"In all thy works remember thy last end, and thou shalt never sin" (Ecclus. 7, 40).

CHAPTER XLVII.

THE DANGER OF RICHES AND THE REWARD OF VOLUNTARY POVERTY.—A PARABLE.

[Mat. 19, 16—30. Luke 18, 18—30; 12, 13—34.]

ON one occasion a young man came to Jesus, and, kneeling before Him, said: "Good Master, what good shall I do that I may have life everlasting?" Jesus answered: "If thou wilt enter into life, keep the commandments." He asked: "Which commandments?"[1] Jesus said to him: "Thou shalt not kill; thou shalt not commit adultery; thou shalt not steal; thou shalt not bear false witness; honour thy father and thy mother; and thou shalt love thy neighbour as thyself."

The youth replied: "All these I have kept[2] from my youth." Jesus, knowing that this was true, looked tenderly[3] upon him, and said: "*If thou wilt be perfect*, go, sell what thou hast, and give it to the poor, and thou shalt have treasure in heaven[4]; then come and follow Me." Hearing these words, the young man went away sorrowful[5], for he was very rich.

Then Peter said: "Behold, we have left all things and have followed thee. What therefore shall we have?" And Jesus said to them: "Amen I say to you, that you who have followed me, in the regeneration, when the Son of Man shall sit on the seat of His

---

[1] *"Which commandments?"* The young man asked this, because he really wished to know to which of the commandments our Lord's answer chiefly applied. Our Lord enumerated the last half of the commandments, which treat of our duty to our neighbour, because these were the commandments most frequently transgressed by the Jews.

[2] *I have kept.* "What is yet wanting to me?" he added. He put this question, because his soul had not found full satisfaction in the mere observance of the law, and he felt inwardly drawn by grace to serve God more perfectly.

[3] *Looked tenderly.* Scripture tells us that "Jesus, looking on him, loved him". It gave Him joy to see this young man's yearning after a higher perfection, and He sought to encourage him to follow the secret movements of grace.

[4] *Treasure in heaven.* "If you renounce your fortune you will, indeed, be poor in this life, but you will lay up in heaven a rich treasure of merits."

[5] *Sorrowful.* His heart was too set on his riches to give them up and obey the call of grace, and become a poor disciple of Jesus Christ. Had the young man despised his wealth and followed Jesus, he would now be a Saint in heaven, and even renowned on earth; as it is, we cannot tell whether he died in the grace of God or not.

Majesty, you also shall sit on twelve seats judging the twelve tribes of Israel. And every one that hath left house or brethren or sisters or father or mother or wife or children or lands, for my name's sake, shall receive an hundredfold, and shall possess life everlasting" (Mat. 19, 27—29).

Again one day one of the multitude said to Him: "Master, speak to my brother that he divide the inheritance with me." Jesus replied: "Man, who hath made me a judge or a divider over you?"

Then, addressing the multitude, He said: "Take heed, and beware of all covetousness, for a man's life doth not consist in the abundance of things." Then He spoke a parable to them as follows: "The land of a certain rich man brought forth plenty of fruits. So he thought within himself: 'What shall I do, because I have not where to lay up together my fruits?' This will I do: I will pull down my barns, and build greater ones, and into them I will gather all things that are grown to me, and my goods. Then I will say to my soul: 'Soul, thou hast many goods laid up for many years; take thy rest, eat, drink, make good cheer!' But God said to him: 'Thou fool! this night do they require thy soul of thee, and whose shall those things be which thou hast provided?'" Then the Divine Master added: "So is he that layeth up treasure for himself, and is not rich towards God."[1]

COMMENTARY.

Faith alone will not save us; for the observance of God's commandments is also necessary. In other words, he who desires to be saved must not only have faith, but must live up to his faith. His faith must be living, and active in love.

---

[1] *God.* Our Lord warned the disciples of the danger of riches by these words: "Amen I say to you, that a rich man shall hardly enter into the kingdom of heaven. And again I say to you: It is easier for a camel to pass through the eye of a needle than for a rich man to enter into the kingdom of heaven." (This was a figure of speech which meant that a thing was, naturally, impossible.) When the disciples heard this, they wondered very much, saying: "Who then can be saved?" for they knew how much rich people cling to their riches, and how much poor people desire to possess them. And Jesus said to them: "With men this is impossible, but with God all things are possible", i. e. by his own strength no man can free himself of his love of the world and its possessions, but he can do so by the help of God's grace.

The Necessity of Grace. Man, being weak and sinful, cannot pos-sibly keep the commandments and save his soul of himself. He requires the assistance of God's grace.

The Evangelical Counsels. The young man had kept the com-mandments from his youth up; and yet he did not feel satisfied. He wished to do even more than was commanded, or was absolutely neces-sary; in other words, he wished to reach a higher state of perfection. Our Lord, seeing this, gave him this counsel: "If thou wishest to be perfect, become voluntarily poor, and follow Me." There is no desire more noble, or more pleasing to God than the desire for perfection; and as our Lord looked at the young man, He loved him for this yearning of his soul.

Resistance of grace. The rich young man was called to a state of perfection by the longing for it which had arisen in his heart, by the impulse of divine grace, and by our Lord's express invitation. Had he corresponded with grace, he would have been a Christian, a Saint, and perhaps even an apostle in the place of Judas. We may well ask ourselves what became of him after he resisted our Lord's gracious invitation, because of his too great attachment to the things of this world. Does he now gaze in heaven on that Divine Face from which, on earth, he turned away? The solemn words uttered by our Lord as the young man went away: "Amen I say to you, that a rich man shall hardly enter into the kingdom of heaven", lead us to fear that, after his rejection of the invitation of Jesus, he may have lost all faith in Him, and therefore all hope of heaven.

Why riches are dangerous. A rich man very easily grows proud, and often uses his wealth as a means of gratifying his evil inclinations. He feels, moreover, so comfortable and satisfied with his possessions that he has no desire for grace and the treasures of heaven. Riches turn a man's heart away from the things of God (see chapter XXI). Now the rich man can avoid these dangers only by the grace of God; he must therefore pray fervently, take to heart the truths of faith, frequent the Sacraments, and use his riches in the service of God, in alms-giving &c., if he does not wish to lose his soul.

APPLICATION. Could you say what the young man said: "All the commandments have I kept from my childhood?" Against which of the commandments have you most sinned? What is wanting to you now? (See chapter XLVI.)

CHAPTER XLVIII.

JESUS GIVES SIGHT ON THE SABBATH TO THE MAN BORN BLIND.

[John 9.]

AS Jesus was one day going out of the Temple[1], He saw a man who had been blind from his birth. The disciples who were with Jesus therefore asked Him: "Master, who hath sinned[2], this man or his parents, that he should be born blind?" Jesus answered: "Neither hath this man sinned, nor his parents; but that the works of God[3] should be made manifest in him."

When Jesus had said this, He spat on the ground and made clay with the spittle, and rubbed the clay[4] on the eyes of the man, and said to him: "Go, and wash[5] in the pool of Siloe." He went, washed, and came away seeing[6].

Now the neighbours that had known him wondered, and some of them said: "Is not this he that sat and begged?" But the others denied it, saying: "No, but he is like him." The man himself, however, exclaimed: "I am he." Then the blind man was

---

[1] *Out of the Temple.* Our Lord had come up to Jerusalem for the Feast of Tabernacles (John 7, 1—14), and had been teaching in the Temple, where many people were gathered together. Once more he came to offer grace to the unbelieving city, and once more it was rejected.

[2] *Who hath sinned?* The Jews believed that every misfortune was the consequence of some particular sin. They believed that a man might be inculpated even before his birth. (See further on, how the Pharisees cast this reproach at the man born blind: "Thou wast wholly born in sins!") So now the disciples wished to know whether the affliction of the blind man was a consequence of his own sin, or of some sin on the part of his parents before his birth.

[3] *The works of God.* It has been permitted by God's Providence that this man should have been born blind, so that he might be cured by Me, and that by this cure My Divine Power might be manifested, and the man himself brought to believe and thus be saved.

[4] *The clay.* The natural effect of covering a man's eyes with clay would be to shut out the light even if he saw already, and so this anointing could of itself have no power to restore the man's sight. It was therefore from our Lord that the healing power proceeded.

[5] *Go, and wash.* Our Lord imposed this command on the blind man in order to test his faith. The water from the pool (which lay to the south between Mount Moria and Mount Sion) could do no more than wash the clay from his eyes, the sight being given by Jesus, Who sent him to the pool.

[6] *Seeing.* Picture to yourselves the man's joy and thankfulness, as he now saw for the first time earth, sky, city and Temple!

brought[1] before the Pharisees, and they asked him how he had received his sight. Then the man told them how it had happened. Then they asked him again: "What sayest thou of Him that hath opened thy eyes?" The man replied: "He is a prophet." [2]

But they, still unbelieving, and not satisfied with the man's own testimony, called his parents, and asked them: "Is this your son who you say was born blind? How, then, doth he now see?" The parents replied: "We know that this is our son, and that he was born blind. But how he now seeth we know not. Ask himself; he is of age, let him speak for himself." The parents said this, because they were afraid of the Jews, who had already agreed among themselves that if any man should confess Jesus to be the Christ he should be put of the synagogue.

Then the Pharisees called again the man who had been blind, and said to him: "Give glory to God. We know that this man is a sinner:" But he replied: "Whether He be a sinner or not, I know not. One thing I know, that, whereas I was blind, now I see." Then they inquired again: "What did He do to thee? How did He open thy eyes?" The man answered: "I have told you already, and you have not heard. Why would you hear it again? Will you also[3] become His disciples?"

Then they reviled him, saying: "Be thou His disciple, but we are the disciples of Moses. We know that God spoke to Moses. But as to this man we know not whence He is." [4] The man

---

[1] *Was brought.* Apparently by the neighbours and relatives, who wished to bring the extraordinary occurrence to the notice of the spiritual authorities, and so led the cured man before the Sanhedrim, which at that time was almost entirely composed of Pharisees.

[2] *"He is a prophet".* As the cured man bore such open and unwavering testimony that He who had performed the miracle was a prophet, or one sent by God, the unbelieving Jews had recourse to another line. They first denied the existence of a miracle, affirming that the whole thing was a deception, and that the man before them had never been blind at all, only bearing a close resemblance to the man born blind; and when that was no longer possible, they had recourse to a theological argument, saying: Sinners cannot do miracles, and Jesus is a sinner [breaker of the Sabbath].

[3] *Will you also?* The blind man's scornful retorts are as keen as his honesty and courage are admirable.

[4] *Whence He is.* The fact that the man born blind adhered thus to his simple, truthful account, from which nothing could make him swerve, put the Pharisees into a dilemma; and when he, not without scorn, asked them: "Will you also be His disciples?" they vented their vexation in abuse of him, and thus

answered and said to them: "For in this is a wonderful thing, that you know not from whence He is, and He hath opened my eyes. From the beginning of the world it hath not been heard that any man hath opened the eyes of one born blind. Unless this man were of God[1], He could not do anything." Then they, being angry, said to him: "Thou wast wholly born in sins[2]; and dost thou teach us?" Thereupon they cast him out[3].

But Jesus met him and said to him: "Dost thou believe in the Son of God?" He answered: "Who is He, Lord, that I may believe in Him?" Jesus replied: "Thou hast both seen Him, and it is He who talketh with thee." Then the man said: "I believe, Lord!" and falling down he adored Him.

COMMENTARY.

Our Lord's testimony to His own Divinity. Jesus revealed Himself to the man born blind, as the Son of God: "He who is talking to thee is He—the Son of God." Moreover, when the man fell down before Him and worshipped Him as God, Jesus suffered him to do it. Jesus is, then, the true Son of God, to whom divine worship is due.

Proof of our Lord's Divinity. Jesus said He was the Son of God, and He proved the truth of His words by a stupendous miracle. His enemies examined this miracle judicially, and hoped to disprove its existence, by entrapping the man with cross-questionings into some contradiction of his own words, which would have shown that the whole thing was a deception. But they could not succeed in their design, and the wonderful deed could not be denied by any one.

The prophecy of Isaias was literally fulfilled by our Lord's cure of this man born blind, as well as by those of the deaf and dumb man, and of the man infirm for thirty-eight years, and also by many other cures: "Then shall the eyes of the blind be opened, and the ears of

---

betrayed their passionate hatred of our Lord. When, however, they pretended not to know whence Jesus was, the blind man gave them a scornful but very solid answer.

[1] *Of God.* Unless He were sent by God, He could not perform such an unheard-of miracle. This reply put the whole Sanhedrim to shame, and as they could not answer the man's reasoning, they were filled with rage and took refuge in abuse.

[2] *Born in sins.* How dare you, a sinner (because punished for your sins from your very birth) teach us just men?

[3] *Cast him out.* Of the synagogue. This was a sign of his exclusion from all spiritual intercourse with Israel. No doubt this brutal conduct wounded the good man. But Jesus comforted and rewarded him by fully revealing to him who He was.

the deaf shall be unstopped. Then shall the lame man leap as a hart, and the tongue of the dumb shall be free" (Is. 35, 5. 6).

The cause of unbelief. In spite of all their efforts, the Pharisees could not disprove the miraculous cure of the man born blind. Why, then, did they not believe in it? Because they had not the will to believe and receive the truth. The great truth that Jesus is God was, it may almost be said, forced on them with violence, but they resolutely shut their eyes to it. Why did they thus refuse to see and believe? Because they hated our Lord. They had got it once for all into their heads that the Messias would come as a great liberator and conqueror who would enable them to realize their political aspirations. Jesus was poor and humble, redeeming the people only from sin and death, and their sensual nature refused to acknowledge any such Messias. Added to this there must be taken into consideration their own personal interests. They had been, hitherto, the acknowledged leaders of the people, who honoured them as the models of virtue and justice. Jesus would not admit this justice of theirs, and ruthlessly showed up their hypocrisy. The greater the following of Jesus, the less was their own; and thus it was that their self-interest as well as their pride made them hostile to our Lord. Under no circumstances would they themselves acknowledge Him as the Messias, and they used every means to prevent the people from doing so. Thus, even before this miracle and their examination of it, they had issued an edict that any one who should say that our Lord was the Christ should be put out of the synagogue. They *would* not believe; nor would they have believed, if Jesus had worked even greater miracles than He did.

Increase of faith. The man born blind corresponded with grace. He obeyed Jesus, believing that He was able to cure him by the washing of his eyes in the pool of Siloe. The cure, when obtained, increased his faith, and he was convinced that Jesus was a prophet sent by God, who had received power from Him. He suffered persecution on account of his faith, and thus obtained the further grace of hearing from our Lord's own lips that He was the Son of God. The man born blind received not only the natural gift of sight, but with it the supernatural gift of faith. Our Lord's miracle was the cause of salvation to him, whereas it was the cause of ruin to the Pharisees, and served only to harden them in their obstinacy.

Confession of faith. The man born blind confessed his faith in Jesus most courageously and unwaveringly. His parents allowed themselves to be intimidated, but he feared neither the anger nor the threats of the Pharisees, and permitted nothing to turn him from the truth, or lead him to contradict his own words.

Effects of holy Baptism. The pool of Siloe, by washing in which the blind man received his sight, was a type of Baptism, by the washing of which those who are born spiritually blind through original sin, receive their sight, and the light of faith. Whence Baptism used to be called the Sacrament of "illumination".

The outward signs of the Sacraments. The outward means used by our Lord for the cure of the man born blind, namely the anointing with clay and the washing with water, could not, of themselves, have restored his sight. But it was our Lord's almighty will that these ceremonies should be the means by which He gave sight to the blind man. They were types of the outward signs in the Sacraments, which are the means chosen by God for imparting the inward and supernatural graces which are given to us in the holy Sacraments.

Confidence in Divine Providence. The poor man's life-long blindness was apparently a very great misfortune. It was not so really; for God ordained that this blindness should not only tend to the glory of His Son, but should be the cause of the salvation of him for whom it was apparently a terrible affliction. We should never murmur against what is sent to us by God, but should always be satisfied, and say to ourselves: "The All-wise God alone knows to what good end such and such an apparent misfortune may lead."

APPLICATION. Sight is the greatest and most precious of God's natural gifts to us. To understand its value you must try to imagine what it would be like had you been born blind. Have you ever thanked God for your good eye-sight? Show your gratitude by keeping a guard over your eyes. Do not let them wander about when you are in church; and above all things do not use them for any unworthy purpose.

But you must thank God still more for the supernatural light of faith, and resolve that all your life through you will bravely confess the holy Catholic Faith by word and by deed.

CHAPTER XLIX.

THE LORD'S PRAYER.

[Luke 11, 1—13. Mat. 6, 9—13.]

JESUS having on one occasion retired to a desert place to pray, one of His disciples said to Him: "Lord, teach us how to pray[1], as John also taught his disciples!" Then Jesus said to them: "When you pray, say: Our Father, who art in heaven,

---

[1] *How to pray.* Probably the disciples had watched our Lord when praying, and the wish had arisen in them: "Would that we could pray like that." According to St. Matthew this prayer formed part of the Sermon on the Mount.

hallowed be Thy Name; Thy Kingdom come; Thy Will be done on earth as it is in heaven. Give us this day our daily bread; and forgive us our trespasses, as we forgive them that trespass against us. And lead us not into temptation, but deliver us from evil. Amen."

He then said to them: "Which of you shall have a friend, and shall go to him at midnight, and shall say to him: 'Friend, lend me three loaves, because a friend is come off his journey to me, and I have not what to set before him'; and he from within should answer and say: 'Trouble me not; the door is now shut, and my children are with me in bed; I cannot rise and give thee.' Yet if he shall continue knocking, I say to you, although he will not rise and give him, because he is his friend, yet because of his importunity, he will rise and give him as many as he needeth. And I say to you, ask, and it shall be given you; seek, and you shall find; knock[1], and it shall be opened to you, for every one that asketh, receiveth; and he that seeketh, findeth; and to him that knocketh, it shall be opened.

"What father among you, if his son shall ask him for bread, will give him a stone! or if he ask a fish, will instead of a fish give him a scorpion? If you, then[2], being evil, know how to give good gifts to your children, how much more will your Father who is in heaven give the good spirit[3] to them that ask him.

"Again, I say to you, that if two of you shall consent upon earth, concerning anything whatsoever they shall ask, it shall be done to them by My Father who is in heaven. For where there are two or three gathered in My Name[4], there am I in the midst[5] of them."

COMMENTARY.

Prayer is an art which must be learnt and practised. Our Lord teaches this by showing us 1. *for what* we are to pray, and 2. *how*

---

[1] *Ask, seek, knock.* The perseverance of prayer is well expressed by these three words.

[2] *If you, then.* If even sinful men grant the requests of their children, how much more will God, your heavenly Father, listen to the prayers of you, His children.

[3] *The good spirit.* All the best gifts and graces of God are spiritual and make our spirit (soul) good.

[4] *In My Name.* i. e. when My honour and the confession of faith in Me is the object of the assembly.

[5] *In the midst.* Making their prayer one with mine and thus pleasing to God and efficacious.

we are to pray. Jesus tells us what we are to pray for, in the Our Father; and in the same prayer He partly tells us how we are to pray, for by the very first words He teaches us that we should pray to God with the confidence of children, while the fifth petition reminds us of our sins, and, therefore, warns us to pray with deep humility. By His exhortations, similes and parables which we have just read our Lord urges us to pray 1. with perseverance; 2. with confidence; and 3. in common.

Perseverance in prayer and its necessity are taught us by the parable of the importunate friend, who though he presented his petition at a time most inconvenient to his friend, and therefore very unfavourable to his cause, got what he wanted, simply because he asked persistently. This example, taken from human life, was given by our Lord to show the necessity of persistence and perseverance in prayer. God is our best friend, and He will undoubtedly hearken to us if we pray without ceasing. The man in the parable at last granted his friend's request, simply to be rid of his importunity: but is this the case with God? Certainly not! God hearkens to us out of pure love; but He often suffers us to plead for a long time in order that, by reason of our perseverance, we may become more worthy to receive what we ask for. Our prayers to God can never be inopportune, because He is ready at all times to hearken to us.

Confidence in prayer is urged on us by our Lord's grand and distinct promise: "Every one that asketh, receiveth; and he that seeketh findeth; and to him that knocketh, it shall be opened." Every one, therefore, without any exception, is heard when he asks for right things, in a right way. "Every real prayer, that is, every prayer which proceeds from the inward needs of the heart, and which is offered up to obtain what is really good and necessary, is heard by God. He is always ready to give us what we need, and only desires what is good for us" (Bisping). And if, sometimes, we do not receive that which we in our short-sightedness have asked for, God gives us something else instead, which it is better for us to have. Our Lord explains this in His simile of the child who asks his father for bread &c. If no earthly father, hearing and understanding his request, would be so cruel to his child as to give him something useless or hurtful instead of the thing for which he asks; how much less would our heavenly Father do such a thing. He will always listen to our prayer, and give us those things which conduce to our welfare.

Prayer in common is recommended by our Lord in these words: "If two of you shall consent upon earth concerning anything whatsoever they shall ask, it shall be done to them by My Father who is in heaven." No matter, therefore, how few people meet to pray together, their united prayer will be heard. Household and family prayers; all general, public worship, and meetings of confraternities, guilds &c. &c., are pleasing to God.

The necessity of prayer. The words: ask! seek! knock! convey a command. We *must*, therefore, pray, because our Lord Jesus Christ has commanded us to do so.

APPLICATION. If you will examine what are the qualities of prayer, you will find that you have very seldom prayed well. Your prayers rarely come from your heart, being mostly lip-service. In order to pray with devotion you ought to meditate on the words which your lips utter. St. Elizabeth often took a whole hour to say one Our Father, weighing each single word in her heart. As she pronounced the word "Father", she meditated on the goodness of God, and excited in her heart feelings of love towards Him. The word "our" made her remember that all men are the children of God, and ought to love one another. The word "heaven" awakened in her heart a longing desire for ever-lasting happiness, and she resolved to win heaven at any price. And so she went on to the end. You too might, sometimes, medi-tate in this sort of way on the words of the Our Father, which are so rich in meaning; and remember that *one* Our Father said with devotion is worth *twenty* said carelessly.

CHAPTER L.

THE PHARISEE AND THE PUBLICAN.

[Luke 18, 1—14.]

JESUS spoke also the following parable in order that He might show forth the difference between true and false prayer: "Two men went up into the Temple to pray, the one a Pharisee, and the other a publican. The Pharisee, standing[1], prayed thus with himself[2]: 'O God, I give Thee thanks that I am not as the rest of men[3], extortioners, unjust, adulterers, as also is this publican[4]. I fast twice[5] in the week: I give tithes[6]

---

[1] *Standing.* Upright and self-conscious.

[2] *With himself.* i. e. within himself, not loud, because even he would have been ashamed to utter such a prayer aloud.

[3] *The rest of men.* He set himself on a pinnacle above all other men, and implied that all except himself were sinners.

[4] *This publican.* For whom he had the utmost contempt.

[5] *I fast twice.* Which was not commanded.

[6] *Tithes.* The law only commanded tithes to be given of the fruits of the field; but the Pharisees paid tithes of the most insignificant garden-produce such as "mint, anise, and cummin". He meant, therefore, to say: "Whereas others do

of all that I possess.' But the publican, standing afar off[1], would not so much as lift his eyes[2] towards heaven, but struck his breast[3], saying: 'O God, be merciful to me a sinner!' I say to you, this man went down to his house justified[4] rather than the other. Because every one that exalteth himself shall be humbled, and he that humbleth himself shall be exalted."

COMMENTARY.

Pride. The Pharisee sinned by pride: 1. He thought too highly of himself. 2. He did not give due glory to God. 3. He despised his fellow-men. His prayer, therefore, was no prayer; it was nothing but a discourse in praise of himself. With the utmost pride and self-righteousness he related to God all the good works he had performed (of which, however, he was only able to enumerate two), and implied that Almighty God must be very glad to have such a valuable servant as himself! Is it not loathsome and irritating to see a wretched man dare to extol himself before God in such a manner! Is not pride like this stupid and despicable! Of what good could his fasts be if he did not practise them with a conviction of his guilt before God, and in a spirit of penance? He had no longing for the Redeemer. He asked not for pardon, because he imagined himself to be a perfect servant of God, without sin, and therefore without need of pardon! This shows us how completely pride can blind a man.

Rash judgment. In his pride the Pharisee not only despised his fellow-men, but judged them rashly, putting them all down, collectively, as great sinners. He congratulated himself on not being a robber, and yet, all the while, he was robbing his neighbours of their good name! Pride makes a man uncharitable, for a proud man is so full of self-love that he cannot find room for the love of his neighbour!

A good intention. The Pharisee performed certain good works; but the good which he did lost all merit in the sight of God, because

---

not even observe the commandments, I practise more than is commanded." First he enumerated the grave sins which he had not committed, and then the good works which he had been careful to perform.

[1] *Afar off.* Behind the other worshippers, not considering himself worthy to go near them.

[2] *Lift his eyes.* Casting down his eyes with a deep consciousness of his sinfulness.

[3] *Struck his breast.* This was to express his sense that he was worthy of punishment at the hands of God. By beating his breast publicly, he made an open confession that he was a great sinner. He neither extolled nor excused himself, but confessed his guilt and implored pardon. He did not trust in himself, but in the grace of God.

[4] *Justified.* The publican obtained pardon and grace from God on account of his humility and contrition.

it was not done for love of Him, but only for the gratification of his own pride; and he had therefore no good intention in doing it.

We must pray with humility. The prayer of the Pharisee was worthless before God, because he extolled himself, and judged his fellow men uncharitably. Only humble prayers please God, and obtain a hearing.

The necessity of humility. The chief lesson to be learnt from this parable is contained in the words with which our Lord concluded it: "Every one that exalteth himself shall be humbled, and he that humbleth himself shall be exalted." Without humility there can be no forgiveness of sins, no grace, no future happiness. It is, therefore, an indispensable virtue. Even as pride lies at the root of all sin, so is humility the foundation of all true virtue (chapter XXXIX). "God resisteth the proud, and giveth grace to the humble" (James 4, 6).

APPLICATION. Ask yourself whether you are proud or self-willed? Do you give glory to God when you succeed in anything? Do you boast? Are you fond of talking about yourself? Do you take pleasure in praising others, or is it more pleasing to you to find fault with them? No other virtue is of any value in God's sight, without humility. You owe to God everything that you are, or have, or can do; therefore, thank God and do not offend Him by pride. Be very careful to-day to utter no word in self-praise. Do not tell an untruth nor feign piety.

CHAPTER LI.

TEN MEMORABLE SAYINGS [1] OF OUR LORD.

I. "My doctrine is not mine [2], but His that sent Me. If any man will do the will of Him, he shall know [3] the doctrine, whether it be of God, or whether I speak of Myself." [4]

II. "I am the Light of the world; he that followeth Me [5], walketh not in darkness, but shall have the light of life." [6]

---

[1] *Ten Sayings.* During the three years of our Lord's public life He uttered many wonderful and beautiful maxims and sayings. Ten of these, rich in the most precious meaning, are here given.

[2] *Not mine.* Not the product of any human knowledge.

[3] *He shall know.* By his own inner experience.

[4] *Speak of Myself.* i. e. by mere natural human reason and knowledge.

[5] *Followeth Me.* i. e. My teaching and example, or, in other words, he who obeys My words and follows My example.

[6] *The light of life.* Which will guide him to eternal life, to the unfading light of glory, the splendour of heaven, and the Vision of God.

III. "If any man will come after Me, let him deny himself[1], and take up his cross[2] and follow Me."

IV. "The foxes have holes[3], and the birds of the air nests, but the Son of Man[4] hath not where to lay His head."

V. "He that loveth father or mother more than Me is not worthy[5] of Me; and he that loveth son or daughter more than Me is not worthy of Me."

VI. "He that loveth his life shall lose it, and he that hateth his life in this world keepeth it unto life eternal."

VII. "The kingdom of heaven suffereth violence[6], and the violent bear it away."

VIII. "What doth it profit[7] a man, if he gain the whole world, and suffer the loss of his own soul? Or what exchange[8] shall a man give for his soul?"

IX. "No man can come to Me[9], except the Father who hath sent Me, draw him[10]; and I will raise him[11] up at the last day." — "If any man keep My word[12], he shall not see death[13] for ever."

X. "Come to Me all you that labour and are burdened[14], and I will refresh you[15]. Take up My yoke[16] upon you and learn of

---

[1] *Deny himself.* All that is bad in himself, pride, avarice, luxury and so forth.

[2] *His cross.* Whatever trials, troubles, or sufferings God may send him

[3] *Holes.* In which to take refuge.

[4] *But the Son of Man.* Does not possess on earth even enough space whereon He could rest His Head.

[5] *Not worthy.* Is not worthy to be My disciple, or to have a share in the Redemption wrought by Me.

[6] *Violence.* Is only to be obtained by means of violent effort.

[7] *Doth it profit?* Or what would it profit &c.

[8] *Exchange.* How shall it be redeemed, once it is lost?

[9] *Come to Me.* Can become My disciples, believing in and loving Me.

[10] *Draw him.* By his grace.

[11] *Raise him.* Him, that is, who, by corresponding with grace, becomes and remains My disciple.

[12] *Keep My word.* Receives it with faith and lives in accordance with it.

[13] *Not see death.* His soul and body shall live for ever, so that the death of his body will not be a terror to him, but will be welcome, as being his introduction to a better and everlasting life.

[14] *Burdened.* Either with grief or with the weight of sin.

[15] *Refresh you.* With consolations and peace.

[16] *My yoke.* My law of love.

Me, because I am meek and humble of heart, and you shall find rest for your souls. For My yoke is sweet, and My burden is light."

COMMENTARY.

Test of Divine Doctrine. He whose heart is bent upon serving God, doing His will and practising the moral precepts of our Lord, will soon recognise and feel within his mind and heart that the doctrine proposed by our Lord is and must be divine. The true faith comes to those of good will. Virtue protects, increases and strengthens faith; whereas vice weakens it, and produces an aversion to its grand teachings, which leads the sinner ultimately into unbelief.

True light. The light of life is the faith taught by Jesus Christ. Without this faith nobody can be saved. True enlightenment, certainty and conviction can only come by faith. Darkness, uncertainty, and the want of all comfort follow unbelief.

Self-denial is necessary for every Christian, for without self-denial there can exist no virtue. Our Lord Jesus Himself went before us to show us the way, and His whole Life on earth was one great act of self-renunciation and self-denial.

The poverty of our Lord was very great. He was born in a stable, and possessed no dwelling-place of His own all the time He dwelt on earth; and He often spent the night praying in the open air. He wandered about as a stranger, living on alms. His only death-bed was the Cross (on which, in very truth, He had not where to lay His Head), and His Body was buried in another man's sepulchre. The words: "Blessed are the poor in spirit" apply to all true followers of Jesus Christ.

The love of God above all things. Because Jesus is God and has loved us even unto death, we, on our side, must love Him above all things—more than father or mother, more than our own lives. He who loves this life more than God, and who, if the choice is given to him, forsakes God rather than lose his life, is sure to lose his life in eternity. But he who esteems this life as little compared with eternal life and will give it for Christ's sake, will certainly gain everlasting life. The Church teaches that the holy martyrs pass straight to heaven, without tasting of Purgatory. "If those who prefer this earthly life (the most precious of natural gifts) to the service of God, forfeit all claim to eternal life, how much more do those endanger their salvation who refuse to mortify the lusts of the flesh, and give up faith, love, and the service of God for the basest pleasures and possessions of this world!" (St. Chrysostom.)

Temperance and fortitude. He who wishes to win heaven must steadfastly restrain his evil inclinations and passions, fight against all external temptations, and never be turned from what is right by any difficulties or persecutions.

The greatest loss. "What will it profit a man if he gain the whole world and suffer the loss of his own soul?" It would profit a man nothing if he possessed all the power, honour and riches that it was possible for him to have, and injured his soul thereby. All sin, and especially mortal sin, does injury to the soul. If, therefore, a man could gain the whole world by committing one mortal sin, would it be of any profit to him? None at all, for death would take all his possessions from him, and he would then be punished for ever in hell.

Once lost, for ever lost! "Or what can a man give in exchange for his soul?" What can he do or give to redeem his soul from hell? Nothing! Once a man's soul is lost, it remains lost, and nothing can redeem it from everlasting damnation. The care of our soul is our one important business in life, "the one thing needful".

The necessity of grace. Grace "draws" us, by enlightening us and awakening in us a desire for salvation; but it does not compel us. God leaves us at perfect liberty either to obey or resist the attractions of grace.

The resurrection of the body. On the last day our Lord Jesus Christ will raise to life the bodies of the dead (Eleventh article of the creed).

Life everlasting (Twelfth article of the creed).

The law of Jesus is sweet and easy 1. because the purport of it is love, and love makes all duties light and pleasant; 2. because Jesus does not merely impose duties on us, but helps us by His grace to fulfil them; 3. because Jesus has gone before us, showing us an example. He Himself has done everything which He requires us to do, and that in the most perfect manner, as, for example, showing love to our enemies. His law is sweet and easy 4. because an exceeding great reward is promised to us if we obey it, namely, peace and joy of heart on earth, and inconceivable glory and happiness in heaven.

Gentleness and humility are especially taught us by the example of our Lord Jesus. The sins contrary to these virtues are the two capital sins of anger and pride.

Devotion of the Sacred Heart of Jesus. Our Lord Himself directs us to His Sacred Heart and invites us to imitate its virtues of love, mercy, gentleness, humility, obedience, patience, fortitude &c. The Heart of Jesus is the model of all virtues and the fountain of all grace, and must therefore be loved and adored by all who love Jesus. The Feast of the Sacred Heart of Jesus is kept on the Friday [in some places, on the Sunday] after the Octave of Corpus Christi.

APPLICATION. Examine your conscience on the subject of gentleness; make acts of contrition, and good resolutions.

Happiness can only be found with Jesus. As long as you follow Him, and are obedient and innocent, you will have peace and joy of heart. But if you do what is wrong, you will feel discontented, restless and troubled. Keep, therefore, away from sin; it will make you very unhappy.

CHAPTER LII.

JESUS AT THE FEAST OF THE DEDICATION CLEARLY ASSERTS HIS DIVINITY.

[John 10, 22—42.]

JESUS assisted at the Feast of the Dedication[1] of the Temple. As He walked through the Porch of Solomon, a number of Jews[2] surrounded Him and said: "How long[3] dost Thou hold our souls in suspense? If Thou be the Christ, tell us plainly." Jesus answered: "I speak[4] to you, and you believe not. The works that I do in the name[5] of My Father, they give testimony[6] of Me. But you do not believe, because you are not of my sheep. My sheep hear my voice, and I know them and they follow me. And I give them life everlasting, and they shall not perish for ever, and no man[7] shall pluck them out of my hand. That which my Father hath given me, is greater than all, and no one can snatch them out of the hand of my Father. I and the Father are one."

---

[1] *Dedication.* This Feast was kept in commemoration of the purification of the Temple and consecration of the altar by Judas Machabeus (Old Test. LXXXV).

[2] *Jews.* The unbelieving leaders of the people, and especially the members of the Sanhedrim.

[3] *How long?* It was no love of the truth which made them speak thus. They wished to force our Lord to declare Himself to be the Messias openly and before many witnesses. They meant then to accuse Him of making Himself a king; for most of the people believed that the Messias would be an earthly king.

[4] *I speak.* I have told you that I am the Messias (see chapter XXVI).

[5] *In the name.* In the power of the Father.

[6] *Testimony.* That the Father hath sent Me.

[7] *No man.* No one, that is, has the power of separating them from Me, for "I and the Father are one", and, therefore, His power is My power.

The Jews then took up stones[1] to stone Him. But He said to them: "Many good works I have shown to you from My Father; for which[2] of those works do you stone Me?" They replied: "For a good work we stone Thee not, but for blasphemy[3]; because that Thou, being a man, makest Thyself God."

Jesus said to them: "If I do not the works of My Father[4], believe Me not. But if I do, though you will not believe Me, believe the works[5], that you may know, and believe that the Father is in Me, and I in the Father." Hearing this, they tried to seize Him[6], but He escaped[7] out of their hands.

COMMENTARY.

Our Lord's Divinity is proved in several ways in this chapter. It is proved: 1. by His own distinct testimony, 2. by His miracles, 3. by the holiness of His life.

1. *Our Lord's own testimony.*

He called God His Father: therefore He is the Son of God.

He says: "I give My sheep life everlasting." God alone can give everlasting life: therefore Jesus is God.

---

[1] *Stones.* In their blind fury they actually attempted to stone the Son of God for blasphemy against God! But Jesus remained calm and unmoved in their midst, and, cowed by His look, they did not venture to cast at Him the stones which they held in their hands.

[2] *For which?* "You can reproach Me with no evil. I have done nothing but good to you; and is it for that you wish to stone Me?"

[3] *Blasphemy.* They could not deny His good works, but reviled Him as a blasphemer, in spite of the many and wondrous miracles by which the Father testified to Him.

[4] *Of My Father.* The same works as My Father. My works, my miracles testify that I have the power of the Father, and that therefore I am one with Him.

[5] *The works.* Which bear unimpeachable witness to My Divine power. They ought to make you believe that the Father is in Me &c.

[6] *Seize Him.* Such was the only response which these stiff-necked people vouchsafed to our Lord's glorious revelation of Himself. They thought now of proceeding to extremities, and tried to seize Him, so as to thrust Him out of the Temple, and drag Him before the Sanhedrim.

[7] *Escaped.* As they were on the point of laying hands on Him, Jesus disappeared from their midst. They surrounded Him on all sides, and yet they could not capture Him! "He went beyond the Jordan", Holy Scripture says, "into that p'ace where John was baptizing first; and many resorted to Him, and said: 'All things whatsoever John said of this Man were true.' And many believed in Him." The memory of the holy Baptist's words still lived in those parts. The people there believed now, not only on John's testimony, but on account of our Lord's holiness and miracles.

He says again: "No man shall pluck My sheep out of My Hand." No one is stronger than He; and therefore He ascribes to Himself a might superhuman or divine.

He says, lastly: "I and the Father are one"; one in power, one in nature. There are two Persons, indeed, I and the Father; but only One Being, One God. The same truth of the unity of nature of the Father and the Son is further expressed by the words: "The Father is in Me, and I in the Father." On these words St. Cyril writes thus: "The effect of this unity of the Divine Nature is that the Son is in the Father, and the Father in the Son. Even as the sun is in the ray which proceeds from it, and the ray is in the sun from which it proceeds, so is the Son in the Father and the Father in the Son; and they, being two Divine Persons, are One God, existing for and in one another by the unity of their Divine Nature."

The Jews understood perfectly well that by these words our Lord ascribed to Himself the Divine Power and Nature, or, in other words, that He called Himself the real Son of God. They reproached Him with making Himself God, and wished to stone Him as a blasphemer. Had the Jews understood His words wrongly, He would have said "I am not God", in the same way as St. John the Baptist said "I am not the Christ" (chapter XI). Jesus, however, retracted none of His words, but, on the contrary, reproached the Jews for not believing them.

2. *The testimony of our Lord's miracles.* Our Lord appealed to His wonderful works as a proof of His divine power, and as a means whereby the Jews might know that "the Father was in Him and He in the Father". This shows us that our Lord's chief aim in working miracles was to induce men to believe in His divine mission and in the truth of His doctrine. Even as He spoke, He confirmed His testimony by a fresh miracle, disappearing from the midst of His infuriated enemies when they were on the point of laying hands on Him.

3. *The testimony of our Lord's holiness,* which was a further proof of the truth of His words, and therefore of His divine nature. Even His enemies, who hated Him, could not reproach Him with any evil deed, but admitted by their silence, when He appealed to them, that He had never done anything but good.

APPLICATION. Excite in your hearts a living faith in your Divine Saviour. He is the Eternal Son of God, who, by His Omnipotence, created the world, and for love of you became Man, and suffered Himself to be blasphemed and persecuted! Hold fast to Him, and you will not be lost, but will attain to everlasting life. No power in the world can snatch you from Him, unless you separate yourself from Him by mortal sin. Die rather than commit a mortal sin!

Chapter LIII.

THE LABOURERS IN THE VINEYARD.

[Mat. 20, 1—16]

AMONG the many parables addressed by our Lord to the Jews occurs the following:

"The kingdom of heaven is like to a husbandman, who went out early in the morning to hire labourers into his vineyard. When he had agreed with the labourers for a penny a day, he sent them into his vineyard. And he went out about the third hour[1], and saw others standing idle in the market-place[2]. And he said to them: 'Go you also into my vineyard, and I will give you what shall be just.' And they went. Again he went out about the sixth and ninth hour and did in like manner. And about the eleventh hour he went out and found others standing, and said to them: 'Why stand you here all the day idle?' They answered: 'Because no man hath hired us.' He said to them: 'Go you also into my vineyard.'

"Now when evening was come, the lord of the vineyard said to his steward: 'Call the labourers, and pay them their hire, beginning from the last even to the first.' When, therefore, they came who had come about the eleventh hour, they received every man a penny. But when the first also came, they thought that they should have received more, and they likewise received every man a penny. However, when they received it, they murmured against the master of the house, saying: 'These last have worked but one hour, and thou hast made them equal to us, that have borne the burden of the day and the heat.' But he addressed one of them: 'Friend, I do thee no wrong; didst thou not agree with me for a penny? Take what is thine[3] and go thy way. I will also give to this last even as to thee. Or is it not lawful for me to do what I will? Is thy eye evil because I am good?'"

---

[1] *The third hour.* About nine o' clock in the forenoon.

[2] *The market-place.* Labourers out of employment were accustomed to wait in the market-place to be hired by those who wanted them.

[3] *What is thine.* You have a right to claim as your own that which I promised to pay you.

Then Jesus concluded the parable, saying: "So[1] shall the last be first[2], and the first, last; for many are called[3], but few are chosen."

COMMENTARY.

"So shall the last be first." These words are addressed in the first place to the Jews, who ought to have been the very first to enter into Christ's new kingdom, because the promises were made to them, and they (the many) were all called. In the next place and in a wider sense they are addressed to all men and have a double meaning. a) Many of those who, according to time, are the first to be called, will be the last to receive their reward, having to suffer a long time in Purgatory in expiation of their laxity and lukewarmness on earth; whereas those called later may, on account of their zeal, be received sooner into the kingdom of heaven. b) Many who on earth were esteemed by others to be first, and were first by reason of their position, will enjoy the lowest degree of heavenly happiness; whereas many who were despised and thought very little of on earth will receive in heaven the highest degree of reward.

In the parable the master of the house is *God;* the market-place is *the world;* the vineyard is God's kingdom on earth, *the Church;* the steward is *our Lord Jesus Christ;* the labourers in the vineyard are *the faithful,* who are called by God to believe the one true faith and to live in accordance with it; the day of work is *the life-time of men on earth;* and the pence signify *the eternal reward* of the Vision of God in heaven. Almighty God calls us at different times to work in His vineyard. Some He calls in the early morning, as little children; others, boys and girls, He calls at the sixth hour; others He calls when they are full-grown men and women; and many He calls at the eleventh hour, quite in the evening of life, or old age. The paying of the wages takes place at the close of the day, at the end of our lives, when, after death, those whom God called late in life will receive an everlasting reward as well as those called earlier, if only they, like the labourers in the vineyard, obeyed God's voice when He did call them, and worked with perseverance, living according to their faith, even unto the end of the day.

---

[1] *So.* As in this parable.

[2] *The last be first.* The first to receive their reward. But many receive no reward at all, for many are called (to believe), but few (in comparison with the number called) are chosen (to be saved).

[3] *Many are called.* He said this to warn the apostles against falling into a state of false security on account of His promises, and looking on their reception into heaven as a certainty. Many who, according to time. were the first to be called to follow Christ, might be in the very lowest rank of those judged by Him, for the time of our call signifies nothing; it is only final perseverance which will avail us. Judas was among the first to be called, and yet he lost his soul!

Those called at the eleventh hour were sinners, for till they were called, they lived without God, and neither had faith, nor practised good works. The parable, therefore, teaches us that even the sinner will be saved if, at the end of his life, he opens his heart to God's grace and is converted. Salvation does not depend on when we are called (for that depends entirely on God), but it does depend on how we obey that call, and whether we persevere to the end.

The parable also shows us *God's Goodness and Mercy,* and ought to be a great comfort to the converted sinner, and teach him never to lose hope and give way to despair.

Furthermore, the parable teaches us the necessity and the merit of *good works.* God calls us into His vineyard on purpose that we may labour for His glory and save our souls by observing His commandments, avoiding sin and doing good, by faithfully fulfilling our duties as Christians in that state of life in which He, of His good pleasure, has put us. He who does not thus do his duty is standing idle and sins by sloth. By our labours for God's glory, i. e. by our good works, we merit heaven, because God, in His goodness, has promised us heaven as our reward. Even though the good which we do is not our own work, being at the same time the work of grace, Almighty God has pledged Himself to reward us for it just as if it were all our own work.

Who are the chosen? All men are *called,* because our Lord Jesus Christ died for all, and "God will have all men to be saved" (1 Tim. 2, 4), and gives to all men sufficient grace to be saved. The *chosen* are those who really attain to heaven. The name of "chosen" is given to them, because God, in His eternal counsel, and foreknowing their correspondence with grace, has chosen them for His kingdom of heaven out of the multitude of those whom He calls. Thus *all* those are among the chosen who, by corresponding with grace, make a good use of their calling and of the graces which God gives them. The number of the chosen is, our Lord says, small in comparison with the multitude of those called; for many—very many—of those called are lost by their own fault. This is a solemn and terrible truth! "Wherefore, brethren, labour the more that by good works you may make sure your calling and election" (2 Pet. 1, 20).

The hatefulness of envy. The envious sin 1. against brotherly love, because they do not heartily wish well to their neighbour, but grudge him the good things that he has. They sin 2. against the love of God, for in their hearts they find fault with Him, saying to themselves: "It is not just that God should give such and such things to that man!" Thus an envious man attacks the rights of God's own Majesty.

APPLICATION. You wish indeed to be among the chosen. But is that possible, if you are lukewarm and slothful in the service of God? Do you not stand all the day idle? You cannot excuse yourself by saying that you have not been called, for you were called by God when you were quite a little child to work in His vineyard, to serve Him and to labour for the salvation of your soul. From this day forward try to be more zealous in God's service.

You have no cause to murmur or to be envious when God gives to another as much as or more than He gives to you. But, if you are envious, apply to yourself the reproach which the master uttered against the labourers: "Art thou evil and envious, because God is good to thy brother?" (Overberg.)

CHAPTER LIV.

THE RAISING OF LAZARUS FROM THE DEAD.

[John 11.]

THE two sisters, Martha and Mary, who lived in Bethania, had a brother named Lazarus. Now Jesus loved Martha and Mary, and Lazarus. But Lazarus fell sick, and his sisters sent word to Jesus[1]: "Lord, behold, he whom Thou lovest is sick." Jesus, hearing this, said to His disciples: "This sickness is not unto death[2], but for the glory[3] of God, that the Son of God may be glorified by it."

Two days after, He spoke again to his disciples: "Let us go to Bethania; Lazarus, our friend, sleeps; but I go that I may awake him out of sleep."[4] The disciples answered: "If he sleeps he shall do well."[5] They thought He spoke of the repose of the body, but Jesus spoke of death. Seeing, however, that they did

---

[1] *To Jesus.* He being then in Peræa, to the east of the Jordan (see chapter XLIH), about thirty miles from Bethania.

[2] *Unto death.* Death which will last.

[3] *For the glory.* It is permitted by God, so that His Son may work the great miracle of raising the dead to life, and may thus manifest His divine power. The messenger returned to Bethania with this consoling though mysterious message, and there he found that Lazarus was already dead.

[4] *Sleep.* Our Lord called the death of Lazarus a sleep, because He foreknew that He would raise him from the dead. For Him, therefore, His friend was only asleep, though for others he was dead (St. Augustine).

[5] *Shall do well.* Sleep often shows a crisis in an illness, and is the first symptom of recovery.

not understand what He meant, He told them plainly: "Lazarus
is dead. And I am glad for your sakes[1] that I was not there,
that you may believe; but let us go to him."

When Jesus arrived in Bethania Lazarus had been four days[2]
buried. Now many friends and relatives had come to console the
two sisters, who were in great affliction. As soon as Martha heard
that Jesus was coming, she left her friends and went forth to
meet Him. When she saw Him she exclaimed: "Lord, if Thou
hadst been here, my brother had not died. But now also[3]
I know that whatsoever Thou wilt ask[4] of God, God will give
it to Thee."

Jesus said to her: "Thy brother shall rise again." Martha
replied: "I know that he shall rise again in the resurrection at
the last day." Jesus answered: "I am[5] the resurrection and the
life. He that believeth in Me, although he be dead, shall live[6].
Believest thou this?" She said to Him: "Yea, Lord[7], I have believed that Thou art Christ, the Son of the living God[8], who art
come into this world."

---

[1] *Your sakes.* Had I been by his bedside as he lay dying, I should have
cured him as I have cured so many others. But now he is dead, I will raise him
to life again; and your faith will be strengthened, for you will behold a far greater
miracle than the healing of the sick. So, for the sake of the apostles, Jesus waited
where He was until Lazarus was dead. "He forebore to cure Lazarus", says
St. Augustine, "in order that He might raise him from the dead."

[2] *Four days.* He had, according to the Jewish custom, been buried on the
day of his death. Jesus arrived at Bethania on the evening of the fourth day.

[3] *Now also.* Although he is dead I still have hope, for I know &c.

[4] *Thou wilt ask.* She hoped and believed that our Lord could procure her
brother's return to life by His prayers. Her faith was but imperfect, for she did
not expect that Jesus could work a miracle by His own Omnipotence, but only
by the power of His prayers. It was to combat this error that our Lord said:
"I am the resurrection and the life."

[5] *I am.* I do not need to pray for the restoration to life of your brother,
for I can raise him up myself; for I am the author of life (chapter XXVI).

[6] *Shall live.* His soul will live for ever in heaven—and his body also, after
its resurrection, will attain to life everlasting.

[7] *Yea, Lord.* Her faith was still imperfect when Jesus first arrived; but His
words: "I am the resurrection and the life" increased and perfected it.

[8] *The Son of the living God.* Her answer is most apt and complete. He
had asked: "Believest thou that I am the resurrection and the life?" Martha
answered: "I believe that Thou art the Son of the living God, and that, therefore, not only canst Thou raise the dead to life, but also do everything that
Thou willest."

Then Martha, going into the house, called her sister secretly[1], and told her: "The Master is come, and calleth for thee." Mary rose up quickly and went to Him. The Jews who were in the house followed her, saying: "She goeth to the sepulchre to weep there." As soon as Mary came to Jesus, she fell at His Feet, exclaiming: "Lord, if Thou hadst been here, my brother would not have died."

Fig. 81. So-called tomb of Lazarus at Bethania. (Phot. Bonfils.)

When Jesus saw her weeping[2], and the friends who had come with her, He groaned in spirit, and troubled Himself, and said: "Where have you laid him?" They answered: "Come and see." And Jesus wept[3]. Seeing this, the Jews exclaimed: "Behold how He loved him!"

---

[1] *Secretly.* So as not to let any of our Lord's enemies who might be present know of His arrival. Jesus remained outside the village, where was the burial-place of the dead.

[2] *Weeping.* She could say no more, nor frame any petition by reason of her weeping. But, in reality, her tears pleaded her cause better than any words could have done.

[3] *Jesus wept.* When Jesus saw Mary's deep grief, and heard the sobs and wailing of those present, His tender Heart was moved, and He wept. Picture this

Jesus, having come to the vault or cave (Fig. 81, p. 597), in which the body of Lazarus was laid, said: "Take away the stone!" Martha told Him that the body of her brother must be already putrid, knowing that he had been four days[1] in the grave. Jesus said to her: "Did I not say to thee that if thou wilt believe[2] thou shalt see the glory of God?"[3] They then removed the stone.

And Jesus, lifting up His eyes, said: "Father, I give Thee thanks[4] that Thou hast heard Me[5]. And I know that Thou hearest Me always, but because of the people who stand about have I said it[6], that they may believe that Thou hast sent Me."

Then crying out with a loud voice, He said: "Lazarus, come forth!"[7] And immediately he that had been four days buried came forth, wrapped in the winding-bands[8]. And Jesus said: "Loose him, and let him go!"[9]

---

scene to yourselves: Mary sobbing at the Feet of Jesus, and our Lord Himself shedding tears in the sight of all present! No doubt Mary's deep grief made Jesus think of that sword which was so soon to pierce the heart of His own Mother.

[1] *Four days.* When she realised that her brother had been already four days in the grave, and that the corruption of his body must have begun, Martha's faith wavered, and she said to herself that he could not possibly be raised up. But our Lord's word once more strengthened her faith.

[2] *Believe.* Jesus had not said explicitly, I will raise your brother up, but He had signified that He would do so by His words: "Thy brother shall rise again", and again: "I am the resurrection and the life."

[3] *The glory of God.* Manifested by the wonderful calling back to life of your brother.

[4] *Thanks.* Our Lord uttered this prayer of thanksgiving aloud, so that those who heard it might know that the miracle which they were about to witness was not, as His enemies maintained, the work of the devil, but of the power of God; and that they might thereby be moved to believe in His divine mission.

[5] *"Thou hast heard Me"*, said our Lord, for His prayer was granted the moment it was uttered. He, being One with the Father, granted as God that which He asked as Man.

[6] *I said it.* I have uttered this prayer of thanksgiving.

[7] *Come forth!* Imagine to yourselves what must have been the state of suspense of the on-lookers, as they peered into the open grave and heard this mighty command given to a mouldering corpse!

[8] *Winding-bands.* He was tied up, so that, naturally, he could not move or use his hands to undo for himself the bands in which he was swathed. That he stepped forth bound hand and foot was a scarcely less great miracle than his coming forth at all (St. Chrysostom). Think of the astonishment of the bystanders, and the joyful thanksgiving of the sisters!

[9] *Let him go!* This command proves that he could not move, or of himself remove his bonds.

Many of the Jews who were present when Jesus raised Lazarus from the dead, believed in Him. Some of these went to the Pharisees and told them what Jesus had done. Then the Scribes and Pharisees assembled together, and said one to another: "What do we, for this man doth many miracles? If we let Him alone so, all men will believe in Him." From that day they resolved to put Jesus to death. But Jesus, knowing their thoughts, walked no more openly among the Jews [1].

COMMENTARY.

The Divinity of our Lord Jesus. Throughout all this story our Lord spoke and acted as God.

a) He called Himself the Son of God, and said that He was the (author of the) resurrection and the life.

b) He solemnly addressed God as His Father, thanking Him for having always heard Him; for the will of God the Father is one with the will of God the Son.

c) He accepted Martha's confession of faith: "I believe that Thou art Christ, the Son of the living God."

d) He manifested His Omniscience by knowing that Lazarus was dead, though He was far from Bethania, and no one had brought Him the news of his death.

e) He revealed His Omnipotence in the most glorious way, by calling back to life, by His sole word, a man who had been four days in the grave, and whose body was already corrupt [2]. He called Lazarus not only from the grave but from corruption, overcoming death in the very midst of its work of devastation, and thus revealing Himself to all present as the very Lord of life and death—as the resurrection and the life. Our Lord worked this miracle before many witnesses. They had all known Lazarus, and they all knew that he was dead: many of them had seen him laid in the tomb, and the mouldering decay of his body was perceptible to their senses, as they stood around the open grave: and, behold, by the mighty power of one omnipotent word he who was dead stood alive and in the full vigour of his manhood in their midst! Not even our Lord's bitterest enemies could deny the miracle!

The especial object of this miracle. The time of our Lord's Passion and Death was at hand, and He wrought this mighty miracle before-

---

[1] *Jews.* He hid himself from these deadly enemies, retiring to the wilderness near Jericho, because His hour, that is the time pre-ordained for His Sacrifice and Death, was not yet come.

[2] Jesus raised up the daughter of Jairus, but a few moments after she had died; the young man of Naim, as he was being taken out to be buried; and Lazarus, after he had lain four days in the grave.

hand in order that the faith of His disciples, and more especially of His apostles, might be strengthened, and "that they might believe" and not doubt when they saw their Lord and Master in the hour of His abasement; and most of all to enable them to hope, when they saw His Body laid in the sepulchre, that He who had raised up Lazarus would Himself rise again.

The necessity of faith. "He that believeth in Me, although he be dead, shall live." It follows, therefore, that he who does not believe will not attain to eternal life.

The causes of unbelief. The impressions produced by the miracle of the raising of Lazarus from the dead were very different. Many believed in Him now who had not believed before; and for them the miracle worked salvation. The Pharisees and their followers could not deny the fact of the miracle, but they believed none the more in our Lord's divine mission, and the wonderful miracle only served to harden them in their obstinate incredulity—once more grace knocked at their hearts for the last time by means of this stupendous miracle which even they could not deny; but so blinded were they by their hatred and envy of Jesus, that they resisted and shut out the true knowledge of Him which was, as it were, forced on them. They had to admit that our Lord did "many miracles"; but this undeniable fact so increased their hatred, that they could not even bring themselves to pronounce His name, but called Him "this man". Though they owned that He worked the miracles they did not draw the logical conclusion that there-fore they must believe in Him, but, on the contrary, the illogical conclusion that therefore they must kill Him! However wonderful the miracles He might work, one thing was certain, they would not believe in Him! The Messias must die, or else their own position would be injured, and their hypocrisy unmasked! "If we let Him alone", said they, "all men will believe in Him." They even wished to put Lazarus to death, "because many of the Jews by reason of him went away and believed in Jesus" (John 12, 11). Pride, envy and love of power com-bined to blind these men, and destroy their souls by reason of their unbelief. Pride and envy are capital sins.

The chief doctrine of Christianity is the doctrine of the Divinity of Jesus Christ. It was because Martha believed that Jesus was the Son of the living God that she also believed His words: "I am the resurrection and the life", although she probably did not understand their full meaning.

The compassion of the Heart of Jesus. "And Jesus wept."

The consolation of faith. The words: "I am the resurrection and the life", are used at the service for the burial of the dead. They console us wonderfully for the loss of those dear to us, for they convince us that we shall all rise and meet again.

APPLICATION. Jesus loved Martha and Mary, and yet He put off helping them, and let their brother die! He did this to prove their faith and their resignation to God's will, and also because their trial would tend to the glory of God and to their own salvation. Be sure that Almighty God's motive is one of love when He visits us with trials. Do not murmur, but use the trial for your salvation by bearing it patiently, because God wills it, and for so long as He wills it.

CHAPTER LV.

JESUS FORETELLS HIS PASSION AND IS ANOINTED BY MARY AT BETHANIA.

[Mat. 20, 17—19; cf. 17, 21—22. Mark 9, 29—31. Luke 9, 21—22. John 12, 1—11. Mat. 26, 6—13.]

THE Paschal feast[1] of the Jews was approaching, and Jesus set out for Jerusalem. At the beginning of this His last journey to the holy city, He said to the twelve: "Behold, we go to Jerusalem, and the Son of man shall be betrayed to the Chief Priests and to the Scribes and Ancients, and they shall condemn Him to death and shall deliver Him to the gentiles[2], and they shall mock Him and spit on Him and scourge Him and kill Him; and the third day He shall rise again." But the apostles understood none of these things[3].

On his way He passed by Jericho, where He cured a blind man sitting by the wayside, and entered into the house of Zacheus, the chief of the publicans [Luke 19, 1—10].

Six days before Easter He came to Bethania, the home of Lazarus, Mary and Martha. There a supper was prepared for Him in the house of Simon the Leper[4], and Lazarus was one of those who sat at table with Him. Martha waited upon the Lord, but Mary brought an alabaster box, a pound of most precious

---

[1] *Paschal feast.* This was the fourth Easter since the beginning of His public life.

[2] *Gentiles.* Pontius Pilate and his soldiers were heathens.

[3] *None of these things.* They heard the words, but could not understand or believe their truth. How could He, the Messias and Son of God, end His life in such a way?

[4] *Simon the "Leper".* A near relative of Lazarus and his sisters. From the name given to him it is evident that he had been a leper, and had probably been cured by Jesus.

ointment[1], and she poured it on the Saviour's head[2] as He was at table.

Now the whole house was filled with the perfume of the ointment. But Judas Iscariot said: "Why was not this ointment sold for three hundred pence[3] and given to the poor?" Then the other disciples also had indignation, and said: "For what purpose is this waste?" Now Judas made this remark, not because he cared for the poor, but because he was a thief and carried the purse[4], and was already possessed by the love of money which, a few days later, led him to betray his Master.

But Jesus, knowing what was going on among His disciples, exclaimed: "Why do you trouble this woman? for she hath wrought a good work[5] upon Me. For the poor you have always with you[6], but Me you have not always. For she, in pouring this ointment upon My Body, hath done it for My burial[7]. Amen, I say to you, wheresoever this gospel shall be preached in the whole world, that also which she hath done, shall be told for a memory of her."

COMMENTARY.

Our Lord's prophecies. He foretold, in detail, His sufferings and death. He also foretold His burial, and His resurrection on the third day.

---

[1] *Precious ointment.* Spikenard, a very precious and sweet-smelling ointment, which is prepared from the root of a tree which grows in India. It was the custom to keep it in boxes of alabaster, with a long, narrow neck, which was sealed at the top.

[2] *Head.* Scripture adds that she also "anointed the Feet of Jesus and wiped His Feet with her hair". The anointing of His Feet was a mark of her especial reverence for Him.

[3] *Three hundred pence.* Nearly £ 10. The ointment would have fetched quite this sum, for according to Pliny the usual price of a pound of spikenard was 400 pence.

[4] *The purse.* The apostles had a purse in common, from which was drawn the money required to procure the necessaries of life, as well as for almsgiving. All the proceeds of the sale of their various possessions, besides the contributions from our Lord's friends, were put into this one purse of which Judas had the charge. He, however, used to take money from it for his own use, and is therefore called "a thief".

[5] *A good work.* And not an act of extravagance.

[6] *Always with you.* So that you can always be charitable towards them, but I shall leave you very soon.

[7] *My burial.* "To embalm Me for My burial". After our Lord's death Mary Magdalen sought vainly for His Body, that she might embalm it. Jesus was willing to receive now before His death this service of love which, by reason of His resurrection, could not be paid to Him in the tomb.

The Divinity of our Lord. These prophecies prove that our Lord knew future things, that He is Omniscient and is therefore God.

Jesus suffered willingly; for though He knew the future, and what awaited Him at Jerusalem, He nevertheless went there to meet His Passion and Death.

Jesus suffered all His Life; for He knew beforehand the terrible sufferings and death which He would endure. These were before His eyes all through His life, and it may be said that, in a certain measure, He suffered a living death.

The Gospel is to be preached throughout the whole world. Our Lord foretold that this was to be, and at the same time He foretold that Mary's service of love would be known and honoured throughout the length and breadth of Christendom. This prophecy has been, and is still being, fulfilled. Each of the three Evangelists, St. Matthew, St. Mark and St. John relate the incident; and on Palm-Sunday the Passion according to St. Matthew, which begins with this story, is read in every Catholic church throughout the world, and thus all Christians hear what Mary did to show her love for Jesus.

Covetousness is a capital sin. Judas had an inordinate love of money, or, in other words, was covetous or avaricious. He did not resist this evil passion, and therefore fell by degrees into greater sins. He began by stealing, first small, and then greater sums from the money entrusted to his care. He then displayed the most shameful hypocrisy by making out that the interests of the poor were his only care, whereas his real object in blaming Mary's extravagance was to facilitate his thefts. In the hardness of his heart he robbed the poor of the alms due to them, and from treachery to them, proceeded to treachery towards his Lord and Master.

Generous love. By this anointing of our Lord Mary wished to give expression to her deep love for Him, and her gratitude for the raising up of her brother. She used the most costly ointment which could be procured, to signify that she was ready to offer up every thing she most valued for His sake.

Care for God's honour, and care for the poor. Mary's example teaches us that we should not economize when it is a question of the worship of God, and the building or beautifying of His churches. The praise bestowed on her by our Lord shows that such offerings in His honour are well pleasing to Him, if they are made in a spirit of love and reverence. There will always be men who, like Judas, will blame such generosity in God's honour, and call it a needless extravagance, saying that the money would be far more usefully spent were it given to the poor—and yet such men as these care little or nothing for the poor. Christianity teaches that we ought to do the one, but not leave the other undone.

APPLICATION. When our Lord Jesus shed tears at the grave of Lazarus, the Jews said: "See how He loved him!" But Jesus has done far more for you. He has shed His Precious Blood for you, and given His Life for you. Can you not see how Jesus loves you? And how much do you love Him? How do you show your love?

Have you ever been a thief? Have you ever pilfered sugar, fruit, cakes &c. from your parents; or taken apples &c. which did not belong to you? If you have, you are a thief. Do you not know the Seventh Commandment?

CHAPTER LVI.

TRIUMPHAL ENTRY OF JESUS INTO JERUSALEM.

[Mat. 22, 1—11.   Mark 11, 1—10.   Luke 19, 29—38.]

ON the following morning[1] Jesus left Bethania and went to Jerusalem. When He had come to Bethphage[2], on the Mount of Olives, He sent two of His disciples, saying: "Go ye into the village that is over against you, and immediately you shall find an ass and a colt[3] with her. Loose them and bring them to Me. And if any man shall say anything to you, say ye that the Lord hath need of them."

So the disciples went and found the colt standing as Jesus had said. They therefore brought the ass and the colt[4] to Jesus, and, laying their garments upon it, they made Jesus sit thereon. Now many wished to see Jesus, because He had raised Lazarus from the dead. When, therefore, Jesus was near the city, His disciples and a great multitude[5] spread their garments in the way:

---

[1] *Following morning.* Jesus had passed Friday and Saturday (Sabbath) at Bethania, where He was anointed by Mary. On the next day, Sunday, He made His triumphal entry into Jerusalem.

[2] *Bethphage.* A little village situated to the west of Bethania, on the summit of the Mount of Olives, and not far from Jerusalem.

[3] *A colt.* "On which no man hath sitten", added our Lord. Therefore the first service performed by this beast was dedicated to Him.

[4] *The ass and the colt.* The disciples brought the ass as well as the colt to Jesus, because this last, having never been separated from its mother, might have proved unmanageable without her.

[5] *A great multitude.* The news of the raising of Lazarus had spread through Jerusalem, and had kindled in the crowd of pilgrims, who had flocked thither for the Paschal Feast, the belief that Jesus was indeed the Messias. They therefore prepared this triumphal entry for Him.

while some cut down branches[1] from the trees and strewed them along the road. And a vast multitude went before and followed after, crying: "Hosanna[2] to the Son of David![3] Blessed is He that cometh in the name[4] of the Lord, Hosanna in the highest!"[5]

There were also in the crowd some Pharisees, who, being filled with envy and hatred, never lost sight of Jesus. Seeing the honours that were now paid to Him, they indignantly[6] asked: "Hearest Thou[7] what these say?" Jesus replied: "If these should hold their peace, the stones[8] will cry out." The nearer He came to the city, the greater the crowd became, and the more the enthusiasm of the people increased.

Then was fulfilled the prophecy of Zacharias, that Jerusalem should be visited by her king as a Saviour; that He should be poor and riding on an ass [Zach. 9, 9].

But seeing[9] Jerusalem, Jesus wept over it, saying: "If thou also[10] hadst known, and that in this thy day[11], the things[12] that are for thy peace, but now they are hidden[13] from thy eyes! For the days shall come upon thee, and thy enemies shall cast a trench

---

[1] *Branches.* It was the custom to carry and wave palm-branches as a sign of joy and victory.

[2] *Hosanna.* This exclamation is the equivalent of our "Hurrah!" and means "Save, we pray".

[3] *To the Son of David.* To the Messias.

[4] *In the name.* Sent by the Lord God.

[5] *The highest!* They appealed to the angels to share the joy with which they greeted their Messias.

[6] *Indignantly.* At the sight of the people's exultation. As they did not dare to impose silence on the populace, they turned on Jesus and rebuked H m.

[7] *Hearest Thou?* How they greet you as the Messias! Do you accept this homage without protest?

[8] *The stones.* The truth that I am the Messias cannot be suppressed; it must be proclaimed; and if men did not bear witness, God would miraculously testify to this truth by means of the very stones. When, at our Lord's death, His disciples, crushed by fear and grief, held their peace, the quaking earth and the rent rocks bore witness to their Lord and Creator (St. Ambrose).

[9] *Seeing.* From the Mount of Olives. He wept over the blindness and obstinacy which must draw down such a terrible judgment on the city.

[10] *Thou also.* As well as this shouting crowd.

[11] *Thy day.* On this day which is so important for you and so decisive of your fate.

[12] *The things.* Namely the belief in the Messias, which would bring you salvation.

[13] *Hidden.* By your own fault, your wilful blindness.

about thee, and straiten thee[1] on every side, and beat thee flat to the ground, and thy children who are in thee, and they shall not leave in thee a stone upon a stone, because thou hast nto known the time of thy visitation."[2]

As Jesus rode through the streets directly to the Temple, the whole city was moved[3]. Then the sick, the blind and the lame were brought to Him from every side, and He cured them all. At this sight the children began to cry out again: "Hosanna to the Son of David!" But the Pharisees, becoming furious, told Him to rebuke them. Jesus answered them: "Have you never read the words: Out of the mouths of infants and sucklings Thou hast perfected praise?"[4]

COMMENTARY.

Jesus, the Promised Redeemer. Hitherto our Lord had avoided all tokens of veneration on the part of the people (see chapter XXXIII); but now that He was approaching Jerusalem to suffer and die for the Redemption of the world, it was His will to enter its walls solemnly, as *Messias* and *King.* He desired that thousands of voices should proclaim in the presence of the unbelieving people of Jerusalem, that He was indeed their promised Redeemer. But He did not make this entry in battle-array, and mounted on a war-horse: He rode in, meek and gentle, sitting on an ass, the type of peace, to signify that He was not the Founder and King of an earthly city, raised by force of arms, such as most of the Jews fondly expected, but the Prince of Peace, whose kingdom was one of truth and grace.

---

[1] *Straiten thee.* Our Lord saw in spirit the terrible fate which would ere long overtake the unbelieving city; how it would be surrounded by enemies, and utterly destroyed.

[2] *Thy visitation.* You refuse to see that God is visiting you at this moment, when your Saviour is entering within your walls.

[3] *Moved.* Scripture adds: "When He was come into Jerusalem, the whole city was moved, saying: 'Who is this?' And the people said: 'This is Jesus, the Prophet from Nazareth of Galilee.'" The multitude which had formed the joyous and triumphant procession was principally composed of pilgrims from Galilee and Peræa. The exultation of these strangers roused even the inhabitants of Jerusalem out of their indifference, and they asked: "Who is this Man? Why is He so honoured and praised?" They quite ignored or forgot the miracles He had worked in their midst: they would not know Him, and thereby betrayed that unbelief over which Jesus had but just before shed such bitter tears.

[4] *Perfected praise.* Jesus applied the passage (Psalm 8, 3) to Himself, saying thus to His adversaries: "These children, by shouting in praise of Me, do but fulfil that which the Prophet foretold they would do."

Jesus, the Son of God. Jesus showed Himself to be God, and this in a fourfold way. 1. He knew that His disciples would find the ass and her colt tied up, as described, in the village of Bethphage, and He knew the disposition of their owner. 2. He foretold the siege and destruction of Jerusalem (for the account of which see chapter LVIII). He knew the things which were invisible, as also those things which had not yet taken place, and the secret thoughts in the hearts of men. He was, therefore, omniscient. 3. He applied to Himself the passage in Psalm 8: "Out of the mouths of infants" &c. This Psalm relates to the adoration paid by all creation, and even little children, to the Lord God. By applying it to Himself, Jesus claimed to be the Lord and God of creation. 4. He showed His divine Omnipotence by healing the lame, blind and sick who were brought to Him.

The tears of Jesus. All in the midst of the joy of the people and the homage paid to Him, Jesus burst into tears at the sight of the holy city! He who had dried the tears of so many, and had said to the mourners: "Weep not", now wept Himself. "This scene is so moving that it defies all attempts at description. The soul alone can try to discern what passed through the mind of Jesus, and weep with Him as a child weeps with its mother, the reason of whose tears it cannot understand. And in truth the tears of Jesus are a mystery to us, so incomprehensible is the love which brought Him from heaven to this vale of tears. He prayed for those who persecuted Him, but it is infinitely more that He should have wept over their misfortunes" (Schegg). Let us try to penetrate the mystery of these tears! He gazed at the Temple, both the erection and the services of which pointed to Him, the Redeemer, whom, in spite of all, this highly favoured city refused to acknowledge! That day was the last day of grace for both city and people. His solemn entry was for them the last warning and the time of visitation: and Jesus knew but too well that this last grace would be passed by, unused, as all the rest had been, and that His chosen people would blindly reject salvation, while hatred and envy of their Saviour filled the hearts of their leaders. Jesus wept therefore 1. over the blindness and obstinacy of the chosen people; for He, the Saviour, was bringing no salvation to the impenitent city which, by its final rejection of Him, would fill the measure of God's wrath, and draw down on itself speedy and terrible judgment. This knowledge drew bitter tears from Him. He wept 2. over the coming downfall of Jerusalem, and the calamities which its people would bring on themselves; and still more over the eternal woe which would overtake this unfaithful and impenitent city. He therefore wept especially 3. over the eternal loss of so many souls which He had come to save. How very great is the love of the Divine Heart of Jesus, that it should make Him shed bitter tears over those who repaid His love with such ingratitude, and who were ruined by their own fault!

Resistance to grace. We see by the case of the unbelieving city of Jerusalem how possible it is to resist grace.

Sins against the Holy Ghost. The Pharisees and those under their influence envied Jesus on account of the wonderful works which He did, and resisted the known truth that Jesus was the Messias; and thus deliberately persevered in impenitence.

Palm-Sunday, with the blessing of palms and its solemn procession, is thus celebrated 1. in memory of our Lord's triumphal entry into Jerusalem; 2. in thankful remembrance of the victory of faith over unbelief; and 3. as a salutary warning to us that we must overcome sin if we desire to enter heaven triumphantly.

APPLICATION. To neglect the hour of grace, and to resist grace are the most terrible of misfortunes. Will you suffer such a misfortune to overtake you? Will you be obstinate, impenitent, and lose your soul? A man's heart becomes bad little by little, not all at once; and he who in his youth refuses to listen to warnings, and resists God's grace, is likely to grow up leading an evil life, and is on the high road to obstinacy in sin and final impenitence. Apply this to yourself!

CHAPTER LVII.

THE PARABLE OF THE MARRIAGE-FEAST.

[Mat. 22, 1—14. Luke 14, 16—24.]

IN the evening Jesus returned from Jerusalem to Bethania. Next morning, however, He went back to the city and taught in the Temple[1]. What grieved Him most was the fickleness of the Jews and their hardness of heart. Wherefore He spoke to them this parable:

"The kingdom of heaven is like to a king who made a marriage[2] for his son. He sent his servants to call them[3] that were invited to the marriage; and they would not come[4]. Again he sent other servants, saying: 'Tell them that were invited:

---

[1] *The Temple.* He cleansed it again of buyers and sellers, driving them out as He had done previously (see chapter XV).

[2] *A marriage.* Who provided a bride and a nuptial feast for his son.

[3] *To call them.* To fetch those who had been already invited.

[4] *Would not come.* The bride chosen did not please them. They wished the king to choose another.

Behold, I have prepared my dinner [1], my beeves and fatlings [2] are killed and all things are ready; come ye to the wedding.' [3] But they [4] neglected and went their ways, one to his farm and another to his merchandise. And the rest laid hands [5] on his servants, and having treated them contumeliously, put them to death.

"But when the king heard of it, he was angry, and sending his armies, he destroyed those murderers, and burnt their city [6]. Then he saith to his servants: Go ye, therefore [7], into the highways [8], and as many as you shall find, invite to the marriage. So his servants, going out into the highways, gathered together all that they found, both bad and good, and the wedding was filled with guests.

"Then the king went in to see the guests, and he saw there a man who had not on a wedding-garment [9]. He saith to him: 'Friend, how camest thou in hither not having on a wedding-garment?' But he was silent [10]. Then the king said to the waiters: 'Having bound his hands and feet, cast him into exterior darkness; there shall be weeping and gnashing of teeth.' For many are called, but few are chosen!"

COMMENTARY.

The Parable of the Marriage-feast. The king signifies God the Father; and therefore his son is the Son of God, our Lord Jesus Christ.

---

[1] *Dinner.* The principal meal in the evening.

[2] *Fatlings.* Fatted poultry.

[3] *The wedding.* Which is fixed without any possibility of change.

[4] *But they.* "What does this marriage signify to us!" said they to themselves, and so saying, they went about their various occupations, although the date of the wedding had been fixed for some time, and they might have arranged their business accordingly.

[5] *Laid hands.* They looked on the king's persistence in inviting them to a marriage of which he knew they did not approve, as a personal insult, and showed their resentment by ill-treating and murdering his messengers.

[6] *Their city.* It is evident that those invited lived in a town not far from the king's palace.

[7] *Therefore.* In order that the meats may not be wasted.

[8] *The highways.* Where usually travellers and tramps are to be found. All were invited indiscriminately, no inquiry being made as to what sort of lives they had led previously.

[9] *Wedding-garment.* In the east kings used to provide their guests with wedding-garments, to ensure them all being suitably attired. This man ought to have clothed himself in his wedding-garment, as all the others had done.

[10] *He was silent.* For he had no excuse to offer.

The bride is the Church, and the marriage-feast is our Lord's spiritual union with the Church: the invited guests are those who are called to believe. Those who accept the invitation are those who are spiritually united to our Lord, and who have a share in the treasures of His grace. Those guests who were first invited are the Jews, who were called by God's servants (i. e. His prophets down to St. John the Baptist) to prepare themselves by penance for the coming of the Messias. They did not obey the call; for a kingdom, the condition of belonging to which was penance, did not please them. Then God, when the work of Redemption was completed, and the Church founded, sent out other servants, namely His apostles and disciples, to warn the Jews that "all things were now ready", and that now was the time to enter His kingdom. But, sunk as they were in carnal notions, given over to avarice, pleasure-seeking and the love of dominion, the Jews had no relish for the idea of a kingdom of grace and salvation, and paid no heed to the urgent call; and many of them—the Scribes and Pharisees—persecuted, maltreated and killed God's servants for daring to deliver God's message. The apostles were imprisoned, scourged &c., and St. Stephen was stoned to death, as you will see. Then Almighty God sent the Roman army to execute His judgments on the ungrateful people. The Romans killed a million of Jews and destroyed and burnt their city of Jerusalem. Then God sent His apostles among the Gentiles who had hitherto been wandering about, faithless and homeless, in the highways of the world, and invited them to the feast. These accepted His invitation, are still accepting it, and will go on doing so till, at the end of time, the Church is "filled with guests".

In the *first part* of the parable our Lord relates in a few words the history of His kingdom on earth, the Church militant, up to the time of His return. He foretold that Israel, taken as a whole, would reject the Gospel, and would therefore be rejected by God; but that the Gentiles would believe, and would, little by little, be received into His Church. It is only when the wedding is completely furnished with guests that the real marriage-feast, of which the *second part* of the parable treats, can take place. Eternal happiness is to be understood by this marriage-feast. This, however, must be preceded by the *judgment*, which will prove each one, whether he has on his wedding-garment, i. e. sanctifying grace. Whosoever is not found in a state of grace will be shut out of the kingdom of heaven, and cast into the exterior darkness where there shall be weeping and gnashing of teeth. Only one man is cited in the parable as being found without a wedding-garment, to show that not even *one* will escape the test. To obtain salvation it is not enough to believe and to be members of the Church: we must be clothed with, and be able to present, before the judgment-seat of God, the robe of innocence, sanctifying grace, which we received in holy Baptism, and which we must either have preserved, or been re-clothed with in the Sacrament of Penance.

Hell is a place of punishment into which no ray of grace or glory can penetrate, and which our Lord, therefore, calls a place of exterior darkness. The lost souls are imprisoned; they cannot get free, but are shut in without help and without hope. In hell there is nothing but weeping and gnashing of teeth, pain, rage and despair!

The excuses of sinners. The rejected guest was silent, for he could bring forward nothing in excuse. Here, upon earth, careless Christians are always excusing themselves, both to themselves and to others. But before the judgment-seat of the All-knowing and All-holy God they will have to keep silence.

The despisers of the Church and her ministers. Those who persecute and speak evil of the bishops and priests of the Church, are like those rebels who ill-treated the servants of the king, and who thereby drew down on themselves his anger and vengeance. With such as these Almighty God will hold a strict account, for our Lord has said: "He that despiseth you, despiseth Me!"

Holy Communion is a Feast in which the Divine Saviour entertains Himself with the individual soul. The Church, by her ministers, invites us to this Feast, commanding us to receive Holy Communion once a year at Easter, and urging us to more frequent Communion. He who does not partake of this Feast on earth, will find himself shut out from the marriage-feast in heaven. But only he who has on a wedding-garment, only he who is in a state of grace, may receive the Bread of Angels; for he who presumes to receive Holy Communion in a state of mortal sin, will be cast, if he does not repent, into hell, where there is wailing and gnashing of teeth.

APPLICATION. Have you a high idea of sanctifying grace? Do you bear in mind what a beautiful garment of the soul it is, and how our Lord recognises his spouses by it? Take care of it as your greatest treasure, and never lose it by mortal sin. The best way to preserve it is to pray and to practise your religion. Never make vain excuses.

CHAPTER LVIII.

THE TRIBUTE TO CÆSAR.

[Mat. 22, 15—22. Mark 12, 13. Luke 20, 20.]

THE Scribes and Pharisees, understanding that the parable of the marriage-feast was meant for them, hated our Lord more than ever. They went, therefore, and consulted together, how they could lay hold of some of His words[1], in order to accuse Him publicly. For this purpose they sent some of their disciples, with the Herodians[2], to ask Him, by way of satisfying their doubts, whether it were lawful to pay tribute[3] to Cæsar, or not. Now, by Cæsar, was meant the Roman Emperor, to whom Judæa was then subject. They thought that, if He answered "Yes", He would make Himself odious to the Jews, and that, on the other hand, if He answered "No", He would draw down on Himself the revengeful hatred of Herod and the Romans.

But Jesus, knowing their malice, said: "Why do ye tempt Me, ye hypocrites?[4] Show Me the coin[5] of the tribute." They showed Him a penny (Fig. 82). And He said to them: "Whose image and inscription is this?" They said: "Cæsar's". Then He said to them: "Render, therefore[6], to Cæsar the things[7] that are Cæsar's, and to God the things that are God's." The messengers could find no opening for

Fig. 82. Roman Penny.

accusing Him, and went away. But again the Pharisees laid a snare for Him. One of them, a doctor of the law, asked Him, tempting Him: "Master, which is the great commandment of the law (i. e. the greatest of the six hundred and thirteen command-

---

[1] *His words.* Which they hoped to twist into a means of bringing Him into disfavour either with the populace, or with the state authorities.

[2] *Herodians.* These were in favour of the Roman rulers and of Herod their creature, whereas to the Pharisees and to most of the Jews his government was abhorrent. The Herodians and Pharisees were thus political adversaries, but they were united in their hatred of Jesus, and were willing to form an alliance to injure Him.

[3] *To pay tribute.* They prefaced their question with artful flattery. "We know", said they, "that Thou art a true speaker, and teachest the way of God in truth, neither carest Thou for any man, for Thou dost not regard the person of man. Tell us, therefore, is it lawful to give tribute to one who is a Gentile?"

[4] *Ye hypocrites.* Such did Jesus call them, because they acted as if they had sought Him for the sole purpose of learning the truth as to what was God's will, whereas their real wicked purpose was to "tempt" Him, or lay a snare for Him. By these words He showed that He penetrated their evil design.

[5] *The coin.* In which the tribute was always paid, and on which was the image of the Emperor with his name.

[6] *Render, therefore.* For you use coins on which is his image, and therefore practically acknowledge him to be your sovereign, even though your state of subjection be a punishment permitted by God.

[7] *The things.* Such as tribute, taxes &c.

ments)?" This being a point of dispute among the Jewish Scribes, he hoped that, whatever our Lord's answer might be, He would give offence to some one. Jesus said to him: "Thou shalt love the Lord thy God with thy whole heart, and with thy whole soul, and with thy whole mind. This is the greatest and first commandment. And the second is like to this (i. e. as great and important): Thou shalt love thy neighbour as thyself. On these two commandments dependeth the whole law [1] and the prophets."

COMMENTARY.

Obedience to temporal authority. We are not only allowed, but commanded to obey the authority of the state, and to pay such taxes &c. as are a due; for the authority of the state is ordained by God to protect the lives and property of subjects. If there were no temporal authority, disorder, robbery, murder &c. would be rampant; and, therefore, as the authority of the state exists for the good of subjects, it is the duty of these last to pay those taxes &c. without which it cannot be kept up.

The Worship of God. We are to be equally particular to give to God what is due to Him: faith, hope, love, thanksgiving, worship, and obedience to His commandments.

The Veracity of our Lord. Even His enemies bore witness that He taught in truth. "Master, we know that Thou art a true speaker, and teachest the way of God in truth." This very testimony condemned them, for, in spite of their saying this, they did not believe what He taught.

Unbelief is, as we see in the case of the Pharisees, untiring in its efforts to find objections to faith, and to forge fresh weapons against the Christian religion, showing its enmity sometimes openly, sometimes veiled under hypocritical flattery. It deals with the Church and the faithful to this day exactly as it dealt with the Divine Founder of the Church.

The two commandments, to love God and to love our neighbour, form, in fact, only one commandment. Without the love of God there can be no true love of our neighbour; and he who does love God must, of necessity, love his neighbour as an image of God.

For the love of God there exists no measure, for we must love Him as much as we can, and more than we love anything else, because He is infinitely worthy to be loved.

The measure of our love of our neighbour is to be found in our love of ourselves, which God has implanted in the heart of each one of us. We are, our Lord says, to love our neighbour as ourselves.

---

[1] *Dependeth the whole law.* i. e. even as anything which hangs on a prop falls to the ground, if the prop be removed, so would all other commandments fall, if these two were removed.

Self-love is, as we have just seen, part of our human nature; but our nature having been corrupted by the Fall, our self-love easily degenerates into a sinful love of self, if it is not limited and regulated by the love of God and of our neighbour.

APPLICATION. Do you love God with all your heart? You will very likely answer: "I do indeed love God! Who could help loving so good a God!" But I ask you: Could you not love Him still more? If you do not love Him with every power that you possess, you do not love Him enough. And how do you show your love for God? Have you a horror and hatred of sin? Would you rather die than commit a mortal sin?

CHAPTER LIX.

THE WOES AGAINST THE PHARISEES, AND THE WIDOW'S MITES.

[Mat. 23, 13—39.   Mark 12, 41—44.]

JESUS, filled with indignation at the hard-heartedness and hypocrisy of the Pharisees, once more, on the eve of His Passion and Death, warned the people against them and pronounced divers woes upon their head. "But woe to you Scribes and Pharisees, hypocrites, because you shut the kingdom of heaven against men, for you yourselves do not enter in, and those that are going in, you suffer not to enter. Woe to you, because you go round about the sea and the land to make one proselyte[1], and when he is made, you make him the child of hell twofold more than yourselves. Woe to you, because you tithe mint[2] and anise and cummin and have left the weightier things of the law, judgment and mercy and faith. Blind guides, who strain out a gnat[3] and swallow a camel! You make clean the outside of the cup and of the dish, but within you are full of rapine and uncleanness. You are like to whited sepulchres[4] which outwardly appear to men beautiful,

----

[1] *Proselyte.* i. e. one convert.

[2] *Tithe mint.* Which is not prescribed by the law.

[3] *Strain out a gnat.* i. e. you are particular and rigorous in small insignificant matters, and wholly careless in important matters.

[4] *Whited sepulchres.* Jewish teachers of the law had prescribed that every year before Easter the sepulchres should be whitened so that they could easily be seen by the passers-by, and all danger of uncleanness avoided by them.

but within are full of dead men's bones and of all filthiness. Fill ye up then the measure of your fathers. You serpents, generation of vipers, how will you flee from the judgment of hell?"

While Jesus remained in the Temple, He saw many making their offerings, and He noticed the way in which each one made the offering. Several rich persons put much into the treasury[1], but one poor widow put in two mites[2]. Then Jesus called His disciples and said to them: "Amen, I say to you, this poor widow hath cast in more than all they who have cast into the treasury; for they all did cast in of their abundance; but she, of her want, has cast in all she had, even her whole living."[3]

COMMENTARY.

The most important Duties. Our Saviour says that the most important duties are those of justice, mercy and faith. External religion must be the expression and practical exercise of internal religion, which consists in the spirit of justice and mercy and faith.

Hypocrisy. The wish to appear religious and God-fearing before men, while your heart is full of ungodly sentiments, is hypocrisy. This is a great sin, forbidden by the eighth commandment.

Good Intention. From the words of our Lord spoken in praise of the poor widow, we learn that in our good works everything depends upon the intention. The widow had given more than all the rich; for she parted with her whole fortune. She intended to give all she had to God. This was an act of perfect love and sacrifice.

APPLICATION. Are you sincere in all your religious practices? In your confession, do you look more to what is in your heart, than outside it? Do you always make a good intention and often say: "All for the greater glory of God"?

---

[1] *The treasury.* The treasury was fixed in the wall of the outer court of the women, and had thirteen trumpet-shaped openings or mouths, into which the money was thrown.

[2] *Two mites.* The widow might easily have reserved one mite for herself, but no, she gave both—all that she had—for the glory of God.

[3] *Her whole living.* God does not look to the greatness of the gift, or else only the rich could gain merit, but to the good-will, or good intention, of the giver.

CHAPTER LX.

JESUS FORETELLS THE DESTRUCTION OF JERUSALEM AND THE END OF THE WORLD.

[Mat. 24, 1—51.]

AS Jesus was leaving[1] the Temple some of His disciples called His attention to the rich materials[2] of which it was built. But He told them[3] that the day would soon come when there should not be left one stone upon another of that gorgeous edifice. They asked Him when these things should come to pass, and what signs should precede the end of the world[4]. He said to them:

"When you shall see Jerusalem compassed about with an army, then know that the desolation thereof is at hand. Then let those that are in Judæa flee to the mountains[5]. And he that is in the field[6], let him not go back to take his coat[7]. For there shall be then great tribulation, such as hath not been from the beginning of the world until now, neither shall be. There shall be wrath upon this people. They shall fall by the edge of the sword, and shall be led away captives into all nations. Jerusalem shall be trodden down by the Gentiles till the times of the nations[8] be fulfilled.

---

[1] *Leaving.* After visiting it for the last time.

[2] *The rich materials.* For a description of the Temple see chapter VII. Some of the stones of which the Temple was built were as much as thirty feet long, and six or seven feet thick. Anyone looking at its construction might have thought it would stand for ever.

[3] *Them.* As they sat on the Mount of Olives, facing the Temple.

[4] *The end of the world.* The apostles thought that the end of the world, and the establishment of the Messias' kingdom would begin soon after the destruction of Jerusalem. They therefore asked in one breath when the Temple would be destroyed, and what signs would herald the end of the world. Our Lord answered their question by telling them, first, what signs would precede the destruction of Jerusalem, and, afterwards, what signs would precede the end of the world.

[5] *To the mountains.* For there would be no security for them behind the walls of the city.

[6] *In the field.* Where, for facilitating labour, a man wears only his under-clothing.

[7] *His coat.* His upper garments.

[8] *The times of the nations.* Until the time comes when the heathen will be heathen no more, on account of their conversion to Christianity.

"Many will come in My name, saying: 'I am Christ', and they shall seduce[1] many. You shall hear of wars and rumours of wars; nation shall rise against nation, kingdom against kingdom, and there shall be pestilences, and famines, and earthquakes in places. These are but the beginning of sorrows. And this Gospel of the kingdom shall be preached in the whole world[2]. And immediately after the tribulation of those days, the sun shall be darkened, and the moon shall not give her light, the stars shall fall from heaven, and the powers of the heavens shall be shaken[3]. And upon the earth, distress of nations, by reason of the confusion of the roaring of the sea and of the waves; men withering away for fear and expectation of what shall come upon the whole world.

"Then shall appear the sign[4] of the Son of Man in heaven, and all the tribes of the earth shall mourn; and they shall see the Son of Man coming in the clouds of heaven with great power and majesty. He shall send His angels with a trumpet and a great voice, and they shall gather together His elect from the four winds, from the farthest part of the heavens to the utmost bounds of them. Heaven and earth shall pass away, but My word[5] shall not pass away."

"Watch therefore", said our Lord in conclusion, "praying at all times that you may be accounted worthy to escape all these things that are to come, and to stand before the Son of Man."

COMMENTARY.

The Destruction of Jerusalem. Our Lord's discourse forms a wonderful prophecy about the destruction of Jerusalem, the end of the world, and the signs which were to herald both. The destruction of

---

[1] *Shall seduce.* "And many false prophets shall arise, and shall seduce many", our Lord said a little further on in His discourse; "and because iniquity hath abounded, the charity of many shall grow cold. But he that shall persevere to the end, he shall be saved."

[2] *The whole world.* The gospel will be preached all over the face of the earth "for a testimony to all nations". At the last judgment, therefore, the unbelievers will not be able to excuse themselves, because the Faith will have been proclaimed to every one: "and then", added our Lord, "shall the consummation come"

[3] *Shaken.* The laws of our solar system, as they are now, will cease to act.

[4] *The sign.* A cross of fire.

[5] *My word.* But what I promise to my faithful disciples shall not pass away, for it is life everlasting.

Jerusalem took place thirty-seven years after our Lord spoke these words (A. D. 70), and the circumstances of it were exactly those foretold by Him. A Jewish priest, by name Josephus, who was an eye-witness of the sad events, has in his seven books of *"The Jewish War"* described the siege, conquest and destruction of the holy city, as well as the signs which preceded them; and all the world can know by his description that our Lord's prophecy was exactly fulfilled.

Among the signs which preceded the destruction of Jerusalem, the following are quoted. According to the Acts of the Apostles several false prophets appeared in Jerusalem; first Theudas, and after him an Egyptian. In the year 64, when Nero was emperor, a great persecution of the Christians broke out, in which, among many others, SS. Peter and Paul suffered martyrdom. Throughout the Roman empire princes were murdered; and there raged civil wars, plagues, pestilences, and earthquakes which swallowed up whole towns. For an entire year a comet, in the form of a sword, was to be seen over Jerusalem. The great iron door of the Temple, which it took twenty men to move on its hinges, opened one night of itself. On the Feast of Pentecost the priests heard mysterious voices in the night, saying: "Let us depart".

In the year 65, the Jews in Jerusalem rose up in open rebellion against the Roman government, and put to the sword the Roman garrison. The emperor Nero then sent his able general, Vespasian, to subdue the Jews. In the course of three years Vespasian conquered all the strong places of Judæa, and was on the point of marching on Jerusalem itself, when he was chosen emperor, and returned home, resigning the command of the army to his son Titus. Meanwhile the Christians in Jerusalem, mindful betimes of our Lord's warnings, fled to Pella in Peræa (see Map).

In the interval civil war broke out in Jerusalem, and three powerful parties were fighting against each other. The principal citizens were executed or assassinated. Bloodshed took place in the streets, and even in the outer courts of the Temple. A part of the city was reduced to ruins, and thousands lost their lives. Each party destroyed the supplies of the others, and thus provisions which might have sustained the inhabitants for several years were lost. In the spring of the year 70 Titus appeared with his army, and pitched his camp before the city. Earth-works were thrown up, and a breach was made in the third or outer wall by the battering-rams of the Romans. After this outer wall had been destroyed, Titus succeeded, notwithstanding the gallant resistance of the Jews, in overthrowing the second wall, and then, after a hard fight of four days, he made his way into the city, and took possession of Fort Antonia, in spite of the heroic defence made by its garrison. By this time the famine in the city was very great. The siege had begun at the time of the Pasch, when Jerusalem was crowded with pilgrims, so that at the time that the enemy surrounded the city, there were more than a million people within its walls. Some of them tried to steal out at night to search for herbs and roots, but such as were surprised were scourged and crucified by the Romans, and before long the crosses on which they were put to death stood like a forest round the Roman camp. To prevent any attempt at escape from the doomed city, and to ensure its reduction by starvation, Titus caused a wall to be built all round it. The famine was so great, that the inhabitants devoured the most loathsome things, old leather, mouldy hay, and even cow-dung. One mother killed and ate her own child! Added to the famine, there raged a devastating plague, and in the course of seven weeks no less than 716,000 dead bodies were carried away or thrown over the walls into the enemy's camp.

After the storming of Fort Antonia, the attack was directed against the mount on which the Temple was built. After vain efforts to take the Temple by storm, Titus commanded that its gates and colonnade of cedar wood should be set on fire. He wished to save the actual Temple, but, in the excitement of the battle, a soldier threw a burning brand into the Sanctuary, and soon the glorious Temple was a heap of ruins. The fight was so furious that blood flowed literally in streams down the steps of the Temple. Finally, the upper city on Mount Sion was taken. Every Jew whom the conquerors met was cut down, and the houses with their inhabitants within were burnt. For two days and two nights the conflagration lasted, and on the third day nothing remained of the holy city but a heap of ashes.

Over a million people perished during the siege, and 97,000 were carried away into captivity and slavery. The ruins of the city and of the Temple were cleared away and the ground levelled. As our Lord foretold, there did not remain one stone upon another. And the Jews were scattered over the face of the earth.

In the year 363 A. D., the Roman emperor, Julian the Apostate, wished to rebuild the Temple, in order to bring to nought the prophecy of Jesus; but an earthquake shattered what foundations remained, and fire was vomited from the earth, killing many heathen and Jewish workmen and making the place unapproachable; so that the work had to be given up. Not long afterwards Julian was killed in an expedition against the Persians, and he died with these words on his lips: "Galilean (meaning our Lord), Thou hast conquered."

The Divinity of Jesus Christ. His prophecy about the destruction of Jerusalem, which was so exactly fulfilled, is a proof of His Divinity, for only God could foreknow all that would occur both before and at the destruction of the holy city.

The End of the World. The exact fulfilment of our Lord's words about the destruction of Jerusalem is a pledge that what He foretold about the end of the world and His second coming will be equally fulfilled. The signs which will precede the end of the world will be similar to those which preceded the destruction of Jerusalem: wars, sedition, and earthquakes. The Gospel will first be preached to all nations (although our Lord does not say that all will accept it); but there will be a great apostasy before the end of the world: false Christs and false prophets shall appear, and many shall be seduced. The laws of the universe will be upset, and then shall be seen the Cross in the heavens, and the Divine Judge will come in power and glory. All the dead will be called from their graves to appear before Him, and heaven and earth shall pass away—or be changed. "The fashion of this world passeth away", says St. Paul (1 Cor. 7, 31); while St. Peter writes thus: "For we look for new heavens and a new earth according to His promises" (2 Pet. 3, 13). God will not destroy either heaven or earth, and then create a new heaven and a new earth, but He will transform and renew them.

The Justice of God. This is revealed to us by the terrible judgment which overtook Jerusalem and the unbelieving Jews.

The Grace of Perseverance. "He that shall persevere to the end, he shall be saved." The end—the death of individuals, is, as far as the time of it is concerned, quite as much a secret as is the end of the world. Blessed is he whom death does not come upon unawares, in a state of sin. As a man dies, so will he appear before the judgment-seat of God at the Last Day. We ought to pray very earnestly for the grace of final perseverance; for this most important of all graces can only be obtained by prayer.

APPLICATION. Our Lord Himself points out the application which we ought to make of this prophetic discourse of His: "Watch and pray!" We must not spend our lives carelessly and frivolously like those who do not believe, but we must be watchful and always prepared for death. We must be on our guard against the drowsiness of tepidity and the deadly sleep of mortal sin. Are you not lax in the service of God? Is not your love for Him cold? Pray fervently: "From sudden and unprepared death, O Lord, deliver me!"

CHAPTER LXI.

THE PARABLE OF THE TEN VIRGINS.

[Mat. 25, 1—13.]

JESUS warns His followers not to seek the things of this world with too much anxiety, and to make a provision of good works, while they yet have time; for that death will come like a thief in the night when least expected. To make them better understand this great truth, He gave them the following parable:

"Then[1] shall the kingdom of heaven be like to ten virgins, who, taking their lamps[2], went out to meet the bridegroom and the bride. And five of them were foolish, and five were wise. But the five foolish, having taken their lamps, took no oil with them; but the wise took oil in their vessels with the lamps. While the bridegroom tarried they all slumbered and slept[3]. And at midnight there was a cry made: 'Behold, the bridegroom cometh; go ye forth to meet him!' Then all those virgins arose and trimmed[4] their lamps. And the foolish said to the wise: 'Give us of your oil, for our lamps are gone out.' The wise answered, saying: 'Lest there be not enough for us and for you, go you, rather, to them that sell, and buy for yourselves.'

"Now, while they went[5] to buy, the bridegroom came, and they who were ready went in with him to the marriage, and the door was shut. But at last came also the other virgins, saying: 'Lord, Lord, open to us!' But he, answering, said: 'Amen, I say to you, I know you not.'[6] Watch ye, therefore, because ye know not the day nor the hour."[7]

COMMENTARY.

The necessity of good works. The ten virgins represent the faithful in general. The bridegroom is our Lord: the marriage-feast is ever-lasting happiness: the arrival of the bridegroom signifies the judgment, both the particular judgment after death, and the general judgment at the end of time. It is the duty of all the faithful to be ever expecting the arrival of the Divine Bridegroom, who will come to take his own servants to the heavenly banquet. We must be ready to go with him at any time or moment. The wise virgins are those Christians who

---

[1] *Then.* i. e. when the time comes for the faithful to be admitted into the kingdom of heaven, it will be with them as it was with the ten virgins.

[2] *Their lamps.* Wedding-processions among the Jews usually took place in the evening, by torchlight.

[3] *Slept.* In the house where they awaited the arrival of the bridegroom.

[4] *Trimmed.* Pouring fresh oil into them, so that their light might burn brightly. The lamps of the foolish virgins gave a very dim light, because they had not enough oil in them.

[5] *While they went.* At that hour the shops were closed, and some time elapsed before those who kept them could open them and attend to the foolish virgins' wants.

[6] *I know you not.* I cannot acknowledge you to be my servants. You are strangers to me, and have no claim to a share in the marriage-feast.

[7] *The hour.* When your bridegroom will come.

stand ready, holding not only the *lamp of faith,* but also the *oil of good works* in their hands. The foolish virgins are those bad Christians who have indeed the lamp of faith, but to whom is lacking the oil of active love, and whose faith is therefore dead. They pass their lives carelessly, taking no thought of that eternally decisive moment which is before us all. At midnight, when none of the virgins were expecting him, the bridegroom came! In other words, death took them unawares. Wise or good Christians, even though death may take them by surprise, are always ready to meet the Lord, and enter into eternity; for they have not only kept the faith, but also gained merit. Foolish, careless Christians do not live in accordance with their faith, but put off their conversion till the hour of death. Death comes on them unawares, and then they find out with terror that their faith is dead, and that there is lacking to them the oil of good works. The merits of their fellow-Christians can avail them nothing, and they have no time to gain merits of their own by the performance of good works. For them, indeed, the night has come "when no man can work"! (John 9, 4.) They may wail and cry out "Lord! Lord!" but they will find themselves shut out from heaven, for our Lord Jesus has said: "Not every one that saith to me, Lord, Lord, shall enter into the kingdom of heaven; but he that doeth the will of My Father who is in heaven, he shall enter into the kingdom of heaven" (Mat. 7, 21).

Watchfulness. Our Lord Himself points the moral of this parable by His concluding words: "Watch you, therefore, because you know not the day nor the hour (of your death)." We ought to live on the watch, and be always ready for the coming of our Divine Judge, because 1. we know not when we shall be called away; 2. the hour of death is, as a rule, too late for conversion and the gaining of merit; and it is therefore a mischievous act of carelessness to put off conversion till the hour of death.

Prudence is one of the four cardinal virtues. The wise or prudent virgins desired to be admitted to the heavenly marriage-feast; therefore they took pains to become worthy of admission by virtues and good works. They avoided sin, and persevered in grace and in the practice of the love of God, and were therefore found ready when death surprised them. The foolish virgins also wished to take part in the banquet, but they did not use those means by which alone they could gain admission. The virtuous are prudent, but sinners are fools!

Dead faith. Even as a lamp goes out when it is not fed with oil, so does faith die, if it is not nourished and sustained by works of piety, mortification and brotherly love.

Humility. It was not from selfishness that the wise virgins refused to share their oil with those who were foolish. Humility made them act thus, because they feared that they would not have enough for themselves. The just do not rely on their good works, but "work out their salvation with fear and trembling". However much good they have done, they confess that they are unprofitable servants, and that their only ground for hope lies in the mercy of God.

APPLICATION. Picture to yourself the consternation and despair of those who are shut out for ever from the happiness of heaven. "We fools!" they will say, "for we might have been saved! We had so many means of grace, so many opportunities of doing good. But we wasted them, and are now, by our own fault, lost for ever!" Do you wish to be one of these unhappy ones? No! Then begin at once, while you are young, to be zealous in the service of God.

CHAPTER LXII.

THE PARABLE OF THE TALENTS.

[Mat. 25, 14—30; of. Luke 19, 11—28.]

JESUS also spoke another parable to the same effect, showing the necessity of making good use of the time and the talents confided to us.

"For even as[1] a man going into a far country called his servants, and delivered to them his goods. To one he gave five talents[2], and to another two, and to another one; to every one according to his proper ability: and immediately he took his journey. Now, he that had received the five talents went his way and traded with the same, and gained other five. And in like manner, he that had received the two gained other two. But he that had received the one, went away, and hid his lord's money in the earth.

"After a long time, the lord of those servants came and reckoned with them. And he that had received five talents, coming, brought other five talents, saying: 'Lord, thou didst deliver to me five talents; behold, I have gained other five over and above.' His lord said to him: 'Well done, thou good and faithful servant; because thou hast been faithful over a few things, I will set thee over many things: enter thou into the joy[3] of thy lord.'"

---

[1] *For even as.* i. e. for the kingdom of God is even as a man who, going into a far country, called his servants &c.

[2] *Talents.* One talent is equal to £ 390.

[3] *Into the joy.* Come to me, and share my joy and possessions.

And to the servant who, having received two talents, came back with four talents, their lord spoke in like manner.

"But he that had received the one talent came and said: 'Lord, I know that thou art a hard man[1]; and, being afraid, I went and hid thy talent in the earth: behold, here thou hast that which is thine!' Then his lord, answering, said: 'Wicked and slothful servant, thou knewest that I was a hard man. Thou oughtest, therefore, to have committed my money to the bankers, and, at my coming, I should have received my own with usury. Out of thy own mouth I judge thee. Take ye away, therefore, the talent from him, and give it to him that hath ten talents. For to every one that hath, shall be given, and he shall abound; but from him that hath not, that also which he seemeth to have shall be taken away. And the unprofitable servant cast ye out into exterior darkness. There shall be weeping and gnashing of teeth.'"

COMMENTARY.

In the Parable of the Talents, the man who delivered his goods to his servants is our Lord Jesus Christ. His goods are the gifts bestowed on us by Him as our Creator, and all those graces which He as our Redeemer left with us when He returned to His Father and "went into a far country". The talents, therefore, signify life, health, memory, understanding, fortune &c. as well as faith, sanctifying and actual grace, and all means of grace, especially His own Body and Blood in the Most Blessed Sacrament. All these gifts, natural as well as supernatural, are talents given to us, of which we are to make good use. We can "trade with them" by using them for the glory of God and the salvation of our own souls.

Almighty God distributes *His* gifts (for they are His, and we are only His stewards) in different measure, as He pleases. He does not, therefore, require an equal return from all, but only a good will and strenuous effort to serve Him and advance His glory. "Unto whom much is given, of him (when our Lord comes to judge) much shall be required" (Luke 12, 48); and it follows that of him who has received less, less will be required, though he who by trading with two talents gained other two, received the same signs of approbation as did he who had gained five more with the five entrusted to Him. Both made a good use of their gifts, and by corresponding with grace and performing good works merited an increase of grace. *The reward* given to the faithful

---

[1] *A hard man.* i. e. hard to satisfy and hard to deal and reckon with. "The wrong-doer generally turns an excuse into an accusation" (Schegg).

servant of God is so exceeding great, that in comparison with it even the five talents appear as "few". The just man will receive a "good measure (of reward) pressed down and shaken together" (Luke 6, 38), and will have a share in the eternal joy and majesty of our Lord Jesus, whom he served faithfully on earth.

The slothful servant did not correspond with grace and made no use of it, and used his natural gifts only in the service of the world. His faith was a dead faith, without love and without zeal. He excused himself by pleading that Almighty God was "hard", that His commandments were too difficult to keep, and that He required what it was impossible to give. His harangue and excuses, however, profited him nothing, because the very fact of his knowing that God's judgments are severe, ought to have made him exert himself to keep His laws. If he had corresponded with the grace he had received, he would have merited further grace, and would have been praised and rewarded. But he was slothful, did not profit by grace, and thus lost what grace he had (as we see lukewarm Christians lose even the gift of faith), and was thrust out of the kingdom of grace into the exterior darkness of hell.

The chief lessons to be learnt from this parable are as follows:

1. *Faith alone does not suffice for salvation,* which must be won by good works.

2. At the judgment every Christian will have to *give an account* of the use he has made of his natural and supernatural gifts. The slothful servant was called wicked and was condemned, simply because he left undone that which he ought to have done.

3. *God is our Lord and Master,* and we are His servants. He is a most gracious Lord, for He gives His servants more and more grace as they need it, and rewards them with everlasting happiness.

Almsgiving. The poor are God's bankers. Alms are a safe investment and bring in the highest interest, for God rewards them with an eternal recompense.

APPLICATION. Everything you have is a gift of God, and a talent committed to your charge. Even your good works are not your own, because without God's grace you can do nothing. Only your sins are quite your own and your own work. Do not therefore boast of your understanding, memory &c., but be humble, and remember that you will one day have to give an account of them. "And what hast thou that thou hast not received? And if thou hast received, why dost thou glory as if thou hadst not received it?" (1 Cor. 4, 7.) Make a resolution not to say one word to-day in your own praise.

CHAPTER LXIII.

THE LAST JUDGMENT.

[Mat. 25, 31—46.]

AFTER Jesus had admonished His disciples to prepare for the Last Judgment, He described it to them in these words:

"When the Son of Man shall come in His majesty, and all His angels with Him, then shall He sit upon the seat of His majesty [1]. All nations shall be gathered together before Him; and He shall separate them one from another, as the shepherd separateth [2] the sheep from the goats [3]. And He shall set the sheep on His right hand [4], but the goats on the left.

"Then the King shall say to them that shall be on His right hand: 'Come, ye blessed [5] of My Father, possess the kingdom prepared for you from the foundation of the world. For I was hungry, and you gave Me to eat; I was thirsty, and you gave Me to drink; I was a stranger, and you took Me in; naked, and you clothed Me; sick, and you visited Me; I was in prison, and you came to Me.' — Then shall the just answer Him, saying: 'Lord, when have we done these things to Thee?' The King shall answer and say to them: 'Amen, I say to you, as long as you have done it to one of these, My least brethren, you did it to Me.'

"Then shall He say to them on His left hand: 'Depart from Me, ye cursed, into everlasting fire which was prepared for the devil and his angels. For I was hungry, and you gave Me not to eat; I was thirsty, and you gave me not to drink; I was a stranger, and you took Me not in; naked, and you clothed Me not; sick and in prison, and you did not visit Me.' Then shall they also answer Him, saying: 'Lord, when did we see Thee

---

[1] *The seat of His majesty.* On His judgment-seat.

[2] *Separateth.* When, in the evening, he pens them in the fold.

[3] *Goats.* The gentle, docile, patient and harmless sheep are taken as a figure of the just; whereas the wild, unruly, quarrelsome and unclean goats are a type of the wicked. This separation of the evil from the good will be made by the angels of God, as we learnt in the parable of the seed and the cockle (chapter XXVIII).

[4] *His right hand.* Which is the place of honour.

[5] *Ye blessed.* They are styled thus, because the Father has called them through His Son to be heirs of His kingdom, and has showered blessings and graces on them.

hungry, or thirsty, or a stranger, or naked, or sick, or in prison, and did not minister to Thee?' Then He shall answer them: 'Amen, I say to you, as long as you did it not to one of these least ones, neither did you do it to Me.' And these shall go into everlasting punishment, but the just into life everlasting."

COMMENTARY.

Jesus our Judge. The judgment at the end of the world will be held by our Lord Jesus Christ; and our Redeemer will then be our Judge. The Son of God came into the world the first time in poverty and lowliness: when He comes again to judge us, He will come in power, glory and great majesty. Then those will tremble who have not believed in Him, or who have despised His commandments, His Church, and His Sacraments.

The Angels also will take part in accusing the wicked, and bearing testimony to the just. Then, after the judgment, they will take God's chosen ones, whose guardians and protectors they were on earth, into the eternal joy of the heavenly marriage-feast.

The judgment will be general. All men, though they have been already judged privately, will stand before God's judgment-seat, and be judged together and openly.

The Divine Judge will equally *make known* the good works of the just and the evil deeds of the wicked, so that the former may publicly receive their merited praise and reward, and the latter may be put to open shame; and men and angels may know and confess the justice of the Divine Judge.

The law by which men will be judged is that first commandment of Christ, the *law of love,* which contains in itself all the other commandments. He who for the love of our Lord has, according to his ability, done good to his fellow-men, and practised a real love of his neighbour springing from his love for God, will be rewarded for what he has done, just as if he had done it to our Lord Himself. But he. who has either performed no works of charity, or has not performed them for our Lord Jesus Christ's sake, will stand condemned, because such an one has neither true love nor living faith. We shall therefore be judged not only for the evil which we have done, but also for the good which we have omitted to do.

The sentence will be publicly pronounced. This sentence will be twofold: To the just will be adjudged everlasting life, while the unjust will be banished to hell; both reward and punishment being carried out immediately after the judgment.

Heaven. The just will go to God. They will live for ever in His sight, having that perfect union with Him which fills them with inconceivable joy and glory.

The punishment of hell consists in this, 1. that the damned are cursed and rejected by God, and deprived of His Vision, in the possession of which alone happiness lies; 2. that they will suffer in fire unquenchable and in the company of devils. The punishment of the damned will be certainly as unending as the happiness of the just.

A comparison of the two sentences shows that the one is the exact opposite of the other:

Come	*Depart from Me*
Ye blessed of My Father	*Ye cursed.* (Not, ye cursed *of the Father,* because the sinner himself, not God, is the author of the curse of the unjust.)
Possess ye the kingdom	*into everlasting fire*
Prepared for you from the foundation of the world.	*Prepared for the devil and his angels.* (Our Lord does not say "prepared for you", for God created hell only for the devils, and He "wills that all men be saved". Moreover hell was not prepared from the beginning of creation, being created only at the time when the angels fell.)

Faith alone cannot save. In the parable of the virgins our Lord taught us plainly that the oil of good works is necessary in addition to the lamp of faith; and He related the parable of the talents for the sole purpose of showing us that he only can be saved who uses the gifts and graces given to him by God, for the practice of works pleasing to God. Now, in the account we have read to-day, our Lord tells us that at the judgment those will be condemned who do not practise works of mercy, and that good works alone can claim the eternal reward of heaven. It is therefore our Lord's distinct doctrine, that good works are necessary for salvation, and it is almost inconceivable that the comfortable idea that faith alone will save us, should ever have been proclaimed to be the doctrine of Christ!

APPLICATION. You also, with the rest of mankind, will be called before the judgment-seat of God. On which side of our Lord do you mean to be? Shall you be among the sheep who have obeyed the voice of their Good Shepherd, or among the goats who have lived according to their own lusts? What a terrible misfortune if you found yourself on the left hand, cursed and rejected by your Lord, separated from those dear to you, and cast into everlasting fire with the devils! To be rejected and cursed by Jesus, and separated for ever from God, who is the source of all happiness, would be such a terrible disaster, that we cannot even picture it to ourselves!

Do you wish to escape this awful fate? Then judge yourself severely now in the holy tribunal of Penance. Accuse yourself sincerely and with a contrite heart both of the sins you have committed, and of the good which you have omitted to do, and make a very firm resolution of amendment. The Sacrament of Penance is the tribunal of God's mercy. If you present yourself at that tribunal often and with a good preparation, you will not be rejected when you appear before God's Tribunal at the Last Day.

CHAPTER LXIV.

THE LAST SUPPER: THE WASHING OF THE FEET.

[Mat. 26, 17—19. Mark 14, 12—16. Luke 22, 14—18. John 13, 1—20.]

ON the first day of the Azymes[1], or unleavened bread, when the Paschal lamb was to be sacrificed, the disciples[2] went to Jesus and said to Him: "Where wilt Thou that we prepare for Thee to eat the Pasch?"[3] He said to Peter and John: "Go ye into the city[4], and there shall meet you a man carrying a pitcher of water: follow him. And wheresoever he shall go in, say to the master of the house: 'The Master saith: Where is My refectory[5], where I may eat the Pasch with My disciples?' He will show you a large dining-room, furnished[6], and there prepare ye for us."

---

[1] *The Azymes.* The Paschal feast was also called the feast of unleavened bread, because on it only unleavened bread might be eaten (Old Test. XXXIII). The "first day of unleavened bread" was the day preceding the Pasch, i. e. a Thursday, because in that year the Pasch fell on a Friday. On the eve of the feast the head of every family had to kill, or have killed, a lamb in the outer court of the temple. In the evening it was roasted whole and eaten.

[2] *The disciples.* Who, being the spiritual sons of our Lord, formed with Him a family.

[3] *The Pasch.* The Paschal lamb.

[4] *The city.* Jesus was at that time at Bethania (Mat. 26, 6), but the pasch had to be eaten in Jerusalem.

[5] *My refectory* (Mark 14, 14). i. e. the room which is already prepared for Me (Fig. 83, p. 630). Our Lord speaks as if He had previously made arrangements with this man to eat the Pasch at his house.

[6] *Furnished.* With cushions. It was the custom among the Jews to eat the Pasch reclining on cushions, and clad in festal garments. The Scribes and doctors

The disciples went into the city, found all as He had told them, and prepared the Pasch. In the evening [1], Jesus came with the other apostles. And when they were at table Jesus said to them: "With desire I have desired to eat this Pasch with you before I suffer. For I say unto you that I will not eat of it, till [2] it be fulfilled in the kingdom of God."

He then rose from supper, and laid aside His garment, and having taken a towel, He girded Himself. After that, He poured water into a basin, and began to wash the feet of his disciples,

Fig. 83.   Cœnaculum at Jerusalem (upper room as at present).

and to wipe them with the towel. But when He came first to Peter, the apostle said in surprise: "Lord, dost Thou wash my feet?" [3]

of the law had decided that the command to eat the pasch standing, and girt ready for a journey, only applied to the time of Israel's servitude.

[1] *In the evening.* For the Pasch might not be eaten till after sunset.

[2] *Not till.* This is the last time I eat the Jewish Paschal lamb [the type and shadow] with you, because now the time has come when the true Paschal lamb [the fulfilment and reality] is given for you: the old Paschal lamb will henceforth be eaten new in the kingdom of God, i. e. the Church.

[3] *Wash my feet!* What! You, the Son of God, to wash the feet of me, a poor sinner, as if you were my servant!

Jesus answered and said: "What I do thou knowest not now, but thou shalt know hereafter." Peter continued to resist, saying that his Divine Master should never wash his feet. Then Jesus said to him: "If I wash thee not, thou shalt have no part with Me."[1] Thereupon Peter humbly replied: "Lord, not only my feet, but also my hands and my head." Jesus saith to him: "He that is washed needeth not but to wash his feet, but is clean wholly. And you are clean[2], but not all."[3]

After He had washed the feet of the twelve apostles, He sat down again at the table, and told them that since He, their Lord and Master, had given them such an example, they were to imitate Him in practising humility.

COMMENTARY.

Omniscience of our Lord. He knew beforehand that Peter and John would meet a man in the city, carrying a pitcher of water, who would go straight into the house where Jesus had arranged to eat the Pasch. He also saw into the heart of Judas, and knew that he was meditating His betrayal.

The last Pasch. Jesus had a great desire to eat "this", the last typical Pasch, with His disciples. When He had eaten this Paschal lamb with them, the Old Covenant was closed, and the New Covenant of grace began; for immediately after the Paschal feast our Lord instituted the Holy Eucharist, in which the true Lamb of God is offered up, and given to the faithful to be the Food of their souls. The loving Heart of Jesus longed to institute the New Covenant of grace, to offer Himself up in the Sacrament of His Body and Blood for our salvation, and to give Himself to us for the nourishment of our souls. Therefore He said: "With desire I have desired to eat this Pasch with you."

The Real Presence. Our Lord tells His disciples beforehand what is the holy Eucharist which He will presently institute. It is the fulfilment of the Paschal lamb. Therefore the Eucharist must be His own Self, His own Body and Blood, the real Lamb of God, and must be a sacrifice.

The object of the washing of feet. Firstly, our Lord wished to cleanse His disciples perfectly from sin, and prepare their souls for the

---

[1] *No part with Me.* No part in the graces given by Jesus, and especially in the Most Holy Sacrament of the altar, which He intended to institute immediately after the washing of feet. This threat had its effect on Peter, for he could conceive nothing more terrible than to be separated from his beloved Lord.

[2] *Clean.* i. e. from sin, for by your faith and love you have obtained pardon, and now you only require to be cleansed of your small daily faults.

[3] *Not all.* Meaning Judas the traitor, who was not clean from sin.

reception of His Body and Blood, teaching us by this ceremony that we must wash our souls in the holy Sacrament of Penance before we receive Holy Communion. Secondly, our Lord desired by this washing of their feet to give to His apostles and to all Christians an example of humility and brotherly love. St. John (13, 3) says that Jesus washed the disciples' feet "knowing that the Father had given Him all things into His hands, and that He came from God and goeth to God". It was, therefore, in the full consciousness of His divine power and majesty that our Lord laid aside His upper garment, girded Himself with a towel, poured water into the basin, knelt down on the ground before each of His apostles, and washed their feet, as if He had been their servant! What self-abasement! What love! Let us remember that He gave us this example that we too might be humble and serve one another.

Virtues shown by St. Peter on this occasion. Humility. Love of our Lord. Obedience.

In commemoration of the washing of the feet, Bishops wash the feet of twelve poor men on Maundy-Thursday. This ceremony is called the *Mandatum,* i. e. the Commandment.

––––––––––

APPLICATION. You could show to others—to your parents, brothers, neighbours &c., far more love than you have hitherto shown. Consider no service or labour for them humiliating. Do it cheerfully, and in imitation of our dear Lord. Never say, when any disagreeable service is required of you: "Oh, such and such an one ought to do this"; but say: "Dear Lord, I will do it for love of Thee!"

CHAPTER LXV.

JESUS INSTITUTES THE MOST HOLY SACRAMENT.

[Mat. 26, 26—29. Mark 14, 22—26. Luke 22, 19—20.]

HAVING washed the feet of His disciples, Jesus sat down[1] again at table, and having loved His own, He loved them to the end" (St. John), i. e. to the end of all times. He desired with great desire to leave them an everlasting memorial and pledge

––––––––––

[1] *Sat down.* The sequence of the events of that evening is as follows: After sunset on Thursday, the vigil of the Pasch, which fell on Friday, our Lord ate the typical Paschal lamb with His apostles. After the Paschal feast He rose, washed the disciples' feet, and then sat down again at table and instituted the Sacrament of His love, as the Pasch of the New Testament.

of His love. He therefore took bread [1] in His holy and venerable Hands, and, raising His Eyes to heaven, He blessed the bread, broke it, and gave it to His apostles, saying: "Take ye and eat; this [2] is My Body, which is given [3] for you; do this [4] for a commemoration [5] of Me." In like manner, taking the chalice, He gave thanks, and blessed it, saying: "Drink ye all [6] of this [7]. For this is My Blood of the New Testament [8], which shall be shed for many, for the remission of sins." [9]

COMMENTARY.

The Real Presence of our Lord in the Blessed Sacrament. A year before (as you learnt in chapter XXXIV), our Lord had promised to give to His disciples His Flesh to eat and His Blood to drink; and now, at the Last Supper, He fulfilled His promise. By His almighty and efficacious words: "This is My Body; this is My Blood", Jesus changed the bread into His Body, and the wine into His Blood, and gave them to be partaken of by His apostles. The appearances, the shape, colour, taste &c., of the bread and wine remained, therefore our Lord gave His Body and Blood to be received by the apostles under the form of bread and wine. The apostles neither doubted nor questioned His words, for the promise of the Blessed Sacrament made a year before as well as the preceding promise that "He would eat the Paschal lamb new in His kingdom", had already prepared them for the mystery. As Jesus solemnly took bread, raised His Eyes to heaven &c., they said within themselves: "Now the Master is going to perform that which He promised to do, a year ago in the synagogue at Capharnaum." By

---

[1] *Bread.* The unleavened, wheaten bread, which alone could be used for the Pasch (Old Test. XXXIII). This bread was made in the form of cakes, and was broken, not cut. The Jews call it "mazzah" (sweetness).

[2] *This.* What I am now holding in my hands and handing to you.

[3] *Given.* Or sacrificed for you.   [4] *Do this.* What I have just done.

[5] *For a commemoration.* "To show forth the death of the Lord till He come" (1 Cor. 11, 26).

[6] *Drink ye all.* Our Lord says expressly, "drink ye all"; for He handed it to one only, and this one had to pass it on. All were to drink out of *one* chalice, as was customary at the Paschal feast.

[7] *Of this.* Namely what is contained in the chalice.

[8] *The New Testament.* In chapter XXXVI Old Test. we saw that Moses sealed the institution of the Old Covenant with the blood of victims; so now, at the Last Supper, our Lord Jesus Christ instituted a New Covenant and sealed it with His Precious Blood. The words: "This is My Blood of the New Testament" mean, therefore: Through this My Blood, present in the chalice, I seal and confirm My New Covenant.

[9] *For the remission of sins.* Shed for the salvation of men, who, through the merits of My Most Precious Blood, shall obtain forgiveness of their sins.

the words: "Do this in commemoration of Me", our Lord gave to the apostles and their successors, the bishops and priests of the Church, the power of changing bread and wine into His Body and Blood, and of distributing them to the faithful; so that, to this day, in the holy Mass, bishops and priests change the bread and wine into the Body and Blood of Jesus when, speaking in His name, they pronounce the words: "This is My Body; this is My Blood." The Sacrament, in which the Body and Blood of our Lord are thus present and received, is called the Most Holy Sacrament, because it is more holy than the other Sacraments; Jesus Himself, and not only His grace, being therein received.

The holy Sacrifice of the Mass. Our Lord did not give His Sacred Body and Blood, under the form of bread and wine, only to be *received* by His apostles; He offered them, first, as a *sacrifice* to His heavenly Father. That the most holy Sacrament is a Sacrifice is shown by the separation of the Blood from the Body, as also by the words of institution: "This is My Body, which is *given for you*", which is offered up for your salvation [1]. Our Lord therefore instituted the Most Holy Sacrament to be a Sacrifice, and commanded the apostles and their successors to continue to offer this unbloody Sacrifice, which we call the Holy Sacrifice of the Mass. Our Lord offered up the first Mass at the Last Supper, and in it we can distinguish the three principal parts of the Mass. First, "He took bread, gave thanks, and blessed it": that was the Offertory. Then He said: "This is My Body—This is My Blood", and by these almighty words changed the bread into His Sacred Body, and the wine into His Precious Blood: that was the Consecration. Finally, the apostles ate His Body and drank His Blood: that was the Communion.

Institution of the Priesthood. To offer sacrifice is the office of a priest, as you have already learnt in the Old Testament. When our Lord Jesus Christ, by His words: "Do this in remembrance of Me", gave to His apostles the power to change the bread and wine, and to offer up the spotless Sacrifice of the New Testament, He instituted the priesthood of the New Covenant.

Institution of the New Covenant. Moses confirmed and consecrated the Old Covenant by the blood of victims. Our Lord refers to this

---

[1] In the Greek text of St. Luke (22, 20) our Lord's words when He gave the chalice to the apostles bear the same meaning: "This is My Blood which *is* shed for you", (not "*shall be* shed for you"). The shedding of the blood for them takes place here under the appearances of bread and wine; in other words, the blood is sacrificed blood. St. Paul's account of the institution of the Blessed Sacrament conveys the same meaning. The passage (1 Cor. 11, 24) can be thus translated: "This is My Body, which is broken for you." Now, on the Cross, the Body of our Lord was not broken (see chapter LXXV), therefore the word "broken" can only be understood of His Sacred Body, present under the appearance of bread.

when He said: "This is My Blood of the New Testament." I institute a new and eternal Covenant, and in confirmation of it I give my own Blood as a sacrifice, to be drunk by you. The blood of victims with which Moses sprinkled the people of Israel could not, of itself, deliver men from sin, and make them pleasing to God, for its whole efficacy lay in its being the type of the Precious Blood of Jesus, which taketh away the sins of the world. That which Moses did, as a visible type, our Lord did in reality. By giving His Precious, Sin-cleansing Blood, He instituted the New Covenant of grace which redeemed man, and by the Sacrament and Sacrifice of His Body and Blood, He gave him a lasting memorial of His love, and an inexhaustible source of grace.

The true Paschal Lamb. Now you can understand why our Lord instituted the Blessed Sacrament immediately after the Paschal feast. The Jewish Paschal lamb was the most perfect type of the Blessed Sacrament. Our Lord first ate the typical Paschal lamb, and by so doing *closed* the Old Testament: having done so, He instituted the Blessed Sacrament, the true Paschal Feast, and with it instituted the New Testament of grace: thus at the Last Supper we see shadow and substance together, type and antitype. Jesus Christ, in the Blessed Sacrament, is our Paschal Lamb, because He first sacrifices Himself for us, and then gives Himself to us as our Food; and it is for this reason that the words: "Lamb of God, who takest away the sins of the world, have mercy on us", are said in the Mass just before the priest's Communion. The Jewish Paschal lamb was sacrificed and eaten first as a means and then as a memorial of the deliverance from the bondage in Egypt: our Paschal Lamb is sacrificed and eaten as a perpetual means and memorial of our deliverance from the slavery of sin and Satan, and in thanksgiving for the grace of Redemption.

Types which find their fulfilment in the Blessed Sacrament as the Food of our souls: 1. The Tree of Life in the garden of Paradise; 2. The Paschal lamb; 3. The manna in the wilderness; 4. The wonderful food of Elias. 5. Our Lord Himself prefigured the Blessed Sacrament by two miracles: when He changed the water into wine, and multiplied the loaves and fishes.

Types which find their fulfilment in the Holy Sacrifice of the Mass: 1. The sacrifice of Melchisedech; 2. The unbloody sacrifices of the Old Law, especially the meat-offerings.

Prophecies which have been fulfilled by the Holy Sacrifice of the Mass: 1. The prophecy spoken by the mouth of David (Ps. 109, 4): "The Lord hath sworn, and He will not repent. Thou art a priest for ever according to the order of Melchisedech." 2. The prophecy of Malachias (Mal. 1, 11): "In every place there is sacrifice; and there is offered to My name a clean oblation."

The Feast of Corpus Christi. The Blessed Sacrament being the Church's most precious treasure, and the centre of all her worship of

God, it is fitting that she should every year solemnly commemorate the institution of this most holy mystery. Now, since we cannot keep Maundy-Thursday as a feast of joy, because it is a day of fasting, and devoted to the memory of our Lord's sufferings, the Church has selected another Thursday, the Thursday after the Feast of the Most Holy Trinity, to be observed as a solemn Feast of thanksgiving for the institution of the Blessed Sacrament. This glorious Feast is called the Feast of Corpus Christi, or of the Body of our Lord Jesus Christ.

The love of Jesus as shown in the Most Holy Sacrament. Jesus, having loved His own unto the end, bequeathed Himself to them in this Sacrament of His love, as the most priceless of memorials, to dwell always with them, to be sacrificed for them, and to be united to them in the most intimate way by Holy Communion. As a solemn testament He gave to us His Body and Blood, His Humanity and Divinity, in short *Himself*, with all His graces and merits; thus the Holy Eucharist is the abiding memorial of our Lord's infinite and inconceivable love. The circumstances under which our Lord Jesus instituted the Blessed Sacrament reveal His unbounded love. He instituted It "the same night in which He was betrayed" (1 Cor. 11, 23), and therefore at the very time when the hatred of His enemies was at its highest pitch, and when they were actually making their preparations to put Him to death. He instituted It, though He knew that there was a vile traitor among His chosen followers, and that many, many Christians would despise and dishonour Him in this Sacrament. Neither the deadly hatred of His enemies, nor the ingratitude of the faithful, could deter Him from giving them this final and enduring proof of His love. Oh, how mighty, how deep is the love which our Lord and Saviour has for ungrateful man! The Sanhedrim had met to resolve upon the death of Jesus: the soldiers were all ready to seize Him: His traitor apostle was about to betray Him. Surely all this will abate His love even at the last moment! Yes, if His love be human, it will; but His love was the love of God, and it was not quenched. He responded to the hatred and treachery of men by the institution of the Most Holy Sacrament, thus giving to the human race a proof of love so intense, that it never could have entered into the hearts of men to conceive it. And—as St. Paul says—this wonderful love was shown by our Lord on the night when He was betrayed. At the very moment that faithless men were betraying their God, He invented a new means of proving His love for them. While they were preparing for Him a most cruel death, He gave to them the means of attaining eternal life. Just when human hatred was doing all it could to remove Him from the world, He discovered a new way of remaining always in the world. He wrought the most astounding miracle of Omnipotence, that He might remain with them. Even as He went forth from the Father without leaving Him, so did He go forth from the world without leaving it. And this He did "on the night when He was betrayed", just as if nothing had occurred to quench His love, but rather as if man had done everything he could to kindle it! Then, having done this for us, He went forth to give Himself up into the hands of His enemies—to die for them!

In the Holy Mass a little water is mixed with the wine. This is done, because the wine changed by our Lord at the Last Supper was mixed with water, this mixture being strictly prescribed for the wine used at the Paschal feast. The mixture of water with the wine at Mass has also a symbolical meaning, and is intended to remind us that in Jesus Christ there are two natures in One Divine Person.

APPLICATION. In the Most Holy Sacrament of the altar our Lord and Saviour is present under the appearances of bread and wine. You ought therefore to worship Jesus in the Blessed Sacrament with living faith and the deepest adoration. Have you done so? Have you always genuflected, as you ought, on entering a church? Do you always kneel down during the Elevation? Have you, finally, a devotion to Jesus in the Blessed Sacrament? Never forget when you are in church that you are in the presence of your Divine Saviour, who will one day come back to this earth in great power and majesty to be your Judge! Be very reverent and devout in the House of God, and repeat these words as often as you can: "Blessed and praised be Jesus in the Most Holy Sacrament of the altar!"

CHAPTER LXVI.

JESUS FORETELLS THE TREASON OF JUDAS.

[Mat. 16, 21—25. Mark 14, 18—21. Luke 22, 21—23. John 13, 21—30.]

WHILST they were eating, He told the apostles: "Amen, I say to you, that one of you[1] who eateth with Me shall betray Me."[2] They, being much troubled, asked Him with one

---

[1] *One of you.* He was, Scripture says, "troubled in spirit", thinking of the base ingratitude with which Judas would repay His love, and of the traitor's eternal doom. He, therefore, full of love, tried to save the wretched disciple by warning and threatening him, without mentioning his name.

[2] *Betray Me.* Satan had put it into the heart of Judas to betray his Master. Before the Pasch he had gone to the chief priests who, ever since the raising of Lazarus, had resolved to kill Jesus, and offered to betray Him into their hands. Our Lord's triumphal entry into Jerusalem and the woes which He pronounced on the Pharisees had confirmed them in this resolution, and all they waited for was an opportunity to secretly seize and condemn Him. They did not dare to use open force, for they feared that the people would rise and defend Jesus. The longed-for opportunity was given to them by Judas. "What will you give me",

voice: "Is it I, Lord?" He answered and said: "One of the twelve[1], who dippeth[2] his hand with Me in the dish." Then He added: "The Son of Man goeth, indeed, as it is written of Him[3], but woe to that man by whom the Son of Man shall be betrayed. It were better[4] for that man if he had not been born!"

Then Judas, who betrayed Him, said: "Is it I[5], Rabbi?" But Jesus replied[6]: "Thou hast said it."[7] Then Judas rose from the table and went out[8], and, going immediately to the High Priest, sold His Master for thirty pieces of silver, and promised to betray Him into the hands of the High Priest's servants. When he was gone Jesus said to His disciples: "Now is the Son of Man glorified, and God is glorified in Him."

---

said he, "and I will deliver Him to you"—for if I help you, you can do the deed quite secretly. They promised to give him thirty pieces of silver. This sum was the price or compensation-money given, according to the Old Law (Ex. 21, 32), for a slave who had been killed, and probably the chief priests fixed on this sum to show their contempt for Jesus, whom they professed to esteem of no greater value than a slave. And for this paltry sum Judas consented to betray his Master!

[1] *One of the twelve.* It grieved them to think that anyone of their number could act so wickedly and ungratefully towards their beloved Master: in fact they could not conceive such wickedness possible. Then Jesus indicated the traitor more directly, saying: "One of the twelve &c."

[2] *Who dippeth.* On the table at the pasch there stood dishes containing a mess of cooked fruit, such as dates, figs &c. In this mess each person dipped his bread before eating it. Among those who were dipping their bread into the same dish with Jesus, was Judas; but as several of the other apostles were also dipping into the same dish, our Lord did not make it plain that He meant Judas. To obtain certainty in the matter, St. Peter beckoned to St. John, who was next to Jesus, and whom our Lord especially loved on account of his virginal purity, bidding him ask who it was of whom our Lord spoke. John, "leaning on the breast of Jesus", saith to Him: "Lord, who is it?" Jesus answered: "He it is to whom I shall give bread dipped." And when He had dipped the bread He gave it to Judas. And after the morsel Satan entered into Judas.

[3] *Written of Him.* In the prophecies relating to His sufferings and death (Old Test. LV and LXXII).

[4] *It were better.* Rather than suffer the everlasting punishment which will be his on account of his wickedness.

[5] *Is it I.* He saw that he was unmasked, but instead of repenting and giving up his evil project, he became more wicked and more obstinate, and fell completely under the dominion of Satan.

[6] *Replied.* In a low tone so that the other apostles could not hear what He said.

[7] *Thou hast said it.* i. e. "it is thou", and He added: "That which thou dost, do quickly", i. e. if you still persist in doing this wicked deed, do not put it off.

[8] *Went out.* "And it was night", says St. John (13, 30)—night, dark night in the street outside, dark night in the soul of Judas, from which the grace of God had departed.

COMMENTARY.

The devil, and the avarice of Judas. Satan hated Jesus, the Most Holy One, and had been trying to outwit God ever since the creation of man. The covetousness of Judas gave him the apparent means of attaining his end. The bad apostle, by resisting grace and indulging his ruling passion, gave the devil an increasing influence over him; till at last, blinded by avarice, and disappointed in his hopes of an earthly Messias, he listened to the suggestions of the spirit of evil, and decided to sell his Lord and Master for a paltry sum. Covetousness is a capital sin. "There is", says the Son of Sirach, "no more wicked thing than to love money, for such an one setteth even his own soul to sale" (Ecclus. 10, 10). Judas set even his God and Saviour to sale! See how sin grows! Our Blessed Lord, who knew the wicked purpose of Judas' heart, tried to win him back from the road to hell. He washed the feet of him, the most unworthy of men; but in spite of his Master's love and humility, the heart of Judas remained untouched, and he persisted in his fiendish purpose of delivering up his Lord into the hands of His bitterest enemies! Oh, what wickedness and hardness of heart!

Jesus suffered death of His Own Will. "The Son of Man, indeed, goeth, as it is written of Him."

God can bring good out of evil. Although our Lord died of His own will, still Judas was guilty of His Death, and on that account Jesus pronounced "woe" on him. But even as once God turned the crime of Joseph's brethren to good account, so did He suffer the wickedness of Judas and of the unbelieving Jews to enter into the plan of Redemption, and allow their sin to be the cause of that Death which brought salvation to the world.

Unworthy Communion. Judas received the Body and Blood of our Lord as well as the other apostles, for according to the Gospel of St. Luke he did not go out till after the institution of the Holy Eucharist. He made an unworthy Communion, for he had, in his heart, already agreed to betray his Master, and neither the humility with which Jesus had washed his feet, nor the love which made Him give His own self to be the Food of the disciples, had served to turn him from his vile purpose. After his unworthy Communion his heart became hardened. The love of Jesus did not move him; the threat of everlasting punishment did not deter him; our Lord's solemn words of warning made no impression on him; he remained obstinate, and gave himself over to the dominion of Satan, who drove him to commit a crime so terrible that a man could not have committed it unaided. See the consequences of an unworthy Communion! To this day, alas, unworthy Communions lead very many to blindness and hardness of heart!

APPLICATION. You can see by the case of Judas how low a man can fall who despises warnings and resists the inspirations of grace. By degrees he becomes so hardened and indifferent, that he is capable of any sin. Examine yourself! Do you take good advice to heart, and act on it? or do you prefer listening to the suggestions of bad companions rather than to the inspirations of the Holy Ghost, and the advice of those set over you? Do not harden your heart and follow the example of Judas!

CHAPTER LXVII.

JESUS FORETELLS THE DENIAL OF PETER AND THE FLIGHT OF THE APOSTLES.

[John 13, 33—38. Luke 22, 31—34. Mat. 26, 31—35.]

HAVING given His apostles this great proof of His love— His own Body and Blood, Jesus vouchsafed to give them also a new commandment of love. "Little children"[1], said He, "yet a little while I am with you. I give you a new commandment, that you love one another, as I have loved you. By this shall all men know that you are My disciples, if you have love one for another."

Simon Peter said to Him: "Lord, whither goest Thou?" Jesus answered: "Whither I go, thou canst not follow Me now, but thou shalt follow Me afterwards." Peter said to Him: "Why cannot I follow Thee now? I will lay down my life[2] for Thee." Jesus answered Him: "Wilt thou lay down thy life for Me? Amen, amen, I say unto thee, the cock shall not crow twice before thou deny Me thrice!"

Then the Lord addressed Peter: "Simon, Simon[3], behold, Satan hath desired to sift you as wheat[4]. But I have prayed for

---

[1] *"Little children"*. As soon as our Lord was relieved of the presence of the traitor who had given himself over to Satan, He poured forth His loving and fatherly heart to His other apostles, whom He called His "little children", and spoke to them the striking farewell words which are contained in the chapters of St. John.

[2] *I will lay down my life.* And "although all shall be scandalized in Thee, yet not I!" It was love which prompted St. Peter to speak thus, but he spoke too self-confidently.

[3] *Simon, Simon.* In order to warn the apostle who, in his self-confidence, forgot his human weakness, our Lord emphasised His warning, by the repetition of the apostle's name.

[4] *As wheat.* Wheat is sifted by being shaken and tossed about, and in this way the good grain is separated from the empty husk. In the same way, by

thee [1] that thy faith fail not; and thou, being once converted, confirm thy brethren. All of you shall be scandalized [2] in Me this night. For it is written: 'I will strike [3] the shepherd, and the sheep of the flock shall be dispersed.'" [4]

COMMENTARY.

The Omniscience of Jesus. Our Lord exactly foretold both that Judas would betray Him, and that, in the same night before the second cockcrow, St. Peter would deny Him three times, and that all the apostles would desert Him. Only the omniscient God can know beforehand what man, gifted with free-will, will do. St. Peter himself thought it quite impossible that he could deny his beloved Master, and yet our Lord foretold in detail all that would occur. This proves that our Blessed Lord was omniscient, or, in other words, that He is God.

St. Peter's self-confidence. We have repeatedly had occasion to admire St. Peter's faith, and love of our Lord. Even in the story we have just read, the chief of the apostles evinced great love and great faith, declaring that he would never take scandal at anything that Jesus did, and was ready to lay down his life for His sake. Peter seriously and honestly meant what he said, but he trusted too much in himself, overrated his own strength and, forgetting the weakness of his human nature, believed himself capable of remaining faithful to his Master under all circumstances, simply because he wished to do so. His will was good, but he was wanting in that humility which comes from a knowledge of one's own frailty. He ought to have thought and said: "With Thy help I will never fail"; but, instead of this, he put himself on a different level from the other apostles, and implied that, although they might very easily go astray, he never could! This high opinion of himself, and his undue self-confidence led him to the fall which will be related in chapter LXXII. We should never forget that, without the assistance of God's grace, we can neither keep the commandments nor persevere in well-doing.

The Pope is the Supreme and Infallible Teacher of Faith. Our Lord foretold to St. Peter that he would deny Him, but at the same time

---

temptation and pressure, Satan would upset the apostles, in the hope of shaking their faith, and leading them to deny our Lord.

[1] *I have prayed for thee.* This prayer of our Lord was efficacious. He knew that Peter, though he might fall through weakness, would not lose his faith, but would rise up again after his fall, with faith as strong as ever. He knew this beforehand; for He said: "and thou, being once converted, confirm thy brethren."

[2] *Scandalized.* You will be offended, and staggered by what you will see to-night.

[3] *I will strike.* i. e. suffer Him to be put to a violent death. Almighty God knew beforehand that this would happen, and foretold it by the mouth of the prophet Zacharias.

[4] *Dispersed.* Those who are His followers will flee hither and thither helplessly.

He gave him the assurance that his faith would not fail, and entrusted him with the office of confirming his brethren in faith. As a matter of fact Peter's faith never did waver, for he did not cease to believe, even when he lacked the courage to confess his faith. Our Blessed Lord destined him to be the foundation of His Church, and on that account prayed that his faith might ever be firm and untarnished, so that he might act as a prop to the faith of his brethren. By so doing our Lord Jesus Christ appointed St. Peter to be the supreme teacher of His Church, his office being to maintain and confirm all members of His Church in the true faith; and He gave to him moreover the special grace that his faith should never fail; in other words, that he should be infallible in the exercise of this office. How could Peter confirm his brethren in the true faith, unless he himself were preserved from error in matters of faith? His infallibility in the exercise of his office has, together with the office itself, descended from Peter to his successors, the Supreme Pontiffs of the Catholic Church. An infallible teacher who can maintain his brethren, his fellow-Christians, in the true faith, is as necessary to the Church now as it was in the days of St. Peter. The Roman See has always proved itself to be the guardian and protector of the true faith, by giving, in virtue of the divine office committed to it, unerring decisions in matters of dispute, and rejecting all false doctrines.

APPLICATION. What happened to St. Peter ought to make you guard very carefully against over-confidence in yourself, and make you pray fervently: "Lead us not into temptation!"

CHAPTER LXVIII.

THE LAST DISCOURSE AND PONTIFICAL PRAYER OF OUR LORD.

[John 14—17.]

JESUS, seeing that they were sad at what He said[1], consoled them, saying: "In My Father's house[2] there are many mansions[3]; I go to prepare a place for you[4]. I will come again[5] and will take you[6] to Myself, that where I am you also may be. And where I go you know, and the way you know." But Thomas

---

[1] *Said.* "The Son of Man, indeed, goeth &c."
[2] *My Father's house.* i. e. in heaven.
[3] *Many mansions.* So that there is room for all.
[4] *A place for you.* So that you may really find admission there.
[5] *Come again.* At the end of the world.
[6] *Take you.* With your souls and bodies.

said to Him: "Lord, we know not whither Thou goest, and how can we know the way?"

Jesus replied: "I am the Way, the Truth, and the Life [1]; no man cometh to the Father but by Me [2]. And I will ask the Father, and He shall give you another Paraclete [3], that He may abide with you for ever—the Spirit of Truth, the Comforter, the Holy Ghost, whom the Father will send in My name—He will teach you all things [4], and bring all things to your mind whatsoever I shall have said to you.

"Peace I leave with you, My peace I give to you; not as the world giveth, do I give to you. But I will not now speak many things with you. For the prince of this world [5] cometh, and in Me he hath not anything. But that the world may know that I love the Father, and as the Father hath given Me commandment, so do I. Arise, let us go hence.

"I am the true vine, and my Father is the husbandman. As the branch cannot bear fruit of itself unless it abide in the vine, so neither can you [6], unless you abide in Me. I am the vine; you are the branches: he that abideth in Me, and I in Him, the same beareth much fruit: for without Me you can do nothing [7]. If any-

---

[1] *The Life.* Jesus is the Way, for by His commandments and example He has shown us the way to heaven. He is the Truth, for He has taught us the one true and saving faith. He is the Life, for He has won for us eternal life, and that grace which is the supernatural life of the soul.

[2] *By Me.* He only can be saved who believes in Jesus Christ and His doctrine, follows His example, and dies in His grace.

[3] *Another Paraclete.* Knowing that His apostles were sad at the thought of His leaving them, our Lord promised that they and their successors should have, in His stead, another Comforter, even the Spirit of Truth, who would never leave them, but remain with them for ever. "The Father will send Him in My name", i. e. on account of My merits.

[4] *Teach you all things.* He will not teach anything new, but, by His interior inspirations, He will interpret to you and the faithful all that I have taught you.

[5] *The prince of this world.* i. e. Satan, who by the hands of his tools, Judas and the wicked Jews, will deliver Me up to be put to death. Our Lord calls the devil the prince of this world, because the children of this world, or, in other words, sinners, serve him and follow his leadership. Jesus knew that His enemies were making ready to seize Him, and went of His own will to meet them.

[6] *Neither can you.* Bring forth fruit, i. e. do any meritorious works, unless you are united to Me by sanctifying grace. By these words our Lord, in a sort of parable, conveys the doctrine that we stand in the same connexion with Him as the branches of a vine with the vine itself.

[7] *Do nothing.* Our Lord now spoke plainly, not using any figure: "without My grace you can do no good thing".

one abide not in Me, he shall be cast forth as a branch, and shall wither[1], and they shall gather him up[2], and cast him into the fire[3], and he burneth."

"This is My commandment[4], that you love one another, as I have loved you. Greater love than this no man hath, that a man lay down his life for his friends."

"In the world you shall have distress: but have confidence, I have overcome the world. Amen, amen, I say to you: if you ask the Father anything in My name, He will give it to you. Ask, and you shall receive."

Then, lifting up[5] His eyes to heaven, Jesus said: "Father, the hour[6] is come, glorify[7] Thy Son, that Thy Son may glorify Thee[8]. As Thou hast given Him power over all flesh, that He may give eternal life to all whom Thou hast given Him[9]. Now this is[10] eternal life: that they may know Thee, the Only True God, and Jesus Christ whom Thou hast sent. I have glorified Thee on the earth[11]: I have finished[12] the work which Thou gavest Me to do. And now glorify Thou Me, O Father, with Thyself,

---

[1] *Wither.* He shall be cut off from the communion of the Saints and of the faithful. He will die spiritually, and become a useless member of the Church of God.

[2] *Gather him up.* These withered branches, these dead members of the Church.

[3] *Into the fire.* Into hell, where he burns for ever without being consumed.

[4] *My commandment.* A new commandment hitherto unknown to you, which I, as your Redeemer, now give to you. The next sentence shows with what measure of love He loved His own.

[5] *Lifting up.* Our Lord offered up this prayer as our High Priest. As High Priest of the New Covenant, He had just instituted the unbloody Sacrifice of the Mass, and was about to offer Himself for the salvation of the world in a bloody manner on the Cross: and now, before consummating His Sacrifice, He offered up this prayer; first that He Himself might be glorified; next, for His apostles; and finally for all the faithful, and His whole Church.

[6] *The hour.* For my Passion and Death.

[7] *Glorify.* That I may rise from the grave, ascend into heaven, and send the Holy Ghost to the Church.

[8] *Thee.* That through my Church millions of men may learn to know Thee and love Thee.

[9] *Given Him.* To all who through Thy grace believe in Him and become His disciples.

[10] *This is.* This is what leads to eternal life.

[11] *On the earth.* By My obedience and My teaching.

[12] *Finished.* For the work of Redemption was already accomplished in *will*, by our Blessed Lord's determination to suffer death willingly.

with the glory which I had[1], before the world was, with Thee. I have manifested Thy Name to the men[2] whom Thou hast given Me out of the world. I pray for them. Holy Father, keep them in Thy Name[3]: that they may be one[4], as we[5] also are. I pray that Thou shouldst keep them from evil. Sanctify[6] them in truth.

Fig. 84. Mount of Olives, Jerusalem. (Phot. Bruno Hentschel, Leipzig.)

And not for them only do I pray, but for them also[7] who through their word shall believe in Me: that they may be one in us, that the world may believe[8] that Thou hast sent Me[9]. Father, I will

---

[1] *Which I had.* i. e. give Me as Man the full glory of the Son of God; in other words, glorify Me by My resurrection, ascension and sitting at Thy right hand in heaven.

[2] *To the men.* Those whom Thou hast chosen by Thy grace to be My disciples.

[3] *In Thy Name.* In holy faith in Thee.

[4] *One.* One in faith and love.

[5] *As we.* Are one in nature.

[6] *Sanctify.* Make them holy by Thy truth.

[7] *Them also.* Those, therefore, who would, in all ages, believe in our Lord, i. e. the whole Church.

[8] *May believe.* By reason of their wonderful unity.

[9] *Sent Me.* And that My work, the Church, comes from Thee.

that, where I am, they also whom Thou hast given Me may be with Me[1], that they may see My glory."

And having said the Hymn[2], they went forth to the Mount of Olives (Fig. 84, p. 645).

COMMENTARY.

Our Lord's Divinity. In His prayer: "Father, glorify Thy Son &c.", Jesus calls God His Father, and Himself the Son of the Divine Father. He also speaks of His glory which He had with the Father before the world began, thus teaching most clearly that, before His Incarnation, He was from all eternity with the Father. For our Lord to speak in this way He must be the only-begotten and co-equal Son of God.

Jesus Christ our Mediator. The chapter we have just read shows us that our Lord gave His life for love of us; that it is only through Him that we can come to the Father; that He prepares a place for us in the House of His Father; that He gives everlasting life to His followers; that the Holy Ghost is sent in His name; and that whoever prays in His name will be heard. It follows from all these passages that Jesus Christ is our Mediator with the Father; that through Him we are reconciled to God; and that it is only through Him that we can obtain grace and glory.

The Holy Ghost is the Third Person of the Blessed Trinity. Our Lord calls Him "another Paraclete", who would, in His own stead, enlighten, sanctify, strengthen and comfort the apostles and those who came after them, till the end of all things. This shows us that the Holy Ghost must be a Divine Person, distinct from the Father and from the Son. We have just read our Lord's words: "The Father will send Him in My Name"; and in another passage He speaks of "the Paraclete, the Spirit of Truth, whom I will send you from the Father". The Holy Ghost is, therefore, the Spirit of the Father and the Son, who proceeds from all eternity from the Father and the Son, and who in time was sent by the Father and the Son.

The Infallibility of the Church. Our Lord knew well that the apostles did not fully understand what He taught them, and He knew moreover that, owing to the weakness of human nature, much that He had taught them would, in the course of time, be forgotten, without the aid of a higher and supernatural assistance. He therefore promised to send the Holy Ghost, the Spirit of Truth, to abide with

---

[1] *With Me.* In the glory of heaven.

[2] *The Hymn.* This hymn consisted of the six Psalms of praise (112—117), the first two of which were sung before, and the others after the paschal feast. The head of the family, and therefore, in this case, our Lord, said or sang each verse, and the rest responded: "Alleluia". (Hence this is called the great Hallel.)

the apostles, to teach them all things, and to bring to their remembrance all that He had said to them. This Spirit of Truth was to abide with them "for ever"; but as the apostles were not to live for ever on this earth, the promise was not meant to apply only to them individually, but to their successors, the Popes and Bishops of the Church. The Spirit of Truth which, according to the promise, abides for ever in the Church, preserves intact in her the Truth taught by Jesus Christ, keeps her from error, and therefore renders the Church infallible.

The wonderful Unity of the Church. For nothing did our Lord, before His death, pray more earnestly than that all who believe in Him might be *one;* and this unity for which He prayed was to be an outward unity such as could be recognised by the whole world. Our Lord willed to found a united Church; so that only a Church which is inwardly and outwardly, invisibly and visibly *one,* can be the true Church founded by Jesus Christ. There is but one Church which has all these marks! It is indeed a marvellous thing how the Catholic Church can be universal and at the same time one; for the enduring unity under one head of the faithful, of all ages, climes, and languages, could never have been brought about by natural means. The unity of the universal Church proves her to be the creation of God, and proves that He who founded her, our Lord Jesus Christ, is indeed the Son of God.

The Necessity of Faith. "No man cometh to the Father but by Me", said our Lord. It follows from this that no one who does not believe in Him can come to the Father, or attain to life everlasting. "This is eternal life", Jesus went on to say, "that they may know Thee the only true God, and Jesus Christ whom Thou hast sent."

The Necessity of Grace. Only that vine-branch which is united to the vine, and which is nourished by sap from it, can bear fruit. In like manner we must be united to our Lord Jesus Christ by sanctifying grace, if we wish to bring forth good and meritorious works; for only sanctifying grace can give to our actions a higher and supernatural value. He who is not in a state of grace can, indeed, perform good actions, such, for instance, as almsgiving, but his good actions have not the full supernatural value, and cannot merit heaven; and he who dies out of the grace of God, that is, who is not united to our Lord by sanctifying grace, will be lost, and must be punished for ever in hell. For doing good works and winning heaven, the state of sanctifying grace is, therefore, an elementary necessity; but beyond this habitual state we need the help of God's grace for the performance of every thing that we do; for, says our Lord "without Me (i. e. without My help and grace) you can do nothing (to merit heaven)". This grace is called *actual* and *assisting* grace.

The commandment to love our neighbour was given in the Old Law, but the Jews limited its practice to those of their own nation and religion; their brotherly love was, therefore, by no means universal. But our Lord has commanded us to love all men, giving His own love for us as a model for our imitation. He showed love in the most perfect form, by laying down His life for all men, just and unjust, friends and enemies; and by His death He has won for us grace to overcome self-love and to practise a supernatural love of our neighbour.

Heaven. There is a heaven, and our Lord in the most distinct terms promises the possession of it to those who love Him. He promises that where He is, in the glory of heaven, there shall His own be also. "What the Almighty Son asked of the Almighty Father *as His will* ('I will') cannot be unfulfilled; for the will of the Father and of the Son is one" (St. Augustine). The happiness of heaven will consist principally in this, that we shall gaze for ever on the glory of our God and Saviour.

Hell. He who does not "abide in Jesus", that is, he who is not united to Him by sanctifying grace, but is separated from Him by mortal sin, shall be cast into the fire like a withered vine-branch. Our Blessed Lord does not say that the dead branch, cast into the fire, "is burnt", but "burneth", i. e. burns for ever without being consumed.

Prayer in the Name of Jesus. Our Lord solemnly asseverates ("Amen, amen, I say unto you") that we shall be heard if we pray in His name. We pray in the name of Jesus when we pray with full confidence in His merits, and in the mind and spirit of Jesus. This promise of our Lord ought to impel us to pray to Almighty God with great confidence.

APPLICATION. Are you a living branch of the vine? Are you in a state of grace? If you are in a state of mortal sin and have thus forfeited sanctifying grace, and if you die in that state, you must go to hell. If you are so unhappy as to commit a mortal sin, remain not in a state of sin, but do penance, and confess your sin as soon as ever you can, so that you may become once more a child of God, and a living branch of the vine.

As we can do nothing without the assistance of God's grace, we require many graces every day of our lives. Now, since we can obtain grace only by prayer, you see how necessary prayer is. Pray, therefore, devoutly every day that you may obtain grace and be saved. You must be especially careful about your morning and night prayers.

CHAPTER LXIX.

THE AGONY OF JESUS IN THE GARDEN.

[Luke 22, 39—46.]

WHEN Jesus had said these things, He went forth with His disciples over the brook Cedron[1] to a place called Gethsemani, on the Mount of Olives, where there was a garden[2], into

Fig. 85. Garden of Gethsemani, Jerusalem. (Phot. Bonfils.)

which He entered (Fig. 85). Then He said to His disciples: "Sit you here[3] while I go yonder and pray." And taking with Him

---

[1] *Cedron.* The ravine to the east of Jerusalem, through which this brook runs, separates the city from the Mount of Olives. Jesus crossed the brook by a bridge to reach the Mount of Olives. David crossing the brook and going up the Mount, weeping (Old Test. LVI), was a type of what our Lord did on this night of His agony.

[2] *A garden.* This formed part of an estate or farm, called Gethsemani.

[3] *Sit you here.* At the entrance of the garden. The eight apostles were not allowed to see our Blessed Lord in the hour of His abasement, lest they should be scandalized.

Peter, James and John [1], He advanced into the garden. He began to be sorrowful and said to them: "My soul is sorrowful even unto death [2]; stay ye here and watch with Me!"

Fig. 86. Grotto of the Agony, Jerusalem. (Phot. Bonfils.)

Then going a little further (Fig. 86), He fell upon His Face, saying: "My Father, if it be possible, let this chalice [3] pass from. Me. Nevertheless, not as I will, but as Thou wilt."

---

[1] *Peter, James and John.* These three were permitted to witness the abasement of Jesus, as they had beheld His glory in the Transfiguration (chapter XXXVII), and had heard the Father's testimony to His Godhead: "This is My beloved Son!"

[2] *Unto death.* "I am brought nigh unto death by the anguish of my soul." In this hour of need our Blessed Lord was deprived of all divine consolation, and bade His three disciples to stay near Him, and watch and pray with Him. He was so entirely destitute of all interior consolation, that He even sought for exterior consolation from His own creatures, and wished to have them near Him. We all know the comfort of having loving friends near us when we are in sorrow and fear.

[3] *This chalice.* "Spare Me the bitter Passion and Death which await Me!" The figure of a cup full of bitter gall, revolting as it is to the nature of man to drink, is used to describe the awful anguish of Body and Soul which Jesus suffered until the moment when He bowed His Head and gave up the ghost. In His prayer He called it *this* chalice, because He saw before Him most clearly every

And rising up, He came to His disciples, and finding them asleep[1], He said to Peter[2]: "Could you not watch one hour with Me? Watch ye and pray, that ye enter not into temptation[3]. The spirit[4], indeed, is willing, but the flesh is weak."

And going a second time, He prayed, saying: "My Father, if this chalice cannot pass away, except I drink it, Thy will be done!" He came back and found His disciples sleeping; and leaving them, He went away again, and prayed a third time in the same words as before. Then He fell into an agony, and His sweat[5] became as drops of blood, trickling down to the ground. And, behold, an angel[6] appeared to Him from heaven, strengthening Him[7].

---

terrible detail of His Passion and Death. He knew the decree of the Eternal Father, that the world was to be redeemed by His Sufferings and Death, and He was, therefore, ready to suffer and die for us, and drink the bitter cup; but the vision of the greatness of His Sufferings and the terrible manner of His Death filled His human nature with fear, and He shrank from "this" chalice, so brimful of bitterness, and prayed to be spared the drinking of it. At the same time, He committed everything to His Father, and full of submission to His will added: "not as I will, but as Thou wilt—I am ready to endure this fearful torment if it really be Thy will."

[1] *Asleep.* While Jesus prayed they had fallen asleep from sorrow and exhaustion. His prayer had lasted a long time, for only the general purport of it is given us in the Gospel. His disciples slept, and left their Master all alone, to pray and wrestle with His deadly anguish; none but His enemies watched, and made their preparations for His destruction. This sleep of the apostles at that solemn and all-important moment was full of danger to them; so our Blessed Lord awakened them and solemnly warned them to prepare for the temptations which were about to assail them.

[2] *Peter.* Jesus addressed Himself to Peter, firstly, because he was the chief of the apostles, and ought to have set an example to the others of watchfulness and fervour; secondly, because Peter considered himself to be stronger than the others, and had said: "Though all be scandalized in Thee, yet not I!"

[3] *Temptation.* Into the temptation of failing in faith, and denying Me. If you will not watch and pray for love of Me, at least do so for love of yourself.

[4] *The spirit.* Your will, indeed, is good, but do not forget that you are frail, fleshly minded men. Strengthen yourselves, therefore, by prayer and watchfulness.

[5] *His sweat.* His terrible anguish and fear of death impressed themselves on His tender Body, and forced from its pores not only sweat but blood, and so abundantly that the sweat, mingled with and reddened by the Precious Blood, fell down in drops upon the ground. St. Bernard says that our Lord wept blood, and shed tears not only from His Eyes, but from His whole Body.

[6] *An angel.* Sent by the Eternal Father, to whom our Lord had so fervently prayed.

[7] *Strengthening Him.* We may suppose that the very appearance and presence of the Angel, besides his words of encouragement, gave strength to Christ in this hour of desolation. (E. E.)

Then, going a third time to His apostles, He found them still asleep. He said to them: "Sleep now, and take your rest. Behold, the hour is at hand, and the Son of Man shall be betrayed into the hands of sinners [1]. Rise, let us go [2]. Behold, he is at hand that will betray Me!"

COMMENTARY.

Our Blessed Lord suffered in His human nature. Contemplate Jesus in the garden of Gethsemani, lying on His face under the olive-trees, in the darkness of night, sighing, praying and sweating blood! Behold Him who fills earth with gladness, and heaven with wonder, in deepest anguish. He who but a short time before was consoling His apostles is now Himself full of sorrow. He who promised help to them is now weak Himself, and asks them to help Him. He who has dried the eyes of so many now sheds tears of Blood. The mighty Wonder-worker is prostrate and trembling, and His Heart is well-nigh breaking for very woe. The Soul of Him who commanded the winds and the waves is now overwhelmed with trouble and anguish. How is this extraordinary change to be explained? In order to understand our Lord's Agony in the garden, and His Sufferings which followed it, you must remember that the divine nature of our Lord Jesus Christ could not suffer, and that it was only His human nature which could suffer and die; and, moreover, that His human nature, being inseparably united to His divine nature, could only suffer as much, and for as long, as He willed it to suffer. He entered on His Passion of His own will, and did not allow torment and fear to take possession of His Heart till He had left His eight apostles at a distance, and had near Him only those three who had been prepared for the sight of Him in His hour of abasement, by the vision of His glory on Mount Thabor. But in order that the human nature might suffer, the Divinity abandoned it to itself and, as it were, withdrew from it, and deprived it of all inward consolation, as we see in the narrative. To such an extent did He abase Himself that He even sought consolation from creatures, the apostles and angels. At the very beginning of His Passion He wished to leave us no room for doubt that He as Man felt and suffered everything acutely, and that fear, pain and horror caused Him as

---

[1] *Of sinners.* First into the hands of the High Priest's servants; then into the power of the Sanhedrim, and, lastly, into that of the heathen governor and his soldiers.

[2] *Let us go.* Our Blessed Lord spoke thus resolutely, for He felt impelled to complete His work, and went forth to meet death, both voluntarily and courageously. The victory was won! The result of His wrestling, and the answer to His prayer was this, that once more the most ardent desire of His Sacred Heart was to suffer and die for the glory of His heavenly Father, and the salvation of mankind.

much anguish as they could cause an ordinary man. He therefore testified to His heavenly Father that His human nature abhorred its fearful torments, and wished to be freed from them; the thrice repeated prayer: "Take this chalice from Me!" shows this to us.

The *causes* of our Lord's profound sadness and terrible agony of mind were as follows:

1. He saw before Him the many and inhuman torments which awaited Him. He pictured all these terrible sufferings, enduring them in anticipation. How would you feel at this moment if you were told that you were to be slowly tortured to death to-morrow? Human nature shrinks from death, and especially from a violent death. The most painful as well as the most ignominious of deaths awaited our Lord, the prospect of which filled His Soul with horror, for He was truly man, like to us in all things, sin only excepted. As Man, He prayed to His Father: "Let this chalice pass"; but there being no sinful rebelliousness in His human will, it remained in full submission to the divine will, and He added: "Nevertheless, not as I will, but as Thou wilt".

2. Our Blessed Lord took the sins of men on Himself, so as to offer satisfaction to the divine justice in their stead. Now that He was on the point of completing His work of Redemption, the horrible mass of evil, abomination and guilt came before His holy Soul and filled it with abhorrence and aversion. "Him, that knew no sin, for us God hath made sin, that we might be made the justice of God in Him" (2 Cor. 5, 21). What a horror it must have been to the Most Holy, the Most Pure One, to feel Himself laden with the sins of the whole world, the sins of pride, lust, avarice &c.! If sorrow for the shameful ingratitude of sin could make Magdalen and Peter weep bitter tears, what a detestation of sin must He have felt who alone knew its malice to the full! "Jesus saw all our individual sins, and grieved over them as if He Himself had committed them, for He had taken on Himself the burden of them all. Truly, the grief of this alone would have killed Him, if He had not held back His soul, in order that He might endure still more, and drink the chalice of suffering to the very dregs. He would not die on the Mount of Olives, because His life was to be sacrificed on Calvary; but He shed His Blood, the bloody sweat of His agony, in order to show us that sin alone, without the help of any executioner, was sufficient to strike His death-blow" (Bossuet). Many indeed are the tears which have been caused, since the Fall of our first parents, by sin and the consequences of sin, but never such tears as these; for "His sweat became as drops of blood trickling down upon the ground". No one can understand, as did our Blessed Lord, the utter malice, baseness, and ingratitude of sin. Oh, would that the sweat of blood, forced from our dear Lord's veins by His sorrow for the sins of men, could serve to make us more sorry for having sinned, and more determined to hate and avoid sin for the future!

3. Our Lord knew beforehand how many souls would be eternally lost in spite of His bitter Passion and Death, because they would not believe in Him and would not love Him. This knowledge made the chalice most bitter, and tortured His Sacred Heart, for He loved men's immortal souls so dearly that He had come down from heaven to save them from eternal damnation. This was why He sighed and prayed in such an agony; it was not for Himself alone, but for His brethren, so many of whom, whatever He might do, would cast themselves into hell. He was willing to be bound, scourged, crowned with thorns, and nailed to the Cross to save the souls which were made to His own image; and yet He knew that for very many His Precious Blood and His Sufferings would be wasted. This it was that caused the keenest anguish to the Heart of Jesus, all on fire with love for men!

How to bear suffering. Look at our dear Lord, suffering such agony of soul for love of us! There He lies, with His Face on the ground, groaning in spirit and trembling in His agony. Around Him is the darkness of night, and within His Heart unspeakable woe. He is alone. His disciples are asleep, and nowhere can He find consolation! Now what did Jesus do in this time of extreme affliction and abandonment? He *prayed* to His heavenly Father, and resigned Himself entirely to His will. Thus should we do. If we are in grief, or fear, or need, we ought to turn to God, from whom alone we can obtain comfort and help, and humbly submit ourselves to His holy will.

The Qualities of prayer. Our Blessed Lord's example teaches us also *how* we ought to pray. In the Garden of Gethsemani He prayed with *devotion,* — *humility,* — *confidence,* — *submission to God's will,* — and *perseverance:* 1. *with devotion;* for He prayed from the very bottom of His Heart, and retired a little way from His apostles so that He might pray undisturbed; 2. with exterior and interior *humility;* for He fell on His Face, humbling Himself in the dust before the majesty of His Eternal Father; 3. with *confidence;* for He began His prayer with the loving words: "My Father"; 4. with *submission* to the will of God; for He left the granting of His petition entirely in the Hands of His heavenly Father: "Not as I will", said He, "but as Thou wilt"; 5. with *perseverance;* for He said the same prayer over and over again. Even though He received no visible answer to His petition, He did not leave off praying, but rather "prayed the longer".

Watchfulness. In the midst of His agony Jesus thought more of His own than of Himself. He went back several times to His disciples and urgently exhorted them to watch and pray, that they might not enter into temptation. This exhortation given by our Lord such a short time before His Death is a very important one, and applied not only to the apostles, but to all Christians. You have been told over and over again that prayer is necessary; but prayer alone is not sufficient,

unless it be united to watchfulness. Watch and pray! This is what
Jesus, the great Searcher of hearts, tells us we must do. We are very
weak and very prone to evil; so we must keep a careful watch over
our thoughts and imaginations, over the movements and desires of our
hearts, and over our senses, especially over our eyes. By so doing we
shall either avoid what is sinful, or else be able to overcome it in its
very beginnings. By watchfulness we shall escape many temptations,
and come victorious out of those struggles with sin which are un-
avoidable.

Could the chalice have passed? Yes! Satisfaction could have been
made to the divine justice without such terrible suffering on the part
of our Blessed Lord; for each act of expiation, each suffering of Jesus,
He being God, had an infinite value. His very smallest suffering would
therefore have been sufficient to pay off the whole debt of sin and
appease the justice of God. But what was sufficient to reconcile us to
God, was not sufficient to cleanse us inwardly from sin and make us
keep from sin. Not only has the guilt of sin to be removed, but sinful
man, who is steeped in evil, must be completely cured. What would
the satisfaction made for us by our Divine Lord avail us, if we still
loved and cherished sin in our hearts, and persisted in sinning more
and more till we died in our sins? Nothing! Thus the bitter chalice
did not pass, and our Blessed Lord suffered indescribable agony in
Soul and Body, in the first place, to put before our eyes in a startling
manner the evil and horror of sin. Isaias (55, 4 &c.) had said of Him:
"Surely He hath borne our infirmities and carried our sorrows; and we
have thought Him as it were a leper, and as one struck by God and
afflicted. But He was wounded for our iniquities, He was bruised for
our sins: the chastisement of our peace was upon Him, and by His
bruises we are healed. All we like sheep have gone astray, every one
hath turned aside unto his own way, and the Lord hath laid on Him
the iniquity of us all." The scourges which tore the Flesh of Jesus, the
thorns which lacerated His Sacred Head, the nails which pierced His
Hands and Feet, in short, all the tortures which He endured for our
sake, teach us more impressively than could anything else what a terrible
evil sin is, and what a heavy punishment it deserves. Who can contemplate the Sufferings of Jesus without being moved to contrition and
hatred of sin? Who does not feel constrained to love God, when he
remembers that the Father gave His Son, and the Son gave His Life
for our sakes? This brings us to the consideration of the *second*
reason why the chalice was not removed. Our Blessed Lord drank
its bitterness to the very dregs, to kindle the fire of divine love in
the hearts of men. There is no one sufficiently degraded not to
appreciate, and in a measure to feel grateful for, any sacrifice made
for his sake. "Oh, immeasurable love and goodness of God", says
the Church on Holy Saturday, "who to redeem a slave hast delivered
up Thine own Son!" It almost looks as if the Father loved man

more than He loves His Son, in that He delivered Him up so that we might be saved! And the Incarnate Son of God Himself gave up all for us, and sought out sufferings which He would endure, to prove to us the excess of His Love by the very excess of His Sufferings! Nothing could better reveal the love of God for us than the Sufferings and Death of the Son of God. Even the angels in heaven, on whom God has so lavishly poured proofs of His love, if they wish to contemplate the highest possible proof of God's goodness, must cast down their glances to this earth of ours, where the Creator suffered for the creature, and He who was offended died on the Cross for those who had offended Him. St. Paul writes thus with reference to Christ's Passion: "Walk in love, as Christ also hath loved us, and hath delivered Himself for us, an oblation and sacrifice to God, for an odour of sweetness" (Eph. 5, 2). What has been said may be briefly summed up thus: The divine justice could have been satisfied with a lesser expiation, and thus the chalice would have been removed from our Lord; but that which would have satisfied the divine justice was not sufficient to satisfy the divine love which knew no measure in its desire to draw us away from sin, and move our hearts to a grateful love in return.

APPLICATION. It was for you that Jesus endured His agony and shed His Precious Blood on the Mount of Olives. The Eternal God suffered for *you*, ungrateful, sinful creature that you are! Will you not for the future try to love Him more, and serve Him better?

Think what grief of soul your sins caused your Divine Saviour! And yet you pay so little heed to your sins, and have so very little sorrow for them. Reflect on the number and grievousness of your sins, confess your ingratitude and indifference, and ask our dear Lord—for the sake of His bitter agony—to instil into your heart a great hatred of sin. Let us now kneel down and make a good act of contrition!

CHAPTER LXX.

JESUS IS APPREHENDED AND BOUND.

[Mat. 26, 47—56. Mark 14 43—49. Luke 22, 47—54. John 17, 3—12.]

WHILE Jesus was yet speaking, Judas[1] came with a great crowd of soldiers[2] and servants from the chief priests and ancients. Now the traitor had given them a sign, saying:

---

[1] *Judas.* He came in the capacity of leader of the troop (Luke 22, 47), the strength of which was out of proportion to its purpose; but the enemies of our Lord were determined that Jesus should not escape by any neglect on their part. The troop consisted of the Temple guard, and the armed servants of the High Priest and the Sanhedrim.

[2] *Soldiers.* "With swords and lanterns". They carried lanterns to make sure that Jesus should not escape them in the darkness of the night.

"Whomsoever I shall kiss, that is He; hold Him fast!" As soon as he saw Jesus, he approached Him, saying: "Hail, Rabbi!" and he kissed Him[1]. Jesus said to him: "Friend[2], whereto art thou come? Judas, dost thou betray the Son of Man with a kiss?"

Then, advancing towards the troop, He said: "Whom seek ye?" They answered: "Jesus of Nazareth". He said to them with a look of majesty: "I am He!" At the sound of His Voice they started back, and fell[3] to the ground as though they had been struck by lightning. When they had raised themselves up, He asked them again: "Whom seek ye?" They spoke as before: "Jesus of Nazareth". He answered: "I have told you that I am He. If, therefore, you seek Me, let these[4] go their way."[5] They then laid hold of Him.

The apostles, seeing this, asked their Lord if they might not strike with the sword in His defence. But Peter[6], without waiting for permission, struck a servant of the High Priest, called Malchus, and cut off his right ear. Then Jesus said to Peter: "Put up thy sword into the scabbard. Thinkest thou[7] that I cannot ask My Father, and He will give Me presently more than twelve legions[8]

---

[1] *Kissed Him.* A kiss is the token of love, faithfulness and reverence; but Judas made use of it for purposes of treachery. The hypocrite did not wish to appear a traitor in the eyes of Jesus and His apostles, but our Lord let him know at once that He saw through his hypocrisy.

[2] *Friend.* I have always treated you as My friend, and yet now you come to Me with the vile purpose of betraying Me! You abuse the token of friendship to betray the Messias! Our Lord wished to move the hard heart of Judas by these words, and to bring him to realise the vileness of his deed. Judas might even then have been saved if he had contritely implored our Lord's forgiveness; but, in spite of all, he remained obstinate, and returned defiantly to the band of soldiers and servants.

[3] *And fell.* All fell flat on the ground, and Jesus remained alone standing in the midst of His powerless enemies. He could have fled had He wished it; but He remained where He was, and having commanded the troop of ruffians not to injure His apostles, He gave Himself into their hands.

[4] *These.* The apostles.

[5] *Their way.* He implied by these words that they were at liberty to seize *Him,* and therefore encouraged them to lay hands on Him.

[6] *Peter.* His love for Jesus made him rash.

[7] *Thinkest thou.* If I wished to resist by force the violence which is about to be done to Me, many thousands of angels would come to My aid; so I do not need your help.

[8] *Twelve legions.* i. e. twelve times 6,000.

of angels? How then shall the Scriptures[1] be fulfilled that so it must be done?" So saying, He touched the ear[2] of Malchus and healed him. He then held out His Hands, and they bound Him[3] and led Him away. Then the disciples all fled[4], leaving Him alone in the hands of His enemies.

COMMENTARY.

The Divinity of our Lord Jesus Christ. Before our Blessed Lord gave Himself up into the hands of His enemies, He manifested His Godhead in several ways: 1. By casting His enemies to the ground by His words: "I am He!" The power of these simple words sufficed to fell to the ground a whole troop of rough soldiers and servants who were thirsting to capture Him. Jesus required no help from outside, no legions of the heavenly host; His word alone sufficed to render his enemies powerless, and their weapons harmless; for it was the word of Him who "shall strike the earth with the rod of His mouth, and with the breath of His lips shall slay the wicked" (Is. 11, 4). By thus over-throwing the troop and bidding them rise again, our Lord proved that no human force, but only the excess of His love could chain Him. He manifested His Divinity 2. in the effect produced by His command that His disciples should be left untouched. Although He was Himself a captive in the hands of the ruffians who had seized Him, He spoke to them as a Master to his slaves, as a conqueror to those he had vanquished; and they, full of hatred as they were both towards Himself and His doctrine, obeyed Him without demur, and did not dare

---

[1] *The Scriptures.* The Old Testament Scriptures, which by their prophecies and types so clearly show that the Redeemer must suffer and die. It is the will of My Father that I should suffer, and therefore I give Myself up, of My own will, into the hands of My enemies.

[2] *The ear.* And, by a wonderful miracle, completely restored his ear to its right place.

[3] *Bound Him.* Like a criminal! Truly this was a deed which cried to heaven for vengeance! Picture to yourself how roughly and cruelly these soldiers and servants treated our Divine Saviour! They were exasperated at having been cast to the ground by the very sound of His Voice, and now they vented their rage on Him who so patiently gave them His Hands to be bound. They thrust Him here and there, abused Him, and secured Him as tightly as they could with their chains and ropes.

[4] *Fled.* When they saw that Jesus would not hear of resistance, and even voluntarily gave His Hands to be bound, they lost all courage, and fled in a panic, lest they too should be seized. But Peter and John did not quite forsake Him, but "followed Him afar off" so as not to lose sight of Him, and to learn what would become of Him. Fear and love struggled within their hearts. Love drew them on to follow Jesus, while fear kept them from following Him too closely. Peter, who but a few hours before had declared that he would lay down his life for Him, now discreetly kept at a distance!

to lay a finger on any of those men who, after their Master's death, were destined to spread His doctrine over the face of the earth. They did not even venture to touch Peter, or take vengeance on him for attacking and wounding Malchus. Was not this a wonderful thing? Our Blessed Lord manifested His Divinity 3. by His miracle, which instantaneously cured the wounded Malchus; 4. by calling God His Father, who was ready at His request to send legions of angels to His aid; and 5. in the proof afforded of His Omniscience by the way in which His disciples, through their cowardice and flight, fulfilled that which He had foretold of them: "All you shall be scandalized in Me this night, for it is written: I will strike the shepherd, and the sheep of the flock shall be dispersed."

1. *His Goodness to Judas was also divine.* He did not refuse his treacherous kiss: He suffered His sacred Face to be touched by the lips of this vile traitor, and He even called him: "Friend!" "I have always treated you as My friend", He meant to imply, "why therefore do you come now at the head of My enemies, and betray Me to them by a kiss!" This loving treatment on the part of our Lord was to the ungrateful traitor a last hour of grace. Jesus gave him to understand that He still loved him in spite of his vile crime, and was ready to forgive him even now, if he would repent; but Judas resisted this last grace, and remained hardened and unmoved.

2. *His Goodness to the eleven Apostles.* Full of loving care for them, though willing Himself to be taken captive and led away to death, He desired to assure freedom and life to His disciples. His enemies might rage against Himself, but they must not lay a finger on those whom He loved, and it was only on this condition that He gave Himself into their hands. Oh, how loving is the Heart of Jesus!

3. *His Goodness to Malchus.* He exercised His Omnipotence and healed Malchus, who, like his master, Caiphas, was one of our Lord's bitterest enemies, and who had pressed forward so as to be the first to seize Him. Jesus has taught us not only by His word, but by His example, that we are to return good for evil, and to love even our enemies.

The voluntary and vicarious Sufferings of our Lord Jesus. Jesus gave Himself up to His enemies, of His own will. He went to meet them, encouraged them to seize Him, and offered His Hands to be bound. He gave up His liberty, to atone to God for our abuse of the liberty He has given us. He gave Himself up as a prisoner, to save us from the everlasting prison of hell. He let Himself be bound, that we might be delivered from the bonds of sin and Satan.

The malice, ingratitude and depravity of Judas. Our Blessed Lord had loaded this man with benefits and graces. He had chosen him to be an apostle; He had let him witness His miracles and the holiness of His life; He had imparted to him His divine doctrine; He had borne with him patiently and warned him lovingly, had washed his feet and given him His own Body and Blood to be his Food; and yet he repaid his Master's love with the basest treachery, placed himself at the head of His enemies, feigned friendship for Him, called Him Master, and betrayed Him with a kiss! But Christians behave quite as basely and ungratefully when they make an unworthy Communion!

APPLICATION. When we contemplate Jesus, bound and taken prisoner, we feel as if we could cry out to these Jews: "Hold! How can you bind the Hands of Him Who has shed such blessings on you! Unbind Him, for He is your God Who delivered you from the bondage of Egypt, Who went before you in a pillar of cloud, and led you into the Promised Land. Woe to you if you lay a hand on Him!" Thus would we fain cry out, but faith says to us: "Spare your indignation! The Jewish servants and pagan soldiers could not have held and bound Jesus if it had not been for your sins! Be not angry with those men, for they knew not what they did; but rather be angry with yourself and your sins, and bear in mind that, each time you sin, you are forging new bonds to bind Jesus and lead Him away to death!"

You are quite right to detest the black ingratitude of Judas; but remember how often you too have been ungrateful to your Creator, Redeemer and Sanctifier. Bear in mind, especially, that every mortal sin is a shameful act of ingratitude towards God, your Father, and a dark act of treachery towards Jesus, your Redeemer.

CHAPTER LXXI.

JESUS BEFORE ANNAS AND CAIPHAS.

[Mat. 26, 57. Mark 14, 53. Luke 22, 54. John 18, 13.]

THE troop of soldiers and servants first led Him bound [1] before Annas [2], a former High Priest, and the father-in-law of

---

[1] *Led Him bound.* What a tale of ignominy and ill-treatment is contained in these few words! Both the soldiers and the chief priests' servants knew how intensely their employers hated Jesus, and that the best way to gain favour with them was to maltreat our Blessed Lord. They bound His Hands together tightly and cruelly, and having put a rope round His neck dragged Him by it into the city, abusing and maltreating Him all the way. The road to Annas' house took about half an hour to traverse, and during that half-hour our Lord, according to tradition, fell to the ground seven times in consequence of the inhuman treatment to which He was subjected.

[2] *Annas.* The Romans were in the habit of setting up and deposing the High Priests in the most arbitrary manner. At the time of our Lord's Death

Caiphas, the High Priest of that year. Annas questioned [1] Jesus concerning His disciples and His doctrine. Jesus calmly told him that He had spoken openly [2], and he might question those who had heard Him. Then one of the servants who stood by gave Jesus a blow [3], saying: "Answerest thou the High Priest so?" Jesus meekly [4] replied: "If I have spoken ill, give testimony of the evil; but if well, why strikest thou Me?"

Annas sent Jesus bound to Caiphas [5], who had meanwhile assembled the Great Council of the Jews. Now he and the whole council would willingly have found some pretext for putting Jesus to death; but they could find none, although many false witnesses [6] had appeared against Him.

At last there came two false witnesses who affirmed that they had heard Jesus saying He would destroy the Temple, and after three days build it up again. But they still contradicting each

---

there were therefore several High Priests, for even those who were deposed kept the title. Caiphas was the fourth High Priest since Annas' deposition, but Annas still exercised great influence, for Caiphas had married his daughter, and Caiphas himself had no strength of character. Annas and Caiphas both lived on Mount Sion, about a hundred and seventy yards apart. To reach the house of Caiphas they had to pass that of Annas, so the troop led Jesus there on the way, both to curry favour with him, and because the Sanhedrim had not yet had time to assemble at the High Priest's house.

[1] *Questioned.* Although he had no authority to put the questions. His interrogation was, moreover, superfluous, as both the disciples and doctrine of Jesus must have been well known to him.

[2] *Openly.* Our Blessed Lord attempted no defence; He merely appealed to the many impartial witnesses before whom He had openly preached.

[3] *A blow.* Annas, who hated our Lord, allowed this man's brutal conduct to pass without even reproof.

[4] *Meekly.* In order to bring the ruffian to a sense of his injustice.

[5] *To Caiphas.* Annas was in a great dilemma, for he could not answer our Lord's calm words; and, moreover, he had no authority to pass sentence on Him. The only thing he could do was to have our Blessed Lord's bonds replaced, and send Him to Caiphas, at whose house part of the Sanhedrim had assembled as soon as the news of the capture of Jesus had reached its members. It was now about three o'clock in the morning, yet the chief priests and Pharisees were but too willing to give up their night's rest in order to gratify their hatred of Jesus.

[6] *False witnesses.* They had already made up their minds to put Jesus to death, but they called witnesses in order to preserve some appearance of justice, and to enable them to pass a legal sentence; for, by the Jewish law, sentence of death might not be pronounced unless the offence of the accused were proved by the unanimous testimony of at least two witnesses. If the testimony of witnesses did not agree, the evidence was adjudged false (see the story of Susanna, Old Test. LXXVI).

other, the High Priest arose and said to Jesus: "Answerest Thou [1] nothing to the things which these witness against Thee?" Jesus was silent [2]. Then the High Priest said to him: "I adjure [3] Thee by the living God, that Thou tell us if Thou be the Christ [4], the Son of the living God?" Jesus answered [5]: "Thou hast said it. I say to you, hereafter you shall see the Son of Man sitting at the right hand of the power of God, and coming in the clouds of heaven." [6]   Then the High Priest rent [7] his garments, saying: "He hath blasphemed [8]; what further need have we of witnesses? Behold, now you have heard the blasphemy; what think you?" They answered: "He is guilty of death." [9]

---

[1] *Answerest Thou.* Their evidence did not agree as to the exact expressions used by our Lord. He had not said "I will destroy this Temple", but "Destroy this Temple", or in other words, if you destroy it. Moreover He had not said: "Destroy *the* Temple", but *this* temple, meaning His Body (chapter XV). Finding that the evidence of the false witnesses did not serve his purpose, the High Priest induced Jesus to speak, in the hope that His own words would incriminate Him and afford ground for accusation.

[2] *Silent.* He would not answer false evidence, or defend Himself against the lies of men. Had it been really the truth which His judges desired to ascertain, they could have easily seen that the evidence was absolutely worthless, by reason of the contradictions contained in it. The silence of our Blessed Lord filled the judges with despair, for it took from them all pretext for condemning Him. Then it was that Caiphas resorted to a final measure, by adjuring our Lord, in the holy and terrible name of God, to speak, and thus forced an oath on Him. The way in which a judicial oath was applied in those days was this: the judge suggested the oath to the accused, who accepted it by replying to the question put, by a simple "yes" or "no". This was how Caiphas applied an oath to our Lord.

[3] *I adjure.* I demand of Thee under a solemn oath to tell me &c.

[4] *The Christ.* The Messias, and the Son of God in the fullest sense of the word. Our Lord no longer kept silence, for the High Priest was justified in putting this question to Him. The question was put in the name of God, and its subject was one of the last importance to the whole world. Therefore Jesus gave to this solemn question an equally solemn answer.

[5] *Answered.* "I am the true Son of God." And as He knew that this assertion, made even on oath, would obtain no credence, He added as a proof of the truth of His words: "Hereafter you shall see the Son of Man &c."

[6] *Of heaven.* As Judge. One day their own eyes would convince them that He was the Almighty Son of God.

[7] *Rent.* As a sign of his indignation.

[8] *Blasphemed.* By making Himself out to be the Son of God, and God Himself. And without further loss of time Caiphas (by his words: "What think you?") put it to the vote as to what punishment our Blessed Lord deserved.

[9] *Of death.* For by the Jewish law the punishment of blasphemy was death by stoning (Lev. 24, 16). Without even considering whether our Lord's solemn assertion on oath might not, after all, be true, they pronounced His words to be blasphemy, and with awful blindness and malice, pronounced on the All Holy One the most unjust sentence that has ever been pronounced!

COMMENTARY.

Our Blessed Lord's own testimony to His Divinity. In the face of death Jesus affirmed on oath that He was the promised Redeemer and the Son of God, and in the most solemn manner possible ascribed to Himself divine power and majesty! To the question put to Him on oath by the High Priest He replied, not as an accused man might address his judge, but as a ruler would address his subject, and threatened His hardened accusers with the divine judgments He would hold in His Hand when coming again in the clouds of heaven! Truly that was not the speech of a man, but of God! The members of the Sanhedrim quite understood that Jesus declared Himself to be God, for it was on this plea that they condemned Him to death for blasphemy. And later on, when they accused Him to Pilate, they said: "We have a law, and according to the law He ought to die, because He made Himself the Son of God!" So it was on account of His own testimony that our Blessed Lord was condemned to death. As His enemies could prove nothing against Him, they turned His testimony that He was the Son of God into a crime, for which they put Him to death. He met His Death, therefore, for bearing testimony to His Divinity!

The Gentleness of Jesus. Our Blessed Lord had proved His Godhead not only by His great miracles (and especially by the raising of Lazarus, which not even His enemies could contest), but by the extraordinary holiness of His life and by His truly divine virtues. When He was brought before Annas, Jesus showed a gentleness which has never been equalled. The ruffianly servant struck the Face of the Most High, with an unjust, painful and shameful blow; and Jesus bore this horrible treatment with patience. He did not upbraid or threaten the man, but pointed out to him the injustice of his action, with calm and gentle words. "Learn of Me, for I am meek and humble of Heart!"

Sharing the guilt of the sins of others. Annas sinned in this way by not punishing, nor even blaming, his servant for his unjust and illegal treatment of Jesus.

False witness. The two witnesses sinned against the eighth Commandment; and they sinned grievously, because they gave false evidence on a very important matter.

Oaths. The example of Jesus, Who accepted the oath applied to Him by the High Priest, teaches us that it is lawful and right to take an oath when it is required of us in a court of justice, by those in authority.

———

APPLICATION. It was for love of us that Jesus let Himself be bound, buffetted, struck in the Face, abused, blasphemed, and sentenced to death! He suffered all this to make satisfaction for our sins, and turn away from us the sentence of everlasting punishment which they had drawn down on us. Thank your Redeemer for His unbounded love, and prove, this very day, by your patience and gentleness, that you love Him in return.

Every wilful sin we commit is, so to speak, a blow struck on the Face of our Divine Lord. Whenever you are on the point of sinning, your conscience says to you: "Do not do it! God has forbidden it!" But then, perhaps, you reply: "All the same I will do it. What is it to me that God has forbidden it!" Do you not see that to act in this way is to strike the Face of God with a blow? And if you go on to commit the sin really, those words of our Blessed Lord are in truth addressed to you: "Why strikest thou Me?" O Lord Jesus, for love of Thee, I will never more commit a wilful sin!

CHAPTER LXXII.

THE DENIAL AND REPENTANCE OF PETER.—THE DESPAIR OF JUDAS.

[Mat. 26, 69. Mark 14, 66. Luke 22, 55. John 18, 15]

PETER and John had followed Jesus at a distance, even to the house of the High Priest, in order to see the end[1]. In the court-yard there was a fire[2], which Peter approached to warm himself. While there, Peter was noticed by one of the maid-servants of the High Priest. She looked at him, and said: "This man also[3] was with Jesus of Nazareth." Peter denied Him, saying: "Woman, I know Him not[4]." Immediately the cock crew.

After a little while a man, coming to Peter, exclaimed: "Thou also art one of them." But Peter said: "O man, I am not." Now, after the space of an hour, a certain servant saw Peter, and pointing him out to the others, affirmed: "Surely, thou art also one of them,

---

[1] *To see the end.* St. John was known to the household of Caiphas, on which account the woman at the door let him in by the gate which was closed to the crowd outside; and at his request she also admitted Peter. After this, John left the house to go and tell all that had occurred to the Mother of Jesus, but Peter remained in the outer court to watch the issue of the examination.

[2] *A fire.* The nights in the spring are very cold in Palestine.

[3] *Also.* i. e. he as well as John.

[4] *I know Him not.* He feared that he might be arrested and condemned on account of being our Lord's disciple. After this challenge, Peter, although the servants paid no further attention to the woman's words, thought it more prudent to leave the court, and went and stood by the door.

for even thy speech [1] doth discover thee!" But Peter swore [2] that he knew not the man! [3]   Then the cock crew a second time.

And the Lord, turning [4], looked [5] at Peter. That look pierced his heart. Remembering the words of his Divine Master: "Before the cock crow twice, thou shalt deny Me thrice", he went out [6], and wept [7] bitterly.

During that fearful night, Jesus was guarded in the court by the soldiery [8], who amused themselves by inflicting upon Him all manner of insults; they spat upon Him [9], blindfolded Him, and struck Him [10] in the Face. Early in the morning [11],

---

[1] *Thy speech.* The accent of the Galileans was broader than that of the inhabitants of Judæa. Among the men-servants standing by was a cousin of Malchus, whose ear Peter had cut off, and this man said that he had seen him in the garden.

[2] *Swore.* "He began to curse and to swear." Now that the servants actually recognised him, and as by this time his Master had been sentenced to death by she Sanhedrin, Peter's fear increased, and he not only denied being our Lord', follower, but denied that he even knew Him. He even confirmed his lie by an oath!

[3] *The man.* Thus did he style his Lord and Master, of Whom he had once confessed: "Thou art the Christ, the Son of the living God!" Now he made out that Jesus was an absolute stranger to him!

[4] *Turning.* Our Blessed Lord was at that moment being led away from the council-chamber. It was not the unjust sentence of the Sanhedrim, or the brutal treatment of the attendants which caused Him then His bitterest pain—but the denial given by His chosen apostle!

[5] *Looked.* With a glance which, while full of sorrow and compassion, was one of light and grace. This one telling look from the eyes of his suffering Saviour pierced the very heart of Peter, who, in spite of what he had done, loved his Lord most dearly. He at once saw the greatness of his sin, and an unspeakable sorrow filled his heart.

[6] *Went out.* Unobserved, for all eyes were now fixed on Jesus.

[7] *Wept.* There he stood outside, in the darkness of the night. His heart was weighed down by the bitterest grief, and the tears gushed irresistibly from his eyes. Truly it must have been a moving sight!

[8] *The soldiery.* Having been condemned to death on the charge of blasphemy our Blessed Lord was given over to these ruffians to treat Him as they liked.

[9] *Spat upon Him.* As a sign of utmost contempt. The face is the noblest part of a man; and therefore any insult directed against it, especially spitting, has been, in all ages, regarded as the very extreme of indignity. And yet our Lord suffered this indignity, not once, but repeatedly!

[10] *Struck Him.* Saying: "Prophesy, who is it that struck Thee?" or, in other words: "Surely, if Thou art the Messias, as Thou sayest Thou art, Thou must know, without seeing, who is striking Thee!" They wished to imply that Jesus was a deceiver, and did not know who it was that struck Him. Jesus made no reply to their questionings, which was interpreted by His tormentors to mean that He was unable to reply, and they met His silence by a fresh shower of insults, ridicule and ill-treatment; and blaspheming, many other things they said against Him.

[11] *In the morning.* On Friday morning.

the council[1] assembled[2] to pronounce sentence of death on Jesus.

Then Judas[3] began to be sorry for having betrayed his Divine Master, and going to the chief priests, he would have given back the thirty pieces of silver he had received as the price of his treason, saying: "I have sinned[4] in betraying innocent blood." But they replied: "What is that to us?[5] Look thou to it." Then, being filled with remorse, and losing all hope, he cast down the pieces of silver in the Temple, and went and hanged himself[6] with a halter.

---

[1] *The council.* i. e. the full and entire council, including those who had not been there during the night. Probably the previous scene of the mock-trial was re-enacted once more.

[2] *Assembled.* It assembled again because, to be legal, a sentence had to be pronounced by daylight, so that the one they had passed in the night was invalid. They wished, moreover, to consult together how they could best ensure the carrying out of their sentence. The Romans had taken away from the Sanhedrim its power of life and death, so that the sentence they had pronounced could not be executed unless the Roman governor of Judæa, Pontius Pilate, confirmed it.

[3] *Judas.* Judas knew perfectly well how bitterly the chief priests and Pharisees, who formed a majority in the Sanhedrim, hated Jesus, and he might have foreseen that they would condemn Him to death, once they had Him in their power. But his greed for money blinded him, and deprived him of the use of his reason; so that it was only after he had received the blood-money, and his passion was appeased, that the voice of his conscience made itself heard, and reproached him with being guilty of the death of his Master. The thirty pieces of silver for which he had so eagerly craved no longer gave him any pleasure; they burnt his fingers and constantly reminded him of his terrible crime. In the hope of obtaining peace of mind, he resolved to return the money to those from whom he had received it, and, by openly confessing his guilt, he hoped to get the sentence of death against our Lord repealed.

[4] *I have sinned.* By betraying an innocent Man for money. His conscience continually tormented him with the thought that it was through his crime that innocent blood would be shed.

[5] *What is that to us?* They did not even reply: "What! is He not guilty? Does He not deserve death?" No, with cold contempt they merely said: "What is it to us whether He be innocent or not! See you to that, and reconcile it with your conscience as best you can!" They did not accept back the blood-money, because to do so would have been a tacit confession of the injustice of what they had done; and nothing would have persuaded them to set Jesus free. When Judas, therefore, saw that nothing could avert the consequences of his deed, he fell into despair, and hanged himself. He committed the sin of suicide, and crowned his criminal life by a criminal death.

[6] *Hanged himself.* The rope with which he hanged himself broke, and he fell to the ground; and, says St. Peter (Acts 1, 18): "Being hanged, he burst asunder in the midst, and all his bowels gushed out."

COMMENTARY.

Our Blessed Lord's Omniscience. When, the evening before, our Lord said to His disciples: "All of you shall be scandalized in Me this night", Peter would not admit the possibility of such a thing in his case: "Although all shall be scandalized", he protested, "I will never be scandalized!" In spite of his protest, our Lord then distinctly told him: "To-day, even in this night, before the cock crow twice, thou shalt deny Me thrice"; and so it came to pass. He knew beforehand precisely how many times, and exactly at what hours Peter would deny Him; and, though He could not possibly have seen with His eyes at the time, what was happening in the outer court of the High Priest's house, He knew exactly what was occurring. Our Blessed Lord proved Himself to be Omniscient, i. e. God.

Peter's sin was a very grievous one. Out of fear of man, Peter lied three times, and denied his faith; and the third time he even swore falsely. The sin of Peter grew, and became more grievous each time he committed it. At his first denial, he simply said of our Lord: "I know Him not." The second time, he asserted: "I know not the Man", thus repudiating as a disgrace any connexion with Jesus; and the third time he confirmed this assertion by an oath. He contemptuously called his Lord and Master "the Man", acting as if he did not even know His Name! And this was the same Peter who, but a few hours before, had declared that he was ready to lay down his life for his Lord!

The following circumstances may serve as *a partial excuse for Peter.* He was thoroughly exhausted, excited, confused, and half out of his mind with sorrow at the events of that terrible night. Moreover, from the moment he joined the company of his Master's fierce enemies, he was in a very real danger of death. Finally, he did not sin from malice, but from weakness and panic; and he did not lose his faith, although he outwardly denied it.

The causes of Peter's fall were these: 1. He did not avoid the proximate occasions of sin; for at the time of his fall he was associating with the enemies of Christ. If he had left their company even after his first denial, he would not have fallen so low. "He that loveth danger shall perish in it" (Ecclus. 3, 27). 2. He had paid too little attention to our Lord's warning words: "Satan hath desired to sift you as wheat ... This night thou shalt deny Me thrice"; and he trusted too much in himself: "Though all shall be scandalized, yet not I. I will lay down my life for Thee!" When he said those words he meant them, for Peter had a very firm faith in our Lord, and an ardent love for Him; but he ought not to have forgotten that he was a weak man, and that without God's grace he could not remain faithful. Our Lord had said to him but a very short time before, as they were walking up the Mount of Olives: "Without Me you can do nothing!" 3. He fell, therefore, through over self-confidence, and by neglecting our Lord's exhortation: "Watch and pray, that ye enter not into temptation!"

Peter's fall should be a warning to us, to carefully avoid bad companions, and the occasions of sin; to remember our weakness and instability; and not to trust too much in ourselves, but to ask humbly for the assistance of grace. It was not without reason that our Lord taught us to pray: "Lead us not into temptation!" St. Paul says (1 Cor. 10, 12): "He that thinketh himself to stand, let him take heed lest he fall!"

The conversion of Peter was the work of the preventing grace of our Lord Jesus Christ. The cock crew immediately after his first denial; and this was intended to remind him of his Lord's warning words, and of his own promise to lay down his life for Him. However, he paid no heed to this first cock-crow, and fell deeper into sin; for an outward warning is of no avail without the inward voice of grace. Even the second cock-crow would not have moved him in his distraction, had not our Lord at the same moment cast his gracious glance on the fallen apostle. With that one look which met his eye, grace penetrated the soul of the unfaithful apostle, and gave him light to see how low he had fallen, and how grievously he had sinned. His heart and will were moved, he detested his sin, and bitterly repented of it. Peter corresponded with the helping grace which was given to him; he opened his heart to it, obeyed its promptings, and was therefore converted. To Judas also great grace was given, in the Garden of Gethsemani, but he resisted it, and therefore perished in his sins.

The repentance of Peter was both real and supernatural. So great was his grief of soul for the sin which he had committed, that bitter tears of contrition flowed from his eyes. His contrition was also supernatural, and was indeed a perfect contrition, for he was sorry purely because he had offended his beloved Lord, and because he had increased His sufferings; for of all our Lord's sufferings the one that pained Him most was that Peter, His highly-favoured and chosen apostle, should be ashamed of Him and deny Him in such a cowardly manner. Peter repented of his fall from perfect love for his Divine Master, whose countless benefits and graces he had repaid with such base ingratitude. Let us, too, if we fall into mortal sin, do penance at once, as Peter did, and awaken a perfect contrition in our hearts. His repentance, furthermore, was no passing one: his sorrow for his sin oppressed him all his life, and it is said that each time he heard a cock crow he was moved to a sense of contrition for his sin, and that his eyes were always red with weeping. All his life long he worked mightily for the glory of his Master and the salvation of souls, and unceasingly preached the Gospel, till at last he gave up his life for Jesus. Great was his fall, but still greater was his penance: and he has by his contrition and life-long satisfaction become the model of a true penitent.

The compassion of Jesus. In the midst of His sufferings Jesus, while tormented by His enemies and unjustly condemned to death, forgot Himself and thought of His fallen apostle, and sought to recall and convert him by His glance. He did not upbraid him, nor punish him, but cast on him one look of love and compassion to bring him to a knowledge of his sin, and to kindle in him the hope of forgiveness. O, how unfathomable is the love of the Sacred Heart of Jesus!

Divine wisdom permitted Peter's fall 1. so that Peter might become very humble, and, as the vicar of the Good Shepherd, might be gentle and considerate to those under his charge; 2. that all men might learn to know the mercy of God and the power of grace, and that no sinner might give himself up to despair.

What the Sufferings of Jesus were. It is with deep emotion and compassion that we approach the thought of what our Lord Jesus suffered that night. For hours together a low, ruffianly rabble amused itself by mocking the Son of God! These men abused Him and insulted Him in every way that they could think of: they struck Him with their brutal fists, they tore out His hair, they spat on His Sacred Face; and Jesus bore all silently and without complaint. His Sacred Face, full of gentleness and grace, was marred with bruises, and dishonoured by the spittle of the very scum of humanity! Truly and terribly were David's words of prophecy fulfilled (Ps. 21, 7): "I am a worm and no man, the reproach of men, and the outcast of the people!" If we contemplate our Saviour in this state of deep abjection, we too could almost put the question to Him: "Art Thou the Christ? Art Thou the Son of God? Why dost Thou suffer this terrible treatment?" This is His answer: "I suffer this for love of thee; to make satisfaction for thy sins, and to give to thee an example of humility and patience."

The repentance, confession, and despair of Judas. When Judas perceived the consequence of his treachery, his conscience reproached him with the awful thought: "I am guilty of the murder of my God!" And then Satan, who had taken possession of his heart by reason of his obduracy, drove him to despair. Before the deed was done, he induced Judas to sin, blinding him so that he did not perceive the heinousness of his crime, nor consider its consequences; but once the sin had been committed, he showed its full horror to the wretched sinner, and whispered to him as he had once whispered to Cain, that his sin was too great to be forgiven. Judas might have obtained pardon even then, had he possessed the proper dispositions. It is true that "he repented himself", and that he made a really good resolution of amendment, for at no price would he have committed the sin again. He confessed his guilt by the words: "I have sinned in betraying innocent blood"; and he made what satisfaction he could, for he gave back the blood-money; and tried to get the sentence of death reversed—but, for all this, he was wanting in true penance. Now, what did he lack? The sorrow of Judas was wanting in hope, and such a sorrow does not lead back to God, but rather leads to despair and to an eternal separation from God. Judas' sin in betraying our Lord was a terribly grievous one; and yet the worst sin he committed was that of despairing of the grace and mercy of God. His first sin might have found forgiveness, but there exists no forgiveness for the sin of despair; for he who despairs of God's pardon denies the infinite mercy of God, and cannot therefore benefit by it. To despair of God's mercy is one of the sins against the Holy Ghost, and it is said of these sins that they will not be forgiven either in this world or in the world to come (see chapter XXVII). Furthermore, Judas' confession of his sin availed him nothing. If, full of confidence in his Saviour, the God of love and mercy, he had thrown himself at His Feet, confessed his guilt to Him, and implored His forgiveness, he would most surely have obtained it; but, as it was, in his despair of God's mercy, he sought for consolation from men, and confessed his guilt merely to the members of the Sanhedrim. When they rejected him contemptuously, and laid all the responsibility on him, his last comfort was torn from him, and the burden of his guilty life was so heavy, that he had not the courage to bear it any longer. He felt that he had nothing more to hope for from heaven, and could find no peace on earth, so he hanged himself between heaven and earth, and to the crime of deicide added that of suicide.

Suicide is a terrible sin, for he who commits it does not only kill his body, but also his soul, since at the very moment of his death he is committing a mortal sin, and flinging his soul into hell.

Continued resistance of grace leads to eternal ruin. When our Lord chose Judas to be an apostle, no doubt he was full of good intentions and worthy of the choice. But by degrees he became the cause of great sorrow to his Divine Master, for his passions gained more and more dominion over him. Jesus bore with him, and repeatedly and solemnly warned him. When, a year before His death, and just after He had promised the Blessed Sacrament, our Lord gave to His apostles the choice whether to leave Him or not, Peter, in the name of the others, confessed his faith in Him as the Son of God, and pledged his allegiance to Him. But Jesus answered: "Have I not chosen you twelve, and one of you is a devil." In these words He alluded to Judas, and distinctly gave it to be understood that he would be unfaithful to Him, and a tool of the devil. Judas, however, dissembled and remained with Jesus, hoping to turn his service of Him to his own advantage; and when he quite lost all hopes of an earthly Messias, and consequent prosperity for himself, he compensated himself for his disappointment by frauds and thefts. Thus he persisted in sin, and abused the patience, gentleness and love of Jesus, by continuing in his evil mode of life, instead of being moved and converted. The unworthy apostle believed that, because his Master was so kind, he could go on sinning with impunity, and he sinned therefore against the goodness and mercy of his Lord. Thus he sank deeper and deeper, until at last he sold his Master, and bartered away his own soul; and when he realized the consequences of his vile treachery, his presumption changed suddenly to despair. God's mercy is, indeed, infinitely great, but meanness and baseness had grown to such dimensions in the heart of the traitor by reason of his long course of deceit and hypocrisy, that he had lost all sense of what is great and noble, and could not form the idea of God's infinite mercy, than which nothing greater or more noble can be imagined. And thus it was that the once loved and chosen apostle of Jesus became a "son of perdition" (John 17, 12), and went "to his own place" (Acts 1, 25).

Sin bears two aspects. Before sin is committed it bears a pleasant, attractive aspect, so that the foolish sinner scarcely fears it at all, and even expects to be made happy by it. But hardly is the sin committed than it shows its true colours, which are hideous and horrible. Once a man has gratified his evil passions, he finds out with dismay that far from being the happier for it, he is robbed of all joy of heart and peace of conscience; and he bitterly reproaches himself, for he now perceives that sin is indeed the greatest of all evils. Thus it was with our first parents, and thus it was with Judas.

APPLICATION. You too have denied Jesus in deed if not in word. Whenever you sin wilfully you act as if you were not a disciple of Jesus Christ, and knew nothing of His love and holiness, and as if you had never promised fidelity to Him. If, however, you have become like Peter by your sin, be like him also in your penance. Have you ever bewailed your sins as sincerely and bitterly as did Peter?

Contemplate with deep emotion of heart how, during that long night, your Saviour was the butt of rude and wanton men, and how he was ill-treated, scoffed at, and loaded with ignominy. Do not forget that He who bore all this for love of you was the Incarnate Son of God! Excite in your heart a deep feeling of compassion for your despised Lord, and promise Him that you will always love Him and will never despise His holy commandments.

If it is ever your misfortune to commit a mortal sin, do not follow the example of Judas, who lived in a state of sin till he became hardened in it; but follow the example of Peter, who immediately repented and was converted for good and all.

Never sin by a presumptuous confidence in God's mercy, for the fact of His being so infinitely good and merciful ought to make you love Him with your whole heart, and keep you from ever offending Him.

CHAPTER LXXIII.

JESUS BEFORE PILATE AND HEROD.

[Mat. 27, 2. Mark 15, 1. Luke 23, 1. John 18, 28.]

THE great council of the Jews, called the Sanhedrim, could not pronounce the final sentence of death without the permission of the Roman governor. Therefore the chief priests and the ancients of the people led Jesus before Pontius Pilate, who then governed Judæa for the Roman emperor. Pilate went out [1] to the excited crowd, and asked: "What accusation [2] bring you against this Man?" They answered [3]: "We have found Him perverting our nation [4], and forbidding to give tribute to Cæsar, saying that He is Christ the King." [5]

---

[1] *Went out.* The chief priests and ancients would not enter the hall of justice, for fear of being defiled; for to enter the house of the Gentile Pilate would have made them legally unclean, and excluded them from the paschal sacrifices.

[2] *What accusation.* These words showed the Jews that Pilate would not consent to confirm their sentence without further investigation as to its justice. This vexed them, and they answered impatiently: "If He were not a malefactor, we would not have delivered Him up to thee", or, in other words: "Do not stand on ceremony, but just confirm our sentence, and let it be executed." Pilate, therefore, answered them back: "Take Him, and judge Him according to your law." The proud Roman meant to say: "If you will not prove the justice of your sentence before my judgment-seat, He deserves no more punishment than you yourselves can inflict." But the Jews replied: "It is not lawful for us to put any man to death"—"We cannot be satisfied with any petty punishment; and on that account we have brought Him to you, so that you may have Him put to death."

[3] *They answered.* They now saw that it would be necessary to bring a valid accusation against Him, if they wished to ensure His being put to death. They themselves had condemned Him on account of His presumed blasphemy, the punishment of which was, by the Jewish law, death by stoning. Our Lord's enemies, however, did not wish Him to be stoned, but preferred His dying the death of the Cross, which was universally recognized as the most ignominious of deaths. If they could secure this, they made sure that His memory would be branded with infamy, and that every person would be ashamed to be counted as a follower of one crucified. They now, therefore, changed their accusation to that of seducing the people from their allegiance to the emperor, such an offence being, in the Roman law, punishable by death on the cross.

[4] *Perverting our nation.* From their allegiance to Rome.

[5] *Christ the King.* This accusation was totally false, for Jesus had said only a few days before: "Render to Cæsar the things that are Cæsar's, and to God the things that are God's." He had, indeed, said that He was the Christ, the Messias, but He had never declared Himself to be king of the Jews; on the contrary, He had escaped from the hands of the people when, after the miracle of the loaves, they wished to make Him their king. The Pharisees, moreover, refused to recognise Him as the Messias, for the very reason that He claimed no temporal or political power.

Hearing this, Pilate went into the hall[1] where Jesus was, and asked Him: "Art Thou the King of the Jews?" Jesus answered[2]: "My kingdom is not of this world."[3] Then Pilate went out again to the Jews, and said that he found no cause[4] for condemning the person whom they had brought before him.

But they insisted that Jesus was guilty of sedition, stirring up the people from Galilee even to Jerusalem. To this charge Jesus made no answer. Then Pilate, seeing that He remained silent, asked Him: "Answerest Thou nothing? Behold in how many things[5] they accuse Thee!" Still Jesus was silent[6], and His silence surprised the governor exceedingly.

But as soon as Galilee was mentioned, Pilate asked if the accused were a Galilean[7], and being told that He was, he remembered that Herod, king of Galilee, was then in Jerusalem. Now, Pilate wished to rid himself of a case, in which he was obliged either to go against his conscience or to displease the Jews. He, therefore, sent our Saviour to Herod[8], that Herod might set Jesus free or condemn Him.

---

[1] *Into the hall.* So as to be alone with Him, and be able to carry on his investigation quietly and undisturbed by the clamours of the Jews.

[2] *Answered.* Jesus answered: "Thou hast said it (i. e. I am a king), but My kingdom &c. &c."

[3] *Of this world.* It is not a political kingdom, but a kingdom of truth; and, he added, "for this cause I came into the world that I should give testimony to the truth", i. e. that I should proclaim truth to the world.

[4] *No cause.* Pilate was quite convinced both by our Lord's words and by His calm and dignified bearing that He was absolutely innocent, and had no thought of undermining the Roman authority, and without any delay he declared to the chief priests that this was his conviction.

[5] *How many things.* What grave accusations they bring against Thee.

[6] *Silent.* Our Lord, by His silence, wished to imply that His innocence required no defending. This eloquent silence made such an impression on Pilate that he was seized with wonder and admiration.

[7] *A Galilean.* Jesus was from Galilee, in the sense that He had lived there from His childhood.

[8] *To Herod.* He said to himself: "I cannot condemn Him, because He is innocent. But the chief priests are so urgent that I should condemn Him to death that it would be best for me to wash my hands of the whole affair. In fact, Herod ought to judge Him, for he is prince of Galilee." This was the same Herod Antipas who had caused St. John the Baptist to be beheaded, and it was by the unjust and cruel murderer of His precursor that Jesus was to be judged. The road along which Jesus went from Pilate's house to that of Herod was thronged with pilgrims, and this was painful and humiliating for Him.

Herod was glad[1] to see Jesus, of whom he had heard many wonderful things. He hoped to witness some great miracle. When Jesus was brought before him he asked many questions, prompted by idle curiosity. But our Lord, knowing his motive, made no answer[2] to any of his questions. Then Herod and his court mocked Jesus, and treated Him as a fool, and, clothing Him in a white garment[3], sent Him back to Pilate. And "Herod and Pilate were made friends[4] that same day, for before they were enemies one to another."

COMMENTARY.

The Love of Jesus. Contemplate Jesus led about from one judgment-seat to the other, from Annas to Caiphas, from Caiphas to Pilate, from Pilate to Herod, and from Herod back again to Pilate; how much He suffered from false accusations, scoffs, mockery and ill-treatment, and then remember that He suffered all this for love of you, and to make satisfaction for your sins, whereby you have despised and offended God.

Jesus suffered patiently, and has taught us by His example that we too should be ready patiently to suffer scorn and persecution for His sake, for faith and for virtue.

Jesus suffered undeservedly. The traitor Judas was not the only one to affirm his Lord's innocence. The Roman governor openly declared: "I find no cause in this Man"; neither could Herod discover any guilt in Jesus, although the chief priests and scribes "earnestly accused Him"; and not being able to condemn Him, he treated Him

---

[1] *Glad.* This pleasure-seeking, worldly-minded prince expected to be amused and distracted by his interview with Jesus, and hoped that He would work wonders before him and his court, just as any juggler might do.

[2] *No answer.* Because Herod only wished to amuse himself and satisfy his vain curiosity. He cared nothing about the truth, nor did he trouble his head about the accusations brought against our Lord by the Pharisees (Luke 23, 10). His pride, however, was nettled by the silence of Jesus, which was so complete that he did not even hear the sound of His voice. He revenged himself by treating our Blessed Lord like a fool, and his officers and retainers did the same.

[3] *White garment.* This was done to make Jesus appear like a ridiculous, half-witted would-be-king.

[4] *Friends.* Pilate had offended Herod by encroaching on his rights, but his action in sending Jesus to him flattered Herod, who took it as an act of courteous attention and deference to his position. Our innocent Lord had to pay the price of this selfish friendship between His unjust judges, neither of whom cared to do justice to Him. Jesus had much to suffer on His road to Herod's house, and still more on His return to Pilate; for it was now broad daylight, and as He passed along, dressed in His robe of mockery and surrounded by Herod's myrmidons, a crowd of people gathered round Him, at whose hands he had to suffer countless insults and injuries.

with frivolous contempt and "set Him at nought" as a harmless fool! The Eternal Father suffered His only-begotten Son to be ill-treated and insulted, but He did not suffer even a shadow of guilt to rest ·on the Most Holy.

God turns even evil to His glory. The chief priests and scribes were obeying the dictates of hatred when they demanded that our Blessed Lord should be crucified. But while they thought to gratify their evil passions, they were unwillingly and unwittingly carrying out the decrees of God, and were the instruments of His compassionate and divine love. It was the eternal counsel of the Most Holy Trinity that the Incarnate Son of God should die on the Cross to work for us "a plentiful Redemption"; and not only the prophets, but our Blessed Lord Himself foretold distinctly that this was to be (see chapter XV and LV). Thus, while His enemies desired to obtain at any price that Jesus should be condemned to the ignominious death of the Cross, believing that they would thereby destroy His work for good and all, they in reality helped to complete it, and to fulfil the prophecies.

The kingdom and royal dignity of Jesus Christ. Jesus, the humbled and suffering captive, spoke truly when He said to the representative of the emperor of world-wide Rome: "I am a king!" His kingdom is a priestly kingdom, of which He is both Priest and King, and which He governs by offering Himself up, and conquering the hearts of men. He who had not where to rest His Head declared: "I have a kingdom, but it is not of this world!" This kingdom of Jesus Christ is His holy Church. She is in the world, and for the world, but not of the world; she comes from heaven, and is the kingdom of divine truth and grace. When our Lord Jesus Christ stood before Pilate this kingdom was very small, but, since then, He has conquered to Himself lands and nations over the whole face of the earth, not by force of arms, but by the power of the Cross, on which the God-Man offered Himself, and which is the sceptre with which He, as King, rules over His Church. Still the Church is a kingdom not of this world, for her object is no worldly or natural one, but one entirely supernatural, namely the salvation and sanctification of souls.

The hypocrisy of the Pharisees. The chief priests and ancients pretended that it was against their conscience to enter the house of the Gentile governor, but it did not give their false consciences even a qualm to accuse Jesus wrongfully, or to demand the death of One who was innocent. They guarded against any exterior defilement, but it never occurred to them to cleanse their hearts from hatred, envy and bloodthirstiness. We see how just was our Lord's denunciation of the Pharisees: "Woe to you .. who leave judgment and mercy and faith." Those Christians who are outwardly pious, but who nurse hatred and enmity in their hearts, are very like the Pharisees!

APPLICATION. See how patiently your Saviour suffered! He was falsely accused, but He answered not a word! He was mocked at and scoffed, but yet He was silent! And yet you are impatient and angry the moment anything disagreeable is said or done to you! Imitate your Lord for the future, and do not return evil for evil. Whenever you feel moved to anger, or impatience, keep silence and say to yourself: "O Jesus, I will bear this for love of Thee!"

CHAPTER LXXIV.

JESUS IS SCOURGED, CROWNED WITH THORNS, AND CONDEMNED TO DEATH.

[Mat. 27, 11. Mark 15, 1. Luke 23, 1. John 18, 33.]

PILATE well knew that it was through envy[1] that the chief priests and the ancients had brought our Saviour before him, and therefore he wished to save[2] Jesus from their hands. So he went out to the people again and said: "You have a custom[3] that I should release to you one of the prisoners[4] at the Pasch. Will you, therefore, that I should release to you Jesus or Barabbas?"[5] Now this Barabbas was a murderer, who had been taken prisoner in a sedition of the people. Immediately the people, instigated by the chief priests and the ancients, cried out: "Away[6] with this Man, and release unto us Barabbas!"

---

[1] *Envy.* At the respect in which Jesus was held by the people.

[2] *Wished to save.* Moreover, his wife, whose name was Procla, and who, though a Gentile, was much impressed by the Jews' faith in one God, and had an ardent longing for the truth, sent to her husband, saying: "Have thou nothing to do with that just Man, for I have suffered many things this day in a dream because of Him." This warning, given through his wife, strengthened Pilate's desire to set Jesus free.

[3] *Custom.* This custom was established in memory of the deliverance of the people of Israel from the captivity in Egypt. As the choice of the prisoner to be liberated rested with the populace, Pilate hoped that the people would ask for Jesus, to whom he thought they were attached, seeing with what joy they had greeted his entry into Jerusalem only a few days before. He thought they would choose Jesus all the more eagerly because Barabbas was a dangerous assassin, and was feared and hated throughout the whole city.

[4] *Prisoners.* Belonging to their own country.

[5] *Jesus or Barabbas.* By putting this choice Pilate abandoned the path of rectitude, for he classed together Jesus whom he knew to be innocent, and the notorious criminal who was indeed worthy of death.

[6] *Away.* "Put Him out of the way! Kill Him!" So intense was their hatred of Jesus that they would not even bring themselves to pronounce His Name. They impetuously demanded that the criminal should be pardoned, and that He who was innocent should be condemned.

Then Pilate said to them in amazement: "What shall I do then with Jesus who is called Christ?"[1] They[2] cried out with savage fury: "Crucify Him! Crucify Him!" Pilate, still endeavouring to save Jesus, asked again: "Why, what evil[3] hath He done? I find no cause of death in Him. I will chastise[4] Him, therefore, and let Him go."

He then caused Jesus to be scourged[5]. Immediately the whole cohort[6] was assembled. They stripped Jesus of His clothes, tied Him to a pillar, and scourged Him. Then, covering Him in derision with a purple garment[7], they plaited a crown of sharp thorns, placed it on His Head, and pressed it down, so that the thorns pierced the flesh and entered into the Sacred Head.

Then, placing a reed in His right Hand, by way of sceptre, they bent the knee before Him in mockery, saying: "Hail[8], King of the Jews!" Others spat upon Him, and took the reed that

---

[1] *Christ.* Instead of saying outright and decidedly: 'I cannot put Him to death, because it would be unjust, seeing He has done no evil', Pilate in the most cowardly manner left the fate of Jesus in the hands of the people.

[2] *They.* It was not only the chief priests and ancients who said this, but also the people, at their instigation.

[3] *What evil.* At least tell me why you wish to have him crucified, for I can find no cause of death in Him.

[4] *Chastise.* Have Him scourged, just to satisfy you. In order to appease the bloodthirstiness of the clamouring mob, the unjust judge ordered that a man whom he knew to be innocent should be cruelly scourged! This compliance on his part, at the expense of justice, only made our Lord's enemies more bloodthirsty than ever.

[5] *Scourged.* These few words describe a terrible amount of suffering! A man sentenced to be scourged was secured by both hands to a pillar, and then several executioners together struck blows on his naked body with rods or scourges, made of knotted leather, into which sharp spikes were fastened. This mode of chastisement was so severe that very often those on whom it was inflicted, succumbed, and died under the strokes. We may assume that the scourging of our Lord was of a most severe description, judging from the wanton tortures inflicted on Him by the rough soldiery after the scourging. Moreover, it suited Pilate's purpose that the chastisement inflicted on Jesus should be severe, as, the more tortured and suffering He was, the better chance would there be of the Jews taking compassion on Him, and renouncing the desire to crucify Him.

[6] *Whole cohort.* All the soldiers who were in the hall of justice or about the premises.

[7] *Purple garment.* This old red cloak was put on His shoulders in mockery of His claim to be king, it being the custom of kings to wear a purple robe on solemn occasions.

[8] *Hail.* They crowned Him with thorns and paid homage to Him in the same spirit of mockery.

was in His Hand, and with it they struck His Head, driving the thorns still deeper into the flesh and bone. Every torment and every insult that malice could invent was then inflicted on His Sacred Person. At last they blindfolded Him, and then they renewed all manner of insult and injury.

By this time the Saviour was reduced to a state so pitiable that Pilate thought the sight of Him would inspire the Jews with compassion. He, therefore, took Jesus out on the balcony and showed Him to the people, saying: "Behold the Man!" (Fig. 87.)[1] But they[2] cried out: "Crucify Him! Crucify Him!"

Fig. 87. Ecce-Homo Arch at Jerusalem.   (Phot. Bonfils.)

Pilate exclaimed: "Take you Him and crucify Him, for I find no cause in Him." The Jews cried out: "We have a law[3], and

---

[1] *Behold the Man.* "Behold, how pitiable He is! See, His Body is covered with wounds and streaming with blood, His Head is pierced with thorns, and disfigured with bruises and blood." It was, indeed, a sight to have softened the very stones, and Pilate felt sure that the Jews must spare Him when they 'saw how terribly He had been punished.

[2] *But they.* i. e. the chief priests and scribes. The people themselves were, doubtless, moved to compassion by the sight of the sorrowful, thorn-crowned Figure, but the chief priests and their adherents cried out the more vehemently: "Crucify Him!" for they feared lest mercy should gain the day.

[3] *We have a law.* They now dropped the accusation of disloyalty to Cæsar, for Pilate had declared it to be unfounded, and returned to their first accusation of blasphemy. "He has offended against our religious law", they said, "and in the case of such a crime you cannot be judge. We have already examined the case and sentenced Him to death; all you have to do is to confirm the sentence, and see it carried out."

according to that law He ought to die, beause He made Himself the Son of God."

Pilate, fearing still more [1], entered the hall, and said to Jesus: "Whence [2] art Thou?" Jesus gave him no answer [3]. Then Pilate continued: "Speakest Thou not to me? Knowest Thou not that I have power [4] to crucify Thee, and that I have power to release Thee?" Jesus answered: "Thou shouldst not have any power against Me, unless it were given thee from above."

Now Pilate sought to release [5] Jesus, but the high priests and ancients, seeing that Pilate was disposed to favour Him, cried out: "If thou releasest this man, thou art no friend of Cæsar." [6] Pilate, roused by this sickening hypocrisy of the Jews, retorted: "Behold your king; shall I crucify your king?" The maddened crowd replied: "We have no king but Cæsar." [7] Hearing this, Pilate was afraid lest he should lose the emperor's favour.

But being still convinced of the innocence of Jesus, he took water in a basin and washed his hands [8] before the whole people, saying: "I am innocent of the blood of this just Man; look you [9]

---

[1] *Fearing still more.* His wife's message had already made Pilate uneasy, and the calm dignity and heavenly patience of Jesus had inspired him with a feeling of awe. Never before had such a prisoner been brought to his judgment-seat. When he now learnt that Jesus made Himself the Son of God, his awe increased, and he suspected that He might, indeed, be some supernatural Being.

[2] *Whence.* Are you from earth or from heaven?

[3] *No answer.* Because He did not wish to increase the guilt of Pilate.

[4] *I have power.* By these words Pilate declares his own responsibility and therefore condemns himself. Our Lord's words: "Thou shouldst not have" &c. bring this responsibility home to him with terrible force.

[5] *Sought to release.* Our Lord's words made a deep impression on Pilate, and he made a final effort to release Him, though in what this effort consisted, the Gospel does not tell us.

[6] *Friend of Cæsar.* Again they return to political intimidation, accusing this time Pilate himself of disloyalty to the emperor. This idea filled Pilate with fear, for the emperor Tiberius was a cruel and capricious man.

[7] *No king but Cæsar.* The Pharisees avowedly detested the Roman yoke and the emperor, but now their hatred of Jesus made them explicitly acknowledge that supremacy which they had hitherto refused to recognize. "We will have no king but Cæsar!" they cried, "We will not even have the Messias as king!" With these words the representatives of God's chosen people solemnly renounced their Messias, repudiated the "Son of David" and rejected Jesus Christ, declaring that the pagan Cæsar was their only lord, and the sole leader of their people. This was national apostasy.

[8] *Washed his hands.* So as to express that none of the guilt of condemning Jesus could attach itself to him.

[9] *Look you.* Reconcile your deed to your own consciences as best you can.

to it." The Jews cried out: "His Blood be upon us[1], and upon our children." Then Pilate released Barabbas, and delivered Jesus[2] to be crucified (Fig. 88).

COMMENTARY.

"*He suffered under Pontius Pilate.* The words of the Apostles' creed do not merely mean that our Blessed Lord suffered during the time that Pontius Pilate was governor of Judæa, but are meant to show that Pontius Pilate was guilty of our Lord's Passion and Death by his cowardly compliance with the Pharisees' demands.

The Innocence of Jesus was supernaturally revealed a short time before His Death; for the dream of Pilate's wife was a supernatural dream. In it God revealed to her that Jesus was a just Man, and that Pilate would incur a heavy punishment if he condemned Him to be crucified.

The Abasement of Jesus. It was a great humiliation to our Lord Jesus not only to be named in the same breath as Barabbas, but to have this ill-famed malefactor preferred before Him. Judas had valued his Lord at the price of a slave, and now the blinded people bartered away the life of their Messias for the liberty of an utter scoundrel who had robbed the peaceful inhabitants of Jerusalem of safety, possessions and life! Could a greater insult be offered to the Most Holy? Why did Almighty God suffer His Son to be so grievously insulted? The answer is this: It was our Blessed Lord's will to be "reputed with the wicked", and to be treated as if He were the worst of men, because

---

[1] *Upon us.* You shall answer for nothing! We take all responsibility on ourselves. We and our children will bear the guilt and the punishment, if innocent blood (which cries to heaven for vengeance) is shed.

[2] *Delivered Jesus.* Pronouncing the sentence of death on Him. It was now "about the sixth hour", or near the end of the second quarter of the day. The Jews divided their day of twelve hours into four quarters, each quarter being known by the name of the hour which began it (or, rather, of the last hour which preceded it). Thus the "first hour" was the quarter from 6 to 9 o'clock a. m. of our time; the third hour was from 9 to 12 o'clock; the sixth hour from 12 to 3 p. m.; the ninth hour from 3 to 6 o'clock. Pilate's first examination of Jesus, which was followed by his sending Him to Herod, began about six o'clock in the morning. When Herod sent our Lord back, and the second examination began, it must have been about nine o'clock. He was scourged, crowned with thorns, and presented to the people between nine and half-past ten, and the sentence of death must have been pronounced a short time before eleven o'clock. During the whole night, and up to that hour, Jesus was being ill-treated, dragged about from one judgment-seat to another, loaded with ignominy, scorned, mocked, and tortured with scourges and thorns! Not for one moment had He been allowed to rest; no one had given Him even a drop of water to revive Him. If all this took place before He was condemned to death, we can imagine what sort of treatment He was likely to receive after Pilate had pronounced sentence.

He had taken the sins of all men upon Him, in order to make satis-faction for them to the divine justice. He took upon Himself the curse which rested on mankind, in order to bring to all men that blessing which Almighty God promised to Abraham, when He said: "In thee shall all the nations of the earth be blessed" (Old Test. IX).

The vicarious Satisfaction of Jesus Christ. The divine plan of salvation is visibly presented to our understanding by the rejection of our Lord in favour of Barabbas, whereby the Innocent suffered for the guilty. We sinful men are so many Barabbasses, for we have robbed God of His honour, and have deserved death. But the Incarnate Son of God has taken our sins upon Himself, and has made satisfaction for

Fig. 88. Place at Jerusalem where Jesus was condemned to death (1st station).

them to the divine justice as our representative, in order that we might be freed from guilt, and delivered from everlasting death.

Our Blessed Lord was scourged for us. The scourging was a terrible torture to our Lord Jesus. The very fact of being stripped of His clothes and exposed to the gaze and laughter of the rough soldiers was an untold shame and pain to the Most Pure. Then followed the countless blows of the cruel scourges. Our Divine Lord's tender Body was covered with wounds and bruises, and the Precious Blood flowed on to the ground. But He uttered no complaint; no cry of pain crossed His lips. He was silent, He endured and prayed, offering each stroke to His Heavenly Father in satisfaction for our sins. Our Lord suffered this chastisement especially to make satisfaction for all our sins against purity and chastity. How grievous and shameful must sins against the sixth Commandment be, if Jesus had to expiate them so terribly!

He was crowned with thorns for us. In order to prove to us the greatness of His love and the grievousness of our sins, our Blessed Lord allowed tortures, unthought-of till then, to be invented on His account. Such a torment, contrived with devilish cruelty, was the crowning with thorns, by means of which tortures were inflicted on the noblest part of His Body, His Sacred Head. Being accused of making Himself king, He was thus crowned in mockery and subjected to the malicious homage of His tormentors, who drove the thorns into His Head, striking Him with the reed which fell from His Hands, spitting in His Divine Face, and adding the sting of their scoffing words to this cruel treatment. Truly no son of Adam had ever endured such pain as Christ, the second Adam, endured, when He suffered the sharp cruel thorns to pierce His Sacred Head, in order to save us from the eternal ruin which the pride and disobedience of the first Adam had brought on us. Jesus, the King of everlasting glory, bore this for us, and carried the crown of thorns even unto death, to make satisfaction to the divine justice for our pride and all the sins which spring from it.

The following prophecies were fulfilled by those sufferings of Jesus about which you have just heard: 1. David's prophecy: "I am a worm (i. e. despised and trodden under foot like a worm) and no man: the reproach of men, and the outcast of the people" (Ps. 21, 7). 2. The prophecy of Isaias: "There is no beauty in Him, nor comeliness. Despised, and the most abject of men, a man of sorrows. He was wounded for our iniquities, He was bruised for our sins, the chastisement of our peace was upon Him, and by His bruises we are healed" (Is. 53, 2 &c.). 3. The prophecy of our Lord Himself (Mat. 20, 18): "The Son of Man shall be betrayed to the chief priests and the scribes (as was done by Judas), and they shall condemn Him to death, and shall deliver Him to the Gentiles (Pilate and his soldiers) to be mocked, and scourged and crucified."

Mortal sin in its true aspect. Nothing is so calculated to show us the fearful evil of mortal sin as that horrible cry of the Jews: "Away with this Man! Give unto us Barabbas!" Any Christian who commits a mortal sin thinks, speaks and acts just as did those blinded Jews. Whenever there is a question between observing or transgressing God's commandments in any important matter, then, we may say, Almighty God with His promises and Satan with his allurements are placed face to face, and man has to choose between them. The choice is put to you. Will you choose God, the most gracious, the most holy God, the source of true joy and of all noble happiness, His grace, His friendship, and His heaven so full of inconceivable bliss; or will you choose the prince of darkness, the liar and the murderer from the beginning, and the sinful pleasures which are all that he holds out to you? Whenever a man consents to sin, he, as it were, says to God: "I have compared together Thy service and that of the devil, and I find that Satan is a better master than Thou art, and that I can gain more from him than from Thee; and that the sinful pleasures by which he allures me are dearer to me than Thy friendship and promises." Thus the sinner insults his Lord and God in exactly the same way as did the Jews, when they cried out: "Not this Man, but Barabbas!" Nay, more; the Christian who commits a mortal sin offers a much greater insult to our Lord than did the Jews when they preferred Barabbas to Him; for 1. he sins against greater knowledge, and therefore with greater malice. He believes and knows that Jesus Christ is His God and Saviour, and has, moreover, pledged both faith and obedience to Him. Nevertheless he despises His Commandments, and prefers the service of His enemy, Satan. 2. The Jews despised our Lord at the time of His abasement, but the Christian sinner despises Him now that He is sitting at the right hand of the Father. 3. Barabbas, whom the Jews preferred to our Lord, was, at least, a man, made to the image of God; but the Christian who sins prefers to the Author of all good the most despicable things, the works of darkness, base lusts and passions. Mortal sin on the part of a Christian is, therefore, a horrible offence, an undervaluing of God, and a shameful want of gratitude towards Him.

Resistance to grace. The divine warning by means of Procla's dream was a grace which Pilate, indeed, wasted; but by corresponding with it his noble wife obtained the gift of faith in our Lord Jesus, and as most ancient fathers tell us, the grace to die a happy death. Pilate, on the other hand, was degraded by the emperor, and was banished to Vienne, where he ended his guilty life by suicide.

Ingratitude and fickleness of the people. They one and all voted in favour of Barabbas: not one raised his voice for Jesus. Ingratitude is the world's recompense for benefits!

"Behold the Man!" These words were spoken to us as well as to the Jews, and demand that we should contemplate the sufferings of our Divine Lord, admire His gentleness and patience, and take to heart the infinite love which made Him suffer so much for us. The contemplation of the sufferings of Jesus Christ is one of the chief devotions we can practise, and is calculated to fill us with a hatred of sin and love of Jesus, and to comfort and strengthen us in all our sufferings and trials.

The Innocence of Jesus. Pilate said repeatedly: "I find no fault in Him", and spoke of Him as "this just Man". When he could find no more words to express his belief in the innocence of Jesus, he affirmed it anew by the solemn action of washing his hands, by which he meant to say: "He whom I am condemning against my will is guiltless of any fault." In other cases where a man, though innocent, has been condemned, the judge has always based his sentence on, at least, some appearance of guilt; but in this case the judge solemnly and publicly declared that He who was accused was innocent on every charge. Jesus was condemned to a disgraceful death, avowedly, in spite of His innocence: no breath tarnished the fair fame of His holiness. No act of justice or law condemned Him to death; He was the Victim of those who hated Him, and who savagely and imperiously demanded His death.

Who was guilty of our Lord's Sufferings and Death? — 1. Pilate bore a guilt which the washing of his hands could not wash away. He knew and testified that Jesus was innocent, and was not worthy of death—and yet he condemned Him to be crucified. By doing this he abused his power and violated the laws of justice. He sinned against the fifth commandment by condemning Jesus unjustly, and thereby causing His death. 2. The Jews, and especially the chief priests and ancients, were even more guilty than Pilate. They delivered their Messias to death, and killed Him with their sharp tongues, by means of false accusations. It is true that they did not quite know that Jesus was the Son of God, as St. Peter testified in his discourse after he had healed the man born lame: "Brethren, I know that you did it through ignorance" (Act. 3, 17). But their ignorance and unbelief were both wilful, because they let themselves be blinded by pride and envy, and shut their eyes to the light of faith which streamed on them from the life, words, and wonderful works of Jesus. 3. However, neither the malice of the Jews nor the weak compliance of Pilate could have caused our Lord's death, had not the eternal counsel of God decreed that His Incarnate Son was to die to redeem us from sin and eternal punishment. It is, therefore, our sins which bear the real burden and guilt of our Blessed Lord's sufferings and death, and cry out louder than His bitterest enemies: "Crucify Him! Crucify Him!" Let us, then, beat our breasts and say with S. Alphonsus: "Mercy and pardon, O eternal God, for by our sins we have nailed Thee to the Cross!"

Temporal authority is from God. "Thou shouldst not have any power against Me, unless it were given thee from above", said our Lord to Pilate. God is the Lord of heaven and earth, and from Him comes all authority and power; so that all those whose duty it is to command others ought to exercise their authority in the name of God, and according to His will.

Fear of man led Pilate to condemn our Blessed Lord against his convictions, for he feared the displeasure of Cæsar more than the displeasure and vengeance of heaven. It was fear of man which also caused St. Peter's fall, and which is, every day, the cause of countless sins. The true fear of God drives out human fear, and bestows fortitude; and he who cares for the praise or blame of men more than for the praise or blame of God, acts in a cowardly manner and has no living faith. Our Lord warns us against human respect in the strongest terms: "Fear not them that kill the body and are not able to kill the soul", He says (Mat. 10, 28), "but rather fear Him who can destroy both soul and body in hell", i. e. the infinitely Holy and Just God.

Israel is no longer the people of God. With wilful blindness God's chosen and highly-favoured people disowned and rejected the Anointed of the Lord, the Messias, for whom their fathers, the patriarchs and prophets, had yearned. Ever since that accursed cry "Crucify Him" was uttered, Israel has ceased to be the chosen people of God and of the Messias; for it proved itself unfaithful to its God, its calling, its history, and its past. The fate of Israel has been a very marvellous and striking one. God prepared this people during two thousand long years for the coming of the Messias. Every type and prophecy pointed to Him, and each day the Israelites prayed that He who was promised might speedily come. And yet when He came, full of grace and truth, to fulfil the law and the prophets, His people disowned, rejected, persecuted and killed Him! However, the delusion and passions of men could not frustrate the loving plans of divine wisdom; on the contrary, under the guidance of Providence, they served to carry them out. The chosen people killed the Messias and would not believe in Him, but Almighty God reserved to Himself a sufficient number of "true Israelites", that through them, that is, through the apostles, salvation might be proclaimed to the whole world. Salvation came out of Israel, and through her gave life to the nations of the world, even though, by their own fault, it turned to the destruction of the unbelieving Jews themselves. The vengeance which they desired and called down, fell upon them.

The Blood of our Blessed Lord has indeed been on the Jews and their children. In the year 70 A. D. the judgment of God which they challenged overtook them, as has been described in chapter LX. The Jews had rejected their Messias and killed Him "by the hands of wicked men", acknowledging the Gentile Cæsar as their sole lord; and now this Cæsar, by sending his army against Jerusalem, became the instrument of the divine vengeance. Many of those very men who had cried out: "Crucify Him, crucify Him!" were alive at the time of the siege and taking of Jerusalem, and themselves experienced its bloody horrors. Many thousand Jews died on the cross under Titus; a million perished partly by the sword, partly by famine and disease; about 92,000 were sold as slaves for a nominal price (thirty being sold for one piece of silver); and the remaining few were scattered over the face of the earth. Israel might have been the first among the nations if it had believed in Christ; but, as it is, it has simply ceased to exist as a nation. The Jews are dispersed, and are without home and country and temple, and for more than eighteen hundred years have been vainly waiting for another Messias. Every nation has its own prince or king, but the Jews, since the rejection of their true king, have had no king of their own; scattered about among all nations, they have as many rulers as there are rulers upon earth, but not one whom they can call their own! Thus was accomplished the fate of Israel, prefigured by that of Cain, affording to all the world a most clear proof that Jesus Christ, whom Israel rejected, is the true Messias and Redeemer.

APPLICATION. Fear and detest sin, for it is a terrible evil! If you are ever tempted to commit a mortal sin, put to yourself this question: "Whom shall I choose, Jesus or Barabbas?" Make a firm resolution never to commit a grievous sin for any price which the world could offer you, never to prefer anything to Jesus, but to serve Him lovingly, who for love of you suffered such shame and torments.

When Pilate asked the Jews: "Why, what evil hath He done?" they knew not what to answer. Let us ask our Divine Saviour: "What evil hast Thou done to be so inhumanly treated, and to die such a cruel death?" And His answer would be: "I loved you, therefore did I suffer these things. Behold the greatness of My sufferings, and you shall behold the greatness of My love. Will you not respond to this love, by loving Me in return?"

"I am a king", said Jesus, though He knew that His royal dignity would procure Him no other crown but a crown of thorns, and no throne but the Cross. Look at Him earnestly, and with deep compassion. Look at this king crowned with thorns! See how He suffers, how He is ill-treated, scoffed at and mocked! See what majesty is His! Behold, the eternal King wears a crown of thorns for love of us, that He may kindle in us love in return. He suffered nameless torments to merit everlasting joy for us. He endured endless indignities to win for us eternal honour. He wore the robe of scorn to clothe us with imperishable glory. His royal dignity is one of love, for He desires to be king of our hearts. Shall He not, then, be our king? Cast yourself at His Feet, and promise Him that you will love Him ever more; and that you will follow His steps in humility and patience.

Think what a cowardly and disgraceful thing human respect is, and examine your conscience whether you have ever done evil or omitted what is right for fear of the wicked of unholy people. Fear God, and be afraid of no man.

CHAPTER LXXV.

JESUS CARRIES HIS CROSS TO MOUNT CALVARY. HE IS CRUCIFIED.

[Mat. 27, 31. Mark 15, 20. Luke 23, 26. John 19, 17.]

THEN the soldiers of the governor, tearing[1] from the Body of Jesus His purple robe, clothed Him again in His own garments, and laid the Cross, whereon He was to be crucified, upon

---

[1] *Tearing.* They tore off his purple robe, but not his crown of thorns. We may imagine what pain the process involved for His wounded Body.

His bruised and mangled shoulders. Bearing this heavy burden, He advanced [1] through the streets [2] of Jerusalem towards the place of punishment, which was called Golgotha, or Calvary [3]. Two robbers [4] were also led out to be crucified with Him.

But Jesus, exhausted by long fasting and loss of blood, fell under the weight of the Cross (Fig. 89). Then the Jews, fearing that Jesus might die on the way, forced a certain man, named Simon of Cyrene [5], who was passing by, to help Him to carry the Cross to the place of execution.

Fig. 89. Place where Simon of Cyrene was forced to carry the Cross. (5th Station).

[1] *Advanced.* Although He was completely exhausted, first from the effects of His agony and bloody sweat in the garden, and then by His scourging, crowning with thorns, and all the other ill-usage which He had received.

[2] *The streets.* The procession was a long one. Four soldiers had to undertake and see to the execution of our Lord, and besides these there was a troop of soldiers to serve as an escort. This troop was headed by a Roman centurion on horseback, while two soldiers marched on each side of Jesus. Behind Him came the two robbers who were to be crucified with Him, and who are commonly known as the two thieves.

[3] *Calvary.* Golgotha is the Hebrew, and Calvary the Latin word for "the place of a skull". The spot on which our Lord was crucified was called thus on account of the likeness which its shape bore to a human skull. It lay to the west of the city, near the walls, and was of no great height. It served as the place of execution of criminals, and it took about a quarter of an hour to get there from Pilate's house. Jesus carried the Cross unaided until He broke down under its weight.

[4] *Two robbers.* As if Jesus were a common malefactor like these men.

[5] *Simon of Cyrene.* Cyrene was a commercial town of considerable importance on the north coast of Africa, where there resided a number of Jews. He was

Among the vast crowd[1] that followed Jesus there were some pious women[2], who shed tears[3] of compassion on seeing Him reduced to such a state. But Jesus, turning towards them, said: "Daughters of Jerusalem, weep not for me, but weep for yourselves and for your children. For, behold, the days[4] shall come when they shall say to the mountains: 'Fall on us', and to the hills: 'Cover us'. For if in the green wood[5] they do these things[6], what shall be done in the dry?"[7]

When[8] Jesus reached the top of the hill of Calvary, the soldiers offered Him wine mingled with myrrh[9], but He refused[10] to drink. They then tore the clothes from His already mangled

---

returning to Jerusalem from the country, and when he met the procession he wished to pass on, but the soldiers stopped him, and compelled him to carry the Cross, for they feared that Jesus would not reach Calvary alive, if He carried the heavy burden any longer. None of those accompanying the procession would touch it, for to carry a cross was the very type of ignomiry. Even the rude soldiers, who would do almost anything for money, considered themselves above such a task. They, therefore, unjustly compelled Simon, a casual passer-by, to take the Cross on his shoulders, and, after that, he and our Lord carried it together, though, according to tradition, Jesus fell to the ground twice more before He reached Calvary.

[1] *Crowd.* The common people knew Jesus, and had hitherto venerated Him on account of His miracles, some even believing Him to be the Messias. But now that they were told He was proved to be a deceiver, and that He was condemned to death on this account, their love turned to hatred, their veneration to contempt, and they hastened to see Him put to death, accompanying Him with scoffs, derision and curses.

[2] *Women.* From Jerusalem, for our Lord addressed them as "Daughters of Jerusalem". Among them was Veronica, who handed the sudarium (cloth) to Jesus. Mary also, the sorrowful Mother of God, was on her road to Golgotha, accompanied by St. John, to share the shame and suffering of her Divine Son. The meeting of Jesus with His Mother filled both their hearts with grief.

[3] *Tears.* These tears of theirs reveal to us how horrible must have been the spectacle which they saw. In spite of the furious crowd, these pious women could not restrain their tears, for the torments and humiliation of Jesus deeply affected them.

[4] *The days.* Days so full of terror that men will welcome a violent and sudden death as a boon.

[5] *The green wood.* To Me who am just and innocent.

[6] *These things.* These sufferings of Mine which you behold.

[7] *The dry.* To the guilty and godless. Our Lord was thinking of the terrible judgment which would fall upon Jerusalem and the people of Israel.

[8] *When.* It was then about noon.

[9] *With myrrh.* It was the custom to offer this bitter drink to the condemned, so that their senses might be deadened, and they might not feel the pain of their crucifixion so acutely. The myrrh mixed with the wine gave to it a stupefying strength.

[10] *He refused.* He would not have His senses dulled, for He willed to feel the tortures of crucifixion to their full extent.

Body, and nailed[1] His Hands and His Feet to the Cross. They crucified Him with two thieves[2], one on the right, the other on the left. Naked and bleeding He hung upon the Cross, raised aloft[3] between heaven and earth. Pilate wrote a title[4] in Hebrew, Greek, and Latin, and put it on the Cross. The writing was: "Jesus of Nazareth, the King of the Jews" (Fig. 90). Many of the Jews were dissatisfied; they came to Pilate

Fig. 90. Inscription of the Cross (kept in the church of S. Croce in Gerusalemme, Rome).

and said: "Write not[5]: 'The King of the Jews', but that He said: 'I am the King of the Jews'." But Pilate answered: "What I have written, I have written."[6] And the soldiers cast lots for His garments[7], even as the prophets had foretold.

---

[1] *Nailed.* Our Lord was crucified in the following way: He was first stripped of all His clothing, with the exception of a cloth round His loins. The tearing of His clothes from His Body re-opened His smarting wounds and renewed the pain of His scourging; but His greatest torment was in having His Sacred Body stripped and exposed to the gaze of the multitude. Then our Blessed Lord was extended on the Cross as it lay on the ground, and His Arms were stretched and fastened to the Cross by nails, driven through His Hands with a heavy hammer. Both His Feet were secured, one over the other, with *one* long nail, driven through both, into the Cross. The torture of this piercing and nailing of His Hands and Feet was indescribably great; the bones and nerves cracked, the blood streamed out. The whole Body was racked with pain. Then the Cross on which the Lamb of God was nailed was raised up, and fastened in the ground.

[2] *Two thieves.* Our Lord being in the middle, as if He were the greatest criminal of the three.

[3] *Raised aloft.* There He hung, covered with wounds and blood, and His Head crowned with thorns, the nails through His Hands and Feet being His only support, while His Precious Blood slowly trickled down on this earth of ours, to cleanse it from sin.

[4] *A title.* It was the custom to fix over the head of each one crucified an inscription telling the cause of the sentence. Hebrew was the language of the Jews, while Greek and Latin were the most widely spread languages of those days. The four letters I N R I which are placed over our Lord's Head on crucifixes are the first letters of the four words of the Latin inscription "Iesus Nazarenus, Rex Iudæorum".

[5] *Write not.* The wording of the inscription vexed the chief priests, for it was an outrage on the Jews to call a crucified man their king, such an one being considered dishonoured and accursed.   [6] *I have written.* i. e. it shall remain written.

[7] *His garments.* Namely, His linen under-garment, His cloak, and His girdle. Jesus hung on the Cross in utter poverty and abasement. He was robbed even of His clothes, and had to witness how His tormentors divided them among themselves.

COMMENTARY.

The reason why our Lord chose the death of the Cross. 1. Because He thereby offered the most complete satisfaction for our sins. Man had offended God by a disobedience which sprang from pride, when he desired to "be like unto God". The Divine Redeemer atoned for this pride by choosing the most painful and ignominious of deaths. Under the Old Law, the body of an executed criminal was hung upon a cross as a token that such a man was cursed of God and rejected by the people; and yet Jesus suffered Himself to be hung on the Cross when alive! For this reason St. Paul writes thus (Gal. 3, 13): "Christ has redeemed us from the curse of the law (i. e. from sin), being made a curse for us: for it is written (Deut. 21, 23): 'Cursed is every one that hangeth on a tree'." By thus dying on the Cross, our Divine Saviour abased Himself as far as He could, so as to offer satisfaction for our pride. In like manner He atoned for our disobedience, for He became "obedient unto death, even to the death of the Cross" (Phil. 2, 8). 2. Our Lord chose to die on the Cross to show His unbounded love for us in a way which we could not mistake, and to move our hearts to love Him in return. When on the Cross, our Blessed Lord suffered the severest torments of Soul and Body, pouring out His Blood for our sakes, slowly, and drop by drop. "He hath loved us," writes St. John," and washed us from our sins in His Blood" (Apoc. 1, 5). "See", says St. Augustine, "see the wounds of the Crucified, the Blood of the dying, the ransom paid by the Redeemer; His Head is bowed down to kiss us; His Heart is opened to love us; His Arms are spread to embrace us; His whole Body is given to save us!"

The Cross the Sign of Redemption. It stands upon the earth and raises itself towards heaven, to signify that our Lord, when lifted up and hanging on the Cross between heaven and earth, purified this sinful earth and reconciled it to heaven. The four arms of the Cross signify the universality of Redemption, all men being saved by Christ crucified. They are symbols of the four parts of the world, pointing, when the Cross is laid down, to the north and south and east and west, and signifying that all men, all over the face of the globe, have a share in the fruits of Redemption. In the Cross alone is salvation, and from it flow all graces and blessings. Thus it is that in all her benedictions the Church makes use of the sign of the Cross: and whenever a Catholic makes the sign of the Cross, he confesses his faith in the crucified Son of God.

Prophecies fulfilled by the Death of Jesus on the Cross:

1. That of *David* (Ps. 21, 17 19): "They have dug My Hands and My Feet. . . . They parted My garments amongst them, and upon My vesture they cast lots."

2. That of *Isaias* (Is. 53, 7): "He was offered because it was His own will, and He opened not His mouth. He shall be led as a sheep to the slaughter, and shall be as dumb as a lamb before his shearer."

3. That of *our Lord Himself* (Mat. 20, 19): "They (the Gentiles) shall crucify Him."

Types fulfilled by our Lord crucified: 1. The tree of knowledge of good and evil (Old Test. III). 2. Isaac, who himself, going up the hill, carried the wood on which his father bound him, to sacrifice him (Old Test. XIII). 3. The paschal lamb (Old Test. XXXII). 4. The brazen serpent (Old Test. XLII).

The Compassion of the Sacred Heart of Jesus. Even as it was with our Lord, when He made His triumphal entry into Jerusalem, so was it with Him in the midst of His sufferings, when He was being led out to death; He did not think of Himself, but of the dreadful judgment which would ere long overtake Jerusalem and all its people. On the former occasion, He wept over the blindness and inevitable overthrow of the holy city; and now again He thinks with sorrow and compassion of the misery of the people. "Weep not for Me," He exclaimed to the weeping women of Jerusalem, "but weep for yourselves and for your children." Having on the first occasion warned ungrateful Jerusalem in vain, He now, in the midst of His Passion, strove to save His very tormentors from the coming judgments. He bore no rancour in His Heart at the ingratitude of His people, who had loaded Him with injuries and were dragging Him to a shameful death, but mourned over the temporal and eternal woe of those who were so blinded by their passions. There could be no heart so noble and loving as the Sacred Heart of Jesus.

God's judgments on impenitent sinners. Our Blessed Lord's words: "If in the green wood they do these things, what shall be done in the dry?" have a deep meaning. If God thus punished His beloved Son for the sins of others, how will He punish men for their own sins! What will those suffer who are rejected by God, if He whom He loves suffered so much! The bitter Passion of our Lord Jesus is a practical warning of the terrible judgments which will overtake sinners.

The two mysteries of the holy Rosary, the Carrying of the Cross and the Crucifixion, serve to remind us of the indescribable agony of Soul and Body which our Blessed Lord suffered on His way to Calvary.

The compassion and courage of the pious women. The vast crowd which was following Jesus was chiefly composed of His enemies, who were hooting, scoffing at Him and blaspheming, as He passed along. There were, however, among them some few pious women, who, in their great compassion for Him, pressed through the yelling crowd, so as to be near Him. They paid no heed to the abusive words of the furious crowd, they did not fear the violence of the soldiers, but let nothing keep them back from showing their compassion for their suffering Saviour. According to a reliable tradition, Veronica, who handed to our Lord a cloth wherewith to wipe the sweat from His brow, was one of these weeping women. When she received back the cloth from Him, the Sacred Face of Jesus was wonderfully imprinted on it.

Carrying the Cross is both necessary and meritorious. It was to all men that our Lord said (Mat. 16, 24): "If any man will come after Me, let him deny Himself and take up his cross and follow Me." Whoever, therefore, wishes to be a true disciple of Jesus Christ must take up his cross daily and follow our Lord, or, in other words, he must patiently bear all labours, burdens, and sufferings. The story of Simon of Cyrene shows us what a blessed and meritorious thing it is to carry the cross after Jesus. At first he strove against the honour imposed on him, considering it to be an indignity. Soon, however, he was seized with compassion for the Divine Sufferer, and from that moment he carried the Cross with joy. By the labour of love which he performed for our Lord, he obtained the gift of faith, and was consecrated bishop by St. Peter.

The devotion of the Way of the Cross places before us for our devout contemplation the sufferings of our Lord divided into fourteen stations, from His condemnation to death to His being laid in the sepulchre. The Church recommends this devotion very much, and he who devoutly practises it in a state of grace may obtain the same indulgences that are granted to the faithful who visit in person the sacred places in Jerusalem. The fourteen stations are as follows: 1. Jesus is condemned to death by Pilate; 2. The Cross is laid on the shoulders of Jesus; 3. Jesus falls under His Cross the first time; 4. Jesus meets His Mother; 5. Simon of Cyrene is compelled to help Jesus to carry the Cross; 6. St. Veronica wipes the Face of Jesus with a cloth; 7. Christ falls under His Cross the second time; 8. The women of Jerusalem mourn for our Lord; 9. Jesus falls the third time under the weight of the Cross; 10. Jesus is stripped of His garments; 11. Jesus is nailed to the Cross; 12. Jesus dies upon the Cross; 13. Jesus is laid in the arms of His most afflicted Mother; 14. Jesus is laid in the tomb.

APPLICATION. Contemplate the Passion of our Lord Jesus Christ very often and very devoutly, that you, like the pious women, may be moved to tears. Do not, however, be content with a merely natural compassion for your Saviour so cruelly nailed to the Cross, but let it call forth within you a deep love for the Son of God, who offered up His sufferings for you. Let it awaken in your heart a great horror of sin, which brought all this suffering on your sinless Saviour. Weep for yourself and for your sins which caused our Lord's bitter Passion, and pray to your crucified God that His Precious Blood may not have been shed for you in vain. Never miss the opportunity of doing the Stations of the Cross, especially during Lent.

CHAPTER LXXVI.

THE SEVEN LAST WORDS ON THE CROSS AND THE DEATH OF OUR LORD.

[Mat. 27, 46. Mark 15, 34. Luke 23, 34—46. John 19, 26—30.]

1. The First word.

MANY of those who passed that way, and saw Jesus hanging on the Cross (Fig. 91, p. 694), blasphemed Him [1] and said: "Thou that destroyest the Temple of God, and in three days buildest it up again, save Thyself. If Thou be the Son of God [2], come down from the Cross." The chief priests also, and the scribes and the ancients mocked Him, saying: "He saved others [3], Himself He cannot save." But Jesus prayed [4]: *"Father, forgive them, for they know not [5] what they do"* (Luke).

---

[1] *Blasphemed Him.* Jesus was hanging on the Cross, with His Arms unnaturally extended, His Hands and Feet pierced, His Body covered with wounds and bruises, and His Face pale and streaming with Blood. A burning pain ran through all His limbs, each slightest movement caused Him unspeakable anguish, and each breath that He drew was a labour. His Precious Blood trickled slowly down to the ground, His very life flowing out drop by drop. It was a long, weary death-struggle, and our Blessed Lord retained His consciousness to the very moment when He drew His last breath. Truly it was a sight to move the very stones. "O all ye who pass by the way, attend and see if there be any sorrow like unto My sorrow!" (Lam. I, 12.) Those, however, who did pass by had no compassion, but blasphemed the crucified Son of God, scoffing at His Divinity, and wagging their heads as an expression of their scorn and unholy joy.

[2] *Son of God.* Thus assuming to Thyself divine power.

[3] *Saved others.* They knew, therefore, and could not deny, that Jesus had saved many in a wonderful way, but their only gratitude was scorn: "Himself He cannot save!" said they, and blasphemed Him on account of His good works. How this ingratitude and malicious raillery must have pained the Sacred Heart of Jesus, and increased His sufferings!

[4] *Prayed.* He neither threatened nor upbraided them, but prayed for them.

[5] *They know not.* How grievously they are sinning. Our Divine Saviour pleaded the cause of His tormentors with His heavenly Father, and excused their sin on the score of ignorance. They did not know that they were blaspheming against the Son of God, because they did not believe in Him. "With the bulk of the people it was the blindness of indifference, with the Pharisees and ancients it was the blindness of selfishness and pride which kept them from believing in

COMMENTARY.

Even as a dying father's last words are indelibly imprinted on his children's memory as a precious legacy, so ought we to observe and take to heart the words which our Lord spoke on the Cross. His first word thus uttered was one of intercession for His deadly enemies. Robbed of His liberty of action, and nailed to the Cross, it might have

Fig. 91.   Golgotha in the Church of the Holy Sepulchre.
(Phot. Bruno Hentschel, Leipzig.)

been thought that He was powerless to do anything more for His people. His Hands, which had distributed benefits, are made fast to the Cross; His Feet, which went about so untiringly in search of sinners, can move no more; His Head is incapable of further movement, being bowed

---

Jesus, and led them on step by step, until, literally, they did not know what they did. Their ignorance was, indeed, their own fault, but, such as it was, love used it as a plea for mercy" (Schegg). It was at any rate an excuse for the common people, that they were misguided by their authorized leaders.

down under His crown of thorns. But His bleeding Heart is till uncon-
quered, still beats with love for His tormentors; His Eyes, too, are free,
and are raised pleadingly to His Father; His Tongue is unfettered, and
with that He prays aloud for His enemies. In the midst of the turmoil
of mockery and blasphemy, Jesus prays that His murderers may be
forgiven. His Blood, innocently shed, cries to heaven for vengeance,
but His loving Heart cries out for pardon. He does not remember that
it is *through* His murderers that He is suffering, He only remembers that
He is suffering and dying *for* them, and prays that even for them His
Precious Blood may not be shed in vain. This first utterance of our Lord
on the Cross shows us, then, 1. that He is the Redeemer of all men, and
that He suffered and died as our Advocate and Mediator with the Father;
2. that Jesus is the Son of God, for even on the Cross He speaks as
a Son to His Father, and the consciousness of His divine dignity never
left Him even when He was brought most low. He suffered and died
as the Son of God. It shows us 3. the infinite love of Jesus for His
enemies. By forgiving His enemies and praying that they might be
forgiven, He proved Himself to be the Son of God, more than if He
had come down from the Cross; for love such as this had never been
seen on earth, and did not spring from earth but from heaven, from
the bosom of the Eternal Father. Our Blessed Lord thus teaches us
not only by His words, but also by His example, that we should "love
our enemies, do good to them that hate us, and pray for them that
persecute and calumniate us".

The fruit of our Lord's prayer was that the Jews were given a
long reprieve (till the year 70), in which interval many thousands were
converted to the Christian faith, and were saved. Only a few weeks
later, on the Feast of Pentecost, three thousand were baptized, among
whom were, no doubt, many of those who scoffed at Jesus on the Cross,
and for whom He had therefore especially prayed.

Blasphemy. The scoffers spoke contemptuously of the power of
Jesus, of His Divinity, and of His royal dignity as the Messias or king
of the Jews.

Unbelief. Now, would the chief priests and scribes have believed
if Jesus had come down alive from the Cross? No! They saw the
wonders which accompanied His death, and were convinced of the truth
of the most wonderful of all miracles, namely His Resurrection from the
dead, but in spite of all, they hardened their hearts and would not
believe.

2. *The Second Word.*

And one of the thieves who were crucified with Him, blasphemed Him like the others, saying: "If Thou be Christ, save

Thyself and us!" [1] But the other rebuked him, saying: "Neither dost thou fear God, seeing thou art under the same condemnation. We, indeed, justly [2], for we receive the due reward of our deeds; but this Man hath done no evil." Then he said to Jesus: "Lord [3], remember me when Thou shalt come into Thy kingdom!" Jesus replied: *"Amen, I say to thee, this day [4] thou shalt be with Me in paradise"* [5] (Luke).

COMMENTARY.

The Conversion of the penitent thief was a miracle of grace won by the merits of Jesus Christ. When this great criminal saw the patience and gentleness with which Jesus suffered, and how He repaid injuries with love, and when he heard Him address God as His Father, he opened his heart to grace and believed that Jesus was the Messias and the Son of God. With this *faith* there was awakened in him *hope* and confidence in the power of the Redeemer to pardon him, and he prayed Him to have mercy on him. He had committed very great crimes in his past life, and had done no penance for them; but now, though he was on the point of dying, he hoped to receive pardon and eternal life from Jesus. *Love* for Jesus also entered his heart, and impelled him to do what he could to protect Him from the insults of the other thief, whom he upbraided for his blasphemies. From a robber and murderer he suddenly became zealous for God's glory and the welfare of his companion's soul. From his love for Jesus proceeded a deep *contrition,* which he made known by a sincere *confession* of his great guilt, whereby he had deserved the punishment of death. He accepted his punishment and suffering willingly and resignedly, in *satisfaction* for his sins. He did not ask to be delivered from his temporal punishment, but acknowledged that his sufferings were no more than his due. His

---

[1] *Save Thyself and us.* This wretched man only thought of saving the life of his body, caring nothing for judgment or eternity. As Jesus did not use His power to save either Himself or His companions, this robber turned against Him, and joined in the blasphemies of the bystanders.

[2] *Justly.* "Companions in misery ought to comfort each other, not to torment each other. Add to this that you and I have deserved our punishment, but this Man is innocent. Do you not fear to scoff, in the very face of death, at this innocent Man?"

[3] *Lord.* The Jews addressed God alone by this Name. This thief (at the right hand of Jesus) believed therefore that our Blessed Lord was God, and would reign in His kingdom. His faithful and contrite prayer was heard, as the next words of Jesus show:

[4] *This day.* Therefore, immediately after his death.

[5] *In paradise.* With the souls of the just in Limbo.

conversion therefore was very real and perfect, and our Lord remitted all his sins, and promised him the immediate possession of paradise. The fervour of his penance shortened its duration.

The Divinity of our Lord. This wonderful conversion of the thief crucified at His right hand is a further proof of our Lord's Divinity. His enemies purposely crucified Him between two thieves, so as to increase the ignominy of His Death; but their intentional insult turned to His honour and glory, and Jesus, while still hanging on the Cross, drew the hearts of men to acknowledge Him as their Lord and King. "This thief", says St. Chrysostom, "saw our Saviour in torments, but prayed to Him as if He were in glory. He saw Him stretched on His Cross, and prayed to Him as if He were seated on His throne in heaven. He saw One condemned, and called Him Lord. He saw One crucified, and confessed Him to be a King. O wonderful conversion!" All in a moment Jesus turned the sinner, whose crimes had merited death, into a Saint! This conversion shows, indeed, the might of the divine grace of our Lord Jesus Christ! And how, moreover, could He have promised paradise to the penitent thief, had He not been God?

To convert sinners is a spiritual work of mercy.

He who corresponds with grace will be saved, while he who resists grace will be lost. This important truth is illustrated by the conduct of the two thieves, in the same way that it is illustrated by the conversion of St. Peter and the despair of Judas. The thief on the left hand received quite as much grace as did the other, for Jesus prayed for both, and shed His Precious Blood for both. He saw the patience and love of Jesus as well as the other, but he resisted grace, hardened his heart, and thus died in his sins, and was eternally lost. On the contrary, the thief on the right hand corresponded with grace and was thereby saved. He left the cross for paradise, whereas the other left it for hell.

3. The Third Word.

Near the Cross stood Mary, the Mother of Jesus, and John, His beloved disciple[1], and Mary Magdalen. Looking upon them with tender affection, He said to His Mother: *"Woman, behold thy son!"*[2] Then, addressing John, He said: *Behold thy Mother!"*[3] (John.)

---

[1] *Beloved disciple.* He was especially dear to Jesus on account of his virginal purity.

[2] *Thy son.* This man, John, shall from henceforth be to you as a son; for I am going to leave you, and depart from this world.

[3] *Thy Mother.* Mary will be to you a mother, and, as such, you shall honour and cherish her. John fulfilled with joy this last testament of his beloved Master, and "from that hour took her to his own".

COMMENTARY.

The Mother of sorrows. Words cannot describe what Mary suffered when she heard of the scourging and condemnation of her Divine Son; when she saw Him dragging the Cross along and heard the strokes of the hammer which were driving the nails through His Hands and Feet; and when, finally, she stood beneath the Cross, watching His Precious Blood trickling down to the ground, and heard the words of blasphemy which were hurled at Him. No mother's heart has ever suffered so much as did Mary's, for never did mother love her son with such a holy love as that with which Mary loved her Son, who was at the same time her God. To see His sufferings, and to be separated from Him, gave her unspeakable pain. Truly Simeon's prophecy was now fulfilled: "Thine own soul a sword shall pierce" (see chapter VII).

Mary's fortitude. In spite of the furious crowd, raging with hatred and envy, Mary fearlessly avowed herself to be the Mother of the Crucified One, and was eager to share His shame. She did not sink down, fainting and helpless, but "stood by the Cross", and with a perfect resignation offered up her Son to the heavenly Father. It was as if she said to God: "Take Him, even if my heart break! Only let the world be saved, and Thine honour restored!" Under the Cross Mary won the title of Queen of Martyrs.

The love for parents. Peter and John were the two Apostles singled out and most confided in by Jesus. To the former He committed the charge of His Church, and to the care of the latter He consigned her who was to Him the dearest on earth, His Mother. To the last moment of His life Jesus observed the fourth commandment, and left an example to all children how they are to love their parents even unto death, and do for them all they can.

Mary our Mother. In the person of John, who at the foot of the Cross represented the apostles and the whole Church, Jesus gave Mary to be the spiritual mother of all Christians, of the whole Church and of all its members. In a far higher sense than Eve she is the mother of all the living, for she is the mother of all those who by the Blood of Christ are born again to eternal life. We ought therefore to love and honour Mary and turn with confidence to her as our mother.

4. The Fourth, Fifth, Sixth, and Seventh Words.—The Death of Jesus, and the Wonders which accompanied His Death.

Now from the sixth hour [1] there was darkness [2] over the whole earth until the ninth hour [3], while Jesus was in His agony. That He might drink the chalice of sorrow even to the dregs, our Divine Lord was abandoned at that awful moment by His Eternal Father. This was the crownir.g point of His terrible agony; for He exclaimed: "Eli, Eli [4], lamma sabacthani", that is *"My God, My God, why hast Thou forsaken Me ?"* (Matthew, Mark.)

After a few moments' silence, He said: *"I thirst."* [5] (John.) Then one of the soldiers took a sponge, and steeping it in vinegar

---

[1] *The sixth hour.* i. e. from noon.

[2] *Darkness.* This was not a natural eclipse of the sun, for the Jewish Pasch was kept at the time of full moon, when a natural eclipse is an impossibility. This wonderful darkening of the sun lasted three hours. It began soon after our Lord was crucified, and only ended when He died. Darkness in the middle of the day is a very terrible thing. Men feel very uneasy, and even the wild beasts creep into their dens.*

[3] *The ninth hour.* Till three o'clock in the afternoon.

[4] *Eli, Eli.* Jesus had borne all His torments and insults without uttering a word. The impression might have been thereby given that though, as was the case with so many of the holy martyrs, He was outwardly tormented, He was inwardly full of joy and consolation. This opinion would be quite wrong. The terrible darkness that covered the whole earth was but a weak picture of the more terrible darkness and absence of all comfort which reigned in the Heart of Jesus. As His bodily sufferings increased, so did His Soul become more and more oppressed by the burden of sin which He had taken on Himself, and by the ingratitude of His people. His divine nature left it to His human nature to endure all this pain of soul and body, until, deprived of all help and consolation, His Soul sank into the feeling of being abandoned by God—the greatest of all sufferings for any soul which loves God. In order to make known this full measure of His interior and invisible pain, and with it the greatness of His love for us, He cried aloud to His heavenly Father: "My God, My God, why hast Thou forsaken Me!"

[5] *I thirst.* The loss of Blood suffered by Jesus, first on the Mount of Olives, then when He was scourged, and finally on the Cross, must have produced the most violent thirst. The first cry of a soldier lying wounded on the battle-field is, not to have his wounds dressed, but for some cooling drink. Moreover, the wounds of Jesus, being exposed to the open air, were inflamed, and caused a burning pain. He cried aloud: "I thirst", to show us that He was not spared even this suffering. Even as the sense of abandonment by God was the greatest pain to His Soul, so was this raging internal fire the climax of His corporal sufferings.

* The darkness was observed beyond the confines of Palestine. The pagan Phlegon mentions in his Annals that the greatest eclipse of the sun ever known occurred in the year of our Lord's Death; and that at the sixth hour of the day it became so dark that the stars could be seen in the heavens. The Christian writer, Tertullian, who lived in the second century of our era, referred the pagans to the archives of the Roman State, wherein this extraordinary darkness was described as an "event which had astonished the whole world". (*Schuster-Holzammer,* Hand-buch zur Bibl. Gesch.[7] II 549.)

and gall, put it on the end of a reed and presented it to His lips[1]. But when He had tasted the vinegar, He said: *"It is consummated!"*[2] (John.)   Then He cried out with a loud voice[3]: *"Father, into Thy Hands I commend My spirit!"* (Luke.)   And bowing down[4] His Sacred Head, He expired.

And behold[5] the veil[6] of the Temple was rent in two from the top even to the bottom, and the earth quaked, and the rocks[7] were rent.   And the graves[8] were opened, and many bodies of the Saints[9] that had slept arose.   Now the centurion and they that were with him, watching Jesus, were sore afraid[10], saying:

---

[1] *His lips.* That He might at least moisten His parched lips.

[2] *Consummated.* i. e. the work of Redemption.

[3] *A loud voice.* This loud cry was miraculous, as was everything which surrounded and accompanied the death of Jesus. We who are of the earth die speechless; but He who came to this earth from heaven died, crying with a loud voice, to show that He had triumphed over death. In a general way men lose their strength before they die, and the tongue usually refuses its service, for those who are dying can either not speak at all, or else very feebly. But Jesus cried out His last words with a loud, far-sounding voice. It was as if death did not dare to lay hold of the Author of life, until He Himself bade it come. This loud cry was something so surprising that the bystanders, and especially the centurion, were deeply struck by it. In fact, He who had the strength to cry out so loudly, had the strength to go on living, and when He died, it was only because He willed to die.

[4] *Bowing down.* When the soul leaves the body, the head sinks down on the breast, because the muscles have no more power to hold it up; but Jesus, before He died, voluntarily bowed His Head in token of obedience and resignation to His Father's will.

[5] *Behold.* This word implies that the following wonders occurred at the very moment when Jesus died.

[6] *The veil.* Which separated the Sanctuary from the Holy of Holies. The hand of God tore the veil in two, and the Holy of Holies, into which even the High Priest was only allowed to enter once a year, was exposed to the gaze of everyone.

[7] *The rocks.* Especially on Mount Calvary *.

[8] *The graves.* Which were hewn in the rocks.

[9] *The Saints.* The souls of the departed just rose and appeared to many at the time of the Resurrection of Christ.

[10] *Afraid.* All the marvels that accompanied our Lord's Death, and especially His loud cry as He gave up the ghost, made a deep impression on the Roman

---

* There exists to this day on Mount Calvary a deep cleft twenty feet broad, about which a Protestant explorer, after having examined, it writes thus: "I am convinced that this cleft was the result of no ordinary or natural earthquake, the shock of which might have rent the strata on which the mass of rock rests. Such a fissure would have shown the line of stratum, the rent would have occurred at the weakest part; but here, on the contrary, the rock is rent obliquely, and the fissure crosses the line of stratum in a wonderful and unnatural manner. It is evident that the rent is the effect of a miracle, such as neither nature nor art could produce. I thank God, therefore, who brought me here to behold this witness to His miraculous power, which so clearly reveals the Divinity of Jesus Christ." (*Schuster-Holzammer,* Handbuch zur Bibl. Gesch.[7] II 552).

"Indeed this was the Son of God." And all the multitude of them that were come together to that sight [1] returned to Jerusalem striking their breasts [2].

COMMENTARY.

The vicarious Sacrifice and Death of Jesus. The great work entrusted by the Eternal Father to His Son is consummated! That which the types foreshadowed, which the just longed for, and the prophets foretold, is accomplished! Jesus Christ was born in poverty and humility, lived a life of toil and hardship, poverty and persecution for thirty-three years, and at the end of it died a painful and disgraceful death. Those Eyes which beamed with gentleness and kindness are shut; that Mouth which spoke comfort to the afflicted and peace to all men is closed; those Hands which bestowed benefits all around are powerless; those Feet which left traces of blessings wherever they went are stiff; that Heart which beat with love for all men is cold and dead! The Good Shepherd has given His life for His sheep; the true Paschal Lamb has been slain, and has delivered us from the slavery of sin and of Satan, and opened to us the way into the Promised Land of heaven. He gave Himself over to a violent death in the very prime of His Manhood and in the height of health and strength, to redeem us from sin and eternal death, and to win for us grace and eternal life. The guiltless died for the guilty; and the Most Holy for the sinner. We have indeed been "bought with a great price" (1 Con. 6, 20).

The Divinity of our Lord was made manifest at His Death by His words and His deeds. a) Jesus, when dying, addressed God as His Father, and thus, with His last words, testified to His Divinity. b) Inanimate nature bore witness that the most terrible of crimes, even the murder of God, had taken place on Calvary. The sun hid itself so as not to witness the death agony of the "Sun of justice"; the earth heaved and the rocks rent themselves asunder, for He who laid the foundations of the earth and built the mountains was dying! Even the kingdom of the dead (by the opening of the graves) testified that the Lord of life had conquered death by His Death.

The abandonment by God was suffered by our Lord in satisfaction for our sins, whereby we have forsaken God and deserved to be eternally

---

centurion and soldiers, who were keeping watch over Him. The soldiers had seen many people die, but never had they witnessed such a Death as this. They confessed that Jesus was "a just man" (and therefore innocent) and "the Son of God", and they were "seized with fear", because they knew they had crucified an innocent Man, and hence they dreaded the punishment of God.

[1] *Sight.* The people who had flocked to see the Crucifixion of Jesus, and who had scoffed at Him.

[2] *Striking their breasts.* As a sign of compunction for having crucified and insulted Jesus.

separated from, and rejected by Him. By this suffering He merited precious graces for us, by means of which we can overcome temptations to faint-heartedness or despair.

The thirst of Jesus. The cry: "I thirst", revealed not only the torturing bodily thirst which our Blessed Lord was suffering, but also His burning desire for our salvation and our love. The desire for our salvation was the cause of all our Lord's pain. It is our business—not that of His executioners—to quench His burning thirst by appreciating and responding to His infinite love, and by caring for the salvation of our own souls.

The wonderful rending of the veil of the Temple showed 1. that Jesus by His Death had opened to all men the way into the real Holy of Holies, even heaven; 2. that the Temple of the Old Covenant, with its typical laws and sacrifices, had lost its meaning, and that from henceforth substance and fulfilment would take the place of shadows and types.

The rending of the rocks gives us an idea of the effect which the contemplation of our Lord's sufferings and death ought to produce on us. At the sight of our crucified Saviour, our hearts ought to "quake" with terror at the evil of sin, and "heave" with pain at the thought of His sufferings; and they ought to be "rent" with contrition, even if they be as hard as stone! They ought to open and cast off their dead works and sins by a good confession, and rise to a new life with Jesus Christ (St. Bernard).

Holy week. Good Friday is a day of mourning and penance, for on that day sin caused the death of the Incarnate Son of God. On the sixth day of Creation God made man; and on the sixth day of the week, God Incarnate redeemed fallen man.

A summary of the Passion of our Lord Jesus Christ. The sufferings of our Blessed Lord were caused by *men*, Jews, Gentiles and even His own apostles (Peter and Judas); by the *light* which revealed His nakedness; and by the *air* which inflamed His wounds. He suffered in His *honour*, by false accusations, insults, and unjust judgment; in His *liberty*, by being seized, bound and fastened with nails. His *Soul* suffered from fear, sadness and complete desolation, and from the scorn, mockery and ignominy that were heaped upon Him; His whole *Body* was tortured by the innumerable bruises and wounds of the scourging; His *Head* by the crown of thorns; His *Face* by the blows and spittle; His *Hands and Feet* by being pierced with nails; His *Knees* by being wounded and torn by His falls; and His *Neck* by the halter laid round it. His *Eyes* were wounded by the looks of His enemies who hated Him, as well as by the sight of His sorrowful Mother; His *Ears* were lacerated by the curses, cries of execration and blasphemy of His tormentors. Truly "from the sole of His Foot unto the top of His Head, there is no soundness therein" (Is. 1, 6). Added to all these sufferings we must remember this, that the Body of our Blessed Lord, conceived by the Holy Ghost in a wonderful and perfect manner, was much more sensitive to pain than our bodies; and that the more innocent, holy and noble a person is, the more intolerable to him is ingratitude, injustice, and malice. The sufferings of Jesus were, therefore, inconceivably great. All this ought to serve to fill us with a *horror* of sin, on account of which our dear and blessed Lord suffered so much, and impress us with the greatness of His love, which made Him endure all this for us!

To die a good death, we must do as our Lord Jesus did, i. e. resign ourselves entirely to the will of God, and commend our souls to the care of our heavenly Father, with a childlike love and confidence.

APPLICATION. Just think what it cost your Saviour to redeem you! Will you not, therefore, make some effort to save your own soul? Jesus accomplished His work; He gave His Blood and His Life to save you. Do your part now: watch and pray; avoid and resist sin.

Our Lord suffered all this for you individually, as much as if you were the only human being on earth. You can, therefore, say with St. Paul (Gal. 2, 20): "He (my Saviour) hath loved me (a sinful, ungrateful creature), and delivered Himself for me." But how have you hitherto loved Him? "If any man love not our Lord Jesus Christ", says St. Paul, let him be anathema" or accursed (1 Cor. 16, 22). And if you picture to yourself all that your Saviour has done and suffered for you, you will understand the meaning of the Apostle's words. In order that this curse may not fall on you, try (especially when you are looking at a crucifix) to awaken in your heart a deep love for your crucified Lord.

CHAPTER LXXVII.

JESUS IS LAID IN THE SEPULCHRE.

[Mat. 17, 57. Mark 15. 42. Luke 23, 50. John 19, 38.]

IN order that the bodies of those who were crucified might not remain on the Cross during the Sabbath[1], the soldiers came and broke[2] the legs of the two thieves, but coming to Jesus, they

---

[1] *The Sabbath.* This Sabbath was doubly holy, being a "great Sabbath-Day", as it came in the paschal week.

[2] *Broke.* If one who had been crucified had to be taken down from the cross before he was dead, his arms and legs were broken with a club, and then, out of so-called mercy, he was pierced through the heart with a lance.

found Him already dead. Hence there was no need to break His legs. Fearing, however, that some vestige of life might still remain in Him, one of the soldiers pierced His side [1] with a spear, and immediately blood and water [2] came forth.

There was among the secret disciples of Jesus a rich man named Joseph of Arimathea [3], a member of the council [4]. He went to Pilate and asked for the Body of Jesus, that he might bury it. Pilate granted his request. Then Joseph, together with Nicodemus [5], took down [6] the Sacred Body from the Cross, and wrapped it up, with costly aromatic spices, in a linen shroud.

It so happened that Joseph had a garden near the place where Jesus was crucified, and in the garden was a new sepulchre, hewn from the rock, wherein no one had yet been buried. In

---

[1] *Pierced His side.* The opening made by the lance was so wide and deep that Thomas was able to put his hand in it (see chapter LXXXI). The spear reached the Sacred Heart of Jesus and pierced it through, for the intention was to inflict an absolutely mortal wound, supposing that Jesus had been still alive. But there was no life left in our Crucified Lord, as was proved to the soldiers by the outpouring of blood and water, which was a clear sign of death. To the four sacred wounds which Jesus bore in His Hands and Feet, there was now added a fifth, in His Side. This was about four o'clock in the afternoon. The bodies of the two thieves were thrown into an empty pit near at hand, and the Sacred Body of our Lord would have been thrown in there likewise had not His disciples, in union with His holy Mother, provided another and more honourable burial for it.

[2] *Blood and water.* The water and the blood that flowed from the Side of Jesus are figures of two great Sacraments; the blood referring to the Holy Eucharist, and the water to Holy Baptism.

[3] *Arimathea.* A town to the north-west of Jerusalem (see Map).

[4] *The council.* Or the Sanhedrim. Scripture says that "he had not consented to their counsel and doings" against Jesus, "because he was a disciple of Jesus, but secretly, for fear of the Jews". Now, however, he came forward openly as a disciple of the Crucified One, and besought Pilate that he might take away the Body of Jesus.

[5] *Nicodemus.* "Who at the first came to Jesus by night" (see chapter XV). Nicodemus helped Joseph both to take down our Lord's Body from the Cross, and to bury it. It stands to reason that our Lord's holy Mother, as also St. John and Mary Magdalen were there.

[6] *Took down.* And laid Him in the arms and on the knee of His Mother. His Head rested on her breast as it used to do in the days of His infancy, no longer, however, in sleep, but in death. Mary contemplated the countless wounds of her beloved Son with unspeakable and silent grief. Magdalen fell on her knees, and for the second time (see chapter XXV) clung to, kissed, and wept over the Feet of her Lord. Then Joseph and Nicodemus took the Body from the Mother's arms, wrapped it in a new clean linen cloth, inside which they laid about a hundred pounds' weight of sweet smelling spices, myrrh and aloes. They postponed the real embalming of the Body to another day, for time failed them now, as the Sabbath began with the setting of the sun.

Fig. 92. Church of the Holy Sepulchre at Jerusalem. (Phot. Dr. Trenkler & Co., Leipzig.)

this they laid the Body of Jesus, and rolled a great stone to the door of the sepulchre (Fig. 92)[1].

<hr />

[1] *The sepulchre,* or cave in the rock, was about fifty paces from the spot of the Crucifixion. It was hewn out of the solid rock, and consisted of an outer cave,

On the following day, the chief priests[1] and the Pharisees went to Pilate and said: "Sir, we have remembered that that seducer said, while He was yet alive: 'After three days I will rise again.' Command, therefore, the sepulchre to be guarded until the third day, lest His disciples come and steal Him away, and say to the people: 'He is risen from the dead'." Pilate gave them guards[2] to watch the sepulchre, and they moreover sealed[3] the stone.

COMMENTARY.

The Soul of Jesus Christ, immediately after His Death, went to Limbo, to announce to the spirits of the just the glad tidings that the work of Redemption was accomplished, and that they would soon ascend with Him to heaven. It was for this reason that our Lord said to the penitent thief: "This day shalt thou be with Me in paradise." Our Lord's Divinity was inseparably joined to His Soul.

Our Paschal Lamb. Our Divine Saviour, crucified on the Jewish paschal feast, is the true Paschal Lamb; and therefore St. Paul says: "Christ, our Pasch, is sacrificed" (1 Cor. 5, 7). No bone of the typical lamb might be broken (Old Test. XXXIII), and this law was meant to typify that no bone would be broken of the true Paschal Lamb, our Redeemer. This, as you have read, came to pass.

The Sacred Heart of Jesus. God did not suffer the bones of His crucified Son to be broken; and in order that no one might attribute this fact to chance, He announced, fifteen hundred years before, by

---

through which a low opening led to the sepulchre itself, which was destined for the burial of only one person. Joseph and Nicodemus carried the Sacred Body to this sepulchre, Mary, John and Magdalen following. It was indeed a striking funeral procession, at which the tears that were shed were most holy. Only the Mother followed the bearers into the outer cave, and remained until the two disciples had laid her Son's Body in the grave. "The setting sun threw feeble, tremulous, blood-red rays on the silent group of men and women who sat on the ground outside the cave, and whose grief was unfathomable as the ocean" (Schegg). After the Sacred Body had been deposited in the grave, they rose and took the sorrowful Mother away from the terrible place.

[1] *The chief priests.* When they learnt how honourably Jesus had been buried, their suspicions were aroused. They did not believe that Jesus could really rise from the dead, but the badness of their own hearts made them suspect that the disciples would steal His Body.

[2] *Guards.* Of Roman soldiers. A guard usually consisted of sixteen men, divided into watches of four, each watch having to keep guard for three hours.

[3] *Sealed.* Our Lord's enemies could not content themselves with an ordinary guard. They could not trust the soldiers implicitly, and feared that they might be suborned by the disciples of Jesus, and allow these latter to steal the Body. To guard against this they sealed the stone which closed the entrance to the sepulchre, by stretching a cord across it, the two ends of which were secured by seals.

the type of the paschal lamb, that it would be so. Why, then, did God permit the Sacred Body of His Only-Begotten Son to be pierced with a lance, and His Sacred Heart to be laid open? The Crucifixion being such an all-important event to the whole world, each circumstance of it, however small, must have a meaning, and have been provided for in the plan of Redemption; so that the lance-thrust which transfixed the Sacred Heart must in the wisdom of God have been meant to serve some special end. The end was this: a) to confirm our faith; b) to kindle our love.

a) The wound inflicted by the lance was, by its nature, absolutely mortal, and left no possible room for doubt that our Lord really did die on the Cross, and that, consequently, His Resurrection was really and truly an awakening from death to life.

b) When the lance pierced the Heart of Jesus, Blood and Water flowed out. Our Blessed Saviour, therefore, shed His Heart's Blood for us, thereby giving us the greatest proof of His love. It was the love of the Sacred Heart of Jesus which impelled Him to suffer all the pain and shame that He endured, and to die for us on the Cross; so now, after His Body was completely covered with wounds, and had been tortured to death, He willed further to give His very Heart's Blood for us, and permitted it to be pierced, so that it might pour out its last drops of Blood for us. The Church speaks thus in her Office for the Feast of the Sacred Heart of Jesus: "For this was His Heart pierced, that we by means of this visible wound might perceive the invisible wound of His love. How could this love be better proved than by allowing His Heart to be wounded by the lance? Who could help loving this Heart thus wounded?" "Sacred Heart of Jesus, I implore grace to love Thee more and more."

The Blood and the Water which flowed from the opened Side of Jesus are figures of the holiest and the most indispensable of the Sacraments, namely the Most Holy Sacrament of the Altar, and of Baptism. These two Sacraments (and with these two greatest, the other five also) proceeded from the Sacred Heart of Jesus, for it was the love of His Sacred Heart which moved Him to institute these Sacraments for our salvation. In this sense, therefore, the Sacred Heart of Jesus is the source of all sacramental grace.

The sorrowful Mother of God. The grief of Mary at the Crucifixion of her Son was immeasurably great. She felt in her own heart all the torments which He suffered, without being able either to help or relieve Him. And now He was dead! Her beloved Son was taken from her, and even His Body belonged to His enemies. She could not tear herself away from the scene of His Death, but remained by the Cross to keep guard over His Body, and, if possible, to assist at its Burial. Full of anxious suspense as to what would be done with that Sacred Body, she implored the help of the heavenly Father. The executioners were already making their preparations to take It down from the Cross and cast It into the pit with the bodies of the two thieves, when Joseph of Arimathea came up, and showed to her Pilate's order that the Sacred Body should be given to him. And when he had taken down the beloved Body from the Cross, he gave It to the holy Mother, and laid It in her arms where It had so often rested in childhood. The faithful friends helped her with loving hands to wash the Body of the Most Holy, so disfigured, torn, and blood-stained; and now for the first time the sorrowful Mother was able to examine the number of His wounds and bruises, and to picture to herself the extent of the horrible torments which Jesus had endured. His wounds bled afresh in her own heart, and her grief was deep as the sea. But while we contemplate this sorrowful picture, let us not forget that sin alone is responsible for the torments of Jesus, and the sorrow of His Mother. Let us awaken within us a deep sense of contrition, and a heartfelt horror of our own sins; and let us make a firm resolution never again to commit a wilful sin!

The courage of Joseph of Arimathea is expressly mentioned in Scripture. "He went in boldly to Pilate and begged the Body of Jesus" (Mark 15, 43). He feared neither the hatred of the Scribes and Pharisees, nor the scorn and ridicule which, as a member of the Sanhedrim, he would draw on himself by taking down One Crucified from the Cross with his own hands, and by laying Him in his own sepulchre. Moreover he shewed Pilate, by his very petition, that he considered Jesus to have been unjustly put to death; and he openly confessed himself to be an adherent and disciple of the Crucified One.

The generosity of Nicodemus also deserves praise. He brought with him a hundred pounds' weight of very precious spices, to lay on the Body of our Lord. He considered nothing too precious for Jesus. Love made him generous.

The sins of our Lord's enemies. The chief priests and Pharisees sinned by falsely suspecting the disciples of intending to steal the Body of their Master. They also committed the sin of calumny by imparting their unfounded suspicions to Pilate, representing to him the disciples of Jesus as deceivers and thieves. They also sinned by blasphemy, in calling our Lord a seducer.

The devices to which the enemies of Jesus resorted to keep His Body in the grave, and to destroy all belief in Him, tended against their will to His glory, and manifested to the whole world that it was by His own power alone that Jesus came forth from the sealed and guarded grave. Thus, by God's wisdom, good can be made to come out of evil.

The poverty of Jesus was extreme. Neither in life nor in death had Jesus a place where to lay His Head; and after He died, His Body did not belong to those who loved Him, but to His executioners and tormentors; and was given away by them to the first asker as a thing of no value. Jesus renounced everything in the world, even His Body, made of the earth; He only kept for Himself the sins of the world, to make satisfaction for them. He had no grave of His own in which His Body might lie: it was buried in the grave of a stranger, by the charity of him who owned it.

Patience in suffering. Our Divine Saviour remained hanging on the Cross till men came to take Him down. Ought we, then, to consider it too much to remain hanging on the cross (of suffering) till it pleases God to take us down?

The opening of the Side of Jesus, sleeping the sleep of death on the Cross, was, according to the Fathers of the Church, a fulfilment of the type presented by the creation of the first woman from the side of the sleeping Adam. From the Side of Jesus Christ, the second Adam and our spiritual Father, there proceeded the Church, which is the second Eve, the true mother of the living.

Preparation for Holy Communion. Even as Joseph of Arimathea and Nicodemus wrapped the Sacred Body of Jesus in clean linen, and laid it in a tomb fragrant with sweet spices, so ought we to receive the Body of our Lord in Holy Communion with hearts cleansed from sin, and fragrant with devotion and the perfume of virtues.

The Holy Sepulchre in Jerusalem was visited by many pilgrims even in the first centuries of the Christian era. In the year 325, St. Helen, the mother of the Emperor Constantine the Great, discovered the True Cross, together with the Nails and Title. But as the crosses of the two thieves were found together with and in the same place as the Cross of Jesus, it was a matter of uncertainty which of the three crosses was that of our Lord. St. Macarius, Bishop of Jerusalem, caused a poor woman, afflicted with a mortal complaint, to touch the three crosses in turn. The touch of the first two had no effect on her; but as soon as she had touched the third, she arose perfectly cured. This miracle made it plain which was the true Cross of Jesus. Fragments of the Holy Cross have been distributed among the faithful in almost every Catholic country. Constantine built a large church on Calvary over the Holy Sepulchre.

APPLICATION. Would you not consider yourself very happy, if you could go to Jerusalem and visit the Church of the Holy Sepulchre, and pray on the two spots where your Saviour was crucified and buried? Your heart would glow with devotion and grateful love, and tears of emotion would flow from your eyes. But in the tabernacle on the altar your Divine Saviour is present with His divine and human natures, under the appearances of bread; and every morning at the holy Mass the Sacrifice on the Cross is renewed in an unbloody manner; and yet you behave so thoughtlessly and indevoutly in church, and are so unwilling to hear Mass!

CHAPTER LXXVIII.

JESUS RISES FROM THE DEAD.

[Mat. 28, 1. Mark 16, 1. Luke 24, 1. John 20, 1.]

EARLY in the morning of the third day[1], there was a great earthquake[2]. At the same moment Jesus rose and came forth from the tomb, glorious[3] and immortal. And an angel came down from heaven. His face shone[4] like lightning, and his garments were white as snow. So terrified were the guards at his appearance that they swooned away, and became as dead men. But the angel rolled[5] the stone from the door of the sepulchre and sat upon it.

As soon as the guards recovered from their terror, they ran[6] in great haste to the city to tell what they had seen.

Towards sunrise, Mary Magdalen, and Salome, and Mary Cleophas brought spices to the sepulchre, intending to embalm[7] the Body of Jesus. As they drew near the sepulchre they said one to another: "Who shall roll us back the stone from the door of the sepulchre?"

When they came to the place they found that the stone had already been rolled away. Surprised and alarmed, they entered in, and behold the Body of Jesus was not there! Great, then,

---

[1] *The third day.* Counting from the time of our Lord's Burial, and therefore, early on Sunday morning. Jesus lay in the grave for two nights and one day, that is, from the evening of Good Friday till the early morning of Easter Sunday.

[2] *Earthquake.* At the moment of the Resurrection there was a violent earthquake around the sepulchre. The cause of the earthquake is explained in the next sentence, "for", says Holy Scripture, "an angel descended from heaven". The earthquake, therefore, announced the arrival of God's messenger, and made the soldiers on guard observant of all that was done by the angel.

[3] *Glorious.* Conqueror of death and the grave!

[4] *Shone.* So that he could be recognised by anyone to be an angel— a messenger from heaven.

[5] *Rolled.* The angel rolled back the stone so that the soldiers on guard, and all who came to the sepulchre, might go inside, and convince themselves with their own eyes that the tomb was empty.

[6] *They ran.* They went "and told the chief priests all things that had been done" (Mat. 28, 11).

[7] *To embalm.* They wished to perform one last service of love for our Lord, which they had had to leave undone on Friday evening, as the Sabbath was just beginning. Their words: "Who shall roll us back the stone?" show us that they knew nothing about the guarding or sealing of the sepulchre.

was their sorrow and distress, for they knew not what had become of the Body of their Lord. But immediately two men in shining garments stood[1] before them. Seeing this, the women were afraid[2]. But one of the angels said to them: "Be not affrighted. You seek Jesus of Nazareth who was crucified. He is not here. He is risen. Go, tell His disciples and Peter."[3] The women went with joy, and told the disciples what they had seen and heard.

In the mean time the chief priests[4] consulted with the ancients, and then they gave the soldiers who had been at the sepulchre a great sum of money, and told them: "Say you[5] that His disciples came by night and stole Him when you were asleep." The soldiers took the money and did as they were told.

COMMENTARY.

How our Lord rose from the dead. On the third day after His Death our Lord came forth from the grave, alive and with a glorified Body, having risen from the dead by His own power. His Soul rejoined His Body, and His Body itself was glorified, so that He was able to go out from the closed sepulchre, and afterwards appear in the midst of the apostles, having passed through the closed doors (chapter LXXXI).

These prophecies were fulfilled by the Resurrection of our Lord Jesus Christ: 1. "Thou wilt not leave My soul in hell, nor wilt Thou give Thy Holy One to see corruption" (Ps. 15, 10, Old Test. LV); 2. "The Gentiles shall beseech Him, and His sepulchre shall be glorious" (Is. 11, 10, Old Test. LXXII); 3. "Destroy this temple, and in three days I will raise it up" (John 2, 19, New Test. XV); 4. "As Jonas was in the whale's belly three days and three nights, so shall the Son of man

---

[1] *Stood.* Standing, the one at the head, and the other at the foot of the empty tomb.

[2] *Afraid.* And "bowed their countenances to the ground", or looked down, being blinded by the brightness of the angels.

[3] *And Peter.* To Peter especially, because he was the chief of the apostles.

[4] *The chief priests.* Having been, as already stated, informed by the soldiers of all that had taken place, namely that there had been an earthquake, that an angel had appeared, that the tomb was empty, and that the angel had rolled back the stone.

[5] *Say you.* The consistent narrative of the soldiers placed the chief priests in a dilemma, out of which they could see no escape except by heavily bribing the soldiers to tell a lie. At the same time they agreed to stand surety for the safety of these men, saying: "If the Governor hear of this (of your pretended sleep while on guard) we will persuade him, and secure you (from punishment)." For to sleep while on guard was forbidden under pain of the severest penalty.

be in the heart of the earth three days and three nights" (Mat. 12, 40, New Test. XXVII); 5. "He shall be mocked and scourged, and crucified, and the third day He shall rise again" (Mat. 20, 19).

The great significance of the Resurrection. That Jesus Christ should rise from the dead by His own power, and call Himself back from death to life, is the greatest of all miracles, a very miracle of miracles. The Resurrection of our Lord Jesus Christ is therefore:

1. *the clearest proof of His Divinity,* for He thereby showed that He is; a) the absolute Lord of life and death, possessing, therefore, Divine Omnipotence; and b) that He is a true Teacher; for His distinct prophecy that He would rise from the dead on the third day came to pass, and proved the truth of his teaching; and if His teaching be true then must His oft repeated assertion that He was the Son of God be equally true. His own testimony to His Godhead is absolutely trustworthy, for not only did He die for this testimony, but He confirmed it by His glorious Resurrection, proving thereby that He is the Truth and the Life.

2. The Resurrection is to us the *proof and pledge of our redemption,* since it shows that His Passion and Death were pleasing to God (for otherwise they would not have been rewarded by the wonderful Resurrection), and that the satisfaction He offered has infinite value, being offered by the Incarnate Son of God. In this sense St. Paul writes (1 Cor. 15, 17. 20): "If Christ be not risen again, your faith is vain, for you are yet in your sins . . . but now Christ is risen from the dead, the first-fruits of them that sleep." The apostle's meaning is this: "If Christ had not overcome death by His Resurrection, He would not have overcome sin; for death is the punishment and consequence of sin; but the fact of His having overcome the consequence of sin, death, gives us the certitude that He has overcome the cause of death, sin."

3. The Resurrection of Jesus Christ is the *pledge of our own future resurrection,* "for by a man came death, and by a man the resurrection of the dead. And as in Adam all die, so also in Christ all shall be made alive" (1 Cor. 15, 21. 22). Compare with this passage the words: "I am the resurrection and the life: he that believeth in Me, although He be dead, shall live: and every one that liveth and believeth in Me shall not die for ever" (John 11, 25. 26), and "The hour cometh wherein all that are in the graves shall hear the voice of the Son of God; and they that have done good things shall come forth unto the resurrection of life; but they that have done evil unto the resurrection of judgment" (John 5, 28. 29). See the eleventh Article of the Creed.

The glorified Body. At His Resurrection our Lord's Sacred Body was transformed, or glorified. The glorious Body is 1. immortal and impassible, i. e. it can neither die nor suffer; 2. it is bright, or full of light; 3. it is subtle, i. e. it can pass through any substance like a spirit; and 4. it is agile, or swift as thought. The bodies of all the just shall one day be thus transformed, and made like unto our Lord's glorious Body. "He (Christ) will reform the body of our lowness, made like to the body of His glory" (Phil. 3, 21). The dead body of the just man is laid in the grave, as a grain of corn is laid in the earth, that it may spring up glorious. "It (the body) is sown in corruption, it shall rise in incorruption; it is sown in dishonour, it shall rise in glory; it is sown in weakness, it shall rise in power; it is sown a natural body, it shall rise a spiritual body" (1 Cor. 15, 42—44).

Service of the Angels. Even as, thirty-three years before, angels announced the Birth of our Lord, so rich in blessings to man, so now did they announce and bear testimony to His glorious Resurrection. They take most active part in all that concerns our salvation.

Mary, the Holy Mother of God, was the first to behold the risen Lord, for, according to the most ancient tradition, He appeared first to her, to console her, and to reward her for her faithful love and deep compassion.

Generosity. Magdalen and the other women bought costly spices, and got up before the break of day to visit the grave of Jesus and render Him their last service of love. As a reward, they were the first of all our Lord's followers to learn the glad tidings of the Resurrection, and to be charged with the honourable embassy of carrying the good news to the apostles.

Easter (the first Sunday after the first full moon in spring) is the greatest feast in the ecclesiastical year.

Paschal Communion (the soul's resurrection). "As Christ is risen from the dead, so may we also walk in newness of life" (Rom. 6, 4).

The terror of sinners. When the soldiers on guard saw the angel they trembled with fear, and fell to the ground, as though they were dead; and yet they were brave soldiers, who had never trembled on the field of battle! How will sinners tremble when the Lord of the heavenly hosts comes to judge the world.

One sin leads to another. The chief priests and scribes were not a little terrified when the soldiers came and told them of our Lord's Resurrection. The voice of their consciences cried to them: "He whom you have killed is, then, after all the Son of God! Do penance and believe in Him!" But they suppressed this inner voice and obeyed their wicked impulses. They hated Jesus, and resolved to prevent at any price the people from believing in Him; and therefore they bribed the soldiers to support them in their wicked lie, that the Body of Jesus had been stolen by His disciples.

The obduracy of His enemies was the reason why our Blessed Lord did not show Himself to them after His Resurrection. They would not believe in Him before, and they would not have believed in Him even had He appeared to them: their guilt would only have been increased.

The lies of the chief priests as to the Resurrection were very malicious, but they were also very stupid. If the watchers were asleep, how could they have seen the disciples stealing the Body? And if they had not seen it done, how could they bear witness to the fact? Sleeping witnesses are no witnesses. Besides this, the disciples were so crushed and cowed that they scarcely dared to show themselves at all; so how could they have had the courage to force their way into a sepulchre closely guarded by soldiers? Why did they not do so during the first night while the tomb was unguarded? And had the soldiers been really asleep, would they not have been awakened by the moving, in the silence of the night, of the heavy stone which closed the door of the Sepulchre? And why, finally, did not the chief priests and scribes arrest the disciples and put them on trial for the alleged violation of the grave and stealing of the Body? Why did they institute no inquiry as to where the Body had been taken?

APPLICATION. You have been spiritually raised from the dead by holy Baptism; therefore you ought to walk in the newness of a holy life, in order that you may some day rise up with a glorified body, and live for ever with Christ. "Let not, therefore, sin reign in your mortal body", says St. Paul, "so as to obey the lusts thereof. Neither yield ye your members as instruments of iniquity unto sin: but present yourselves to God as those that are alive from the dead, and your members as instruments of justice unto God" (Rom. 6, 12—13). Hold your body in honour, resist evil passions, and do not use the members of your body for sinful purposes, but use them for the practice of good works.

CHAPTER LXXIX.

JESUS APPEARS TO MARY MAGDALEN AND PETER.

[John 20, 1—18. Mat. 28, 1—15. Mark 16, 1—10. Luke 24, 1—12.]

NOW, Mary Magdalen, seeing that the stone was rolled away from the Sepulchre, and noticing that the Body was not there, hastened[1] back to Jerusalem, to tell the news to the

---

[1] *Hastened.* She left the other women at the Sepulchre. A great fear seized her as she looked into the tomb and saw that her Lord's Body was not there. Without waiting a moment she hastened to find Peter and John to tell them the terrible news: "They (His enemies) have taken away the Lord out of the Sepulchre, and we know not where they have laid Him!" It never seemed to occur to her that He had risen from the dead.

apostles. Whereupon Peter and John likewise hastened to the grave, and, entering in, saw the linen cloths in which the Body had been wrapped, each in its right place, the head-cloth where our Lord's Head had lain, and the foot-cloths where His Feet had been; but the Sacred Body itself had vanished. They could perceive that no one had stolen the Body, for had they done so, they would have taken It away wrapped in the cloths, or else they would have torn these off and cast them aside. It began to dawn upon them that their Lord had really risen from the dead. But where was He? Why did He not show Himself? And full of such thoughts they returned home.

Mary Magdalen, following the two apostles, returned herself to the grave. And while she stood there weeping, she saw the two angels. One of them said to her: Woman, why weepest thou?" Mary sorrowfully replied: "Because they have taken away my Lord, and I know not where they have laid Him."

When she had said this she turned back, and saw Jesus standing! but she knew not[1] that it was Jesus. He said to her: "Whom seekest thou?" She, thinking it was the gardener[2], replied: "Sir, if thou hast taken Him, tell me where thou hast laid Him, and I will take Him away." Jesus said to her: "Mary!"[3] Immediately recognising Him, she fell down at His Feet, and exclaimed: "Rabboni!" that is to say, "Master!" He said to her: "Do not touch Me[4], for I am not yet ascended to My Father, but go to My brethren, and say to them: I ascend to My Father, and to your Father, to My God and to your God." He then disappeared.

Meanwhile the other women had returned from the Sepulchre, and to them also our Lord appeared and gave the same message: "Go and tell My brethren[5], that they go into Galilee, there they shall see Me." On the same day also He appeared to Simon Peter (Luke 24, 34).

---

[1] *She knew not.* Just as, later in the day, the two disciples walking to Emmaus did not know Him (chapter LXXX).

[2] *Gardener.* In the employ of Joseph of Arimathea.

[3] *Mary.* This one word was said in a tone which pierced her heart, and opened her eyes to know Him. Truly, no other voice could equal the voice of the Incarnate Son of God for beauty and majesty.

[4] *Touch Me.* Mary had stretched out her hands to detain Him, lest He should leave her again.

[5] *Tell My brethren.* But when the women delivered the message, the disciples would not believe them, but thought they were under a delusion.

COMMENTARY.

Proofs of our Lord's Resurrection. To the proof mentioned in the last chapter the following may be added: 1. Peter and John convinced themselves by the evidence of their own senses that the tomb was empty, and that the Body of Jesus could not have been taken away by any person. 2. Our Lord appeared to Magdalen, and then to the other women, speaking with them, and foretelling His Ascension. These last two form the first and second apparitions of our Lord after His Resurrection that are mentioned in Holy Scripture.

The disciples of Jesus were by no means credulous. On the contrary they refused at first to believe in our Lord's Resurrection, in spite of His having appeared to the holy women.

The reward of true love. Magdalen's sorrow at the loss of the Sacred Body is very touching. She stood before the empty grave, dis- consolate, and weeping bitter tears. To her was given the great consolation of being the first to whom our Lord appeared. He had forgotten all her sins, and thought only of her true love and true sorrow. O how good and merciful is Jesus!

We are the brethren of Jesus and the Children of God. Our Blessed Lord called His disciples His "brethren", and said, moreover, to them: "I ascend to My Father and to your Father." God the Father, who is, by nature and from eternity, the Father of Jesus Christ, by the atoning death of His Son, becomes our Father as well. For the sake of His beloved Son, Jesus, He has admitted us to the grace of sonship and to be the brethren of, and "heirs with", Jesus.

APPLICATION. We can see by the case of Magdalen how precious in the sight of the Lord are tears of contrition and of the love of God. Do you feel this kind of love for Jesus? Does it cause you pain when you are prevented for any length of time from visiting Him in the church? And have you ever shed tears of contrition?

CHAPTER LXXX.

JESUS APPEARS TO TWO DISCIPLES ON THE WAY TO EMMAUS.

[Luke 24, 13—35. Mark 16, 12.]

IT also happened that in the course of the same day two of the disciples[1] went to Emmaus[2], and talked together of the

---

[1] *Disciples.* Not apostles. Most likely the home of one of them, at all events, was at Emmaus.

[2] *Emmaus* (Fig. 93). This little town lay about eight miles to the west of Jerusalem (see Map).

events[1] that had taken place in Jerusalem. Jesus suddenly joined them under the form of a stranger. He walked on with them, but they knew Him not[2]. He asked them what these events were of which they spoke, and why they appeared so sad.

Then one of them, whose name was Cleophas, answered: "Art Thou alone[3] a stranger in Jerusalem, and hast not known

Fig. 93. Emmaus. (Phot. Bonfils.)

the things that have been done there in these days?" Then Jesus asked: "What things?" They replied: Concerning Jesus of Nazareth, who was a Prophet[4], and concerning our chief priests

---

[1] *The events.* About our Lord's death, and about what Magdalen and the other women had that same day reported that they had seen.

[2] *Knew Him not.* He did not wish to make Himself known at once, so that the disciples might unrestrainedly speak out the thoughts of their hearts, and that He might instruct them. They thought that He was a pilgrim, returning home from the feast. Our Lord blinded the eyes of their body, so that He might gradually open the eyes of their soul.

[3] *Thou alone.* "Even the strangers and pilgrims in Jerusalem must have heard all about these things. Are You the only one who has heard nothing?" Their hearts were so entirely occupied with all that had taken place concerning Jesus, that they thought nobody could be thinking of anything else.

[4] *A Prophet.* "We hoped", they said, "that it was He that should have redeemed Israel; and now besides all this, to-day is the third day" &c. They had

and rulers who crucified Him. Now to-day it is the third day since these things were done. Yea, some women, also of our company, who have been at the sepulchre, say He is alive.

When Jesus had heard these words, He said to them: "O foolish and slow of heart to believe all[1] the things which the prophets have spoken! Ought not Christ to have suffered these things, and so enter into His glory?" Then, beginning with Moses and the prophets, He explained to them everything[2] in the Scriptures that was said in relation to Himself.

When they reached Emmaus, He made as though he would go farther, but they pressed Him to remain with them, as the day was far spent. He remained accordingly. But when they sat down to table, He took bread, and blessed, and broke[3], and gave it to them. And immediately their eyes[4] were opened, and they knew Him. But He vanished[5] from their sight. They then said to one another: "Was not our heart burning[6] within us whilst He was walking in the way?"

---

hoped that He would prove to be the Messias, but their hopes in the Messias, like those of the rest of their people, were principally earthly. The Pharisees explained the prophecies relating to the Messias in a very one-sided way. They ignored the passages which treated of the humiliations and sufferings of the Redeemer, giving exclusive prominence to those which described His power and majesty, and even these they interpreted in a sense entirely earthly. Therefore our Lord, in His answer, emphasized: "Should you not have believed all that the prophets have said? i. e. not only what they said about His glory, but also what they said about His humiliation?"

[1] *Believe all.* How imperfect is your understanding of the Scriptures! You have, indeed, the will to believe, and are not stiff-necked like the Pharisees, but you have much to do before you can rid yourselves of your false hopes about the Messias, and can believe all that has been written concerning Him.

[2] *Everything.* i. e. all the types which foreshadowed the Messias (such as Isaac, the brazen serpent, the paschal lamb &c.), and all the prophecies, which showed that Christ *ought* to have suffered what He did suffer, and enter into His glory through His sufferings.

[3] *And broke.* He did exactly as He had done at the Last Supper, and therefore gave them His own Body under the form of bread, to be the Food of their souls.

[4] *Their eyes.* Were opened as soon as they had received the Holy Eucharist.

[5] *Vanished.* For the object of His apparition was accomplished, as soon as they had recognised Him, and were convinced of the reality of His Resurrection.

[6] *Burning.* They had felt so wonderfully drawn to Him while He was speaking with them, that now they felt they ought, by their feelings, to have recognised who He was.

The same evening[1] they returned to Jerusalem, where they found the eleven gathered together, who exclaimed: "The Lord is risen indeed[2], and hath appeared to Simon." The two disciples now told the apostles how they also had seen the Lord, and how they had known Him in the breaking of bread.

COMMENTARY.

Further proofs of the Resurrection. The Lord had risen indeed, for He had appeared a) to Peter, and b) to the two disciples on the road to Emmaus, conversing with these two last for a considerable time, and instructing them in the Faith. These form the *third* and *fourth* apparitions of Jesus after His Resurrection. His sudden mode of disappearance proved that His Body was glorified, subtle and agile.

The apparition to Peter. Our Lord appeared to St. Peter before any of the other apostles 1. to distinguish him as the chosen head of His Church; 2. to repay him for the greater love he bore Jesus than the others; 3. to assure him of His forgiveness, and to show to the whole world how pleasing to Him were Peter's tears of contrition, and how willing He is to forgive repentant sinners.

The doctrine of the apostles is the doctrine of Jesus Christ. We see in this chapter how our Lord Himself instructed His apostles and disciples in the understanding of the Scriptures. All the explanations of the types, prophecies &c. which are to be found in the writings and discourses of the apostles are, therefore, to be regarded as the explanations of our Lord Himself.

Jesus Christ is the promised Redeemer, for in Him and through Him was fulfilled all that the prophets foretold about the Redeemer.

Faith must be entire. Our Lord rebuked the disciples because they, like the rest of the people who were misguided by the Pharisees, believed only in those prophecies which treated of the glory and power of the Messias, and ignored those which related to His humiliations, sufferings and death; and He expressly demanded of them that they should believe *all* that God had revealed through the prophets. So now God requires of us Catholics to believe, not only the truths which suit our inclinations, nor again only such truths as the Church has

---

[1] *The same evening.* Although it was already evening, and the way was long. They wished to lose no time in announcing to the apostles the good news that Jesus was really alive and had appeared to them.

[2] *Is risen indeed.* "It is no delusion, as we thought it was earlier in the day, when the women told us that He was risen. He has really risen and has appeared unto Simon (Peter)." Where our Lord appeared to Peter, and what He then said to him, the Gospel does not inform us.

defined in the past, but every truth which the Church teaches now and may teach in the future.

The human nature of Jesus Christ obtained its glorified state (its Resurrection, Ascension, and place at the right hand of the Father) by the merits of its humiliations and sufferings. "Ought not Christ to have suffered these things, and so enter into His glory?" asked our Lord of the two disciples. Through His sufferings, the human nature of Jesus Christ won a share in that glory which the Son of God had with the Father before the world began (chapter LXVIII). St. Paul says (Phil. 2, 8—11): "He humbled Himself, becoming obedient, even to the death of the Cross. For which cause, also, God hath exalted Him, and hath given Him a Name which is above all names, that in the Name of Jesus every knee should bow, of those that are in heaven, on earth, and under the earth. And that every tongue should confess that the Lord Jesus Christ is in the glory of God the Father." We, in the same manner, must win heaven by humility, patience and obedience. The way of the cross is the way to heaven.

Communion under one kind. Jesus gave His Body and Blood to the two disciples under the one form of bread, to be the Food and Nourishment of their souls.

Our hearts ought to burn within us each time we find ourselves in a church, in the Presence of our Lord in the Blessed Sacrament, and still more when we receive Him in Holy Communion.

The two disciples corresponded with grace, and therefore obtained further grace. When Jesus, whom they considered to be a stranger, asked them about what they were speaking together so earnestly, they confessed their belief that He whom the chief priests had given over to be crucified was no malefactor, but the promised Messias. And when our Lord reproached them for their want of faith, they accepted His reproof humbly. They thus made themselves worthy that our Lord should explain to them the types and prophecies, and so confirm their faith. And when, prompted partly by a kind solicitude for Him, and partly by a desire to profit further by His instructions, they invited the unknown stranger to eat and sleep at their house, our Lord gave them His Body to be the Food of their souls, and made Himself known to them "in the breaking of bread". Thus all their doubts were set at rest, their faith was confirmed, and an unspeakable joy filled their hearts. "God resisteth the proud, and giveth grace to the humble" (James 4, 6).

———————

APPLICATION. If our Lord were to ask you what you were talking about as you walked along with your companions, what could you answer? Perhaps you were talking boastfully, or untruthfully, or immodestly, or abusing and ridiculing others, even those set in authority over you. "Let no evil speech proceed from your mouth, but that which is good to the edification of faith, that it may administer grace to the hearers" (Eph. 4, 29).

CHAPTER LXXXI.

JESUS APPEARS TO THE ASSEMBLED APOSTLES, AND INSTITUTES THE SACRAMENT OF PENANCE.

[Luke 24, 36. Mark 16, 14. John 20, 19.]

WHILE the apostles and disciples were thus assembled together[1] in a room in Jerusalem, the doors of which were closed, Jesus came[2] and stood in their midst, saying to them: "Peace[3] be to you! It is I, fear not!" They trembled with fear, thinking it was a spirit[4]. But He said to them: "Why are you troubled? See My Hands and Feet! A spirit hath not flesh and bones as you see Me to have." Then He showed them His Hands, His Feet, and His Side[5]. But they still wondered[6], and were scarcely able to believe their senses, when Jesus asked: "Have ye here anything to eat?"[7] They gave Him broiled fish and some honeycomb. And when He had eaten in their presence, He took what remained, and gave it to them. "Then He opened their understanding that they might understand the Scriptures."[8]

---

[1] *Assembled together.* On the evening of the day of the Resurrection, when, as was related in the last chapter, the eleven apostles and the other disciples were assembled together. In this chapter further particulars are given, and we are told that they were in a room—probably the room which Jesus had sanctified by the institution of the Holy Eucharist.

[2] *Came.* Suddenly, and without passing through the door.

[3] *Peace.* This salutation, which Jesus repeated, had since the consummation of His Sacrifice on Calvary acquired an especial significance and force. By these words our Blessed Lord imparted to His disciples the fruits of His saving death, i. e. a complete reconciliation with God and a forgiveness of all their sins.

[4] *A spirit.* They believed that His Soul was visiting them with only the appearance of a body, instead of with His real Body.

[5] *His Side.* The wound in His Side.

[6] *Wondered.* For very joy, just as, of old, Jacob (Old Test. XXVI) could not believe the good news that his son Joseph was still alive. They could not realise the truth, so great was their joy, but went on saying to themselves: "Is it possible? Can it be true? Is it not a delusion?"

[7] *To eat.* In order to convince them that His Body was real and not merely an apparition. The glorified body *can* eat, though it *need not* eat, for it does not require earthly nourishment.

[8] *Scriptures.* i. e. what was written in the law of Moses, and in the Prophets, and in the Psalms concerning Him (Luke 24, 44. 45).

Again He said: "Peace be to you! As[1] the Father hath sent Me, I also send you." When He had said this He breathed upon them[2], saying: "Receive ye the Holy Ghost. Whose sins you shall forgive, they are forgiven them; and whose sins you shall retain, they are retained."[3]

Now it so happened that Thomas was not with the other apostles when Jesus appeared to them. Therefore they told Thomas afterwards that they had seen the Lord. But Thomas declared that he would not believe unless[4] he saw in His Hands and in His Feet the print of the nails.

Eight days after, the apostles were again assembled, Thomas being in their midst. And Jesus suddenly appeared to them, saying: "Peace be to you!" Then He told Thomas to put his finger in the print of the nails in His Hands and Feet, and to put his hand into His Side. Thomas did so, and exclaimed with fervour: "My Lord and my God!"[5] Jesus replied: "Because thou hast seen Me, Thomas, thou hast believed. Blessed[6] are they that have not seen, and have believed."

COMMENTARY.

Proof of the Resurrection of our Lord Jesus Christ. Jesus appeared in the midst of the assembled apostles, let Himself be touched by them,

---

[1] *As.* With the same power, and for the same end.

[2] *Breathed upon them.* As a sign that He imparted to them His own Spirit, i. e. the Holy Ghost, to enable them to forgive the sins of men on earth.

[3] *Retained.* i. e. are not forgiven by God. By these words our Lord actually imparted to His apostles the power of binding and loosing which He had previously (chapter XXXVI) promised that He would give them.

[4] *Unless.* Thomas had repeatedly proved his love for, and faithfulness to Jesus, but he could not believe that He had risen bodily from the dead. He thought the other apostles were under a delusion, so he demanded not only to see the wounds cf our Lord, but actually to touch them, before he would yield his faith.

[5] *My God.* Our Lord knew that Thomas had the will to believe, and therefore He appeared to him as he wished, so as to remove all doubts from the mind of this apostle who would have to bear testimony to His Resurrection before Jews and Gentiles. Thomas, as our Lord commanded him, put his finger into the marks of the wounds in His Hands and Feet, and his hand into the wound in His Side; and then all doubt vanished! Not only did he believe that our Lord was standing before him in His own risen Body, but the wonderful Resurrection made him recognise His Divine Omnipotence as he had never done before, and he sank on his knees before Jesus, and worshipped Him; thus atoning for his former scepticism by the most explicit act of faith.

[6] *Blessed.* Greater would have been his merit, if Thomas had believed the trustworthy testimony of the other apostles.

and ate with them. He imparted to His apostles various gifts and instructions for the good of His Church; gave them the power to forgive and retain sins; and opened their minds to understand the types and prophecies relating to the Messias.

The apostles as witnesses to the Resurrection. It was not without reason that our Lord sought to convince the apostles by the evidence of their senses that He had risen from the grave with the same Body which had died on the Cross. He did this because they were to testify before Jews and Gentiles to the fact of His Resurrection. Thus, Peter was able to say on the day of Pentecost, when speaking to ten thousand men: "This Jesus hath God raised again, whereof all we are witnesses!" and not one man could contradict him. St. John was able to write with equal truth: "That which was from the beginning, which we have heard, which we have seen with our eyes, which we have looked upon, and our hands have handled, of the Word of life (Jesus Christ, the Eternal Word, made Man) we declare unto you" (1 John 1, 1).

The mission of the apostles and their successors. Our Lord's words: "As the Father hath sent Me, so send I you", are full of very deep meaning. Even as God the Father had sent the Son into the world, so did God the Son send the apostles. Their mission therefore is divine, and the end for which they were sent forth is the same end as that for which Jesus Christ was sent. Now, what was the end for which our Lord was sent into the world? He Himself answers the question thus, in His discourse with Nicodemus: "God sent His Son into the world, that the world might be saved by Him." This was the mission which He transferred to the apostles. The work of Redemption was accomplished, and the office of the apostles was to apply the fruits of Redemption to men, in order that they might be saved. This was the office of the apostles, and this is the office of the Church. To her has our Lord bequeathed the treasures of His doctrine and of His merits, to administer them for Him, and it is only through her that we can receive a share in these treasures. For this reason our Lord said: "He that heareth you heareth Me, and he that despiseth you despiseth Me!" (Luke 10, 16.)

The holy Sacrament of Penance. Jesus Christ, by His Passion and Death, obtained for the world the forgiveness of sin. But this forgiveness has to be applied to each individual. Now, in order that individual men might actually receive this pardon, and with it the peace of God, our Lord gave to His apostles the power of remitting sins in His stead, and equally of retaining them should the sinner be unworthy of forgiveness. By doing this our Lord instituted the holy Sacrament of Penance, whereby all sins, without exception, can be remitted, provided the sinner be contrite. Our Lord left it to the apostles to decide whether the sinner was or was not worthy of absolution: but since they were not omniscient as He was, they could not decide unless the sinner

revealed or confessed his sins to them; and thus, while our Lord imposed on the apostles the duty of deciding as to the condition of the
sinner, and of acting as judges, He equally imposed on the faithful the
duty of revealing the condition of their souls, and of confessing their
own individual sins.

*The peace of God, and the consolation given by the holy Sacrament
of Penance.* When our Saviour was born into the world, the angels
sang: "Peace on earth to men of good will." And now that the work
of Redemption was accomplished, and He was on the point of returning
to heaven, our Lord imparted peace to His own; and, in order that
all might receive this peace of soul, He instituted the holy Sacrament
of Penance. By means of this Sacrament any poor, anxious sinner can
receive pardon and grace, and with these peace for his uneasy soul—that
peace of God which, according to St. Paul (Phil. 4, 7), "surpasseth all
understanding", and is the greatest treasure on earth. The Sacrament
of Penance was not instituted to torment us, but to console us. It is
the tribunal of God's mercy, and will enable us to stand one day before
the tribunal of His justice, and obtain everlasting peace. We cannot
possibly thank our loving Saviour sufficiently for having instituted this
holy Sacrament.

The Divinity of our Lord stands out prominently in the chapter
we have just read, for only God could impart the Holy Ghost, and
only God could give to mortal men the power of forgiving sins. It
would have been impossible for our Lord to have said: "Receive ye
the Holy Ghost, and whose sins you shall forgive they are forgiven",
had He not been God. The sixth apparition of our Lord (to Thomas)
is a further and incontestable proof both of our Lord's Resurrection
and of His Divinity. 1. He knew the thoughts of Thomas, and knew
that he had said: "Unless I see the marks of the nails. . . I will not
believe." He was, therefore, omniscient, as God alone can be. 2. When
Thomas worshipped Him and called Him his Lord and his God, Jesus
did not say: "What are you doing, Thomas? I am not God!" No, He
accepted the apostle's homage, and called those blessed who believed
without, however, requiring ocular evidence.

The faith of Thomas was not without merit. We might be inclined
to think that Thomas' faith was not a virtue and had no merit, because
he only believed after he had seen and touched the risen Saviour. But
we should be mistaken. It was only the Body and the wounds of our
Lord that Thomas could see; he could not see His Godhead. As, however, Thomas had the will to believe, the tokens of our Lord's marvellous
Resurrection enabled him to recognise His Divinity, and believe in it.
His faith, therefore, was a gift of God, and a true and meritorious
faith. The chief priests and scribes, even had they seen and touched
the risen Lord, would not have believed in Him, because the will to
believe was wanting to them.

The unbelief of Thomas was unreasonable, and was therefore rebuked by our Lord. He ought to have trusted the testimony of His fellow-apostles. Thomas, as an apostle, had himself to be an eye-witness of the Resurrection of Jesus Christ, and as an eye-witness can only give evidence of what he himself has seen, Jesus, the Good Shepherd, went after the wandering sheep, and appeared to Thomas to convince him of the reality of His Resurrection, so that he might declare it to all the world, as an eye-witness.

The unbelief of Thomas has, by the Providence of God, been rendered *very useful to us.* "By touching the Lord's wounds, the apostle has healed for ever the wounds of unbelief in our hearts; and thus the unbelief of Thomas is a greater help to belief than the faith of the other apostles" (St. Gregory the Great).

Sunday. It was on a Sunday that our Lord rose from the dead; and on the following Sunday the apostles and disciples were once more assembled together. We can see by this that from the very beginning the faithful kept this day holy, as being the day on which our Lord rose from the dead. Again, it was on a Sunday that the Holy Ghost came down on the apostles. Thus Christians have always kept holy the Sunday instead of the ancient Sabbath, it being the day on which God both completed and confirmed the work of Redemption—the new spiritual creation.

Our Lord retained the marks of His five wounds in His glorified Body, and ascended into heaven with them: 1. as a witness that He rose from the dead with the same Body which was crucified and laid in the grave; 2. as a sign of His victory over sin, hell, and death; 3. as a token of His everlasting office of High Priest and Mediator with the Father; for His wounds are ceaselessly interceding for us with the Father, and imploring Him to have mercy on us for the sake of our Lord who suffered for us; 4. as a proof of His infinite love for us. They are a consolation to the penitent sinner, but a terror to the impenitent, for Jesus will show them to these last at the Day of Judgment, and will say to them: "All this I suffered for you, but you would not love Me nor be converted!"

The five grains of incense are placed in the Paschal Candle in remembrance of the five wounds of the risen Saviour.

APPLICATION. Are you one of those ignorant Christians who regard the Sacrament of Penance as a burden rather than a boon? Did it ever occur to you how much it cost your Saviour to obtain the pardon of your sins? Thank Him, then, from the bottom of your heart for having instituted this Sacrament of mercy. Receive it with the most careful preparation, and never neglect to make a fervent thanksgiving after receiving it.

Throw yourself with Thomas at the Feet of Jesus, and worship Him as your Lord and your God. If Jesus is your God, His doctrine is divine truth, and His Church is a divine institution. Keep a firm hold on your holy Catholic Faith, and pray to God to increase your faith, and to make it more firm and living.

CHAPTER LXXXII.

JESUS APPEARS TO THE DISCIPLES BY THE SEA OF GALILEE, AND CONFERS UPON PETER THE PROMISED SUPREMACY.

[John 21, 1—17.]

AT the command[1] of their Lord, the apostles left[2] Jerusalem and went into Galilee.

"There were together Simon Peter and Thomas, who is called Didymus, and Nathanael, who was of Cana of Galilee, and the sons of Zebedee, and two others of his disciples. Simon Peter saith to them: 'I go a fishing.' They say to him: 'We also come with thee.' And they went forth and entered into the ship, and that night they caught nothing. When the morning was come Jesus stood on the shore: but the disciples knew not that it was Jesus. Jesus, therefore, said to them: "Children, have you any meat?" They answered Him: "No!" He saith to them: "Cast the net on the right side of the ship, and you shall find." They cast therefore; and now they were not able to draw it for the multitude of fish. Then John said to Peter: "It is the Lord!" When Peter heard this, he cast himself into the sea, and swam to the shore. But the other disciples came in the ship, dragging the net with the fishes. On the land they saw hot coals lying, and a fish laid thereon and bread[3]. Jesus saith: "Bring hither the fishes which you have now caught." Peter went up, and drew the net to land with one hundred and fifty-three great fishes in it, and yet the net was not broken. Jesus saith: "Come and dine"; and He giveth them first bread and then fish.

---

[1] *The command.* Conveyed to them by the pious women (chapter LXXVII).

[2] *Left.* The apostles' work was not to begin till after the Descent of the Holy Ghost; meanwhile they turned to their former occupation as fishermen.

[3] *Bread.* This meal had been miraculously prepared by our Lord, in the exercise of the same omnipotent will which had produced the wonderful draught of fishes.

And after they had eaten, our Lord said to Simon Peter: "Simon, son of John, lovest thou Me more[1] than these?" Peter answered: "Yea, Lord, Thou knowest[2] that I love Thee." Jesus said to him: "Feed My lambs!"[3] Then our Lord said to him again: "Simon, son of John, lovest thou Me?" Peter again replied: "Yea, Lord, Thou knowest that I love Thee." And Jesus spoke to him again: "Feed My lambs!" Then Jesus, as though to try His apostle still further, asked him a third time: "Simon, son of John, lovest thou Me?" Peter was grieved[4] because His Divine Master seemed to doubt his love, and he answered warmly and earnestly: "Lord, Thou knowest all things, Thou knowest that I love Thee!" Then our Lord said to him: "Feed My sheep." "Amen, amen, I say to thee, when thou wast younger thou didst gird thyself, and didst walk where thou wouldst; but when thou shalt be old thou shalt stretch forth thy hands[5] and another shall gird thee, and lead thee whither thou wouldst not."[6]

COMMENTARY.

The Divinity of Jesus Christ is proved by this, His *seventh* apparition after His Resurrection: 1. by the threefold miracle which He worked, namely the miraculous draught of fishes, the marvellous feast, and the unnatural strength of the net which remained unbroken in spite of the weight of the 153 large fishes; 2. by the prophecy of Peter's martyrdom, which was literally fulfilled by his crucifixion in the year 67. St. Peter also testified to our Lord's divinity when he exclaimed: "Lord, Thou knowest all things!" for He who knows all things, and can read the secrets of the heart, is omniscient, and must be God, Who alone is omniscient.

---

[1] *More.* Than James and John and the others.

[2] *Thou knowest.* Peter answered humbly and without comparing his love with that of the other apostles. Before his fall he volunteered the statement, without even waiting to be asked, that he would be more true and devoted to our Lord than any of the others (chapter LXVII). Now, however, he had grown humbler and more prudent, and, while confessing his love, was careful not to set himself above the other disciples.

[3] *My lambs.* Or young sheep. The lambs and the sheep together represent the whole flock of the Good Shepherd, i. e. the Church.

[4] *Grieved.* Because the question thrice repeated reminded him of his threefold denial of his Lord, and he feared that Jesus did not trust his faithfulness.

[5] *Hands.* On the cross.

[6] *Wouldst not.* Namely to a violent death, from which the weak nature of man shrinks.

The wonderful draught of fishes has a typical meaning. On the occasion when our Lord first called Peter to be an apostle, He worked a similar miracle (see chapter XIX). Now that He was about to confer on Peter the Chief Pastorship over His Church, He worked another miracle of the same kind, in order to bring home to him the work which he, as Chief Shepherd, would have to perform. The miracle worked before the Chief Pastorship was conferred on Peter is, therefore, full of typical and prophetical meaning. The lake signifies the world; the ship, the Church; the net, the doctrine of the Church. There was only one ship, even as there is only one Church of Christ. It was the ship of Peter; he governed it, and he drew the fish to land and brought them to our Lord. This signifies that Peter (with his successors, the Popes) is the visible head of the Church, and that, as such, he brings the faithful to our Lord in heaven (on the eternal shore). The number of the fishes caught shows that Peter (the Pope) and the apostles (the bishops and priests), working under his guidance, will gain many souls for Christ. The apostles had toiled the whole night and had caught nothing, till Jesus came and helped them in a wonderful way. This should serve as an indication to priests and teachers in the Church that none of their labours will produce any result, unless Jesus directs and blesses them. That the net, in spite of the number of fishes in it, was not broken, signifies that the Church of Peter will receive multitudes and nations into her fold and will be strong enough to contain and maintain them all in the unity of faith. The miraculous feast indicates that our Blessed Lord will comfort and strengthen His apostles in the midst of their labours, by His grace, and will some day refresh them at His heavenly banquet.

Peter's Pastoral Office. Gradually and slowly our Lord prepared St. Peter for his high office. When Jesus saw him first, He promised him a change of name. "And Jesus looking upon him, said: Thou art Simon, the Son of Jona, thou shalt be called Cephas, which is interpreted Peter" (John 1, 42). Then He placed him at the head of the twelve and preferred him on many occasions. And when Peter had made his solemn profession of faith in the Divinity of Christ, Jesus fulfilled His first promise, saying: "Thou art Peter", and added a further promise: "And on this rock I will build My Church, and to thee will I give the keys of the kingdom of heaven" etc. Again, at the Last Supper Jesus told him that He had prayed for him especially that his faith might not fail, in order that he might confirm his brethren. And now we have reached the climax. Our Lord commits to Peter the full and final charge of His whole flock, which comprises sheep and lambs, i. e. pastors or bishops and the ordinary faithful. Thus Peter was made the Vicar of Christ upon earth and Head of the Church.

Jesus Christ is our Lord. Jesus, speaking of the faithful, calls them "*My* lambs". We are His people; we belong to Him, He is our Lord, because He has bought us with His Precious Blood. "You are not your own", says St. Paul, (for) "you are bought with a great price" (1 Cor. 6, 19).

Proof of true love. Each time that Peter assured our Lord that he loved Him, Jesus replied: "Feed my lambs." Peter, therefore, was to prove his love for his Master by directing and teaching the faithful, i. e. the flock of Christ. In the same way parents, priests and teachers ought to prove their love for our Lord by leading those placed under their charge to the knowledge and imitation of our Lord, by instruction, discipline, and good example. He who loves the Good Shepherd must look after His lambs.

APPLICATION. Are you really grateful for being in the true Church of Christ? What sort of an answer could you give if our Lord asked you: "Lovest thou Me?" How do you show your love for Jesus? Are you fond of prayer? Do you faithfully fulfil the duties of your state in life, and your duty towards your parents, teachers &c.? Do you bear suffering with patience and resignation, for love of Jesus?

CHAPTER LXXXIII.

THE ASCENSION OF JESUS CHRIST.

[Mark 16, 19. Luke 24, 50—51. Acts 1, 1—12.]

JESUS having appeared to His apostles many times[1] and spoken[2] to them of the kingdom of God, that is to say, of all that was requisite for the foundation and government of His Church, appeared to them for the last time[3], on the fortieth day after His Resurrection. He commanded them to wait in Jerusalem until they had received the Holy Ghost[4], and then He added:

---

[1] *Many times.* Up to now we have heard of *seven* apparitions of our Lord after His Resurrection, five of which took place on the same day that He rose from the dead. After these seven we are told (Mat. 28, 16; 1 Cor. 15, 6) that He appeared to more than five hundred disciples at once. This was the *eighth* apparition of which we are told, and this was followed by the last, and *ninth* related in Scripture, the account of which is given in this chapter, and which was immediately followed by His Ascension. Probably, however, He appeared many more than nine times to His apostles and disciples, though these nine are the only apparitions related in Scripture.

[2] *Spoken.* These discourses about the institution, spread and government of the Church are not related in Holy Scripture.

[3] *The last time.* "As they were eating." He ate with them, and then commanded them to remain in Jerusalem.

[4] *The Holy Ghost.* After the Descent of the Holy Ghost they were to preach to the whole world—Jews, Samaritans and Gentiles, beginning with the Jews.

"All power is given[1] to Me[2] in heaven and on earth. As the Father hath sent Me, I also send you. Go ye, therefore[3], and teach all nations, baptizing them in the Name of the Father, and of the Son, and of the Holy Ghost, teaching them to observe all things whatsoever I have commanded you. And, behold, I am with you[4] all days, even to the consummation of the world. He that believeth[5] and is baptized, shall be saved; but he that believeth not, shall be condemned. And these signs shall follow them that believe. In My name they shall cast out devils; they shall speak with new tongues; they shall take up serpents; and if they shall drink any deadly thing, it shall not hurt them."

Then He took them out to Mount Olivet[6], raised up His Hands and blessed them. He began to ascend[7] upward, and soon a cloud hid Him from their sight (Fig. 94). Whilst they stood looking sorrowfully after Him, two angels appeared to them in shining white garments, saying: "Ye men of Galilee[8], why stand you looking up to heaven? This Jesus, who is taken up from you into heaven, shall so come[9], as you have seen Him going into heaven."

Hearing these words the apostles fell down and adored God, and returned to Jerusalem with joy[10], praising and blessing God.

Many other things which Jesus did are not related in the Gospel; for St. John thinks that if they were all written, the world itself would not be able to contain all the books. But

---

Jerusalem, which was the centre of God's kingdom under the Old Covenant, was to be the birthplace but not the centre of the Church of the New Covenant. The apostles, as we shall see further on, exactly followed this prescribed order in their preaching.

[1] *Given.* By God the Father.   [2] *To Me.* The Incarnate Son of God.

[3] *Therefore.* By virtue of My power which I have over the whole world, I give you the mission and the authority to teach the whole world.

[4] *I am with you.* You need not lose courage at the magnitude of the task, for behold I am with you.

[5] *Believeth.* Whatever you teach in My name.

[6] *Mount Olivet.* He willed to ascend into heaven from the same mount where His Passion had begun.

[7] *Ascend.* Rising slowly and with great majesty.

[8] *Of Galilee.* Thus did the angels address them, because all the apostles present were Galileans.

[9] *Come.* In the same visible and glorious way.

[10] *With joy.* They rejoiced, 1. on account of Jesus, because He was glorified and raised to heaven, and 2. on their own account, because both their faith and hope were confirmed by the Ascension of our Lord.

thus much[1] has been written, that we may believe that Jesus is the Son of God; and that, believing, we may have life[2] in His Name[3].

COMMENTARY.

The Ascension of our Lord Jesus Christ. Our Lord went up Body and Soul into heaven in the sight of His apostles, by His own power, to take possession of His glory, and to be our Advocate and Mediator in heaven with the Father. He ascended as Man, as Head of the

Fig. 94. Church on the place from which Christ ascended on Mount Olivet. (Phot. Bonfils.)

redeemed, and has prepared a dwelling in heaven for all those who follow in His steps (Sixth article of the Creed).

The Feast of our Lord's Ascension, forty days after Easter. On this day after the Gospel at the High Mass the Paschal Candle is put out, as a sign that He who had risen was no longer visible on earth.

---

[1] *Thus much.* The preceding chapters have been gathered from the four Gospels, according to St. Matthew, St. Mark, St. Luke, and St. John; whereas those that are to follow will be taken from the Acts of the Apostles. The words quoted from St. John form a very fitting conclusion to the Life of our Lord Jesus Christ on earth.

[2] *Life.* The life of grace here on earth, and eternal life hereafter.

[3] *In His Name.* i. e. by His merits.

The universal dominion of Jesus Christ. All power in heaven and earth is given to our Lord, not only as the only-begotten Son of God, but as Man, for He merited this dominion by His Passion and Death. As God made Man, he is the supreme King and Ruler of this world. He governs it invisibly from heaven, and on the Last Day will return visibly, and in glory, to judge the just and the wicked.

The Divinity of Jesus Christ is shown forth by the fact of His ascending into heaven by His own power, as all the apostles could testify; and is, moreover, proved 1. by Jesus Himself in His discourse prior to His Ascension; for how could He have promised the Holy Ghost, and His own protection to the apostles even to the end of the world; how could He have said: "All power is given to Me in heaven and earth", unless He had been God? 2. It is proved by the adoration paid to Him by the apostles. They would not have worshipped Jesus, had they not been convinced of His Divinity. 3. It is proved, especially, by the holy Evangelist St. John, who writes in so many words that "Jesus is the Son of God".

The threefold office of the apostles and their successors. When He left this world, our Lord handed over to His apostles His threefold office. 1. The office, or the right and duty of teaching the Christian faith ("Go ye and teach all nations"). 2. The priestly office, or the right and duty of sanctifying the souls of men by the Christian Sacraments ("baptizing them in the Name of the Father and of the Son and of the Holy Ghost"). 3. The pastoral office, or the right and duty of guiding and maintaining the faithful in the observance of the commandments ("Teach them to observe all things whatsoever I have commanded you"). Our Lord did not commit this threefold office to the apostles only, but also to their successors, as is to be plainly inferred from the words: "Go and teach all nations", and: " I am with you all days even unto the end of the world." The eleven apostles could not themselves have taught all nations, nor were they to live till the end of the world; but their office was to continue after their death, in their successors, the Bishops of the Catholic Church. Hence the *prophetical, priestly* and *royal* offices of Christ must continue in the Church till the end of time. This ruling power given to the Church is divine and not subject to any civil or earthly power. Within her own sphere the Church is supreme and independent.

The Church of Christ must necessarily be Catholic or universal. Our Lord said that "all nations" were to be received into the Church by Baptism, and instructed in the Christian life by her. The Church of Christ must therefore be, firstly, universal in *place :* she must be not a national Church, but a universal Church. Secondly, seeing that she was to be protected by her Divine Founder, for "all days even to the end of the world", she must be equally Catholic as to *duration.* Being upheld by our Lord Jesus Christ in all ages, there is no time when she could fall away or decay, for, if she did, our Lord would not be fulfilling His promise to be always with her. All Protestant sects are based upon the false supposition that the Church of Christ has fallen into error and corruption. But according to Christ's clear promise this can never be. The Church can neither teach nor believe false and corrupt doctrine. The infallible authority of the Church is a fundamental Christian dogma and inseparably connected with the Divinity of Christ.

The necessity of faith. "He that believeth (what the apostles and their successors teach) shall be saved, but he that believeth not shall be condemned" (Mark 16, 16).

The necessity of Baptism. "He that believeth and is baptized shall be saved" (Mark 16, 16).

Faith alone will not save, for we must also observe the commandments. Our Lord, therefore, says: "Teach them to observe all things that I have commanded you."

The Most Holy Trinity. The Mystery of the Blessed Trinity is most expressly laid down in the words with which holy Baptism is to be administered. Although three Divine Persons, Father, Son and Holy Ghost, are enumerated, yet it is in their *Name,* not in their *Names* that Baptism is to be administered. The word 'Name' being used in the singular is intended to signify that the Being to whom it applies is One God, though in Three Persons.

The prophecies were fulfilled by our Lord's Ascension into heaven: 1. That of David: "The Lord said to My Lord: Sit Thou at My right hand till I make Thy enemies Thy footstool" (Ps. 109, 1). 2. Those of our Lord Himself: "Then you shall see the Son of Man ascend to where He was before" (John 6, 63; chapter XXXIV), and: "Hereafter you shall see the Son of Man sitting at the right hand of the power of God, and coming in the clouds of heaven" (Mat. 26, 64; chapter LXXI).

Holy Scripture is not the only source of faith. St. John says in so many words, that all that Jesus did is not contained in the Gospels: and still less do they contain all that He said. During the forty days that passed between His Resurrection and His Ascension our Lord spoke to His apostles about the kingdom of God, but only a small fraction of what He said on these occasions is contained in Holy Scripture. This shows us that the entire Divine revelation through Jesus Christ is only partially contained in the Bible.

APPLICATION. Heaven is our eternal home. There is a place prepared for you there, where you can be for ever with God. Whenever you say: "Our Father who art in heaven", long ardently for eternal happiness, and make a firm resolution to perform all your duties on earth faithfully, and to avoid sin, so that you may be worthy of heaven.

SECOND SECTION.

THE ACTS OF THE APOSTLES.

CHAPTER LXXXIV.

THE ELECTION OF MATTHIAS.—DESCENT OF THE HOLY
GHOST.

[Acts 1, 12 to 2, 47.]

RETURNING from Mount Olivet on the day of the Ascension, the apostles repaired to the upper chamber, or supper-room, of the house in which they usually assembled. There they remained in prayer[1] for ten days, with Mary, the Mother of Jesus, several other holy women, and a great number of disciples, the number of persons being about one hundred and twenty.

During those ten days[2] of prayer, Peter, rising up, said it was necessary, according to the scripture which the Holy Ghost spoke before by the mouth of David concerning Judas (Ps. 68, 26 and 108, 8), that a new apostle should be chosen in his stead, one of those "who had companied with us all the time[3] that the Lord Jesus came in and went out among us from the baptism of John until the day wherein He was taken up from us." Two[4] of the disciples were then proposed: Joseph, called Barsabas,

---

[1] *In prayer*. All exciting in their hearts the same desire for the Holy Ghost, and the same confidence that the promise of His Coming would be fulfilled.

[2] *Ten days*. Between our Lord's Ascension and the Day of Pentecost.

[3] *All the time*. In other words, one who had known our Lord and been with Him during His public life, for he had to be, equally with the other apostles, a witness to the words and actions of our Lord, and especially to His Resurrection.

[4] *Two*. Who, in the opinion of all present, had the necessary qualifications for the apostleship. However, as the call to be an apostle could only proceed from our Lord Himself, they prayed to Him to decide by lot and show them which of the two He had chosen.

and Matthias. After praying [1] for light from above, they cast lots, and the lot fell upon Matthias, who was numbered with the eleven apostles, and filled the place left vacant by the lamentable fall of Judas.

Ten days after the Ascension, the Jews celebrated the feast of Pentecost [2].

On that day the apostles were assembled [3] together, persevering in prayer, when suddenly there came a sound from heaven as of a mighty rushing wind, and it filled the whole house where they were sitting. There appeared to them parted tongues, as it were, of fire [4], and it sat upon every one of them. And they were filled [5] with the Holy Ghost, and began to speak in divers tongues [6].

Now there were at that time in Jerusalem Jews from every nation under heaven, who had come for the celebration of the feast. These, having heard of what had taken place, hastened with a great number of the inhabitants of Jerusalem to the house wherein the apostles were assembled. Each one was astonished [7] to hear them speak in his own tongue. But some of the people mocked them, saying that they were full of new wine.

Then Peter, going forth from the house with the other apostles, lifted up his voice, and spoke: "These are not drunk, as you suppose, but this is that which was spoken by the prophet Joel: 'In the last days I will pour out My Spirit upon all flesh, and your sons and your daughters shall prophesy.' Ye men of Israel,

---

[1] *After praying.* "Thou, Lord", they prayed, "who knowest the hearts of all men, show whether of these two Thou hast chosen!" The "Lord", to whom they thus prayed, was our Blessed Lord, Jesus Christ, of whom St. Peter had just been speaking.

[2] *Pentecost.* About this feast see Old Test. XXXIX. This year it fell on the first day of the week, Sunday.

[3] *Assembled.* In the same upper chamber which has been mentioned before.

[4] *Of fire.* These cloven tongues had the appearance of fire, but it was no natural fire.

[5] *Filled.* They now received the Holy Ghost with all the fulness of His grace and gifts: before this they had only received single and isolated gifts, such, for example, as the priesthood and the power to forgive sins.

[6] *In divers tongues.* Up to that moment each had been able to speak only his own native language. The Holy Ghost imparted to them the marvellous gift of being able to speak various languages which they had never learnt.

[7] *Astonished.* "What meaneth this?" they said one to another. They felt that what was occurring before their eyes could not be anything natural.

hear these words: Jesus of Nazareth, a man approved of God among you by miracles, and wonders, and signs, which God did by Him in the midst of you, as you also know; Him you have crucified and put to death by the hands of wicked men. God hath raised Him up, whereof we all are witnesses. Being exalted therefore, by the right hand of God, and having received of the Father the promise of the Holy Ghost, He hath poured forth this which you see and hear[1]. Therefore, let all the house of Israel know most assuredly[2] that God hath made both Lord and Christ, this same Jesus, whom you have crucified."

The words of Peter had a divine power that penetrated all hearts, and many, repenting of their sins, asked Peter and the other apostles what they ought to do[3]. Peter said to them: "Do penance, and be baptized[4], every one of you, in the Name of Jesus Christ, for the remission of your sins, and you shall receive the gift of the Holy Ghost." They received his words with joy, and, on that day, about three thousand persons were baptized.

COMMENTARY.

The Divinity of Jesus Christ. Not only did Peter call Him 'Lord' (i. e. God), but they supplicated Him as One who is omniscient, and knows the hearts of all men. This shows us how living and real was the belief of the first Christians in our Lord's Divinity.

Mary is especially mentioned as being one of those who were assembled together in expectation of the coming of the Holy Ghost. It was but natural that the early Christians should hold the Mother of Jesus in the highest honour.

The Primacy of Peter. We can see that St. Peter, immediately after our Lord's Ascension, entered on his office of visible head of the

---

[1] *Which you see and hear.* You can recognise the action of the Holy Ghost by its effects, by our courage and inspiration, and by the miracle of the gift of tongues.

[2] *Most assuredly.* For it is proved by His Resurrection and Ascension, and by the Descent of the Holy Ghost, that Jesus is "the Christ", i. e. the promised Messias, and "the Lord", i. e. the Son of God, of whom David prophesied: "The Lord said to my Lord: sit Thou at My right hand &c."

[3] *They ought to do.* They were confounded and horrified by the thought that they had killed the Messias, sent by God. They now addressed the apostles, whom they had despised, as "brethren", anxiously asking them: "What shall we do, men and brethren?" i. e. what shall we do to make amends for the evil we have done, and to avert God's judgments from us?

[4] *Be baptized.* Not with John's baptism, but with the baptism instituted by Christ. By this baptism you shall receive forgiveness of your sins, and the indwelling of the Holy Ghost.

Church. He declared in the presence of a hundred and twenty of the faithful that another apostle must be chosen in the place of Judas, and they did exactly as he told them, without seeing any pretension or arrogance in his thus putting himself forward; for they, one and all, knew that our Blessed Lord had appointed him to be the chief pastor of His Church.

Let us see what *virtues* were exercised by the apostles and disciples in the history of the election of Matthias, and in their conduct, while waiting for the coming of the Holy Ghost.

1. *Obedience,* for they obeyed our Lord's command to remain in Jerusalem, until He should send the Holy Ghost.

2. *Hope* (and confidence), for they trusted the word of the Lord that He would send the Holy Ghost, although He had not told them at what time He would come.

3. *Piety,* for they prayed earnestly and perseveringly that the Holy Ghost might come.

4. *Brotherly unity,* for they kept together in unity of spirit.

The number (twelve) of the apostles (see also chapter XXXI). So significant was this number that the gap made by the apostasy of Judas had to be filled up before the Holy Ghost descended, and before the preaching of the apostles began.

Preparation for the Sacrament of Confirmation. The earnest preparation made by the disciples for the Descent of the Holy Ghost ought to serve as an example of how we ought to prepare ourselves for receiving the Sacrament of Confirmation.

The Holy Ghost was sent to the Church to maintain her in her threefold office, doctrinal, priestly and pastoral, and to impart to individual souls the graces won by Jesus Christ. He preserves the Church free from all error in the exercise of her doctrinal office, and blesses the preaching of the word of God, making it penetrate the hearts of men for the improvement of their lives. He works in the priestly office of the Church by bestowing grace through the holy Sacraments, and by thus enlightening, sanctifying and strengthening individual souls. He protects and governs her in her pastoral office by giving to her a supernatural vitality, so that the gates of hell cannot prevail against her.

The outward signs of inward graces. The effects of the Holy Ghost were signified by the outward signs which accompanied His coming. Fire, which enlightens, warms and purifies, and under the form of which He descended, was intended to show that the Holy Ghost inwardly illuminated the apostles (and through them the faithful) with the light of faith, inflamed their hearts with love, and purified them from sin. The gift of tongues proved that the Holy Ghost could make the uneducated apostles eloquent in speaking to the hearts of men. In the holy Sacraments also He makes use of outward and visible signs, by which He imparts inward and invisible graces and gifts.

The wonderful workings of the Holy Ghost were made manifest: 1. in the apostles themselves, and 2. in the people.

1. The uneducated fishermen of Galilee, who had so often misunderstood our Lord, were suddenly illuminated, so that they were able to understand the great truths of the Christian Faith, and to expound the prophecies contained in Scripture. They, who had been so timid, were all at once filled with courage and holy zeal, and boldly confessed their faith in Jesus Christ, before thousands of people. Peter, who but a short time ago was afraid to confess his faith before a maid-servant, now openly preached faith in Him who was crucified and who had risen from the dead.

2. The very people who seven weeks before had cried out: "Crucify Him! Crucify Him!" were now impelled to believe in our Lord and repent of their share in His crucifixion, and were received by holy Baptism into His Church. So wonderfully can the Holy Ghost transform the hearts of men!

The effects and necessity of grace. How came it that the words of Peter made such an impression on his hearers? How came it that the Jews, who but a short time before cried out in their frenzy against our Blessed Lord: "Crucify Him! Crucify Him!" were suddenly converted and were ready meekly to do whatever the apostles prescribed? The reason was that the Holy Ghost, with whom Peter was filled, enlightened with His grace the understanding of those who heard his words, and moved their hearts and wills to believe and to do what was right. He enlightened the understanding of the unbelieving Jews by His grace, to enable them to believe in the Godhead of Jesus Christ, by means of His Resurrection and Ascension, by the Descent of the Holy Ghost and the gift of tongues. He moved their hearts to repent of their wickedness towards Jesus, for Scripture says: "They had compunction in their heart"; and He moved their wills to humbly ask the apostles: "Brethren, what shall we do?" This question of theirs proved that they *desired* to do what was right, and they proved their good *intention* by doing penance and being baptized. If the Holy Ghost had not enlightened and moved the hearts of the hearers, St. Peter's discourse would have borne no fruit.

Resistance to grace. All the assembled Jews were witnesses of the gift of tongues, all heard the mighty, rushing sound, and all heard St. Peter's inspired discourse; but not all were baptized, some remaining obstinate and satirical. These men resisted grace, because they hated Jesus and were resolved not to believe in Him.

Pentecost (fifty days after Easter). In the liturgy of the Church the season of Pentecost lasts till the end of the ecclesiastical year, in the same way that the workings of the Holy Ghost abide in the Church, and will abide till the end of time.

The meaning of Pentecost. The Jewish Pentecost, as explained in Old Test. XXXVI, was a type of the Christian Pentecost. The object of the Jewish feast was to remind the people of the giving and writing on stone of the Ten Commandments upon Mount Sinai. The Christian Whit-Sunday, or Pentecost, is to remind us that God the Holy Ghost came down on the Church, and inscribed the law of love on the hearts of the faithful. The Jewish Pentecost was also the harvest festival, on which the first-fruits of the harvest were offered to God. The Christian Pentecost is also a harvest festival, though in a much higher sense, for on that day the apostles, as their Lord had commanded them (chapter LXXXI), came forward openly to teach and to baptize, and by the assistance of the Holy Ghost reaped a rich harvest, converting and baptizing three thousand on that one day. Whit-Sunday may well be called the birthday of God's holy Church, because 1. it was upon that day that the Holy Ghost came down on the Church to remain with her and assist her in her threefold office till the end of time, and 2. because on that day the Church was first openly made manifest, and won several thousands of souls for Christ. The seed of corn, watered by the Holy Ghost, sprang up, and began to spread itself.

What aspect did the Church bear in those days? She appeared as a visible body of believers, gifted and governed by the Holy Ghost, with Peter as her visible head. And for what end was she made manifest among men? To bring them salvation by the preaching of the faith and the administration of the Sacraments.

The Primacy. On Whit-Sunday Peter came forward as the supreme head of the Church. As chief pastor, he was the first to preach and to bring the sheep into the fold.

Proofs of the Divinity of Jesus Christ were drawn by Peter 1. from His Resurrection, when he said: "That God hath raised Jesus from the dead, we all (apostles and disciples) are witnesses", and not one of the unbelieving Jews ventured to contradict this assertion, or to deny our Lord's Resurrection; 2. from His Ascension into heaven, where He sitteth at the right hand of God; and 3. by His sending down the Holy Ghost; for were Jesus not God, He could not have sent forth the Holy Spirit.

All sins are remitted by Baptism. St. Peter declares this in his exhortation to his hearers: "Be baptized for the remission of your sins."

The following prophecies were fulfilled by the outpouring of the Holy Ghost: 1. That of Joel 2, 28; 2. that of Jeremias: "I will give My law in their bowels, and I will write it in their heart. I will forgive their iniquity, and I will remember their sin no more" (Jer. 31, 33. 34; Old Test. LXXV); 3. that of Ezechiel: "I will put My Spirit in you, and you shall know that I am the Lord" (Ezech. 37, 13. 14; Old Test. LXXV); 4. that of our Lord Himself: "I will ask the Father, and He shall give you another Paraclete, that He may abide with you for ever, the Spirit of Truth" (John 14, 16. 17; New Test. LXVI).

The gift of tongues bestowed by the Holy Ghost on the Apostles was a great marvel. Why was this wonderful gift bestowed? 1. To enable the apostles to proclaim the Gospel to all nations and in all languages. 2. To signify that, by the preaching of the Gospel, all men of all nations and languages were to be bound together in one family and one universal Catholic Church. (For the contrast between the gift of tongues at Pentecost, and the confusion of tongues of Babel see Old Test. VIII.) The gift of tongues was often bestowed during the first Christian centuries, so as to facilitate the rapid spreading of the Faith; but once the Faith had been spread by means of miracles, and sealed by the blood of martyrs, the gift of tongues became more rare. It has, however, never entirely ceased in the Church, for St. Francis of Assisi, St. Dominic, St. Anthony of Padua, St. Francis Xavier, and others possessed this wonderful gift.

APPLICATION. How happy were the first Christians to have Mary in their midst, praying with them, interceding for them, and supporting them by her merits. Share their happiness! Ask her intercession, and implore her to present your petitions at the throne of God. You will pray far more humbly and confidently, if you obtain the intercession of Mary.

How immeasurably great is the love of our God! Not only did He give His only-begotten Son for us, but He also sent the Holy Ghost to remain with us till the end of time. Just think how many graces both the Church and individuals owe to the Holy Ghost! Whenever you say the third glorious mystery of the Rosary, the Descent of the Holy Ghost, thank God with all your heart for this priceless gift.

Most of you have received the Holy Ghost in the Sacraments of Baptism, Penance, and Confirmation. Have you kept Him in your hearts, or driven Him from you? It would be a terrible sin to drive away the Holy Ghost from us. St. Paul says (Eph. 4, 30): "Grieve not the Holy Spirit of God!" Do not resist His grace! Obey His inspirations! Thank Him for all the precious gifts which He has bestowed on you, and pray to Him daily to enlighten and govern you. "Come, Holy Ghost, fill the hearts of Thy faithful" &c.

The Holy Ghost is the Spirit of Truth: the evil spirit is the spirit of lies. Which of the two governs your life? Whom do you obey? Whenever you tell lies you obey the devil, who is the father of lies, and you "grieve the Holy Ghost". Hold, therefore, to the truth, for it is shameful and sinful to tell lies. St. Augustine says that we may not tell a lie, even if by the lie we could save a man's life.

CHAPTER LXXXV.

A LAME MAN CURED BY PETER AND JOHN.—THEY ARE BROUGHT BEFORE THE COUNCIL.

[Acts 3, and 4 to 22.]

ONE day, Peter and John were going up to the Temple to pray. There was at the gate called the Beautiful, a man who was lame from his birth, and who was carried every day to the gate of the Temple to beg alms from those who went in. Seeing Peter and John, he asked them for an alms. But Peter said to him: "Silver and gold I have none, but what I have I give thee: In the Name of Jesus Christ of Nazareth, rise up and walk!" Then having taken the man by the right hand, Peter lifted him up, and immediately his feet and soles became firm. Then leaping up, he stood and walked, and entered with them into the Temple, praising and blessing God.

All the people[1] were filled with amazement to see the lame man leaping and walking.

But Peter said to them: "Ye men of Israel, why wonder you[2] at this? or why look you upon us as if by our strength we had made this man to walk? The God of our fathers[3] hath glorified[4] His Son Jesus, whom you delivered up to death, but Pilate judged He should be released; but you[5] denied the Holy One and the

---

[1] *All the people.* Who followed them into the inner court of the Temple, when Peter seized the opportunity to preach to them faith in Jesus Christ.

[2] *Why wonder you?* You need not look at us with astonishment, for this miracle was not worked by our own power, but by the power of God.

[3] *Of our fathers.* That is to say, God who revealed Himself of old to our father Abraham, and did great things for him.

[4] *Glorified.* He has cured this man in order that glory may be given to His Son, and that you may recognise the Divine Power and Majesty of Jesus.

[5] *But you.* Thus St. Peter, in order to bring home to the Jews the enormity of the crime of which they had been guilty, recapitulated to them the following circumstances: a) you delivered up Jesus to the Gentiles to be crucified, but God has glorified Him; b) even the Gentile Pilate wished to release Him, but you, the Messias' own people, denied Him, and would not recognise Him as the Christ;

Just, and desired a murderer to be granted unto you, but the
Author of life you killed, whom God hath raised from the dead,
of which we are witnesses. The faith which is by Him[1] has
given this perfect soundness in the sight of you all. I know that
you did it through ignorance[2]. Be penitent, therefore, and be
converted[3], that your sins may be blotted out!" Many[4] of those
who heard these words were converted.

And while the apostles were yet speaking to the people,
the priests and the officers of the Temple came and laid hands
on them and cast them into prison, where they remained till the
following day.

Then the chief priests and the ancients had the apostles
brought before them and asked: "By what power[5] or in whose
Name have you done this?" Peter answered: "Be it known to
you all, and to all the people of Israel, that in the Name of our
Lord Jesus of Nazareth whom you crucified, whom God raised
from the dead, even by Him doth this man stand before you
whole. This (Jesus) is the stone which was rejected by you the
builders[6]: which is become the head of the corner. Neither is

c) you desired the release of Barabbas, and refused to acknowledge Jesus, though
the former was a criminal and a destroyer of life, whereas Jesus was the Holy One,
the Just, and the Author of life.

[1] *By Him.* The faith which is from Him and unto Him.

[2] *Through ignorance.* To prevent the Jews from falling into despair on
account of what they had done to our Lord, Peter tried to make excuses for their
crime. He addressed them lovingly as "brethren", and told them that it was
through ignorance that they had delivered up Jesus to be crucified. Our Blessed
Lord Himself while hanging on the Cross had cried out: "Father, forgive them,
for they know not what they do"; and St. Paul writes thus (1 Cor. 2, 8): "Which
none of the princes of this world knew: for if they had known it, they would
never have crucified the Lord of glory." The ignorance of the Jews was, all the
same, culpable, for they could have recognised Jesus to be the Messias, had they
not been blinded by their own passions.

[3] *Converted.* To faith in Jesus Christ.

[4] *Many.* "The number of men (converted) was made 5,000". On the Day
of Pentecost the Christians numbered 3,000, men, women and children included;
while, after the miracle performed on the man born lame, the number of men
alone reached 5,000. The Church, therefore, even in those few days had increased
by thousands. Now, however, persecution against her broke out, and Peter and
John were cast into prison.

[5] *By what power* have you healed the man born lame? The members of
the Sanhedrim did not attempt to deny that the man had been cured.

[6] *You the builders.* i. e. you, the leaders of the chosen people, ought to have
worked with God in the building up of His new kingdom, but instead of that you
rejected Jesus, as if He were a stone unfit for the building, and yet He, by His

there salvation in any other. For there is no other Name under heaven given to men whereby we must be saved."

The chief priests and the ancients ordered Peter and John to be taken out, and said one to another: "What shall we do to these men? for a miracle, indeed, hath been done by them, conspicuous to all the inhabitants of Jerusalem; it is manifest, and we cannot deny it. But that it may be no further divulged among the people, let us threaten them, that they speak no more in this Name to any man."

Then, calling the two apostles, they charged them not to speak at all in the Name of Jesus. But they answered them, saying: "If it be just in the sight of God to hear you rather than God, judge you, for we cannot[1] but speak the things which we have seen and heard."

COMMENTARY.

The doctrine of the Divinity of Jesus Christ was taught by Peter in word and deed. He called Him the Son of God, and the Author of life; and he proved it by the great miracle worked in His Name, for were He not God, His Name would have been powerless to work the miracle.

The difference between our Lord's own miracles, and those of the apostles. Jesus worked miracles in His own Name, and by His own power. He said to the young man of Naim: "Young man, I say to thee, arise!" and by the power of His almighty word the dead came back to life. The apostles, on the contrary, did not work miracles in their own name, but in the Name of Jesus. Thus Peter said to the lame man: "In the Name of Jesus Christ of Nazareth, rise up and walk!" This word of Peter was not almighty, but on account of Peter's faith Jesus willed to use His Omnipotence to cure the lame man.

The object of the apostolic miracles. God willed, by the miracles which the apostles worked, or rather which He worked through them,

---

Passion, Death and Resurrection, has become that one stone which holds together the walls of the building, and on which, therefore, the whole building depends. Then, abandoning this figure of the key-stone, Peter explained his meaning in clear words, declaring that pardon and salvation were to be obtained through Jesus Christ alone, He being the only source of salvation.

[1] *We cannot.* The apostles boldly declared that they could not obey this command; and gave as their reasons a) that God Himself, namely Jesus, the Son of God, had commanded them to teach; b) that they were only teaching what was true, namely the things which they had seen Jesus do, and heard Him speak. The threats of punishment had no effect on the apostles, as you will see in the following chapters.

to prove to the world that they were sent by Him, and taught the truth in His Name. Their miracles were intended to confirm their doctrine, so that by them the world might believe this doctrine. "They (the apostles), going forth, preached everywhere: the Lord working withal, and confirming the word with signs that followed" (Mark 16, 20).

Jesus is the Author of life. He is the only Saviour of the world, and it is only through faith in Him and His teaching that we can obtain grace and salvation. He Himself said: "I am the Way, the Truth, and the Life. No man cometh to the Father but by Me!" (John 14, 6.)

The limit of obedience to temporal authority. Jesus Himself submitted to authority and by His example taught obedience to His apostles. And yet, when summoned before the Council, both apostles declared that it would be wrong for them to obey the command given them to preach no more in the Name of Jesus! How was this? Why did they refuse obedience to this command? Because the Council required obedience in a matter which was obviously against the will of God. Jesus, to whom was given all power in heaven and earth, before His Ascension, had expressly commanded them to preach faith in Him to Jews, Samaritans, and Gentiles; and had, by the wonderful cure of the man born lame, testified that they were sent by Him to teach with His authority. The command of the Council was, therefore, in direct contradiction to the command of their Divine Lord, and on that account they refused to obey it, saying that they must obey God rather than men; and they continued to preach and teach as Jesus had commanded them to do.

The following Virtues were exercised by the apostles in the story we have just heard:

1. *Firm faith.* Peter did not doubt for an instant that all he had to do to cure the lame man was to invoke the holy Name of Jesus. He trusted implicitly in the truth of our Lord's words: "Amen, amen, I say to you, if you ask the Father anything in My Name, He will give it you" (John 16, 23).

2. *Courageous confession of their faith* before the Sanhedrim.

3. *Humility.* The apostles declined all glory for themselves, proclaiming loudly that it was not they, but the Lord Jesus, who had cured the lame man. They therefore gave glory to God.

4. *Zeal for God's glory and for the salvation of souls.* This zeal drove them to preach faith in Christ Jesus before the assembled multitude, to declare their sins, and urge them to do penance. It was no blind or harsh zeal, but was united with

5. *Prudence and indulgence.* They called these Jews their "brethren", and for fear of driving them to despair judged their crime leniently, and did what they could to excuse it.

6. *Fortitude.* The apostles suffered no threats to turn them from the exercise of their apostolic office.

APPLICATION. See how zealous the apostles were for God's glory! Do you rather seek God's glory than your own? Are you not full of vanity about your capabilities? Suppress every movement of vanity; say nothing in praise of yourself, and often renew this intention in all your actions: "O Jesus, I will do everything for Thee!"

CHAPTER LXXXVI.

THE HOLY LIFE OF THE FIRST CHRISTIANS.—ANANIAS
AND SAPHIRA.

[Acts 4, 23 to 5, 11.]

WHEN Peter and John were dismissed by the Council, they returned and related to the disciples all that the chief priests and ancients had said to them. The disciples saw and understood that they were not above the Master, and that the kings of the earth would ever stand up, and the princes assemble together against the Lord and against His Christ. And lifting up their voice to God they prayed: "And now, Lord, behold their threatenings and grant unto Thy servants that with all confidence they may speak Thy word, by stretching forth Thy hand to cures and signs and wonders to be done by the name of Thy Holy Son Jesus. And when they had prayed, the place was moved wherein they were assembled, and they were all filled with the Holy Ghost; and they spoke the word of God with confidence."

"And the multitude of believers had but one heart and one soul." For they persevered in the doctrine of the apostles, in prayer, and in the breaking of bread[1]; that is, the apostles

---

[1] *The breaking of bread.* This was the name for the holy Sacrifice of the Mass and Holy Communion, because, when our Lord instituted the Blessed Sacrament, He broke the bread which He changed into His Sacred Body, before giving It to His apostles. The celebration of the Mass took place in the houses of the Christians, but at the stated hours of prayer and praise, the faithful went to the

celebrated the Holy Sacrifice of the Mass, and the faithful received Holy Communion. Thus they became so perfect that, of their own accord, they sold all they had, and brought the price thereof to the apostles to distribute among the poor.

But among the good seed sown, there was also some cockle. A certain man, named Ananias, with his wife Saphira, sold a piece of land, and brought a portion of the price to the apostles, pretending[1] that they were giving the whole price, while they concealed a part for themselves.

But Peter said: "Ananias, why hath Satan[2] tempted thy heart that thou shouldst lie to the Holy Ghost[3], and by fraud keep part of the price of the field? Whilst it remained, did it not remain to thee? And being sold, was it not in thy power? Why hast thou conceived this thing in thy heart? Thou hast not lied to men, but to God." Ananias, hearing these words, fell down and expired. Great fear came upon all who heard it; and the young men[4], rising up, carried away the body.

About three hours after, Saphira[5], the wife of Ananias, came in, and Peter addressed her, saying: "Tell me whether you sold the land for so much?"[6] She answered: "Yea, for so much." Then Peter rebuked her sharply: "Why have you agreed together to tempt the Spirit of the Lord? Behold, the feet of those who

---

Temple. Of course they took no further interest in the sacrifices which were offered there, because they possessed the spotless and unbloody Sacrifice of which the Jewish sacrifices were but types.

[1] *Pretending.* Ananias and Saphira wished to appear as generous as their fellow-Christians, and sold a field for the benefit of the common fund, but, instead of giving the whole price, they avariciously kept a part for themselves. Ananias took the remainder to the apostles, acting as if it were the whole price. By the inspiration of the Holy Ghost, Peter was aware of the deception.

[2] *Satan.* Why have you allowed yourself to be seduced by Satan to tell this lie?

[3] *Holy Ghost.* Ananias knew the apostles to be the representatives of God and under the guidance and inspiration of the Holy Ghost. Therefore his lie was an offence against the Holy Ghost.

[4] *Young men.* Who attended to, and maintained order at the religious services of the Christians.

[5] *Saphira.* Came to the assembly of the faithful, hoping to be praised by the apostles for her generosity and self-sacrifice.

[6] *For so much.* In order to lead her to make a contrite confession of her guilt, St Peter asked her, pointing to the money which Ananias had brought, and which still lay beside him: "Did you sell the field for so much?"

have buried thy husband are at the door, and they shall carry thee out."

Immediately she was struck dead at his feet, and the young men, coming in, carried her out also, and buried her with her husband. "And there came a great fear upon the whole Church", because the faithful saw the justice of God in the sudden death of Ananias and Saphira.

COMMENTARY.

The Worship of God consisted in the earliest days of the Church, as it does now, in the preaching of Christian doctrine, in prayer said in common, in the offering of the Holy Sacrifice of the Mass, and in Holy Communion. The love and devotion of the first Christians to the Holy Eucharist was so great that, as a rule, they received Holy Communion at every Mass.

The Internal Unity of the Church. A common proverb says: "Many heads, many minds"; but the first Christians proved the fallacy of the saying. The Christian flock counted many thousand heads, but they were all of one mind, as if they had one heart and one soul. This wonderful unity was the work of the Holy Ghost, whose grace changed the hearts of the faithful, and made them all ready to obey the Apostolic teaching. Thus was granted the prayer of our great High Priest for His Church: "I pray that all may be one, that the world may know that Thou hast sent Me" (John 17, 21).

The External Unity of the Church can equally be traced in the days of the first Christians. They all professed the same faith, had the same worship, and the same government. They all reverenced the apostles as the chosen servants of God and their spiritual fathers and superiors, and all acknowledged Peter as the chief pastor and visible head of the Church. We can see in what light the apostles were regarded, by the fact that the faithful reverently laid at their feet the price of the possessions which they had sold, to be distributed by them as they thought fit. The Church, to be the true Church of Christ, must be internally and externally one, as it was in the days of the apostles.

The Primacy of Peter. St. Peter shines forth unmistakably as the supreme pastor of the Church. He it was who interrogated Ananias and Saphira, and it was to him that the Holy Ghost revealed their deceit. He too exercised the supreme authority of the Church, in punishing the hypocrites with the penalty of death.

The love of God and the love of our neighbour. The first Christians observed in a sublime manner that first and greatest commandment which contains in itself all the other commandments, namely the love of God and of our neighbour. They proved their love for God by their constant prayer, by their delight in hearing the word of God, and by devoutly receiving Holy Communion. Their love for their neighbour was active and self-sacrificing. The rich willingly gave up all their fortune for the support of their poorer brethren in the faith. Selfishness, which is so deeply ingrained in the human heart, was driven out by Christian love.

Hypocrisy. The sin of Ananias and Saphira consisted in hypocrisy, or an assumption of piety which proceeded from pride and avarice. They wished to appear generous and charitable in the eyes of men, but were too avaricious to be so in reality. Therefore they kept back a part of the price of their field, and lied to the head of the Church. Their sin was all the greater, because no one compelled them either to sell the field or to give the price of it to the apostles; and since their lie was planned and premeditated, it contained a certain insolence towards those in authority in the Church. Had their sin remained unpunished, the pharisaical hypocrisy against which our Lord had so urgently warned His followers would have crept into the Church. Therefore Almighty God punished Ananias and his wife by a sudden death, in order that all Christians might see the sinfulness of lies and deceit, and of contempt for ecclesiastical superiors.

The Holy Ghost is the Third Person of the Blessed Trinity. St. Peter said to Ananias: "Thou hast lied to the Holy Ghost." Therefore the Holy Ghost is a Person, for you can lie only to a person. Then St. Peter continued: "Thou hast not lied to men, but to God." Therefore the Holy Ghost, to whom Ananias lied, is God.

The Necessity of Grace. Holy Scripture (in the Acts of the Apostles) does not say that many Jews were converted to the Christian faith by the zealous preaching of the apostles, or by the holy lives of the Christians; but it says that "the Lord increased daily together such as should be saved". The preaching of the apostles and the holy example of the Christians would have produced no result whatever, had not the Lord enlightened the understanding of the unbelievers and drawn their hearts to Him by His inward grace.

The Holiness of the Church. The lives of the first Christians show the ennobling and blessed influence of the Christian religion. Being penetrated by the leaven of Christianity (see chapter XXVIII), they loved God above all things, and their neighbour as themselves. They served God with zeal, and conscientiously observed all the commandments. Such things as injustice, theft, or enmities were unknown amongst them, and they all loved and supported one another, so that not one of them suffered want. Even the unbelievers were compelled to respect and honour the Christians on account of their fear of God, and the holiness of their lives. To-day human society would be far better off, and there would be less crime, less misery, less want, if all who call themselves Christians were more imbued with the spirit of Christianity. Moreover, unbelievers and heretics would have perforce to respect and honour the Catholic religion, if all Catholics would live up to their faith.

———

APPLICATION. Are you of one heart and one soul with your brothers, sisters and comrades? Or do you live at enmity with them and quarrel with them? If so, you have not the spirit of Christianity. You ought to observe the commandment to love your neighbour, especially your brothers, sisters and companions.

You can see by the punishment of Ananias and his wife how very much God hates lies and hypocrisy; and yet you make so little account of telling lies! It is especially sinful to tell lies to your parents, or others set in authority over you, for by so doing you show contempt for them. Have you ever acted thus? "Put away lying", says St. Paul, "speak ye the truth every man with his neighbour" (Eph. 4, 25).

It is a terrible sin to tell a lie or to conceal a sin in confession. St. Peter's words: "You have not lied to men, but to God", apply to such a one; for a priest, in the holy Sacrament of Penance, is the representative of God. To conceal a mortal sin in confession is a hateful act of hypocrisy, and a sign of great hardness of heart, and he who does so makes a useless, and, still worse, a sacrilegious confession, receives no absolution of his sins, and commits a fresh and most grievous sin. If any of you have been so blind as to make a bad confession, make a good confession as soon as possible, or else you cannot be a child of God nor have any peace of conscience.

CHAPTER LXXXVII.

THE TWELVE APOSTLES IN PRISON.—GAMALIEL'S COUNSEL.

[Acts 5, 12—42.]

THE apostles wrought many signs and wonders among the people. The sick were brought out into the streets on beds and couches, so that at least the shadow[1] of Peter might fall upon them, and they might be cured. By the daily repetition of these prodigies, the number of believers was wonderfully increased. "Then the High Priest[2] rising up and all they that

———

[1] *The shadow.* Of Peter it is recorded that even his shadow sufficed to work a miracle upon those who believed. This is noteworthy.

[2] *High Priest.* Caiphas.

were with him (which is the heresy of the Sadducees) were filled with envy. And they laid hands on the apostles and put them in the common prison."

But an angel of the Lord came by night, and opening the doors of the prison led them forth, saying: "Go, and, standing, speak in the Temple to the people the words of life!"[1] Hearing this they went into the Temple, at the dawn of day, and taught.

The chief priests were enraged when they heard that the apostles were again teaching in the Temple. They gave orders to have them immediately arrested, and put in prison. Then the apostles were again brought before the Council, and the elders said: "We commanded you that you should not teach in this Name[2]. Behold you have filled Jerusalem with your doctrine." Peter[3] and the apostles answered: "We ought to obey God rather than men. The God of our fathers hath raised up Jesus whom you put to death, hanging Him upon a tree. Him God hath exalted with His right hand to be Prince and Saviour, to give repentance to Israel[4], and remission of sins."

When the priests and ancients heard these things they were filled with anger[5], and thought to put the apostles to death. But one of the Council, named Gamaliel, a doctor of the law, and respected by all the people, rising up, commanded the men to be removed for a little time. He then addressed the Council, saying: "Ye men of Israel, consider with yourselves what you are about to do with these men. If this work[6] be of men, it will fall to nothing. But if it be of God, you are not able to

---

[1] *The words of life.* Namely, the Gospel of Jesus Christ, which is life, and gives life to all who believe.

[2] *In this Name.* They spoke in this way, because they hated Jesus so much that they could not bring themselves to pronounce His Name.

[3] *Peter* answered in the name of the other apostles. He now boldly confessed our Lord before the High Priest himself, whereas, but a few weeks before, he had not had the courage to confess Him before one of his maid-servants.

[4] *To Israel.* Our Lord was primarily the Saviour of Israel, that people being called before all others to receive remission of their sins, to do penance, and be converted.

[5] *With anger.* They remained hardened, and resolved to kill the apostles. And they would have carried out their resolution, had not Gamaliel warned them against doing anything rash.

[6] *This work.* The apostles' mission and doctrine.

destroy it [1], lest, perhaps, you be found to oppose God." They agreed with Gamaliel, and calling in the apostles, they scourged them [2] and charged them to speak no more in the Name of Jesus.

But the apostles went forth from the presence of the Council rejoicing that they were accounted worthy to suffer reproach for the Name [3] of Jesus. They went daily to the Temple, and from house to house, teaching and preaching to the people, proclaiming everywhere the glory and power of the Crucified Saviour of the world.

COMMENTARY.

Jesus is King and Lord of all the redeemed, and the Supreme Head of the Church, Militant, Suffering, and Triumphant. Jesus being our Lord and King, it follows that we ought to serve Him, do His will in all things, and follow His example.

The Primacy and Supremacy of Peter. God gave special miraculous powers to Peter, so as to distinguish him as the supreme head on earth of His Church. If the sick were brought near him — even within reach of his shadow — they were cured. There is nothing less substantial or less real than a shadow, and yet our Lord worked miracles by even the shadow of His vicar. The primacy of Peter was also signified by his being always the one to speak in the name of the other apostles.

The Indestructibility of the Church is a proof of her divine origin, or, in other words, that she is founded by God. The wise Gamaliel's words were very true! "If this work be of men, it will come to nought: but if it be of God, you cannot overthrow it." All human works, doctrines and contrivances pass away in time, and only those which have their foundation in the Eternal God endure. The Church of Christ has survived all persecutions, all heresies, and all the divisions of kingdoms and races, and is spreading herself continuously, in spite

---

[1] *Not able to destroy it.* Even if you kill the apostles. Gamaliel, therefore, admitted the possibility that the teaching of the apostles came from God. Tradition tells us that Gamaliel himself subsequently became a Christian.

[2] *Scourged them.* To satisfy their hatred to some extent they had the apostles scourged. The Jewish scourging was not such a terrible punishment as the Roman scourging which was inflicted on our Blessed Lord, but nevertheless it was painful and degrading. As the Jewish law (Deut. 25, 3) prescribed that the number of strokes given was not to exceed forty, the scourge used was divided into three thongs, with which thirteen strokes were given, so that the total number of strokes received was thirty-nine.

[3] *For the Name.* On account of their faith in Jesus.

of antagonism and pressure from without. She is at this day, after more than nineteen hundred years of existence, as full of vigour as ever, and in a wonderful state of unity and stability. She is the pillar and ground of Christian truth, and is deeply loved by the millions who have the happiness of being her children. She has no armies to protect her; but she is overshadowed by the protection of the Most High, whose only-begotten Son founded and built her on the rock of Peter. As, then, the Church is indestructible, and as the gates of hell cannot prevail against her, she must be a divine work and institution.

How a Christian ought to regard sufferings. The apostles did not merely suffer *patiently,* for the sake of Jesus, but they suffered *joyfully.* Sufferings were a joy to them, and they esteemed ignominy an honour! That which the children of this world would look on as a misfortune, the holy apostles considered to be a happiness! And why? 1. Because faith taught them that Christ would reward their present sufferings with eternal happiness. "Blessed are they that suffer persecution for justice' sake; for theirs is the kingdom of heaven." 2. Because their love of Jesus made all suffering sweet to them. As their Lord had suffered so much shame and pain for them, they were willing to suffer something for Him, in order to return love for love, and to be like their Master even in His sufferings.

Courageous performance of duty. The council first threatened the apostles, and then, when they persisted in preaching, cast them into prison, and finally scourged them. They could plainly see that they would be persecuted and punished further still, unless they refrained from preaching the Gospel, but all the same they fearlessly continued to do the work which their Lord had given them to do. They did not allow threats, or punishment, or even the fear of death to turn them from doing the will of their Divine Master.

The Liberty of the Church. By His miraculous deliverance of the apostles from prison, Almighty God showed it was His will that they should be free to preach the Gospel, and that no human power was to interfere. The Church in her threefold office is instituted by God, and is independent of all human authority; and therefore St. Peter solemnly affirmed: "We ought to obey God rather than men." "This solemn and authoritative repudiation of obedience in face of the synagogue was", says Reischl, "one of the most splendid episodes in the world's history. By it the Church, on God's authority, asserted her independence. At the same time she challenged the secular power, and opened the chapter of her long history of martyrdom."

APPLICATION. Is Jesus King of your heart? Do you love Him above all things? Do you do His holy will in all things? Does the Spirit of Christ reign in your heart, or the spirit of worldliness, pleasure and pride? Each morning at Mass, during the priest's communion, say: "Come, O Jesus, into my heart; reign in it, and drive from it all that is displeasing to Thee. Make it humble, pure, and holy."

CHAPTER LXXXVIII.

ELECTION AND ORDINATION OF DEACONS.—STEPHEN THE FIRST MARTYR.

[Acts 6 to 7.]

AS the number of the disciples increased, it happened that some poor widows were neglected in the daily distribution. Hence [1] it was that the apostles, calling together the multitude of the disciples, said: "It is not fit that we should leave the word of God, and serve tables [2]. Therefore, brethren, look out among you seven men of good reputation [3], full of the Holy Ghost and of wisdom, whom we may appoint [4] over this business."

This proposal was pleasing to the disciples. They chose Stephen, a man full of faith and of the Holy Spirit, with Philip and five others. These they presented to the apostles, who prayed over them, and imposed hands [5] upon them.

Stephen, full of grace and power, did great wonders amongst the people. Some of the most learned of the doctors, envying his fame, began to dispute with him [6], but even they were no match for the marvellous wisdom [7] with which he spoke.

---

[1] *Hence.* In order to guard against similar oversights in the future.

[2] *Serve tables.* Hitherto the apostles, as the rulers of the Church, had super-intended the distribution of alms; but as the number of the faithful increased daily, they no longer had time to look after the temporal needs of the poor without neglecting the preaching of the word of God, the instruction of those who were preparing for baptism, and the worship of God in the several quarters of the city.

[3] *Of good reputation.* Being respected and trusted by everyone. Those chosen had also to be "full of the Holy Ghost", for the office which it was the intention of the apostles to confer on them was not a civil but an ecclesiastical and spiritual office. The deacons were to combine instruction and preaching with the distribution of alms, and were to minister not only to the bodily, but also to the spiritual wants of the poor. They were to be men of "wisdom", so as to be able to direct and do everything in the best way.

[4] *Appoint.* Giving them full discretion as to the distribution of alms (money, food and clothing).

[5] *Imposed hands.* Having approved the choice, they consecrated or ordained them by prayer and the imposition of hands.

[6] *Dispute with him.* About matters of faith.

[7] *Wisdom.* For the Holy Ghost put into his heart what he should say.

Ashamed [1] of their defeat, they stirred up the people against him. He was seized and brought before the Council. They then brought up false witnesses, who testified that he ceased not to speak against the holy place and the law. All the members of the Council looked angrily upon him, but they saw his face [2] shining like that of an angel.

Filled with divine love and the Spirit of God, Stephen reminded them of the wonders which God had wrought for their fathers in Egypt and other places. After showing them how ungrateful [3] their fathers had been, he concluded with these words: "With a stiff neck [4] and uncircumcised heart and ears, you always resist the Holy Ghost, as your fathers did. Which of the prophets have not your fathers persecuted? And they have slain those who foretold the coming of the Just One, of whom you have been now betrayers and murderers."

When they heard him speak thus, they raged and gnashed their teeth with fury. But Stephen, being filled with the Holy Ghost, looked steadfastly [5] into heaven, and saw the glory of God, and Jesus standing at the right hand [6] of God. When the Jews heard him tell his vision [7], they cried out with a loud voice, and stopped their ears, and rushing upon him with one accord, drove him out [8] of the city and stoned him.

---

[1] *Ashamed.* As they could not answer him, they had recourse to lies and violence.

[2] *His face.* So innocent and joyous that it looked, as it were, glorified. St. Hilary says: "The fulness and beauty of the Holy Ghost, which were in the heart of Stephen, shone on his countenance, and made his face look like the face of an angel."

[3] *Ungrateful.* Towards God and His messengers.

[4] *Stiff neck.* A neck that will not bend to the yoke of God.

[5] *Looked steadfastly.* Amid the raging tumult, Stephen stood like a lamb in the midst of wolves, and raised his eyes and heart to heaven, the home of everlasting peace.

[6] *The right hand.* Rapt in the Holy Ghost, his spirit gazed into heaven, and there he saw our Lord in glory, at the right hand of the Father. Our Lord vouchsafed this vision to his servant, in order to give him courage and strength to meet the martyrdom which was awaiting him.

[7] *His vision.* They looked on his words as a horrible blasphemy.

[8] *Drove him out.* Without waiting either to try him, or to have their sentence of death confirmed by the Roman authorities. Stoning to death was the punishment decreed by the Jewish law for blasphemy. The punishment had to be executed outside the walls of the city, because a blasphemer was regarded as one unclean and excommunicated from the people of God. Thus the holy deacon, like his

Whilst Stephen was being put to death, a young man[1], named Saul[2], held the garments[3] of the murderers. But Stephen, falling on his knees[4], cried with a loud voice[5]: "Lord, lay not this sin to their charge!"[6] When he had said these words, he expired[7].

COMMENTARY.

The Divinity of Jesus Christ. St. Stephen testified to our Lord's Divinity in three ways: by his prayer, by his vision, and by his blood. 1. He confessed Jesus to be his "Lord" or his God, and prayed to Him to receive his soul into heaven; and he prayed to Him also not to condemn his murderers, but to forgive them. 2. He declared that he saw Jesus standing at the right hand of God in heaven. He was therefore an eye-witness of our Lord's glory in heaven. 3. On account of this testimony he suffered a violent death, bearing witness with his own blood to the Divinity of Jesus, and being therefore a martyr for his faith. Being, moreover, the first disciple to give his life and blood for Jesus, he is known and venerated as the proto-martyr, or first martyr.

The Diaconate. The word "deacon" means minister or helper. The diaconate is a spiritual office, and is a stepping-stone to the priesthood; for a man must be a deacon before he can be a priest. We are told how the apostles ordained the deacons. The outward sign of their sacramental ordination was the imposition of hands, with prayer; and thereby the seven men received grace and authority to perform

---

Divine Master, was condemned to a shameful death on the score of blasphemy. Who can describe what the holy martyr endured as he was driven to the place of execution in the valley of Cedron?

[1] *A young man.* Under thirty years of age.

[2] *Saul.* Saul was among those who were carrying out the sentence of death. He was held in high esteem by the Jews on account of his fiery zeal for the Jewish faith, and he had agreed that Stephen ought to be stoned. He was born in Tarsus of Cilicia, in Asia Minor, and had come to Jerusalem to study and qualify as a scribe or doctor of the law. He was a disciple of Gamaliel, whose wise counsel was mentioned in the last chapter.

[3] *The garments.* They had taken off their upper garments to have more freedom in their movements.

[4] *On his knees.* Once more confessing his faith, he joyfully gave over his body to be killed, and commended his immortal soul to the care of his Divine Saviour. "These men have rejected me; do Thou, O God, accept me!" (St. Augustine.)

[5] *A loud voice.* With supernatural strength.

[6] *To their charge!* The prayer of St. Stephen for his enemies was very pleasing to God, and some say that through this prayer Saul received, later on, the grace of conversion.

[7] *Expired.* "He fell asleep in the Lord." He died in the love and grace of God. Gamaliel buried the body of the holy martyr on his own property.

their sacred duties. The duty and office of the deacons consisted in helping the apostles not only in the care of the poor, but also in the cure of souls. In the chapter we have just read, we have seen that Stephen the deacon taught and preached, and in the following chapter we shall see that Philip, another deacon, baptized. Deacons are still ordained in the Catholic Church by the bishop, as successor of the apostles; and the order is conferred in the same way as the apostles conferred it, namely, by the imposition of hands with prayer. Deacons are assistants to bishops and priests, having authority to preach, to baptize, to assist the priest at the holy Sacrifice of the Mass, and to give Holy Communion; but they have not the power to change bread and wine into the Body and Blood of our Lord, or to remit sins. This power belongs to priests alone.

The Virtues shown by Stephen are as follows:

1. *Living faith,* in virtue of which he performed great signs and wonders.

2. *Love of God;* for he loved God more than his own life.

3. *Love of his neighbour,* and especially of the poor. In his death-agony he thought more of the sins of his enemies than of his own sufferings. While their sins were crying to heaven for vengeance, Stephen cried to the Lord of heaven to have mercy on his tormentors.

4. *Zeal for souls,* which proceeded from his love for God and his neighbour.

5. *Wisdom,* as shown in his explanation and defence of his faith.

6. *Patience under suffering.* He stood like an angel in the midst of his furious enemies, and no word of complaint crossed his lips.

7. *Fortitude,* in the strength of which he confessed his faith without fear, and sealed it with his blood.

The Gifts of the Holy Ghost. It is said of Stephen that he was "filled with the Holy Ghost"; consequently he possessed all the gifts of the Holy Ghost. The story which we have read proves that he did, indeed, possess them, and especially the gifts of wisdom, fortitude, piety and holy fear.

Happy death. Holy Scripture says that Stephen "fell asleep in the Lord". As regards the body, death is a sleep, as was explained in reference to the raising to life of Jairus' daughter (chapt. XXX). But, further, Stephen fell asleep "in the Lord". Such a death is truly happy, for the soul which leaves the body in a state of grace is sure to go to heaven. "Blessed are the dead who die in the Lord. From henceforth now, saith the Spirit, that they may rest from their labours, for their works follow them" (Apoc. 14, 13). The souls of the just do not all go to heaven immediately after death, not being quite purified. St. Stephen, however, went immediately to heaven, for not only did he die *in* the Lord, but also *for* the Lord. All stains of sin and all temporal punishment are wiped away by martyrdom, and the soul of a martyr goes at once to God in heaven, and is rewarded with an especial degree of glory—a martyr's crown.

Comparison between the Martyrdom of Stephen and our Lord's Death on the Cross. 1. Our Blessed Lord was sentenced to death on the charge of blasphemy, because He had affirmed on oath: "I am the Son of the living God, and hereafter you will see the Son of Man sitting at the right hand of God." In the same manner Stephen was stoned on the assumption that he was a blasphemer, and because he professed his belief in the Divinity of Jesus, and said: "I see heaven open, and Jesus standing at the right hand of God." 2. Both our Blessed Lord and St. Stephen were treated as outcasts, and put to death outside the city. 3. Both, when dying, prayed for their enemies: "Father, forgive them, for they know not what they do."—"Lay not this sin to their charge." 4. Both, before dying, commended their souls to God: "Father, into Thy hands I commend My spirit."—"Lord Jesus, receive my soul!"

The Feast of St. Stephen. The first Christian martyr has from the beginning of our era been highly honoured by the Church on account of his great holiness. From the earliest times the Church has kept a special feast in his honour, on the day after Christmas Day.

The power of prayer. Stephen's dying prayer for his enemies was not offered up in vain. God granted it by giving the grace of conversion to Saul, the fiery persecutor of Christians. St. Augustine writes thus: "If a Stephen had not prayed, the Church would not have had a Paul." We ought therefore to have great confidence in the power of prayer.

The Invocation of the Saints. If Stephen and other Saints could obtain so much from God by their prayers even while they were on earth, how much more efficacious must their prayers be now that they are in heaven and united by love to God? It is, therefore, right and reasonable to ask the Saints in heaven to intercede for us.

Sins against the Holy Ghost. How did the unbelieving Jews resist the Holy Ghost? St. Stephen, inspired by the Holy Ghost, proved to them the truth of the Christian faith, and answered all their objections, so that they had nothing more to say, and could bring forward no arguments against him. Added to this, the incontestable miracles of the apostles and of the holy deacon bore irresistible testimony to the truth of Christianity. Nevertheless, the Jews wilfully resisted the truth. They hardened their hearts against all exhortations, and remained resolutely impenitent. Thus they sinned against the Holy Ghost in three ways: they resisted the known truth, they remained obstinate in sin, and were finally impenitent.

False witness. Those witnesses who brought false accusations against Stephen sinned against the eighth commandment.

Wilful murder is one of the sins which cry to heaven for vengeance.

Sharing the guilt of the sins of others. Did Saul actually cast stones at Stephen? No! Was he, then, guiltless of the death of Stephen? No! He was guilty of it, because he consented to it, and therefore shared the guilt of those who actually stoned him.

Care of widows. The early Christians always took especial care of them.

Comfort in suffering. A glance at heaven can give us courage and consolation in suffering and adversity. Heaven is open for us, as well as for Stephen, if we too persevere to the end in what is good. Jesus looks down on us from heaven as we strive and suffer, and assists us by His grace if we put our confidence in Him.

Lies and violence have, from the beginning, been the weapons of the enemies of Jesus Christ and His Church. We see that they were so in the case of Stephen.

APPLICATION. Stephen gave his life and blood for love of Jesus. Jesus does not ask for your life and blood, but He does ask for your heart. "Son (or daughter), give Me thy heart!" (Prov. 23, 26.) Stir up within your heart great love for Jesus, and perform all your duties in life faithfully, for His sake; and pay Him homage even unto death.

CHAPTER LXXXIX.

THE SACRAMENT OF CONFIRMATION.—BAPTISM OF THE OFFICER OF QUEEN CANDACE.

[Acts 8, 1—40.]

AFTER the death of Stephen, the disciples of Jesus Christ were grievously afflicted[1] in Jerusalem. Among the worst of the persecutors was Saul, the same who had held the garments of those who put Stephen to death. He went from house to house, dragging out[2] men and women who professed to be

---

[1] *Afflicted.* The plain speaking of Stephen in his discourse had inflamed the hatred of the Jews; their obstinacy increased, and far from being satisfied with the blood which they had shed, they wished to destroy the whole Christian body.

[2] *Dragging out.* It is obvious that Saul acted in conjunction with the Sanhedrim, for without its authority he could never have made his way into private houses, and taken off the Christians whom he found to prison.

followers of Christ, and threw them into prison. On account of this fierce oppression the disciples were scattered[1] abroad through all Judæa and Samaria, preaching everywhere the Gospel[2] of Jesus Christ.

Philip[3] the deacon went to Samaria, where he cured all manner of diseases. The inhabitants of that city received the Gospel with joy, believed and were baptized.

When the apostles heard this[4], they sent Peter and John to confirm[5] the newly-baptized. The two apostles went to Samaria and prayed for the new Christians. Then they imposed hands upon them, and they received the Holy Ghost. After Peter and John had preached the Gospel in Samaria and the country round about it, they returned to Jerusalem.

But an angel appeared to Philip, saying: "Arise and go towards the south to the way that goeth from Jerusalem down to Gaza[6]. Philip went immediately[7]. While journeying along he was overtaken on the road by an officer of Candace, queen of Ethiopia[8], who was returning from Jerusalem, where he had gone to worship[9].

As he rode along, sitting in his chariot, he read aloud the prophecy of Isaias. Then the Spirit said to Philip: "Go near, and

---

[1] *Scattered.* They did not hide, but scattered themselves about.

[2] *The Gospel.* Or the doctrine of Jesus, which was the Word of God. The apostles remained in Jerusalem, to tend, from that centre, the increasing flock of Christ.

[3] *Philip.* It seemed as if the hatred of the persecutors was especially directed against the brother deacons of St. Stephen. They, therefore, had to leave Jerusalem. Philip went to Samaria. His wonderful work among the Samaritans is described in the Acts of the Apostles.

[4] *Heard this.* That the Samaritans had accepted the faith.

[5] *To confirm.* By the baptism bestowed on them by Philip they had received sanctifying grace, but they had not yet received the Holy Ghost with the fulness of His gifts.

[6] *Gaza* is situated to the south of Palestine (see Map), on the Mediterranean. It used to be the chief city of the Philistines (see Old Test. XLVI).

[7] *Immediately.* Although he was not told what he was to do when he got there. While he was travelling along, full of thought, he was overtaken by the chariot.

[8] *Ethiopia.* Ethiopia was a kingdom in Africa to the south of Egypt, now called Nubia and Abyssinia. The Ethiopians are descended from Cham, and are negroes.

[9] *To worship.* He believed therefore in the One True God. He was a Jew or a proselyte of the Jews, and took part in their worship.

join thyself to that chariot!" He did so, and heard the officer reading the words: "As a sheep[1] He was led to the slaughter; and, like a lamb dumb before his shearer so opened He not His mouth." Philip asked him: "Thinkest thou that thou understandest[2] what thou readest?" The officer replied: "How can I, unless some one show me?"

He then requested Philip to come up into the chariot and sit with him. Philip did so, and, beginning with the text which had puzzled the officer, he explained[3] to him all the Scriptures relating to Jesus Christ, instructing him in the mystery of Redemption.

As they rode on they came to a stream, and the stranger said to Philip: "See, here is water, what hindereth me[4] from being baptized?" Philip replied: "If thou believest with thy whole heart, thou mayest." He answered: "I believe that Jesus Christ is the Son of God." He then stopped the chariot, and they both went down into the water; and Philip baptized the officer. But when they came up out of the water, the Spirit of the Lord took away Philip[5], and the officer saw him no more. Praising and blessing God, he went back joyfully to his own country.

COMMENTARY.

The holy Sacrament of Confirmation. The Sacrament which St. Peter and St. John administered to the baptized Samaritans was the Sacrament of Confirmation, the outward sign of which is the imposition of hands with prayer. The anointing with chrism which accompanies the imposition of hands is not explicitly alluded to in the account given, but it can

---

[1] *As a sheep.* This prophecy was quoted and explained in Old Test. LXXII.

[2] *Understandest.* "Do you understand of whom the prophet is speaking in this passage?"

[3] *He explained* to him that the passage in question related to the Messias, and that Jesus Christ was that Messias, the Incarnate Son of God, and that through Him all those who believed and were baptized would be saved.

[4] *Hindereth me.* The words of Philip kindled in the heart of the Ethiopian a great desire for the Sacrament of Regeneration, so that when they reached a stream he eagerly seized the opportunity, and cried out: "See, here is water &c.!" He was eager to receive the holy Sacrament of Baptism at once, before his return home.

[5] *Took away Philip.* The Holy Ghost, in a wonderful manner, carried him away to a distant place. This marvel confirmed the faith of the Ethiopian, for he knew thereby that it was God Himself who had sent Philip to him. Thus, rejoicing at the great grace which he had received, he returned to his own country. According to tradition he himself sowed the first seed of the Gospel in Ethiopia.

be proved from many sources that from the most ancient times anointing formed part of the outward sign of Confirmation. The inward grace imparted by Confirmation is the receiving of the Holy Ghost, with the strength given by Him to confess the Faith boldly, and to live in accordance with it. This Sacrament was instituted by our Lord, or else the apostles would not have administered it. The deacon, Philip, could not administer it, but only the apostles, who had received from our Lord the power and authority to apply to the faithful all the graces of Redemption. Hence bishops, as the successors of the apostles, are the ordinary ministers of Confirmation.

God knows how to bring good out of evil. The great persecution of the Christians in Jerusalem, far from destroying the Church, served by the wise Providence of God to increase her sphere of action and her glory. The persecuted Christians themselves became richer in merits, and many Jews and Samaritans were converted to the faith; and the Church was extended throughout Judæa and Samaria. Just as the storm which shakes the trees carries their seed to a distance, even so did the storm of persecution which broke over the Church in Jerusalem serve to scatter the seed of the Gospel, and propagate it in distant regions. "The blood of the martyrs", writes Tertullian, "is the seed from which spring up new Christians".

The conversion of the Samaritans was a very significant fact in the Church's history. The Samaritans were, avowedly, outside the pale of faith, and did not belong to the chosen people of God, but stood, as it were, between the Jews and the Gentiles. By now calling them into His Church, God gave it to be known that His was to be no national Church, limited to the Jews, but a Universal, Catholic Church, intended for all countries and nations; and for this reason the head of the Church, St. Peter, went himself to Samaria to unite this new and important flock to the Mother Church. The conversion of the Samaritans prepared the way for the conversion of the Gentiles.

The object of miracles. The Samaritans paid heed to the words of Philip, and believed them, "for they saw the miracles which he did".

The Universality, or Catholicity of the Church. God sent the messenger of the Gospel to the Ethiopian officer, although he lived in a Gentile country. Thereby God showed that the heathen also were called to have a share in Redemption, and that the Church was to be indeed Catholic. The curse which rested on the race of Cham (see Old Test. VII) was removed in the person of this Ethiopian: and in him the descendants of Cham, who had fallen away from God into the very lowest depths of idolatry, were now called into God's Church, and offered salvation by her means.

He who corresponds with grace will obtain salvation. The Ethiopian was a man of good will. In spite of his wealth and high position, he made the pilgrimage to Jerusalem, and diligently studied the Holy

Scriptures. God, by His preventing grace, first awakened in his heart a longing for the truth and for a right understanding of the prophecies, and then sent Philip to help him. The Ethiopian corresponded with grace, by humbly owning that he could not understand what he was reading, by begging Philip to explain it, and by accepting the instruction given him by the teacher whom God had sent to him. And as soon as he understood the necessity of Baptism, he did not postpone indefinitely the receiving of it, but seized the first opportunity that presented itself to be baptized. To him can be applied the words: "Blessed are they that hunger and thirst after justice, for they shall have their fill."

The necessity and properties of grace. "If thou believest with all thy heart thou mayest be baptized (or born again to eternal life)", replied Philip to the Ethiopian. And our Lord said: "He that believeth and is baptized shall be saved" (chapter LXXXIII). Faith is the root and ground of justification (Council of Trent); and he who does not believe cannot be justified or saved. We must, moreover, "believe with all our hearts"; we must grasp the doctrines of faith, not only with the understanding, but also with the heart and will, and shape our lives in accordance with our faith.

The chief Doctrine of Christianity is that of the Divinity of our Lord Jesus Christ. When the Ethiopian declared: "I believe that Jesus Christ is the Son of God", Philip asked no more, but gave him holy Baptism on the strength of this confession of faith. He who believes in the divinity of our Lord, believes also in the Holy Trinity, and in all that Jesus taught. He especially believes that the Church was founded by Jesus Christ, and that He has sent to her the Spirit of truth.

Holy Scripture and the Infallible Teaching of the Church. The Ethiopian read the Holy Scriptures without prejudice and with a sincere desire to understand them; but he could not glean the truth from them, because there was nobody to expound them to him. The Scriptures are not clear, nor easy for everybody to understand. They form a divine and mysterious book, "in which (as St. Peter says about the Epistles of St. Paul) are certain things hard to be understood, which the unlearned and unstable wrest to their own destruction" (2 Pet. 3, 16). Wherefore St. Augustine says: "From whence arise so many heresies, but because Holy Scripture, which is good in itself, is misunderstood?" But was the interpretation of Holy Scripture which Philip gave to the Ethiopian correct and reliable? Yes! And why was it so? Because Philip interpreted Holy Scripture as the apostles had taught it to him. But why was the interpretation of the apostles infallibly correct? Because they were instructed by the Holy Ghost in the right understanding of the Scriptures, and were by Him preserved from all error. Only the Holy Ghost, under whose inspiration the Holy Scriptures were written, can infallibly interpret their meaning. For that purpose the Holy Ghost was sent to the Church, that He might explain both Scripture and tradition to the faithful, and declare to them the true faith. The Holy

Ghost, however, did not impart directly to the Ethiopian's mind the true explanation of what he was reading, but He sent to him Philip, who had received from the apostles power and authority to proclaim the true faith. Thus faith did not come to the Ethiopian by the reading of the Scriptures, but by hearkening to the interpretation of them given to him by Philip. "Faith cometh by hearing; and hearing by the word of Christ" (Rom. 10, 17).

APPLICATION. The first Christians confessed their faith boldly, and no persecution could frighten them out of it. Do you courageously confess your holy faith, or do you fear the ridicule of the unbelieving and foolish? Are you ashamed to make the sign of the cross, or to genuflect before the Blessed Sacrament, when others are present? Do you neglect to raise your hat to a crucifix, or to join aloud in public prayers, for fear of criticism? Be ashamed of such despicable cowardice, and pray to the Holy Ghost, whom you received in your Confirmation, to give you strength to overcome all human respect.

Are you as anxious to know your holy religion as was the Ethiopian officer? Do you, like him, pay great attention to the instruction which is given you? Are you willing to listen to the Word of God, and take what you hear to heart? Are you careful to learn your catechism? Do you take pleasure in reading spiritual books?

The Ethiopian went on his way rejoicing after he had learnt to know the true faith, and had been made a child of God. The purest and noblest joy is that which is spiritual and supernatural. Do you not feel a heavenly joy in your heart, when you have made either a good confession, or a fervent Communion? Is not your soul filled with a joyful sense of exultation, when you are assisting devoutly at any of the splendid religious ceremonies of the Catholic Church? Thank God that you are a child of His holy and infallible Church, and resolve that you will do honour to your holy Church by the piety and goodness of your life!

CHAPTER XC.

THE CONVERSION OF SAUL (about A. D. 37).

[Acts 9, 1—30.]

SAUL, still [1] breathing threats and slaughter against the disciples of our Lord Jesus Christ, went to the High Priest, and

---

[1] *Still.* It is said that he was "still" full of fury against the Christians, because this hatred had already been alluded to (see chapter LXXXVIII and LXXXIX).

asked[1] him for letters to Damascus[2], that he might bring the disciples whom he found there prisoners[3] to Jerusalem.

As he journeyed on the road[4] to Damascus, suddenly a great light[5] from heaven shone around him. Struck as if by lightning, he fell to the ground. At the same moment, he heard a voice saying: "Saul, Saul, why[6] dost thou persecute Me?" Saul asked: 'Who art Thou, Lord?"[7] The voice replied: "I am Jesus[8], whom thou dost persecute." Trembling with fear, and much astonished, Saul said: "Lord, what wilt Thou have me to do?" The Lord replied: "Arise, and go into the city[9], and there it shall be told thee what thou must do."

Saul rose up from the ground and opened his eyes, but he had lost his sight[10]. His companions then took him by the

---

[1] *Asked.* He had not, therefore, been commissioned by the High Priest to act as he was doing, but volunteered his services, and in fact begged as a favour to be allowed to take the measures he proposed. He now received a commission from the Sanhedrim, and with it a company of armed men to serve as an escort and to help him in his deeds of violence.

[2] *Damascus.* This, the chief city of Syria, is seven days' journey from Jerusalem (see Map). Many thousands of Jews lived there; and when the persecution against our Lord's disciples broke out in Jerusalem, a number of them fled to Damascus, there being constant commercial intercourse between that populous city and Jerusalem. Saul, therefore, made sure that he would find there a great many Christians. The fact that he was ready to go so far out of his way to persecute them, shows the intensity of his hatred of the followers of Jesus Christ.

[3] *Prisoners.* He intended to arrest all Christians, regardless of age or sex, and take them bound to Jerusalem, there to be judged by the Sanhedrim. Our Lord Himself, however, set a limit to his vindictive career.

[4] *On the road.* According to tradition he was within an hour's journey of Damascus.

[5] *Great light.* Which, according to the Acts of the Apostles (26, 13), was brighter than the sun, for it was the glory which surrounded the glorified Redeemer. The vision occurred in the brightness of mid-day (Acts 22, 6), and in the glimpse vouchsafed to him Saul beheld our Lord Himself, in His glorified Body (1 Cor. 9, 1 and 15, 8).

[6] *Why.* "What have I done to you that you persecute Me?"

[7] *Lord.* He said "Lord", for he perceived very well that the wonderful vision could proceed from God alone.

[8] *I am Jesus.* This reply stirred Saul's heart to its very depths. What! had he then been persecuting his Redeemer? He "trembled" at the sight of our Lord's divine majesty, and he "was astonished", because Jesus of Nazareth, whom he considered to be dead, now appeared to him, clothed with divine glory. He perceived that he had been living in a state of awful blindness. But now he believed, and addressed Jesus as "Lord', i. e. God, and declared himself ready to obey Him humbly and do everything that He commanded him to do.

[9] *The city.* i. e. to Damascus.

[10] *His sight.* For his eyes were blinded by that glimpse of the glory of heaven. *Within* him, all was bright with the light of faith, but all *without* was dark

hand[1] and led him[2] into the city. There he remained[3] three days without eating[4] or drinking.

Now, there dwelt in Damascus a certain disciple of Jesus, named Ananias[5]. The Lord appeared to him in a vision[6], saying: "Arise, and go into the street that is called Strait, and seek, in the house of Judas, Saul of Tarsus, for, behold, he prayeth."

Ananias answered: "Lord[7], I have heard from many of this man, how great evils he hath done to Thy saints[8] at Jerusalem." The Lord said to him: "Go, for this man is a vessel[9] of election to Me, to carry My Name before the Gentiles[10], and kings, and the children of Israel. For I will show him how great things he must suffer[11] for the sake of My Name."

---

[1] *By the hand.* Like a helpless child.

[2] *Led him.* How different was this entry into Damascus from that which he had anticipated! "He, who had intended to lead away men and women captive from the city, was himself led into it dependent on the compassion of others" (St. Chrysostom).   [3] *Remained.* In a state of complete blindness.

[4] *Without eating.* But praying earnestly. Who can tell what passed in Saul's great soul during those three days? Hitherto, he had hated Jesus for being, as he thought, a false Messias, and had, on that account, persecuted His disciples. He had believed that he was acting rightly, and was pleasing God by thus zealously opposing the Crucified One and His followers. Now, however, he had seen Jesus in His divine glory and had heard His voice; he knew that He had risen from the dead and was in heaven; and he knew that He was in truth the Messias and the Son of God. He recalled to mind all the prophecies with which he, as a scribe, was well acquainted; grace enlightened his understanding, so that he now perceived their real meaning, and that they were all fulfilled in Jesus. He could not understand his previous blindness of heart; deep contrition filled his soul; the blood of the innocent Stephen rose up in judgment against him, and all his cruel violence towards the followers of Jesus accused him. He had persecuted the friends and beloved of God, yea, even the Son of God Himself, and the words of his Divine Redeemer: "Why persecutest thou Me", rang continually in his ears. He could not touch food; he could only humble himself, and pray earnestly to God to forgive him, to grant him still more light, and to give him the grace to make amends for the wrong he had done. His prayer was heard.

[5] *Ananias.* According to tradition Ananias was one of our Lord's seventy disciples, and, later on, died a martyr's death.

[6] *A vision.* While he was praying.

[7] *Lord.* Ananias was amazed at the commission entrusted to him, and, in his astonishment, remonstrated in the words that follow.

[8] *Thy saints.* Thy disciples.

[9] *Is a vessel.* He is no longer a persecutor of My followers, but a believer and a vessel of election to Me.

[10] *Before the Gentiles.* I have chosen him, especially, to proclaim the Gospel to the pagan world.

[11] *He must suffer.* So complete is his conversion that he, the former persecutor, will in his turn be persecuted, and will suffer much for My sake.

Ananias went, and entering into the house where Saul was, he laid his hands upon him, and said: "Brother Saul[1], the Lord Jesus hath sent me, He who appeared to thee in the way as thou camest, that thou mayest receive thy sight, and be filled with the Holy Ghost." And suddenly there fell from the eyes of Saul, as it were, scales, and he received his sight[2], and, rising up, was baptized[3]. Immediately he began to preach[4] in the synagogues that Jesus was the Son of God[5].

COMMENTARY.

The Divinity of Jesus Christ. The story of Saul's conversion bears testimony in several ways to the divinity of our Lord. 1. Saul himself saw our Lord Jesus in glory, and was thus, like Stephen, an eye-witness of His Godhead. 2. Saul repeatedly addressed Jesus as "Lord", that is, God, and preached in Damascus that "Jesus is the Son of God". 3. The marvellous and sudden conversion of Saul shows the omnipotence of Jesus, for only God can turn the hearts of men. 4. Our Lord also appeared to Ananias, and foretold to him certain things which afterwards came to pass, namely, that Saul would preach the Name of Jesus before Jews and Gentiles, and that he would suffer much for His sake. 5. Ananias confessed Him to be God, addressing Him as "Lord", and saying to Saul: "The Lord Jesus hath sent me." 6. Ananias was sent by Jesus, and in His Name he worked a great miracle, for by the touch of his hand Saul recovered his sight. He who, in spite of all these proofs and testimonies, does not believe in the divinity of Jesus Christ, is indeed inexcusable.

The Mercy of Jesus. Our Lord loved Saul, who hated and persecuted Him. He sought him out and enlightened him at the very moment when he was most thirsting for blood and was least deserving of grace. He did not speak to him in a terrifying manner, but with

---

[1] *Brother Saul.* Ananias lovingly addressed him as brother, for he knew that Saul had become his brother in the faith.

[2] *Received his sight.* And was, by this miracle, confirmed in faith.

[3] *Was baptized.* Because he had by prayer and fasting prepared himself for Baptism.

[4] *To preach.* Saul later took the name of Paul, while preaching the Gospel in the Roman empire. It is, therefore, said: "From (the unbelieving) Saul proceeded (the believing and holy) Paul."

[5] *The Son of God,* and promised Messias. Paul proved his words from the prophecies which relate to the Messias, and showed that they all found their fulfilment in Jesus. The Jews, who could not answer his arguments, tried to kill him, and kept guard over the gates of the city lest he should escape them; but the disciples lowered him down over the walls in a basket, and thus he escaped. We shall next hear of him at Antioch (XCIV).

loving words of expostulation. He did not punish him, but forgave him all his sins, accepted him as a disciple, and even raised him to be an apostle. When He was on earth, Jesus was merciful to sinners, and lovingly went in search of His lost sheep; and, now that He is in glory in heaven, He is as full as ever of compassion and mercy towards sinners.

The power of divine grace. Our Blessed Lord prevented Saul with His grace, enlightened his understanding, moved his heart, and prepared his will to do all that was commanded him. In the very midst of his sinful career grace called to Saul to stop, and changed his heart so completely that the bitter enemy of Jesus Christ was transformed into an apostle, all aglow with love; and the persecutor of the Christian faith became its indefatigable defender and advocate. Thus St. Paul was able to say of himself: "By the grace of God I am what I am; and His grace in me hath not been void, but I have laboured more abundantly than they all: yet not I, but the grace of God with me" (1 Cor. 15, 10).

We must correspond with grace if we wish to be saved. In the passage just quoted St. Paul says: "God's grace in me hath not been void." In other words, it was effectual because, instead of resisting it, he co-operated with it. He did not shut his soul to the light of grace, but believed and submitted himself to the will of God. He repented of his sins, fasted, prayed, and prepared himself for holy Baptism. And after he was a Christian he did not fear the scorn and hatred of the Jews, but fearlessly confessed and preached the Christian faith.

Prayer for sinners. The Church has always held the belief that the conversion of Saul was in answer to the prayer of St. Stephen. Thus St. Augustine writes: "Stephen's prayer was already granted even while Saul was still raging." We should, therefore, never despair of the conversion of a sinner, be he never so far removed from God, for the mighty grace of God can change his heart at any moment. Let us then pray for sinners with zeal and with confidence, that God may grant to them the grace of conversion.

Whoever persecutes the Church, persecutes Jesus Christ. It was the disciples of Jesus whom Saul was persecuting, and yet our Lord said to him: "Why persecutest thou *Me?*" Did Saul, then, in any way injure our Lord in the glory of heaven? No, but he was persecuting the disciples on account of their Lord, and because they believed in Him and loved Him. Now, in the same way that our Blessed Lord regards the smallest act of kindness done to his disciples for His sake, as done to Himself, so does He count the injuries done to His followers on His account, and because of their faith in Him, exactly as if they were done personally to Himself.

Sanctifying grace. Saul received sanctifying grace, if not by his perfect contrition, certainly by his Baptism, and was justified by it;

that is, after his Baptism he was no longer a sinner, but a child and friend of God, and an heir to heaven.

Good works performed in a state of sin. During the three days before he was baptized, Saul fasted rigorously and prayed without ceasing. He was perhaps all this time in a state of sin, for he had not yet received holy Baptism and with it sanctifying grace. Were then his works of prayer and penance of no value? No! they were not without value, for they obtained for him the grace of a greater know-ledge of himself, a deeper sense of contrition, and an ardent desire for Baptism and reconciliation with God; all of which prepared him better for the reception of the holy Sacrament of regeneration.

Christians should be Saints. Ananias called the disciples in Jeru-salem "saints". And why? Because they had been made holy in Baptism, and led holy lives.

APPLICATION. You too have persecuted and injured your Divine Lord by sins against your neighbours who are His disciples. Have you deeply repented of these sins as Saul did, and amended your ways as sincerely as he did? Make a firm resolution never again to commit a wilful sin. Remember whom you offend when you sin, even your Lord and Saviour, the King of everlasting glory. Often make the ejaculation: "My Jesus, mercy!"

CHAPTER XCI.

PETER'S JOURNEY.—HE RAISES TABITHA TO LIFE.

[Acts 9, 32—43.]

AFTER[1] the conversion of Saul, the Church enjoyed peace for a while throughout Judæa and Samaria and Galilee. Peter went about among the faithful, making a general visitation, encouraging and confirming them in the faith. During this journey he performed two great miracles.

At Lydda[2] there was a man, named Eneas, who had kept his bed for eight years, being afflicted with palsy. Peter said to him: "Eneas[3], the Lord Jesus Christ healeth thee[4]. Arise, and

---

[1] *After.* And on account of his conversion, he having been the chief per-secutor of the Church.

[2] *Lydda.* A small town not far from the Mediterranean, and about one day's journey west of Jerusalem (see Map).

[3] *Eneas.* Apparently Eneas was already a Christian.

[4] *Healeth thee.* Now, at this moment, by my words.

make thy bed!"[1] Immediately he arose. Seeing this great miracle, all the inhabitants of Lydda were converted to the Lord.

While Peter remained at Lydda, he was sent for in haste[2] by some of the disciples in Joppe[3], not far distant[4], because a certain holy woman, named Tabitha[5], had just died there.

Peter, rising quickly, went to Joppe. They brought him to an upper chamber, where Tabitha lay dead. Many poor widows stood around weeping[6], and showed him the garments which Tabitha had made for them[7]. Peter was touched at the sight, and, ordering all to leave the room, he knelt down and prayed[8]. Then[9], turning to the corpse, he said: "Tabitha, arise!" She opened her eyes, and when she saw Peter, sat up. The fame of this miracle converted very many to the Lord Jesus Christ[10].

And Peter "abode many days in Joppe", instructing those who were newly converted, and confirming them in their faith.

COMMENTARY.

The meaning of "the Church". When the disciples fled from Jerusalem on account of the persecution there, they proclaimed the Christian faith in many towns in Judæa, Galilee, and Samaria, and thus Christian communities sprang up in these towns. Now, in the story we have just been reading, it is said (Acts 9, 31): "The Church had peace throughout all Judæa, and Galilee, and Samaria." What is here meant by the word "Church"? Simply, all the Christian communities united under one Head. All Christian communities form together one great community, or communion, i. e. the Church.*

---

[1] *Make thy bed.* Which had hitherto been made for him by others.

[2] *In haste.* This urgent message to Peter shows what great faith the Christians had in their chief pastor's miraculous powers. They believed that Peter could restore their benefactress to them.

[3] *Joppe.* A town on the sea-coast, now known by the name of Jaffa.

[4] *Distant.* About nine miles.

[5] *Tabitha.* Who had been a true mother to the poor.

[6] *Weeping.* Because they had lost so great a benefactress.

[7] *Made for them.* In olden times rich and noble women used to weave stuffs and make clothes. We read that the emperor Augustus, when at home, wore only such clothes as were made by his wife and daughter.

[8] *Prayed.* He was moved with compassion for these poor people who had lost their mother, and wished to implore God's help for them. In order to pray without disturbance, and in imitation of his Divine Master (chapter XXX), he caused everybody to leave the room, and then knelt down and prayed.

[9] *Then.* Full of confidence that his prayer was granted.

[10] *Jesus Christ.* In whose name Peter had called the dead back to life, by which action they recognised that Jesus was Lord over life and death.

---

* By "Christian communities" is meant "Catholic communities." The early Christians were all Catholics.
—*Publisher*, 2003.

The chief Pastorship of Peter. The account we have been reading shows us that St. Peter exercised a supervision over the whole Church. As chief pastor, he moved about, visiting the various churches or communities, so as to keep them in the unity of faith and practice, to administer the Sacrament of Confirmation, and to appoint pastors over every flock. St. Chrysostom writes thus about St. Peter's journeys: "Peter moved to and fro among the churches, as a general moves about in his army, to prove and see what part is weak, and what part is prepared, and to discover where his presence is most required. Everywhere do we see him moving about, and everywhere placing himself at the head."

The object of miracles. Jesus worked these great miracles through Peter in order to show the world that He had sent Peter, and that the doctrine taught by him was divine and true. These miracles were the cause of the conversion of multitudes to the Christian faith.

The "Fear of God", or the "Fear of the Lord" consists in this, that we fear to offend Almighty God by even one sin, because He hates and punishes sin. Fear of God proceeds from a living faith in the holiness and justice of God.

The Holy Ghost, the Comforter. The Holy Ghost consoles Christians by giving them a quiet conscience, peace of heart, joy in well-doing and patience under suffering; and by inspiring them with a confident hope of obtaining everlasting happiness.

Works of mercy. In Tabitha we come across one of the first of that great host of spouses of Christ, whose only family are His poor, and whose lives are one unbroken chain of holy practices and works of mercy (Reischl). We might justly call Tabitha the first Sister of Mercy. She was wealthy, but she did not live for the world, but loved our Lord with all her heart, and served Him in the person of His poor. She gave abundant alms and employed her time in making clothes for those in need. She devoted herself especially to the care of widows, as being the most forsaken and unprotected among the poor. To her we can apply the words of St. James (1, 27): "Religion clean and undefiled before God and the Father is this, to visit the fatherless and the widows in their tribulation, and to keep oneself unspotted from the world."

APPLICATION. A kind, generous heart like Tabitha's is very beautiful. Look into your heart, and see whether it be selfish and self-seeking, or filled with love and compassion. Is it a pleasure to you to do good to others? Even if you are unable to give anything, still you can show kindness to the poor. You could always perform some little service for a widow, or visit the sick &c. Make a resolution not to let this day pass without performing some act of love towards your neighbour.

CHAPTER XCII.

THE CONVERSION OF CORNELIUS.

[Acts 10, 1—48.]

THERE lived in Cæsarea[1] a man named Cornelius[2], a Roman centurion, a devout and God-fearing man, who gave much alms to the poor, and prayed continually. One day an angel appeared to him and said: "Thy prayers and thy alms have ascended for a memorial in the sight of God. Send men to Joppe[3], and call hither one Simon, who is surnamed Peter. He will tell thee what thou must do." Then the angel disappeared, but Cornelius sent three men, who feared the Lord, to Joppe.

On the following day, as these men were drawing near the city, Peter, waiting for his mid-day meal, went up to the house-top to pray. During his prayer he was rapt[4] in ecstasy. He saw heaven opened, and behold, a great sheet, as it were, was let down by the four corners from heaven to earth. In the sheet there were all manner of four-footed beasts, and creeping things of the earth, and birds of the air. Then a voice came from heaven, saying[5]: "Arise, Peter, kill and eat!"[6] Peter replied: "Far be it from me, Lord, for I have never eaten any common and unclean thing."[7] But the voice spoke to him again: "That

---

[1] *Cæsarea.* Cæsarea Palæstinæ (so called to distinguish it from Cæsarea Philippi, mentioned chapter XXXVI) was situated on the Mediterranean, about a day and a half's journey north-west of Jerusalem (see Map). This town was the residence of the Roman governor, and was garrisoned by Roman soldiers.

[2] *Cornelius.* Cornelius belonged to one of the noblest families of Rome. He was a Gentile, for though he worshipped one God he was neither a Jew (not having been circumcised), nor was he a proselyte or affiliated to the Jews, like the Ethiopian officer of queen Candace.

[3] *To Joppe.* Where Peter had remained, as mentioned in last chapter, after the raising of Tabitha.

[4] *Rapt.* His spirit was, as it were, removed from the earth, and he was entirely absorbed in supernatural things.

[5] *Saying.* To Peter, who was still kneeling, absorbed in prayer.

[6] *Eat.* "Whatever you fancy". Peter knew that the voice came from God, and thought that God was putting him to the test whether he were faithful in the observance of the Mosaic laws regarding food. Therefore he answered: "Far be it from me, Lord &c."

[7] *Unclean thing.* Anything forbidden by the law to be eaten (see Old Test. VI).

which God hath purified [1] do not thou call common!" This was done three times [2], after which the vision disappeared.

Whilst Peter was wondering [3] what this vision might signify, the Spirit of God [4] spoke within him, saying: "Behold, three men seek thee; arise, therefore, go down, and go with them, doubting nothing, for I have sent them." [5] Immediately Peter went down and met the men whom Cornelius had sent.

Next day he set out with them, and with some of his own disciples, for Cæsarea. Here he was met by Cornelius, who, bowing down before Peter, told his vision and all that the angel had said.

Peter then understood his own vision about clean and unclean animals; that is to say that the Gentiles, who had hitherto been considered as unclean, were to be received henceforth into the Church of Christ. Whereupon he announced to Cornelius and his household the doctrine of Jesus Christ.

And opening his mouth, he said: "In very deed I perceive [6] that God is not a respecter of persons [7]. But in every nation he that feareth Him [8], and worketh justice, is acceptable to Him. God sent the word [9] to the children of Israel, preaching peace [10] by Jesus Christ (He is Lord of all [11]). You know [12] the word which hath been published through all Judæa: for it began from Galilee,

---

[1] *Hath purified.* God has purified all things by the blood of His Son.

[2] *Three times.* In order to remove all doubt from Peter's mind. This vision signified to Peter that all distinctions between clean and unclean food were removed under the New Covenant; and that likewise the distinction between clean and unclean men, between Jew and Gentile, was to cease in the kingdom of God.

[3] *Wondering.* For he did not feel at all clear about it. But as soon as the three Gentile messengers came to invite him to go to Cornelius, he understood what the vision had meant, and that the Gentiles as well as the Jews had direct access to the grace of the kingdom of heaven.

[4] *Spirit of God.* The Holy Ghost.

[5] *I have sent them.* For I have commanded Cornelius, through an angel, to send some one to fetch you.

[6] *I perceive.* By experience, by the fact that God has sent me to you.

[7] *A respecter of persons.* Whether they be descended from Abraham or not.

[8] *Feareth Him.* And obeys the voice of his conscience.

[9] *The word.* i. e. the revelation of Jesus Christ or the Gospel.

[10] *Peace.* Redemption and reconciliation.

[11] *Of all.* All people, not only the people of Israel.

[12] *You know.* For Cornelius and his friends, who were, like him, Roman officials, lived in Judæa and often visited Jerusalem, and must have heard a good deal about Jesus.

after the baptism which John preached, Jesus of Nazareth: how God anointed Him with the Holy Ghost, and with power, who went about doing good, and healing all that were oppressed[1] by the devil, for God was with Him. And we are witnesses[2] of all things that He did in the land of the Jews, and in Jerusalem; whom they killed, hanging Him upon a tree. Him God raised up the third day, and gave Him to be made manifest, not to all the people, but to witnesses pre-ordained[3] by God, even to us who did eat and drink with Him after He arose again from the dead, and He commanded us to preach to the people and to testify that it was He who was appointed by God to be the Judge of the living and of the dead. To Him all the prophets[4] give testimony, that by His Name all receive remission of sins who believe in Him."

Whilst Peter was yet speaking, the Holy Ghost[5] came upon all who heard him. Peter and his disciples[6] were astonished to hear these Gentiles speak in divers tongues, even as the apostles had done on the day of Pentecost. Then Peter said: "Can any man forbid water, that these should not be baptized, who have received the Holy Ghost as well as we?" And he commanded[7] them all to be baptized in the Name of the Lord Jesus Christ.

From that time forth the Gospel was preached to the Gentiles in various other places. Paul, as Saul was now called, and Barnabas,

---

[1] *Oppressed.* Or possessed.

[2] *Witnesses.* What you know about Jesus you know only by hearsay, but we, the apostles, know it by experience, having seen with our eyes and heard with our ears all that occurred. Moreover we are not only eye-witnesses, but we are official public witnesses, because sent by Christ to bear witness before the world.

[3] *Pre-ordained.* The apostles were pre-ordained by God, i. e. were chosen from all eternity to be witnesses to the Resurrection of Jesus Christ.

[4] *All the prophets.* The prophets foretold this, as, for example, in that passage quoted in Old Test. LV: "In His days shall justice spring up, and abundance of peace", and again in Old Test. LXXV: "I will forgive their iniquity, and I will remember their sin no more."

[5] *The Holy Ghost.* When Cornelius and his friends accepted with faith Peter's words, Almighty God visibly interposed to confirm what His apostle said, and sent down the Holy Ghost in the same manner as He had been sent on the Day of Pentecost.

[6] *His disciples.* Who had been Jews, and were known as the Jewish-Christians.

[7] *Commanded.* This may mean that he ordered his assistants (perhaps deacons) to baptize the household of Cornelius.

his companion, preached especially at Antioch [1], the ancient capital of Syria. There the number of the faithful increased very much; and there, for the first time, the believers in Christ were called Christians [2], after the Name of their Divine Master and Founder Jesus Christ.

COMMENTARY.

The Catholicity of the Church. The events just related were of the highest importance for the development of the Church. The apostles had known that the Gospel was to be preached to the Gentiles. Soon after their Lord's Birth, Gentiles had come from afar to worship Him and hail Him as the Saviour of the world; and just before His Ascension Jesus had commanded His apostles to "go and teach all nations"; but the manner and conditions under which Gentiles were to be made Christians, were not yet clearly and distinctly perceived by the apostles. A further and special revelation was necessary to shew that nothing but sincere faith was required, and that none of the ceremonial laws of the Old Testament were to be imposed on them. Peter, therefore, was taught by this wonderful vision that the Jewish ceremonial law was done away with by our Lord; and God's marvellous and direct interposition in the case of the call of Cornelius taught the apostle that the Gentiles were to be admitted directly into the Christian Church, without first submitting to the rite of circumcision. Thus the reception of Cornelius and his friends into the Church was a most important and decisive moment in her history, for it proved not only her Catholicity, but also her entire independence of Judaism. Moreover, by the conversion of the Roman centurion and his friends a link was formed between the Christian Church and Rome, the capital and mistress of the ancient world, and a road to the centre of civilisation was thrown open to the vicar of Jesus Christ; the development of the infant Church into the Church of the whole world being thus facilitated. God, by giving the impulse to her further development, by His direct intervention in the conversion of the first Gentiles, proved that He ever governs her, and that our Lord was faithful to His promise: "Lo, I am with you all days, even unto the consummation of the world."

The Primacy of Peter. Why was the revelation that the Old Law was done away with, and that Gentiles were to be received into the Church, given to Peter only, and not to the other apostles? And why

---

[1] *Antioch.* See Old Test. LXXXIV. The inhabitants of this city numbered about 700,000.

[2] *Christians.* The pagans had hitherto regarded the Christians as a mere Jewish sect, but they now perceived that theirs was a religion by itself, and an independent Church, to which the Jews were opposed, and into which both Jews and Gentiles were received. To make, therefore, a distinction between Judaism and Christianity, they gave the name of Christians to the followers of Jesus Christ.

did Almighty God refer Cornelius to Peter for instruction, and not to the other apostles, or even to the deacon Philip, who was living in the very same town (Cæsarea)? He did so, because to Peter was given the power of the keys of His kingdom, the Church. Peter was the chief pastor of the Church, so to him was assigned the office of receiving the first Gentiles into her fold, even as he had been appointed to admit the first Jews on the Day of Pentecost. He it was who had authority to throw open the gates of salvation to the pagan world.

The graces of Redemption can be received only through the Church. When our Lord Jesus revealed Himself to Saul, He might Himself have imparted to him all necessary instruction, and the grace of regeneration. He did not, however, do so, but sent to him the priest Ananias to teach him and baptize him. Our Blessed Lord acted in the same way regarding the conversion of Cornelius. He neither taught him directly Himself, nor by the mouth of an angel, but commanded him to send for Peter, and hear his words. Nor did the wonderful outpouring of the Holy Ghost on Cornelius and his companions make Baptism superfluous; for each one had to be baptized, and be thus received into the Church by her ministers. It is only by the exercise of the threefold—teaching, pastoral, and priestly—office of the Church, that men can be united and reconciled to our Lord Jesus Christ. He who despises and neglects the means of grace entrusted to the Church cannot receive grace; and he who says that the priesthood is unnecessary, falls into a most fatal error. St. Paul writes thus (1 Cor. 4, 1): "Let a man so account of us as the ministers of God, and the dispensers of the mysteries of God."

Baptism is the first and most necessary of the Sacraments. The Holy Ghost descended visibly on Cornelius and his companions, and imparted to them the gift of tongues, in order to convince the Jewish Christians that the Gentiles need not first become Jews before they could receive the gifts of the Holy Ghost. This outpouring of the Holy Ghost prepared them for a worthy reception of holy Baptism, but it was only by their Baptism that they received the grace of regeneration, and became members of the Body of Christ, that is, His Church.

The good works of sinners. Cornelius was convinced of the nothingness of the pagan gods, and believed in One Invisible God, the Creator of heaven and earth. He also observed the moral law which God has written in the hearts of men, and which He revealed in the ten Commandments. He constantly prayed to God for guidance and knowledge of the truth; and he supplemented his prayers by works of mercy and almsgiving. Now, these good works of prayer and almsgiving were indeed *supernatural* good works, but still could not directly merit for Cornelius everlasting happiness, for only those good works which are performed in a state of sanctifying grace have meritorious value for heaven. Because Cornelius corresponded with divine grace, he received the further gift of faith, and by Baptism received sanctifying grace.

The following virtues are to be found in Cornelius:

1. He was *religious,* for he prayed continually, and honoured God, and according to his lights strove after religious truth.

2. He was *conscientious,* for, as far as his conscience taught him, he observed God's commandments, obeyed the will of God, and kept himself from sin.

3. He was *charitable* and *compassionate,* working for the good of his neighbour. He practised not only the corporal but also the spiritual works of mercy, by inviting his friends to hear the words of Peter, and thus leading them to the true faith.

4. He was *obedient* to God's command to send for Peter, and he thereby obtained salvation.

5. He was *humble.* If he had said to himself: "What can an uneducated fisherman like Peter do for me, a cultivated Roman?" he would not have obtained the gift of faith in Jesus Christ.

6. He *believed* the word of God, as it was announced to him by Peter, and therefore he received the gift of faith from the Holy Ghost, and the grace of Baptism.

Indifferentism in matters of faith. The sentence in Peter's discourse: "In every nation he that feareth God and worketh justice is acceptable to Him", has been interpreted by people either indifferent about, or weak in faith, to mean: "It is all the same what people believe, or what religious creed they profess, if only they live good lives." Now is this principle, that religion and faith are matters of indifference, correct? No! it is utterly false and un-Christian, and that for these reasons: 1. Peter did not say: "Faith does not signify"; for he was, on the contrary, most anxious to convert Cornelius to the true faith; but his words meant rather that nationality does not signify—it does not matter what nation a man belongs to, for all nations are called to believe in Jesus Christ, and all persons, to whatever nation they may belong, are acceptable to Him, if, as Cornelius did, they keep the commandments and strive after a knowledge of the truth. Such men, being acceptable to God, are called by Him to believe the true faith, and thereby obtain salvation. 2. Peter, at the end of his discourse, expressly teaches that no one can obtain forgiveness of sins but through faith in Jesus (compare with this his words in chapter LXXXV: "There is no other Name under heaven given to men, whereby we must be saved"; Acts 4, 12). 3. If no account was to be made of holding the true faith, St. Peter need not have preached to Cornelius, and need not have baptized him. 4. If it be a matter of indifference what faith a man holds, then the whole revelation of God would have been unnecessary, and it would have been quite superfluous for our Lord Jesus Christ to have come into the world, to have taught the true faith, and founded His Church. 5. The principle that it does not signify what a man believes is in direct opposition to the teaching of the Gospels, in which we find our

Blessed Lord so often demanding faith in Himself and His doctrine (see, for example, chapter XV). There is only one true God, one Saviour, and one true faith, which Jesus Christ taught and bequeathed to the Church that He founded. Any indifference in matters of faith, or any admiration of it in others must come from a want of firm religious convictions, and is a grievous sin against faith.

The name of Christian means a disciple and adherent, a follower of Jesus Christ. It is a glorious title to bear, and is a continual exhortation to us who do bear it, to cling to our Lord by a firm faith and true love, to keep His commandments, and to follow His example.

APPLICATION. You may take example from the centurion Cornelius. He was not a Christian, and yet he feared God; he prayed continually, and did good to his neighbour. You are a Christian, and yet how lukewarm and negligent you are in your prayers! How little account you make of sin! How little love you bear to your neighbour!

CHAPTER XCIII.

PETER IN PRISON (A. D. 42).

[Acts 12, 1—25.]

HEROD Agrippa [1], grandson of that Herod who had caused the little children of Bethlehem to be slaughtered, was now reigning in Judæa. Wishing to find favour with the Jews, he began to persecute the disciples of Jesus; and having put James [2] the brother of John to death, he caused Peter [3] to be arrested and thrown into prison.

As it was the time of the Jewish Passover, Herod gave the apostle in charge to four files [4] of soldiers, that they might guard him till after the festival time, when he meant to put him to

---

[1] *Herod Agrippa.* Was a brother of the wicked Herodias (see chapter XXXII). He had been brought up in Rome, and was the friend of the Roman emperors Caligula and Claudius. These emperors gradually gave him complete dominion over Palestine, as well as the title of king. The Jews detested him both for his pagan tendencies and for the favour in which he stood at Rome; and it was in order to make himself more popular with them that he persecuted the Christians.

[2] *James.* Known as St. James the Greater. He was the first among the apostles to give his life for his Master.

[3] *Peter.* Who, as supreme pastor of the Church, was especially hateful to the unbelieving Jews.

[4] *To four files.* Each file consisting of four soldiers.

death publicly. But prayer[1] was made unceasingly by the infant Church for Peter.

Now, on the night preceding the day on which he was to be put to death, Peter, being bound with two chains, slept between two soldiers[2]. The other soldiers kept watch at the door of the prison. And behold, an angel of the Lord appeared to Peter, and a bright light shone all around. The angel struck Peter on the side and awakened him, saying: "Arise quickly!" He did so, and the chains fell from off his hands. Then the angel spoke to him: "Gird thyself, and put on thy sandals and follow me!" Peter obeyed, not knowing, however, whether it[3] were a dream[4] or a reality.

Going out, they passed through the first and second ward or watch, and came to the iron gate leading to the city, which opened of itself before them. But when they came out of the prison yard, and had passed along one street, the angel disappeared.

Then Peter, coming to himself[5], found it was not a dream, and exclaimed: "Now I know in very deed that the Lord hath sent His angel, and hath delivered me out of the hand of Herod, and from all the expectation[6] of the people of the Jews."

He then went to the house of Mark[7], where many Christians were assembled in prayer. When Peter knocked at the door, a young girl named Rhode came to listen[8]. On hearing and recognising Peter's voice the girl was so delighted that she forgot to open the door, and ran in haste to tell the others. But they supposed that she had lost her mind. Yet she insisted that

---

[1] *Prayer.* That he might be delivered from death.

[2] *Two soldiers.* With one hand chained to each soldier. He slept soundly and calmly, in spite of the knowledge that he was to be put to death next morning; for his conscience was at peace, and he was entirely resigned to the will of God.

[3] *It.* i. e. what he saw and heard.

[4] *A dream.* For he was still heavy with sleep, and had not quite come to the right use of his senses.

[5] *To himself.* To a full and clear consciousness.

[6] *The expectation.* From all that the Jews expected to happen to him, i. e. his execution.

[7] *Mark.* Or of Mary the mother of Mark, in whose house a number of the faithful had assembled, in the stillness of the night, in order to pray for their chief pastor. This Mark was in later years one of the Evangelists, and was the special follower or disciple of St. Peter.

[8] *Listen.* Who was outside.

Peter was really at the gate. Then they said that it must be his angel[1].

Meanwhile Peter continued knocking. When the door was at length opened, and they saw that it was indeed Peter, every one was struck with amazement. Their wonder increased when they heard how the angel of the Lord had delivered him from prison.

When morning came, and Peter was not be found, the guards were filled with consternation. And well they might be, for Herod, hearing of Peter's escape[2], caused them all to be put to death.

Herod himself did not long escape the punishment which his impiety and cruelty deserved. He had gone to Cæsarea[3] and was seated on his throne in kingly state, to receive some foreign ambassadors[4]. He delivered an oration which drew from the people[5] the wildest acclamation. They said he spoke as a god and not as a man. This absurd and senseless flattery was very acceptable to the tyrant. He was well pleased to be considered as a god[6]. But immediately the angel of the Lord struck him with a terrible and loathsome disease, and he expired in fearful torments. "But the word of the Lord increased and multiplied."[7]

COMMENTARY.

God's protection of His Holy Church. Herod and the Jews thought that by putting her head to death they would deal a death-blow to the

---

[1] *His angel.* His guardian angel. The assembled Christians thought it far more probable that the apostle's guardian angel should have assumed his voice for the purpose of delivering some last message from him, than that Peter himself should be standing outside, alive and free.

[2] *Peter's escape.* Peter had, at once, gone to "another place". As he was not safe in any part of Herod's territory, he left Palestine (A. D. 42) and went to Rome, where he preached the Gospel to the many Jews who lived there, and founded a Christian community in the capital of the pagan world.

[3] *Cæsarea.* Cæsarea Palestinæ (see chapter XCII).

[4] *Ambassadors.* From Tyre and Sidon.

[5] *The people.* The pagans who were present.

[6] *As a god.* Herod took pleasure in this fulsome and blasphemous flattery, instead of repudiating it and giving the glory to the One True God. So the angel of the Lord struck him with a loathsome disease similiar to that of which his grandfather (chapter IX) and, earlier still, the tyrant Antiochus (Old Test. LXXXV) had died.

[7] *Increased and multiplied.* That is, the Christian faith increased in power and in the numbers of its adherents.

Church of God. But God confounded their wicked plans by miraculously freeing Peter from prison on what was meant to be the last night of his life, and when everything was made ready for his execution. Every precaution had been taken to prevent his escape; he was actually chained to two soldiers; a guard stood before the door of his prison, and a little further off there was placed a second guard; and the iron gate which led into the outer street was firmly barred and bolted. The unbelieving Jews were looking forward with jubilation to the coming morning, when the apostle whom they so bitterly hated was to be put to death; they never even thought of his rescue and escape as a possibility! However, man proposes, but God disposes. The Lord God exercised His almighty power, the chains fell from Peter's hands, the iron gate was thrown open, and Peter, guided by an angel, passed out of the prison into the city, without anyone being able to stop him! This great miracle increased the number of believers, and was the cause of the further extension of the Church.

The power of prayer. Peter's wonderful deliverance was the fruit of the common and persevering prayer of the Christians. The captivity and approaching death of its Supreme Pastor was a terrible trial to the infant Church. The faithful, however, did not give themselves over to sadness and discouragement, but prayed earnestly and confidently to the Lord of the Church to help them in their distress. The Christians of Jerusalem sent the sad news of the danger which threatened their common father to all the other Christian communities at Samaria, Joppe, Damascus, Antioch, and so forth; and everywhere the faithful joined together to pray in common for the head of the Church. The whole Church was on her knees supplicating Him who had said to her: "Lo, I am with you all days, even unto the consummation of the world." Scripture says that the faithful prayed without ceasing. They prayed by day and by night, and did not lose hope although the days were running by without, apparently, bringing help. Then—in the middle of the very last night—Peter was set free and given back to the sorrowing Church. When the need is greatest, God is nearest!

The sins of Herod Agrippa. Herod sinned grievously, 1. by mercilessly persecuting the Church of God; 2. by allowing divine honour to be paid him, without protest. Although he was a Jew and knew the true God, yet, blinded by a senseless pride, he complacently accepted the blasphemous flattery that he was a god and not a man! This filled the measure of his sins, and the punishment of divine justice overtook him. Hardly had he accepted the blasphemous adulation before he was seized with the most intense physical pains, and died after five days of terrible agony. Thus Almighty God proved to him and his flatterers that he was no supernatural being, but a truly miserable mortal man.

Sharing the guilt of the sins of others. The Jews, by expressing satisfaction at the murder of St. James, made themselves participators in Herod's sin, and incited him to proceed to violent measures against the prince of the apostles.

Guardian angels. It is evident that the very earliest Christians believed in guardian angels, this being proved by the words which escaped from the lips of those assembled in the house of Mary, the mother of Mark: "It is his angel!"

The depravity of paganism. The pagans of the Roman Empire had, at this time, sunk to such a depth of depravity that they paid divine honour not only to the emperors who were dead, but also to those who were living, and even to the favourites, dancers, and wrestlers of the emperor, no matter how debased and immoral they were.

APPLICATION. You should learn from the example of the first Christians how great a duty it is for all the faithful to pray for their bishops and priests, and especially for the supreme head of the Church, our Holy Father the Pope. Our present Holy Father (Pius X.) is also surrounded by enemies. He is outraged, calumniated, hated, robbed of his possessions and liberty, and is virtually a prisoner. He needs the prayers and assistance of all his children.

CHAPTER XCIV.

PAUL'S FIRST MISSION (A. D. 45—48).

[Acts 13 to 14.]

NOW there were in the Church which was at Antioch (Fig. 95, p. 782) prophets and doctors, among whom were Barnabas and Simon, who was called Niger, Lucius of Cyrene, Manahen, who was the foster-brother of Herod the tetrarch, and Saul[1]. And as they[2] were ministering to the Lord and fasting, the Holy Ghost said to them: "Separate[3] me Saul and Barnabas for the work whereunto I have taken[4] them." Then they, fasting and praying and imposing hands upon them, sent them away. So they, being sent by the Holy Ghost, went to Seleucia, and from thence they

---

[1] *And Saul.* Saul, having come to Jerusalem to see Peter, was after 15 days sent by the brethren to Tarsus, his native place (Acts 9, 30; Gal. 1, 21), and from thence he was after some time brought to Antioch by Barnabas in order to help in the work of the Church. There he taught a whole year with great success (Acts 11, 25—26).

[2] *They.* i. e. the bishops and priests and deacons.

[3] *Separate.* By consecrating them bishops.

[4] *Taken.* i. e. called them.

sailed to Cyprus.[1] After they had preached throughout the whole island, the pro-consul, Sergius Paulus[2], sent for them, that he might hear from their mouth the word of God.

There was with Sergius a Jew, a magician, named Bar-Jesus. This man resisted them to the utmost, and endeavoured to dissuade Sergius from becoming a Christian. But Paul, full of the Holy Ghost, looked at him and said: "O thou, full of all guile and all deceit, son of the devil, enemy of all justice; thou dost not cease to pervert the right ways of the Lord. And now,

Fig. 95. Antioch. (Phot. Bonfils.)

behold, the Hand of the Lord is upon thee, and thou shalt be blind, not seeing the sun for a time."

Immediately a thick mist came before his eyes, and he went about groping for some one to take him by the hand. The pro-consul, seeing this miracle, believed in the Lord Jesus Christ.

From Cyprus, Paul and Barnabas sailed[3] for Asia Minor. Having come to Antioch, in Pisidia, they entered into the synagogue

---

[1] *Cyprus.* An island in the Mediterranean to the west of Antioch.

[2] *Paulus.* The Roman pro-consul quite perceived the folly of paganism, and was sincerely searching for the true religion.

[3] *Sailed.* They went by ship in a northerly direction to Asia Minor, stopping first in Pamphylia. From thence they passed, further north, to Pisidia.

on the Sabbath-day, and preached to the people Jesus crucified and risen again from the dead, with the remission of sins through Him alone.

Paul's discourse pleased the people[1] so much that he was requested to come on the following Sabbath and preach again. But the Jews were filled with envy, seeing the multitude that came on the second Sabbath to hear Paul, and they blasphemed[2] and contradicted all he said. Then Paul and Barnabas spoke boldly: "To you it behoved us to speak first the word of God; but seeing that you reject it, and judge yourselves unworthy of eternal life, behold! we turn to the Gentiles."

The Gentiles, hearing this, rejoiced, and the Gospel was proclaimed throughout the whole land. The Jews, however, incited a persecution against Paul and Barnabas, and they were expelled from that country. The two apostles, shaking the dust[3] from their feet, went to Lycaonia[4], where Paul preached the Gospel in a city called Lystra.

Among those who heard him was a man who had been a cripple from his birth, and had never walked. Paul, looking at him, perceived that he had faith, and said with a loud voice: "Stand upright on thy feet!" The cripple leaped up and walked. The multitude, seeing this, cried out: "The gods, in the likeness of men, are come down to us!" And they called Barnabas, on account of his height, Jupiter, and Paul they called Mercury, because of his eloquence. And the priest of Jupiter, bringing oxen with garlands of flowers to the gate, would have offered sacrifice[5] with the people to Paul and Barnabas.

But they, seeing what was going on, rent their garments[6], and ran among the people crying out: "O men, why do ye these things? We also are mortals, men like unto you, preaching to you to be converted from these vain things[7] to the living God,

---

[1] *The people.* These were Jews and "strangers who served God", or, in other words, those Gentiles who worshipped the God of Israel.

[2] *Blasphemed.* Denying that Jesus was the promised Redeemer of all nations.

[3] *The dust.* Even as our Lord had commanded His disciples to do (chapter XXXI).

[4] *Lycaonia.* To the east of Pisidia.

[5] *Offered sacrifice.* To them as gods.

[6] *Rent their garments.* As a sign of pain and indignation at the heathenish abomination.

[7] *Vain things.* From this vain worship of false gods.

who made heaven and earth, and the sea, and all things that are in them: who in past generations suffered all nations to walk in their own way. Nevertheless, He left not Himself without testimony, doing good from heaven, giving rains and fruitful seasons, filling our hearts with food and gladness."

Having heard this, many believed in the word of God. But some Jews who had come from Antioch and Iconium stirred up[1] the people against Paul. They stoned him until they thought he was dead, and cast him out[2] of the city.

But while the disciples of the city, who had gone out, stood weeping around him, he arose[3] and went back[4] with them to the city. Then he and Barnabas, having announced the Gospel in Derbe, returned to the cities where they had already preached. They exhorted the disciples to persevere, ordained priests for them in every church, and with fasting and prayer commended them to the Lord. Finally, they returned to Antioch[5], and related the great things which God had done through them, and how He had opened the door of faith to the Gentiles.

COMMENTARY.

God the Creator of heaven and earth. "God", in St. Paul's words, "made heaven, and earth, and the sea, and all things that are in them."

The Justice and Mercy of God. The avenging hand of God (Acts 14, 11) struck the sorcerer with blindness. He was deprived of the light of the sun, because he shut his eyes to the heavenly light of truth. God, however, showed mercy towards him as well as justice, for he was not deprived of sight for the rest of his life, but only "for a time". His blindness was intended by God to be the means of his salvation, and, having served for his conversion, was removed.

The ordination of priests and bishops. Our Lord Himself called Paul to be an apostle, even as He had Himself directly converted him to the true faith. We have seen that, in spite of his conversion by the direct intervention of God, it was necessary that he should be baptized and received into the Church by one of her ministers; for which purpose our Lord sent Ananias to him. Now in the same way that Paul

---

[1] *Stirred up.* By bribery and calumny directed especially against St. Paul, who was the chief spokesman.

[2] *Cast him out.* Bleeding from a hundred wounds, they did not even carry him, but threw out his body, to be devoured by the wild beasts.

[3] *Arose.* Well and strong.   [4] *Went back.* Full of confidence in God.

[5] *Antioch.* In Syria, the Antioch from whence they had started.

became a Christian only by the prescibed rite of Baptism, so could he become an apostle of Christ only through the rite of consecration, administered to him, at the command of the Holy Ghost, by the chief pastors of the Church of Antioch, whom the apostles had already ordained by prayer and the imposition of hands. By this consecration Paul was ordained to be a bishop, and received the power, in his turn, to consecrate other bishops, and to ordain priests. Thus we see Paul on his return journey exercising this power, and appointing pastors in all the various churches.

Ember-days. We read that the apostles who were to be consecrated, and those commanded to consecrate them, fasted in preparation for the holy rite. True to this apostolic practice, the Church still commands the bishop who is about to ordain priests, as well as those who are going to be admitted to the priesthood, to prepare themselves by prayer and fasting. She also commands all the faithful to fast on the ember-days, at which season holy orders are, as a rule, conferred, and she desires that on those days the faithful should be asked to offer up prayers to God, to send good priests into His Church.

The object of miracles. Holy Scripture says that "the pro-consul, when he had seen what was done (that is, the miracle worked on the sorcerer), believed, wondering at the doctrine of the Lord". He had hitherto given ear to the sorcerer, because of his assumption of supernatural knowledge. Now, however, by means of the miracle worked by St. Paul, he perceived that God was with the holy apostle, and that what he taught came from God, and was, therefore, "the doctrine of the Lord".

Faith is the primary condition of justification. This is shown to us in the words used by St. Paul in his first sermon at Antioch in Pisidia (Acts 13, 39): "In Jesus Christ every one (whether Jew or Gentile) that believeth (in our Lord Jesus Christ and His doctrine) is justified."

Sins against faith. This chapter puts before us several examples of the various ways of sinning against faith.

1. *Idolatry.* This sin was committed by the Lystrians, when they wished to offer sacrifice and pay divine honour to the two apostles.

2. *Superstition.* This was the sin both practised and taught by the Jewish sorcerer, who claimed supernatural knowledge for himself, and ascribed supernatural power to his magical arts.

3. *Unbelief.* After St. Paul's first sermon the Jews of Antioch in Pisidia seemed inclined to accept the Christian faith; but when, at his second sermon, they perceived that the Gentiles were flocking into the Christian Church, they set themselves against the faith, and persisted in unbelief. The cause of their unbelief was jealousy, born of pride. Their Jewish dignity was offended, because the despised Gentiles were

offered the same chances of salvation as the "children of Abraham". They wanted to have a special redemption for themselves, and refused to have anything to do with a Redeemer who offered salvation to all alike. Many of the so-called enlightened men of our own time have rejected the saving faith preached by the Church, for the very same cause, namely, jealous pride, and have thereby made themselves unworthy of everlasting life.

4. *Speaking against faith.* The sorcerer sinned in this way by seeking, for his own interests, to set the pro-consul against the Christian faith. The Jews of Antioch in Pisidia committed the same sin when they contradicted the doctrine of St. Paul, and even uttered blasphemies against it.

Sacrifice can be offered to God alone. The two apostles were, therefore, justly indignant when the Lystrians wished to offer sacrifice to them. Filled with righteous anger they rushed into the midst of the idolaters, to stay them in their sin.

To convert the sinner, and prevent him from sinning, is one of the spiritual works of mercy. It is an act of love of God, because an offence against Him is prevented; and it is an act of love of our neighbour, because his soul is thereby saved from injury. Herod Agrippa complacently accepted his deification by his flatterers, whereas Paul and Barnabas were indignant at the attempt to pay them divine honour, and cried out: "We are mortals, men like unto you!"

Among the many great virtues of St. Paul, the following shine forth conspicuously in this chapter:

1. He was full of *zeal for the glory of God,* which made him oppose the Jewish sorcerer, and forbid the idolatry of the Lystrians.

2. Being armed with *patience* and *fortitude,* he did not shrink from the fatigue of his long journeys, nor did he fear the hatred of the Jews, or let even the fear of death restrain him from preaching faith in Jesus Christ.

3. His *humility* made him seek God's glory in all things, and declare, after his return to Antioch, that it was God who had done such great things through him and Barnabas; thus giving God the glory, and taking none to himself.

APPLICATION. Do you seek God's glory in all things? Do you perform the duties of your state of life faithfully, or neglect them from a slothful dread of exertion? Be careful to direct your intention to God every morning!

CHAPTER XCV.

THE COUNCIL OF JERUSALEM (about A. D. 50).

[Acts 15.]

SOME disciples[1] who came from Jerusalem to Antioch said to the Christians[2] there: "Unless[3] you be circumcised after the manner of Moses, you cannot be saved." Paul and Barnabas opposed this doctrine; but in order to settle the question, they went up to Jerusalem, to consult[4] with Peter and the other apostles.

When Paul and Barnabas arrived in Jerusalem, the apostles and elders or priests[5] assembled in council to consider the matter. After much discussion, Peter[6] rose up and said:

"Men, brethren, you know that in former days[7] God made choice among us, that the Gentiles[8], by my mouth, should hear the word of the Gospel, and believe. And God, who knoweth the hearts, gave them testimony, giving to them the Holy Ghost as well as to us, and made no difference between us[9] and them[10], purifying their hearts by faith. Now, therefore, why tempt you[11] God to put a yoke upon the necks of the disciples, which neither our fathers nor we were able to bear. But by the grace[12] of the Lord Jesus Christ we believe to be saved, even as they." When

---

[1] *Some disciples.* Who had belonged to the sect of the Pharisees.

[2] *The Christians.* Who had been Gentiles.

[3] *Unless.* You observe the law of Moses, generally, in all its regulations as to food, purifications &c.

[4] *To consult.* The matter in dispute being a very important one, it was decided to submit it to the apostles as a body. It is easy for us to see the importance of the subject in question. If the opinion held by these Jewish Christians had been generally accepted, the admission of Gentiles into her fold would have been complicated to an extraordinary degree, and her growth would have been much fettered, and the Old Testament itself would have lost its real character as "a mere preparation and introduction" to Christianity. The matter was therefore a vital question for the welfare of the Church.

[5] *Priests.* All those whom the apostles had ordained.

[6] *Peter.* Peter had left Rome a short time before and returned to Jerusalem.

[7] *In former days.* About nine years previously.

[8] *The Gentiles.* Cornelius and his companions.

[9] *Us.* Who were circumcised Jews.

[10] *Them.* The uncircumcised Gentiles.

[11] *Why tempt you.* God has already decided the question through me both theoretically and practically. He has bidden the shadows that lay so heavily upon us, to depart from the new Israel. Why then do you tempt Him to alter His decree?

[12] *By the grace.* And not by circumcision.

Peter had finished speaking, "all the multitude held their peace" [1] (Acts 15, 12).

Then James [2], bishop of Jerusalem, spoke to the same effect. It was then [3] decreed by the whole Council of Jerusalem that the Christians of Antioch, or elsewhere, were no longer bound to observe the law of Moses. This decree [4] commenced with these remarkable words: "It hath seemed good to the Holy Ghost and to us to lay no further burden upon you."

COMMENTARY.

General Councils. The assembly at Jerusalem was the first General Council, and has been the pattern of all succeeding Councils. Let us, therefore, examine: 1. how this Council was held; 2. what was the subject or matter discussed by it; 3. what was the significance of the decision arrived at by it.

1. How was the Council of Jerusalem held?

St. Peter presided over it and conducted its discussions. His discourse was listened to with respect, and all opposition was silenced by it. All present took part in the discussion, but the decision was made by the apostles and bishops.

Thus has it been at every General Council. The successor of St. Peter, the Pope, or some one delegated by him to represent him, has presided over it. During the discussion, learned priests take their part as well as bishops, but only the bishops, as successors of the apostles, have the right of voting in the final decision.

---

[1] *Held their peace.* The Council received the decision of its head with a respectful silence; and even those who had formerly opposed the view he took, ventured on no answer.

[2] *James.* This apostle, known as St. James the Less, was bishop of Jerusalem. As the kinsman of our Lord, he was held in high esteem in the Church. He spoke "to the same effect" as the prince of the apostles, although he himself was a close observer of the Jewish law.

[3] *Then.* After Paul and Barnabas had related all the signs and wonders which God had wrought among the Gentiles by their means. They related these things to show that the uncircumcised Gentiles were acceptable to the Lord if only they believed in Him.

[4] *This decree.* To give greater finality to the decision, it was written down and sent to the Christians at Antioch, "which when they read they rejoiced for the consolation" that no barriers, such as circumcision, were to be put in the way of their salvation. We see that even in the first Council, in which the apostles were assembled, the word and voice of Peter ended the doubt and dispute. But as the doctrine of Peter was infallible, so the teaching of his successors in Rome is also infallible

2. What was the subject, or matter discussed by the Council?

There was no question of setting up a new doctrine, but simply of explaining and defining that which God had revealed about the point in dispute.

Thus has it been with all General Councils. They have never set up new doctrines, but they have defined and explained the doctrines of divine revelation, in answer to the objections and denial of unbelievers and heretics, so that the members of the Church may be guarded against error and seduction.

3. What was the significance of the decision arrived at by the Council of Jerusalem?

The decision of the Council was not merely the result of a consultation of a number of wise and holy pastors, but it was a decision made under the guidance of the Holy Ghost. The apostles were convinced that the Holy Ghost had conducted their discussion and decision, and preserved them from error. When, therefore, they announced their decision to the Christian Church, they did not say: "*We* have decided in such and such a way", but: "It hath seemed good to the Holy Ghost and to us" so to decide.

The same applies in matters of doctrine to the decisions of every General Council which has been held, because it was to the Church in her office of teacher that our Lord promised to send the Spirit of Truth, to be with her and guide her unto all truth, and to direct her definitions of what it is that God has revealed on any point of doctrine.

The Infallibility of the Church is a great consolation for all the faithful. The Gentile Christians at Antioch "were filled with consolation" when they learnt the decision of the Council: for now all their doubts and fears were set at rest, and they knew exactly what God required of them. So also is it a great joy and consolation for us, living as we do in the midst of the errors and false doctrines of the age, to know that we have a guiding star by which we can steer our course, namely the infallible teaching of the Holy Church of God, which is, in the words of St. Paul (1 Tim. 3, 15), "the pillar and ground of the Truth", being unerringly guided by the Holy Ghost. We live at rest, protected from all anxious doubts, for by believing in the Church we believe in the Spirit of Truth, and we know that our faith does not rest on human but on divine authority. By yielding our faith to the teaching of the Church we submit our finite reason and our erring spirits to the Supreme Reason and Spirit of God, who is the Eternal Truth.

APPLICATION. I thank God every day for the gift of the holy Catholic faith! Have you been in the habit of doing so? O never neglect this in the future; for the safe possession of divine truth is the greatest of all blessings! And the greatest joy is that of being a Catholic.

CHAPTER XCVI.

THE SECOND MISSION OF ST. PAUL (A. D. 51—54).

[Acts 15, 35 to 18, 18.]

SOME time after, Paul set out on his second apostolic journey, taking with him Silas instead of Barnabas, who with Mark sailed to Cyprus. Paul published the decree of the Council and preached with great zeal in Syria, Cilicia, Phrygia, Lycaonia, Galatia, Mysia, and nearly all Asia Minor. At last he came to Troas. There he doubted where he should go next; but God made it known to him in a vision. During the night he saw, as it were, a man of Macedonia[1], who said to him: "Pass over into Macedonia, and help us!"

Immediately Paul set out for Europe, with three companions, Silas, Luke[2], and Timothy[3], and landed safely in Philippi, the capital of Macedonia. On the Sabbath-day Paul preached the Gospel of Christ. Among his hearers was a God-fearing woman named Lydia, a seller of purple. Opening her ears and her heart to the divine word, she received it with joy and was baptized with her whole family.

Very soon, however, a storm was raised against the apostle. As Paul and Silas were going, as usual, to the place of prayer, they were met by a certain girl who had a spirit of divination, and was, therefore, a source of great gain to her masters. She persisted in following the apostles, crying out: "These men are the servants of the Most High God, who show to you the way of salvation." Paul, turning round, said to the spirit that possessed her: "I command thee in the Name of Jesus Christ to go out of

---

[1] *Macedonia.* The name then given to the present European Turkey.

[2] *Luke* was born of Greek parents in Antioch. He was a physician by education and profession. After his conversion to Christianity he accompanied St. Paul on his second great missionary journey, sharing the toils and labours, and even the captivity of the great apostle of the Gentiles. After St. Paul's death, he preached the Gospel in Gaul, Dalmatia, and Egypt, and was martyred in Achaia.

[3] *Timothy,* whose father was a Greek, and whose mother was a Jewess, had already been converted to the true faith A. D. 45, when St. Paul preached in Lystra (chapter XCII). When the apostle returned to Lystra on his second journey, Timothy, who was still quite a youth, attached himself to the apostle as his companion. St. Paul consecrated him and appointed him to be first bishop of Ephesus, and while still holding that see he was martyred in the reign of Domitian.

her." And the spirit left her. Then her masters, seeing that the hope of their gain was gone, seized Paul and Silas, and brought them into the market-place before the magistrates, saying: "These men, being Jews, disturb our city."

Then the people rose against them, their garments were torn off, and the magistrates commanded them to be beaten with rods, and then to be thrown into prison. At midnight Paul and Silas were praying and praising God, and suddenly there was a great earthquake, so that the walls of the prison were shaken to their foundations. Immediately the doors flew open, and the bonds of the prisoners were rent asunder.

The keeper of the prison, awaking in terror from his sleep, and seeing the doors open, drew his sword to kill himself, because he thought that the prisoners had fled. But Paul cried out to him: "Do thyself no harm, for we are all here!" Upon this the jailer, calling for a light, went in trembling, and fell down at the feet of Paul and Silas. Then he brought them out, and said to them: "Masters, what must I do that I may be saved?" They answered: "Believe in the Lord Jesus, and thou shalt be saved!" That same hour he took them and washed their wounds, and he and all his household were baptized.

Next morning the magistrates sent orders to the jailer to release Paul and Silas, but when they learnt that the two apostles were Roman citizens, they came themselves to ask pardon for having ill-treated them.

After this, Paul and his companion visited many cities of Macedonia.

From there Paul went to Athens (Fig. 96, p. 792)[1], the most celebrated city of Greece. Seeing that city wholly given up to idolatry, his heart was stirred within him; he disputed publicly in the synagogues with the Jews, and in the market-place every day with all who were present.

There came to Paul certain philosophers, who conducted him to the Areopagus[2], saying: "May we know what this new doctrine

---

[1] *Athens.* The centre of pagan philosophy and art. "Here", says St. Augustine, "here in the home of the greatest poets, orators and philosophers, whose proud renown filled the world, and governed the schools, here did the apostle preach Christ crucified, who was to the Gentiles foolishness, and to the Jews a stumbling-block."

[2] *Areopagus.* The great Athenian Court-house on the hill of Mars where the assizes were held. The Acropolis lay on the hill opposite.

is, which thou speakest of?" And Paul, standing in the midst of the Areopagus, said:

"Ye men of Athens, passing and seeing your idols, I found an altar[1] on which was written: *'To the unknown God'*. What, therefore, you worship without knowing it, this I preach to you—God who made the world and all things therein. He, being Lord of heaven and earth, dwelleth not in temples made with hands; neither is He served with men's hands, as if He needed anything, seeing it is He who giveth to all life and breath and all things. He hath made of *one*, all mankind to dwell upon the whole face of the earth, that they should seek God, if happily they may feel after Him and find Him, although He be not far

Fig. 96. View of Athens.

from every one of us: for in Him we live and move and be: as some also of your own poets said: 'For we are also His offspring.' Being, therefore[2], the offspring of God, we must not suppose the divinity to be like gold and silver, or stone, the graving of art and device of man. And God, indeed, having winked at[3] the

---

[1] *An altar.* This altar had been dedicated to "the unknown God", because many among the pagans had a suspicion that over and above their own gods there was another God whom they did not know.

[2] *Being, therefore.* The purport of St. Paul's words is this: Even pagan poets have proclaimed that mankind is sprung of a divine race, being near to God, and like to Him. If man be like unto God, then senseless and lifeless objects made by man cannot be like unto Him, for these are much lower than man himself, and it follows that the "devices of men" made of gold and silver and stone could not be gods, as was taught by the pagans.

[3] *Winked at.* i. e. has tolerated the long continued ignorance of the true God.

times of ignorance, now declareth unto men that they should everywhere do penance[1]. Because He hath appointed a day wherein He will judge the world in equity by the Man whom He hath appointed, giving faith to all by raising Him up from the dead." St. Paul wished to teach them more about our Lord, but he was interrupted and could proceed no further.

The result was that only a few of them believed. Among these few was Dionysius the Areopagite[2], one of the most learned men of his time. After Paul had preached the Gospel at Athens, he went to Corinth.

There he preached first to the Jews, but they would not hear him, but rather blasphemed and contradicted all he said. Then Paul, filled with a holy indignation, spoke to them: "Your blood be upon your own heads; I am clean. From henceforth I will go to the Gentiles." He then preached to the pagans of Corinth, many of whom were converted. Having remained in Corinth a year and six months, teaching and preaching, he returned to Antioch via Cæsarea and Jerusalem.

COMMENTARY.

The necessity of revelation. Athens was the most cultured city of the ancient pagan world. All arts and sciences flourished there to a high degree, but in religious matters there reigned the grossest superstition and most senseless idolatry, the inhabitants paying divine honour to images made by themselves. This shows us that even those among the pagans of the old world who were most advanced in civilization had fallen very far short of the knowledge of the True God, and that, in spite of their progress in art and science, they would never have arrived at knowing God, had He not, in an extraordinary and supernatural way, revealed Himself in Jesus Christ. Without this supernatural revelation, the world would have sunk deeper and deeper into the abyss of superstition, impiety, and immorality.

Sorrow for the sins of others. "The spirit of Paul was stirred within him" when he saw that Athens was wholly given over to idolatry. His feeling of grief proceeded from his love both of God and of his

---

[1] *Do penance.* And be converted to Him, the Only True God. To move the Athenians to do penance, the apostle put before them the judgment of the world, which God will hold by "One Man", i. e. Jesus Christ, whom He raised from the dead.

[2] *Dionysius the Areopagite.* Who later on was made bishop, and died a martyr's death.

neighbour (see the holy anger of Moses. Old Test. XXXVII). "Blessed are they that mourn, for they shall be comforted!" At this moment there are many millions of heathens who do not know God. Let us pray for their conversion.

The causes of unbelief. Most of those who heard St. Paul's words at Athens remained in their unbelief. They had neither the will to believe, nor any earnest desire to know the truth. They invited the apostle to speak, out of a mere spirit of curiosity (Acts 17, 21); but as soon as he entered on the great doctrines of the Resurrection and the Judgment, they refused to listen to him any more. Some of them, instead of examining his words, simply mocked at them, while the rest put him off with the excuse that they would hear him some other time. Frivolity, superficiality and religious indifference were then, as they are now, the principal causes of unbelief.

In his discourse to the Athenians St. Paul taught them 1. about God; 2. about men; 3. about Jesus Christ.

1. "God", he said, "dwelleth not in temples", in the sense that He can be shut in a temple. He is an infinite, immeasurable Spirit, to whom no limits of space can be allotted. He is "the Lord of heaven and earth"!

"He is not served with men's hands, as though He needed anything." He is infinitely perfect of Himself, so that He needs nothing and depends on nothing.

"He is not far from every one of us", being near to each person, "for in Him we live and move and be." He is in us, and about us, and everywhere present.

He "hath made the world and all things therein". He "giveth to all life and breath and all things". Without Him we could not be, nor live, nor move; for our being, our life, and our movement depend entirely on Him, who is the First Cause of all things.

He is indulgent and patient, and did not at once punish the errors of the pagans, but invited them to do penance. He is, however, just, and will one day "judge the world in equity".

2. St. Paul proclaims the origin, dignity, and end of man.

Man, he says, was created by God, and in such a way that all men were made from one, that is, from Adam, and that all men are, therefore, brethren.

Man is far above all other visible creatures. He is, so to speak, "the offspring of God", having an immortal soul made to the image of God.

God is the end of man, for He created him "that he should seek Him". Man, therefore, is made to know God, to love God, and to be happy for ever with God in heaven.

3. Of our Lord Jesus Christ St. Paul says that God "raised Him up from the dead", and that thereby He hath "given faith to all",

because by that miracle He has furnished a solid ground of belief for all men; and that on a day fore-ordained and known to God, He will judge all men in equity.

———

APPLICATION. God is never far from you! He is always with you! Remember His holy Presence, especially when you are tempted to sin, and do not dare to do wrong in His sight. Remind yourself of His holy Presence during the day, and often make the ejaculation: "O my God, I love Thee with my whole heart!"

CHAPTER XCVII.

ST. PAUL'S THIRD MISSION (A. D. 55—58).

[Acts 18, 19 to 20.]

AFTER Paul had remained some time at Antioch, he passed a third time[1] through the greater part of Asia Minor, and came to Ephesus, the capital of the Roman province of Asia (Fig. 97, p. 796). Here he met some twelve disciples, and said to them: "Have you received the Holy Ghost?" They answered him: "We have not so much as heard whether there be a Holy Ghost." Paul asked them again: "In what, then, were you baptized?" They replied: "In John's baptism." Then Paul said: "John baptized the people with the baptism of penance, saying that they should believe in Him who was to come after him, that is to say: Jesus." Hearing this they were baptized in the name of the Lord Jesus. Then Paul laid his hands upon them, and they received the Holy Ghost, and prophesied.

Paul remained two years at Ephesus, so that all those who dwelt in the Roman province of Asia heard the word of the Lord. Moreover, God was pleased to work many wonderful miracles by the hand of the holy apostle, and no sooner were handkerchiefs or aprons[2] that had touched his body applied to the sick, than they were instantly cured. Seeing these things a great fear came upon all the people, and they magnified the name of Jesus.

———

[1] *A third time.* On his third journey Paul was accompanied by Titus, who was born of heathen parents either at Antioch or Corinth. He was a spiritual son of St. Paul, having been converted by him to the true faith. He was consecrated by him bishop of Crete, and died at the advanced age of ninety-four.

[2] *Aprons.* Or girdles.

Many of those who had dealt in magic brought their books, which were of great value, and burned them before the apostle and the whole people. But a certain man named Demetrius, a silversmith, who made little idols and miniature models in silver of the famous temple of Diana, called together his fellow-craftsmen and told them that Paul, by his preaching, was destroying their trade, turning the people away from the worship of Diana, on which their living depended. When the silversmiths heard this they cried out: "Great is Diana of the Ephesians!" And a tumult was raised throughout the whole city. The people were about

Fig. 97. Site of ancient Ephesus. (Phot. Bonfils.)

to lay hold on Paul and his disciples, with intent to kill them; but, happily, the town-clerk, by wise persuasions, succeeded in appeasing their wrath, so that peace was speedily restored.

The tumult being quelled, Paul assembled the Christians of Ephesus, and having exhorted them to persevere, sailed for Macedonia. Thence he returned to Troas, where he remained seven days. On Sunday he assembled all the faithful in an upper chamber, where he offered up the Holy Sacrifice, and preached to the people till midnight. The sermon being so long, a young man named Eutychus, who sat in the window, having fallen asleep, fell from the third story to the ground, and was taken up dead. Paul, hearing of the accident, immediately went down and restored the young man to life.

From Troas, Paul repaired to Lesbos, Chios, Samos, and Miletus. From the latter place he sent for the clergy of Ephesus, and bade them a last tender farewell, saying: "Now, behold, bound in the spirit I go to Jerusalem[1], not knowing the things that shall befall me there." He then told them that he feared nothing, but was willing to lay down his life for his Divine Master.

To the bishops he said: "Take heed to yourselves, and to all the flock over which the Holy Ghost has placed you bishops to rule the Church of God, which He hath purchased with His own Blood. I know that after my departure ravenous wolves will enter in among you, not sparing the flock." Then, kneeling down, he prayed with them all. And there was much weeping among them; and falling on Paul's neck, they embraced him, and accompanied him to the ship, sorrowing that they should see his face no more.

COMMENTARY.

The Divinity of Jesus Christ has been proved by St. Paul in many of his epistles to the faithful. It may be well to quote a few of the most important passages in them.

In his Epistle to the Romans St. Paul writes thus: "God is my witness, whom I serve in my spirit in the Gospel of *His Son,* that without ceasing I make commemoration of you always in my prayers" (I, 9). And again: "If, when we were enemies, we were *reconciled to God by the Death of His Son,* much more, being reconciled, shall we be saved by His Life" (5, 10). "If God be for us, who is against us? He that *spared not even His own Son,* but delivered Him up for us all, how hath He not, also with Him, given us all things" (8, 31. 32)? "Of whom (the Israelites) is *Christ,* according to the flesh, *who is over all things, God blessed for ever*" (9, 5).

To the Galatians St. Paul writes: "And I live, now not I, but Christ liveth in me. And that I live now in the flesh, I live in the faith of the *Son of God, who loved me and delivered Himself* for me" (2, 20). "When the fulness of the time was come, *God sent His Son,*

---

[1] *To Jerusalem.* Thus ended his third great missionary journey. Well might St. Paul say (1 Cor. 15, 10): "The grace of God in me hath not been void (or inefficacious); but I have laboured more abundantly than they all (i. e. than the other apostles): yet not I, but the grace of God with me."

made of a woman, made under the law, that He might redeem them that were under the law, that we might receive the adoption of sons" (4, 4. 5).

In his Epistle to the Colossians the apostle says: "We cease not to pray for you, that you may give thanks to God the Father who hath delivered us from the power of darkness, and hath translated us into the kingdom of the *Son of His love*, in whom we have redemption through His Blood, the remission of sins: who is *the image of the invisible God, the first-born of every creature.* For *in Him were all things created* in heaven and on earth, visible and invisible, whether thrones or dominations, or principalities, or powers: all things were created by Him and in Him: and He is before all, and by Him all things consist" (1, 13—17). "Beware lest any man cheat you by philosophy and vain deceit, according to the tradition of men, according to the elements of the world, and not according to Christ. *For in Him dwelleth all the Fulness of the Godhead corporally*" (2, 8. 9).

To the Philippians he writes: "That *in the Name of Jesus every knee should bow*, of things that are in heaven, on earth, and under the earth, and that every tongue should confess that the *Lord Jesus Christ is in the glory of God the Father*" (2, 10, 11).

St. Paul's Epistle to the Hebrews begins by these words: "God who, in sundry times and in divers manners, spoke in times past to the fathers by the prophets, last of all in these days hath spoken to us by *His Son*, whom He hath appointed heir of all things, *by whom also He made the world.* Who, being the brightness of His glory, and the figure of His substance, and upholding all things by the word of His power, making purgation of sins, sitteth on the right hand of the majesty on high" (1, 1—3).

The Relics of the Saints. We give the name of relics to the bones, or any objects that are connected with the Saints, and we venerate them, because God has often worked miracles by them. In the Old Testament (chapter LXV) we learnt how a dead man was raised to life by the bones of the prophet Eliseus; and in the chapter we have just read we are told how the sick were healed, and those who were possessed by the devil were delivered by the touch of St. Paul's handkerchief or girdle. We must not suppose that there lies in the relics of the Saints a hidden virtue which works miracles, for it is not the relics themselves which work the miracles, but God who works through them, in order to testify and bring honour to the virtues and merits of His Saints.

St. Paul's virtues, and especially his love for Jesus. In chapter XCIV we examined some of St. Paul's virtues, and especially admired his zeal, fortitude and humility. The chapter we have just read also shows us his indefatigable *zeal*, which came from his love of Jesus. He journeyed about from town to town, from country to country, everywhere proclaiming the Gospel, and not ceasing to do so even when he was a prisoner.

His deep *humility* is expressed by his words to the Corinthians (1 Cor. 15, 9 &c.): "I am the least of the apostles, who am not worthy to be called an apostle, because I persecuted the Church of God. But by the grace of God I am what I am, and His grace in me hath not been void." He corresponded faithfully with the grace of God, which was the reason why he was able to accomplish so much.

His *fortitude* and *patience* are proved by what he suffered and endured on his five great missionary journeys. He himself thus describes what he endured. "(I have suffered) by prisons more frequently, in stripes above measure, in deaths often. Of the Jews five times did I receive forty stripes save one. Thrice was I beaten with rods, once was I stoned, thrice I suffered shipwreck; a day and a night I was in the depth of the sea. In journeying often, in perils of waters, in perils of robbers, in perils from my own nation, in perils from the Gentiles, in perils in the city, in perils in the wilderness, in perils in the sea, in perils from false brethren. In labour and painfulness, in much watchings, in hunger and thirst, in fastings often, in cold and nakedness" (2 Cor. 11, 23—27).

And what was it that constrained the holy apostle to endure all this? It was *the love of Jesus!* "The charity of Christ presseth us!" he says himself (2 Cor. 5, 14). The love for his Crucified Saviour drove him to renounce all the rest, and to proclaim faith in Jesus to all men, wherever he could. Love strengthened him in all his labours and sufferings, comforted him in prison, and finally impelled him to give his life joyfully for Jesus. Of this love he writes thus: "Who, then, shall separate us from the love of Christ? Shall tribulation? or distress? or famine? or nakedness? or danger? or persecution? or the sword? In all these things we overcome because of Him who hath loved us. For I am sure that neither life, nor death, nor angels, nor principalities, nor powers, nor things present, nor things to come, nor any other creature shall be able to separate us from the love of God which is in Christ Jesus our Lord" (Rom. 8, 35—39). This love has made St. Paul a model of Christian perfection.

APPLICATION. (See Application, chapter XCVIII.)

CHAPTER XCVIII.
LAST YEARS OF THE LIVES OF THE APOSTLES.

[Acts 21 to 28.]

WHEN Paul had returned to Jerusalem, he was seized by the Jews, and cast into prison. After two years' imprisonment he was sent, at his own request, to Rome, to be judged by the emperor. On his way to the great city he was shipwrecked at Malta, but was saved in a miraculous manner. Arrived in Rome, he was kept two years more in prison, but was allowed the freedom of preaching the Gospel to those who came to see and hear him during this his first Roman captivity.

At the same time the other apostles were journeying in various countries[1], preaching[2] as they went, and working all manner of signs and wonders. Peter, in his capacity of head of the Church, visited the various churches, confirming them in the faith. It was *in this capacity* that he had gone before Paul to the capital[3] of the ancient world, and had there established his episcopal see; thither he returned after each of his apostolic journeys, or visitations; and in his last years he remained there permanently.

Peter and the other apostles everywhere established bishops as their successors. These bishops were to govern the faithful, and to teach[4] them the same doctrine that they had learnt from the apostles. As to the Scriptures of the New Testament, we must bear in mind that they were written later, and collected later still. Hence the apostles and the first followers of the apostles had no written books wherewith to convert the world. It was all done by preaching. The apostles preached what they had seen and heard, and their successors preached what they had learnt from the apostles. Much of what the apostles preached was afterwards written down in the books of the New Testament[5],

---

[1] *Countries.* Even in the most distant lands known in those times.

[2] *Preaching.* In accordance with the command of their Divine Master (chapter LXXXIII) they preached first to the Jews, then to the Samaritans, and, finally, to the Gentiles.

[3] *The capital.* The whole vast empire was governed from its centre, Rome, where the emperor resided. It was an enormous city, containing about 4,000,000 inhabitants.

[4] *To teach.* Being guided by the Holy Ghost, and having by their consecration received those gifts of His which were necessary to them for the exercise of their pastoral office.

[5] *The New Testament.* Some of the apostles wrote epistles or letters, and others caused books to be written under their supervision. Thus St. Mark, at St. Peter's bidding, wrote his Gospel, or the public life of our Lord; and St. Luke, under similar direction from St. Paul, wrote his Gospel, and also the book of the Acts of the Apostles. St. Matthew and St. John also wrote Gospels. Besides these five books, St. Peter, St. Paul, St. James, St. John and St. Jude or Thaddæus wrote letters or epistles to the various churches. Finally, St. John wrote the Apocalypse,

but not all. Yet even the unwritten teaching has come down to us, and is called tradition.

All the apostles, with one exception, sealed with their blood [1] the Gospel which they announced to the world. In the year of our Lord 67, Paul returned to Rome, where he and Peter gloriously suffered martyrdom under Nero [2]. Paul, being a Roman citizen, was beheaded; Peter died on a cross, with his head downwards [3]. James the Greater suffered under Herod, about the year 42 of the Christian era.

John, the beloved disciple, who had been thrown into a caldron of boiling oil and been miraculously preserved, was the only one who died a natural death, which event took place about the year 100.

Mary, the Mother of our Lord, died at Jerusalem in the year 47, and was, according to ancient tradition, assumed into heaven with her body as well as her soul. The Church historian, Nicephorus, thus describes her Assumption: "When the time came for Mary to die, the apostles who were scattered in different lands came to Jerusalem. But her Divine Son came to the Blessed Virgin at her death, and took her soul to heaven. Her holy body was laid in a sepulchre near Gethsemane (Fig. 98, p. 802), amid the songs of angels and apostles. But when, on the third day, the grave was opened, they found that the sacred body was no longer there; only her grave-clothes were left, which emitted an indescribably

---

or Book of Revelations, in which he recorded that which God revealed to him in a vision concerning the destiny of the Church on earth, and of the heavenly abode of the blessed. This book is full of prophecies and secret revelations, hard to understand or expound. These sacred writings or books, twenty-seven in number, all written under the inspiration of the Holy Ghost, are known by the name of the New Testament.

[1] *Sealed with their blood.* Andrew, Philip, Simon Zelotes, and Matthias were crucified; Bartholomew, who preached the Gospel in Armenia and India, was flayed alive, and then beheaded. Thomas was killed with a lance, and Matthew with a sword. Jude was martyred in Phenicia. James the Less was bishop of the Church in Jerusalem for thirty years, and was held in high veneration on account of his severe and holy life. He was cast down from a pinnacle of the Temple by command of the Scribes and Pharisees, and, life not being quite extinct, he was despatched with a club.

[2] *Nero.* Emperor of Rome. He was a cruel tyrant, who caused a multitude of Christians to be put to death with every refinement of cruelty. St. Peter and St. Paul were among the last victims of his barbarity.

[3] *Head downwards.* At his own humble request, for he did not think himself worthy to die by the same death as his Divine Master. The church of St. Peter's at Rome, the largest church in the world, is built over the tomb of St. Peter, and the bones of the great prince of the apostles lie under the high altar (Fig. 99, p. 803).

sweet perfume. The apostles closed the sepulchre, knowing that the Lord had endowed the most pure and holy body of Mary with immortality, before the day of the general resurrection, and had sent His angels to carry it up to heaven."

COMMENTARY.

The Persecution of the Church. When our Blessed Lord first sent forth His apostles and disciples to preach, He said to them: "Behold I send you as sheep in the midst of wolves. Beware of men, for they will hate you and persecute you for My name's sake. The disciple is

Fig. 98. Tomb of our Lady at Jerusalem. (Phot. Bonfils.)

not above his master, nor the servant above his lord." That which our Lord foretold was completely verified in the case of the apostles, for they were all persecuted and martyred; and even now it is still being realised in the Church, for her faithful children and servants are continually hated, calumniated and persecuted by the world on account of their steadfast confession of their holy faith. This very fact that the Catholic Church and her bishops and priests are reviled and persecuted by the world, is a proof that she is the true Church of the persecuted Saviour; for she does but share the fate of her Divine Master. What Jesus prophesied of His own is fulfilled in her: "If the world hate you, know that it hath hated Me before it hated you. Because you are not of the world, the world hateth you" (John 15, 18. 19). The Church of God is hated by the world because she is not of the world.

The omniscience of our Lord. He foretold to Peter what death he should die (chapter LXXXII), and what He foretold came to pass.

The Feast of the holy Apostles Peter and Paul is kept on the 29th of June, because on that day both of them glorified God by their martyrdom, and won the crown of justice. Peter is the chief, and Paul is the greatest of the apostles. The former is the rock of the unity of the Church, the latter is the representative of her Catholicity. Their

Fig. 99   St. Peter's Church at Rome.   (Phot. Anderson, Rome.)

blood has consecrated Rome, the ancient capital of the pagan world, to be the capital of the Christian world, the mother and teacher of all churches.

Steadfast faith. The holy apostles were steadfast in faith, preferring to suffer death, rather than deny their holy faith.

The witness borne by the Apostles and martyrs to the truth of the Christian faith. The holy apostles did not testify to the truth of Christianity by word only, that is, by preaching and writing, but also by their blood, for they joyfully gave their lives for the truth of what they taught, sealing their testimony with their blood. In like manner, many of their successors, Popes, bishops and priests, especially in the first

three centuries, have died as witnesses for the faith.   In the course of
the centuries of the Christian era 13,000,000 martyrs have attested with
their life-blood the truth of the Catholic faith.   Could there exist a
greater or more incontestable witness to the truth?

The red vestments used on the feasts of the apostles and martyrs
ought to remind us how they gave their life and blood for love
of Jesus.

The Growth of the Church.   When the apostles died, a multitude
of believers already existed in the various countries of the then known
world, extending from India on the one side to the Atlantic Ocean on
the other, and from the Upper Nile to the Danube.

Holy Scripture was written under the inspiration of the Holy Ghost,
Who put into the minds of the apostles and their disciples that which
they wrote down in the sacred books.   When the Holy Scriptures of
the New Testament were written, our Blessed Lord partly fulfilled His
promise: "The Paraclete, the Holy Ghost, whom the Father will send
in My name, He will teach you all things, and bring all things to your
mind, whatsoever I shall have said to you" (see chapter LXVIII).

The Holy Scriptures and the Teaching of the Church.   1. Before
any of the New Testament Scriptures existed, there were a great many
Christians in Judæa, Samaria and the pagan world, for the Christian
faith was not spread by the reading of the Scriptures, but by the living
word and teaching of the apostles and their disciples, or, in other words,
by the Church as a teacher.   2. If the infallible Church were not at
hand to enlighten us, we could not know for certain what books belong
to the inspired Scriptures, nor could we be sure that the Bible, as we
have it, is complete and unfalsified.   St. Augustine says: "I would not
believe the Gospel itself, were I not directed thereto by the authority
of the Catholic Church."   3. That Church alone in which the Holy
Ghost dwells can interpret the true meaning of the Scriptures.   4. Holy
Scripture contains only a portion of the Christian revelation, for we
know that the apostles did not write down everything that they taught.
Therefore, the Scriptures are not the only source of faith, for there
exists another alongside of it, namely the Tradition of the Church.   From
these two sources, Scripture and Tradition, the Church draws the doctrines
of Christianity, and delivers them to us for our acceptance.

APPLICATION.   Let us admire and venerate the holy apostles,
for they were the friends of God, the truest benefactors of mankind,
and the greatest, noblest and most devoted men who have ever
lived.   They accomplished a gigantic work, since as God's messengers they converted the world, and laid the foundation for the
raising and renovating of mankind.   In spite of danger, persecution,
and suffering they accomplished the great work which their Master
had given them to do, and remained true to their calling even

unto death. Each one of them might have said with St. Paul: "I have fought a good fight, I have finished my course, I have kept the faith. As to the rest, there is laid up for me a crown of justice, which the Lord, the just Judge, will render to me in that day" (2 Tim. 4, 7. 8). By means of their glorious martyrdom they entered into the joy of their Lord, and were crowned as princes of heaven with the crown of justice. Reverence them, therefore, and imitate their faithful love of Jesus, and thus you will obey the words of our Blessed Lord and obtain the promise they contain: "Be thou faithful unto death, and I will give thee the crown of life!" . (Apoc. 2, 10.)

CHAPTER XCIX.

THE PERPETUITY OF THE APOSTOLIC CHURCH.

WITH marvellous rapidity did the Church of Jesus Christ grow from a small grain of mustard-seed to a great and mighty tree overshadowing all nations. Nor was her development in any way checked by the death of the apostles. For they had left successors of their office and work, the bishops of the various churches. These continued with unwearying zeal the work which the holy apostles had commenced. And as the faithful were obedient to their bishops, so the bishops were obedient to the successor of St. Peter, that is the Pope, who is the chief pastor of the Church. In this manner there was a bond of union and unity between the faithful and their priests, between the priests and their bishops, and between all the bishops and the Pope. And it has been the work of Popes and bishops in all ages to spread the Gospel, sending forth missionaries all over the world, "to enlighten them that sit in darkness, and in the shadow of death". Such a messenger of the Gospel was St. Augustine for England, St. Boniface for Germany &c. &c. And to this day the Holy See is sending forth missionaries into every known country, to India, China, Africa &c.

Thus was established the One, Holy, Catholic and Apostolic Church, which, built by Christ upon the rock of Peter, and guided by the Holy Ghost, has now existed for nineteen centuries, and will exist to the end of time[1], in spite of all that the powers

---

[1] *The end of time.* Our Blessed Lord has ever kept and ever will keep His promise contained in the words: "Thou art Peter, and on this rock I will build My Church, and the gates of hell shall not prevail against it."

of hell can do against it. Happy are they who belong to that Church, who believe as she believes, and who observe her commandments.

Yea, happy are they who belong to the Church and are her living members[1]. Jesus Christ, the King of kings, will own them as His brethren. They shall dwell with Him and His Saints in a new heaven and a new earth[2], and shall eat of the Tree of Life[3] in the Paradise of heaven.

COMMENTARY.

The wonderful preservation and growth of the Church prove 1. that Jesus Christ is God, and 2. that the Church is a divine institution.

1. Our Lord Jesus Christ Himself foretold that the powers of hell should not prevail against the Church, and that she would grow and spread like a tree springing from a small grain of mustard-seed (see chapter XVIII). This prophecy has been in a perpetual state of fulfilment for nineteen hundred years; therefore He who uttered it must be Omniscient, i. e. God.

2. During the first three centuries the Church was persecuted in the most cruel way, and yet, far from being destroyed, she throve and grew. Even in the centuries which followed, down to the present day, she has been continually opposed, oppressed, and persecuted. She would have infallibly succumbed to the combined forces of heresy and the civil power, if Almighty God had not protected and sustained her. That after nineteen centuries she still exists is a great miracle, and a tangible proof that she is the work, not of man, but of God.

The Papacy. Peter is dead, but his chief pastorship continues. Peter having died bishop of Rome, his present successor in the See of Rome is the chief bishop, the supreme pastor of the Church. As such he is called the Pope, or Father of Christendom.

The Bishops. The other apostles likewise died, but their pastoral office did not cease, having been continued to this day in an unbroken chain of bishops.

The Priests. The bishops are. aided and supported by the priests in the exercise of their pastoral office.

---

[1] *Living members.* Living in God's grace, and according to their faith.

[2] *A new earth.* For, at the end of the world, heaven and earth will be transformed and renewed.

[3] *The Tree of Life.* This Tree of Life is Jesus Christ Himself, whose glory the blessed shall share. The words: "They shall eat of the Tree of Life" are taken from the Apocalypse (2, 7), where our Lord says: "To him that overcometh (temptation), I will give to eat of the Tree of Life, which is in the Paradise of My God."

The Church is One. One in doctrine, one in worship, one in discipline, and one in government. The unity of government which includes the power of infallible teaching secures her unity of doctrine, worship and discipline. Therefore the Supremacy of the Pope is the one efficacious and necessary means of unity.

The Church is Holy, for she was founded by the Most Holy Son of God, and makes holy all those who live in accordance with her sublime teaching.

The Church is Catholic. Catholic as *to time;* for she has existed at all times since the days of our Lord. Catholic as *to place;* for she exists in every part of the world as a matter of fact and as a matter of right. Catholic as *to character;* for she is not national, but international and supernational. Her charter is: "Go and teach *all nations,* baptizing them in the Name of the Father and of the Son and of the Holy Ghost".

The Church is Apostolic. Our Lord Jesus Christ founded the Church, and His apostles disseminated her doctrines; and it is on the doctrine and tradition of the apostles that the Church of God rests; the Pope and bishops, the pastors of the Church, being the lawful successors of the apostles. Even as the Israel of the Old Testament sprang from the twelve Patriarchs, the sons of Jacob, so does the Israel of the New Testament spring, in a spiritual manner, from the twelve apostles of Jesus Christ.

In the Church alone there is salvation, for she alone was founded by Jesus Christ and is protected and sustained by Him for the purpose of saving the souls of men. She was instituted by God for the salvation of mankind, and all those will be saved who live in accordance with her doctrines and precepts.

Confession of faith. Those members of the Church will be saved who steadfastly confess their faith by word and deed. We confess our holy faith by deed if we live up to its teaching. If we do this, then we are living members of the Church, and so far those words of our Lord apply to us: "Every one that shall confess Me before men, I will also confess him before My Father who is in heaven" (Mat. 10, 32).

The transformation of the world. In the Apocalypse (21, 1) St. John says: "I saw a new heaven and a new earth. For the first heaven and the first earth was gone." And St. Peter writes in his second Epistle (3, 10): "The day of the Lord (that is, the day of Judgment) shall come as a thief (suddenly), in which the heavens (the firmament of stars) shall pass away with great violence, and the elements (the matter of which the world is made) shall be melted with heat, and the earth and the works which are in it shall be burned up", and (in verse 13): "We look for a new heaven and a new earth according to His promises in which justice dwelleth." Nature, upon which the curse of God has fallen on account of man's sin, longs for redemption ("The expectation of the creature waiteth for the revelation of the sons of God"; Rom.

8, 19), and it also will have its share in the Redemption of Jesus Christ, "for the fashion (the present form) of this world passeth away" (1 Cor. 7, 31), and nature will be, not destroyed, but transformed and glorified. The earth on which once the Son of God dwelt visibly, and on which He now dwells invisibly in the Blessed Sacrament, will be transformed into an everlasting Paradise. It has been for a long time the abode of sin, misery and death, a vale of tears; but after the Last Judgment it will become the abode of immortality, joy and rapture. So all-embracing is the work of Redemption that it will obliterate all the consequences of sin, will entirely remove the curse which rests upon nature, and will impart to all creation a higher and eternal life!

APPLICATION. We have now arrived at the conclusion of the Bible History, and how beautiful and magnificent this conclusion is! You have been taken back to the beginning of Sacred History, and reminded how in the beginning God created heaven and earth, and made for man an earthly Paradise. This Paradise was lost to man by his sin, and from henceforth the earth was stained with sin and every kind of abomination. Some day, however, all that has been marred by sin will be restored by the Divine Redeemer; the whole of creation will be transformed and renewed, and the earth converted into a Paradise. God grant that, some day, you too may be glorified and received into the heavenly Paradise!

In order to attain to this, your last end, you must hold fast to the Holy, Catholic, and Apostolic Church. This last Chapter of the Bible History which we have just read places before you the wonderful constitution, preservation and development of the Church, and reminds you that the Church is God's work, instituted by Him for the salvation of souls. She was foreshadowed, and the way was prepared for her, in the Old Testament; and when the fulness of time came she was founded by Jesus Christ as a means of salvation for the whole world. She is the Bride of Jesus Christ, won by Him through His Most Precious Blood. Our Lord delivered to her His doctrine and the treasury of the graces of Redemption, and only through her can you partake of the fruits of Redemption, and be pardoned and saved. Thank God, therefore, that you are members of His saving Church. Honour, reverence and love her, obey her precepts, and diligently receive those means of grace which were committed to her; and then you will be saved!

Let us, as we finally close this Bible History, fervently renew our baptismal vows.

APPENDIX.

CONCORDANCE

OR

SCRIPTURE AIDS TO THE CATECHISM.

INTRODUCTION.

THE END OF MAN.

The end of man is to know, love and serve God here on earth in
order to obtain everlasting life and happiness with God in heaven
hereafter. This end is supernatural. Hence man must know, love and
serve God not only according to natural reason, but also according
to supernatural Revelation. He must have *faith, hope* and *charity,*
and must be in a state of *sanctifying grace.* By wilfully refusing to
know, love and serve God, i. e. by grievous sin, man loses his last
end. All this is well illustrated in the chapters on the Creation of
Man 13—28. See also David's words to Solomon 248, and St. Paul's
to the Athenians 794. To serve God is the highest honour 329.
Examples: The three youths in the furnace; Daniel; the Machabees;
all the Martyrs.

Life a pilgrimage 117; a journey to the Promised Land 190; towards
home 328.

The things of this world cannot give happiness 261. "What doth it
profit a man to gain the whole world" 588. "One thing is needful"
560. Sin is the cause of misery. Examples: Adam and Eve; the
people at the time of the Flood; the Israelites in the desert; the
prodigal Son; Judas.

Man must work for his salvation 621 624. Parable of the labourers
in the vineyard 594; of the talents 624.

FIRST PART.

§ 1. THE NATURE OF FAITH.

Faith is a free act of our mind and will by which we believe all that
God has ever revealed through His special messengers, the Patriarchs,
Prophets, Christ and the Apostles, and proposes to our belief by

His infallible Church. God's messengers have delivered the word of God to men chiefly by word of mouth (Tradition); but some of them also by writing (Holy Scripture). Hence the Church, in teaching us what is revealed, draws her doctrine from two sources: Tradition and Holy Scripture 38 312 446 723. Holy Scripture is inspired 804; requires interpretation 762. Faith is a gift of God and an act of virtue 460 507 530. The *object* of faith is the unalterable Word of God who is Truth and Truthfulness itself 54 60 (Abraham); 187 (Balaam). The causes of unbelief 507 600. Doubts about faith 183. Indifference 776. Sins against faith 785.

§ 2. THE NECESSITY OF FAITH.

Faith is the very beginning and root of our supernatural life and our justification 54 184 448 487.

"Without faith it is impossible to please God" (Hebr. 11, 6). No salvation without faith in Jesus Christ 448 (Mark 16, 16).

Faith to be bought at any price 512 (The precious pearl).

§ 3. THE QUALITIES OF FAITH.

Faith must be:

1. *entire* 54 186 719.
2. *firm*, like that of Abraham 54 60 68; Job 126; Josue 195; the widow of Sarepta 268; Elias 273; Simeon and Anna 409; the Magi 414.
3. *steadfast*, as that of Abraham, Moses, Ruth, Daniel, Eleazar, Machabees, the Man born blind, St. Stephen, the Apostles.
4. *living* 54 414 (Magi); 621 (Wise virgins); dead faith 460 622.
5. *openly and fearlessly confessed* 234 (David); 339 (Three youths); 427 (John the Baptist); 579 (Man born blind). "He who shall confess me before men" &c. (Matth. 10, 32). The Apostles and St. Stephen after Pentecost.

FIRST ARTICLE OF THE CREED.

§ 1. GOD.

His Divine Attributes:

1. *Eternity* 7 134 ("I am who am"); 332 (Prayer of Susanna).
2. *Immutability* 134. In His designs and decrees 78 289 (Ninive).
3. *Omnipotence.* Illustrated by the Creation of heaven and earth through His sole word 7; the deluge; the ten plagues; the Exodus of the people of Israel &c. 282 289.
4. *Omnipresence.* Illustrated by the history of Adam and Eve in Paradise, and the life of the Patriarchs 44 61 267 332 475; by the words of St. Paul 794.

5. *Omniscience.* Illustrated by the history of Adam and Eve, of Abel and Cain; by every prophecy of the O. T. Proclaimed by Samuel 221; by David 243 248; by Susanna 332. God knew the secret sins of David 243; of Achab 276; testified to by our Lord in the Sermon of the Mount 475.

6. *Wisdom.* In Creation 7; in the story of Jacob 78; of Joseph 103; of the people of Israel 117—176; in the history of mankind 376; in the work of redemption 287 310.

7. *Holiness.* Lev. 21, 8; 31 39 135. "Holy and terrible is His Name". Ps. 110, 9. "Hallowed be Thy Name". "Holy Father, keep them in Thy Name" 644.

8. *Goodness.* All good things come from Him 83 126 252 478; Manifested in His lavish gifts to Men and Angels 9—19; in the preservation of the human race through Noe; in the repeated promise of a Redeemer; in the special election and guidance of the people of Israel; in the case of individuals as Joseph, Solomon, Elias, Tobias, Daniel; finally and fully in the Incarnation of His Only-begotten Son 401 452.

9. *Justice.* Manifested in the sin of the Angels 11; of our first parents 26; of Cain 31; in the deluge 39; in the destruction of Sodom 64; in the history of Esau and Jacob; of Joseph and his brethren; in the ten plagues; in the sedition of Core; in the destruction of the Chanaanites, of the kingdoms of Israel and Juda, of Jerusalem; in the parable of Lazarus and Dives; in the punishment of Herod the Great and Herod Agrippa; of Ananias and Saphira.

10. *Mercy and Compassion.* Manifested in the promise of a Redeemer 26; in the deluge 39; in the sin of the golden calf 160; in the brazen serpent 182—184; in the case of the judges 200—203; in forgiving the sin of David 243; in promising to forgive all, even the greatest, sins 312 ("If your sins be as scarlet &c."); in the deliverance from Babylonian captivity 326 338 349. — The Mercy and Compassion of Jesus manifested in the cure of the paralytic 467; of the leper 487; of Mary Magdalen 496; of the prodigal son 568; in feeding the hungry multitude 528; in the repentance of Peter 669; in the conversion of Saul 766; in the institution of the Sacrament of penance 723.

§ 2. THE THREE PERSONS OF GOD.

The Holy Trinity. A plurality of divine persons signified in the O. T. 7 17; clearly revealed in the N. T. 432 447 646 733. The Father sent His Son into the world (Incarnation), and the Son sent the Holy Ghost, visibly once (on Pentecost), invisibly whenever a soul is sanctified by grace. By sanctifying grace the Holy Ghost with Father and Son dwells in our hearts.

§ 3. GOD THE CREATOR OF HEAVEN AND EARTH.

1. THE CREATION AND GOVERNMENT OF THE WORLD.

God the *Creator* of the world 1—9; words of the Machabee brothers 365; of St. Paul at Lystra 784; at Athens 794.

God *maintains* the world: "Behold the birds of the air, for they neither sow" &c. 478; God works continuously 500; the annual multiplication of bread 529.

God *gove. ns* the world 110 202. See "Providence".

God suffers evil and knows how to turn it to good: Guidance of Jacob 78; Joseph 93; Joseph's words 114; destruction of Israel 294; the cockle among the wheat 508; the sin of Judas 637; the hatred of the Pharisees 675; the unbelief of Thomas 724; the sealing of our Lord's sepulchre 708; the persecution of the Christians in Jerusalem 761. *Why there is so much suffering:* Abraham 69, Joseph in Egypt 98; his brethren 107; Job 126; oppression of the Israelites 182 201; David's trials 245; Solomon's magnificence 260; overthrow of Israel 294; of Juda 326; trials of Tobias 296 306; the paralytic man 467; persecution of the Christians 761.

Divine Providence: Esau and Jacob 78; Joseph 103 114; Jacob in Egypt 117; Ruth 208; Saul 218; Aman's murderous plot frustrated 355; guidance of mankind 376; the enrolment at Bethlehem 400; rescue of the Child Jesus 419; our Lord's word's: "Be not solicitous" &c. 478; and "The hairs of your head" &c. 522.

2. THE ANGELS.

Creation and fall of angels 9—13. The sin of angels greater than that of Adam 27.

Office of the good angels: They are God's messengers 10; Gabriel's message to Zachary 382; to Mary 385; to Joseph 387 417; message of the angel to the shepherds 402; and to Philip the deacon 759. They praise God 402 ("Glory to God in the highest").

They come to our aid: Lot 66; Tobias 298; the three children 336; Daniel in the lion's den 344; Judas Machabeus 369; Peter in prison 778.

They pray for us: Jacob's ladder 83; words of Raphael 305.

They exhort us to what is right: Raphael's words to young Tobias 300.

Belief in *guardian angels:* Tobias the elder 299 305; Judith 321. The doctrine taught by our Lord 548 550; and believed by the first Christians 779.

The *evil spirits* lay snares for us out of hatred and envy: Fall of Adam and Eve 19; Job 122 127. Our Lord's temptation 429; the possessed 458; Judas Iscariot 639. They cannot, however, injure us, if we, following our Lord's example, resist their temptations 433.

3. THE FIRST MAN.

Creation of man 13. Made to the image of God 15 792 (St. Paul's discourse at Athens). Immortality of the soul 93 371. Free-will 16 17 31.

The fall of man 19. Original sin 22 447 (discourse with Nicodemus).

Mary conceived without sin: First promise of the Redeemer 27. Types of the immaculate Virgin: Gedeon's fleece 203; Esther 356.

Consequences of sin: Adam and Eve after the fall 22; the sentence 24; Cain 32; corruption of man 35; idolatry 48; and repeated falls of Israel 201. *Figures of the corruption of man:* 327 (destruction of the city and Temple); 537 (the man deaf and dumb); 558 (the Jew wounded and plundered by robbers); 670 (Judas).

SECOND ARTICLE OF THE CREED.

The holy Name of *Jesus* 404.

The name of *Christ* (the Anointed). In the Old Testament high priests 173, kings 220, and prophets 278, were anointed with oil; but Jesus is the supreme Priest, King and Prophet, as was signified in the Old Law 190, and as such He was anointed immediately by the Holy Ghost, and after His Baptism in the Jordan was manifested to the world 432.

We are the *children of God* 716.

Jesus Christ is *our Lord* 562 590 673 732 736 751.

§ 1. JESUS CHRIST THE PROMISED REDEEMER.

Promises of the Redeemer: to our first parents 26; to Abraham 54 70; to Jacob 83; through Jacob 120; through Balaam 186; Moses 190; David 238; Isaias 313; Jeremias 326; vision of Ezechiel 327; Nabuchodonozor's dream 337; Aggeus 350; Zacharias 350; Malachias 359.

Personal types of Christ: Adam 27; Abel 33; Noe 45; Melchisedech 58; Isaac 70; Joseph 104 114; Job 127; Moses 160; Josue 195; Gedeon 203; Samson 203; David 249; Solomon 260; Elias 283; Jonas 291.

Material types of Christ: Tree of knowledge 18; the ram in the thicket 70; Jacob's ladder 84; the paschal lamb 143; the rock in the wilderness 152; the sacrifices of the Old Law 170; the brazen serpent 183; Gedeon's fleece 203.

That Jesus is the promised Redeemer is shown:
a) by Himself 452 (to the Samaritan woman); 456 (in the synagogue at Nazareth); 663 (before the Sanhedrim).
b) by the apparition of Moses and Elias at the Transfiguration 544;
c) by the angel who appeared to the shepherds 402.
d) by John the Baptist 428 437.
e) by the first disciples 437; especially by Peter 533 540.
f) by the crowd when Jesus entered Jerusalem 606.

g) by the fact that all the promises of the Messias were fulfilled in Him, especially in those things foretold by the prophets:

1. concerning the time of His Birth 376; the place of His Birth 413; His descent from David (and the virginity of His Mother) 239 313 387.

2. the circumstances of His Life 454 494 606 (His solemn entry into Jerusalem); as well as the circumstances and details of His Passion and Death 690 701 706.

3. about His Resurrection 711; Ascension 733; and the descent of the Holy Ghost 739.

4. about the foundation and everlasting duration of His Church 540 806.

Preparation of the Gentiles for the Redeemer: the deluge 38; destruction of Sodom 64; the plagues of Egypt 139; Balaam 186; Naaman 284; Jonas 290; overthrow of Israel 294; dream of Nabuchodonozor 337; Daniel 345 377.

Condition of the world at the Advent of Christ: 338 (despotism); 346 (idolatry); 554 (slavery); 783 785 (deification of men). A picture of the misery of mankind before Christ 501.

§ 2. JESUS CHRIST TRUE GOD.

The *Divinity of Christ* is attested:

a) by the prophets 239 313 (Isaias: "God Himself will come and save you"); especially by John the Baptist 426 ("He will baptize with the Holy Ghost"); 435 ("Behold the Lamb of God ... He was before me ... I give testimony that He is the Son of God"). By the angel Gabriel 382 ("He shall convert many to *the Lord their God.* And he shall go before *Him*"); 386 ("He shall be called the Son of the Most High ... He shall be called the Son of God ... He shall save the people from their sins"). By the angel to the shepherds 402 ("A Saviour who is Christ the Lord"). By Elizabeth 390 ("Whence is this to me that the Mother of my Lord should come to me?"). By Zachary 395 ("Thou child shalt be called the prophet of the Highest, for thou shalt go before the face of the Lord").

b) by God the Father at the Baptism in the Jordan 429 ("This is My beloved Son" &c.); and at the Transfiguration 543.

c) by Christ Himself:

1. by His words 421 ("Did you not know that I must be about my Father's business?"); 442 446 ("Make not the house of My Father a house of traffic"); 447 ("God so loved the world as to give His Only-begotten Son ... God sent His Son into the world"); 500 ("Whatsoever things the Father doth, these the Son also doth in like manner ... For as the Father raiseth the dead &c. ... that all men may honour the Son as they

honour the Father"); 538 (when in response to Peter's confession: "Thou art the Christ, the Son of the living God", Jesus answered: "Blessed art thou, Simon, for flesh and blood hath not revealed it to thee, but My Father who is in heaven... And I will give to thee the keys of the kingdom of heaven" &c.); 553; 578 ("It is He—the Son of God—who speaketh with thee"); 589 ("I and the Father are one...the Father is in Me and I in the Father"); 595 ("This sickness is ... for the glory of God, that the Son of God may be glorified by it...I am the resurrection and the life" &c.); 644 ("Father, glorify Thy Son...glorify Thou Me with the glory which I had before the world was"); 662 (Jesus attested on oath: "I am the Christ, the Son of the Blessed God, and you shall see the Son of Man sitting on the right hand of the power of God"); 662 (To the question of the Sanhedrim: "Art Thou therefore the Son of God?" Jesus answered: "I am"); 693 ("Father, forgive them" &c.); 696 ("Amen, I say to thee, this day shalt thou be with Me in Paradise"); 700 ("Father, into Thy hands I commend My spirit"); 722 ("Receive ye the Holy Ghost; whose sins ye shall forgive" &c.); 722 (Jesus accepted the homage of Thomas when he cried out: "My Lord and my God!"); 730 ("All power is given to Me in heaven and earth... and behold I am with you all days even unto the consummation of the world")

2. by His divine works. See "Third Article" under "Miracles", 816.

3. by His Blood, for He died for the confession of His divinity 661 675 694.

d) by the apostles: 533 ("We have believed and have known that Thou art the Christ, the Son of God"); 538 (Peter confesses: "Thou art Christ, the Son of the living God"); 543 723 (the apostles were witnesses to the Transfiguration and Resurrection of Jesus); 722 (Thomas cries out: "My Lord and My God!"); 727 (Peter says: "Lord, Thou knowest all things"); 731 (St. John writes that "Jesus Christ is the Son of God"); 736 (the disciples pray to Jesus as the omniscient Lord); 739 (Peter preaches that "Jesus was exalted to the right hand of God, and had sent the Holy Ghost"); 742 (Peter calls Jesus the Son of God and the Author of ife); 755 (Stephen testifies to the divinity of Christ by his vision, his prayer and his blood); 766 (Paul preaches at Damascus that "Jesus is the Son of God"); 773 (Peter preaches at Cæsarea that "Jesus is the Judge of the living and the dead", and that "through His name all receive remission of sins"); 797 (testimony of St. Paul to the divinity of Christ); 803 (the apostles bore witness to it with their blood).

e) by the Catholic Church 736 762.

THIRD ARTICLE OF THE CREED.

The *Incarnation of the Son of God* was foreshadowed 203 (Gedeon's fleece); foretold by Isaias 313; announced by Gabriel 385.

There are *two natures in Christ*: Declaration of David 239; Isaias 313. The Annunciation 385; the Nativity 400; the Child Jesus in the Temple 422; our Lord's discourse with Nicodemus 447; the storm on the lake 514.

Mary is the Mother of God: 385 (the Annunciation); 390 (the Holy Ghost speaks through Elizabeth).

Mary has co-operated in our salvation 385 698; power of her intercession 441.

Types of Mary: 27 389 (Eve); 320 (Judith); 356 (Esther).

Virtues of Mary: 389 393 410 419 423 441 560.

Sorrows of Mary: 410 698 707. Her death and assumption into heaven 801.

St. Joseph: 419 (his virtues and his high place in the kingdom of God); 441 (his blessed death).

Type of St. Joseph: 108 ("Go to Joseph").

The reason why the Son of God became incarnate: 84 (the heavenly ladder); 401; 447 (Jesus Himself told Nicodemus); 655 (Agony in the garden); only God can redeem us 558.

Christmas 404.

Adoration of the shepherds 402; the Magi 411; 416 (signification of their gifts); 416 (Feast of the three kings)..

Circumcision of Jesus 403.

Presentation of Jesus in the Temple 405.

Jesus subject at Nazareth 423.

His Baptism 428; fasting and temptation 429.

Jesus teaches: 447 (Nicodemus); 449 (the Samaritan woman); 454 (the Nazarites); 458 (in Galilee); 435 (He gathers disciples round Him); 518 (chooses twelve of them to be apostles).

Jesus proved the divinity of his doctrine by:
1. the *holiness of His Life* 590 ("Believe the works" &c.); 669 675 (gentleness of Jesus); 658 683 (His patience, innocence &c.); 676 (Procla's dream); 741 (the holy One and the just); 773 ("Who went about doing good").
2. by *miracles*: 438 446 452 (He knew secret and distant things); 439 (He changes water into wine); 442 (drives the buyers and sellers out of the Temple); 458 (drives out devils, cures Peter's wife's mother and many other sick). 461 (He proves He has dominion over nature by the miraculous draught of fishes); 465 (cure of the man sick of the palsy); 484 (by mere force of will He cures the leper and centurion's servant; 489 (He proves His dominion over life and death by raising up the young man of Naim); 495 (He reads the thoughts of Simon the Pharisee); 498 (He heals the infirm man);

512 (He proves His dominion over nature by stilling the tempest). 515 (the raising of Jairus' daughter, and the cure of the infirm woman by the touch of His garments); 519 (He transfers His power of working miracles to His apostles, who heal many sick); 525 (the multiplication of the loaves manifests His creative omnipotence); 530 (the four miracles the day after the miracle of the loaves prove that Jesus is independent of the laws of nature); 536 (He delivers from a devil the absent daughter of the Chanaanite woman, and cures a man deaf and dumb); 543 (by His Transfiguration He reveals His indwelling divine majesty); 576 (the cure of the man born blind is judicially examined and authenticated); 589 (Jesus appeals to His miracles as proofs of His Divinity, and vanishes suddenly from the midst of His enraged enemies); 595 (raising to life of Lazarus); 657 (Jesus strikes the ruffians to the ground by a word, and heals the wounded Malchus); 696 (the wonderful conversion of the penitent thief); 702 (the miracles attendant on His death); 710 (the miracle of all miracles, the Resurrection); 724 (Jesus reveals His omniscience); 728 (the miraculous draught of fishes); 732 (the Ascension); 734 (Jesus sends the Holy Ghost); 741 (Peter in the name of Jesus heals the lame man); 755 (Jesus appears to Stephen); 766 (He appears to Saul, converts and cures him); 769 (through Peter He cures Eneas and raises Tabitha to life); 778 (through the angel He frees Peter from prison); 782 795 797 (He works many miracles through St. Paul); 521 806 (the maintenance and spread of the Church proves the divinity of Christ).

Object of our Lord's miracles 440 446 599; object of the Old Testament's miracles 139 149 194 272 284 346.

Witnesses of our Lord's miracles 491 599.

Object of the apostles' miracles 743 761 770 785; difference between our Lord's miracles and those of the apostles 743.

3. by *prophecies*: Jesus foretold the treason of Judas and the denial of Peter 637 640; His Passion and Death 444 445 531 562; His Resurrection 444 503 (the sign of Jonas); His Ascension 532 642 ("In My Father's house there are many mansions, I go to prepare a place for you"); 715 ("I ascend to my Father"); the martyrdom of St. Peter 727 802; the descent of the Holy Ghost 643; the destruction of Jerusalem 605 616; the spread of the Church 486 510 (the grain of mustard-seed); 539 ("the gates of hell shall not prevail against it"); 561 (the sheep-fold), 806.

FOURTH ARTICLE OF THE CREED.

The *Passion* of Christ *foretold:* 238 (by David); 313 (by Isaias); 435 (by John the Baptist); 444 533 601 602 (by Christ Himself).

Types of the crucified Saviour: Isaac 70; the paschal lamb 142 701 706; the brazen serpent 183 445.

Types of the Cross of Christ: the Tree of knowledge 18; the wood which made the bitter water sweet 150; the budding rod of Aaron 180.

Jesus suffered as man: 652; throughout His whole life 410; (even in the manger) 401 447; finally, He was seized 656; mocked 674; scourged and crowned with thorns 676; sentenced to death by Pilate 679; and nailed to the Cross 686 702 706.

The *miracles* accompanying the Death of Jesus prove His divinity 696 700.

The *way of the Cross* 692; *Good Friday* 171 702; the *dolours of Mary* 406 410 698 707.

Jesus suffered *willingly:* 313 (Isaias); 401 601 639 659; in order to atone for our sins 313 (Isaias); 650 669 674 681 682 690 695 701; and to redeem us and open heaven to us 447 655 690 701.

Jesus suffered *innocently* 674 679 680.

Only *God* could redeem us 558.

Why not all men are saved 177 592 (Many are called &c.); 654.

FIFTH ARTICLE OF THE CREED.

The Resurrection of Jesus Christ foretold 238 (by David); 313 (by Isaias); 503 (the sign of Jonas).

Type: Jonas 291.

Limbo: 75 524 571.

"He descended into hell" 706; on the third day He rose again from the dead 710.

Significance of our Lord's Resurrection 712 794.

Proofs of the Resurrection of Christ: He appears 1. to Magdalen; 2. to the other women, 3. to Peter, 4. to the two disciples on the road to Emmaus, to whom He expounds the Scriptures, 5. to the apostles, eats with them, explains the Scriptures, bequeaths His mission, and institutes the Sacrament of Penance, 6. to the eleven, and lets Thomas touch Him, 7. to seven disciples on the Sea of Galilee, and confers the chief pastorship on Peter, 8. to more than five hundred disciples on a mountain in Galilee, 9. to the apostles in the room at Jerusalem, and confers on them His teaching, priestly and pastoral office. Stupid lies of the chief priests 714 729.

The apostles are witnesses to the Resurrection 723.

The marks of the five wounds on Jesus' glorified Body 725.

The Paschal Feast in the Old and New Testament 144 713; the true Paschal Lamb 635 706.

SIXTH ARTICLE OF THE CREED.

Type of the glorified Redeemer: Solomon 260.

He ascended into heaven, sitteth at the right hand of God the Father Almighty 729.

He ascended, 1. to take possession of His glory 646 ("Glorify Thou Me with the glory which I had before the world was"); 2. in order to send the Holy Ghost (see Eighth Article); 3. to be our Advocate with the Father 646; 4. to prepare a place for us 642 ("In My Father's house are many mansions").

The human nature of Christ merited its glory 720

SEVENTH ARTICLE OF THE CREED.

Type of the Last Judgment: the deluge 40.

Jesus Christ will judge the world 500 ("The Father hath given all judgment to the Son"); 503 ("The men of Ninive" &c.); 508 (the parable of the cockle); 510 (the parable of the net); 616 (signs preceding the judgment); 623 (Jesus describes the judgment); 732 (the universal dominion of Jesus); 794 (St. Paul at Athens); 807 (a new heaven and a new earth).

The glory of the just and *the shame of the wicked* at the Last Judgment: Esau weeps aloud 78; terror of Joseph's brethren 114; the false accusers of Susanna 333; the man without a wedding-garment 610; the manifestations of all sins 626; "What shall be done in the dry wood" &c; 691; terror of sinners 713

EIGHTH ARTICLE OF THE CREED.

The Holy Ghost: allusion to Him in the Old Testament 7; "The Holy Ghost will overshadow thee" 386; Elizabeth filled with the Holy Ghost 390; the Holy Ghost under the form of a dove 429; sins against the Holy Ghost 502; promise of the Holy Ghost 643; the Holy Ghost is the Third Person of the Blessed Trinity 646 737 748; descent of the Holy Ghost 735.

Pentecost: type 157 739.

The Holy Ghost teaches the Church 643 646 ("He will teach you all things"); 740 (therefore manifested under the appearance of tongues); 762 789 (Council of Jerusalem). He *sanctifies* the Church: 738 (conversion of the Jews); 745 (the holy lives of the first Christians). He *governs* the Church: 772 (the Holy Ghost sends Peter to Cornelius); 781 (the Holy Ghost commands the sending out of Paul and Barnabas).

The Holy Ghost enlightens and comforts 390 (Elizabeth); 411 (Simeon); 646 770.

The gifts of the Holy Ghost: Solomon 253 (gift of wisdom); 738 (the apostles); St. Stephen 754; (Holy Fear) 764.

NINTH ARTICLE OF THE CREED.

§ 1. THE IDEA AND INSTITUTION OF THE CHURCH.

Pentecost is the feast of the *institution* or rather of the *dedication* of the Church 739; after it the apostles went forth, preached, established

Christian communities and consecrated bishops 769 774 781 784 788 800; the Church proceeds from the Side of Jesus 707.

What is the Church? 739 747 751 769.

Christ is the *invisible Head*, Lord and Protector of the Church: 463 514 (Christ in St. Peter's little ship); 673 ("I am a king"); 774 (Christ governs the Church); 779 (St. Peter delivered from prison); 806 (Christ protects the Church).

Peter is the *visible Head* of the Church: 436 (Simon is called Peter); 518 ("The first Simon who is called Peter"); 539 ("Thou art Peter" &c.); 641 ("Confirm thy brethren"); 726—728 (the chief pastoral office conferred on Peter); He stands forth as the chief pastor 734 (at the election of Matthias); 735 (at Pentecost); 746 (when he questioned and punished Ananias); 750 (when he acted as spokesman before the Council); 768 (when he undertook a visitation); 774 (when he received a revelation and admitted the first Gentiles into the Church); 787 (by presiding at the Council of Jerusalem).

The Pope is the successor of St. Peter as chief pastor 541 807.

The bishops are the successors of the apostles 555 805 806 (Titus, Timothy &c.).

Types of the Church: 40 (the Ark of Noe); 463 728 (the ship of Peter).

§ 2. MARKS OF THE CHURCH.

Christ founded only *one*, and that one a *visible* Church 551 ("Tell it to the Church"); 540 ("On this rock I will build My Church"); 562 ("There shall be one fold and one shepherd"); there is only one truth 512.

The Church of Christ must be: 1. *one* 645 (Christ prays for the unity of the Church); 2. *holy* 645 ("Keep them from evil . . . . Sanctify them in truth"); 3. *catholic or universal* 337; 510 (the grain of mustard-seed); 562 730 ("Teach all nations . . . to the consummation of the world"); 761 (the Ethiopian); 4. *apostolic* 522 (the apostles are the patriarchs of the Church); 761 (the Church to be spread by the apostles and their successors).

The *Roman Church is the true Church*, founded by Christ, for she is:

1. *one* 49 562 745.
2. *holy* 510 511 745 (the holy lives of the first Christians).
3. *universal* 761 774 807.
4. *apostolic* 799 807.

In her alone are the types of the Old Testament fulfilled 173 337. According to our Lord's prophecy 518 647; she is hated and persecuted by the world 751 754.

§ 3. THE OFFICE OF THE CHURCH.

The *prophetical, priestly and royal office* of the Church instituted by God 541, 723 (Jesus confers His own mission on the apos); 774 (only by means of this threefold office can man have part in the grace of redemption).

The *Church as a teacher is infallible* 646 732 762; whether its decisions are made by a general council 789; or by the Pope as chief pastor 541 641 728 when the matter is one of faith or morals.

The infallibility of the Church is a consolation to the faithful 789.

In the Catholic Church *alone is salvation:* 463 (the draught of fishes); 471 ("You are the light of the world"); 722 ("As the Father hath sent Me" &c.) 728 730 732 806. The Ark of Noe a type of the Church in which alone is salvation 40.

The Church is *indestructible:* 386 ("Of His kingdom there will be no end"); 514 (the ship of Peter); 521 541 751 805.

We owe obedience to the Church 541 551 747 (Ananias and Saphira); 767.

§ 4. THE COMMUNION OF SAINTS.

Jesus is the king of all the redeemed 562. All who belong to Him shall be called Saints 768. The blessed in heaven pray for us 372 563. Prayers for the holy souls 371.

TENTH ARTICLE OF THE CREED.

Remission of sins 722 (institution of the Sacrament of Penance); 730 ("He that believeth and is baptized shall be saved"); 736 ("Be baptized for the remission of your sins").

ELEVENTH ARTICLE OF THE CREED.

At *death* the soul is separated from the body, and the latter returns to the earth 13 25 269 301 517; death is a sleep 517 756; it comes unexpectedly 622.

The *resurrection of the body:* Job's faith 125; the vision of Ezechiel 324; faith of the Machabee brothers 365; death a sleep 517; "I am the resurrection and the life" 596; the Resurrection of Christ is the cause and pledge of our resurrection 712.

The *glorified body* 712.

TWELFTH ARTICLE OF THE CREED.

The *particular judgment* 343 (numbered, weighed and judged); 365 588 756.

Purgatory 371 505.

Hell: the destruction of Sodom a type of hell 66; cruelty of Satan 461 486 (weeping and gnashing of teeth); 478 (cast into the oven); 548 ("everlasting fire"); 570 (a glimpse of hell); 611 628 ("depart from Me"); 648 (the withered vine-branch burneth, but is not burnt).

It lasts for ever 505 571 628.

Who go to hell? 481 (the broad way); 571 (the impenitent); 611 628 (he who has done no good works); 648 (he who is not in a state of grace).

Heaven: its type 17 (Paradise); "I am thy reward" 59; Joseph's exaltation 104; faith of Job 126; of the Machabee brothers 365. "The just shall shine like the sun in the kingdom of their Father" 509; joy of the apostles at the Transfiguration 544; "Come ye blessed" &c. 628; promise of heaven 642 648; the Tree of life in the heavenly Paradise 806; degrees of bliss 481; a glimpse of heaven gives consolation 806.

The *transformation* of the world 807.

SECOND PART.

THE TEN COMMANDMENTS.

The Ten Commandments: 154 156; the law of Jesus is sweet and light 624; he who will be saved must keep the commandments 54 (Abraham); "Not every one that saith unto me, Lord, Lord" &c. 482 624 628; "Teaching them to observe all things" &c. 730; perfection of the Christian law 472.

The commandments are a benefit 156 484.

FIRST COMMANDMENT.

§ 1. OF THE LOVE OF GOD.

Models of the love of God: Abraham 69; Solomon 252; the three youths in the furnace 339; Eleazar 362; the seven Machabees 365; Mary and Martha 560; the first Christians 747; Stephen 756; Paul 799; the apostles 801.

The love of God above all thing 587 613. Motives for the love of God (see "The goodness and mercy of God" 811).

§ 2. OF THE LOVE OF OUR NEIGHBOUR.

The commandment to love our neighbour: 472 479; 558 (the good Samaritan); 640 648.

Models of the love of our neighbour: Noe 40; Abraham 57 60; Moses 160; Booz 209; Tobias 295; Jeremias 326; Mary 393; the first Christians 747; Stephen 756; Tabitha 770; Cornelius 776.

Our love of our neighbour ought to be

1. *sincere:* Abraham 57; Joseph's love for his brethren 112; Moses' love for his people 160; Mary's for Elizabeth 393; Elizabeth's neighbours 396; the centurion 487; the good Samaritan 558.

2. *disinterested:* Abraham 57; Rebecca 74; Booz 209; David and Jonathan 227; Tobias 300; Mary ministering to Elizabeth 393; "With what measure" &c. 479; the good Samaritan 558; Stephen 756; Tabitha 770; Cornelius 776.

3. *entire:* Joseph's love for his enemies 110 112; David 231 245; the good Samaritan 558; Stephen 756.

Jesus has *commanded* us to *love our enemies* 473 ("I say to you, love your enemies" &c.); 551 (parable of the unmerciful servant); He taught the same by His example 659 (by healing the wounded Malchus); 693 (by praying on the Cross for His enemies).

It is *noble to forgive:* 89 (Esau); 112 (Joseph).

Love of the poor, widows &c.: the king's daughter and the infant Moses 130; Booz and the poor Ruth 209; Tobias 300; Jesus with the widow of Naim 491; the centurion 487; the widows of the early Christians 758; Tabitha and the widows 770.

The corporal works of mercy:

1. to feed the hungry: Abraham 57; Joseph 108; Booz 209; the widow of Sarepta 267; Jesus multiplies the loaves 526; Martha 560;
2. to give drink to the thirsty: Abraham 57; Rebecca 74; the woman of Samaria 453.
3. to clothe the naked: Tabitha 770.
4. to harbour the harbourless: Abraham 60; Martha and Mary 560; the two disciples at Emmaus 720.
5. to visit the imprisoned: Abraham 56; Daniel saves Susanna 331.
6. to visit the sick: Job's friends 124; the disciples of John the Baptist 492; the good Samaritan 558; Peter visits Eneas 768.
7. to bury the dead: Tobias 305; the inhabitants of Naim 489; Joseph of Arimathea and Nicodemus 704.

The spiritual works of mercy:

1. to convert the sinner: Henoch 35; Noe 36; Joseph 107; Elias 271; John the Baptist 425; the thief on the right hand 696; Paul and Barnabas at Lystra 783.
2. to instruct the ignorant: Jesus in chapters XV—XVII; Peter on day of Pentecost 735; at Cæsarea 772; Philip and the Ethiopian 760; Paul at Athens 792.
3. to counsel the doubtful: Joseph 102; Roboam's old advisers 262; Naaman's servants 280; the counsel of Gamaliel 750.
4. to comfort the sorrowful: Joseph 99; Tobias 296; Jesus in chapt. XXIII (the young man of Naim), XXV (Magdalen), XXX (Jairus' daughter), LIV (the raising of Lazarus), LXVIII (parting words).
5. to bear wrongs patiently: Job, his wife and his friends 126; David's magnanimity 231; Tobias and his wife's reproaches 294; Eleazar 361; Jesus in His Passion 656 701.
6. to forgive injuries: Esau 89; Joseph 112; David 228 246; Jesus 693; Stephen 757.
7. to pray for the living and the dead: Abraham intercedes for Sodom 62; Moses for his people chapt. XXXVII XL, Samuel XLVIII; Solomon LIX, Elias LXIII, Judas Machabeus LXXXV (for the dead); the disciples pray for Peter's mother-in-law 460; Jesus for His apostles 520; for the unity of the Church 265; for His enemies 645; Stephen prays for his murderers 755; the Church for Peter 780.

§ 3. OF CHRISTIAN SELF-LOVE

Inordinate self-love: Lot 55; Jacob 76; Achab 274; the Pharisees 545.
Christian self-love cares more for the soul and for what is eternal than
for the body and for what is temporal: folly of sinners 87 (Esau);
301 ("Enemies of their own souls"); the Machabee brothers 363;
Jesus heals first the soul of the paralytic man 465; 477 ("Lay not up
to yourselves treasures upon earth &c. . . . Seek you first the kingdom of God &c."); 548 (the value of a soul); 560 (the one thing
needful); 571 (why the rich man was eternally punished); 586 ("He
that loveth his life shall lose it"); 586 ("What doth it profit a man &c.").

§ 4. OF THE WORSHIP OF GOD.

Models of the worship of God: Abraham 52; Joseph 94; David 222;
Tobias 295 301; Judith 319; our Lord's words: "Render to God
the things that are God's" 612.

Gratitude to God: Noe after leaving the Ark 44; the three young men
in the furnace 339; Zachary 395; Simeon 408; the man born lame 741.

Resignation to God's will: Abraham 52; Job 126; Heli 214; Samuel
221; Tobias 297; Mary and Joseph at the flight into Egypt 417;
John the Baptist 428; Lazarus 571; Jesus in the Garden 654.

Unbelief: the men before the Flood 35; Pharao 140; the Nazarites 425;
the proud Pharisees 498; many disciples when the Blessed Sacrament
was promised 532; the rich man and his brethren 572; the chief
priests 695 785.

Causes of unbelief: 40 160 309 456 504 579 584 600 785 794.

The weapons of unbelief: 505 714 754 (lies); 578 749 754 757 758 763
777 782 796 801 (violence); 693 734 794 (scorn); 639 714 (bribery).

Heresy: the Samaritans 451.

Doubt: Moses and Aaron 183; Zachary 384.

Religious indifference: Solomon 260; its blameworthiness 776.

Denial of faith: Solomon 260 339; Peter 667.

Sins against hope: the murmuring Israelites 153 176 182; Moses and
Aaron 183; presumption of the Pharisees 425; despair of Cain 30;
of Judas 669.

Sins against charity: Job's wife 127; the Israelites in the desert 151
176 182.

External worship of God: Moses 133; the sacrifices of the Old Law
170; David 234; dedication of the Temple 256; Tobias 293; Jesus,
Mary and Joseph go up to the Temple 420; worship of God in
spirit and in truth 453; Jesus in the synagogue of Nazareth 454;
the publican in the Temple 583; religious worship of the early
Christians 747; religious music 235.

Sins against religion: Heli's sons 214; Jesus cleanses the Temple 442.

Idolatry: tower of Babel 46; the golden calf 158; the Chanaanites 194; Nabuchodonosor 335; Babylon 344; the Roman empire 781; the men of Lystra 783; of Athens 791.
Superstition: dreams 90; Balak 185; the sorcerer at Cyprus 783.
Sacrilege: Heli's sons 214; Baltassar's banquet 343; desecration of the Temple 361.

§ 5. OF THE VENERATION OF SAINTS.

The veneration and invocation of Saints: Job's intercession 127; Moses' 151 160 177; Judith's 320; Onias' 372; the apostles' 460; St. Stephen's 757.
The Angels and Saints know about us and our prayers: Raphael's words to Tobias 306; vision of Judas 372; the joy of the angels over the conversion of one sinner 568.
We honour God in His Saints: the veneration of the Blessed Virgin 392; of St. Joseph 419.
The worship of Mary: the angel's reverential greeting 385; St. Elizabeth's greeting 390; the dignity of the Mother of God 392; her prophecy 391 504; the power of her intercession 441; Mary our Mother 698; the feeling towards her of the first Christians 736.
Veneration of pictures: 166 (the pictures of Cherubim in the Tabernacle).
Veneration of relics: the mantle of Elias 278; the bones of Eliseus 284; the girdle &c. of St. Paul 798.

SECOND COMMANDMENT.

Blasphemy: the Israelites in the desert 177; the Pharisees 466; the Jews at the Crucifixion 693 708.
Curses (imprecations): the people in the desert 177; Balak 185; the Jews 679 685.
Oaths: our Lord's words 474; His oath 662.
Sinful oaths: Esau makes an unnecessary oath 79; Herod also 523; Peter's false oath 667.
Vows: Jacob 82 84 88; Anna 213; Mary 389.
Zeal for God's glory: Moses 160; David 234 250; Elias 272; Daniel 343; the Machabees 372; Mary 423; Jesus 446; Peter 738 744; Paul 798.

THIRD COMMANDMENT.

Institution of the Sabbath 7; commandment to keep it holy 154; example of Jesus 458; keeping holy Sunday instead of the Sabbath 725; divine worship of the early Christians 747.
Desecration of the Sabbath: manna did not fall on Sabbath 149; the Sabbath-breaker 180.
Permission to do work on the Sabbath 501 ("Take up thy bed and walk").

FOURTH COMMANDMENT.

Good children: Joseph 89 112; Ruth 208; Tobias 301; Jesus 423 698.

Parents are the representatives of God: Jacob's words 89.

Love of parents for their children: Jacob 118; the parents of Moses 129; David 245; Tobias 300 304; Mary and Joseph 417 419; dolours of Mary 410; the widow of Naim 491.

Reverence for parents: Sem and Japhet 43; Joseph 117; admonition of Tobias 304. Sins against it: Cham 43; Absalom 245.

Love for parents: Joseph 110 113 117; Juda 112; Tobias 304; Jesus 697. Sins against it: Joseph's brethren 90; Absalom 244.

Punishment of bad children: Cham 43; the sons of Heli 214; Absalom 245.

Reward of good children: Sem 45; Joseph 121; Tobias 304.

Conduct towards foster-parents: Ruth 208; Samuel towards Heli 214; the disciples of Elias 283; Jesus towards Joseph 423. Conduct towards masters: Eliezer 74.

Authority ordained by God: Aaron's budding rod 179; Saul 230; our Lord's words 722 ("As the Father hath sent Me" &c.); divine right of kings 228; distinction between spiritual and temporal authority 310; Nabuchodonosor's dream 337; our Lord's words 589 612 ("Render to Cæsar" &c.); 684 ("Thou shouldst not have power" &c.).

Sins against spiritual authority: The revolt of Core 180; Ozias 309; the boys at Bethel 285; Ananias 746; *against temporal authority:* the murmuring of the Israelites against Moses 150 178; the revolt of Core 180; Absalom's rebellion 244; the ten tribes 262.

Lawful disobedience: Tobias 294; the high priest and Ozias 309; Daniel 325; the young men in the furnace 339; the Machabee brothers 363; the apostles before the Council 744.

Duties of parents and superiors: Abraham 71; the exhortation of Moses 189; Heli's sons 214; Tobias 304; "Suffer the children to come unto Me" 549.

Respect for old age: Pharao pays honour to Jacob 117; the boys of Bethel 285.

FIFTH COMMANDMENT.

Injury to our neighbour's body and soul: Cain 31; Joseph's brethren embitter their father's life 92; Samson's eyes put out 200; David causes the death of Urias 240; Naboth unjustly put to death 275; Eleazar 361; the Machabee brothers 363; the holy Innocents 416; beheading of John the Baptist 523; Passion and Crucifixion of Jesus, the scourging of the apostles, stoning of Stephen &c.

When the taking of life is lawful: 159 224.

Evil intentions against our neighbour: our Lord's words 472; the envy of Cain 31; the hatred of Esau 77; the envy of Joseph's brethren 90; envy of Saul 227; anger of the Nazarites 457; hatred of Herodias 523; hatred of the Pharisees towards Jesus 684 &c.

Suicide: Saul 231; Judas 670.

Desire for death: Elias 282.

Giving scandal: Putiphar's wife 95; Job's wife 127; the spies 177; David 243; Absalom 244; Jeroboam 264; Jezabel 276; our Lord's words 482 ("Beware of false prophets" &c.); 550.

Concord with our neighbour: Abraham's love of peace 55; the first Christians 747; our Lord's words 469 ("Blessed are the peacemakers").

Cruelty to animals: 16 44 291.

Zeal for souls: Henoch 35; Noe 40; Moses 160; Samuel 212; Elias 272 282; Tobias 301; Isaias 313; John the Baptist 425; Andrew and Philip 438 472 563 (the Good Shepherd); 702 (the thirst of Jesus); 738 744 771 (Peter); 751 (the apostles); 756 (Stephen); 765 786 799 (Paul).

SIXTH COMMANDMENT.

Sins against chastity: Cham 45; David 243; exhortation of Tobias 298 ("Keep thyself from all fornication").

Their shamefulness: Sodom 65.

Their bad consequences: Putiphar's wife 94; David 243 244; Susanna's accusers 330; Herod and Herodias 492.

Means of resisting them: Joseph 94; Susanna 332; purity of heart 470; the living temples of God 446.

SEVENTH COMMANDMENT.

Robbery: Achab seizes Naboth's vineyard 277; the robbers near Jericho 556.

Deceit: Giezi 281; what is found must be restored: Jacob 111; stolen goods must not be received: Tobias 296.

Beneficence: see "Corporal works of mercy" 823.

Economy: Joseph in Egypt 108; Jesus at the miracle of the loaves 529.

EIGHTH COMMANDMENT.

False witness: the witnesses against Naboth 276; against Susanna 332; against Jesus 663 672; against Stephen 754.

Lies: Satan 20; Jacob 76; the spies 177; the woman before Solomon 253; Giezi 285; Peter 664; the stupid lies of the chief priests 714; Ananias and Saphira 746.

Detraction: 45 (Cham); 480.

Calumny: Putiphar's wife 95; the Pharisees about Jesus 505 (saying that he was in league with the devil); 708 (the chief priests saying that the apostles meant to steal the Body of Jesus).

Hypocrisy: Joseph's brethren 91; Herod 415; Eleazar scorns it 361; the Pharisees 546 675; Judas 639 659; Ananias 748.

False suspicions: Job's friends 127; the chief priests 708.

Rash judgment: Putiphar 95; the proud Pharisee in the Temple 583; our Lord's words 480 ("Judge not" &c.).
Models of sincerity: Samuel 214; Eleazar 361.

NINTH AND TENTH COMMANDMENTS.

To covet another's wife: David 243; Herod Antipas 492 524.
To covet another's possessions: Achab 277.

FIRST AND SECOND COMMANDMENTS OF THE CHURCH.

Feasts: types of them 171; Christmas 401; Circumcision 404; Epiphany 416; Candlemas 410; Palm-Sunday 608; Corpus Christi 635; Good Friday 702; Easter 713; Ascension 731; Whit-Sunday 738; Feast of St. Stephen 757; the Assumption 801; SS. Peter and Paul 803.
Behaviour at divine worship: example of Solomon 255; Jesus 423; punishment of the sons of Heli 214; purification of the Temple 446.
Necessity of worship 256 477.
Holiness of God's house: Jacob's exclamation 82 ("How terrible is this place" &c.). Comparison between our churches and the Tabernacle 165; and the Temple of Solomon 257; Jesus cleanses the Temple 442 ("Make not my Father's house a house of traffic").
Zeal in hearing the word of God: the example of Jesus 423; the crowd on the shores of the lake 464; at the Sermon on the Mount 468; the first Christians 745.

THIRD COMMANDMENT OF THE CHURCH.

Ember-days: 785.
Abstinence from flesh-meat: example of Daniel and his friends 325; Eleazar 361; the Machabee brothers 366.
Fasting: recommended by the angel Raphael 303 ("Prayer is good with fasting and alms more than to lay up treasures of gold"); the example of Moses 158 161; the Israelites 213; the Ninivites 288; Judith 320; Jesus 434; Saul 768; the ancients of Antioch 781.

FOURTH AND FIFTH COMMANDMENTS OF THE CHURCH.

Necessity of confession 723.
Holy Communion: necessity of receiving it 534; frequent Communion of the first Christians 746; our Lord's words: "Suffer the children to come unto Me!" 549; Easter Communion 713.

ON BREAKING THE COMMANDMENTS.

§ 1. OF SIN GENERALLY.

What is sin? Adam and Eve 21; Noe's drunkenness not a sin 45; *conscience admonishes us* 22; Saul 222.
Sins *of thought:* Eve 21; the Pharisees 467; *of desire:* Eve 21; Cain 31; Esau wishes to kill Jacob 77; Herod purposes to kill the Child Jesus

420; *of word:* curses, lies &c.; *of deed:* killing, stealing; *of omission:* Ruben 93; the slothful servant 625.

Sin is the greatest of all evils: sin of the angels 11; sin of our first parents 22; evil consequences of one venial sin 93; Joseph's words: "How can I do this wicked thing" &c. 94; the severe punishment of Moses' doubt 183 189; our Lord's words: "If thy hand scandalize thee" &c. 548 553 (an inconceivably great guilt); 566 (dissipation and slavery); "What doth it profit a man" &c. 588; sin bears two aspects 671; Punishment of the fallen angels 11; of our first parents 24; the bitter Passion and Death of Jesus 652 655 659 669 674 680 681 690 701 702.

Sin is an act of ingratitude 22 99 112 244 567.

The folly of sinners: Esau sells his birthright 79 301 (enemies of their own souls); the prodigal son 566.

The consequences of mortal sin: the angels 11; our first parents 22; Cain's pangs of conscience 30; Samson 204; Saul 218; the city laid waste 327; the loss of Jesus 423; sin a leprosy 488; the prodigal son wastes his substance 566. The punishment of Sodom 65; the rich man in hell 571.

§ 2. THE DIFFERENT KINDS OF SIN.

When is sin mortal? Examples: the sin of our first parents 21; the lie told by the woman before the judgment-seat of Solomon 253; the false witnesses against our Lord 663.

The name of "mortal sin": God's threat "in what day soever thou shalt eat of it, thou shalt die the death" 15. The father's words in the parable: "This my son was dead" 568.

When is a sin venial? Examples: Jacob 93; doubt of Moses 183; Zachary 384.

Capital sins are the sources of all other sins:
Cain 31; Joseph's brethren 92; the avarice of Judas 639.

Pride: the fallen angels 11; our first parents 21 26; the Tower of Babel 48; Pharao 140; Core &c. 180; Saul 218; Goliath 225; Absalom 246; Solomon 260; Roboam 263; Tobias warns his son against it 298; Ozias 309; Aman 355; Herod 415; Simon the Pharisee 498; the rich glutton 571; the Pharisee in the Temple 584; the Pharisees 579; Herod Agrippa 780; the Jews of Antioch 785.

Avarice (covetousness): it is an idolatry 161; Achab 276; Giezi 285; Jesus warns against the worship of mammon 478; Judas 639 669; Ananias 748.

Lust: see the Sixth Commandment.

Envy: the devil 18; Cain 31; Laban 89; Joseph's brethren 93; Saul 227; the cruel woman before Solomon 253; the labourers in the vineyard 594; the Pharisees 713.

Gluttony: Noe 45; Esau 79; the Israelites in the desert 149 160; it is hurtful to the health 328; Baltassar 343; Herod 525; the rich man 571.

Anger: Esau 79; Nabuchodonosor 338; Aman 353; Herod 419; the Nazarites 457; Herodias 523. Righteous or holy anger (zeal): Moses 160; Jesus 442; Paul and Barnabas 783.

Sloth: work a means of resisting sin 26; David's tepidity 244; Solomon 260; Jesus works 423; the labourers in the vineyard 594; the foolish virgins 621; the slothful servant 624.

The six sins against the Holy Ghost:

1. *Presumption:* the men before the Flood 36; the inhabitants of Sodom 62; Judas 670.
2. *Despair:* Cain 30; Judas 670.
3. *Resisting the known truth:* the Pharisees 504; the reproach of St. Stephen against the unbelieving Jews 754 757.
4. *Envy of another's spiritual good:* Cain 29; the Pharisees 504 608; the Jews of Antioch in Pisidia 783.
5. *Obstinacy in sin:* Cain 29 32; Pharao 145; the kingdom of Israel 295; the kingdom of Juda 326; the Pharisees at the preaching of John the Baptist 425; at the preaching of Jesus 505; Jesus weeps over Jerusalem 607.
6. *Final impenitence:* the devil 12; Pharao 140; the Pharisees 425 504 579 684 713 738.

The four sins crying to heaven for vengeance: 31.

1. *Wilful murder:* Cain 30 ("The voice of thy brother's blood crieth to Me"); Herod's massacre of the Innocents 419; stoning of Stephen 754 758.
2. *The sin of Sodom:* the unchaste city of Sodom 62 ("The cry of Sodom and Gomorrha is multiplied").
3. *Oppression of the poor, widows and orphans:* Pharao oppresses the Israelites 128; Jesus cries woe on the Pharisees 545.
4. *Defrauding labourers of their wages:* Tobias' warning against it 301.

The nine ways in which we share in the sins of others:

1. By *counsel:* the young advisers of Roboam 264; the compassionate advisers of Eleazar 362; Herodias 524.
2. By *command:* Eve 21; Rebecca 76; David 244; Jeroboam 264; Jezabel 277; the chief priests and the watch at the sepulchre 714.
3. By *consent:* Achab 276; Saul 758.
4. By *provocation:* Putiphar's wife 94; Job's wife 127; Roboam 264; the accusers of Susanna 330; the Pharisees before Pilate 676.
5. By *praise or flattery:* The Jews after the murder of St. James 780.
6. By *concealment:* Joseph 92; Ruben 93; Herod's guests 524. *The lawful revealing of the sins of others:* Joseph 92; Mardochai 356.

7. By *being a partner in the sin:* Heli 214; Annas 663.
8. By *silence:* Aaron 161; the adherents of Core 178; of Absalom 240; Dalila 200.
9. By *defending the ill done:* the Pharisees defend the trafficking in the outer court of the Temple 444; Saphira confirms her husband's lie 746.

THE CHRISTIAN VIRTUES.

§ 1. THE THEOLOGICAL VIRTUES.

Faith is a gift of God: 409 (Simeon and Anna); 579 (the man born blind); 540 (Peter); 724 (Thomas); 764 (Saul); it is consoling 409 789; it is a precious treasure 512; heavenly light 587.

Models of faith: Abraham 53 60 68; the widow of Sarepta 268; Elias 273; Mary 389 419; the three kings 414; Simeon and Anna 409; Peter 464 540; the leper and the centurion 487; the man born blind 579; Cornelius 776.

Grounds of hope: 312 (God, through Isaias, promises forgiveness of the most grievous sins); 326 (the same through Jeremias); 589 642 648 (our Saviour promises heaven to His disciples).

Models of hope: Abraham 52 59; Moses when pursued by Pharao's host 147; the Machabee brothers and their mother 366; Judas Machabeus 372; Jairus and the infirm woman 517; the apostles after our Lord's Ascension 737; the Church when St. Peter was in prison 780.

Charity: see above 822—824.

§ 2. THE CARDINAL VIRTUES.

Prudence: David 233; Esther 356; our Lord's words: "Be ye wise as serpents" &c. 519; the wise virgins 622; Peter 745.

Justice: Jacob 111; Tobias 296; Assuerus 356; Zachary 383; John the Baptist preaches its necessity 426; "Render to Cæsar" &c. 232; want of justice in the Pharisees 545; Pilate 684.

Temperance: "The lust of sin be under thee" 31; Gedeon 202; want of it in Esau 79; the Israelites 182; Samson 203; Daniel 328; Assuerus 356; "The kingdom of heaven suffereth violence" 587.

Fortitude: Noe 40; Elias 273 283; Tobias 296; Judith 320; Susanna 332; the three young men in the furnace 339; Esther 356; Eleazar 362; the Machabee brothers 365 372; John the Baptist 396 427 494; the weeping women 691; the sorrowing Mother 698; Joseph of Arimathea 708; Peter 738 744 752; Stephen 756; Paul 786 799.

§ 3. THE CONTRARY VIRTUES TO THE SEVEN DEADLY SINS.

1. *Humility:* Joseph 99 102; Moses 135; Gedeon 202; Ruth 208; David 225 231; Solomon 252; Naaman 285; the archangel Raphael 305; Judith 320; Daniel 338; Mary 389 393 410; John the Baptist

427 428 432; Peter 463 ("Depart from Me" &c.); 744 "Blessed are the poor in spirit"; 469 the centurion 487 ("Lord, I am not worthy"); Jairus 517; "Whosoever shall humble himself as this little child" 548; the publican in the Temple 584 ("God, be merciful to me a sinner"); exhortations and example of Jesus 431 549 585 588; the wise virgins 622; Paul 786 799 ("I am the least of the apostles" &c.).

2. *Liberality:* Abraham's hospitality 58; Booz 209; Tobias 297; Mary Magdalen 494 713; the poor widow 615; Nicodemus 708; the first Christians 746. See the corporal works of mercy above 823.

3. *Chastity:* Sem and Japhet 45; Joseph 94; Ruth 208; Judith 320; Susanna 332; Mary 393.

4. *Brotherly love:* Abraham 56 60; Rebecca 73; Ruth 208; Booz 209; Jonathan 227 232; Tobias 295; the relatives of Elizabeth 396; Jesus and Mary at Cana 440; Jesus weeps over Jerusalem 605 ("Weep not for Me" &c.).

5. *Temperance* (moderation in eating and drinking): Judith 320; Daniel and his companions 328; John the Baptist 396 427.

6. *Meekness:* David towards Saul and Absalom 228 245 264 282; our Lord's words 587 ("Learn of Me, because I am meek" &c.); example of Jesus 663.

7. *Diligence:* Moses' last words 189; David 233 247; Elias 265; Isaias 311; the Machabees 367; the widow Anna 409; our Lord's exhortation 560 ("One thing is needful"); the labourers in the vineyard 594; the wise virgins 621; parable of the talents 623.

Industry: Jacob 82; Ruth 208; Mary 393; Jesus 423 457; the apostles 464.

CHRISTIAN PERFECTION.

Perfection: commanded by our Lord 474 573; models of perfection: Jesus, Mary 389 393 &c.; Paul 798.

The following of Jesus Christ 464.

The eight Beatitudes 469.

The spirit of the world and the spirit of the Christ 470.

Self-denial: its necessity 202; Samson 203; Tobias 305; Judith 320; Daniel and his friends 328; John 396 427; Jesus 434; our Lord's words 481 ("Enter ye in at the narrow gate"); 586 ("If any man will come after Me, let him deny himself").

Conduct in adversity: Job 126; Tobias 296; Lazarus 571; Jesus on the Mount of Olives 654; the apostles 751; Stephen 755 756.

The evangelical counsels 575 (difference between the commandments and counsels):

1. *Voluntary poverty:* Abraham, Job, Mary, John the Baptist; poor Lazarus 571; the apostles 464 ("Behold we have left all and followed Thee"); advocated by Jesus 573; His example 401 586 ("The foxes have holes" &c.) 708.

2. *Perpetual chastity:* Mary 387; St. Joseph 388 419; St. John 697.
3. *Entire obedience under a religious superior:* Samuel's words: "Obedience is better than sacrifice" 219; our Lord's words: "If any man will come after Me, let him deny himself" 586.

THIRD PART.

GRACE AND THE MEANS OF GRACE.

§ 1. ACTUAL GRACE.

How grace works: Cain 32; leaven 511; the prodigal son 567; conversion of Peter 668; discourse of Peter 738; conversion of Saul 767.

The necessity of assisting grace: God leaves the idolaters to their own devices 48; Jeremias' words: "Convert us, O Lord" &c. 326; 327 (vision of Ezechiel); parable of the lost sheep 563; the prodigal son 567; our Lord's words: "Flesh and blood hath not revealed it to thee, but My Father who is in heaven" 538; also: "With men it is impossible" &c. 574; "No man can come unto Me" &c. 586; 647 ("Without Me ye can do nothing"); the fall and conversion of Peter 668; conversion of unbelievers 738 741.

Correspondence with grace: Samuel 215; Eliseus 283; Naaman 285; the shepherds 403; the three kings 415; the Samaritan woman 453; parable of the sower 506; of the talents 624; the man born blind 579; Peter 668; the wife of Pilate 683; the good thief 696; the two disciples on the road to Emmaus 720; the Ethiopian 761; Saul 767; Paul 799.

Resistance of grace: Cain 32; Pharao 140; Heli's sons 215; the kingdom of Israel 295; the Nazarites 456; the Pharisees 446 504 507 579; the rich young man 575; Jerusalem 607; the Jews 604; Judas 659 669; the thief on the left hand 697; the scoffers at the Feast of Pentecost 738.

§ 2. SANCTIFYING GRACE.

The grace of sanctification or justification: the healing of Naaman 285; the living water 450; the great treasure &c. 510; the new robe for the prodigal son 568; the wedding garment 610; the parable of the vine and the branches 643 647; the justification of Saul 767.

Justification of sinners: Magdalen 497 563; the prodigal son 568; conversion of Peter 668; the penitent thief 696; Saul 767.

§ 3. GOOD WORKS.

Works meritorious only in a state of grace: parable of the vine 647.

Good works of sinners not useless: the widow of Sarepta 266; the Ninivites 290; the centurion of Capharnaum 485; the rich man 571; Saul 767; Cornelius 775.

Meritorious works rewarded by God: the treasure in heaven 305 477; even the gift of a cup of cold water will be rewarded 520; the labourers in the vineyard 594; the good and faithful servant 623; the just at the Last Judgment 626.

Necessity of good works: Isaias 311 ("Learn to do good" &c.); preaching of penance by John the Baptist 425 ("Every tree that doth not yield good fruit shall be cut down"); our Lord's words "Lay up for yourselves treasure in heaven" &c. 477; "Every good tree bringeth forth good fruit" 482 520; the sentence at the Last Judgment 626.

Prayer, fasting and almsgiving: specially recommended by the examples of Moses 158 161: the Israelites 213; the Ninivites 290; Tobias 306; the prophetess Anna 409; Jesus 429; Saul 768; Tabitha 770; and by the words of the angel Raphael "Prayer with fasting and alms" &c. 305.

Necessity of good intention: the sacrifice of Cain and Abel 33; our Lord's words in the Sermon on the Mount 475; the Pharisee in the Temple 584; the poor widow's mite 615.

THE HOLY SACRAMENTS.

The use of outward signs and ceremonies, in order to convey material or spiritual benefits: in the cure of the man born blind 580; the descent of the Holy Ghost 737; Elias at the raising up of the widow's son 269; the cure of the deaf and dumb man 537.

BAPTISM.

Types of Baptism: circumcision 61; the passage of the Red Sea 148; of the Jordan 195; the cure of Naaman 285; the baptism of John 431; the pool of Bethsaida 501; the pool of Siloe 579.

Institution of Baptism 431; the commandment to baptize 730.

The necessity of Baptism: discourse with Nicodemus 447; 733; Peter's discourse on the Day of Pentecost 736; Baptism of the Ethiopian 760; of Cornelius 775.

The effects of Baptism: signified by the wonders that occurred at the Baptism of Jesus in the Jordan 432; by the cure of the deaf and dumb man 537; of the man born blind 579.

The covenant of Baptism 189 ("Beware lest thou ever forget the covenant" &c.); feast-day 397.

Baptism by blood 420.

CONFIRMATION.

The typical signification of oil 84.

Confirmation: in Samaria 760; the sign of the Cross 690.

Preparation for it 737.

Effects of it: the effects of the Holy Ghost on the Day of the Pentecost 738.

Life a warfare 373.

THE MOST HOLY SACRAMENT OF THE ALTAR.

§ 1. THE REAL PRESENCE OF JESUS CHRIST IN THE BLESSED SACRAMENT.

Types of the Blessed Sacrament: the Tree of Life 18; the paschal lamb 144 635; the Manna 151; the pillar of cloud on the Tabernacle 166 257; the miraculous food of Elias 284; the changing of water into wine 440; the miracle of the loaves 528.

Promise of the Holy Eucharist 533.

Its Institution 632.

The love of Jesus in the Most Holy Sacrament 636.

Reverence for the Most Holy 306 (Tobias, father and son, "being seized with fear fell upon the ground on their face" before the angel Raphael); 416 (the three kings before Jesus).

Corpus Christi 635.

§ 2. THE HOLY SACRIFICE OF THE MASS.

Sacrifice, as a supreme act of divine worship, is as old as man and has been of universal practice. Sacrifice of Cain and Abel 28; of Noe 43; Abraham 52 67; Melchisedech 56; Jacob 87 115; the friends of Job 125; the sacrifices instituted by God under the Old Law 169; their typical signification 170 701.

Types of the unbloody Sacrifice: the offering of Melchisedech 56; the unbloody sacrifices of the Old Law 170.

Promises of the Holy Sacrifice of the Mass: through David 236 ("Thou art a Priest for ever according to the order of Melchisedech"); through Malachias 360; through our Lord at the well of Jacob 453.

Institution of the Mass at the Last Supper 632.

§ 3. HOLY COMMUNION.

The whole of Jesus Christ is present under the form of bread 533 720.

Effects of Holy Communion 534; prefigured by the paschal lamb 144; the Manna 151; by the miraculous food of Elias 284; by the virtue that went out of our Lord 461 529.

Unworthy Communion: Tree of life 28; the ark of the covenant in the days of Samuel 215; the king's wedding feast 611; Judas 638 639.

Necessity for preparation: preparation of the Israelites for receiving the Commandments 153; the wedding garment 611; the washing of the feet 630; the Entombment of Jesus 709; the preparation of the apostles before receiving the Holy Ghost 734; the preparation of Saul for receiving Baptism 766.

Holy Communion should be received with

1. *living faith:* Simeon 410; Nathaniel 437; Peter 538.
2. *humility:* Elizabeth 393; Peter 464; the centurion 487; the prodigal son 567; the publican in the Temple 585.

3. *contrition:* the paralytic 466; Mary Magdalen 497; the publican 585;
4. *hope:* the leper 484; the infirm woman 515;
5. *love:* Martha and Mary 560; the two disciples at Emmaus 718 ("Was not our heart burning within us");
6. *desire:* the man infirm thirty-eight years 498; Peter 530; the Ethiopian 762.

PENANCE.

The necessity of penance 214 313 460.

Models of true penance or conversion: David 244; the Ninivites 290; the man sick of the palsy 466; Magdalen 497 716; the prodigal son 566; the penitent thief 696; Saul 767.

Types of true penance: the cure of Naaman 285; the leper 488; the raising of the young man of Naim 491. Putting off conversion 371.

Institution of the Sacrament of Penance: 539 (the promise of it); 721.

All sins can be remitted: God's promise through Isaias: "If your sins be as scarlet" &c. 312; 723.

Effects of the Sacrament of Penance: the reception of the prodigal son 568; the peace of God 724.

Conditions of Worthy Reception:

1. *Examination of conscience:* the prodigal son returned to himself 567.
2. *True contrition:* David ("I water my couch with my tears") 244; Isaias' preaching of penance 310; the man sick of the palsy 466; Magdalen 497; the prodigal son 567; Jesus in the Garden 653; Peter "wept bitterly" 665 668; 723; the contrition of Antiochus was not supernatural 371.
3. *Hope of pardon:* its ground 324 ("I will forgive their iniquity, and I will remember their sin no more"); the prodigal son 567. He who gives up hope is lost: Cain 30; Judas 669.
4. *Sincere purpose of amendment:* Jonas 290; Isaias 312; 551 ("I will pay thee all"); the prodigal son 568; Saul 765; Pharao's resolution was not sincere 140 148; relapse into sin 501.
5. *Avoiding the proximate occasion of sin:* Eve 19; the temptation of Jesus 434; our Lord's words "If thy right hand scandalize thee" &c. 548; Peter's fall 668.
6. *Confession:* God requires a confession from Adam 21; from Cain 29 31; a confession of sin required at sin-offerings 171: at the baptism of John 427; from the leper 485 ("Show thyself to the priest"); the prodigal son 565 ("I will say, father, I have sinned"). Concealment of sins in confession 506 749.
7. *Satisfaction:* Jonas 290; the fellow-servant 552; the prodigal son ("Make me as one of thy hired servants") 565; Saul 765. *Temporal punishment of sin must be suffered:* Lot 66; Rebecca and Jacob 78; the Israelites in the desert 177; David 244; the man infirm thirty-eight years 501.
8. *Thanksgiving* after receiving this Sacrament 466.

INDULGENCES.

The power of the Church to grant indulgences: 540 ("Whatsoever thou shalt loose upon earth" &c.).

The necessity of a state of grace in order to gain an indulgence: 467.

Jubilee-indulgence: its type 172.

EXTREME UNCTION.

Typical signification of oil 84.

Type of Extreme Unction: the anointing of the sick by the disciples 522.

HOLY ORDER.

The priesthood of the Old Law taken as a type of the priesthood of the *New Law* 173; punishment of Core &c. 180; Ozias 310.

Ordination of priests: instituted by Jesus Christ 523 634; given to St. Paul 784; the *diaconate* 755.

Office of the priesthood under the New Law 471 521 723 732.

The priestly state to be honoured 520 ("He that receiveth you &c. He that heareth you, heareth Me" &c.); 608 (parable of the marriage-feast).

Prayer for good priests 273 555 785 (Ember-days).

MATRIMONY.

Institution and sanctification of marriage 18 441 (marriage at Cana).

Unity of married people 18; the Holy Family 423.

Duty of married people towards their children: Moses' last words 189; Heli's punishment 214; Tobias 300; the mother of the Machabees 366; our Lord's words 548 729.

Preparation for the holy state of matrimony: Raphael's words to Tobias 301.

Mixed marriages not approved: Abraham seeks a wife for Isaac 71; the Israelites among the Chanaanites 201.

SACRAMENTALS.

The curse resting on the lower creatures 24 is removed by the blessing of the Church 27. The healing of the water by Eliseus a type of the blessing of water by the Church (holy water) 286. Blessing of palms on Palm-Sunday 608.

The evil influence of the devil is warded off by exorcisms 127 458 461.

PRAYER.

Prayer of praise and thanksgiving: 56 (Melchisedech); 72 (Eliezer; 125 (Job); 255 (the dedication of the Temple); 297 (Tobias "thanked God all the days of his life"); 318 (Judith); 339 (the young men in the furnace); 391 (the Magnificat); 395 (the Benedictus); 402 ("Gloria in excelsis").

The necessity of prayer: command of Jesus 581 ("Ask and it shall be given you"); 620 651 ("Watch ye and pray that ye enter not into temptation"); our Lord's example 460 520 654; Saul 767.

The fruits of prayer:

1. it *unites us to God* and makes us heavenly-minded: Henoch 35; the rays on Moses' countenance 161; John the Baptist 396; Simeon and Anna 409;
2. it *strengthens us* against evil, and helps us to do right: Judith 320;
3. it *obtains* for us *comfort in affliction:* Anna 213; Tobias 296; Jesus in the Garden 654; *help in need:* Jacob 88; Moses 152; Josue 195; in the time of the Judges 202 213; Ezechias 315; Susanna 333; Daniel 338; Judas Machabeus 372; Peter in prison 780;
and the *grace of final perseverance:* Noe 40; Lot 65; 620.

The power of prayer: besides Abraham's intercession for Sodom already cited 66; Moses 161; Elias 269 273; Zachary 383; *intercession* 460 488; Stephen's prayer 757 767.

The qualities of prayer. We must pray with

1. *devotion:* worship in spirit 453; prayer in common 476 582; Jesus in the Garden 654.
2. *humility:* Abraham 65; Solomon 252; Jairus 517; the Chanaanite woman 536 582; the publican in the Temple 585; Jesus in the Garden 654.
3. *confidence:* Josue 195; Elias 273; Susanna 333; our Lord's promise 582; Jairus 515 648; the thief 696.
4. *submission to God's will:* Judith and the people of Bethulia 319; the young men in the furnace 339; Jesus in the Garden 654.
5. *perseverance:* Abraham 65; Jacob's wrestling 88; Zachary 383; our Lord's exhortation 477 582; the Chanaanite woman 537; the importunate friend 582; Jesus in the Garden 654.

How we can pray without ceasing: example of David 222; of Mary 423 560.

We should especially pray

1. *morning and evening:* the morning and evening sacrifice of the Israelites 167.
2. *before and after meals:* Daniel in the lion's den 346; Jesus 529.
3. *in time of temptation:* Susanna 332; the example of Jesus 434 514.
4. *in need:* Eliezer 71; Jacob 88 118; Anna 213; Solomon 252; Jesus before the choice of the apostles 520.
5. *in times of private and public tribulation:* Jacob 88; Ezechias 316; the Church during the imprisonment of Peter 780.

Where we should pray: 256 451 475.
The Lord's Prayer 580.
The Angelical Salutation 385 389; *the Angelus* 389.

PROCESSIONS, PILGRIMAGES AND CONFRATERNITIES.

Processions : the marching round Jericho 195; transfer of the Ark of the Covenant 235 256; the entry of Jesus into Jerusalem 608.

Pilgrimages: the feasts of the Jews 172; the example of Jesus, Mary and Joseph 423.

Confraternities: prayer said in common 582.

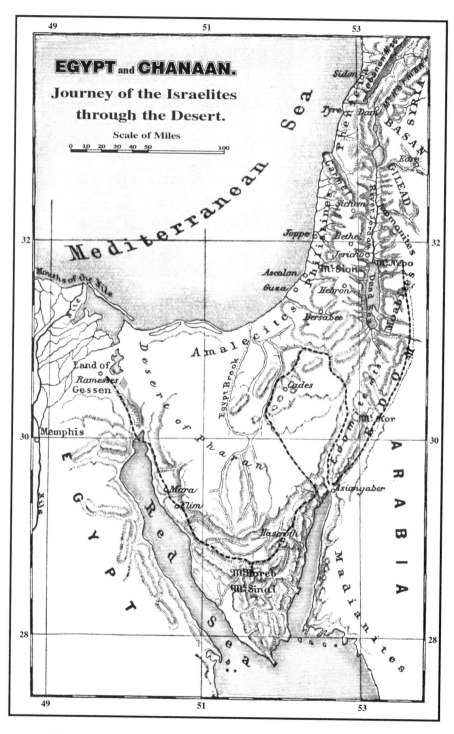

The dashed ----- *line indicates the journey of the Israelites.*

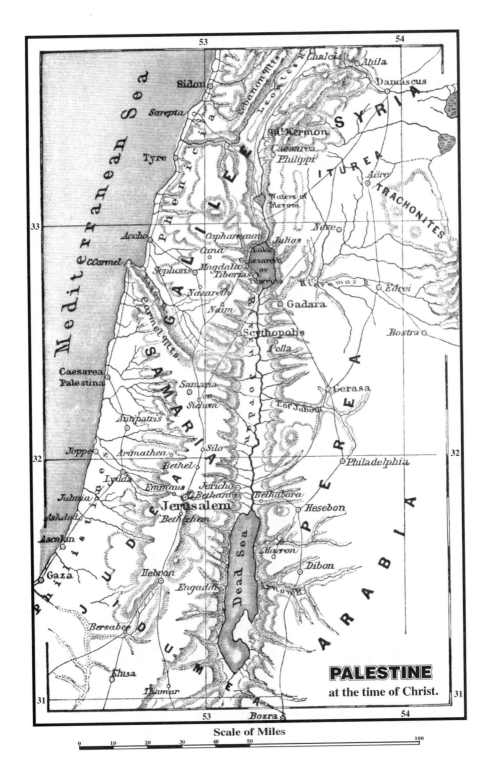

PALESTINE
at the time of Christ.

Scale of Miles

841

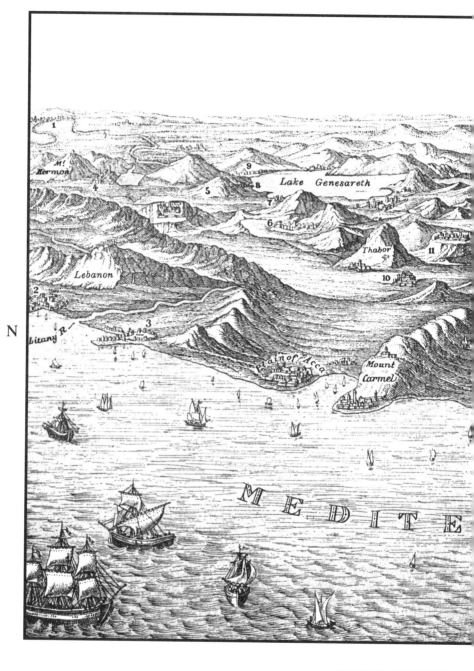

N

BIRD'S EYE VIEW

1. Damascus
2. Siden (now Saida)
3. Tyre

4. Caesarea Philippi (Ruins)
5. Mount of the Beatitudes
6. Nazareth

7. Tiberias
8. Capharnaum (Ruins)
9. Bethsaida

10. Naim
11. Samaria
12. Mount Gerizim

E

Dead Sea

Torrent of Cedron

15

13

18
17
19

20
21

22

16

S

u of Saron

Canah R.

Plain of

Ascalon

Sephela

14

Sorek R.

RANEAN

W

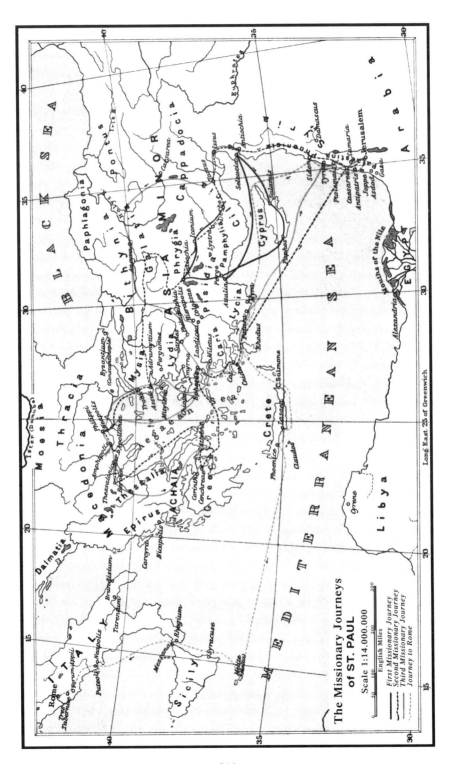

The Missionary Journeys
of ST. PAUL

Scale 1:14.000.000

English Miles

First Missionary Journey
Second Missionary Journey
Third Missionary Journey
Journey to Rome

If you have enjoyed this book, consider making your next selection from among the following . . .

Bible History. (Grades 6-10). *Johnson, Hannan, Dominica* 24.00
Bible History Workbook. (Companion to above). *Marie Ignatz* 21.00
Set of Bible History and Workbook. ($45.00 value) 35.00
Life and Revelations of St. Gertrude the Great. 24.00
School of Jesus Crucified. *Fr. Ignatius* 13.50
Devotion to the Holy Spirit. 3.00
Shroud of Turin. *Fr. Guerrera* 15.00
Ven. Francisco Marto of Fatima. *Cirrincione*, comp. 2.50
Ven. Jacinta Marto of Fatima. *Cirrincione* 3.00
St. Philomena—The Wonder-Worker. *O'Sullivan* 9.00
The Facts About Luther. *Msgr. Patrick O'Hare* 18.50
Little Catechism of the Curé of Ars. *St. John Vianney.* 8.00
The Curé of Ars—Patron Saint of Parish Priests. *Fr. B. O'Brien* 7.50
Saint Teresa of Avila. *William Thomas Walsh* 24.00
Isabella of Spain: The Last Crusader. *William Thomas Walsh* 24.00
Characters of the Inquisition. *William Thomas Walsh* 16.50
Blood-Drenched Altars—Cath. Comment. on Hist. Mexico. *Kelley* 21.50
The Four Last Things—Death, Judgment, Hell, Heaven. *Fr. von Cochem* 9.00
Confession of a Roman Catholic. *Paul Whitcomb* 2.50
The Catholic Church Has the Answer. *Paul Whitcomb* 2.50
The Sinner's Guide. *Ven. Louis of Granada* 15.00
True Devotion to Mary. *St. Louis De Montfort* 9.00
Autobiography of St. Anthony Mary Claret 13.00
I Wait for You. *Sr. Josefa Menendez* 1.50
Words of Love. *Menendez, Betrone, Mary of the Trinity* 8.00
Little Lives of the Great Saints. *John O'Kane Murray* 20.00
Prayer—The Key to Salvation. *Fr. Michael Müller.* 9.00
Sermons on Prayer. *St. Francis de Sales* 7.00
Sermons on Our Lady. *St. Francis de Sales* 15.00
Passion of Jesus and Its Hidden Meaning. *Fr. Groenings, S.J.* 15.00
The Victories of the Martyrs. *St. Alphonsus Liguori* 13.50
Canons and Decrees of the Council of Trent. *Transl. Schroeder* 16.50
Sermons of St. Alphonsus Liguori for Every Sunday 18.50
A Catechism of Modernism. *Fr. J. B. Lemius* 7.50
Alexandrina—The Agony and the Glory. *Johnston* 7.00
Life of Blessed Margaret of Castello. *Fr. William Bonniwell* 9.00
The Ways of Mental Prayer. *Dom Vitalis Lehodey* 16.50
Catechism of Mental Prayer. *Simler* 3.00
Fr. Paul of Moll. *van Speybrouck* 13.50
St. Francis of Paola. *Simi and Segreti* 9.00
Abortion: Yes or No? *Dr. John L. Grady, M.D.* 3.00
The Story of the Church. *Johnson, Hannan, Dominica* 22.50
Reign of Christ the King. *Davies* 2.00
Hell Quizzes. *Radio Replies Press* 2.50
Indulgence Quizzes. *Radio Replies Press* 2.50
Purgatory Quizzes. *Radio Replies Press* 2.50
Virgin and Statue Worship Quizzes. *Radio Replies Press* 2.50
Holy Eucharist—Our All. *Etlin* 3.00
Meditation Prayer on Mary Immaculate. *Padre Pio* 2.50
Little Book of the Work of Infinite Love. *de la Touche* 3.50
Textual Concordance of The Holy Scriptures. PB. *Williams* 35.00
The Way of Divine Love. *Sister Josefa Menendez* 21.00
The Way of Divine Love. (pocket, unabr.). *Menendez* 12.50
Mystical City of God—Abridged. *Ven. Mary of Agreda* 21.00

Prices subject to change.

Dolorous Passion of Our Lord. *Anne C. Emmerich*............................ 18.00
Priest in Union with Christ. *Garrigou-Lagrange, O.P.*.......................... 16.50
Purgatory—The Two Catholic Views. (From *All for Jesus*). *Fr. Faber* 6.00
Shroud of Turin: A Case for Authenticity. *Fr. Guerrera* 15.00
33 Doctors of the Church. *Fr. Christopher Rengers* 33.00
Creation Rediscovered. *Keane* 21.00
Hail Holy Queen (from *Glories of Mary*). *St. Alphonsus*...................... 9.00
Novena of Holy Communions. *Lovasik* 2.50
Brief Catechism for Adults. *Cogan*... 12.50
The Cath. Religion—Illus./Expl. for Child, Adult, Convert. *Burbach* 12.50
Eucharistic Miracles. *Joan Carroll Cruz*..................................... 16.50
The Incorruptibles. *Joan Carroll Cruz* 16.50
Pope St. Pius X. *F. A. Forbes* 11.00
Self-Abandonment to Divine Providence. *Fr. de Caussade, S.J.*.................... 22.50
The Song of Songs—A Mystical Exposition. *Fr. Arintero, O.P.* 21.50
Prophecy for Today. *Edward Connor* 7.50
Saint Michael and the Angels. *Approved Sources* 9.00
Modern Saints—Their Lives & Faces, Book I. *Ann Ball*........................ 21.00
Modern Saints—Their Lives & Faces, Book II. *Ann Ball* 23.00
Our Lady of Fatima's Peace Plan from Heaven. *Booklet*........................ 1.00
Divine Favors Granted to St. Joseph. *Père Binet*.............................. 7.50
St. Joseph Cafasso—Priest of the Gallows. *St. John Bosco*...................... 6.00
Catechism of the Council of Trent. *McHugh/Callan* 27.50
The Foot of the Cross. *Fr. Faber*... 18.00
Padre Pio—The Stigmatist. *Fr. Charles Carty* 16.50
Why Squander Illness? *Frs. Rumble & Carty*................................. 4.00
The Sacred Heart and the Priesthood. *de la Touche* 10.00
Fatima—The Great Sign. *Francis Johnston* 12.00
Heliotropium—Conformity of Human Will to Divine. *Drexelius* 15.00
Charity for the Suffering Souls. *Fr. John Nageleisen* 18.00
Devotion to the Sacred Heart of Jesus. *Verheylezoon* 16.50
Who Is Padre Pio? *Radio Replies Press* 3.00
Child's Bible History. *Knecht*... 7.00
The Stigmata and Modern Science. *Fr. Charles Carty* 2.50
The Life of Christ. 4 Vols. P.B. *Anne C. Emmerich* 60.00
St. Anthony—The Wonder Worker of Padua. *Stoddard*......................... 7.00
The Precious Blood. *Fr. Faber* 16.50
The Holy Shroud & Four Visions. *Fr. O'Connell* 3.50
Clean Love in Courtship. *Fr. Lawrence Lovasik* 4.50
The Prophecies of St. Malachy. *Peter Bander*................................. 9.00
St. Martin de Porres. *Giuliana Cavallini*.................................... 15.00
The Secret of the Rosary. *St. Louis De Montfort*.............................. 5.00
The History of Antichrist. *Rev. P. Huchede*.................................. 4.00
St. Catherine of Siena. *Alice Curtayne* 16.50
Where We Got the Bible. *Fr. Henry Graham* 8.00
Hidden Treasure—Holy Mass. *St. Leonard*.................................. 7.50
Imitation of the Sacred Heart of Jesus. *Fr. Arnoudt* 18.50
The Life & Glories of St. Joseph. *Edward Thompson*........................... 16.50
Humility of Heart. *Fr. Cajetan da Bergamo* 9.00
The Curé D'Ars. *Abbé Francis Trochu*...................................... 24.00
Love, Peace and Joy. (St. Gertrude). *Prévot* 8.00

At your Bookdealer or direct from the Publisher.
Toll-Free 1-800-437-5876   **Fax 815-226-7770**
Tel. 815-226-7777   **www.tanbooks.com**

Prices subject to change.